SABAEAN INSCRIPTIONS FROM MAḤRAM BILQÎS (MÂRIB)

Publications of the American Foundation for the Study of Man,
edited by William F. Albright
with the assistance of Ray L. Cleveland and Gus W. Van Beek

VOLUME III

SABAEAN INSCRIPTIONS

BALTIMORE: THE JOHNS HOPKINS PRESS

FROM MAḤRAM BILQÎS (MÂRIB)

by A. JAMME, W.F.
S.T.D., D.Or. (Louvain), Lic. Bibl. St. (Vatican City),
Research Professor, The Catholic University of America (Washington, D.C.)

with foreword by WENDELL PHILLIPS
Sc.D., Litt.D., J.D., L.H.D., D.C.S., H.H.D., LL.D.
President, American Foundation for the Study of Man

Published with grants from the
A. W. Mellon Educational and Charitable Trust
and the Sarah Mellon Scaife Foundation

The Johns Hopkins Press, Baltimore 18, Md., 1962

Distributed in Great Britain by Oxford University Press, London
Printed in the U.S.A. by The Murray Printing Co., Forge Village, Mass.
Library of Congress Catalog Card Number 62-10311

THE DIRECTORS OF THE AMERICAN FOUNDATION
FOR THE STUDY OF MAN HAVE THE HONOR OF DEDICATING
THIS VOLUME WITH DEEPEST APPRECIATION TO

E. Roland Harriman

FOREWORD

Of all the ancient kingdoms of South Arabia, great and small, the Kingdom of Saba˒ was the most powerful and enduring. It was established as early as 1000 B.C. and perhaps several centuries before that time; it continued to exist, with only one or two brief periods of waning, until all of South Arabia was united under one ruler about A.D. 300. It was only natural that it was from this state that a royal visitor, the Queen of Sheba, should make her way to Jerusalem to be received at the court of Solomon and that the fame of the Sabaeans would be recorded by Classical writers. The capital of this ancient kingdom, a caravan city more prosperous and magnificent than its rivals, was known by the Sabaean name Maryab, which appears in the ancient Greek sources as Mariaba. In this city were centered the commerce, cult, crafts, and administration of the Kingdom.

But it has been the decision of history that the Kingdom of the Sabaeans should disappear long since and that its great capital, Maryab, should fall into ruin. Like hundreds of splendid cities of yore, so this one stands only as a great mound of debris, on one end of which survives a relatively unimpressive town called Mârib. It was at this place that an advance exploratory party of the American Foundation for the Study of Man, including Dr. Albert Jamme and the writer among others, first arrived during April of 1951. We were there for only a brief inspection to determine the requirements both for scientific work and for suitable living quarters. Even this brief survey was enough to convince us that none of the earlier visitors to the site (only three Europeans, Arnaud, Halévy, and Glaser, had visited it, all in the nineteenth century) had overstated the archaeological attractiveness of the ruins. (I have described the principal visible monuments in Chapter 24 of my book, *Qataban and Sheba.*) It was some time later, however, after I had again talked to H.M. Imâm Aḥmed in Taᶜiz and to other Yemeni officials in Ḥodeida and Sanᶜā, that my expedition was able to move to Mârib to begin work.

Dr. Jamme arrived in Mârib to begin work on November 2, 1951. Without the slightest hesitation or delay, he began, with his characteristic energy and enthusiasm, the formidable task of recording the inscriptions uncovered by the expedition before his arrival. Laboring under very difficult conditions, including continuous harassment by local officials, he was nevertheless able to obtain prodigious results. In addition to copying inscriptions discovered by the excavators and making latex squeezes of them, he also searched the area around Mârib for other inscriptions and graffiti. After placing a series of obstacles in his way, the local officials finally ordered Dr. Jamme to cease all work on January 12, 1952, and he was confined to his room by Yemeni soldiers. After my arrival at Mârib in February, he was able to work for several more days, but under nearly impossible conditions.

The great collection of inscriptional material which Dr. Jamme was able to make during the difficult campaign at Mârib has occupied much of his time during the ensuing years, as he has carefully studied his hand copies and photographs in the greatest detail. (The latex squeezes, some of which were damaged while in the storeroom at Mârib, had to be abandoned.) The present volume from the hand of Dr. Jamme presents the results of his labors. Part I contains the texts of the inscriptions in transliteration, accompanied by translations and detailed notes on textual and grammatical points. Part II presents the results of Dr. Jamme's historical studies of this new inscriptional material and demonstrates the great importance of this material for South-Arabian history. The appended concordance, glossary, and indexes also exhibit the energy and time which Dr. Jamme devoted to this volume; the concordance and glossary are in themselves substantial contributions.

It would be an unfortunate oversight if I failed to take this opportunity to thank the foremost Orientalist of our time, Professor W. F. Albright, for his personal contribution toward the work of the American Foundation for the Study of Man. He has generously given of his time in co-ordinating the research being done by various scholars collaborating in the publication of our South-Arabian materials, and his part, as General Editor, in making the present series of scholarly publications of the highest quality possible cannot be over-emphasized. When overwork and an eye operation made it impossible for Dr. Albright to continue reading the manuscript of this volume, Professor Richard M. Frank of the Catholic University in Washington gave generously of his time and skill. At the same time, the editorial work was largely taken over by my fellow Arabian explorer, Dr. Ray L. Cleveland of the Johns Hopkins University, working in his capacity of Assistant Editor.

On behalf of the Directors of the American Foundation for the Study of Man, I wish to express grateful appreciation to the field staff of our expeditions and to the contributors – government and academic organizations, corporations, companies, and individuals – who made this Arabian endeavor possible. In particular, I wish to record again my deep gratitude to Mr. E. Roland Harriman for his continuing interest and generous support of our work both in the field and at home. It is our pleasure and honor to dedicate this volume to him.

WENDELL PHILLIPS

2969 Kalakaua Avenue,
Honolulu, *June, 1961*

CONTENTS

PART I: TEXTS

PART II: HISTORICAL STUDIES

Chapter I: Three groups of inscribed stones re-used in the entrance hall

Chapter II: Research on the mural inscriptions: Ja 550-557

SABAEAN INSCRIPTIONS
FROM MAḤRAM BILQÎS (MÂRIB)

INTRODUCTION

This volume brings to publication all the texts which the writer copied during the campaign of excavation carried out in the winter of 1951-1952 by the American Foundation for the Study of Man, in the entrance hall of Maḥram Bilqîs (near Mârib, Yemen)[1], which was the temple ᵓAwwâm dedicated to the moon god ᵓIlumquh, the patron of the city Mârib itself and also of the Sab state. To these are added several other texts from the same excavations, known to me only through photographs or copies made by F. P. Albright and J. Rubright. A few texts from various other places are also given, as required for the comparative study of the Maḥram Bilqîs inscriptions.

The period of inactivity imposed upon me by the ᶜÂmil of Mârib, ᶜAbdulraḥmân, from the 13th of January until the 8th of February, while the field work was in progress, explains not only why all the inscriptions unearthed by excavators were not copied, but also why even the approximate number of uncopied inscribed stones excavated remains unknown. However unfortunate it may be that we were not able to record all the material to be found at Maḥram Bilqîs, I yet feel fortunate for having possession of my notebooks and those photographs which I was able to take on Fridays[2]. Without these, the results of my own work would have been void, and those of the excavation campaign disastrously limited. Finally, the loss of the latex squeezes which I made is a very painful handicap for my research and for South-Arabian science as well. At least, I succeeded in saving ten small ones (Ja 603, upper part; 637; 648; 662, upper part; 673; 694; 698; 704 and 718, right part[3]) which were hidden in the personal belongings of the members of the expedition. The loading on the truck of all the squeezes, which occupied about 2.5 cubic m. in my small bedroom, would doubtless have aroused the attention of the Yemeni sentry; and even having escaped his notice, such a mass could not possibly have escaped from the inquisitive eyes of the two Yemeni officials who inspected the truck before departure. Our flight had to be accomplished without further difficulties with the Yemeni authorities and so the latex squeezes were left behind. It is, however, with great pleasure that I recall the friendly welcome and the help given me by the population of Mârib during the few days I spent in the city, recording the inscribed stones re-used in recent buildings, and also the kindness of the workmen and soldiers during the first weeks of the campaign. Even when it became obvious to

[1] The results of these excavations have been published by *AlEMY* and F. P. Albright, "Catalogue of Objects Found in Mârib Excavations", in *BoAlADSA*, pp. 269-75.

[2] All the photographs printed here, except those of Ja 550, No. 1, 552 and 671, were taken by me.

[3] MaPI is an Ethiopic fragmentary text, which will be published by A. Caquot.

everyone that friendly relations no longer existed between myself and the ᶜÂmil of Mârib, most of them maintained their previous attitude of kindness and hospitality and tried to be of some help in my work. I am very thankful to all of them.

The present work is divided into two parts, viz., the publication of the texts and the historical studies made in connection with these inscriptions.

Part I. The texts are classified on a logical basis, viz., their content, which does not affect in any way their dating or their relative chronology. The translation follows the very wording of the original text as far as possible, even if several expressions prove to be rather awkward. In the commentary which follows the translation, the study of a term is normally given at its first occurrence in the collection; otherwise, the exact place where the study is published is indicated at the first occurrence of the word. Finally, my evaluation of the degree of probability of the translations suggested in the work must be found in the commentary and not at all in the glossary.

Part II. The second part of this publication is focused on historical research. The first chapter, which deals with the location of four groups of inscribed stones and which completes a study previously published, forms no exception, since this chapter offers important historical information with regard to the dating of successive transformations made in the entrance hall.

The understanding and evaluation of the texts belonging to a historical period requires the study of the previously published inscriptions dating from the same period. All this material must be treated afresh, independently of interference from any foreign literature or tradition which so often misrepresents the actual historical picture [4]. It is for this reason that I have concentrated on the study of the epigraphical material as carefully as possible and on reconstructing historical events on that basis. A general study of palaeography obviously is out of place in the present work; nevertheless the facsimiles here reproduced and the palaeographical descriptions of many texts will be, it is hoped, a not-insignificant step toward a more extensive and definitive study of South-Arabian palaeography.

My historical studies offer, in many instances, new interpretations and solutions of problems which are by no means final, but which, it is my hope, will be helpful for further study. The studies of dynasties or isolated rulers are presented in ten chapters (Chapters II-XI), and their dating is offered in Chapter XII.

A great number of questions could have been pointed out and treated in relation to the texts of this collection. However, the complete study of such a large epigraphical collection is almost endless, since each question can easily be taken as a subject for a separate monograph. On the other hand, I am very anxious to put this collection of inscriptions at the disposal of South-Arabian scholars, for they will surely find in it useful material for their own research.

I wish to express my deep gratitude to the American Foundation for the Study of Man for the opportunity given me to work in the field as a member of its expeditions, and also to all those who helped me in any way in my work since the beginning of

[4] Cf., e.g., A. F. L. Beeston's remark on the Islamic traditions, in *BiO*, 12 (1952), p. 216.

these expeditions, and especially among them, my former professor at the Catholic University of Louvain, René Draguet, whose inspiring example and friendship are to me more than can be expressed by words alone. Finally, may my Mother find in each page of this publication a humble homage of admiration and of love.

SYSTEM OF TRANSLITERATION

𐩱	ا	ʾ	𐩷	ط	ṭ	𐩶	غ	ġ
𐩨	ب	b	𐩼	ظ	ẓ	𐩰	ف	f
𐩴	ج	g	𐩺	ى	y	𐩮	ص	ṣ
𐩵	د	d	𐩫	ك	k	𐩳	ض	ḍ
𐩹	ذ	ḏ	𐩡	ل	l	𐩤	ق	q
𐩠	ه	h	𐩣	م	m	𐩧	ر	r
𐩥	و	w	𐩬	ن	n	𐩦	ش	š
𐩸	ز	z	𐩪	(س)	s	𐩯	س	ś
𐩢	ح	ḥ	𐩲	ع	ʿ	𐩩	ت	t
𐩭	خ	ḫ				𐩻	ث	ṯ

SIGNS USED IN THE TRANSLITERATION

[ ] : letter destroyed and restored.
⌈⌉⌊⌋ : missing part of the letter flanked by one of these half brackets.
( ) : letter badly damaged, but certain.
⟨ ⟩ : letter not engraved but restored, or engraved but suppressed in the transliteration.

Part I

Texts

— A —

INSCRIPTIONS ON THE WALL: Ja 550–557

550 – Inscription engraved on the south-west part of the wall; nine photographs in Plates 1–3, a small part of which is reproduced in *AlEMY*, pl. 209. – MaMB 3+4+5=CIH 375 (cf. *CIH*, II, pp. 25-28 and III, pp. 354-55): *RhSLG*, II, pp. 15-25; cp. *FaAJY*, I, pp. 93 and 99.

MaMB 3: line 1 (from ⌊*mrydʿ* of *ḏmrydʿ* to *wʿs* of *wʿsmt*, and from *ḏn* of *mḥḏn* to *h* of *h*[*wfyhw*]): 13.75 m. × 23 cm. + 1.25 m. × 23 cm.; distance to the upper edge of the stones: from 3 cm. to 6.5; Fakhry 92+91+90. Line 2 (from the beginning to *y*⌉ of *yṯʿʾmr* in the final invocation): 24.26 m. × 21 cm.; distance to the upper edge of the stones: 3 cm.; Fakhry 89.

MaMB 4: fallen stone (from *ʿʾmr* in the final invocation to *krb*⌉ of *krbʾl*); 1.07 m. × 30 cm.; text: 1.065 m. × 22.5 cm.; distance to the upper edge of the stone: 3.2 cm.; Fakhry 93.

MaMB 5: fallen stone supporting the last two signs of line 2.

SYMBOLS: simple and triple symbol at the beginning of lines 1 and 2, respectively; cf. Plate C, Fig. 2.

1 **Single symbol** → *tbʿkrb/ršw/ḏt/ġḍrn/qyn/sḥr/*
wqyn/ydʿʾl/byn/wykrbmlk/wtr/wyṯʿʾmr/byn/bn/
ḏmrydʿ/bn/mḏmrm/hqny/ʾlmqh/kl/tmlʾ/gnʾn/ln/
ʾʾwdn/ʾly/sṭrn/ʿd/šqrm/wkl/mġbb/wmḥfdt/ḏn/
mhyʿn/wbnhw/ḏmrydʿ/wsmhʾmr/wkl/wldhw/
wqnyhw/wkl/ʾnẖlhw/bʾḏnt/ktm/wwrq/wḏ/trd/
wwġmm/wʿsmt/wbrʾm/⟨⟩wzmn/wḥgrw/wgdlm/
wsḥm/wmṭrn/bysrn/mflqn/wrdmn/bysrn/mḥmyn/
wmẖḏn/byhdl/ywm/h[*wfyhw/ʾlmqh*. . .

2 **Triple symbol** ← *ḏt/tnbʾhw/lwldm/wywm/*
hwṣthw/ykrbmlk/wtr/wyʿqb/bkbtn/bʿly/sbʾ/wʾšʿbn/
ẖmst/ẖrfn/bḍr/qtbn/whwfy/ʾlmqh/kl/sbʾ/wʾšʿbn/
wkl/ʾrgl/hwrd/ʿd/hgrn/thrgb/bkl/ẖrfy/hrs/bkbtn/
bʿly/sbʾ/wʾšʿbn/wʾtw/ʿd/mryb/bslm/sbʾ/wqtbn/
whṯb/lhw/yṯʿʾmr/byn/wsbʾ/tʾmnm/bʿṯtr/wb/hwbs/
wb/ʾlmqh/wb/ḏt/ḥmym/wb/ḏt/bʿdnm/wb/ḏt/ġḍrn/
wb/ydʿʾl/byn/wb/ykrbmlk/wtr/wb/yṯʿʾmr/byn/wb/
krbʾl/wtr/wb/ʾbhw/ḏmrydʿ/bn/mḏmrm/

1 **Single symbol** Tabaʿkarib, priest of Ḏât-Ġaḍarân, administrator for Saḥar, and administrator for Yadaʿʾil Bayyin and for Yakrubmalik Waṭar and for Yaṯaʿʾamar Bayyin, son of Ḏamaryadaʿ, people of [the clan] Maḏmarum, has dedicated to ʾIlumquh the whole mass of the enclosing wall from the lines which [belong to] this inscription to the top, and all the recesses and towers of this wide wall and his sons Ḏamaryadaʿ and Sumhuʾamar and all his children and his slaves and all his palm groves in ʾAḏanat: Kutum and Warq; and of Tarid and Waġimum and ʿAsmat and Baraʾum and Zimmân and Ḥagarû and Gadilum and Siḥum and Maṭrân in Yasrân, irrigated by the sluice-ways, and Radmân in Yasrân, irrigated by the deflector-dam, and Maẖḏan in Yuhdil, when [ʾIlumquh had granted to him. . . .

2 **Triple symbol** what He has promised him [Tabaʿkarib] concerning a child; and when Yakrubmalik Waṭar had appointed him and he then had stayed in the hostilities against Sabaʾ and the tribes for five years during the war of Qatabân; and ʾIlumquh had saved all Sabaʾ and the tribes and all the foot-soldiers [whom] he had conducted against the town Tahargab during the two whole years he was in command in the hostilities against Sabaʾ and the tribes, and he came back to Mârib after making peace

between Sabaʾ and Qatabân, and [after] Yaṯaᶜʾamar Bayyin and Sabaʾ presented him with a testimony of confidence. By ᶜAṯtar and by Hawbas and by ʾIlumquh and by D̲ât-Ḥimyâm and by D̲ât-Baᶜdânum and by D̲ât-Ġaḍarân and by Yadaᶜʾil Bayyin and by Yakrubmalik Watar and by Yaṯaᶜʾamar Bayyin and by Karibʾil Watar and by his [Tabaᶜkarib] father, D̲amaryadaᶜ, descendant of Mad̲marum.

L. 1: *tbᶜkrb*, and not *krbᶜt̲t* (as *CIH*, II, p. 27: transliteration in Hebrew characters); e.g., Ja 217, Qat. – *ršw* (e.g., Ja 852/7, Qat) indicates the function of the priesthood; *ršwt* means "family of priests" (e.g., Ja 540 A/4, Qat). – *d̲t/ġḍrn*, female sun deity (cf. *JaP*, p. 105 and *JaRSAP*, p. 267). – *qyn*, e.g., RÉS 3540 b/1 (concerning RÉS 3540 a and b, cf. *JaPSAP*, pp. 101-02 and 117-18); pl. *ʾqyn*, e.g., RÉS 4963/1 and construct dual *qyny* in Ja 556; noun derived from the same root as that of the name of the deity *qynn* "Qaynân", who probably was, according to Semitic cognates, the god of the smiths (cf. *JaP*, pp. 133-34 and *JaRSAP*, p. 273; cf. also *MoNTA*, p. 343). *qyn* (cf. *PiPISA*, p. 139, note 5) indicates a high-ranking official in charge of economic matters which may belong, e.g., to a ruler (e.g., Ja 550, 552, and 555) or temple (here), and in itself has nothing to do either with the priesthood or politics. The function of *qyn* is very well illustrated by Ja 555/4; *d̲mrkrb* was *qyn* of four *mukarribs* (cf. *JaPSAP*, p. 139; contrast *LuYFS*, pp. 8 and 14, note 27) and one of his functions is described as follows: "he prepared all skin cover(s) and garments and all preparations of [for] the war of Sumhuᶜalay". Further, there is no reason to believe that the *qyn* function here was military (as *RycIMAM*, p. 146). On the contrary, *tbᶜkrb*'s appointment, mentioned in line 2 as given to him by *ykrbmlk/wtr*, is independent from his function as *qyn* which he already had during the reign of *ydᶜʾl/byn*, the father of the above-mentioned ruler. The opposition between the *qyn* function and a military job is parallel to the opposition between *ršw* "priest" and *qyn*, two different functions held by the same *tbᶜkrb*. Compare the Qat parallel *rby*, who was an economic administrator of a temple, but not necessarily a priest (cf. *JaRSAP*, pp. 292-93). – *sḥr*: probably deity according to *RhSLG* (II, p. 18), but clan name according to *CIH* (II, p. 27 A), followed by *RyNP* (I, p. 306 A); however, on the basis of the references mentioned by *CIH* and *RyNP*, one would expect *qyn/d̲sḥr* (cp. *bny/d̲sḥr* in CIH 457/2); on the other hand, it would be surprising to find a clan name preceding the names of three rulers; *sḥr* is the name of the Sab stellar god (cf. *JaP*, p. 99 and *JaRSAP*, p. 266); the preceding interpretation explains the fact that *sḥr* precedes the mention of three rulers. Cf. also commentary on Ja 567/3: *sḥr*, clan name. – *ydᶜʾl*, very well-known name of a man; e.g., Ja 540 A/1, CIH 979 (cf. *JaPSAP*, pp. 63, 82, 85-86, and 175), RÉS 3120 (cf. *JaPSAP*, pp. 111-12 and 158-59), and Gl 1703/3: *y(d)*[*ᶜʾl*], cf. *l.c.*, pp. 112-13. The decipherment published in this reference was thoroughly checked on the squeezes themselves (on July 15, 1960, during a research trip sponsored by the *American Philosophical Society*, Philadelphia). Furthermore, the important palaeographic remarks stated in *l.c.*, p. 143, are also confirmed by the squeezes themselves. One cannot expect that all the measurements taken from small photographs would be exactly identical with those of the squeezes. However, the most important point in this case is that the general conclusion based on the first measurements is confirmed by the second ones. The first column of the following scheme mentions several letters of Gl 1703; the second gives the proportion between the letter height and its width based on my measurements from photographs, and the third the same proportion (cf. *l.c.*) followed by my measurements (in cm.) taken from the squeeze A 590c.

m of line	7	2.727	2.5;	6 cm. × 2.4;
	8	2.666	2.8;	7 cm. × 2.5;
d of line	6	2.307	2.407;	6.5 cm. × 2.7;
k of line	8	2.307	2.285;	6.4 cm. × 2.8;
b of line	6	2.142	2.248;	6.3 cm. × 2.9;
	7	2.357	2.333;	7 cm. × 3;
	8	2.166	2.460;	6.4 cm. × 2.6;
line 12:	*m*	1.857	1.781;	5.7 cm. × 3.2;
	d	1.625	1.6;	5.6 cm. × 3.5;
	k	1.857	1.838;	(5.7 cm.) × 3.1;
	b	1.857	1.838;	(5.7 cm.) × 3.1;
m of line	9	1.866	1.842;	7 cm. × 3.8;
b of line	11	1.437	1.388;	5 cm. × 3.6.

Cf. also the clan name *ydᶜ*, e.g., in Ja 404/1, Min. – *wtr*: *UlSLE* (p. 156 and note 5) proposes translating *wtr* as "lasting, eternal"; it is difficult to admit such an idea in South Arabian (cf. also

MoNTA, p. 359); the verb *wtr* is attested, e.g., in Ja 541/3. – *bn*: cf. *CoRoC*, p. 115 A; for the Western Semitic cognates, cf. *JeHoDISO*, p. 37: bn_{I}. – *ḏmrydᶜ* is the name of both the father and the first listed son of *tbᶜkrb*; the latter and his son *ḏmrᶜly* are not to be identified with *tbᶜkrb/wḏmrᶜly*, the authors of Gl 1131+1132+1133 (cf. *HöDSP*, pp. 40-41; the interchange of the numbers of this reference in Gl 1132+1133+1131 [as *PiPISA*, pp. 167, 188, and 189] is not correct nor is adequate "Gl 1131+1131+1134" in *LuYFS*, p. 12, note 15) in spite of another possible common mention, that of *ytᶜᵓmr* and *ydᶜᵓl* in the latter and *yṯᶜᵓmr/byn* and *ydᶜᵓl/byn* in the first, because the ancestor is different in each case: *ḏmrᶜly* here, but *b*(?)[...in the other inscription. It is true that the first letter of the name of the ancestor in Gl 1131+1132+1133 does not seem certain according to M. Höfner. However, in case of doubtful reading, *ḏ* would be much closer to *b* than *d*. *ḏmr* enters as component into many proper names; e.g., *ḏmrwqh* (Ja 540 A/3) and in the present collection *ḏmr*, *ḏmry*, *ḏmrᶜly*, and *ḏmrkrb*. – *mḏmrm*, family name (e.g., *RhSLG*, II, p. 18) and not personal name (e.g., *CIH*, I, p. 77, commentary on CIH 46/5, *RyNP*, I, p. 70 and II, p. 82 B, and *RycIMAM*, p. 156). On the one hand, its onomastics differ entirely from that of the other personal names mentioned in the texts engraved on the enclosing wall of ᵓAwwâm, these names being composed of two (verbal+verbal or verbal+pronominal) elements. On the other hand, its onomastics fit perfectly that of the other family or clan names which are composed of only one verbal element. – *hqny*, cf. *JaASAB*, p. 157, commentary on CIH 407/5. – *ᵓlmqh*, cf. *JaP*, pp. 62-67, *JaRSAP*, p. 260, *JaISAR*, p. 107 (commentary on Ja 510) and *JaASAB*, pp. 157-58, commentary on CIH 407/5. The present collection also offers the following spellings of the name of the Sab moon god: *ᵓlmw* (Ja 699/9), *ᵓlmq* (e.g. Ja 708/4), *ᵓlmqw* (Ja 733/9) and *lmqh* (Ja 579/13) (cf. *JaAGM*, p. 300, and A. Jamme, in *BiO*, 14 [1957], p. 80 A); cf. also *ᵓlqhw* in RÉS 4938/4. In *Atti della Accademia dei Lincei. Rendiconti. Classe di Scienze morali, storiche e filologiche* (13 [1958], p. 354), P. Boneschi proposes his own interpretation: "la mia ultima [the thirty-fourth one indicated in his study based exclusively on philology] ipotesi, secondo la quale *al-qahwān* sarebbe un vocabolo sudarabico... *ᵓīl-mā-qáhū*...'*Deus ille* [, qui caelestis] *ibex* [est]'". It suffices to note here that the South Arabian word for "ibex" is *wᶜl*. – *kl*: cf. *CoRoC*, p. 168 B; for the Western Semitic cognates, cf. *JeHoDISO*, pp. 118-20: Kl_{I}. – *tmlᵓ*, cf. *RhSLG*, II, p. 13 and note 2. – *gnᵓ* is either a noun (here and also, e.g., in Ja 404/4, Min) or verb (e.g., Ja 514); cf. the masculine personal name *gnᵓn* in Ja 558/3 (cf. *JaPSAP*, pp. 163-64 and 191, note 76). – *ln/ᵓᵓwdn/ᵓly/sṭrn* (lit. "from the lines, these of the inscription"), cf. the singular formula *ln/ᵓwdn/ḏsṭrn* in Ja 551 and *ln/ḏn/sṭrn* in Ja 539/1; the basic meaning of the root *sṭr* is "to mark"; the verb *sṭr* "to write" is attested, e.g., in Ja 540 A/3; two meanings of the noun *sṭr* are actually known: "script" or "document" and "patch (of grazing land)" (cf. Ist 7630/6; cf. *BeFSTI*, pp. 277-82). *ln...ᶜd=ln...ᶜdy* (e.g., Ja 551): composite preposition "from...to" (cf. *HöASG*, p. 150); the preposition *ln* is also attested alone (e.g., Ja 633/16); for the conjunction *ln*, cf. commentary on Ja 584/7. – *mġbb*, as well as *mġb*, plural (cf. the dual *mġbtnhn* in Ja 556; contrary to *MoMiSI*, p. 33) of *mġbt* (e.g., RÉS 4795, Ist 7628/2 [cf. *BeFSTI*, p. 276] and Ja 556); *CIH* (II, p. 25): "vallum"; *RhSLG* (II, p. 12 in CIH 374 and p. 22 in CIH 375): "Wall (Graben)" (cf. also *RhSLG*, II, p. 13 and note 13) and also *HöASG*, p. 129, and finally *RÉS*: "remblai (digue)" in RÉS 2654 and "barrage" in RÉS 4794; the noun refers to the parts separated from each other by towers, according to the Arabic verb indicating both ideas of interval and recess (cf. also *LaH*, p. 668). – *mḥfd*, pl. *mḥfdt*, e.g., Ja 857/2 and Ja 403, Min; cf. the Ḥaḍr parallel *mgdl* in RÉS 4852/6 (cf. the proper name *gdlm*, below). – *mhyᶜ*, cf. *CIH*, I, p. 394 B; *RhSLG* (II, p. 14) translates it as "Tempel" (cf. also *HöASG*, e.g., p. 97); *mhyᶜ* (from *hyᶜ*; cf. Ja 643/15 and commentary) refers to the wall and emphasizes the thickness of the masonry according to the Arabic verb *hâᶜa* I "to be spread" and its derived terms *mahyaᶜ* and *mahyâᶜ* "opened and wide (road)" and also *mahyaᶜ* "large road" (cf. also *DoSDA*, II, p. 775 A). – *smhᵓmr*, e.g., RÉS 2726/23; the expression *smh* "his name" is frequently used in proper names; e.g., *smhwtr* (e.g., Ja 832), *smhyfᶜ* (e.g., Ja 615/16-17), *smhkrb* (e.g., Ja 567/7), and also *ydᶜsmh(w)*, name of a Sab deified king (cf. *JaP*, p. 144; the personal pronoun *h*[*w*] indicates that the man bearing the preceding name belonged to Sabaᵓ, contrary to

RycIMAM, p. 112). – *qny* "slave" or (collect.) "slaves"; cf. *BeSI*, p. 78 and *HöASG*, p. 184; contrary to *RycIMAM* (p. 144), who identifies *ᶜbd* and *qny* (cf. A. F. L. Beeston, in *BiO*, 9 [1952], p. 215 B; for *ᶜbd*, cf. the commentary on Ja 557); pl.: *ʾqny*, e.g., RÉS 3966/7 and *HöASG*, p. 34. – *nḫl*, pl. *ʾnḫl*, e.g., Ja 541/9-10; in RÉS 4781/1, 1-2 and 3, read *nḫlnhn* instead of *nḫlhn*. – *ʾḏnt*: Wâdî Ḏanah (cf. *RhSLG*, II, p. 23 and *JaAGM*, p. 291, note 1, where *ḏnh* must be read instead of *dnh*); *ʾḏnt* is probably a feminine personal name in RÉS 4966/2; cf. also the masculine personal name *ʾḏnm* (e.g., RÉS 4860/3-4, Ḥaḍr), the clan name *mʾḏnm* (e.g., Ja 564/12) and the second masculine name *yhʾḏn* in Ja 489 A/1 (cf. *JaPSAP*, pp. 10, 11, 13, 43, and 185, note 26); cf. also the Arabic name of a man *ʾibn ʾuḏaynat* (cf. *WüID*, e.g., 106/12-13). – *ktm*, cf. *CIH*, II, p. 27 A, and also the Arabic personal name *kittâm* (cf. *SlGaVNPA*, p. 30 A). – *wrq*, cf. *CIH*, II, p. 27 and the noun, e.g., in RÉS 3910/7; cf. also the Arabic names of men *waraqat* and *warqāʾ* (cf. *WüID*, 102/5 and 280/10 respectively). – *trd*, also name of a palm-grove in RÉS 3889/3. – *wġmm*, cf. CIH, II, p. 27 B; in RÉS 5036/3, Ḥaḍr, read *bn/nġm* "son of Naġim" (instead of *bn yġm*) – *ᶜsmt*, RÉS 3945/4, name of a mountain; cp. *ᶜsmy* in Ja 682/2 and *ᶜsmm* in NaNN 57/2. – *brʾm*, cf. *CIH*, *l.c.*, personal name in Ja 484/1, Qat (cf. *JaAFEQ*, p. 191), and the feminine personal name in Ja 195, Qat (cf. *JaDME*, p. 18); cf. also *brʾn*, temple of ʾIlumquh, e.g., in Ja 534/2 and 535/7. – *ẓmn*, name of a man (NaNN 5/1) and of a person in Safaitic (cf. *LiSI*, p. 313 B) and in Thamudic (cf. *vdBrIT*, pp. 164-65: HU 772/2); cf. also *zimânî* (cf. *SlGaVNPA*, p. 51 B). – *ḥgrw*, same nominal formation as that, e.g., of *nrw*, Sab name of the stellar deity (cf. *JaP*, p. 100 and *JaRSAP*, p. 266), and also of *rbḥw* (RÉS 4608, instead of *rbḥ w*..., as *RÉS*, VII, p. 272); cf. the name of group *ḥgr/lmd* in Ja 616/25 and the name of a valley *ḥgrn* in RÉS 4351/1. – *gdlm*, cf. the name of group *gdlt* in Ja 616/25; cf. also the Arabic names *ğdylt* (person and clan; cf. *SaIS*, p. 38 B), *mğîdil* (man) and *ğidlā* (woman) (cf. *HeBN*, p. 14 B), *miğiddil* (person; cf. *SlGaVNPA*, p. 36 B), and also the Safaitic personal name *gdlt* (cf. *LiSI*, p. 304 A); cf. also the Ḥaḍr noun *mgdl* (cf. above). – *sḥm*, cf. the Arabic personal names of a woman *siḥmah*, of men *siḥmân* (cf. *HeBN*, p. 28 B) and *suḥaym* (cf. *WüID*, e.g., 62/22). – *mṭrn*, also name of palm-grove in RÉS 3913/3 and masculine personal name in RÉS 4546/1; cf. the noun *mṭr* "irrigated field", e.g., in Ja 735/6. – *ysrn/mflqn*, *ysrn/mḥmyn* (RÉS 3943/5) and *yhdl: ysrn* (RÉS 5096/2 and *bysrn* in RÉS 4793 and Ja 555/3) and *yhdl* are the names of two parts of *ʾḏnt*, and the first is specified by *mflqn* and *mḥmyn* (cf. *RhSLG*, II, p. 23). The interpretation of these two adjectives is clarified by RÉS 4626/2: *mḥmtm/wṣᶜtm/wmflqm* translated by *RhSLG* (II, p. 120) as follows: "Eindämmung und Überflutung und Öffnung (Durchlassen des Wassers)" and by *HöIAI* (p. 81) as: "Führung (des Wassers) mittels Dammsystem und Überflutung und Öffnung (Durchlassen des Wassers)". For *mḥmt*, cf. Arabic *muḥâmin* "clôture" (cf. *DoSDA*, I, p. 330 A); for *ṣᶜt*, cp. Arabic *ṣâᶜa*, II "to divide two things by separation", and for *mflq*, cf. *CoRoC*, p. 218 B: Arabic *falq* "crevice, split" (cf. also *MoNTA*, pp. 318-19). It seems that *mḥmt*, *ṣᶜt*, and *mflq* indicate three different parts of the irrigation system, namely the deflector dam itself characterized by its lateral walls, the canal system of distributing water, and finally the sluice-ways. I would therefore suggest translating the two adjectives in the present text respectively as "irrigated by the dam itself" and "irrigated by the system of sluice-ways". – *rdmn*, name of a well-known tribe (e.g., Ja 576/3); cf. also the personal name *rdmyn* in Ja 755/1 and the proper name *rdmw* in Ja 513/1. – *mḫdn*, for the root *mḫd* and the noun *mḫdn*, cf. commentary on Ja 555/4. – *yhdl*, cp. the following personal names *hdl* in Safaitic (cf. *LiSI*, p. 309 A) and in Thamudic (cf. *vdBrIT*, p. 332: HU 624), and in Arabic *al-hadl* (cf. *SaIS*, p. 242 B) and *hadîl* (cf. *SlGaVNPA*, p. 22 B). – *ywm*: we have no indication with respect to the contemporaneity of the two facts mentioned in the phrases introduced by *ywm* (cf. *JaIMT*, p. 145) just as it occurs in Semitic cognates (cf. also *JeHoDISO*, pp. 107-08: jm_{II}).

End of line 1: according to *RhSLG* (II, pp. 23-24), the end of line is possibly missing, in spite of E. Glaser's notebook. The two lines of the inscription were almost certainly of equal length (cf. also Ja 553 and 556). But, line 1 is actually much shorter than line 2, and the construction *ywm/hwfy/dt/tnbʾhw* is unusual (cf. *RhSLG*, II, p. 23). The end of the line is certainly missing; at least the name of *ʾlmqh* (cf. Ja 555/3) and possibly also *yhwfyn* (cf. Ja 551 and 558/5) and other terms.

L. 2: *tnbʾhw*, cf. *RhSLG*, II, pp. 15 and 22, and also *HöASG*, p. 149 β. – *hwṣt*/ – – /*wtr*, cf. *RhSLG*, II, p. 22 and *HöIAI*, p. 96; for *hwṣt*, cf. also *RhSLG*, II, p. 8 and RÉS 4966/4; the noun *mwṣt* is mentioned, e.g., in CIH 338/5; *RyISA* reads (XII, pp. 299 and 300) and translates (p. 301) Geukens 1/27-28 as follows: – /*w*(28)[*b*]⌊ʾ⌋*brṯ*/*bhw*/*yhwṣthmw*/*mrʾhmw*/ – "– et [dans] les expéditions qu'entreprendrait leur seigneur – "; with regards to *bhw*, the commentary suggests "faute pour *bhmw*?" (p. 307). However, *bhw* suggests reading – *w*/[*b*](28)[*kl*]/*brṯ*/ – ; the preceding restoration is possible if the end of line 27 and the beginning of line 28 are compared with their parallels in the preceding and following lines; besides, *hmw* in *hwṣthmw* is not translated. The whole expression may be translated as follows: "– and [in every] expedition in which their lord shall appoint them –". – *ʿqb*, RÉS 4450; cf. *CoRoC*, p. 211 B; cf. also the nouns *ʿqb* "representative," e.g., in Ja 577/10, and *ʿqbt*, "slope" in Ja 649/31; the meaning of the verb is also attested in the collective Ḥaḍr noun *msʿqb* "equipage" (Ingrams 1/5; for the latter, cf. A. J. Drewes, in *BiO*, 11 [1954], pp. 93-94; cf. *JaIHI*, p. 101) and in Sab *mʿqbt* with the same meaning (RÉS 5085/10; cf. *UlSLE*, p. 156. – *kbt*, cf. *CoRoC*, p. 167 A. – *bʿly*=*bʿl*=*bʿlw* in Qat (cf. *HöASG*, p. 158) and Sab (Ja 643/29). – *šʿb*, cf. *HöBAI*, pp. 61-62. – *ḫmst*, cf. *StSESA*, p. 522. – *ḍr* means either "war" (here) or "foe" (e.g., Ja 564/25); cf. *StSESA*, p. 517. – *rgl* (cf. *CoRoC*, p. 237 B), *rgly* (construct dual; e.g., CIH 351/6), and plurals *ʾrgl* (e.g., Ja 576/14) and *rgl* (Ja 577/5). In CIH 375/2, *ʾrgl* is commonly translated "men" (e.g., *CIH* and *RÉS*, VI, p. 279, in the commentary on RÉS 3695/9; cf., e.g., in Ẓofâr *rajjâl* "Mann"; cf. *RhVDD*, p. 21 A.) However, the context being military, one should expect *ʾ*(*n*)*s* or *ʾsd*. On the basis of the military context, I translate *rgl* in Ja 550/2, 576/14, 577/5, and 665/24, as "foot-soldier" (cf. Arabic *rağil* and *rağîl* "pedestrian, footman", as opposed to *râkib*). Cf. also *rgly* (Ja 566/1), that may be related to *raglî* "who walks on foot" in Hebrew (cf. *KoBaLVTL*, p. 873 A) and "footman, runner" in post-Biblical Hebrew (cf. *JaDT*, p. 1449 B), where the expression *rgly*/*mlkn* is comparable to *ʿbd*/*mlkn* in South Arabian. – *hwrd* "to lead, conduct, guide", 4th form of *wrd* "to come down" (cf. *CoRoC*, p. 140 B). – *thrgb*, cf. the Arabic personal name *riğib* (cf. *SlGaVNPA*, p. 44 A). – *bkl*/*ḫrfy*/*hrs*: this expression is certain on the stone; F. Fresnel's copy (cf. *JA*, 6 [1845], p. 181) has *bklḫrfy*/*hrs*, which is accepted by *CIH* (II, p. 26) in his transliteration in South-Arabian letters; however, *CIH* writes *bkl*[/]*ḫrfy*/*hrs* in his transliteration in Hebrew characters (p. 26) and also *bkl*/*ḫrfy*/*hrs* both in his commentary (p. 27) and his final transliteration of the text (p. 28). In *RhSLG*'s (II, p. 15) transliteration, *ḫrfy* has disappeared: *bkl*/*hrs*. *ḫrfy* is normally interpreted as a dual construct. The two-year campaign against the town Tahargab is a part of the five-year military activity of Tabaʿkarib during the Sab-Qat war; cf. the identical expression *bkbtn*/*bʿly*/*sbʾ*/*wʾšʿbn*. – *hrs*: the equation Hebrew *hrs* = the present form *hrs*, accepted by *StSESA* (p. 533), was discarded by *BeSI*, who relates it to *rsy* (p. 74), but mentions it under *rs* (p. 147); it was re-stated very recently by *UlCSH* (p. 196) and *LeESAC* (p. 18). *hrs* and *strs* (Ja 561 bis /9) are respectively the 4th and 10th forms of *rys*, and may be translated "to be in command" and "to be chosen as chief" respectively. – *ʾtw*/*ʿd*/*mryb*/*bslm*/*sbʾ*/*wqtbn*: *CIH* (II, p. 28): "venit ad Maryabum in pace Sabaeorum et Ḳatabânitarum"; *CoRoC* (p. 196 A) has about the same translation: "rediit usque ad (urbem) Maryab in pace cum Sabaeis et Qatabānensibus"; *RhSLG* (II, p. 22): "(TBʿKRB) nach Mârib gebracht hat den Frieden zwischen Sabaʾ und Ḳatabān"; the preceding translation distorts the grammatical value of *bslm*; *HöASG* (p. 141 δ) probably felt this difficulty and therefore writes: "'ʾ*tw*' '*bslm*' 'und er brachte' 'den Frieden' (wörtl. 'kamm mit den Frieden')". The interpretation of *slm* as noun (cf. all the preceding translations and also *BeSI*, p. 130) makes these translations rather complicated and distorts the syntax of the phrase. I propose interpreting *slm* as a denominative verb, as in CIH 308 bis (cf. *BeSI*, *l.c.*) (cp. *bhwfyn* in RÉS 4176/13), of the 2nd form (cf. *CoRoC*, *l.c.*). For *ʾtw* (e.g., RÉS 4842/1), two variants of which are *ʾty* (e.g., Ja 577/11) and *wtw* (attested in the 4th form in Ja 560/4), cf. *CoRoC*, p. 110 A; Arabic *ʾatā* (*i*). – *mryb* and later *mrb* (e.g., CIH 407/10 and Ja 576/2); cf. *JaISAR*, pp. 104-05, note 1; cf. also the beautiful expression *ʾlmqh*/*ḏmryb* in Ja 533. On a stone fallen from the enclosing wall and found in the sand, there are only three letters: . . . *m*]*ryb* "*Mâ*]*rib*", which is identical with the contents of RÉS 4442 (Gl 583). Any identification between these two texts is however very difficult since the fallen stone was not and very probably has never been "verkehrt eingemauert" as is the case of Gl 583 according to *GrKFG* (p. 78). – *ḥṯb/lhw/–/tʾmnm*, cf. commentary on Ja 555/4, where the context is more elaborate; *hṯb*, 4th form of *ṯwb* (cf. *StSESA*, p. 527 and *JaFSR*, pp. 16-17) means "to present" in Ja 506 A/2; *hṯb* is also a masculine personal name in RÉS 4617; for [*h*]*ṯb* in RÉS 4612, cf. commentary on Ja 585/1: *hᶜll*; proper names with the 4th verbal form are frequent; e.g., *hyṯᶜ* in Ja 741/6 and also *hṣrḥ* in RÉS 4972/1 (instead of *hṣmḥ*); *tʾmn* may be translated "testimony of confidence" (cf. commentary on Ja 555/4); this testimony was given to Tabaᶜkarib by "Yaṯaᶜʾamar Bayyin and Sabaʾ" and neither by "Karibʾil et Saba" or "Yaṯaᶜʾamar seul" (as *RycIMAM*, pp. 13 and 156 respectively). – *b*...introducing a nominal list; J. Walker translates this preposition as "in the name of" in RÉS 4842/11; there is no reason to believe that *b* is equivalent to *bsm*. Furthermore, several expressions occurring in Sab inscriptions have been studied by *RycIMAM* (pp. 139-43) and are interpreted indistinctly as "Les invocations" (*l.c.*, p. 138). Yet, they are three different things. The first two formulas, *brᶜẓ* (*l.c.*, p. 139) and *bmq*(*y*)*m*(*t*) (*l.c.*, p. 140) attested in some texts commemorating the construction of buildings indicate (as already pointed out in *JaCD*, p. 3), particular interventions of certain deities in human activities described in the texts. The third formula (cf. *RycIMAM*, p. 139) is composed of a list, more or less elaborated, and introduced by the preposition *b* "by"; it normally characterizes the end of dedicatory inscriptions (cf. *JaCD*, p. 32); the whole formula, usually called final invocation, is to be interpreted as a petition connected with oath and directed to the persons, divine or human, mentioned in the list. Contrary to the preceding formula, the present one has no syntactic connection with the rest of the text. The fourth formula "employée dans les dédicaces ne varie guère. En voici le texte: *lsᶜdhmw rḍw mrʾhmw X mlk sbʾ*" (cf. *RycIMAM*, p. 141). After mentioning that the noun *ḥẓy* may also follow *rḍw*, the same author writes: "On connaît un seul exemple d'une formule plus étendue encore: *ltʾzl sᶜḏhmw ḥẓy wrḍw mrʾyhmw*" (*l.c.*) with reference to note 23 which reads as follows: "Yarîm ʾAymân et Karibʾil Watar: RES 4190, 13-14." The first quoted formula is still the only one occurring in the texts of the present collection and belonging to the beginning of the Hamdanid period which is dealt with by the author, and is but one kind of petition mentioned in those dedicatory inscriptions. Further, the text of RÉS 4190/13-14 is different from that reproduced by *RycIMAM*, where *ltʾzl* and *sᶜḏhmw* should in any event be corrected to *ltẓʾn* and *sᶜdhmw* respectively; it reads as follows: (line 11)...*/wl/sᶜ* (line 12) *dhmw/.../ḥẓy/w* (line 13) [*r*]*ḍw/mrʾyhmw/yrm/ʾymn* (line 14) *wkrbʾl/wtr*. I suspect that the author has mixed RÉS 4149/4-5: *lt*()*ẓʾn/sᶜ*[*dhmw/ḥẓy/wrḍw/mrʾh*]*mw*, which mentions *śᶜrm/ʾwtr/mlk/sbʾ/wḏrydn* (line 3), with RÉS 4190/11-14. – *ᶜṯtr*, cf. *JaP*, pp. 85-96, *BePESA*, p. 21, note 1, *JaIMT*, p. 129 and commentary on Ja 559/18. Note that *MoNTA* (p. 324) refers to the root *ᶜṯr*. A. van den Branden remarks that no "tutto soddisfacente" etymology has ever been presented (cf. *Bibbia e Oriente*, 2 [1960], p. 42 A and *vdBrHT*, p. 109). This author however neither expresses his objection/s to any etymology previously suggested nor attempts to propose his own solution. Further, *LuYFS* (p. 6) states: "habituellement, on admet que même les inscriptions les plus anciennes ne gardent que les traces de l'ancien culte d'ᶜAṯtar", with the only reference to W. Caskel in *Le antiche divinità semitiche* (Rome, 1958), pp. 105-06. But, W. Caskel does not make such a statement. The problem which is probably alluded to by *LuYFS*, is discussed in *JaP* (p. 147) and *JaRSAP* (p. 277, last paragraph). However, W. Caskel inaccurately affirms that ᶜAṯtar is the first-ranking deity in Sabaʾ and Maᶜîn (cf., e.g., *JaP*, *l.c.* and *JaRSAP*, pp. 276-77). Furthermore, the Qat rock inscriptions from the country of Mukérâs present other spellings of this name: *ᶜśtr*, *ᶜśt*, and *ᶜtr* (cf. *JaIRM*, pp. 309-10). – *hwbs*, cf. *JaP*, pp. 68-69, *JaDME*, p. 5 and *JaRSAP*, p. 261. – *ḏt/ḥmym* and *ḏt/bᶜdnm*, names of the female sun deity characterized as the sun in summer and winter time respectively (cf. *JaP*, pp. 103-05, *JaRSAP*, pp. 266-67 and commentary on Ja 618/35-36; cf. also *MoNTA*, p. 105 for *ḏt/bᶜdn*, and p. 115 where *ḏt/ḥmym* is related to the root *ḥmm*; it seems strange that one of the three *principal* deities would have as name a *diminutive* form: *ḥumaym*). For *ḏtḥ*[*mym*], cf. Ja 863/5, Qat. My identification of these two divine names is considered as "précaire" by J. Ryckmans (cf. *BiO*, 17 [1960], p. 206 B) because of two reasons which need to be discussed here. The *first* reason is composed of two parts: "il n'est pas établi que les termes *d̲t ḥmym* et *d̲t bᶜdn* aient désigné la déesse solaire Šams, avec laquelle ils ne sont jamais confondus" and "il est peu probable que la seconde se réfère à l' 'éloignement' d'hiver du soleil, puisque c'est en plein été que se situe l'aphélie de la terre, ce qui fut établi dès l'antiquité". The *second* reason is that the "appellations des divinités...sont empruntées à un texte étranger aux lionnes et même à la maison Yafaš". With regard to the *first reason*, it is regretful that the author did not take advantage of his review to publish at least a summary of his own identification of both *d̲t/ḥmym* and *d̲t/bᶜdn* and also of his own interpretation of *d̲t/bᶜdn*, as he did for the Qat noun *ᵓḫ̲tb* (p. 206 B; his suggestion is already disproved by *JaIRHY*, p. 184 A). Furthermore, the true meaning of his remark, "avec laquelle ils ne sont jamais confondus", remains unknown. Finally, the reason for rejecting that *d̲t/bᶜdn* characterizes the sun in winter, is surprising and anachronic. The name *d̲t/bᶜdn* was used by Sabaeans, even according to the chronology accepted by the author, *several centuries* before the time of the discovery of the aphelion by Greek science. Moreover, the origin of this name as well as that of the other divine appellations must be sought in popular beliefs. The *second reason* is rather amazing. The author denies any importance to Ja 122, a text which was found only a few meters east from the house Yafaš, and also to another *Qat* text, RÉS 4332, which he does not even mention. But, he favors a suggestion based on *Greek* stylistic parallels.

551 – Inscription engraved on the same masonry course as the 2nd line of Ja 550 and on the right of the latter; the two texts are separated from each other by 5.55 m.; four partial photographs; cf. *PhQS*, p. 219. – MaMB 2 (from *ᶜdy/šqrm* to the end, including the double symbol) = CIH 374 (cf. *RhSLG*, II, pp. 12-15); mentioned as Fakhry (88) (cf. *FaAJY*, I, p. 92).

INSCRIPTION: 13.75 m. × 27 cm.; distance to the upper edge of the stones: 1 cm. – SYMBOLS: single and double at the beginning and the end of the text respectively; distance from the double symbol to the last letter: 5 cm.; cf. Plate C, Fig. 2.

Single symbol *ᵓlšrḥ/bn/smhᶜly/d̲rḥ/mlk/sbᵓ/*
hqny/ᵓlmqh/kl/tmlᵓ/gnᵓn/ln/ᵓwdn/d̲sṭrn/ᶜdy/šqrm/wkl/
mġbb/wmḥfdt/bᶜly/d̲n/mhyᶜn/ḥgdt/wqh/ᵓlmqh/
ᵓlšrḥ/bmsᵓlm/bd̲t/hwfyhw/ᵓlmqh/wyhwfyn/d̲t/
tnbᵓhw/bᶜt̲tr/wb/hwbs/wb/ᵓlmqh/wbd̲t/ḥmym/wbd̲t/
bᶜdnm/wb/ᵓbhw/smhᶜly/d̲rḥ/mlk/sbᵓ/wb/ᵓḫ̲hw/krbᵓl
Double symbol

Single symbol ᵓIlšaraḥ, son of Sumhuᶜalay D̲ariḥ, king of Sabaᵓ, has dedicated to ᵓIlumquh the whole mass of the enclosing wall from the line of the inscription to the top and all the recesses and towers on this wide wall, as ᵓIlumquh had ordered to ᵓIlšaraḥ through an oracle, because ᵓIlumquh had granted him and shall grant what He has promised to him. By ᶜAt̲tar and by Hawbas and by ᵓIlumquh and by D̲ât-Ḥimyâm and by D̲ât-Baᶜdânum and by his father Sumhuᶜalay D̲ariḥ, king of Sabaᵓ and by his brother Karibᵓil. **Double symbol.**

For the palaeography of the text, cf. *JaPSAP*, pp. 121, 162-64, 174, 191, note 71. – *ᵓlšrḥ*, frequently used name; e.g., Ja 860, Qat. – *smhᶜly/d̲rḥ*, e.g., Ja 540 A/1. – *mlk*: this noun also means "property, estate" (e.g., Ja 577/7); the verb *mlk* means "to become king" (RÉS 3945/1; cf. *JaPSAP*, pp. 146-50), "to reign over" (RÉS 3878/3, Qat; cf. *JaPSAP*, pp. 21, 36 and 165-66) and "to possess (?)" (CIH 505/1). – *ḥgdt/wqh/ᵓlmqh/–/bmsᵓlm*: ordinary formula (cp. *ḥgn/wqhhmw ᵓlmqh/bmsᵓlhw* in Ja 563/4-5) indicating that the deity himself took the initiative of ordering a gift (cf. *BeSI*, pp. 2-3). – *wqh*, e.g., Ja 541/3 and *yqh* in the feminine form *yhqt* in NaNN 74/5. – *krbᵓl*, e.g., Ja 541/3-4.

The inscription Ja 551 bis = AM 207 is spurious; lines 1-13 and 14-17 were copied from Ja 551 and 534 (cf. *JaPSAP*, pp. 48, 50-51 and 73) respectively. STONE: limestone; average thickness: 8 cm.; front: 25.5 cm. × 45.3. – INSCRIPTION: letters and spaces between the lines are so irregular that no measurement, even approximative, can be given, except that line 17 is about 7 cm. from the lower edge of the stone. Line 1 is preceded by a symbol composed of the letter *ṣ* of late period (thus, with only two vertical strokes in the lower part); the letter is upside down but aslant at about 45° to the left; between the two lower vertical strokes, a sign which may be compared with a capital *I*.

1 **Symbol** *ʾlšrḥ/bn/smhʿly/ḏr⌉*
2 *ḥ/mlk/sbʾ/hqny/ʾlm*
3 *qh/kl/tmlʾbnʾn/ln/*
4 *ʾwdn/ḏsṭrnʿdy/šqrm*
5 */wkl/mġbb/wmḥfdt/bʿ/y*
6 */ḏn/mhyʿn/ḥgḏt/wqh/*
7 *ʾlmqh/ʾlšrḥ/bmsʾ/m/bḏ*
8 *t/hwfyhw/ʾlmqh/wyh*
9 *wfyn/ḏt/tnbʾhw/bʿṯ*
10 *tr/wb/hwbs/wb/ʾlmqh/*
11 *wḏt/ḥmym/wbḏt/bʿdnm/*
12 *wb/ʾbhw/smhʿly/ḏrḥ/m*
13 *lk/sbʾ/wb/ʾẖhw/krbʾl*
14 *ẖḏwʾl/śn/hʿzgn/whr*
15 *ʾšn/bn/krbl/ṣrf/ʾmq*
16 *h/bʿl/brʾn/mḥrmn/*
17 *brʾn*

552 – Inscription on the northwest wall; two masonry courses below Ja 550 and 6.86 m. to the north of the end of the 2nd line of the latter; photograph in Plate 3. – MaMB 6.

The text is engraved on four stones in two courses; the lower left-hand corner of the left stone in the lower course has been cut off and two small stones have been added. – STONES: total length: 2.67 m.; total height: 60.3 cm. (28.8 cm. for the upper range and 31.5 for the lower one). – INSCRIPTION: boustrophedon; each line presents three horizontal lines superficially traced (cf. Ja 127). L. 1: 2.47 m. × 11.6 cm.; distance to the upper edge of the stones: 2.5 cm., to the right edge: 17 cm., to the symbol: 1.6 cm., and to line 2: 2.3 cm. L. 2: 2.56 m. × 11.3 cm.; distance to the right edge of the stone: 9.3 cm., and to the lower edge: 1 cm. L. 3: 2.54 m. × 11.6 cm.; distance to the right corner of the stone: 7.6 cm., to the upper edge: 1 cm., and to line 4: 2.5 cm. L. 4: 2.415 m. × 11.3 cm.; distance to the right edge: 33.3 cm. – SYMBOL: at the beginning of lines 1 and 2; cf. Plate C, Fig. 2.

1 **Sym-** ← *ʾbkrb/kbr/kmdm/bn/ʿmkrb/bn/[š]wḏbm/ qyn/ydʿʾl/byn/wsmh[ʿl]*
2 **bol** → *[y/]⌈ynf/hqny/ʾlmqh/bnhw/smhʾmr/ wʾbʾmr/whlkʾmr/wkl/wldh*
3 ← *w/wbythw/yhr/wkl/qnyhw/wkl/ mbny[/]ẖẖnhn/wmḏqntn/bʿṯtr*
4 → *wb/ʾlmqh/wb/ḏtḥmym/wb[/]ḏtbʿdn/ wb/ydʿʾl/wb/smhʿly*

1 **Sym-** ʾAbkarib, leader of [the clan] Kamidum, son of ʿAmmkarib, people of [the family Ša]wḏabum, administrator for Yadaʿʾil Bayyin and for Sumhu[ʿala-]
2 **bol** [y] Yanûf, has dedicated to ʾIlumquh his sons Sumhuʾamar and ʾAbʾamar and Halakʾamar and all his chil-
3 dren and his house Yahar and all his slaves and all the construction of the two passages and of the oratory. By ʿAṯtar
4 and by ʾIlumquh and by Ḏât-Ḥimyâm and by Ḏât-Baʿdân and by Yadaʿʾil and by Sumhuʿalay.

L. 1: *ʾbkrb*, e.g., RÉS 3908/3, Ja 548/1, 862, Qat and 404/1, Min. – *kbr* (cf. also *MoNTA*, pp. 342-43 and *JeHoDISO*, p. 115: *kbr*$_{II}$), this noun may indicate several different kinds of leadership (cf. *RhSLG*, II, p. 150); here, the leadership of a clan; *krb* may thus be translated as "leader" (cf. *BePC*: "chief" in RÉS 4877/2-3, Ḥaḍr, and *RÉS*: "chef", e.g., in RÉS 4798 A); however, the noun is more often only transcribed (e.g., *RÉS*: "Kabir", e.g., in RÉS 3022/1, or "kabîr", e.g., in RÉS 4963/1); the plural of *kbr* with the preceding meaning is *kbwr* (e.g., RÉS 2633/6 and Ja 547/2) and *ʾkbrw* (e.g., CIH 618/1). Very often, *kbr* is an abstract noun indicating the "leadership" (e.g., RÉS 2771/7, Min); *kbr* is also an adjective, "great" (RÉS 2695/6). The verb *kbr* usually means "to be the leader of" (e.g., RÉS 2742/2, 2743/8, and 3535/2, where *RÉS* respectively translates in "exercer le Kabirat", "diriger" and "gouverner comme Kabir"). Finally, *kbrm* is a second masculine name in RÉS 2717/1. – *kmdm*, cf. the following personal names: Arabic *kimmâd* (cf. *VNIA*, p. 210 B) and Safaitic *kmd* (cf. *LiSI*, p. 321 A); the decipherment *ʾk(?)md* in Safaitic CIS 1 (cf. *CIS*, pp. 1-2) must be discarded; the personal name is formed of five letters and one could read *ʾlnmd* (as Abel) or *ʾbkmd*. – *bn/–/bn*, cf. *JaPEHA*, pp. 20-23, formula G. – *ʿmkrb*, e.g., Gl 1575+1130+1134/1 (cf. *HöDSP*, p. 39; concerning this text, cf. *JaPSAP*, pp. 115-17) and Ja 852/5, Qat; same nominal formation as that of *ʿmyṯʿ* (e.g., Ja 555/2), *ʿmsmʿ* (e.g., Ja 404/1, Min), *ʿmrfʾ* (e.g., Ja 767/6) and *ʿmšfq* (e.g., Ja 674 B/1), and also *ʿmšrr* "ʿAmšarr" in RÉS 5040 bis B. *RÉS* (VII, p. 488) notes that "à part quelques exceptions, ces graffites ne sont susceptibles d'aucune interprétation." His reading *ḥsrm*, whose dextrograde direction is not mentioned, is A. On the photograph listed as

"Freya Stark 52(3)" (cf. *RyISA*, VI, plate VIII, upper left corner), there are five other graffiti which are not deciphered either by *RyISA*, *l.c.*, p. 303) or *RÉS* (*l.c.*). B (see above) is dextrograde and is located below and to the right of A. Immediately to the right of B, and engraved almost vertically, the graffito C: *ᶜšš/bn lḥwd* "ᶜAšš, son of Laḥûd". To the right of the end of C, the dextrograde graffito D reads *ʾbẕr* "ʾAbzar". In the lower left corner of the photograph, the senestrograde graffito E is engraved aslant: *ḫlys* "Ḫulays"; and immediately below E, the senestrograde graffito F reads *ʾslb* "ʾAslab". – *šwḏbm*, the first letter is restored on the basis of Ja 553. *šwḏb* and its *scriptio defectiva šḏb* are known by the inscriptions from the Persian Gulf region; the first is in RÉS 4685/6-7 (=BM 130541) and probably in ᶜAin Jawan 1/4 (cf. F. V. Winnett, in *BASOR*, No. 102 [April, 1946], p. 4), and the second in Qatif 1/5 (cf. P. B. Cornwall, in *The Geographical Journal*, 107 [1946], p. 44 and Pl. 12).

Ll. 1-2: *smhᶜly*, e.g., Fakhry 24 (cf. *JaPSAP*, pp. 4, 7, and 83).

L. 2: *ʾbʾmr*, e.g., RÉS 3902 bis, No. 131/1. – *hlkʾmr*, e.g., RÉS 3099/2 (cf. *JaPSAP*, pp. 31, 40, 41, 42, and 44) and RÉS 4905/1 (the 2nd name of the man mentioned in this text is probably *ḫdyb* "Ḫudayb", instead of *h(?)dᶜ(?)b* or *ʾ(?)dᶜ(?)b* in *BeAIP*, p. 446, and of *ᶜ(?)dyb* in *RÉS*, VII, p. 411); same nominal formation as that of *hlksmᶜ* in Ja 682/1.

L. 3: *byt*, cf. remark in *JaDME*, p. 10, and the Western Semitic Cognates in *JeHoDISO*, pp. 35-36: *byt*$_{I}$. – *yhr*, well-known proper name, especially in Min, e.g., Ja 404/2: tower, RÉS 2771/5: house, and RÉS 3060/3: temple of ᶜAṯtar (cf. *JaP*, p. 91); in Sab, clan name in RÉS 3932/2. – *mbny*, e.g., Gl 1575+1130+1134/1 and Ja 404/2, Min. – *ḫh*: the simple form *ḫw* is attested in Qat RÉS 3854/10 (cf. *RhKTB*, II, p. 23); cf. Arabic *ḫawḫat* "aperture...in a wall,...admitting the light...to a house, *or* chamber; passage...between any two houses, not having a door, *or* gate" (cf. *LaAEL*, p. 820 B). The building of small windows in a wall does not seem important enough to be mentioned with that of an oratory. – *nhn*, ending of the absolute dual; cf. *JaASAB*, p. 158, commentary on CIH 407/26. – *mḏqnt*, e.g., RÉS 4342/2; place for prostrations (cf. *RhIAI*, pp. 48-49). RÉS 4905/3 has *ḏn/mḏ[qn]n*. In the commentary of this text, *BeAIP* (p. 446) says that "one would therefore have to assume" *mḏqn* "to be a parallel form to the more usual *mḏqnt*", and *RÉS* (VII, p. 411) comments as follows: "*mḏ[qn]n*, restitution la plus probable". The proposed restoration is not the only possible one and contradicts the fact, pointed out by *BeAIP* himself, that *mḏqn* "has been considered plural to singular *mḏqnt*". The noun *mḏbḥ* "altar for sacrifice", known as singular in RÉS 3570/2, Min, perfectly fits the text; so I propose reading *ḏn/mḏ[bḥ]n*.

L. 4: *ḏtḥmym* is also found in RÉS 4678 which reads as follows:

1 *šbmm/bn[/]ʾbš*
2 *bm/mrṯd[/]ʾl*
3 *wḏtḥmym/⌊w⌉*
4 *[b]⌊nhw/wʾlyhn*
5 *ḏyšr/sbyw/*

1 Šibâmum, son of ʾAbši-
2 bâm, entrusted to ʾIl
3 and Ḏât-Ḥimyâm, and
4 his [s]on and ʾAlayhân,
5 he of Yašur, have captured.

Below and between *y* and *š* (line 5), there is a divine symbol composed of two parallel lines (cf. *GrGST*, p. 35, fig. 74 a) whose curve might be compared with the reverse drawing in *l.c.*, p. 8, fig. 6 f.

553 – Inscription located at 30.2 cm. (width of the stone) below Ja 552; engraved on the inset panel over the west door; photograph. – MaMB 8.

This boustrophedon inscription is engraved on two stones of which the inscribed part is covered with red paint; same disposition of lines as in Ja 552. The upper stone (88.6 cm. × 28.7) supports the first two lines of the text. L. 1: 69.2 cm. × 9.7; distance to the upper edge of the stone: 3.2 cm, to the right edge: 9.7 cm, and to line 2: 3 cm. L. 2: 68 cm. × 9.8; distance to the right corner: 3 cm. – The lower stone (88.6 cm. × 30.3) supports the third line of the text the letters of which border the upper edge. L. 3: 82 cm. × 9.7; distance to the right edge: 4 cm.; on both ends of line 2, a round hole; the stone was first cut for another door.

1 ← *ʾbkrb/bn/ᶜmkrb/bn/*
2 → *šwḏbm/hqny/ʾlmqh/*
3 ← *kl/wldhw/wqnyhw/bʾlmqh*

1 ᵓAbkarib, son of ᶜAmmkarib, descendant of [the family]
2 Šawḏabum, has dedicated to ᵓIlumquh
3 all his children and his slaves. By ᵓIlumquh.

Same author as in Ja 552.

554 – Inscription engraved at 3.15 m. north of Ja 552, but two masonry courses above; four incomplete photographs; cf. *PhQS*, p. 278. – MaMB 9.

INSCRIPTION: 11.44 m. × 23.5 cm. (without the symbol); distance to the lower edge of the stones (width: 30.5 cm.): between 4 and 5 cm. – SYMBOL: same height as that of the letters; its upper left corner is at 3 cm. from the upper right corner of the first letter, and its lower left corner at 11.5 cm. from the lower right corner of the same letter; width: 4.5 cm.; distance to the right edge of the stone: 12.5 cm. (top) and 3.5 (bottom); cf. Plate C, Fig. 2.

Symbol *ḏmrkrb/bn/ᵓbkrb/bn/šwḏbm/wmshᵓmr/*
bn/tbᶜkrb/bn/ršwn/mᶜhdy/qyn/ᵓlmqh/bᵓwm/bnyy/
whḥdṯ/ᵓlmqh/tmlᵓ/gnᵓn/ln/mḥfdn/ᶜd/sṭr/whqnyt/
ḏmrkrb/bn/šwḏbm/ln/ᵓwdn/ḏsṭrn/ᶜd/šqrm/bn/mbᶜl/
ᵓlmqh/

Symbol Ḏamarkarib, son of ᵓAbkarib, descendant of [the family] Šawḏabum, and Sumhuᵓamar, son of Tabaᶜkarib, descendant of [the family] Rašwân, both "sworn men" of the administrator for ᵓIlumquh in ᵓAwwâm, have built and renewed for ᵓIlumquh the mass of the enclosing wall from the tower to the inscription and [to] the dedication of Ḏamarkarib, descendant of Šawḏabum, from the line of the inscription to the top, belonging to the property of ᵓIlumquh.

ḏmrkrb/bn/ᵓbkrb/bn/šwḏbm, cf. Ja 555/1. – *ršwn*, also family name, e.g., in Ja 703/2; RÉS 4766/2 and 4815/7 and 8, but *ršyn* in lines 3 and 4 of the latter. – *mᶜhdy*, construct dual of the participle of the 3rd form of *ᶜhd*; for *ᶜhd* as verb and substantive, cf. CIH 376/1 and 541/47 respectively. – *bnyy*, dual form, e.g., RÉS 3902 bis, No. 130/2; *bnyy/whḥdṯ*, cp. *bny/wsḥdṯ* in RÉS 3881/1, Qat, and 2831/1, Min; for *bny*, cf. *CoRoC*, p. 115 A and the Western Semitic cognates in *JeHoDISO*, p. 38: *bny*1. – *hqnyt*, in Qat *sqnyt*, e.g., Ja 865/4. – *ᵓwdn/ḏsṭrn*, cp. the plural parallel *ᵓᵓwdn/ᵓly/sṭrn* in Ja 550/1. – *mbᶜl*, e.g., RÉS 3892/4.

555 – Inscription engraved on the left of Ja 554, so that its vertical final stroke (end of line 4) may also be considered as part of both texts; partial photograph. – MaMB 10.

INSCRIPTION: boustrophedon. L. 1: 10.53 m. × 21.5 cm.; stone height: 29.2 cm.; distance to the upper edge of the stones: between 3 and 4 cm. L. 2: 10.69 m. × 21.5 cm.; stone height: 31.5 cm.; distance to the upper edge of the stones: between 3.5 cm. and 4.5. L. 3: 10.65 m. × 21.5 cm.; stone height: 34 cm.; distance to the upper edge of the stones: between 4 and 5 cm. L. 4: 10.50 m. × 21.5 cm.; stone height: between 31 and 32 cm.; distance to the upper edge of the stones: 4 cm. – SYMBOL: same height as the letters; width: 4 cm. distance to the right edge of the stone: 11 cm. and 7; and to the first letter of line 1: 2 cm. and 6; cf. Plate C, Fig. 2.

1 **S** ← *ḏmrkrb/bn/ᵓbkrb/bn/šwḏbm/qyn/yṯᶜᵓmr/*
y *wykrbmlk/wsmhᶜly/wydᶜᵓl/wykrbmlk/*
m *hqny/ᵓlmqh/kl/mbny/wtmlᵓ/gnᵓn/ln/*
b *ᵓᵓwdn/ᵓly/sṭrn/ᶜd/šqrm/wbnhw/šrḥᵓl/*
o *bn/ykrbmlk/wtr/wkl/bnhw/smhᵓmr*
l

2 → *whlkᵓmr/wyṯᶜkrb/wẖyrhmw/wnšᵓkrb/bny/šwḏbm/*
wᶜmyṯᶜ/wyṯᶜkrb/bny/ṣbḥrym/wḥmᶜṯt/ḏḏkr/wkl/
wldhw/wbythw/yhr/wᵓnẖlhw/ḏṣwm/wḏ/
rmdn/wḏ/ᵓnwyn/wḏ/mqldn/wšrwn/wᶜgntn/
wḏmsqmm/wymlᵓṣḥl

3 ← *wᵓḥṭbn/bysrn/mflqn/wnẖlhw/ḏmšmn/bbḍᶜ/*
nšqm/wbythw/ḥrwr/bhgrn/ghrn/
wᵓbythw/wᶜbrthw/wᵓrḍthw/wᵓġylhw/bbḍᶜ/
šᶜbnhn/mhᵓnfm/wybrn/ywm/hwfyhw/ᵓlmqh/
ḏt/tnbᵓhw/wywm/tᵓbhhw/qyn/mryb/

4 → *wywm/ḍbᵓ/bᶜm/smhᶜly/ynf/ᶜd/ᵓrḍ/qtbn/whwfᵓ/*
kl/nṭᶜ/wkśwy/wkl/mwfᵓ/ḍbᵓ/smhᶜly/whṯb</>
lhw/smhᶜly/tᵓmnm/wšrᶜtm/wmẖḍnm/bᶜṯtr/
wb/ᵓlmqh/wb/ḏtḥmym/wb/ḏtbᶜdn/wb/ykrbmlk/
wtr/wb/yṯᶜᵓmr/byn/

1 **Symbol** Ḏamarkarib, son of ᵓAbkarib, descendant of [the family] Šawḏabum, administrator for Yaṯaᶜᵓamar and for Yakrubmalik and for Sumhuᶜalay and for Yadaᶜᵓil and for Yakrubmalik, has dedicated to ᵓIlumquh all the construction and the mass of the wall, from the lines which [belong to] this inscription, to the top, and his son Šaraḥᵓil, son of Yakrubmalik Watar, and all his sons Sumhuᵓamar
2 and Halakᵓamar and Yaṯaᶜkarib and Ḫayrhumû and Našaᵓkarib, descendants of [the family] Šawḏabum, and ᶜAmmyaṯaᶜ and Yaṯaᶜkarib, of [the family] Ṣabaḥriyyâm, and Ḥammᶜaṯat, him of [the family]

Ḏakir, and all his children and his house Yahar and his palm-groves of Ṣawâm and of Ramdân and of ʾAnwayân and of Maqladân and Šarwân and ʿAgantân and of Masqamum and Yamlaʾṣaḥal

3 and ʾAḥṭabân in Yasrân, irrigated by the sluice-ways, and his palm-grove of Mašâmân in the district of Našqum and his house Ḥarûr in the town Gaharân and his houses and his river-side fields and his lands and his stream beds in the district of the two tribes Muhʾanifum and Yabrân, when ʾIlumquh granted to him what He had promised him, and when He appointed him as administrator of Mârib,

4 and when he waged war with Sumhuʿalay Yanûf in the land of Qatabân and made ready all skin cover and garment and all preparation of [for] the war of Sumhuʿalay, and Sumhuʿalay presented him with a testimony of confidence and administration and management. By ʿAṯtar and by ʾIlumquh and by Ḏât-Ḥimyâm and by Ḏât-Baʿdân and by Yakrubmalik Watar and by Yaṯaʿʾamar Bayyin.

L. 1: *šrḥʾl*, e.g., RÉS 4527 and more frequently *ʾlšrḥ* (e.g., Ja 243, Qat); cf. also *yšrḥʾl* in Ja 536 (cf. *JaPSAP*, pp. 39, 48-51, and 73) and *šrḥm* in Ja 863/1, Qat.

L. 2: *yṯʿkrb*, e.g., RÉS 2886/2, Min, 2661 and 3878/19, Qat. – *ḫyrhmw* confirms *CIH*'s translation in CIH 937/1, where *RÉS* considers it as a noun (cf. commentary on RÉS 4126/1, where *ḫyrhmw* may also be a proper name and not a noun); cf. also the masculine name *ḫyry* in RÉS 4859/1, Ḥaḍr, and the personal name *ḫyrm* in Ja 259/1 (Qat; cf. commentary); nominal form identical with that of *ṣbḥhmw*, e.g., in CIH 383/2-3 (cf. *JaPSAP*, pp. 22-23, 26, 73-76, and 79) and of *rʾshmw* in RÉS 4226/2, which *RÉS* translates as "leur personne", and on which *RycIMAM* (p. 84) comments as follows: "famille" (cf. *JaASAB*, p. 182). In RÉS 4859 referred to above, read *ḏmtryn* (line 2; instead of *ḏmtr*(?) *m*(?)*n*), *kšdyyhn* (line 3; there is no room for *n* before *hn*; same formation as in *hndyyhn* in line 4), and *k*(4)*nhm* (lines 3-4; instead of *b*(4)*nd*(?)..). – *nšʾkrb*, e.g., RÉS 2726/18-19 and also *nšʾkryb* in RÉS 2724/13. – *ʿmyṯʿ*, e.g., Ja 285 B/1 (Qat; cf. commentary). – *ṣbḥrym*, cp. the masculine personal names *ṣbḥkrb* in Ja 212, Qat, *smhrym* in RÉS 3103 and the personal names *ṣbḥ*[*t*] (woman) in Ja 213/1 (Qat; cf. commentary and *JaDME*, pp. 18-19) and *ṣbḥm* (man) in Ja 852/3, Qat. – *ḥmʿṯt*, e.g., Ja 393, Qat; cf. also the Qat family name *ḥm* in RÉS 4975. – *ḏkr*, e.g., RÉS 3771 and the masculine personal name *ḏkrm* in Ja 349/1, Qat. The root *ḥmm* is also attested in *tḥm* in RÉS 5076 A: *tḥm* 1 Taḥamm
ytd 2 Yatid.

RÉS 5076 B (to the right of A, and vertically engraved): *tmmr* "Tammar". – *ṣwm*, place name; cp. the Arabic adjective *ṣawâm* "arid and unprovided with water (land)". – *rmdn*, e.g., name of a city in RÉS 2789/3, Min, and the Arabic personal name *rumîdî* (cf. *SlGaVNPA*, p. 45 A). – *ʾnwyn*, family name in RÉS 4229/2; *ʾaqtalân* form, as well as *ʾḥṭbn* in line 3; to be related to Arabic *nawâ* "to intend, plan", and not to the root *ʾnw* (cf. *RyNP*, I, p. 285 B). – *mqldn*, cp. the Arabic verb *qalada* "to gather, collect, pick up, reap". – *šrwn*, cp. Arabic *šarân* "country of the Mount Salma, abundant in lions". – *ʿgntn*, cp. the Arabic verb *ʿaǧana* "to knead". – *msqmm*, cp. Arabic *sawqam* (collective) "high trees". – *ymlʾṣḥl*, composite proper name including the well-known verb *mlʾ* and also *ṣḥl*; in Arabic *ṣaḥila* means "to be hoarse, have a hoarse voice".

L. 3: *ʾḥṭbn*, *ʾaqtalân* form; cp. Arabic *ḥaṭab*, pl. *ʾaḥṭâb* "fire-wood", the personal name *al-ḥaṭṭâb* (cf. *SlGaVNPA*, p. 25 A), and the expression *bḥr/ḥṭbn* in Ja 564/27. – *mšmn*, cp. Arabic *mašâmmun* "odors, scents". – *bbḏʿ*, e.g., RÉS 3607/2. – *nšqm*, very well-known city; e.g., RÉS 3945/14; probably al-Baiḍâ (cf. *WiHöBGS*, p. 14), about 110 km. northwest of Mârib. – *ḥrwr*, name of an incense sanctuary in CIH 41/2 (not personal name, as *RyNP*, I, p. 99 A), of a place (Ja 576/12) and also noun (e.g., RÉS 3911/3); probably to be related to Arabic *ḥirâr*, pl. of *ḥarrat* "stony tract" (cf. *CoRoC*, p. 153 A). – *ghrn*, RÉS 3605 bis/2 (cf. *JaPSAP*, pp. 113-15, 196, and 197); cp. (*ḏ*)*ghrm* in RÉS 4594 B. – *ʿbrt*, pl. of *ʿbr*, e.g., Ja 514 (commentary), *RoVSAY*, p. 308, and RÉS 4514/2; *ʿbr* also means "canal" which irrigates the fields (e.g., RÉS 4351/1). – *ʾrḍ*, cf. *StSESA*, p. 516, and the Western Semitic cognates in *JeHoDISO*, pp. 25-26: *ʾrṣ*. In CIH 432/4, *ʾrḍy* is dual, not plural as suggested by *RyHE* (p. 234), who also translates erroneously the singular *ʾrḍ* in RÉS 4069/6 (not 4096) as a plural; the same error is already on p. 233, where *ʾtmrm/hnʾm/bn* and CIH 67/17-18 must be corrected: *ʾt*[*mrm/hnʾm/*]*bn* and CIH 67/16-18 respectively. Further, in the expression, *b*[*ʾ*]*rḍ/wgblt* (AM 206/4), *ʾrḍ* is not a part of *gblt* (contrary to *l.c.*, who gratuitously inserts the preposition *b* before *gblt*). – *ʾġylhw*, RÉS 3899; for the expression *ḥrn ġyl/wd* in RÉS 2774/6,

Min, cf. *JaP*, p. 77 and A. Jamme, in *Oriente Moderno*, 33 (1953), p. 110 B; *ġyl* or *ġl* in *scriptio defectiva* (RÉS 5085/5) means either the stream irrigating a valley (e.g., Ja 670/29) or the irrigated valley itself (e.g., here); in modern Yemeni, cf. *RoAS* (p. 209 A): "fiume d'acqua incanalata *ġayl* pl. *ġiyûl*". – *mhʾnfm*, tribe name, e.g., in CIH 40/1-2 (for the left monogram, cf. *JaJEQH*, p. 133, note 1). – *ybrn*, also tribe name in CIH 368/2; from the root *brr* (cp. *yhbr*) rather than from *bry*(?) (as *RyNP*, I, p. 288 B). – *tʾbhhw*, 5th form of *ʾbh*; cf. Hebrew *ʾâbâh* "to want, be willing" (cf. *KoBaLVTL*, p. 3 B) and Arabic *ʾabā* (i) "to will, request" (cf. also in Daṯînah in *LaGD*, p. 11).

L. 4: *ḍbʾ*, feminine noun (cf. Ja 577/16 and 636/6-7), cf. *JaASAB*, p. 161, commentary on CIH 407/18. – *hwfʾ* and *mwfʾ*, cf. Syriac *yifô* in Aphel "to bring to an end, complete" (cf. *PaSmCSD*, pp. 194-95) and "*rem* confecit, perfecit" (cf. *BrDSL*, p. 213 A), and Arabic *wafâ* 4th form "to accomplish, fulfil"; the verb *wfʾ* (cf. also the noun *wfʾ* in RÉS 3610/3; *JaSaMA*, [p. 239] refer to Arabic *wafâʾ* "integrity, perfection", the root *wfʾ* being connected with *wfy*) in the 4th form, *hwfʾ*, seems to have the meaning of "to prepare" and the derived noun *mwfʾ* "preparation". – *nṭʿ*, cf. M. Höfner, K. Mlaker and N. Rhodokanakis, in *WZKM*, 41 (1934)[1], pp. 88-90, and *RoVSAY*, p. 307; the noun *nṭʿ* has several meanings, e.g., "plantation" (e.g., RÉS 3858/7, Qat [cf. *JaPSAP*, pp. 33, 64, 65, 104, and 169-70], and Hebrew *nĕuṭaʿ*, cf. *KoBaLVTL*, p. 613 A and *UlCSH*, p. 196), "bastion" (e.g., Ja 557), etc.; the noun *kśwy* mentioned immediately after *nṭʿ* suggests for the latter the comparison with *naṭʿ* in Arabic as well as in Daṯînah (cf. *LaGD*, p. 2782): "skin or leather cover", and in modern Yemeni "*naṭāʿah* pelle per coprire bagagli su cavalcature; *naṭaʿ* tovaglia di pelle che si stende per terra e sulla quale sono deposti i recipienti e i cibi" (cf. *RoVSAY*, *l.c.*). – *kśwy*, cp. *kśw* in RÉS 3427/2, Min, and *ʾkswt* in CIH 523/5 "garments"; cf. Arabic *kiswat* or *kuswat*, pl. *kasâwî* "vestment, garment, clothing, clothes" (cf. *DoSDA*, II, p. 468 B), and in Daṯînah, cf. *LaGD*, p. 2574: "les fournitures en habits étaient auparavant très fréquentes; les princes les distribuaient à leurs favoris, comme encore dans l'Arabie du Sud"; cf. also *StSESA*, pp. 523 and 524, and *BePESA*, pp. 11 and 17. – *ḥṯb*</>*lw*/–/*tʾmnm*/*wšrʿtm*/*wmḫdnm*, cf. *ḥṯb*/*lhw*/––/*tʾmnm* in Ja 550/2, *yḥṯb*/*krbʾl*/––/*ʿšrn*/*wmʾtn*/*lmʿhrm*/*tʾmnm* in RÉS 4624/8-9, and also the following Min expressions: *sṯb*/––/*ksʿd*/––/*tʾmn*/*wmḫdn* in RÉS 3535/3[2] and *sṯb*/––/*kʿlmn*/*tʾmn*/*wsšrʿ* in RÉS 2774/3. In spite of the similarity of the expressions, *RhSLG* proposes different translations of *tʾmn*: "Vertrauen" (II, p. 22, in CIH 375/2) and "Verwaltung" (II, p. 56, in RÉS 2774/3); the first interpretation is accepted by *CIH* (II, p. 28). In the inscriptions referred to above, *tʾmn* (cf. *BeSI*, p. 20 and *CoRoC*, p. 106 B) is a noun and the direct complement of *ḥṯb*; besides, the personal pronoun *hw* refers to the author of the text (cf. *RhSLG*, II, pp. 24-25) and not to the deity (cf. *CIH*, II, p. 27 B). Three parallel texts make a better translation of *tʾmn* possible: RÉS 4193/12: *ḥṯb*/*lḫyl*/*wmqm*/*tʾlb*/*tʾmnm*, practically identical with Ja 716/9: *ḥṯbw*/*lḫyl*/*wmqm*/*ʾlmqh*/––/*tʾmnm*, and a variant of Ja 651/34-36: *hgbʾ*/*ʿbdʿm*/–/*tʾmntm*/*lḫyl*/*wmqm*/–/*ʾlmqh*. The equivalence of meaning between *ḥṯb* and *hgbʾ*, and RÉS 4193/12 is not referred to by *RycIMAM* (p. 137). The last three quotations justify the translation of *tʾmn*, pl. *tʾmnt* (Ja 651/34-35) as "testimony of confidence", which may be given either to men or deities. Finally, *tʾmn* was a civic, not military (as *RycIMAM*, *l.c.*) award which may be granted in recognition of outstanding performance during a military campaign for either fighting activity (e.g., Ja 550) or army service corps (e.g., here) as well as after the opening of a mountain road (e.g., RÉS 4624). – *šrʿt* (cf. *RhSLG*, II, p. 67); cp. Ethiopic *śĕrĕʿăt* "administratio, dispensatio" (cf. *DiLLA*, col. 243-44). – For *mḫdn*, e.g., RÉS 2774/6, Min, cf. *CoRoC*, p. 177 A; also *smḫd*, e.g., in RÉS 2774/3; *mḫdn* is the proper name of a palm-grove in Ja 550/1. The verb *mḫd*, "to strike" (cf. *CoRoC*, *l.c.* and *BeSI*, p. 66) is used with the meaning of "to defeat" (e.g., RÉS 3945/3), "to pierce" a mountain road (RÉS 3550/3, Qat; [cf. *JaPSAP*, pp. 31, 33, 36, 167-69, and 190, note 46]; this text is erroneously referred to by *RyISA* [X, p. 283] as mentioning "marteler

[1] *RyET* (p. 69, commentary on Fakhry 119/12) interchanges this article with the following: M. Höfner, "Zur Interpretation altsüdarabischer [not altsüdarabischen; cf. *l.c.*, p. X] Inschriften, II."

[2] *RÉS* (VI, p. 194) translates as plural the following singular nouns: *ʾl*, *šym* and *mlk* (line 3) and does not translate the expression *ymt*/*hgrn*/*qrnw* (line 4; *l.c.*, p. 195) which means "during the days of the city Qarnâwû".

(une inscription)"), and "to pierce" the barrage of a reservoir (RÉS 3943/5; cf. *RhSLG*,, II pp. 98-99; for the palaeography of this inscription and its relation with CIH 622 and 623, cf. *JaPSAP*, pp. 63, 89, 91-92, 105, 155-62, and 190); furthermore, the noun *mḫḏ* in CIH 570/2 might refer to a kind of official measure (cf. *BeSI*, p. 58).

556 – Inscription engraved on the left of line 4 of Ja 555. – MaMB 11.

INSCRIPTION: 9.92 m. × 24 cm.; distance from the first letter to the upper left corner of the symbol: 4 cm.; distance to the upper edge of the stones: 4 cm. – SYMBOL: at 27.5 cm. on the left of Ja 555; vertical height: 26 cm.; width: 3.5 cm.

> **Symbol** *lḥyᶜṯt/bn/ḥywm/wḥywm/bn/lḥyᶜṯt/ḏy/*
> *ʾrbᶜnhn/ḏy/ḫwln/bny/myṯᶜm/qyny/hwbs/wʾlmqh/*
> *hqnyy/ʾlmqh/tmlʾ/gnʾn/ln/ḏn/ʾwdn/ḏsṭrn/ᶜd/šqr/*
> *mḥfdn/wmġbtnhn/bʾlmqh*

> **Symbol** Laḥayᶜaṯat, son of Ḥayûm, and Ḥayûm, son of Laḥayᶜaṯat, both of [the tribe] ʾArbaᶜnahân, both of [the clan] Ḫawlân, both descendants of [the family] Muyaṯiᶜum, both administrators for Hawbas and ʾIlumquh, have dedicated to ʾIlumquh the mass of the enclosing wall from the line of this inscription to the top of the tower and of the two recesses. By ʾIlumquh.

lḥyᶜṯt, cf. Ja 400 B/1-2 in *JaSIBS*, p. 32 A; cf. also *lḥyᶜt*, e.g., in Ja 881 F/1, Qat (cf. *JaPEQL*, p. 210). – *ḥywm*, e.g., Ja 542 A/1 and Fakhry 13 (cf. *JaISAR*, p. 106, note 1); cf. also *ḥywn*, e.g., in Ja 882 O, Qat (cf. *JaPEQL*, p. 216), and *ḥywnly* in Ja 525/3. The formula of the present text is equivalent to the common *lḥyᶜṯt/bn/ḥywm/wbnhw/ḥywm*; nevertheless the independence of the second person is pointed out in the first expression and not in the second. – *ḏy*, relative dual (cf. *HöASG*, p. 42). – *ḏy/ʾrbᶜnhn*, cf. *ḏʾrbᶜnhn* in RÉS 3951/7, where mention is made of another *lḥyᶜṯt*, who is *bn/mlḥn*; same nominal formation as that, e.g., of *hgrnhn* in Ja 335/1, Qat (cf. commentary and *JaPSAP*, pp. 48 and 115-16). *RhSLG* (I, p. 74, note 3) is inclined to think that *ʾrbᶜnhn* were the two most outstanding families of *ʾrbᶜn* (e.g., RÉS 2726/25). A connection between the two texts might appear possible, since both texts come from Ṣirwâḥ, and belong to the beginning of the *mlk/sbʾ* period. However, it would seem obvious that *ʾrbᶜn/ḏbrtn* (RÉS 2726/25), because of *ḏbrtn*, was a part of *ʾrbᶜnhn*. On the other hand, *RyET* (p. 40) presents as possible the identification of *ʾrbᶜn* in RÉS 2726/25 and *ʾrbᶜm* in Fakhry 69/1 [3]. Although *JaP* (p. 94, note 320) points out that in several cases, the endings *n* and *m* are not important at all as far as the meaning of terms is concerned, I think that the distinction must be preserved in the present case for the following reasons. *ʾrbᶜm* in Fakhry 69/1, confirmed by CIH 487/1, is not identical with *ʾrbᶜn/ḏbrtn*, and *ʾrbᶜm* is mentioned in two texts from Mârib and *ʾrbᶜn/ḏbrtn* is found in an inscription from Ṣirwâḥ. Furthermore, it is rather difficult to understand why *RyET*, after proposing the identification of *ʾrbᶜm* and *ʾrbᶜn*, writes: "Ces rois de ʾArbaᶜum devaient être des souverains locaux sans grande importance", since the peoples belonging to *ʾrbᶜ*(*m* or *n*) were living in two large cities such as Mârib and Ṣirwâḥ. – *ḫwln*, cp. *ḫwlm* in CIH 443/2 and Ja 649/2; cp. also the Qat personal name *ḫlrm* in Ja 279/1 (cf. commentary and also *JaDME*, p. 17); for *ḫwln* in RÉS 3954/2, cf. commentary on Ja 846/2. – *myṯᶜm*, cf. commentary on *myṯᶜ* in Ja 401/1 in *JaSIBS*, p. 34 B; before mentioning the official function of the authors of the inscription, the beginning of the text gives a very accurate, yet rather unusual description of their social affiliations: the tribe *ʾrbᶜnhn*, the clan *ḫwln* and finally the family *myṯᶜm*. The presence of the same social organization has been pointed out in Qatabân by *JaSQI*, pp. 44-45. – *qyny*, dual, cf. Ja 550/1. – *hwbs/wʾlmqh*, e.g., CIH 487/2. – *hqnyy*, dual (cf. *JaIAA*, p. 316, commentary on Ja 532), e.g., RÉS 4191/5. In both RÉS 4347/3 and 4459/1, *hqny* is interpreted as dual by *RÉS*. The first text is complete and has two subjects; but this fact does not justify his hypothesis, since *hqny* is singular and refers only to the first subject as principal author of the dedication; the latter acts in the name of the subjects mentioned in the text; this grammatical construction is far from being unusual (cf. in the present collection of texts

[3] For the palaeography of Fakhry 69, cf. *JaPSAP*, pp. 4 and 54-57. In Fakhry 69/1, *hqny/hwbs* is certain; in spite of A. Fakhry's copy where the end of line 2 is *ḏtḥ*, *RyET* (p. 39) restores *ḏtḥ*[*m*]; on the stone, the upper quarter of *m* is on the beginning of line 3; line 3, there is a word divider before *ydᶜʾl*; *yṯᶜʾmr* in A. Fakhry's copy, but *yṯtʾmr* in *RyET*'s transliteration. Referring to the text, G. Ryckmans (cf. *Le Muséon*, 61 [1948], p. 229) writes: "dédicace faite au dieu ʾAlmaqah", and *RycIMAM* (p. 85): "une dédicace à Hawbas"; this inscription actually mentions a dedication to both ʾIlumquh and Hawbas. On the other hand, *RycIMAM* (*l.c.*) writes: "l'invocation est au nom de Yadaᶜʾil, ainsi que de ᶜAmmʾamin, père du dédicant", although the third line mentions *wb/ydᶜʾl/wb/yṯᶜʾmr/wb/ᶜmʾmn/ʾbhw*. Incidentally, the end of the text may be compared with Gl 1131 + 1132 + 1133/3 (cf. *HöDSP*, p. 41) *wb/yṯᶜ*]*ʾmr/wb/ydᶜʾl/wb/ʾbhmy/b*... (the first two names are interchanged) and also with Gl 1128+1129/11-12 (cf. *HöDSP*, p. 39).

Ja 590/4, 608/4, 609/3-4, 611/4, 619/3-4, etc.). In the second text, both the end and the beginning of line 1 are missing, so that the number of author(s) is unknown; furthermore, Ja 551 which mentions only one subject, offers a perfect parallel for restoring the beginning of RÉS 4459/1; in the case of several subjects, the rule pointed out above also applies. – *tmlʾ/– –/šqr*, cf. Ja 551. – *mġbtnhn*, dual, Ja 550/1; this term obviously indicates the two parts of the enclosing wall on each side of the *mḫfd*.

557 – Inscription engraved on the left of Ja 556; end is missing. – MaMB 12.

INSCRIPTION: 18.25 m. × 21.5 cm.; distance to the upper edge of the stones: 4 cm. – SYMBOL: at 1 cm. from the lower extremity of the last letter of Ja 556, and at 4.5 cm. (bottom) and 10 (top) from the beginning of the present text; vertical height: 22.5 cm.; width: 4 cm.; cf. Plate C, Fig. 2.

Symbol *ʾbkrb/bn/nbṭkrb/ḏzltn/ʿbd/ydʿʾl/byn/*
wsmhʿly/ynf/wyṯʿʾmr/wtr/wykrbmlk/ḏrḥ/wsmhʿly/
ynf/hqny/ʾlmqh/kl/wldhw/wqnyhw/wbny/wmlʾ/
tmlʾ/nṭʿ/hmlʾn/whwśqn/gnʾ/ʾwm/ln/ḏn/ʾwdn/
ḏsṭrn/wrymm/kl/blqhw/wʿḏhw/wklʾy/mḫfdnhn/yʾzl/
wdrʿ/wmġbbhmy/ʿd/šqrm/whqm/ʾqnyt/ʾbhhw/bny/
ḏzltn/bʿṯtr/wb/ʾlmqh/wbḏtḥmym/wbḏtbʿdn/wwḍʾ/
ʾbkrb/bʾḏn/ʾlmqh/wmlk/mryb/š[. . .

Symbol ʾAbkarib, son of Nabaṭkarib, of [the family] Zaltân, servant of Yadaʿʾil Bayyin and of Sumhuʿalay Yanûf and of Yaṯaʿʾamar Watar and of Yakrubmalik Ḏariḥ and of Sumhuʿalay Yanûf, has dedicated to ʾIlumquh all his children and his slaves and has built and completed the mass of the bastion [by which] he has completed and filled up the enclosing wall of ʾAwwâm from the line of this inscription and in addition, all its masonry of hewn stones and its woodwork and the two towers Yaʾzil and Daraʿ and their [the two towers] recesses, to the top, and he has raised up the possessions of his ancestors, the descendants of Zaltân. By ʿAṯtar and by ʾIlumquh and by Ḏât-Ḥimyâm and by Ḏât-Baʿdân. And ʾAbkarib has made known, in submission to ʾIlumquh and to the king of Mârib, Š[. . .

ʾbkrb, e.g., Ja 552/1. – *nbṭkrb*, e.g., in Min Ja 403 and 404/1, and RÉS 2754/1. – *zltn*, cp. the clan name *zlt* in RÉS 2681. – *ʿbd*, cf. *JaASAB*, pp. 158-59, commentary on CIH 407/9. *ʿbd* is also found in RÉS 4542 A, which may be read as follows: . . . /*b*]*n/mʿnf* (line 2) *m*[/]*ʿ*(*b*)*d*(/)*ʾ*(*b*)*y*(*dʿ*) ". . . ,s]on of Muʿanifum, se(rv)ant of ʾA(b)ya(daʿ)". – *bny/wmlʾ*, RÉS 4766/2; *bny* is also verb in Ja 538/2 (cf. commentary on the latter and *JaSAI*, pp. 506-07, No. 2). P. Boneschi gives his own Latin translation of Ja 538, 539, 540 A, 542 A, and 544 in *RSO*, 34 (1959), pp. 27-32 and 137-40. – *nṭʿ*, cf. commentary on Ja 555/4; pl. *nṭʿt* in RÉS 4663/3, where the translation as "bastion" may also be accepted and where ʿAṯtar Šarqân indicates the temple dedicated to that deity. – *hmlʾ*, 4th form of *mlʾ*; in Ja 631/20 and 671/16, with the probable meaning of "to favor"; here with a material sense such as "to complete". – *hwśq*, 4th form of *wśq* (cf. *CIH*, I, p. 197 B and *CoRoC*, p. 141 B); cf. Arabic *wasaqa* "to fill (up)" (cf. also *MoNTA*, pp. 360-61), probable allusion to the fact that the space between the two exterior walls, which are connected to each other by small retaining walls, is filled with loose stones and cinders (cf. also *AlEMY*, p. 218 B). – *rym*, cf. *CoRoC*, p. 241 A, and Arabic *raym* "surplus, increase"; here, in the indefinite state; this term equals an expression such as "in addition". – *blqhw/wʿḏhw*, RÉS 3027/1, Min; *blq/wʿḏm*, *RoVSAY*, p. 301, and *RÉS* (V, p. 22) which describes *blq* as a kind of hewn stones; here, *kl* and the pronoun *hw* referring to *gnʾ*, indicate that *blq* and *ʿḏ* (also, e.g., Ja 404/2, Min) are not merely common nouns but are collective nouns referring respectively to masonry in hewn stones and woodwork. In connection with irrigation works, *blq* means "opening, exit" (e.g., RÉS 2650/2). – *klʾy* (cf. also *JeHoDISO*, p. 120: *klʾ*$_{II}$) and *klʾty* (Ja 672/1), respectively masculine and feminine construct dual of *klʾ*; cf. Ugaritic *klʾ* = *klat* (cf. *GoUM*, p. 278 A, No. 909), Hebrew *kilʾayim* (cf. *UlCSH*, p. 194), Arabic *kilâ* and *kiltâ* and Ethiopic *kĕlĕʾu* and *kĕlĕʾtu* (cf. *DiLLA*, col. 820 and 821) "two". – *yʾzl*, well-known proper name especially illustrated by the brother of the king ʾIlšaraḥ Yaḥḍub. – *drʿ*, name of a citadel in RÉS 4626/2; cf. also the following personal names in Arabic *dirʿ*, *dâriʿ*, and *dirʿân* (cf. *HeBN*, p. 22 B), in Safaitic *drʿ* (cf. *LiSI*, p. 308 A), and *drʿm* in RÉS 4446/2. – *hqm*, e.g., RÉS 3946/6 (cf. *JaPSAP*, pp. 16, 32, 126-28, 131-32, 143-46, 149-50, 187, note 7, and 189, note 38) and 4646/16; the ordinary meaning, "to build up", may be taken in a derived sense, such as "to extend". – *ʾqnyt*, CIH 95/3. – *ʾbhhw*, CIH 37/6 and *CIH*, I, p. 59. – *wḍʾ/ʾbkrb/bʾḏn/ʾlmqh/wmlk/mryb/š*[. . ., cp. Ḥaḍr *tḍʾ/ṣdqdkr/bʾḏn/syn* in RÉS 2693/4-5 "a voué Ṣadiqdakar en sujétion à Sin" (cf. *RÉS*, V, p. 46). According to *RhSLG* (II, p. 40), "*wḍʾ* bezeichnet die Absonderung (des Geweihten) für den Gott". The present formula does not agree with this interpretation, for it mentions a living king to whom an offering is never presented. Furthermore, a parallel such as *qny* "to possess" – *hqny* "to dedicate", indicates that a secondary verbal form may have a dedicatory meaning, although its 1st form has only a profane sense (cf. *JaRIH*, p. 150, remarks on Hamilton 7/3). For *wḍʾ*, cf. *StSESA*, pp. 516-17 and *CoRoC*, p. 139 B: on *yḍʾwn* in RÉS 3566/18 "evulgabunt (?)"; this interpretation may be retained here; cf. Ethiopic *wăḍĕʾă* II, 1 "exire facere *vel* jubere...in vulgus efferre, evulgare" (cf. *DiLLA*, col. 945). *bʾḏn/ʾlmqh*, e.g., *bʾḏnh/ʿṯtr* in RÉS 2869/7, Min (cf. *RhSLG*, II, pp. 40-41), *bʾḏn/ʿm* in RÉS 5014/1-3, Qat (cf. M. Höfner, in *BiO*, 10 [1953], p. 152 B) and Qat *bʾḏn/ʿm/wʿṯtr*, *bʾḏn/šmsm* and *bʾḏn/ʿm/wšmsm/wʿśt*, Qat, in *JaIRM*, pp. 310-11, and *bʾḏn ḏtḥ[mym]* in Ja 863/5, Qat; for other meanings of *ʾḏn*, cf. commentary on Ja 558/4; cf. also *StSESA*, p. 512. – *š*[..., initial of the name of an unknown king of Mârib.

— B —

INSCRIPTIONS MENTIONING ROYAL NAME(S): Ja 558–671

1 – PERIOD *mlk/sbʾ*: Ja 558-566

a – Karibʾil Bayyin: Ja 558

558 – Yellowish, slightly grayish sandstone. – MaMB 201.

STONE: thickness: 47.5 cm. – *Front:* upper edge badly damaged (line 1 completely destroyed); lower edge slightly damaged; the inscribed surface is covered with red paint; 2.7 m. × 42 cm. – INSCRIPTION: each line of the text is located between two horizontal lines finely traced (cf. Ja 559), plus a small vertical line immediately on the right of the first sign of each line; letter height: 3.8 cm.; space between the lines: 1.1 cm. – SYMBOL: facing the first two lines of the text; cf. Plate C, Fig. 2.

1 **[Sym-** *ʾlʿt̲t/wʾwsʿt̲t/w . . .   /wšrḥʾl/bnw/ʿblm/ wbnyhmw/ʾlwhb/wdrsm/wdwsm/wgnʾn/ bny/ʿblm/hqnyw/mrʾhmw]*

2 **bol** *ʾlmqh/bʿl/ʾwm/. . . . t . m . . .   ʿn/ wt̲mntn/ʾmt̲ln/ʾly/d̲hbn/ʾly/ stwk(lh)w⌜/ʾl⌝[ʿ]t̲t/wʾws[ʿ]t̲t⌜/ ⌝[w . . .   t . . . /w]*

3 *šrḥʾl/bnw/ʿblm/wl/bnyhmw/ʾlwhb/wdrsm/wdwsm/ wgnʾn/bny/ʿblm/lwfyhmw/wwfy/ʾnfshmw/ wbnyhmw/wʾw*

4 *ldhmw/wqnyhmw/wbd̲t/yśfnhmw/ʾlmqhw/wldm/ wqnym/hnʾm/wbry/ʾd̲nm/wmqmm/wbd̲t/ yhʿnnhmw/wmtʿ/ʾlm*

5 *qh/bn/bʾstm/wnkytm/wbn/ʿdqm/wqmtm/wbn/mlʾ/ wḥf/šnʾm/wbd̲t/hwfyhmw/wyhwfyn/ʾlmqh/d̲t/ tnbʾhw/b*

6 *ʿt̲tr/wb/hwbs/wb/ʾlmqh/wbd̲t/ḥmym/wbd̲t/bʿdnm/ wb/mrʾyhmw/ydʿʾl/bn/krbʾl/byn/mlk/sbʾ/wʾh̲hw/ʾl*

7 *šrḥ/bn/smhʿly/d̲rḥ/wb/šʿbhmw/fyšn⟨/⟩wrt̲dw/bnw/ ʿblm/ʾlmqh/hqnythmw/bn/hkrnh/wʾh̲rnh*

8 *⟨w⟩ḍrynh*

1 **[Sym-** ʾIlʿat̲at and ʾAwsʿat̲at and . . . and Šaraḥʾil, descendants of ʿAblum, and their sons ʾIlwahab and Darisum and Dawsum and Ganaʾân, descendants of ʿAblum, have dedicated to their lord]

2 **bol** ʾIlumquh, master of ʾAwwâm, . . . and these eight representations, which [are] in bronze, by which ʾIl[ʿa]t̲at and ʾAws[ʿa]t̲at [and . . .] have shown their confiden[ce in H]im [. . .   . . . t . . . and]

3 Šaraḥʾil, descendants of ʿAblum and for their children ʾIlwahab and Darisum and Dawsum and Ganaʾân, descendants of ʿAblum for their own safety and the safety of their persons and of their sons and of their children

4 and of their slaves; and that ʾIlumquhû may add to them pleasing children and slaves and [also] the strength of understanding and of power; and that ʾIlumquh may help and save them

5 from misfortunes and sufferings and from press and harsh treatment and from the gathering and encirclement of [any] enemy; and because ʾIlumquh has granted to them and shall grant to them what He has promised him. By

6 ʿAt̲tar and by Hawbas and by ʾIlumquh and by D̲ât-Ḥimyâm and by D̲ât-Baʿdânum and by their two lords Yadaʿʾil, son of Karibʾil Bayyin, king of Sabaʾ, and his cousin ʾIl-

7 šaraḥ, son of Sumhuᶜalay Ḏariḥ, and by their tribe Fayšan; and the people of ᶜAblum have entrusted to ᵓIlumquh's care their offering against [whomever would] either change it or put it aside
8 [or] hide it.

L. 1: restoration based on lines 2 and 3. – *hqnyw*: obviously pl. of *hqny*, and not dual (as *RyET*, p. 30, commentary on Fakhry 53 and 54); cf. commentary on Ja 532 and 556.

L. 2: *ᵓlmqh/bᶜl/ᵓwm*, e.g. RÉS 3624/1: *ᵓwm/byt/ᵓlmqh*; for *bᶜl*, cf. C. Rabin, *Ancient West-Arabian*, London, 1951, p. 26; for *bᶜl* and *mrᵓ*, cf. *JaIAA*, p. 322; note that *bᶜlt* in NaNN 74/6 means "spouse [of the god]" (cf. *JaCRR*, p. 9); for the Western Semitic cognates of *bᶜl*, cf. *JeHoDISO*, p. 40: *bᶜl*$_{\text{I}}$. – *ṯmntn*, e.g., RÉS 3856/3, Qat, and *HöASG*, pp. 131-32, §112. – *ᵓmṯl*, cf. commentary on Ja 401/3 in *JaSIBS*, p. 34 A. – *ḏhb*, cf. *JaFSR*, p. 13, *JaQISA*, pp. 3-4 and *JaSIBS*, pp. 32-33. *BeTMS* still translates *ḏdhb* as "golden". In the reading of Ashmolean Museum 1957-16/1, insert a word divider (the lower half of it still on the stone) before *hqny*, and suppress the word divider before *bᶜl* (line 2). – *stwk(lh)w*, e.g., CIH 336/5-6; in Fakhry 88/2-3; *mṯln/ḏstwklhw/* [not *ḏstwklw*, as *RyET*, p. 58] *lwfy/bnhw* is a perfect parallel of Ja 726/3-4: *ṣlmn/ḏstwklhw/lwfy/bnhw*, and of RÉS 3908/2-3: *ṣlmn/ḏstwklhw/lwfy/ᵓbkrb*; in the present text, the formula is plural: *ᵓmṯln/–/ᵓly/stwk[lh]w/–/lwfyhmw*. In other similar texts, *ḏ* or *ᵓly* is replaced by the conjunction *ḥgn*, which thus clarifies the value of *ḏ* or *ᵓly*; e.g., CIH 336/5-6, 348/7-8, Ja 605/4-5, 704/3-4 and also RÉS 4148/1-2. In RÉS 3908/3, *RÉS* (VI, pp. 377-78) translates *stwkl* as "confier aux soins de"; but in RÉS 4148/2, *MoMiHI* (pp. 40-41) prefer "gelobt haben" and are followed by *RyET* (p. 58, in Fakhry 88/2): "promettre". The first translation, giving the 10th form of *wkl* the same meaning as that of the 1st, practically identifies *stwkl* with *rṯd*, and the second *stwkl* with *šft* (cf. *RyET*, p. 63, in Fakhry 102/3). J. H. Mordtmann und D. H. Müller (cf. *Sabäische Denkmäler*, Vienna, 1883, p. 29) already had proposed the equivalence of *stwkl*, *rṯd*, and *šft*. On the other hand, *NaNAG* (II, p. 41) identifies *stmlᵓ* with *stwkl*, translating both by the Arabic verb *ṭalaba* "to beseech, implore". The personal pronoun *hw* attached to *stwkl* refers to the deity (cf. *CoRoC*, p. 137 A) and not to the statue (as *CIH*, II, p. 243 B, in CIH 336/5-6) nor to the author of the inscription (as *CIH*, II, p. 247 A, in CIH 531/3). Further, *ᶜbdhw/nšᵓkrb* in CIH 336, as well as the personal names immediately following *stwklhw* here are the subject of the verb, and not its direct complement (cf. *CIH*, II, p. 243 B and *CoRoC*, *l.c.*). According to N. Rhodokanakis (cf. "Die Inschriften Os. 10 und 16," in *WZKM*, 29 [1915], p. 352), *stwkl* means "den Gott um seine Fürsorge und Hilfe bitten, indem man ihm dafür ein Gelübde macht" and "zuletzt 'als Preis für die Stellvertretung und Fürsorge geben'" (*l.c.*, note 3). With reference to the preceding explanation, *RyET* (p. 58) writes: "*stwklhw* X° forme de *wkl*, 's'en remettre à la protection (du dieu), à son secours', et aussi 'prendre un engagement'"; nevertheless, there is no argumentation supporting the last translation and *RyET* translates *stwkl* as "promettre". It is noteworthy that the ideas of vow, promise, help, protection, etc., are not directly or immediately involved either in Arabic *wakala* or in Ethiopic *wăkălă*, both roots indicating the idea of "trust, confidence". It is also interesting to note that both the 4th and the 8th forms of Arabic *wakala* have practically the same meaning, "to confide (in), trust entirely (in)", and the 1st form has a fundamentally active meaning, "to confide (to), trust (to)". Thus, I suggest translating *stwkl* in the above mentioned expressions as "to show one's confidence in" and, consequently, *ḏstwklhw* (e.g., Ja 726/3 and 816/4) or *ᵓly/stwk[lh]w* (here) as "by which he has shown his confidence in Him", *ḥgn/stwklhw* (Ja 605/4) or *ḥgn/ḏt/stwklhw* (Ja 704/3) as "as he has shown his confidence in Him", and *bḏt/stwkl/bᶜmhw* (Ja 655/5) as "because he has shown his confidence in Him". In other texts (e.g., Ja 568/6-7), the meaning of *stwkl* is "to bind oneself to". – *ᵓl[ᶜ]ṯt*, badly damaged; cp. *ᵓlᶜṯ* (RÉS 4186 B/2, Ḥaḏr; cf. commentary on Ja 711/1), which *RyNP* (I, pp. 244-45) mentions as a compound proper name derived from the root *ᶜṯṯ*; however, it should be noted that the interpretation of *ᶜṯ* as a diminutive of *ᶜṯtr* is also possible; *RyNP* (II, p. 16 A) quotes *ᵓlᶜṯ* among the names derived from *ᶜṯtr* and does not mention it among those from the root *ᶜṯṯ*. – *ᵓwsᶜṯt*, e.g., Ja 380/2, Qat and RÉS 4752; in RÉS 3099/2, read *ᵓlᶜz* instead of *ᵓlᶜṯ*.

L. 3: *ᶜblm*, e.g., RÉS 4595 C and Ja 585/3-4; for *bnw/ᶜblm*, cf. *JaPEHA*, p. 29. RÉS 4595 A reads as follows: *mbgmm* **stylized bucranium** *mrdᶜm*

"Mabgamum – Marda^cum". – *ʾlwhb*, e.g., RÉS 3902 bis, No. 138/1; the form *whbʾl* is more frequently used; e.g., RÉS 3087/22. – *drsm*, cf. in Daṯînah *daris* "être souillé, impur, sale" and its derived adjective *darîs* "souillé, impur" (cf. *LaGD*, pp. 750 and 757 respectively), and the personal Thamudic name *drs* (cf. *HaLiSTI*, p. 15, No. 64) and the Arabic name of a man *dirwâs* (cf. *WüID*, 327/2). – *dwsm*, e.g., RÉS 3111; cf. also the personal names in Arabic *daws* (cf. *SaIS*, p. 73), *dûyisî* (cf. *VNIA*, p. 187 A), and *dûwâs* (cf. *HeBN*, p. 24 A), and the adjective *dawwâs* in Daṯînah (cf. *LaGD*, p. 882), as well as in Arabic "brave, courageous". – *gnʾn*, noun in CIH 40/4 (cf. *BeSI*, p. 9) and not personal name (as *RyNP*, I, p. 62 A); cp. *gnʾm*, e.g., in Ja 286/1, Qat. – *lwfyhmw*/*wwfy*, a very common expression; e.g., RÉS 3966/4; *wfy* is also a noun in RÉS 3535/2, Min. – *ʾnfshmw* = *ʾfshmw* (e.g., Ja 750/9); *nfs* (cf. *StSESA*, p. 522) and *grb* (pl. *grbt*, e.g., in Ja 594/7, and *grybt*, e.g., in CIH 535/5 and Ja 567/10) indicate the human being in many texts. *nfs* in Condé 16/3 is erroneously translated "vie" (cf. *RyISA*, XVIII, p. 20). – *bḏt*, e.g., RÉS 4150/3 (cf. *HöASG*, pp. 163-64); very often mentioned in the formula *ḥmdm*/*bḏt* "in praise, because" (cf. *JaRIH*, p. 149, commentary on Hamilton 7/2); *bḏt* may have the same value as *lḏt*, e.g., *bḏt*/*hwfy*[*hmw*] in RÉS 4138/3 and *lḏt*/*hwfyhmw* in RÉS 4148/4-5.

L. 4: *wlḏt*/*yśfnhmw*, e.g., CIH 565/3-4 "ut augeat ipsos"; for *lḏt*, cf. *HöASG*, pp. 169-70; for *wśf*, cf. *BeSI*, p. 15, *BeFSTI*, p. 280, Soqoṭri *sef* "venir après, augmenter" (cf. *LeLS*, p. 283), Hebrew *yâsaf* "to add" (cf. *KoBaLVTL*, pp. 386-87 and *UlCSH*, p. 196) and the Western Semitic cognates in *JeHoDISO*, p. 109: *ysf*; the verb *wśf* is followed by two accusatives in RÉS 3946/8 (cf. *RhAST*, I, p. 99), but only by one in Ja 570/5; *RyET* (p. 58, in Fakhry 88/3) and *RyISA* (X, pp. 270-72 [on p. 271, the last line should be suppressed and the order in the translation of lines 5 and 6 restored], in JM 9+7/7) translate it as "enrichir"; but the idea of enriching is secondary; *BeFSTI* (p. 281, in Ist 7630/3) rightly translates as "to add"; cf. also *StSESA*, p. 524 and *BePESA*, p. 12. – *ʾlmqhw*: *w* might be a dittography: *ʾlmqhw*/*wldm*, since *ʾlmqh* is attested elsewhere in the text, viz. lines 2, 4-5, 5, 6 and 7. – *wld*, for the Western Semitic cognates, cf. *JeHoDISO*, p. 107: *yld*$_{\text{II}}$. – *hnʾ*, cf. *JaASAB*, pp. 171-72, commentary on CIH 352/10, *JaSASA*, pp. 176-79 and *JaSAAA*, pp. 264-66. *BeTMS* translates *hnʾ* as "good", and *RyHE* (p. 233) as "excellent". – *bry*/*ʾḏnm*/*wmqmm*, a very well-known formula (cf. *BeSI*, p. 15), e.g., CIH 76/8-9: "plenitudinem potentiae et auctoritatis" and in plural form *bry*/*ʾʾḏnm*/*wmqymtm*, e.g., CIH 152+.+151/2: "Fülle von Ansehn und Macht" (cf. *MoMiSI*, p. 54); cf. also *bry*/*ʾʾḏnm* in CIH 408/13-14: "plenitudinem facultatum ipsorum" and "mit Klugheit ihrer Sinne (Ohren)" (cf. *RhIAI*, p. 76). *CoRoC* (p. 118 A) refers *bry* to Accadian *barû* "fett sein, strotzen. III/II 2 übervoll sein, überreich sein" (cf. *BeBAG*, p. 92 B) and *RhIAI* (*l.c.*, note 4) to *bērtu* "Blick, offener Sinn, Klugheit" from *barû* "sehen, schauen, blicken" (cf. *BeBAG*, p. 92 A); cf. also *BeSI* (p. 15), who prefers the 1st opinion, "abundance", and is followed by *RyET* (p. 60, in Fakhry 95+94/3) and *RyISA* (X, p. 272, and XII, p. 301). One might refer *bry* to Hebrew *bârîʾ* "fat". For *ʾḏn*, *CoRoC* (p. 100 B) refers to Arabic *ʾuḏn* "ear" and translates as "potentia"; *RhIAI* (*l.c.*, note 4) mentions Accadian *uznu* "Sinn, Aufmerksamkeit, Verstand" (cf. *BeBAG*, p. 21 B); *BeSI* (*l.c.*) hesitates as to the etymology of *ʾḏn* and translates as "authority (or, understanding)"; and finally, G. Ryckmans: "puissance" (RÉS 4724 [Ja 420]/4, 4962/5 and *RyISA*, X, p. 272), "pouvoir" (e.g., RÉS 4648/4) and "autorité" (cf. *RyET*, p. 60, in Fakhry 95+94/3 and *RyISA*, XII, p. 301 and XV, p. 101) on the basis of *BeSI*, p. 15. There is no reason why *ʾḏn* and *mqm* (cf. below) should be synonymous; it seems preferable to keep *RhIAI*'s opinion. For *mqymt* (e.g., Ja 528/3), which is, as well as *mqmt*, pl. of *mqm* (cf. *CoRoC*, p. 230 B: "potestas"), G. Ryckmans translates as "les pouvoirs" (RÉS 3972/2), "pouvoir" (cf. *RyET*, p. 60, in Fakhry 95+94/3, *RyISA*, X, p. 272, XII, p. 301 and XV, p. 101), "autorité" (RÉS 4994/3) and finally "biens" (Ja 420/4); the latter interpretation (also proposed by *NaNAG*, II, p. 31, in Ja 602/15-16) is erroneous; *BeSI* (p. 14) translates as "might". Finally, *RycSD* translates *mqm* as "aide" (p. 345, in RÉS 4964/9; for this inscription, cf. *JaFSR*), thus confounding *mqm* and *rdʾ*. The expression *bry*/(ʾ)ʾ*ḏnm*/*wmq*(*y*)*m*(*t*)*m* may be translated "the strength of understanding and of power" (cf. also below, the commentary on line 5). *NaNAG*'s (*l.c.*) translation, "an increase of their goods", is an over-simplification of the South-

Arabian expression and adds a gratuitous personal pronoun. In the late text Ḥimâ/11 (cf. *RyISA*, X, p. 287), *ʾḏn/ʾsdn* certainly means "the strength of the soldiers"; the translation of *ʾḏn* as "understanding" also fits in RÉS 4336/4, Qat. According to *RycIHS* (pp. 321-22), JM 9+7 (see above) and RÉS 4658 would belong to the same original. First of all, the palaeography of JM 9+7 is much clearer in the photograph printed in *The Geographical Magazine* (London, July, 1954, p. 133, bottom) than in the one published in *Le Muséon* (cf. *l.c.*, pl. I). The letters in JM 9+7 are a little wider than those in RÉS 4658; the relation between height and width is 2.5 in *y*, *r*, and *ṯ* in the first, but 2.8 in the latter; the same relation is 3.33 in *d* in the first text but 3.48 in the second. Further, the letter height is 3.7 cm. in RÉS 4658 but 4 cm. in JM 9+7 (cf. *RyISA*, X, p. 270). Furthermore, the insertion of an expression such as *wbʿmhw/ḫm*...into the formula which precedes the verb of the principal phrase, as suggested by *RycIHS*, (p. 322), is quite unusual. Finally, *RycIHS*'s correction of RÉS 4658/6 is erroneous;...*krb*...is certain and is preceded by...]ₗ/*w*ₗ. Note that the beginning of RÉS 4658/5 reads...*gwn* before *yṯl*, instead of *h*]*g*?[*r*]*n*, and also that one *h* is still visible in line 7. – *yhʿnnhmw/wmtʿ*, cf. *JaASAB*, p. 158, commentary on CIH 407/7-8. *BeTMS* gives *mtʿ* in AshM 1957-17/4 the meaning "to protect".

L. 5: *bn/bʾstm/wnkytm*, e.g., CIH 82/9-10; in the present collection, *bʾst* is mentioned in all the texts, except Ja 615/26 and 670/17, where *bʾs* is attested. For a complete discussion of the expression, cf. *JaASAB*, pp. 165-66, commentary on CIH 407/32; for the repetition *nky* – *nkyt* in CIH 82/9-10, cf. that of *nkyt* in Ja 650/32-33, and also that of *hʿn* in Ja 700/16-17. For *bʾst*, cf. the Western Semitic cognates in *JeHoDISO*, p. 31: *bʾyš*. – *ʿdq*, cf. post-biblical Hebrew *ʿădaq* "to stick to" and Pael "to bring close" (cf. *JaDT*, p. 1045 B); *ʿdq* could be translated "press". – *qmt* may be derived from the root *wqm*; cf. Arabic *waqama* "to treat with violence and hardness, to debase"; *qmt* could be translated "harsh treatment". It seems to me that *bry/ʾḏnm/wmqmm* has some antithetic connection with *bn/ʿdqm/wqmtm*; there may be a paronomia in the words *mqm* and *qmt*. – *mlʾ*, cf. *JaASAB*, p. 159, commentary on CIH 407/10-11. – *ḥf*, cf. *ḥff* "faire qc. en rond, tout autour de qc, entourer" (cf. *LaGD*, p. 439 and also *LaH*, p. 553); here, encirclement. – *šnʾ*, cf. *CoRoC*, p. 250 and *MoNTA*, pp. 132-33. – *ḏt/tnbʾhw*: the singular pronoun *hw* is related to ʾIlʿaṯat as the leader of the persons mentioned in line 1.

L. 6: *mrʾyhmw*, cf. e.g., Ist 7628/4 (instead of the singular [*mr*]ʾ*hmw* as in *BeFSTI*, pp. 276-77).

L. 7: *fyšn*, a very well-known tribal name; e.g., RÉS 2726/3; cf. S. Smith, in *Vetus Testamentum*, II (1952), p. 287 and A. F. L. Beeston, in *BrBeSIS*, pp. 52-53; contrast *JaRIH*, p. 147 and note 3. – *rṯd*, e.g., *JaCD*, p. 68. The expression *rṯdw/– –/ʿṯtr/šrqn/wldhmw/ḥmyt/wʾhlht/hrmm* in Fakhry 127/3-4 is translated by *RyET* (p. 78) as follows: "Et ont placé – – sous la protection de ʿAṯtar Šariqân, leurs enfants du district et des clans (urbains) de Harimum". In his review of *RyET*, A. F. L. Beeston (cf. *BSOAS*, 16 [1953], p. 396) rightly corrects the preceding grammatical interpretation by considering the subjects of the inscriptions as the subjects of *rṯdw*. However, *RyHE* (p. 227) simply maintains his inaccurate interpretation, and omits the translation of *ʿṯtr/šrqn*. Further, "leurs enfants du district" is surely not correct; *ḥmyt* is a proper name as indicated by A. F. L. Beeston (cf. *l.c.*), who suggests reading *wgdhmw* "their ancestor" instead of *wldhmw*. Here again, *RyHE* simply maintains his previous translation, as follows: "their children of the district". Although *RyET* (p. 78) states that "la copie de Fakhry a été collationnée sur une photographie lisible", the decipherment of the end of line 4 needs to be revised. I suggest that the original contains some formula like *wwd/wḏt/ḥmym/wʾlʾlt/hrmm* "and Wadd and Ḏât-Ḥimyâm and the deities of Haramum". – *ʾlmqh/hqnythmw*, RÉS 4139/12, where the present order of the terms is inverted. – *hkrnh*: *hnkrhw* in Ja 562/21 (cp. *hqḏ* from *nqḏ* in CIH 353/12; cf. also *HöASG*, p. 94, §79); 4th form of *nkr* and parallel to Min and Qat *snkr* "to change" (cf. *JaPEHA*, p. 198); cf. the noun *nkr* in RÉS 5094/4; the pronoun *h* in *hkrnh* as well as in *ʾḫrnh* and *ḍrynh* obviously refers to the feminine noun *hqnyt*. – *ʾḫrnh*, RÉS 2695/1 (cf. *RhSLG*, II, pp. 151-52); cf. *DoSDA* (I, p. 13 A): "II destituer, déposer" and the derived meaning "s'en aller, s'écarter, se détacher de" (cf. *LaGD*, p. 70); cf. also the Hebrew Piel *ʾêḥar* "to detain someone, keep back" (cf. *KoBaLVTL*, p. 31 B; cf. RÉS 4230/10 and *JaASAB*, p. 186); the Hebrew Qâl of *ʾḥr* "to stay on" is attested, e.g., in Ja 601/17; *ʾḫr* is an adjective, e.g., in Ja 633/12.

L. 8: *ḏrynh*, cf. Arabic *ḏaraʾa* "to be hidden, to hide one's self"; *ḏry* may be considered as a 2nd form with an active meaning.

b – Našaʾkarib Yuhaʾmin: Ja 559-561

559 – Yellowish, slightly grayish sandstone; cf. Chapter I, A; partial photograph in *Aramco Handbook* (Haarlem, 1960), p. 309. – MaMB 221.

STONE: thickness: 42 cm. (top) and 39.5 (bottom). – *Front:* upper left corner broken; a large piece is splintered off on the left edge; 1.482 m. × 53.3 cm. (top) and 53 (bottom). – INSCRIPTION: same disposition of lines as in Ja 123; letter height: from 6.5 cm. (top) to 5.5 (bottom); space between the lines: between 0.6 cm. and 0.4. – SYMBOL: the drawing in my notebook does not mention any particular details, since I expected to have both photograph and squeeze of the text; cf. Plate A; cp. *GrGST*, p. 6A, Fig. 1.

1 **Sym-** *bnw/grt/ʾq[wl/šᶜbn/ḏmry]*
2 **bol** *wšᶜbhmw/smhrm/hq⌜ny⌝[w]*
3 *ʾlmqh/bᶜl/ʾwm/ṣlmnhn/ḏy/ḏh*
4 *bn/ḥmdm/bḏt/sᶜdhmw/ʾlmqh*
5 *wfy/mrʾhmw/nšʾkrb/yhʾmn*
6 *mlk/sbʾ/bn/ḏmrᶜly/ḏrḥ/wbḏ[t]*
7 *sᶜd/ʾlmqh/bᶜl/ʾwm/mrʾhm[w/n]*
8 *šʾkrb/stqḥn/mqyḥt/ṣdqm⌜/b⌝*
9 *kl/ʾbrṯ/bhmw/hwṣl/lbytn*
10 *slḥn/bʾḍrrm/wbslmm/wl/w*
11 *zʾ/ʾlmqh/sᶜd/mrʾhmw/nšʾk*
12 *rb/wfym/wᶜztm/wkhltm/wbry*
13 *ʾḏnm/wmqmm/wl/sᶜdhmw/ʾlmqh*
14 *wfy/bytn/slḥn/wʾbᶜlhw/wwfy*
15 *ʾdmhw/bny/grt/wqlhmw/bᶜṯtr*
16 *šrqn/wᶜṯtr/ḏḏbn/whwbs/wʾlmqh*
17 *wḏt/ḥmym/wḏt/bᶜdnm/wbšms/m*
18 *lkn/tnf/wb/ʾlyhmw/ᶜṯtr/ᶜzzm*
19 *wḏt/ẓhrn/bᶜly/ᶜrn/knn/wrṯdw/h*
20 *qnytn/ᶜṯtr/šrqn/wʾlmqh/bᶜl/ʾwm*

1 **Sym-** The people of Garat, ru[lers of the tribe] Ḏamrî,]
2 **bol** and their tribe Sumhurâm, [have] dedicated
3 to ʾIlumquh, master of ʾAwwâm, these two statues, both in bronze,
4 in praise because ʾIlumquh has made them happy
5 with the safety of their lord Našaʾkarib Yuhaʾmin,
6 king of Sabaʾ, son of Ḏamarᶜalay Ḏariḥ, and becau[se]
7 ʾIlumquh, master of ʾAwwâm, has made happy thei[r] lord [Na-]
8 šaʾkarib with drawing perfect profit from
9 all the places which he [the king] has entrusted to the house
10 Salḥân in wars and in peace; and that
11 ʾIlumquh may continue to make happy their lord Našaʾka-
12 rib with safety and vigor and might and [with] the strength
13 of understanding and of power: and that ʾIlumquh may make them happy
14 with the safety of the house Salhân and of its masters and with the safety
15 of His worshippers, the people of Garat, and of their ruler. By ᶜAṯtar
16 Šarqân and ᶜAṯtar, Him of Ḏabân, and Hawbas and ʾIlumquh
17 and Ḏât-Ḥimyâm and Ḏât-Baᶜdânum and by Šams of the
18 king, Tanûf, and by their two gods ᶜAṯtar ᶜAzîzum
19 and Ḏât-Ẓahrân, the two masters of the citadel Kanin. And they have entrusted the
20 offering to the care of ᶜAṯtar Šarqân, and of ʾIlumquh, master of ʾAwwâm.

L. 1: *bnw/grt*, cp. *bnw/ᶜblm* in Ja 558/3; *grt*, family name as, e.g., in RÉS 4818/4; cf. also CIH 985/3 (masculine personal name) and RÉS 4627/3 (name of a palm-grove). At the end of the line, *ʾq[wl/šᶜbn/ḏmry]* is certain; according to Ja 561/1-2, text identical with Ja 559, *ʾq[wl/šᶜbn]* must be read in Ja 559/1 and the last two letters of the following tribal name are *ry*; but Ja 606 and 607 also mention the clan name *grt*, the tribal names *smhrm* and *ḏmry* (line 3; cf. also Ja 650/2 and 24-25); the latter fits the blank perfectly in Ja 561/1-2 and also here; the restoration of *ḏmry* is certain, for the photograph of Ja 561 shows that the lower part of the first letter of the tribal name is composed of the extremities of two vertical strokes, those of a *ḏ*; cf. also Ja 568 and 753 A; *ḏmry*, proper name with *nisba* ending, cf. *ḏḏmryn* in Ja 516/5 (cf. commentary in *JaISAR*, p. 114), and *ḏmr*, name of a town (e.g., Ja 576/14). – *qwl* (e.g., Ja 489 A/1), *ql* or *qyl* (e.g., CIH 314 + 954/2), pl. *ʾqwl* (e.g., CIH 648/2, where *CIH* [III, p. 82] rightly reads [ʾ]*qwl*, contrary to *BeSI* [p. 144], who mentions *qwl* as plural in this text, and also RÉS 4712/3); in Ḥimâ/1, *RyISA* (X, pp. 285-86) reads *ʾql* as plural; the photograph of this passage (upper left corner of pl. III, between pp. 312 and 313) is so obscure that it is impossible to check this reading; *ʾqwl* is, however, mentioned in line 2 of the same inscription. The noun *qwl* has been variously interpreted; e.g., *CIH*: "princeps" (in CIH 37/6, 40/1, and 645/3) and "dux" (in CIH 599/2 and 648/2); this opinion is the same as that of N. Rhodokanakis: "Vogt (Führer)" (cf. *RhSLG*, II, p. 151, in RÉS 2695 [CIH 599]/2, and *RhIAI*, p. 25, in RÉS 4624/6), and also of M. Höfner in RÉS 4190/8 (cf. *HöSSE*, p. 9) and *HöASG*, p. 26: "Vogt"; *CoRoC* (p. 230 A): "princeps"; *KeHYNI* (p. 371): "prince" and also *BeSI*: "prince" (pp. 8-9, in CIH 40/1, and pp. 76-77, in RÉS 4176/5) and "prince" and "lord" in the same line of CIH 37/6 (pp. 6-7); there is no reason for using two different terms in CIH 37/6; G. Ryckmans: "chef" (RÉS 2633/9), then "préposé" (e.g., RÉS 3300 A and 4658/1), again "chef" (RÉS 4712 [Ja 495]/3) and then again "préposé" (RÉS 4771/1 and Fakhry 3/2). Finally, some authors only transliterate the noun, e.g., *MoMiSI*: "Qail" (p. 38, in RÉS 3990/1-2), *MoMiHI*: "Qail" (p. 13, in RÉS 4127/4) and E. Mittwoch and H. Schlobies in RÉS 4677/2 and 4638/1, indifferently "Qail" or "Qaul". Translations such as "prince" are certainly much too precise; others, such as "préposé", allude to the root *qdm* rather than to the root *qwl* "to speak", here "to give commands". Since the noun "commander" has some military connotation, I propose translating *qwl* as "ruler", someone who, by his words, issues orders.

L. 2: *smhrm*, name of a man in RÉS 4763/2; personal name in the unpublished Qat text TC 809; name of an ancient city in the region of Ṣalâlah, presently Ḫôr Rôrî (cf. Ja 402/4 and *JaNA*); cf. also the masculine name *smhrym*, e.g., in Ja 831/1.

L. 3: *ṣlmnhn*, cf. *JaASAB*, p. 158, commentary on CIH 407/7.

L. 4: *ḥmdm/bḏt*, cf. *JaASAB*, *l.c. BeTMS* translates the whole expression, e.g., in AshM 1957-16/3-4, as "in gratitude because". – *sʿd*, cf. *JaASAB*, p. 171, commentary on CIH 352/9; cf. also *MoNTA*, pp. 126-27; *BeTMS* translates the verb in AshM 1957-16/7 as "to prosper". *sʿdhmw/ʾlmqh/wfy/mrʾhmw* is parallel to *sʿdhmw/[ʾ]lmqh/ḥẓy/wrḍw/mrʾ[y]hmw* translated by J. Walker in RÉS 4842/8-10 as follows: "Ilmakah may felicitate with favour and grace their two Lords"; but *hmw* in *sʿdhmw* is not translated; *mrʾyhmw* is erroneously interpreted as direct complement of *sʿd*, and "two" must be placed between brackets.

L. 8: *stqḥn/mqyḥt/ṣdqm: stqḥ*, 10th form of *qwḥ* (cf. the 4th form *hqwḥ* in CIH 40/2 and *hqḥ* in CIH 520/2), and *mqyḥt*, derived from the same root; for *mqyḥt/ṣdqm*, cf. CIH 137/1; cf. *RhKTB* (II, pp. 21-23), who relates *qwḥ* to Arabic *qâḥa* (o, i) "to sweep, clean (a house)" and *qâḥat* "court (of a house)". The present expression is also attested in Ja 561/8-9, and *stqḥ* followed by the preposition *b* also mentioned in Ja 644/19. The present collection of Sab texts mentions *mq(y)ḥ(t)* along with *wfy* "safety" (e.g., Ja 601/11), *mhrgt* "war trophies" (e.g., Ja 561 bis/7), *mlt* "riches" (Ja 643 bis/6), *mngt* "security" (e.g., Ja 601/11) and *ġnmt* "booty" (e.g., Ja 561 bis/7-8). In these contexts, there is no question of building, as in the inscriptions studied by *RhKTB* and, e.g., RÉS 4648/6. On the basis of Ja 602/11, *NaNAG* (II, p. 31) translates *mqḥ* as "felicity, welfare", but his commentary also suggests "gain, profit" (p. 33), although there is no etymological commentary. According to the present text, *stqḥ/mqyḥt* is considered as a blessing for the king, and *mqyḥt* are *bkl/ʾbrṯ* "in *or* from all the places" entrusted by the king to the house Salḥân. I should suggest considering the 1st meaning of Arabic *qâḥa* "to suppurate (a wound)", which seems to allude to the idea of a thing coming out from something else, and thus translating *mq(y)ḥ(t)* as "profit, advantage" and *stqḥ* as "to draw (profit)". – *ṣdqm*, cf. *JaASAB*, p. 171, commentary on CIH 352/10, *JaSASA*, pp. 180-81 and *JaSAAA*, pp. 266-67, cf. the noun *ṣdq* in Ja 567/11 and 12.

Ll. 8-9: *bkl: b* has the same value as that of *bn* "from"; e.g., *bkl/ʾrḍthmw* (Ja 618/23) and *bnkl ʾrḍhmw* (Ja 628/22-23), *btʾwln-/bkl/sbʾ[t]* (Ja 586/11-13) and *btʾwln/-/bnkl/sbʾt* (Ja 635/8-9); *b* or *bn* are often replaced by *ʿdy*.

L. 9: *ʾbrṯ*, pl. of *brṯ*, the primary meaning of which is "place, site" (cf. *JaPEHA*, pp. 197-99 [commentary on Ja 350/4, Qat], *JaDME*, pp. 15-16 and *JaISAR*, pp. 114-15 and note 1 [commentary on Ja 516/8]); this meaning is attested, e.g., in Qat Ja 350/4 and RÉS 4336/6, and in Sab RÉS 4962/17-18 (cf. *BeNL*, V, p. 109 and *JaDME*, pp. 26-27, note 21, contrary to G. Ryckmans: "[military] expedition"); secondary meanings of *brṯ* are "military campaign" (e.g.,

RÉS 4842/2 and Ja 635/19) and "proclamation" (e.g., Ja 516/8; in RÉS 4986/3, the text is too fragmentary to justify the translation "destination"); cf. the verb *brṯw* in Ja 651/27-28. – *hwṣl*, 4th form of *wṣl*; cf. *JaRIH*, pp. 149-50 (remark on Hamilton 7/3); *bkl/ʾbrṯ/bhmw/hwṣl/lbytn slḥn/bʾḏrrm/wbslmm* with Našaʾkarib as subject has a meaning slightly different from that of the following expression in spite of their material resemblance: *bkl/ʾbrṯ/ʿdyhmw/hwṣlw/lḏrm* (Ja 561 bis/10-11). The form *hwṣl* originally means "to join"; however, in the first above-mentioned expression, the preceding meaning implies the secondary idea of committing one's self; cf. Arabic *waṣala*, 4th form "to intercede, intervene" with the preposition *l*; in this expression, *hwṣl* may thus be translated "to entrust". In the second expression, however, *hwṣl* simply indicates the fact of joining. Thus, the two expressions mean respectively "in all the places which he [the king] entrusted to the house Salḥân in wars and in peace" and "in all the military campaigns in which they intervened for war". The second expression is similar to [ʾ]*brṯ/bhmw/yhwṣlnn* (JM 9+7/6) "the military campaign[s] which they will join" and not "les ex]péditions [*sic*] par lesquelles il réunisse(?)" (cf. *RyISA*, X, p. 271), *yhwṣlnn* being plural and not singular. The meaning "to assemble, regroup" fits Ja 576/4, 578/25, and 665/24, indicating the effect of joining (cf. *LaAEL*, pp. 3054C-55B, and *FrLAL*, p. 677 B and *LaGD*, pp. 2924-25).

L. 10: *slḥn*, e.g., RÉS 3946/5; 2nd name of a man in RÉS 2687/1, Ḥaḍr, and of a family in RÉS 3902, No. 17, Qat; in Sab, *slḥn* is the name of the royal fortress in Mârib (cf. *CIH*, I, p. 303 and Ja 644/6-7); cf. also the proper name *slḥm* in RÉS 4528/2. – *bʾḏrrm/wslmm*, cp. Min *bḏrm/wslmm* (e.g., RÉS 2831/3) and *bḏr/wslm* (RÉS 2774/3); *slm* is also a noun in RÉS 3535/2, Min; for the verb *slm*, cf. commentary on Ja 550/2.

Ll. 10-11: *wl/wzʾ*, cp. *wlwzʾ* in RÉS 4233/11 (cf. *JaSAA*, p. 154 A); in RÉS 4842/6, *wzʾ* is not translated.

L. 12: *wfym/wʿztm/wkhltm/wbry/ʾḏnm/wmqm*, cf. CIH 326/3; for *ʿzt*, cf. Arabic *ʿizzat* "gloria" (cf. *CIH*, I, p. 365 B); the translation "power, might" is certainly to be preferred; cf. also *LeLS* (p. 304): "*ʿzz*, raffermir, donner de la force" and the Semitic parallels mentioned there. – *khlt*, cf. *CIH*, *l.c.*; in Soqoṭri, cf. *LeLS*, (p. 214): "*khl*, *kol*, pouvoir, connaître...*kohóte* 'force'"; in Daṯînah, cf. *LaGD* (p. 2590): "*kahil*, a, dans le Sud, pouvoir...*kâhil*, puissant"; in Aramaic *kâhêl* "to be able" (cf. *KoBaLVTL*, p. 1084 B and *JeHoDISO*, pp. 115-16).

L. 14: *wfy/bytn/slḥn*, Fakhry 9/4-5. – *ʾbʿlhw*, e.g., RÉS 3966/5.

L. 15: *ʾdmhmw*: for *ʾdm*, cf. commentary on Ja 557: *ʿbd*; *RyISA* (XII, p. 300, in Geukens 1/1) gives *ʾs* the meaning of "gens de", that is also given both to *ʾdm* and *ʾsd* by *RyET*, e.g., p. 4, in Fakhry 3/1 and 7 respectively; *ʾdm* in relation with deities may be translated as "worshippers". – *qlhmw*, RÉS 3990/9; the clan of Garat was dependent on the fortress of Salḥân, and its authority upon the clan was exercised by a man bearing the title of *ql* "ruler".

L. 16: *šrqn*, cf. *JaP*, p. 88, and *JaRSAP*, p. 265. – *ḏbn*, name of a mountain (cf. *JaP*, p. 94 and note 322).

Ll. 17-18: *šms/mlkn/tnf*, cf. *JaP*, pp. 101-03, 96, and 106, and *JaRSAP*, pp. 266-67; for *šms*, cf. also *StSESA*, p. 530.

L. 18: *ʾly*, construct dual of *ʾl*; for the Western Semitic cognates, cf. *JeHoDISO*, p. 13: $ʾl_{VI}$. – *ʿzzm*=*ʿzzn* (e.g., Ja 631/20; cp. *ʿm/ryʿm*=*ʿm/ryʿn*, cf. *JaSASA*, p. 178 and *JaSAAA*, p. 265), cf. Arabic *ʿazîz*, pl. *ʿizâz* "powerful, mighty", the family name *ʾʿzz* in Ja 702/2 and the noun *ʿzt* in line 12. The new qualification *ʿzz*(*m* or *n*) of ʿAṯtar perfectly suits (cf. *JaRSAP*, p. 265 and note 2) the etymology of *ʿṯtr* proposed in *JaP*, p. 85, note 229, whose original text is restored in *JaIAA*, p. 317: *ʿṯtr* is related to Arabic *ʿattâr* "strong, brave, courageous"; *ʿzzm* is also personal name, e.g., in RÉS 5081; the root *ʿzz* is frequently used in proper names, e.g., *ʾlʿz* (RÉS 3958/8), *bʿzhmw* (RÉS 3959/3), *ʿzz*[] (CIH 406/8), *ʿzm* (Ja 186; cf. commentary and *JaDME*, p. 18), *ʿztm* (CIH 816), *ʿzyz* (RÉS 2773/1, Min); cf. also the following Arabic names of men (*ʾabû*) *ʿzyz* (cf., e.g., *SaIS*, p. 160 A), *ʿûzîz*, *ʿizayyiz* (cf. *HeBN*, p. 39 B), *ʿazîzî* (cf. *WüR*, p. 555), *ʿzyzt* (cf. *GoAT*, p. 384), *ʿazzat* (cf. *WüR*, *l.c.*) and of a place *ʿazâz* (cf. *WüR*, p. 151 A).

L. 19: *ḏt/ẓhrn*, cf. *JaP*, pp. 107-08 and note 454, and *JaRSAP*, p. 267: a name of the Qat sun goddess, probably with the meaning "she who appears in her splendor". – *bʿly*, cp. *ʾly* in line 18; both ʿAṯtar and Ḏât-Ẓahrân are worshipped in the same place; cp. *šrqn/wḏt/ḥmym/bʿly/mḥrmn/rydn* (CIH 41/3) "Šarqân and Ḏât-Ḥimyâm, the two masters of the temple Raydân" (cf. *JaP*, p. 92): in the two preceding texts, the deities are distinct from each other; in other inscriptions, it is the same deity under different names; e.g., *ʿṯtr/wsḥr/bʿly/nfqn* "ʿAṯtar and Saḥar [cf. *JaP*, p. 99 and *JaRSAP*, p. 266], the two masters of Nafqân" (cf. *JaP*, p. 92) and *ʾlmqh/ṯhwn/wṯwr/bʿlm/bʿly/ʾwm*, e.g., in Ja 563/19-20 (cf. commentary). – *ʿr*, e.g., CIH 5/2 and *ʿrnhn*, e.g., in Ja 564/30-31; cf. *CoRoC*, p. 213 A: a mountain with a citadel on top of it and hence the citadel itself (cf. also *HöASG*, p. 43; "Burg", *HöTPK*, pp. 30-31: Gl 1142/8: "Berg"(and *ʿurr* "montagne (isolée)" in both Daṯînah (cf. *LaGD*, p. 2276) and modern Ḥaḍr (cf. *LaH*, p. 653); cf. also Ugaritic *ġwr=ġr* (cf. *GoUM*, p. 309 A, No. 1471); the translation as "ville" (cf. *RÉS*, in RÉS 3551/3, Qat and in the commentary on RÉS 4904/2) is not correct. For the palaeography of the latter, cf. *JaPSAP*, pp. 38, 62, and 120. The ordinary writing is *ʿr*; however, the full writing of it, *ʿrr*, is attested in RÉS 4907/7-8: *ṣwd/ʿrrm* translated by *BeAIP* (p. 448) as follows "a hillside (plantation) of cypresses (?)", *ʿrr* being related to Arabic *ʿarʿar*; I translate *swd/ʿrrm* as "the side of a mountain". Further, in RÉS 4904/2, Ḥaḍr, *gnʾ/ʿrrtm/ḥrb* is translated by *BeAIP* (p. 445) as "walled with fortifications ḤRB"; but, the verb *gnʾ* is ordinarily followed immediately by the proper name of the building or of the city (e.g., RÉS 3624/1, 3948/2, 3950/2; for the palaeography of RÉS 3948, cf. *JaPSAP*, pp. 76-79, 126-28, 130-32, 150, and 187, notes 5 and 7). On the other hand, the nouns mentioning the material from which the building is made (here, parts of the building), usually follow the name of the building (e.g., RÉS 2771/2-3, Min, 3869/2-3, Ḥaḍr, and 3880/5-6, Qat). It thus seems better to consider *ʿrrtm* as the proper name of the building or the city or whatever it may be, and *ḥrb* as name of a valley attested in Ja 649/25. – *knn*, name of a mountain (cf. *CIH*, I, p. 227), 2nd personal name in Ja 882 U, Qat, and also the name of a tomb in RÉS 4836/1, Min, which reads *ḏ]n/qbrn/knn/ṯm[n...* "...has added...to th]is tomb Kanin eigh[t...". *RÉS*'s translation, "...Tham...a achevé ce tombeau" is impossible because of the invertion of all the terms. – *rṯdw/hqnytn*, e.g., Ja 558/7.

560 – Yellowish, slightly grayish sandstone; cf. Chapter I, A. – MaMB 222.

STONE: thickness: 33.5 cm. (top) and 36 (bottom). – *Front:* right edge badly damaged; 1 m. × 57.2 cm. – INSCRIPTION: same disposition of lines as in Ja 559; letter height: from 4.7 cm. to 3.5; space between the lines: 0.5 cm.; reading sometimes very difficult.

1 **[Sym-** *ġw]ṯm/...r/[w]ʾslm/wbnyhmw/[ʾbk]*
2 **[bol** *r]b/ḏʿ[y]nwm/bnw/gmyln/ʿrgn/ʾk*
3 *[br/]šʿbn/mydʿm/wʿlt/ʾḏnt/hqnyw/ʾ*
4 *[l]mqh/ṯhwn/bʿl/ʾwm/ṣlmnhn/ḏbhmy*
5 *[ḥmd]/ġwṯm/mqm/ʾlmqh/bḏt/hwfy/ʾlmqh*
6 *[bkl/ʾ]mlʾ/stmlʾw/bʿmhw/lnkl/bythmw*
7 *[sl]ḥn/ḏgmyln/wbḏt/stwfy/ṣry/bnhw*
8 *⌞ʾ⌟bkrb/wbḏt/stwfy/sbʾt/wbltw/blt*
9 *[hw/]mrʾhw/nšʾkrb/yhʾmn/mlk/sbʾ/bn*
10 *[ḏmrʿ]ly/ḏrḥ/ʿdy/ʾrḍ/ʿrbn/lstwkbn*
11 *[whn]qḏn/ʾṣḥb/ṣḥbw/h̲lfn/hgrn/mryb*
12 *[wst]wkbw/w⌜h⌝nqḏn/wʾh̲ḏ/hmt/ʾsdn/ʾṣ*
13 *[ḥb]h(mw)/whnbw/rkbhmw/wʾh̲[ḏ]w/ʾsdn/ʾ*
14 *rḍn/wrkbhmw/whwtwhmw/ʿdy/hgrn/mr*
15 *[yb/...../mrʾhw]/nšʾkrb/mlk/sbʾ/w*
16 *[ḥmd]/ġwṯm/mqm/ʾlmqh/bḏt/hwfyhmw/b*
17 *ʾmlʾ/stmlʾ/bʿmhw/wl/wẓʾ/ʾlmqh/s*
18 *ʿd/ʿbdhw/ġwṯm/nʿmtm/wḥẓy/mr⟨ʾ⟩hmw*
19 *nšʾkrb/yhʾmn/mlk/sbʾ/bn/ḏmrʿly/ḏ*
20 *rḥ/bʿṯtr/whbs/wʾlmqh/wbḏt/ḥmym/wbḏt*
21 *bʿdnm/wb/šms/mlkn/tnf/wb/ʾlmqh/ḏgblm*

1 **[Sym-** Ġaw]ṯum...r [and] ʾAslam and their son [ʾAbka-]
2 **[bol** ri]b, of [the clan] ʿA[y]nawum, people of Gumaylân ʿArgân, lead-
3 [ers of] the tribe Muyaddaʿum, bringing fame to ʾAḏanat, have dedicated to ʾI-
4 [lu]mquh Ṯahwân, master of ʿAwwâm, these two statues by both of which
5 Ġawṯum [has praised] the power of ʾIlumquh, because ʾIlumquh has granted
6 [all the] favor[s for which] they had besought Him for the decoration of their house
7 [Sal]ḥân of Gumaylân, and because He has given counsel to his son
8 ʾAbkarib, and because He has given protection in the military campaign and (military) duties [which] has imposed
9 upon [him] his lord Našaʾkarib Yuhaʾmin, king of Sabaʾ, son of
10 [Ḏamarʿa]lay Ḏariḥ, in the country of the Arabs in order to bring back
11 [and res]cue the friends [who] accompanied the countrymen of the city [of] Mârib;
12 [and] they [brought] back and rescued and seized these soldiers, the(ir)
13 fri[end]s and they replaced their riding animals and the soldiers se[iz]ed the

14 land and their riding animals and they sent them back to the city [of] Mâr[ib,

15 ...his lord] Naša'karib, king of Saba'; and

16 Gawṯum [has praised] the power of 'Ilumquh, because He has granted to them

17 the favors [for which] he has besought Him; and that 'Ilumquh may continue to

18 make His worshipper Ġawṯum happy with prosperity and [with] the esteem of their lord

19 Naša'karib Yuha'min, king of Saba', son of Ḏamarᶜalay Ḏa-

20 riḥ. By ᶜAṯtar and Hawbas and 'Ilumquh and by Ḏât-Ḥimyâm and by Ḏât-

21 Baᶜdânum and by Šams of the king, Tanûf, and by 'Ilumquh, Him of Gablum.

L. 1: the symbol is missing. – [*ġw*]*ṯm* is restored on the basis, e.g., of line 5: cf. Gl 1131+1132+1133/2 (cf. *HöDSP*, pp. 40-41), RÉS 3902, No. 63, Qat; cf. also *ġwṯ*, 2nd personal name in RÉS 3870/1, Qat (the reading of this name in CIH 985/4 is uncertain), *ġṯm*, name of a woman in ᶜAin Jawan 1/1 (cf. F. V. Winnett, in *BASOR*, No. 102, April, 1946, p. 4), *'ġwṯm*, masculine personal name in RÉS 4205/1-2, 4854 B/1-2, and 4867/3, Ḥaḍr, *yġṯ*, 2nd personal name in RÉS 5002, and *ġwṯ'l*, name of a man in Ja 340/1, Qat, and RÉS 2837/1, Min, or its equivalent *ġwś'l* (cf. *StSESA*, p. 528). *ġwṯ* is attested either as a verb ("to improve"; e.g., RÉS 2814/2, Min) or as a noun ("improvement"; e.g., RÉS 2869/2, Min). RÉS 4205 reads as follows: *nṣb/smbyn/'ġ* (line 2)*wṯm/ġrḥyn* "stela of Sumbayyin 'Aġ (line 2)waṯum, the Ġaraḥite". RÉS 4854, Ḥaḍr, is composed of two texts which are separated from each other by a crevice in the rock; A on the right and B on the left. A reads as follows:

nhdm/bn/m	1	Nahdum, son of Mu-
l'nmm	2	la'imum.

– *'slm*, e.g., Hamilton 12a, Ḥaḍr (cf. *JaRIH*, p. 155), and *'slmm* in Van Lessen 9/3, Qat.

Ll. 1-2: *'bkrb* is completed on the basis of line 8. The nominal formation *'aqtal* is frequently attested in South-Arabian onomastics, e.g., in RÉS 4696 (Ḥaḍr)/1-2: *–/'r* (line 2) *nb/bnt/f* (line 3) *lšm* "–'Ar (line 2) nab, daughter of Fa (line 3) lašum".

L. 2: ᶜ[.]*nwm* could be restored as ᶜ[*n*]*nwm*; cf. the verb ᶜ*nw*, e.g., in RÉS 3956/8 and Ja 525/3-4 "to humble one's self". The preceding hypothetical restoration is difficult for the orthographic reduplication of the 2nd radical is extremely rare. The proper name ᶜ*ynm* (Ja 575/6) suggests ᶜ[*y*]*nwm*; the ending *wm* in a proper name is already attested, e.g., in *ḥlzwm* (Ja 629/27). – *bnw/gmyln*, cp. *ḏgmyln* in line 7; the *qutaylân* form is especially found in the Qat texts from Ḥeid bin ᶜAqîl (cf. *JaPEHA*, p. 11); cf. *gmwln* in RÉS 4127/1[1]; and the Arabic personal names *ǧimîl*, *ǧimîlat*, *ǧimîli*, and *bû ǧimlîn* (cf. *SlGaVNPA*, p. 17 B); *bnw/gmyln/ᶜrgn*, cf. *bnw/ᶜrgn/gmwln* in AM 206/3, where *RyISA* (VIII, pp. 60-61) translates *gmwln* as "ensemble" and interprets it as a common noun; this author may have been misled by his transliteration of *gmwlN* as *gmwlM* (cf. commentary on p. 61); cf. also the 2nd personal name *gml* in Ja 881 E/1, Qat (cf. *JaPEQL*, p. 209) and personal name *gmlm* in Ja 878/1, Qat. For ᶜ*rgn*, cf. Arabic ᶜ*arǧân*, ᶜ*araǧân*, *maṣdar* of the 1st form of ᶜ*rǧ* (and not an adjective; cf. *l.c.*, p. 61) "gait of a lame person"; the adjective is 'aᶜ*raǧu*, pl. ᶜ*urǧ* and ᶜ*urǧân* "lame"; cf. also the following proper names: ᶜ*rgn* in Safaitic (cf. *LiSI*, pp. 336-37), ᶜ*rǧ* in Thamudic (cf. *vdBrIT*, p. 290: Jsa 500) and in Arabic ᶜ*arǧûn*, *al-*ᶜ*ariǧ* (cf. *SlGaVNPA*, p. 6 B) and ᶜ*ar*(*r*)*ûǧ* (cf. *VNIA*, p. 18); cf. also the noun ᶜ*rg* in Safaitic (cf. *LiSI*, p. 336 B) and al-ᶜarǧîyu (cf. *WüID*, 48/22).

L. 3: *myd*ᶜ*m*, RÉS 3156/6; name of a territory in RÉS 3945/2; cf. also *myd*ᶜ, proper name in Serjeant-Hûd 1 (G. Ryckmans transcribes *myd*ᶜ*m* in his commentary; cf. *Le Muséon*, 67 [1954], p. 181), and clan name in *RyGSAS*, p. 561: *ḏmyd*ᶜ, and the name of a man *yd*ᶜ*m* (RÉS 4945, Qat) which is related to the root *d*ᶜ*m* by *RÉS* (VII, p. 445). – *w*ᶜ*lt*, feminine participle (cf. *w*ᶜ*l* in RÉS 3427/2, Min, according to *CoRoC*, pp. 86 and 138 A); cf. Arabic *wa*ᶜ*ala* "eminuit, prominuit" (cf. *FrLAL*, p. 681 A); here, with an active meaning, such as "to bring fame, do *or* give honor"; *w*ᶜ*lt/'ḏnt* indicates the outstanding situation of the tribe in the country of Mârib.

L. 4: *ṯhwn*, very probably "the speaker" (cf. *JaP*, p. 63 and note 20).

Ll. 4-5: *ṣlmnhn/ḏbhmy* [*ḥmd*]*/ġwṯm/mqm/'lmqh/bḏt*, cp. *ṣlmn/–/ḏbhw/ḥm*[*dw*] *ḫyl/wmqm/'lmqh/– –/bḏt*

[1] The restorations at the beginning of lines 2 and 4 are purely hypothetical, and the reference to CIH 70 mentioned in the commentary on line 4 has no value for the restoration of the latter.

in RÉS 4962/4-6 [2], where *ḏbhw* is rightly referred to *ṣlm*. However, previously, in RÉS 3884 [Ja 115]/1-2: [*ṣlm*]*n*/–/*ḏbhw*/*ḥmdm*[/*bḏt*], G. Ryckmans had simply accepted (though he says "je traduis" in *RyET*, p. 71, l. 20) *JaIH*'s (p. 568) French translation of *MaTSAI* (p. 4): "en témoignage de gratitude parce que". This interpretation is preferred (cf. *RyET*, pp. 70-71; but "de ce que" replaces "parce que") to the 1st one in Fakhry 120/3-4 [3]: [*ṣlm*]*nhn*/*ḏḏhbn*/*ḏbhw*/*ḥ*[*mdm* (not *ḥdm*)/*bḏt*] "ces de(ux) [sta-(])tues d'or, en témoignage de gra[titude de ce que]". First, "statues" and not only a part of it must be placed between brackets. Secondly, "en témoignage de gratitude parce que" or "en témoignage de gratitude de ce que" cannot be considered as a translation of the entire expression *ḏbhw*/*ḥmdm*/*bḏt*, because *ḏbhw* is not translated; for *ḥmdm*/*bḏt*, cf. commentary on Ja 559/4. Thirdly, the argumentation presented by *RyET* (p. 71) in support of his translation of RÉS 3884/2 is worth mentioning: "dans le contexte qui se présente ici [Fakhry 120/3-4; cf. above], *ḏbhw* ne peut être en relation avec *ṣlmnhn* qui est au duel; on ne peut donc traduire comme le fait Rhodokanakis dans RÉS 3884, à supposer même qu'un terme tel que *mśndn* soit sous-entendu". One may be surprised that *RyET* did not quote, instead of N. Rhodokanakis' translation, his own one of RÉS 2724/8: *bn*/(ʾ)*smʿn*/*ḏbhw* "en vertu des protocoles par lesquels", where both *ḏ* and *hw* of *ḏbhw* are referred by the translator to the plural (ʾ)*smʿ*. However, in the following quotations, both *ḏ* or *ḏt* and *hw* are in agreement with the preceding noun: ʿ*d*/*ḏʾbhy*/–/*ḏbhw* (RÉS 2726/10-11), *ṣlmn*/(–/)*ḏbhw* (Ja 564/3, 739/4-5, and also RÉS 4962/4), *mngwm*/*ḏbhw* (Ja 564/4), *gnʾm*/*ḏbhw* (RÉS 3945/14) and *ṣlmtn*/*ḏt*/*ḏhbn*/*ḏt*/*bhw* (Ja 751/3-4); but in the following quotation, *hmy* is in agreement with the preceding noun, but *ḏ* is not: *ṣlmnhn*/*ḏbhmy* (here). Consequently, the agreement of *hw*, and especially that of *ḏ*, although respected in several cases, is looser than admitted in *RyET*'s (p. 71) argument, and expressions like *ḏbhw*/*ḥmdw*/*bḏt*, *ḏt*/*bhw*/*ḥmdt*/*bḏt* or *ḏbhmy*/*ḥmd*/*bḏt* mean "by which he (*or* she *or* they) has (*or* have) praised because". Furthermore, the preposition *b* in these expressions does not mean "upon" (cf. *MaTSAI*, *l.c.*) or "auf" (cf. *RhIMG*, p. 48), but corresponds to *b* in *bḏ*(*t*).

Ll. 5-6: *hwfy*/– – – –/*bʿmhw*, cp. CIH 88/7-9: *hwfyhmw*/*bklʾmlʾ*/*stmlʾw*/–/*bʿmhw*, and also, e.g., RÉS 3992/4-6 and 4150/3-4; cf. *JaASAB*, p. 160, commentary on CIH 407/14-15.

L. 6: *nkl*, cf. *CoRoC*, p. 186 B; the fundamental meaning of the root *nkl*, "to be clever, skilful", has been developed in Accadian *nakālu* in two different ways: "to act with artifice, to be cunning" and "to decorate (palace)" (cf. *BeBAG*, p. 197 B); Hebrew *nkl* has only preserved the moral meaning, "to act cunningly" (cf. *KoBaLVTL*, p. 617); here, *nkl* with the material meaning of "artistic work, decoration", as well as, e.g., in RÉS 4050/2 and 4194/6.

L. 7: *stwfy*, cf. *JaASAB*, pp. 170-71, commentary on CIH 352/7-9. – *ṣry*, pl. of *ṣryt*: *CoRoC* (p. 226 A) and *BeSI* (p. 18) consider both nouns as singular. However, the distinction between singular and plural is evident in A. F. L. Beeston's translations in *Le Muséon*, 62 (1949), p. 219; *ṣryt* means "guard, watch" and "decision, advice"; the expression *stwfy*/*ṣry* means "to give counsel to".

L. 8: *sbʾt* (cf. *CoRoC*, p. 193 A), feminine noun, singular (e.g. *hyt*/*sbʾtn* in Ja 585/10 and *bḏt*/*sbʾtn* in Ja 649/11) or plural (e.g., *bn*/*hnt*/*sbʾtn* in Ja 578/13); another plural form is *sbyʾ* (cp. *ḥtyʾ* and *ḍbyʾ*), e.g., Ja 577/16; dual: *sbʾtnhn* (e.g., Ja 629/39); "military campaign, encounter". *sbʾ*, pl.: ʾ*sbʾ* (Ja 562/8): "(professional) warrior, fighter" (cf. commentary on Ja 562/8: *ḥms*); to be referred to Arabic *sabâ* (1): "captivum fecit, captivavit" (cf. *FrLAL*, p. 270 B), "envahir" (cf. *DoSDA*, I, p. 631 A), "*śobi* emporter, ravir" (cf. *LeLS*, p. 280) and "faire *qn* captif, emmener en captivité" (cf. *LaGD*, p. 1898) and its derived noun *misbā* ("attaque par surprise", cf. *LaGD*, p. 1899) = *msbʾ* "military expedition" (e.g., CIH 2/10-11) and "military service" (e.g., RÉS 3951/4); cf. *RhAST*, I, p. 106 and *CoRoC*, p. 193 A; cf. also ʾ*sbʾ*, e.g., in Ja 562/8. The root *sabaʾa* "to buy, travel" is related to *masbaʾ* "mountain road" = *msbʾ* ("watering place", cf. *LaGD*, p. 1887) "tank" (e.g., RÉS 4815/2; cf.

[2] *RyISA* (VIII, p. 59) points out three modifications to his 1st reading of AM 165 after receiving C. H. Inge's copy of the text; the new transliteration is published as RÉS 4962. Other corrections must be made (cf. the drawing in *l.c.*, p. 89), in lines 11-12, read ʾ*lšrḥ*(12)*yḥḍb*; in line 16, *ystmlʾn* instead of *stmlʾn*; in lines 20-21, read *mlky*/*s*(21)*bʾ*; in lines 24-25, *mngt* instead of *mnlt*, and finally in line 28, *bnyhmy* instead of *bnyhmw*.

[3] *RyET* (p. 70) indicates "Hauteur maxima: 35, 5 cm.; largeur: 17 cm.," although *FaAJY* (I, p. 118) writes "36.5 cms. high, but having a preserved width of only 13 cms."

RhSLG, II, pp. 112-13) or "pass" (e.g., CIH 418/1). In this text, the expression *msbᵓ/sbᵓ* is translated by *RyET* (p. 21, end of the commentary on Fakhry 30/1) "la conduite (d'eau) qu'il a menée"; but the whole expression is *kl/mnqltn/wkl/msbᵓ/sbᵓ*; *mnql* also means "mountain road" (cf. *CoRoC*, p. 191 A); there is no question of "conduite (d'eau)" in CIH 418/1 because of the parallelism between *mnqlt* and *sbᵓ*; the above-mentioned expression means "all the mountain roads and every pass [which] he has made".

Ll. 8-9: *bltw/blt[hw]*; for *blt*, cf. *CoRoC*, p. 114 B and *BeSI*, p. 30, where the verbal formation of *blt* (from *wbl*) is discussed, and the double meaning of "tax, duty, tribute" and "gift" (*bltn*; cf. also Ja 750/5) is pointed out; *bltw*, pl. of *blt* (cf. *HöASG*, p. 104, §87); the plural *bltt* is attested in Fakhry 102/10. Because of its connection with *sbᵓt*, *blt* in the present text means "(military) duty" (also in Ja 578/39) which is an application on the military field of the first meaning "duty, tribute"; *bltw/blt[hw/]mrᵓhw* means "the (military) duties [which] his lord has imposed upon him". The verb *blt* cannot be considered as a synonym of *ysr*, both verbs (Geukens 7/2 and 3, respectively) are translated by *RyISA* (XIV, pp. 383-84) "envoyer". Furthermore, Fakhry 102/7-11 mentions *ḥmd/rṯdm/ḫyl/wmqm/ᵓlmqh/bḏt/ᵓtw/bwfym/wġnmm/wmhrgm* which is immediately followed by *bkl/ᵓbrṯ/sbᵓ/*... and *wbkl/bltt/blthw/mrᵓhw/*... *RyET*'s translation (p. 63) reads as follows: "Raṯadum a loué la force et la puissance de ᵓAlmaqah, en ce qu'il est revenu en bonne santé, et butin, et carnage, dans toutes les expéditions où il a fait campagne... ...et en toutes les faveurs que lui a octroyées son seigneur". First, *b* in *bkl* here (twice) means "from", like *bn* (cf. commentary on Ja 559/8-9). Secondly, because *bkl/ᵓbrṯ* and *bkl/bltt* equally depend on the verb *ᵓtw*, it is rather difficult to understand a phrase such as the following: "en ce qu'il est revenu en bonne santé, et butin, et carnage... ...en toutes les faveurs que lui a octroyées son seigneur"; the preceding expression, parallel to that of the present text must be translated as follows: "because he came back in safety and [with] booty and war trophy... ... from all the (military) duties [which] his lord has imposed upon him". In the present collection of texts, the verb *blt* is attested with the meaning of "to impose a duty" in Ja 578/22 and 633/6, and "to impose a (military) duty" in Ja 575/2; the noun *blt* means "(military) duty" (Ja 578/39 and 631/15) and "rent" (e.g., Ja 591/2); cf. also the 4th form *hblt* (Ja 631/16) and the 5th form *tblt* (Ja 643/11).

L. 10: *ᶜrb*, collective noun (e.g., CIH 343/14) [and also singular noun according to the plural *ᵓᶜrb*, e.g., CIH 540/2 and Ja 546/3] indicating the Arabic population (cf. *CIH*, I, pp. 123-24); cf. Arabic *ᶜurb* or *ᶜarab* "collective Arabs, Arabic population in towns *or* in the deserts"; *ᵓrḍ/ᶜrbn*, cf. *ᵓrḍt/ᶜrbn* in Ja 561 bis /12-13. These (ᵓ)ᶜ*rb* were, in my opinion, native Bedouins (cf. also *HöBAI*, pp. 60-68). All graffiti known so far from South-Arabian countries are written in native dialects and scripts (cf. also A. van den Branden, in *Studia Islamica*, 7 [1957], p. 27). The preceding fact does not support the hypothesis of the Thamudic origin of these (ᵓ)ᶜ*rb* (as suggested by J. Ryckmans, in *l.c.*, 6 [1956], p. 16 and accepted by *vdBrHT*, p. 27), because this opinion should assume that the emigrant Thamudaeans would have abandoned their native writing (also A. van den Branden, *l.c.*) *as soon as* they went southwards so that they apparently never used it again. Such an assumption does not seem very probable. – *stwkb*, 10th form of *wkb*; cf. commentary on Ja 567/11; the 10th form may be translated "to bring back".

L. 11: three letters are missing at the beginning of lines 11 and 12, and two at the beginning of line 13. – *[hn]qḏ*, cf. line 12; cf. Arabic *naqaḏa* 1st, 4th, and 10th forms "to save somebody, deliver somebody from danger; to conquer (a city), to sweep away (treasures from enemy)"; here, with a favorable meaning, but unfavorable in Ja 643 bis/2; cf. *hqḏ*, also 4th form (cp. *hkr* from *nkr* in Ja 558/7) in CIH 353/12 and Ja 586/22 or *hnqḏ* in RÉS 4386 and Ja 643 bis/2; for the 10th form *stqḏ*, cf. Ja 665/39 or *stnqḏ*, cf. Ja 644/20; cf. also the adjective *nqyḏ* in Ja 665/45-46. – *ᵓṣḥb/ṣḥbw*, cf. Arabic *ṣaḥaba* "to accompany" and its derived noun *ṣâḥib* "friend, companion" and also "enemy" in Daṯînah (cf. *LaGD*, p. 2118); the latter meaning is excluded by the two verbs *stwkl* and *nqḏ*, the first meaning is also attested in CIH 26/4 (cf. *HöSSE*, p. 11) and Geukens 1/21. – *ḫlfn/hgrn/mryb*, cp. *ḫlfn/ḏmhrmm* in RÉS 4176/6, where *RhAST* (II, p. 202 and note 6) translates as "Nachkommenschaft (der Tiere)"; however, *BeSI* (pp. 77 and 80) translates as "doorkeepers" on the basis of "the usual meaning of *ḫlf* in SA 'door'"; the *ẖlfn* are certainly human beings, but, *ẖlf* having the double meaning of "gate" and "country (contiguous to the gate)" (cf. commentary on Ja 567/8), I would rather suggest connecting *ẖlfn* with the second meaning and translating as "countrymen", that is to say the population living in the country; for in RÉS 4176/6, there is no question of city, but of clans. In the present text, the city of Mârib is mentioned; but, it seems that the "doorkeepers" had to stay in the city and not to go elsewhere.

L. 12: reading particularly difficult. – *[wst]wklw*: the restoration of the first three letters perfectly fits the blank. – *ʾẖd* has the ordinary meaning of Arabic *ʾaẖaḏa* "to take, seize" (e.g., Gl 1143/3; cf. *HöTPK*, pp. 32-33 and *JaITDL*, pp. 185-86); the verb is often used in describing military expeditions with the meaning of "to capture" (e.g., here and Ja 576/2) and the derived noun *ʾẖd* means "prisoner" (e.g., Ja 576/10; cf. commentary); for the Western Semitic cognates, cf. *JeHoDISO*, pp. 9-10: *ʾḥz*. – *hmt/ʾsdn*, e.g., RÉS 4134/4; *hmt*, masculine plural demonstrative pronoun (cf. *HöASG*, pp. 37-38, §34 *β* and *UlSLE*, p. 157); for *ʾsd*, noun, cf. *JaASAB*, p. 163, commentary on CIH 407/25.

L. 13: *hnbw*, 4th form of *nwb*; cf. Arabic *nâba* "to take the place of" and 4th "to let one be replaced by another"; from the same root, the preposition *nb* with the meaning of "instead of, for" (cf. *HöASG*, p. 155). – *rkb* has different meanings according to the contexts of the inscriptions. In expressions such as *frsm/wrkbhw* (Ja 666/4-5) and *frsn/wrkbhw* (Ja 745/4; cf. also CIH 306/4-5), *rkb* may be translated "saddle" (cf. Arabic *rikâb* "stirrup"). According to *RyISA* (XIII, p. 154), *rkb* in CIH 306/5 "doit s'entendre du harnachement du cheval". However, judging from the bronze horse of the Dumbarton Oaks (cf. my paper "Inscriptions on the Sabaean Bronze Horse of the Dumbarton Oaks Collection", in *Dumbarton Oaks Papers*, 8 [1954], pp. 317-30, pl. 37; cf. also my booklet *Note on the Dating of the Bronze Horse of the Dumbarton Oaks Collection*, Washington, 1957), *rkbhmw*, which refers to *frsy[nh]n* in line 3 of Ja 489 A, inscription engraved on the left shoulder of the remaining horse, cannot be translated as "the harness of them both" since the statue does not have any blinder, headstall, nose-band, collar, or crupper; yet all these elements are parts of a harness. The small bronze horse of CIH 504 bis has indeed both a headstall and a nose-band; but that does not prove at all that *rkb* means the whole harness (cf. Arabic *ğihâz*). In all the other references in the present collection, *rkb* is either a singular or a collective singular noun, referring either to men or animals. The meaning of "cameleer" (cf. Arabic *râkib*, pl. *rukkâb* and *rukûb*) is attested in Ja 665/23 (singular) and Ja 577/15, 665/16, 17, 19, 30, 33 (collective singular; "camelry"); in Ja 665/33, *nḫl/rkbn* may be translated "commissioner of the camelry". The expression *ʾfrsm/wrkbm/wgmlm* (Ja 576/3) is to be compared with the two following *ʾfrshmw/wrkbhmw/wbʿrhmw* (Ja 644/20) and *ʾfrsm/wrkbm/wġnmm* (Ja 665/46). There is every reason to believe that these three parallel expressions designate different classes of animals, the meanings of *frs*, *bʿr* and *ġnm* are beyond any doubt; for *gml*, cf. commentary on Ja 576/3; therefore, the translation of *rkb* as "harnachement" (as *RyISA*, *l.c.*, in Ja 576/3) is inaccurate. Besides, the perfect parallel between the first two expressions suggests giving both *gml* and *bʿr* the same general meaning: "camels"; A. F. L. Beeston's translation of *rkb* as "riding camels" (cf. *JSS*, 3 [1958], p. 144, note 1) introduces a common idea between the last two nouns of the first expression; this idea is not suggested by either one of the last two expressions. I suggest translating *rkb* in each case as "beasts of burden"; this translation seems to be confirmed by the following expression: *rwthmw/wrkbhmw* (Ja 665/43), which seems to designate the two main classes of animals used in the service corps: the specialized "water-carrier beasts" (*rwt*) and all the other "beasts of burden" (*rkb*). However, in Ja 649/40 and 665/39, *rkb* designates riding camels, since the whole expression *rkbm/brḥlhn* alludes to saddled camels. In lines 13 and 14 of the present text, *rkb* is better translated as "riding animals" (cf. Arabic *rakûb*, pl. *rakâʾib*) in order to meet the imprecision of the second reference (the *rkb* of the land = of the land of the Arabs). As for the last two texts mentioning *rkb*, Ja 649/40 and 586/22, *rkb* in the first indicates the riding camels and in the second the beasts of burden.

Ll. 13-14: *ʾrḍn* (cf. *ʾrḍ/ʿrbn* in line 10), here for its inhabitants.

L. 14: *hwtw*, 4th form of *wtw*, variant of *ʾtw*, cf. commentary on Ja 550/2; the 4th form *hwtw* corresponds to *hʾtw* (e.g., RÉS 3945/6) and may be translated as "to return, send back"; *wtw* is a preposition of direction in RÉS 3310 B/2, Min (cf. commentary in *RÉS*, VI, p. 95 and *HöASG*, p. 154); for *hwtwhmw/ʿdy/mryb*, cp. *ʾtw/ʿd/mryb* in Ja 550/2. For *wtw*=*ʾtw*, cp. on the one hand *wh̲r* (RÉS 2876/6)=*ʾh̲r* (e.g., Ja 601/17), and on the other hand *ṣlʾ* (in *tṣlʾ* in RÉS 4964/4)=*ṣlw* (in *ṣlwt*, e.g., in RÉS 3013/1, Min). The graffito Serjeant-Hûd 2 (cf. *Le Muséon*, 67 [1954], p. 183) is not, in my opinion, certain enough as to give any definitive proof of the equivalence *ydʿ*=*ʾdʿ*. In the commentary of this text, as well as in that of Ḥimâ/7, *RyISA* (X, p. 292) refers to *MoMiSI* (p. 214), who claim that South-Arabian *ẓʾd* – *ẓyd* and *rʾb* – *ryb* may have alternated. The examples referred to by these two authors are not convincing; for the four above-mentioned roots do exist in Arabic with different meanings; there is thus no evidence that the situation was different in South Arabian. Entirely different is the case of the three pairs of terms mentioned at the beginning of the present note, since the first form of each pair is attested as having the meaning of the other form. Hamdânî's transcription of South-Arabian *ẓʾdm* by *zwd* follows a well-known rule of equivalence; e.g.,

South Arabian	*ṣnʿw*	– Arabic	*ṣnʿʾ*;
	mẓʾ		*mẓy*;
	ẓwr		*ẓʾr*;
	sdʾ (Ḥimâ/7) –		*sdw* and
Aramaic *gnʾ* –	*gnw*	–	*gny*.

L. 15: at least, fourteen characters are missing.

L. 16: almost identical to line 5.

L. 18: *nʿmt*, cf. *CoRoC*, p. 188 B and Arabic *naʿama* "to live in prosperity" and its derived nouns *nuʿm* and *naʿamat* "prosperity, plentifulness, happiness". Translations such as "grace" (cf. *BeSI*, p. 25, in CIH 88/9) and "grâce" (cf., e.g., *RyET*, p. 60 and *RyISA*, XV, p. 105) are incorrect; in RÉS 3956/6-7: *fl/yśwbnh/nʿmtm* "qu'il la restitue en grâce" (*RÉS*); this translation of *nʿmt* does not seem to fit the context, for if it were the right meaning of the inscription, the text would have *nʿmthw*, the *hw* referring to the god D̲û-Samâwî, to whom the confession is addressed; the above mentioned expression may be translated as follows: "that He [D̲û-Samâwî] may reward her with happiness". – *ḥẓy/wrḍw*, cf. *JaASAB*, pp. 164-65, commentary on CIH 407/29-30. *BeTMS* translates *rḍw/wḥẓy* in AshM 1957-16/6 as "the favour and the good-pleasure". – *mr* 〈ʾ〉: the ʾ is mentioned in my notebook as missing on the stone.

L. 21: *gblm*, proper name indicating a sanctuary, a tribe or a place; cf. the masculine personal name *gblt* in CIH 541/91; in Arabic, the masculine personal and clan name *ǧblt* (cf. *SaIS*, p. 38 A) and the masculine personal name *Ǧabâlî* (cf. *VNIA*, p. 183 A); cf. also the noun *gblt* "territory, district" (e.g., Ja 526/4).

561 – Grayish sandstone; photograph; cf. Chapter I, C. – MaMB 313.

SYMBOL, cf. *GrGST*, p. 9, Fig. 8c; cf. Plate E.

1 **Sym-** *bnw/grt/ʾqwl/šʿbn/[d̲m]*
2 **bol** *ry/wšʿbhmw/smhrm/hqnyw*
3 *ʾlmqh/bʿl/ʾwm/ṣlmnhn/d̲y/d̲h*
4 *bn/ḥmdm/bd̲t/sʿdhmw/ʾlmq⌊h⌋*
5 *wfy/mrʾhmw/nšʾkrb/yhʾmn*
6 *mlk/sbʾ/bn/d̲mrʿly/d̲rḥ/wb*
7 *d̲t/sʿd/ʾlmqh/bʿl/ʾwm/mrʾ*
8 *hmw/nšʾkrb/stqḥn/mqyḥt/ṣdq*
9 *m/bkl/ʾbrt̲/bhmw/hwṣl/lbytn*
10 *slḥn/bʾḍrrm/wbslmm/wl/wzʾ*
11 *ʾlmqh/sʿd/mrʾhmw/nšʾkrb/wf*
12 *ym/wʿztm/wkhltm/wbry/ʾd̲nm/w*
13 *mqmm/wl/sʿdhmw/ʾlmqh/wfy/by*
14 *tn/slḥn/wʾbʿlhw/wwfy/ʾdmhw*
15 *bny/grt/wqlhmw/bʿt̲tr/šrqn/wʿt̲t*
16 *r/d̲d̲bn/whbs/wʾlmqh/wd̲t/ḥmym*
17 *wd̲t/bʿdnm/wb/šms/mlkn/tnf/w*
18 *b/ʾlyhmw/ʿt̲tr/ʿzzm/wd̲t/ẓh*
19 *rn/bʿly/ʿrn/knn/wrt̲dw/hqny*
20 *tn/ʿt̲tr/šrqn/wʾlmqh/bʿl/ʾwm*

1 **Sym-** The descendants of Garat, rulers of the tribe D̲am-]
2 **bol** rî, and their tribe Sumhurâm, have dedicated to
3 ʾIlumquh, master of ʾAwwâm, these two statues, both in bron-
4 ze, in praise because ʾIlumquh has made them happy
5 with the safety of their lord Našaʾkarib Yuhaʾmin,
6 king of Sabaʾ, son of D̲amarʿalay D̲ariḥ, and be-
7 cause ʾIlumquh, master of ʾAwwâm, has made happy their
8 lord Našaʾkarib with drawing perfect profit
9 from all the places which he [the king] has entrusted to the house
10 Salḥân in wars and in peace; and that may continue.

11 ʾIlumquh to make happy their lord Našaʾkarib with safe-
12 ty and vigor and might and [with] the strength of understanding and
13 of power; and that ʾIlumquh may make them happy with the safety of the hou-
14 se Salḥân and of its masters and with the safety of His worshippers,
15 the descendants of Garat and their ruler. By ʿAṯtar Šarqân and ʿAṯtar,
16 Him of Ḏabân, and Hawbas and ʾIlumquh and Ḏât-Ḥimyâm
17 and Ḏât-Baʿdânum and by Šams of the king, Tanûf, and
18 by their two gods ʿAṯtar ʿAzîzum and Ḏât-Ẓah-
19 rân, the two masters of the citadel Kanin. And they have entrusted the offer-
20 ing to the care of ʿAṯtar Šarqân and of ʾIlumquh, master of ʾAwwâm.

This text is identical with Ja 559, except *hbs* in line 16 in *scriptio defectiva* (cf. *JaP*, p. 68) instead of the *scriptio plena* in Ja 559/16; the repartition of the lines is identical in both texts only in lines 3, 4, and 5.

c – Wahabʾil Yaḥûz: Ja 561 bis

561 bis. – Yellowish, grayish sandstone; photograph; cf. Chapter I, A. – MaMB 204.

STONE: thickness: 36.5 cm.; upper left corner broken. – *Front:* 45.1 cm. × 1.775 m. – INSCRIPTION: same disposition of lines as in Ja 552, plus one vertical line on each lateral edge; letter height: 4.9 cm. and 5; space between the lines; 0.5 cm. – *Symbol:* the photographs are not clear enough to allow an accurate drawing; about 1/3 wider than that of Ja 559.

1 **Sym-** *yrm/ʾymn/wʾẖ[yhw/brg]*
2 **bol** *yhrḥb/wbnhw/ʿl[hn/bny]*
3 *ʾwslt/rfšn/bn/hmdn/ʾqwl/šʿ*
4 *⌊bn/smʿy/ṯlṯn/ḏḥšdm/hqnyw/ʾl*
5 *mqh/ṯhwn/bʿl/ʾwm/ṣlmn/ḥmdm/bḏ*
6 *t/hwšʿ/whwfyn/ʾlmqh/ʾdmhw/bny*
7 *hmdn/wšʿbhmw/ḥšdm/bmqyḥt/wm*
8 *hrgt/wġnmt/ṣdqm/bkl/ʾbrṯ/bhm*
9 *w/strsw/bʾḍrr/kwnw/byn/ʾmlk/s*
10 *bʾ/wbny/ḏrydn/wbkl/ʾbrṯ/ʿdyhm*
11 *w/hwṣlw/lḍrm/bʿly/ḏbn/ʾʿrbn/b*
12 *ʾwṯn/šʿbn/ḥšdm/wbḏbn/ʾrḍt/ʿr*
13 *bn/ʾʿrb/ẖṭʾw/bʾmrʾhmw/ʾmlk*
14 *sbʾ/wbḏbn/ʾrḍt/ʾšʿb/mlk/sbʾ*
15 *wbḏt/ṣdqhmw/whwfynhmw/ʾlmqh*
16 *bkl/ʾmlʾ/stmlʾw/bʿmhw/wlḏt/y*
17 *zʾn/ṣdqhmw/ʾlmqh/kl/ʾmlʾ/ystm*
18 *lʾnn/bʿmhw/wl/sʿdhmw/ḥẓy/wrḍw*
19 *mrʾhmw/whbʾl/yḥz/mlk/sbʾ/wl/sʿd*
20 *hmw/ʾwldm/ʾḏkrwm/hnʾm/wʾṯmr/wʾ*
21 *fql/ṣdqm/ʿdy/kl/ʾsrrhmw/wʾrḍhmw*
22 *wl/ẖrynhmw/bn/bʾstm/wnḍʿ/wšṣy/šn*
23 *ʾm/wl/wḍʿ/wṯbr/ʾlmqh/ḍrhmw/wšnʾhm*
24 *w/bʿṯtr/wʾlmqh/wšymhmw/tʾlb/rymm*

1 **Sym-** Yarum ʾAyman and [his] brother [Barig]
2 **bol** Yuharḥib and his son ʿAl[hân, descendants of]
3 ʾAwsalat Rafšân, people of Hamdân, rulers of the tri-
4 be Sumʿay, the third of Ḥâšidum, have dedicated to ʾIl-
5 umquh Ṯahwân, master of ʾAwwâm, this statue in praise because
6 ʾIlumquh has assisted and protected His worshippers, the descendants of
7 Hamdân and their tribe Ḥâšidum with profit and war
8 trophies and booty perfect from all the military campaigns in which
9 they have been chosen as chiefs during the wars [which] were between the kings of Sa-
10 baʾ and the descendants of Raydân, and from all the military campaigns in which
11 they intervened for war against some of the Arabs on
12 the borders of the tribe Ḥâšidum and against some of the lands of the Arabs,
13 Arabs [who] had acted wrongfully toward their lords, the kings
14 of Sabaʾ, and against some of the lands of the tribe of the king of Sabaʾ;
15 and because ʾIlumquh has bestowed upon them and granted to them
16 all the favors [for which] they besought Him; and that
17 ʾIlumquh may continue to bestow upon them all the favors [for which] they shall beseech
18 Him; and that He may make them happy with the esteem and grace
19 of their lord Wahabʾil Yaḥûz, king of Sabaʾ; and that He may make
20 them happy with pleasing, male children, and (with) fruits and
21 harvests perfect in all their wâdî-side valleys and their land;
22 and that He may preserve them from misfortunes and (from) the hostility and wickedness of [any] ene-

23 my; and that ʾIlumquh may humiliate and crush their foe and their ene-

24 my. By ʿAṯtar and ʾIlumquh and their patron Taʾlab Riyyâm.

Ll. 1-4: the present text confirms the restoration of *CIH* at the end of CIH 315/1 and is even clearer than the latter because of the mention of *ʾh*[*yhw*] introducing [*brg*] *yhrḥb*; it also mentions *yrm*/*ʾymn*'s son, namely *ʿlhn*. *yrm*, also name of man in RÉS 4994/1 and 2d name of a man in Geukens 2/1; cf. also the names of men *hymn* in RÉS 5042, Ḥaḍr (instead of *hqmr*) and *yrmʾl* in RÉS 4787/1. *yhrḥb* is the name of a family or clan in RÉS 4632/2. *hmdn*, also Ja 544/2 and *šʿb*/*ḏhmdn* in Ja 547/3. *ʾwslt*, cp. *bʾws* in RÉS 4568 and *JaSAA*, p. 153 B.

L. 3: *hmdn*, cf. the Arabic personal name *hamdân* (cf. *SlGaVNPA*, p. 25 B).

L. 4: *smʿy*/*ṯlṯn*/*ḏḥšdm*, cp. *smʿy*/*ṯlṯn*/*ḏhgrm* (e.g., Ja 616/3-4, e.g., in RÉS 3990/2-3, *šlṯ* instead of *ṯlṯn*) and *smʿy*/*ṯlṯn*/*ḏḥmln* (e.g., RÉS 4718/2 and Ja 562/2-3); the clan *smʿy* was divided into three parts, each belonging to another larger tribe; the people of *smʿy* ordinarily offer to the god Taʾlab whose name is mentioned in the final invocation. The restoration *ḥmdn* at the end of RÉS 4022 is not more probable than either *hgrm* or *ḥšdm*.

L. 6: *hwšʿ*, 4th form of *wšʿ* (e.g., RÉS 4137/9); *CoRoC*, p. 141 B and *StSESA*, p. 537 refer to Hebrew *hôšîaʿ*; but the form *hwṯʿ* would be expected. Cf. *BePESA*, p. 16: "*wšʿ* is a doublet-form with metathesis of the root *šwʿ*". *RhIAI* (p. 42, note 4; cf. also *RhIMG*, p. 48 and note 2) compares *hwšʿ* with Ethiopic *ʾawšeʾa* (cf. *DiLLA*, col. 895), but does not present any explanation for the change of the radical ʿ to ʾ; and *RyISA* (XII, p. 30) avoids the preceding difficulty by transcribing the Ethiopic form as *ʾawšeʿa*. Besides, the expression "les exaucer en abondance d'autorité et de pouvoir" (cf. *l.c.*, p. 301) as translation of *hwšʿhmw*/*bbry*/*ʾʾḏnm*/*wmqymtm* (Geukens 1/27) is not extremely clear. Cf. the 10th form *stwšʿ*, e.g., in Ja 700/7; for *šwʿ*, cf. commentary on Ja 564/8-9.

L. 7: *ḥšdm*, cp. the Qat personal name [*ḥ*]*šdm* in Ja 146.

Ll. 7-8: *mhrgt*, pl. of *mhrg* (e.g., Ja 575/7). The interpretation of CIH 407/25-26 presented by *JaASAB*, pp. 163-64, must be revised in the light of Ja 644/24-25 and 649/11-12 and 36-40, which describe the comprehension of the noun *mhrg* respectively as follows: *ʾḫll* "animals" and horses; beheaded soldiers and one prisoner; and finally beheaded soldiers, prisoners, captives, and riding camels. The description of the third passage covers thus that of the first two and adds something to it. The noun *mhrg* may thus be translated "war trophy"; the meaning "slaughter" is doubtless excluded, as it is already by an expression such as *lfy*/*mhrg* "to bring back..." (e.g., Ja 576/4). Therefore, an expression such as *hrg*/*bnhmw*/*mhrgm*/*ḏʿsm* (cp. Ja 575/7) may be translated "to take from them *or* to deprive them of a war trophy which was desired"; the meaning of *hrg* in such instances must be related to Arabic *harraǧa* (and *ʾahraǧa*) (cf. *JaASAB*, p. 164). Contexts such as Ja 635/30-32 positively exclude the translation of *hrg* as "to kill".

L. 8: *ġnmt*, plural of *ġnm*, cf. *CoRoC*, p. 216 B: Arabic *ġanama*, 2nd form "to give someone a part of booty", and *ġanîmat*, plural *ġanâʾimu* "booty, prey"; for the comparison between *ġnm* and *ʾḫll*, cf. commentary on Ja 574/9; in Fakhry 102/3-4, read *ġnmh*(4)*w*/*bn* instead of *ġnmm*(4)*wbn* (cf. *RyET*, p. 62). – *bhmw*, cp. *ʿdyhmw* in lines 10-11.

L. 9: *strs*, 10th form of *rys*; RÉS 3306 A/1-2, Min, translated "to put (in), set, place" but "to be chosen as chief" by *CoRoC*, p. 241 B, who refers to *strʾs*(?); cf. modern Ḥaḍr *rys* "se rendre maître de" (cf. *LaH*, p. 595), and Arabic *raʾasa*=*râsa* "to be chief" (cf. *RhIAI*, p. 24). – *bʾḏrr*/*kwnw*, cf. e.g., *bḏr*/–/.*kwn* (CIH 315/7), where *RyHE* (p. 235) inaccurately translates *kwn* as "to rage"; for the Western Semitic cognates of *kwn*, cf. *JeHoDISO*, p. 117: kwn_{III}. – *byn*, cf. *CoRoC*, p. 113 A and *JeHoDISO*, p. 34: byn_{II}.

L. 10: *rydn*, cf. the Arabic personal name *rîdân* (cf. *SlGaVNPA*, p. 45 A).

L. 11: *hwṣl*, cf. commentary on Ja 559/9. – *ḏbn*, e.g., RÉS 3566/8, Qat; literally "those from"; cf. *ḏbnhw* in commentary on Ja 571/7-8.

L. 12: *ʾwṯn*, e.g., Ja 541/6-7 with the ordinary meaning of "boundaries" (cf. also *RoVSAY*, p. 304); here, "borders" of a country or of a tribe. – *bḏbn* (also line 14) = *bʿly*/*ḏbn* (line 11).

L. 13: *ḫṭʾ*, cf. *StSESA*, p. 516 and Daṯînah *ḫaṭâ* "erreur" (cf. *LaGD*, p. 609) and Soqoṭri *ḫaṭôʾoh* "péché" (cf. *LeLS*, p. 477 B); cf. also *hḫṭʾ*, 4th form, e.g., in Ja 577/9; the meaning of moral transgression is more often attested, e.g., CIH 532/3-4; here, as well as the noun, e.g., in RÉS 3854/9, Qat, and Ja 601/8, the verb means "to commit a fault against his own duty, to fail", that is to say "to fail in his own duty" toward the king (cf. *HöASG*, p. 171); however, in Ja 720/10, the noun *ḫṭ*ʾ means "the fine, penalty" incurred by and resulting from a fault.

L. 15: *bḏt* depends on *ḥmdm* in line 5.

Ll. 15-16: *ṣdqhmw/–/bkl/ʾmlʾ/stmlʾw/bʿmhw*, cp. CIH 84/9-10: *ṣdq/ʿbdhw/–/bʾmlʾ/ystmlʾn/bʿmhw*; cf. *CoRoC*, p. 222 A; *ṣdq* also means "to finish, accomplish" (e.g., RÉS 3945/2, Sab, and 4836/2, Min) and "to be justified" (cf. *JaFSR*, p. 14).

L. 18: *rḍw*, cf. commentary on Ja 560/18.

L. 20: *ḏkr*, cf. *CoRoC*, p. 129 A and the Western Semitic cognates in *JeHoDISO*, p. 77: *zkr*$_{III}$. – *ṯmr*, cf. *CoRoC*, p. 260 B: Arabic *ṯamar* coll., plural *ʾaṯmâr* "fruit" and *RoAS* (p. 210 A): "frutta *ṯämäreh*." *BeTMS* translates *ʾṯmr* in AshM 1957-16/7 as "crops". Cf. also *ṯṯmr*, 5th form of the verb *ṯmr* in RÉS 4815/5, and *ʾṯmrm*, name of a river flat in Ja 514.

Ll. 20-21: *ʾfql*, cf. *CoRoC* (p. 219 B), *LaH* (p. 678) and *LaGD* (p. 2427): "*faqal*, pl. *fiqâl*, *ʾafqâl*, produit de la récolte, saison", and *RoVSAY* (p. 310): "*fagal* [*g* for *q*] ventilare il grano". G. Ryckmans erroneously translates *ʾfql* as "légumes" in RÉS 4938/18, and restores *ʾ*[*b*]*ql* in Fakhry 102/11-12, with reference to RÉS 3958/4, which gives no support to his restoration; (*ʾ*)*fql* is always mentioned with (*ʾ*)*ṯmr* and must be restored in Fakhry 102/11-12. *RyHE* translates *ʾfql* as "agricultural products" (p. 233).

L. 21: *ʾsrr*, pl. of *sr*, cf. *JaASAB*, p. 162, commentary on CIH 407/20-21 and *RoVSAY*, p. 308. The translation of *ʾsrr* as "slopes" (cf. *RyHE*, p. 233) is not correct.

L. 22: *wl/ḫrynhmw*, cf. *JaASAB*, pp. 165-66, commentary on CIH 407/32. *BeTMS* translates *ḫry* in AshM 1957-16/8 as "to deliver". – *bn/nḍʿ/wšṣy*, cf. *JaASAB*, pp. 166-67, commentary on CIH 407/33. *BeTMS* translates the whole expression in AshM 1957-16/8-9 as "from humiliation and evil-eye".

Ll. 23-24: *wl/wḍʿ/wṯbr/–/ḍrhmw/wšnʾhmw*, cp. CIH 2/17-18, where the verbs *wḍʿ*, *ṯbr* and *ḍrʿ* (because of the form *ḍrʿn*) depend on the conjunction *l* mentioned before *sʿd* in line 16 (cf. the parallel in RÉS 4190/16-18). For *wḍʿ*, e.g., RÉS 5099/2 and Ja 489 A/9: *ydʿ*; cf. *CoRoC*, p. 140 A, *RhIMG*, p. 48 and note 3, and Arabic *waḍaʿa* "to humiliate, abase, humble." For *ṯbr*, cf. *CoRoC*, p. 258 B, *RhIMG*, p. 48 and note 5, and *LaGD*, p. 245; *ṯbr* is passive in RÉS 4912/2, Ḥaḍr (cf. *JaSAI*, pp. 512-13, No. 21), and also in Ja 671/11; cf. also the noun *ṯbr* and *mṯbr* in Ja 643 bis/4 and 671/24, respectively.

L. 24: *šym*, cf. *StSESA*, p. 530. – *tʾlb/rym*, cf. *JaASAB*, p. 169, commentary on CIH 352/3.

d – ʾAnmarum Yuhaʾmin: Ja 562

562. – Grayish sandstone. – MaMB 279.

STONE: thickness: 35.8 cm. – *Front*: upper right corner slightly broken; the lower half of the right edge is largely splintered off; 1.47 m. × 49 cm. – INSCRIPTION: same disposition of lines as in Ja 552; letter height: from 4.2 cm. to 4.4; space between the lines: from 0.5 cm. to 0.6; distance from line 1 to the upper edge: 1.3 cm. – *Symbol*, cf. Ja 559.

1 **Sym-** [*sḫ*]⌜*mn*⌝/⌜*y*⌝*hṣbḥ/bn/btʿ/ʾbʿl/byt*
2 **bol** *n/wklm/ʾqwl/šʿbn/smʿy/ṯlṯn/ḏḥ*
3 *mln/hqnyw/ʾlmqhw/bʿl/ʾwm/ṣlmn/ḥ*
4 *mdm/bḏt/hwšʿhmw/bstwfyn/ʾtyt/m*
5 *rʾhmw/ʾnmrm/yhʾmn/mlk/sbʾ/bn/w*
6 *hbʾl/yḥz/mlk/sbʾ/ʿdy/bytn/slḥ*
7 *n/bn/byt/bny/dġymn/ḥgn/tqnʿhw/ʾ*
8 *dmhw/ʾsbʾn/wʾqwln/wḫmsn/wl/sʿd*
9 *ʾlmqhw/bʿl/ʾwm/ʿbdhw/sḫmn/bn/bt*
10 [*ʿ*]/*rḍw/wḥẓy/mrʾhmw/ʾnmrm/yhʾmn/ml*
11 [*k*]/*sbʾ/bn/whbʾl/yḥz/mlk/sbʾ/wls*
12 [*ʿd*]*hmw/ʾlmqhw/bʿl/ʾwm/ʾṯmr/wʾfql/ṣ*
13 [*dqm*]/*bn/kl/ʾrḍhmw/wʾsrrhmw/wmšym*
14 [*thmw*]/*wlḏt/nʿmt/wtnʿmn/lsḫmn/wbny/*[*b*]
15 [*tʿ/w..*]*lw/ḥmln/wl/ḫrynhmw/ʾlmqhw*
16 [*wmtʿnhmw/*](*b*)*n/bʾstm/wnkym/wnḍʿ/wšṣy*
17 [*šnʾm/ḏr*]*ḥq/wqrb/bʿṯtr/whbs/wʾlm*
18 [*qhw/wb*]*ḏt/ḥmym/wbḏt/bʿdnm/wbšms*
19 *mlkn/tnf/wbšymhmw/tʾlb/rymm/bʿl/š*
20 *ṣrm/wrṯdw/hqnythmw/ʿṯtr/šrqn/wʾlmqh*
21 *w/bʿl/ʾwm/bn/hnkrnhw/bn/brṯ*⟨.⟩*hw*

1 **Sym-** [Suḫ]mân Yuhaṣbiḥ, descendant of [the clan] Bataʿ, masters of the hou-
2 **bol** se Wakilum, rulers of the tribe Sumʿay, third of Ḥu-
3 mlân, have dedicated to ʾIlumquhû, master of ʾAwwâm, this statue in
4 praise because He has helped them in giving protection for the return of
5 their lord ʾAnmarum Yuhaʾmin, king of Sabaʾ, son of Wa-
6 habʾil Yaḥûz, king of Sabaʾ, to the house Salḥ-

7 ân from the house of the people of Ġaymân; so have pleased Him

8 His worshippers, the warriors and the rulers and the army; and that may make happy

9 ʾIlumquhû, master of ʾAwwâm, His worshipper Suḫmân, descendant of Bat-

10 [aʿ] with the grace and esteem of their lord ʾAnmarum Yuhaʾmin, kin-

11 [g] of Sabaʾ, son of Wahabʾil Yaḥûz, King of Sabaʾ; and that

12 ʾIlumquhû, master of ʾAwwâm, may ma[ke] them [happy] with fruits and harvests per-

13 [fect] in their every land and (all) their wâdî-side valleys and [their] arable fields;

14 and that it may have been pleasant and be pleasant for Suḫmân and the people of [Ba-]

15 [taʿ and...] of Ḥumlân; and that ʾIlumquhû may preserve them

16 [and save them] (fr)om misfortunes and suffering and (from) the hostility and wickedness

17 [of (any) enemy, who is re]mote and near. By ʿAṯtar and Hawbas and ʾIlum-

18 [quhû and by] Ḏât-Ḥimyâm and by Ḏât-Baʿdânum, and by Šams

19 of the king, Tanûf, and by their patron, Taʾlab Riyyâm, master of Ša-

20 ṣṣarum. And they have entrusted their offering to the care of ʿAṯtar Šarqân and of ʾIlumquh-

21 û, master of ʾAwwâm, against removing it from its place.

L. 1: *sḫmn* (also in line 9): also proper name in CIH 224/3; derived from the same root as the *quṭaylum* form, *sḫymn*, well-known tribe name. – *yhṣbḥ*: e.g., RÉS 4128 and 4976/2, Qat; cf. also *ṣbḥkrb* in Ja 212, Qat (see commentary) and *ṣbḥrym* in Ja 555/2. – *bn* introducing a family or clan name, cf. *JaPEHA*, pp. 25-26; *bn/btʿ*, cf. *bny/btʿ*, e.g., in CIH 187/2 and *bnw/btʿ*, e.g., in RÉS 4016/1 (cf. Chapter V, F); cf. also the name of a person *btʿ* in Ja 225/1, Qat, of a family *btʿn* in RÉS 4741/2, and of a clan *btʿt* in RÉS 3977/2. – *ʾbʿl* to be referred to *btʿ*; the people of *btʿ* were masters of the house *wklm* and rulers of the clan *smʿy/ṯlṯn/ḏḥmln*.

Ll. 1-2: *bytn/wklm*, cp. *bytn/slḥn*, e.g., in Ja 561/9-10.

L. 2: *wklm*, name of a sanctuary dedicated to *mnḏḥ* "the deity of irrigation" (cf. *JaP*, p. 126).

Ll. 2-3: *ʾqwl/– –/ḏḥmln*, cf. CIH 187/2-3; cf. also the Arabic personal names *ḥamlânî* and *ḥûmil*, *ḥamlat*, *ḥamlânî* (cf. *SlGaVNPA*, pp. 5 B and 23 B respectively).

L. 3: *ʾlmqhw*: for an explanation of the final *w*, cf. *JaP*, p. 62, note 73.

L. 4: *ʾtyt*: from the verb *ʾty* (e.g., CIH 290/5: *yʾtyn*) or *ʾtw* (e.g., RÉS 2861/17 and Ja 550/2) or *wtw* (Ja 560/14; cf. commentary); cf. Arabic *ʾatā(i)* "to come" (cf. also *LaGD*, p. 62) and its derived nouns *ʾatiyat* "what must happen" and *ʾityân* "arrival, coming", and the modern Ḥaḍr expression: "*ābā yaytî* il refusa de venir" (cf. *LaH*, p. 520); cp. *ʾtwtm*, name of a mountain on top of which was built the sanctuary *rymm* dedicated to the god Taʾlab (cf. *JaP*, p. 139); for *ʾtw* = *ʾty*, cf. commentary on Ja 560/18: *rḍw* = *rḍy*.

L. 5: *yhʾmn* is engraved in a hollow; the worker had probably engraved a wrong name, which he completely erased.

L. 7: *bny/ḏ*, cf. *JaPEHA*, p. 28. – *ġymn*, e.g., Ja 489 A/2 and 1: tribe name mentioned as third element of the masculine personal name *hwfʿṯt/yhʾḏn/ġymn*. –*ḥgn*, cf. *HöASG*, p. 167, Ja 535/3 and Gl 1142/9-10 (cf. *HöTPK*, pp. 30-31 and *JaITDL*, pp. 184-85). – *tqnʿ*, 5th form of *qnʿ*, CIH 315/8; cf. *CoRoC*, p. 233 A: Arabic *qanaʿa*, 4th form "to satisfy, please"; cf. also *LaGD*, p. 2533, and the noun *qnʿ* in Ja 643/10.

L. 8: *ḫms*: the latest study of *ḫms* was written by *BeNL* (IV, pp. 140-41, and an additional rectification in V, p. 122). This opinion is first simply mentioned, but later accepted by *RyISA* (XII, p. 302, and XIII, p. 151, respectively). On the basis of E. Glaser's testimony (cf. *MüRhGRM*, p. 24 B) according to which *ʾhl al-ḫums* is composed of "altangesessene Araber oder Sklavenabkömmlinge", *BeNL* suggests (p. 141) "that this modern usage of the term *ʾahl al ḫums* is derived unchanged from the pre-Islamic period", and also that "*ḫms* in the inscriptions denotes the non-tribal element of the population as opposed both to the tribal element designated *ʾšʿb*...and to the purely bedouin *ʾʿrb*". However, *BeNL* does not allude at all to *LaGD*'s (pp. 645-47) remarks on E. Glaser's statement, according to which these persons "accompagnent la tribu à la guerre et portent...l'eau, les munitions de guerre et les vivres: ce sont les ravitailleurs des soldats" (p. 645), "ce sont les clients de la tribu...On leur donne la *cinquième* partie du butin qu'on fait...; ces gens ont véritablement le nom de *ʾhl al-ḫums*, et le pluriel en est *ʾḫmûs*" (p. 646). The ancient *ḫms* represents thus something different from the present *ʾhl al-ḫums*: the first was composed of true fighting men, and the

second was a kind of service corps; besides, "les clients de la tribu" actually were a part of the tribe. Furthermore, how could "the non-tribal element" have had a great power such as that of *ḫms* in the inscriptions, in a social organization based on tribe? *BeNL* presents two objections against *HaAF*'s (p. 448) translation of *ḫms* as "Berufsheer", namely "I regard it as highly doubtful whether a «Berufheer» can ever have existed in the social condition of Ancient South Arabia" (p. 140), and "it would be difficult to account for [CIH 334/2-3: *mrʾhmw/š*[*ᶜrm*]*ʾwtr/ wḫmsyhw/sbʾ/wḥmyrm*] if *ḫms* meant ...«army»" (p. 141). In this text, Ḥimyar is the ally of Sabaʾ, and the Sab king is waging war against Ḥaḍramawt, with two armies under his command, one of Sabaeans and the other of Ḥimyarites. Further, why would the Sab crown not have had any regular army? Even in the present time, for instance, the *šerîf* of Beiḥân has one, besides the tribal fighting groups. I propose to recognize the professional soldiers in *ʾsbʾ*, which precedes *ʾqwl* and *ḫms* in the three texts of the present collection, Ja 562, 564 and 643, and to translate *ḫms* as "army, army corps" (cf. also *DoSDA*, I, pp. 404 and 405, and *HöBAI*, p. 62: "'Heervölkern' *ʾḫms*"), that is to say the soldiers gathered either by the king or by the ruler of a tribe (cf. Ist 7608 bis 4: *ḫmshmw/ mlykym/wqylym*). Both the size and the composition of *ḫms* is variable in each case; this fact is illustrated by some examples. In Ja 577/15, the pericope *hwʾ/wʾqwlhw/wḫmshw/wʾfrshmw/wrkbhw/ wḥṣqhmw* designates the king ʾIlšaraḥ Yaḥḍub, the tribal leaders as commanding officers, the infantry, the cavalry, the camelry and the prisoner-keeper corps. On the contrary, in both CIH 334/2-3 (see above) and Ja 577/18, *ḫms* indicates the entire contingent of fighters. *ḫms* with the preceding meaning may be divided in two (e.g., NaNN 72+73+71/3) or several (e.g., Ja 722/a-b) corps. In Ja 612/9, *ḫms* indicates the soldiers of any kind, by opposition with their officers (*ʾqwl*). Then, *šᶜb* would mean a "tribal fighting group" under the command of the tribal leader or of his delegate, and *gyš* the "non-regular troop" probably composed of Bedouins. The relation between *ḫms* of a *qwl* and the latter's *šᶜb* can also be understood in the same line of thought: *ḫms* is the regular army (small, of course) and *šᶜb* the tribal men fighting along with *ḫms*.

Ll. 13-14: e.g., RÉS 4013/4; four letters are missing at the beginning of line 14. – *mšymt* (e.g., RÉS 4646/8) or *mšmt* (e.g., Ja 650/14), pl. of *mšm* (e.g., CIH 352/12; cf. *JaASAB*, p. 172, commentary), cf. *CoRoC*, p. 249 A, *StSESA*, p. 530 and *DoSDA*, I, p. 709 A: *sawwâmat* (from the root *swm*) "arable field" (cf. also *BeSI* pp. 3-4). The translation of *mšm* as "demesne" (cf. *RyHE*, p. 233) is incorrect.

L. 14: *wldt/nᶜmt/wtnᶜmn/l*: stereotyped formula mentioned at the end of dedicatory inscriptions; e.g., CIH 79/12. The feminine ending *t* in *nᶜmt* proves that *ḏt* was considered as a "fully functional relative" feminine "pronoun" (cf. *BeSI*, p. 16) in the original formula; but it is doubtful that this particular meaning was still kept in mind later; and it seems natural to translate *ḏt* of this expression as "it". The expression mentioned above may be compared with *wl/sᶜd*[*hmw/*]*ḏt/nᶜmt/wtnᶜm*[*n*] (RÉS 3990/9-10; cf. also Ja 528/5), equivalent to *wl/sᶜdh*[*mw*]/ *nᶜmtm* (RÉS 3993/5-6 [cf. Ja 421/3-4]) and [*wl/sᶜdh/ḏt/nᶜm*]*t* (Ja 489 A/8-9), and may also be compared with *wlḫmr/../ḏt/nᶜmt/wtnᶜmn* (RÉS 4962/23-25; where the two verbs are erroneously translated by the present subjunctive).

Ll. 14-15: the last letter of line 14 is missing; it is practically impossible to know the exact number of missing letters at the beginning of line 15; for 29, 30, 31, 32, 33, 34, and 35 characters are attested in lines 6, 4 (and 5, 8, 11, 17, 18, and 21), 3 (and 7, 9, and 13), 10, 12 (and 19), 14, and 20, respectively. For *bny/btᶜ*, cf. *bn/btᶜ* in line 1.

L. 16: for the number of missing characters, cf. remark on lines 14-15. For the restoration of *mtᶜ* after *ḫry*, cf. Ja 567/26 and 654/14; in Fakhry 120/4-5, the restoration of *ḫry* is much more probable than that of *hᶜn*, which is suggested by *RyET*, p. 70.

L. 17: *šnʾm/ḏrḥq/wqrb* (e.g., CIH 95/7-8) equals *šnʾm/rḥqm/wqrbm* in Ja 737/4-5; cp. *b*[*rṯm*]*/qrbm/ wrḥqm* in RÉS 4962/17-18. For *rḥq*, cf. *CoRoC*, p. 240, *LeLS*, p. 398 and *LaGD*, pp. 1181-82; for *qrb*, cf. *CoRoC*, p. 233 B, *LaGD*, p. 2470 and *BiSSS*, IV, p. 46.

L. 19: *šym*, cf. commentary on Ja 611/16-17.

Ll. 19-20: *šṣrm*, name of a temple dedicated to Taʾlab (cf. *JaP*, p. 138). *WeCGC* (p. 138 and maps) mentions the city of Šeṣṣarîm located about 20 km. northeast of Raydat and about 63 km. north of Ṣanᶜâʾ.

L. 21: *bn/hnkrnhw*, cf. *bn/hkrnh* in Ja 558/7. – *brṯ⟨.⟩hw* (copy: *brṯnhw*): the error of adding *n* at the end of *brṯ* and before *hw* is probably due to *hnkrNhw*.

e – Karibʾil Watar Yuhanᶜim: Ja 563 and 564

563. – Stone re-used in the western pavement; cf. Chapter I, B. – MaMB 269.

Front: upper right corner badly damaged. – INSCRIPTION: same disposition of lines as in Ja 559; letter height: from 4.5 cm. to 4.8; space between the lines: from 0.7 cm. to 0.8.

1 **[Sym-** *swdm/ʾs]⌜ʾ⌝r/wyhᶜn/.*
2 **[bol** *..]m/wbnyhmw/klbm/b*
3 *[ny/ᶜṯkl]n/hqnyw/ʾlmqh/ṯhwn*
4 *[bᶜ]l/ʾwm/ṣlmn/ḥgn/wqhhmw*
5 *ʾlmqh/bmsʾlhw/lwfyhmw/w*
6 *wfy/bnhmw/klbm/bn/ᶜṯkln*
7 *wl/sᶜdhmw/ʾlmqh/nᶜmtm/ww*
8 *fym/wmngt/ṣdqm/wḥẓy/wrḍw*
9 *mrʾhmw/krbʾl/wtr/yhnᶜm/m*
10 *lk/sbʾ/bn/whbʾl/yḥz/mlk*
11 *sbʾ/wl/ẖmrhmw/ʾlmqh/ṯhwn*
12 *bᶜl/ʾwm/ʾṯmr/wʾfql/ṣdqm/b*
13 *n/kl/ʾrḍthmw/wl/ẖrynhmw*
14 *ʾlmqh/bn/bʾstm/wnkym/wn*
15 *ḍᶜ/wšṣy/šnʾm/wl/ḏt/nᶜmt/w*
16 *tnᶜmn/lswdm/wyhᶜn/wklbm/b*
17 *ny/ᶜṯkln/wl/sᶜdhmw/ʾlmqh/ʾ*
18 *wldm/ʾḏkrwm/hnʾm/bᶜṯtr*
19 *whbs/wʾlmqh/ṯhwn/wṯwr/bᶜl*
20 *m/bᶜly/ʾwm/wḥrwnm/wbḏt/ḥ*
21 *mym/wbḏt/bᶜdnm/wbšms/mlkn/tnf*

1 **[Sym-** Sawdum ʾAs]ʾar and Yuhaᶜîn.
2 **[bol** ..]um and their son Kalbum, peo-
3 [ple of ᶜAṯkalâ]n, have dedicated to ʾIlumquh Ṯahwân,
4 [mas]ter of ʾAwwâm, this statue as has ordered them
5 ʾIlumquh through His oracle for their safety and
6 the safety of their son Kalbum, descendant of ᶜAṯkalân;
7 and that ʾIlumquh may make them happy with prosperity and sa-
8 fety and security perfect and [with] the esteem and grace
9 of their lord Karibʾil Watar Yuhanᶜim,
10 king of Sabaʾ, son of Wahabʾil Yaḥûz, king
11 of Sabaʾ; and that may vouchsafe to them ʾIlumquh Ṯahwân,
12 master of ʾAwwâm, perfect fruits and harvests in
13 all their lands; and that may preserve them
14 ʾIlumquh from misfortunes and suffering and [from] the hos-
15 tility and wickedness of [any] enemy; and that it may have been and
16 be pleasant for Sawdum and Yuhaᶜîn and Kalbum, peo-
17 ple of ᶜAṯkalân; and that ʾIlumquh may make them happy with
18 pleasing, male children. By ᶜAṯtar
19 and Hawbas and ʾIlumquh Ṯahwân and Ṯawr Baᶜal-
20 um, the two masters of ʾAwwâm and Ḥirwânum, and by Ḏât-Ḥi-
21 myâm and by Ḏât-Baᶜdânum and by Šams of the king, Tanûf.

L. 1: the monogram and the first personal name are missing; *swdm* is restored on the basis of line 16. – [..]. *r*; the letter preceding *r* is either ʾ or *s*; therefore, I propose restoring *ʾsʾr*, a well-known second proper name, cf., e.g., CIH 339 bis/1 and Ja 703/1. The hypothesis of *ʾsʾr* instead of *ʾsʾn* in Ḥîma/3 (cf. *RyISA*, X, p. 289) is disproved by the remains of the lower half of *n* (cf. *l.c.*, p. 286); cf. also the commentary on Ja 578/8-9, *ʾsʾr* may be found also as the 2nd name of a man in RÉS 4875/1, Ḥaḍr [cf. also RÉS 4891/1 of the same collection] which may be read as follows: *(h)fḥ[/]ʾsʾr/ḏqyḥn/b(n)/(b)ḏ(l)t/–* "(Ha)faḥḥ ʾAsʾar, he of Qîḥân, son of (Ba)ḏ(la)t, –". The beginning of this line might also be read *(h)fḥʾ[/]sʾr/–* "(Ha)fḥaʾ Saʾr, –". – *yhᶜn*, also name of a man in RÉS 4038(136) and 4624/6, and of a clan in RÉS 4629; cf. also *hᶜn*, name of a place (Ja 575/6) and of a person (Ja 733/1). – Of the last letter of line 1 only two broken vertical strokes remain.

L. 2: *bnyhmw* equals *bnhmw* in line 6; cf. *RhAST*, I, p. 72. – *klbm*, also masculine personal name in RÉS 4856/1, Ḥaḍr, and Ja 244 and 871/1, Qat; cf. also the following personal names: *klb* (RÉS 3902, No. 43, Qat), *klbn* (Ja 348/4, Qat, and 582/1) and *klbt* (e.g., Ja 240/1, Qat), and also the masculine personal name (diminutive *qutaylum*) *klybm* (e.g., Ja 852/4-5, Qat).

L. 3: *ᶜṯkln*, also clan name in RÉS 4549 (instead of *ᶜṯk/n*), where RÉS 4564 is erroneously referred to for the gratuitous correction to *ᶜṯ(ʾl)n*; this reading must be discarded; in Fakhry 52, the restoration of *ᶜṯkln* proposed by *RyET* (pp. 29-30) is not justified by the stone where I read *ᶜṯ(kʾ)n* (cf. *JaIAA*, p. 317, commentary on Ja 533).

Ll. 7-8: *n*ᶜ*mtm/wwfym/wmngt/ṣdqm*, cf. *n*ᶜ*mtm/wwfy wmngt/ṣdqm* in RÉS 4187/5-6; these two references prove the mention of *mngt* in the two following parallels: RÉS 4216/2 (contrary to *MoMiASI*, p. 46. followed by *RÉS*: *mnlt*; as commentary of *mnlt*, the latter refers to RÉS 4187/6, which has *mnGt* and not *mnLt*), and Fakhry 95+94/3, where the reason pointed out by *RyET* (p. 70) is not valid. For *mngt* (also in NaNN 75/9 and RÉS 4962/24-25 [not *mnlt* as in *RÉS*]), *scriptio defectiva* of *mngwt* (e.g., Ja 626/6) or *mngyt* (e.g., CIH 308/26 and Ja 568/16) and *mngw* (Ja 564/4), cf. *CoRoC*, p. 183 B, *BeSI*, p. 125, *CIH*, I, p. 331, Soqoṭri *ngy* "délivrer" (cf. *LeLS*, p. 256), and Ẓofâr *nǧw* "II. erretten" (cf. *RhVDD*, p. 57 B); ordinarily connected with the verb *s*ᶜ*d* (e.g., CIH 335/3), but also with *wśf* (e.g., CIH 544/7), the noun *mng*(*w* or *y*)*t* is commonly translated "deliverance" or some synonym. This interpretation is contradicted by the texts of the present collection. FIRST, the expressions *mngwt/ṣdqm/bḏrm/wslmm* in Ja 652/17-18 and *lmngt/y*ᶜ*krn/mlk/ḥdrmwt* in Ja 643/11 exclude the meaning of "deliverance" because of *slm* "peace time" in the first quotation, and in the second, because there is no possibility that this Ḥaḍr king was actually prisoner. The same remark must be made about Ja 564/4-6, where there is no indication that the Sab king was actually prisoner; he most probably was in great danger and was well pleased by the reliability shown to him by his own people in the recovery of his security which was granted to him by the god ᵓIlumquh. SECONDLY, the texts mentioning *mng*(*w* or *y*)*t* may be divided into three categories. The texts belonging to the first series (here and Ja 567, 604, 605, 606, 607, 626, 627, 628, 630, 643, 645, 652, 690, 707, 726, 732, 747, and 753) contain no mention whatsoever either of military activities or razzia, which could have put an end to the liberty of someone; thus there cannot be question of deliverance. The texts belonging to the second series (Ja 581, 587, 601, 602, and 623) mention military activities, it is true; however, this mention only occurs independently from the occurrence of *mng*(*w* or *y*)*t* and, in all the texts, this noun is a part of stereotyped expressions (e.g., *n*ᶜ*mtm/wwfym/wmngt/ṣdqm* or more simply *n*ᶜ*mtm/wmngt/ṣdqm*), which must be interpreted as having no relation with the military activities referred to in the text. The third series contains three texts, Ja 564, 568, and 610, which deal with non-military activities; e.g., Ja 564 alludes to decrees for the protection and the preservation of the authority of the king. In all the above-mentioned texts, the meaning of "deliverance" does not fit. I suggest translating *mng*(*w* or *y*)*t* as "security"; cf. Daṯînah *nǧw* "se réfugier" (cf. *LaGD*, pp. 2749-50) and Arabic *naǧâᵓ* "refuge" (cf. also *njy* in *MoNTA*, p. 350). In Min, the verb *ngw* is ordinarily followed by a noun such as *sṭr* "script" and means "to make known, promulgate". In Ja 564/14, *mngt* may be translated "security measures". However, *mng*(*w*)*t* in Ja 564/23 and 645/18-19, has a hostile meaning (cp. ᵓ*rḫ*; cf. commentary on Ja 567/24) as well as *mngw* in Fakhry 71/9. In the latter, *RyET* (pp. 42 and 44) translates it as "ravage"; *NaNAG* (II, p. 40) identifies *mngw*(*t*) (Ja 645/18-19 and Fakhry 71/9) with Arabic *talaf* (loss, perdition) = *ḫasârat* (loss, damage) = *nâzilat* (accident, calamity), and he uses the last Arabic noun in his translation (p. 38). In Fakhry 71, the context is well defined: it deals with crops and irrigated lands; therefore, I prefer to relate *mngw* to Arabic *naǧw* = *naǧâᵓ* "violent rain", and translate *mng*(*w*)*t* as "storms". A similar context precedes the mention of *mngt* in Ja 564 (see lines 20-21), but does not in Ja 645; I wonder whether the meaning of "storm" does not apply to the last text, as well as to the two others.

L. 11: *ḫmr*, cf. *JaASAB*, pp. 159-60, commentary on CIH 407/11, and also commentary on Ja 559/4: *s*ᶜ*d*, and *RhIMG*, p. 48 and note 1. *BeTMS* translates it as "to grant" in AshM 1957-16/5.

L. 16: *swdm*, also masculine personal name in RÉS 4791/1 and Ja 660/12; cf. the name of a man *sydn* in RÉS 4197/5, the proper name *swdn* in RÉS 5070, the clan name *swd* in Wâdî Maᵓsil 1/10 (cf. *RyISA*, X, pp. 303-04, where this name is not mentioned in the commentary; cf. p. 307); cf. also commentary on Ja 660/12.

Ll. 19-20: *ṯwr/b*ᶜ*lm* "Bull Patron" (cf. *JaP*, pp. 67-68 and *JaRSAP*, p. 261) is another denomination of the Sab lunar god; *b*ᶜ*ly* refers to the nominal distinction between ᵓ*lmqh* and *ṯwr*. Both *ṯwrm* (or *śwrm*) and *b*ᶜ*lm* are also personal names in the rock inscriptions from the country of Mukérâs (cf. *JaIRM*, pp. 309 and 313 respectively); *ṯwrm* is also name of a man, e.g., in RÉS 4867/2, Ḥaḍr, and Altounyan 1 A (not that of the lunar god as proposed by *BeOSA*, pp. 22-23).

564 – Grayish sandstone; photograph; cf. Chapter I, C. – MaMB 314.

STONE: upper right corner broken; left edge splintered off in three places. – INSCRIPTION: letter height twice as small as that of Ja 568.

1 [**Sym-** *ᵓnmrm/... ...]⌜ġ⌝ymn/ᵓ⌜b⌝[ᶜ]l/bytn⌝*
2 [**bol** *slḥn]⌜/ᵓq⌝wl/š⌜ᶜb⌝n/ġymn/hqny/ᵓlmqh*
3 *[ṯhwn]⌜/b⌝ᶜl/ᵓwm/ṣlmn/ḏbhw/ḥmd/ᵓnmrm/mqm*
4 *[ᵓ]⌜lmqh/bḏt/stwfy/mngwm/ḏbhw/tqnᶜw/wst*
5 *ydᶜn/ᵓsbᵓn/wᵓqwln/wẖmsn/mrᵓhmw/krbᵓl*
6 *⌞wtr/yhnᶜm/mlk/sbᵓ/bn/whbᵓl/yḥz/mlk/sbᵓ*
7 *⌜hyhr/mrᵓhmw/krbᵓl/bythmw/slḥn/wḥmdm*
8 *bḏt/stwfy/ᶜbdhw/ᵓnmrm/ḏġymn/wkl/ᵓsd/šw*
9 *ᶜhw/bn/šᶜbhmw/ġymn/bgzyt/gzyw/bhgrn/m⌟[ry]*
10 *b/bn/ryt/mrᵓhmw/krbᵓl/wtr/yhnᶜm/mlk/sbᵓ/bn*
11 *whbᵓl/yḥz/mlk/sbᵓ/ḥgn/wqhhmw/lnẓr/wtn⌞ṣ⌟f*
12 *n/qhthw/bhgrn/mryb/hᵓ/wᵓẖhw/rṯdm/ḏmᵓḏnm/b*
13 *mlᵓ/ẖmst/ᵓwrẖm/wḥmdm/bḏt/stwfy/wštrḥn*
14 *wstkmln/lmrᵓhmw/krbᵓl/kl/mngt/wqhhmw/⌞b⌟*
15 *kl/hmt/ᵓwrẖn/wlsᶜd/ᵓlmqh/ᶜbdhw/ᵓnmrm/ḏġ[ym]*
16 *n/nᶜmtm/wwfym/wmngt/ṣdqm/wḥẓy/wrḍw/mrᵓ[hm]*
17 *w/krbᵓl/wtr/yhnᶜm/mlk/sbᵓ/bn/whbᵓl/yḥz⌝[/ml]*
18 *k/sbᵓ/wlsᶜd/ᵓlmqh/ᶜbdhw/ᵓnmrm/ḏġymn/ᵓw⌜ld⌝[m]*
19 *ᵓḏkrm/hnᵓm/bᵓbyt/ġymn/wlsᶜd/ᵓlmqh/ᶜbd[hw]*
20 *ᵓnmrm/ḏġymn/nᵓd/ᵓṯmrm/wᵓfqlm/bn/kl/ᵓrḍt*
21 *hmw/wᵓsrrhmw/wᵓġylhmw/wmfnthmw/wlhᶜ[nn]*
22 *wšwf/wẖryn/ᵓlmqh/bᶜl/ᵓwm/ᶜbdhw/ᵓnmrm/w⌜bny⌝*
23 *⌞ḏġymn/wšᶜbhmw/ġymn/bn/bᵓstm/wmngt/swᵓ*
24 *m/wbn/nḍᶜ/wšṣy/šnᵓm/wlwḍᶜ/wṯbr/ᵓlmqh/bᶜl/ᵓ*
25 *⌞wm/kl/ḍr/wšnᵓ/ᵓnmrm/wbny/ḏġymn/wšᶜbhmw/ġ*
26 *ymn/wlḏt/nᶜmt/wtnᶜmn/lᵓnmrm/wbny/ḏġymn/w*
27 *šᶜbn/ġymn/bᶜṯtr/ḏḏbn/bᶜl/bḥr/ḥṭbm/*
28 *whbs/wᵓlmqh/ṯhwn/wṯwr/bᶜlm/bᶜly/ᵓwm/wḥrw*
29 *nm/wᵓlmqh/bᶜl/mskt/wyṯw/brᵓn/wbḏt/ḥmy*
30 *m/wbḏt/bᶜdnm/wbšymhmw/ḥgrm/qḥmm/bᶜl/ᶜr*
31 *nhn/tnᶜ/wlms/wbytn/ᵓḥrm/wbšmsyhmw/bᶜlty/nhd*
32 *..ᵓm/wrṯdw/hqnythmw/ᶜṯtršrqn/wᵓlmqh/bᶜl/ᵓwm*

1 [**Sym-** ᵓAnmarum ... ...] Ġaymân, ma[s]ters of the house
2 [**bol** Salḥân,] rulers of the tribe Ġaymân, has dedicated to ᵓIlumquh
3 [Ṯahwân,] master of ᵓAwwâm, this statue by which ᵓAnmarum has praised the power
4 [of ᵓIl]umquh because He has assured security in which have given satisfaction and proved
5 their reliability the warriors and rulers and the army to their lord Karibᵓil
6 Watar Yuhanᶜim, king of Sabaᵓ, son of Wahabᵓil Yaḥûz, king of Sabaᵓ;
7 their lord Karibᵓil has exalted their house Salḥân; and in praise
8 because He has given protection to His worshipper ᵓAnmarum, him of Ġaymân, and to everyone [who] has assisted
9 him from their tribe Ġaymân, in the edict [which] they have issued in the city [of] Mâ[ri]b
10 under obligation to their lord Karibᵓil Watar Yuhanᶜim, king of Sabaᵓ, son of
11 Wahabᵓil Yaḥûz, king of Sabaᵓ, as he had commanded them in order to protect and to preserve
12 his authority in the city [of] Mârib, himself and his brother Raṯadum, him of Muᵓḏinum, during
13 five full months; and in praise because He has given protection and made successful
14 and terminated happily for their lord Karibᵓil all security measures [which] he has ordered them during
15 all these months; and that ᵓIlumquh may make His worshipper ᵓAnmarum, him of Ġ[aym]ân happy
16 with perfect prosperity and safety and security and [with] the esteem and grace of [th]eir lord
17 Karibᵓil Watar Yuhanᶜim, king of Sabaᵓ, son of Wahabᵓil Yaḥûz, [kin]g
18 of Sabaᵓ; and that ᵓIlumquh may make His worshipper ᵓAnmarum, him of Ġaymân, happy with pleasing, male children
19 in the houses of Ġaymân; and that Ilumquh may make happy [His] worshipper
20 ᵓAnmarum, him of Ġaymân, with the magnificence of fruits and harvests in all their lands
21 and their wâdî-side valleys and their stream beds and their lands irrigated by canals; and that may assist
22 and take care of and preserve ᵓIlumquh, master of ᵓAwwâm, His worshipper ᵓAnmarum and [also] the people
23 of Ġaymân and their tribe Ġaymân from disastrous misfortunes and storms
24 and from the hostility and wickedness of [any] enemy; and that may humiliate and crush ᵓIlumquh, master of ᵓA-
25 wwâm, every foe and enemy of ᵓAnmarum and of the people of Ġaymân and of their tribe
26 Gaymân; and that it may have been pleasant and be pleasant for ᵓAnmarum and the people of Ġaymân and
27 the tribe Ġaymân. By ᶜAṯtar, Him of Ḏabân, master of Baḥr Ḥaṭabum
28 and Hawbas and ᵓIlumquh Ṯahwân and Ṯawr Baᶜalum, the two masters of ᵓAwwâm and Ḥirwâ-
29 num and ᵓIlumquh, master of Maskat and Yaṯaw Baraᵓân and by Ḏât-Ḥimy-
30 âm and by Ḏât-Baᶜdânum and by their patron Ḥagarum Qaḥamum, master of the two cita-

31 dels Tani^c and Lamas and [master] of the house ʾAḥram and by their two Šams, the two mistresses of Nahd

32 [..]ʾm. And they have entrusted their offering to the care of ʿAṯtar Šarqân and of ʾIlumquh, master of ʾAwwâm.

L. 1: symbol missing; *ʾnmrm* restored on the basis, e.g., of line 3.

Ll. 1-2: *bytn/slḥn*, cf. line 7.

L. 3: *ḏbhw*, cf. *ḏbhmy* (commentary on Ja 560/4).

L. 4: *tqnʿw*, cf. *tqnʿhw* in Ja 562/7.

Ll. 4-5: *stydʿ*, cf. *JaFSR*, pp. 15-16 and *JaPDSM*, pp. 178-79; for the Western Semitic cognates of *ydʿ*, cf. *JeHoDISO*, pp. 104-05: *ydʿ*.

L. 7: *hyhr*, 4th form of *yhr*; cf. CIH 82/5, 408/11, and Ja 668/13, and the noun *yhr* in Ja 616/19; for the etymology, cf. *BeSI*, p. 21, who refers to Hebrew *yhr* "to be exalted", a meaning already pointed out by *CIH* (III, p. 359 B), which translates *hyhr* (CIH 408/11) as "triumphus". The verb *hyhr* has an active meaning such as "to exalt, raise up; elevate"; the noun *yhr* in Ja 616/29 may be translated "exaltation". The verb *yhr* must not be confounded with the verb *whr*, the 10th form of which seems to be attested in Ja 527/3 (cf. *JaISAR*, pp. 124-25). – No letter is missing either at the end of line 6 or at the beginning of line 7.

L. 8: *ʾsd*, relative pronoun (cf. *HöASG*, p. 53, §45-46).

Ll. 8-9: *šwʿhw*: the first two letters, although damaged, are still certain; for *šwʿ*, cf. *JaASAB*, pp. 160-61, commentary on CIH 407/15; and also commentary on Ja 561 bis/6.

L. 9: *bgzyt/gzyw* confirms the etymology of *gzwt* from *gzy* (e.g., *CoRoC*, p. 122 B, *BeSI*, p. 101, and *BeFSTI*, p. 274) contrary to *RÉS* (VII, p. 92: from *gzz*; in commentary on RÉS 4131/6); *gzz* (cf. *StSESA*, p. 514) and *gzy* are morphologically close to each other; however, their meaning is not quite alike; the first means "to cut" and the second "to separate, discriminate, attribute" (cf. also *LeLS*, p. 106 and *MoNTA*, p. 109: *jzy* "partager").

L. 10: *ryt*: H. Grimme (cf. *Le Muséon*, 37 [1924], p. 183) relates this noun to the Arabic root *rwy* and to its derived noun *rawîyat* "obligation, what must be done". In Min, *ryt* (or *rt* in *scriptio defectiva*; cf. RÉS 3697/9) is translated "penitential offering"; *ryt* is also attested in Sab (RÉS 4010/3), but this text is too fragmentary to be of any help as to the meaning of the noun. In the present text, *bn/ryt* means "under obligation to" or "following an order from".

Ll. 11-12: *lnẓr/wtnṣfn*, also in Ja 651/16; *lnẓr*, e.g., CIH 334/7 and *CoRoC*, p. 186 B: "to protect". *tnṣf*, 5th form of *nṣf*, cf. *CoRoC*, p. 190 A: cf. Arabic *naṣafa*, 5th form "to submit to someone"; here, with the meaning of "to preserve"; cf. also the noun *mnṣf* "minister" (CIH 338/6; cf. *BeSI*, p. 37 and *HöASG*, p. 167); for *nṣf* and NaNN 74/3, cf. *JaFSR*, p. 16.

L. 12: *qht*: e.g., *BeSI*, pp. 32-33 and 108: from the root *wqh*; in the present text and in Ja 578/39; *qht* certainly means "authority"; however, in Ja 565/6, this noun means "obedience" as well as Arabic *waqhat* "obedience, docility" (cf. also *MoNTA*, p. 361). – *hʾ* (cf. *HöASG*, pp. 36-37), also sing. m. separate dem. pron. in Ja 525/4: *whʾ* "quant à lui" (cf. *JaISAR*, p. 121), but feminine in Ja 584/7; *hʾ/wʾẖhw* equals *hʾ/wʾẖyhw* in Ja 584/11; *hʾ*, *scriptio defectiva* of *hwʾ*, e.g.: *hwʾ/wʾqwlhw* in Ja 577/15, but adjective in Ja 585/15.– *rṯdm*, also masculine personal name in RÉS 4632/1 and Ja 888/1, Qat; *rṯd* is frequently used in the composition of proper names; e.g., *mrṯdm* (e.g., Ja 182, Qat; cf. commentary in *JaPEHA*, p. 73). – *mʾḏnm*, e.g., Ja 489 A/2.

Ll. 12-13: *bmlʾ* "in the fullness of", equals the adverbial expression "all...through"; the idea of "fullness" is also expressed by *mlʾ* "muster" (Ja 558/5; cf. commentary), "favor" (Ja 560/6), "potentiality" (Ist 7630/6; cf. *BeFSTI*, p. 281), and also by the verb *mlʾ* "to fill" (e.g., Ja 735/13).

L. 13: *ʾwrḫ*, pl. of *wrḫ*, cf. *CoRoC*, p. 140 B and the Western Semitic cognates in *JeHoDISO*, p. 111: yrh_{II}. – *štrḥ*, 8th form of *šrḥ* (Ja 570/13); cf. *CIH* (I, p. 380 B), who mentions J. H. Mordtmann's opinion: Ethiopic *tašareḥa* "prosperum successum habuit", followed by *CoRoC*, p. 252 B, *BeSI*, p. 43, and *RhIAI*, p. 25, note 3.

L. 14: *stkml*: 10th form of *kml*; e.g., CIH 308/4.

L. 20: *nʿd/ʾṯmrm/wʾfqlm*, cp. CIH 174/1-2, where *nʿd* is a noun (*CIH*) and not a verb (cf. *CoRoC*, p. 182 B: "concessit[?]") or an adjective (possibility suggested by *BeSI*, p. 41: "excellent"); however, *nʿd* is adjective in, e.g., CIH 99/4 and 343/4. In the present collection of Sab texts, *nʿd* is also an adjective; e.g., Ja 567/23-24 (cp. *qll* as noun in Ja 750/9 and as adjective in CIH 547/10). The interpretation of *nʿd* has been a subject of much controversy. *CIH* translates it as "taste" and "tasty"; *CoRoC* (*l.c.*) relates *nʿd* to Ethiopic *neʿeda*, Assyrian *naʾādu* "glorify, magnify, exalt"; *BeSI* (p. 40) accepts the Assyrian parallel, mentioning its derived adjective *nāʾidu* (read *naʾidu*) "high". However, *MoMiHI* (p. 20): "rain" and *MoMiSI* (p. 118): "humidity", referring *nʾd* to Arabic *nʾd* "humidity which comes up from the soil". *HöIAI* (p. 90) rejects *MoMiSI*'s interpretation, for *nʾd* is always attested along with fruits and harvests, and therefore reaffirms the etymology presented by *CoRoC*. In spite of this argument, *RyET* (p. 36) simply accepts *MoMiSI*'s etymology and translates *nʾd* as "fertilité" (Fakhry 63/1) and *RyISA* (XV, pp. 101 and 102): "saveur" (Geukens 9/12). The root *nʾd* seems to have as fundamental meaning: "to elevate" (contrast *MoNTA*, p. 351: "accabler, porter envie"), which is connected either with a moral sense (cf. Accadian *naʾādu*) or with water, cf. Arabic *naʾd* "gushing water", Soqoṭri *nʾd* "apporter de l'eau" (cf. *LeLS*, p. 254), and then Accadian *nâdu*, Hebrew *nʾôd* and Šhauri *niʾd* (cf. *BiSSS*, IV, p. 53): "leather bottle"; however, El-Amarna *naʾâdu* "erhaben sein" (cf. J. A. Knudtzon, *Die el-Amarna-Tafeln*. II: *Anmerkungen und Register*, Leipzig, 1915, p. 1476) either with a moral or a material meaning. The term *nʾd* may thus be translated as "magnificent" (adjective) and "magnificence" (substantive); and expressions like *nʾd/dṯʾ*, *nʾd/qyẓ* (both, e.g., in RÉS 4013/3) and *nʾd/ḫrf* could, in my opinion, indicate the magnificence of fruits and harvests respectively during spring, summer, and autumn. Cf. also the masculine personal names *nʾdm* (e.g., RÉS 4864/3, Ḥaḍr; cf. commentary on Ja 584/4) and *ʾlnʾd* (RÉS 3902, No. 119; the same stela is also dealt with in RÉS 4637).

Ll. 20-21: *ʾrḍthmw/-/wʾġylhmw*, cf. Ja 555/3 and 562/13-14.

L. 21: *mfnt, scriptio defectiva* of *mfnyt* (Ja 645/25), derived from the root *fnw* (cf. *CoRoC*, p. 218 B); cf. Arabic *ʾarḍ mafnat* "territory, place which is the best located for meeting from every direction". But, because of South-Arabian *fnwt* "canal" (e.g., Ja 842/3), *mfn(y)t* may have the meaning of "lands irrigated by canals". – *lhʿ[nn]*, the last two letters are missing; cf. CIH 282/5 and commentary on Ja 558/4.

L. 22: *śwf*: CIH 82/8 "tueri" (cf. *CIH* and *CoRoC*, p. 248 B) and "to assist" (cf. *BeSI*, p. 21); *ś(w)f*: RÉS 3991/11 and 14: "retten" (cf. *MoMiSI*, p. 44); cf. Arabic *šâfa* "to look at" (cf. also *MoNTA*, p. 133); in the derived meaning attested by the 5th form in Daṯînah *tašawwafa* "to take care of" (cf. *LaGD*, p. 2099). The Ḥaḍr masculine name *śfsy* in Ja 402/1 has nothing to do with the root *ś(w)f* (cf. *JaDME*, p. 21). In Geukens 2/4: *-/wwfy/ʾfshmw/wnẓrhmw wś.[...*, *RyISA* (XII, p. 309) omits one *w* in *wwfy* in his transcription in South-Arabian letters, restores the end as *wśw[fhmw*, and (p. 310) interprets both *nṣr* and *św[f]* as verbs and *wfy* as a noun. However, the author points out (p. 312) that the letter following *ś* is either *w* or *ʿ*; therefore, *ś(w)[ʿ]*, *ś(ʿ)[b]* and *ś(w)[ft]* (cf. Ja 686/6) are as probable as *ś(w)[f]*. Further, *nẓr* could also be a noun (cf. commentary on Ja 616/22) depending on *wfy*; this opinion would perfectly fit the text in the hypothesis of the reading either of *ś(w)[ʿ]* (cf. commentary on Ja 629/17) or *ś(ʿ)[b]*.

Ll. 23-24: *mngt/swʾm*, already in CIH 581/19, where the reading of *mnyt* is proposed by *CIH* (II, p. 375) and accepted by *BeSI* (p. 123) and *RhASI*, p. 468. – *swʾ*, cf. *CoRoC*, p. 194 A.

L. 27: *bḥr/ḥṭbm*: *bḥr/ḥṭybm* (Fakhry 55/2), cf. *JaP*, p. 90; according to *LaH* (p. 548), *baḥr al-ḥadab* is the name of the Gulf of ʿAden used in several countries of South Arabia; cf. also *ʾḥṭbm*, name of a palm grove in Ja 555/3 and *ḥṭb*, name of a slope in RÉS 4351/3.

L. 29: *bʿl/mskt/wyṯw/brʾn* (contrary to *JaP*, p. 66: *yṯ* instead of *yṯw*) confirms CIH 404/1 (*br[ʾn]*, and not *br[ʾyn]*). The etymology and the meaning of *yṯw* remain unknown.

L. 30: *ḥgrm/qḥmm*, Sab name of ʿAṯtar (cf. *JaP*, pp. 96-97, *JaRSAP*, p. 265 and *JaIMS*, p. 335 (commentary on Ja 500 A). *ḥgrm* is personal name in the unpublished Qat graffito WB 4-20. In his publication of Walker 5, Qat, *RyISA* (XV, p. 126) publishes several statements which need to be corrected. Line 1 of Walker 5 has *ḥlrm* rather than *ḥgrm*. *RyISA* refers to Ja 234, Qat, which has "(*ḥ*?)*grm*" (cf. *JaPEHA*, p. 107) and not *ḥgrm*. Ja 279, Qat reads *ḥlrm* and *ḥgrm*, as stated by *RyISA*, is erroneous. In support of his theory, *RyISA* refers to one of his articles but, as usual, fails to point out that the answer to his affirmations was published in *JaDME*, pp. 16-17. He also refers to a paragraph (pp. 167-68, and not "p. 167") in a review of M. Höfner; this author discusses a question totally irrelevant to the present question, viz., *ḥwlʿm*. In his commentary on Walker 5/2, *RyISA* makes a remark on Ja 309, Qat, without apparently remembering that he already published it in 1953. Further, he erroneously states that "le commentaire... est sans objet", for the commentary refers to RÉS 3902, No. 166, Qat, which indeed mentions *sbḥm*.

L. 31: *tnʿ* and *lms*: names of citadels, where a temple was built dedicated to the god Ḥagarum. *tnʿ*, proper name derived from the root *nwʿ* "to ask, implore" (rarely used); cf. the Thamudic personal name *nʿ* (cf. *vdBrIT*, p. 122: HU 209). For *lms*, cf. Arabic *lamasa* "to touch, palpate" and the following personal names: Thamudic *lms* (cf. *vdBrIT*, p. 107: HU 182) and Arabic *lamîs* (woman; cf. *SaIS*, p. 200 B; not *lamîš*, as *vdBrIT*, *l.c.*). – *ʾḫrm*, name of a tomb in CIH 619/4, and of a man, e.g., in RÉS 3965/1, Qat. – *šmsy*, cf. *JaP*, p. 102: in NaNN 74/6, *bʿlt* means "spouse (of the god)" (cf. commentary on Ja 558/2).

Ll. 31-32: *nhd...ʾm*: the shadow of the lower part of Ja 568 hides the beginning of lines 26-32; I am not able to read the beginning of line 32; for *nhd*, cf. Arabic *nahada* "to rush upon somebody"; cf. also *nhdm*, Ḥaḍr masculine personal name in RÉS 4852/1 and 4854 A/1 (cf. commentary on Ja 560/1), and also the Arabic clan name *banû nahd* (cf. *SaIS*, p. 240 A and *WüID*, 320/4).

L. 32: *ʿṯtršrqn*: no word divider as in RÉS 4091/3-4.

f – Yarum ʾAyman and Karibʾil Watar: Ja 565

565 – Stone re-used in the western pavement; cf. Chapter I, B. – MaMB 266.

FRONT: upper left corner, left edge and lower part badly damaged. – INSCRIPTION, same disposition of lines as in Ja 561 bis; letter height: 5.2 cm.; space between the lines: 0.8 cm. – SYMBOL, cf. *GrGST*, p. 16, Fig. 27 f.

1 **Sym-** *rṯdṯwn/ʾzʾd/w⌈h⌉[wfʿ]ṯt*
2 **bol** *yhšʿ/wwhbʾwm/wsʿdṯwn*
3 *bnw/gdnm/hqnyw/ʾlmqh/ṯhwn*
4 *bʿlʾwm/ṣlmn/ḥmdm/bḏt/h[wf]*
5 *yhmw/bʾmlʾ/stmlʾw/bʿmhw/*
6 *bn/sbʾt/sbʾw/bqht/ʾmrʾhm*
7 *w/ʾmlk/sbʾ/wlḏt/yzʾn/ʾlm*
8 *qh/hwfyn/ʾdmhw/rṯdṯwn/whwf*
9 *ʿṯt/wwhbʾwm/wsʿdṯwn/bʾmlʾ*
10 */stmlʾnn/bʿmhw/wl/sʿdhmw*
11 *rḍw/wḥẓy/mrʾyhmw/yrm/ʾymn/w*
12 *ʾḫyhw/krbʾl/wtr/mlky/sbʾ/w*
13 *l/sʿdhmw/n(ʿ)mtm/wmngt/ṣdq*
14 *m/wl/sʿdhmw/ʾṯmr/wʾfql/ṣd*
15 *qm/bn/kl/ʾsrrhmw/bʿṯtr/whb*
16 *s/wʾlmqh/wbḏt/ḥmym/wbḏ*
17 *t/bʿdnm/wbšms/mlkn/tnf*

1 **Sym-** Raṯadṯawân ʾAzʾad and H[awfʿa]ṯat
2 **bol** Yuhašiʿ and Wahabʾawwâm and Saʿadṯawân,
3 people of Gadanum, have dedicated to ʾIlumquh Ṯahwân,
4 master of ʾAwwâm, this statue in praise because He has g[ran-]
5 ted to them the favors [for which] they have besought Him
6 during the military campaign [which] they fought in obedience to their lords,
7 the kings of Sabaʾ; and that may continue ʾIlum-
8 quh to grant to His worshippers Raṯadṯawân and Hawf-
9 ʿaṯat and Wahabʾawwâm and Saʿadṯawân the favors [for which]
10 they have besought Him; and that He may make them happy
11 with the grace and esteem of their two lords, Yarum ʾAyman and
12 his ally Karibʾil Watar, both kings of Sabaʾ; and
13 that He may make them happy with perfect pr(os)-perity and security;
14 and that He may make them happy with perfect fruits and harvests
15 from all their wâdî-side valleys. By ʿAṯtar and Hawbas
16 and ʾIlumquh and by Ḏât-Ḥimyâm and by
17 Ḏât-Baʿdânum and by Šams of the king, Tanûf.

Ll. 1-3: CIH 1/1-3 mentions the father of the persons recorded in the present text; this father is called *whbʿṯt/yfd*. For *ʾzʾd* (also in RÉS 4649/1), cp. *ʾḏʾd* (e.g., Ja 566/1). For *hwfʿṯt*, e.g., CIH 960/2 (cf. *JaPSAP*, pp. 31, 40, 41, 42, and 44) and Ja 489 A/1; cf. the Ḥaḍr form *hwfʿśt* (RÉS 3512/2) and the Qat forms from Mukérâs: *hwfʿtt*, *hwfʿtr*, and *hwfʿt* (cf. *JaIRM*, p. 313); compare also *hwfʿṯt/bn/ʿw*(line 2)*ṯm/*– "Hawfʿaṯat, son of ʿAwṯum, –" in RÉS 4853/1-2, Ḥaḍr.; same nominal formation as that of *hwfʿm* (family name in Ja 870/2, Qat) and *hwfʾl* (Ja 620/1-2); cf. also the personal name *hwf* in Ja 489 B. The full name of *whbʾwm* (cf. also Ja 506 A/1 and C) is *whbʾwm/yrḥb*. For *sʿdṯwn*, e.g., Ja 506 A/1-2; same nominal formation as *sʿdʾwm* (Ja 590/4), *sʿdʾl* (e.g., Ja 404/1, Min), *sʿdwdm* (Ja 605/1-2), *sʿdšmsm* (Ja 566/2) and *sʿdtʾlb* (Ja 665/1); parallel to *hnʾṯwn* (Ja 797 B/3; cf. commentary on *sʿdwdm*); cf. also *sʿdm* (Ja

594/5). According to D. Nielsen ("Der sabäische Gott ᵓIlmukah", in *MVAG*, 14 [1909], p. 51, note 1), *ṯwn* may be considered as *ṯhwn* in *scriptio defectiva*. – *gdnm*, e.g., Ja 509 and 541/9 (family name) and *gdn* (name of a horse) in Ja 745/7.

Ll. 6-7: *sbᵓt/sbᵓw/bqht/ᵓmrᵓhmw*: CIH 332/2 and RÉS 4138/4-5; in a parallel inscription, RÉS 3877, *RÉS* erroneously translates *bqht* as "sous la protection de"; for *qht*, cf. commentary on Ja 564/12; the verb *sbᵓ* has a metaphorical meaning in Ja 735/7. In Geukens 1/4, *sbᵓ[w]* must be read instead of *sbᵓ*; there is a haplography of *w/w* between the two verbs (cf. lines 5 and 21-22); the subject of the two verbs is the persons recalled by *hmw* which is repeated twice before *bkn*.

L. 13: *w* instead of ᶜ in *nᶜmt* is certain on the stone (cf. my notebook).

g – Fariᶜum Yanhub: Ja 566

566 – Yellowish sandstone; photograph in Plate 3. – MaPI 2[1].

STONE: thickness: 7 cm.; right lateral face broken. – *Front:* a hollow (diameter 6.5 cm.) in the lower half; 34.6 cm × maximum of 16.6. – INSCRIPTION: several letters are more or less effaced in the lower half; some other signs are entirely obliterated; one or two letters are missing at the beginning of lines 3 and 5-12. The width of *t* at the beginning of line 4 makes unnecessary the restoration of one letter. – SYMBOL: lower half destroyed; the upper horizontal line (and thus also the lower one) is concave; a small vertical stroke hangs from it and there was probably no small stroke inside the center; cf. Plate A.

1 **Sym-** *rbšms/ᵓḏᵓd/rgly/ml*
2 **[bol]** *kn/wᵓẖyhw/sᶜdšmsm*
3 *[w]bnyhmw/rṯdṯwn/bnw/ṯn*
4 *⸢t⸥/hqnyw/ᵓlmqh/bᶜl/ᵓwm/ṣ*
5 *[l]⸢mn/wṣlmtn/ḏḏhbn/lḏ*
6 *[t/]hwfyhmw/bmlᵓ/stmlᵓ*
7 *[bᶜ]mhw/wlẖmrhmw/bᶜl/ᵓw*
8 *[m/]ḥẓy/wrḍw/mrᵓhmw/fr*
9 *[ᶜm]/yn(hb/)wbnyhw/ᵓlšrḥ*
10 *[y]⸢ḥḏb/wyᵓ(z)⸤l/mlk/⸥sbᵓ/wlw*
11 *[zᵓ]/ᵓlmqh[/bᶜlᵓwm/hw]fynhmw*
12 *[bk]⸢l/ᵓmlᵓ[/ystmlᵓnn/]⸢b⸣ᶜmhw/bᵓ*
13 *lmq⸢h/b⸣ᶜlᵓwm*

1 **Sym-** Rabbšams ᵓAḏᵓad, orderly of the king,
2 **[bol]** and his brother Saᶜadšamsum,
3 [and] their son Raṯadṯawân, descendants of Ṯaniat,
4 have dedicated to ᵓIlumquh, master of ᵓAwwâm, this sta-
5 [tu]e and this female statue which [are] in bronze, becau[se]
6 He has bestowed upon them the favor [for which] he besought
7 Him; and that the master of ᵓAww[âm] may vouchsafe to them
8 the esteem and grace of their lord Fari-
9 [ᶜum] Yan(hub) and his two sons ᵓIlšaraḥ
10 [Ya]ḥḍub and Yaᵓ(zi)l, the king of Sabaᵓ; and that may [con-]
11 [tinue] ᵓIlumquh, [master of ᵓAwwâm, to be]stow upon them
12 [al]l the favors [(for which) they shall beseech] Him. By ᵓI-
13 lumquh, master of ᵓAwwâm.

L. 1: *rbšms*, RÉS 3250/5 and 4899, Ḥaḍr, and *rbšmsm* (Ja 578/1); same nominal formation as that, e.g., of *rbnsrm* (Ja 605/5), *rbtnf* (Ja 669/1), and *rbṯwn* (Ja 701 A/8); the double *b* is sometimes written, cf., e.g., *rbbᵓwm* (Ja 698/1), *rbbᵓl* (Ja 619/6-7), *rbbḥgrm* (Ja 747/8), and also *rbbm* (Ja 683/4). – *ᵓḏᵓd*, cp. *ᵓzᵓd*, Ja 565/1 and very probably CIH 742/2 (the doubtful *b* is easier corrected to *ḏ* than to *z*); *ḏ*=*z*, cf., e.g., *StSESA*, p. 513, and the graffiti discovered by Freya Stark in Wâdî Raḥbe (e.g., RÉS 5043). – *rgly*, cf. commentary on Ja 550/2: *rgl*.

Ll. 3-4: *ṯnt*, probably in CIH 289/1 and possibly in CIH 144/1; cf. also *ṯnyn* (e.g., CIH 289/24) and *ᶜm/ṯntm* (cf. *JaP*, p. 79;) *ṯnyt* is a well-known Thamudic personal name (cf., e.g., *vdBrIT*, p. 387: Jsa 61).

Ll. 5-6: *lḏ[t/]hwfyhmw*, cp. *l/ḏt/hᶜn* in CIH 82/5-6; the value of *lḏt* introducing either a petition (normal case; cf. *HöASG*, p. 169) or a reason for gratitude (here, also, e.g., in Ja 576/2) is determined by the tense of the following verb, either imperfect or perfect. In CIH 352/6 and 7, *lẖmrh(m)w*, *l* equals *lḏt* with the second of the above-mentioned meanings (cf. *JaASAB*, p. 170, commentary on CIH 352/6, 7, 9).

Ll. 8-9: *frᶜm*, also 2nd clan name in RÉṢ 4938/2.

L. 10: the name of *ᵓlšrḥ/yḥḏb*'s brother is badly damaged; the following decipherment of it is based on a further study of my two black and

[1] At a later period, I was told that this inscribed stone was found in front of the Maḥram Bilqîs.

color photographs. The first two letters, although very much effaced, are *yʾ*. From the last letter, remain both the upper extremity of a vertical stroke with a triangle-shaped end, and a triangle-shaped end with a short oblique line directed toward the top of the above-mentioned fragmentary stroke; such remains belong to *l*. However, such an upper end in the vertical stroke of *l* requires that the worker made a mistake: he first forgot the letter *l* and thus engraved the following word divider. Finally, the letter between *yʾ* and ⌊*l*⌋ is *z* of which remain the lower extremities of the two upper oblique lines.

2 – PERIOD *mlk/sbʾ/wḏrydn: Ja 567-655*

a – ʾIlšaraḥ Yaḥḍub

1° – ALONE: Ja 567-573.

567 – Grayish sandstone; partial photograph; cf. Chapter I, C. – MaMB 291.

STONE: thickness: 20.5 cm. – *Front:* upper left corner broken; 1.128 m. × 36.9 cm. – INSCRIPTION: same disposition of lines as in Ja 552; letter height: from 3.2 cm. to 3.9; space between the lines: from 0.6 cm. to 0.4; distance from line 1 to the upper edge: 0.9 cm. – SYMBOL, cp. Ja 565; but six small (instead of three long) lines inside the design; cf. Plate A.

1 **Sym-** *ʾbʾmr/ʾṣdq/ḏṣryhw/mʿdkrb[/wb]*
2 **bol** *nyhw/brlm/ḏṣryhw/mʿdkrb[/wkrb]*
3 *ʿṯt/ḏṣryhw/nšʾkrb/bnw/ḏsḥr/hq[nyw]*
4 *ʾlmqhṯhwnbʿlʾwm/ṯlṯtn/ʾṣlmn/ʾl[y/ḏh]*
5 *bn/ḥgn/ḏt/hrʾy/ʾlmqhṯhwnbʿlʾwm/ʿbd*
6 *hw/brlm/bwsṭ/snthw/bkn/ḥlẓ/bwrẖ/ḏʿ*
7 *ṯtr/ḏẖrf/smhkrb/bn/ʾbkrb/bn/ḥḏmt/kyrʾynh*
8 *w/byn/ṯrnhn/ḏẖlf/mṣrʿy/qsdm/ḏygwnhw/kly*
9 *hqnynn/ʾlmqhbʿlʾwm/ṯlṯt/ʾṣlmm/ḏhbm/l*
10 *wfy/grybthmw/wrʾ/kstmlʾ⟨⟩w/bʿm/ʾlmqh/k*
11 *hmy/bṣdqm/whkn⟨/hkn⟩/hwt/ḥlmn/wwkbw/bʿm*
12 *ʾlmqh/kbṣdqm/whkn/hkn/hwt/ḥlmn/wrʾ/kh*
13 *qnyw/ḏt/hqnytn/ḥgn/kwqh/ʾlmqhṯhwnbʿlʾ*
14 *wm/lwfy/grybt/ʾdmhw/ʾbʾmr/wbnyhw/brlm/w*
15 *krbʿṯt/bny/ḏsḥr/wlwzʾ/ʾlmqhṯhwnbʿlʾwm/h*
16 *ʿnn/wmtʿn/wfrqn/grybt/ʾdmhw/ʾbʾmr/wbny*
17 *hw/brlm/wkrbʿṯt/bn/mwtm/wnkytm/wḥlẓ/swʾ*
18 *m/wlẖmrhmw/hwfynhmw/bkl/ʾmlʾ/wmydʿ/yzʾn*
19 *n/stmlʾn/wstydʿn/wtḍʿn/bʿmhw/wlẖmrhmw/ṣ*
20 *ḥ/lbhw/wḥẓy/wrḍw/mrʾhmw/ʾlšrḥ/yḥḍb/mlk/s*
21 *bʾ/wḏrydn/bn/frʿm/ynhb/mlk/sbʾ/wlwzʾ/wśfh*
22 *mw/wsʿdhmw/ʾlmqh/nʿmtm/wwfym/wḥẓym/wkr*
23 *btm/wʾwldm/hnʾm/ʾly/kwkbt/ṣdqm/wʾṯmrm/n*
24 *ʾdm/hnʾm/bn/kl/ʾrḍthmw/wʾʾrẖ/wmngt/ṣdqm*
25 *wḏt/nʿmt/wtnʿmn/lgrybthmw/wʾwldhmw/wḏqn*
26 *yw/wlẖrynhmw/wmtʿnhmw/wfrqnhmw/bn/kl/bʾstm*
27 *wnkytm/wʿbṭm/wtlftm/wẖybtm/wqlmtm/wbn/nḍʿ*
28 *wšṣy/wsyb/wtṯʿt/šnʾm/bʾlmqhṯhwnbʿlʾwm*

1 **Sym-** ʾAbʾamar ʾAṣdiq, he of Ṣarayhû Maʿadkarib [and] his two
2 **bol** [s]ons Barlum, he of Ṣarayhû Maʿadkarib [and Karib-]
3 ʿaṯat, he of Ṣarayhû Našaʾkarib, descendants of Saḥar, [have] dedi[cated to]
4 ʾIlumquh Ṯahwân, master of ʾAwwâm, these three statues, whi[ch (are) in bron-]
5 ze, as ʾIlumquh Ṯahwân, master of ʾAwwâm, has shown to His worshipper
6 Barlum during his sleep, when he was overwhelmed by oppression in the month of ʿAṯ-
7 tar, in the year of Sumhukarib, son of ʾAbkarib, descendant of [the family] Ḥaḏimat, in order that He shows him
8 between the two bulls of the region of the two arena fields of Qâsidum, what He desires intensely from him, so that
9 they would dedicate to ʾIlumquh, master of ʾAwwâm, three statues in bronze for
10 the safety of their persons; and now they have besought ʾIlumquh that
11 [it would] ever [be] in reality; and the realization of this dream came to pass; and they have received from
12 ʾIlumquh that [it became] in reality; and the realization of this dream came to pass; and consequently, they
13 have dedicated this offering, as has ordered ʾIlumquh Ṯahwân, master of ʾA-
14 wwâm for the safety of the persons of His worshippers ʾAbʾamar and his two sons Barlum and
15 Karibʿaṯat, descendants of Saḥar; and that ʾIlumquh Ṯahwân, master of ʾAwwâm, may continue to
16 assist and save and deliver the persons of His worshippers ʾAbʾamar and of his two sons
17 Barlum and Karibʿaṯat from death and sufferings and ill oppression;
18 and that He may vouchsafe to them to grant them all the favors and requests [for which] they shall continue
19 to beseech and confide in (Him) and implore Him; and that He may vouchsafe to them
20 the best of His heart and the esteem and grace of their lord ʾIlšaraḥ Yaḥḍub king of

21 Sabaʾ and Raydân son of Fariʿum Yanhub, king of Sabaʾ; and that ʾIlumquh continue to add to them
22 and to make them happy with prosperity and safety and esteem and blessings
23 and (with) pleasing, numerous, perfect children, and (with) magnificent,
24 perfect fruits from all their lands, and (with) perfect undertakings and security;
25 and that it may have been pleasant and be pleasant for their persons and their children and what they have in possession;
26 and that He may preserve them and save them and deliver them from all misfortunes
27 and sufferings and calamity and ruin and failure and insect-pests, and from the hostility
28 and wickedness and irruption and fear of [any] enemy. By ʾIlumquh Ṯahwân, master of ʾAwwâm.

L. 1: *ʾbʾmr*, e.g., RÉS 3902 bis, No. 131/1. – *ʾṣdq*: *ʾaqtal* form; also second masculine name, e.g., in Ja 506 A/1. – *mʿdkrb*, e.g., Ja 303, Qat, and 400 A and RÉS 4226/1; cf. also *mʿdʾl* in Condé 11, where it is translated "Wahabʾil" (cf. *RyISA*, XVIII, p. 17).

Ll. 1-2: *bnyhw*: for the drawing of Ja 506 A/1, cf. *JaPSAP*, p. 174.

L. 2: *brlm*; also personal name in RÉS 3908/1 (*brlm*, so *RyISA*, I, p. 162, who points out that "la 3e lettre présente les caractéristiques du *l*"; there is thus no reason for transcribing *brg*(?)*m* in RÉS 3908/1), RÉS 4479/2 (transcribed *brg*(?)*m* by *RÉS*), family name in Ja 863/2, Qat, and second personal name in Ja 692/1. Judging from the copy reproduced by *RyISA* (V, p. 107), the reading of *brg* in RÉS 4994/1 is as uncertain as that of *brl*, and *NaNN*'s (p. 33, No. 21/1) reading as *brg* cannot be checked; cf. also the feminine personal name *brlt* in Ja 700/7-8.

Ll. 2-3: *krbʿṯt*, cf. commentary on Ja 401/5 in *JaSIBS*, p. 34 A.

L. 3: *nšʾkrb*, e.g., RÉS 2726/18-19. – *bnw/ḏsḥr* = *bny/ḏsḥr* in RÉS 4135/1 (cf. *JaPEHA*, p. 28); *ḏsḥr*, cf. also Ja 540 A/4, 542 A/1 and the monograms C and D (E only mentions *sḥr*).

L. 4: *ṯlṯtn*, cf. *HöASG*, p. 131, §112.

Ll. 5-6: *ḥgn/ḏt/hrʾyn/–/ʿbdhw/–/bwsṭ/snthw*, cp., *ḥgn/khrʾyhw/bsnthw* in RÉS 3929/5 "selon qu'il lui a manifesté par son ordre" (*RÉS*). For *bwsṭ*, cf. *JaASAB*, p. 159, commentary on CIH 407/9-10. Two texts are important for the translating of the above-mentioned expression: *ḥgn/wqhhmw/bms lhw/lḥmdhw/bhrʾyt/hrʾy/lhm*[*w*] (CIH 357/8-12) and [*ḥ*]*g*/[*ḏt*/]*wqhhmw/ʿṯ*[*tr*/–]/*bmsʾlm/wlf/hrʾyt/hrʾy* (RÉS 4052/3-4). *HöIAI* (p. 105) writes about the first quotation: "das Orakel bestand diesmal nicht in einem Spruch, sondern in einem sichtbaren Zeichen, einer Vision"; and *BeNL* (IV, p. 145) expresses the same idea: "in C.357 the divine oracle is manifested by means of a 'vision'". The preceding interpretation does not reflect the text which means that, through an oracle, the god gives several persons the order to praise him because of a sign sent to them by himself; *msʾl* and *hrʾyt* are two different things which occurred separately; it is therefore difficult to accept the opinion that *hrʾyt* helps determine the nature of *msʾl*. In the second quotation, *hrʾyt* can scarcely be a repetition to explain the nature of *msʾl*. The two preceding texts, together with the fact that *bmsʾlm* "through an oracle" or *bmsʾlhw* "through His oracle" is very often related to a verb expressing an order, a command (e.g., very often *wqh*, e.g., RÉS 3884 bis/10, ʾAwsânite, 4052/4 and 3902, No. 137/5, Qat; but also *ktʾ* in RÉS 2693/4, Ḥaḍr, and *ʾmr* in RÉS 3551/4, Qat; however, cf., e.g., *ḫmr*, cf. commentary on Ja 563/11) seems to indicate that the oracle *msʾl* was given in the form of a verbal decision. The noun *hrʾyt* (or also *rʾy*, cf. Hamilton 9/5) implies some visual fact explained as follows by A. F. L. Beeston (cf. *BrBeSIS*, p. 58): "'vision', scilicet a dream interpreted as an oracular sign from the deity". However, *rʾy* fundamentally means "to see", and thus (*h*)*rʾy*(*t*) does not necessarily mean a "vision, dream"; I prefer to translate (*h*)*rʾy*(*t*) as "sign", something visible, which was interpreted as an "omen", since it is believed to be sent by the deity (cf. *JaRIH*, p. 152). The form *hrʾy*, 4th form of the verb *rʾy*, means "to let see, show" and does not agree with the translation of *snt* as "order"; for one expects some kind of sign; for *snt*, cf. commentary on line 6 (below).

L. 6: *bkn* (cf. *HöASG*, p. 163) = *kn* (Hamilton 7/4, Qat), temporal conjunction, *kn* being the infinitive of *kwn*; cf. also, e.g., RÉS 4765/2, and Philby-Tritton 135 a/2 (cf. *BeNL*, VI, p. 312) and 103/2; for these two texts, cf. *JaDN*. – *snt*: ordinarily referred to Arabic *sunnat* "custom, habit, law" (cf. commentary on RÉS 2876/4 and 3929/5; cf. *JaCD*, p. 26, note 348). Here, cf. H. Schlobies (in *Orientalia*, 5 [1936], p. 60) who refers to Arabic *sinat* and Hebrew *šênâh* (from the verb *yâšân*) "sleep". – *ḥlẓ*, cf. *JaASAB*, p. 159, commentary on CIH 407/9.

Ll. 6-7: *bwrḫ/dᶜṯtr* (CIH 547/7-8): the month *ᶜṯtr* was especially dedicated to the star god ᶜAṯtar.

L. 7: *dḫrf* introduces the names of an eponym; the real function of the latter is still unknown. – *smhkrb/bn/ʾbkrb/bn/ḥḏmt*, cf. *JaPEHA*, pp. 20-23, formula G; *ḥḏmt* is a family (also RÉS 4505/1) to which belong several eponyms; one of them, Biᶜaṯtar, is still isolated (RÉS 2726/10-11 does not mention his father's name); the present *smhkrb* is different from that of CIH 83/5-6 (*smhkrb/bn/tbᶜkrb*), but the present *ʾbkrb* could be identified with the person mentioned in CIH 380/5 (*wddʾl/bn/ʾbkrb*).

Ll. 7-8: *kyrʾynhw*, for the temporal conjunction *k*, cf. *HöASG*, pp. 167-68; for *RycSD*'s (p. 347) translation of *k* in NaNN 74/3, cf. *JaFSR*, pp. 15-16.

L. 8: *byn*, preposition (cf. *HöASG*, p. 143); cf. the noun *byn*, e.g., in Ja 846/2-3 – *ṯrnhn*, *scriptio defectiva* (CIH 671/2-3) of *ṯwrnhn*; cp. the clan name *ṯwrnhn* in CIH 601/24. – *ḫlf*: after having mentioned *CoRoC* (p. 156), which gives both "gate" and "district" as translations of *ḫlf*, *BeNL* (VI, p. 318, note 23) translates quotations from five texts where "the rendering 'gate' is possible, and sometimes decidedly better" (*l.c.*) and then concludes "We ought therefore definitively and finally to abandon the rendering 'district' for *ḫlf*". In good logic, a "possible" translation certainly does not require the rejection of another one, quite the contrary. Besides, in the preceding argument, one would have expected to find the reference to *BeSI*, which translates (pp. 16 and 42, respectively) *ḫlf* in CIH 79/10 and 350/6 (texts quoted by *BeNL*), as "neighborhood", and also to the same *BeSI*, which proposes (p. 84) the same translation in RÉS 4193/7-10 (text not quoted by *BeNL*). Finally, *BeNL*'s opinion, which is not even mentioned by *RyISA* (XII, p. 302, commentary on Geukens 1/3), simplifies the facts and it is advisable to maintain the translation of *ḫlf* as "region (facing the gate)" in several texts of the present collection (e.g., Ja 576/5); cf. also *ḫlfn* "countrymen" (Ja 560/11). The verb *ḫlf* (10th form *stḫlfw*, and not *stḫlfhw*, as *RyISA*, X, p. 284, in CIH 541/11-12) and its derived noun *ḫlft* (CIH 541/11) refer to *ḫlf* "to govern a province, a country". – *mṣrᶜy*, construct dual (e.g., CIH 1/3-4) of *mṣrᶜ* "leaf of a folding door". I suggest to refer *mṣrᶜy* in the expression *ḏḫlf/mṣrᶜy/qsdm* and *mṣrᶜt* (pl.; CIH 448/4) to Arabic *maṣraᶜ* "arena field, field" and to make *qsdm* a tribal name (cf. also Wâdî Maʾsil 2/5, where *qsdm* is translated "colons militaires" by *RyISA*, *l.c.*, p. 308, who also mentions the possibility that *qsdm* is the name of a tribe of *qsd*; p. 310); for the verb *qsd*, cf. commentary on Ja 577/8. *qsdm* could be identified with Bânû Qâsid of the tribe Yâfiᶜ (cf. *MüHG*, 89/8), in the Wâdî Sulub (cf. *FoSA*, p. 137, note 1), that is to say between J. Ṯamar and J. Šaᶜb (cf. *l.c.*, p. 136, note 8). – *ḏygwnhw*, from the verb *gwy*; cf. Arabic *ǧawiya* "to have a great passion, a violent affection"; here, with the meaning "to desire intensely *or* the most".

Ll. 8-9: *klyhqnynn*: *kl* (*k*+*l*; cf. *HöASG*, p. 169) + *yhqnynn*. Cp. *ḏygwnhw/klyhqnynn/ʾlmqhbᶜlʾwm//ṯlṯt ʾṣlmn* with CIH 105/2-3: *ḥgn/wqᶠhˀ[hw/b]msʾlhw/kl/yqnynhw/ṣlmm* "sicut jussit eum oraculo suo ut consecraret sibi statuam" (cf. *CIH*, III, p. 329 B). This translation supposes *yhqnyn* instead of *yqnyn*; this correction, proposed by *CIH* (*l.c.*, p. 329 A), is confirmed by the present text. In CIH 105/2-3, *h* may have been omitted by haplography; for *y* and *h* are close enough in form especially if the stone is damaged.

L. 9: *ṯlṯt/ʾṣlmm/ḏhbm*: a relative pronoun would normally be expected between *ʾṣlm* and *ḏhb*; cp. *ṯlṯt/ʾṣlmn/ʾl[y/ḏh]bn* in lines 4-5.

L. 10: *grybt*, pl. of *grb*; cf. commentary on Ja 558/3 and *JaASAB*, p. 158, commentary on CIH 407/8. – *rʾ*, very often followed by *k* (e.g., here and line 12), but sometimes mentioned alone (e.g., Ja 619/9-10); cf. *HöASG* (p. 173): "die deiktische Partikel *rʾ* hat meist stark adversativen Charakter" and *BeFSTI* (p. 275): "assertive particle"; these two descriptions must be put together and it must be added to them that *rʾ*(/*k*) introduces an act presented as a consequence of the preceding facts mentioned in the texts (e.g., lines 10 and 12). – *kstmlʾ⟨⟩w* instead of *kstmlʾhw* in copy; the complement of *stmlʾ* is introduced by *bᶜm* (e.g., Ja 560/17); cp. also the plural verb *wkbw* in the following line.

Ll. 10-11: *khmy*: *k*+*hmy* (cf. also an analogous context in Ja 729/8-10); *hmy*, Sab form of Qat *hmw* (cf. *HöASG*, p. 165); *khmy* has the same meaning as that of *kmhnmw* (e.g., Ja 669/10; cf. *JaPDSM*, pp. 176-80); for the alternance *-mw*=*-my*, cp. *k[m](ᶜ)nmy* in CIH 336/6-7 and *kmᶜnmw*, e.g., Ja 693/6; cf. *JaPDSM*, *l.c.*).

L. 11: *bṣdqm*, cf. *kbṣdqm* in the following line; infinitive phrases with *kwn* understood. *khmy/bṣdqm* and *kbṣdqm* refer to the contents of the dream; the authors of the text besought the god that it would become reality; cf. *maṣdar ṣadq* or *ṣidq* "truth" and in Ẓofâr *ṣúdg(a)* "Wahrhaftigkeit" (cf. *RhVDD*, p. 33 A, under *ṣdq*). – *whkn/hwt/ḥlmn* in copy; however, the number of letters varies from 30 to 32 in lines 8-10 and 12-14; the copy of line 11 shows only 27 letters; the parallel of line 12, *whkn/hkn/hwt/ḥlmn*, suggests restoring *hkn* here; *hkn*, 4th form of *kwn*, e.g., CIH 609/5; the second *hkn* is the *maṣdar* in construct state; for *hkn/hkn*, cp. *ḥlẓ/ḥlẓ* (e.g., Ja 613/9) and *mrḍ/mrḍ* (e.g., Ja 572/7) in reverse position; the repetition of the verb *kwn* also occurs in the well-known expression *ḏkwn/kwnhmw* (e.g., Ja 575/5; cf. commentary) = *ḏkyn/kwnhmw* (e.g., Ja 601/10) = Qat *ḏm/kwn/kwnsm* (e.g., RÉS 3566/3). – *hwt*: masculine singular demonstrative adjective (not pronoun as *RyISA*, XIV, p. 379, commentary on Geukens 6/22-23); cf. also *UlSLE*, p. 157. – *ḥlm* (cf. *JeHoDISO*, p. 89: *ḥlm*$_{II}$): masculine noun (cf. *hwt*); in NaNN 74/6, *ḥlmt* is rendered by *NaNN* (p. 100) "chieftains", but by *BeNL* (IV, p. 145) "seeress, prophetess" and by A. F. L. Beeston (cf. *BrBeSIS*, p. 58) "dream-seeress"; *ḥlmt* is a female dreamer.

Ll. 11-12: *wkbw/bʿm ʾlmqh*, e.g., CIH 314+954/11-12; for *wkb*, cf. A. Jamme, in *BiO*, 14 (1957), p. 77, and *JaCRR*, pp. 5-7.

L. 16: *frq*, e.g., CIH 79/8; cf. the 5th form *tfrq*, e.g., in Ja 644/22.

L. 17: *mwt*, e.g., RÉS 3910/6; for the verb *mwt* "to die"; cf. Ja 735/7; *mtw*, pl. of *mwt*, is attested in Ḥimâ/5 (cf. *RyISA*, X, pp. 285-86). The translation of *mwt* as "pestilence" (cf. *RyHE*, p. 235) is incorrect.

L. 18: *mydʿ*, cp. Arabic *muwaddaʿ* "what is entrusted, confided"; the noun may be translated "request".

L. 19: *tḍʿ* (e.g., RÉS 4150/4, 4217/3 and Ja 590/19), contracted writing of *tnḍʿ* (e.g., CIH 571/3-4 and Ja 657/4); *stmlʾ* is also mentioned with *tḍʿ*, e.g., in RÉS 4150/4, where J. H. Mordtmann and E. Mittwoch rightly translate *tḍʿ* as "erflehen"; in another context, *tḍʿ* means "to humiliate" (Ja 581/8).

Ll. 19-20: *lẖmrhmw/ṣḥ/lbhw/wḥẓy/wrḍw/mrʾhmw*, cp. *lẖmr/– –/ḥẓy/w[rḍw]/wṣḥ/ʾlbb/mrʾyhw* in RÉS 4962/9-11, where *RÉS* translates *ṣḥ* as "fidélité"; but this meaning departs from the normal senses of the root *ṣḥḥ* (cf. *JaISAR*, p. 125, commentary on Ja 528/3, where the noun may be translated "perfection"); here, "the best" seems to fit both the context and the root *ṣḥḥ* "to be good, in perfect health"; in Ja 525/4, the verb *ṣḥḥ* means "to be restored"; *hw* of *ṣḥhw* refers to the god himself; for *lẖmrhmw/ṣḥ/lbhmw*, cp. *lẖmrhmw/–/rḍw/lbhw* (CIH 535/7) and *[lẖmr/–]rḍw/lbh* (Ja 489 A/8); cf. also *bṣḥm/wʾmnm* (CIH 308/13): "in perfection and security"; "safety" (*BeSI*'s [p. 28] interpretation of *ṣḥ*) is not very fortunate. For *lb*, cf. commentary on Ja 468 for the etymology of the Qat personal name *lbʿm* in A. Jamme, *Les antiquités sud-arabes du Museo Nazionale Romano* (Rome, 1955), p. 82 B.

Ll. 22-23: *krbt*, plural of *krb*, also mentioned in Ja 692/10 before *ʾṯmr* and *ʾfql*; the present context legitimates referring to Accadian *kerebtu* "blessing" (cf. *BeBAG*, p. 148 B).

L. 23: *ʾwldm/hnʾm/ʾly/kwkbt/ṣdqm*, cp. *ʾwldm/ʾḏkrm/ʾly/kwkbt/ṣdqm/hnʾm* in RÉS 4938/15-17, where *RÉS* refers *kwkbt* to Arabic *kawkabat* "troupe nombreuse, foule" (cf. *RÉS*, VII, p. 441); cf. also *ʾwldm/ʾḏkrwm/hnʾ(m)*⌊*/ḏk*⌋*[w]kbt/ṣdqm* (NaNAG 3/7-8), and Ja 655/12 and 703/5, where *ḏkwkbt* replaces *ʾly/kwkbt*.

L. 24: *ʾrẖ*, pl. *ʾʾrẖ*, feminine noun, cf. the feminine demonstratives *hyt* in Ja 669/23, 25 and *hnt* in Ja 712/10; cf. *JaASAB*, p. 169, commentary on CIH 352/5; *ʾrẖ* fundamentally means "way" (cf. especially Hebrew *ʾôraḥ*). In the present collection, *ʾrẖ* indicates either something good (e.g., here: always plural) or something bad (e.g., Ja 669/23: singular, and, e.g., Ja 620/6: plural).

L. 27: *ʿbṭ*, also in Geukens 9/9, where *RyISA* (XV, p. 101) translates as "exaction", with reference (p. 102) to Ethiopic *ʿabaṭa* "to force someone to do something" and Hebrew *ʿabôṭ* (not *ʿâbhôṭ*). However, the first meaning of the Hebrew noun is not "Strafpfand" (as *RyISA*, p. 102), but "Pfand *pledge*", the only one meaning given by *KoBaLVTL*, p. 674 A. Further, the meaning of Ethiopic *ʿabaṭa* implies some authority in the person who imposes something on someone, and consequently would imply some authority in the enemy of the author of the text; such an interpretation must be discarded. I relate *ʿbṭ*, pl. *ʿbṭt* (e.g., Ja 598/5-6) to Arabic *ʿawbaṭ* "calamity". – *tlft* confirms Mayer Lambert's reading in RÉS 4272/5, Qat, against M. Cohen (*Documents sudarabiques*, Paris, 1934, p. 24), followed by

RÉS (VII, p. 173); it must be pointed out that the oblique strokes of *t* are still visible on the photograph reproduced by M. Cohen (*l.c.*, phot. XII, No. 6); *tlf* is noun in RÉS 3566/20, Qat, and verb in Ja 700/14; cf. also the 4th form, *htlf*, in CIH 155/4 and Fakhry 71/19; cf. Arabic *talafa* "to perish, pass away" and *talaf* "loss, ruin, perdition", and Mehri *telûf* "verderben, vertilgen" (cf. *JaMSSA*, p. 230 A). – *ẖybt*, also noun in RÉS 4966/2: *ḏt/ẖybt*; cf. Arabic *ẖaybat* "failure, check", from verb *ẖyb* [cf. imperfect in RÉS 3945/3], Arabic *ẖâba* (i) "to fail", Mehri *ẖayôb* "böse, schlecht" (cf. *JaMSSA*, p. 195 and Ẓofâr *ẖyb* "schlecht, böse sein" (cf. *RhVDD*, p. 17 B). – *qlmt*, e.g., CIH 74/20 and the singular *qlm* in RÉS 4230/10; cf. *BeSI*, p. 14, for the etymology, which leads to the translation "insect-pest"; cf. also Ẓofâr "*qml gámel* Läuse" (cf. *RhVDD*, p. 50 A), with the metathesis of the last two consonants.

L. 28: *syb*, cp. Arabic *sâba* (i) "to walk, move forward rapidly"; here, with a hostile meaning; read *sʿd* instead of *syb* in CIH 140/8. – *ṯṯʿt*: RÉS 4139/10; *CIH* (II, p. 90 A) proposes relating this word to Hebrew *tešûʿâh* and translating it as *victoria*. But, the idea of "victory" does certainly not fit the context, and the Hebrew noun means "deliverance, salvation, help". *RhSLG* (II, p. 66) proposes relating *ṯṯʿt* to Arabic *at-ṯâʿî* and *at-ṯâʿatu* from the root *ṯwʿ*; the preceding opinion is accepted by *RyISA* (XII, pp. 301 and 308, in Geukens 1/30), who translates as "outrage" (also XIV, p. 376, and XV, p. 101). However, the fact that *Lisân* (quoted by *RhSLG*) must explain the two Arabic terms by other terms with which they have no etymological relation, indicates that they are not Arabic at all. Further, a South-Arabian singular noun with both prothesis and apodosis of *t* is extremely rare. The preceding remark is also true with regard to *NaNAG*'s (II, p. 23) opinion, according to which *ṯṯʿt* is translated by Arabic *siʿâyat* (from the root *sʿy*) "detraction, evilspeaking". Finally, South-Arabian *ṯ* corresponds to Arabic *ṯ* and not *s*. Cp. the metathesis of the first two consonants, Ugaritic *ṯṯʿ* "to fear" (cf. *GoUM*, p. 339 B, No. 2086).

568 – Grayish sandstone; photograph; cf. Chapter I, C. – MaMB 295.

STONE: thickness: 39.7 cm. (top) and 38 (bottom); height: 1.592 m. – *Front:* upper corners badly broken; lower right corner broken; three large places on the left edge are splintered off; 1.53 m. × 47.5 cm. (top) and 47.9 (bottom). – INSCRIPTION: line 1 is missing.

1 [**Sym-** *sʿdšmsm/ʾsrʿ/wbnhw/mr]*
2 [**bol** *ṯdm/yh]⌈ḥm⌉d/bny⌈/⌉[grt/ʾqw]*
3 *[l/šʿbn/]⌈ḏmry⌉/hqnyw/ʾlmqh/b⌉[ʿl/ʾ]*
4 *[w]m/ṣlmn/ḥgn/kwqh/ʾlmqh/bms*
5 *ʾlhw/ʿbdhw/ʾlšrḥ/yḥḍb/mlk*
6 *sbʾ/wḏrydn/lqbly/hwkl/stw⌉[k]*
7 *[l]/mlkn/ʾlšrḥ/lʿbdyhw/sʿd[šms]*
8 *m/wbnhw/mrṯdm/bny/grt/bʿ⌉[m/ʾl]*
9 *mqh/bʿl/ʾwm/wḥmdy/sʿdšmsm/[wb]*
10 *nhw/mrṯdm/bny/grt/bḏt/hwfy/ʾ*
11 *lmqh/ʿbdhw/ʾlšrḥ/mlk/sbʾ/w⌊ḏ⌋*
12 *r⌋ydn/wʿbdyhw/sʿdšmsm/wm⌊r[ṯdm]*
13 *bny/grt/ḥgn/hnt/hwkln/[wlwz]*
14 *ʾ/ʾlmqh/sʿd/ʿbdyhw/sʿdšm[sm/w]*
15 *bnhw/mrṯdm/bny/grt/wqlhmw/w[š]*
16 *ʿbhmw/smhrm/nʿmtm/wmngyt[/ṣd]*
17 *qm/wbry/ʾʾḏnm/wmqymtm/w[lsʿ]*
18 *d/ʾlmqh/ʾdmhw/bny/grt/wšʿ[bhmw]*
19 *⌈s⌉m⌈h⌉rm/ḥẓy/wrḍw/ʾmrʾhmw/ʾm⌈lk/s⌉*
20 *⌊bʾ/wl/wḍʿ/wṯbr/ʾlmqh/ḍr/wšnʾ/ʾ⌋*
21 *⌊mrʾhmw/ʾmlk/sbʾ/wḍr/wšnʾ/ʾd⌊m⌋*
22 *hmy/bny/grt/bʿṯtr/whbs/wʾlm*
23 *qh/wbḏt/ḥmym/wbḏt/bʿdnm/w*
24 *bšms/mlkn/tnf/wb/ʾlyhmw/ʿṯ*
25 *trʿzzm/wḏt/ẓhrn/bʿly/ʿrn/k*
26 *⌊nn⌋/wrṯdw/hqnythmw/ʿṯt⌊ršrq⌋*
27 *[n]⌊/⌋wʾlmqh/b[ʿ]l/ʾwm*

1 [**Sym-** Saʿadšamsum ʾAsraʿ and his son Mar-]
2 [**bol** ṯadum Yuh]aḥmid, people of [Garat, rulers]
3 [of the tribe] Ḏamrî, have dedicated to ʾIlumquh, ma[ster of]
4 [ʾAww]âm, this statue, as ʾIlumquh has ordered through His ora-
5 cle to His worshipper, ʾIlšaraḥ Yaḥḍub, king of
6 Sabaʾ and Raydân, because of the recommendation [by which] bound himself
7 the king ʾIlšaraḥ to his two servants Saʿad[šams]um
8 and his son Marṯadum, people of Garat, un[der ʾIl-]
9 umquh, master of ʾAwwâm; and have praised Saʿadšamsum [and] his
10 [s]on Marṯadum, people of Garat, because has protected
11 ʾIlumquh His worshipper ʾIlšaraḥ, king of Sabaʾ and
12 Raydân and His two worshippers Saʿadšamsum and Mar[ṯadum,]
13 people of Garat, as regards these recommendations. [And that may conti]nue

14 ʾIlumquh to make happy His two worshippers Saʿadšam[sum and]
15 his son Marṯadum, people of Garat, and [also] their ruler and their
16 [t]ribe Sumhurâm with [perfe]ct prosperity and security
17 and (with) the strength of understanding and of power; and that [may make]
18 happy ʾIlumquh His worshippers, the people of Garat, and [their] tri[be]
19 Sumhurâm with the esteem and grace of their lords, the kings of Sa-
20 baʾ; and that ʾIlumquh may humiliate and crush the foe and enemy of their
21 lords, the kings of Sabaʾ, and [also] the foe and enemy of the
22 servants of them both, the people of Garat. By ʿAṯtar and Hawbas and ʾIlum-
23 quh, and by Ḏât-Ḥimyâm and by Ḏât-Baʿdânum and
24 by Šams of the king, Tanûf, and by their two deities ʿAṯ-
25 tar ʿAzîzum and Ḏât-Ẓahrân, the two masters of the citadel
26 Kanân. And they have entrusted their offering to the care of ʿAṯtar Šar-
27 q[ân] and of ʾIlumquh, ma[s]ter of ʾAwwâm.

Preliminary remarks. The first sixteen lines have been copied from the stone, but I never again had the opportunity to continue my work; the end of the text is copied from a photograph; cp. Ja 606, 607, and 753 A, which were used for the restoration of the beginning; cf. also commentary on Ja 559/1.

Ll. 1-2: the symbol is missing. – []*ḥmd* could be restored as, e.g., *ʾḥmd* and *yḥmd* (e.g., RÉS 4994/1); but the first is commonly an isolated name (e.g., Ja 690/2) or first personal name (e.g., Ja 587/1); the same remark may be made about *yḥmd* (e.g., isolated in Ja 656/3-4 and first personal name in Ja 623/10-11). I propose restoring [*yh*]*ḥmd*, since it is a very well-known second personal name (e.g., RÉS 4334/1, Qat, and Ja 515), and also because the persons listed in lines 1-2 have the same names as the Sab kings mentioned, e.g., in Ja 626/9-10. The proposed restoration of lines 1-2, which have the same number of signs, reckons with the fact that the letters of line 2 are wider than those of the following lines.

L. 3: *ḏmry*, cp. the name of the city *ḏmr* in Ja 576/14, etc.

L. 4: *ḥgn/kwqh*, Ja 567/13.

L. 6: *lqbly*, cf. *JaPDSM*, pp. 176-80. – *hwkl*, plural *hwklt* (Ja 611/7); cf. *CoRoC*, p. 137 A; *NaNAG* (II, p. 42) inexactly translates as "protection".

L. 7: *ʿbdy*, noun here as well as in Geukens 13/1, where *RyISA* (XV, p. 112) comments on his interpretation of this term as personal name by referring to Fakhry 30/2-3 where *ʿbdy* is also a noun.

L. 8: *bʿ*[*m*], cf. RÉS 3688[1]/9, Qat, and *RhKTB*, I, p. 38: *bʿm* = *bn*/*tḥt*.

L. 10: after *bny*/*grt*, the name of the deity would be expected.

L. 13: *hnt*, plural feminine of the demonstrative adjective; cf. Fakhry 76/4.

Ll. 21-22: *ʾdmhmy*, *sic* on the stone; the dual is a mistake: the personal pronoun refers to *ʾmlk*/*sbʾ*; the *y* may be explained by the final letter of the following term, *bny*.

L. 24: *ʾly*, construct dual of *ʾl*.

569 – Upper part of an inscription; yellowish sandstone; photograph in Plate 3. – MaMB 188.

STONE: maximum thickness: 13.5 cm. – *Front:* upper corners badly damaged; covered with red paint; length: 14 cm.; width: 16 cm. – INSCRIPTION: same disposition of lines as in Ja 552; letter height: from 1.6 cm. to 1.7; space between the lines: from 0.25 cm. to 0.3. – SYMBOL: cp. Ja 565, but the inside lines are more elaborate; cf. Plate A.

1 **Sym-** *⌜lḥy⌝ʿṯt/wl*[. . . . . ./*wb*]
2 **bol** *nyhmw/mrṯd⌜m/⌝*[*wḥy*]*w⌜ʾ⌟*
3 *wm/wḥywʿṯtr/bnw⌜/⌝⌜mrbʾ⌟*
4 *n/hqnyw/ʾlmqhbʿlʾwm/ṣ*
5 *lmtm/lḫmrhmw/ḥẓy/wrḍw*
6 *mrʾhmw/ʾlšrḥ/yḥḍb/mlk⌟*
7 *sbʾ/wḏrydn/bn/frʿm/yn⌜h⌝*
8 *b/mlk/sbʾ/wlwzʾ/hw⌞fy⌟*[.]
9 . . .]*⌞h.tt⌟*[. . .

1 **Sym-** Laḥayʿaṯat and L[. . . . . .and] their
2 **bol** [s]ons Marṯadum [and Ḥay]ûʾa-
3 wwâm and Ḥayûʿaṯtar, descendants of Marbaʾ-
4 ân, have dedicated to ʾIlumquh, master of ʾAwwâm, a
5 female statue in order that He may vouchsafe to them the esteem and grace of
6 their lord ʾIlšaraḥ Yaḥḍub, king of
7 Sabaʾ and Raydân, son of Fariʿum Yanh-
8 ub, king of Sabaʾ; and that He may continue to grant
9 . . .]. . . .[. . .

[1] Both RÉS 3688 and 3689 come from J. Labaḫ, and not from Mablaqah.

The present text and Ja 595 do not seem to belong to the same original; the number of signs is slightly different in each case (20 and 21 in the 1st text, but 24 and 26 in the 2nd); the front of the 1st is covered with red paint, and that of the 2nd is not; however, the difference in personal pronouns (*hmw* in the 1st and *hw* in the 2nd) would not be a reason against the re-union of the two inscriptions for such a change in the number of personal pronouns is well known. – Ja 804 is not a part of Ja 569 because of the difference in the gender of the personal pronouns. – Ja 813 does not belong to the present text for the letters are thicker in the 1st than in the 2nd; each left ornament of *š* almost equals a third of the letter height in the 1st text, but less than one fourth in the 2nd; finally; the color of the stone is different in each case. – Ja 839 is not to be re-united with the present inscription because the height of the triangular ornament located at the end of each vertical stroke is much smaller in the 1st than in the 2nd; that is especially visible in *q*.

L. 1: the 1st half of the 1st name is badly damaged; nevertheless, its remains require the reading of *lḥy*.

Ll. 1-2: *bnyhmw*, plural, cf. Ja 558/3.

Ll. 2-3: *ḥywʾwm*, cp. *ḥyʾwm*, e.g., in RÉS 4084/1.

L. 3: *ḥywʿṯtr*, cf. Kensdale 3 (cf. *KeHYNI*) = RÉS 3194.

Ll. 3-4: *mrbʾn*, cp. the personal name *rbʾ* in Thamudic (cf. *vdBrIT*, p. 476: HU 817) and Safaitic (cf. *LiSI*, p. 342 B) and also Ραββανης (cf. H. Wuthnow, *Die semitischen Menschennamen in griechischen Inschriften und Papyri des vorderen Orients*, Leipzig, 1930, p. 96).

L. 9: the top of *t* is preceded by a circle, which belongs to *y*, *ṣ*, or *ṯ*, and by two monumental triangles, which belong to *h*; to the left of *t*, there is the upper extremity of another *t*.

570 – Yellowish sandstone; broken at the right side; photograph in Plate 4. – MaMB 227.

STONE: maximum thickness: 8.5 cm. – *Front:* 11.5 cm. (top) and 14.8 (bottom) × 27.7. – INSCRIPTION, same disposition of lines as in Ja 552; letter height: from 1.2 cm. to 1.4: space between the lines: from 0.2 cm. to 0.3.

1 **[Sym-** . . .]⌊*m/rkbn/ʿbd/mlkn/hqny*
2 **[bol** *ʾlm*]⌊*qhbʿlʾwm/ṣlmn/ḏšft*
3 [*hw/lqbl*]*y/ḏʾl/tgn/bywm/ṯmny*
4 [*m/. . .*]⌊*l/*⌋*bʿm/ʾsd/mḫtnhw/wh*
5 [*. . . . . mḥ*]*rmn/wyrʾyn/ḏśfhw/bk*
6 [*l/. .   . ./*]*wġwy/ʿnhw/wrʾ/kstyf*
7 [*ʿ/ʾlmqh/w. . .*]*ysr/ṯny/ʾsn/wyqrʾnh*⌉*w/k*
8 [*. . .   . . .*]*/lgtnn/lʾlmqh/kśʿ/y*[.]
9 [*. . .   . . . h*]*my/bn/gtnnn/lʾlmqh/wh*
10 [*. .   . . /hq*]*nytn/wlḫmrhw/ʾlmqh/ḥ*
11 [*ẓy/wrḍ*]*w/mrʾhw/ʾlšrḥ/yḥḍb/m*
12 [*lk/sb*]*ʾ/wḏrydn/bn/frʿm/ynhb*
13 [*mlk/s*]⌊*bʾ/wlšrḥ/ydhw/wlsnhw*
14 [*wlḫry*]*nhw/bn/nḍʿ/wšṣy/šnʾm*
15 [*wlḫ*]⌊*m*⌋*rhw/ʾlmqh/brwm/hnʾm*
16 *bʾlmqhbʿlʾwm*

1 **[Sym-** . . .]um Rakbân, servant of the king, has dedicated to
2 **[bol** ʾIlum]quh, master of ʾAwwâm, this statue, which he has promised
3 [to Him, because] of this: he did not collect the garden products on the eighth day
4 [. . .   . . .] with these of his ceremonial place, and.
5 [. . .   . . .] the [tem]ple(?) and he shall see what He added to him in al[l]
6 [. . .   . . .], but he went away from Him. But now, he has exalted
7 [ʾIlumquh . . .] sent two men, and he shall call on Him in order that
8 [. . .   . . .] to collect the garden products for ʾIlumquh so that. .
9 [. . .of both] of them from the collecting of the garden products for ʾIlumquh, and
10 [. . .   . . .] the [of]fering; and that ʾIlumquh may vouchsafe to him the es-
11 [teem and gra]ce of his lord ʾIlšaraḥ Yaḥḍub,
12 k[ing of Sabaʾ] and Raydân, son of Fariʿum Yanhub,
13 [king of Sa]baʾ; and that He may give success to his hand and his tongue;
14 [and that He may preserve] him from the hostility and wickedness of [any] enemy;
15 [and that] ʾIlumquh [may vouchsa]fe to him a pleasing child.
16 By ʾIlumquh, master of ʾAwwâm.

L. 1: the first three letters of the first personal name are missing; any restoration is entirely conjectural. – *rkbn*, personal name in RÉS 2633/5; the *k* of *rkbn* in Ist 7627/1 is complete; cp. the gentilic *rkb*[*y*]*n* in CIH 441/1-2; cf. also the Arabic names of a man *ar-rakb* and *ar-rakbîyûn* (cf. *MüHG*, p. 145 A) and of a place *ar-rakab*, *rakbat* and *ar-rukbat* (cf. *l.c.*, p. 52 B) and *ar-rikâbîyat*, *rakabân* (cf. *WüR*, p. 102 B), and the Thamudic names of a man *rkb* and *rkbʾl* (cf. *vdBrIT*, p. 82: HU 116 and *vdBrTTPN*, p. 131: Ph 366 v respectively); cf. also *rkbtn* in Ja 577/12 and commentary.

L. 2: *šfthw*, e.g., Ja 535/3-4; for a discussion of the verb *šft*, cf. *BeSI*, pp. 17-18: "to promise" when the subject is a human being (e.g., here), and "to grant" when the subject is a deity (e.g., Ja 633/13). Cf. also A. F. L. Beeston in *Vetus Testamentum*, 8 (1958), pp. 216-17; *šft* does not simply mean "to give" (cf. *UlCSH*, p. 197). The noun *šft* connected with *mᶜd* "help" is translated by *RÉS* "contribution volontaire" (RÉS 2663), but "ordre" (RÉS 4370 and 4477/1), with reference to RÉS 3945/14, where *RhAST* (I, p. 29) suggests "Entscheid"; in the latter text, however, *BeSI* renders *šft* as "grace" (p. 64) and admits that *RhAST*'s translation is supported by RÉS 4370. But, such a short text is practically of no help in the study of the exact meaning of a term. Further, the building by a *mukarrib* of the enclosure wall of Mârib *bšft/ᶜṯtr* does not require giving *šft* the meaning of "order, decision". We thus are left with the ordinary meaning of the verb *šft*, and because the subject of the noun *šft* is a deity, we only have one possibility: a meaning synonymous with "grant", a noun such as "kindness".

L. 3: the restoration [*lqbl*]*y* fills the blank perfectly. – *tgn*: 5th form of the denominative verb *gn* (cf. the noun *gnw* in Ja 574/6); cf. also the infinitive of the 8th form *gtnn*(*n*) in ll. 8, and 9, and their parallel in CIH 74/13-14: *gtnnn/lhmt/ ʾsrrn/bn/mrṯdm* "dass die Gartenernte nehmen solle von jeden Talgründen (ʾRHḲm) der Marṯadite" (cf. *RhGO*, pp. 13 and 15, followed by *HöASG*, pp. 149-50, who adds to the translation "(=aberntе jene Talgründe)"; cf. also *BeSI*, pp. 13-14; in spite of being fragmentary, the present text indicates that *l* introduces the possessive (cf. D. S. Margoliouth). The denominative verb *gn* must not be confused with the verb *gnn*, the 4th form (*hgn* "to assist") of which is attested in Kawkab 2/1 (cf. *RyISA*, X, p. 311). – *bywm/ṯmny*[*m*], RÉS 2726/8; cp. *bywm/tsᶜm* in RÉS 3104/3-4.

L. 4: *mẖtn*, e.g., RÉS 3534 B, Qat (cf. *JaPSAP*, pp. 30-31, 36, 99-101, 102, 167-69, and 190, note 46); *RhSLG* (II, p. 35) relates to an alleged Assyrian *ẖutnû* "knife" and Arabic *ẖatana* "to circumcise" (cf. also Ẓofâr *ẖtâna* in *RhVDD*, p. 15 B, Mehri *ẖtôn* in *JaMSSA*, p. 198 A, Soqoṭri *ḥéton* in *LeLS*, p. 195, and Šẖauri *ẖtn* and *ẖtenít* in *BiSSS*, IV, p. 42, with the same idea as that of Arabic) and affirms that *mẖtn* was a temple for sacrifices or for circumcision; *BeSI* (p. 49) writes: "the contexts in which this word occurs make it clear that it indicates a cult building" and translates as "shrine". *BeSI* is right when he points out that the idea of circumcision would "give the word too restricted a meaning". But, the interpretation of the noun as "temple" or "shrine" is not justified by inscriptions. Qat texts like RÉS 3354 B and 3550/4-5 indicate at the same time a distinction and a connection between the temple itself and the *mẖtn*; these two texts also attest the existence of a *mẖtn/mlkn*. This expression is translated by *GhNQI* (p. 8, note 3) as "the king's banqueting hall" with reference to Arabic *ẖitân* "'the making of a feast...' (Lane, *Lexicon*)". However, the same *Lexicon* points out clearly that the *first* meaning of *ẖitân* is "circumcision", and the preference given to the second meaning rather than to the first remains unexplained by the author. Further, that this *mẖtn* would be the place where the king was sacrificing victims is neither indicated by the etymology of the root *ẖtn* nor fitting RÉS 3104 which explicitly mentions a *mḏbḥt* "altar for sacrifice" which was reserved for the use of the king at the ninth day of the month of Ṯawr. In Assyrian *ẖatānu* (*ẖatnu*) means "relative by marriage, son-in-law, brother-in-law" (cf. *The Assyrian Dictionary*, Chicago, 6 [1956], p. 148). Cf. also Hebrew *ḥtn* "whose son-in-law he is" and *ẖâtân* "daughter's husband, son-in-law. Bridegroom" (cf. *KoBaLVTL*, p. 344), post-biblical Hebrew *hithattên* and *nithatten* "to become connected, to enter into the family, to intermarry" and *ẖâtân* "connection, son-in-law; bridegroom" (cf. *JaDT*, p. 514 A) and also *JeHoDISO*, p. 98: *ḥtn*I, II. The preceding idea fits the verb *ẖtn/b-* in Ja 651/14, "to ally by marriage"; therefore, *mẖtn* may be interpreted as "ceremonial place" (either a room or an apartment), whose primary purpose was for holding wedding ceremonies. A place of that nature may also be used for banquets, or any kind of ceremony.

L. 5: *ḏśfhw*: for the verb *wśf*, cf. commentary on Ja 558/4.

L. 6: *ġwy*, cp. Arabic *ġawâ* (i): "to lose one's way, go out of one's way" and modern Ṣanᶜâʾite "perdere la strada" (cf. *RoAS*, p. 226 B); but, the active meaning is preserved in modern Ḥaḍr and Daṯînah "to mislead, seduce" (cf. *LaH*, p. 671, and *LaGD*, p. 2386, respectively); cf. the feminine adjective *ġwyt* in CIH 563+956/5; here, *ġwy* has the derived meaning of "to go away". – *ᶜn*: RÉS 3351/6, Min, or *ᶜnn*, e.g., in RÉS 3341/1, Min; cf. the Arabic preposition *ᶜan*, the primitive meaning of which is to indicate the removal or the separation from something or someone (cf. *HöASG*, pp. 155-56); cf. also Š̱hauri *ēn=men* "von" (cf. *BiSSS*, IV, p .9).

Ll. 6-7: *styfᶜ*, cf. *JaFSR*, pp. 15-16: discussion of the opinions presented by *RycSD*, pp. 347-48 and summarized later by J. Ryckmans, in *Le Muséon*, 69 (1956), p. 92.

L. 7: *ysr*: CIH 308/18; cf. *BeSI*, p. 31, *CoRoC*, p. 163 B, *BePESA*, p. 13 and *JeHoDISO*, pp. 112-13: *yšr*$_1$; cf. also the 4th form *hysr* in Ja 576/6. – *ṯny*, cf. *StSESA*, p. 527. – *ʾs*, e.g., Ist 7626/4 (cf. *BeFSTI*, p. 273; for Bo 6/3 referred to on p. 273, cf. *JaDME*, p. 14: "man, husband") and Ja 541/3; cf. also *ʾlʾs* in RÉS 4626/2 or *ʾl/ʾs* in Ja 541/3; cf. commentary on Ja 577/6 (*ʾys*) and 559/15 and *JeHoDISO*, pp. 26-27: *ʾš*. – *qrʾ* "to call (on someone)"; cf. *CoRoC*, p. 233 B; for the 10th form *stqrʾ*, cf. *BeSI*, p. 73.

L. 8: *lgtnn*, cf. commentary on *tgn* in line 3. – *kśᶜ*; for *śᶜ*; cp. *śwᶜ* in RÉS 4194/2, connected by *HöSSE* (p. 20) to Arabic *ṯâwa* "to run (water)"; here, *śᶜ* could be related to Arabic *sâᶜa* (o) "to be loosened and in liberty to graze freely".

L. 9: *h*]*my*: isolated personal pronoun; cf. *hmw*, e.g., in Ja 574/8.

L. 13: *šrḥ*: RÉS 4624/5 and 6, and *CoRoC*, p. 252 B: "prosperare fecit, auxit". Judging from the contents of the following pericopes, Ja 586/10, 670/15-16, 692/5, 750/9, and 751/5-6, the primary meaning of *šrḥ* is "to keep healthy". The other texts of the present collection require a derived sense according to the different contexts. Note that the meaning "to give success" is also, in my opinion, attested in RÉS 4624/5 and 6 where I consider the deity as the subject of the two verbs *šrḥ* (contrary to *RhIAI*, p. 25). For the 8th form, cf. commentary on Ja 564/13. – *lsn*, cf. Arabic *lisn* or *lisân* "speaking, tongue"; the expression *ydhw*/*wlsnhw* indicates the acting and the speaking of the author of the inscription.

L. 14: [*ẖry*]*nhw*: the verb *ẖry* ordinarily precedes the expression *ndᶜ*/*wšsy*: e.g., in Ja 562/15, where, as well as in Ja 567/26, 654/14, and 815/6, *ẖry* is followed by *mtᶜ*.

L. 15: *brw*, singular, CIH 105/3, NaNN 20/8, Ja 576/2, 641/8, and 648/5; dual: *brwy* (cp. *bnwy* in RÉS 3691/2 and 3, Qat) in Ja 716/7-8; plural: *ʾbrw* in RÉS 3316/4, Min, and Ja 591/9; cf. *JeHoDISO*, pp. 41-43: *br*. In CIH 105/3-4, *brwh*[*w*] is followed by the personal name [*ḥ*]*ywᶜṯtr*. The expression *lwfy*/*brwhmw*/*rṯdt*/*tʾlb* in NaNN 20/8-9 is translated by *NaNN* (p. 33) as follows: "for the security of their children (or, their constructions) under the guard of Taʾlab". G. Ryckmans (cf. *Le Muséon*, 54 [1947], pp. 162-163) only remarks that the meaning of "house, building", and not that of "son", best fits the context, because the children are mentioned later in the text. It is quite unusual for *lwfy* to introduce a noun designating an inanimate thing. Further, "son" is not exactly the same as "child"; the presence of one of these two terms may certainly go along with that of the other. Finally, Ja 576/2 mentions in the same series *brw* and *bny* with the meaning of "son(s)". The key of the above-mentioned quotation is the interpretation of *rṯdt*. *NaNN* does not make any comment on it, and his translation seems to consider *rṯdt* as a noun; but in this hypothesis, the South-Arabian text should have a preposition introducing this noun. The hypothesis of a verb (3rd person feminine) is excluded, whether with an active meaning – the subject of the text is masculine – or with a passive one – for *brw* is masculine. The term *rṯdt* is not a participle either; the latter is *mrṯd* (RÉS 4043/2 and 4678/2; cf. commentary on Ja 552/4). The original of NaNN 20 cannot be checked, for *NaNN* does not publish any photograph of it. But, in any case, the otherwise surprising *rṯdt* may easily be explained and translated if one admits the dittography of *t* in *rṯdT*/*Tʾlb*, and reads the masculine personal name *rṯdtʾlb*; cp., e.g., on the one hand *rṯdʾl* (e.g., RÉS 2773/5, Min), *rṯdʾlw* (e.g., RÉS 3929/1 and Ja 618/1). *rṯdṯwn* (e.g., CIH 1/1 and Ja 565/1), and on the other hand *sᶜdtʾlb* (e.g., Ja 665/1) and *rbtʾlb* (CIH 289/5?). The expression *brwhmw*/*rṯd*⟨⟩*tʾlb* "their son Raṯadtaʾlab" in NaNN 20/8-9 is a good parallel to *brwh*[*w*/*ḥ*]*ywᶜṯtr* "hi[s] son [Ḥa]yûᶜaṯtar" in CIH 105/3-4. Finally, the element *br* is attested in the following masculine personal names: *brhmw* (Ja 541/8-9) and *brnṭm* (Ja 349/1, Qat).

571 – Lower part of an inscription; grayish, porous sandstone; photograph in Plate 4. – MaMB 189.

STONE: maximum thickness: 8.7 cm. – *Front:* 21.2 cm. × 17.6 (left) and 15 (right). – INSCRIPTION: same disposition of lines as in Ja 552; letter height: 1.5 cm.; space between the lines: from 0.2 cm. to 0.3; distance from line 8 to the lower edge: 3.1 cm. (right) and 2.7 (left).

1 *. . . /wlẖmrhw/ʾ]⌜lmqhṯh⌝wnb*
2 *⌜ʿlʾ⌝wm[/]⌜ḥẓy/wrḍw/mrʾhmw/ʾl*
3 *šrḥ/yḥḍb/mlk/sbʾ/wḏrydn*
4 *wlsʿdhw/wfy/grbhw/wʾṯmrm*
5 *wʾfqlm/ṣdqm/ḏyhrḍyn/ʿbdh*
6 *w/hwfʿṯt/ʾzʾd/bn/yṣḥm/wlẖ*
7 *rynhw/bn/nḍʿ/wšṣy/šnʾm/wḏd*
8 *ʿw/wʾl/dʿw/bʾlmqhwṯhwnbʿlʾwm*

1 . . .; and that may vouchsafe to him ʾI]lumquh Ṯahwân, mas-
2 ter of ʾAwwâm, the esteem and grace of their lord ʾIl-
3 šaraḥ Yaḥḍub, king of Sabaʾ and Raydân;
4 and that He may make him happy with the safety of his person and (with) perfect
5 fruits and harvests, which will please His worshipper
6 Hawfʿaṯat ʾAzʾad, son of Yaṣḥum; and that He may pre-
7 serve him from the hostility and wickedness of [any] enemy and those who are
8 known and [those who] are not known. By ʾIlumquhû Ṯahwân, master of ʾAwwâm.

L. 1: the restoration of the singular pronoun in [*ẖmrhw*] instead of the plural is suggested by *sʿdhw* (line 4) and *ẖrynhw* (lines 6-7). – The remains on the stone forbid restoring *w* after *ʾlmqh*; cf. *ʾlmqhw* in line 8.

L. 2: *mrʾhmw*: the plural pronoun *hmw* refers to Hawfʿaṯat ʾAzʾad, whose name was written at the beginning of line 1 of the missing part, as well as to the persons mentioned along with him and belonging to his family or clan.

L. 5: *ḏyhrḍyn* (e.g., CIH 397/13 and Ja 580/6) = *ḏyhrḍwn* (e.g., Ja 615/22), cf. *JaASAB*, p. 164, commentary on CIH 407/26.

L. 6: *hwfʿṯt/ʾzʾd* was mentioned at the beginning of the text, and was, immediately or not, followed by *hqny(w)/mrʾh(m)w/ʾlmqhṯhwnbʿlʾwm*. – *yḥṣm*, cp. Arabic *ṣaḥama*, 8th form "to rise" and the Thamudic personal name *ṣḥm* in *HaLiSTI*, p. 12, No. 28.

Ll. 7-8: *šnʾm/wḏdʿw/wʾl/dʿw*: another formula is more frequent: *šnʾm/ḏbnhw/dʿw/wḏbnhw/ʾl/dʿw* (found in RÉS 4139/10-11; Ja 614/19-20, 615/27-28, 617/14-15, 661/9, and 703/11). Several variants are known: instead of *wḏbnhw/ʾl*, see *wḏʾl* (Ja 619/20 and 758/20) or simply *wʾl* (Ja 647/33). The parenthetical phrase *ḏrḥq/wqrb* may be inserted either immediately after *šnʾ* (Ja 578/41, 616/39-40, 623/23, and 650/34) or after the entire formula (Ja 647/34). Two other parallels are important for the interpretation of *dʿw*: *šnʾm ḏrḥq/wqrb/ḏbnhw/ġrbw/wḏbnhw/ʾl/ġrbw* in Ja 651/53-55 and *hrbqn/lʾlʾltn/wlʾnsn/wḏbnhw/ʾl/dʿw/wšʿrw* in CIH 429/6-7. *CIH* (II, p. 90 A) relates the form *dʿw* to Arabic *daʿâ* "to call, call for help"; for this meaning, cf. also *LaGD*, p. 796; in the same line of thought, *CoRoC* (p. 126 B) gives the meaning of RÉS 4139/11 as "qui contra ipsum invocet et qui (= sive) contra ipsum non invocet (?)" and *HöASG* (p. 146): "das, um dessen Abwendung (wört. von dem Weg) er gebeten hat, und das, um dessen Abwendung er nicht gebeten hat". However, *CIH* (III, p. 359 B for CIH 411 and p. 360 B for CIH 429) translates *dʿw* as "noverint" or "noverunt", referring to *yâdaʿ* "to know" (p. 359 B). Finally, *BeSI* (p. 102) lists the root *dʿw* in connection with the texts RÉS 4139/11 and CIH 429/7. *NaNAG* (II, p. 36) also refers to RÉS 4139/11, where he considers *dʿw* to be an active verb in the singular, and translates *ḏbnhw/dʿw/wḏbnhw/ʾl/dʿw* as "whom he knows amongst them (that is to say amongst his adversaries) and whom he does not know" (p. 35; cf. also p. 36). For *ḏbn*, cf. commentary on Ja 561 bis/11; for *ḏbnhw*, cp. *ḏbn/šʿbn* in RÉS 3566/8, Qat; *bn* is not an adversative preposition, but a partitive one; *ḏbn* is a collective expression, with which the plurals *dʿw*, *šʿrw*, and *ġrbw* are in accord; and finally, *hw* refers not to the author of the inscription, but to *šnʾ* which, though singular in form, designates a class of people as a collectivity. Furthermore, the repetition *ḏbnhw. . .ḏbnhw* indicates that they mean "those. . . those", that is to say the enemies are divided into two series opposed to each other according to the viewpoint expressed by the verbs *dʿw* and *ġrbw*. I thus translate the present formula, the more developed one, Ja 651/53-55 and CIH 429/6-7 respectively as follows: "[any] enemy and those who are known and [those who] are not known", "every enemy, who is remote and near, those who come from abroad and those who do not come from abroad", and "[who] was a cause of torment for the gods and the men and those who are not known and known".

572 – Fragmentary inscription, broken into five parts; yellowish, slightly grayish sandstone; left part = MaMB 112 = Ja 593; upper right corner (broken into two parts) = MaMB 133 = Ja 573 A; central right part = MaMB 85, and lower right part = MaMB 134 = Ja 573 B; four photographs in Plates 4-5.

The front of the stone was painted in red before being engraved; almost constant thickness: 9.8 cm. (MaMB 112) and 10 (other parts). – INSCRIPTION: same disposition of lines as in Ja 552; letter height: 2 cm., but 2.1 in lines 14 and 16; at 0.4 cm. below line 16, another horizontal line is traced.

MaMB 112 (left part of lines 2-16): 41.1 cm. × 24.5 (top) and 19 (bottom).

MaMB 133 (right part of lines 1-5): measurements of the engraved part: 16.5 cm. × 12; distance from line 1 to the upper edge: 0.7 cm.; the small fragment includes the left part of lines 2-4.

MaMB 85 (right part of lines 6-10, plus the center of lines 5, 11, and 12-13): maximum length: 17.9 cm., and width: 22.7; photograph in Plate 5.

MaMB 134 (right part of lines 11-16): maximum length: 23.3 cm., and width: 18; a vertical line at 1 cm. from the right edge and at 0.2 from the 1st letter of each line.

1		*ʾʿrq]⌜m/yqbl/⌝[. . .*	
2		*sʾr]⌜n/⌝wmḥylm/m⌟][qtw]⌜yy/⌝[ʾ]*	*⌜lšrḥ/y⌝[ḥḏb/mlk/sbʾ/w]*
3		*[ḏry]⌞d⌟n/bn/frʿm/yn[hb]/ml⌞k⌟]*	*⌜k/sbʾ/hqnyy/⌜ʾlm⌝[qhṯwn]*
4		*[bʿl]⌞ʾwm/ṣlmn/ḏṣr⌞fn/ḏ⌟]*	*⌜/⌝⌜ḏmdlthw/ṯlṯ/mʾnm/rḍ⌜fm⌝[. .]*
5		*]⌞ḥmd⌟m⌞/bḏt⌟ ⌜t⌝/hʿ*	*n/wmtʿn/wẖlwn/grb/mrʾhmw/ʾ*
6		*[lšrḥ/yḥḍ][⌞b/⌝mlk/s⌟*	*bʾ/wḏrydn/bn/frʿm/ynhb/mlk*
7		*[sbʾ/bn][⌞m⌝rḍ/mrḍ/b*	*⌞h⌟grn/mrb/wʾlmqhbʿlʾwm/fly*
8		*[ẖm]⌜r⌝⌜n/wmtʿn/wrt⌜ṯdn⌝*	*⌞ṯdn⌟/grb/mrʾhmw/ʾlšrḥ/yḥḍb/m*
9		*[lk/s]⌜b⌝ʾ/wḏrydn/bn/frʿ⌜m/⌝*	*[⌞m/⌟ynhb/mlk/sbʾ/wlyhʿnn*
10		*[hw/][⌞bn/bʾstm/wnkytm⌜/⌝*	*⌞/⌟wbn/ḥlẓm/wmyqẓm/wn*
11	*[ḍʿ]⌜/⌝wšṣ⌟]*	*⌞šṣ⌟y/šnʾm/wʾlmqhbʿ⌜l⌝*	*⌞l⌟ʾwm/flyẖmrn/ʿbdyh*
12	*[⌞w/ʾʿrqm/⌜yqb⌝*	*⌞yqb⌟l/w[. . .*	*⌞/ḥ⌟ẓy/wrḍw/mrʾhmy/ʾl*
13	*šrḥ/yḥḍb/mlk/⌜sbʾ⌝*	*⌜sbʾ/⌟wḏrydn*	*[b]n⌟]/frʿm/ynhb/mlk*
14		*sbʾ/wlysʿdnhmy/nʿmt⌜m/w⌝*	*wfym/wlẖrynhmy/b*
15		*n/bʾstm/wnkytm/wbn/nḍʿ⌟]*	*[⌞ʿ/wšṣy/šnʾm/ḏbnhw/d*
16		*ʿw/wḏʾl/dʿw/bʾlm⌟]*	*[⌞mqhṯwnbʿlʾwm*

1 ʾAʿarqu]m Yuqbil [. . .
2 Suʾr]ân and Miḥîlum, [the] two hi[gh offici]als of [ʾI]lšaraḥ Ya[ḥḍub, king of Sabaʾ and]
3 [Ray]dân, son of Fariʿum Yan[hub,] king of Sabaʾ, have dedicated to ʾIlum[quh Ṯahwân,]
4 [master of] ʾAwwâm, this statue which [is] in brass, the weight of which [is] three hundred *raḍaf* [. . .
5 ,] in praise because He has assisted and saved and acted pleasingly toward the person of their lord ʾI-
6 [lšaraḥ Yaḥḍ]ub, king of Sabaʾ and Raydân, son of Fariʿum Yanhub, king of
7 [Sabaʾ, in] the illness [which] he was suffering in the city [of] Mârib; and as for ʾIlumquh, master of ʾAwwâm, may He
8 [vouch]safe and save and preserve the person of their lord ʾIlšaraḥ Yaḥḍub,
9 k[ing of Sa]baʾ and Raydân, son of Fariʿum Yanhub, king of Sabaʾ; and that He may assist
10 [him] from misfortunes and sufferings and from oppression and sleeplessness and the hos-
11 [tility] and wickedness of [any] enemy; and as for ʾIlumquh, master of ʾAwwâm, may He vouchsafe to His two worshippers
12 ʾAʿarqum Yuqbil and [. . .] the esteem and grace of the lord of them both ʾIl-
13 šaraḥ Yaḥḍub, king of Sabaʾ and Raydân, [so]n of Fariʿum Yanhub, king of
14 Sabaʾ; and that He may make them both happy with prosperity and safety; and that He may preserve them both from
15 misfortunes and sufferings and from the hostility and wickedness of [any] enemy, those who are

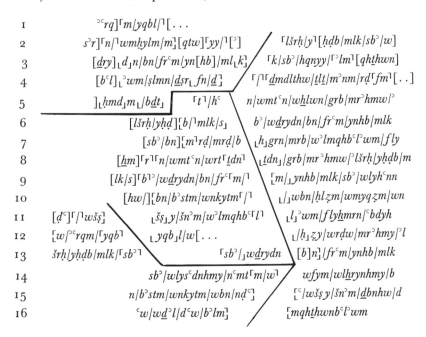

16 known and those who are not known. By ʾIlumquh Ṯahwân, master of ʾAwwâm.

Preliminary remarks. The signs are not equally distributed among the lines; e.g., they are more numerous in line 8 than in line 9. Similarly, the ends of the lines are not equally close to the left edge of the stone; e.g., compare lines 7 and 9.

L. 1: *ʾʿrqm*, known as noun in CIH 67/18; *CIH* (I, p. 95 B): "littus"; cf. Arabic *ʿirâq*, plural *ʾaʿriqat* "coast (of the sea), bank (of a river)"; the preceding parallel must be preferred to that suggested by *RyISA* (X, p. 309): "*ʿarq* 'opened way,'" which does not fit Wâdî Maʾsil 2/4; the plural *ʾʿrq* may be translated "coast lands"; cf. the Arabic name of a man *ʿâriq* (cf. *WüID*, 235/4). – *yqbl*, RÉS 4069/1.

L. 2: *sʾr*]*n/wmḥylm*, cf. *NaNN*, p. 77, commentary on NaNN 59/1; cf. also commentary on Ja 578/1. – *m*[*qtw*]*yy*, dual of *mqtwy* (e.g., RÉS 4892/2, Ḥaḍr); cf. the apocopated form *mqtw* (e.g., Kawkab 3/1); the feminine *mqtwy*(*t*) (e.g., Bo 6/1; it is important to note that the 2nd *t* is not restored; the lower half of the left oblique stroke is still visible) and the plural forms *mqtwt* (Wâdî Maʾsil 1/8) = *mqtyt* (e.g., Ja 577/7) = *mqtt* (e.g., CIH 287/10 and Ja 576/14); cf. *JaASAB*, pp. 156-57, commentary on CIH 407/2-3 and *RhIGC*, p. 74, note 3.

L. 4: *ṣrf*, cf. my discussion in *JaIAA*, pp. 320-21. – *ḏmdlthw*, cf. *ḏmdlt* in RÉS 2693/2-3, Ḥaḍr, and 4191/6, where the expression is respectively preceded by *sqnyt/ḏhbn* and *ṣlmn*]*ḏṣrfn*; cf. also *UlSLE*, p. 156. – *ṯlṯ/mʾnm*, cp. *ẖms/mʾm* in RÉS 3945/13; *mʾn* is also attested in CIH 353/13; cf. Arabic *miʾyat*, plural *miʾûna* and *muʾûna*; the common South-Arabian form is *mʾt* (e.g., Ja 649/27-28) and sometimes *mʾ* (cf. *CoRoC*, p. 174 and *HöASG*, p. 134, §115); cf. also the form *mʾh* in Ingrams 1/3, Ḥaḍr. — *rḍf*, weight unit; cp. Arabic *raḍf*, coll. (sing. *raḍfat*) "stones reddened by fire" (cf. also *LaGD*, p. 1293).

L. 5: *ḥlw*, cf. Arabic *ḥlw* "mild, pleasing" and the verb *ḥalâ* (o), 1st form "to be mild, pleasing; to do something pleasing, make oneself mild toward someone"; cf. also *JeHoDISO*, p. 88: *ḥly*I. – *mrʾhmw*, as in line 8, but *mrʾhmy* in line 12.

L. 7: *bn/mrḍ/mrḍ*, e.g., RÉS 4215/2; cf. *CoRoC*, p. 181 B and also *mrḍyt* "sick people" in Ja 544/4; the verb *mrḍ* is also attested in RÉS 4839 B (for the decipherment and the translation of RÉS 4839, cf. commentary on Ja 671/16). – *fl*, e.g., CIH 547/11.

Ll. 7-8: *fly*[*ẖm*]*rn*, cf. line 11.

L. 8: *rṯṯdn/grb*, cf. *rṯṯdn/grybt* in Ja 586/10; *rṯṯd*, 8th form of *rṯd* both the 1st and the 5th forms are known; the contexts suggest translating *rṯṯd* as "to preserve"; cf. also commentary on Ja 558/7.

L. 10: *myqẓ*, cf. Arabic *yaqiẓa* "to be awake" and its derived noun *yaqaẓat* "wakefulness"; *NaNAG* (II, p. 23) translates *myqẓ* as "calamity" or "partial sleeplessness".

L. 12: after *yqbl/w*, the personal name was first corrected and then damaged.

L. 16: *ḏʾl/ḏʿw* = *ʾl/ḏʿw* in Ja 571/8.

573 A and B = MaMB 133 and 134 = upper right corner and central right part of Ja 572 respectively.

2° – WITH HIS BROTHER YAʾZIL BAYYIN: Ja 574 – 600

574 – Yellowish, slightly grayish sandstone plaque; photograph in Plate 5. – MaMB 153.

STONE: constant thickness: 17.3 cm. – *Front:* covered with grayish paint; upper edge badly damaged; 79.5 cm. (top) and 78.9 (bottom) × 54 cm. (right) and 53 (left). – INSCRIPTION, same disposition of lines as in Ja 552; letter height: from 2.9 cm. to 3.3; space between the lines: from 0.5 cm. to 0.9; distance from line 1 to the upper edge: 1 cm. – SYMBOL (cp. Ja 567); five lines inside, and the triangle of the upper one is left unfinished; cf. Plate A.

1 **Sym-** *ʾlšr*⌈*ḥ/yḥḍb/*[*w*]⌈*ʾẖyh*⌉[*w/yʾzl/byn/mlky/*
sbʾ/w](*ḏ*)⌈*ryd*⌉*n/bny/frʿm/y*
2 **bol** *nhb/mlk/sbʾ/hqnyy/ʾlmq*⌈*hṯ*⌉*hwnbʿlʾwm/*
⌈*ṣlm*⌉*ynn/ḏṣrfn/ḥmdm/b*
3 ⌊*ḏt/ẖmr/whwšʿn/ʿbdhw/ʾlšrḥ/yḥḍb/mlk/sbʾ/*
wḏrydn/bnqm/ʾḥbšn/wḏs
4 *hrtm/bḥrbt/ḥrbw/bqrhmw/bsrn/ḏshm/wbʿdhw/*
fyḍbʾ/ʾlšrḥ/yḥḍb/m
5 *lk/sbʾ/wḏrydn/wbʿmhw/ḏbn/ẖmshw/wʾqwlhw/*
bʿly/ʾḥzb/ḥbšt/wʾʿṣdhm
6 *w/ʿdy/ʾgnw/srn/śrdd/wyḥrbw/hmt/ʾḥbšn/wḏshrtm/*
bkdnn/ḏwdftn/wwdyfn
7 *wfršt/lqḥ/wḥrbw/bhmyt/ʾkdnn/ẖmst/wʿšry/ʾdwrm/*
bn/ʾdwr/ʾksmn/wgmdn/wʿ
8 *km/wḏbn/ʾdwr/ḏshrtm/wḥmdm/bḏt/tʾwlw/hmw/*
wʾqwlhmw/wẖmshmw/wʾ
9 *frshmw/bwfym/wḥmdm/wʾḥllm/wsbym/wmltm/*
wġnmm/ḏʿsm/ḏhrḍwh
10 *mw/wbʿd/ḏtʾwlw/ʿdy/hgrn/ṣnʿw/fhdrkhmw/*
tnbltm/ʿmn/gmdn/tḍ

11 *rᶜm/wᶜrbtm/wwhbw/ᵓwldhmw/ᵓwṯqm/wkwnw/ lmlk/sbᵓ/whgrn/lq*
12 *ḥ/fwhbw/ᵓwṯqm/wmqblhmw/wlwzᵓ/ ᵓlmqhṯhwnbᶜlᵓwm/hwšᶜnhmw/bwḍ*
13 *ᶜ/wṯbr/whms/whkms/kl/ḍrhmw/wšnᵓhmw/ bᵓlmqhṯhwnbᶜlᵓwm*

1 **Sym-** ᵓIlšaraḥ Yaḥḍub [and] hi[s] brother [Yaᵓzil Baÿyin, the two kings of Sabaᵓ and] Raydân, the two sons of Fariᶜum Ya-
2 **bol** nhub, king of Sabaᵓ, have dedicated to ᵓIlumquh Ṯahwân, master of ᵓAwwâm, these two statues which [are] in brass, in praise be-
3 cause He has vouchsafed and assisted His worshipper ᵓIlšaraḥ Yaḥḍub, king of Sabaᵓ and Raydân, in taking vengeance from the Ḥabašites and (the tribe) Sa-
4 haratum during the battle [which] they fought in their fixed settlements in the wâdî-side valley of Sahâm; and after that, waged war ᵓIlšaraḥ Yaḥḍub, king of
5 Sabaᵓ and Raydân, and with him, some of his army and his rulers against the fighting bands of Ḥabašat and their gangs
6 in the gardens of the wâdî-side valley Śurdad; and they fought these Ḥabašites and (the tribe) Saharatum in the two ploughed plains of Wadfatân and Wadîfân
7 and (in) the green field of Laqaḥ; and they fought in these ploughed plains twenty-five Bedouin campings from the Bedouin campings of ᵓAksûman and Gumdân and
8 ᶜAkkum and several Bedouin campings of Saharatum; and [also] in praise because they went back, themselves and their rulers and their army and their
9 horsemen, in safety and praise and (with) animals and captives and riches and booty, which was desired, [and] which pleased them;
10 and after that, they went back to the city [of] Ṣanᶜâᵓ, so that messengers from Gumdân reached them in
11 submission and (with) pledge; and they gave their children [as] firm pledges, and they belonged to the king of Sabaᵓ and to the city [of] Laqaḥ,
12 for they gave firm pledges and their peace-offerings. And that ᵓIlumquh Ṯahwân, master of ᵓAwwâm, may continue to assist them in humiliating
13 and crushing and breaking down and withering their every foe and enemy. By ᵓIlumquh Ṯahwân, master of ᵓAwwâm.

L. 2: *ṣlmynn: ynn*, primitive form of *ynhn* (cf. *HöASG*, p. 114).

L. 3: *nqm*, cf. Arabic *naqima* "to revenge, take vengeance" and *LeLS*, p. 274; cf. also *MoNTA*, pp. 354-55; e.g., RÉS 3945/18. – *ᵓḥbš*, cf. Arabic *ᵓaḥbaš*, pl. *ᵓaḥâbiš* "Abyssinian"; cf. *ḥbšt* in line 5, and the personal name *ḥbš* in Ist 7630/2; cf. also my review of *Annales d'Ethiopie, II*, in *BiO*, 17 (1960), pp. 263-64, and the Arabic personal names *ḥabbuš*, *ḥabbušî*, *al-ḥabšî*, *ḥabiš*, *ḥabîbîš*, especially *ḥabšîyat* (cf. *SlGaVNPA*, p. 22 A) and also *ḥubšîyu* and *banû ḥubšîyata* (cf. *WüID*, 236/2 and 276/11 respectively).

Ll. 3-4: *ḏshrtm*, cf. *JaASAB*, p. 161, commentary on CIH 407/18-19.

L. 4: *ḥrbt*, cf. *l.c.*, commentary on CIH 407/20; and *JeHoDISO*, p. 95: *ḥrb*$_{\text{I}}$ – *bqrhmw*: there is no question of interpreting *bqr* either as "bovines" (Ja 649/40-41) or "cows" (Ja 665/26); nor is the meaning of "cowherd" (cf. Arabic *baqqâr*) more suitable. I propose relating *qr* to Arabic *qarr* "fixed settlement", from the root *qarra* "to stop and stay a while in a place". The noun *qr* is also attested in Kawkab 1/6-7: *bn qrm/bn/ ᵓzᵓn[n]* where *RyISA* (X, p. 300) refers to Arabic *qarm* "tribal chief"; according to that opinion, however, one would expect *qrmn*. – *ḏshm*, cf. Arabic *sâhim* "lean", and the Arabic names of a man *saham*, *as-sahâm* and *as-sihâm* (cf. *WüID*, 74/2 and 1). – *bᶜdhw/f* (e.g., CIH 308/23), temporal conjunction more frequently used than its equivalents *bᶜdnhw/f* (e.g., Ja 658/14) or simply *bᶜdnhw* (Murayġân/7); these forms correspond respectively to *bᶜd/ḏ* (e.g., CIH 314+954/17 and here, line 10), *bᶜdn/ḏ* (e.g., CIH 541/76; cf. *HöASG*, p. 172) and *bᶜdn* (e.g., CIH 541/46).

L. 5: *ḏbn/ḫmshw*, cf. Ja 576/8, and *ḏbn/ḫmshw/ wᵓqwlhw*, cf. *ḏbn/ᵓqwlhw/wḫmshw*, e.g., in Ja 576/5. – *ḥzb*, pl. *ᵓḥzb*, cf. *StSESA*, p. 514, and note 81. *CIH* (I, p. 344 A) considers *ḥzb* as the equivalent of *šᶜb*, and thus translates it as "tribus"; this equivalence is accepted by *RhIG* (p. 54, note 1) and *RyISA* (XIII, p. 154). However, *BeSI* (p. 34, in CIH 314+954/14, 17, and 19) translates it as "clan", but does not comment on it. The Qurᵓân (referred to by *CIH*) as well as the inscriptions have in common the fact that *ᵓḥzb* is used to indicate some groups of men (cf. Arabic *ḥizb*, pl. *ᵓaḥzâb*) who actually are the enemy. Furthermore, in the Sab inscriptions *ᵓḥzb* (never the singular form) is always connected with the Ḥabašites. It seems thus logical to suppose that *ᵓḥzb* has a pejorative meaning, as *gyš* often does. Finally, there is so far not the slightest clue leading to the equivalence with *ʾšʿb*. I suggest translating *ʾḥzb* as "fighting bands". – *ḥbšt*, cf. Arabic *ḥabašat* "the Abyssinians, Abyssinia"; I prefer to translate *ḥbšt* as "Ḥabašat", leaving "the Ḥabašites" for *ʾḥbš*. – *ʾʿṣd*, pl. of *ʿṣd*, cf. Arabic *ʿaṣwada* "to fight" and *qawmun ʿaṣâwîdu* "band of men rushing altogether, for instance in a hand to hand fight"; I translate *ʿṣd* as "gang, horde"; the plural *ʾʿṣd* is also mentioned in Ja 575/3, where *RyISA* (XIV, p. 384) erroneously translates it as a proper name.

L. 6: *ʾgnw*, pl. of *gnw* (or *gny*, Ja 650/6); cf. Arabic *ǧannat* and Hebrew *gan* "garden" and also Arabic *ǧanâ* (i) "to gather fruits"; cf. the denominative verb *gn* in commentary on Ja 570/3; cf. also commentary on Ja 560/14 and *JeHoDISO*, p. 52: *gnh*. – *śrdd*, cf. *JaASAB*, p. 156, commentary on CIH 407/2. – *yḥrbw* depends on *bʿdhw*/*f* (line 4), as well as *ydbʾ* (same line). – *kdn*, pl. *ʾkdn* (line 7), masculine noun; cf. Arabic *kadana* "to put (oxes) to the plough" and its derived noun *kadnat* "one day's ploughing"; note the opposition between *kdn* and *fršt* (line 7). A series of proper names may be introduced by a singular noun which indicates that the following names are those of cities, places, or clans; some examples taken from this collection: *hgr* introduces 2 and 3 names of a city, e.g., Ja 585/5 and 577/17 respectively; *byt* is followed by 2 clan names in Ja 651/13; *šʿb* precedes 2 and 3 clan names, e.g., in Ja 628/2 and 649/3 respectively; *ʿšrt* introduces 13 clan names in Ja 616/24; *kdn* is followed by 2 names of places here. In order to make the translation clearer, the noun itself will be translated as a dual or plural according to the context. – *wdftn* and *wdyfn*, derived from the root *wdf*; cp. Arabic *wadfat* and *wadîfat* "flower garden; meadow"; the two places were called after their peculiarity, the meadows.

L. 7: *fršt*, cf. Arabic *farš* "field, plain, field all covered with plants and herbs"; this noun, as well as *kdn*, depends on the preposition *b* (line 6). – *lqḥ*, name of a city (cf. lines 11-12); the verb *lqḥ* is attested in CIH 155/4. – *hmyt*, *scriptio plena* of the ordinary form *hmt*. – *ʾdwr* or *ʾdyr* (Ja 577/4), pl. of *dwr* (or *dr* in *scriptio defectiva*, in Ingrams 1/2, Ḥaḍr; cf. *JaIHI*, p. 100); cf. Arabic *dâr*, pl. *ʾadwur*, *ʾadwâr*, or *diyâr* "settlement with a few houses or tents, tribe of Bedouins"; cf. also the proper name *dr* indicating a place in Gl 1142/5; the noun *dr* is also well known in Safaitic (cf. *LiSI*, pp. 307-08) and attested in Thamudic (cf. *vdBrIT*, p. 374: Jsa 243). – *ʾksmn*, same name as that of the Abyssinian capital. – *gmdn* (also in line 10), name of a place; e.g., CIH 293/3; for *gmd* in RÉS 4594 A/1 and *gmdm* in RÉS 4623 A/2, cf. commentary on Ja 616/25: *ḥgr*/*lmd*.

Ll. 7-8: *ʿkm* (also personal name in Ja 614/1): tribe, cf. *SpAGA*, pp. 259-61, and W. Caskel, in *Encycl. of Islam* (2nd ed.), I, fasc. 6 (1956), pp. 340-41.

L. 8: *tʾwl*, 5th form of *ʾwl*, "to come back, go back"; cf. also commentary on Ja 567/11-12: *wkb*.

Ll. 8-9: *ʾfrshmw*: *frs* (cf. *CoRoC*, p. 220 A), horse (cf. Arabic *faras*), either a bronze statue dedicated to some deity (e.g., Ja 666/4) or in most of the cases the living animal itself, which may be known through its proper name (e.g., Ja 649/20). In most of the references, *frs* is in the plural form, *ʾfrs*, which more often designates "horsemen" (cf. Arabic *fâris*) or "cavalry" depending on the context. *frs* as "mare" (cf. Arabic *furaysat*) is attested, e.g., in Ja 752/7.

L. 9: *ʾḥll* (pl. of *ḥll*), always in plural form. In his commentary on Geukens 1/15, *RyISA* (XII, p. 305) agrees with *RhIG*'s opinion (p. 59 and note 2), according to which *ʾḥll*, objects retained by the army chiefs, must be distinguished from *ġnm* and *sby*, both of them becoming property of the state or the king. Such an opinion is at first sight difficult to understand. Army chiefs as such are as a matter of fact always acting both in the name of and for the state or the king, therefore there is no basic difference between *ʾḥll* on the one hand and on the other *sby* and *ġnm* as far as the army commanders are concerned, because the objects indicated by these three nouns belong in the beginning and necessarily to the sender, the authority and not to his envoy, the agent. Further, the texts mentioning these three nouns do not present any indication leading to a distinction such as the above-mentioned one. On the contrary they rather suggest that appointments as army commander and even as officers implied for these military leaders the right to retain for themselves what was taken away from the enemy by soldiers under their command. Two examples among many others. In Ja 632/4-6, a tribal chief brought back *ʾḥll* and *ġnm* from battles in which he had helped his king; in Ja 632/7, two servants of the preceding chief thank the deity for *ġnm* that pleased them both.

These two references do not mention at all any explicit permission granted by the king in their cases but rather suggest that no special permission was required from the king. As one would have expected, the king had the right to appropriate to himself whatever pleased him from the general war booty, as suggested by Ja 586/22-23. It is in the light of the two preceding references as well as of many other equivalent parallels that we must interpret Geukens 1/10-11: *sbym/wġnmm/ ḏhrḍwhmw/bn/*[*mr*](*ʾh*)*mw/š*ʿ*rm* [for *RyISA*'s translation of *hrḍw* (XII, p. 300), cf. commentary on Ja 571/5] "captives and booty, which pleased them, from (t)heir [lor](d) Šaʿirum". The expression *bn mrʾhmw* alludes, in my opinion, to an unusual and extraordinary gift from the king to his military officers.

The distinction mentioned above is, in my opinion, incorrect not only with regard to military officers or commanders, but also to ordinary persons. Two examples. In CIH 79/5-8, an individual mentions the gain of *ʾḫll* and *ʾsby* in military expeditions undertaken for his master Yufriʿ of the clan of Marṯadum. Ja 634 deals with two persons who are not even referred to as military officers; they could have simply been plunderers or robbers. Nevertheless, they speak of *ġnm* brought back by them from a city. These two texts do not allude to any authorization granted to the three persons to retain some part of the booty.

Another question is the meaning of *ʾḫll*; e.g., *CoRoC* (p. 149 A): "bona" (cf. also *LaH*, p. 555), *BeSI* (pp. 15-16): "booty" (also *RÉS* in RÉS 3884 [cf. Ja 115]/10); note that the verb *ḫll* in Wâdî Maʾsil 1/5 (cf. *RyISA*, X, pp. 303-04) means "to take possession". *JaASAB* (pp. 163-64, commentary on CIH 407/26) already studies several words, *ʾḫḏ*, *ʾsd*, *sby*, and *ġnm*, which are mentioned with *ʾḫll*. It seems hard to believe that common expressions such as that in line 9 of the present text, if understood according to translations proposed by scholars, would never mention any animals since victorious armies or raiders should have taken away camels, horses, etc., as well as prisoners and captives. This remark is confirmed by Ja 643 bis/2-3 and 644/24-25, two passages which mention explicitly animals and which deal with activities of victorious persons. I should thus suggest to translate *ʾḫll* as "animals" in general. Sometimes however the meaning is restricted as, e.g., in Ja 635/30-31 and 644/25, where horses are listed separately. It is difficult to say whether or not the noun *ʾḫll* in these two texts refers exclusively to camels, and also to explain why *ʾḫll* is always listed first in the series of nouns which describe the practical results of a victory.

Therefore, according to my interpretation, *ʾḫll* and *sby* in the present text refer to living beings on the one hand, and on the other *mlt* and *ġnm* to things. The meaning of *ġnm*, when not listed with *mlt* (e.g., Ja 632/5-6), seems to refer to all kinds of things which can be taken away by victorious men. When listed with *mlt* (e.g., here), *ġnm* would indicate all common things by opposition to *mlt* "riches", which would refer to certain kinds of goods such as for instance precious or expensive things (cf. *CIH* in CIH 174/1: "resources, riches"; contrast *MoMiHI* in RÉS 4137/13: "booty"). – *ḏʿsm*: relative phrase which is attested no less than 24 times in the present collection, and always depending on nouns. In Murayġân/6, *ḏʿsm* depends on the verb *ġnmw*, and is translated by *RyISA*: "Et quiconque prit le fuite" (X, p. 278; also "se ruer en fuite" on p. 283); this opinion is rightly discarded by A. F. L. Beeston (in *BSOAS*, 16 [1954], p. 390). In his commentary (p. 282), *RyISA* refers to "CIH 429, 8: *yʿsm*"; correct this form to *yhʿsmn*, which is referred to in XII (p. 306). He also refers to *BeSI* (p. 48) as saying *ʿsm/ġlmm/ʾḏkrw* "desire of children"; the term *ʾḏkrm* (not *ʾḏkrw*) must be omitted. Further, he notes that *RhSLG* (III, p. 48) relates *ʿsm* to Arabic *iʿtasama* (read *ʾiʿtasama*); *RhSLG* suggests this Arabic form in relation with *hʿsm* (not *ʿsm*) in CIH 429/8. In the same Murayġân/6, *ḏʿsm* is translated by *RycIHS* as "de ce que...avait acquis" (p. 340, note 28); this translation confuses *ʿsm* and *ʿsy*. *RyISA* (XII, p. 300, in Geukens 1/15, and XIII, pp. 147-49, in Ja 576/5, 7, 8, 9, 11, 13, and 14) translates *ḏʿsm* as "qui étai[en]t à souhait", but as "qui donnait satisfaction" (in Ja 576/4; *l.c.*, p. 147). The latter interpretation comes from A. F. L. Beeston (*l.c.*, who adopts the two following translations: "which is satisfactory" and "that which is desirable"), and must be discarded, because it is the translation of *ḏhrḍw* or *ḏhrḍy* (cf. commentary on Ja 571/5, and Ja 576/6: *ḏhrḍwhmw* "qui leur donnait satisfaction"; cf. *RyISA*, XIII, p. 147). The noun *ʿsm* "desire" is also attested, e.g., in Ja 578/11, with the same meaning and construction as, e.g., in CIH 350/15: *ᶜsm/ġlmm/ᵓḏkrm* "optatos liberos masculos" (cf. also *CIH*, I, p. 422 A and *BeSI*, p. 42: "wished-for male children"). In Ja 585/10, the noun *ᶜsm* has an entirely different meaning. Finally, in *šfqm/ᵓsyṭm/ᶜsmm* (Ja 735/14), as well as in *ᵓfql[m/hn]ᵓm/ᶜsmm* (RÉS 3966/10-11), the latter being a perfect parallel of *ᵓfqlm/ṣdqm/hnᵓm* (Ja 738/10), *ᶜsm* is an adjective; contrast for RÉS 3966/10-11, *RhSLG* (III, p. 48): "*ᶜsmm*, 'wie man es wünscht,"; and A. F. L. Beeston (*l.c.*): "that which is desirable". The use of *ᶜsm*[noun]/– and –/*ᶜsmm*[adjective] is a perfect parallel of *nᵓd*[noun]/– and –/*nᵓdm*[adjective].

L. 10: *ṣnᶜw*, cf. personal name *ṣnᶜ* (RÉS 4623 B/1); cf. remark on *ḥgrw* in Ja 550/1. – *hdrkhmw*, cf. *CoRoC*, p. 126 B. – *tnblt*, plural of *tnbl*, e.g., CIH 314+954/14.

Ll. 10-11: *tḏrᶜ*, 5th form of *ḏrᶜ*, e.g., CIH 314+914/15; cf. *CoRoC*, p. 227 B.

L. 11: *ᶜrbt*, cp. Syriac *ᶜreb* "to promise solemnly..., pledge oneself" (cf. *PaSmCSD*, p. 426 B) and *ᶜarbutô* "pledge" (cf. *l.c.*, p. 427 B); e.g., CIH 308/23-24. – *whbw*, e.g., RÉS 4134/1 and *JeHoDISO*, pp. 105-06: *yhb*. – *wṯq*, plural *ᵓwṯq*; cf. Arabic *waṯâq* or *wiṯâq* "band, tie, bond" from *waṯuqa* "to be firm, act firmly"; cf. the 4th form *hwṯq* (RÉS 2724/4) and *swṯq* (RÉS 3610/7, Min) and the 10th form *stwṯq* (CIH 291/4).

L. 12: *mqbl*, plural *mqblt*, e.g., in RÉS 2876/2, with the meaning of "thing ascribed to someone for rent"; in the present text, cf. Arabic *maqbûl* "accepted; agreeable, welcome", Syriac *muqbôlô* "price for acceptance, admission" and Soqoṭri *qóbol* "être content" (cf. *LeLS*, p. 366); *mqbl* probably means the tribute given for peace and the security of their donation is proved by *ᵓwṯq* "pledges".

L. 13: *hms*, cf. Arabic *hamasa* "to break down". – *hkms*, 4th form of *kms*, e.g., CIH 314+954/22; Mayer Lambert, followed by *BeSI* (p. 36), relates this verb to Arabic *kamasa* "to frown"; cf. Syriac *kmas* "to let fade *or* languish, to languish, wither" (cf. *PaSmCSD*, p. 217 B); the 4th form in the present text as well as in CIH 314+954/22 may very well be translated "to wither (someone)".

575 – Yellowish, slightly grayish sandstone. – MaMB 224 = Geukens 7.

STONE: thickness: 24 cm. (left) and 23 (right.) – *Front:* upper left corner broken; 1.081 m. × 32 cm. (right) and 24.6 (left). – INSCRIPTION: same disposition of lines as in Ja 559; letter height: from 3.2 cm. to 2.9; space between the lines: from 0.5 cm. to 0.4. – SYMBOL, cf. Ja 559.

1 **Sym-** *ᵓlšrḥ/yḥḍb/wᵓḫyhw/yᵓzl/byn/mlky/sbᵓ/*
wḏrydn/bny/frᶜm/ynhb/mlk/sbᵓ⌈*/*
h⌉[*nyy/*19 or 20 signs */b*]
2 **bol** *n/sḫymm/wᶜlyn/bn/yqnᶜm/wᵓsdhmy/bkn/*
blthmw/mrᵓhmw/ᵓlšrḥ/yḥḍb/mlk/sbᵓ/
wḏrydn/⌈*lgzmn/h*⌉*mt/ᵓḥbšn/*[*...* *...m*]
3 *lk/sbᵓ/wḏrydn/wḫmshw/wḏbn/ᵓqwlhw/lnqm/bhyt/*
ḥrbtn/whbrrw/lḍbᵓ/bn/hgrn/ṣnᶜw/wysrw/
bqdmyhmw/dlwlm/ldll/ᵓᶜṣd[*...*
4 *bklm/wwrdw/shrtn/bᶜly/ᵓᶜṣd/dllw/lhmw/whḏrw/hmt/*
ᵓᶜṣdn/bn/kfl/ᶜrn/wḥdt/wẓᶜnw/lbḥrn/whdrkhmw/
bᵓṯrhmw/wḥrbw/h[*mt/...* *.../h*]
5 *mt/ᵓḥbšn/wᶜkm/wḏkwn/kwnhmw/ḏshrtm/mwṯbtm/*
bᶜd/ᵓwldhmw/wqnyhmw/wyᵓttmw/wtqdmn/
wrtḍḥn/bᶜm/hmt/ᵓḥbšn/w[*...* *.../wᵓ*]
6 *wldhmw/wᵓᵓnṯhmw/fhrgw/wsbyw/wbnhw/ftᵓwlw/*
wḥrbw/bᶜynm/whᶜn/lḏmḫrm/bᶜlyhmw/ḏsᵓr/bn/
hmt/ᵓḥbšn/wᶜkm/wḏstṣrw/b[*n/...*
7 *ᵓwm/bḥsm/whrg/whsḥtn/ᶜnt/hmt/ᵓḥbšn/wᶜkm/wkl/*
ḏkwn/kwnhmw/bn/ḏᵓšᶜb/ḏshrtm/wyhrgw/bnhmw/
mhrgm/ḏᶜsm/wḏsᵓ[*r...*
8 *ytᵓwlw/bwfym/wḥmdm/wmhrgm/wsbym/wmltm/*
wġnmm/ḏᶜsm/wḥmdm/bḏt/wkb/ᵓḫhw/yᵓzl/byn/
mlk/sbᵓ/wḏrydn/bṣnᶜw/wslḥn/wb[*...*

1 **Sym-** ᵓIlšaraḥ Yaḥḍub and his brother Yaᵓzil Bayyin, the two kings of Sabaᵓ and Raydân, the two sons of Fariᶜum Yanhub, king of Sabaᵓ, [have] de[dicated to... ...descen-]
2 **bol** dants of Suḫaymum and ᶜAlayân, descendant of Yaqunᶜamm and the soldiers of both of them, when their lord ᵓIlšaraḥ Yaḥḍub, king of Sabaᵓ and Raydân, imposed upon them to destroy these Ḥabašites [...
3 [k]ing of Sabaᵓ and Raydân and his army and some of his rulers in order to take vengeance in this battle; and they agreed to fight from the city [of] Ṣanᶜâᵓ, and sent before them guides to indicate the gangs [of...
4 of Bakîlum, and they went down to Saharatân against the gangs [which] had been indicated to them, and these gangs were scattered from the steep brink of the citadel [of] Waḥadat; and they fled to the sea, and they reached them because of their tracks, and they fought against the[se...the-]
5 se Ḥabašites and ᶜAkkum and those who were with them from Saharatum [who were] camping far from their children and their slaves, and they mustered and attacked and slew these Ḥabašites and [...and]

6 their children] and their wives, so that they were either killed or captured; and from there, they went back and fought in ᶜAynum and Huᶜân in order to oppose those of these Ḥabašites and ᶜAkkum who remained and those whom they called for help fr[om...

7 ᵓAwwâm in cutting to pieces and killing and destroying the reinforcements of these Ḥabašites and ᶜAkkum and everyone who was with them from the tribes of Saharatum; and they deprived them of a war trophy which was desired, and those who rem[ained...

8 they went back in safety and praise and (with) war trophy and captives and riches and booty, which was desired; and in praise because his brother Yaᵓzil Bayyin, king of Sabaᵓ and Raydân, was received in Ṣanᶜâᵓ and Salḥân and in(?) [...

Preliminary remarks. The opinion according to which line 8 is the last one (cf. *RyISA*, XIV, pp. 382 and 389) is unfounded. In the transliteration of the text proposed by *RyISA*, *l.c.*, pp. 382-83, read *lgzmn* (line 2) instead of *lhzmn(?)*, *bᶜly* (line 4) instead of *ᶜly*, *bᶜm* (line 5) instead of *ᶜm*, *fhrgw* (line 6) instead of *whrgw*, *wdsᵓ*[*r* (line 7) instead of *wds*. [..., and *ytᵓwlw* (line 8) instead of [*w*]*tᵓwlw*. Finally, *RyISA* omitted *wᶜkm* after *ᵓḥbšn* in line 6, and at the end of the same line, read *b* after *wdstṣrw*/.

L. 2: *shymm*, e.g., Gl 1142/3 and 13 (cf. *HöTPK*, pp. 30-31). – *ᶜlyn*, e.g., CIH 308/20 and the Arabic name of a man *ᶜilyân* (cf. *LöHSM*, p. 75 A); cf. the personal names *ᶜlym* (Ja 689/4) and *ᶜlyt* (Ja 156, Qat). – *yqnᶜm*, name of person (Ja 332/1, Qat), of a clan (e.g., RÉS 4727 [=Ja 417]/5 and 7) and of a tribe (RÉS 4677/1-2 and 3). – *blt*, cf. commentary on Ja 560/8-9; the translation of this verb as "envoyer" (cf. *RyISA*, XIV, p. 383) is inaccurate. – *gzm* (cf. *StSESA*, p. 514: *CoRoC*, p. 122 B and *RhIGC*, p. 73, note 4): the upper part of the letters is missing; the ordinary meaning is "to declare upon oath"; also in Mehri (cf. *JaMSSA*, p. 182 B: *jizôm*) and Soqoṭri (cf. *LeLS*, p. 106); here, to be related to Arabic *ǧazama* "to cut" and Soqoṭri *megzímoh* "ruine" (cf. *LeLS*, *l.c.*).

L. 3: *hyt*, cf. *UlSLE*, p. 157. – *hbrr*, 4th form of *brr*; cp. Min *sbrr* "to give, assign to" (e.g., Ja 403) and Sab *hbrr* (e.g., CIH 581/10) "to decide" (cf. *RhASI*, p. 468), and *brr* "to perforate" (RÉS 3550/3, Qat); here, cf. Hebrew *brr* "to purge out, select" and thus the 4th form *hbrr* may be translated "to agree, accept"; cf. however Ja 644/8; *RyISA* (XIV, p. 384) translates *hbrr* as "se lancer" with reference to "Ry 535, 8, etc." (*l.c.*, p. 385). In the commentary of the latter text, the same author (XIII, pp. 159-60) first refers to RÉS 4053/2, and on the basis of Ethiopic *barara* "pervadere, transire", writes: "nous traduisons, eu égard à la préposition *bᶜly* qui suit: 'se lancer contre'." The verb in RÉS 4053/2 is partially restored and is not in the 4th form, [*br*]*ry*; such a reference is thus useless. Further, the meaning of Ethiopic *barara* is that of the 1st form of *brr*, which is attested in RÉS 3550/3 (cf. above). *hbrr* alludes to a decision taken during a meeting in which the course of action was discussed. – *bqdmy*, composite preposition (e.g., RÉS 3951/5); equals *bqdm* or *qdm* (cf. *CoRoC*, p. 229 B); in Murayġân/5, *qdmy* is the dual of *qdm* "attack [military] corps". – *dlwl*, intern plural (cf. Arabic plural in *qutûl*) of *dll*; cf. Arabic *dalîl*, plural *ᵓadillâᵓu* "guide", from the root *dalla* "to show, indicate, point out"; (cf. also *MoNTA*, p. 119); in RÉS 4782/2, in *bdlt* (*b*+*dlt*), *dlt* means "flattery" (cf. *JaIHI*, pp. 106-07).

L. 4: *bklm*: well-known tribe; e.g., Ja 547/5 and *WiHöBGS*, pp. 19-20. – *shrtn*, cf. *JaASAB*, p. 161, commentary on CIH 407/18-19. – *hḏr*, 4th form of *ḏrr*; the verb *ḏarra* both in Arabic and Daṯînah (cf. *LaGD*, p. 925) = Syriac *drō* (cf. *PaSmCSD*, p. 97 A) "to scatter, sprinkle"; cf. also *MoNTA*, p. 119; cf. *mhḏr* in Fakhry 71/5-6: *sqym*/*mhšfqm* *bmrb*/*wsryhw*/*mhḏrm* "une irrigation abondante à Mârib et ses deux districts, en répandant partout (?)" (cf. *RyET*, p. 42); *mhḏr* is thus considered as an active participle; but the commentary (*l.c.*) adds: "*mhḏrm* est peut-être le n. pr. des deux districts". At first sight, it is difficult to admit that two districts would have only one name. The term *mhḏr*, as well as *mhšfq*, is a passive participle qualifying *sqy* (cf. Ja 851/7) and means "spread"; the whole expression indicates the amplitude of the irrigation, and may be translated as follows: "a plentiful, extensive irrigation in Mârib and in its country"; cf. also the participles *ḏr* (Ja 735/13) and *mnḏr* (Ja 643/26) and the *maṣdar* *tḏr* (Ja 720/5); for *sryhw*, cf. commentary on Ja 577/13. – *kfl*, cf. Soqoṭri *kaféleh* "steep brink of a valley" (cf. *LeLS*, p. 223); this parallel fits *ᶜr* "citadel" built on top of a hill. – *wḥdt*, cf. *wḥd*[..?] in Ja 516/2 and commentary in *JaISAR*, p. 114; cf. also the Arabic place names *waḥdat*, *al-waḥîdân*, and *al-waḥîdat* (cf. *WüR*, p. 226 C). – *ẓᶜn*, CIH

547/4-5 and *CoRoC*, p. 161 A; here, with the meaning "to flee, fly". – *bḫr*, cf. *CoRoC*, p. 112 A and *RoVSAY*, p. 301; for the meaning of country, cf. Ja 489 A/5. – *bʾṯrhmw*, cf. Min composite preposition *bʾṯrh* "toward, in the direction of" (RÉS 3310 A/2, *CoRoC*, p. 110 B, and *HöASG*, p. 161); here, *b* (cf. *HöASG*, p. 142, η) and *ʾṯr* "track, trail".

L. 5: *RyISA*'s (XIV, p. 384) translation of this line must be discarded as inaccurate; further, it implies a victory of the Ḥabašites, which contradicts the following line which mentions "those of these Ḥabašites who remained". – *ḏkwn/kwnhmw* (also line 7, and Ja 629/12, 15, 635/22-23, 24-25) = *ḏkyn/kwnhmw* (Ja 601/10, 602/10, and JM 9+7/4). *ḏkwn/kwnhmw/ḏshrtm*, cp. *kl/ḏkwn/kwnhmw/bn/ḏʾšʿb/ḏshrtm* (line 7), which must be related to *ḏm/kwn/kwnsm/bnḏʾsrrn* (RÉS 3566/8, Qat) and also to [*ḏ*]*kyn/bkl/ʾrḍn* (RÉS 4138/7) and *ḏkyn/kwnhmw/bn/ʾʿrbn* (JM 9+7/4). According to *RyISA* (X, p. 273), "*ḏkyn* doit être en relation avec le verbe *kwn*. Faut-il y voir un passif? 'Et ce qui était compté (*kyn*) de leurs pareils en fait d'Arabes'"; the last phrase being the translation of JM 9+7/4. The relation between *kyn* and *kwn* is unfortunately not explained, and no reason is given to support the hypothesis of *kyn* being a passive verb. Further, *MoMiHI* (p. 26) thought of "ein Versehen des Steinmetzen für *kwn*"; and *HöIGT* suggests "arabisch 'schlechte Lage', etwa von der Seuche, *ẖum*, die schlimmm wütete im ganzen Land" (p. 16). In all the above-mentioned texts, *kyn* is the verb *kwn* "to be", a passive form of which is impossible; cf. in Mehri, the infinitive *kiyûn* (cf. *JaMSSA*, p. 202 B) and in Arabic, *kiyân*, *maṣdar* of the 1st form of *kwn*; cf. also the South-Arabian parallel *qwl* = *qyl* (cf. commentary on Ja 559/1). The expression *ḏkwn/kwnhmw/bn*(/*ḏ*) simply means "those who were with them from". – *mwṯbt*, plural of *mwṯb*; the verb *wṯb* means "to stay, settle" (e.g., RÉS 4782/3; cf. *JaIHI*, pp. 104-05 and Ist 7626/2, cf. *BeFSTI*, pp. 271-72; for *RycSD*'s opinion (p. 348) on the verb *wṯb*, cf. *JaFSR*, pp. 16-17; the noun *mwṯb* is attested, e.g., in Ja 600/8 and means "the place where the people stay"; here, participle; cf. Arabic *mîṯab* "sitter". – *bʿd* (cf. *HöASG*, p. 146): preposition indicating the removal, absence, "far from"; cf. Arabic *baʿdakum* "when you will be far from us"; the same idea of absence is also attested in the name of the female divinity *ḏt/bʿdn*(*m*). – *yʾttmw*, 8th form of *ʾtm* (cf. *RhSLG*, III, p. 19); cf. Arabic *maʾtam* "meeting of men and women". – *tqdm*, 5th form of *qdm*; cf. commentary on Ja 576/5. – *rtḍḫ*, 8th form of *rḍḫ*; compare *yʾttmw/wtqdmn/wrtḍḫn* (here) with *bkn/tʾtmw/wrtḍḫn/wtqdmn/bsrn/ḏʾẓwr* (Ja 578/19), to which [*bkn*] *tʾtmw/wrtḍḫn/bbrrn/ḏḥq*[. .] (RÉS 3884 [cf. Ja 115]/4-5) must be related. The latter was translated as follows by *MaTSAI* (p. 4): "they sued for peace and offered apologies with the gift of Ḥaql". This translation is simply rendered into French by *JaIH* (p. 568) and G. Ryckmans (cf. *RB*, 36 [1927], p. 383) mentions only *tʾtmw* "ont proposé un accord" and *bbrrn/ḏḥq*. . . "dans la plaine Ḏû-Ḥq . . ."; *MoMiSI* (p. 228) translate "sich mit ihnen vertrugen und um Entschuldigung baten in B-r-rān ḏū Ḥ-q . ." and suggest interpreting *brrn* as the name of the temple dedicated to Ḏât-Baʿdân, and to see in *ḥq* the ancient name of present Ḥuqqa; finally, *RÉS* translates "ont entamé des négociations de paix (cf. also in *RycIMAM*, p. 187) et se sont justifiés à Bararân de Ḥuqqa" (note that *brrn* is now considered as a proper name, contrary to the opinion suggested in *RB*, see above). The ideas of peace negotiations and of submission (cf. also *RhIMG*, p. 49 and note 2) proposed by the preceding translations are contradicted by the context and especially by Ja 115/4 and 6, and also by the context of the present inscription, as well as by Ja 578/19, where *rtḍḫ* is coupled with *tqdm/bʿm* "to attack"; cf. Arabic *raḍaḫa* "to break, bruise, crush" and Hebrew *râṣaḥ* "to kill" (cf. *KoBaLVTL*, p. 907 A). On the basis of the contexts, I translate *rtḍḫ* as "to slay". Further, since *bbrn/ḏḥq*[. .] in Ja 115/5 is parallel to *bsrn/ḏʾẓwr* in Ja 578/19, and *brr* (also Fakhry 3/8 [cf. *JaDME*, pp. 15-16], and Ja 576/6 and 12) equals *br* "flat country, plain" with the orthographic reduplication of the second radical, Ja 115/4-5 means "[when] they gathered together and were slain in the plain of Ḥq[. .]". I consider *rtḍḫ* as a passive verb, for lines 4-5 were most probably dealing with the enemies of ʾIlšaraḥ Yaḥḍub.

L. 6: *ʾʾnṯ*, plural of *ʾnṯ*; cf. *StSESA*, p. 527. – *hrgw/wsbyw*: the subjects are the Ḥabašites and their associates; same change of subject occurs in line 4: *ẓʿnw*. In expressions such as *ẖm*[*r*]*hmw/ʾlmqh/hrg/ʾlẓʾd* (Ja 586/21), which is perfectly parallel to *ẖmrhw/ʾlmqh/hrg hwʾ/lbʾn* (Geukens 6/23-24), *hrg* is a verb and not a noun (as suggested by *RyISA*, XIV, p. 375), where the commentary refers to *RhAST*'s (I, p. 24) translation of RÉS 3945/5-6: *hrgm*, as "Tötung". However, *hrg* in this text is also an infinitive with a passive meaning. It might be somewhat easier to use the noun in the translation; but, the actual value of the word cannot be misunderstood. For *hrg*, cf. *CoRoC*, p. 133 B, *JeHoDISO*, p. 69, and *JaASAB*, pp. 163-64. *sbyw* is also attested in RÉS 4678/5 (cf. commentary on Ja 552/4). – *bnhw|f* (cf. *HöASG*, p. 171), cp. *bn|hgrn|nʿḏ|f* in Ja 576/10; this expression, which is especially used in Ja 576, introduces an event as posterior as that (or those) related before and which is considered as the starting point of the next event. – *ʿynm*, cp. the clan name *ʾʿyn* in CIH 287/10, and also the Arabic place names *al-ʿayn* (cf. *WüR*, p. 157 A) and *ʿAina* (cf. *PhAHL*, p. 403) and the name of a man *ʿuyaynat* (cf. *WüID*, 173/1). – *whʿn|lḏmẖrm|bʿlyhmw|ḏsʾr|——|wḏsṯṣrw* "Et vint au secours de Ḏû-Muẖârim contre eux ce qui restait——Et ceux qui tentaient une poussée" (cf. *RyISA*, *l.c.*, p. 384). The preceding translation dissociates *ḏsṯṣrw* from *ḏsʾr*; yet, both verbs are introduced by *ḏ* which refers to *hmw* of *bʿlyhmw*. Further, *hʿn* is a proper name (cf. the masculine personal name in Ja 733/1) and not a verb; in the latter hypothesis, one would expect *hʿnw* and not *hʿn*; cf. in the immediately preceding context *fhrgW|wsbyW* and *ftʾwlW|wḥrbW*. *lḏmẖrm* (and not *ḏmẖrmn*, *sic* in *RyISA*, *l.c.*, p. 388), infinitive; e.g., CIH 555/2 and Ja 649/41 (*lḏmẖr*); cf. *RhSLG*, II, pp. 75-76: *maẖaru* "entgegenstehen"; the Accadian verb is also used with a hostile meaning, which corresponds to South-Arabian *mẖr|bʿly* "to oppose, combat". *ḏsʾr*, cf. *CoRoC*, p. 192 B, Ugaritic *šir* (*šʾr*) "remnant" (cf. *GoUM*, p. 326 A, No. 1796) and the noun *sʾr* in Ja 735/11. *sṯṣr*, 10th form (e.g., CIH 314+954/17) of *nṣr* (e.g., Ja 577/10); cf. also the 4th form *hnṣr*, e.g., in CIH 308/20; cf. *CoRoC*, p. 190 A.

L. 7: *ḥsm*, cf. Arabic *ḥasama* "to cut (off)"; according to the context, I translate as "to cut to pieces"; cf. also *RhIMG*, p. 48 and note 5. – *hsḥt*, 4th form (e.g., RÉS 4988/1; cf. C. Rathjens, *Sabaeica*, I, Hamburg, 1953, p. 29, Fig. 15) of *sḥt* (cf. commentary on Ja 578/8); in Arabic, both the 1st and 4th forms mean "to destroy, annihilate, crush"; for *sḥt* in Bellerby-Habban 2d (cf. *RyISA*, VIII, p. 107), cf. *JaDME*, pp. 14-15. – *ʿnt* (also in Ja 670/11), feminine noun (cf. *hyt|ʿntn* in Ja 643/25) derived from *ʿwn*, which is very well attested in the 4th form *hʿn* "to aid, help" (e.g., Ja 567/15-16). In Ja 670/11, whose context does not deal with military questions, *ʿnt* means simply "aid, help". Elsewhere, in the military contexts, *ʿnt* means either "reinforcements" (e.g., Ja 575/7) or "auxiliary operation" (Ja 635/20). Cf. also *JaDSY*, pp. 15-16, commentary on Ja 876 (=RÉS 4969)/5.

576 – Yellowish, slightly grayish sandstone. – MaMB 212 = Geukens 3; cf. *JaDCR*.

STONE: thickness: 26.1 cm. (right) and 26.8 (left). – *Front:* covered with red paint; the right part of the upper edge is largely splintered off, and the center of the lower edge as well; the right part of the lower edge is also splintered off; 1.814 m. (top) and 1.811 (bottom) × 36.7 cm. (right) and 36.1 (left). – INSCRIPTION: letter height: from 2 cm. (top) to 1.8 (bottom); space between the line: from 0.3 cm. to 0.4; continued by Ja 577. – SYMBOL, probably somewhat like Ja 574.

1 **S** *ʾlšrḥ|yḥḍb|wʾ⌈ẖ yhw⌉[|yʾzl|byn|mlky|sbʾ|*
]wḏrydn|bny|frʿm|ynhb|mlk|sbʾ|[hqnyy|
y *ʾlmqhṯhwnbʿlʾwm|{ts/sb}]ʿtn|ʾṣlmn|ʾly|ṣrfn|*
ḥmdm|bḏt|hwšʿ|whrdʾn|ʿbdhw|ʾlšrḥ|yḥḍb|
m *bškr|kl|ʾẖms|wʾšʿb|tnšʾw|bʿlyhmw|ḍrm|bn|*
ʾšʿb|šʾmt|wymnt|wb[ḥ]
2 *rm|wybsm|wlḏt|hwšʿhmw|⌈ʾlmqh|bʾẖḏ⌉|mlkm|*
b *mlk|kdt|wšʿbn|kdt|bẖfrt|hẖfr|mlkm|ʾlmqh|*
wm⌈l⌉k⌈nhn⌉|mrʾlqs|bn|ʿwfm|mlk|ẖṣṣtn|
o *wʾẖḏhw|hwt|mlkm|wʾkbrt|kdt|bhgrn|mrb|ʿdy|*
hgbʾw|hwt|ġlmn|mrʾlqs|wwhbw|ʾwṯqm|bn|
l *šʿbn|kdt|brwhw|wbny|mrʾs|wʾkbrt|kdt|whb*
3 *w|ẖfrt|ʾlmqh|wmlknhn|ʾfrsm|wrkbm|wgmlm|*
wḥmdm|bḏt|hwšʿ|ʾlmqh|ʿbdhw|ʾlšrḥ|yḥḍb|
bẖrʾn|wškr|wnqm|ʾḥzb|ḥbšt|wḏshrtm|wšmr|
ḏrydn|wʾšʿb|ḥmyrm|bḥbl|ḥblw|bʿd|slm|wgzm|
gzmw|wyśmkw|bn|hgrn|mryb|ʿdy|hgrn|ṣnʿw|
lḍbʾ|whṣrn|bʿly|šmr|ḏrydn|wʾšʿb|ḥmyrm|
wrdmn|wmḍḥym
4 *wyʿdwn|mlkn|ʾlšrḥ|wḏbn|ʾqwlhw|wẖmshw|wʾfrshw|*
ʿdy|ʾrḍ|ḥmyrm|wṯbrw|whbʿln|wqmʿ|whsbʿn|byt|
ḏšmtn|whgrn|dll|wbyt|yhr|whgrn|ʾẓwr|bwṯnn|
bʾrḍ|qšmm|bywm|hġrw|wylfyw|bn|hnt|hgrn|
mhrgtm|wsbym|wġnmm|ḏʿsm|wbnhw|fhwṣlw|
ʿdy|byn|hgrnhn|wbnhw|fybḥḍn|mlkn|ʾlšrḥ|yḥḍb

5 wbʿmhw/ḏbn/ʾqwlhw/wẖmshw/wʾfrshw/wybḥḍw/
ʿdy/ẖlf/hgrn/bʾsn/wqdmhmw/ʾsd/hysr/šmr/
ḏrydn/bn/ʾšʿb/ḥmyrm/lhʿnn/ʿdy/wṯnn/wytqdmw/
bʿmhmw/bẖlf/hyt/hgrn/bʾsn/wẖmrhmw/ʾlmqh/
hsḥtn/hmt/ʾsdn/ʾḥmrn/wyhrgw/bnhmw/mhrgm/
ḏʿsm/wtmlyw/sby/wqny/hyt/hgrn/bʾsn/wbnhw/
fhṣrw/ʿdy

6 ḏt/mẓʾw/ʿdy/brrn/ḏdrgʿn/wtflw/mṣr/ḏrydn/wʾl/
qdmhmw/wbʿdhw/fyṣbʾw/bʿly/ʾrḍ/mhʾnfm/
wyhysrw/bḥḍm/ḏbn/ẖmshmw/bʿly/ʾrḍt/mhʾnfm/
wlfyw/bhw/mhrgtm/wsbym/wġnmm/ḏhrḍwhmw/
wbnhw/fśmkw/mqln/ḏylrn/wnḥbw/hgrn/tʿrmn/
wẖmrhmw/ʾlmqh/hbʿln/hyt/hgrn/tʿrmn/wylfyw/
bhw/mhrgtm/w

7 ysbyw/kl/ʾwld/wʾnṯhw/wymtlyw/kl/ʾbʿlhw/wbnhw/
fytʾwlnn/ʿdy/hgrn/nʿḍ/wrtʿ/bʿmhw/ḏbn/
ẖmshmw/wyhṣr/mlkn/ʾlšrḥ/yḥḍb/wʾsd/qrbw/
bśnhw/bn/ẖmshmw/wʾfrshmw/wyhṣrw/bʿly/
mšrqt/ʾrḍ/qšmm/wyhsbʿw/whśln/hgrn/ʾyḍmm/
wybḥḍw/kl/mšrqt/qšmm/wylfyw/bhw/mhrgtm/
wsbym/ḏʿsm/wbnh

8 w/fygbʾw/ʿdy/hgrn/nʿḍ/wbnhw/fyhṣrn/mlkn/
ʾlšrḥ/yḥḍb/wḏbn/ẖmshw/wʾfrshw/ʿdy/ʾrḍ/
mhʾnfm/wyqmʿw/whbʿln/hgrnhn/ʿṯy/wʿṯy/
wylfyw/bhw/mhrgtm/wsbym/wmltm/wġnmm/
ḏʿsm/wbnhw/fytʾwlw/bʿly/hgrn/ḍfw/wykbnn/
bhw/ḏmḏrḥm/wšʿbn/mhʾnfm/wyhbrrw/šʿbn/
mhʾnfm/bʿly/mqdmthm

9 w/whsḥthmw/mqdmthmw/ʿdy/ḏt/ḥmlhmw/hgrn/
ḍfw/wyhrgw/bnhmw/mhrgm/ḏʿsm/wbnhw/
fytʾwlw/ʿdy/ẖlf/hgrn/yklʾ/wykbnn/bhw/ḏbn/
ʾqwl/ḏrydn/wmṣr/ḥmyrm/whbrrw/wtqdmn/
bʿmhmw/whsḥthmw/bn/mrḥḍn/ʿdy/ḏḥmlhmw/
śʾd/yklʾ/wlfyw/bnhmw/mhrgtm/ḏʿsm/wbnhw/
ftʾwlw/ʿdy/h[g]

10 rn/nʿḍ/wyʾdbhmw/hmt/ʾḥmrn/klyqdmnn/lmhrgtm/
ʿdy/sr/ngrrm/wyhṣrn/mlkn/ʾlšrḥ/yḥḍb/wḏbn/
ʾqwlhw/wẖmshw/wʾfrshw/ʿdy/ḏt/mẓʾw/śʾd/
yklʾ/wʾl/hbrrw/hmw/ʾḥmrn/lmhrgtm/wgbʾw/
wtʾwlw/ʿdy/hgrn/nʿḍ/wbn/hgrn/nʿḍ/fytʾwlw/
ʿdy/hgrn/ṣnʿw/bhwbltm/wmhrgtm/wʾẖyḍtm/wsb

11 ym/wġnmm/ḏʿsm/wbʿdhw/fnbl/bʿbrhmw/šmr/
ḏrydn/lmḥkm/bḥblm/whʾ/šmr/ḏrydn/fnbl/bʿbr/
ʿḏbh/mlk/ʾksmn/lnṣrm/bʿly/ʾmlk/sbʾ/wyhṣrn/
mlkn/ʾlšrḥ/yḥḍb/wʾqwlhw/wẖmshw/wʾfrshw/bn/
hgrn/ṣnʿw/drm/ṯntm/bʿly/šmr/ḏrydn/wʾšʿb/
ḥmyrm/wrdmn/wmḍḥym/wybḥḍn/mlkn/ʾ

12 lšrḥ/yḥḍb/wḏbn/ʾqwlhw/wẖmshw/wʾfrshw/brrn/
ḏhrwr/wʿrṣm/wdrgʿn/wylfyw/bhmw/mhrgtm/
wsbym/wġnmm/wmltm/ḏʿsm/whdrkthmw/
ḥyrthmw/ʿdy/qrb/wqrs/wwṯrw/kl/ʾbʾrhmy/
wqmʿw/hgrn/qrs/wbnhw/fybḥḍw/mlkn/ʾlšrḥ/
yḥḍb/wḏbn/ʾqwlhw/wẖmshw/wʾfrsh

13 w/ʾrḍt/yhbšr/wmqrʾm/wšddm/wlfyw/bhw/
mhrgtm/wsbym/wġnmm/ḏ(ʿ)sm/whbʿlw/bytn/
rʾs/wkl/mḥfdt/kwnw/ʾwmrhw/wqdmthmw/
ḥyrthmw/ʿdy/ẖlf/[. . 12 characters . .]/sbʿw/
hyt/hgrn/rʾsw/wbyt/ḏsnfrm/wynblnhmw/kl/
qrn/šym/bhw/ḏrydn/wbnhw/fhṣrw/ʿdy/ẖlf/
hgrn/ẓ

14 lm/wyhwkbnn/bhw/mqtt/wʾrgl/wqrn/ysr/šmr/
ḏrydn/lšrḥhw/wfẖrhmw/lsbʾ/wṯhbhmw/nkfm/
wgbʾw/wnḥbw/hyt/hgrn/wẖmrhmw/ʾlmqh/
ṯbr/hyt/hg[rn/. . 15 characters . ./wylfyw/bhyt/
]hgrn/mhrgtm/wsbym/wġnmm/ḏʿsm/wbnhw/
fyhṣrw/ʿdy/byn/hgrnhn/hrn/wḏmr/wyśmkn/
mlkn/ʾ

15 lšrḥ/yḥḍb/wbʿmhw/ḏbn/ʾqwlhw/wẖms/mʾnm/
wʾlfm/ʾsdm/wʾrbʿy/ʾfrsm/wykbnn/šmr/ḏrydn/
wbʿmhw/sṯt/ʿšr/ʾʾlfm/ʾb[lm/wʾšʿb/ḥmyrm/
w]rdmn/wmḍḥ[ym/. . 33 characters . .]krʾ/
ḏrydn/wmṣyrt/ḥmyrm/bwsṭ/hgrn/ḏmr/wśmkw/
bn/ḥyrthmw/mhsknm/wʾfrshmw/bʾnḥ

16 rm/wṭrydm/whmw/ʾḥmrn/fʾsyw/lhmw/wkym/ʿdy/
ḏt/mẓʾw/ẖlf/[hg]r[n]/whbrr/ḏrydn/wmṣyrt/
ḥmyrm/bʿlyh[mw/. . 29 characters . .]hm[w]/
m[. . 28 characters . .]m/šmr/ḏrydn/wmṣyrt/
ḥmyrm/wldʿm/whsḥthmw/ʿdy/ḏḥmlhmw/mṣrʿt/
hgrn/ḏmr/wšmr/ḏryd

SECOND STONE:

1 [n/. . . .   .]

1 **Sym-** ʾIlšaraḥ Yaḥḍub and his brother [Yaʾzil Bayyin, the two kings of Sabaʾ] and Raydân, the two sons of Fariʿum Yanhub, king of Sabaʾ, [have dedicated to ʾIlumquh Ṯahwân, master of ʾAwwâm,] these [(ni-)/(se-)]ne/ven statues which [are] in brass, in praise because He has helped and assisted His servant ʾIlšaraḥ Yaḥḍub in defeating all the armies and tribes [which] rose up against them in war, from the tribes of the north and of the south and of the s[e]a

2 **bol** and of the land, and because ʾIlumquh has helped them in capturing Malikum, the king of Kindat, and the tribe Kindat because of the assistance Malikum extended against ʾIlumquh and the two kings to Maraʾlaqas, son of ʿAwfum, king of Ḫiṣâṣatân, and [in] his capture of this Malikum and of the leaders of Kindat in the city [of] Marab until they gave over this youth Maraʾlaqas and [until] they presented firm pledges from the tribe Kindat: his [Malikum's] son and the sons of the chiefs and of the leaders of Kindat; they [also] gave

3 to the familiars of ʾIlumquh and the two kings horses and beasts of burden and camels; and in

praise because ʾIlumquh has assisted His worshipper ʾIlšaraḥ Yaḥḍub in opposing and defeating and taking vengeance on the fighting bands of Ḥabašat and Saharatum and Šamir, him of Raydân, and the tribes of Ḥimyarum because of the revolt they perpetrated after the peace and the oath they swore; and they went up from the city [of] Mârib to the city [of] Ṣanʿâʾ in order to fight and to fall upon Šamir, him of Raydân, and the tribes of Ḥimyarum and Radmân and Muḏḥayum;

4 and the king ʾIlšaraḥ and some of his rulers and his army and his cavalry went over to the land of Ḥimyarum and they crushed and seized and subjugated and plundered the house of [the tribe] Šamatân and the city [of] Dalâl and the house of Yahar and the city [of] ʾAẓwar, at the boundary, in the land of Qašamum, when they made a raid and brought back from these towns war trophies and captives and booty, which was desired; and from there, they assembled in [the district which lies] between the two cities; and from there, abruptly attacked the king ʾIlšaraḥ Yaḥḍub

5 and along with him some of his rulers and his army and his cavalry and they went to the region of the town [of] Baʾsân; and [there] preceded them the soldiers [which] Šamir, he of Raydân, had sent from the tribes of Ḥimyarum in order to be of protection at the boundary; and they attacked them in the region of the city [of] Baʾsân; and ʾIlumquh vouchsafed to them to destroy these soldiers, the Ḥimyarites; and they deprived them of a war trophy, which was desired; and they enjoyed [taking away] the captives and the slaves of the city [of] Baʾsân; and from there, they set out until

6 they arrived in the plain of Dargaʿan, and the expeditionary force of Raydân went away and did not precede them; and from there, they proceeded against the land of Muhaʾnifum and they sent (in) a sudden attack some of their army against the lands of Muhaʾnifum and they brought back from there war trophies and captives and booty, which pleased them; and from there, they went up through the pass of Yalrân, and harassed the city [of] Taʿramân; and ʾIlumquh vouchsafed to them to seize this city, Taʿramân; and they brought back from there war trophies and

7 they captured all [its] children and its wives, and they enjoyed [taking away] all its husbands; and from there, they went back to the city [of] Naʿiḍ and some of their army were duly established under [the control of] it; and set out the king ʾIlšaraḥ Yaḥḍub and the soldiers [who] were close to him from their army and their cavalry, and they fell upon the eastern parts of the land of Qašamum and they plundered and emptied the city [of] ʾAyḏamum; and they raided all the eastern parts of Qašamum and they brought back from there war trophies and captives, which was desired; and from the-

8 re, they returned to the city [of] Naʿiḍ; and from there, the king ʾIlšaraḥ Yaḥḍub and some of his army and his cavalry set out for the land of Muhaʾ-nifum and they subjugated and seized the two towns [of] ʿAṯay and ʿAṯay and they brought back from there war trophies and captives and riches and booty, which was desired; and from there, they returned against the city [of] Ḍâffaw where they met with Maḏraḥum and the tribe Muhaʾnifum; but the tribe Muhaʾnifum decided itself against their vanguard

9 and their vanguard continued to destroy them until the city [of] Ḍâffaw took them up; and they deprived them of a war trophy, which was desired; and from there, they returned to the region of the city [of] Yaklaʾ where they met with some of the rulers of Raydân and the expeditionary corps of Ḥimyarum and they agreed and attacked them and crushed them from Marḥiḍân until the prince of Yaklaʾ took them up; and they brought back from there war trophies, which was desired; and from there, they returned to the ci[t]y [of]

10 Naʿiḍ; and these Ḥimyarites persuaded them to move forward to [make] war trophies in the wâdî-side valley of Nagrarum; but the king ʾIlšaraḥ Yaḥḍub and some of his rulers and his army and his cavalry set out until the prince of Yaklaʾ arrived and they did not agree with these Ḥimyarites to war trophies; and they returned and went back to the city [of] Naʿiḍ: and from the city [of] Naʿiḍ, they went back to the city [of] Ṣanʿâʾ after [making] successful pursuits and (with) war trophies and prisoners and captives

11 and booty, which was desired; and after that, Šamir, he of Raydân, sent [messengers] to them concerning [his] quarrel in [his] revolt; and he, Šamir, he of Raydân, sent [messengers] to ʿAḏbah, king of ʾAksûman, [asking] for some support-troops against the kings of Sabaʾ, and the king ʾIlšaraḥ Yaḥḍub and his rulers and his army and his cavalry fell again from the city [of] Ṣanʿâʾ upon Šamir, him of Raydân, and upon the tribes of Ḥimyarum and Radmân and Muḏḥayum; and abruptly attacked the king ʾIl-

12 šaraḥ Yaḥḍub and some of his rulers and his army and his cavalry the plain of Ḥarûr and ʿArṣum and Dargaʿan; and they brought back from them war trophies and captives and booty and riches, which was desired, and their camp reached them in Qarîb and Qarîs; and they leveled all the wells of them both [the two cities] and they subjugated the city [of] Qarîs; and from there, the king ʾIlšaraḥ Yaḥḍub and some of his rulers and his army and his cavalry abruptly attacked

13 the lands of Yahbašir and Muqraᵓum and Šadâdum, and they brought back from there war trophies and captives and booty, which was (de)sired; and they seized the house Raᵓs and all the towers [which] were its posts of command, and their camp moved forward into the region of [*12 characters*] they sacked this city, Rasᵓaw, and the house of Sanfarum and so was given over to them every rebel [whom] Raydân had hidden there; and from there, they set out toward the region of the city [of]

14 Ẓalm and so he forced there the high military officials and the foot-soldiers and the rebel [whom] Šamir, he of Raydân, had summoned to reinforce himself and he assembled them for battle and returned them in good order; and they returned and harassed this city; and ᵓIlumquh vouchsafed to them to crush this cit[y *15 characters* and so they brought back from this] city war trophies and captives and booty, which was desired; and from there they set out into [the region] between the two cities [of] Hirrân and Ḏamar, and so went up the king

15 ᵓIlšaraḥ Yaḥḍub and along with him some of his rulers and 1500 soldiers and 40 horsemen and they met with Šamir, him of Raydân, and with him 16,000 ca[mels and the tribes of Ḥimyarum and] Radmân and Muḏḥa[yum *33 characters*].. Raydân and the expeditionary forces of Ḥimyarum in the midst of the city [of] Ḏamar, and [the] wretched ones and their horsemen went up from their encampment into ᵓAnḥa-

16 rum and Ṭuraydum; and as for these Ḥimyarites, they sent them support (?) until they arrived in the region of [the cit]y; and Raydân and the expeditionary forces of Ḥimyarum decided [.] against t[hem *29 characters*] thei[r].[*28 characters*]. Šamir, him of Raydân and the expeditionary forces of Ḥimyarum, children of ᶜAmm; and they continued to destroy them until the arena fields of the city [of] Ḏamar took them up; and Šamir, he of Rayd-

SECOND STONE:

a [ân,...

L. 1: the two restorations fit the blanks perfectly. – [...].*ᶜtn*: the lower part of a vertical stroke which belongs either to *b* or *s* is visible on the right of *ᶜ*; *sbᶜtn* or *tsᶜtn*; for *sbᶜ*, cf. *StSESA*, p. 523 and *BePESA*, p. 8. – *hrdᵓ*, 4th form of *rdᵓ*; cf. CIH 543/2 and the formula *brdᵓ* "with the help of" (e.g., Ja 857/2-3); cf. Arabic *radaᵓ*, 4th form, "to help, assist"; cf. also the noun *mrdᵓ* "depravation" in RÉS 5094/4 (cf. *JaFSR*, pp. 15-16). – *škr*, cf. *BeSI*, p. 31, – *tnšᵓ*, 5th form of *nšᵓ* (cf. *StSESA*, p. 529 and *BePESA*, p. 2); e.g., CIH 611/3 and RÉS 3858/3, Qat, which is parallel to the present text; cf. *CIH*, I, p. 329 A and *BeSI*, p. 66; cf. the noun *mnšᵓ* "(military) expedition" (e.g., Ja 643/5).

Ll. 1-2: *šᵓmt/wymnt/wb[ḥ]rm/wybsm*, cf. Ja 577/18; cf. *JaASAB*, pp. 153-54. *šᵓmt/wymnt*, cf. RÉS 3022/2, Min; *RyISA* (XIII, pp. 140 and 144) reads *šᵓmtn*; but the *n* does not exist and is excluded by the mimation of both *b[ḥ]r* and *ybs*; for the absence of mimation in both *šᵓmt* and *ymnt*, cf. *HöASG*, pp. 126-27, §106 β); cf. the adjectives *šᵓmyt* and *ymnyt* in *RyGSAS*, p. 561. – *b[ḥ]rm/wybsm*: *RyISA* (*l.c.*, p. 140) reads "*b*(line 2)⌊*ḥ*⌋*rm*" and comments as follows (p. 152): "les traits verticaux du *ḥ* apparaissent" (p. 152); but the first three letters of line 1 (*ᵓlš*) are exactly above *rm/* (line 2); there is thus no space at the beginning of line 2. Further, the end of line 1 is damaged and has space for one letter. *RyISA* also writes: "l'expression *bḥr/wybs* pourrait signifier 'campagne', c.-à-d. la région cultivable, 'et steppe', c.-à-d. la région aride, désertique," with reference to E. Ullendorff's article in *Africa*, 1955, p. 156. The latter affirms "the special E[pigraphic] S[outh-]A[rabian]-Gəᶜəz affinity" (cf. note 3) between *bḥr* and Ethiopic *bəḥer* "region, country, earth". But Ullendorff fails to prove that *bəḥer* is to be preferred to *bāḥĕr* "sea, great lake, western coast" (cf. *DiLLA*, col. 493). Further, the ideas of "steppe, desert" are only secondary to the root *ybs* which primarily means "dry, absence of water"; such a concept also applies to desert as well as to arable ground. There is thus no need to think that expressions such as *šᵓmt/wymnt/wbḥrm/wybsm* designate the four cardinal points. Here, for instance, *šᵓmt/wymnt* are not exactly opposed to *bḥrm/wybsm*, as if "north and south" and "west and east", because no powerful enemy of Sabaᵓ was living on the east where the great desert stretches; the expression primarily indicates the universality of the coalition against the Sab kings.

L. 2: *ld̲t* here equals *bd̲t*, when followed by a perfect tense. – *mlkm*, personal name (e.g., RÉS 4356/1); cf. also the clan name *mlkn* (e.g., Ja 859/2 and 306/2, Qat). – *kdt*: the reading *kdt* in Wâdî Maᵓsil 1/10 (cf. *RyISA*, X, pp. 303-04) is not justified by the photograph (cf. also *RycPCH*, pl. 4), which suggests *sn*(?)*rt*. – *ḫfrt*, e.g., RÉS 4646/8-9 "familiars" (also in line 3), in Ḥîma/10: "protector, patron", and in Kawkab 1/11: *ḫfr* "protection, patronage" (both related to Arabic *ḫufrat* from *ḫafara* "to protect"); *ḫfrt/hḫfr* means "the assistance he has extended to". – *mlknhn* refers to ʾIlšaraḥ and his brother Yaʾzil; *idem* in RÉS 4134/4. – *mrʾlqs*, cp. the four ʾImruʾlqays and alsoʾ Imruʾlqays mentioned by *WüID*, 222/13, 14, 259/11, 285/8, and 258/19 respectively. – *ʿwfm*, the names of a man *ʿwfm* (NaNN 15/1) and of a clan *ʿfm* (Ja 727/1-2 and commentary); cf. Arabic *ʿâfa* "to adhere, stick on" and *ʿAwf*, name of a person (cf. *LöHSM*, p. 75 B and *SaIS*, p. 179) or of a clan (cf. *SaIS*, *l.c.*,) and the personal name *ʿf* both in Safaitic (cf. *LiSI*, p. 336 B) and in Thamudic (cf. *vdBrIT*, pp. 224-25: HU 693 and *HaLiSTI*, p. 49, No. 521) and also the Arabic name of a man *ʿuwâfat* (cf. *WüID*, 150/16). – *ḫṣṣtn*, cf. Arabic *ḫiṣâṣ* or *ḫuṣâṣ*, pl. of *ḫaṣṣat* "réservoirs, bassins" (cf. *DoSDA*, I, p. 375); cf. also the Arabic clan name *banû l-ḫaṣâṣîyat* (cf. *WüID*, 212/1). – *ʿdy*, cf. *HöASG*, p. 171; *ʿdy*=*ʿdy*/*d* (e.g., line 9) and *ʿdy*/*dt* (e.g., lines 5-6). – *hgbʾw*: *RyISA* (*l.c.*, pp. 140 and 144) erroneously reads *hll*/*ʾwd*⟨/⟩; cf. *JaFSR*, pp. 14 and 15 and Ja 506 A/2: "to offer". – *ġlm*, e.g., CIH 19/7; cf. Arabic *ġulâm* "youth"; here with the intention of belittling the person involved. – *wbny*/*mrʾs*/*wʾkbrt*: *RyISA* (*l.c.*, p. 144) erroneously reads *wbnyhw*/*bn*/*ʾkbrt* (but *ʾkrbt* on p. 140); the noun *mrʾs* here precedes *ʾkbrt* but follows *ʾqwl* in Ḥîma/1, where *RyISA* (X, p. 288) refers to Arabic *mtrʾûs* "subalternes". The fact that *mrʾs* follows *ʾqwl* in Ḥîma/1 does not justify interpreting *mrʾs* as second-rank chiefs since it precedes *ʾkbrt* here. Same nominal formation as that of *mśwd*. – *ʾkbrt*, pl. of *kbr*, as well as *ʾkbr* (e.g., Ja 560/2-3), *ʾkbrw* (e.g., RÉS 3951/5) et *kbwr* (e.g., RÉS 2633/6).

L. 3: *gml*, cf. Arabic *ǧâmil* "(coll.) camels" and *ǧamal* "(unity) camel"; cf. *JeHoDISO*, p. 51: *gml*; also in Ḥimâ/9, where *RyISA* (X, p. 293) remarks that it is the first occurrence of that noun. *gml* was previously attested in Philby-Djebel ʿUbaid 7/2, published by *RyISA*, VIII, p. 100, without commentary. The meaning of *gml* seems to be very general, that is to say without any allusion to any specification (cp. *bʿr*), as indicated by *gmlm*/*wbqrm*/*wḏʾnm* (Ja 649/40-41) "camels and bovines and sheep"; this expression may be compared with the following: *ʾʾblhmw*/*wḥmrthmw*/*wkl*/*grḥ* (Ja 643 bis/3), "their camels and their asses and every carnivorous animal." – *ḫrʾ*: *RyISA* (XIII, p. 154) affirms its identity with *ḫry*. But the verbs *ḫrʾ*, *škr*, and *nqm* depend on the preposition *b* and form only one series with *ʾḥzb*/*ḥbšt* as direct object; *ḫrʾ* cannot thus mean "to protect"; I propose to relate *ḫrʾ* to Syriac *ḥrʾ*, ethpael "to oppose." – *nqm* instead of erroneous *nfm* (cf. *RyISA* , *l.c.*, pp. 140 and 144). – *ʾḥzb*; the *z* is certain, contrary to *RyISA*, *l.c.*, pp. 140, 144 [where it is followed by *ḳbšt*; read *ḥbšt*] and 154. – *šmr*, also Ja 516/6; cf. also *šmrm*, name of a man (RÉS 4749), of a woman (Ist 7630/2) and also *šmyr* (Ja 394, Qat), and *hšmr* (e.g., Ja 882 L/1, Qat; cf. *JaPEQL*, p. 215). – *bḥbl*/*ḥblw*, cf. *CoRoC*, p. 144 B and Arabic *ḥabala* "to catch with a net"; *ḥibl* "sly" and *ḥabl* "rope, dissimulation, deceit"; *ḥbl* means a revolt started in spite of a sworn peace. *RyISA* reads *ḏḥbl* (pp. 140 and 144) instead of *bḥbl*, and comments "*ḏḥbl*/*ḥblw*, infin, absolu et parfait, comme en cananéen?" (p. 154), and translates the whole expression as follows: "qui ont engagé des hostilités" (p. 147). This translation is inaccurate for it does not express the fact of the rebellion; and the true reading of *bḥbl*/*ḥblw* renders the suggested reference to Canaanite superfluous. For the formula *kl*/*ʾlʾlt*/*wʾšʿbm*/*ḏʾlm*/*wšymm*/*wḥblm*/*wḥmrm*, "all the deities and the tribes (united) by a god and a patron and an agreement and a secret stipulation (?)", cf. *JaP*, pp. 117-18 and note 524, and *JaPSAP*, p. 122; contrast *GhNQI*, pp. 13-16. – *slm*, e.g., Ja 545/4: exclamation repeated twice. – *gzm*/*gzmw*, e.g., CIH 435/1; *RyISA* (*l.c.*, p. 147) dissociates *slm* and *gzm*; both terms depend on the preposition *bʿd* here as well as in Ja 577/4: *bʿd*/*gzm*/*wslm*/*kwn*, and *gzmw* as well as *kwn* refer to both words. – *yśmkw*, the infinitive of the 1st form is attested in CIH 314+954/12; cf. Arabic *samaka* "to raise, rise, arise"; cf. also *MoNTA*, p. 129. – *ḥṣr*, RÉS 4176/7 and *BeSI*, p. 80; cf. Soqoṭri *ṣer*(*r*) "jeter" (cf. *LeLS*, p. 358) and Arabic *ṣarrat* "rage (of the fight), tumult (of the fighters)"; *ḥṣr*, used either alone or with *bʿly*, may be translated "to set out" and "to fall upon (an adversary)" respectively. – *rdmn* and *mḏḥym* are two very well known Qat tribes; *mḏḥym*=*mḏḥyn* (e.g., Ja 739/10)=*mḏḥy* (Geukens 1/6).

L. 4: *yʿdw*, cf. *JaASAB*, p. 163, commentary on CIH 407/23. *hbʿl*, 4th form of *bʿl*, e.g., RÉS 3945/3 and Ja 526/3. – *qmʿ*, e.g., CIH 308/22; cf. Arabic *qamaʿa* "to subjugate, subject". – *hsbʿ*, 4th form of *sbʿ*; cf. *CoRoC*, p. 193 B. – *ḏšmtn* (*RyISA* transcribes it both as *ḏšmtm* on p. 162, and as *ḏšmtn* on pp. 141, 144, and 156, and translates it both as "Šamatum" on pp. 147 and 150, and as "Ḏû-Šamatim" on pp. 156-57), cp.

šmtm, clan name mentioned in Bellerby-Habban 5h from Wâdî Habban, about 190 km. northeast of ʿAden; in RÉS 5040/1, *šmtm* may be the name either of a man or of a clan; *šmt* in RÉS 5083 and 5086 must be corrected: *šrrt*. – *dll*, not *dln* (as *RyISA*, pp. 141, 144, 147, and 156); cf. the Arabic personal name *dillâl* (cf. *SlGaVNPA*, p. 16 A). – *ʾẓwr*, name of a city; also in Ja 578/19; for *ẓwr* either as noun "pilaster(s)" or verb "to besiege", cf. Ja 859/4-5 and 577/8 respectively. – *wṯn*, e.g., Ja 540 A/2. – *bʾrḍ*, not *ḏʾrḍ* (as *RyISA*, *l.c.*, pp. 141 and 144). – *qšmm*, tribe name mentioned in RÉS 4196/1 with *mḏḥym* of the preceding line. – *bywm*, also in RÉS 4966/1, instead of *y*(?)*.wm*. – *hġr*, 4th form of *ġwr* (cf. *CoRoC*, p. 215 A), CIH 350/2 (and not 9 as in *RyISA*, X, p. 292) "to make a raid"; in Ḥimâ/7, *s*[*t*]*ġrw* [neither *st*(*ġ*)*rw* as in *l.c.*, p. 285, nor *s*(*t*)*ġrw* as in *RyISA*, XIII, p. 156]/*ʿlhmw*/*mgrmtm* "ils se jetèrent contre eux criminellement" (cf. *l.c.*, p. 287). In this expression, *stġr*, 10th form of *ġwr*, is a transitive verb, and *mgrm* a noun and not an adverb; the expression means "they sent criminals against them for a raid". – *lfy*, cp. Arabic *lafaʾa* "to strip off, peel off" (cf. *LaAEL*, p. 2665 B); here, with the meaning "to deprive of"; *bn* introduces the mention of the losing party. *RyISA* (XIII) reads *gfy* instead of *lfy* every time this verb occurs in the present text; *lfy* is certain. Further, the grammatical difficulty arising from the reading of *gfy* (cf. *RyISA*, *l.c.*, p. 156) does not exist with *lfy*. – *hgr*, also plural in Ja 577/14; *RyISA*'s reading (pp. 141 and 144) and commentary (p. 156): *hntʾhgrn* are erroneous; the ʾ does not exist. – *fhwṣlw*: *RyISA* (*l.c.*, pp. 141, 144, and 156) erroneously reads *whwṣlw* in spite of the fact that *bnhw*, which precedes *fhwṣlw*, is always followed by a verb introduced by the conjunction *f*; e.g., line 4: *bnhw*/*fybḥḏn*, line 5: *bnhw*/*fhṣrw*, line 6: *bnhw*/*fšmkw*, lines 7-8: *bnhw*/*fygbʾw*, etc. – *fybḥḏn*: *bḥḏ* is verb here (also in RÉS 3884/12, where *RÉS* and also *RyNP* [I, p. 286 B] consider it as a proper name) and noun, e.g., in line 6. *RyISA* (*l.c.*, p. 157) writes that *bḥḏ* "doit signifier 'envahir' (cf. also commentary on line 6). Nous ne connaissons pas de racine sémitique à laquelle ce verbe puisse se rattacher". With the metathesis of the last two radical letters, *bḥḏ* may be related to Ethiopic *băṣĕḥa* "pervenire, advenire, attingere...invadere" (cf. *DiLLA*, col. 545-46). The verb *bḥḏ* may thus be translated "to attack abruptly", and the noun (e.g., Ja 578/10), pl. *bḥḏt* (Ja 578/10) as "sudden attack".

L. 5: *wbʿmhw*: *RyISA* (*l.c.*, pp. 141 and 144) erroneously reads lines 4-5 as follows: /[ʾ*l*] (line 5)*y*/*ʿmhw*; there is no place at the end of line 4 and the proposed reading of the beginning of line 5 is erroneous. – *bʾsn*, name of a city connected with ʿAṯtar (e.g., CIH 510/7); cp. the feminine personal name *bʾst* (RÉS 4361), the family name *bʾs* (e.g., RÉS 2814/3, Min) and the noun *bʾs*(*t*) "misfortune" (cf. commentary on Ja 558/5). – *qdm*, cf. *JaDN*, p. 168; the 2nd form of *qdm* is attested, e.g., in line 6, and means, as in Arabic, "to proceed"; another meaning of the same form is "to offer, present" (e.g., RÉS 4830/2; cf. E. Littmann, in *ZDMG*, 101 [1951], p. 376). – *hysr*, 4th form of *ysr*; cf. *BeSI*, p. 31: Hebrew *yiššîr*. – *tmly*, 5th form of *mly*, cf. the 1st form *mly* in Ja 649/40, the 8th form *mtly* in line 7, the 10th form *stmly* in RÉS 3945/13 and the adjective *mly* in Ja 653/8; cf. Arabic *malâ* (i), 5th form and *muliya* "to enjoy". – *fhṣrw* and not *fyhṣrw* (*sic RyISA*, *l.c.*, pp. 141 and 144).

Ll. 5-6: *ʿdy*/*ḏt*, cf. commentary on line 2. *ʿdy ḏt*/*mẓʾw*/*ʿdy*/*brrn*, cp. *ʿd*/*mẓʾ*/*bḥrn* in RÉS 3945/5; cp. Soqoṭri *mṯy* "venir, arriver, atteindre" (cf. *LeLS*, p. 241); for another meaning of *mẓʾ*, cf. Ja 750/9-10 and commentary.

L. 6: *brr*: e.g., Ja 115/5 (cf. end of the commentary on Ja 575/5); for Fakhry 3/8, cf. *JaDME*, pp. 15-16. – *drgʿn*, also in line 12; a few quadriliterals beginning with *drğ* are known in Arabic, such as *drğb*, *drğl*, and *drğn*, but *drğʿ* is unknown. I wonder whether *drgʿn* is not a compound name: *dr*+*gʿn*; for *dr*, cf. *JaIHI*, p. 100; cf. the Arabic names of a clan *banû d-dâr* and of a man *ğaʿwanat* (cf. *WüID*, 226/5 and 179/7 respectively). – *ṯflw* (e.g., CIH 204/4) = *ṯfl* (Ja 633/9-10); 5th form of *flw*, cf. Ethiopic *tăfalăyă* or *tăfalăwă* "alium ab alio separari, dissidere" (cf. *DiLLA*, col. 1344). – *mṣr*, pl. *mṣyrt* (e.g., Ja 576/15) and *ʾmṣr* (Ja 512/5); cf. *CoRoC*, p. 180 and *BeSI*, p. 30. The identity of meaning given both to *mṣr* and *ḫms* (as *MoMiHI*, p. 41) is disproved by Ja 643/24, according to which *mṣr* is a part of *ḫms*. However, this relation is not always indicated (e.g., Ja 578/1). The proper name which qualifies *mṣr* is usually the name of a hostile neighboring population; e.g., *mṣr*/*ʾḥbšn* (e.g., CIH 308/12) and *mṣr*/*ḥḏrmwt* (Ja 665/29). When used in connection with Sabaʾ, it always is in relation to a military campaign against a foreign enemy. The preceding remarks suggest agreeing with N. Rhodokanakis (cf. *WZKM*, 28 [1914], p. 114), who refers to Accadian *miṣru* and Arabic *miṣr* "partition, limit, boundary between two lands"; *mṣr* may be translated "expeditionary corps" (cf. also *RhIGC*, p. 73: "Grenztruppen", with the remark that they were sent abroad; *l.c.*, note 3) or "expedition abroad" according to the context. The preceding interpretation seems to be illustrated by *mᶜn/mṣrn* (e.g., RÉS 3022/1, Min), where *mṣrn* is a proper name, but could have originally meant "the expeditionary corps". – *yṣbʾw* and not *ysbʾw* (cf. *RyISA*, *l.c.*, pp. 141 and 145); cf. Arabic *ṣabaʾa* "to guide a troop against the enemy". – *yhysrw/bḥdm/d̲bn/ḫmshmw* "ils envoyèrent une reconnaissance d'entre leur troupe" (cf. *RyISA*, *l.c.*, p. 147) with the following commentary: "*bḥd* se traduirait par 'reconnaissance' d'une troupe armée qui pénètre dans un territoire" (p. 158) (cf. also commentary on line 4). But, the French military term "reconnaissance" means an action of small scale with the purpose of obtaining information on either the position or the movement of the enemy; such is not the case of the operation mentioned in the text. *bḥd/d̲bn/ḫmshmw* means "a sudden attack (involving) some of their army" or "in a sudden attack, some of their army". – *lfyw/bhw*, cp. *ylfyw/bn/hnt/hgrn* in line 4; *b*=*bn* (origin); *hw* refers to the place indicated by *ʾrḍt*; *RyISA* (*l.c.*, pp. 141 and 145) reads *bhmw* instead of *bhw*. – *d̲hrḍwhmw*: there is no reason for translating the perfect tense *hrḍw* as an imperfect (cf. *RyISA*, *l.c.*, p. 147: "donnait satisfaction"). – *mql*: *mnql* "pass in the mountain" (e.g., RÉS 3550/3, Qat, and *CoRoC*, pp. 190-91); cf. the preposition *mqly* "through, toward" (e.g., CIH 541/29). *RyISA* (*l.c.*, pp. 141 and 145) erroneously reads *msl* and writes (p. 158) that "le bas de la hampe du *l* se confond avec la hampe gauche du *s*". The second letter is quite clear and quite separated from the third letter. – *d̲ylrn* (not *d̲ygrn* as in *RyISA*, *l.c.*, pp. 141, 145, and 147; the commentary on p. 158 is erroneous) corroborates *ylr* in Ja 295/2, where *JaPEHA* (p. 148) transliterates *ILR* and suggests that *l* could be a mistake for *g*; *RyISA* (XI, p. 106) accepts this hypothesis. – *nhb*, cf. Arabic *nahaba*, 1st and 2nd forms, means "to hasten"; here, with a direct object "to press, harass". – *tᶜrmn*, and not *trgmn* (cf. *RyISA*, XIII, pp. 141, 145, 147, 150, and 158); cf. *tᶜrm*, name of a Min hall in RÉS 2999/2; cf. also the Arabic name of a man *ᶜarmân* (cf. *WüID*, 287/12).

L. 7: *ysbyw*, and not *sbyw* (cf. *RyISA*, *l.c.*, pp. 141, 145, and 158). – *ʾwld/wʾnt̲hw*: the personal pronoun also qualifies the noun *ʾwld*. – *ʾbᶜl* (cf. *CoRoC*, p. 116 A): *RyISA* (*l.c.*, pp. 147 and 158) translates it as "propriétés" with reference to CIH 291/7. However, this text has not yet been translated; therefore, line 7 of it cannot be used as the basis for a translation which remains otherwise unsupported. Further, *RyISA* quotes the partial translation proposed both by *CIH* (I, p. 308 B) and *RhKTB* (II, p. 11). But, these two authors translate *bᶜl* as "master" and in spite of that, *RyISA* translates it as "estates". Such a translation may be explained as follows. *RhKTB* with some hesitation proposes "Eigentümer"; this German noun means either "estates" or "owner(s)"; but the first meaning is obviously excluded since *RhKTB* deals with a term which is "von Menschen gesagt". *RyISA*'s opinion about *bᶜl* must be discarded, since the ordinary words for "estate" are *qny* and *mlk*. Furthermore, the context does not require giving *bᶜl* a meaning different from the ordinary one: the Sab soldiers seized all the children and wives of the city and enjoyed having all its married men. The contents of the expression *hyt/hgrn/tᶜrmn/–/kl/ʾwld/wʾnt̲hw/–/kl/ʾbᶜlhw* are to be compared with those of *byt/d̲ᶜmrt/wʾbᶜlhw/ʾsdm/wbntm* (RÉS 3966/4-6) in as far as both expressions describe the population of two communities; but their point of view differs. In RÉS 3966/4-6, *ʾbᶜl* alludes to the land-owners, man and woman; in the present inscription, the population is presented as composed of children, wives and husbands; both meanings of *bᶜl* are quite common in the Semitic languages (cf., e.g., *JeHoDISO*, p. 40). – *mtly*, 8th form of *mly*; cf. commentary on line 5. – *rtᶜ/bᶜmhw/d̲bn/ḫmshmw* "se rangèrent avec lui ceux d'entre leur troupe" (cf. *RyISA*, *l.c.*, pp. 147-48) and the commentary points out that "les troupes de Naᶜḍ prennent le parti du roi" (cf. *l.c.*, p. 159), relating *hw* of *bᶜmhw* and *hmw* of *ḫmshmw* to ʾIlšaraḥ and the city Naᶜiḍ respectively. First of all, the plurals mentioned in the preceding part of line 7 as well as in lines 5-6 (and especially *d̲bn/ḫmshmw* in line 6) refer to both ʾIlšaraḥ and his army; it is thus highly improbable that ʾIlšaraḥ would be referred to here by a singular pronoun. The king is mentioned just after the above-quoted pericope, but the expression *mlkn/ʾlšrḥ/yḥḏb* in the present text always introduces a new part of the story or another campaign. On the other hand, the pronoun *hw* is frequently related in the present text to a city; e.g., *hyt/hgrn/tʿrmn/wylfyw/bhw* at the end of line 6. For *rtʿ*, cf. RÉS 4176/4 and *BeSI*, p. 79 and *HöASG*, p. 171: here as well as in Ja 658/11-12 and 745/10, cf. Ethiopic *ʾărteʿă* "erigere, stabilire...dirigere" (cf. *DiLLA*, col. 289-90); for *bʿmhw*, cf. *bʿm* in Ja 568/8. Thus I translate the pericope as follows: "and some of their army were duly put under [the control of] it [the city]"; a part of ʾIlšaraḥ's army was left behind in Naʿiḍ as a reserve. – *ʾsd/qrbw/bśnhw*, cp. parallel *ʾsd/qrbw/bʿmhw* in Ja 643/31; this expression means "the soldiers which were at the hand of the king and were able to answer to his order". *śn*, verb, e.g., in Ja 534/1 (cf. commentary in *JaIAA*, pp. 319-20) and the 5th form in Gl 1142/10-11 (cf. *JaITDL*, p. 185). – *mšrqt*, pl. of *mšrq*; cf. Arabic *mašriq* "east, country in the east"; cp. *bmšrqn* (CIH 541/20) "eastward". – *hśl*, 4th form of *śll* "to take out, make lean, emaciate"; it may be translated "to empty"; in Ja 669/13 and 24 with the meaning "to drive, lead (cattle)". – *ʾyḏmm*, *ʾaqtalum* form; cf. Arabic *waḏama* "to lay something on a *waḏam* (a wooden board)"; *RyISA* (pp. 142, 145, nothing in the commentary on p. 159) reads *ʾyḏmm* and translates it as "ʾAyḏamum" (p. 148) or as "ʾAyḏam" (p. 150).

L. 8: *gbʾ*: cf. *BeFSTI*, p. 273 (commentary on Ist 7626/2); here, with the meaning of "to return"; cf. *UlCSH*'s erroneous affirmation: "in South Arabian the root *gbʾ*..means 'to collect'" (p. 193). – *qmʿ*, e.g., RÉS 4536/2 and *CoRoC*, p. 232 B. – *ʿṯy*, cp. Arabic *ʿaṯā(i, o)* "to commit crimes and be cause of unhappiness". – *ylfyw/bhw*: *bhw* equals *bnhw* in *lfyw/bnhw* in line 12. – *ḏfw*, name of a pasture-land in CIH 516/14 (cf. *CIH*, II, p. 226 A, contrary to III, p. 364 A); cf. the Arabic place name *ḏafwā* (cf. *WüR*, p. 140 C). – *ykbnn*, imperfect of *wkb*. – *mḏrḥm*, clan name mentioned also in CIH 40/1 along with the tribe name *mhʾnfm*; cf. also Ja 489 A/4.

Ll. 8-9: *mqdmthmw*: *RyISA* (*l.c.*, p. 160) rightly refers to Arabic *muqaddamat* (or *muqaddimat*); the letter *w* is certain on the stone (contrary to *l.c.*, pp. 142 and 145).

L. 9: *ʿdy/ḏt/ḥmlhmw* = *ʿdy/ḏḥmlhmw* (end of the same line); cf. *JaASAB*, p. 163, commentary on CIH 407/22. – *yklʾ*, cf. the noun *klʾ* "young herbage, ground" (e.g., Ja 653/9). – *mrḥḏn*, name of place; cp. Arabic *raḥaḏa* "to wash, clean (hands, clothes)". *RyISA* (*l.c.*, p. 160) mentions "*mḥḏm*, territoire de tribu?" between "*hkbnn*" and "*śʾ[m]*" in line 9. Such a proper name does not exist; *RyISA*' *mḥḏm* is probably a remnant from his first decipherment. – *śʾd* and not *śʾ[m]* (cf. *l.c.*, pp. 142, 145, and 160); cf. Arabic *sâʾid*, pl. *sâdat* or *sayâʾidu* "chief, prince", from *sâd* "to be chief". – In the same line, *RyISA* (*l.c.*) erroneously reads *whkbnn* and *ʿmhmw* instead of *wykbnn* and *bʿmhmw*.

Ll. 9-10: instead of *hg* (line 10)*rn* proposed by *RyISA* (*l.c.*, pp. 142 and 146), read *h[g]* (line 10)*rn*.

L. 10: *ʾdb*, cp. the noun *mʾdb* "hireling" (RÉS 4336/4, Qat) and *ʾdb* "beautiful work(?)" (Ja 540 A/2); the verb *ʾdb* may be translated "to engage, persuade"; *hmw* is related to *śʾd/yklʾ*; according to *RyISA* (*l.c.*, p. 160), *hmw* would be "suffixe explétif"; but the two parallels presented by the author are not convincing for the subject of the verb is mentioned between the latter with the pronoun and the direct object. – *klyqdmn*, cp. *klyhqnynn* (Ja 567/8-9). – *ngrrm* (not *ngfrm* as read by *RyISA*, *l.c.*, pp. 142 and 145; the commentary on p. 160 is erroneous), *qatlal* form, cp. the name of a place *nagr* (cf. *MüHG*, p. 113 A) and the Arabic personal name *niğâr* (cf. *SlGaVNPA*, p. 40 A). – *hmw*, pl. masc. demonstrative adjective (cf. *HöASG*, p. 37, §33); cp. *hmy*, the dual masc. demonstrative pronoun, (e.g., in Ja 651/14); *RyISA* (*l.c.*, p. 148) translates it as a personal pronoun. – *hwblt*, cp. *wbl* (CIH 518/4) "Bodenzins (Abgabe)" (cf. *RhSLG*, II, p. 121) and *mwbl* (RÉS 3688/5, Qat) "Pachtzins" (cf. *RhKTB*, I, pp. 9 and 14-15); *hwblt* must be maintained in CIH 289/15, where it is connected with *ḥmd*; in the latter as well as here, cf. Arabic *wabala* "to pursue one's prey"; the context shows that the pursuit was successful. – *ʾhḏ*, cf. *JaASAB*, pp. 163-64, commentary on CIH 407/26. – In the same line, read *mẓʾw/śʾd* and *fytʾwlw* instead of *mẓʾ/w[ś]tʾd* and *ftʾwlw* suggested by *RyISA*, *l.c.*, pp. 142, 145, and 160.

L. 11: *bʿdhw*, temporal adverb (cf. *HöASG*, p. 146); for the conjunction, cf. *l.c.*, p. 171. – *nbl/bʿbrhmw*, CIH 308/17; for *bʿbr* "against" in RÉS 4233/6 (cf. *JaSAI*, p. 507 B, No. 5) and not "de la part de" (cf. *RÉS*, VII, p. 160). – *mḥk*, and not *mḥ[ś]* (cf. *RyISA*, *l.c.*, pp. 142, 145, and 161), cf. Arabic *maḥaka* and *maḥika* "to quarrel with". –

ᶜd̲bh, same nominal formation as that, e.g., of *ʾh̲rh* (RÉS 3699/2, Min); cf. the proper name *bhᶜd̲b* (RÉS 3093) and the verb *hᶜd̲b* (Ja 542 A/2). – The root *nṣr* means "to help, assist, aid" (cf. also *MoNTA*, pp. 352-53); therefore, the noun *nṣr* means "help" (e.g., RÉS 4069/11), "body guard" (RÉS 4855/2-3, Ḥaḏr) and "royal guard" (RÉS 5085/9 and Ḥaḏr, Ingrams 1/3; for the latter, cf. *JaIHI*, pp. 99-101). In the present text, *nṣr* could simply mean "help" (also *RyISA*, *l.c.*, p. 148). However, Ja 577/11 and 647/22 suggest the meaning "support troops; auxiliaries". – *dr*, *scriptio/defectiva* for *dwr*, cf. *CoRoC*, p. 125 B; this *dr* must not be confounded with *dwr* "bedouin camp" (e.g., Ja 574/7); *drm/t̲ntm* means "a second time".

L. 12: *ḥrwr*, and not *ḥw*[*t*] (cf. *RyISA*, *l.c.*, pp. 143 and 145), "*ḥwt* ou *ḥwr*?" (p. 161), "Ḥawt" (p. 149) or "Ḥawt(?)" (p. 150); name of a house in Ja 555/3. – *h̲yrt*=*h̲rt* (CIH 334/7), cf. *JaDN*, pp. 165-66. This publication is not referred to by *RycPRSA*, p. 91, note 38. – *qrb* and *qrs*: place names; notice the alliteration; for *qrb*, cf. *qurb* in *WüR*, p. 171 A; for *qrs*, cf. *qurâs* in *l.c.*, p. 170 B; *qrb* is also known as personal name in Thamudic (cf. *vdBrIT*, e.g., p. 58: HU 42: *hqrb*) and in Safaitic (cf. *LiSI*, p. 342 A). – *wt̲r*: the 4th form is frequently mentioned in inscriptions commemorating buildings and with the meaning "to lay the foundation of" (e.g., RÉS 4196/2); cf. *BeSI*, pp. 9-10; here, cf. Arabic *wat̲ara* "to flatten, tread, trample upon"; *ʾwt̲r* "flat ground" (RÉS 4351/3) must be compared with the preceding form. – *bʾr*, cf. *CoRoC*, p. 111 A and *JeHoDISO*, p. 32: *bʾr*.

L. 13: the first letter of the line, *w*, is certain (contrary to *RyISA*, *l.c.*, pp. 143 and 146). – *yhbšr*, cp. the clan name *ybšr* (CIH 939/2). – *šddm*, CIH 326/2 and the Arabic personal name *šidâd* (cf. *SlGaVNPA*, p. 12 A). – *lfyw/bnhw*=*ylfyw/bhw* in line 8. – *d̲*(ᶜ)*sm*: the *w* instead of ᶜ is certain on the stone (contrary to *RyISA*, *l.c.*). – *bytn/rʾs* and *hyt/hgrn/rʾsw* (*sic* on the stone): the determinative adjective *hyt* indicates that there is question of only one proper name which was the name of both the clan and the city. However, both *rʾs* and *rʾsw* are followed in the text by /*w*; it is therefore not possible to decide between haplography (for *rʾs/w*...) or dittography (for *rʾsw/w*...). *rʾs* "head, top", is frequently used in compound proper names (cf. *WüR*, p. 97 B-C and *PhAHL*, p. 758 A); cf. also the Arabic personal names (*bin ar-*)*raʾîs* (cf. *SlGaVNPA*, p. 10 B); for the ending *w*, cf. *ʾlmqhw* (cf. *JaP*, p. 62, note 13) and *nrw* (cf. *l.c.*, p. 100, note 375); cf. also the first name *rʾshw* in CIH 110/1 (cf. commentary on Ja 752/9-10: *mhrt*). – *ʾwmr* (not *ʾ*[*n*]*mr*, as proposed by *RyISA*, *l.c.*, pp. 143, 146, and 162), internal plural of *ʾmr* (cp. Arabic *ʾamr*, pl. *ʾawâmiru* "command, order") with the meaning of "post of command"; cf. *ʾmr*, either a verb "to command" (e.g., Ja 520/5) or noun "order" (Ja 671/16); cf. also *JeHoDISO*, pp. 17-18: *ʾmr*$_{\text{I}}$. – *sbᶜw* is preceded by the dividing stroke and not by *h* (cf. *RyISA*, *l.c.*, pp. 143 and 146); cf. *CoRoC*, p. 193 B. – *snfrm*, and not ....*rm* (cf. *RyISA*, *l.c.*,), tribe name the plural *nisba* of which is *snfrtn* (RÉS 4919+CIH 537/3). – *qrn*, cf. *CoRoC*, p. 234 A and also Ḥimâ/10; pl. *ʾqrn* (Ja 660/17); for the verb, cf., e.g., Ja 643/23. – *šym*, for the etymology, cf. *CoRoC*, p. 248 B and *StSESA*, p. 530: "to place, set up"; e.g., Ja 874, Qat; RÉS 4845 bis is too fragmentary to justify *RÉS*' translation as "préposer"; cf. plural *šmw*, e.g., in RÉS 4632/2 and Kawkab 1/2, or *šymw* (*scriptio plena*) in Ja 120, Qat; the dual *šmy* in Ja 491/1 "to inaugurate"; the meaning of "to assure" is attested, e.g., in CIH 349/6 and Ja 611/16-17. According to *BeSI* (p. 2), "the semantic relation" of the noun *šym* "patron" (cf. also *MoNTA*, p. 133) to the verb *šym* "to place" "is not clear". But, the Arabic verb *šâma* (*i*) has both the material and moral meaning; the 1st form "to place, insert" and "to hope (for the favors of someone)" and the 4th form "to cause to hope"; cf. also the expression *ǧamîl aš-šiyam* "a good-natured man" (cf. also *DoSDA*, I, p. 812 A). *LaGD* (p. 2110) also mentions *šâma* "to insert" and notes that ᶜOmânî *šîmat* means "help, aid".

Ll. 13-14: *ẓlm*, and not *nʾḏ* (cf. *RyISA*, *l.c.*, pp. 143, 146, 149, and 151), name of a city mentioned in RÉS 4815/2, 4, and 8 (cf. *WiHöBGS*, p. 29 and note 3), as a point of orientation (cf. A. F. L. Beeston, in *JRAS*, 1948, pp. 177-80 and in *AfO*, 17 [1954-1955], p. 162 B, who practically denies the existence of the city *ẓlm*); the city of Yat̲il was also used with the same purpose.

L. 14: *hwkb*, cf. *JaASAB*, p. 162, commentary on CIH 407/21. – *mqtt*, and not *mftt* (cf. *RyISA*, *l.c.*, pp. 143, 146, and 163). – *ysr*, and not *hṣr* (cf. *RyISA*, *l.c.*) – *šrḥ*, and not *štrḥ* (cf. *RyISA*, *l.c.*), cf. commentary on Ja 570/13; here, with the meaning of "to reinforce", operation intended to give him success. – *fẖrhmw*, and not...*hmw* (cf. *RyISA*, *l.c.*, pp. 143 and 146); cf. Accadian *paḫāru*, 2nd form "to gather together, muster" (cf. *BeBAG*, p. 220 B) and Ẓofâr *fóẖra* "zusammen" (cf. *RhVDD*, p. 45 A and commentary); *hmw* after *fẖr* relates to *mqtt*, etc. – *lsbʾ*, and not *lsbᶜ* (cf. *RyISA*, pp. 143, 146, and 163). – *ṯhb*, also in Ja 577/9, 616/18, 20, 631/14, and 643/8; the form *ṯhb* must thus be maintained and not be corrected to *(y)hb* (cf. *RyISA*, *l.c.*): "le lapicide a gravé fautivement *wṯhbhw*" (p. 163). The metathesis of the first two radical letters cannot be applied here, as in *wšᶜ* = *šwᶜ* (cf. commentary on Ja 561 bis/6), for the metathesis *ṯhb* = *hṯb* would imply the first radical letter and the preformant *h*. I suggest considering *ṯhb* as the 1st form of *ṯwb* (*h* = *w*), which is always used in the 2nd form. The meaning of *ṯwb*, 1st form "to return", is identical with that of *ṯhb* in the present text as well as in Ja 643/8; in Ja 577/9, 616/18, 20, and 631/14, *ṯhb* has the derived meaning of "to return according to the expectation of someone", that is to say "to satisfy someone". – *nkf* (not *nkśm*, as in *RyISA*, *l.c.*, pp. 143, 146, and 163), also in Ja 643/9: cf. both Daṯînah (cf. *LaGD*, p. 2823) and modern Ḥaḍr (cf. *LaH*, p. 726): "réunir, mobiliser (terme militaire)"; *nkf* is a *maṣdar* and could be translated "in good order" as opposed to "in disarray, in confusion". – *wgbʾw* instead of *w....w* (cf. *RyISA*, *l.c.*, pp. 143 and 146). – *nḥbw* instead of *h[s]bᶜw* (cf. *RyISA*, *l.c.*). – *ṯbr/hyt/hg[rn/*15 signs*/wylfyw/bhyt/]hgrn* instead of "*hʾ*[30 caractères]" (cf. *RyISA*, *l.c.*). – *byn*, e.g., CIH 609/3; cf. Arabic *bayn* "distance between two things" or *bîn* "land, borders, frontiers". – *hrn*, and not *hdn* (cf. *RyISA*, *l.c.*, pp. 143, 146, 149, 151, and 163); a city of the same name is located about 30 km. southwest of Qarnâwû. – *ḏmr*, cf. *WiHöBGS*, e.g., p. 21. *ḏmr* is second personal name in RÉS 4856/1, Ḥaḍr: *–/klbm/ḏmr/whwfᶜ*(line 2)*ṯt/–*. – *wyśmkn* instead of *whš......* (cf. *RyISA*, *l.c.*, pp. 143 and 146).

L. 15: *mʾnm/wʾlfm/ʾsdm/wʾrbᶜy/ʾfrsm* instead of *.ʾ.m⌈/⌉wʾl../ʾsd⌈m⌉/..........rsm* (cf. *RyISA*, *l.c.*); for *ʾlf*, cf. the Western Semitic cognates in *JeHoDISO*, p. 15: *ʾlf*$_{\text{III}}$. – *sṯ(t)* or *sdṯ(t)* are the two ordinary forms (cf. *CoRoC*, pp. 200 B and 193-94, and *HöASG*, pp. 131-32); cf. also *st* (Ingrams 1/3, Ḥaḍr), which is closer to Arabic (cf. *JaIHI*, p. 100). – *ᶜšr*, cf. *StSESA*, pp. 529-30 and *BePESA*, p. 2. – *ẖms/mʾnm*, cf. commentary on Ja 572/4. – *ʾb[lm/wʾšᶜb/ḥmyrm/w]rdmn/wmḏḥ[ym/* 33 signs*]krʾ* instead of "[60 caractères]*rʾ*" (cf. *RyISA*, *l.c.*). *ʾbl* (cf. *CoRoC*, p. 99 B), either singular (e.g., Ja 535/2), pl. *ʾʾbl* (e.g., Ja 665/26). 16 signs are missing between *ʾb* and *rdmn*; the proposed restoration perfectly fits the blank. – *bwsṭ*, cf. Ja 567/6 and commentary on lines 5-6. – *śmkw* instead of *yṣrhw* (cf. *RyISA*, *l.c.*, pp. 144 and 146). – *mhsknm* instead of *mh.⌈t⌉.m* (cf. *RyISA*, *l.c.*, pp. 144, 146, and 163), participle of the 4th form of *skn*; cf. Arabic *sakana*, 4th form "to render *or* be poor, miserable"; here, probably with a meaning such as in Arabic *miskîn* "wretched".

Ll. 15-16: *bʾnḥ*(line 16)*rm/wṭrydn* instead of ⌈*bn/hgrn*⌉(line 16)*.rf/wb/rydn* (cf. *RyISA*, *l.c.*).

L. 16: *ṭrydm*, cf. the Arabic names of a man *ṭarîd* (cf. *SlGaVNPA*, p. 49 A), *ṭarûd*, *maṭrûd*, and of a clan *banû maṭrûd* (cf. *WüID*, 318/4, 279/9, and 187/4 respectively). – *ʾḥmrn* instead of *ʾḥbšn* (cf. *RyISA*, *l.c.*, pp. 144, 146, and 149). – *fʾsyw* (instead of *wʾsyw*, as *RyISA*, *l.c.*, pp. 144 and 146) (e.g., RÉS 4356/4), cf. *CoRoC*, p. 108 B, *StSESA*, p. 535 and *BeSI*, p. 85 (commentary on RÉS 4193/8). In RÉS 4084/8, *tʾsynhw* "seine Genesung" (so *MoMiHI*, p. 42), but "sa consolation(?)" (as *RÉS*, VII, p. 75), must be related to Arabic *ʾasiya* "to grieve, mourn" and *ʾāsin*, *ʾaswânu* and *ʾasyânu* "grieving, mourning", and was preceded by a verb such as "to take away" or "to alleviate". – *wky*, cf. Arabic *wikâyat* "leaning-stick"; *wky* could be translated "support(?)". – *lhmw/wkym/ᶜdy/ḏt* instead of *lk....ḏt* (cf. *RyISA*, *l.c.*). – *mẓʾw/ẖlf/[hg]rn/* instead of *m..f/w.. ../* (cf. *RyISA*, *l.c.*). – *bᶜlyh[mw/*20 signs*]hl[w]/m[*28 signs*]m* instead of "*bᶜly*[60 caractères]" (cf. *RyISA*, *l.c.*). – *mṣrᶜt*, cf. commentary on Ja 567/8.

577 – Yellowish slightly grayish sandstone. – MaMB 219.

STONE: thickness on the right side: 28 cm. (top) and 26.1 (bottom), on the left side: 28.3 cm. (top) and 26.3 (bottom). – *Front:* slightly damaged; 1.57 m. × 45.9 cm. (right) and 45.5 (left). – INSCRIPTION: letter height: 1.8 cm.; and space between the lines: 0.4 cm.; end of the continuation of Ja 576.

1 *fhrg/frshw/wḥ(ẓ)/fᶜdww/lhgrn/ẕḫnm/whrgw/bn/*
mṣyrt/ḥmyrm/wrdmn/wmḏhym/mhrgm/ḏᶜsm/
wmlkn/ʾlšrḥ/yḥḏb/wʾsd/sttqf/(.)nm[..]/bn/

ẖms[hw/]wʾfrshw/ftʾwlw[/ᶜ]dy/[...h]mw/
ḏtrznn/bwfym/wḥmdm/wmhrgtm/ḏᶜsm/[...
2 *bᶜm/ḥyf/ḥyfhmw/šmr/ḏrydn/wʾšᶜb/ḥmyrm/wldᶜm/*
wfẖrw/bᶜbr/šmr/ḏrydn/wmṣrhw/ltqdm(n)/kl/
hmt/ymtn/wtṣnᶜw/bwṣt/hgrn/ḏmr/wgbʾw/
wtʾwlw/ᶜdy/hgrn/nᶜḍ/wbn/hgrn/nᶜḍ/fgbʾw/
whṣrw/ᶜdy/byn/hgrnhn/wlfyw/bhw/mh[rgtm/
wsbym/wġnmm/ḏᶜsm/wbnh]
3 *w/ftʾwlw/ᶜdy/hgrn/ṣnᶜw/bwfym/wḥmdm/wʾḥllm/*
wsbym/wġnmm/wmltm/ḏᶜsm/wbᶜdhw/fᶜdw/
grmt/wld/ngšyn/wbᶜmhw/ʾḥzb/ḥbšt/wḏshrtm/
ḍrm/bᶜly/ʾmlk/sbʾ/ḥgn/kstṣrhmw/šmr/ḏrydn/
wẖmrhmw/ʾlmqhṯhwnbᶜlʾwm/ḥsm/kl/hm[t/
... .../šmr]
4 *ḏrydn/wbᶜdhw/fhdrkhmw/mlkn/ʾlšrḥ/yḥḍb/*
wbᶜmhw/ḏbn/ʾqwlhw/wʾlfm/ʾsdm/bn/ẖmshmw/
wsṯ/wᶜšry/ʾfrsm/lnqm/bḥrbt/ḥrbw/whṣrn/šmr/
ḏrydn/bᶜḏ/gzm/wslm/kwn/byn/ʾmlk/sbʾ/
wḥbšt/wḥrbw/ẖmst/ʾdyrm/bn[/... .../wlfy]
5 *w/bnhmw/mhrgtm/wsbym/wmltm/wġnmm/ḏᶜsm/*
wyhᶜnw/bᶜlyhmw/ḏbn/ʾḥbšn/wḏshrtm/
wyhdrkhmw/ᶜnt/hmt/ʾḥbšn/bkdnn/ḏʾḥdqm/
wytqdmw/bᶜmhmw/rglm/wẖmrhmw/ʾlmqh/
hsḥtn/wṯbr/ᶜnt/hmt/ʾḥbšn/wytʾwln/mlkn/ʾlšrḥ/
yḥḍb/[wʾqwlhw/wẖms]
6 *hw/ᶜdy/hgrn/ṣnᶜw/bwfym/wḥmdm/wʾḥllm/*
wsbym/wmltm/wġnmm/ḏᶜsm/wḥmdm/bḏẖmrhmw/
ʾlmqh/škr/wnqm/grmt/wld/ngšyn/mlk/ʾksmn/
btnblt/ḥbl/ʾsd/nbl/bᶜbrhw/ʾmlk/sbʾ/wḥmdm/bḏt/
hwšᶜhmw/ʾlmqh/bškr/ʾysn/ṣḥbm/bn/[gyšm/...
7 *ys/bn/mlk/ʾlmqh/wyhysrw/mqtwyhmw/nwfm/bn/*
hmdn/wḏġymn/wbᶜmhmw/ḏbn/mqtythmw/
wḏbn/šᶜbynhn/ḥšdm/wġymn/wẖmrhmw/ʾlmqh/
tʾwln/mqtwyhmw/nwfm/bwfym/wʾsd/sttqf/
bᶜmhw/wškr/hwt/ʾysn/ṣḥbm/bn/gyšm/wʾwlw/
rʾshw/wy[dyhw/w...
8 *šᶜbn/ẖwln/gddm/wḥmdm/bḏt/hwšᶜhmw/ʾlmqh/*
bwḏᶜ/šᶜbn/ngrn/bkn/qsdw/wnzᶜ/ydm/bn/
ʾmrʾhmw/ʾmlk/sbʾ/bᶜbr/ʾḥbšn/wyḍbʾn/bᶜlyhmw/
mlkn/ʾlšrḥ/yḥḍb/wḏbn/ʾqwlhw/wẖmshw/
wʾfrshw/wyẓwrw/hgrn/ẓrbn/ṯny/wrẖn/wfẖr[w/
bᶜbr/...
9 *ṯhbhmw/kyṣwynn/ʾmrʾhmw/ʾmlk/sbʾ/khᶜsmw/*
hẖṯʾn/wwᶜdhmw/kyṣrynhmw/mlk/ḥḍrmwt/
bᶜbr/ʾmrʾhmw/ʾmlk/sbʾ/wwᶜdhmw/šᶜbn/ngrn/
ṯny/wrẖyn/ltṣryn/bᶜbr/ʾmrʾhmw/ʾmlk/sbʾ
wytʾwln/mlkn/ʾlšrḥ/yḥḍb/wʾqwlhw/wẖmshw/
ᶜdy/hgr[n/... ...ng]
10 *rn/wysmᶜw/knblw/hmw/ʾgrn/bᶜbr/ʾḥzb/ḥbšt/*
lhᶜnn/ᶜqb/ngšyn/bhgrn/ngrn/wšᶜbn/ngrn/whmw/
fnẓrw/mwᶜd/ʾgrn/ltṣryn/bᶜbr/ʾmrʾhmw/ʾmlk/
sbʾ/whẖwhw/bmwᶜdhmw/lnṣr/ᶜnt/ʾḥbšn/
wbᶜdhw/fysrw/mqtwyyhmw/nwfm/bn/hmdn/
wḏġymn/wk[... ...h]
11 *mw/wnṣrhmw/wḏbn/šᶜbnhn/ḥšdm/wġymn/wʾrbᶜ*
ᶜšrhw/ʾfrsm/wyḥrbhmw/bsrnhn/ngrn/wyʾtyw/
bᶜbr/mrʾyhmw/mlknhn/ᶜdy/hgrn/ṣnᶜw/bwfym/
wḥmdm/wmhrgtm/wsbym/wġnmm/ḏᶜsm/
wbᶜdhw/fyḍbʾn/bᶜlyhmw/mlkn/ʾlšrḥ/yḥḍb/
wbᶜmhw/[... .../bywm/h]
12 *ġrw/bᶜlyhmw/bn/mġwnhmw/ḏsrn/rkbtn/wylfyhmw/*
kl/mrʾs/wʾḥrr/šᶜbn/ngrn/bmslmn/wyhrgw/bn/hmt/
ʾgrn/mhrgm/ḏᶜqdm/wbṯlṯm/ywmm/ffẖrw/hmw/
ʾgrn/ṯdrᶜm/bᶜbr/mrʾhmw/ʾlšrḥ/yḥḍb/mlk/sbʾ/
wḏrydn/wᶜqbhmw/ḥbšyn/sbqlm/s[... ...h]
13 *w/wʾsd/hbʾsw/whštʾw/qsdtn/fnblw/bᶜmhw/wwhbw/*
bnyhmw/wbnthmw/ʾwṯqm/wḥmlw/ᶜdy/hgrn/
ṣrbn/ᶜqb/wqh/mrʾhmw/mlkn/ʾlšrḥ/yḥḍb/lᶜqb/
bhyt/hgrn/ṣrbn/wsryhw/ngrn/wtgᶜr/kl/ḏhḍrᶜ/
bn/hgrn/ṣrbn/wsryhw/[ngrn/...
14 *ʾmlk/sbʾ/bḍbyʾ/ḍbʾ/bᶜlyhmw/mlkn/ʾlšrḥ/yḥḍb/*
wʾgyš/wġzwy/hysr/lḍbʾ/bᶜlyhmw/wyhrgw/bn/
šᶜbn/ngrn/ʾrbᶜt/wᶜšry/wtsᶜ/mʾnm/ʾsdm/wṯny/
wsṯy/wẖms/mʾnm/ʾsbym/wyqmᶜw/bsrnhn/ngrn/
ṯmn/wsṯy/hgrm/wygbḏ[w/... ...s]
15 *ṯy/ʾʾlfm/ʾᶜmdm/wytrw/sbᶜ/wtsᶜy/ʾbʾrm/wḥmdm/bḏt/*
hwšᶜ/ʾlmqhṯhwnbᶜlʾwm/ᶜbdhw/ʾlšrḥ/yḥḍb/mlk/
sbʾ/wḏrydn/stʾwln/hwʾ/wʾqwlhw/wẖmshw/
wʾfrshw/wrkbhw/wḥṣqhmw/bn/kl/hn[t/ḍbyʾn/
...
16 *sbʾw/bᶜly/ʾmlkm/wẖmsm/wʾšᶜbm/ḏtnšʾw/bᶜlyhmw/*
ḍrm/wytʾwlw/bn/kl/hnt/ḍbyʾn/wsbyʾn/bwfym/
wḥmdm/wmhrgtm/wsbym/wġnmm/ḏhrḍw/ᶜbdhw/
ʾlšrḥ/yḥḍb/mlk/sbʾ/wḏrydn/wḥmdm/bḏt/
ẖmrhmw/ʾ[lmqhṯhwnbᶜlʾwm/... ...bytn/sl]
17 *ḥn/wġndn/wmḥrmnhn/whgrn/mryb/wṣnᶜw/wnšqm/*
wkl/mqwlhmw/bwfym/bn/kl/ʾḍrr/tnšʾ/
bᶜlyhmw/wlḏt/yzʾn/ʾlmqhṯhwnbᶜlʾwm/hwšᶜn/
ᶜbdyhw/ʾlšrḥ/yḥḍb/wʾẖyhw/yʾzl/byn/mlky/sbʾ/
wḏrydn/wẖmshmw/ẖm[s/sbʾ/... .../ᶜbd]
18 *yhw/ʾlšrḥ/yḥḍb/wʾẖyhw/yʾzl/byn/mlky/sbʾ/*
wḏrydn/bwḏᶜ/wṯbr/whmsn/whkmsn/kl/ḍrm/
ḏyzʾn/yfᶜhmw/bn/šʾmt/wymnt/wbḥrm/wybsm/
wḥmdm/bḏhwšᶜhmw/bmqyḥt/ṣdqm/wḥmdm/
bḏt/ẖmr/ʾlmqh/ᶜbdhw/ʾlšrḥ/yḥḍb/bnᶜm/ʾlbb/
ẖmshw/ẖms/sbʾ/b[...
19 *ʾlšrḥ/yḥḍb/wlḏt/nᶜmt/wtnᶜmn/l(h)mw/wlbytn/*
slḥn/wġndn/wlṯbr/wwḏᶜ/wḏrᶜn/whms/whkmsn/
kl/ḍr/wšnʾ/ʾlšrḥ/yḥḍb/wʾẖyhw/yʾzl/byn/mlky/sbʾ/
wḏrydn/bny/frᶜm/ynhb/mlk/sbʾ/bᶜṯtr/whbs/
wʾlmqhṯhwnbᶜlʾwm/wbḏt/ḥmym/wb[ḏt/bᶜdn...

1 so] his horse Wâḥi(ẓ) was killed; and they then went to the city [of] Zaẖnum and they deprived the expeditionary forces of Ḥimyarum and Radmân

and Muḏḥayum of a war trophy, which was desired; and as for the king ʾIlšaraḥ Yaḥḍub and the soldiers he took along. .from [his] army and his cavalry, they went back to [t]heir [. . .] of Taraznân in safety and (with) praise and war trophies, which was desired [. . .

2 because of the injustice [which] Šamir, he of Raydân, and the tribes of Ḥimyarum, the children of ʿAmm, had committed against them; and they gathered together with Šamir, him of Raydân, and his expeditionary corps in order to move forward during all those days; and they retrenched in the midst of the city [of] Ḏamar; and they returned and went back to the city [of] Naʿiḍ; and from the city [of] Naʿiḍ, they turned and set out toward the territory between the two cities, and they brought back from there war [trophies and captives and booty, which was desired; and from the]re

3 they went back to the city [of] Ṣanʿâʾ in safety and [with] praise and animals and captives and booty and riches, which was desired; and after that, Garmat, the child of the Neguš and with him the fighting bands of Ḥabašat and Saharatum went to war against the kings of Sabaʾ just as Šamir, he of Raydân, had called them for help; and ʾIlumquh Ṯahwân, master of ʾAwwâm, had vouchsafed to them to cut into pieces all the[se. . . . . .Šamir,]

4 him of Raydân; and after that, the king ʾIlšaraḥ Yaḥḍub and with him some of his chiefs and one thousand soldiers from their armies and twenty-six horsemen reached them to take vengeance in the battle [in which] they fought and fell upon Šamir, him of Raydân, after the oath and the peace [which] had been between the kings of Sabaʾ and Ḥabašat; and they fought five camps of Bedouins from [. . . . . .; and] they [brought back]

5 from them war trophies and captives and riches and booty, which was desired; and some of the Ḥabašites and Saharatum have assisted against them and reinforcements of these Ḥabašites reached them in the ploughed plain of ʾAḥdaqum, and so they attacked them [with] foot-soldiers; and ʾIlumquh has vouchsafed to them to destroy and crush the reinforcements of these Ḥabašites; and the king ʾIlšaraḥ Yaḥḍub [and his rulers and] his [army] went back

6 to the city [of] Ṣanʿâʾ in safety and (with) praise and animals and captives and riches and booty, which was desired; and in praise because ʾIlumquh has vouchsafed to them to defeat and take vengeance on Garmat, the child of the Neguš, the king of ʾAksûman, because of the messengers [who] have deceived those [whom] the kings of Sabaʾ sent to him; and in praise because ʾIlumquh has assisted them in defeating the adversary Ṣaḥbum, son of [Gayšum,. . .

7 . .from the property of ʾIlumquh; and they sent their high military official Nawfum, of Hamdân and Ġaymân, and with them some of their high military officials and some of their two tribes Ḥâšidum and Ġaymân; and ʾIlumquh has vouchsafed to them [that] their high military official Nawfum came back in safety along with those [whom] he took along with him; and [that] he defeated this adversary Ṣaḥbum, son of Gayšum; and they brought back his head and [his] (hands?) [. . .

8 the tribe Ḫawlân Gaddum; and in praise because ʾIlumquh has assisted them in humiliating the tribe Nagrân, when they revolted and rebelled against their lords, the kings of Sabaʾ, on behalf of the Ḥabašites; and the king ʾIlšaraḥ Yaḥḍub and some of his chiefs and his army and his cavalry fought against them and so they besieged the city [of] Ẓarbân for two months and gathered together [with. . .

9 satisfied them, so weakened their lords, the kings of Sabaʾ by obstinately continuing to seduce into acting wrongfully and in their assurance that the king of Ḥaḍramawt would give them protection against their lords, the kings of Sabaʾ; and the tribe Nagrân assured them for two months that they would supply them with a guard against their lords, the kings of Sabaʾ; and thus the king ʾIlšaraḥ Yaḥḍub and his chiefs and his army went back into [the] city [. . . . . .Na-]

10 grân, and so they agreed that they would send these mercenaries to the fighting bands of Ḥabašat in order to assist the representative of the Neguš in the city [of] Nagrân and the tribe Nagrân; and so as for them, they took care of gathering the mercenaries in order to provide a guard against their lords, the kings of Sabaʾ, and [they took care of] his association with their gathering in order to help the reinforcements of the Ḥabašites; and after that, their two high military officials Nawfum, of Hamdum and Ġaymân, and K[. . . . . .] sent

11 [t]heir [. . . . . .] and their support troop and some of the two tribes Ḥâšidum and Ġaymân and fourteen of his horsemen, and he fought them in the two wâdî-side valleys [of] Nagrân, and they came back to their two lords, the two kings, into the city [of] Ṣanʿâʾ in safety and (with) praise and war trophies and captives and booty, which was desired; and after that, the king ʾIlšaraḥ Yaḥḍub and with him [. . . . . .] fought against them [when]

12 they [ma]de a raid against them from their hiding-place, that of the wâdî-side valley [of] Rakbatân and deprived them of all the chiefs and the freemen of the tribe Nagrân in Maslamân and they deprived these mercenaries of a war trophy according to [their] oath; and the third day they gathered them,

these mercenaries, in submission to their lord ʾIlšaraḥ Yaḥḍub, king of Sabaʾ and Raydân, and the Ḥabašite Sabqalum .[...] watched them [...] his [... ...]

13 and the soldiers [who] acted harmfully and initiated this revolt; so they were sent with him and gave their sons and their daughters [as] firm pledges and they were taken up into the city [of] Ṣarbân after their lord, the king ʾIlšaraḥ Yaḥḍub had ordered [them] to be guarded in this city [of] Ṣarbân, and its two wâdî-side valleys, Nagrân; and he has kept under guard all that he had subjugated from the city [of] Ṣarbân and its two wâdî-side valleys [Nagrân...

14 the kings of Sabaʾ in the engagements [that] the king ʾIlšaraḥ Yaḥḍub and the troops and the two raid-corps [whom] he sent to fight against them, fought against them; and so they killed from the tribe Nagrân nine hundred and twenty-four soldiers and [took away] five hundred and sixty-two captives and they subjugated in the two wâdî-side valleys [of] Nagrân, sixty-eight towns and plundered [... ...six-]

15 ty thousand naturally watered fields and they leveled ninety-seven wells; and in praise because ʾIlumquh Ṯahwân, master of ʾAwwâm, has assisted His worshipper ʾIlšaraḥ Yaḥḍub, king of Sabaʾ and Raydân, in bringing back him and his chiefs and his infantry and his cavalry and his camelry and their prisoner keepers from all tho[se engagements...

16 they] fought against kings and armies and tribes which rose up against them in war; and so they came back from all these engagements and encounters in safety and (with) praise and war trophies and captives and booty, which pleased His worshipper ʾIlšaraḥ Yaḥḍub, king of Sabaʾ and Raydân; and in praise because ʾI[lumquh Ṯahwân, master of ʾAwwâm] has vouchsafed to them [... ...the two houses Sal-]

17 ḥân and Ġandân and the two temples and the cities [of] Mârib and Ṣanʿâʾ and Našqum and every ruler of them in safety from all the wars [which] arose against them; and that ʾIlumquh Ṯahwân, master of ʾAwwâm, may continue to assist His two worshippers, ʾIlšaraḥ Yaḥḍub and his brother Yaʾzil Bayyin, the two kings of Sabaʾ and Raydân, and their army, the ar[my of Sabaʾ,... ...] His two [worshippers]

18 ʾIlšaraḥ Yaḥḍub and his brother Yaʾzil Bayyin, the two kings of Sabaʾ and Raydân, in humiliating and crushing and breaking down and withering every enemy who would continue to raise up against them, from north and south and sea and land; and in praise because He has assisted them with perfect profits; and in praise because ʾIlumquh has vouchsafed to His worshipper ʾIlšaraḥ Yaḥḍub to please the hearts of his army, the army of Sabaʾ .[...

19 ʾIlšaraḥ Yaḥḍub; and that it may have been pleasant and be pleasant for them and the two houses Salḥân and Ġandân; and that He may crush and humiliate and humble and break down and wither every foe and enemy of ʾIlšaraḥ Yaḥḍub and his brother Yaʾzil Bayyin, the two kings of Sabaʾ and Raydân, the two sons of Fariʿum Yanhub, king of Sabaʾ. By ʿAṯtar and Hawbas and ʾIlumquh Ṯahwân, master of ʾAwwâm, and by Ḏât-Ḥimyâm and by [Ḏât-Baʿdânum...

L. 1: *wḥ*(.): from the last letter remains a rectangle without bottom; thus ʾ, *ẓ*, *k*, *s*, or *ṣ*; I propose restoring *wḥ*(*ẓ*); cf. the Arabic names of a place, of a clan, and of a man *wuḥâẓat* (cf. *WüR*, p. 226 C, p. 261 A and *LöHSM*, p. 82 B respectively); the proper name *wḥk* is attested in Thamudic (cf. *vdBrTTPN*, p. 101: Ph 346 a). – *z̲h̲nm*, cf. *z̲h̲nn*, name of a man (RÉS 3878/16, Qat) and of a family (Ja 290, Qat). – *stṯqf*, 10th form of *ṯqf*; the 4th form of which is mentioned in CIH 350/13 (cf. *BeSI*, p. 43); cf. Arabic *ṯaqifa* "to meet, find, get"; the 10th form may be translated "to take to one's self; select for one's self". – (.)*nm*[..]: from the 1st sign only remains the lower half of a vertical stroke belonging to a letter such as *g*, *y*, *l*, or *n*. – *trznn*, cf. the names of a man *rznm* (RÉS 3470; D. H. Müller's reading as *rbnm* is erroneous) and *rzn* (e.g., Ja 811/1) and of a clan *mhrzn* (CIH 287/1; cf. *NaNN*, p. 72); cf. also the Arabic names of a clan *razân* (cf. *WüR*, p. 245 B), of a man *razîn* (cf., e.g., *GoAT*, pp. 193-94), (*ʾibn*) *razîn* (cf. *WüR*, p. 430), *ruwayzin* (cf. *HeBN*, p. 25 B) and *abû razîn* (cf. *SaIS*, pp. 77-78) and of a woman *raznah*, *ruzînah*, *ruzûn* (cf. *HeBN*, *l.c.*).

L. 2: *ḥyf*; for the verb, cf. RÉS 3958/2 which mentions several heavy construction works; here, cf. Arabic *ḥâfa* (i) "to act wrongfully, unjustly" and *ḥayf* "hostility, injustice"; *ḥyf*/*ḥyfhmw* "the injustice by which he has acted unjustly against them" or "the injustice he has committed against them". – *ymt*, pl. of *ywm*; cf. *HöASG*, p. 106. – *tṣnʿ*, 5th form of *ṣnʿ* (e.g., CIH 353/6 "to retrench"); the 4th form, *hṣnʿ*, is mentioned in Ja 585/6; cf. *CoRoC*, pp. 224-25 for a summary on *ṣnʿ*; cf. also *RoVSAY*, p. 310. Further, for the 2nd form *ṣnʿ*, cf. Ḥimâ/10 and Kawkab 1/8 "to strengthen"; the preceding interpretation is in the line of the already known forms, either verb or noun. However, the 4th form, *hṣnʿ* (Ja

585/6) must be related to Aramaic *ṣâna*ᶜ "to hide, retire" and hiphîl *hiṣnîᶜa* "to withdraw" (cf. *JaDT*, p. 1292 B) and be translated "to hold back" (cf. also introduction on *ṣn*ᶜ in *KoBaLVTL*, p. 809 A). – The restoration at the end is probable; *ḏhrḏwhmw* (e.g., Ja 576/6) instead of *ḏᶜsm* is less probable, since *ḏᶜsm* is much more often mentioned in the present text.

L. 3: *grmt*, personal name, but family name in RÉS 3735/2, Min; *grmt/wld/ngšyn*, cf. perfect parallel *bygt/wld/ngšyn* (Ja 631/21); cf. also the Arabic names of a man *ǧarm*, and of a clan *banû ʾaǧram* and *banû ǧârim* (cf. *WüID*, 314/6, 305/5 and 117/14 respectively); *ngšy*, cp. the Arabic name of a man *an-naǧâšîy* (cf. *WüID*, 239/6).

L. 4: *ḫmshmw*: the personal pronoun refers to *ʾqwl*.

L. 5: *bkdnn/ḏʾḥdqm*, cp. *bsrn/ḏʾẓwr* in Ja 578/19 (cf. commentary on Ja 575/5).

L. 6: *ḥmdm/bḏ*=*ḥmdm/bḏt* (cf. commentary on Ja 559/4). – *bᶜbrhw*: *hw* refers to *grmt*. – *ʾys* (also in line 7 and *ʾs*, e.g., in Ja 585/14): *CIH* (I, p. 329 B, commentary on CIH 308/17; cf. *RhIGC*, pp. 69-75; for CIH 308/17, cf. *HöASG* p. 157) affirms that *ʾys*, as Hebrew *ʾîš* (cf. also, e.g., W. S. LaSOR, in *The Jewish Quarterly Review*, 48 [1957], p. 165, and *LeESAC*, p. 10) is another form of *ʾns*=Hebrew *ʾĕnôš*; cf. also *BeSI* (p. 31), *BeFSTI* (p. 278), *BeNL*, VI, pp. 316-17 and note 20, and *UlCSH*, p. 196. However, the verb *ʾys* is attested in RÉS 4193/8 (cf. *BeSI*, p. 85), where it is related to Arabic *ʾayisa* "to despair" and translated "to be at a disadvantage". Further, the 5th form, *tʾys* "to give help" is mentioned, e.g., in Ja 629/35. Furthermore, in all the texts from Maḥram Bilqîs, CIH 429/6 and RÉS 3992/14, *ʾys*, or *ʾs* in *scriptio defectiva*, indicates an "opponent, adversary". Since some words have two opposite meanings (e.g., *ʾrḫ*), *ʾys*, whether noun or verb, in all probability refers to Arabic *ʾâsa* or *āsa* "to give a present, a retribution" (*maṣdar*: *ʾaws* and *ʾiyâs*); 10th form "to ask for gift, help". In a text such as CIH 308/17, *ʾys* has the favorable meaning as the 5th form *tʾys*, and may be translated "ally". Cf. also the 1st name of a man *ʾysn* (RÉS 4107/1, where the beginning of the line is *ʾysn/⌈ʾby⌉dᶜ*). – *ṣḥbm*: *ṣḥb*, verb and noun in Ja 560/11; cf. the Arabic names of a man *ṣâḥib* (cf., e.g., *VNIA*, p. 337 B), *(aṣ-)ṣâḥib* (cf. *WüR*, p. 475), of a person *ṣiḥâb* (cf. *SlGaVNPA*, p. 46 B and of a place *ṣâḥabat* (cf. *MüHG*, p. 68 B); cf. also the Thamudic *ṣḥb* (cf. *vdBrTTPN*, p. 99: Ph 345 bis f). – *gyšm*, cf. the noun *gyš* "(irregular) troop" (cf. commentary on line 14, below) and Arabic *ǧayšân*, name of a man (cf. *SaIS*, p. 44 B), of a tribe (cf. *WüR*, p. 242 B) and of a place (cf. *l.c.*, p. 64 C), *ʾal-ǧayš*, place name (cf. *l.c.*), and also *ʾabû l-ǧayš*, name of a man (cf. *l.c.*, p. 369); cf. also the Thamudic personal name *gyšhd* (cf. *vdBrIT*, p. 303: Jsa 549).

L. 7: *mlk* with the meaning "property, estate" is rendered as plural, "possessions" by both A. F. L. Beeston (cf. *Orientalia*, 22 [1953], p. 417) and *RycIMAM* (p. 115), and as singular, "domaine" by *RyET* (p. 10, in Fakhry 9/5); but the latter (cf. *RyISA*, X, p. 287, in Ḥimâ/11) translates *mlkt* also by the same singular noun, and does not mention the form *mlkt* in his commentary (cf. *l.c.*, p. 295). The form *mlkt*, as well as *ʾmlk* (Ja 816/9), may be considered as the plural of *mlk* "property". – *nwfm*, CIH 645/1; for *nwfn* in CIH 125/1-2 (cf. *CIH*, III, p. 330 B and *RyNP*, I, p. 138 A), cf. *JaISAR*, p. 126. – *šᶜbynhn*, *scriptio plena* of *šᶜbnhn* (line 11). – *hwt/ʾysn*=*hwʾ/ʾysn* (Ja 644/10) =*hʾ/ʾsn*(*scriptio defectiva*; Ja 585/15). – *twʾln*, here infinitive as well as in RÉS 3884/6, where it is translated by *RÉS* "l'expédition de"; the restoration at the end of the same line must be discarded, because *bwfym* is followed on the stone by a word divider and the right half of *w*, which introduces another noun. – *ʾwlw*, plural of the 2nd form; cf. CIH 500/1: *b*]*ḏt/ʾwly/bᶜmhmy* "be]cause they brought back with them both". – *y*[..: one might conjecturally propose *ydyhw* "his two hands"; for *yd*, cf. *CoRoC*, p. 162 and *JeHoDISO*, pp. 103-04: *yd*.

L. 8: *gddm*, Ja 616/12; cf. *gddn* in Ja 601/5. – *qsdw*: agreement *ad sensum* with the collective noun *šᶜb*; cf. CIH 541/9-10 and recently Murayǧân/3; cf. *CoRoC*, p. 233 and especially *BeSI*, p. 69, who rightly disregards both *RhAST*'s (II, p. 222) and *RhKTB*'s (I, p. 78, note 4) opinion, which nevertheless is recently accepted again by *RyISA* (X, p. 310), without any reference to *BeSI*'s argumentation. *BeSI* (*l.c.*) suggests translating *qsd* as "yeomen". However, we must reckon with the fact that, in the present collection of texts, both the verb *qsd* (here) and the noun *qsdt* (e.g., line 13) are mentioned as involving the idea of rebellion, revolt; cf. also *CIH*, II, p. 287 A. – *nzᶜ* has nothing to do with *nzᶜ*=*nḍᶜ* (cf. commentary on Ja 561 bis/22), *nzᶜ/ydm/bn* equals Arabic *naza*ᶜ*a yadahu min* (cf. *CIH*, II, p. 289 A): "he drew his hand back from", that is to say "he revolted, rebelled against"; cf. also Arabic *nâzi*ᶜ "deserter, fugitive" (cf. *DoSDA*, II, p. 658 A). – *ẓwr*, cf. Arabic *ẓa*ʾ*ara* "to force, coerce" and Hebrew *ṣwr*, 1st form "to bind, shut in (besieging), besiege" (cf. *KoBaLVTL*, p. 799 A); the South-Arabian noun *ẓwr* is known with the meaning of "column" (cf. *CoRoC*, p. 160 B: Arabic *ẓi*ʾ*r*). – *ẓrbn*, cf. the name of the city *ẓrbm*, e.g., in NaNN 20/5-6.

L. 9: *yṣwynn*, cf. Semitic root *ṣwy* "to dry up, wither" (cf. Arabic and Daṯînah *ṣawā* (i) [cf. *LaGD*, pp. 2158-59], Aramaic *ṣewê* [cf. *JaDT*, p. 1267 A] and Syriac *ṣwô* [cf. *BrDSL*, p. 537 B]); *ṣwy* may be translated "to weaken". – *h*ᶜ*smw*, cf. CIH 429/8. – *hḫṯ*ʾ, 4th form of *ḫṯ*ʾ (cf. *StSESA*, p. 516); CIH 532/3-4 and 612/5; *CIH* (II, p. 249 A) correctly translates it as "to cause, induce to sin"; *BeSI* (p. 49): "to act wrongfully", which is the meaning of the 1st form. – *w*ᶜ*d*: the imperfect of the 1st form is probably attested in RÉS 3703/6, Min "to promise" (cf. also *RoVSAY*, p. 304), and the 4th form *h*ᶜ*d*, e.g., in CIH 541/39 "to give back". – *ṯny*/*wrḫ yn* = *ṯny*/*wrḫn* in line 8. – *tṣry*, 5th form of *ṣry*; cf. commentary on Ja 560/7; here, "to supply with a guard" and "to ask for advice" in Ja 877/7.

L. 10: ʾ*gr*, cf. *JaIMT*, p. 136. – *sm*ᶜ "to listen to, hear" (e.g., Ja 876/5 and 866) and thus "to agree with, accept"; for the ordinary meaning of the noun *sm*ᶜ "witness", cf. *BeFSTI*, p. 273. – ᶜ*qb*, e.g., RÉS 4230/2-3, and the verb, e.g., in RÉS 5040/2, Ḥaḍr; ᶜ*qb*/*ngšyn*, cf. *wld*/*ngšyn* (line 6); cf. Arabic ᶜ*aqb*, plural ʾ*a*ᶜ*qâb* "child, posterity, descendants" and especially Ethiopic "ᶜ*ăqabe mangešt* διάδοχος τοῦ βασιλέως vicarius regis, procurator regni" (cf. *DiLLA*, col. 980); cf. also *BeSI*, p. 86, *HöIAI*, pp. 95-6 and Ja 619/2-3. – *mw*ᶜ*d*, e.g., CIH 541/95; cf. Arabic *maw*ᶜ*id* "meeting, place of the meeting". – *hḫwhw*: 4th form of ʾ*ḫw* "to be brother" (cf. *CoRoC*, p. 102); the personal pronoun is related to ᶜ*qb*/*ngšyn*. – *lnṣr*, for the verb *nṣr* (also, e.g., in Kawkab 1/10: *lyṣrn*), cf. commentary on Ja 576/11.

L. 11: *š*ᶜ*bnhn*, cf. *š*ᶜ*bynhn* in line 7. – ʾ*rb*ᶜ, cf. *JeHoDISO*, p. 23: ʾ*rb*ᶜ. – ᶜ*šrhw*: the pronoun refers to the subject of the sentence as also in *yḫrbhmw*, in opposition to the two tribes mentioned before. – *y*ʾ*tyw*, cf. CIH 290/5; ʾ*ty* (cf. *JeHoDISO*, p. 29: ʾ*ty*) = ʾ*tw* (e.g., Ja 550/2). – *mr*ʾ*yhmw*/*mlknhn*, cf. RÉS 4134/4, also related to the same two kings.

L. 12: *mġwn*, cf. Hebrew *mâ*ᶜ*ôn* "hiding-place, dwelling" (cf. *KoBaLVTL*, p. 545) and Arabic *ma*ᶜ*ân* "place, spot, space". – *rkbtn*, cf. *rkbn*, 2nd name of a man in Ja 570/1, and the Arabic place names *ar-rukbat* and *ar-rkbtyn* (cf. *MüHG*, p. 52 B). – ʾ*ḥrr*, plural of *ḥr*, e.g., RÉS 4912/1, Ḥaḍr; for *ḥr* in Ja 404/3, cf. *JaIMT*, pp. 135 foll.; cf. *CoRoC*, p. 152 B, *BeSI*, p. 18 and *JeHoDISO*, p. 95: *ḥr*. *mslmn*: *mslm* is the name of a man in RÉS 3833, Min, and also in Thamudic (cf. *vdBrTTPN*, p. 134: Ph 367 p/1) and Safaitic (cf. *LiSI*, p. 325 A). – *ḏ*ᶜ*qdm*, cf. Arabic ᶜ*aqd* "pact, alliance, contract, convention" and also the passive participle of the 3rd form *m*ᶜ*qd* "fixed according to contract"; here, the *maṣdar* of ᶜ*aqada* "to take an oath"; *mhrgm*/*ḏ*ᶜ*qdm* means a killing which they bound themselves by oath to do, "killing in fulfilment of an oath". – *ḥbšy*, family name in RÉS 5063; cf. also commentary on Ja 574/3. – *sbqlm*, cf. the verb *sbql* in RÉS 2743/9, Min.

L. 13: *hb*ʾ*s*, 4th form of *b*ʾ*s*; e.g., CIH 494/2. – *hšt*ʾ*w*, 4th form of *št*ʾ, e.g., CIH 308/19 and RÉS 4193/8-9 and *BeSI*, p. 31: "to bring about, initiate". – *qsdt*, noun derived from *qsd*; cf. commentary on *qsd* in line 8. – *bnt*, cf. the Qat expression *bnt*(*y*[/])ʾ*l* in Ja 868/2, 869/2, 871/3, and 872/3 (cf. *JaSQI*, pp. 39-46 and especially 45-6) which may be compared with ᶜ*bdy*/ʾ*lmqh* in RÉS 4967/2-3; for Ja 350/1, Qat. cf. also *JaDME*, pp. 20-21. – The restoration of *t* in *bn*[*th*]*w* in RÉS 4189/3-4 is not, as it is suggested by *GhNQI*, p. 4, note 1, "called for by the name KLBT, taken for a female's name." The lower third of the vertical stroke of *l* (end of line 2) and the upper left corner of *m* (beginning of line 3) are still on the stone; the major part of these two letters must thus be restored. Therefore, *t* and *h*, below *l* and *m* respectively, must also be restored at the end of line 3 and at the beginning of line 4 respectively. Additional note to RÉS 4189: maximum thickness: 9.2 cm.; front: (maximum) 34 cm. × 29.5 cm.; letter height: 5 cm. – *ṣrbn*, cf. the place name *ṣarbat* (cf. *WüR*, p. 135 C), the month *ṣrbn* (RÉS 5085/10) and the noun *ṣrb* "fruits of autumn" (e.g., Ja 617/9). – ᶜ*qb*, conjunction; cf. Arabic ᶜ*uqayba* "a little after; after". – *sryhw*: Fakhry 71/6 interpreted by *RyET* (p. 43) as the dual of *sr* (from the root *syr*) with reference to CIH 506/3 and 546/4 and 10-11, and also to *RhSLG*, I, p. 57 (read 57-58) and III, p. 7 and note 5. The two following expressions, *sr/wmwfr/hgrn* (CIH 506/3) and *syr/wmfr/hgrn* (CIH 546/2) seem to be identical, and *s(y)r* is supposed to indicate the lands belonging to a community (cf. *HaAF*, p. 401; this opinion is accepted by *BeSI*, p. 45 and *RyET*, p. 43). The interpretation of *sr* in the text depends thus on its form and also on the context which indicates whether there is or is not a question of a belonging either to a community or an individual. For instance, *sr* attested twice in CIH 546/4 and 10-11, contrasting with *syr* in line 2 does not seem to be accidental. In Fakhry 71, the two expressions *sq ym/mhšfqm bmrb/wsryhw* (lines 5-6) seems to be recalled by *sqym/mhšfqm/lmryb/wʾsrrhw* (lines 17-18) (notice the difference in writing between *mrb* and *mryb*). Both expressions seem to be identical; and I do not see any reason for giving *sry* and *ʾsrr* two different interpretations (as *RyET*, who translates *sry* in "deux districts" [p. 42] and *ʾsrr* as "versants" [p. 43], without any explanation), since *sry* and *ʾsrr* may very well be the construct dual and plural of *sr* respectively. – *tgʿr*, 5th form of *gʿr* (cf. 2nd masculine personal name *ygʿr* in RÉS 3990/1); cf. Arabic *taǧaʿʿara* "he bound upon his own waist a rope of the kind called *ǧiʿâr*". The context of Ja 665/14-15, *tgʿr/wʾttmn*, suggests the retention for *tgʿr*, of the meaning "to tie, fasten together; to keep tied together". Here, the verb has an adverse meaning, however not in Ja 665/14. The meaning of Hebrew (cf. *KoBaLVTL*, p. 191 A), post-biblical Hebrew (cf. *JaDT*, p. 261 B), and Ugaritic (cf. *GoUM*, p. 252 A, No. 428), "to rebuke" does not fit the two contexts. – *hḍrʿ*, 4th form of *ḍrʿ*; with the usual meaning of "to humble one's self"; cf., e.g., Ja 525/2-3: *hḍrʿt* (feminine); cf. Arabic *ḍaraʿa*, 4th form "to humiliate, win, subjugate" (cf., e.g., RÉS 4190/17).

L. 14: *bḍbyʾ*, e.g., CIH 299/2 and commentary on Ja 555/4. – *gyš* (e.g., RÉS 4658/4 and Ja 616/20), pl. *ʾgyš* (e.g., CIH 26/4 and here) is translated, e.g., "copia" (*CIH*, in CIH 541/25), "Heer" (*HöSSE*, in RÉS 4193/9) and "host" (*BeSI*, p. 84, in RÉS 4193/9); *gyš* alludes indeed to the idea of a band, troop (also *RyISA*, X, p. 271, in JM 9+7/4); cf. also Daṯînah (cf. *LaGD*, p. 331) and Safaitic (cf. *LiSI*, No. 146/4: *gš*). The meaning of "armée" (*RÉS* in RÉS 4658/4), although it could be referred to modern Šanʿâʾite "*ǧäyš esercito*" (cf. *RoAS*, p. 147), is not accurate. The noun *gyš* often has a pejorative meaning (e.g., RÉS 4193/9), but not always (e.g., CIH 541/25 and here). The present context, where *ʾgyš* is mentioned in connection with *ġzwy*, suggests interpreting *gyš* as "(irregular) troop", this opinion seems all the more probable in view of its use by the author of Ja 665, who went fighting with his men, being leader of the Arabs of the king of Sabaʾ, etc. This irregular troop could have been composed only of Bedouins. – *ʾgyš/wġzwy*, cf. *ʾgyš/wġzw* (CIH 26/4; cf. *HöSSE*, p. 11) with the same meaning as here. *ġzw*, cf. Arabic *ġazâ* "to raid" (cf., e.g., *CoRoC*, p. 215 B); *ġzw* is singular (cf. also *HöSSE*, p. 11, in CIH 26/4; cf. also *BeSI*, p. 138) as indicated by the dual constructus *ġzwy* (e.g., here), pl. *ġz(w)t*; *CoRoC* (*l.c.*) interprets *ġzw* and *ġzwt* as plural and singular respectively; *RyISA* (X, pp. 278 and 280, in Murayġân/3) also considers *ġzwt* as a singular. In RÉS 4336/6, the space between the word divider after *ʾlhw* and *zwm* is 18 mm.; the upper side both of the horizontal stroke and the appendix of the *ġ* as well as the upper extremity of the right vertical stroke of that letter, whose width is 15 mm., are visible on my paper squeeze; there is thus no space for *ʾ*; the end of RÉS 4336/6 reads as follows: *ʾlhw*⌊*/ġz*⌋*w*⌋⌊*m*⌋. According to the context, *ġzw* means either a raid (e.g., Ja 586/14) or raiders, raid corps (here). – *gbd̲*, e.g., CIH 308/23.

L. 15: *ʿmd*, plural *ʾʿmd*; e.g., CIH 308/6-7, RÉS 4815/5 and *BeSI*, p. 29; cp. *ygbd̲[w/..* *../s]ṯy/ʾʾlfm/ʾʿmdm* with *wgbd̲w/kl/ḥblthw* in CIH 308/23. – *hwʾ*, cf. commentary on Ja 564/12: *hʾ*; here, pronoun but adjective in Ja 644/10. – *yṯr*, imperfect of *wṯr*; cf. commentary on Ja 576/12. – *sbʿ*, cf. *StSESA*, p. 523 and *BePESA*, p. 8. – *stʾwl*, 10th form of *ʾwl*; cf. 5th form *tʾwl* in CIH 95/1 and *BeSI*, p. 25. – *ḥṣq*, also in JM 9+7/3; cf. Soqoṭri "*ḥáṣaq*, tordre (une corde); voir sous *ḥázaq*" (cf. *LeLS*, p. 187), Šh̲auri "*ḥazóq* festbinden" (cf. *BiSSS*, IV, p. 39) and "*añḥazéq* Strick" (cf. *l.c.*, I, p. 33, and IV, p. 10). In the three contexts, here, Ja 586/22-23 and 644/20-21, *ḥṣq* is always mentioned the last in the list of terms, and these nouns are either plural or collective terms; therefore, *ḥṣq* is probably a collective plural (*ḥuṣûq*) and its etymology suggests translating it as "prisoner-keepers". Further, the enumeration of the present text by mentioning *ḥṣq* with the plural pronoun *hmw* on the one hand and on the other the nouns *h̲ms*, *ʾfrs*, and *rkb* with the singular pronoun *hw*, as well as *hwʾ*, suggests that the *ḥṣq* were divided between the king himself and the three major army corps, the infantry, the cavalry, and the camelry. However, the reason why *ḥṣq* is always listed last, even after the mention of animals (Ja 586/22), is not apparent. In JM 9+7/3: ...*wḥṣq/sbʾ/bʿm/hwt/gyšn/–* is translated by *RyISA* (X, p. 271) "...et Saba avait fait cause commune avec cette troupe..." (cf. also *RycIHS*, p. 322, where "armée" replaces "troupe"). Since *gyš* is the enemy, it would be quite abnormal to find Sabaʾ mentioned in a Sab text as the ally of the enemy; and since the verb *hlqḥ* (line 4) also alludes to bond, fetters (cf. commentary on Ja 601/9), I propose translating the expression mentioned as follows: "...and the prisoner-keepers of Sabaʾ against this troop...".

L. 17: *ġndn*, fortress in Ṣanʿâʾ; cf. CIH 429/10; presently called Ġumdân. – *hgrn/mryb/wṣnʿw/wnšqm*, cp. *hgrn/mrb/wnšqm/wnšn* in Fakhry 76/7 (*RyET*, p. 52: "la ville de..."). – *mqwl* may be considered as a synonym of *q(w)l*; cf. Arabic *miqwal*, pl. *maqâwilu* "Kinglet (among the Ḥimyarites)".

L. 18: *yfʿhmw*, e.g., CIH 88/5. – *nʿm/ʾlbb/ẖmshmw*, cp. *rḍw/ʾlbbhmw* in NaNN 75/6.

L. 19: *lḥmw* instead of *lhmw*; *ḥ* is certain on the stone.

578 – Stone re-used in the western pavement; cf. Chapter I, B. – MaMB 263.

INSCRIPTION: letter height: from 2 to 2.2 cm.; space between the lines: 0.4 cm. – SYMBOL: cf. Ja 559.

1 **Sym-** *rbšmsm/yzd/wʾẖy[hw/krbʿṯt/ʾsʿd/bny/sʾrn/..]*
2 **bol** *wmḥylm/wśmkm/ʾqwl/šʿbn/b⌜kl⌝m/rbʿn/ḏrydt/mq*
3 *twyy/ʾlšrḥ/yḥḍb/wʾẖyhw/yʾzl/byn/mlky/sbʾ/wḏrydn/b*
4 *ny/frʿm/ynhb/mlk/sbʾ/hqnyy/ʾlmqhṯhwnbʿlʾwm/ḏn/ṣl*
5 *mn/ḏḏhbn/ḥmdm/bḏt/hwšʿ/whrdʾn/mrʾhmw/ʾlšrḥ/yḥḍb*
6 *mlk/sbʾ/wḏrydn/bsbṭ/wṯbr/whṯlʿn/whsḥtn/krbʾl/ḏrydn*
7 *wkl/mṣr/wʾšʿb/wẖms/ḥmyrm/wldʿm/bkn/tqdmw/wrtḍḥn/b*
8 *ḥql/ḥrmtm/wsḥt/krbʾl/ḏrydn/wʾšʿbhw/wẖmshw/bn/ʿrn/ʾ*
9 *sʾy/wqrnnhn/ʿdy/ʿrwštn/wẓlmn/whkrbm/wḥmdm/bḏt/hwšʿ*
10 *whwfyn/mrʾyhmw/bn/kl/bʿwt/wbḥḍt/sbʾy/wbʿw/wbḥḍ*
11 *wtḥbn/wwḍʿ/whrg/wmtlyn/ʿsm/sbʾtm/wbʿwtm/whgm/w*
12 *mṣnʿm/wʾbytm/wmhrgtm/wsbym/wġnmm/wmltm/ḏhrḍw*
13 *mrʾyhmw/bn/hnt/sbʾtn/ḏsbʾy/wḍbʾ/mrʾyhmw/ʾlšrḥ/yḥḍb*
14 *wʾẖyhw/yʾzl/byn/mlky/sbʾ/wḏrydn/bny/frʿm/ynhb/mlk/sbʾ*
15 *ʿdy/ʾrḍ/ḥmyrm/wḥmdm/bḏt/hwšʿ/whrdʾn/ʾlmqhṯhwnbʿlʾ*
16 *wm/mrʾyhmw/ʾlšrḥ/yḥḍb/wʾẖyhw/yʾzl/byn/mlky/sbʾ/wḏry*
17 *dn/bny/frʿm/ynhb/mlk/sbʾ/bṯbr/wwḍʿ/whsḥtn/whṯlʿn/k*
18 *rbʾl/ḏrydn/wʾqwlhw/wẖmshw/wʾšʿbhw/wʾfrshw/wldʿm*
19 *bkn/tʾtmw/wrtḍḥn/wtqdmn/bsrn/ḏʾẓwr/wʾtw/krbʾl/ḏry*
20 *dn/wẖmshw/bsḥtm/ʿdy/hgrnhn/yklʾ/wʾbwn/wbnhw/ftʾwlw*
21 *ḏsʾr/bn/mṣrhmw/ʾysm/ʿbrhw/sḥtm/ʿdy/ʾrḍthmw/wbʿdhw/f*
22 *blt/krbʾl/ḏrydn/tʿrbm/wsfḥ/ʿqbthw/tḥt/mrʾyhmw/ʾlš[r]*
23 *ḥ/yḥḍb/wʾẖyhw/yʾzl/byn/mlky/sbʾ/wḏrydn/bny/frʿm/ynhb*
24 *mlk/sbʾ/wbʿdhw/fḍbʾy/mrʾyhmw/ʾlšrḥ/yḥḍb/wʾẖyhw/yʾ*
25 *zl/byn/mlky/sbʾ/wḏrydn/ʿdy/ʾrḍ/ḥmyrm/whwṣlw/ʿdy/ẖlf*
26 *hgrn/hkrm/wʾsyw/bhw/krbʾl/ḏrydn/wẖmshw/wẓwryhmw/m*
27 *rʾyhmw/ʾlšrḥ/yḥḍb/wʾẖyhw/yʾzl/byn/mlky/sbʾ/wḏryd*
28 *n/bhyt/hgrn/hkrm/ʿdy/sbʿ/wtḍrʿn/krbʾl/ḏrydn/wʾqwlhw/w*
29 *ʾšʿbhw/tḥt/mrʾyhmw/ʾlšrḥ/yḥḍb/wʾẖyhw/yʾzl/byn/mlky*
30 *sbʾ/wḏrydn/wḥmdm/bḏt/ẖmr/ʾlmqhṯhwnbʿlʾwm/ʿbdyh*
31 *w/rbšmsm/yzd/wkrbʿṯt/ʾsʿd/btʾwln/hmy/wšʿbhmy/bklm*
32 *[r]bʿn/ḏrydt/bwfym/w(m)hrgtm/wsbym/wʾẖḏtm/wġnmm/wmltm*
33 *ḏhrḍw/ʿbdyhw/wḥmdm/bḏt/mtʿ/ʾlmqhṯhwnbʿlʾwm/ʿbdhw*
34 *krbʿṯt/ʾsʿd/bn/sʾrn/bn/kl/tšynt/šyn/bḥql/ḥrmtm/w*

35 *[lw]zʾ/ʾlmqhṯhwnbʿlʾwm/ẖmr/ʿbdyhw//rbšmsm/ wkrbʿṯt/b*

36 *[ny/sʾrn]/ḥẓy/wrḍw/mrʾyhmw/ʾlšrḥ/yḥḍb/ wʾẖyhw/yʾzl/byn*

37 *mlky/sbʾ/wḏrydn/bny/frʿm/ynhb/mlk/sbʾ/bʾhnmw/ yqhnn*

38 *hmy/mrʾyhmw/ʾlšrḥ/yḥḍb/wʾẖyhw/yʾzl/byn/mlky/ sbʾ*

39 *wḏrydn/lbltm/wmqrnm/wqhtm/wbʾl/ʾbrṯ/yqhnhmw/ mrʾy*

40 *⌈h⌉mw/lsbʾ/wtnṣfn/wl/ẖrynhmy/ʾlmqhṯhwnbʿlʾwm/ bn/nḍʿ*

41 *wšṣy/wʿbṭ/wzʾt/wtṯʿt/šnʾm/ḏrḥq/wqrb/wḏbnhw/ dʿw/w*

42 *⌊ḏbnhw/ʾl/dʿw/wbn/ʾlhtm/ḏytʾlhnhmy/šnʾhmw/ bʿly/ḥ*

43 *⌊ṣ⌋y/mrʾyhmw/bʿṯtr/wʾlmqhṯhwnbʿlʾwm/wb/ šymyhmw/ʿṯ*

44 *[t]rwʾlwzʿlnbʿlyʿrnbyfʿ/wb/mrʾyhmw/ʾlšrḥ/yḥḍb/ wʾẖyhw*

45 *[y]ʾzl/byn/mlky/sbʾ/wḏrydn/bny/frʿm/ynhb/mlk/ sbʾ*

1 **Sym-** Rabbšamsum Yazid and [his] brother [Karibʿaṯat ʾAsʿad, people of Suʾrân,...

2 **bol** and Miḥîlum and Śamkum, rulers of the tribe Bakîlum, the fourth of Raydat, both high military offi-

3 cials of ʾIlšaraḥ Yaḥḍub and his brother Yaʾzil Bayyin, the two kings of Sabaʾ and Raydân, the two

4 sons of Fariʿum Yanhub, king of Sabaʾ, have dedicated to ʾIlumquh Ṯahwân, master of ʾAwwâm, this sta-

5 tue which [is] in bronze, in praise because He has helped and assisted their lord ʾIlšaraḥ Yaḥḍub,

6 king of Sabaʾ and Raydân, in throwing down and crushing and breaking and destroying Karibʾil, him of Raydân,

7 and all the expeditionary corps and the tribes and the army of Ḥimyarum, the children of ʿAmm, when they moved forward and sowed death in

8 the country of Ḥurmatum; and Karibʾil, he of Raydân, and his tribes and his army were destroyed from the citadel ʾA-

9 sʾay and Qarnnahân as far as ʿArwaštân and Ẓalmân and Hakrabum; and in praise because He has helped

10 and protected their two lords from all acts of treachery and the sudden attack [against which] the two of them had to fight, and [from] treachery and sudden attack

11 and violence and humiliation and killing and the rejoicing of desirable encounters, and [from] acts of treachery and unexpected assault and [He has granted to them]

12 fortresses and houses and war trophies and captives and booty and riches, which pleased

13 their two lords, from these military campaigns which fought and waged war their two lords ʾIlšaraḥ Yaḥḍub

14 and his brother Yaʾzil Bayyin, the two kings of Sabaʾ and Raydân, the two sons of Fariʿum, Yanhub, king of Sabaʾ,

15 in the land of Ḥimyarum; and in praise because has helped and assisted ʾIlumquh Ṯahwân, master of ʾA-

16 wwâm, their two lords ʾIlšaraḥ Yaḥḍub and his brother Yaʾzil Bayyin, the two kings of Sabaʾ and Ray-

17 dân, the two sons of Fariʿum Yanhub, king of Sabaʾ, in crushing and humiliating and destroying and breaking Ka-

18 ribʾil, him of Raydân, and his rulers and his army and his tribes and his cavalry, the children of ʿAmm,

19 when they joined and sowed death and moved forward in the valley of ʾAẓwar; and came back Karibʾil, he of Ray-

20 dân, and his army in defeat into the two cities [of] Yaklaʾ and ʾAbwân; and from there went back

21 those of their expeditionary corps who remained, as an adversary in defeat, into their lands; and after that,

22 Karibʾil, he of Raydân, was forced to give pledges of submission and to place his representatives under the control of their two lords ʾIlša[ra]ḥ

23 Yaḥḍub and his brother Yaʾzil Bayyin, the two kings of Sabaʾ and Raydân, the two sons of Fariʿum Yanhub,

24 king of Sabaʾ; and after that, fought their two lords ʾIlšaraḥ Yaḥḍub and his brother Yaʾ-

25 zil Bayyin, the two kings of Sabaʾ and Raydân, in the land of Ḥimyarum and assembled at the gate of

26 the city [of] Hakirum; and Karibʾil, he of Raydân, and his army took refuge in it; and besieged them their

27 two lords ʾIlšaraḥ Yaḥḍub and his brother Yaʾzil Bayyin, the two kings of Sabaʾ and Raydân,

28 in this city, Hakirum until was plundered and submitted Karibʾil, he of Raydân, and his rulers and

29 his tribes under their two lords ʾIlšaraḥ Yaḥḍub and his brother Yaʾzil Bayyin, the two kings

30 of Sabaʾ and Raydân; and in praise because ʾIlumquh Ṯahwân, master of ʾAwwâm, has vouchsafed to His two worshippers

31 Rabbšamsum Yazid and Karibʿaṯat ʾAsʿad to come back, both of them and their tribe Bakîlum,

32 the [fo]urth of Raydat, in safety and (with) war trophies and captives and prisoners and booty and riches,

33 which pleased His two worshippers; and in praise because ʾIlumquh Ṯahwân, master of ʾAwwâm, has saved His worshipper

34 Karibʿaṯat ʾAsʿad, descendant of Suʾrân, from all the diseases [which] he suffered in the country of Ḥurmatum; and

35 [that] ʾIlumquh Ṯahwân, master of ʾAwwâm, [may con]tinue to vouchsafe to His two worshippers Rabbšamsum and Karibʿaṯat, des-

36 [cendants of Suʾrân], the esteem and grace of their two lords ʾIlšaraḥ Yaḥḍub and his brother Yaʾzil Bayyin,

37 the two kings of Sabaʾ and Raydân, the two sons of Fariʿum Yanhub, king of Sabaʾ, in whatever shall command

38 to both of them their two lords ʾIlšaraḥ Yaḥḍub and his brother Yaʾzil Bayyin, the two kings of Sabaʾ

39 and Raydân, with regard to military duty and military expedition and authority and leadership of [military] campaigns [which] shall command to them their two

40 lords in order to fight and subdue; and that ʾIlumquh Ṯahwân, master of ʾAwwâm, may preserve them both from the hostility

41 and wickedness and calamity and constraint and fear of [any] enemy, who is remote and near, and those who are known and

42 those who are not known, and from the adulations that their enemy might give them against the es-

43 teem of their two lords. By ʿAṯtar and ʾIlumquh Ṯahwân, master of ʾAwwâm, and by their patrons ʿAṯ-

44 [ta]r and ʾIlwuzaʿilân, the two masters of the citadel in Yâfiʿ, and by their two lords ʾIlšaraḥ Yaḥḍub and his brother

45 [Ya]ʾzil Bayyin, the two kings of Sabaʾ and Raydân, the two sons of Fariʿum Yanhub, king of Sabaʾ.

L. 1: *rbšmsm/yzd*, CIH 314+954/1; *rbšmsm*, also, e.g., RÉS 4577/1; *yzd*, cf. also commentary on Ja 615/1-3. – *krbʿṯt* (e.g., Ja 567/15) and *ʾsʿd* (e.g., CIH 24/2), where it is related to a personal name composed of *krb*, scl. *ʾbkrb*) are restored on the basis of lines 31 and 34. – *sʾrn*, Ja 544/2 and commentary on Ja 572/2; epithet in RÉS 4889/1, Ḥaḍr; cf. also the family name *sʾr* in Qat Blaymires 2 (cf. *BeOSA*, p. 21, and pl. IV, left), instead of the personal name *sʾr*[*n*].

L. 2: *śmkm* and *mhylm* are attested as personal names in CIH 314+954/25, where *rb*[*šmsm*] is read on line 24; in Fakhry 132, I read the monogram as *śbk* rather than *śmk*(?) (so *RyET*, p. 80). – *rydt*, town in the Wâdî Mayfaʿ, about 55 km. north-northwest of Ṣanʿâʾ (cf. *WiHöBGS*, p. 86).

L. 6: *sbṭ*, cf. *CoRoC*, p. 193 A; the meaning of Accadian *šabāṭu* "schlagen, erschlagen, niederschlagen" (cf. *BeBAG*, p. 264 A; cf. also in Daṯînah, *LaGD*, pp. 1890-91) is attested here; for *sbṭ* in Ja 700/11-12, cf. Ethiopic *zăbăṭă* "verberare" (cf. *DiLLA*, col. 1050); cf. also the 5th form *tsbṭ* in Ja 669/19, and the noun *sbṭ* in Ja 665/34. – *hṯlʿ*, 4th form of *ṯlʿ*; cf. Arabic *ṯalaʿa* "to break, smash (the head)".

L. 8: *ḥql*, cf. *CoRoC*, p. 151 B, *BeSI*, p. 7, *RhVSAY*, p. 305 and *JeHoDISO*, p. 95: *ḥql*. – *ḥrmtm*, cf. *ḥrmt* in RÉS 4176/10. *ḥrmtm* in CIH 366α (cf. *JaPSAP*, pp. 63 and 89-92) is also the name of a city, and not that of some kind of incense (so *LuYFS*, p. 6). – *sḥt*, cf. *CoRoC*, p. 194 B; here in passive form, as well as in Philby-Tritton 135 a/2 (cf. *JaDN*, pp. 169-70); for the 4th form *hsḥt*, cf. commentary on Ja 575/7; for the noun *sḥt*, cf., e.g., line 20 and CIH 334/12.

Ll. 8-9: *ʾsʾy*, name of a citadel; cf. Arabic *saʾā* (o) "to intend, plan"; cf. the name of a man *mrṯdʾsʾy* (Ja 692/8-9).

L. 9: *qrnnhn*, cp. the Arabic names of a man *qaran*, *qurayn*, of a clan *banû qaran* (cf. *WüID*, 247/9, 209/16, and 245/11-12 respectively), and of a place *al-qurayyinayn* and *al-qarînayn* (cf. *WüR*, p. 173 A); same nominal formation as that, e.g., of *ʾrbʿnhn* (Ja 556 and commentary). – *ʿrwštn*, the root *ʿrš* is attested in several place names (cf. *WüR*, p. 149 C); cf. also the Arabic name of a man *al-ʿarâyiš* (cf. *WüID*, 168/8).

L. 10: *bʿwt*, plural of *bʿw*; cf. the verb in RÉS 4324/4, Qat and Ja 631/29; cf. Arabic *baʿā* "to commit a crime *or* a treason; betray" and *baʿw* "crime, felony, treachery, act of treachery".

L. 11: *tḥbn*, *maṣdar* of the 5th form of *ḥbn*; cf. Arabic *ḥabina* "to become angry against someone"; *tḥbn* could be translated "violence". – *ʿsm*, cf. commentary on Ja 574/9: *ḏʿsm*. – *hgm*, cf. *hağama* "to attack with fury" in Arabic, Ẓofâr (cf. *RhVDD*, p. 61 B), and Mehri (cf. *JaMSSA*, p. 186 B: *hijôm*) and in Arabic *hağmat* "unexpected assault". – Between lines 11 and 12, *hwfyn/mrʾyhmw*, without *bn* "from", is understood.

L. 12: *mṣnʿt*, pl. *mṣnʿ*; cf. *CIH*, II, p. 288 A, *CoRoC*, pp. 224-25, and *RÉS*, in RÉS 3250/3, Ḥaḍr; *RyISA* considers *mṣnʿ* both as plural (e.g., X, pp. 287 and 291, in Ḥimâ/5, and p. 298, in Kawkab 1/4) and as singular (XII, pp. 301 and 307, in Geukens 1/20).

L. 19: *tʾtm*, 5th form of *ʾtm*; cf. *RhIMG*, p. 48 and note 1.

L. 20: *ʾbwn*, name of a city; cf. *ʾabawā*, Arabic place name (cf. *WüR*, p. 4 A).

L. 21: *ʾsym/ʿbrhw/sḥtm*, circumstantial phrase; "adversary [having] with him defeat" or "as a defeated enemy". – *sḥt*, cf. commentary on line 8.

L. 22: *tʿrb*, 5th form (also Ja 735/9) of *ʿrb* "to give pledges of submission" confirms the restoration in CIH 308/23-24; cf. *CoRoC*, p. 212 A, *BeSI*, p. 31, and RÉS 4337 A/8 and probably 4767/5. RÉS 4337 is the subject of A. F. L. Beeston's booklet, *The Mercantile Code of Qataban* (London, 1959). It is rather surprising that the author is satisfied with his "amended" (p. 3) text which needs to be corrected and completed, without mentioning that the *American Foundation* uncovered the *whole* inscription (cf. A. Jamme, in *Oriente Moderno*, 33 [1953], p. 138), and "made our squeezes available to her [M. Höfner] for a more complete publication" (cf. *AlCAS*, p. 8, note 20, and A. Jamme, *l.c.*). – *sfḥ*, e.g., RÉS 3689/1, Qat; here, coupled with *tḥt* (cf. Arabic *taḥta*) "under". – *ʿqbt*, pl. of *ʿqb*, cf. commentary on Ja 550/2.

L. 26: *hkrm*, name of a city (cf. *WiHöBGS*, p. 61, note 3: city located in the region of Mayfaʿ and Radâʿ); another *hkr* existed in the area of Mukérâs, at the foot of J. Hakar, near ʿArieb (northwest of Mukérâs). – *ʾsyw*: the ordinary meaning "to send" does not fit here; cf. K. Mlaker's opinion (cf. *WZKM*, 34 [1927], pp. 74-75), according to which *ʾsy* equals *ʿsy*; the present text requires a meaning such as "to take refuge".

L. 32: *mhgrtm*; copy: *bhgrtm*.

L. 34: *tšynt/šyn*, cp. *tšyn/šyn* in RÉS 3991/7 with the meaning of "the disease [which] he suffered"; *tšyn* is also attested in AshM 1957-17/7-8 (cf. *BeTMS*); in Ja 865/11, *šynt* means "dishonor" (cf. *JaQISA*, pp. 3 and 5).

L. 37: *ʾhnmw*, cf. *JaASAB*, p. 164, commentary on CIH 407/28.

Ll. 37-38: *yqhnn*, energic form of *wqh*; e.g., RÉS 4137/5.

L. 39: *mqrn*; the root *qrn* means "to make war against someone", and the noun "warrior, rebel"; cf. *CoRoC*, p. 234 A; *mqrn*, pl. *mqrnt* (Kawkab 1/8) may be translated here "military expedition". – *bʾl*, cp. Arabic *bâla* (o) "faire attention" (cf. *DoSDA*, I, p. 129 B) and *bâl* "a state, condition, *or* case, for which one cares" (cf. *LaAEL*, p. 277 A); the context requires a meaning such as "leadership, direction, care"; *brṯ* must be translated "[military] campaign" on account of the context.

L. 41: *zʾt*, from *wzʾ* (cp. *qht* from *wqh*); cf. Daṯînah *wzʾ* "serrer (un sac)" and "Zwang" (cf. *LaGD*, p. 2920) and Ẓofâr **ūẓâ (wẓy)* "bedrängen, belästigen" (cf. *RhVDD*, p. 64 A); *zʾt* may be translated "constraint".

L. 42: *ʾlhtm/ḏytʾlhnhmy*; *ʾlht* is the *maṣdar* (cf. Arabic *ʾilâhat*) of the verb *ʾlh*, 1st and 5th forms: "to adore"; the context requires for both the verb (5th form) and the *maṣdar* a moral secondary meaning, such as "adulation, flattery"; cp. Arabic *ʾlh*, 2nd form, "to deify", but also "to glorify someone"; the two authors demand to be preserved from adulations, flatteries which their enemies might give them against the esteem of their lords.

Ll. 43-44: *ʿṯ[t]rwʾlwzʿlnbʿlyʿrnbyfʿ* without any word divider. The correction of *ʾlwzʿln* to *ʾl(/t)ʿl(y)* must be discarded, for this reading supposes a word divider, which is contrary to the whole expression which does not have any, and also because three characters must be changed. I suggest interpreting *ʾlwzʿln* as a new name of the moon god by comparison with *hlʾly* "the favor rises up" (cf. *JaP*, p. 70). Both *ʾly* (cf. Arabic *ʾily*) and *ʾlw* (e.g., Ja 615/5, cf. Arabic *ʾilw*) mean "favor, benefit". For *zʿln*, cp. Arabic *zaʿila* "to be gay"; this parallel must be preferred to Ẓofâr *zʿl*, I, "zürnen" and *zaʿâlân*, *zaʿlên* "zornig, verdriesslich" (cf. *RhVDD*, p. 23 B); *ʾlwzʿln* "favor of gaiety" or "cheerful favor", idea close to that of *hlʾly*; cf. also the Arabic clan name *banû ziʿl* (cf. *WüID*, 298/16). For the name of the city *yfʿ*, cf. *WiHöBGS*, p. 52, note 2; *yfʿ* is name of man in Ja 746/1 and *yfʿm* in RÉS 4613; *yfʿn* and *yfʿm* in NaNN 14/1-2 are names of a family and not of a temple (so G. Ryckmans, in *Le Muséon*, 60 [1947], p. 162, followed by *RycIMAM*, p. 146).

579 – Grayish sandstone. – MaMB 281.

STONE: thickness: 14.7 cm. – *Front:* covered with red paint; 22.5 cm. (top) and 22.7 (bottom) × 36.7. – INSCRIPTION, same disposition of lines as in Ja 552; letter height: 1.6 cm.; space between the lines: 0.3 cm.; distance from line 1 to the upper edge: 0.5 cm. – SYMBOL: cf. Ja 565.

1 **Sym-** *dwmn/bn/ṯly/mqtwy/ʾlšrḥ*
2 **bol** *yḥḏb/wʾḫyhw/yʾzl/byn/ml*
3 *ky/sbʾ/wḏrydn/bny/frʿm/ynhb/ml*

4 *k/sbʾ/hqny/ʾlmqhṯhwnbʿlʾwm/ṣlmn*
5 *ḏḏhbn/ḥmdm/bḏt/tʾwl/mrʾhmw/ʾlšrḥ*
6 *yḥḍb/mlk/sbʾ/wḏrydn/bwfym/bn/sb*
7 *ʾt/wḍbyʾ/sbʾ/wḍbʾ/bʿly/ḏshrtm/wʾ*
8 *rḍ/ḥmyrm/wngrn/wl/ẖmrhw/ʾlmqhbʿlʾ*
9 *wm/ḥẓy/wrḍ⟨w⟩/mrʾyhw/ʾlšrḥ/yḥḍb/w*
10 *ʾẖyhw/yʾzl/byn/mlky/sbʾ/wḏrydn*
11 *bny/frʿm/ynhb/mlk/sbʾ/wlhʿnnhmw/ʾl*
12 *mqhṯhwnbʿlʾwm/bn/nḍʿ/wšṣy/šnʾ*
13 *m/blmqh/ṯhwn/bʿlʾwm*

1 **Sym-** Dawamân, son of Ṯalî, high official of ʾIlšaraḥ
2 **bol** Yaḥḍub and his brother Yaʾzil Bayyin, the two
3 kings of Sabaʾ and Raydân, the two sons of Fariʿum Yanhub, king
4 of Sabaʾ, have dedicated to ʾIlumquh Ṯahwân, master of ʾAwwâm, this statue
5 which [is] in bronze, in praise because has returned his lord ʾIlšaraḥ
6 Yaḥḍub, king of Sabaʾ and Raydân, in safety from the encounters
7 and the engagements [in which] he fought and combatted against (the tribe) Saharatum and the
8 land of Ḥimyarum and Nagrân; and that may vouchsafe to him ʾIlumquh, master of ʾA-
9 wwâm, the esteem and grace of his two lords ʾIlšaraḥ Yaḥḍub and
10 his brother Yaʾzil Bayyin, the two kings of Sabaʾ and Raydân,
11 the two sons of Fariʿum Yanhub, king of Sabaʾ; and that may assist them ʾIl-
12 umquh Ṯahwân, master of ʾAwwâm, against the hostility and wickedness of [any] enemy.
13 By ʾIlumquh Ṯahwân, master of ʾAwwâm.

L. 1: *dwmn*, e.g., CIH 69/2, and the adverb *dwmm* "always" (e.g., RÉS 2726/3); cf. also the Arabic personal names *al-dûmî* and *bin-dûmat* (cf. *SlGa-VNPA*, p. 18 B). – *ṯly* (also in the following text): RÉS 4080, No. 93: this spurious inscription could have reproduced a genuine text mentioning *ṯly*; personal name with the *nisba* ending; cf. the Arabic personal names *ʾaṯâl* and *ʾibn ʾaṯâl* (cf. *GoAT*, p. 12); cf. Arabic *ṯâla* "to be or become stupid, foolish" and the derived adjective *ʾaṯwalu* "mad, possessed".

L. 9: the writing *rḍ* instead of *rḍw* is certain (cf. my notebook).

L. 13: the writing *lmqh* is certain (cf. my notebook).

580 – Yellowish sandstone inscription, broken at the bottom; photograph in Plate 6. – MaMB 184.

STONE: constant thickness: 15 cm. – *Top:* hollow: 9.5 cm. × 4.7 × 2.1 (depth); upper part of another hollow: length: 10.3 cm., and depth: 2.3. – *Front:* the width (21.5 cm. on the top) grows wider toward the bottom; a hollow in the center; maximum width: 24.6 cm. – INSCRIPTION: same disposition of lines as in Ja 559; letter height: from 1.4 cm. to 1.5; space between the lines: 0.3 cm. – SYMBOL: cf. Ja 559.

1 **Sym-** *bqlm/bn/ṯly/mqtwy/ʾlšrḥ/yḥḍb*
2 **bol** *wʾẖyhw/yʾzl/byn/mlky/sbʾ/wḏ*
3 *rydn/bny/frʿm/ynhb/mlk/sbʾ/hqny/ʾ*
4 *lmqhṯhwnbʿlʾwm/ṯwrn/ḏḏhbn/ḥmd*
5 *m/bḏhwfyhw/bmsʾlhw/kyʾtyn/bwf*
6 *ym/wmhrgm/wġnmm/ḏyhrḍyn/lbhw/b⌋*
7 *kn/sbʾ/wšwʿn/mrʾ⌊yhmw/⌋[ʾlšrḥ/]⌊y⌋ḥḍb⌋*
8 *wʾẖyhw/yʾzl/by[n/mlky/sbʾ/wḏryd]⌊dn/[ʿ]*
9 *⌊dy/ʾrḍ/ḥmyrm/wbḏ⌈t⌉⌈/ẖmrh⌉[w]⌈/ʾlm⌉[qh/]bʿ⌋[l]*
10 *⌊ʾ⌋wm/hwfyn/ʾẖhw/ʾsdm/bn/ṯly/wʾw[ld]*
11 *[h]⌊m⌋y/wẖmrhmw/mhrgm/wġnmm/bkl/⌊h⌋[nt]*
12 *[sbʾ]⌊t⌋n/wlwzʾ/ʾlmqhbʿlʾwm/ẖmr/ʿb⌊dh⌋[w]*
13 *[bqlm/bn/]⌊ṯl⌋y/hwfynhw/w⌊ẖmrh⌋w/mhrgm[/ wġnmm]*
14 *[wl/ẖrynhw/bn]⌈/bʾ⌉[stm/wnkym/wnḍʿ]/w[šṣy/šnʾ]*
15 *[m/. . . .*

1 **Sym-** Baqilum, son of Ṯalî, high official of ʾIlšaraḥ Yaḥḍub
2 **bol** and his brother Yaʾzil Bayyin, the two kings of Sabaʾ and
3 Raydân, the two sons of Fariʿum Yanhub, king of Sabaʾ, have dedicated to ʾI-
4 lumquh Ṯahwân, master of ʾAwwâm, this bull, which [is] in bronze, in praise
5 because He has granted him through His oracle that he would come back in safe-
6 ty and (with) war trophy and booty, which would please his heart,
7 when he fought and assisted their two lords, [ʾIlšaraḥ] Yaḥḍub
8 and his brother, Yaʾzil Bayy[in, the two kings of Sabaʾ and Ray]dân,
9 [i]n the land of Ḥimyarum, and because has vouchsafed to hi[m] ʾIlum[quh], mas[ter of]
10 ʾAwwâm, to protect his brother ʾAsdum, son of Ṯalî, and the chi[ldren]
11 [of th]em both and [because] He has vouchsafed to them war trophy and booty from all the[se]
12 [encoun]ters; and that ʾIlumquh, master of ʾAwwâm, may continue to vouchsafe Hi[s] worshipper
13 [Baqilum, son of] Ṯalî, to protect him and to vouchsafe to him war trophy [and booty;]

14 [and that He may preserve him from] misfor[tunes and suffering and the hostility] and [wickedness of (any) enemy,]

15 . . .

L. 1: *bqlm*, e.g., CIH 146/1 and RÉS 4852/3-4, Ḥaḍr; another member of the family *ṯly* already mentioned in Ja 579.

L. 4: *ṯwrm/ḏḏhbn*, e.g., CIH 343/3.

L. 7: *sbʾ/wšwʿn*, cp. *sbʾw/wšwʿn* in CIH 407/15; for *šwʿ*, cf. commentary on Ja 564/8-9.

L. 10: *ʾsdm*, e.g., CIH 303/1, and Ist 7630/2; cf. also *ʾsdn* (e.g., RÉS 4210/2) and the *nisba* nouns *ʾsdyn* (RÉS 4869/2, Ḥaḍr; cf. commentary on Ja 684/1) and *ʾsdyhn* (RÉS 4878/1-2, Ḥaḍr).

L. 11: two or three letters are missing at the end; for the restoration of lines 11-12, cf. Ja 578/13.

Ll. 11-12: *bkl/h[nt sbʾ]tn* equals *bkl/hnt/sbʾt* in Ja 650/22.

581 – Yellowish, slightly grayish sandstone. – MaMB 254.

STONE: thickness: 26.6 cm. (left) and 25.8 (right). – *Front:* 33 cm. (top) and 32 (bottom) × 47 (right) and 47.2 (left). – INSCRIPTION: same disposition of lines as in Ja 561 bis; letter height: from 1.7 cm. to 1.9; space between the lines: 0.3 cm. and 0.4; distance from line 19 to the lower edge: 0.9 cm. (right) and 1 (left). – SYMBOL: cf. Ja 559. – DOUBLE DESIGN: cf. Plate B.

1 **Sym-** *ʾsdm/ʾsʿd/bn/mhdmm/wqrḍn/mqtwy/ʾlš*
2 **bol** *rḥ/yḥḍb/wʾẖyhw/yʾzl/byn/mlky/sbʾ*
3 *wḏrydn/bny/frʿm/ynhb/mlk/sbʾ/hqny/ʾlm*
4 *qhṯhwnbʿlʾwm/ṯlṯtn/ʾṯwrn/wṣlmn/ʾly/ḏhb*
5 *n/ḥmdm/bḏt/tʾwly/mrʾyhmw/bwfym/wḥmdm*
6 *bn/kl/sbʾt/wḍbyʾ/wtqdmt/sbʾy/wḍbʾ/w*
7 *tqdmn/mrʾyhmw/bʿm/ʾšʿb/wmṣyrt/ḥmyrm*
8 *wbḏtbry/wtḍʿn/ḍrhmy/wḥmdm/bḏhmr/ʾl*
9 *mqhṯhwnbʿlʾwm/ʿbdhw/ʾsdm/ʾsʿd/bn/mh*
10 *dmm/wqrḍn/btʾwln/bwfym/wmhrgtm/wʾẖyḏt*
11 *m/wġnmm/ḏhrḍwhw/bn/kl/sbʾt/wtqdmt/b*
12 *hmw/šwʿw/mrʾyhmw/wḥmdm/bḏt/hwfyhw/ʾ*
13 *lmqh/bkl/ʾmlʾ/stmlʾ/bʿmhw/wlwzʾ/ʾlm*
14 *qh/ẖmr/wsʿd/ʿbdhw/ʾsdm/nʿmtm/wwfym/wm*
15 *ngt/ṣdqm/wḥẓy/wrḍw/mrʾyhmw/ʾlsrḥ/yḥ*
16 *ḍb/wʾẖyhw/yʾzl/byn/mlky/sbʾ/wḏrydn/wlsʿ*
17 *dhw/ʾṯmr/wʾfql/ṣdqm/hnʾm/wlẖrynhw/ʾlm*
18 *qh/bn/bʾstm/wnkytm/wnḍʿ/wtṯʿt/wšmt/šn*
19 **Design** *ʾm/bʾlmqhṯhwnbʿlʾwm* **Design**

1 **Sym-** ʾAsdum ʾAsʿad, descendant of Mahdumum and Qarḍân, high official of ʾIlša-
2 **bol** raḥ Yaḥḍub and his brother Yaʾzil Bayyin, the two kings of Sabaʾ
3 and Raydân, the two sons of Fariʿum Yanhub, king of Sabaʾ, has dedicated to ʾIlum-
4 quh Ṯahwân, master of ʾAwwâm, these three bulls and this statue which [are] in bronze,
5 in praise because their two lords have come back in safety and (with) praise
6 from all the encounters and the engagements and the attacks [in which] have fought and combatted and
7 attacked their two lords against the tribes and the expeditionary forces of Ḥimyarum;
8 and because both of them have crushed and humiliated the enemy of the two of them; and in praise because has vouchsafed ʾIl-
9 umquh Ṯahwân, master of ʾAwwâm, to His worshipper ʾAsdum ʾAsʿad, descendant of Mah-
10 dumum and Qarḍân, to come back in safety and (with) war trophies and prisoners
11 and booty, which pleased him, from all the encounters and attacks in
12 which they assisted their two lords; and in praise because has showered upon him ʾIl-
13 umquh all the favors [for which] he besought Him; and that may continue ʾIlum-
14 quh to vouchsafe to and make happy His worshipper ʾAsdum with prosperity and safety and se-
15 curity perfect and [also] (with) the esteem and grace of their two lords ʾIlšaraḥ Yaḥ-
16 ḍub and his brother Yaʾzil Bayyin, the two kings of Sabaʾ and Raydân; and that He may make him
17 happy with perfect, pleasing fruits and harvests; and that may preserve him ʾIlum-
18 quh from misfortunes and sufferings and [from] the hostility and fear, and abuse of [any] ene-
19 **Design** my. By ʾIlumquh Ṯahwân, master of ʾAwwâm. **Design**

L. 1: *ʾsdm/ʾsʿd*, Geukens 1/1. – *mhdmm*, RÉS 4604 (instead of *mhdmr*); cf. the personal *ʾhdm* "ʾAhdam" in RÉS 5067 (instead of *ʾdb*?), and *hdym* (Ja 750/12), and also the Arabic names of a place *al-hudum*, *al-hidam* (cf. *WüR*, p. 230 B), of a clan *banû hidm* (cf. *WüID*, 154/7), and of a man *hidm* (cf. *SaIS*, p. 242 B); for *mhdmm*, cp. Arabic *mahdûm* "demolished, broken down"; the root *hdm* (cf. Arabic *hadama* "to crush; break someone's back; demolish") must be preferred to that of *dwm* (cf. Ja 579/1), 4th form. – *qrḍn*, e.g., Ja 339/2, Qat; for the left monogram in Fakhry 72 = MaN 19, cf. *JaJEQH*, p. 132, note 4.

L. 7: *bʿm* = *bʿly*.

L. 10: *ʾẖydt*, plural of *ʾẖ(y)ḏ*; cf. Arabic *ʾaẖîḏ*.

L. 18: *šmt*, RÉS 4139/10; cf. the Arabic noun *šamît* "one who abuses a person"; cf. also *RhSLG*, II, p. 66.

L. 19: on both sides of line 19, an ornament; the one on the left is the reverse of that of the right; description of the left one: (1) on the extreme left, a flower, cf. Ja 506 (1st and 3rd from the top on each side), but here only the 4 petals which point to the corners, are engraved; (2) on the right of the preceding flower, a design composed of two leaves (one on each end), which look like rose leaves; in between these two leaves, a design which may be considered as a schematization of that of CIH 442, or Ja 507 and 508.

582 – Yellowish, slightly grayish sandstone; photograph in Plate 6. – MaMB 163.

STONE: constant thickness: 12.7 cm. – *Front:* covered with red paint; mutilated at the lower edge and damaged at the upper corner; 18.8 cm. (top) and 19.3 (bottom) × 24 (right) and 25.4 (center) and 21 (left). – INSCRIPTION: same disposition of lines as in Ja 552; letter height: from 2 cm. to 2.2; space between the lines: from 0.3 cm. to 0.4. – SYMBOL: cf. Ja 561, but four inside lines; cf. Plate A.

1 **Sym-** *ʾwlṭ/bn/klbn⌜/mqtwy⌝*
2 **bol** *ʾlšrḥ/yḥḍb/wʾḫy*
3 *⌞⌜hw/yʾzl/byn/mlky/sbʾ/wḏr*
4 *ydn/bny/frʿm/ynhb/mlk/sb*
5 *ʾ/hqny/ʾlmqh/ṯhwnbʿlʾwm*
6 *ṣlmn/ḏḏhbn/ḏšfthw/lwfy*
7 *hw/wlḫmrhw/ḥẓy/wrḍw/mr*
8 *ʾyhw/ʾlšrḥ/yḥḍb/wʾḫyhw*
9 *yʾzl/byn/mlky/sbʾ/wḏryd*
10 *n/bʾlmqh/bʿlʾw⌞m⌟*

1 **Sym-** ʾAwlaṭ, son of Kalbân, high official of
2 **bol** ʾIlšaraḥ Yaḥḍub and of his brother
3 Yaʾzil Bayyin, the two kings of Sabaʾ and Ra-
4 ydân, the two sons of Fariʿum Yanhub, king of Sabaʾ,
5 has dedicated to ʾIlumquh Ṯahwân, master of ʾAwwâm,
6 this statue which [is] in bronze, which he has promised to Him in order that He may protect
7 him and that He may vouchsafe to him the esteem and grace of his
8 two lords ʾIlšaraḥ Yaḥḍub and his brother
9 Yaʾzil Bayyin, the two kings of Sabaʾ and Rayd-
10 ân. By ʾIlumquh, master of ʾAwwâm.

L. 1: *ʾwlṭ*, 2nd name in Ja 658/1. – *klbn*, cf. commentary on Ja 563/2.

583 – Yellowish, slightly grayish sandstone; photograph in Plate 6. – MaMB 167.

STONE: thickness: 13 cm. (top) and 10.4 (bottom). – *Front:* the upper edge is splintered off; left edge badly broken; 14.4 cm. (top) and 10.4 (bottom) × 25.3 (right) and 7.5 (left). – INSCRIPTION: same disposition of lines as in Ja 552; letter height: from 1.2 cm. to 1.3; space between the lines: from 0.2 cm. to 0.3; distance from line 15 to the lower edge: 1.9 cm. (right) and 1.8 (left). – SYMBOL: cf. Ja 565, but the inside lines are more elaborate; cf. Plate A.

1 **Sym-** *⌜ʾlkrb/b⌝[n/. . . ./m]⌜q⌝tw⌜y/ʾ⌝*
2 **bol** *lšrḥ/yḥḍ⌝⌜b/⌝wʾḫyhw/⌞y⌟*
3 *ʾzl/byn/mlky/sbʾ/wḏr⌜y⌝[d]*
4 *n/bny/frʿm/ynhb/mlk/sbʾ/h⌝*
5 *qny/ʾlmqhbʿlʾwm/ṣlmn/⌞ḏ⌝*
6 *ḏhbn/ḥgn/wqhhw/bmsʾ⌞l⌟[h]*
7 *w/bkn/ḥlẓ/rglyhw/w⌞l⌟[wzʾ]*
8 *ʾlmqh/hʿnhw/bn/mr⌞ḍ/⌟[mrḍy]*
9 *rglyhw/wlḫrynhw⌞/⌟[bn/nḍʿ]*
10 *wšṣy/šnʾm/wlsʿ⌝[dhw/ʾlm]*
11 *⌜q⌝hbʿlʾwm/ḥẓy/wr[ḍw/mrʾyh]*
12 *w/ʾlšrḥ/yḥḍb/wʾ[ḫyhw/yʾ]*
13 *zl/byn/mlky/sbʾ⌜/⌝[wḏrydn]*
14 *bny/frʿm/ynhb/ml[k/s]*
15 *bʾ/bʾlmqhbʿlʾ[wm]*

1 **Sym-** ʾIlkarib, so[n of..., o]fficial of ʾI-
2 **bol** lšaraḥ Yaḥḍub and his brother Ya-
3 ʾzil Bayyin, the two kings of Sabaʾ and Ray[d-]
4 ân, the two sons of Fariʿum Yanhub, king of Sabaʾ, has de-
5 dicated to ʾIlumquh, master of ʾAwwâm, this statue which [is] in
6 bronze, as He had ordered him through [H]is oracle,
7 when his feet were suffering; and that may [continue]
8 ʾIlumquh to protect him from the disease [with which were suffering]
9 his two feet; and that He may preserve him [from the hostility]
10 and wickedness of [any] enemy; and that may ma[ke him happy ʾIlum-]
11 quh, master of ʾAwwâm, with the esteem and gr[ace of hi]s [two lords]
12 ʾIlšaraḥ Yaḥḍub and [his] br[other Yaʾ-]
13 zil Bayyin, the two kings of Sabaʾ [and Raydân,]
14 the two sons of Fariʿum Yanhub, kin[g of Sa-]
15 baʾ. By ʾIlumquh, master of ʾA[wwâm.]

L. 1: *ʾlkrb*, e.g., RÉS 3991/9 and Gl 1575+1130+1134/1 (cf. *HöDSP*, pp. 39-40).

L. 7: *rgl*, e.g., CIH 351/9: *rgly* also in line 9.

584 – Yellowish, slightly grayish sandstone. – MaMB 246.

STONE: thickness: 9.2 cm. (top) and 11 (bottom). – *Front:* 21.6 cm. (top) and 21.5 (bottom) × 24.8 (right) and 25.2 (left). – INSCRIPTION: same disposition of lines as in Ja 552; letter height: between 1.5 cm. and 1.8, and 1.3 in line 12; space between the lines: from 0.3 cm. to 0.5; line 12 is just on the lower edge. – SYMBOL, cf. Ja 567.

1 **Sym-** *sʿdṯwn/tly/ʾfrs/mlkn/hqny*
2 **bol** *ʾlmqh/bʿlʾwm/ṣlmn/ḏḏhbn/*
3 *ḥmdm/bḏt/mtʿhw/ḏlf/ḏmr/hwt/wbn*
4 *hw/ddʾl/wlyzʾn/ʾlmqh/hwfynhmw*
5 *bkl/sbʾt/sbʾnn/wšwʿn/mrʾyhmw(/)*
6 *ʾlšrḥ/yḥḍb/wʾẖyhw/yʾzl/byn/mlky*
7 *sbʾ/wḏrydn/šwf/ḏt/lnhʾ/hqnyt/ʾ*
8 *lmqh/bʿlʾwm/ṣlmtn/ḏt/ḏhbn/ḥmd*
9 *m/bḏt/hydʿhw/bʿl/ḥrnm/bʿbr/ʾẖyh*
10 *w/wrʾ/khqnythw/ḥgn/⟨.⟩wqhhw/bḏ(/b)ṯṯ*
11 *thw/whʾ/ẖmrhw/h(nw)lhw/hʾ/wʾẖyhw*
12 *bʾlmqh*

1 **Sym-** Saʿadṯawân, equerry of the horses of the king, has dedicated
2 **bol** to ʾIlumquh, master of ʾAwwâm, this statue which [is] in bronze,
3 in praise because He of the people of Ḏamar has saved him, him and his
4 son Dôdʾil; and that ʾIlumquh may continue to protect them
5 in all the encounters [in which] they will fight and assist their two lords
6 ʾIlšaraḥ Yaḥḍub and his brother Yaʾzil Bayyin, the two kings of
7 Sabaʾ and Raydân; he applied himself to it until this was offered to
8 ʾIlumquh, master of ʾAwwâm, [that is to say] this female statue which [is] in bronze, in praise
9 because the master of Ḥirwânum has given him some information through his brother;
10 but now, it [the statue] has been offered to Him as He had ordered him in what was communicated
11 to him; and with regard to Him, He has vouchsafed to him to lead him with care, him and his brother.
12 By ʾIlumquh.

Preliminary remarks. My notebook points out that *hmwm* instead of *hmw(/)* at the end of line 5 is certain on the stone; read also *hydʿhw(/b)ʿl* instead of *hydʿhwṭʿl* (line 9), *wqhhw* instead of *wwqhhw* (line 10) and *bḏ(/b)ṯṯ* instead of *bḏṯṯ* (also in line 10). Since I have no photograph of the stone, I do not know whether these three mistakes are mine or not.

L. 1: *tly*, pl. *ʾtly* (Wâdî Maʾsil 1/8-9) = *tlwt* (CIH 743/1), pl. *ʾtlwt* (Ja 745/2); cf. the verbal form *ytlwn* in Ja 851/6. *RyISA* translates *ʾtly* as "suivants, sujets" (X, pp. 304 and 307), and *CIH* (III, p. 155) renders *tlwt* as "submissus"; these authors as well as *BeSI* (p. 151) refer the noun to the root *tlw*. The suggested translations are not suitable here nor in Ja 745/2: *ʾtlwt/ʾfrs/mlkn*. I consider *tly* and *tlwt* as *maṣdar* of the 8th form of *wly* (cf. *HöASG*, pp. 93-94, §77 and 78); cf. Arabic *wly* "to hold command (authority) *or* have charge as a commander, administrator, or manager", and the 5th form "to undertake" (cf. *LaAEL*, p. 3060 C). The nouns *tly* or *tlwt* in association with *ʾfrs* may thus be translated "equerry"; this meaning also fits Wâdî Maʾsil 1/8-9. When related to an individual (CIH 743/1), *tlwt* may be translated "praeceptor". Therefore, *wʾrḏ/ytlwn/lmlk/sbʾ* (CIH 518/4) may be translated as follows: "and the land [which] he shall administer for the king of Sabaʾ". The fragmentary condition of CIH 588 makes it very difficult to determine the value of *b* introducing *mrṯd*[...(b/7), and therefore also that of *ytlwn* (b/6). RÉS 3869/6, Qat, is also very difficult because the definitive reading of line 6 is not published yet. First of all, A. F. L. Beeston (cf. *AfO*, 17 [1954-1955], p. 164 A) refers to that inscription as being "SE 43 (45)"; yet SE 45 is RÉS 3966. N. Rhodokanakis' translation, "und es möge herr(schen) weiterhin der König von Ḥaḍramaut" (cf. *WiHöBGS*, p. 86) supposes the following text: *wl/yml(k)/tlw/mlk/ḥḍrmt*; therefore, *RÉS*' reading, *wl/yʿ[n]/wtlw/mlk/ḥḍrmt* (cf. VI, p. 326), which is still maintained by A. F. L. Beeston (cf. *l.c.*), since he prefers *RÉS*' translation to that of N. Rhodokanakis, must be discarded once and for all. On the basis of N. Rhodokanakis' translation, *RycSD* (p. 341) transcribes as follows: *wl y(mlk) tlw mlk ḥḍrmt*, which requires "(herrschen)" in N. Rhodokanakis' text instead of "herr(schen)" and he translates the expression as follows (cf. *l.c.*, p. 342): "Et que continue à régner le roi de Ḥaḍramawt". This translation is incorrect, for it requires a text such as follows: *wl/ytlw/mlk/mlk/ḥḍrmt*, and also because Arabic *talā* means "to follow" and not "to continue". Since the inscription deals with repairs in two walls and a tower, I refer the verb *mlk* to Arabic *malaka ʾamrahu* "He had the ruling, or ordering, of his affair, or case" (cf. *LaAEL*, p. 3023 B), and translate *wl/yml(k)/tlw/mlk/ḥḏrmt* in "and that the king of Ḥaḍramawt may take charge of the administration of"; in other words, the author of the text wishes that the king himself would take over the administration of the buildings mentioned in the inscription.

L. 3: *ḏlf*; for *ḏ*, indicating the god himself, cf. *JaP*, p. 91; cp. *bʿl* in line 9; *lf*, cf. Arabic *liff* "crowd, multitude". – *hwt*, also Ja 649/27; isolated demonstrative pronoun (cf. *HöASG*, p. 47).

L. 4: *ddʾl*: RÉS 4103/1-2, Qat, and *d(dʾ)l* in RÉS 4864/1, Ḥaḍr (instead of *d..l*; cf. also in the same collection RÉS 4883/1 and 4898/1); the drawing of the text suggests taking *dṯynm/* (considered as line 4 by both *BePC*, p. 322 and *RÉS*, VII, p. 399; note that these two authors do not allude to the word divider) as the beginning of line 3 which therefore reads *dṯynm/nʾdm*, "Dutaynum Naʾdum". For *[d]dʾl* in Ingrams 1/3-4, cf. *JaIHI*, p. 100.

L. 7: *ln*: temporal conjunction (cf., e.g., *CoRoC*, p. 173 A), which is also attested in the composite form *ln/ḏ* (e.g., CIH 95/1 and Ja 633/5). According to *CIH* (I, p. 156 A), *ln* must be considered as identical with Arabic *lammâ* "when". Such an interpretation does not at all take into consideration the meaning of the prepositions *ln* "from" and *ln...ʿd(y)* "from...to" (cf. commentary on Ja 550/1); contrast *BeSI* (p. 26) who accepts *CIH*'s translation. CIH 95/1 is of no help due to the missing context. However, in Ja 651/27 as well as in Geukens 6/31, where *RyISA* (XIV, p. 376), apparently under *CIH*'s influence, translates *ln* as "lorsque" without any commentary (p. 380). The event mentioned in the phrase introduced by *ln* is the final act of the whole operation described in the phrase introduced by *bkn* "when"; *ln* means thus "until", that is to say, has the meaning of the composite preposition *ln..ʿd(y)*. The same idea is also found in the present text, although *bkn* is missing. Further, the comparative study, in Ja 633, of lines 10-12 and 14-15, the end of which being in both cases *ln/tkwn/ḏt/hqnytn*, shows that *ln* means "until" in line 12, but "as soon as" in line 15 (thus, the meaning of the isolated preposition *ln*). The most attested meaning for *ln* is thus "until", which is to be retained unless the context positively indicates the other one. At any rate, the translation of *ln* as "when" is inaccurate for it simply does not render the temporal characteristics of the conjunction. – *hʾ*: isolated demonstrative pronoun; here, feminine, but masculine in line 11.

L. 10: *bṯṯ*, 2nd passive form; cf. Arabic *baṯṯa* "to divulge (a secret), communicate (news)"; cp. RÉS 3306 A/7.

L. 11: *hnwl*, cf. Arabic *nâla*, 1st and 2nd form, "to give" and Hebrew *nhl*, piel, "to lead (with care)".

585 – Yellowish sandstone inscription, broken at the bottom; photograph in Plate 6. – MaMB 137.

STONE: thickness: 23.5 cm. (top) and 22 (bottom). – *Front:* covered with red paint; 45.3 cm. × 35.8. – INSCRIPTION: same disposition of lines as in Ja 552; letter height: 2 cm.; space between the lines: 0.3 cm. – SYMBOL, cf. Ja 583, but four inside lines (cp. Ja 582); cf. Plate A.

1 **Sym-** *yṣbḥ/ʾšwʿ/wʾẖyhw/ʿrbm/bnw/ḏʿblm/whʿll/hqn*
2 **bol** *yy/ʾlmqhṯhwnbʿlʾwm/ṣlmnhn/ḏy/ḏhbn/ḏšfthw/*
3 *ḥmdm/bḏẖmr/ʿbdyhw/yṣbḥ/ʾšwʿ/wʾẖyhw/ʿrbm/bny/ʿbl*
4 *m/whʿll/btʾwln/ʾbhmy/hwfʿṯt/ʾṣḥḥ/ḏġymn/bwfym/bn*
5 *hgrn/śwm/wshrtn/bkn/nblhw/mrʾyhmw/ʾlšrḥ/yḥḍb/wʾẖ*
6 *yhw/yʾzl/byn/mlky/sbʾ/wḏrydn/bʿbr/ʾḥbšn/whṣnʿw/ʾb*
7 *hmy/hwfʿṯt/ḏġymn/ʾḥbšn/bhgrn/śwm/brqm/wṯny/ẖrfn/wk*
8 *ydw/ʾḥbšn/hgzn/grb/ʾbhmy/hwfʿṯt/ḏġymn/wḥmdy/yṣb*
9 *ḥ/wʿrbm/ẖyl./wmqm/ʾlmqhṯhwnbʿlʾwm/bḏt/tʾwl/ʾbhmy/h*
10 *wfʿṯt/ʾṣḥḥ/ḏġymn/bwfym/bn/hyt/sbʾtn/wbn/ʿsm/ḥlẓ/w*
11 *mrḍ/mrḍ/ʾbhmy/bhyt/hgrn/śwm/wḥmdm/bḏẖmr/ʾlmqhṯhwn*
12 *bʿlʾwm/mrʾyhmw/ʾlšrḥ/yḥḍb/wʾẖyhw/yʾzl/byn/mlky/s*
13 *bʾ/wḏrydn/bny/frʿm/ynhb/mlk/sbʾ/bwḍʿ/kl/ʾḍrr/yfʿhmw*
14 *bʿltm/wsfylt/bḥrm/wybsm/wbḏt/škr/ʾsn/grmt/wld/n[g]*
15 *šyn/mlk/ʾksmn/bkn/ʿdw/bḍrm/wtškr/hʾ/ʾsn/grmt/wʾ⌜ḥ⌝*
16 *zb/ḥbšt/wlwzʾ/ʾlmqhbʿlʾwm/hwšʿn/mrʾyh⟨m⟩w/ʾlšrḥ/yḥḍ*

17 *b/wʾh̲yhw/yʾzl/byn/mlky/sbʾ/wd̲rydn/bwḍʿ/kl/ḍr/ wšnʾ/mrʾy*

18 *hmw/wlwzʾ/ʾlmqh/hwfyn/ʿbdyhw/yṣbḥ/ʾšwʿ/ wʾh̲yhw/ʿrbm/bny*

19 *ʿblm/whʿll/bkl/ʾmlʾ/ystmlʾnn/bʿmhw/wlh̲mrhmw/ ʾlmqht̲h*

20 *⌞wnbʿlʾwm/ḥẓy/wrḍw/mrʾyhmw/ʾlšrḥ/yḥ⌟ḍ⌞b/ ⌟wʾh̲yhw/y⌞ʾ⌟zl/b*

21 *[yn/mlky/sbʾ/wd̲rydn/. . . .*

1 **Sym-** Yaṣbaḥ ʾAšwaʿ and his brother ʿArbum, descendants of [the clans] ʿAblum and Haʿlal, have de-

2 **bol** dicated to ʾIlumquh Ṯahwân, master of ʾAwwâm, these two statues, both in bronze, which he has promised to Him

3 in praise because He has vouchsafed to His two worshippers Yaṣbaḥ ʾAšwaʿ and his brother ʿArbum, descendants of ʿAblum

4 and Haʿlal that the father of them both, Hawfʿaṯat ʾAṣḥaḥ, he of [the tribe] Ġaymân, come back in safety from

5 the two cities [of] Śawum and Saharatân, when have sent him their two lords ʾIlšaraḥ Yaḥḍub and his

6 brother Yaʾzil Bayyin, the two kings of Sabaʾ and Raydân, against the Ḥabašites and (when) have held the father

7 of them both, Hawfʿaṯat, him of Ġaymân, the Ḥabašites in the city [of] Śawum for one lightning season and two years; and

8 the Ḥabašites have plotted to shave the body of their father Hawfʿaṯat, him of Ġaymân; and have praised Yaṣbaḥ

9 and ʿArbum the strength and power of ʾIlumquh Ṯahwân, master of ʾAwwâm, because came back their father Hawf-

10 ʿaṯat ʾAṣḥaḥ, he of Ġaymân, in safety from that military campaign and from the stiffness (?) of the oppression and

11 of the disease [which] their father was suffering in this city, Śawum; and in praise because has vouchsafed ʾIlumquh Ṯahwân,

12 master of ʾAwwâm, to their two lords ʾIlšaraḥ Yaḥḍub and his brother Yaʾzil Bayyin, the two kings of Sa-

13 baʾ and Raydân, the two sons of Fariʿum Yanhub, king of Sabaʾ, to humiliate all the enemies [who] rose against them

14 in the higher lands and in the lower countries of the sea and of the land; and because was defeated the adversary Garmat, the child of the Ne[gu]š,

15 the king of ʾAksûman, when he went to war, and were defeated this adversary Garmat and the fighting

16 bands of Ḥabašat; and that ʾIlumquh, master of ʾAwwâm, may continue to assist (their) two lords ʾIlšaraḥ Yaḥḍub

17 and his brother Yaʾzil Bayyin, the two kings of Sabaʾ and Raydân, in humiliating every foe and enemy of their

18 two lords; and that ʾIlumquh may continue to shower upon His two worshippers Yaṣbaḥ ʾAšwaʿ and his brother ʿArbum, des-

19 cendants of ʿAblum and Haʿlal, all the favors [for which] they shall beseech Him; and that may vouchsafe to them, ʾIlumquh Ṯah-

20 wân, master of ʾAwwâm, the esteem and grace of their two lords ʾIlšaraḥ Yaḥḍub and of his brother Yaʾzil Ba-

21 [yyin, the two kings of Sabaʾ and Raydân,. . .

L. 1: *yṣbḥ*; CIH 544/1 and *ṣbḥ* in Ja 308, Qat (and commentary on Ja 161/1). – *ʾšwʿ*, well-known second personal name; e.g., CIH 145/1 and Ja 489 A/2, Qat. – *ʿrbm*, e.g., name of a man, e.g., in RÉS 3945/17, and of a tower in RÉS 3552/3, Qat (cf. *JaPSAP*, pp. 101, 102, and 170-71). – *ʿblm*, e.g., RÉS 4387/1. – *hʿll*, CIH 6/2; cf. also the 2nd name of a man *yhʿll* in RÉS 3996; in RÉS 4612, read *ʿyll*, family name, instead of *yṣ*(?)*ll*; read RÉS 4612 as follows: (line 1) *ḍbḥ*[/]*ʿyll* (line 2) *nḥ* "Ḍabaḥ ʿAylal (line 2) has a deep voice"; instead of "*h*]*t̲b*. . *ʿṣ*(?)*ll* (Lecture très douteuse)" (*RÉS*, VII, p. 273).

L. 2, end: the worker started to engrave first *ḥ*; the extremities of the two upper right strokes are not erased.

L. 4: *ʾṣḥḥ*, Ist 7630/1, and the Arabic personal name *ṣaḥîyiḥ* (cf. *SlGaVNPA*, p. 46 A).

Ll. 4-5: *bn hgrn/śwm/wshrtn*, CIH 314+954/14.

L. 6: *ḥṣnʿ*, cf. commentary on Ja 577/2; cp. Aramaic *ṣânaʿ* "to hide, retire" and piel *ṣînnêʿa* "to restrain" (cf. *JaDT*, p. 1292 B); here, with the meaning of "to withhold, hold back, restrain".

L. 7: *brq*, CIH 282/6; cf. Arabic *baraqa* "to shine, gleam (with lightning)". *brq* is feminine; cf. e.g., *bhyt/brqn* in Ja 610/9. The two rainy seasons, *d̲tʾ* and *h̲rf* (cf. *BeESACD*, p. 19) are the only ones connected with *brq* in the present collection of texts (cf. *brq/h̲rf* in Ja 610/6, 653/5, 735/4, and *ʾbrq/d̲tʾ/whh̲rf* in Ja 610/14, 627/11-12, and 628/12-13); cf. also *brq/d̲tʾ* in CIH 282/6. *brq* means either the lightning storm (e.g., Ja 610/14) that occurs during the rainy season and usually accompanies the rain storm (cf., e.g., Ja 627/12-13), or the lightning season itself (e.g., here). *brq* does not allude to rain as indicated by etymology: this fact is confirmed by

Ja 735, especially line 4: *sqy/brq/ḫrf* "(that He would) irrigate the lightning season of autumn".

Ll. 7-8: *kyd*, cf. the 5th form *tkyd* in RÉS 3992/13 (cf. *BeNL*, VI, pp. 313-16); cf. Arabic *kâda* "to plot, deceive, circumvent".

L. 8: *hgzn*, 4th form of *gzz* (RÉS 2865/1 and *BeSI*, p. 100; for the palaeography of RÉS 2865 = CIH 610, cf. *JaPSAP*, pp. 136-39 and 183, note 4); cf. *ǧazza* in Arabic "to shear, crop (the hair)", in Datînah "to cut" (cf. *LaGD*, p. 281) and modern Ḥaḍr "to cut (corn, mustache)" (cf. *LaH*, p. 542).

L. 9: *ẖyl/wmqm*, very well-known expression; e.g., RÉS 4142/7; cf. also commentary on Ja 558/4; for *ẖyl*, cf. *JeHoDISO*, p. 87: *ḥyl$_{I}$*.

L. 10: *ʿsm*: the ordinary meaning of *ʿsm* (cf. commentary on Ja 574/9) is not suitable here; cf. Arabic *ʿasima* "to be, *or* become distorted (man's hand, and his foot)" (cf. *LaAEL*, p. 2047 B); this *maṣdar* may allude to the stiffness or some paralysis resulting from injury and disease.

L. 14: *bʿltm/wsfylt*, cp. in singular *bʿlym/wsflm* in RÉS 3566/17, Qat, and *ʿlyhmw/wsflthmw* in RÉS 3966/10; for *ʿly*, pl. *ʿlt*, cf. Arabic *ʿulw* and *ʿulâwat* "the higher, *or* highest part" (cf. *LaAEL*, p. 2144 B); for *sfylt*, broken plural of *sfl*, cf. the ordinary plural *sflt* in RÉS 3966/10; *StSESA* (p. 525) rightly relates both *sfl* and *śfl* to the same root (contrary to *BePESA*, p. 18); for the parallel *mś(n)d-msnd*, cf. commentary on Ja 669/6. – *ʾs*, *scriptio defectiva* of *ʾys*; cf. commentary on Ja 577/6.

L. 15: *tškr*, 5th form of *škr*; here, passive form as well as in CIH 308/18 (cf. *BeSI*, p. 31).

L. 16: *mrʾyh⟨m⟩w* instead of *mrʾyhw* (on the stone), according to lines 5, 12, and 20.

586 – Stone re-used in the western pavement; broken on the top and at the bottom; cf. Chapter I, B. – MaMB 262.

Front: right edge badly damaged. – INSCRIPTION: same disposition of lines as in Ja 552; letter height: from 1.7 cm. to 2; space between the lines: from 0.3 cm. to 0.4.

1 **[Sym-** *ẓbym/yrzḥ/...   ...]*
2 **[bol]** *m/ʾʿ[....]/hqnyw/ʾlmqhṯhwnbʿlʾw[m]*
3 *[ṣlm]n/ḏḏ[hbn/ḥmdm]/b[ḏ]t/ẖmr/whwšʿn/[wh]*
4 *[ʿnn/m]rʾyhmw/ʾlšrḥ/yḥḍb/wʾẖyhw/yʾz[l]*
5 *byn/mlky/[sb]ʾ/wḏrydn/bny/frʿm/ynhb/mlk/s*
6 *bʾ/b[šk]r/w⸤ṯ⸥[br/ws]bʿn/ʾšʿb/wmṣyrt/ḥmyrm/wy*
7 *[tʾ]wln/mrʾyhmw/bwfym/wḥmdm/wbḏrḍwhm*
8 *[w/]bn/kl/sbʾt/wtqdmt/sbʾy/wtqdmn/bʿm*
9 *[kr]⸤b⸥ʾl/ḏrydn/wmṣyrt/ḥmyrm/wlwzʾ/ʾl*
10 *[mqh/]šrḥ/wrtṯdn/grybt/mrʾyhmw/wḥmdm*
11 *[bḏ]ẖmr/ʾlmqh/ʿbdhw/ẓbym/yrzḥ/btʾwln*
12 *[bwf]ym/wʾḥllm/wsbym/wmltm/wġnmm/bkl/sbʾ*
13 *[t/w]tqdmt/bhmw/šwʿ/mrʾyhmw/wbkl/sbʾt/w*
14 *ġzw(y)/wʾ(ḍ)[bʾ]/sbʾ/wtqdmn/ḥgn/wqhy/mrʾy*
15 *hmw/ʿdy/ʾrḍ/ḥmyrm/wysbʾ/ġztm/bʾrbʿ*
16 *(y)/ʾsdm/ʿdy/ẖlf/srʿn/wytqdmw/bʿm/ʾrbʿ*
17 *m[ʾnm]/ʾsdm/bn/ḥmyrm/[w]hwšʿhmw/ʾlmqh/bh*
18 *[bʿl* or *sḥt]n/wṯbr/hmt/ʾḥmrn/whrgw/bnhmw/sbʿt/wʿšry*
19 *[ʾs]bʿm/wb[n]hw/fysbʾ/ẓbym/ġztm/bẖmsy/ʾ*
20 *sdm/ʿdy/⸤ẖ⸥lf/srʿn/wtqdmw/bʿm/šʿbn/qšmm/wy*
21 *[m]tʿ/wẖm[r]hmw/ʾlmqh/hrg/ʾlzʾd/ḏrbḥm/wḏ*
22 *bn/ʾsdhw/ʾḥd/wẖmsy/bḍʿm/wyhqḏw/rkbhmw/wḥ*
23 *ṣqhmw/ḏtrbʿ/mrʾyhmw/wbʿdhw/fysbʾ/ẓbym*
24 *bṯn(y)/lwḍ[ʿ..]/ʾṣ[..]/wysʿḍw/bmq[r](n)/ḏẓbym/..*

1 **[Sym-** Ẓabîum Yarzaḥ,...
2 **[bol]** m, the ʿ...s, have dedicated to ʾIlumquh Ṯahwân, master of ʾAww[âm,]
3 this [statue] which [is] in br[onze, in praise] be[cau]se He has vouchsafed to and assisted [and helped]
4 their two [lo]rds ʾIlšaraḥ Yaḥḍub and his brother Yaʾz[il]
5 Bayyin, the two kings of [Sab]aʾ and Raydân, the two sons of Fariʿum Yanhub, king of Sa-
6 baʾ, in [def]eating and c[rushing and plund]ering the tribes and the expeditionary forces of Ḥimyarum; and so
7 their two lords [ca]me back in safety and praise; and because He has favored
8 the[m] in all the encounters and attacks [in which] the two of them fought and attacked
9 [Kari]bʾil, him of Raydân, and the expeditionary forces of Ḥimyarum; and that may continue ʾIl-
10 [umquh] to keep healthy and preserve the bodies of their two lords; and in praise
11 [because] ʾIlumquh has vouchsafed to His worshipper Ẓabîum Yarzaḥ to come back
12 [in safe]ty and [with] animals and captives and riches and booty from all the encoun[ters]
13 [and] attacks in which he has assisted their two lords, and from all the encounters and
14 the (two) raids and (the en)[gagement]s [in which] he fought and attacked as ordered their two
15 lords in the land of Ḥimyarum; and so he made raids with for(ty)
16 soldiers in the region of Sâriʿân and they attacked four

17 h[undred] soldiers from Ḥimyarum [and] ʾIlumquh assisted them in
18 [seizing *or* destroying] and crushing these Ḥimyarites, and of them they killed twenty-seven
19 pillagers; and fr[om] there, Ẓabîum made raids with fifty sol-
20 diers in the region of Sâriʿân and they attacked the tribe Qašamum and so,
21 ʾIlumquh saved and vouchsafed to them to kill ʾIlzaʾad, him of [the family] Rabḥum, and some
22 of his soldiers, fifty-one beheaded; and so they carried away their beasts of burden and
23 prisoner keepers whom their two lords arrogated for themselves; and after that Ẓabîum fought
24 two [years] in order to humiliate...]...[...] and so they...in the military expedition of Ẓabîum..

L. 1, cp., e.g., line 11.

L. 6: *bškr*, cf., e.g., Ja 576/1.

Ll. 7-8: *wḥmdm/wbḏrḍwhmw*: there is no reason to suppose that *w* introducing *bḏ* is a mistake, since the expression *bwfym/wḥmdm* is attested several times (e.g., Ja 574/9) and *bḏ*, as well as *b*[*ḏ*]*t* in line 3, depends on [*ḥmdm*] in the same line. – *rḍw*, 2nd form of the verb, has the same meaning as the 4th form *hrḍw* or *hrḍy*; also in Ja 691/10.

L. 8: the subject of *sbʾy* is *mrʾy*, the two kings.

L. 11: *ẓbym*, Ja 147/1, Qat, and name of a horse in Ja 745/9. – *yrẓḥ*, cp. *rẓḥn* in Ja 165/1, Qat.

L. 14: *ġzw*(*y*): *ġzwṯ* in the copy. – *ʾ*(*ḏ*)[*bʾ*], cp. Ja 832/2.

Ll. 15-16: *bʾrbʿm* (copy): the number 4 is ridiculously small compared with the 400 soldiers who were attacked by them; I read *bʾrbʿ*(*y*); cp. *bẖmsy* in line 19.

L. 16: *srʿn*: cp. *srʿm*, masculine personal name in, e.g., CIH 84/1; cf. also the name of a terrace *srʿ* in RÉS 3856/2, Qat.

L. 17: *m*[*ʾnm*], e.g., Ja 572/4.

Ll. 17-18: *hbʿl* and *hsḥt* are mentioned with *ṯbr* in Ja 576/4 and 577/5, respectively.

L. 18: */bnhmw*: the worker had first engraved */b/bnhw* with the dittography of */b*; the last four characters have not been erased and *nhmw* was engraved on top of them.

L. 19: [*s*]*bʿm*, participle from the root *sbʿ* "to plunder".

L. 21: *ʾlzʾd*, CIH 695/1. – *rbḥm*, name of a man, e.g., in RÉS 3871/1, Qat, and of a clan *rbḥ* in Ja 347/1, Qat; cf. also the Arabic personal names *râbaḥ*, *rabḥî*, and *ribîḥ* (cf. *SlGaVNPA*, pp. 43 A and 44 A respectively).

L. 22; *bḍʿ*, cf. *JaASAB*, p. 163, commentary on CIH 407/25.

L. 23: *trbʿ*, 5th form of *rbʿ*, with the same meaning as that of the 1st Arabic form "to claim, arrogate for one's self".

L. 24: *bṯn*(*y*); copy: *bṯnṯ*. – *lwḏ* is followed in the copy by the mention of three missing letters.

587 – Yellowish, slightly grayish sandstone; photograph in Plate 7. – MaMB 149.

STONE: almost constant thickness: 15 cm. – *Front*, left edge slightly damaged; 21.8 cm. (top) and 21.9 (bottom) × 35.7. – INSCRIPTION, same disposition of lines as in Ja 552; letter height: 1.8 cm.; space between the lines: 0.3 cm.; distance from line 1 to the upper edge: 0.8 cm. – SYMBOL, cf. Ja 561, but the two extremities are concave; cf. plate A. – FLOWER: on both ends of line 13; the one at the beginning has 10 petals; the other only 9; cf. Plate B; cf. CIH 73.

1 **Sym-** *ʾḥmd/ʾẓlm/bn/fḍlm/hqny*
2 **bol** *ʾlmqhṯhwnbʿlʾwm/ṣlmn/ḏḏhbn*
3 *ḏšfthw/lḏt/ẖmrhw/hwfynhw/bn/kl/s*
4 *bʾt/sbʾw/wšwʿn/mrʾhmw/ʾlšrḥ/y*
5 *ḥḍb/mlk/sbʾ/wḏrydn/bn⟨⟩/frʿm/ynhb/m*
6 *lk/sbʾ/wlwzʾ/ʾlmqhṯhwnbʿlʾwm/hwfy*
7 *n/ʿbdhw/ʾḥmd/wlẖmrhw/ḥẓy/wrḍw/mrʾ*
8 *yhw/ʾlšrḥ/yḥḍb/wʾẖyhw/yʾzl/byn/mlky*
9 *sbʾ/wḏrydn/bny/frʿm/ynhb/mlk/sbʾ*
10 *wlsʿdhmw/nʿmtm/wmngt/ṣdqm/wʾṯmrm/hnʾ*
11 *m/ʿdy/ʾrḍhmw/wlẖmrhw/ʾlmqhṯhwnbʿlʾ*
12 *wm/hʿnnhw/wẖrynhw/bn/bʾstm/wnḍʿ/wšṣy*
13 **Flower***šnʾm/bʾlmqhṯhwnbʿlʾwm***Flower**

1 **Sym-** ʾAḥmad ʾAẓlam, descendant of Faḍlum, has dedicated
2 **bol** to ʾIlumquh Ṯahwân, master of ʾAwwâm, this statue which [is] in bronze,
3 which he has promised to Him because He has vouchsafed to him to protect him in all
4 the encounters [in which] they fought and assisted their lord ʾIlšaraḥ
5 Yaḥḍub, king of Sabaʾ and Raydân, son of Fariʿum Yanhub,
6 king of Sabaʾ; and that ʾIlumquh Ṯahwân, master of ʾAwwâm, may continue to protect
7 His worshipper ʾAḥmad; and that He may vouchsafe to him the esteem and grace of his two
8 lords ʾIlšaraḥ Yaḥḍub and of his brother Yaʾzil Bayyin, the two kings

9 of Sabaʾ and Raydân, the two sons of Fariᶜum Yanhub, king of Sabaʾ;
10 and that He may make them happy with perfect prosperity and security and (with) pleasing fruits
11 in their land; and that may vouchsafe to him ʾIlumquh Ṯahwân, master of
12 ʾAwwâm, to assist him and to preserve him from misfortunes and (from) the hostility and wickedness
13 **Flower** of [any] enemy. By ʾIlumquh Ṯahwân, master of ʾAwwâm. **Flower**

L. 1: *ʾẓlm*, e.g., CIH 78/1 and RÉS 4664/3. *-fḏlm*, name of a man in RÉS 5037, Ḥaḏr, and of a family in Ja 511/1 (cf. commentary in *JaISAR*, p. 108); cf. also the Arabic personal names *al-faḍlâwî*, *fiḍûl*, and *fuḍil* (cf. *SlGaVNPA*, pp. 19 A, 19 B, and 20 B respectively).
L. 4: *sbʾw* and *mrʾhmw*: the plural refers to both *ʾḥmd* and *fḏlm*.
L. 5: *bny* instead of *bn* (e.g., Ja 567/21).
Ll. 10-11: *ʾṯmrm/hnʾm*, also *[ʾṯ]mrm/hnʾm* in NaNN 65/1.

588 – Yellowish, slightly grayish sandstone; the right side is missing; photograph in Plate 7. – MaMB 152.

STONE: thickness: 12.7 cm. (top) and 11.7 (bottom). – *Front:* upper left and lower right corners are broken; upper right corner damaged; 15.2 cm. (top) and 13.7 (bottom) × 18.6 (left) and 22.2 (right); the stone has been re-used in a building, for several letters are filled with cement. – INSCRIPTION: same disposition of lines as in Ja 552; letter height: 1.1 cm.; space between the lines: 0.2 cm. – SYMBOL: the right half is completely destroyed; the left half is so badly damaged that it is practically impossible to see anything.

1 **[Sy]m-** *⌈m⌉ᶜ⌈d⌉krb/wbnyhw/ʾlw[h](b)[/ bn/ḏh]*
2 **[bo]l** *ẓfn/hqnyw/ʾlmqh⌈b⌉ᶜ⌈l⌉ʾwm/⌈ṣlm⌉*
3 *[n]⌊hn/ḏḏhbn/ḥmdm/bḏt/ẖmrhw/ʾlm*
4 *[q]⌊hbᶜlʾwm/wldm/ḏkrm/ḥgn/ktbš*
5 *[r/]ᶜbdhw/mᶜdkrb/bmlʾhw/wlwzʾ/ʾ*
6 *[lm]qh/bᶜlʾwm/ẖmr/ᶜbdhw/⌈m⌉ᶜdkrb/ʾ*
7 *[wl]dm/hnʾm/wlẖmrhmw/ḥẓy/wrḍw/⌈m⌉*
8 *[rʾ]yhmw/ʾlšrḥ/yḥḍb/wʾẖ yhw/y[ʾ]z*
9 *[l/]⌊byn/mlky/sbʾ/wḏrydn/bny/frᶜm/y*
10 *[n]⌊hb/mlk/sbʾ/wlsᶜdhmw/ʾlmqh/m⌋*
11 *[ngt/]ṣdqm/wwfy/grybthmw/wlhᶜ*
12 *[nnh]mw/bn/nḍᶜ/wšṣy/šnʾm/bʾl*
13 *mqhbᶜlʾwm*

1 **[Sy]m-** Maᶜadkarib and his son ʾIlwa[ha](b), [descendants of (the family) Ḏa-]
2 **[bo]l** zfân, have dedicated to ʾIlumquh, master of ʾAwwâm, [the]se two statues
3 which [are] in bronze, in praise because has vouchsafed to him ʾIlum-
4 [qu]h, master of ʾAwwâm, a male child as He announ[ced] to
5 His worshipper Maᶜadkarib in His generosity; and that may continue ʾI-
6 [lum]quh, master of ʾAwwâm, to vouchsafe to His worshipper Maᶜadkarib
7 pleasing [chil]dren; and that He may vouchsafe to them the esteem and grace of
8 their two l[ord]s ʾIlšaraḥ Yaḥḍub and his brother Ya[ʾ]z-
9 [il] Bayyin, the two kings of Sabaʾ and Raydân, the two sons of Fariᶜum Ya-
10 [n]hub, king of Sabaʾ; and that ʾIlumquh may make them happy with
11 perfect se[curity] and the safety of their persons; and that He may pro-
12 [tect t]hem from the hostility and wickedness of [any] enemy. By ʾIlu-
13 mquh, master of ʾAwwâm.

L. 1: *mᶜdkrb*, e.g., The Hombrechtikon Plaque published by A. M. Honeyman (cf. *Iraq*, 16 [1954], pp. 23-28); this personal name, a monogram in relief, is interpreted as the subject of *sq*[...], the only two letters of the inscription, which are completed as *sq[ny]* by the publisher. Such a relation between a monogram and an inscription is unknown in South Arabic; therefore, *mᶜdkrb* must be interpreted as separated from the inscription itself and *sq*[...] as the first two letters of another personal name, which is the beginning of the text and can be restored as follows: e.g., *sq[rn]*, e.g., in Ja 683/1); furthermore, the plaque is Sab.
Ll. 1-2: after *bnyhw*, 10 or more probably 11 signs are missing (cp. lines 2 and 3); the second personal name is *ʾlw[h](b)*; at the end of line 1, I restore *bn/ḏh* and read *bn/ḏhzfn*, expression attested in Ja 660/13; my restoration fills up the blank perfectly.
Ll. 4-5: *tbšr*, cf. *CoRoC*, p. 119 B and *BePESA*, p. 2; also verb in CIH 333/6. CIH 333 = Ist 7480 is a whitish limestone; maximum thickness: 17 cm.; the front measures 65 cm. × 22.

589 – Yellowish, slightly grayish sandstone inscription, broken at the bottom; photograph in Plate 7. – MaMB 179

STONE: constant thickness: 26.5 cm. – *Front:* the upper edge is splintered off; 35.8 cm. (right), 37 (center) and 36 (left). – INSCRIPTION, same disposition of lines as in Ja 552; letter height: from 2 cm. to 2.3; space between the lines: from 0.3 cm. to 0.4. – SYMBOL, some kind of unattractive combination of Ja 582 and 585; cf. Plate A.

1 **Sym-** *yhᶜn/ʾẖṭ⌜r/ḏṣ⌝ryhw/ʾbkrb/wbn*
2 **bol** *yhw/hḥyᶜṯt/ḏṣryhw/mᶜdkrb/w⌝*
3 *šfᶜṯt/ḏṣryhw/wddʾl/wwhbʾwm/ḏ*
4 *ṣryhw/smhkrb/bnw/ᶜṯkln/ᶜṣyt/hq*
5 *nyw/ʾlmqhṯhwnbᶜlʾwm/ṣlmn/ḏḏh*
6 *bn/ḥmdm/bḏẖmr/whwšᶜn/mrʾyhmw*
7 *ʾlšrḥ/yḥḍb/wʾẖyhw/yʾzl/byn/ml*
8 *ky/sbʾ/wḏrydn/bny/frᶜm/ynhb/mlk*
9 *sbʾ/bwḍᶜ/wṯbr/whṯlᶜn/whsḥtn/krb*
10 *ʾl/ḏrydn/wʾšᶜb/wmṣyrt/ḥmyrm/wldᶜm*
11 *bḥbl/wḍr/hštʾw/wtnšʾn/bᶜbr/mrʾ*
12 *yhmw/ʾlšrḥ/yḥḍb/wʾẖyhw/yʾzl/byn*
13 *mlky/sbʾ/wḏrydn/wrʾ/kẖmr/ʾlmqh*
14 *bᶜlʾwm/⌞t⌟⌞ʾwln/mrʾyhmw/bwfym/wḥ⌞m⌟*
15 *[dm/... ...]⌜/ḏ⌝[ᶜ]⌜sm⌝/[...*

1 **Sym-** Yuhᶜîn ʾAẖṭar, he of Ṣarayhû ʾAbkarib, and his
2 **bol** sons Haḥayᶜaṯat, he of Ṣarayhû Maᶜadkarib, and
3 Šûfᶜaṯat, he of Ṣarayhû Waddʾil, and Wahabʾawwâm, he of
4 Ṣarayhû Sumhukarib, descendants of ᶜAṯkalân ᶜUṣayyat, have
5 dedicated to ʾIlumquh Ṯahwân, master of ʾAwwâm, this statue which [is] in bron-
6 ze, in praise because He has vouchsafed to and assisted their two lords
7 ʾIlšaraḥ Yaḥḍub and his brother Yaʾzil Bayyin, the two
8 kings of Sabaʾ and Raydân, the two sons of Fariᶜum Yanhub, king of
9 Sabaʾ, in humiliating and crushing and breaking and destroying Karib-
10 ʾil, him of Raydân and the tribes and the expeditionary forces of Ḥimyarum, the children of ᶜAmm,
11 in the revolt and the war they started and rose up against their two
12 lords ʾIlšaraḥ Yaḥḍub and his brother Yaʾzil Bayyin,
13 the two kings of Sabaʾ and Raydân; but now, has vouchsafed ʾIlumquh,
14 master of ʾAwwâm, that their two lords come back in safety and prai-
15 [se... ...], which [was de]sired, [...

L. 1: *ʾẖṭr*, e.g., CIH 457/1; cf. also the Arabic personal name *al-ẖâṭir* (cf. *SlGaVNPA*, p. 31 B).

L. 2: *hḥyᶜṯt*, e.g., CIH 536/2; compare *ṯḥyʾb* in Ja 864/1, Qat.

L. 3: *šfᶜṯt*, e.g., CIH 353/11 and RÉS 4673/2; for *šfsy* in Ja 402/1, Ḥaḍr, cf. *JaIHB*, p. 161, *JaNA* and *JaDME*, p. 21. – *wddʾl*, e.g., RÉS 4610 B and Ja 613/10 (cf. also *wdd* in RÉS 5059 and *wddm* in RÉS 4596/1); more frequently, *wdʾl* in, e.g., RÉS 5098/1 and Ja 852/1, Qat; cf. also *wdyġl* in Ja 549.

L. 4: *ᶜṣyt*: masculine name in CIH 450/4. Cf. the Arabic names *ᶜuṣayyat* of men (cf. *WüID*, e.g., 187/4 and *GoAT*, p. 385; also "'Oçajja" in F. Wüstenfeld, *Register zu den genealogischen Tabellen der arabischen Stämme und Familien*, Göttingen, 1853, p. 348) and of a clan (cf. *WüR*, p. 252 A), and *al-ᶜuṣayyat* of a man (cf. *GoAT*, *l.c.*).

Ll. 5-6: *ḏhbn*, the *n* is engraved on top of an *m*.

L. 15: ⌜*ḏ*⌝[ᶜ]⌜*sm*⌝ is certain under *hmw* of *mrʾyhmw* and is preceded by an empty space of 15 or 16 characters; the first three signs are *dm/*; the 12 or 13 others might be restored as follows *wʾḥllm/wsbym* (Ja 574/9) or *wmhrgm/wsbym* (Ja 575/8).

590 – Yellowish sandstone inscription, cut in order to be re-used in a wall; lower fifth of the right side broken; photograph in Plate 7. – MaMB 181.

STONE: almost constant thickness: 13.5 cm. – *Front:* 9.5 cm. (top) and 9.3 (center) and 7.2 (bottom) × 35.2. – INSCRIPTION: first line is missing; and end of lines 7, 10, and 11 is damaged; same disposition of lines as in Ja 552; letter height: from 1 cm. to 1.3; space between the lines: 0.2 cm. – *Symbol:* combination of Ja 561 and 589; cf. Plate A.

1 **[Sym-** *whbʾwm/..../wsᶜdʾwm/...]*
2 **bol** *⌜bn⌝w⌜/krbm/⌝w⌜m⌝ᶜ⌜dnm⌝/hqny/ʾlmqh⌝*
3 *ṯhwnbᶜlʾwm/ṣlmn/ḏḏhbn/ḥmdm/bḏt*
4 *ẖmr/(ᶜ)bdyhw/whbʾwm/wsᶜdʾwm/tʾwl*
5 *n/bwfym/bn/shrtn/bkn/sbʾw/wšwᶜn/m*
6 *rʾhmw/ʾlšr(ḥ)/yḥḍb/mlk/sbʾ/wḏrydn*
7 *wbḏt/ẖmrhmw/ʾlmqhbᶜlʾwm/tʾwln/[b]*
8 *wfym/bn/ʾrḍ/ḥmyrm/bkn/sbʾw/wšwᶜn*
9 *mrʾhmw/ʾlšrḥ/yḥḍb/mlk/sbʾ/wḏryd*
10 *n/bkn/tqdmw/bᶜm/mṣr/ḏrydn/bḥql/ḏ⌝rm*
11 *tm/wbḏt/ẖmr/ʾlmqhbᶜlʾwm/ᶜbdhw/[w]*
12 *hbʾwm/tʾ⌟wln/bn/hwt/tqdmn/bwfym/w*
13 *mhrgm/wsbym/wġnmm/ḏhrḍw/ᶜbdhw/w*

14 *hbʾwm/wlwzʾ/ʾlmqh/ẖmr/ʿbdhw/w*
15 *hbʾwm[/]hwfynhw/bkl/sbʾt/ysbʾn/w*
16 *šwʿn/mrʾyhmw/ʾlšrḥ/yḥḏb/wʾḫy*
17 *hw/yʾzl/byn/mlky/sbʾ/wḏrydn/wlḫ*
18 *mrhw/ʾlmqh/hwfynhw/bkl/ʾmlʾ/y*
19 *stmlʾn/wtḍʿn/bʿmhw/wlḫmrhw/ḥẓ*
20 *⌊y/⌋wrḍw/mrʾyhmw/ʾlšrḥ/yḥḏb/wʾḫyhw*
21 *[y]⌈ʾ⌉⌊ ⌋zl/byn/mlky/sbʾ/wḏrydn/bny/frʿ*
22 *[m/y]nhb/mlk/sbʾ/wlḫryn/ʾlmqh/ʿbd[y]*
23 *[hw/]whbʾwm/wsʿdʾwm/bny/krbm/wmʿ*
24 *[d][nm/bn/bʾstm/wnkytm/wnḍʿ/wš*
25 *[ṣ]y/šnʾm/bʾlmqhṯhwnbʿlʾwm*

1 **[Sym-** Wahabʾawwâm...and Saʿadʾawwâm...]
2 **bol** descendants of Karibum and Maʿdanum, has dedicated to ʾIlumquh
3 Ṯahwân, master of ʾAwwâm, this statue which [is] in bronze, in praise because
4 He has vouchsafed to His two worshippers Wahabʾ-awwâm and Saʿadʾawwâm to come back
5 in safety from Saharatân, when they fought and helped
6 their lord ʾIlšara(ḥ) Yaḥḍub, king of Sabaʾ and Raydân;
7 and because ʾIlumquh, master of ʾAwwâm, has vouchsafed to them to come back [in]
8 safety from the land of Ḥimyarum, when they fought and helped
9 their lord ʾIlšaraḥ Yaḥḍub, king of Sabaʾ and Rayd-
10 ân, when they attacked the expeditionary corps of Raydân in the country of Rayma-
11 tum; and because ʾIlumquh, master of ʾAwwâm, has vouchsafed to His worshipper [Wa-]
12 habʾawwâm to come back from this attack in safety and
13 (with) war trophy and captives and booty, which pleased His worshipper Wa-
14 habʾawwâm; and that ʾIlumquh may continue to vouchsafe to His worshipper Wa-
15 habʾawwâm to protect him in all the encounters [in which] he shall fight and
16 assist their two lords ʾIlšaraḥ Yaḥḍub and his brother
17 Yaʾzil Bayyin, the two kings of Sabaʾ and Raydân; and that may vouch-
18 safe to him ʾIlumquh to shower upon him all the favors [for which] he
19 shall beseech and implore Him; and that He may vouchsafe to him the es-
20 teem and grace of their two lords ʾIlšaraḥ Yaḥḍub and his brother
21 [Ya]ʾzil Bayyin, the two kings of Sabaʾ and Ray-dân, the two sons of Fariʿ-
22 [um Ya]nhub, king of Sabaʾ; and that ʾIlumquh may preserve [His two] worshippers
23 Wahabʾawwâm and Saʿadʾawwâm, descendants of Karibum and Maʿ-
24 [da]num from misfortunes and sufferings and (from) the hostility and wick-
25 [ed]ness of [any] enemy. By ʾIlumquh Ṯahwân, master of ʾAwwâm.

L. 1: restoration based, e.g., on line 4.

L. 2: *krbm*, cf. the name of a man, e.g., in CIH 601/21. – *mʿdnm*, cp. the masculine name *mʿdn* (e.g., RÉS 4992 A/1); cf. also the Arabic names of a person *ʿadnâm*, *ʿadûnat* (cf. *SlGaVNPA*, pp. 3 A and 3 B respectively), and of a man *ʿadnânu* and *ʾibn ʿadnâna* (cf. *WüID*, 20/17).

L. 4: (ʿ)*bdy*: *w* instead of ʿ is certain on the stone. – *sʿdʾwm*, e.g., RÉS 4188/1, 4770/5-6 and AshM 1957-17/5 (cf. *BeTMS*).

Ll. 10-11: *rmtm*, e.g., CIH 390/2-3.

L. 15: the space before *hwfynhw* exists for a word divider, which was forgotten. – *l* of *bkl* is engraved on top of *n*.

L. 19: *tḍʿn*, e.g., Ja 567/19.

591 – Whitish, slightly grayish sandstone; left part = MaMB 82, right part = MaMB 192 = Ja 596; two photographs in Plate 8.

STONE: almost constant thickness: between 9 cm. and 8.8. – *Front*: the four edges are splintered off; covered with red paint. – INSCRIPTION: same disposition of lines as in Ja 552; letter height: 1.2 cm., but only 1 in line 12; space between the lines: 0.3 cm. – SYMBOL, same general type as that of Ja 585; cf. plate A. – FLOWER: at both ends of line 12; the flower on the left is much better designed and more regular than that on the right; each flower is composed of four petals normally attached to the bud; in each space between the petals, a small curve is engraved; cf. Plate B. – *MaMB* 82: front : 19.1 cm. × 8.5 (maximum). – *MaMB* 192: front: 19 cm. × 3.8 (top) and 9.3 (bottom).

1 **Sym-** *rṯ⌈dšm⌉⌈s⌉[m/yh]⌈t⌉f/bn/rḍw⌈n/ḏ⌉[ḫ]⌈r⌉*
2 **bol** *blt/ʾlš⌈r⌉[ḥ/y]⌈ḥḏb/wʾḫyhw/yʾ*
3 *zl/byn/mlky/s⌉[b]ʾ/wḏrydn/bny/f*
4 *rʿm/ynhb/mlk/⌊s⌋[bʾ/hqny/ʾlmqhṯ*
5 *wnbʿlʾwm/ṣlm⌋[m]⌊/⌋ḏḏhbm/lḫmrhw/ʾ*
6 *lmqhṯhwnbʿl[ʾwm/]⌊ḥ⌋ẓy/wrḍw/mrʾyh⌋*
7 *w/ʾlšrḥ/yḥḏb⌈/w⌉[ʾḫ]⌈y⌉hw/yʾzl/byn/m*
8 *⌊lky/sbʾ/wḏryd[n/bn]y/frʿm/ynhb/m[l]*
9 *[k/]sbʾ/wlḫmrhw/ʾ⌉⌈ṯmrm/hnʾm/wʾbrw*

10 *[ṣ]⌊dqm/ʿdy/byth⌊m⌋[w/]⌊byt/rḍwn/wlẖry*
11 *[n]⌊hw/bn/nḍʿ/wšṣy/⌈š⌉[n]ʾm/ḏrḥq/wqrb/b*
12 **Flower** *ʾlm⌊qh⌉⌊b⌋ʿlʾwm* **Flower**

1 **Sym-** Raṯadšams[um Yah]tuf, descendant of Riḍwân, trea[su]rer of
2 **bol** the rent of ʾIlšar[aḥ Ya]ḥḍub and of his brother Yaʾ-
3 zil Bayyin, the two kings of Sa[ba]ʾ and Raydân, the two sons of Fa-
4 riʿum Yanhub, king of [Sa]baʾ, has dedicated to ʾIlumquh Ṯah-
5 wân, master of ʾAwwâm, [a] statue which [is] in bronze, in order that may vouchsafe to him
6 ʾIlumquh Ṯahwân, master of [ʾAwwâm,] the esteem and grace of his two lords
7 ʾIlšaraḥ Yaḥḍub and of his [brother] Yaʾzil Bayyin,
8 the two kings of Sabaʾ and Rayd[ân,] the two [sons of] Fariʿum Yanhub, k[ing
9 of] Sabaʾ; and that He may vouchsafe to him pleasing fruits and [pe]rfect
10 sons in thei[r] house, the house of Riḍwân; and that He may preserve
11 him from the hostility and wickedness of [any] e[ne]my, who is remote and near. By
12 **Flower** ʾIlumquh, master of ʾAwwâm. **Flower**

Preliminary remarks. Only lines 9 and 12 are complete; the center of the other lines is missing and ranges from one to four signs.

L. 1: *rṯdšms*[ ]*tf*: according to line 2, four signs are missing: I propose restoring *rṯdšms[m/yh]tf*; for the 1st name (same nominal formation as, e.g., that of *rṯdʿzyn* in AshM 1957-17/6; cf. *BeTMS*), cf. Ist 7627/1; for *yhtf*, cf. RÉS 4033/1. – *rḍwn*, RÉS 2687/1, Ḥaḍr; cf. also *rḍyn*, family name in Ja 881 G, Qat (cf. *JaPEQL*, p. 210), *rḍwt* (RÉS 4243) and *rḍn* (Ja 166/1, Qat, and commentary). – *ḏ.r*: I propose restoring *ḏ[ẖ]r* as present participle *ḏâẖir*; cf. Arabic *ḏaẖara* "to hoard, treasure, store, reserve" (cf. *LaAEL*, p. 956 C).

592 – Grayish sandstone; top broken and splintered off; photograph in Plate 8. – MaMB 95.

STONE: constant thickness: 11.5 cm. (top) and 12.8 (bottom). – *Front:* both edges partly splintered off; 28 cm. (right) and 27.2 (left) × 19.6. – INSCRIPTION: same disposition of lines as in Ja 559; letter height: 1.5 cm.; space between the lines: 0.3 cm.; distance from line 10 to the bottom: 11 cm. (right) and 11.3 (left).

0 **[Sym-**
1 **[bol** *.../bnw/ḥḏʾbm/hqnyw/ʾlmqh]*
2 *⌈ṯh⌉[w]⌈n⌉bʿlʾw⌈m/ṣlmnhn/ḏḏhbn/ḏšfth⌉[w]*
3 *ḥmdm/bḏt/ẖmrhmw/mrʾyhmw/ʾlšr*
4 *ḥ/yḥḍb/wʾẖ yhw/yʾzl/byn/mlky/sbʾ/w*
5 *ḏrydn/bny/frʿm/ynhb/mlk/sbʾ/byt/b[ny]*
6 *ḥḏʾbm/wbḏt/hwfyhmw/bkl/ʾmlʾ*
7 *stmlʾnn/bʿmhw/wlwzʾ/ʾlmqh/(ẖ)mrhm*
8 *w/ḥẓy/wrḍw/mrʾyhmw/wlẖrynhmw/ʾ*
9 *lmqh/bn/nḍʿ/wšṣy/šnʾm/wrṯdw/h⟨q⟩*
10 *nythmw/bʾlmqhbʿlʾwm*

0 **[Sym-**
1 **[bol** ..., descendants of Ḥaḏʾabum, have dedicated to ʾIlumquh]
2 Ṯah[w]ân, master of ʾAwwâm, these two statues which [are] in bronze, which he had promised to H[im]
3 in praise because has vouchsafed to them their two lords ʾIlšaraḥ
4 Yaḥḍub and his brother Yaʾzil Bayyin, the two kings of Sabaʾ and
5 Raydân, the two sons of Fariʿum Yanhub, king of Sabaʾ, the house of the des[cendants of]
6 Ḥaḏʾabum; and because He has showered upon them all the favors [for which]
7 they besought Him; and that ʾIlumquh may continue to vouchsafe to them
8 the esteem and grace of their two lords; and that may preserve them
9 ʾIlumquh from the hostility and wickedness of [any] enemy. And they have entrusted their off⟨er-⟩
10 ing [to the care of.] By ʾIlumquh, master of ʾAwwâm.

L. 6: *ḥḏʾbm*, same nominal formation as that of *ḥḏʾr* (RÉS 2829/2, Min).

L. 7: *h* instead of *ẖ* in *ẖmr* is certain on the stone.

Ll. 8-9: ʾ of *ʾlmqh* is engraved on top of the letter *b*.

Ll. 9-10: *q* of *hqnyt* is not engraved although there is space for a letter at the end of line 9. – The formula with *rṯd* is ordinarily followed by the name of a deity; here, this name was probably omitted by haplography, since it immediately follows in the final invocation.

593 = MaMB 112 = left part of Ja 572.

594 – Lower part of a yellow, slightly grayish sandstone inscription; upper two thirds of left side splintered off; photograph in Plate 8. – MaMB 115.

Front: 18.6 cm. (top) and 21.4 (bottom) × 23.5 (left), 23.2 (center) and 9 (bottom). – INSCRIPTION:

same disposition of lines as in Ja 558; letter height: between 1.5 cm. and 2.1; the letters do not follow the horizontal lines; space between the lines: between 0.3 cm. and 0.5.

1 [... .../*ʾlšrḥ/yḥḍb/wʾẖyhw/yʾz*]
2 *l/byn/mlky/sb⸢ʾ/wḏryd〈n〉/bn⸣*[*y/f*]
3 *rʿm/ynhb/mlk/sbʾ/wlḥẓ⸥*[*y/wr*]
4 *ḍw/mrʾyhmw/nmrn/ʾwkn/w*[*ʾẖy*]
5 *hw/gḥḍm/ʾḥṣn/bny/sʿ*(*d*)[*m*]
6 *wl/sʿdhmy/ʾlmqhwṯhw⸣*[*n/b*]
7 *ʿl/ʾwm/wfy/grbthmy/w*[*wf*]
8 *y/ʾmhmy/wʾṯthmy/wwld*[*hm*]
9 *y/wlsʿdhmy/ʾwldm/ḏkwr*[*m*]
10 *hnʾm/wnʾd/qṣ/wṣrb/wʾb*
11 *q/ṣdqm/wl/ẖrynhmw/bn/nḍʿ*
12 *wšṣy/šnʾm/bʾlmqhwṯh*
13 *wn/bʿlʾwm*

1 [... ...ʾIlšaraḥ Yaḥḍub and his brother Yaʾz-]
2 il Bayyin, the two kings of Sabaʾ and Raydân, [the two] son[s of Fa-]
3 riʿum Yanhub, king of Sabaʾ, and for the estee[m and gra-]
4 ce of their two lords Nimrân ʾAwkân and his [brother]
5 Gâḥḍum ʾAḥṣân, the two sons of Saʿ(ad)[um;]
6 and that may make them both happy ʾIlumquh Ṯahw[ân, mas-]
7 ter of ʾAwwâm, with the safety of the persons of them both and [the safe-]
8 ty of the mother of them both, of the wives of them both, and of the children of [them] both;
9 and that He may make them both happy with pleasing male
10 children and (with) the magnificence of the fruits of summer and of autumn and (with) alluvion (?)
11 perfect; and that He may preserve them from the hostility
12 and wickedness of [any] enemy. By ʾIlumquh Ṯah-
13 wân, master of ʾAwwâm.

Cf. the beginning of the commentary on Ja 790. The beginning of the text mentioned *hqnyy* because of the dual personal pronoun *hmy*, and also *ʾlmqhwṯhwn/bʿlʾwm* (cf. lines 12-13).

L. 2: the last four vertical strokes must be interpreted *d/bn*; the distance between the first two strokes does not allow the reading of the first as *n*; this letter is missing; three letters are missing at the end.

L. 3: the use of *l* before *ḥẓy* is quite unusual.

L. 4: *nmrn*, well-known proper name, e.g., of masculine person (e.g., Ja 529/1) and of a city (RÉS 4198/5); cf. also the personal name *nmrm* (e.g., RÉS 4578, RÉS 4854 B/1, Ḥaḍr, and Ja 220/1, Qat. – *ʾwkn*, CIH 130/1; cp. *hwkn* in Ja 867/1, Qat (cf. commentary) and Van Lessen 9/5, Qat. The restoration of *ʾẖ* is based on Ja 684/9.

L. 5: *gḥḍm*, cf. Arabic *ǧâḥiẓ* "having the eyeball, *or* globe of the eye, prominent and apparent" (cf. *LaAEL*, p. 382 C) and the Arabic epithet *al-ǧâḥiẓ* and personal name *ǧḥẓt* (cf. *WüR*, respectively pp. 359 and 360). – *ʾḥṣn*, e.g., CIH 106/1. – *sʿ*(*d*)[*m*]: the ʿ is engraved over and slightly to the right of a word divider, which was supposed to belong to *d*; *sʿd* is excluded for two letters must be restored; *sʿdm*, e.g., RÉS 4890/1, Ḥaḍr, Fakhry 76/3 (and not *sdm*; the ʿ is destroyed), Gl 1142/2, Ist 7626/4 (and not *hʿdm* in *BeFSTI*, p. 271) and Ja 263, Qat; *sʿdm* is more frequently used than *sʿdn* (e.g., RÉS 3476); cf. also *sʿdn/bn/sʿdm* in NaNN 74/2.

L. 6: the *q* of *ʾlmqhw* is engraved on top of a *w*.

L. 8: *ʾm*, e.g., Ja 402/1, Ḥaḍr; cf. also the Western Semitic cognates in *JeHoDISO*, pp. 15-16: *ʾm*$_1$.

L. 9: *ḏkwr*, plural of *ḏkr*; cf. Arabic *ḏakar*, plural *ḏukûr*.

L. 10: *qṣ* of the present text has nothing to do with *qṣ* in RÉS 5085/7, which must be related to Arabic *qaṣṣ* "plaster"; here, *qṣ* is the *scriptio defectiva* of *qyẓ* (e.g., Ja 617/9: "fruits of summer") "summer" (cf. *StSESA*, p. 517 and *BeESACD*, p. 20); cf. also Mehri *qáyṭ* (cf. *JaMSSA*, p. 204 B) and Soqoṭri *qíyaṭ* (cf. *LeLS*, p. 374); cf. also in Ẓofâr *qyẓ* "II. Im Sommer wohin (Akkus.) gehen, fahren" (cf. *RhVDD*, p. 50 B) and Ugaritic *qyẓ*=*qẓ* (cf. *GoUM*, p. 319 B, No. 1678); *qṣ/wṣrb*, cf. *ṣrbm wqyẓm* in RÉS 4230/8; cf. the name of the month *ḏqyṣn* in CIH 448/6; about this reference, *RyISA* (X, p. 301) mentions *MoMiSI*, p. 17; read pp. 176 and 180; a careful examination of the photograph should indicate whether *MoMiSI*'s suggestion (*ḏqyẓn*) is worthy of consideration or not; *ṣrb*, CIH 73/7, *BeSI*, p. 12 and *BeESACD*, *l.c.*; cf. also modern Ṣanʿâʾite *ṣarab* "mietere orzo, grano ecc." and *ṣårâb* "mietitura" (cf. *RoAS*, p. 220 A and *RoVSAY*, p. 310).

Ll. 10-11: *ʾbq*, cf. Hebrew *ʾâbâq* "dust, powder" (cf. *KoBaLVTL*, p. 8 A and also *JaDT*, p. 8 A); *ʾbq* could possibly allude to the dust brought by alluvion, and thus to the alluvion itself.

595 – Fragment of the right part of an inscription; yellowish sandstone; photograph in Plate 9. – MaMB 126.

STONE: maximum thickness: 16 cm. – *Front:* length at the bottom of line 1: 9.6 cm.; height at the right edge: 7 cm. – INSCRIPTION: same disposition of lines as in Ja 552; letter height: 1.7 cm. (lines 2 and 3) and 1.8 (lines 4 and 5); space between the lines: 0.4 cm., 0.3, 0.25 and 0.4.

1 [... .../*wl*]
2 *⌜sʿdh⌝w⌜/⌝⌜ḥẓy/wr*[*ḍw/mrʾyhmw/ʾl*]
3 *šrḥ/yḥḍb/w*[*ʾẖyhw/yʾzl/byn*]
4 *mlky/sbʾ⌟⌞/⌟*[*wḏrydn/bny/frʿm/y*]
5 *nh⌞b/ml⌟*[*k/sbʾ*/...
6 .[...

1 [... ...; and that He may]
2 make him happy with the esteem and gra[ce of his two lords ʾIl-]
3 šaraḥ Yaḥḍub and [his brother Yaʾzil Bayyin,]
4 the two kings of Sabaʾ [and Raydân, the two sons of Fariʿum Ya-]
5 nhub, kin[g of Sabaʾ,...
6 .[...

Cf. the beginning of the commentary on Ja 569 and 791. – The present text and Ja 813 may palaeographically belong to the same original; however, the color of the stone and of its front is different in each case.

L. 2 is engraved on top of another which was not perfectly erased and which can be read as follows: *wlẖryn/mrʾy*[... "and that He may preserve the two lords of...".

L. 6: the first letter, of which only the upper half of the upper circle remains, is *y*, *ẓ*, *ṣ* or *ṯ*, and thus could belong to terms such as [*wf*]*y*,[*ḥl*]*ẓ*, *ṣ*[*dqm*] or [ʾ]*ṯ*[*mrm*].

596 = MaMB 192 = left part of Ja 591.

597 – Lower part of an inscription; yellowish sandstone; photograph in Plate 9. – MaMB 193.

STONE: maximum thickness: 13.2 cm.; a part of the top is preserved; height: 21.8 cm. – *Front:* width: 19.4 cm.; height: 16.8. – INSCRIPTION: same disposition of lines as in Ja 552; letter height: from 1.1 cm. to 1.3; space between the lines: from 0.15 cm. to 0.3. – FLOWER at the end of line 8; eight petals normally attached to the central bud; cf. Plate B.

1 [..*sb*]*⌜ʾt/⌝sbʾ*⟨⟩*/wgnb/⌜ʾbfn⌝*(*d*)*⌜/⌝*[*bʿm*]
2 [*mrʾyh*]*w/ʾlšrḥ/yḥḍb/wʾẖyhw⌜/⌝*[*yʾ*]
3 [*zl*]*⌜/by⌝n/mlky/sbʾ/wḏrydn/bny/frʿ⌜m⌝*
4 *⌜y⌝nhb/mlk/sbʾ/wlẖmrhw/ʾlmqh/⌜ḥ⌝*
5 *ẓy/wrḍw/mrʾyhw/ʾlšrḥ/yḥḍb*
6 *wʾẖyhw/yʾzl/byn/mlky/sbʾ/w⌟*
7 *⌞ḏrydn/wlhʿnnhw/bn/nḍʿ/wšṣy/šn*
8 *ʾm/bʾlmqh/ṯhwn/bʿl/ʾwm* **Flower**

1 [...the enc]ounters [in which] ʾAbfan(ad) fought and battled [for]
2 [hi]s [two lords] ʾIlšaraḥ Yaḥḍub and his brother [Yaʾ-]
3 [zil] Bayyin, the two kings of Sabaʾ and Raydân, the two sons of Fariʿum
4 Yanhub, king of Sabaʾ; and that ʾIlumquh may vouchsafe to him the es-
5 teem and grace of his two lords ʾIlšaraḥ Yaḥḍub,
6 and his brother Yaʾzil Bayyin, the two kings of Sabaʾ and
7 Raydân; and that He may protect him from the hostility and wickedness of [any] ene-
8 my. By ʾIlumquh Ṯahwân, master of ʾAwwâm. **Flower**

Cf. the beginning of the commentary on Ja 791, 792 and 807.

L. 1: *sbʾw/wgnb* on the stone: since the subject of these two verbs is ʾAbfanad and the personal pronoun in the text is always singular, *hw* (lines 2, 4, 5, and 7), the plural of *sbʾw* cannot be explained as an agreement *ad sensum*, but may be considered as the haplography of *w* which introduces *gnb*. – *gnb*, cf. Arabic *ǧanaba* "to break, hit, hurt one's side"; cf. the Western Semitic cognates in *JeHoDISO*, p. 51: *gnb*I, II; *gnb* may be a synonym of *sbʾ*. – *ʾbfn*(.): although beheaded, the first four letters are certain; the 5th cannot be *y*, for the following word divider is too far away; it must be *g*, *d*, or *l*. The proper name *fnd* is known as place name in Arabic (cf. *WüR*, p. 166 C) and also as personal name both in Arabic (cf. *l.c.*, p. 608 and *GoAT*, p. 453) and in Thamudic (cf. *vdBrIT*, pp. 461-62: Jsa 704).

598 – Center of the right side of an inscription; yellowish sandstone; photograph. – MaMB 195.

STONE: maximum thickness: 8 cm. – *Front:* covered with red paint; maximum length: 16.5 cm., and width: 20.5. – INSCRIPTION: same disposition of lines as in Ja 552; letter height: from 2.1 cm. to 2.3; space between the lines: from 0.4 cm. to 0.5.

1 *[...   .../mrˀy]*
2 *⌈h⌉mw/ˀlšrḥ/yḥḏb[/wˀḫ yhw/yˀzl/byn/mlky/sbˀ/wḏry]*
3 *dn/bny/frᶜm/ynh⌈b⌉[/mlk/sbˀ/....../wlḏt/nᶜmt/wt]*
4 *nᶜmn/lhmw/wlḫmrh[mw/...   .../wˀ]*
5 *ḫfd/ṣdqm/wlḫᶜn[nhmw/ˀlmqh/bn/ndᶜ/wšṣy/wtṯˀt/wᶜ]*
6 *bṯt/šnˀm/bˀl⌊m⌋[qhṯhwnbᶜlˀwm/....../wbšymhmw/tˀ]*
7 *lb/rymm/wḥgrm/qḥ*⌉*[mm/...   ...]*

1 [...   ...] their [two lords]
2 ˀIlšaraḥ Yaḥḏub [and his brother Yaˀzil Bayyin, the two kings of Sabaˀ and Ray-]
3 dân, the two sons of Fariᶜum Yanhub, [king of Sabaˀ...; and that it may have been pleasant and be]
4 pleasant for them; and that He may vouchsafe to t[hem...   ..., and]
5 perfect grand-son[s]; and that [ˀIlumquh] may protect [them from the hostility and wickedness and fear and ca-]
6 lamities of [any] enemy. By ˀIlum[quh Ṯahwân, master of ˀAwwâm......and by their patron Taˀ-]
7 lab Riyyâmum and Ḥagarum Qaḥa[mum...   ...]

L. 3: about six characters are still missing.
L. 5: *ḫfd*, cf. Arabic *ḥafîd* "grand-son".
Ll. 5-6: cf. Ja 635/44-46.
L. 6: about seven characters are still missing.
L. 7: *qḥmm*: in RÉS 4993/2, the reading *[b](n)hw* is erroneous; the drawing (cf. *RyISA*, V, p. 107) clearly shows the letter *ḫ*, which indicates *[ˀ]ḫhw*; besides, the reading of *ḏ* as third letter of *qḥ.m* fits the drawing perfectly, and that of *m* supposed an error in the copy; *qḥḏm* is an Arabic personal name (cf. *GoAT*, p. 461).

599 – Lower part of an inscription; yellowish, slightly grayish sandstone; photograph in Plate 9. – MaMB 198.

STONE: maximum thickness: 15 cm. – *Front:* covered with red paint; length: 19 cm., and width: 17.2. – INSCRIPTION: same disposition of lines as in Ja 561 bis; letter height: 1.3 cm.; space between the lines: 0.3 cm.

1 *[...   ...](h)⌈rn/⌉w.*
2 *[...   .../]⌈bn/ngrn/lm*
3 *[rˀyhmw/ˀlšrḥ/yḥ]⌈ḏb/⌉wˀḫ yhw/yˀzl/byn/m*
4 *[lky/sbˀ/wḏryd]⌈n/b⌉ny/frᶜm/ynhb/mlk/sbˀ*
5 *[wlḫmrhmw/ˀlmq]⌊h⌋ṯhwn/ḥẓy/wrḍw/mrˀyhmw/ˀ*
6 *[lšrḥ/yḥḏb/wˀ]ḫ yhw/yˀzl/byn/mlky/sbˀ/w*
7 *[ḏrydn/bny]/⌈frᶜm⌉/ynhb/mlk/sbˀ/wlḫmrhm*
8 *[w/]⌈ˀ⌈lmqh⌉/ˀṯmr/wˀfql/ṣdqm/hnˀm/bn/ˀ*
9 *[rḍ][⌊t⌋hmw/wlḫrynhmw/ˀlmqhbᶜlˀwm/bn/n*
10 *dᶜ/wšṣ⌊y/šnˀ⌋m/bˀlmqh*

1 [...   ...] (Hi)rrân and.
2 [...   ...] from Nagrân for
3 [their two] l[ords] ˀIlšaraḥ Yaḥ[ḏub and his brother Yaˀzil Bayyin, the two]
4 k[ings of Sabaˀ and Rayd]ân, the two sons of Fariᶜum Yanhub, king of Sabaˀ;
5 [and that ˀIlumq]uh Ṯahwân [may vouchsafe to them] the esteem and grace of their two lords
6 ˀI[lšaraḥ Yaḥḏub and] his [brother Yaˀzil Bayyin, the two kings of Sabaˀ and
7 [Raydân, the two sons of] Fariᶜum Yanhub, king of Sabaˀ; and that may vouchsafe to th[em]
8 ˀIlumquh perfect, pleasing fruits and harvests from their
9 fi[eld]s; and that ˀIlumquh, master of ˀAwwâm, may preserve them from the hos-
10 tility and wickedness of [any] enemy. By ˀIlumquh.

Cf. the beginning of the commentary on Ja 807.

600 – Yellowish, slightly grayish sandstone; cut at the bottom; the front part of the top is widely splintered off; photograph in Plate 9. – MaMB 231.

STONE: constant thickness: 12.3 cm. – *Front:* upper edge badly damaged. – INSCRIPTION: same disposition of lines as in Ja 552; letter height: from 1.8 cm. to 1.9; space between the lines: from 0.25 cm. to 0.3; line 1 completely destroyed; four characters still exist from line 2. – SYMBOL: cf. Ja 587.

1 **⌈Sym-⌉** *[...   .../hqny/ˀlmq]*
2 **bol** *[hṯhwnbᶜlˀ]⌈wm⌉/dn*
3 *ṣlmn/⌈ḏḏhbn/ḥ⌉mdm/bḏt*
4 *ḫmrhw/stwfyn/mḏht/mrˀ*
5 *yhw/ˀlšrḥ/yḥḏb/wˀḫ yhw*
6 *yˀzl/byn/mlky/sbˀ/wḏryd*
7 *n/bny/frᶜm/ynhb/mlk/sbˀ/bk*
8 *n/tnḏh/bmwṯbn/yhgl/wlwzˀ*
9 *⌊ˀlmqhṯhwnbᶜlˀwm/ḫmrhw/*
10 *⌊ḥẓy/wrḍw/mrˀyhw/ˀlšrḥ/yḥḏ⌋*
11 *[b/wˀḫ yhw/yˀzl/byn/mlky/sbˀ/wḏ]*
12 *[rydn/bny/frᶜm/ynhb/mlk/sbˀ/..]*

1 ⌜**Sym-**⌝ [... ... has dedicated ʾIlumq-]
2 **bol** [uh Ṯahwân, master of ʾAwwâ]m, this
3 statue which [is] in bronze, in praise because
4 He has vouchsafed to him to give protection to the herd of camels of his
5 two lords ʾIlšaraḥ Yaḥḍub and his brother
6 Yaʾzil Bayyin, the two kings of Sabaʾ and Raydân,
7 the two sons of Fariʿum Yanhub, king of Sabaʾ, when
8 he was pasturing in the place Yuhagul; and that may continue
9 ʾIlumquh Ṯahwân, master of ʾAwwâm, to vouchsafe to him
10 the esteem and grace of his two lords ʾIlšaraḥ Yaḥḍ[ub]
11 [and his brother Yaʾzil Bayyin, the two kings of Sabaʾ and]
12 [Raydân, the two sons of Fariʿum Yanhub, king of Sabaʾ...]

The present text and Ja 813 do not belong to the same original; the letters of the latter are thicker than those of the former; cf. especially *b*.

L. 1: the comparison of the height of the symbol with that of line 2 indicates that only one line of the text is missing. – For the restoration of the latter, the number of the letters in lines 6-10 cannot be taken into consideration, for the letters are more numerous there than in the preceding lines.

Ll. 4 and 8: *mḏht* and *tnḏh*, derived noun and 5th form of the root *nḏh*, respectively; cf. Arabic *nadaha* "to remove; drive (e.g., camels)" and *nudhat* "great number of cattle"; cf. also from the root *ndw*, both Arabic *munaddâ* "kind of pasture for camels; collective: cattle", and Daṯînah *mandā* "pasture" (cf. *LaGD*, p. 2759); for the root *ndy*, cf. CIH 548/7 and commentary; for South-Arabian *ḏ* corresponding to Semitic *d*, cf. *StSESA*, p. 513; the subject of the verb *tnḏh* is the author of the inscription.

L. 8: *mwṯb*, cf. commentary on Ja 575/5. – *yhgl*, also mentioned as *mwṯb* in CIH 308/5 and 308 bis/4.

b – Watarum Yuhaʾmin: Ja 601-607

601 – Yellowish, slightly grayish sandstone; photograph; cf. Chapter I, A. – MaMB 205.

STONE: thickness: 37.7 cm. – *Front*, covered with red paint; upper right corner broken; 61.3 cm. (top) and 61 (bottom) × 1.354 m. – INSCRIPTION: same disposition of lines as in Ja 561 bis; letter height: 5.6. cm.; space between the lines: 0.7 cm. – SYMBOL: cf. Ja 559.

1 **Sym-** *ʾlrm/ygʿr/bn/sẖymm/[qwl]/šʿ*
2 **bol** *bn/smʿy/šlṯn/ḏhgrm/hqnyw/ʾ*
3 *lmqhw/ṯhwn/bʿl/ʾwm/ṣlmnhn/ḥmdm*
4 *bḏt/hwfy/ʾlmqh/ʿbdhw/ʾlrm/bsbʾt*
5 *y/sbʾw/ʿdy/ʾrḍ/ẖwln/gddn/bkn/wqhh*
6 *mw/mrʾhmw/wtrm/yhʾmn/mlk/sbʾ/wḏr*
7 *ydn/bn/ʾlšrḥ/yḥḍb/mlk/sbʾ/wḏrydn/lʿ*
8 *ḏrn/bʿm/ʾšʿbn/ẖwln/bẖṭyʾ/hẖṭʾw/bʾm*
9 *rʾhmw/ʾmlk/sbʾ/wyṯbrw/whlqḥn/hmt*
10 *ʾšʿbn/ẖwln/gddn/wḏkyn/kwnhmw/wyʾtyw*
11 *bwfym/wmqḥm/wmngt/ṣdqm/ḏhrḍw/mrʾh*
12 *mw/wtrm/yhʾmn/mlk/sbʾ/wḏrydn/wlḏt/y*
13 *zʾn/ʾlmqh/sʿd/ʿbdhw/ʾlrm/nʿmtm/wmn*
14 *gt/ṣdqm/wrḍw/mrʾhmw/wtrm/yhʾmn/mlk*
15 *sbʾ/wḏrydn/wlsʿd/ʾlmqh/ʾdmhw/bny/s*
16 *ẖymm/bry/ʾʾḏnm/wmqymtm/wʾṯmr/wʾfq*
17 *l/ṣdqm/bn/kl/ʾrḍhmw/wl/ʾẖrn/ʾlmqh/ʿl*
18 *n/ʾdmhw/bny/sẖymm/bʾstm/wnkym/wnḍʿ/w*
19 *šṣy/šnʾm/bʿṯtr/whwbs/wʾlmqh/wbḏt/ḥ*
20 *mym/wbḏt/bʿdnm/wb/šymhmw/tʾlb/rymm*
21 *wrṯdw/hqnythmw/ʾlmqh/bʿl/ʾwm*

1 **Sym-** ʾIlrâm Yagʿur, descendant of [the tribe] Suẖaymum, [ruler of] the tri-
2 **bol** be Samʿay, third of (the tribe) Hagarum, have dedicated to
3 ʾIlumquhû Ṯahwân, master of ʾAwwâm, these two statues in praise
4 because ʾIlumquh has saved His worshipper ʾIlrâm from the two encounters [which]
5 they fought in the land of Ḫawlân Gaddân, when had ordered
6 them their lord Watarum Yuhaʾmin, king of Sabaʾ and Ra-
7 ydân, son of ʾIlšaraḥ Yaḥḍub, king of Sabaʾ and Raydân, to give
8 help against the tribes Ḫawlân because of the evil deeds [into which] they seduced [others] against their
9 lords, the kings of Sabaʾ; and so they crushed and enchained these
10 tribes, Ḫawlân Gaddân, and those who were with them; and they came back
11 in perfect safety and profit and security, which pleased their
12 lord Watarum Yuhaʾmin, king of Sabaʾ and Raydân; and that
13 ʾIlumquh may continue to make His worshipper ʾIlrâm happy with prosperity and secu-
14 rity perfect and (with) the grace of their lord Watarum Yuhaʾmin, king

15 of Sabaʾ and Raydân; and that ʾIlumquh may make happy His worshippers, the descendants of Su-
16 ẖaymum, with the strength of understanding and of power and (with) fruits and har-
17 vest perfect from their every field; and that ʾIlumquh may go on with causing
18 His worshippers, the descendants of Suẖaymum, to overcome all misfortunes and suffering and [also] the hostility and
19 wickedness of [any] enemy. By ʿAṯtar and Hawbas and ʾIlumquh and by Ḏât-Ḥi-
20 myâm and by Ḏât-Baʿdânum and by their patron Taʾlab Riyyâmum;
21 and they entrusted their offering to the care of ʾIlumquh, master of ʾAwwâm.

L. 1: *ʾlrm*, e.g., RÉS 4118/2, Qat. – *ygʿr*, e.g., CIH 349/1; cf. also the Arabic names *ǧaʿrân*, *ḏû ǧaʿrâna* (cf. *WüID*, 251/2), and of a person *ǧaʿrûn* (cf. *SlGaVNPA*, p. 16 A).

L. 2: *šlṯ*, cf. *StSESA*, p. 530. – *hgrm*, e.g., Ja 514 and commentary in *JaISAR*, p. 112. Weigall 2 (cf. *Le Muséon*, 62 [1949], p. 57) may be read as follows: *dhnym/bn/qśmʾl/hgryhn* "Duhuniyum, son of Qaśamʾil, the Hagrite". For *dhn*, cf. the Arabic names of a clan *banû duhn* (cf. *SaIS*, p. 73 A) and of a place *duhunnâ* (cf. *WüR*, p. 92 B), and probably personal name in Thamudic (cf. *vdBrIT*, p. 55: HU 33). *MüHG* (89/11) mentions the *ʾahǧûr* as being located in Sarw Ḥimyar; the article *-hn*, as well as the form *qśm* (for Sab *qsm*; cf. also CaTh 54/1), indicates that this graffito is Ḥaḍr. – *hqnyw*, agreement *ad sensum*.

L. 5: *gddn*, name of a temple dedicated to Taʾlab in RÉS 4193/4.

Ll. 7-8: *ʿḏr*, e.g., CIH 308/22 and *StSESA*, p. 513.

L. 8: *ẖṭyʾ*, internal plural (also in Ja 602/8 and 720/10) instead of the ordinary form *ẖṭʾt*; cf. also commentary on Ja 560/8, and the Western Semitic cognates in *JeHoDISO*, p. 85: *ḥṭʾ* I, II.

L. 9: *hlqḥ*, e.g., CIH 155/4 and commentary, and recently in JM 9+7/4; cf. *CoRoC*, p. 173 B; cf. the noun *mlqḥ*, e.g., in Ja 643/32.

L. 10: *ḏkyn/kwnhmw* equals *ḏkwn/kwnhmw* in Ja 575/5; the translation of *kyn* as "to rage" (cf. *RyHE*, p. 235; cf. also the commentary on Ja 561 bis/9: *kwn*) is incorrect.

L. 17: *ʾẖr*, cf. commentary on Ja 558/7.

Ll. 17-18: *ʿln*, cf. Arabic *ʿalâ*, 3rd form, "to rise, climb up, raise up, uplift". The 7th form of *ʿly*, *nʿly*, is attested in RÉS 4829 which reads as follows:

ḥgr/ʿzyn/w	1	Ḥagar [to] ʿUzzayin; and
ltnʿly/r	2	that she may be exalted for having
fʾn/hw/b	3	healed him (Ḥagar) from
mhbʾsm	4	mistreatment inflicted by a malefactor.

602 – Yellowish, slightly grayish sandstone; photograph; cf. Chapter I, A. – MaMB 209=NaNAG 7.

STONE: thickness: 40.5 cm. – *Front:* upper corners broken; both the center of the upper edge and the upper part of the right edge are splintered off; covered with red paint; 61.2 cm. × 1.33 m. – INSCRIPTION: same disposition of lines as in Ja 561 bis; letter height: from 5 cm. to 5.3; space between the lines: from 0.6 cm. to 0.8. – SYMBOL: cf. Ja 559.

1 ⌜**Sym-**⌝ *[ʾlrm]/ygʿr/bn/sẖymm[/qwl/š]*
2 **bol** *[ʿbn/]⌜smʿ⌝y/šlṯn/ḏhgrm/⌜h⌝q[nyw]*
3 *ʾlmqhw/ṯhwn/bʿl/ʾwm/ṣlmnhn/ḥmd*
4 *m/bḏt/hwfy/ʾlmqh/ʿbdhw/ʾlrm/bsb*
5 *ʾty/sbʾw/ʿdy/ʾrḍ/ẖwln/gddn/bkn/wqhh*
6 *mw/mrʾhmw/wtrm/yhʾmn/mlk/sbʾ/wḏry*
7 *dn/bn/ʾlšrḥ/yḥḍb/mlk/sbʾ/wḏrydn/lʿḏ*
8 *rn/bʿm/ʾšʿbn/ẖwln/bẖṭyʾ/hẖṭʾw/bʾmr*
9 *ʾhmw/ʾmlk/sbʾ/wyṯbrw/whlqḥn/hmt/ʾšʿb*
10 *n/ẖwln/gddn/wḏkyn/kwnhmw/wyʾtyw/bwfy*
11 *m/wmqḥm/wmngt/ṣdqm/ḏhrḍw/mrʾhmw/wtr*
12 *m/yhʾmn/mlk/sbʾ/wḏrydn/wlḏt/yzʾn/ʾl*
13 *mqh/sʿd/ʿbdhw/ʾlrm/nʿmtm/wmngt/ṣdq*
14 *m/wrḍw/mrʾhmw/wtrm/yhʾmn/mlk/sbʾ/wḏ*
15 *rydn/wlsʿd/ʾlmqh/ʾdmhw/bny/sẖymm/b*
16 *ry/ʾʾḏnm/wmqymtm/wʾṯmr/wʾfql/ṣdqm*
17 *bn/kl/ʾrḍhmw/wl/ʾẖrn/ʾlmqh/ʿln/ʾdm*
18 *hw/bny/sẖymm/bʾstm/wnkym/wnḍʿ/wš*
19 *ṣy/šnʾm/bʿṯtr/whwbs/wʾlmqh/wbḏt/ḥ*
20 *mym/wbḏt/bʿdnm/wb/šymhmw/tʾlb/rymm*
21 *wrṯdw/hqnythmw/ʾlmqh/bʿl/ʾwm*

This text is restored on the basis of Ja 601; the two texts are identical; the repartition of only lines 1 and 2 of the present inscription is identical with that of Ja 601. – *NaNAG*'s (II, p. 30) transliteration and translation do not mention the symbol. In *NaNAG*'s transliteration, line 1:]/ instead of /], [/*qwl/š*] instead of /[ʾ*qwl*]; line 2: omit initial *š*, insert] after ʿ*bn*, omit bracket in *smʿy*, *hq[nyw]* instead of *hq[ny]*; lines 7-8: *lʿḏrn* instead of ʿ*ḏrn*; line 16: *mqymtm* instead of *mqytm*.

603 – Yellowish sandstone plaque, broken into two pieces; photograph (cf. Plate 10) and later squeeze of top part. – MaMB 87.

PLAQUE: maximum thickness: 11.5 cm. – *Front:* length: 31 cm.; width: 46.5 cm. (left) and 46 (right); border at both lateral edges: depth: 2.2 cm. and width: 2.6 cm. (left) and 1.9 (right); the anterior part of the brim is covered with red paint. – INSCRIPTION: in relief of 0.4 cm.; letter height: between 3.1 cm. and 3.7; distance from line 1 to the top: 0.7 cm.; space between the lines: between 0.7 cm. and 0.5. – SYMBOL: same type as that of Ja 587; cf. Plate A.

1 **Sym-** *frᶜm⌜/bn/m⌝qrm/wbnyhw*
2 **bol** *šrḥṯt/whwfᶜṯt/wsᶜdʾw*
3 *m/bnw/ḏᶜqbn/hqnyw/ʾlmqh*
4 *⌜ṯhwn/b⌝* *⌞ṯhwn/b⌟ᶜl/ʾwm/ṣlmn/ḥmdm*
5 *bḏt/br⌜ʾw/wh⌝* *⌞/wh⌟šqrn/wḥẓwn/s*
6 *qh/wmśwd/wṣrḥ⌜t/b⌝* *⌞ḥ⌟⌞t/b⌟ythmw*
7 *ḏᶜqbn/wlsᶜdhmw/ʾlm⌜qh/n⌝* *⌞qh/n⌟ᶜ*
8 *mtm/wḥẓy/wrḍw/mrʾhmw/w*
9 *trm/yhʾmn/mlk/sbʾ/wḏr*
10 *ydn/bn/ʾlšrḥ/yḥḍb/mlk/sb*
11 *ʾ/wḏrydn/wl/hᶜnnhmw/ʾlmqh*
12 *bn/šṣy/šnʾm/bᶜṯtr/wʾlmqh*

1 **Sym-** Fariᶜum, son of Maqrum, and his sons
2 **bol** Šaraḥaṯat and Hawfᶜaṯat and Saᶜadʾaww-
3 âm, descendants of (the tribe) ᶜAqbân, have dedicated to ʾIlumquh
4 Ṯahwân, master of ʾAwwâm, this statue in praise
5 because they have built and covered and repaired the cis-
6 tern and the incense-burner sanctuary and the upper room of their house,
7 that of ᶜAqbân; and that ʾIlumquh may make them happy with pros-
8 perity and (with) the esteem and grace of their lord Wa-
9 tarum Yuhaʾmin, king of Sabaʾ and Ra-
10 ydân, son of ʾIlšaraḥ Yaḥḍub, king of Sabaʾ
11 and Raydân; and that ʾIlumquh may preserve them
12 from the wickedness of [any] enemy. By ᶜAṯtar and ʾIlumquh.

L. 1: *mqrm*, CIH 584/1; this inscription also refers to the building of a construction, and its final invocation also contains the same names of deity; *mqrm* is a family name in RÉS 4469/1 and Ja 700/2.

L. 2: *šrḥṯt*, e.g., RÉS 4151/7.

L. 3: *ᶜqbn*, family name, e.g., in RÉS 4628; cp. *bnw/ḏᶜqbn* (here) with *bny/ḏᶜqbn* in RÉS 4938/2; cf. also the personal name *yᶜqb* (cf. *RyGSAS*, p. 560).

L. 5: *brʾw*: in RÉS 4985/2-3, *RÉS* erroneously translates *brʾ* as "restaurer(?)" and transcribes *brʾy* instead of *brʾw*; this *w* is perfectly clear in A. Fakhry's copy (cf. *FaAJY*, I, p. 16, fig. 6). – *hšqr*, 4th form of *šqr*, e.g., RÉS 4196/2; the 1st form has the same meaning as that of the 4th in RÉS 4627/2. The translations "achever" (cf. *RyET*, p. 78) and "to complete" (cf. *RyHE*, p. 227) are incorrect. – *ḥẓw*, CIH 149/1, Ja 411/2 and *ḥẓy* in Ja 528/2.

Ll. 5-6: *sqh*, cp. Arabic *siqqâyat* "cistern, reservoir".

L. 6: *mśwd*, cf. *JaDME*. p. 10 and *StSESA*, p. 525; e.g., Ja 491/2 and 867/2, Qat. – *ṣrḥt*, e.g., RÉS 4655/3 and Ja 118/3, Qat; cf. also *RoVSAY*, p. 310.

604 – Yellowish, slightly grayish sandstone; photograph; cf. Chapter I, A. – MaMB 207.

STONE: thickness: 30 cm. – *Front:* covered with red paint; 1.08 m. × 37.6 cm. – INSCRIPTION: same disposition of lines as in Ja 561 bis; letter height: from 4.8 cm. to 5.1; space between the lines: 1 cm.; distance from line 1 to the upper edge: 1.5 cm. – SYMBOL: cf. Ja 565.

1 **Sym-** *whbm/ʾṣdq/bn/myṯᶜm/hqny/ʾlmqh/ṯhwn/ bᶜl/ʾwm/šlṯ*
2 **bol** *tn/ʾṣlmn/lwfyhw/wwfy/bnyhw/sᶜdʾwm/ wṯwbn*
3 *wwhbʾwm/bny/myṯᶜm/wl/sᶜdhmw/ʾlmqh/nᶜmtm/ wwfym*
4 *wmngt/ṣdqm/wrḍw/wḥẓy/mrʾhmw/wtrm/yhʾmn/mlk*
5 *sbʾ/wḏrydn/bn/ʾlšrḥ/yḥḍb/mlk/sbʾ/wḏrydn/bᶜṯtr*
6 *whwbs/wʾlmqh/wbḏt/ḥmym/wbḏt/bᶜdnm/wbšms/ mlkn/tnf*

1 **Sym-** Wahbum ʾAṣdiq, descendant of [the family] Muyaṯiᶜum, has dedicated to ʾIlumquh Ṯahwân, master of ʾAwwâm, these
2 **bol** three statues for his safety and the safety of his sons Saᶜadʾawwâm and Ṯawbân
3 and Wahabʾawwâm, descendants of [the family] Muyaṯiᶜum; and that ʾIlumquh may make them happy with prosperity and safety
4 and security perfect, and (with) the grace and esteem of their lord Watarum Yuhaʾmin, king

5 of Sabaʾ and Raydân, son of ʾIlšaraḥ Yaḥḍub, king of Sabaʾ and Raydân. By ʿAṯtar
6 and Hawbas and ʾIlumquh and by Ḏât-Ḥimyâm and by Ḏât-Baʿdânum and by Šams of the king, Tanûf.

L. 1: *whbm*, e.g., RÉS 2707/2-3; cp. *whbn*, e.g., in RÉS 4623 A/1-2.
L. 2: *lwfyhw* = *lwfyh* in Ja 489 A/4-5. – *ṯwbn*, e.g., Ja 287/1, Qat, and commentary; *RyET* (p. 85 B) erroneously mentions *ṯwbm* instead of *ṯwbn* in Fakhry 72/1.
L. 4: *rḍw/wḥẓy*, the reverse order of the two nouns is more ordinarily used.

605 – Top part of an inscription; yellowish, slightly grayish sandstone; photograph in Plate 10. – MaMB 232.

STONE: lower half of the right side broken and cut again; maximum thickness (upper left corner): 20.2 cm. – *Front:* maximum width: 53.7 cm.; length: 29.3 cm. (top) and 24.8 (bottom). – INSCRIPTION: same disposition of lines as in Ja 559; letter height; 3.5 cm.; space between the lines: 0.5 cm. – SYMBOL: same type as that of Ja 603.

1 **Sym-** *tzʾd/ʾṯqf/bn/sʿ*
2 **bol** *dwdm/bn/tzʾd/hqn*
3 *yw/ʾlmqhw/ṯhwn/bʿl/ʾwm*
4 *ṣlmn/ḥgn/stwklhw/lwfy*
5 *bnhw/rbnsrm/bn/tzʾd/wl*
6 *sʿdhmw/nʿmtm/wwfym/wmn*
7 *gt/ṣdqm/wlsʿdhmw/rḍw/w*
8 *[ḥẓ]y/mrʾhmw/wtrm/yhʾmn*
9 *[mlk]/sbʾ/wḏrydn/bn/ʾlšrḥ*
10 *[mlk]/sbʾ/wḏrydn/wlwśfh*
11 *[mw/ʾl]⌞m⌟qhw/ʾwldm/ʾḏkrwm*
12 *[wḥmdm/b]⌞dt/⌟ṣdq/whwfyn/ʾl*
13 *[mqhw/bny/]⌞tzʾd⌟/bkl/⌞ʾ⌟*
14 *[mlʾ/...*

1 **Sym-** Tazʾid ʾAṯqaf, son of Saʿ-
2 **bol** adwaddum, descendants of [the family] Tazʾid, have dedi-
3 cated to ʾIlumquhû Ṯahwân, master of ʾAwwâm,
4 this statue as he has bound himself to Him for the safety
5 of his son Rabbnasrum, descendant of [the family] Tazʾid; and that
6 He may make them happy with prosperity and safety and secu-
7 rity perfect; and that He may make them happy with the grace and
8 [este]em of their lord Watarum Yuhaʾmin,
9 [king of] Sabaʾ and Raydân, son of ʾIlšaraḥ,
10 [king of] Sabaʾ and Raydân; and that may add to
11 t[hem ʾIlu]mquhû male children;
12 [and in praise be]cause ʾIlu[mquhû] has bestowed and showered
13 [upon the descendants of] Tazʾid, all the
14 [favor]s [...

L. 1: *tzʾd*, e.g., RÉS 4132/2. – *ʾṯqf*, second personal name, e.g., in RÉS 4649/1, but clan name in Ja 519/1.
Ll. 1-2: *sʿdwdm*, cp. *sʿdtʾlb* (Ja 665/1) and *ṯʿdlt* (RÉS 4857/1, Ḥaḍr).
Ll. 2-3: *hqnyw*, agreement *ad sensum* (cf. Ja 601/2).
L. 5: *rbnsrm*, e.g., CIH 441/1.
L. 10: the restoration *yḥḍb* is impossible because of lack of space.
Ll. 10-11: the restoration of *h[mw]* is required by the number of missing letters and also by *hqnyw*, *sʿdhmw* and *mrʾhmw*.
L. 12: each line (except lines 1 and 2, because of the symbol) has 18 or 19 letters and 3 or 4 word dividers; there are thus 5 or 6 letters missing at the beginning of line 12; cf. Ja 716/4-5.

606 – Grayish sandstone; partial photograph; cf. Chapter I, C. – MaMB 278.

STONE: thickness: 42.7 cm. in the upper part (1.435 m.) and 26.2 cm. in the rest of the stone. – *Front:* upper corners badly broken; 1.90 m. × 44.1 cm. – INSCRIPTION: same disposition of lines as in Ja 552; letter height: 5.5 cm. (top) and 6 (bottom); space between the lines: 0.6 cm.

1 **[Sym-** *sʿdšmsm/ʾsrʿ/wbnhw/m]*
2 **[bol** *rṯdm/]bny/grt[/ʾqwl/šʿ]*
3 *[bn/ḏmry]/hqnyw/ʾl⌜mq⌝[hw/ṯh]*
4 *[wn/bʿ]l/ʾwm/ṣlmnhn/ḥ⌜gn⌝*
5 *[wqh]hmw/ʾlmqhw/bmsʾl*
6 *[hw]/lsʿdhmw/ʾlmqhw/nʿ*
7 *mtm/wmngt/ṣdqm/wlwfy*
8 *mrʾhmw/wtrm/yhʾmn/mlk*
9 *sbʾ/wḏrydn/bn/ʾlšrḥ/y*
10 *ḥḍb/mlk/sbʾ/wḏrydn/wl*
11 *wfy/ʾdmhw/sʿdšmsm/wbn*
12 *hw/mrṯdm/bny/grt/wqlhm*
13 *w/wš(ʿ)bhmw/smhrm/wlsʿd*
14 *hmw/ʾlmqhw/rḍw/wḥẓy/[m]*
15 *rʾhmw/wtrm/mlk/sbʾ*
16 *wḏrydn/wlḏt/nʿmt/wtnʿ*
17 *mn/lsʿdšmsm/wbnhw/m*
18 *rṯdm/wbny/grt/wqlhmw*
19 *wšʿbhmw/smhrm/bʿṯtr/wh*

20 *bs/wʾlmqhw/wbḏt/ḥmym/wb*
21 *ḏt/bʿdnm/wbʾlyhmw/ʿṯtr*
22 *ʿzzm/wḏt/ẓhrn/bʿly/ʿrn*
23 *knn/wrṯdw/hqnythmw/ʿṯtr*
24 *šrqn/wʾlmqhw/bʿl/ʾwm*

1 [**Sym-** Saʿadšamsum ʾAsraʿ and his son Ma-]
2 [**bol** rṯadum], descendants of Garat, [rulers of the tri-]
3 [be Ḏamrî,] have dedicated to ʾIlumqu[hû Ṯah-]
4 [wân, mast]er of ʾAwwâm, these two statues, as
5 ʾIlumquhû [has ordered] them through [His] oracle
6 in order that ʾIlumquhû may make them happy with prospe-
7 rity and security perfect; and that He may protect
8 their lord Watarum Yuhaʾmin, king of
9 Sabaʾ and Raydân, son of ʾIlšaraḥ
10 Yaḥḍub, king of Sabaʾ and Raydân; and that
11 He may protect His worshippers Saʿadšamsum and his
12 son Marṯadum, descendants of Garat, and their ruler
13 and their tr(i)be Sumhurâm; and that may make
14 them happy ʾIlumquhû with the grace and esteem of their
15 [l]ord Watarum, king of Sabaʾ
16 and Raydân; and that it may have been pleasant and be pleas-
17 ant for Saʿadšamsum and his son Ma-
18 rṯadum and the descendants of Garat and their ruler
19 and their tribe Sumhurâm. By ʿAṯtar and Haw-
20 bas and ʾIlumquhû and by Ḏât-Ḥimyâm and by
21 Ḏât-Baʿdânum and by their two deities ʿAṯtar
22 ʿAzîzum and Ḏât-Ẓahrân, the two masters of the hill-town
23 Kanin; and they have entrusted their offering to the care of ʿAṯtar
24 Šarqân and of ʾIlumquhû, master of ʾAwwâm.

Ll. 1-3: restored on the basis of Ja 607; same subjects as in Ja 568.
L. 2: *ʾqwl*, restored on the basis of Ja 559/1.
Ll. 4-5: *ḥg[n/wqh]hmw* as in Ja 607/4-5; compare *ḥgn/kwqh* in Ja 568/4.
L. 13: the *w* instead of ʿ in *šʿb* is certain on the stone; but its diameter is smaller than that of the other *w*.

607 – Grayish sandstone inscription, broken at the bottom; two partial photographs; cf. Chapter I, C. – MaMB 289.

STONE: thickness: 40 cm. (top) and 17.5 (bottom). – *Front:* upper corners broken; lower part badly damaged; 1.85 m. × 48.5 cm. – INSCRIPTION: letter height: 6 cm. (top) and 5.7 (bottom); space between the lines: 0.5 cm.; distance from line 1 to the upper edge: 1.5 cm. – *Symbol*, cf. Ja 559.

1 ⸢**Sym-**⸣ *sʿdšm[sm/ʾsrʿ/wbnhw]*
2 **bol** *mrṯdm/b[ny/grt/ʾqwl]*
3 *šʿbn/ḏmry/hqnyw/ʾlmqh[w]*
4 *ṯhwn/bʿl/ʾwm/ṣlmnhn/ḥ*
5 *gn/wqhhmw/ʾlmqhw/bmsʾ*
6 *lhw/lsʿdhmw/ʾlmqhw/nʿm*
7 *tm/wmngt/ṣdqm/wlwfy/mr*
8 *ʾhmw/wtrm/yhʾmn/mlk/sbʾ*
9 *wḏrydn/bn/ʾlšrḥ/yḥḍb/m*
10 *lk/sbʾ/wḏrydn/wlwfy/ʾd*
11 *mhw/sʿdšmsm/wbnhw/mrṯd*
12 *m/bny/grt/wqlhmw/wšʿbhm*
13 *w/smhrm/wlsʿdhmw/ʾlmqhw*
14 *rḍw/wḥẓy/mrʾhmw/wtrm/m*
15 *lk/sbʾ/wḏrydn/wlḏt/nʿm*
16 *t/wtnʿm⟨⟩n/lsʿdšmsm/wbnh*
17 *w/mrṯdm/wbny/grt/wql*
18 *hmw/wšʿbhmw/smhrm/bʿ*
19 *ṯtr/whwbs/wʾlmqhw/wb*
20 *ḏt/ḥmym/wbḏt/bʿdnm*
21 *wbʾlyhmw/ʿṯtr/ʿzzm/w*
22 *ḏt/ẓhrn/bʿly/ʿr⸤n/k⸥[nn]*
23 *wrṯdw/hqnythm⸢w/⸣[ʿṯtr]*
24 *šrqn/wʾlmqhw/bʿl/[ʾwm]*

Text identical with Ja 606, with the following differences: 1. the disposition of the lines; 2. *tnʿmtn* in line 16; the expression *ḏt/nʿmt/wtnʿmn* is too well known to accept the present form; further, with the form *tnʿmt*, the *n* is inexplicable; 3. *hwbs* in line 19 instead of *hbs* (*scriptio defectiva*) in Ja 606/19-20; 4. Ja 607 is more complete at the beginning and was used to restore Ja 606/1-3; on the other hand, Ja 606/22-24 gives the complete ending of the inscription and was used to restore the end of Ja 607/22-24.

c – Našaʾkarib Yu(ha)ʾmin Yuharḥib: Ja 608-625.

608 – Slightly grayish sandstone; intact; photograph in Plate 10. – MaMB 109.

STONE: front: the engraved surface is covered with red paint; 1.133 m. (left) and 1.137 m. (right) × 35.4 cm. (bottom) and 38.1 (top.) – INSCRIPTION: same disposition of lines as in Ja 552. – SYMBOL, cf. Ja 561.

1 **Sym-** *nšʾkrb/yʾmn/yhrḥb/ml*
2 **bol** *k/sbʾ/wḏrydn/bn/ʾlš*
3 *rḥ/yḥḏb/wyʾzl/byn/mlky/s*
4 *bʾ/wḏrydn/hqny/ʾlmqhṯhw*
5 *nbʿlʾwm/ṣlmn/ḏṣrfn/ḏmdlt*
6 *hw/ʾl(f)n/rḏym/ḥmdm/bḏt/hwf*
7 *yhw/bʾmlʾ/stmlʾ/wtḏʿn/bʿ*
8 *[mh]w/bqdmy/ḏt/hqnytn/wlwz*
9 *ʾ/ʾlmqhṯhwnbʿlʾwm/ṣdq/w*
10 *hwfyn/ʿbdhw/nšʾkrb/yʾmn*
11 *yhrḥb/mlk/sbʾ/wḏrydn/bkl*
12 *ʾmlʾ/yzʾn/stmlʾn/wtḏʿn*
13 *bʿmhw/wlwfyhw/wwfy/mlkh*
14 *w/wḫmshw/bʾlmqhṯhwnbʿlʾwm*

1 **Sym-** Našaʾkarib Yuʾmin Yuharḥib, king
2 **bol** of Sabaʾ and Raydân, son of ʾIlša-
3 raḥ Yaḥḍub and Yaʾzil Bayyin, the two kings of Sa-
4 baʾ and Raydân, has dedicated to ʾIlumquh Ṯahw-
5 ân, master of ʾAwwâm, this statue which [is] in brass, the weight
6 of which [is] a thousand *raḍay*, in praise because He has showered upon
7 him the favors [for which] he besought and implored
8 [Hi]m prior to this offering; and that may continue
9 ʾIlumquh Ṯahwân, master of ʾAwwâm, to bestow and
10 to shower upon His worshipper Našaʾkarib Yuʾmin
11 Yuharḥib, king of Sabaʾ and Raydân, all
12 the favors [for which] he shall continue to beseech and implore
13 Him; and that He may protect him and protect his property
14 and his army. By ʾIlumquh Ṯahwân, master of ʾAwwâm.

L. 6: *ʾl(f)*: *q* instead of *f* is certain on the stone. – *rḍy*, a measure of weight; in Arabic, *rḍḍ* means "to break into large fragments" and *raḍîḍ* "grossly broken"; Hebrew *rṣṣ* also means "to crush"; cf. Ja 609/6.

609 – Yellowish, slightly grayish sandstone; cf. Chapter I, A. – MaMB 202.

STONE: front: the engraved surface is covered with red paint; 1.1 m. × 39 cm. – INSCRIPTION, same disposition of lines as in Ja 561 bis; letter height: from 3.1 cm. to 3.4; space between the lines: 0.5 cm.; distance from line 1 to the upper edge: 0.6 cm. – SYMBOL, cf. Ja 559.

1 **Sym-** *nšʾkrb/y[ʾmn/y]hrḥb/mlk/s*
2 **bol** *bʾ/wḏrydn/bn/ʾlšrḥ/yḥḏb*
3 *wyʾzl/byn/mlky/sbʾ/wḏrydn/h*
4 *qny/ʾlmqhṯhwnbʿlʾwm/ṣlmn/ḏ*
5 *ṣrfn/ḏmdlthw/ʾrbʿ/mʾnm/wʾ*
6 *ḥd/ʾlfm/rḏym/ḥmdm/bḏt/hw*
7 *fyhw/bʾmlʾ/stmlʾ/wtḏʿn/bʿ*
8 *mhw/bqdmy/ḏt/hqnytn/wlwzʾ*
9 *ʾlmqhṯhwnbʿlʾwm/ṣdq/whwfy*
10 *n/ʿbdhw/nšʾkrb/yʾmn/yhrḥb/m*
11 *lk/sbʾ/wḏrydn/bkl/ʾmlʾ/wn*
12 *ḏʿ/yzʾn/stmlʾn/wtḏʿn/bʿmhw*
13 *wlwfyhw/wwfy/mlkhmw/wḫmsh*
14 *mw/bʾlmqhṯhwnbʿlʾwm*

Text identical with Ja 608, with the following differences: 1. the repartition of the text on the stones is different; 2. on lines 5-6: *ʾrbʿ/mʾnm/wʾḥd/ʾlfm/rḏym* "four hundred, and one thousand *raḍay*"; 3. in lines 11-12: *nḏʿ* "benefit" and in lines 13-14, the personal pronoun is *hmw* (also in Ja 610/15-18) "their" instead of *hw* "his".

610 – Yellowish, slightly grayish sandstone; photograph; cf. Chapter I, A. – MaMB 208.

STONE: thickness: 30.5 cm. – *Front:* not polished; badly damaged before the engraving; covered with red paint; upper edge broken; 52.3 cm. (top) and 52.7 (bottom) × 97.5. – INSCRIPTION, same disposition of lines as in Ja 561 bis; letter height: from 3.8 cm. to 4.2; space between the lines from 0.5 cm. to 0.7. – SYMBOL, cf. Ja 559.

1 **Sym-** *[nšʾkrb/yʾmn/yhrḥb/mlk/sbʾ/w]*
2 **bol** *ḏrydn/b⌈n⌉[/ʾlšrḥ/y]ḥḏb/wyʾ[zl]/⌈by⌉[n]*
3 *mlky/sbʾ/wḏrydn/[hqny/]ʾlmqh/[ṯhwn]bʿl*
4 *ʾwm/ṯny/ṣlmn/ḏḏhbm/ḥmdm/bḏt/ḥmr*
5 *hmw/ʾlmqh/ʾtw/wstwfyn/kl/dʿt/kwn*
6 *bmfnthmw/bbrq/ḫrf/ḏḫrf/nšʾkrb/bn*
7 *mʿdkrb/bn/fḏhm/ṯnyn/whwfyhmw/ʾl*
8 *mqh/bn/brdm/wʾrbym/wʿrglm/wbn/kl*
9 *qlmtm/bhyt/brqn/wlwzʾ/ʾlmqhṯhwn*
10 *bʿlʾwm/hwfyn/ʿbdhw/nšʾkrb/yʾmn/yh*
11 *rḥb/mlk/sbʾ/wḏrydn/bn/ʾlšrḥ/yḥ*
12 *ḏb/wyʾzl/byn/mlky/sbʾ/wḏrydn/bk*
13 *l/ʾmlʾ/wṣry/wtbšr/yzʾnn/stmlʾn*
14 *bʿmhw/lʾbrq/ḏṯʾ/wḫrf/wlḫmrhmw/ʾ*
15 *ʾrḫ/wmngt/ṣdqm/ḏyhrḏwnhmw/wlwf*
16 *yhmw/wwfy/mlkhmw/wḫmshmw/wlṯbr*
17 *wwḏʿ/wḏrʿ/whms/whkms/kl/ḏrh*
18 *mw/wšnʾhmw/bʾlmqhṯhwnbʿlʾwm*

1 **Sym-** [Našaʾkarib Yuʾmin Yuharḥib, king of Sabaʾ and]
2 **bol** Raydân, son of [ʾIlšaraḥ Ya]ḥḍub and Yaʾ[zil] Bayy[in,]

3 the two kings of Sabaʾ and Raydân, [has dedicated to] ʾIlumquh [Ṯahwân,] master of
4 ʾAwwâm, these two statues which [are] in bronze, in praise because has vouchsafed to
5 them ʾIlumquh to come back and to give protection to every *daʿat*-palm [which] was
6 in their lands irrigated by canals during the lightning season of the autumn of the year of Našaʾ-karib, son of
7 Maʿadkarib, descendant of [the family] Faḍḥum, the second; and [because] has protected them ʾIl-
8 umquh from cold and locust and cloud (of flies)(?) and from all
9 insect-pests in this lightning season; and that may continue ʾIlumquh Ṯahwân,
10 master of ʾAwwâm, to shower upon His worshipper Našaʾkarib Yuʾmin Yuh-
11 arḥib, king of Sabaʾ and Raydân, son of ʾIlšaraḥ Yaḥ-
12 ḍub and Yaʾzil Bayyin, the two kings of Sabaʾ and Raydân, all
13 the favors and counsel and announcements [for which] they shall continue to beseech
14 Him concerning the lightning storms of spring and of autumn; and that He may vouchsafe to them
15 perfect undertakings and security, which would please them; and that He may protect
16 them and protect their property and their army; and that He may crush
17 and humiliate and humble and break down and wither their every foe
18 and enemy. By ʾIlumquh Ṯahwân, master of ʾAwwâm.

L. 5: *dʿt*, cf. commentary on Ja 615/9-10.

Ll. 6-7: *nšʾkrb/bn mʿdkrb/bn/fḍḥm/ṯnyn*, cf. *mʿdkrb/bn [s]mhkrb/bn/fḍḥm/rbʿn* (Fakhry 71/14-15). – *ṯnyn* is, as usual, related to *ḫrf* (e.g., RÉS 4133/4-5).

L. 8: *brd*; e.g., RÉS 4230/11; cf. *CoRoC*, p. 118 A and *RoAS*, p. 210 A. – *ʾrby*, cf. Hebrew *ʾarběh* "migratory locust" (cf. *KoBaLVTL*, p. 82 B). – *ʿrglm* is known as proper name in CIH 287/4; *CIH* (I, p. 297 B) suggests relating this term to Syriac *ʿargel*, parallel form ("to be rolled, roll down") of the verb pael *ʿagel* "to roll round"; *ʿrgl* could be translated "whirlwind" and more probably, on account of the context, "cloud (of flies)".

L. 13: *tbšr*, pl. of *tbšrt* (cf. verb, e.g., in Ja 588/4-5, and commentary); also noun in RÉS 3992/5 (cf. also *BeNL*, VII, p. 316; and not verb as in *BeSI*, p. 100).

L. 14: *dṯʾ/wḫrf*, e.g., CIH 2/13 and commentary on Ja 585/7; for the Semitic parallels of *dṯʾ*, cf. *LeLS*, p. 137, *StSESA*, p. 526 and *LaGD*, pp. 699-700 (cf. also *RhVSAY*, p. 302); for *ḫrf*, cf. *LeLS*: *ḫarif* (p. 197) and *ḥorf* (p. 191) and also *LaGD*, pp. 585-86.

611 – Grayish, slightly bluish sandstone; broken in three parts; main part = MaMB 277 = NaNAG 10 (only 18 lines; partial photograph; upper left corner (photograph in Plate 10) = MaMB 21; center of lines 1-2 is missing.

MaMB 277: STONE: thickness: 33 cm. (top) and 22.4 (bottom); front: 88.5 cm. × 37. – MaMB 21: splinter: thickness: (maximum) 13 cm.; front: width: 20.6 cm., and height: 24.6. – INSCRIPTION: same disposition of lines as in Ja 552; letter height: between 2.6 cm. and 3; space between the lines: 0.5 cm. and 0.6; distance from line 1 to the upper edge: 1 cm. – SYMBOL, cf. Ja 603.

1 **Sym-** *nšʾk⌜r⌝ \ [b/y] / ⌜ʾmn/yhrḥb/⌝m⌜l⌝k*
2 **bol** *sbʾ/wḏr \ / ⌞ydn/bn/ʾlšrḥ/y*
3 *⌞ḥḍb/wyʾzl/by⌜n/⌝ \ ⌞n/⌟mlky/sbʾ/w*
4 *ḏrydn/hqny/ʾlmq⌜h⌝ \ ⌞hṯ⌟hwnbʿlʾ*
5 *wm/ḏn/ṣlmn/ḏḏhbn/⌜ḥ⌝ \ ⌞ḥ⌟⌞mdm/bḏ*
6 *t/hwfyhw/bʾmlʾ/stml⌜ʾ⌝ \ ⌞ʾ⌟/wb*
7 *hwklt/stwkl/bʿmhw/lwrḫ⌜/ḏ⌟ \ ⌞/ḏ⌟*
8 *hbs/wʿṯtr/ḏḫrf/nšʾkrb/bn*
9 *mʿdkrb/bn/ḥḏmt/ṯlṯn/wlwz*
10 *ʾ/ʾlmqhṯhwnbʿlʾwm/ṣdq/w*
11 *hwfyn/ʿbdhw/nšʾkrb/yʾmn/y*
12 *hrḥb/mlk/sbʾ/wḏrydn/bn/ʾl*
13 *šrḥ/yḥḍb/wyʾzl/byn/mlky/s*
14 *bʾ/wḏrydn/bkl/ʾmlʾ/whwkl[t]*
15 *yzʾn/stmlʾn/wstwkln/lḫyl*
16 *ʾlmqhṯhwnbʿlʾwm/fly*
17 *šmn/wfy/grb/ʿbhdw/nšʾkrb*
18 *yʾmn/yhrḥb/mlk/sbʾ/wḏr*
19 *ydn/wmlkhmw/wḫmshmw/wlṯ*
20 *br/wwḍʿ/wḍrʿn/whms/whkm*
21 *s/kl/ḍrhmw/wšnʾhmw/bʾl*
22 *mqhṯhwnbʿlʾwm*

1 **Sym-** Našaʾkar[ib Yu]ʾmin Yuharḥib, king of
2 **bol** Sabaʾ and Raydân, son of ʾIlšaraḥ Ya-
3 ḥḍub and Yaʾzil Bayyin, the two kings of Sabaʾ and
4 Raydân, has dedicated to ʾIlumquh Ṯahwân, master of ʾA-
5 wwâm, this statue, which [is] in bronze, in praise becau-
6 se He has showered upon him the favors [for which] he besought and

7 the recommendations [for which] he showed his confidence in Him for the month of
8 Hawbas-and-ʿAṯtar of the year of Našaʾkarib, son of
9 Maʿadkarib, descendant of [the family] Ḥaḏmat, the third; and that may conti-
10 nue ʾIlumquh Ṯahwân, master of ʾAwwâm, to bestow and
11 to shower upon His worshipper Našaʾkarib Yuʾmin Yu-
12 harḥib, king of Sabaʾ and Raydân, son of ʾIl-
13 šaraḥ Yaḥḍub and Yaʾzil Bayyin, the two kings of Sa-
14 baʾ and Raydân, all the favors and recommenda-tion[s] [for which]
15 he shall continue to beseech and to show his confi-dence in the strength of
16 ʾIlumquh Ṯahwân, master of ʾAwwâm, so that He may
17 assure the safety of the person of His worshipper Našaʾkarib
18 Yuʾmin Yuharḥib, king of Sabaʾ and
19 Raydân and their property and their army; and that He may
20 crush and humiliate and humble and break down and wither
21 their every foe and enemy. By ʾIl-
22 umquh Ṯahwân, master of ʾAwwâm.

NaNAG (II, p. 41) does not mention the symbol. Since the upper left corner (MaMB 21) was unknown to the preceding author, it is unnecessary to point out that brackets in his restoration of that part of the text must be omitted; nevertheless, line 1: *yhrḥb* instead of *yhrhb*; line 3: *mlky/sbʾ* instead of *mlky sbʾ*. Besides, line 3: *ḥḏb* instead of *ḥ[db*; line 4: omit the bracket after *ḏ*; line 7: *hwklt* instead of *m]hw/bḏt*, *lwrẖ* instead of *bwrẖn*; line 9: *ṯlṯn* instead of *ṯnyn*; line 14: *hwkl[t]* instead of *hwkl*; line 15: omit the initial point, *lẖyl* instead of *ẖyl/*; line 16: omit *[l]wʾlmqh*, where the 1st *l* is printed instead of /.

L. 9: *ḥḏmt*, e.g., RÉS 2726/10-11.

612 – Yellowish sandstone block; lower left corner damaged; lower right corner broken; photograph in Plate 11. – MaMB 88.

STONE: constant thickness: 12.2 cm. – *Left side:* at 2.3 cm. from the right edge a *š* (1.3 cm. × 2.2) and 0.8 cm. below a reversed *b* (0.8 cm. × 1.6). – *Front*, covered with red paint; 25.3 cm. × 47 (right) and 47.5 (left). – INSCRIPTION, same disposition of the lines as in Ja 561 bis; letter height: 2.1 cm. (line 1), 2.3 (line 13), 1.7 (line 14) and 1.5 (lines 15-20); distance from line 1 to the top: 1.1 cm. (right) and 0.6 (left). – SYMBOL, combination of the type of Ja 585 and that of Ja 589; cf. Plate A.

1 **Sym-** *ʾḥmd/yġnm/bn/nšʾy/mqt*
2 **bol** *wy/nšʾkrb/yʾmn/yhrḥb/m*
3 *lk/sbʾ/wḏrydn/bn/ʾlšrḥ/yḥ*
4 *ḍb/wyʾzl/byn/mlky/sbʾ/wḏr*
5 *ydn/hqny/ʾlmqhṯhwnbʿlʾwm*
6 *ṣlmn/ḏḏhbn/bḏt/ẖmr/ʾlmqhṯ*
7 *hwnb(ʿ)lʾwm/ʿbdhw/ʾḥmd/hwfy*
8 *nhw/bmlʾ/stmlʾ/bʿmhw/bkn/s*
9 *bʾ/wšwʿn/ʾqwln/wẖmsn/ʿdy/ʾrḍ*
10 *ḥḍrmt/wẖmr/ʾlmqhṯhwnbʿlʾw*
11 *m/ʿbdhw/ʾḥmd/ʾtw/bbrytm*
12 *whrg/ṯny/ʾsyn/wlwzʾ/ʾlmqhṯh*
13 *wnbʿlʾwm/ẖmr/ʿbdhw/ʾḥmd/mh*
14 *rgm/wġnmm/wbry/ʾḏnm/wmqmm/wls*
15 *ʿd/ʾlqmhṯhwnbʿlʾwm/ʿbdhw/ʾḥm*
16 *d/bn/nšʾy/ḥẓy/wrḍw/mrʾhmw/nšʾ*
17 *krb/yʾmn/yhrḥb/mlk/sbʾ/wḏryd*
18 *n/bn/ʾlšrḥ/yḥḍb/wyʾzl/byn/ml*
19 *ky/sbʾ/wḏrydn/wlẖrynhw/bn/n*
20 *ḍʿ/wšṣy/šnʾm/bʾlmqhṯhwnbʿlʾwm*

1 **Sym-** ʾAḥmad Yuġnim, son of Našʾay, high military offi-
2 **bol** cial of Našaʾkarib Yuʾmin Yuharḥib,
3 king of Sabaʾ and Raydân, son of ʾIlšaraḥ Yaḥ-
4 ḍub and Yaʾzil Bayyin, the two kings of Sabaʾ and Ra-
5 ydân, has dedicated to ʾIlumquh Ṯahwân, master of ʾAwwâm,
6 this statue which [is] in bronze, because has vouchsafed ʾIlumquh Ṯa-
7 hwân, master of ʾAwwâm, to His worshipper ʾAḥmad to shower
8 upon him the favor [for which] he besought Him when he
9 fought and assisted the rulers and the army in the land
10 of Ḥaḍramawt and [because] ʾIlumquh Ṯahwân, master of ʾAwwâm, has vouchsafed
11 to His worshipper ʾAḥmad to come back in strength
12 and to kill two messengers; and that may continue ʾIlumquh Ṯah-
13 wân, master of ʾAwwâm, to vouchsafe to His worshipper ʾAḥmad war
14 trophy and booty and [also] the strength of understanding and of power; and that may make
15 happy ʾIlumquh Ṯahwân, master of ʾAwwâm, His worshipper ʾAḥmad,

16 son of Našʿay, with the esteem and grace of their lord Našaʾ-
17 karib Yuʾmin Yuharḥib, king of Sabaʾ and Raydân,
18 son of ʾIlšaraḥ Yaḥḍub and of Yaʾzil Bayyin, the two
19 kings of Sabaʾ and Raydân; and that He may preserve him from the
20 hostility and wickedness of [any] enemy. By ʾIlumquh Ṯahwân, master of ʾAwwâm.

L. 1: *yġnm*, e.g., CIH 153/1 and commentary on *ġnm* in Ja 282/1, Qat; in RÉS 2734 R, read *ġnnm* "Ġannam" instead of *ḏnnm*. – *nšʿy*, *nisba* nominal form as in *ršʿy* (RÉS 3945/5); the *y* had first been omitted and engraved later; thus the three characters *ʿy/* are extremely close together.

L. 7: *bwl* instead of *bʿl* is certain on the stone.

L. 11: *bryt*: ordinarily in singular *bry* (cf. line 14); compare the parallels *mqm–mqymt* and *ʾḏn–ʾʾḏn*.

L. 12: *ʾsy*, for the verb, cf. Ja 576/16 and 578/26.

613 – Yellowish, slightly grayish sandstone; photograph in Plate 11. – MaMB 157.

STONE: thickness: 14 cm. (top) and 11.5 (bottom). – *Front:* covered with red paint; 23.4 cm. (top) and 24 (bottom) × 50.7. – INSCRIPTION: same disposition of lines as in Ja 552; a vertical line is traced at 0.5 cm. from the right edge, and another one at 0.3 from the left one; at the bottom, six horizontal lines indicate the space for three more lines, which were never engraved; letter height: 1.6 cm.; space between the lines: 0.4 cm. – SYMBOL: same general type as that of Ja 567, but five inside lines instead of six, and the lower extremity is horizontal; cf. Plate A.

1 **Sym-** *ʿwfm/yġnm/bn/⌈m⌉⌈ḏkrm/wr*
2 **bol** *šdm/mqtwy/nšʾkrb/yʾmn*
3 *yhrḥb/mlk/sbʾ/wḏrydn/bn/ʾ*
4 *lšrḥ/yḥḍb/wyʾzl/byn/mlky/s*
5 *bʾ/wḏrydn/hqny/ʾlmqhṯhw*
6 *nbʿlʾwm/ṣlmn/ḏḏhbn/ḥmdm*
7 *bḏt/hʿn/wmtʿn/grb/ʿbdhw/ʿ*
8 *wfm/yġnm/bn/mḏkrm/wršdm/b*
9 *n/ḥlẓ/ḥlẓ/bhgrn/mrb/bwrẖ*
10 *ḏmlyt/ḏẖrf/wddʾl/bn/ʾbkr*
11 *b/bn/kbrẖll/sdṯn/wlwzʾ/ʾl*
12 *mqhṯhwnbʿlʾwm/hʿnn/wmtʿn/*
13 *grb/ʿbdhw/ʿwfm/yġnm/bn/mḏ*
14 *krm/wršdm/bn/ḥlẓm/wmrḍm/w*
15 *myqẓm/wbn/bʾstm/wnkytm/wʿ*
16 *bṭm/wbn/nḍʿ/wšṣy/šnʾm/wlẖ*
17 *mrhw/ʾlmqhṯhwnbʿlʾwm/ḥẓy*
18 *wrḍw/mrʾhw/nšʾkrb/yʾmn/yh*
19 *rḥb/mlk/sbʾ/wḏrydn/wbry*
20 *ʾḏnm/wmqmm/wʾṯmr/ṣdqm/ḏ*
21 *yhrḍynhw/bn/kl/ʾrḍthmw/w*
22 *mšymthmw/bʾlmqhṯhwnbʿlʾwm*

1 **Sym-** ʿAwfum Yuġnim, son of Maḏkirum and Ra-
2 **bol** šîdum, high official of Našaʾkarib Yuʾmin
3 Yuharḥib, king of Sabaʾ and Raydân, son of
4 ʾIlšaraḥ Yaḥḍub and Yaʾzil Bayyin, the two kings of Sa-
5 baʾ and Raydân, has dedicated to ʾIlumquh Ṯahw-
6 ân, master of ʾAwwâm, this statue which [is] in bronze, in praise
7 because He has assisted and saved the person of His worshipper ʿA-
8 wfum Yuġnim, son of Maḏkirum and Rašîdum, from
9 the oppression [with which] he was overwhelmed in the city [of] Mârib in the month of
10 Malayat, of the year of Waddʾil, son of ʾAbkarib,
11 descendant of the Leader of Ḫalil, the sixth; and that may continue ʾIl-
12 umquh Ṯahwân, master of ʾAwwâm, to assist and save
13 the person of His worshipper ʿAwfum Yuġnim, son of Maḏ-
14 kirum and Rašîdum, from oppression and disease and
15 sleeplessness and from misfortunes and sufferings and ca-
16 lamity and from the hostility and wickedness of [any] enemy; and that may vouch-
17 safe to him ʾIlumquh Ṯahwân, master of ʾAwwâm, the esteem
18 and grace of his lord Našaʾkarib Yuʾmin Yuh-
19 arḥib, king of Sabaʾ and Raydân, and the strength
20 of understanding and of power, and perfect fruits, which
21 would please him from all their grounds and
22 arable fields. By ʾIlumquh Ṯahwân, master of ʾAwwâm.

L. 1: *ʿwfm*, e.g., RÉS 4878/1, Ḥaḍr, and 5064 A/1; for *ʿwfm/yġnm*, cf. the masculine personal name *ḏʿfm/yġnm* in CIH 361/3-4. – *mḏkrm*, cf. *mḏkr* in RÉS 2819/9-10, Min. – *ršdm*, cf. the proper name *ršd* in Serjeant-Hûd 7, and the verb *ršd* in RÉS 3957/7-8 and *ʾlršd* in RÉS 4229/1; cf. also the following Arabic masculine personal names *rašîd* (cf. *WüR*, p. 430, *HeBN*, p. 25 B and *GoAT*, pp. 194-95), *râšid* (cf. *HeBN*, *l.c.*, and *GoAT*, p. 187), *rašdân* (cf. *HeBN*, *l.c.*) and *rašdayn* (cf. *GoAT*, p. 194).

L. 10: *ḏmlyt*, CIH 607/3.

L. 11: *sdṯn*: ordinal number. In Geukens 6/22-23: *bmw/sdṯ/hwt/ywmn*, *sdṯ* is interpreted as a cardinal number by *RyISA* (XIV, p. 375), who translates the expression as follows: "durant ces six jours". Since *ywm* is masculine, *sdṯ* should have the feminine form *sdṯt* (cf. *HöASG*, pp. 131-32, §112). Furthermore, the numbers 3-10 are followed by a plural genitive (cf. *l.c.*); and both *hwt* and *ywm* are singulars. The above-mentioned expression must be translated as "during this sixth day", that is to say during the sixth day of the military campaign.

614 – Yellowish sandstone; photograph in Plate 11. – MaMB 90.

STONE: thickness: 13.5 cm. (top) and 15.4 (bottom). – *Front:* covered with red paint; upper edge damaged; both upper corners broken; 61 cm. (right) and 58.5 (left) × 30 (top) and 30.6 (bottom).– INSCRIPTION: same disposition of lines as in Ja 552; letter height: 2 cm.; space between the lines: 0.4 cm.; below line 20 of the text, another pair of horizontal lines including no letter, and 0.4 cm. below these two lines, another horizontal line. – SYMBOL: cf. Ja 583, but the two extremities are horizontal, and the central inside line is much longer, has sharply pointed extremities, and is divided into two parts by two parallels perpendicular to the frame; cf. Plate A.

1 ⌈**Sym-**⌉ *ʿ⌈km/ʾrym⌉/wb⌈nyh⌉w⌈/ḥywm/⌉[bnw]*
2 **bol** *ʾdfm/mqtwyy/nšʾkrb/yʾmn/y*
3 *hrḥb/mlk/sbʾ/wḏrydn/bn/ʾlšr*
4 *ḥ/yḥḍb/wyʾzl/byn/mlky/sbʾ/w*
5 *ḏrydn/hqnyy/ʾlmqhṯhwnbʿlʾwm/ḏ*
6 *n/ṣlmnhn/ḏḏhbn/ḥmdm/bḏt/hwfy*
7 *ʾlmqhṯhwnbʿlʾwm/ʿbdyhw/ʿkm/ʾ*
8 *rym/wbnyhw/ḥywm/bkl/ʾmlʾ/wtb*
9 *šr/stmlʾ/wtbšrn/bʿmhw/wlwzʾ*
10 *ʾlmqhṯhwnbʿlʾwm/hwfyn/ʿbdy*
11 *hw/ʿkm/ʾrym/wbnyhw/ḥywm/b*
12 *kl/ʾmlʾ/wtbšr/yzʾnn/stmlʾ*
13 *n/wtbšrn/bʿmhw/wlẖmrhmy/ʾl*
14 *mqhṯhwnbʿlʾwm/ḥẓy/wrḍw/mr*
15 *ʾhmy/nšʾkrb/yʾmn/yhrḥb/mlk*
16 *sbʾ/wḏrydn/wbry/ʾʾḏnm/wmqy*
17 *mtm/wlẖrynhmy/ʾlmqhṯhwnb*
18 *ʿlʾwm/bn/ṭwʿ/wnḍʿ/wšṣy/wt*
19 *ṯʿt/šnʾm/ḏbnhw/dʿw/wḏbnhw*
20 *ʾl/dʿw/bʾlmqhṯhwnbʿlʾwm*

1 **Sym-** ʿAkkum ʾAryam and his son Ḥayûm, [descendants of (the family)]
2 **bol** ʾAdfum, the two high officials of Našaʾ-karib Yuʾmin Yu-
3 harḥib, king of Sabaʾ and Raydân, son of ʾIlšaraḥ
4 Yaḥḍub and Yaʾzil Bayyin, the two kings of Sabaʾ and
5 Raydân, have dedicated to ʾIlumquh Ṯahwân, master of ʾAwwâm, the-
6 se two statues which [are] in bronze, in praise because has showered
7 ʾIlumquh Ṯahwân, master of ʾAwwâm, upon His two worshippers ʿAkkum ʾA-
8 ryam and his son Ḥayûm all the favors and announce-
9 ments [for which] he besought and begged of Him; and that may continue
10 ʾIlumquh Ṯahwân, master of ʾAwwâm, to shower upon His two wor-
11 shippers ʿAkkum ʾAryam and his son Ḥayûm
12 all the favors and announcements [for which] they shall continue to beseech
13 and beg of Him; and that may vouchsafe to them both ʾIl-
14 umquh Ṯahwân, master of ʾAwwâm, the esteem and grace of the lord of both of them
15 Našaʾkarib Yuʾmin Yuharḥib, king of
16 Sabaʾ and Raydân, and the strength of understand-ing and of po-
17 wer; and that may preserve them both ʾIlumquh Ṯahwân, mas-
18 ter of ʾAwwâm, from the constraint and hostility and wickedness and
19 fear of [any] enemy, those who are known and those who
20 are not known. By ʾIlumquh Ṯahwân, master of ʾAwwâm.

L. 1: *ʿkm*, already known as tribe name (e.g., Ja 574/7-8); cf. the Thamudic personal name *ʿk* (e.g., *vdBrTTPN*, p. 58: Ph 280 j 3). – *ʾrym*, masculine personal name, e.g., in RÉS 5088 (–/ *ḏqḏn* "–, he of Qaḏân", instead of *ḏq*...), and second masculine personal name, e.g., in Ja 495/1; cf. also the second clan name *ʾrymn*, e.g., in RÉS 4636/4 and the name of a woman *ʾrm* in RÉS 4387/2. – At the end, three characters are missing.

L. 2: *ʾdfm*, e.g., CIH 130/3; for the root *ʾdf*, cf. Arabic *wadafa* "to give very little".

L. 18: *ṭwʿ* (cf. *CoRoC*, p. 159 A) = *ḍwʿ* (e.g., Geukens 6/44), as *nṭʿ* = *nḍʿ* (cf. commentary on Ja 561 bis/22).

615 – Yellow, grayish sandstone; photograph in Plate 11. – MaMB 107.

STONE: thickness: 29 cm. (top) and 17 (bottom). – *Front:* covered with red paint; upper right corner broken; 1.211 m. (left) and 1.052 (right) × 36.7 cm. – INSCRIPTION: same disposition of lines as in Ja 561 bis.

1 [**Sym-** *ʾsʿd/yzd/w]⸢ʾ⸣⸢h̲yhw/smhyfʿ/y*
2 [**bol** *⸢hḥmd/⸣w⸢bnyhmy/ʾsdm/wsʿd*
3 *[m/bn]w/d̲kbrʾqynm/ʾqwl/šʿbn/b*
4 *[kl]⸢m/rbʿn/d̲hgrn/šbmm/d̲ʾʿd̲r/ʿ*
5 *rn/ʾlw/mqtt/nšʾkrb/yʾmn/yhr*
6 *ḥb/mlk/sbʾ/wd̲rydn/bn/ʾlšrḥ*
7 *yḥḍb/wyʾzl/byn/mlky/sbʾ/wd̲r*
8 *ydn/hqnyw/ʾlmqht̲hwnbʿlʾwm/d̲n*
9 *ṣlmn/d̲d̲hbn/d̲ʿšrhw/bn/sqy/wdʿ*
10 *t/fqlw/bn/kl/ʾsrr/wmšymt/wmf*
11 *nt/wkl/hgr/bythmw/byt/d̲kbrʾ*
12 *qynm/lh̲rf/wddʾl/bn/ʾbkrb/bn*
13 *kbrh̲ll/sdt̲n/wlh̲rf/nšʾkrb/b*
14 *n/mʿdkrb/bn/ḥd̲mt/t̲lt̲n/wlwzʾ*
15 *ʾlmqht̲hwnbʿlʾwm/h̲mr/ʾdmhw*
16 *ʾsʿd/yzd/wʾh̲yhw/smhyfʿ/yhḥ*
17 *md/wbnyhmw/ʾsdm/wsʿdm/bny/d̲*
18 *kbrʾqynm/frʿw/lʾmrt/dt̲ʾ/wh̲*
19 *rf/wsʿsʿm/wmlym/wnʾd/ʾt̲mrm/w*
20 *ʾfqlm/bn/kl/ʾrḍ/wʾsrr/wmḟnt/w*
21 *mšymt/bythmw/byt/d̲kbrʾqynm*
22 *d̲yhrḍwn/ʾlbbhmw/wlh̲mrhmw/ʾl*
23 *mqht̲hwnbʿlʾwm/ḥẓy/wrḍw/mrʾh*
24 *mw/nšʾkrb/yʾmn/yhrḥb/mlk/sbʾ*
25 *wd̲rydn/wbry/ʾʾd̲nm/wmqymtm/w*
26 *lh̲rynhmw/bn/bʾsm/wnkytm/wnḍʿ*
27 *wšṣy/wtt̲ʿt/wʿbṭ/wġbṭ/šnʾm/d̲*
28 *bnhw/dʿw/wd̲bnhw/ʾl/dʿw/bʾl*
29 *mqht̲hwnbʿlʾwm*

1 [**Sym-** ʾAsʿad Yazid and] his brother Sumhuyafaʿ Yu-
2 [**bol** haḥmid and their two sons ʾAsdum and Saʿad-
3 [um, descen]dants of [the clan] the Leader of ʾAqyânum, rulers of the tribe Ba-
4 [kîl]um, the fourth of the city [of] Šibamum, settlers of the acro-
5 polis ʾAlw, high officials of Našaʾkarib Yuʾmin Yuhar-
6 ḥib, king of Sabaʾ and Raydân, son of ʾIlšaraḥ
7 Yaḥḍub and Yaʾzil Bayyin, the two kings of Sabaʾ and
8 Raydân, have dedicated to ʾIlumquh T̲ahwân, master of ʾAwwâm, this
9 statue which [is] in bronze, which he had assessed to Him as tithe from [the product of] *saqay-* and *daʿat*-palms [that]
10 they harvested from all the wâdî-side valleys and arable fields and lands irrigated
11 by canals and every city of their house, the house of the Leader of ʾA-
12 qyânum in the year of Waddʾil, son of ʾAbkarib, descendant of [the clan]
13 the Leader of H̲alil, the sixth, and in the year of Našaʾkarib, son
14 of Maʿadkarib, descendant of [the clan] Ḥad̲mat, the third; and that may continue
15 ʾIlumquh T̲ahwân, master of ʾAwwâm, to vouchsafe to His worshippers
16 ʾAsʿad Yazid and his brother Sumhuyafaʿ Yuhaḥ-
17 mid and their two sons ʾAsdum and Saʿadum, descendants of
18 the Leader of ʾAqyânum, optimum crops for the cereals of spring and of au-
19 tumn and of summer and of winter and [also] the magnificence of fruits
20 and of harvests from every ground and all the wâdî-side valleys and lands irrigated by canals and
21 arable fields of their house, the house of the Leader of ʾAqyânum,
22 which would please their hearts; and that may vouchsafe to them ʾIl-
23 umquh T̲ahwân, master of ʾAwwâm, the esteem and grace of their lord
24 Našaʾkarib Yuʾmin Yuharḥib, king of Sabaʾ
25 and Raydân, and the strength of understanding and of power; and
26 that He may preserve them from misfortune and sufferings and [from] the hostility
27 and wickedness and fear and calamity and envy of [any] enemy,
28 those who are known and those who are not known. By ʾIl-
29 umquh T̲ahwân, master of ʾAwwâm.

Cf. preliminary remark on Ja 822.

Ll. 1-3 are restored on the basis of lines 16-18. – *yzd*, e.g., RÉS 3659, Qat, and Kawkab 4/1-2; masculine personal name (e.g., Ja 620/1) and clan name (cf. *RyGSAS*, p. 562); cf. also commentary on Ja 578/1. – *smhyfʿ*, e.g., RÉS 3945/14. – *bnyhmy*, but *bnyhmw* in line 17.

Ll. 3-4: *bn]w / d̲kbrʾqynm / ʾqwl/šʿbn / b[kl]m*, cp. *ʾkbrwʾqynm/ʾqwl/šʿbn/bklm* in RÉS 2695/2 and 3; cp. also *ʾkbrw/h̲ll/[w]ʾqynm* in Ja 711/9-10. An expression such as *kbr(/)h̲ll* is a family name (e.g., Ja 613/11) whose first element, *kbr*, is sometimes treated as a noun (e.g., Ja 711/9, RÉS 2695/2 and 4963/1). It seems thus better to translate *kbr* (as *CIH*, II, p. 189); however, it is simply transliterated "*kabîr*" (e.g., *RÉS*, VII, p. 466, and *RycIMAM*, p. 85, where "Našaʾamar" should be corrected "Našaʾʾamar"). Besides, *ʾqynm*, which is derived from the noun *qyn*, indicates a group of persons (e.g., *BeSI*, p. 18) and therefore is a proper name (e.g., *HaAF*, p. 149) which is not to be translated (as, e.g., *RÉS*, VII, p. 453 and *RycIMAM*, *l.c.*). – *b[kl]m/rb^{c}n/d̲hgrn/šbmm*, compare *bklm/bšbm* in CIH 126/9; for *d̲hgrn/šbmm*, cf. *bhgrn/šbmm* in RÉS 3991/8; *šbmm* is masculine personal name in RÉS 4678/1 (cf. commentary on Ja 552/4).

L. 4: *d̲ʾ^{c}dr*, RÉS 2695/2 and recently BM 104395/5; cf. *CoRoC*, p. 203; in T[imna^{c}] S[outh Gate] p/3-4: *d̲^{c}d̲r* probably has, in my opinion, the meaning "eunuch".

Ll. 4-5: *^{c}rn/ʾlw*, for the Ḥaḍ acropolis ʾAlw, cf. *WiHöBGS*, p. 78.

L. 9: *^{c}šr*, RÉS 2771/3, Min: "first-fruits" or "to deduct the first-fruits"; cf. Arabic *^{c}ašara* "to assess *or* impose someone a tithe".

Ll. 9-10: *d̲^{c}šrhw/bn/sqy/wd^{c}t/fqlw*, cp. *d̲^{c}šrhw/bn sqy wd^{c}t/h̲mrhmw/ʾlmqh* (Ja 617/4-5), *l[s^{c}]dhmw/ʾt̲mrm/šfqm/d^{c}tm [ws]qym* (Ja 691/8-10), *wrqm/wd^{c}tm/wt̲ḥnm* (RÉS 3951/3), *wr]qm/wd^{c}tm/h̲rdm/[w]ʾty[m* (RÉS 4130/1) and *wrqm/wd^{c}tm* (RÉS 3910/7). The first and third expressions clearly indicate that *sqy* and *d^{c}t* are things that can be harvested and consequently justify *MoMiHI*'s interpretation of *wrq* as "greens, vegetables" (p. 14). *BeSI* (p. 74), who accepts the preceding interpretation of *wrq*, refers *d^{c}t* to Arabic *du^{c}â^{c}* "plant. . . used as human food under pressure of famine" and translates it as "cattle-fodder(?)". The preceding translation is far-fetched and cannot be accepted here, for "cattle-fodder" does not grow *bkl/hgr* (line 10). Because both *sqy* and *d^{c}t* are mentioned as growing in *bkl/hgr*, I suggest interpreting these two nouns as indicating two different kinds of palms; cf. Arabic *du^{c}â^{c}* "palms planted separately" and *saqiy* or *saqiyyat* "palm-trees that are irrigated by means of water-wheels" (cf. *LaAEL*, p. 1386 A). – *fql*, e.g., CIH 80/10.

Ll. 12 and 13: *lh̲rf*: the preposition *l* introduces the datation (cf. *HöASG*, p. 149, δ).

Ll. 12-14: the two datations are also mentioned in Ja 613/10-11 and 611/8-9, respectively.

L. 17: *bnyhmw* equals to *bnyhmy* in line 2.

Ll. 18-19: *fr^{c}w/lʾmrt/d̲tʾ/wh̲rf/ws^{c}s^{c}m/wmlym*, cf., e.g., *fr^{c}/d̲tʾ/wh̲rf* in CIH 2/13 and especially *fr^{c}/ʾmyrt/d̲tʾ/wh̲rf/ws<^{c}>s^{c}m/wmlym* in Ja 623/14-15 (also in Geukens 9/14-15). *fr^{c}w*, plural of form *qatlaw* (cf. *HöASG*, p. 104, §87), e.g., *bltw–blt* (cf. commentary on Ja 560/8-9); cf. *CoRoC*, p. 220, and *BeSI*, p. 3; *CIH*'s (I, p. 10) translation of *fr^{c}* as "optimum" is correct according to Arabic *far^{c}* "top, highest point (in anything)" and also "sprout, shoot" (cf. *DoSDA*, II, p. 256 B); *fr^{c}* may thus be translated "optimum crop". *RyISA*'s (XV, p. 102) translation of this noun as "prémices" is inaccurate for "prémices" only designates the first-fruits, which does not imply that they are optimum. However, *fr^{c}* has its abstract meaning of high value in Ja 649/12, 18, 35, and 735/11 where *fr^{c}* is a noun (and not an adjective; cf. Arabic *fâri^{c}* "great, beautiful, and of high value") as it is positively indicated by *d̲* (*d̲ fr^{c}m*) in the first three contexts; the absence of *d̲* in the last one is a common feature; e.g., *ṣlmtm d̲hbm* (Ja 694/4-5) and *ṣlmn/ṣrfm* (Ja 700/3-4). – *ʾmrt* (also in Ja 650/12) and *ʾmyrt* in *scriptio plena* (e.g., Ja 623/14-15), as well as *ʾmr* (e.g., Ja 627/5) are plural forms of *myr*; cf. in both Arabic and Dat̲înah (cf. *LaGD*, p. 2727) *mîrat* "provision" especially wheat, corn, etc.; *myr* may thus be translated "cereal". – *s^{c}s^{c}*, cf. Arabic *sa^{c}sa^{c}a*, 2d form "to pass away (month)", according to its place in the series of seasons, *s^{c}s^{c}* must indicate the "summer" time (cf. also *RyISA*, XV, p. 103). – *mly*, CIH 174/3 and *CoRoC*, p. 178 A and *BeESACD*, p. 20; cp. the name of the month *mlyt*, e.g., in Ja 653/10.

L. 26: *bʾs*, CIH 539/3 and commentary on *bʾst* in Ja 558/5.

L. 27: *ġbṭ*, cf. Arabic *ġibṭat* "envy, desire (without jealousy)"; the restriction about jealousy does not seem acceptable in the present text.

616 – Yellowish, slightly grayish sandstone; top (photograph in Plate 12.) = MaMB 154; bottom = MaMB 199 = Ja 622.

Top: constant thickness: 32.8 cm.; front: 45.5 cm. (top) × 29.3 (right) and 52.5 (left). *Bottom:* upper part of the right edge broken; thickness: 36.4 cm.; front: 98 cm. (right) and 73.8 (left) × 45.5 (top) and 45 (bottom). Total height of the stone: 1.26 m. (left) and 1.27 (right). – INSCRIPTION: letter height: 2.5 cm.; space between the lines: 0.4 cm.; distance from line 1 to the upper edge: 0.6 cm. – SYMBOL: cp. Ja 591; cf. Plate A.

1 **Sym-** whbʾwm/yʾḏf/wʾẖyhw/ydm/ydrm/wbnyhw
2 **bol** ḥmʿṯt/ʾzʾd/wʾbkrb/ʾsʿd/wsẖymm/yzʾn⌉
3 bnw/sẖymm/ʾbʿl/bytn/rymn/ʾqwl/šʿbn/yrsm/ḏs
4 mʿy/ṯlṯn/ḏhgrm/mqtt/nšʾkrb/yʾmn/yhrḥb/mlk
5 sbʾ/wḏrydn/bn/ʾlšrḥ/yḥḏb/wyʾzl/byn/mlky/s
6 ⌊bʾ/wḏrydn/hqnyw/mrʾhmw/ʾlmqhṯhwnbʿlʾwm/ḏ
7 ⌊n/⌋ṣlmn/ḏḏhbn/ḥmdm/bḏt/hwfy/ʿbdyhw/ḥmʿṯt
8 [ʾ]⌈⌊zʾd/wʾbkrb/ʾsʿd/bny/sẖymm/bkl/ʾmlʾ/wt
9 ⌈⌊bšr/⌋wṣry/stmlʾw/wtbšrn/wṣtryn/bʿmhw/bkn
10 [w]⌊qhhm⌊y/⌋mrʾhmy/nšʾkrb/yʾmn/yhrḥb/mlk/s
11 [b]ʾ/wḏr⌈yd⌉ ⌊n/b⌋n/ʾlšrḥ/yḥḏb/wyʾzl/byn/mlky/sbʾ
12 [wḏ]rydn/lsb⌈ʾ/⌉ ⌊/w⌋wfyn/ʾšʿb/wʿšr/ẖwln/gddm/wḥm
13 [dw]/ẖyl/wmqm/mrʾ⌈hm⌉ ⌊hm⌋w⌊/ʾlmqhṯhwnbʿlʾwm/bḏt/tʾ
14 [t]mw/wqtḍn/kl/ʾšʿb/wʿ⌈šr⌉ ⌊šr/⌋ẖwln/gddm/wʾwlw/kl
15 ⌊ʾ⌋ḥrrhmw/ʾwṯqm/wẖbṯhmw/w⌈kl⌉ ⌊kl⌋/ḏwqhhmw/mrʾhm
16 w/nšʾkrb/yʾmn/yhrḥb/mlk/sbʾ/w⌈ḏr⌉ ⌊ḏry⌋dn/ʿdy/hgr
17 n/ṣnʿw/wbmw/hwt/wfyn/ysrw/bhʾthm⌈w/⌉ ⌊/lbh⌋ʾ/lh
18 mw/shrtn/wṯhbhmw/bhʾthmw/ʿdy/hgrn/rḥbm⌈m/⌉ ⌊m/ḏ⌋
19 ʾrḍ/ẖwln/krʾ/khṭbw/lhmw/ʾšʿb/dwʾt/wbmw/y
20 wmn/ḏbhw/ṯbhmw/bhʾthmw/nzʿw/gyšhmw/whbr
21 yw/ʿwfhmw/wtʾtm/gyšhmw/sṯ/wʿšry/ʾfrsm/wṯl
22 ṯ/mʾnm/ʾsdm/bn/šʿbhmw/yrsm/wbn/nẓr/mlkn
23 wḏbn/ẖwln/whġrw/wṣbḥn/wḥrb/bn/ʿšr/dwʾt
24 ʿšrt/ʾbʾs/wʾydʿn/wḥkmm/wḥdlnt/wġmdm/wk
25 hlm/wʾhlny/wgdlt/wsbsm/wḥrmm/wḥgr/lmd/w
26 ʾwmm/wrḍḥtn/bn/ḥrt/wḥrbhmw/bsfl/ʾwdytn
27 ḏbʾrn/wẖlb/wtdḥn/wḥmdw/ẖyl/wmqm/mrʾhmw
28 ʾlmqhṯhwnbʿlʾwm/bḏt/ẖmrhmw/tʾwln/hmw/w
29 ʾfrshmw/wgyšhmw/bwfym/wḥmdm/wyhrm/wʾḥll
30 m/wʾẖyḏtm/wmhrgtm/wsbym/wmltm/wġnmm/šfq
31 m/ḏhrḍw/mrʾhmw/wḏhrḍwhmw/wlwzʾ/ʾlmqhṯhw
32 nbʿlʾwm/ṣdq/whwfyn/ʾdmhw/bny/sẖymm/bk
33 l/ʾmlʾ/wtbšr/wṣry/yzʾnn/stmlʾn/wtbšrn/w
34 ṣtryn/bʿmhw/wlsʿdhmw/mrʾhmw/ʾlmqhṯhwnb
35 ʿlʾwm/ḥẓy/wrḍw/mrʾhmw/nšʾkrb/yʾmn/yhrḥb
36 mlk/sbʾ/wḏrydn/bn/ʾlšrḥ/yḥḏb/wyʾzl/byn/m
37 lky/sbʾ/wḏrydn/wbry/ʾʾḏnm/wmqymtm/wnʾḏ/ʾ
38 ṯmrm/wlẖrynhmw/ʾlmqhṯhwnbʿlʾwm/bn/bʾs
39 tm/wnkytm/wbn/nḍʿ/wšsy/wtṯʿt/wṭwʿ/šnʾm/ḏrḥq
40 wqrb/ḏbnhw/dʿw/wḏbnhw/ʾl/dʿw/bʾlmqhṯhwnbʿlʾwm

1 **Sym-** Wahabʾawwâm Yaʾḏif and his brother Yadum Yadrim and his sons
2 **bol** Ḥammʿaṯat ʾAzʾad and ʾAbkarib ʾAsʿad and Suẖaymum Yazʾân,
3 descendants of [the tribe] Suẖaymum, masters of the house Raymân, rulers of the tribe Yarsum, of [the tribe] Sa-
4 mʿay, the third of [the tribe] Hagarum, high military officials of Našaʾkarib Yuʾmin Yuharḥib, king
5 of Sabaʾ and Raydân, son of ʾIlšaraḥ Yaḥḏub and Yaʾzil Bayyin, the two kings of Sa-
6 baʾ and Raydân, have dedicated to their lord ʾIlumquh Ṯahwân, master of ʾAwwâm, this
7 statue which [is] in bronze, in praise because He has showered upon His two worshippers Ḥammʿa-ṯat
8 [ʾA]zʾad and ʾAbkarib ʾAsʿad, descendants of Suẖaymum, all the favors and ann-
9 ouncements and counsel [for which] they besought and begged of and implored from Him when
10 has [or]dered them both their lord Našaʾkarib Yuʾmin Yuharḥib, king of Sa-

11 [ba]ʾ and Raydân, son of ʾIlšaraḥ Yaḥḏub and Yaʾzil Bayyin, the two kings of Sabaʾ

12 [and] Raydân to fight and to protect the tribes and groups of Ḫawlân Gaddum; and [they have] prais[ed]

13 the strength and the power of their lord ʾIlumquh Ṯahwân, master of ʾAwwâm, because have

14 joi[n]ed and settled down all the tribes and groups of Ḫawlân Gaddum, and they brought back all

15 their freemen [as] firm pledges and their fullers and all [those] whom has ordered them their lord

16 Našaʾkarib Yuʾmin Yuharḥib, king of Sabaʾ and Raydân, in the city [of]

17 Ṣanʿâʾ; and in this protection they have sent their incomes in order that Saharatân would become

18 friendly to them; and their incomes satisfied them in the city [of] Raḥbamum of

19 the land of Ḫawlân; so now the tribes of Dawʾat have made it pleasant to them; however in this very

20 day, in which their incomes satisfied them, they deserted their troop and

21 cut their profit; but have joined their troop twenty-six horsemen and three

22 hundred soldiers from their tribe Yarsum and from the subordinates of the king

23 and some of Ḫawlân; and they made a raid and an incursion in the morning and fought, among the groups of Dawʾat:

24 the groups of ʾAbʾas and ʾAydaʿân and Ḥakamum and Ḥadlanat and Ġumdum and Ka-

25 hilum and ʾAhlânî and Gadlat and Sâbisum and Ḥarmum and Ḥagar Lamad and

26 ʾAwmum and Raḏḥatân from Ḥârat, and they have fought them in the lower country of the wâdîs

27 of Biʾrân and Ḫulab and Tadḥân; and they have praised the strength and power of their lord

28 ʾIlumquh Ṯahwân, master of ʾAwwâm, because He has vouchsafed to them to come back, themselves and

29 their cavalry and their troop in safety and (with) praise and exaltation and animals

30 and prisoners and war trophies and captives and riches and booty plentiful

31 which pleased their lord and which pleased them; and that may continue ʾIlumquh Ṯahwân,

32 master of ʾAwwâm, to bestow and shower upon His worshippers, the descendants of Suḫaymum, all

33 the favors and announcements and counsel [for which] they shall continue to beseech and beg and

34 implore from Him; and that may make them happy their lord ʾIlumquh Ṯahwân, mas-

35 ter of ʾAwwâm, with the esteem and grace of their lord Našaʾkarib Yuʾmin Yuharḥib,

36 king of Sabaʾ and Raydân, son of ʾIlšaraḥ Yaḥḏub and of Yaʾzil Bayyin, the two

37 kings of Sabaʾ and Raydân, and [also] with the strength of understanding and of power and [with] the magnificence of

38 fruits; and that ʾIlumquh Ṯahwân, master of ʾAwwâm, may preserve them from misfortunes

39 and sufferings and from the hostility and wickedness and fear and constraint of [any] enemy, who is remote

40 and near, those who are known and those who are not known. By ʾIlumquh Ṯahwân, master of ʾAwwâm.

Preliminary note. The present text has the same authors as Ja 718 as well as NaNAG 8 the beginning of which must thus be read as follows:

1 **[Sym-** *whbʾwm/yʾḏf/wʾẖyhw/yd*
2 **bol** *⌜m/ydrm/⌝wbnyhw/ḥmʿṯt/ʾ*

NaNAG's transliteration and translation (II, pp. 33-34) do not mention the symbol. In the same transliteration, line 5: *ḏsmʿy* instead of *dsmʿy*; line 8: *ḥmdm* instead of *ẖmdm*; lines 15-16: *wydm* instead of *w..m*; line 16: *ḥmʿṯt* instead of *ḥmʾṯt*; line 19: *ḥẓy* instead of *hẓy*; line 23: *frʿm* instead of *frʾm*; line 27; omit brackets.

Ll. 1-3, cf. CIH 24/1-4+*MoMiSI*, p. 22, note 1, which is needed for completing the family of Wahabʾawwâm; CIH 24 mentions four of his sons of whom the last two and another one are listed in the present inscription; CIH 24, being written by Wahabʾawwâm's oldest son, is posterior to the present text, which is related to the father himself.

L. 1: *ydm*, also, e.g., in RÉS 4909/1, Ḥaḍr; in RÉS 4646/5, read *ydm* instead of *yddm* or *ydmm*.

L. 2: *yzʾn*, also 2nd personal name, e.g., in Ja 495/2 and Ist 7628/1; tribe name, e.g., in RÉS 5085/4; *yzʾn* is also very well known as imperfect of the verb *wzʾ* (e.g., Ja 561 bis/16-17).

L. 3: *rymn*, also name of a house in RÉS 4919+CIH 537/4 and 4979/2; cp. *ḏrymn* in RÉS 4627/4; *rym* is 2nd personal name, e.g., in Ja 404/1, Min, and *rymt* (e.g., Hamilton 12 c, Ḥaḍr, cf. *JaRIH*, p. 155, and Ja 405, Qat). – *yrsm*, e.g., RÉS 4646/7 and 4649/4.

L. 4: *hgrm*, very well known name of a tribe; cf. also the name of a Qat woman *hgrlt* on the necklace (cf. *PhQS*, p. 111).

L. 9: *ṣtry*, 8th form of *ṣry*.

L. 12: *ʿšr*, plural of *ʿšrt* (e.g., line 24), cf. Arabic *ʿašîrat*, plural *ʿašâʾiru* "family, group (subdivision of a tribe)".

Ll. 13-14: *tʾ[.]mw*, cf. *tʾtm* in line 21 and *tʾtmw* in Ja 578/19.

L. 14: *qtḏn*, 8th form of *qḏn*, which I propose to relate to Arabic *qaṭana* "to reside"; the 8th form may be translated as "to settle".

L. 15: *ẖbṭ*, for the etymology, cf. *StSESA*, p. 516; cf. Arabic and Daṯînah (cf. *LaGD*, pp. 559-60) *ẖabaṭa* "to strike, trample under foot" and Hebrew *ḥâbaṭ* "to beat off (fruit), beat out (corn)" and post-biblical Hebrew "to press down...to force, knock open" (cf. *JaDT*, p. 417 A); *bn/ẖbṭn/[ḏ]ẖbṭ* (CIH 575/6-7) means "from the blow which he struck"; in CIH 562/6 as well as in RÉS 3012/15, the meaning is "pastures"; *ẖbṭ* here may be an active participle with a collective meaning.

L. 17: *bmw*, e.g., CIH 350/11 and also, e.g., Ja 618/10; for *mw*, the indefinite pronoun *m* augmented by *w*, the sign of a diphthong and which indicates the strengthening of an idea, cf. *HöASG*, pp. 56-58, §48-49. – *bhʾt*, plural of *bhʾ*; RÉS 2774/4, Min; for the verb *bhʾ* in the same line, cf. Arabic *bahaʾa* "to be, *or* become friendly with someone" (cf. *LaAEL*, p. 263 B); cf. also the use of "to enter, come in" (CIH 548/2, Ja 644/6; and the Western Semitic cognates in *JeHoDISO*, p. 32: *bwʾ*) with sexual implication (CIH 523/4, 4-5) and "to confirm" (RÉS 3951/1).

L. 18: *rḥbmm*, name of a city; cf., e.g., the names of a person *rḥbt* (RÉS 3921) and of a territory *rḥbtn* (RÉS 3951/2); cf. also the Arabic names of men *rḥyb* (cf. *WüR*, p. 429), *ruḥb*, *ar-rḥbt* (cf. *LöHSM*, p. 69 A) *ʾrḥb* (cf. *GoAT*, p. 23), *ar-raḥbat* (cf. *MüHG*, p. 144 B), and of places *ar-rḥbt* (cf. *LöHSM*, p. 85 A), *ruḥâb*, *ar-ruḥâbât*, *(ar-)ruḥâbat*, *raḥb*, *raḥab*, *ruḥbân*, *(ar-)raḥbat* (cf. *MüHG*, pp. 50 B-51 A), *ruḥb*, *raḥbat*, *ruḥbat* (cf. *WüR*, p. 99 C), *ar-raḥûb*, *ar-raḥîb*, and *ar-ruḥayyib* (cf. *l.c.*, p. 100 A); cf. also the names of men in Thamudic *rḥbm* (cf. *vdBrTTPS*, p. 110: Ph 170 g 9) and *bnrḥb* (cf. *vdBrTTPN*, p. 141: Ph 370 m 2) and the Safaitic place name *rḥbt* (cf. *LiSI*, p. 343 A).

L. 19: *hṭb*, 4th form of *ṭwb*; cf. Arabic *ṭâba* (i), 4th form "to render it pleasant, delightful". – *dwʾt* (also in line 23), *shrtn* (line 18) and *ḥrt* (line 26) are also mentioned all together in CIH 407/18-19.

L. 20: *nzʿ*, cf. commentary on Ja 577/8.

Ll. 20-21: *hbry* and *hbrw* (Ja 631/4), 4th form of *brw*; cf. Arabic *barā* (o, i), Daṯînah *bry* (cf. *LaGD*, p. 166) and post-biblical Hebrew *bry* II, *bârâh* (cf. *JaDT*, p. 192 B) "to cut".

L. 21: *ʿwf*, cf. *ʿwfy* in CIH 575/11; cf. Arabic *ʿuwâf* "prey, profit".

L. 22: *nẓr*, cf. *CoRoC*, p. 186 B: official, subordinate. – *ṣbḥ*, also verb in RÉS 4337 C/10, Qat "to come (morning)"; here, "to make a hostile, *or* predatory incursion in the morning" (cf. *LaAEL*, p. 1640 C: 1st form of Arabic *ṣabaḥa*).

L. 24: *ʾbʾs*, Thamudic name; cf. *HaLiSTI*, p. 10, No. 12, with the following commentary: "ʾAbʾas is known from Safaitic sources." However, Saf CIS 5172 reads either *ʾrʾs* (E. Littmann) or *ʾbʾs* (G. Ryckmans). Besides, *RyNP* (I, p. 217 A) interprets *ʾbʾs* as composed of *ʾbʾ* + *s*, the latter being considered as the *scriptio defectiva* of *ʾws*. But, *ʾs* is known as *scriptio defectiva* of *ʾws*, *ʾys*, and *ʾns*; thus it should be preferable to avoid the difficulty in the choice of one of the three possibilities, to refer *ʾs* to *ʾss* (cf. Arabic *ʾassa* "to found, mark the limits of"). I prefer to adopt H. Grimme's opinion according to which *ʾbʾs* is related to the root *bʾs*. — *ʾydʿn*, cf. the Arabic place name *al-ʾaydâʿ* (cf. *MüHG*, p. 10 A). – *ḥkmm*, cf. the personal name *ḥkm* (cf. *RyGSAS*, p. 559), and, e.g., the Arabic names of men *ḥakam*, *al-ḥakamîyûn* (cf. *MüHG*, p. 140 A), *al-ḥâkim* (cf. *WüR*, p. 373), *ḥakîm* (cf. *GeKH*, p. 4 A), *al-ḥakm* (cf., e.g., *SaIS*, p. 59), *ḥkmt*, *al-ḥkymy* (cf. *GoAT*, p. 147), of women *ʾumm al-ḥkm* (cf., e.g., *SaIS*, pp. 59 B-60 A), *ʾumm ḥakîm* (cf. *GoAT*, p. 146), *ḥâkmah* (cf. *HeBN*, p. 19 A), *Ḥikmat* (cf. *LiEHA*, p. 84 A), of places *ḥakam* (cf., e.g., *MüHG*, p. 35 B), *ḥakamân* (cf. *WüR*, p. 73 A), and of a clan *ḥkm* and *ḥakkâm* (cf. *l.c.*, p. 243 B). – *ḥdlnt*, the root *ḥdl* is also attested in the masculine personal name *ʾ(ḥd)l* in RÉS 4866/1, Ḥaḍr; this text may be read as follows:

ʾ(ḥd)l[/]ḏ(y)bn	1	ʾA(ḥda)l Ḏîbân,
[b]n/ḥggt	2	[so]n of Ḥaggat.

Cf. the Arabic names of a man *ḥadâl* (cf. *GoAT*, p. 125), of clans *banû ḥadîlat* (cf. *l.c.*, p. 126), *ḥudaylat* (cf. *WüR*, p. 243 A), and of places *ḥadaylat* and *ḥadaylâʾu* (cf. *l.c.*, p. 67 C); cf. also the Thamudic names of men *ḥdl* (cf., e.g., *HaLiSTI*, p. 47, No. 506) and *ḥdlt* (cf. *vdBrTTPS*, p. 91: Ph 167 q 3). – *ġmdm*, cf. the Arabic names of men *ḏû-ġumdân* (cf. *LöHSM*, p. 66 B), *ġâmid* (cf., e.g., *GoAT*, p. 437), *al-ġâmadîy* (cf. *WüR*, p. 598), and of a place *ġumdân* (cf., e.g.,

MüHG, p. 85 B); cf. also the Safaitic name of a man *ġmd* (cf. *LiSI*, p. 337 B).

Ll. 24-25: *khlm*, also in Ja 634/5; well known proper name, e.g., in RÉS 3943/6 (a tank) and 3902, No. 112 (Qat person); cf. also the monogram on the Qat jar published by G. W. Van Beek (cf. *BASOR*, No. 143, October, 1956, pp. 8-9 and *JaJEQH*, p. 134, note 2.

L. 25: *ʾhlny*, *nisba* formation as, e.g., in *ḏmry* (e.g., Ja 568/3); cf., e.g., *ʾhln* designating the lunar god in the compound name of a house (RÉS 4094/2), Qat; cf. *JaPSAP*, pp. 30 and 170-71); cf. *JaP*, pp. 111-12 and *JaRSAP*, p. 268). – *gdlt*, personal name in *RyGSAS*, p. 559; cf. also the place name *gdlm* in Ja 550/1 (cf. commentary). – *sbsm*, cf. the Arabic place name *sâbus* (cf. *WüR*, p. 112 B). – *ḥrmm*, also clan name in Weigall 1 (cf. *Le Muséon*, 62 [1949], pp. 56-57); this graffito may be read as follows: *flkʾnm/ḏḥrmm/ḥ[š]˻d˼y[n]* "Falakʾanam, he of [the clan] Ḥarmum, [the] Ḥâ[ši]dite"; for *ḥ[š]dy[n]*, cf. the plural *ʾḥšdn* in Ja 704/1-2; Weigall 1 could thus be considered as Sab. *ḥrmm* is also personal name, e.g., in RÉS 3902, No. 165/1, Qat; cf. also *ḥrm*, e.g., in RÉS 3091 and *tḥrmn* on Ja 797 B/1-2. – *ḥgr/lmd*. For *ḥgr*, cf. the name of the stellar god *ḥgrm* (cf. Ja 564/30 and commentary); cf. also *ḥgrw* in Ja 550/1, and the masculine personal name *ḥgr* in RÉS 4829/1 (cf. commentary on Ja 601/17-18) and Ja 520/2; the root *ḥgr* is very frequently used in Arabic onomastics; cf. also the Thamudic names of a man *ḥgr* (cf. *vdBrIT*, e.g., pp. 439-40: Jsa 609) and *ḥgrt* (cf. *HaLiSTI*, p. 52 B). For *lmd*, cf. the name of a city in CIH 541/35; in RÉS 4594 A/1 and 4623 A/2 (cf. *JaPEHA*, pp. 23-24, note 14), *gmd* and *gmdm* are as probable as *lmd* and *lmdm* since the letter characterized as *g* is interpreted as *l* in four graffiti belonging to the same collection, RÉS 4583/1, 4612 (twice), 4614 and 4616; note that *ḏ(g)mdm* in RÉS 4623 A is preceded by *ḏgḏm* "he of Guḏum" (instead of *bgbm*); for *gmd*, cf. *gmdn* (e.g., Ja 574/7; cf. also the Arabic names of men *ǧamd* (cf., e.g., *SaIS*, p. 41 B), *ǧamâd* (cf. *LöHSM*, p. 59 B), and of places *ʾaǧmâd* (cf. *MüHG*, p. 3 A), *al-ǧamad* (cf. *WüR*, p. 60 C), *al-ǧumud* and *ǧumdân* (cf. *l.c.*, p. 61 A); cf. also the Safaitic name of a man *gmd* (cf. *LiSI*, p. 305 A).

L. 26: *ʾwmm*, cp. *ʾwm*. – *rḏḥtn*, cf. the Thamudic name of a man *rḏḥn* (cf. *vdBrIT*, p. 364: HU 545, where it is interpreted as composed of *rḏw* and *ḥnn*). – *ḥrt*, also CIH 407/19. – *ʾwdyt*, pl. of *wdy* (e.g., CIH 540/9; possibly also RÉS 4779/3-4); cf. Arabic *wâdin*, pl. *ʾawdiyat* and *ʾawdâyat*.

L. 27: *bʾrn*, cf. the name of a man *bʾr* in RÉS 3699/2, Min (also in Thamudic; cf. *vdBrTTPN*, p. 56: Ph 279 bh), and the Arabic place name *bârân* (cf. *WüR*, p. 25 C). – *ẖlb*, *ẖlbn*, family name in Van Lessen 10/2 (*GhNQI*, p. 423 considers it as a personal name); cf. also the Arabic place names *ẖulab*, *ẖilab*, *ẖullab* (cf. *MüHG*, p. 40 B), *ẖilibtā*, and *ẖillîb* (cf. *WüR*, p. 82 B and C); cf. also the names of men *ẖlb* in Safaitic (cf. *LiSI*, p. 317 B) and *ẖlbn* in Thamudic (cf. *vdBrIT*, e.g., pp. 390-91: Jsa 79). – *tdḥn*, cf. the Arabic names of men *duḥayyân* (cf. *HeBN*, p. 22 A) and *diḥyat* (cf. *SaIS*, p. 72 B); cf. also the name of a man *dḥ* in both Thamudic (cf. *vdBrIT*, e.g., p. 156: HU 325: related to the root *dḥḥ*) and in Safaitic (cf. *LiSI*, p. 307 A); cf. also the Thamudic clan name *dḥt* (cf. *HaLiSTI*, p. 38, No. 392).

L. 29: *yhr*, cf. commentary on Ja 564/7.

L. 30: *šfq*, e.g., NaNN 75/12 and *CoRoC*, p. 251.

617 – Yellowish, slightly greyish sandstone; broken on top; photograph in Plate 12. – MaMB 237.

STONE: thickness: 36 cm. (top) and 27 (bottom); height: 58.3 cm. – *Top:* a very small part still remains; this excludes the possibility of restoring another line of text and consequently a symbol. – *Front:* 42 cm. (top) and 41.8 (bottom) × 45 (left), 53 (center), and 48 (right). – INSCRIPTION: the line 1 is missing; same disposition of lines as in Ja 561 bis; letter height: from 2.5 cm. to 2.7; space between the lines: from 0.4 cm. to 0.5.

1 *[ʾsʿd/. . . ./wʾẖyhw/smhyfʿ/bnw/ḏḥbb/wsʾryn/ mqtwy]*
2 *[y]˹/nšʾk˺rb/yʾmn/yhrḥb/m˹lk˺[/sbʾ/wḏrydn/bn/ʾ]*
3 *lšrḥ/yḥḍb/wyʾzl/byn/mlky/˹sbʾ˺[/wḏrydn/hqnyw]*
4 *ʾlmqhṯhwnbʿlʾwm/ṣlmn/ḏḏhbn/ḏʿš˹rh˺w/bn/sqy*
5 *wdʿt/ẖmrhmw/ʾlmqh/bn/mšymthmw/wʿbrthmw/bn*
6 *ẖlf/mšr/whynn/wʾṯʾbtm/wlwzʾ/ʾlmqhṯhwnbʿlʾwm*
7 *ẖmr/ʾdmhw/ʾsʿd/wʾẖyhw/smhyfʿ/bnw/ḏḥbb/ws*
8 *ʾryn/ẖrf/wdṯʾ/wsʿsʿm/wmlym/ʿdy/kl/ʾrḍthmw/wʾ*
9 *srrhmw/wmšy⟨m⟩thmw/wmfnthmw/wnʾd/qyẓ/ wṣrb/wlẖmrhm*
10 *w/ʾlmqhṯhwnbʿlʾwm/ʾdmhw/ʾsʿd/wsmhyfʿ/bnw/ ḏḥbb*
11 *wsʾryn/ḥẓy/wrḍw/mrʾhmw/nšʾkrb/yʾmn/yhrḥb/ mlk/s*
12 *bʾ/wḏrydn/bn/ʾlšrḥ/yḥḍb/wyʾzl/byn/mlky/sbʾ/wḏry*

13 *dn/wlẖryn/ᵓlmqh/ᶜbdyhw/ᵓsᶜd/wᵓẖyhw/smhyfᶜ/ bny/ḏ*
14 *ḥbb/wsᵓryn/bn/bᵓstm/wnkytm/wnḍᶜ/wšṣy/wtṯᶜt/šn*
15 *ᵓm/ḏbnhw/dᶜw/wḏbnhw/ᵓl/dᶜw/bᵓlmqhṯhwnbᶜlᵓwm*

1 [ᵓAsᶜad...and his brother Sumhuyafaᶜ, descendants of (the clans) Ḥabab and Saᵓriyân, high offi-]
2 [cials of] Našaᵓkarib Yuᵓmin Yuharḥib, king [of Sabaᵓ and Raydân, son of]
3 [ᵓI]lšaraḥ Yaḥḍub and Yaᵓzil Bayyin, the two kings of Sabaᵓ [and Raydân, have dedicated to]
4 ᵓIlumquh Ṯahwân, master of ᵓAwwâm, this statue which [is] in bronze, which he had assessed as tithe to Him from [the product of] *saqay-*
5 and *daᶜat*-palms [that] ᵓIlumquh vouchsafed to them from their arable fields and their river-side fields in
6 the region of Mašâr and Haynân and ᵓAṯᵓabtum; and that ᵓIlumquh Ṯahwân, master of ᵓAwwâm, may continue
7 to vouchsafe to His worshippers ᵓAsᶜad and his brother Sumhuyafaᶜ, descendants of Ḥabab and Sa-
8 ᵓriyân, the fruits of autumn and of spring and of summer and of winter in all their grounds and
9 their wâdî-side valleys and their arable fields and their lands irrigated by canals and the magnificence of the fruits of summer and of autumn; and that may vouchsafe to them
10 ᵓIlumquh Ṯahwân, master of ᵓAwwâm, to His worshippers ᵓAsᶜad and Sumhuyafaᶜ, descendants of Ḥabab
11 and Saᵓriyân, the esteem and grace of their lord Našaᵓkarib Yuᵓmin Yuharḥib, king of Sa-
12 baᵓ and Raydân, son of ᵓIlšaraḥ Yaḥḍub and Yaᵓzil Bayyin, the two kings of Sabaᵓ and Ray-
13 dân; and that ᵓIlumquh may preserve His two worshippers ᵓAsᶜad and his brother Sumhuyafaᶜ, descendants of
14 Ḥabab and Saᵓriyân, from misfortunes and sufferings and [from] the hostility and wickedness and fear of [any] ene-
15 my, those who are known and those who are not known. By ᵓIlumquh Ṯahwân, master of ᵓAwwâm.

L. 1: *ḥbb*, cf. commentary on *ḥbbt* in Ja 509 (cf. *JaISAR*, pp. 106-07); cf. also the masculine personal names *ḥbm* (e.g., RÉS 4580/1) and *ḥbybm* (diminutive form): Ja 715/8, cf. commentary on line 7.

L. 6: *mšr*, CIH 376/9. – *hynn* cannot be identified with Ḥaḍr *haynan*, wâdî and city (cf. *MüHG*, 85/19, 86/20, and 88/10, *FoSA*, p. 129, note 8 and *WiHöBGS*, especially p. 124); cf. also the Arabic clan name *banû hînat* (cf. *WüID*, 278/11). – *ᵓṯᵓbtm*, cp. *ᵓṯᵓbn*, name of an estate in RÉS 3946/6, and of a palm grove in RÉS 4085/3.

L. 7: *bnw/ḏḥbb* (also in line 10) equals *bny/ḏḥbb* in lines 13-14.

Ll. 7-8: *sᵓryn*, cp. *sᵓrn*, e.g., in CIH 282/1 and commentary on Ja 578/1.

L. 8: *ẖrf/– –/wmlym*: each term of this series indicates not the season itself, but the crops and fruits gathered during these periods of the year.

L. 9: *mšythmw* (on the stone) instead of *mšymthmw*. – *qyẓ/wṣrb* equals *qṣ/wṣrb* in Ja 594/10 (cf. commentary; cf. also *RoVSAY*, p. 311 for *qyẓ*); *qyẓ* is a noun in CIH 323/9, contrary to *CIH* (I, p. 359), who interprets it as proper name and translates it by adding *ḏ* before the noun: *ḏqyẓ*; this opinion which is accepted by *RyISA* (X, p. 301), must be discarded.

618 – Stone re-used in the western pavement; cf. Chapter I, B. – MaMB 259.

Front: left edge and upper left corner badly damaged; 85 cm. × 24.2. – INSCRIPTION, same disposition of lines as in Ja 561 bis; letter height: 1.7 cm.; space between the lines: 0.3 cm.; length of line 36: 8.1 cm. – SYMBOL, cf. Ja 559. – FLOWER: on both ends of line 36; cf. Ja 597, but each flower is framed in a square; cf. also the flower at the end of AshM 1957-16/9 (*BeTMS* does not mention it), where the frame is circular, instead of square; cf. Plate B.

1 **Sym-** *rṯdᵓlw/ᵓzk[n/wb]ny[hw/ḥy]*
2 **bol** *wm/bny/kb[sym/ᵓ]qw[l/šᶜbn]*
3 *tnᶜmm/wtnᶜmtm/hqnyw/ᵓl[m]q⌜h⌝[ṯ]*
4 *hwnbᶜlᵓwm/ṣlmn/ḏḏhb[n/]⌞ḥmd*
5 *m/bḏt/hwfyhmw/ᵓlmqh/b[tbš]rt*
6 *tbšrw/bᶜmhw/kymlᵓn/mnẖthmw*
7 *ḏyfd/bṯny/brqn/[w]ẖmrhmw/ᵓlmq*
8 *h/bᶜl/ᵓwm/ml⌜ᵓ⌝[/mᵓ]d⌜b⌝hmw/ḏyfd*
9 *bsqy/dṯᵓ/wẖrf/ḏẖrf/wddᵓl/b*
10 *n/ᵓbkrb/bn/kbrẖll/rbᶜn/wbmw*
11 *ḏn/ẖrfn/fhfsḥ/bṣlyn/mṣ[ly]*
12 *nn/wlwzᵓ/ᵓlmqh/ṣdq/whwf[y/ᶜ]*
13 *bdyhw/rṯdᵓlw/wḥywm/bny/kb[sy]*
14 *m/bkl/ᵓmlᵓ/ystmlᵓn/bᶜmhw/[wl]*
15 *sᶜdhmw/ᵓlmqh/frᶜ/dṯᵓ/[wẖ]rf/[ww]*
16 *fy/mᵓẖḏhmw/ḏyfd/wmḏhbthw/w[by]*
17 *thw/wmᵓẖḏthw/wmfsḥthw/wls[ᶜdh]*
18 *mw/ᵓlmqh/wfy/kl/ᵓġyl/yfᶜw/[wy]*
19 *tġln/bᵓrḍ/tnᶜmm/ᵓġyl/kwnw/[kw]*
20 *n/rṯdᵓlw/wḥywm/bny/kbsym/[wl]*

21 *ẖmrhmw/ʾlmqh/ʾdmhw/bny/k[bsy]*
22 *m/wšʿbhmw/tnʿmm/wtnʿmtm/[ʾṯ]*
23 *mrm/wʾfqlm/hnʾm/bkl/ʾrḍhmw/*
24 *wmšymthmw/wʾsrrhmw/wlẖmrhm[w]*
25 *ʾlmqh/ʿbdyhw/rṯdʾlw/wḥywm/bn*
26 *y/kbsym/ḥẓy/wrḍw/mrʾhmw/n[šʾk]*
27 *rb/yʾmn/yhrḥb/mlk/sbʾ/wḏry[d]*
28 *n/bn/ʾlšrḥ/yḥḍb/wyʾ[z]l/byn/ml*
29 *ky/sbʾ/wḏrydn/wlsʿdhmw/ʾlmqh*
30 *nʿmt/wwfym/wḥẓym/wlhʿnnhmw/ʾ*
31 *lmqh/bn/bʾstm/wnkytm/wnḍʿ/wš*
32 *ṣy/šnʾm/bʿṯtr/wʾlmqh/bʿlʾwm*
33 *wbšymhmw/ʾlmqh/bʿl/šwḥṭ/wbḏ*
34 *t/ḥmym/wbḏt/bʿdnm/wbšmsyhmw*
35 *bʿlty/qyf/ršm/wbrbʿhmw/ḏt/ḥm*
36 **Flower** *ym/ʿṯtrygr* **Flower**

1 **Sym-** Raṯadʾilû ʾAzk[ân, and his s]on [Ḥay-]
2 **bol** ûm, descendants of [the clan] Kab[sayum,] rul[ers of the two tribes]
3 Tanaʿamum and Tanaʿamatum, have dedicated to ʾIl[um]quh [Ṯa-]
4 hwân, master of ʾAwwâm, this statue which [is] in bronze, in praise
5 because ʾIlumquh has showered upon them the [announce]ment [which]
6 they begged of Him so they might complete their caravan station
7 of Yafid in two lightning seasons, [and because] has vouchsafed to them ʾIlumquh,
8 master of ʾAwwâm, to complete their [beautiful w]ork of Yafid
9 during the irrigation of spring and of autumn of the year of Waddʾil, son
10 of ʾAbkarib, descendant of [the clan] the Leader of Ḫalil, the fourth; and so during this
11 very year, he built an annex in Ṣulaiyân and Maṣ[lî-]
12 nân; and that ʾIlumquh may continue to bestow and to show[er upon]
13 His two [wor]shippers Raṯadʾilû and Ḥayûm, descendants of Kab[say-]
14 um, all the favors [for which] he shall beseech Him; [and that]
15 ʾIlumquh may make them happy with optimum crop of spring [and of au]tumn [and (with) the sa-]
16 fety of their breakwater of Yafid and of its passages and (the safety of) his
17 [hou]se and of its breakwaters and of its annexes; and that may ma[ke th]em happy
18 ʾIlumquh with the safety of all the stream beds [which] have been raised up [and shall]
19 become abundant in the land of Tanaʿamum, stream beds [which] belong
20 to Raṯadʾilû and Ḥayûm, descendants of Kabsayum; [and that]
21 ʾIlumquh may vouchsafe to them, His worshippers, the descendants of Ka[bsay]um
22 and to their two tribes Tanaʿamum and Tanaʿamatum [fr]uits
23 and harvests pleasing from their every land
24 and all their arable fields and their valleys; and that may vouchsafe
25 ʾIlumquh, to the[m,] His two worshippers Raṯadʾilû and Ḥayûm, descen-
26 dants of Kabsayum, the esteem and grace of their lord Na[šaʾka-]
27 rib Yuʾmin Yuharḥib, king of Sabaʾ and Ray[d]ân,
28 son of ʾIlšaraḥ Yaḥḍub and Yaʾ[z]il Bayyin, the two
29 kings of Sabaʾ and Raydân; and that ʾIlumquh may make them happy
30 with prosperity and safety and esteem; and that may protect them ʾI-
31 lumquh from misfortunes and sufferings and (from) the hostility and wick-
32 edness of [any] enemy. By ʿAṯtar and ʾIlumquh, master of ʾAwwâm,
33 and by their patron ʾIlumquh, master of Šawḥaṭ and by Ḏât-
34 Ḥimyâm and by Ḏât-Baʿdânum and by their two Šams,
35 the two mistresses of the monument of [the tribe] Rašam and by their Rubʿ Ḏât-Ḥim-
36 **Flower** yâm ʿAṯtar Yagur. **Flower**

L. 1: *rṯdʾlw/ʾzkn*, RÉS 3929/1.

L. 2: *kbsym*, clan name, RÉS 4779/1; cp. also *kbsyn* in Ja 712/4; in RÉS 4589 D, read *ḏg/mqs* [*rn*] "Ḏâgg Maqsa[rân]" instead of *kb*(*s*).

L. 3: *tnʿmm*, e.g., Ja 233, Qat. – *tnʿmtm*, cp. *tnʿmt* in RÉS 2728 and also Ja 627/1-2.

L. 6: *mnẖt*, cf. Arabic *munâẖ* (from the root *nwẖ*) "relay, station for caravan"; the noun *nẖt* in Ugaritic means "couch" (cf. *GoUM*, p. 295 B, No. 1236).

L. 7: *ḏ yfd*, cp. the proper name *yfd*, e.g., in CIH 53 and Ja 746/5.

L. 8: *ml*(ʾ): the lower half of the third letter is still on the stone; space for three letters follows; and the letter *d* is followed by two vertical strokes which belong to the lower half of a letter; I propose to restore *mʾdb*, which is related to *ʾdb* in Ja 540 A/2 and 3, and not to *mʾdb* (Ja 491/1) "courtier" (cf. *JaIMS*, pp. 324 and 326); the latter translation may also be applied through a synonym in RÉS 4194/5.

L. 9: *sqy*, e.g., RÉS 4781/1.

L. 11: *hfsḥ*, 4th form of *fsḥ*; cf. Arabic *fasaḥa* "to

enlarge" and *fasuḥa* "to be large, spacious"; the noun *mfsḥ* (line 17) is derived from the same root, and may be translated "annex"; compare the Ugaritic proper name *psḥn* (cf. *GoUM*, p. 313 A, No. 1558).

Ll. 11-12: *ṣlyn/wmṣ[ly]nn*, cp. the Arabic place names *aṣ-ṣullayyu* and *al-muṣallā* (cf. *WüR*, pp. 138 A and 205 B respectively); cp. the adjective *ṣly* in Ja 730/4.

L. 15: *frʿ/dṯʾ/wẖrf*, e.g., CIH 2/13.

L. 16: *mʾẖḏ*, pl. *mʾẖḏt*, e.g., RÉS 4775/2. – *mḏhb*, pl. *mḏhbt*, cf. Arabic *maḏhab* "way, passage".

Ll. 16-17: two letters are missing at the end of line 16; one could restore [*by*]*t*.

L. 17: *mfsḥ*, cf. *hfsḥ* in line 11.

Ll. 18-19: *ytġln*, 5th form of *ġyl*; cf. Arabic *ġâla*, 5th form "to become many, abundant"; the root *ġll* (RÉS 4176/5) does not fit the context.

L. 19: *tnʿmm*, personal name in Ja 485/1, Qat (cf. *JaAFEQ*, p. 191).

L. 33: *šwḥṭ*, also in Ja 627/28-29 and 628/28, name of a temple; unit of measure in CIH 570/2 and Ja 539/1-2; in Arabic *šawḥaṭ* means "a kind of tree from which bows are made, when it grows at the foot of a mountain".

L. 35: *qyf*, e.g., CIH 367/1 (cf. *JaPSAP*, pp. 20, 30, 39, 79-81, 126, 132-35, and 143) and RÉS 3958/11; cf. *JaIAM*, p. 268; the *scriptio defectiva qf* is attested, e.g., in Ja 541/7. The translation of *qyf*, *mqf* as "altar" (cf., e.g., *RyHE*, p. 229) is incorrect; the monument, e.g., of Ja 538 is not an altar. – *ršm*, tribe name in Qatabân (e.g., RÉS 3566/23) and also in Ḥaḍramawt (RÉS 3663/1).

Ll. 35-36: *brbʿhmw/ḏt/ḥmym/ʿṯtrygr*, expression mentioning the three principal South-Arabian deities, cf. *JaAGM*, p. 301; *ḏt/ḥmym/ʿṯtr*, also in Qat Jones 2/2 (cf. *Glasgow University Oriental Society Transactions*, 14 [1953], p. 14, fig. 4) and Ja 122/2 (cf. *JaIRHY*, pp. 191 B – 192 B, 190 and 193 B); cf. also commentary on Ja 550/2.

619 – Yellowish, slightly grayish sandstone; photograph in Plate 12. – MaMB 178.

STONE: thickness: 19.3 cm. (top) and 19.7 (bottom). – *Front:* upper edge badly damaged, and lower left corner slightly damaged; covered with red paint; 27 cm. × 54. – INSCRIPTION: same disposition of lines as in Ja 552; letter height: from 3.4 cm. (line 1) to 2.4 (line 21); space between the lines: from 0.4 cm. to 0.3. – SYMBOL, same general type as that of Ja 587, but three small lines instead of the long inside line; cf. Plate A.

1 **Sym-** *r⌜bbʾ⌝[l]⌜/ʾšwʿ/wbnyhw*
2 **bol** *ddʾl/bnw/ḥlḥlm/ʿ*
3 *qbt/mlkn/bhgrn/nšqm/hqn*
4 *y⟨/⟩ʾlmqhbʿlʾwm/ṣlmnhn/ḏḏh*
5 *bn/ḏšfthw/ḥmdm/bḏt/ẖm*
6 *[r/w]⌞mtʿn/ʾlmqh/ʿbdhw/rbbʾ*
7 *l/bn/dqt/wdq/ʿln/ʾblhw/b*
8 *hʾ/byn/krʿ/ʾblhw/klbym*
9 *bẖlf/hgrn/yṯl/bllyn/wr*
10 *ʾ/yfʿ/lhw/ʾlmqh/khʾ/m*
11 *tʿhw/wlḏt/mtʿhw/wkl/ʾḥ*
12 *ṣnhw/bʾbythw/bn/sdm/wmr*
13 *ḍ/mrḍw/bhgrn/nšqm/wlẖmr*
14 *hmw/ʾlmqh/ḥẓy/wrḍw/mr*
15 *ʾhmw/nš(ʾ)krb/yhʾmn/yhr*
16 *ḥb/mlk/sbʾ/wḏrydn/bn/ʾ*
17 *lšrḥ/yḥḍb/wyʾzl/byn/m*
18 *lky/sbʾ/wḏrydn/wlhʿnn*
19 *hmw/ʾlmqh/bn/nḍʿ/wšṣy*
20 *šnʾm/ḏbnhw/dʿw/wḏʾl/d*
21 *ʿw/bʾlmqh/bʿlʾwm*

1 **Sym-** Rabîbʾi[l] ʾAšwaʿ and his son
2 **bol** Dôdʾil, descendants of (the clan) Ḥalḥalum, re-
3 presentatives of the king in the city [of] Našqum, has dedicated
4 to ʾIlumquh, master of ʾAwwâm, these two statues which [are] in bron-
5 ze, which he promised Him in praise because has vouch-
6 [safed to and] saved ʾIlumquh His worshipper Rabîbʾil
7 from the fall [that] happened to his camel, in which
8 the knee of his camel Kalbayum was dislocated
9 in the region of the city [of] Yaṯil during the night; but now
10 ʾIlumquh has raised him up so that He has
11 saved him; and because He saved him and all his stallions [who were]
12 in his houses from lack of appetite and disea-
13 se [which] they suffered in the city [of] Našqum; and that may vouchsafe
14 to them ʾIlumquh the esteem and grace of their
15 lord Naša(ʾ)karib Yuhaʾmin Yuhar-
16 ḥib, king of Sabaʾ and Raydân, son of ʾI-
17 lšaraḥ Yaḥḍub and Yaʾzil Bayyin, the
18 two kings of Sabaʾ and Raydân; and that may protect

19 them ʾIlumquh from the hostility and wickedness
20 of [any] enemy, those who are known and those who are not
21 known. By ʾIlumquh, master of ʾAwwâm.

L. 1: *rbbʾl*, more often *rbʾl* (e.g., Ja 620/1); cp. the masculine personal names *rbb* (RÉS 3079/3) and *rbbm* (e.g., RÉS 2641, Ḥaḍr).

L. 2: *ḥlḥlm*, clan name, e.g., RÉS 3929/1; cp. the name of the city *ḥlḥln* in RÉS 4700/1-2 (for some remarks on the palaeography of this inscription, cf. *JaPSAP*, p. 130); in CIH 351/1, it is either *ḥlḥl*[*m*] or *ḥlḥl*[*n*], and not *ḥlḥl* (as *RyNP*, I, p. 92 A and *RÉS* in the commentary on RÉS 4700/1).

L. 3-4: there is no word divider between *hqny* and *ʾlmqh*.

L. 7: *dqt* (from the root *wdq*), cf. Ethiopic *dĕqăt* "casus, lapsus, ruina" (cf. *DiLLA*, col. 932); for *wdq*, cf. Ethiopic *wădĕqă* "cadere, labi" (cf. *l.c.*, col. 930). – *ʿln*, cf. *HöASG*, pp. 151-52.

L. 8: *byn*, e.g., *CoRoC*, p. 112 B and Arabic *bâna* (i) "to become separated, severed, disunited" (cf. *LaAEL*, p. 285 C); for the 2nd form, cf. Ja 671/12. – *krʿ*, cp. post-biblical Hebrew *kĕraʿ* "knee, leg" (cf. *JaDT*, p. 673 A); in modern Arabic, *kurâʿ* means either the foot or the thinnest part between the knee and the foot in ovine and bovine animals. – *klby*, cp. the name of a man *klbm*, e.g., Ja 563/2; cf. also the Arabic personal names *(al-)kalbîy*, *al-kalbî*, *al-kilâbî*, *al-kilâbîyân*, *al-kilâbîyat*, *kalbîyat*, and *al-kalbîyûn* (cf. *WüR*, p. 623 and *SaIS*, p. 197 B).

L. 9: *ḫlf*: the meaning "gate" could also be accepted. – *bllyn* (also, e.g., in Ja 631/10) equals *bn/llyn* in Ja 631/24; with the 1st expression, cp. Syriac *blîlô* "by night, at night"; *lly* (also CIH 581/8) corresponds to Syriac *llī*; but *lyl* (Ja 649/33 and RÉS 4337 C/9, Qat) or *ll* in *scriptio defectiva* (CIH 532/7; contrast *BeSI*, p. 50) corresponds, e.g., to Hebrew *layil* (cf. also *CoRoC*, p. 172 B).

L. 10: *khʾ*, e.g., RÉS 4964/12.

Ll. 11-12: *ʾḥṣn*, pl. of *ḥṣn*, cf. Arabic *ḥiṣân*, pl. *ḥuṣun* "stallion".

L. 12: *sdm*, cf. Arabic *sdm* "lack of appetite" (cf. *DoSDA*, I, p. 642 B).

L. 15: *nšnkrb* instead of *nšʾkrb* is certain on the stone.

620 – Yellowish, slightly grayish sandstone; photograph in Plate 12. – MaMB 150.

STONE: constant thickness: 11.5 cm. – *Front:* 29.7 cm. × 18.3 (top) and 18.6 (bottom). – INSCRIPTION: same disposition of lines as in Ja 552; letter height: 1.5 cm; space between the lines: from 0.2 cm. to 0.3; distance from line 1 to the upper edge: 0.5 cm. – SYMBOL: in its center a small ornament having the form of a *š*; in both the upper right and lower left corners of the square in which the symbol is in relief, a flower is roughly designed; cf. Plate A.

1 **Sym-** *rbʾl/wʾẖyhw/yzd/whwf*
2 **bol** *ʾl/wbnyhmw/ʾzʾd/bnw/ḏẖ*
3 *rm/hqnyw/ʾlmqhṯhwnbʿlʾwm*
4 *ṣlmn/ḏḏhbn/ḥmdm/bḏt/hʿn/wm*
5 *tʿn/grb/ʿbdhw/rbʾl/bn/tšynt*
6 *hšyn/bn/ʾʾrẖ/nhk/ʿlyhmw/šnʾ*
7 *n/wlwzʾ/ʾlmqh/hwfyn/wmtʿn/ʾ*
8 *dmhw/rbʾl/wyzd/whwfʾl/wbny*
9 *hmw/ʾzʾd/bn/bʾstm/wnkytm/w*
10 *bn/nḍʿ/wšṣy/šnʾm/wlẖmrhm*
11 *w/ʾlmqh/ʾṯmr/wʾfql/ṣdqm/b*
12 *n/ʾʿnbhmw/wʿbrthmw/wlẖmrhmw*
13 *ʾlmqh/ḥẓy/wrḍw/mrʾhmw/nšʾ*
14 *krb/yhʾmn/yhrḥb/mlk/sbʾ/wḏ*
15 *rydn/bn/ʾlšrḥ/yḥḍb/wyʾzl*

1 **Sym-** Rabbʾil and his two brothers Yazad and Hawf-
2 **bol** ʾil and their son ʾAzʾad, descendants of [the family] Ḏaẖa-
3 rum, have dedicated to ʾIlumquh Ṯahwân, master of ʾAwwâm,
4 this statue which [is] in bronze, in praise because He has assisted and sav-
5 ed the person of His worshipper Rabbʾil from the diseases [which]
6 he suffered from the calamities [which] had inflicted upon them the ene-
7 my; and that ʾIlumquh may continue to protect and to save His
8 worshippers Rabbʾil and Yazad and Hawfʾil and their
9 son ʾAzʾad from misfortunes and sufferings and
10 from the hostility and wickedness of [any] enemy; and that may vouchsafe to them
11 ʾIlumquh perfect fruits and harvests from
12 their vineyards and their river-side fields; and that may vouchsafe to them
13 ʾIlumquh the esteem and grace of their lord Nášaʾ-
14 karib Yuhaʾmin Yuharḥib, king of Sabaʾ and
15 Raydân, son of ʾIlšaraḥ Yaḥḍub and Yaʾzil.

L. 1: *rbʾl*, e.g., RÉS 3975/1; cf. also *rbbʾl*, e.g., in Ja 619/1.

Ll. 1-2: *hwfʾl*, e.g., Ja 865/1, Qat.

L. 2: *ʾẓʾd*, e.g., CIH 743/1; for *ʾẓʾd* in CIH 742/2, cf. commentary on Ja 566/1.

Ll. 2-3: *ḏẖrm*, e.g., RÉS 4084/2 and the commentary on Ja 226/1: Qat personal name *ḏẖrt*.

L. 6: *nhk*, RÉS 4090/2-3: *ynhkn* with the meaning "to fall on with rage"; here, connected with the preposition *bʿly*, *nhk* may be translated "to inflict something upon someone."

L. 12: *ʾʿnb*, e.g., CIH 342/11-12.

Ll. 13-15: there is no explanation of the fact that the title of the king remains incomplete, since two more lines could very easily have been engraved below line 15.

621 – Upper part of an inscription; yellowish sandstone; photograph in Plate 13. – MaMB 171.

STONE: constant thickness: 10.5 cm. – *Front:* covered with red paint; 22.3 cm. (top) and 22 (bottom) × 28.7 (right) and 24.8 (left). – INSCRIPTION, same disposition of lines as in Ja 552; letter height: from 2 cm. to 2.2; space between the lines: from 0.3 cm. to 0.4; distance from line 1 to the upper edge: 0.5 cm. – SYMBOL, cp. Ja 589, but only one inside line instead of two; cf. Plate A.

1 **Sym-** *ytd/ʾbkʾ/wbnyhw/bqlm*
2 **bol** *wʾbkrb/bnw/ʿblm/ʾʾḏ*
3 *nn/hqnyw/ʾlmqhbʿlʾwm/ṯwr*
4 *n/ḏḏhbn/ḥmdm/bḏt/hwfyh*
5 *mw/bklʾml/stmlʾw/wyst*
6 *mlʾnn/b(ʿ)mhw/wlsʿdhmw*
7 *ḥẓy/wrḍw/mrʾhmw/nšʾkr*
8 *b/yʾmn/yhrḥb/mlk/sbʾ/w*
9 *ḏrydn/bn/ʾlšrḥ/yḥḍb/w*
10 *yʾzl/byn/mlky/sb⸤ʾ/⸥w⸤ḏry⸥*
11 *dn/wḥẓ⸤y/ʾmr⸥[ʾhmw/wbry/ʾ]*
12 *(ʾ)⸤ḏnm/⸥[wmqymtm/...*

1 **Sym-** Yatid ʾAbkaʾ and his two sons Baqilum
2 **bol** and ʾAbkarib, descendants of [the tribe] ʿAblum, the ʾAḏa-
3 nites, have dedicated to ʾIlumquh, master of ʾAwwâm, this bull,
4 which [is] in bronze, in praise because He has showered upon
5 them all the favors [for which] they besought and shall
6 beseech Him; and that He may make them happy
7 with the esteem and grace of their lord Našaʾkarib
8 Yuʾmin Yuharḥib, king of Sabaʾ and
9 Raydân, son of ʾIlšaraḥ Yaḥḍub and
10 Yaʾzil Bayyin, the two kings of Sabaʾ and Ray-
11 dân, and (with) the esteem of [their] lo[rd]s [and (with) the strength of]
12 (und)erstanding [and of power,...

L. 1: *ytd*: 2nd personal name in RÉS 5076 A/2 (cf. commentary on Ja 555/2: *hmʿṯt*); also known in Thamudic (cf. *vdBrIT*, pp. 47-48: HU 8); derived from the root *wtd*; compare Arabic *watada* "to sink, drive down"; *RyNP* (I, p. 278 A) mentions this proper name among those whose origin he considers as uncertain or unknown. – *ʾbkʾ*, the tracing of the second letter is rather strange; the curved line on top is certain; *ʾaqtal* form; cp. Arabic *bakuʾa* "to become poor; have little wealth" (cf. *LaAEL*, p. 239 A) and the Arabic names of a man *al-bakkāʾ* and of a clan *banû l-bakkāʾa* (cf. *WüID*, 179/16).

Ll. 2-3: *ʾʾḏnn*, same formation as that, e.g., of *ʾḥmrn* and *ʾḥbšn*.

L. 6: *b(ʿ)mhw*: *w* instead of *ʿ* is certain on the stone.

Ll. 11-12: the reading *ʾḏnm* at the beginning of line 12 is certain on the basis of the remains on the stone; this noun usually in plural form follows *bry*; the proposed restoration at the end of line 11 fits the blank since eleven signs are missing.

622 = MaMB 199 = bottom of Ja 616.

623 – Lower part of an inscription; yellowish, slightly grayish sandstone; photograph in Plate 13. – MaMB 238.

STONE: thickness: 23 cm. (right) and 25 (left). – *Front:* covered with red paint; 23 cm. × 74 (left), 75.8 (center) and 72 (right). – INSCRIPTION, same disposition of lines as in Ja 559, plus a vertical line on each end of the line; letter height: 2.5 cm. and 2.6; space between the lines: 0.4 cm. and 0.5.

a [**Sym-** *ʾbkrb/ʾṣḥḥ/wbnyhw/yḥmd/yzʾn*]
b [**bol** *wʾḥmd/yzd/bnw/grt/wʾnbr/...*]
c [*.../hqnyw/ʾlmqhṯhwnbʿlʾwm/... ...*]
1 [*... ...lẖmr/ʾlm*]
2 [*qhṯhwnbʿlʾwm/ʾbkrb/ʾṣḥḥ/wbnyh*]
3 [*w/yḥmd/yz*]⸢*ʾ*⸣*n/wʾḥmd/yzd/bn/grt*
4 *w*⸢*ʾ*⸣*nbr/mhrgtm/wġnmm/ḏyhrḍwn*
5 *hmw/bʾhnmw/yšwʿnn/mrʾhmw/nšʾk*
6 *rb/yʾmn/yhrḥb/mlk/sbʾ/wḏrydn/w*
7 *bʾhnmw/yqhnhmw/mrʾhmw/nšʾkrb*
8 *yhʾmn/yhrḥb/mlk/sbʾ/wḏrydn*
9 *lsbʾ/wlẖmr/ʾlmqhṯhwnbʿlʾwm*
10 *ʾdmhw/ʾbkrb/ʾṣḥḥ/wbnyhw/yḥ*

11 *md/yzʾn/wʾḥmd/yzd/bny/grt/wʾ*
12 *nbr/ḥẓy/wrḍw/mrʾhmw/nšʾkrb/yh*
13 *ʾmn/yhrḥb/mlk/sbʾ/wḏrydn/wlẖm*
14 *rhmw/ʾlmqhṯhwnbʿlʾwm/frʿ/ʾm*
15 *yrt/dṯʾ/wẖrf/ws〈ʿ〉sʿm/wmlym/ḏyhrḍ*
16 *ynhmw/ʿdy/kl/ʾrḍthmw/wmfnthmw*
17 *wʾsrrhmw/wmqyẓhmw/wʿbrthmw*
18 *wmšymthmw/wlsʿdhmw/ʾlmqhṯ*
19 *hwnbʿlʾwm/nʿmtm/wmngt/ṣdqm*
20 *wbry/ʾʾḏnm/wmqymtm/wlẖrynhm*
21 *w/ʾlmqhṯhwnbʿlʾwm/〈bn/〉bʾstm/wnk*
22 *ytm/wmyqẓm/wʾʾrẖ/swʾm/wnḍʿ/wš*
23 *ṣy/wtṯʿt/šnʾm/ḏrḥq/wqrb/ḏbnh*
24 *w/dʿw/wḏbnhw/ʾldʿw/bʾlmqhṯhwn*
25 *bʿlʾwm*

a [**Sym-** ʾAbkarib ʾAṣḥaḥ and his two sons Yaḥmad Yazʾân]
b [**bol** and ʾAḥmad Yazad, descendants of Garat and ʾAnbar, . . .]
c [. . . . . .have dedicated to ʾIlumquh Ṯahwân, master of ʾAwwâm, ...]
1 [. . . . . .that may vouchsafe ʾIlum-]
2 [quh Ṯahwân, master of ʾAwwâm, to ʾAbkarib ʾAṣḥaḥ and his two sons]
3 [Yaḥmad Yaz]ʾân and ʾAḥmad Yazad, descendants of Garat
4 and ʾAnbar, war trophies and booty, which would please
5 them, wherever they may help their lord Našaʾka-
6 rib Yuhaʾmin Yuharḥib, king of Sabaʾ and Raydân, and
7 in whatever may command them their lord Našaʾ-karib
8 Yuhaʾmin Yuharḥib, king of Sabaʾ and Raydân
9 for Sabaʾ; and that ʾIlumquh Ṯahwân, master of ʾAwwâm, may vouchsafe to
10 His worshippers ʾAbkarib ʾAṣḥaḥ and his two sons Yaḥ-
11 mad Yazʾân and ʾAḥmad Yazad, descendants of Garat and
12 ʾAnbar, the esteem and grace of their lord Našaʾ-karib Yuhaʾ-
13 min Yuharḥib, king of Sabaʾ and Raydân; and that may vouchsa-
14 fe to them ʾIlumquh Ṯahwân, master of ʾAwwâm, the optimum crop of
15 cereals of spring and of autumn and of summer and of winter, which would please
16 them, in all their lands and their lands irrigated by canals
17 and their wâdî-side valleys and their summer settlements and their river-side fields
18 and their arable fields; and that may make them happy ʾIlumquh Ṯa-
19 hwân, master of ʾAwwâm, with perfect prosperity and security
20 and (with) the strength of understanding and of power; and that may preserve them
21 ʾIlumquh Ṯahwân, master of ʾAwwâm, 〈from〉 misfortunes and suffer-
22 ings and sleeplessness and disastrous calamities and (from) the hostility and wick-
23 edness and fear of an enemy, who is remote and near, those who are
24 known and those who are not known. By ʾIlumquh Ṯahwân,
25 master of ʾAwwâm.

Cf. preliminary remark in the commentary of Ja 625.

The missing part of the stone contained the beginning of the text, which may be restored at least partly, and also the object of the dedication and the favors received prior to the offering.

L. 1: the verb *ẖmr* is ordinarily mentioned with *mhrg(t)* and *ġnm*.
L. 4: *ʾnbr*, *aqtal* form; personal name in RÉS 4994/1, if *NaNN*'s (p. 33) reading is correct; cf. also the Arabic place name *al-ʾanbar* (cf. *WüR*, p. 19 C) and verb *nabara* "to raise (higher)".
Ll. 4-5: *ḏyhrḍwnhmw*, as well as *ḏyhrḍynhmw* in lines 15-16, is a parenthetical phrase; the complement that follows this phrase must be related to the nouns which precede this parenthesis.
L. 6: *yʾmn*, but *yhʾmn* in lines 8 and 12-13.
L. 7: *yqhnhmw*, cp. *yqhnn* in RÉS 4962/19.
Ll. 14-15: *ʾmyrt*, cf. commentary on Ja 615/18-19.
L. 15: *s*[ʿ]*sʿm*, the first ʿ is missing on the stone.
Ll. 15-16: *ḏyhrḍynhmw*, cf. commentary on lines 4-5.
L. 17: *mqyẓ*, derived noun from *qyẓ*; cf. Arabic *maqîẓ*, or *maqâẓ* "summer camp *or* settlement"; the noun *qyẓ* is attested, e.g., in Ja 617/9.
L. 21: the preposition *bn* is missing on the stone.

624 – White sandstone block with one large reddish stain; found about 20 m. to the north of the columns; broken on top, bottom, and right side; left side damaged; incomplete photograph in Plate 13. – MaMB 26.

Front: maximum length: 19.3 cm.; width: 19.5. – INSCRIPTION: letter height: 2 cm.; space between the lines: 0.5 cm.

1 ...]⌊*bš*⌋*m*⌊/⌋*m*⌋⌊*q*⌉*t*[*wyy*/*nš*]⌈ʾ⌉
2 [*krb*/*yʾmn*/*yhḥrb*/*mlk*/*s*]⌊*bʾ*/*wḏry*(*d*)*n*/*bn*⌉
3 [ʾ*lšrḥ*/*yḥḏb*/*wyʾzl*/]⌊*byn*/*mlky*/(*s*)⌈*bʾ*/*w*⌉
4 [*ḏrydn*/*hqnyy*/ʾ*lmqh*]⌈*ṯh*⌉*wnbᶜlʾwm*/*ṣlmn*
5 [*ḏṣrfn*/*ḏmdlthw*/*s*]*bᶜ*/*mʾnm*/*blṭm*/*wṣl*
6 [*mt*... .../*bḏ*]*t*/*hwfyhm*⌊*y*/*bʾ*⌋[*mlʾ*]
7 [*stmlʾn*/*bᶜmhw*/. ./](*ḥ*)*mdm*/*b*⌊*ḏ*⌋[*t*/..

1 ...] Bašam, [the two] hi[gh] offi[cials of Naša]ʾ-
2 [karib Yuʾmin Yuharḥib, king of Sa]baʾ and Ray(d)ân, son of
3 [ʾIlšarah Yaḥḏub and Yaʾzil] Bayyin, the two kings of (Sa)baʾ and
4 [Raydân, have dedicated to ʾIlumquh] Ṯahwân, master of ʾAwwâm, this statue
5 [which (is) in brass, the weight of which (is) se]ven hundred *balaṭ*, and [. female] sta-
6 [tue.. ..be]cause He has showered upon them both [the favor]s
7 [for which they besought Him.. ..] (in) praise becau[se..

The restoration of lines 2-4 may be considered as certain, since the end of lines 1-3 determines the beginning of each successive line; there is thus no place for the lower part of a symbol at the beginning of line 2. It is impossible to know whether there was a symbol at the beginning of line 1. Further, although badly broken, the top is preserved above *bšm*/*m*; there is thus no line missing on top.

L. 1: *bšm*, cf. the name of a Sab deity *bšmm* (cf. *JaP*, p. 140 and *JaRSAP*, p. 274) and the name of a Qat month *bšmm* (e.g., RÉS 3689/9); however, the first letter(s?) of this proper name may possibly be missing; cf., e.g., *mbšmt* (e.g., Ja 717/5).
L. 3: in *mlky*, *k* is engraved on top of a *y*.
L. 5: cf. Ja 608/5-6. – *blṭ* (cf. *CoRoC*, p. 114 A, *BeSI*, p. 12 and *RhKTB*, II, pp. 25-26), a South-Arabian coin.

625 – Splinter from the upper part of an inscription; grayish sandstone; photograph in Plate 14. – MaMB 66.

SPLINTER: maximum thickness: 6 cm. – *Front:* covered with red paint; length in the center of line 2: 5.8 cm.; diagonal width: 10.6 cm. – INSCRIPTION: same disposition of lines as in Ja 559; letter height: 2.5 cm.; space between the lines: 0.3 cm.

1 ...]⌈*m*./⌉*w*[...
2 .../*h*]*qnyw*/ʾ⌊*l*⌋[*mqh*...
3 ...]⌊/⌉*nš*⌊ʾ*krb*⌉[/...

1 ...]m. and [...
2 ...have de]dicated to ʾIl[umquh...
3 ...] Našaʾkarib [...

Ja 625 is not a part of Ja 623/b, c, and d for many reasons (e.g., the disposition of lines, etc.) and especially because the *w* (end of line 1) and the letter following *m* in the same line should be *y* and *d* respectively. – The present text is not to be reunited with Ja 792, because the lettering of the latter is more perfect (cf., e.g., ʾ and *k*) than that of the first.

L. 1: the letter *m* is followed by a sign such as *g*, *y*, *l*, etc., but not *d*, for the lower left extremity of the triangle of the latter should be visible on the stone; what appears on the photograph is the edge of a damaged spot. The original length of the lines being unknown, the possible restorations of lines 2-3 are too numerous to indicate any greater probability of one over the other.

d – Saᶜadšamsum ʾAsraᶜ and his son Marṯadum Yuhaḥmid: Ja 626-630

626 – Yellowish, slightly grayish sandstone. – MaMB 146.

STONE: constant thickness: 40 cm. – *Front:* upper and left edges badly damaged, and right edge slightly damaged; 1.325 m. (left) and 1.30 m. (right) × 47.7 cm. – INSCRIPTION: same disposition of lines as in Ja 552; letter height: 4.5 cm.; space between the lines: 0.5 cm. – SYMBOL, cf. Ja 559.

1 ⌈**Sym-**⌉ ⌈*y*⌉*nᶜm*/ʾ*ḏrḥ*/*wbnyhw*/ʾ*bkrb*
2 **bol** *wkbrm*/*bnw*/*ḏġymn*/*wḏnʾsm*
3 ʾ*qwl*/*šᶜbn*/*ġymn*/*hqnyw*/ʾ*lmqh*/*ṯ*
4 *hwn*/*bᶜl*/ʾ*wm*/*ṣlmn*/*ḥgn*/*wqhh*
5 *mw*/ʾ*lmqh*/*bmsʾlhw*/*lsᶜdhmw*/ʾ*l*
6 *mqh*/*nᶜmtm*/*wwfym*/*wmngwt*/*ṣdqm*
7 *ḏyhrḍwn*/ʾ*lbbhmw*/*wlsᶜd*/ʾ*lmqh*
8 ʾ*dmhw*/*bny*/*ġymn*/*wḏnʾsm*/*rḍw*
9 *wḥẓy*/*mrʾyhmw*/*sᶜdšmsm*/ʾ*srᶜ*/*w*
10 *bnhw*/*mrṯdm*/*yhḥmd*/*mlky*/*sbʾ*/*w*
11 *ḏrydn*/*bny*/ʾ*lšrḥ*/*yḥḏb*/*mlk*/*s*
12 *bʾ*/*wḏrydn*/*wlwzʾ*/ʾ*lmqh*/*ṣdqhmw*
13 *whwfynhmw*/*bkl*/ʾ*mlʾ*/*ystmlʾn*
14 *bᶜmhw*/*wlẖrynhmw*/ʾ*lmqh*/*bn*/[*bʾ*]
15 *stm*/*wnkym*/*wbnkl*/*nḍᶜ*/*wšṣy*/*š*
16 *nʾm*/*ḏrḥq*/*wqrb*/*wkwnt*/*ḏt*/⌊*hqn*⌋
17 *ytn*/*lḏt*/*nᶜmt*/*wtnᶜmn*/*lynᶜ*[*m*/*w*]
18 *bnyhw*/ʾ*bkrb*/*wkbrm*/*bny*/*ḏġ*⌉[*y*]

19 *mn/wḏnʾsm/wqlhmw/wšʿbhmw/ġ⌝[y]*
20 *mn/bʿṯtr/whwbs/wʾlmqh/wbḏ[t]*
21 *ḥmym/wbḏt/bʿdnm/wbšms/mlkn*
22 *tnf/wbšymhmw/ḥgrm/qḥmm/bʿl*
23 *ʿrnhn/tnʿ/wlms/wrṯdw/hqnyt*
24 *hmw/ʿṯtršrqn/wʾlmqh/bʿl/ʾwm*

1 **Sym-** Yunʿim ʾAḏraḥ and his two sons ʾAbkarib
2 **bol** and Kabrum, descendants of [the two tribes] Ġaymân and Naʾsum,
3 rulers of the tribe Ġaymân, have dedicated to ʾIlumquh Ṯa-
4 hwân, master of ʾAwwâm, this statue, as has ordered to
5 them ʾIlumquh through His oracle in order that may make them happy ʾIl-
6 umquh with perfect prosperity and safety and security,
7 which would please their hearts, and (in order) that ʾIlumquh may make happy
8 His worshippers, the descendants of Ġaymân and of Naʾsum, with the grace
9 and esteem of their two lords Saʿadšamsum ʾAsraʿ and
10 his son Marṯadum Yuhaḥmid, the two kings of Sabaʾ and
11 Raydân, the two sons of ʾIlšaraḥ Yaḥḍub, king of Sa-
12 baʾ and Raydân; and that ʾIlumquh may continue to bestow upon them
13 and to shower upon them all the favors [for which] they shall beseech
14 Him; and that ʾIlumquh may preserve them from
15 [misfor]tunes and suffering and from every [act of] hostility and wickedness of [any] ene-
16 my, who is remote and near; and was [given] this offer-
17 ing so that it may have been pleasant and be pleasant for Yunʿ[im and]
18 his two sons ʾAbkarib and Kabrum, descendants of Ġ[ay-]
19 mân and of Naʾsum, and to their ruler and to their tribe Ġ[ay-]
20 mân. By ʿAṯtar and Hawbas and ʾIlumquh and by Ḏ[ât-]
21 Ḥimyâm and by Ḏât-Baʿdânum and by Šams of the king,
22 Tanûf, and by their patron Ḥagarum Qaḥamum, master of
23 the two citadels Tanaʿ and Lamas. And they have entrusted their
24 offering to the care of ʿAṯtar Šarqân and of ʾIlumquh, master of ʾAwwâm.

L. 1: *ynʿm*, e.g., RÉS 4134/3. – *ʾḏrḥ*, CIH 329/1.
L. 2: *kbrm*, e.g., Ja 149, Qat; cf. the family name *ḏkbrn* in RÉS 5085/4; in RÉS 4595 B, read *ʾbr* instead of *kbr*; cf. also the name of a woman *k[b]rt* in AshM 1957-17/1; see *BeTMS*. – *nʾsm* compare *nʾs* in RÉS 3858/1, Qat.

627 – Yellowish, slightly grayish sandstone; cf. Chapter I, A. – MaMB 210 = NaNAG 6, with incomplete photograph.

STONE: thickness: 39 cm. – *Front:* upper edge badly damaged; covered with red paint; 1.49 m. × 52.8 cm. (top) and 53.5 (bottom). – INSCRIPTION, same disposition of lines as in Ja 561 bis; letter height: from 3.4 cm. to 4; space between the lines: 0.7 cm. – SYMBOL, cf. Ja 603.

1 **Sym-** *hwfʿṯt⌜/y⌝z⌜ʾ⌝[n/wbnw/kbsym/ʾqwl/šʿbn/t]*
2 **bol** *nʿmm/wtnʿmt/hqnyw/ʾlmqhw/ṯhwn/bʿl*
3 *ʾwm/ṣlmn/ḥmdm/bḏt/hwfy/ʾlmqhw/ʿbdhw*
4 *hwfʿṯt/bn/kbsym/bmlʾ/wtbšrt/tbšrhw*
5 *kysqyn/wkbrn/ʾrḍhmw/bn/ʾmrn/ḏmlyn/b*
6 *wrẖ/bhw/stmlʾw/bʿmhw/whwfyhmw/ʾlmq*
7 *hw/bhwt/mlʾn/wtbšrtn/wsqy/sryhmw/ḏy*
8 *ʿd/wʾtb/wḏbn/ʾrḍ/tnʿmm/bhwt/wrẖn/w*
9 *ʾlmqhw/fwzʾ/šft/wtbšrn/ʿbdhw/hwfʿṯ*
10 *t/wbny/kbsym/kysqyn/whšfqn/whʿmmn/m*
11 *ʾẖḏhmw/ḏyfd/wkl/ʾrḍhmw/bkl/ʾbrq/dṯʾ*
12 *wẖrf/mhwtnm/wʾlmqhw/fl/yzʾn/ṣdq/whw*
13 *fyn/ʿbdhw/hwfʿṯt/wbny/kbsym/bkl/ʾm*
14 *lʾ/stmlʾw/wystmlʾnn/bʿmhw/wlsʿd/ʾl*
15 *mqhw/ʿbdhw/hwfʿṯt/bn/kbsym/ḥẓy/wr*
16 *ḍw/mrʾyhmw/sʿdšmsm/ʾsrʿ/wbnhw/mr*
17 *ṯdm/yhḥmd/mlky/sbʾ/wḏrydn/bny/ʾ*
18 *lšrḥ/yḥḍb/mlk/sbʾ/wḏrydn/wlsʿ*
19 *dhmw/ʾlmqhw/nʿmtm/wwfym/wmngyt*
20 *ṣdqm/ḏyhrḍwn/ʾlbbhmw/wlsʿdhm*
21 *w/ʾlmqhw/ʾṯmr/wʾfql/ṣdqm/bn/kl*
22 *ʾrḍhmw/wʾsrrhmw/wlwfyhmw/wwfy*
23 *ʾrḍhmw/wšʿbhmw/tnʿmm/wlḏt/yẖ*
24 *ryn/ʾlmqhw/ʿbdhw/hwfʿṯt/wbny/k*
25 *bsym/wšʿbhmw/bn/bʾstm/wnkym/w*
26 *bn/kl/nḍʿ/wšṣy/šnʾm/bʿṯtr/whwb*
27 *s/wʾlmqhw/wbḏt/ḥmym/wbḏt/bʿdnm*
28 *wbšms/mlkn/tnf/wbʾlmqhw/bʿl/šwḥ*
29 *ṭ/wbšmshmw/bʿlt/qyf/ršm/wrṯdw/hq*
30 *nythmw/ʿṯtršrqn/wʾlmqhw/bʿl/ʾwm*

1 **Sym-** Hawfʿaṯat Yazʾ[ân and the descendants of Kabsayum, rulers of the two tribes Ta-]
2 **bol** nʿamum and Tanʿamat, have dedicated to ʾIlumquhû Ṯahwân, master of
3 ʾAwwâm, this statue in praise because ʾIlumquhû has showered upon His worshipper

4 Hawfʿaṯat, descendant of Kabsayum the favor and the announcement [which] he implored from Him
5 so that He may irrigate and augment their land with the cereals of winter during
6 the month in which they besought Him; and has showered upon them ʾIlumqu-
7 hû in this favor and the announcement and the irrigation of their two wâdî-side valleys of Ya-
8 ʿud and ʾAtab and some part of the land of Tanʿ-amum in this month; and
9 as for ʿIlumquhû, may He continue to promise and announce to His worshipper Hawfʿaṯ-
10 at and to the descendants of Kabsayum that He will irrigate and make abound and fill up
11 their breakwater of Yafid and their every land with all the lightning storms of spring
12 and of autumn with lasting running water; and as for ʾIlumquhû, may he continue to bestow and to sho-
13 wer upon His worshipper Hawfʿaṯat and upon the descendants of Kabsayum all the fa-
14 vors [for which] they besought and shall beseech Him; and that may make happy ʾIl-
15 umquhû His worshipper Hawfʿaṯat, descendant of Kabsayum with the esteem and gra-
16 ce of their two lords Saʿadšamsum ʾAsraʿ and his son Mar-
17 ṯadum Yuhaḥmid, the two kings of Sabaʾ and Ray-dân, the two sons of ʾI-
18 lšaraḥ Yaḥḏub, king of Sabaʾ and Raydân; and that
19 ʾIlumquhû may make them happy with perfect prosperity and safety and security,
20 which would please their hearts; and that may make them happy
21 ʾIlumquhû with perfect fruits and harvests from
22 their every land and all their wâdî-side valleys; and that He may protect them and protect
23 their land and their tribe Tanʿamum; and that may pre-
24 serve ʾIlumquhû His worshipper Hawfʿaṯat and the descendants of Ka-
25 bsayum and their tribe from misfortunes and suffering and
26 from every [act of] hostility and wickedness of [any] enemy. By ʿAṯtar and Hawb-
27 as and ʾIlumquhû and by Ḏât-Ḥimyâm and by Ḏât-Baʿdânum
28 and by Šams of the king, Tanûf, and by ʾIlumquhû, master of Šawḥ-
29 aṭ and by their Šams, mistress of the monument of Rašam. And they have entrusted their offe-
30 ring to the care of ʿAṯtar Šarqân and of ʾIlumquhû, master of ʾAwwâm.

In *NaNAG*'s transliteration (II, pp. 24-25): line 1 does not exist; line 2: *nʿmm/wt* instead of ....../ *bnw/*, omit the 5 brackets; line 4: *bmlʾ* instead of *btmlʾ*; line 5: *ʾrḏ* instead of *ʾrd*; lines 6 and 14: *bʿm* instead of *bʾm*; line 8: *tnʿmm* instead of *tnʿm*; line 18: *mlk/sbʾ* instead of *mlk sbʾ*; line 19: *nʿmtm* instead of *nʾmtm*; line 20: *ʾlbb* instead of *lbb*; line 21: *ʾṯmr* instead of *ʾṭmr*; lines 23-24: *yẖryn* instead of *ybryn*; line 27: omit bracket; line 28: omit bracket; lines 28-29: *šwḥṭ/* instead of *šʿḥ*...; line 29: *bšmshmw* instead of *bšms*, omit bracket, *wrṯdw* instead of *mrṯdw*; line 30: *ʿṯtršrqn* instead of *ʿṯtr/whwbs*, omit bracket, *bʿl* instead of *bʾl*.

L. 1: *hwfʿṯt* is followed by the lower part of two vertical strokes; the first one belongs to a word divider; the restoration of ʾ is thus impossible (*hwfʿṯt/ʾzʾd* is attested in Ja 571/6); the third letter of the second personal name can only be either ʾ or *s*; *hwfʿṯt/yzʾn* is mentioned in Ja 628/1.

L. 5: *ysqyn*, Ja 112/3, where the second *n* is a typographical error. – *kbrn*, infinitive of the 2nd form; CIH 343/11: "to augment"; cf. the Western Semitic cognates in *JeHoDISO*, p. 115: kbr_{I}. – *bn/ʾmrn*, *bn* indicates the origin of the increase; *ʾmr*, cf. commentary on Ja 615/18-19; *ʾmrn/ḏmlyn*, as far as the form is concerned, cp. *ʾṣlmn/ḏḏhbn* (e.g., CIH 308/3) and *ʾṣlmm –/ḏḏhbm* (e.g., Ja 632/2).

L. 7: *sryhmw*, dual of *sr* (cf. commentary on Ja 577/13).

Ll. 7-8: *ḏyʿd*, the proper name *yʿd* is very well known.

L. 8: *ʾtb*, noun in CIH 949/3-4 and the family name *ʾtbt* in RÉS 4267/2, Min.

L. 10: *hšfqn*, CIH 603 B/20; cf. *CoRoC*, p. 251 A: "to enrich"; grammatically, this verb depends on *fwzʾ* in line 9. – *hʿmmn*, infinitive of the 4th form of *ʿmm*; cf. Arabic *ʿamma* 1st form "to spread, stretch" and 8th form "to reach one's full growth"; *hʿmm* may be translated "to let grow, fill up"; the noun *tʿmm* is attested in RÉS 4514/1-2.

L. 12: *mhwtn*, noun from the participle of the 4th form of *wtn* (cf. *CoRoC*, p. 141 B); cf. also Arabic *wâtin* "that runs; flowing (water)"; the nouns *ḏṯʾ* and *ẖrf* being without *m* ending even if not followed by a determinative complement (e.g., Ja 610/14), *mhwtn* is a circumstantial complement.

628 – Yellowish, slightly grayish sandstone; cf. Chapter I, B. – MaMB 211.

STONE: thickness: 36 cm. – *Front*, upper left corner badly broken; lower corners broken; 1.483 m. × 47 cm. – INSCRIPTION, same disposition of lines as in Ja 561 bis; letter height: 4.1 cm.; space between the lines: 0.6 cm. – SYMBOL, cf. Ja 565.

1 **Sym-** *hwfʿṯt/yz⌈ʾn⌉[/wbnw/kbsym/ʾqw]*
2 **bol** *l/šʿbn/tnʿmm/wtnʿ(m)[t/hqnyw]*
3 *ʾlmqhw/ṯhwn/bʿl/ʾwm/ṣlmn/[ḥgn]*
4 *wqhhmw/ʾlmqhw/bmsʾlhw/bkn/t*
5 *flw/bʿmhw/lmʾḫdhmw/ḏyfd/lqbl*
6 *y/ḏtʾl/yʾtwn/ʿdyhw/sqym/wwkbw*
7 *flythmw/kʿbrnmw/ʾlmqhw/bʿl/ʾwm*
8 *kwn/ḫdg/ʾtw/sqym/ʿdy/hwt/mʾḫd*
9 *n/ḏyfd/bqdmy/ḏt/hqnytn/wʾlmqh[w]*
10 *fwzʾ/šft/wtbšrn/ʿbdhw/hwfʿṯt*
11 *wbny/kbsym/kysqyn/whšfqn/whʿm*
12 *mn/mʾḫdhmw/ḏyfd/bkl/ʾbrq/ḏtʾ*
13 *wḫrf/mhwtnm/wʾlmqhw/fl/yzʾn/ṣ*
14 *dq/whwfyn/ʿbdhw/hwfʿṯt/wbny/k*
15 *bsym/bkl/ʾmlʾ/stmlʾw/wystmlʾ*
16 *nn/bʿmhw/wlsʿdhmw/ʾlmqhw/ḥẓy/w*
17 *rḍw/mrʾyhmw/sʿdšmsm/ʾsrʿ/wbnhw*
18 *mrṯdm/yhḥmd/mlky/sbʾ/wḏrydn/b*
19 *ny/ʾlšrḥ/yḥḍb/mlk/sbʾ/wḏrydn*
20 *wlsʿdhmw/ʾlmqhw/nʿmtm/wwfym/w*
21 *mngt/ṣdqm/ḏyhrḍwn/ʾlbbhmw/wlsʿ*
22 *dhmw/ʾlmqhw/ʾṯmr/wʾfql/ṣdqm/bnkl*
23 *ʾrḍhmw/wʾsrrhmw/wlḫryn/ʾlmqhw/ʿ*
24 *bdhw/hwfʿṯt/wbny/kbsym/wšʿbhmw*
25 *bn/bʾstm/wnkym/wbn/kl/nḍʿ/wš*
26 *ṣy/šnʾm/bʿṯtr/whwbs/wʾlmqhw*
27 *wbḏt/ḥmym/wbḏt/bʿdnm/wbšms/m*
28 *lkn/tnf/wbʾlmqhw/bʿl/šwḥṭ/wbš*
29 *mshmw/bʿlt/qyf/ršm/wrṯdw/hqny*
30 *thmw/ʿṯtršrqn/wʾlmqhw/bʿl/ʾwm*

1 **Sym-** Hawfʿaṯat Yazʾân [and the descendants of Kabsayum, rul-]
2 **bol** er[s] of the two tribes Tanʿamum and Tanʿa(m)[at, have dedicated to]
3 ʾIlumquhû Ṯahwân, master of ʾAwwâm, this statue [as]
4 ʾIlumquhû has commanded them through His oracle, when
5 he separated from Him on account of their breakwater of Yafid because of
6 this: irrigation-water does not come back into it [barrier], so they received
7 their ordinances in order that ʾIlumquhû, master of ʾAwwâm,
8 would allow [the] irrigation-water to come back into this breakwater
9 of Yafid before this offering [be made]; and as for ʾIlumquh[û],
10 may He continue to promise and to announce to His worshipper Hawfʿaṯat
11 and to the descendants of Kabsayum that He will irrigate and let abound and fill up
12 their breakwater of Yafid with all the lightning storms of spring
13 and of autumn with lasting running water; and as for ʾIlumquhû, may He continue to be-
14 stow and to shower upon His worshipper Hawfʿaṯat and upon the descendants of Ka-
15 bsayum all the favors [for which] they besought and shall beseech
16 Him; and that ʾIlumquhû may make them happy with the esteem and
17 grace of their two lords Saʿadšamsum ʾAsraʿ and his son
18 Marṯadum Yuhaḥmid, the two kings of Sabaʾ and Raydân, the two
19 sons of ʾIlšaraḥ Yaḥḍub, king of Sabaʾ and Raydân;
20 and that ʾIlumquhû may make them happy with prosperity and safety and
21 security perfect, which would please their hearts; and that may make
22 them happy ʾIlumquhû with perfect fruits and harvests from
23 their every land and all their wâdî-side valleys; and that ʾIlumquhû may preserve His
24 worshipper Hawfʿaṯat and the descendants of Kabsayum and their tribe
25 from misfortunes and suffering and from every [act of] hostility and wick-
26 edness of [any] enemy. By ʿAṯtar and Hawbas and ʾIlumquhû
27 and by Ḏât-Ḥimyâm and by Ḏât-Baʿdânum and by Šams of the
28 king, Tanûf, and by ʾIlumquhû, master of Šawḥaṭ and by their
29 Šams, mistress of the monument of Rašam. And they have entrusted their offer-
30 ing to the care of ʿAṯtar Šarqân and of ʾIlumquhû, master of ʾAwwâm.

Although the repartition of the characters on the lines is different in Ja 627 and 628, lines 1-3 (except the last term) and (the last term of) 9-30 of the present text are identical to lines 1-3 (first two terms) and 8-30 of Ja 627, with the following differences: *wkl/ʾrḍhmw* (line 11), *ʿbdhw/– –/kbsym* (line 15) and *wlwfyhw/– –/tnʿmm* (lines 22-23) in Ja 627 do not exist in Ja 628, and *mngyt* (line 19), *bn/kl* (line 21) and *wlḏt/yḫryn* (lines 23-24) in Ja 627 are respectively mentioned in Ja 628 as follows: *mngt* (line 21), *bnkl* (line 22), and *wlḫryn* (line 23).

Ll. 4-5: *tflw*, cf. commentary on Ja 576/6.

L. 5: for the preposition *l* "with respect to", cf. *HöASG*, p. 149, *β*.

Ll. 5-6: *lqbly/d̲tʾl*, combination of *lqbly/d̲t* (e.g., Ja 648/4) and *[lqbl]y/d̲ʾl* (e.g., Ja 570/3), cf. *JaPDSM*, pp. 176-78.

L. 7: *flyt*, plural of *fly*, cf. *BeSI*, p. 13; same root as *flw* (cf. commentary on Ja 576/6).

L. 8: *h̲dg*, cf. *CoRoC*, p. 154 A for Ja 643/29 and 644/9; here, cf. Ethiopic *h̲ădăgă* "sinere, permittere" (cf. *DiLLA*, col. 617).

629 – Yellowish, slightly grayish sandstone; cf. Chapter I, A. – MaMB 203.

STONE: thickness: 37.7 cm. – *Front:* both the right part of the upper edge and the upper part of the right edge are splintered off; 1.507 m. × 47 cm. – INSCRIPTION: same disposition of lines as in Ja 552; letter height: 2.4 cm.; space between the lines: 0.7 cm.

1 *mrt̲dm/y[...../wb]nhw/d̲rḥn/ʾšwʿ/bny/d̲grfm/ʾq*
2 *wl/šʿbn/yhbʿl/hqnyw/ʾlmqh/t̲hwn/bʿl/ʾwm/ṣlmn*
3 *d̲d̲hbn/ḥmdm/bd̲t/hwšʿ/whwfyn/ʿbdhw/d̲rḥn/d̲grfm/b*
4 *kn/[sbʾw/]lšwʿn/mrʾyhmw/sʿdšmsm/ʾsrʿ/wbnhw/mrt̲dm/y*
5 *[ḥmd]/mlky/sbʾ/wd̲rydn/bny/ʾlšrḥ/yḥḍb/mlk/sbʾ*
6 *[wd̲ry]dn/ʿdy/ʾrḍ/šʿbn/rdmn/bḍr/hštʾ/whbʾl/bn/mʿhr*
7 *[wd̲]h̲wln/wḥḍrmwt/wqtbn/wrdmn/wmḍḥym/wkl/ʾns/wʾʿr*
8 *b/kwn/kwnhmw/bʿbr/ʾmrʾhmw/ʾmlk/sbʾ/wyhṣry/mrʾyhm*
9 *w/sʿdšmsm/wmrt̲dm/wbʿmhmy/ʾdmhmy/d̲bn/ʾsbʾn/wʾqwl*
10 *n/wh̲ms/mlk/sbʾ/ʿdy/h̲lf/hgrn/wʿln/wtqdmw/bʿm/ydʿʾl/m*
11 *lk/ḥḍrmwt/wḥḍrmwt/wnbṭm/mlk/qtbn/wqtbn/wwhbʾl/bn*
12 *mʿhr/wd̲h̲wln/wd̲ḥṣbḥ/wmḍḥym/wkl/d̲kwn/kwnhmw/wḥmdy/mr*
13 *t̲dm/wd̲rḥn/bny/d̲grfm/h̲yl/wmqm/ʾlmqh/bd̲t/hwšʿ/mrʾyhmw*
14 *sʿdšmsm/wmrt̲dm/mlky/sbʾ/⟨.⟩t̲br/whlqḥn/kl/mṣr/ydʿʾl*
15 *mlk/ḥḍrmwt/wwhbʾl/bn/mʿhr/wkl/d̲kwn/kwnhmw/wwẓ*
16 *ʾy/mrt̲dm/wd̲rḥn/bny/d̲grfm/ḥmd/h̲yl/wmqm/ʾlmqh/bʿl*
17 *ʾwm/bd̲t/hwšʿ/ʿbdhw/d̲rḥn/wʾsd/wmqtt/šwʿhw/bn/šʿb*
18 *hmw/fyšn/wyhbʿl/bmhrgt/wġnmt/ṣdqm/d̲hrḍwhmw/bn/ʾš*
19 *ʿb/tqdmw/bʿmhmw/hwt/wymn/wbd̲t/hwfy/ʾlmqh/bʿl/ʾwm*
20 *ʿbdhw/d̲rḥn/wʾsd/wmqtt/šwʿhw/bhwt/ḍrn/wbkl/ʾmlʾ*
21 *[s]tmlʾ/d̲rḥn/bʿm/ʾlmqh/lhyt/sbʾtn/wwẓʾy/ḥmd/mr*
22 *t̲dm/wd̲rḥn/ʾlmqh/bd̲t/mẓʾy/wstwfyn/mrʾyhmw/sʿdšm*
23 *sm/wmrt̲dm/mlky/sbʾ/wh̲mshmy/ʿdy/hgrn/mryb/bwfym*
24 *wwẓʾy/mrt̲dm/wd̲rḥn/bny/d̲grfm/ḥmd/h̲yl/wmqm/ʾlmqhw*
25 *bʿl/ʾwm/bd̲t/hwšʿ/whwfyn/ʿbdhw/d̲rḥn/d̲grfm/wʾsd/wmqt*
26 *t/šwʿhw/bkn/sbʾw/lšwʿn/mrʾyhmw/sʿdšmsm/wmrt̲dm/m*
27 *lky/sbʾ/ʿdy/h̲lf/hgrn/ḥlzwm/wmšrqytn/wẓwrw/wnḥb/h*
28 *grn/ḥlzwm/wgbzw/kl/ʾsrrhmw/wwt̲r/wqmʿ/mḥrmt/why*
29 *klt/wʾbʾr/wmsqy/bh̲lfhy/wbd̲t/hwšʿ/mrʾyhmw/sʿdšmsm*
30 *wmrt̲dm/bhsbʿn/wwḍʿ/hgrn/mnwbm/wkl/hgr/wmṣnʿ/šʿbn*
31 *ʾwsn/whgrn/šyʿn/wwẓʾy/mrt̲dm/wd̲rḥn/ḥmd/h̲yl/wmqm/ʾlm*
32 *qh/bd̲t/hwfy/wmtʿn/ʿbdhw/d̲rḥn/ʾšwʿ/d̲grfm/wrbšmsm/yʿrr*
33 *bn/ʿlfqm/bn/ʿnt/hʿnw/whdrkn/bʿd/ʾḥdr/wʿrb/mẓʾw/ʿdy*
34 *h̲lf/tmnʿ/wwẓʾy/mrt̲dm/wd̲rḥn/ḥmd/h̲yl/wmqm/ʾlmqh/bʿl/ʾ*
35 *wm/bd̲t/stwfy/wtʾysn/mrʾyhmw/sʿdšmsm/wmrt̲dm/ʿdy/hg*
36 *rn/mryb/bwfym/wmqyḥtm/d̲hrḍwhmw/bhyt/sbʾtn/wwẓʾy*
37 *mrt̲dm/wd̲rḥn/ḥmd/ʾlmqh/bd̲t/stwfy/gẓyt/mrt̲dm/d̲grfm*
38 *bhgrn/ṣnʿw/wʾqwl/wqhy/mrʾyhmw/sʿdšmsm/wmrt̲dm/lgẓy/br*
39 *ḥbtn/bhmt/sbʾtnhn/wstwfy/gẓyt/mrt̲dm/wʾqwl/gẓy/bʿmh*
40 *[w/r]ḥʾl/bn/d̲rnḥ/wšrḥt̲t/bn/btʿ/wʾlrm/bn/sh̲ymm/wyrʿd/bn/sʾ*
41 *rn/wyrm/bn/hmdn/wlwẓʾ/ʾlmqh/sʿd/ʿbdyhw/mrt̲dm/wd̲rḥn/bny*
42 *d̲grfm/ḥẓy/wrḍw/mrʾyhmw/sʿdšmsm/wmrt̲dm/mlky/sbʾ/wd̲rydn*
43 *wlsʿdhmw/ʾlmqh/bry/ʾʾd̲nm/wmqymtm/wl/h̲ryn/bn/wʿl*
44 *n/ʾdmhw/mrt̲dm/wd̲rḥn/wšʿbhmw/fyšn/wyhbʿl/bʾstm/wnky*

45 *[m]/wkl/nḍᶜ/wšṣy/šnᵓm/[ḏrḥq/]wqrb/bᶜṯtr/whwbs/ wbᵓ*

46 *lmqh/bᶜl(/)ᵓwm/wḥrwnm/wᵓlmqh/bᶜl⟨⟩/mtbᶜm/ wrwẓn/wbḏt*

47 *ḥmym/(w)bḏt/bᶜdnm/wbšms/mlkn/tnf/wšmshmw/ bᶜlt/ṣyḥyn*

1 Marṯadum Y[.. ..and] his s[on] Ḏarḥân ᵓAšwaᶜ, descendants of [the clan] Garfum, ru-

2 lers of the tribe Yuhbiᶜil, have dedicated to ᵓIlumquh Ṯahwân, master of ᵓAwwâm, this statue

3 which [is] in bronze, in praise because He has helped and saved His worshippper Ḏarḥân, him of Garfum, when

4 [they fought] in order to assist their two lords Saᶜadšamsum ᵓAsraᶜ and his son Marṯadum Yu-

5 [haḥmid], the two kings of Sabaᵓ and Raydân, the two sons of ᵓIlšaraḥ Yaḥḍub, king of Sabaᵓ

6 [and Ray]dân, in the land of the tribe Radmân during the war that brought about Wahabᵓil, descendant of Maᶜâhir

7 [and of] Ḫawlân, and Ḥaḍramawt and Qatabân and Radmân and Muḏhayum and every person and the Arabs

8 [who] were with them against their lords, the kings of Sabaᵓ; and fell their two lords

9 Saᶜadšamsum and Marṯadum and with them both their servants, some of the warriors and the rulers

10 and the army of the king of Sabaᵓ upon the region of the city [of] Waᶜlân; and they attacked Yadaᶜᵓil,

11 king of Ḥaḍramawt and Ḥaḍramawt and Nabaṭum, king of Qatabân and Qatabân and Wahabᵓil, descendant of

12 Maᶜâhir and of Ḫawlân and of Haṣbaḥ, and Muḏhayum and everyone who was with them; and have praised both Mar-

13 ṯadum and Ḏarḥân, descendants of Garfum, the strength and the power of ᵓIlumquh because He has assisted their two lords

14 Saᶜadšamsum and Marṯadum, the two kings of Sabaᵓ, in crushing and enchaining all the expeditionary force of Yadaᶜᵓil,

15 king of Ḥaḍramawt, and Wahabᵓil, descendant of Maᶜâhir, and everyone who was with them; and have conti-

16 nued both Marṯadum and Ḏarḥân, descendants of Garfum, to praise the strength and the power of ᵓIlumquh, master of

17 ᵓAwwâm, because He has assisted His worshipper Ḏarḥân and the soldiers and the high military officials of his train from their two

18 tribes Fayšân and Yuhbiᶜil to perfect war trophies and booty, which pleased them, from the tri-

19 bes which they attacked [at] that time; and because ᵓIlumquh, master of ᵓAwwâm, has protected

20 His worshipper Ḏarḥân and the soldiers and the high military officials of his train in that war and [has showered] all the favors

21 [for which] Ḏarḥân besought ᵓIlumquh for that military campaign; and have continued to praise both Mar-

22 ṯadum and Ḏarḥân ᵓIlumquh because have arrived and were given protection their two lords Saᶜadšam-

23 sum and Marṯadum, the two kings of Sabaᵓ and the army of both of them in the city [of] Mârib in safety;

24 and both Marṯadum and Ḏarḥân, descendants of Garfum, have continued to praise the strength and the power of ᵓIlumquhû,

25 master of ᵓAwwâm, because He has assisted and saved His worshipper Ḏarḥân, him of Garfum, and the soldiers and the high military officials of

26 his train when they fought to assist their two lords Saᶜadšamsum and Marṯadum, the

27 two kings of Sabaᵓ, in the region of the two cities [of] Ḫalzawum and Mašraqîtân; and they besieged and harassed the

28 city [of] Ḫalzawum; and they plundered all their wâdî-side valleys and leveled and destroyed temples and pa-

29 laces and wells and irrigation canals in its region; and because He has assisted their two lords Saᶜadšamsum

30 and Marṯadum in pillaging and humiliating the city [of] Manwabum and all the cities and fortresses of the tribe

31 ᵓAwsân and the city [of] Sayᶜân; and both Marṯadum and Ḏarḥân have continued to praise the strength and the power of ᵓIlum-

32 quh because He has protected and saved His worshipper Ḏarḥân ᵓAšwaᶜ, him of Garfum, and Rabbšamsum Yuᶜirr,

33 descendant of ᶜAlfaqam, from the reinforcement [which] brought help and reached the dwellings and the Arabs [who] arrived in

34 the region of Timnaᶜ; and both Marṯadum and Ḏarḥân have continued to praise the strength and the power of ᵓIlumquh, master of ᵓA-

35 wwâm, because He has given protection and help to their two lords Saᶜadšamsum and Marṯadum in the ci-

36 ty [of] Mârib in safety and (with) profit, which pleased them, in that military campaign; and have continued

37 both Marṯadum and Ḏarḥân to praise ᵓIlumquh because He has given protection to the edict of Marṯadum, him of Garfum,

38 in the city [of] Ṣanᶜâᵓ, and to the rulers [to whom] commanded their two lords Saᶜadšamsum and Marṯadum to decree in Ru-

39 ḥâbatân during those two military campaigns, and [because] He has given protection to the decree of Marṯadum and to the rulers [who] decreed with hi[m:]

40 [R]aḥḥʾil, descendant of Ḏarnaḥ and Šaraḥaṯat, descendant of Bataʿ and ʾIlrâm, descendant of Suḫaymum and Yarʿid, descendant of Saʾ-

41 rân and Yarum, descendant of Hamdân; and that ʾIlumquh may continue to make happy His two worshippers Marṯadum and Darḥân, descendants

42 of Garfum, with the esteem and grace of their two lords Saʿadšamsum and Marṯadum, the two kings of Sabaʾ and Raydân;

43 and that ʾIlumquh may make them happy with the strength of understanding and of power; and that He may preserve from Waʿlân

44 His worshippers Marṯadum and Ḏarḥân and their two tribes Fayšân and Yuhbiʿil [from] misfortunes and suffering

45 and [from] every [act of] hostility and wickedness of [any] enemy, [who is remote] and near. By ʿAṯtar and Hawbas and by

46 ʾIlumquh, master of ʾAwwâm and Ḥirwânum and ʾIlumquh, master of Matbaʿum and Rawẓân and by Ḏât-

47 Ḥimyâm (and) by Ḏât-Baʿdânum and by Šams of the king, Tanûf, and their Šams, mistress of Ṣîḥân.

L. 1: *ḏrḥn*, masculine personal name in NaNAG 3/1; very well-known Qat tribe name (cf. *JaPEHA*, p. 40). – *ḏgrfm*, CIH 528/2 and RÉS 4824/2 (instead of *ḏgrśm*); cp. *ḏgrfn* in Ja 522/2, Min.

L. 4: *sbʾw* is restored on the basis of line 26.

L. 6: *whbʾl*, e.g., Fakhry 72/1. – *mʿhr*, well known Qat tribe name (cf. *JaPEHA*, pp. 118-21) and also Ja 398 and 489 C; cp. the proper name *mʿhrm* in RÉS 4624/9.

L. 7: *ʾns*, cf. *CoRoC*, pp. 107-08 and the Western Semitic cognates in *JeHoDISO*, p. 19: *ʾnš*.

L. 10: *wʿln*, cf. *WiHöBGS*, pp. 38-39.

L. 12: *ḏḥṣbḥ*, RÉS 3878/18, Qat, and *ḥṣbḥ*, also clan name in Van Lessen 25/6, Qat.

L. 14: my copy has *–/sbʾ/wṯbr/–*; the *w* is suppressed to conform the whole expression to the ordinary formula. The number of letters in line 14 compared with that of the preceding and following lines does not suggest any missing verb in the copy.

L. 17: *šwʿhw*, cp. *śʿy* in RÉS 3951/4 and *BeSI*, p. 74.

L. 19: *bʿmhw*: the personal pronoun related to *ʾśʿb*. – *ywm* here has not the strict value of "day", but that of "time" as in the conjunction *bywm*.

L. 24: *ʾlmqhw*, *sic* in the copy instead of *ʾlmqh* mentioned in all other places.

L. 27: *ḫlzwm*, unknown name of a city. – *mšrqytn*, name of a city identical to that of the sun goddess (cf. *JaP*, p. 109).

L. 28: *gbẓ* equals *gbḏ*.

Ll. 28-29: *hykl*, plural *hyklt*, perfect consonantal transcription of Hebrew *hêkal*; cf. also the Western Semitic cognates in *JeHoDISO*, p. 64; *hykl*; here, with the meaning of Assyrian *êkallu* "palace" because of the mention of *mḥrmt* "temples".

L. 29: *msqyt* (RÉS 2754/2, Min), plural *msqy* (RÉS 3945/2) "irrigation canal". – *bḫlfhy*: *hy* is the personal feminine pronoun related to *hgr*.

L. 30: *mnwbm*, name of a city; compare *m(n)bt*, masculine personal name, e.g., in RÉS 4897/2, Ḥaḏr.

L. 31: *ʾwsn*, cf. *WiHöBGS*, e.g., pp. 69-75; the root *ʾws* is frequently used in simple proper names: e.g., *ʾwsm* (cf. *MlHLM*, p. 32), *ʾwys* (*qutayl* form; cf. *l.c.*) and *ʾwysm* (*qutaylum* form; RÉS 4750), *ʾsn* (Ja 364/1, Qat) and theophoric names such as *ʾwsʾl* (e.g., Ja 644/7), *ʾwskrb* (Ja 730/2) and *ʾwslt* (Ja 561 bis/3). – *šyʿn*, RÉS 3945/10 and 12; cf. also the Qat personal name *śʾʿn* in Ja 882 U.

L. 32: *yʿrr*, CIH 339 bis/1; cf. the Arabic names of a person *ʿarâwir* (cf. *SlGaVNPA*, p. 6 B), of a man *maʿrûr* and of a clan *banû ʿirâr* (cf. *WüID*, 273/13 and 254/9 respectively).

L. 33: *ʿlfqm*, RÉS 3915/1; for the 1st component of this name, cf. the Arabic personal names *ʿallif* and *maʿillaf* (cf. *SlGaVNPA*, pp. 5 A and 35 A respectively). – *ʾḥḏr*, plural of *ḥḏr*; cf., e.g., *CoRoC*, p. 151 A: house, dwelling; cf. also the Western Semitic cognates in *JeHoDISO*, p. 95: $ḥṣr_{III}$ and *ḥṣrh*; in modern Yemeni, *ḥaḏîrah* means "giardino" (cf. *RoVSAY*, p. 305).

L. 35: *tʾysn*, cf. commentary on Ja 577/6.

Ll. 38-39: *rḥbtn*, name of a city (CIH 314+954/13); also name of a territory (e.g., RÉS 3951/2).

L. 40: no more than three characters may be restored at the beginning of this line; for [.]*ḥʾl*, one might think of [*r*]*ḥʾl*, masculine personal name in Ja 489 A/2. – *ḏrnḥ*, Ja 491/2. – *yrʿd*, cp. the 2nd name of a man in NaNN 57/2-3, and the clan name *yhrʿd* in RÉS 3902, No. 56, Qat.

Ll. 43-44: *ḫryn/bn/wʿln/——/bʾstm*: the place of the complement *bn/wʿln* and the absence of the preposition *bn* before *bʾstm* are both unusual. One might suggest that *bn* before *wʿln* should be placed before *bʾstm* and thus that *wʿln* be the verb *ʿly* (*ʿln* is attested, e.g., in Ja 601/17-18) introduced by the copula *w*. It is however preferable to preserve the text like it is since *wʿln* is the name of a city in line 10.

Ll. 45-46: *bʾlmqh/bʿl(/)ʾwm/wḥrwnm*: *bʿly* instead of *bʿl(/)* is certain on the stone; the same mistake occurs between *ʾlmqh* and *mtbʿm*; *hwbs* is separated from *ʾlmqh* by *b* and the second *ʾlmqh* is alone; the dual of the two *bʿly* seems explained by the two names of temple which follow the mention of *ʾlmqh*; for *ḥrwn*, cf. *JaP*, p. 66; *mtbʿm* is known as a temple dedicated to the god Ḥalîm (cf. *JaP*, p. 128; cf. also *MoNTA*, pp. 114-15).

L. 47: *ʿḏt* is certain on the stone; the ʿ has the same diameter as that of an ordinary *w*, but there is no vertical stroke inside. – *ṣyḥyn*, cp. *ṣyḥw* in RÉS 3946/3 and *ṣyḥn* in CIH 158/2; cf. also the Arabic names of a person *ṣiyâḥ* (cf. *SlGaVNPA*, p. 47 B), of a man *ṣayḥân*, *aṣ-ṣuwâḥ* and of a clan *banû ṣûḥân* (cf. *WüID*. 199/6, 8, and 10 respectively).

630 – Stone re-used in the western pavement; cf. Chapter I, B. – MaMB 267.

Front: upper and right edges as well as lower part badly damaged. – INSCRIPTION, same disposition of lines as in Ja 559; letter height: 4.8 cm.; space between the lines: 0.4 cm. – SYMBOL, cf. Ja 559, plus a small vertical stroke in the lower part; cf. Plate A.

1 **Sym-** *lḥyʿṯt/ʾṣḥḥl/bn/yhʿn/h*
2 **bol** *qny/ʾlmqh/ṯhwn/bʿl/ʾwm*
3 *ṣlmn/ḥgn/wqhhw/bmsʾlhw/ḥ*
4 *mdm/bḏt/hwfy/ʾlmqh/ʿbdhw*
5 *lḥyʿṯt/bn/yhʿn/bʾmlʾ/stm*
6 *lʾ/bʿmhw/wlḏt/yzʾn/ʾlmqh/b*
7 *ʿl/ʾwm/ṣdq/whwfyn/ʿbdhw/lḥ*
8 *yʿṯt/bn/yhʿn/bkl/ʾmlʾ/ystm*
9 *lʾn/wntbʿn/bʿmhw/wlsʿd/ʾlm*
10 *qh/bʿl/ʾwm/ʿbdhw/lḥyʿṯt/nʿm*
11 *t[m]/wmngyt/ṣdqm/wḥẓy/wrḍw/m*
12 *rʾyhmw/sʿdšmsm/ʾsrʿ/wbnyhw*
13 *[m]rṯdm/yhḥmd/mlky/sbʾ/wḏry*
14 *dn/bny/ʾlšrḥ/yḥḍb/mlk/sbʾ*
15 *wḏrydn/wlḏt/nʿmt/wtnʿmn/lh*
16 *mw/wlbythmw/wlsʿdhmw/ʾlmqh*
17 *ʾṯmr/wʾfql/ṣdqm/bn/kl/ʾrḍt*
18 *hmw/wl/ḫryn/ʾlmqh/ʿbdhw/lḥ*
19 *yʿṯt/wbny/yhʿn/bn/bʾstm*
20 *wnkym/wnḍʿ/wšṣy/šnʾm/bʿṯtr*
21 *whwbs/wʾlmqh/wbḏt/[ḥmym/w]*
22 *bḏt/bʿdnm/wbšms/mlkn/tnf*

1 **Sym-** Laḥayʿaṯat ʾUṣaḥḥil, descendant of [the family] Yuhʿin, has
2 **bol** dedicated to ʾIlumquh Ṯahwân, master of ʾAwwâm,
3 this statue as He has ordered him through His oracle in
4 praise because ʾIlumquh has showered upon His worshipper
5 Laḥayʿaṯat, descendant of Yuhʿîn, the favors [for which] he
6 besought Him, and in order that may continue ʾIlumquh, mas-
7 ter of ʾAwwâm, to bestow and shower upon His worshipper Laḥa-
8 yʿaṯat, descendant of Yuhʿîn, all the favors [for which] he shall be-
9 seech and express to Him; and that may make happy ʾIlum-
10 quh, master of ʾAwwâm, His worshipper Laḥay-ʿaṯat with prosperi-
11 ty and security perfect and with the esteem and grace of their
12 two lords Saʿadšamsum ʾAsraʿ and his son
13 [Ma]rṯadum Yuhaḥmid, the two kings of Sabaʾ and Ray-
14 dân, the two sons of ʾIlšaraḥ Yaḥḍub, king of Sabaʾ
15 and Raydân; and that it may have been pleasant and be pleasant to
16 them and to their house; and that ʾIlumquh may make them happy
17 with perfect fruits and harvests in all their
18 fields; and that ʾIlumquh may preserve His wor-shipper Laḥa-
19 yʿaṯat and the descendants of Yuhʿîn from mis-fortunes
20 and suffering and (from) the hostility and wicked-ness of [any] enemy. By ʿAṯtar
21 and Hawbas and ʾIlumquh and by Ḏât-[Ḥimyâm and]
22 by Ḏât-Baʿdânum and by Šams of the king, Tanûf.

L. 1: *ʾṣḥḥl*, cf. Arabic *ʾaṣḥal* "who has a hoarse voice".

L. 9: *ntbʿn*, infinitive of the 8th form of *nbʿ*; cf. the Semitic root *nbʿ* "to spring, gush" [*nbʿn*, epithet of ʿAṯtar in RÉS 4194/5, cf. *JaP*, pp. 89-90 and note 260; contrast *vdBrDSAMW*, p. 186 and note 23] and the 8th form in Arabic "to burst out"; cf. the tribe name *nbʿt* in Ja 649/10.

e – Šaʿirum ʾAwtar

1° – ALONE: Ja 631-640

631 – Yellowish, slightly grayish sandstone; cf. Chapter I, A. – MaMB 213.

STONE: thickness: 29.7 cm. (top) and 28.5 (bottom). – *Top:* the left edge is splintered off; width: 22.8 cm., and depth: 5 cm. – *Front:* upper left corner broken; 1.338 m. (right), 1.288 (center), and 1.188 (left). – INSCRIPTION, same disposition of lines as in Ja 559; letter height: from 2.3 cm. to 2.4.; space between the lines: from 0.3 cm. to 0.4. – SYMBOL, cf. Ja 567, only four small strokes instead of six; it occupies the beginning of the first three lines, and not only of two, as in most of the cases.

1 **Sym-** *qṭbn/ʾwkn/bn/grt/ʾqwl/šʿ[bn/smhrm/yhwld/hqn]*
2 **bol** *yw/ʾlmqhw/ṯhwnbʿlʾwm/ṯny/ṣlm[n/ḏdhbm/ḥmdm]*
3 *lḏt/hwšʿ/ʿbdhw/qṭbn/ʾwkn/bn/grt[/wšʿb]*
4 *⌜hmw/smhrm/yhwld/bhrg/whbrwn/wṯbr/wḏrʿn/[w]*
5 *hsḥtn/bʿsm/tqdmt/tqdmw/wrtḏḥn/bʿm/ʾmlk/wʾ*
6 *šʿb/štʾw/ḍrm/bʿbr/mrʾhmw/šʿrm/ʾwtr/mlk/sb*
7 *[ʾ]/wḏrydn/bn/ḏbḥrm/wybsm/bkn/šwʿw/mrʾhmw/šʿ*
8 *rm/ʾwtr/mlk/sbʾ/wḏrydn/wbʿdw/whbʿln/whrg/w*
9 *sby/wġnm/wmtlyn/mhrgm/wsbym/wġnmm/ḏʿsm/bʿ*
10 *sm/sbʾt/šwʿw/mrʾhmw/šʿrm/ʾwtr/mlk/sbʾ/wḏry*
11 *dn/wbḏt/hwšʿ/ʿbdhw/qṭbn/ʾwkn/bn/grt/bkn/nb*
12 *lhw/mrʾhmw/šʿrm/ʾwtr/mlk/sbʾ/wḏrydn/ʿdy/ʾr*
13 *ḍ/ḥbšt/b(ʿ)br/gdrt/mlk/ḥbšt/wʾksmn/wtʾw*
14 *lw/bnhw/bwfym/hwʾ/wkl/šwʿhmw/wṯhbw/mrʾhmw/šʿ*
15 *rm/ʾwtr/mlk/sbʾ/wḏrydn/bkl/blthmw/ʿmn/ngšyn*
16 *mṯbt/ṣdqm/ḏhrḍw/mrʾhmw/bn/kl/ḏhbltw/wbḏt/h*
17 *wšʿ/ʾlmqhwṯhwnbʿlʾwm/ʿbdhw/qṭbn/ʾwkn/bn/g*
18 *rt/wšʿbhmw/smhrm/yhwld/bkn/sbʾw/whʿnn/qṭbn*
19 *ʾwkn/bn/grt/wšʿbhmw/smhrm/yhwld/bn/hgrn/nʿḍ*
20 *ʿdy/hgrn/ẓfr/ḥgn/hmlʾhmw/šymhmw/ʿṯtrʿzzn/bk*
21 *n/ʿdw/whṣrn/bygt/wld/ngšyn/wmṣr/ʾḥbšn/ʿdy/h*
22 *grn/ẓfr/wḫyrw/bḫlf/hgrn/ẓfr/wyfṣn/qṭbn/ʾwk*
23 *n/bn/grt/wšʿbhmw/smhrm/yhwld/ʿdy/hgrn/ẓfr/ʿbr*
24 *n/qtr/wʿd/bn/llyn/wʾḥbšn/yʿdwn/bnhmw/ʿbrn/ʿr*
25 *ʾln/wsṭ/hgrn/wʿdw/qṭbn/ʾwkn/bn/grt/wšʿbhmw/s*
26 *mhrm/yhwld/wyʾttmnn/bʿm/lʿzzm/yhnf/yhṣdq/mlk*
27 *sbʾ/wḏrydn/wʾqwl/wʾšʿb/ḏrydn/whrgw/wḏkwn/w*
28 *hsḥtn/ʾḥbšn/bn/wsṭ/hgrn/wltltm/ywmm/ybrrn*
29 *ḏbn/ḏmr/wmnśrt/ḫmsn/wḏbn/ʾšʿb/ḏrydn/wbʿww*
30 *bllyn/ḥyrt/ʾḥbšn/wyhrgn/bn/ʾḥbšn/ʾrbʿ/mʾ*
31 *nm/ʾsdm/bḍwʿm/wltltm/ywmm/fybrrn/qṭbn/ʾwkn*
32 *bn/grt/wšʿbhmw/smhrm/yhwld/wytśbbnn/bʿm/ʾḥb*
33 *šn/wbʿmhmw/bn/ndf/mʿfrm/wyhrgn/bn/ʾḥbšn/b*
34 *tśbbn/wgbʾw/bnhmw/ʾḥbšn/ḥyrthmw/wbʿd/ṯny*
35 *m/ywmm/ftʾwlw/ʾḥbšn/bn/ḫlf/ẓfr/gwʿm/wwrdw*
36 *mʿhrtn/wlwẓʾ/sʿdhmw/ʾlmqhw/ṯhwn/bʿlʾwm/ḥẓ*
37 *y/wrḍw/mrʾhmw/lḥyʿṯt/yrḫm/mlk/sbʾ/wḏr*
38 *ydn/wbry/ʾʾḏnm/wmqymtm/wlṯbr/wwḍʿ/wḍ(r)*
39 *ʿn/ḏrhmw/wšnʾhmw/wlsʿdhmw/ʾlmqhwṯhwn/bʿl*
40 *ʾwm/nʾd/qyẓ/wṣrb/ʿdy/ʾrḍhmw/wʾsrrhmw/wmq*
41 *yẓhmw/wsʿsʿm/wmlym/wlḫrynhmw/bn/nḍʿ/wšṣy*
42 *šnʾm/bʾlmqh⟨w⟩ṯhwnbʿlʾwm*

1 **Sym-** Qaṭbân ʾAwkân, descendant of Garat, rulers of [the] tri[be Sumhurâm Yuhawlid,] have [dedicat-]
2 **bol** ed to ʾIlumquhû Ṯahwân, master of ʾAwwâm, [these] two statues [which (are) in bronze, in praise]
3 because He has assisted His worshipper Qaṭbân ʾAwkân, descendant of Garat [and] their [tribe]
4 Sumhurâm Yuhawlid in killing and cutting and crushing and humbling [and]
5 destroying in the desirable attacks [with which] they assaulted and slew the kings and the
6 tribes [who] started war against their lord Šaʿirum ʾAwtar, king of Saba[ʾ]
7 and Raydân by sea and land when they assisted their lord Šaʿi-
8 rum ʾAwtar, king of Sabaʾ and Raydân; and they repelled and seized and killed and
9 captured and plundered and rejoiced with war trophy and captives and booty, which was desired, in the
10 desirable encounters [in which] they assisted their lord Šaʿirum ʾAwtar, king of Sabaʾ and Raydân; and because He has protected His worshipper
11 Qaṭbân ʾAwkân, descendant of Garat when sent
12 him their lord Šaʿirum ʾAwtar, king of Sabaʾ and Raydân, into the land of
13 the Ḥabašites against Gadarat, king of the Ḥabašites and of ʾAksûman; and they came
14 back from there in safety, he and all their train; and they have satisfied their lord Šaʿi-
15 rum ʾAwtar, king of Sabaʾ and Raydân, in all their military duties against the Neguš,
16 a perfect reward, which pleased their lord, from all that with which they have been endowed; and because
17 ʾIlumquhû Ṯahwân, master of ʾAwwâm, has assisted His worshipper Qaṭbân ʾAwkân, descendant of Ga-
18 rat and their tribe Sumhurâm Yuhawlid when were fighting and helping Qaṭbân
19 ʾAwkân, descendant of Garat and their tribe Sumhurâm Yuhawlid from the city [of] Naʿiḍ

20 to the city [of] Ẓafâr as their patron ^{c}Aṯtar ^{c}Azîzân had favored them, when

21 Baygat, the child of the Neguš and the expeditionary force of the Ḥabašites went forth and set out toward the ci-

22 ty [of] Ẓafâr; and they settled down in the region of the city [of] Ẓafâr; and then departed Qaṭbân ʾAwkân,

23 descendant of Garat and their tribe Sumhurâm Yuhawlid into the city [of] Ẓafâr into

24 Qatr Wa^{c}d during the night; and then the Ḥabašites went from them into the citadel

25 of the god in the center of the city; and went forth Qaṭbân ʾAwkân, descendant of Garat and their tribe Sum-

26 hurâm Yuhawlid and they then associated with Li^{c}azzum Yuhnaf Yuhaṣdiq, king of

27 Sabaʾ and Raydân, and with the rulers and the tribes of Raydân; and they killed and eradicated and

28 destroyed the Ḥabašites from the center of the city; and the third day came to an agreement

29 some of Ḍamâr and the cavalry squadron of the army and some of the tribes of Raydân and they betrayed,

30 the camp of the Ḥabašites during the night; and so they killed from the Ḥabašites four hun-

31 dred soldiers beheaded; and the third day came to an agreement Qaṭbân ʾAwkân,

32 descendant of Garat and their tribe Sumhurâm Yuhawlid and they then turned aside from the Ḥabašites

33 and from them in scattering [in] Ma^{c}âfirum; and so they killed [some] of the Ḥabašites by

34 turning aside; and the Ḥabašites returned from them to their encampment; and after the second

35 day the Ḥabašites [being] famished, withdrew from the region of Ẓafâr, and went down to

36 Ma^{c}âhiratân; and that ʾIlumquhû Ṯahwân, master of ʾAwwâm, may continue to make them happy with the esteem

37 and grace of their lord Laḥay^{c}aṯat Yarḫam, king of Sabaʾ and Ray-

38 dân and [with] the strength of understanding and of power; and that He may crush and humiliate and hum-

39 ble their foe and their enemy; and that may make them happy ʾIlumquhû Ṯahwân, master of

40 ʾAwwâm, with the magnificence of the fruits of summer and of autumn in their ground and their wâdî-side valleys and their summer

41 settlements and (with) the fruits of summer and of winter; and that He may preserve them from the hostility and wickedness of

42 [any] enemy. By ʾIlumquh⟨û⟩ Ṯahwân, master of ʾAwwâm.

L. 1: *qṭbn*, name of a palm grove in RÉS 3911/4. – *ʾqwl* is grammatically related to *grt*; note that all the verbs and pronouns are plural.

L. 2: the end is restored on the basis of Ja 610/4.

L. 3: the end is restored on the basis of lines 17-18.

L. 4: *yhwld*, new proper name from the root *wld*. – *hbrw* = *hbry* (Ja 616/20-21); cf. also the 10th form *stbrw* (Ja 649/17).

L. 6: *šṭʾw*, 2nd form; CIH 325/7 and *CoRoC*, p. 253; the translation "to blaze" (cf. *RyHE*, p. 235) is not correct; the 4th form *hšṭʾ* is attested in, e.g., Ja 577/13. – *š^{c}rm*, cf. the name of a house *mš^{c}rm* in Ja 832.

L. 8: *b^{c}dw*, CIH 380/4; cf. Arabic *ba^{c}uda* "to be distant, remote"; and 2nd form "remove, put away, repel".

L. 9: *ġnm*, verb; cf. the Thamudic active participle *ġnm* (cf. *vdBrIT*, p. 332: HU 657/2).

L. 13: *b*(^{c})*br*, *w* instead of ^{c} is certain on the stone. – *gdrt*, cf. the Arabic names of a man *al-ğadarat* and *al-ʾağdâr* (cf. *WüID*, 301/9 and 317/3 respectively).

L. 16: *mṯbt* means "rescrit, edict" (e.g., CIH 601/17 and RÉS 3306 A/7); here, cf. Arabic *maṯâbat*, *maṯûbat* "reward, compensation" (cf. *CoRoC*, p. 259). – *hbltw*, 4th form of *blt*, RÉS 4779/1; cf. commentary on Ja 560/8-9.

L. 20: *ẓfr*, cf. also the Arabic name of a person *ẓâfir* (cf. *SlGaVNPA*, p. 14 A), and of a clan *banû ẓafar* (cf. *WüID*, 187/4).

L. 21: *bygt/wld/ngšyn* is the perfect parallel *grmt/wld/ngšyn* (e.g., Ja 577/3), who is surely a person; for a more complete treatment of these two expressions, cf. *JaCRR*, pp. 11-12.

L. 22: *ḫyrw*, cf. commentary on Ja 576/12. – *yfṣn*, consecutive imperfect of *fyṣ*; cf. Arabic *fâṣa* (i) "to go away to a place".

L. 24: *qtr/w^{c}d*, probably name of a quarter of the city; cf. *qtrn*, tribe name in Ja 669/4; cf. also the Arabic names of men *qatîr*, *qitrat* (cf. *WüID*, 222/5 and 4 respectively) and of a clan *banû qutayrat* (cf. *WüID*, 222/4).

L. 25: *wsṭ* = *bwsṭ*, cf. commentary on Ja 567/5-6.

L. 26: *ʾttm*, 8th form of *ʾtm*; cf. commentary on Ja 575/5. – *l^{c}zzm*: name composed of *l* and *^{c}zzm*; for the latter, cf. *^{c}zzm* or *^{c}zzn*, determinative of ^{c}Aṯtar. – *yhnf*, e.g., RÉS 4665, where the transliteration indicates that *yhnf* is considered as derived from the 4th form of *nwf*; the root *hnf* is also possible; cf. Arabic *hanafa*, 2nd form "to hasten, hurry".

L. 27: *ḏkwn*, infinitive of *ḏkw*; cf. *CoRoC*, pp. 128-29

and commentary on *hḏkwt* in Ja 541/6; *ḏky* "to establish" is attested in *CIH* (references in *BeSI*, p. 103) and also in Muraygân/4, Ḥimâ/4 (*bᶜ[l]y* is not translated by *RyISA*, X, p. 287, who suggests, on pp. 290-91, the haplography of *ḏ* in *klḏky* instead of *klḏḏky*) and Kawkab 1/3 and 6. In the present text as well as in Ja 665/17 and 19, the preceding interpretation does not fit; I suggest relating *ḏkw* to Syriac *dkô* Pa "to cleanse, purify...purge out" (cf. *PaSmCSD*, p. 91 B).

L. 28: *brr*, cf. commentary on Ja 575/3.

L. 29: *bʾw*, cf. commentary on Ja 578/10. – *mnśrt*, cf. Arabic *mansir* and *minsar* "a portion of an army that goes before the main army" and "a troop of horse *or* horsemen" (cf. *LaAEL*, p. 2790 B). The second meaning seems preferable because of the existence of the term *mqdmt* (e.g., Ja 576/8).

L. 32: *ytśbbnn*, 5th form of *śb*; cf. Ugaritic *sb* "to turn" (cf. *GoUM*, p. 299 B: No. 1308) and Hebrew *sâbab* "to turn around, turn" and in hiphîl "to go off of one's way, turn away" (cf. *KoBaLVTL*, pp. 646-47).

L. 33: *ndf*, cf. Hebrew *nâdaf* "to drive away, scatter" (cf. *KoBaLVTL*, p. 597 B).

L. 35: *gwᶜ*, cf. Daṯînah *ğâyiᶜ* "qui a faim" (cf. *LaGD*, p. 311) and Arabic *ğâʾiᶜ*, from the verb *ğâᶜa* (o), "to be hungry, famished"; cf. also Ẓofâr "*jûᶜi* Hunger" (cf. *RhVDD*, p. 9 B) and Mehri "Hungern *jûya*" (cf. *JaMSSA*, p. 253 B).

L. 36: *mᶜhrtn*, name of a region; cf. the family or clan name *mᶜhrnhn* in CIH 378/1-2 (cf. *CIH*, II, p. 34 A).

Ll. 37-38: *lḥyᶜṯt/yrẖm/mlk/sbʾ/wḏrydn*: an unknown king; cf. *lḥyᶜṯt yrẖm* in RÉS 2633/1-2.

Ll. 38-39: *wwḍᶜ/wḍᶜᶜn*: *sic* on the stone (cf. my notebook); dittography of *wḍᶜ*; the second verb is *ḍrᶜ* (e.g., Ja 577/19).

L. 42: *ʾlmqh*: in the copy, instead of *ʾlmqhw*.

632 – Grayish sandstone. – MaMB 301.

STONE: constant thickness: 13.2 cm. – *Front:* covered with red paint; many places are splintered off; 48.3 cm. (top) and 46.4 (bottom) × 26 (left) and 25.5 (right). – INSCRIPTION: same disposition of lines as in Ja 552; letter height: 2.3 cm; space between the lines: 0.2 cm.; distance from line 1 to the upper edge: 0.6 cm. – SYMBOL, cf. Ja 565.

1 **Sym-** *ḥmᶜṯt/ʾrśl/bn/rʾbm/wmhqbm/bn/wzᶜn/ mqtwyy/ʾsdm/ʾsᶜd/b*
2 **bol** *n/sʾrn/wmḥylm/hqnyy/ʾlmqh/ṯhwn/bᶜlʾwm/ ʾrbᶜt/ʾṣlmm*
3 *wṯwrm/ḏḏhbm/bn/ġnmhmw/bn/šbwt/wbn/hgrn/qnʾ/ ḥmdm/b*
4 *ḏt/tʾwl/mrʾhmw/ʾsdm/ʾsᶜd/bn/sʾrn/bn/kl/sbʾt/sbʾ/ wšwᶜn*
5 *mrʾhmw/šᶜrm/ʾwtr/mlk/sbʾ/wḏrydn/bwfym/wʾḥllm/ wġn*
6 *mm/ḏhrḍw/lb/mrʾhmw/ʾsdm/ʾsᶜd/bn/sʾrn/wḥmdm/ bḏt/ẖ*
7 *mrhmy/ʾlmqhw/mhrgm/wġnmm/ḏhrḍwhmy/wḥmdm/ bḏt/hw*
8 *fyhw/ʾlmqh/bmsʾlhw/wlsᶜdhmy/ḥẓy/wrḍw/ mrʾhmy/ʾsdm*
9 *ʾsᶜd/bn/sʾrn/wlẖrynhmw/bn/nḍᶜ/wšṣy/šnʾm/bʾlmqh/ bᶜlʾwm*

1 **Sym-** Ḥammᶜaṯat ʾArśaf, son of Raʾabum and Muhqabbim, son of Wazaᶜân, military officials of ʾAsdum ʾAsᶜad, descendant of
2 **bol** Suʾrân and Miḥîlum, have dedicated to ʾIlumquh Ṯahwân, master of ʾAwwâm, four statues
3 and a bull which [are] in bronze, from their booty from Šabwat and from the city [of] Qanaʾ, in praise be-
4 cause their lord ʾAsdum ʾAsᶜad, descendant of Suʾrân has come back from all the encounters [in which] he fought and assisted
5 their lord Šaᶜirum ʾAwtar, king of Sabaʾ and Raydân, in safety and (with) animals and boo-
6 ty, which pleased the heart of their lord ʾAsdum ʾAsᶜad, descendant of Suʾrân, and in praise because
7 ʾIlumquhû has vouchsafed to them both war trophy and booty, which pleased them both; and in praise because
8 ʾIlumquh has saved him through His oracle; and that He may make them both happy with the esteem and grace of their lord ʾAsdum
9 ʾAsᶜad, descendant of Suʾrân; and that He may preserve them from the hostility and wickedness of [any] enemy. By ʾIlumquh, master of ʾAwwâm.

L. 1: *ʾrśl*, also 2nd masculine personal name in CIH 352/2. – *rʾbm*, e.g., Ja 248/1, Qat, and commentary; also in RÉS 5095/1; cf. also the names of men *rʾbᶜm* (e.g., Ja 867/1, Qat), *rʾbnᶜm* (RÉS 4214, Ḥaḍr) and *rʾbśl* (Ja 507 C). – *mhqbm*, cf. the *nisba* name *qbymyn* in Ja 493, monogram. Among names of either uncertain or unknown origin, *RyNP* (I, p. 281 B) mentions Safaitic *qbymt* in Vogüé 399 a; this text is CIS 1197 which is read *qrṣmt*, without mentioning *RyNP*'s reading. According to the drawing of Vogüé, the *y* is certain. In *qbm* I suspect a secondary form of the well-known root *qbl*. Cf. Thamudic personal name *mqbl* (cf. *vdBrIT*,

p. 316: Jsa 383). – *wzʿn*, cf. the Arabic names of men *bin wuzaʿ* (cf. *SlGaVNPA*, p. 43 B) and *al-wâziʿ* (cf. *WüID*, 253/3). *wzʿ* is a common noun, e.g., in Ja 660/14; cf. Arabic *wazaʿa* "to contain, incite" (RÉS 2895 A/4, Min). – *ʾsdm/ʾsʿd*, cf. Ja 581/1 which indicates a different person.

L. 3: *qnʾ*, cf. also the personal name *qnʾm* in RÉS 5032, Ḥaḍr (instead of *qrʾm*; note that *RyISA*, VI, p. 299, considers his reading as doubtful); for *qnʾ*, cf. *WiHöBGS*, pp. 89-93, and B. Doe, in *Le Muséon*, 74 (1961), pp. 191-98.

633 – Brownish sandstone. – MaMB 271.

STONE: thickness: 24 cm. (top) and 21.5 (bottom). – *Front:* upper corners broken; a large part of the right edge is splintered off; 39.7 cm. (top) and 39.5 (bottom). – INSCRIPTION: same disposition of lines as in Ja 552; letter height: 3.2 cm.; space between the lines: 0.4 cm.; distance from line 1 to the upper edge: 1.2 cm. – SYMBOL, upper half missing; for the lower part, cf. Ja 565.

1 **[Sym-** *ʾbkr]⌜b⌝/ʾḥrs/b⌜n⌝[/ʿblm]*
2 **bol** *wyḥmḏl/hqny/ʾlmqh/⌜ṯ⌝[hwn]*
3 *bʿlʾwm/ṣlmn/ḏḏhbn/ḥgn/w[q]*
4 *hhw/bmsʾlhw/lwfy/grbhw/wlh[ʿ]*
5 *nnhw/bn/ḥlẓ/ḥlẓ/ln/ḏʾtw/bn*
6 *mqmn/ḏlḥgm/bkn/blthw/mrʾh*
7 *w/lqdmn/wqwm/bʿm/ʾḥmrn/bʾbdt*
8 *m/ḏkwnw/byn/ẖmsnhn/wyḥlẓn*
9 *hwt/ḥlẓn/drm/bẖrfm/ʿdy/ḏt/t*
10 *fl/bʿm/ʾlmqh/wwqhhw/lḏt/hqny*
11 *tn/wlstʿnnhw/drm/bẖrfm/lʿbrhw*
12 *ln/tkwn/ḏt/hqnytn/wlʾẖr/wʾlm*
13 *qh/fšft/whʾmnn/wṣry/wtbšrn/⟨⟩*
14 *ʿbdhw/ʾbkrb/brbẖ/wḥyw/bn/hwt*
15 *ḥlẓn/ln/tkwn/ḏt/hqnytn/wlʾẖ*
16 *r/ln/wrẖ/ḏdnm/ḏẖrf/ʾbkrb/bn*
17 *[mʿ]dkrb/bn/fḍḥm/wlẖmrhw/ʾlmqh*
18 *ḥẓy/mrʾhw/šʿrm/ʾwtr/mlk/s*
19 *bʾ/wḏrydn/bn/ʿlhn/nhfn/mlk*
20 *sbʾ/wlẖrynhw/ʾlmqh/bn/nḍʿ*
21 *wšṣy/šnʾm/bʾlmqh/bʿlʾwm*

1 **[Sym-** ʾAbkar]ib ʾAḥras, descendant of [ʿAblum]
2 **bol** and Yaḥamḏil, has dedicated to ʾIlumquh Ṯa[hwân,]
3 master of ʾAwwâm, this statue which [is] in bronze, as He has or[der-]
4 ed him through His oracle for the protection of his person and because He has [hel]ped
5 him from the oppression [by which] he was overwhelmed until he came back from
6 the place of Laḥgum when his lord charged him
7 with the supervision and care of the Ḥimyarites [who lived] in permanent dwellings
8 [and] who were between the two armies; and he had been overwhelmed by
9 this oppression once a year until he turn-
10 ed to ʾIlumquh; and He ordered to him to [make] this offering
11 and to ask Him for help once a year for himself
12 until he made this offering and the other [things]; and as for ʾIlum-
13 quh, He has granted and protected and guarded and announced
14 to His servant ʾAbkarib for release and life from this
15 oppression as soon as he made this offering and the other [things],
16 from the month of Dînum of the year of ʾAbkarib son of
17 [Maʿa]dkarib, descendant of Faḍḥum; and that ʾIlumquh may vouchsafe to him
18 the esteem of his lord Šaʿirum ʾAwtar, king of Sa-
19 baʾ and Raydân, son of ʿAlhân Nahfân, king of
20 Sabaʾ; and that ʾIlumquh may preserve him from the hostility
21 and wickedness of [any] enemy. By ʾIlumquh, master of ʾAwwâm.

L. 1: *ʾbkrb* is restored on the basis of line 14, *ʾbkrb/ʾḥrs*, RÉS 4143/1; *ʾḥrs* is also second personal name in RÉS 4962/10; cf. also the Arabic personal name *ʾaḥris* (cf. *SlGaVNPA*, pp. 3 B and 6 B).

L. 2: *yḥmḏl*, cf. the personal names *ḏl* in Safaitic (cf. *LiSI*, p. 308 B) and *hḏl* in Thamudic (cf. *vdBrIT*, pp. 372-73; HU 592); *ḏ* may possibly be a mistake for *ʾ* (*yḥmʾl* in Ja 707/2).

L. 6: *lḥgm*, cf. Arabic *lḥǧ*, name of place and clan, and personal name *al-laḥǧî* (cf. *WüR*, pp. 190 B, 257 B, and 626, respectively).

L. 7: *qdm*, 1st form "to be at the head of" (e.g., CIH 309/4). – *qwm*, 2nd form "to direct" or "to erect" (e.g., Ja 538/2 and *JaSAI*, pp. 506-07, No. 2); here "to take care of".

Ll. 7-8: *bʾbdtm*, cf. Arabic *ʾabada* "to remain, abide, dwell permanently" (cf. *LaAEL*, p. 4 A).

L. 9: *drm/bẖrfm*, e.g., CIH 392/8.

Ll. 9-10: *tfl*, cf. commentary on Ja 576/6; *tfl/bʿm*, as in Ja 718/8, "to turn to".

L. 11: *stʿnn*, 10th form of *ʿwn*, RÉS 3710/2, Min, "to ask for help".

L. 12: *ln/tkwn/– –/wlʾẖr*, cf. *bnkn/lʾẖr* in RÉS 3566/11, Qat, and *bnhw/wlʾẖr* in CIH 99/8; cf. the Western Semitic cognates of *ʾẖr* in *JeHoDISO*, p. 10: *ʾḥr* III.

L. 13: *hʾmnn*, RÉS 3960/2 "to confide to, trust"; the 4th form also means "to shelter, protect". – The end of the line mentions *w*; this letter is superfluous, and may be explained either as introducing a verb which has not been engraved, or as a mechanical repetition of the three preceding *w*, or even as a dittography of ʿ in *ʿbdhw*.

L. 14: *rbẖ/wḥyw*, cf. CIH 544/4-5; in both texts these two terms are nouns and not verbs (cf. *CIH*, *CoRoC*, p. 236 A and *BeSI*, p. 111 for *ḥyw* and p. 146 for *rbẖ*). *CIH* (I, p. 33 B) relates *rbẖ* to Arabic *rbẖ* which indicates the idea of "rest" (cf. also *RoVSAY*, p. 311: "riposare sulle ginocchia"); for *rbẖ*, cf. *LaH*, pp. 249-50 "to be soft, slack"; the examples quoted by the preceding author attest the meaning "to relax, be unbent, release the pressure"; this meaning fits the present text: ʾIlumquh has granted both the release from the oppression and life; for the Western Semitic cognates of *ḥyw*, cf. *JeHoDISO*, p. 86: *ḥy*II.

L. 16: *wrẖ/ḏdnm*, CIH 555/8.

L. 17: [*mʿ*]*dkrb*, cf. Fakhry 71/14.

634 – Yellowish sandstone; photograph of the right side with Ja 644. – MaMB 273.

STONE: thickness: 45.9 cm. – *Front:* 28.7 cm. × 48.9. – INSCRIPTION: letter height: 3 cm.; space between the lines: 0.6 cm.; distance between line 1 and the upper edge: 1 cm. – SYMBOL, cf. Ja 603.

1 **Sym-** *šrḥm/bn/ẖḏwt/wrg*
2 **bol** *lm/hqny/ʾlmqhw/ṯ*
3 *hwn/bʿl/ʾwm/ḏn/ṣlmn/b*
4 *n/ġnmhmw/bn/hgrn/qryt*
5 *m/ḏt/khlm/lsʿdhmw/ʾlm*
6 *qhw/ḥẓy/wrḍw/mrʾhmw/šʿ*
7 *rm/ʾwtr/mlk/sbʾ/wḏry*
8 *dn/bn/ʿlhn/nhfn/mlk/*
9 *sbʾ/wl/sʿdhmw/nʿmtm/*
10 *wwfym/wl/hʿnnhmw*
11 *bn/bʾstm/bʾlmqh*

1 **Sym-** Šarḥum, descendant of [the families] Ḫaḏwat and Rig-
2 **bol** lum, has dedicated to ʾIlumquhû Ṯa-
3 hwân, master of ʾAwwâm, this statue from
4 their booty from the city [of] Qaryat-
5 um, that of Kahilum, in order that ʾIlumquhû may make them
6 happy with the esteem and grace of their lord Šaʿi-
7 rum ʾAwtar, king of Sabaʾ and Ray-
8 dân, son of ʿAlhân Nahfân, king of
9 Sabaʾ; and that He may make them happy with prosperity
10 and safety; and that He may protect them
11 from misfortunes. By ʾIlumquh.

L. 1: *šrḥm*, e.g., Ja 863/1, Qat, and commentary; cf. also the diminutive Sab personal name *šryḥm* (cf. *RyGSAS*, p. 561). – *ẖḏwt*, family name, e.g., in RÉS 4151/2 and Ja 511/1; cf. also the clan name *ẖḏwtn*, e.g., in RÉS 4368, and the name of a man *ẖḏwm* in Ja 757 bis/1-2.

Ll. 1-2: *rglm*, probably clan name in CIH 600/1 (cf. *CIH*, III, p. 9 A); cf. also the clan names *rglt* in CIH 256/2, and *rgl* (cf. *RyGSAS*, p. 560: *ḏrgl*).

Ll. 4-5: *qrytm* is indicated by the present text as belonging to the tribe Kahilum; cp. *qrytnhn*, a city in the Wâdî Ḥarîb (Ja 649/26) and the masculine name *qryt* in RÉS 4908/2, Ḥaḍr.

Ll. 10-11: *hʿnnhmw/bn/bʾstm*: the verb *ẖry* is more often mentioned with *bʾst* than *hʿn*.

635 – Brownish sandstone. – MaMB 270.

STONE: thickness: 19.8 cm. (left), 23.5 (right) and 30 (top center). – *Front:* upper and lower right corners badly broken; the center of the right edge is splintered off; 35.7 cm. (top) and 35.5 (bottom). – INSCRIPTION: letter height: 3.1 cm., and space between the lines: 0.3 cm.

1 [**Sym-** *ʾbkrb/ʾ*]⌜*ḥrs/bn/ʿblm/*
2 [**bol** *wyḥmḏl*]*/hqny/ʾlmqh/ṯ*
3 *hwn/bʿl/ʾwm/ṣlmn/ḏḏhbn/ḏ*
4 *tmly/bn/qrytm/wṭnfm/ṭyb*
5 *m/ḥmdm/bḏt/ẖmr/whwšʿn/mr*
6 *ʾhmw/šʿrm/ʾwtr/mlk/sbʾ/w*
7 *ḏṛydn/bn/ʿlhn/nhfn/mlk/s*
8 *bʾ/btʾwln/bwfym/wbrytm*
9 *wḥmdm/bnkl/sbʾt/wḍbyʾ*
10 *sbʾw/wḍbʾ/wmṭw/whʿnn/bʿly/*
11 *kl/ʾẖms/wšʿb/tnšʾw/ḍrm/bʿ*
12 *ly/mrʾhmw/bn/ḏymnt/wbn/ḏšʾ*
13 *mt/wbn/ḏbḥrm/wybsm/wbḏt*
14 *yzʾn/ʾlmqh/ṯbr/wwḍʿ/wḍrʿ*
15 *n/whkmsn/kl/ḍr/wšnʾ/mrʾhm*
16 *w/wḥmdm/bḏt/ẖmr/whwšʿn/ʾlm*
17 *qh/ʿbdhw/ʾbkrb/ʾḥrs/bn/ʿbl*
18 *m/btʾwln/bwfym/wġnmm/wʾḥ*
19 *llm/wsbym/bn/kl/ʾbrṯ/wḍb*
20 *yʾ/wʿnt/sbʾw/wšwʿn/mrʾhmw/šʿr*
21 *m/ʾwtr/mlk/sbʾ/wḏrydn/ʿdy/s*
22 *hrtm/bʿly/ʾšʿrn/wbḥrm/wḏkw*

23 *[n/k]wnhmw/wᶜdy/ẖlf/hgrn/ngrn*
24 *[bᶜl]y/ḍbᵓt/ᵓḥbšn/wḏkwn/kw*
25 *nhmw/wᶜdy/hgrn/qrytm/ḏt/khl*
26 *m/ṯty/ḍbᵓtn/bᶜly/rbᶜt/ḏᵓl*
27 *ṯwrm/mlk/kdt/wqḥṭn/wbᶜly*
28 *ᵓbᶜl/hgrn/qrytm/wḥmdm/b*
29 *ḏt/ẖmr/ᵓlmqh/ᶜbdhw/ᵓbkrb*
30 *btᵓwln/bᵓḥllm/wsbym/wml*
31 *tm/wġnmm/wᵓfrsm/ḏhrgw/wḏᵓẖḏ*
32 *w/ḥym/bkl/ysrhw/mrᵓhw/lsbᵓ*
33 *wqtdmn/ḏbn/ẖwln/ẖḍlm/wḏb*
34 *n/ngrn/wḏbn/ᵓᶜrbn/lḥrb/ᶜš*
35 *[r]t/yḥbr/ᵓsd/kwnw/kwn/bny/yw*
36 *[n]m/wqrytm/wyḥrbhmw/bknf/ᵓrḍ*
37 *ᵓlᵓsd/mgzt/mwnhn/ḏṯml/wyt*
38 *ᵓwl/kl/gyšhmw/bwfym/bn/hwt/b*
39 *rṯn/wḥmdm/⟨⟩bḏt/ẖmr/ᵓlmqh*
40 *ᶜbdhw/ḥẓy/wrḍw/mrᵓhw/šᶜrm/ᵓw*
41 *tr/mlk/sbᵓ/wḏrydn/wbḏt/yzᵓ*
42 *n/ᵓlmqh/ṯhwn/ẖmr/ᶜbdhw/ᶜsm/ᵓḥ*
43 *⟨⟩llm/wᵓẖḏtm/ᵓbrṯ/yzᵓn/šwᶜn*
44 *mrᵓhw/wlẖrynhw/ᵓlmqh/bn*
45 *nḍᶜ/wšṣy/wtṯᶜt/wᶜbṭt/wkf*
46 *⸢ḥ⸣/šnᵓm/bᵓlmqh/bᶜlᵓwm*

1 **[Sym-** ᵓAbkarib ᵓA]ḥras, descendant of ᶜAblum
2 **[bol** and Yaḥamḏil] has dedicated to ᵓIlumquh Ṯa-
3 hwân, master of ᵓAwwâm, this statue which [is] in bronze, which
4 he enjoyed from [the sale of] excellent *qârit*-musk and *ṭanuf*,
5 in praise because He has vouchsafed and helped their
6 lord Šaᶜirum ᵓAwtar, king of Sabaᵓ and
7 Raydân, son of ᶜAlhân Nahfân, king of Sa-
8 baᵓ, in coming back in safety and (with) strength
9 and praise from all the encounters and the engagements [which]
10 they have fought and combatted and [in which] they have taken part and given aid against
11 all the armies and the tribes [which] raised up war against
12 their lord from south and from north
13 and from sea and land; and that
14 ᵓIlumquh may continue to crush and humiliate and humble
15 and wither every foe and enemy of their lord;
16 and in praise because ᵓIlumquh has vouchsafed and assisted
17 His worshipper ᵓAbkarib ᵓAḥras, descendant of ᶜAblum
18 in coming back in safety and (with) booty and
19 animals and captives from all the military campaigns and engagements
20 and the auxiliary operation [in which] they fought and assisted their lord Šaᶜirum
21 ᵓAwtar, king of Sabaᵓ and Raydân, in Sa-
22 haratum against ᵓAšᶜarân and Baḥrum and those who
23 [w]ere with them, as well as in the region of the city [of] Nagrân
24 [agai]nst the fighting men of the Ḥabašites and those who were
25 with them, and [also] in the city [of] Qaryatum, that of Kahilum,
26 [during] the two engagements against Rabîᶜat, him of ᵓIl-
27 ṯawrum, king of Kindat and Qaḥṭân, and [also] against
28 the masters of the city [of] Qaryatum; and in praise be-
29 cause ᵓIlumquh has vouchsafed to His worshipper ᵓAbkarib
30 to come back with animals and captives and riches
31 and booty and horses which they took away and which they captured
32 alive, everywhere his lord has sent him to fight
33 and to take command of some of Ḫawlân Ḫaḍlum and some
34 of Nagrân and some of the Arabs in order to fight the
35 groups [which] have seduced those [who] were the descendants of Yaw-
36 [ân]um and of Qaryatum; and he fought them at the border of the land of
37 ᵓIlᵓasad Magûzat Mawnahân, him of Ṯimâl; and came
38 back all their troop in safety from this
39 campaign; and in praise because ᵓIlumquh has vouchsafed to
40 His worshipper the esteem and grace of his lord Šaᶜirum ᵓAw-
41 tar, king of Sabaᵓ and Raydân; and that may continue
42 ᵓIlumquh Ṯahwân, to vouchsafe to His worshipper desirable
43 animals and prisoners [in (all)] the military campaigns [in which] he will continue to assist
44 his lord; and that ᵓIlumquh may preserve him from
45 the hostility and wickedness and fear and calamities and unexpected attack
46 of [any] enemy. By ᵓIlumquh, master of ᵓAwwâm.

Ll. 1-2; cf. Ja 633/1-2.

Ll. 4-5: *qrytm/wṭnfm/ṭybm*: *qrytm* is also mentioned in lines 28 and 36, but is preceded in the 1st citation by the noun *hgr* "city"; here, *qryt* is a noun; cf. Arabic *qârit* and *qârrât* "excellent musk" and also *qarrât* (cf. *DoSDA*, II, p. 324 B) and *qârit* "light and of higher quality (musk)". *ṭnf*, cf. Arabic *ṭanaf* "a kind of red tree" (cf. *LaAEL*, p. 1886 A). For *ṭyb*, cf. *CoRoC*, p. 159 B and *StSESA*, p. 516. *tmly/--/ṭybm* means that the author of the text was happy to get the statue through the means collected by selling excellent musk and *ṭanuf*; for *ṭyb*, cf. the Western Semitic cognates in *JeHoDISO*, pp. 98-99: *ṭb*.

L. 10: *ḏbʾ/wmṭw*, cf. *mṭww/wḏbʾ* in CIH 397/9 (cf. *CIH*, II, p. 57 A); cf. Arabic *mṭw*, 2nd form "to extend, stretch" (cf. *DoSDA*, II, p. 601 A), post-biblical Hebrew *mĕṭâ* and Aramaic *mĕṭê* and *mĕṭâ* "to stretch, reach, to arrive at; to obtain" (cf. *KoBaLVTL*, pp. 1092-93 and *JaDT*, p. 767 A respectively), and Syriac *mṭô* "to come, arrive at, reach" (cf. *PaSmCSD*, p. 266 A). *CIH* (II, p. 58) translates it, "to reach"; the present context suggests the meaning "to take part".

L. 22: *ʾšʿrn*, cf. Arabic *ʾaš-šaʿr*, name of a place (cf. *WüR*, p. 13 C), of a clan (cf. *l.c.*, p. 238 A) and of a man (cf. *GoAT*, p. 43), the clan name *banû š-šaʿr* (cf. *GoAT*, *l.c.* and *SaIS*, p. 13 B), the names of men *ʾibn* or *ʾabû š-šaʿr* (cf. *GoAT*, *l.c.*), *bin-šâʿir* (cf. *SlGaVNPA*, p. 12 A) and *ʾaš-šaʿrûn* (cf. *SaIS*, p. 14 A), of a person *šaʿrân* (cf. *SlGaVNPA*, *l.c.*) and the *nisba* forms *ʾaš-šaʿrîy*, *ʾaš-šaʿrîyûn* (cf. *SaIS*, *l.c.* and *GoAT*, *l.c.*) and *ʾaš-šaʿrîyat* (cf. *SaIS*, *l.c.*). – *bḥrm*, also clan name, e.g., in RÉS 4248 (cf. *JaSAA*, p. 153 B); cf. also the names of men *bḥrm* (Ja 302, Qat) and *ybḥrʾl* (RÉS 4813/1) and of a family *bḥrn* in RÉS 4606, contrary to G. Ryckmans (cf. *Le Muséon*, 66 [1953], p. 124), who accepts H. Grimme's reading (*b*+*ḥrn*) after having rejected it in *RÉS* (VII, p. 272).

L. 26: *ṯty*, contracted form of *ṯnty* (feminine); cf. *HöASG*, p. 131, §111 b.

Ll. 26-27: *rbʿt/ḏʾlṯwrm/mlk/kdt/wqḥṭn*; *rbʿt*, masculine personal name, e.g., in RÉS 4842/8; *ʾlṯwrm*; this family name does not prove the identity of the god ʾIl with the moon god Ṯawrum for *ʾl* is a noun and not a proper name (cf., e.g., *JaP*, p. 114); *qḥṭn*, copied as *qḥṭʾn* in the spurious inscription RÉS 4304/2; name of a tribe and of a city between Zabîd and Ṣanʿâʾ (cf. *Encyclopédie de l'Islam*, II, pp. 669-71), which still exists at the present time, located north of Ḫawlân (cf. *PhAHL*, e.g., p. 109 and separated map).

L. 32: *ḥym*, cf. *ḥywn* in RÉS 3610/13, Min; *ḥym* (cf. the Western Semitic cognates in *JeHoDISO*, p. 86: *ḥy*I): *ḥâyum*, parallel form to Arabic active participle *bâlin*.

L. 33: *qtdm*: 8th form of *qdm*; e.g., *CoRoC*, p. 229 A. – *ḫḏlm*, cf. Min proper name *ḫḏln* in RÉS 3054.

L. 35: *yḥbr*, cf. the noun *ḥbr* in RÉS 4230/11 (cf. *JaASAB*, p. 189, commentary); the present verb may be translated "to seduce, deceive"; cf. the form *nḥbr* in Ja 702/3.

Ll. 35-36: *yw*[*n*]*m*, probably a Greek colony; already mentioned in Gl 967 (cf. *MlHLM*, pp. 35-36, and *JaSAI*, p. 508 B, introduction to No. 9).

L. 36: *knf*, CIH 407/22 and *CoRoC*, p. 170 A.

L. 37: *ʾlʾsd*: *ʾsd* is frequently used both in simple and theophoric proper names, e.g., *ʾsdm* (Ja 580/10) and *ʾsdkrb* (Ja 842/1-2). – *mgzt*, from the root *gwz*; cf. verb in Ja 711/11 and the Arabic names of a man *miǧûz*, of a woman *miǧûzat* (cf. *VNIA*, p. 270 A), and of a person *ǧûzat* (cf. *SlGaVNPA*, p. 18 A). – *mwnhn*, same nominal formation as that, e.g., of *ʿhrnhn* (CIH 37/8) and *ʾrbʿnhn* (Ja 556; cf. commentary); for *mw* "water", cf. Ja 750/7; there is no reason to believe that *h* is a mistake for *y* (cf. *mwnyn* in RÉS 3951/7). – *ṯml*, personal names *ṯml* in Thamudic (cf. *HaLiSTI*, p. 12, No. 33) and *ṯamâl* in Arabic (cf. *GoAT*, p. 91); cf. also the Arabic clan names *ṯamâlat* (cf. *GoAT*, *l.c.*), *banû ṯumâlat* and *banû m-muṯammalat* (cf. *WüID*, 288/20 and 219/12 respectively).

L. 39: *wbḏt*: *sic* in the copy.

L. 42: *ḫmr*/–/*ʿsm*, e.g., CIH 397/10-12.

Ll. 42-43: *ʾḥḥllm*: two *ḥ* by dittography; same division of the noun as in lines 18-19.

L. 43: before *ʾbrṯ*, an expression like *bn*[/*kl*] would be expected; cf. line 19.

Ll. 45-46: *kf*.(.)/*šnʾm*: according to my notebook, the word divider is preceded, at the beginning of line 46, by either two narrow letters or only a wide one, and the upper left part of the letter immediately on the right of that word divider is a vertical stroke. The preceding remark excludes the restoration of *kl* "every", which may introduce *šnʾ* (Ja 651/53) in an enumeration such as the one in line 45. The letter *ḥ* meets the first requirement pointed out by my notebook. I therefore suggest reading *kfḥ*; cf. Arabic *kafaḥa* "to meet, encounter, face to face, suddenly, *or* unexpectedly" (cf. *LaAEL*, p. 2619 C).

636 – Lower part of an inscription; yellowish, slightly grayish sandstone. – MaMB 245.

STONE: thickness: 14.3 cm. (top) and 14 (bottom). – *Front:* covered with red paint; 47.8 cm. (right) and 48.4 (left) × 22.2. – INSCRIPTION: same disposition of lines as in Ja 552; letter height: from 1.7 cm. to 2; space between the lines: from 0.4 cm. to 0.5.

1 *....⸢t⸣.mᶜ....⸢hg⸣rn/šbwt[/b]*
2 *kn/šwᶜw/mrʾhmw/šᶜrm/ʾw*
3 *tr/mlk/sbʾ/wḏrydn/bn/ᶜ*
4 *lhn/nhfn/mlk/sbʾ/wbkn*
5 *ḍbʾ/ḥḍrmt/ḥmdm/bḏt/t*
6 *ʾwl/mrʾhmw/bn/hnt/ḍbʾ*
7 *tn/bwfym/ᶜdy/hgrn/mryb*
8 *wḥmdm/bḏt/ẖmrhmw/ʾlm*
9 *qh/ʾḥllm/wsbym/wġnmm/*
10 *ḏhrḍwhmw/wlsᶜdhmw/ḥ*
11 *ẓy/wrḍw/mrʾhmw/šᶜrm/ʾ*
12 *wtr/mlk/sbʾ/wḏrydn/bn*
13 *ᶜlhn/nhfn/mlk/sbʾ/wḥ*
14 *mdm/bḏt/ẖmrhmw/wldm/ḏ*
15 *krm/wl/wzʾ/ẖmrhmw/ʾwld*
16 *m/ʾḏkrm/hnʾm/wl/ẖrynh*
17 *mw/ʾlmqh/bn/nḍᶜ/wšṣy/š*
18 *nʾm/wbn/kl/tlftm/bʾl*
19 *mqhwṯhwnbᶜlʾwm*

1 [... ...] the city [of] Šabwat
2 when they have assisted their lord Šaᶜirum ʾAw-
3 tar, king of Sabaʾ and Raydân, son of ᶜA-
4 lhân Nahfân, king of Sabaʾ, and when
5 he fought Ḥaḍramawt, in praise because
6 their lord has come back from these engagements
7 in safety to the city [of] Mârib;
8 and in praise because ʾIlumquh has vouchsafed to them
9 animals and captives and booty
10 which pleased them; and that He may make them happy with the es-
11 teem and grace of their lord Šaᶜirum ʾA-
12 wtar, king of Sabaʾ and Raydân, son of
13 ᶜAlhân Nahfân, king of Sabaʾ; and in
14 praise because He has vouchsafed to them a male
15 child; and that He may vouchsafe to them children
16 male, pleasing; and that may preserve
17 them ʾIlumquh from the hostility and wickedness of [any] e-
18 nemy, and from all ruin. By ʾIl-
19 umquhû Ṯahwân, master of ʾAwwâm.

637 – Upper part of an inscription; yellowish sandstone; photograph (cf. Plate 14) and latex squeeze. – MaMB 60.

STONE: thickness: 34.1 cm. – *Front:* 28.2 cm. × 18. – INSCRIPTION: same disposition of lines as in Ja 559; letter height: 2.7 cm.; space between the lines: 0.4 cm.; distance from line 1 to the upper edge: 0.6 cm. – SYMBOL, cf. Ja 619; cf. Plate A.

1 **Sym-** *ẓbnm/ʾṯqf/bn/ḥlḥ⸣*
2 **bol** *lm/hqny/ʾlmqh/ṯhw*
3 *n/bᶜlʾwm/ṣlmn/ḏḏhb*
4 *n/bn/ġnmhmw/bn/hgrn/š*
5 *⌊bwt/bkn/šwᶜw/mrʾhmw*
6 *⌊š⌋[ᶜ]⌊rm/ʾwtr/mlk/sbʾ/[w]⌊ḏ⌋*
[7 *rydn/bn/ᶜlhn/nhfn/ml]*
[8 *k/sbʾ/...*

1 **Sym-** Ẓabnum ʾAṯqaf, descendant of Ḥalḥa-
2 **bol** lum, has dedicated to ʾIlumquh Ṯahw-
3 ân, master of ʾAwwâm, this statue which [is] in bronze,
4 from their booty from the city [of] Ša-
5 bwat when they assisted their lord
6 Ša[ᶜi]rum ʾAwtar, king of Sabaʾ [and]
[7 Raydân, son of ᶜAlhân Nahfân, king]
[8 of Sabaʾ,...

Palaeography disproves any connection between this inscribed stone and Ja 638.

L. 1: *ẓbnm*, the root *ẓbn* is attested in the second personal name *yhẓbn* (CIH 41/1).
L. 5: *šwᶜw*: agreement *ad sensum* with both *ẓbnm* and the tribe *ḥlḥlm*.

638 – Lower left corner of an inscription; yellowish sandstone; re-cut on the right side; photograph in Plate 14. – MaMB 128.

STONE: thickness: 18 cm. (top) and 16.7 (bottom). – *Front:* covered with cement, proof that this stone had been re-used in a wall; the cement was removed in order to assure the reading of the text; the left side is intact; 11.9 cm. (top) and 11 (bottom) × 26.2 (right) and 24.4 (left). – INSCRIPTION: same disposition of lines as in Ja 552; letter height: 2.5 cm.; space between the lines: 0.4 cm.

1 *...]m[...*
2 *mrʾhmw/šᶜrm/]⸢ʾ⌊wtr/mlk/sb*
3 *ʾ/wḏrydn/bn/ᶜ]lhn/nhfn/ml*
4 *k/sbʾ/wl/ẖry]⌊nhmw/bn/nḍᶜ*
5 *wšṣy/šnʾm/bʾ]lmqh/bᶜlʾwm*

1 ....
2 [their lord Šaᶜirum] ʾAwtar, king of Sab-

3 [aʾ and Raydân, son of ʿA]lhân Nahfân, kin[g]
4 [of Sabaʾ; and that He may preserve] them from the hostility
5 [and wickedness of (any) enemy. By ʾI]lumquh, master of ʾAwwâm.

Cf. the beginning of the commentary on Ja 637 and 792.

639 – Upper right corner of an inscribed yellowish sandstone plaque; photograph in Plate 14. – MaMB 117.

PLAQUE: thickness: top: 6.5 cm. (left) and 7 (right); bottom: 6.7 cm. (left) and 7.3 (right). – *Front:* covered with red paint; slightly damaged on the right; 8.2 cm. (top) and 8.7 (bottom) × 11.9 (right) and 12.2 (left). – INSCRIPTION: same disposition of lines as in Ja 561 bis; letter height: 1.9 cm; space between the lines: 0.4 cm. – SYMBOL, cf. Ja 587, but two small lines instead of the one inside line; cf. Plate A.

1 **Sym-** *ġyln*⌋[...
2 **bol** *bn/ġ.*[... ...*mrʾhw*]
3 *šʿrm/ʾwtr*[/... .../*bkn*]
4 *hbʿl/wqm*⌋[ʿ... ...*mrʾ*]
5 *hw/šʿrm/b*[*n*/...

1 **Sym-** Ġaylân [... ...]
2 **bol** of Ġ.[... ...his lord]
3 Šaʿirum ʾAwtar[... ..., when]
4 he seized and subjuga[ted... ..] his [lord]
5 Šaʿirum fr[om...

L. 1: *ġyln*, very well-known name of a man also in Arabic (cf. *WüID*, e.g., 116/5); cf. also family name in Ja 536 and *wdyġl* in Ja 549.

L. 2: *ġ*[....]: from the second letter only the lower half of a vertical stroke remains; this is too close to *ġ* to belong to *y*.

L. 3: because the actual length of the lines remains unknown, it is impossible to prefer any one of the four titulatures of Šaʿirum, namely Ja 631/6-7, 633/18-20, 640/8-9, or 641/12-14.

640 – Lower part of an inscription; yellowish, slightly grayish sandstone; fragmentary on the left side. – MaMB 250.

STONE: constant thickness: 10 cm. – *Front:* 30.6 cm. (right) and 29 (left) × 24.1 (top) and 20.2 (bottom). – INSCRIPTION: slightly damaged; letter height: from 2 cm. to 2.1; space between the lines: 0.5 cm. and 0.6; distance from line 9 to the bottom: 9.3 cm. (right) and 9.6 (left).

1 [... .../*bn/ġnmh*]
2 ⌊*mw/bn/hgrn/*⌈ʾ⌉*wsrn/ḏt*[/... .../*y*]
3 *wm/šwʿ*[*w*]*/mrʾhmw/š*[ʿ]*rm/ʾwtr/mlk*[*/sb*]
4 *ʾ/wḏrydn/ywm/ḍbʾ/lhʿnn/wnṣr/*[*ʾlʿ*]
5 *z/mlk/ḥḍrmt/bʿly/ʾšʿb/ḥḍrm*[*t/wḥ*]
6 *mdw/bḏt/ẖmrhmw/ʾlmqh/mhrg/w*(*s*)[*by/ṣ*]
7 *dqm/wlsʿdhmw/ʾlmqh/ḥẓy/wrḍw/m*⌋[*rʾ*]
8 *hmw/šʿrm/ʾwtr/mlk/sbʾ/wḏrydn/w*[*ʾẖyh*]
9 *w/ḥywʿṯtr/yḍʿ/wlẖrynhmw/ʾlm*[*qh/b*]
10 *n/bʾstm/wšṣy/šnʾm/bʾ*[*lmqh*]

1 [... ...from th]eir [booty]
2 from the city [of] ʾAwsarân, that of [...
3 [w]hen [they] assisted their lord Ša[ʿi]rum ʾAwtar, king of [Sab]aʾ
4 and Raydân, when he fought in order to help and assist [ʾIlʿa]zz,
5 king of Ḥaḍramawt, against the tribes of Ḥaḍramaw[t, and]
6 they have [pr]aised because ʾIlumquh has vouchsafed to them war trophy and (cap)[tives]
7 [per]fect; and that ʾIlumquh may make them happy with the esteem and grace of their lo[rd]
8 Šaʿirum ʾAwtar, king of Sabaʾ and Raydân and [hi]s [brother]
9 Ḥayûʿaṯtar Yaḍiʿ; and that ʾIlum[quh] may preserve them [fr]om
10 misfortunes and the wickedness of [any] enemy. By ʾI[lumquh.]

Ll. 1-2: cf. Ja 632/3.

L. 2: *ʾwsrn*, *qawtalân* form from the root *ʾsr*; cf. the Safaitic personal name *ʾsr* (cf. *LiSI*, p. 299 B) and the Arabic proper names *al-ʾaysar* (cf. *WüR*, p. 23 A) and *ʾumm al-ʾaysar* (cf. *SaIS*, p. 21 A); *ʾwsrn/ḏt*, cf. *qrytm/ḏt/khlm* in Ja 634/4-5.

L. 4: *šʿrm* is subject of *ḍbʾ*.

Ll. 4-5: the restoration of *ʾlʿz* gives 31 signs to line 4; cf. the same number of signs in both lines 3 and 7; *ʾlʿz*, same nominal formation, e.g., as *ʿlʿz* which must be read instead of *bʿlʿt* in RÉS 4202.

L. 6: (*s*)[*by*]: the copy has *b*[..].

L. 8: the end is restored on the basis of Ja 641/12-13.

2° – WITH HIS BROTHER ḤAYÛ ʿAṮTAR YAḌIʿ: Ja 641

641 – Yellowish, slightly grayish sandstone; broken into two parts; main part = MaMB 206 (cf. Chapter I, A); upper right corner (photograph in Plate 15) = MaMB 49 = Ja 779.

MaMB 206: thickness: 26.1 cm.; *front:* upper right corner slightly damaged; 32.2 cm. (top) and 31.3 (bottom) × 85.9. – MaMB 49: maximum thickness: 9.2 cm.; *front:* 5.4 cm. × 17.8. – SPLINTER: missing; thin plaque the front of which supported one letter of both lines 1 and 2. – INSCRIPTION: same disposition of lines as in Ja 559; letter height: from 3 cm. to 3.5; space between the lines: 0.5 cm. and 0.6; distance to the upper edge: 1.4 cm. – SYMBOL, cf. Ja 559.

1 **Sym-** *qšn/ʾšwʿ/wbn* | [*h*] | ⸤*w/ʾb*
2 **bol** *krb/bnw/ṣʿqn/* | [*h*] | ⸤*q*⸣*nyw*⸥
3 *ʾlmqh/ṯhwn/bʿl/ʾw* | ⸤*m/ṣl*⸣
4 *mn/bn/ġnmhmw/ḏġnmw*⸢*/*⸣ | ⸤*/b*⸥
5 *n/qrytm/bkn/sbʾw/lšw*[*ʿ*]
6 *n/mrʾhmw/šʿrm/ʾwtr/m*
7 *lk/sbʾ/wḏrydn/ḥgn/š*
8 *ftw/ʾlmqh/lwfy/brwhw*
9 *ʾbkrb/wlwzʾ/ʾlmqh/b*
10 *ʿlʾwm/sʿdhmw/nʿmtm/wwf*
11 *ym/wḥẓy/wrḍw/mrʾyhmw*
12 *šʿrm/ʾwtr/wʾẖyhw/ḥyw*
13 *ʿṯtr/yḍʿ/mlky/sbʾ/wḏrydn*
14 *bny/ʿlhn/nhfn/mlk/sbʾ*
15 *wlẖrynhmw/bn/nḍʿ/wšṣy/š*
16 *nʾm/ḏrḥq/wqrb/bʾlmqh*

1 **Sym-** Qašân ʾAšwaʿ and [hi]s son ʾAb-
2 **bol** karib, descendants of Ṣaʿiqân, have [ded]icated to
3 ʾIlumquh Ṯahwân, master of ʾAwwâm, this statue
4 from their booty which they have plundered from
5 Qaryatum, when they fought in order to assi[st]
6 their lord Šaʿirum ʾAwtar,
7 king of Sabaʾ and Raydân, as they
8 have promised to ʾIlumquh for the safety of his son
9 ʾAbkarib; and that may continue ʾIlumquh,
10 master of ʾAwwâm, to make them happy with prosperity and safe-
11 ty and [with] the esteem and grace of their two lords
12 Šaʿirum ʾAwtar and his brother Ḥayû-
13 ʿaṯtar Yaḍiʿ, the two kings of Sabaʾ and Raydân,
14 the two sons of ʿAlhân Nahfân, king of Sabaʾ;
15 and that He may preserve them from the hostility and wickedness of [any]
16 enemy, who is remote and near. By ʾIlumquh.

L. 1: *qšn*, cf. the Arabic adjective *qašwân* "tall and thin" from the root *qašâ* (o); cf. the parallel formation in *rḍn* (e.g., Ja 166/1, Qat) from *rḍw*; cf. also the Arabic place name *qašâwat* (cf. *WüR*, p. 173 C).

L. 2: *ṣʿqn*, e.g., RÉS 4962/1; cf. Arabic *ṣaʿiqa* "to faint" and its derived adjective *ṣaʿiq* "crying, stunned by some crash"; cf. also the Arabic names of a place *ṣuʿaq* (cf. *WüR*, p. 136 B) and of a person *ʾibn aṣ-ṣaʿiq* (cf. *LöHSM*, p. 73 A).

f – Karibʾil Bayyin: Ja 642-643 bis

642 – Stone re-used in the western pavement; cf. Chapter I, B. – MaMB 260.

INSCRIPTION: same disposition of lines as in Ja 552; letter height: from 1.8 cm. to 2.1; space between the lines: from 0.2 cm. to 0.3.

1 [**Sym-** *ḥrb*]⸢*m*⸣*/ynhb/w*[. . .
2 [**bol** .]*ʿr/bny/hllm/*[. . ./*bnw*]
3 [*ḏ*]⸤*ġymn/hqnyw/ʾ*[*lmqhw/bʿl/ʾ*]
4 [*w*]*m/ṣlmn/ḥmdm/bḏt/ḥ*[*my/ḥrb*]
5 *m/bn/mrḍ/bhw/ʾtw/ḥrbm/bh*
6 [*gr*]*n/mryb/bwrẖ/ḏʾlʾlt/wlḏ*[*t*]
7 *ysʿdnhmw/ʾlmqhw/rḍw/mrʾ*[*hm*]
8 *w/krbʾl/byn/mlk/sbʾ/wḏ*[*ry*]
9 [*d*]⸤*n/bn/ḏmrʿly/ḏrḥ/wlḏt/yz*
10 [*ʾ/ʾ*]*lmqhw/mtʿn/ʾdmhw/bny*
11 [*hll*]*m/bn/bʾstm/wnkym/wl*[*w*]
12 [*zʾ/*]*hwšʿnhmw/ʾlmqhw/bqn*[*y*]
13 [*ʾw*]*ldm/ʾḏkrm/hnʾn/ḥgn*[*/w*]
14 [*qhh*]*mw/ʾlmqhw/bmsʾlhw*[*/w*]
15 [*lsʿ*]*dhmw/ʾlmqhw/rḍw/ʾm*[*r*]
16 [*ʾhmw/bn*]⸤*y/ḏġ*⸣[*ymn*. . .

1 [**Sym-** Ḥarb]um Yanhub and [. . .
2 [**bol** .]ʿar, descendants of Hilalum [. . ., descendants of]
3 (the tribe) Ġaymân, have dedicated to ʾI[lumquhû, master of]
4 [ʾAww]âm, this statue in praise because [He has] pr[otected Ḥarb]um
5 from the disease with which Ḥarbum came back to the
6 ci[ty of] Mârib during the month of ʾIlʾilôt; and that
7 ʾIlumquhû may make them happy with the grace of [thei]r lord
8 Karibʾil Bayyin, king of Sabaʾ and [Ray-]
9 [d]ân, son of Ḏamarʿalay Ḏariḥ; and that may conti-
10 [nue ʾI]lumquhû to save His worshippers, the descendants of
11 [Hilal]um from misfortunes and suffering and that may [con-]
12 [tinue] ʾIlumquhû to help them to obta[in]
13 male, pleasing [ch]ild[ren], as [has]

14 [commanded t]hem ʾIlumquhû through His oracle; [and]
15 [that] ʾIlumquhû [may make] them happy with the grace of [their]
16 l[ord]s [, the descend]ants of Ġa[ymân,...

L. 1: *ḥrbm* is restored on the basis of line 5; cf. Ja 145/1, Qat, and commentary; cf. also the Arabic names of men (*ʾabû*) *ḥarb* and *ḥarrâb* (cf. *WüID*, 45/18 and 278/16 respectively).

L. 2: *hllm*, cf. Ja 353/2 and commentary, and also Ja 497; cf. also *hll* (RÉS 4959/2, Qat), *hlm* (Ja 665/32), *hltn* (Ja 772/1).

Ll. 4-5: at least six signs are missing; for *ḥmy*, cf. Ja 651/33.

Ll. 13-14: *ḥgn...bmsʾlhw* is to be related to *hqnyw* in line 3 and mentions the reason of the offering.

L. 16: *ġ*⌉[*ymn* was most probably followed by *wlẖrynhmw*.

643 – Grayish sandstone. – MaMB 275.

STONE: thickness: 45.8 cm. – *Front:* upper corners largely broken; lower left corner broken; 1.177 m. × 50 cm. (top) and 50.6 (bottom). – INSCRIPTION; letter height: 2.6 cm.; space between the lines: 0.4 cm.; distance from line 1 to the upper edge: 1 cm.

1 **[Sym-** *nšʾkrb/... ...]*⌈*/*⌉*ṯwbn/ʾnṭ[... .../bnw/grt/ʾqwl*
2 **[bol** *šʿbn/smhrm/hqnyw/ʾlmqh]/ṯhwn/bʿl/ ʾw*⌈*m*⌉*[/...*
3 *[ḥmdw/nšʾkrb/...]/ḏw[...]bn/bny/grt/ mqm/ʾ[lmqh...*
4 *...](.)n/mrʾhmw/krbʾl/byn/mlk/sbʾ/ wḏ[rydn/...*
5 *...]ẖ/bn/mnšʾ/wštʾ/wmṣr/nšʾ/whštʾn/ whṣrn/[..../y]*
6 *[dʿʾl/mlk/ḥḍr]mwt/wšʿbn/ḥḍrmwt/wʾšʿb/kwnw/ bʿmhw/bn/ʾš[ʿb/...*
7 *...]/wymẓʾw/whndʾn/ydʿʾl/wmṣrhw/ʿdy/ẖlf/ hgrn/ḥnn*
8 *...]w/bʿbr/krbʾl/byn/klm/slmm/mẓʾw/ wṯhbhmw/krbʾl[/byn]*
9 *...]/nkfm/bn/ʿwdnhw/slmm/lqbly/mngt/ḥdṯw/ bhgrn/mryb/wbl*
10 *[..]/mlk/ḥḍrmwt/bʿbr/krbʾl/byn/ẖlfn/hgrn/ḥnn/ qnʿm/lhysrn/b*
11 *ʿbrhw/bn/ʾsbʾn/wʾqwln/lmngt/yʿkrn/mlk/ḥḍrmwt/ tbltn/bʿm*
12 *mlk/sbʾ/whysr/krbʾl/byn/ʿbdhw/nšʾkrb/bn/grt/ wbʿmhw/ṯlṯ/m*
13 *ʾn/ʾsdm/bn/šʿbn/smhrm/wyfʿw/mlk/ḥḍrmt/ʿdy/ ẖlf/ḥnn/wtg*
14 *bʾw/nšʾkrb/bn/grt/lmlk/ḥḍrmt/mṯbt/mngyt/ḏkr/ bʿmhw/ḥgn/stʾ*
15 *ḏn/bʿm/mrʾhmw/krbʾl/byn/wyrʾyn/mlk/ḥḍrmwt/ kʾl/ʿbrnhw/hyʿ/mng*
16 *t/tbšr/bʿly/grybt/ʾns/yfʿhw/bn/mryb/ʿdy/ẖlf/ḥnn/ wgbʾ/lʾḏn/l*
17 *nsʾkrb/bn/grt/wʾns/bʿmhw/wtʾysw/bʿbr/mrʾhmw/ krbʾl/byn/ʿdy*
18 *hgrn/mryb/bwfym/wmlk/ḥḍrmt/wmṣrhw/fbmhwt/ ywmn/sbʾw/ʿdy*
19 *ẖlf/hgrn/yṯl/ksfhw/bʿwhmw/krbʾl/byn/wmṣrhw/ bn/hgrn/mr*
20 *yb/ʿdy/ẖlf/ḥnn/wmẓʾw/ʿdy/ẖlf/hgrn/yṯl/wftḥhmw/ ʾns/stṯqf/b*
21 *hyt/hgrn/yṯl/wḥyrw/bh/wbn/yṯl/fhṣr/mlk/ḥḍrmwt/ wkl/mṣrhw/ʿd*
22 *y/ẖlf/hgrnhn/nšqm/wnšn/wʾdmhmw/ʾbʿl/hmt/ hgrnhn/wqrn/wqh/mlk*
23 *sbʾ/lqrn/bhmt/hgrnhn/wtmnʿhmw/wkrbʾl/byn/fwqh/ ʿbdhw/nšʾkr*
24 *b/bn/grt/wbʿmhw/smhyfʿ/bn/btʿ/wmṣrm/wʾfrsm/ bn/ẖms/mlk/sbʾ/lhʿnn*
25 *ʿdy/ẖlf/hgrnhn/nšqm/wnšn/wbkn/smʿ/mlk/ḥḍrmt/ bn/hyt/ʿntn/fʾtw*
26 *mlk/ḥḍrmwt/wkl/mṣrhw/bn/ẖlf/hgrnhn/nšqm/ wnšn/wmẓʾhmw/mnḏr*
27 *m/ʿdy/yṯl/kyhṣrn/bʿlyhmw/krbʾl/byn/wmṣr/bʿmhw/ bn/mryb/wʾd*
28 *mhw/nšʾkrb/bn/grt/wsmhyfʿ/bn/btʿ/wmṣr/bʿmhmw/ bn/hgrn/nšqm/wsf*
29 *h/mlk/ḥḍrmwt/ʾtmn/bʿlwhw/mṣrnhn/bhgrn/yṯl/ wẖdg/hgrn/yṯl/w*
30 *ʾtw/ʿdy/ẖlf/hgrn/ḥnn/wqdmhmw/mrʾhmw/krbʾl/ byn/mlk/sbʾ/wḏr*
31 *ydn/wʾsd/qrbw/bʿmhw/bhgrn/mryb/wgbʾ/mlk/ ḥḍrmwt/wkl/mṣrhw/ẖl*
32 *fn/ḥnn/bsḥtm/wmlqḥtm/wmẓʾw/ʿdy/mḥrm/ ḏyġrw/wnšʾkrb/bn/gr*
33 *t/wsmhyfʿ/bn/btʿ/wmṣr/bʿmhmw/ftʾysw/bn/nšqm/ ʿdy/hgrn/mryb/lt*
34 *qdmt/mlk/ḥḍrmwt/wgbʾ/mlk/ḥḍrmwt/wkl/mṣrhw/ bn/mḥrmn/ḏy*
35 *ġrw/ʿdy/ẖlf/hgrn/ḥnn/wyhbrrw/bʿlyhmw/mrʾhmw/ krbʾl/by*
36 *n/mlk/sbʾ/wḏrydn/bn/ḏmrʿly/ḏrḥ/wʿbdhw/nšʾkrb/ bn/grt*

1 **[Sym-** Našaʾkarib...]Ṯawbân ʾAnṭ[... ..., descendants of Garat, rulers of]
2 **[bol** the tribe Sumhurâm have dedicated to ʾIlumquh] Ṯahwân, master of ʾAwwâm, [...

3 [... have praised Našaʾkarib and ... ...], he of Wa[...]bân, descendants of Garat, the power of ʾI[lumquh, ...

4 ...]..their lord Karibʾil Bayyin, the king of Sabaʾ and [Raydân,...

5 ...]. from the military expedition and the skirmish and the expedition abroad he undertook and brought about and set out [....Ya-

6 [daʿʾil, king of Ḥaḍra]mawt and the tribe Ḥaḍramawt and the tribes [which] were with him from the tri[bes...

7 ...] and Yadaʿʾil and his expeditionary corps arrived and took...unaware in the region of the city [of] Ḥanan [...

8 ...]. for Karibʾil Bayyin [in] all peace they arrived and Karibʾil [Bayyin] has returned them

9 ...]. in good order because of his bringing peace because of the security they have secured in the city [of] Mârib and [.]

10 [ ] the king of Ḥaḍramawt for Karibʾil Bayyin the countrymen of the city [of] Ḥanan satisfactorily in order to send

11 for him some of the warriors and the rulers [who are] for the security of Yaʿkirân, the king of Ḥaḍramawt to serve for

12 the king of Sabaʾ; and Karibʾil Bayyin sent his servant Našaʾkarib, descendant of Garat and with him three

13 hundred soldiers from the tribe Sumhurâm and they have raised up the king of Ḥaḍramawt in the region of Ḥanan, and

14 Našaʾkarib, descendant of Garat, gave the king of Ḥaḍramawt a security rescript [with which] he has to invest him since he had received

15 [it] from their lord Karibʾil Bayyin; and the king of Ḥaḍramawt decided not to let him build up this security

16 [which] he had announced for the persons of the men whom he had raised up from Mârib in the region of Ḥanan and he has returned to dismiss

17 Našaʾkarib, descendant of Garat, and the men [who were] with him and they have given help to their lord Karibʾil Bayyin in

18 the city [of] Mârib in safety; and as to the king of Ḥaḍramawt and his expeditionary corps, in this very period they fought in

19 the region of the city [of] Yaṯil so that they have foolishly performed their act of treachery [against] Karibʾil Bayyin and his expeditionary corps from the city of [Mâ-

20 rib in the region of Ḥanan and they have arrived at the gate of the city [of] Yaṯil; and have opened to them the men [who] he had selected in

21 this city [of] Yaṯil and they have settled down in it [the city]; and from Yaṯil the king of Ḥaḍramawt and all his expeditionary corps fell upon

22 the region of the two cities [of] Našqum and Našân, and their servants, the masters of these two cities, and rebelled against [what] had ordered the king

23 of Sabaʾ in order to attack these two cities and their system of fortifications; and as to Karibʾil Bayyin, he commanded his servant Našaʾkarib,

24 descendant of Garat, and with him Sumhuyafaʿ, descendant of Bataʿ and [the] expeditionary corps and [the] cavalry of the army of the king of Sabaʾ to lend assistance

25 in the region of the two cities [of] Našqum and Našân; and when the king of Ḥaḍramawt heard about that reinforcement, then went back

26 the king of Ḥaḍramawt and all his expeditionary corps from the region of the two cities [of] Našqum and Našân; and a spy came to them

27 in Yaṯil so that fell upon them Karibʾil Bayyin and [the] expeditionary corps [which was] with him from Mârib and his

28 servants Našaʾkarib, descendant of Garat, and Sumhuyafaʿ, descendant of Bataʿ, and [the] expeditionary corps [who was] with them from the city [of] Našqum; and

29 the king of Ḥaḍramawt acted foolishly in mustering against him [the king of Sabaʾ] the two expeditionary corps in the city [of] Yaṯil; and he left the city [of] Yaṯil and

30 went back into the region of the city [of] Ḥanan and attacked them their lord Karibʾil Bayyin, the king of Sabaʾ and Ray-

31 dân, and the soldiers [who] were close to him from the city [of] Mârib; and the king of Ḥaḍramawt and all his expeditionary corps returned [to] the region

32 [of] Ḥanan in defeat and chains; and they arrived at the temple which they intended to plunder; as to Našaʾkarib, descendant of Ga-

33 rat and Sumhuyafaʿ, descendant of Bataʿ and the expeditionary corps [which was] with them, they gave help from Našqum in the city [of] Mârib for the

34 attacks of the king of Ḥaḍramawt; and the king of Ḥaḍramawt and all his expeditionary corps returned from the temple which they had intended

35 to plunder to the region of the city [of] Ḥanan, and have decided against them their lord Karibʾil Bayyin,

36 the king of Sabaʾ and Raydân, son of Ḏamarʿalay Ḏariḥ, and his servant Našaʾkarib, descendant of Garat,

(continued in Ja 643 bis)

L. 1: the proposed restoration is based also on the information provided both by Ja 643 bis and 631/1. – *ʾnṯ*[: *ʾaqtal* form; the possibilities of restoration are numerous: e.g., from *nṭf*, cf. the Arabic personal name *ʾan-naṭaf* (cf. *GoAT*, p. 596), *nṭl*, cf. the Arabic names of a place *nâṭliyân*, (cf. *WüR*, p. 215 C) and of a woman *manṭûlah* (cf. *HeBN*, p. 50 B).

L. 4:](.)*n*: the letter *n* is preceded by the lower half of a vertical stroke.

L. 5: *mnšʾ*, e.g., RÉS 3945/1; cf. commentary on Ja 576/1: *tnšʾ*. – *šṭʾ*, verb in Ja 631/6; may be translated "skirmish".

L. 7: *hndʾ*, 4th form of *ndʾ*; cf. Arabic *nadaʾa* "to take unaware". – *ḥnn*, city with the temple D̲ahabum dedicated to the sun goddess D̲ât-Baʿdân (RÉS 3943/4); also clan name (CIH 111/2; for this text, cf. commentary on Ja 752/9-10) and masculine name in *RyGSAS*, p. 562; the value of *ḥnn*, which is introduced by *w* "and" and not by a word divider (as *RyISA*, XV, p. 106), is unknown in RÉS 4521/4. Several families of *ʾḥnnn* "Ḥananites" are known (e.g., CIH 535/2), as well as a man called *ḥnnyn* "the Ḥananite" in CIH 401/7. The clan *ḥnn* most probably inhabited the city of the same name. Cf. also the masculine name *mḥnn* in RÉS 4605.

L. 9: *ʿwd*, cf. *CoRoC*, pp. 203-04, and the 4th form *hʿd*, e.g., CIH 541/39. – *ḥdṯ*, 1st form in CIH 80/4 "to befall" (cf. *CoRoC*, p. 145 B and *BeSI*, p. 17) and 4th form (very common) e.g., in Ja 554 "to renew"; here, 2nd form with the meaning of "to perform, execute, assure".

L. 10: before the 1st word divider of the line, a blank precedes the half of a vertical stroke which belongs to the left part of a letter such as *ʾ*, *b*, *d̲*, etc. – *qnʿ*, cf. commentary on Ja 562/7, and Arabic *qânâʿat* and *qunûʿ* "contentedness, satisfaction".

L. 11: *yʿkrn*, cf. the Arabic names of men *abû l-ʿakr* (cf. *SaIS*, p. 162 B), and *al-ʿakrî*, *al-ʿakir*, and *al-ʿakîrî* (cf. *SlGaVNPA*, p. 4 B). *tbltn*, infinitive of the 5th form of *blt* (cf. commentary on Ja 560/8-9).

Ll. 13-14: *tgbʾw*: agreement *ad sensum* with Našaʾkarib and the soldiers who were with him; 5th form of *gbʾ*. – *d̲kr*, cf. *CoRoC*, p. 129 A; cf. Arabic *d̲akara* "to invest someone with (preposition *bi*) something, assign to" and "to speak evil" (in RÉS 5094/5).

Ll. 14-15: *stʾd̲n*, 10th form of *ʾd̲n*; RÉS 3700/13, Min "to obtain, receive".

L. 15: *yrʾyn*/–/*k*, e.g., CIH 396/6 and commentary. – *ʿbrnhw*: from the verb *ʿbr*, cf. *CoRoC*, p. 201 A; here, with a derived meaning such as "to pass someone". – *hyʿ*=*hʿ* (e.g., RÉS 4963/2): for the ordinary meaning, cf. *JaRIH*, pp. 148-49; here, as well as in Ja 831/2, the meaning of "to build up" is analogical. "*hyʿ* signifie 'enduire d'aromates'", according to *LuYFS* (p. 6) who quotes Biberstein-Kasimirski. His quotation is inaccurate.

Ll. 16-17: *lʾd̲n*/*lnšʾkrb*; compare *ʾd̲nw*/*lhmw* in CIH 541/74-75.

L. 18: *fbmhwt* (*f*, consecutive; *b*, preposition; *m*, indefinite, and *hwt*, demonstrative), cf. feminine *bmhyt* in NaNN 74/3; cf. also *bmw*/*hwt* in NaNN 19/7.

L. 19: *sfh*, here as well as in RÉS 5094/5, 3rd form of *sfh*, cf. Arabic *sâfaha* "to act foolishly" (cf. *LaAEL*, p. 1376 C) or here, because of the direct object *bʿwhmw*, "to perform foolishly".

L. 20: *fṯḥ*, cf. *CoRoC*, p. 221 A.

Ll. 22 and 23: *qrn*, for the noun, cf. Ja 576/13 and commentary; *lqrn*/*b* equals *lqrn*/*ʿly* (Kawkab 1/6). – *tmnʿ*, *maṣdar* of the 5th form of *mnʿ*; cf. Arabic *tamannaʿa* "to become strengthened, fortified; to protect, defend (by a fortress)"; here, collective noun with the meaning of "system of fortifications"; the 1st form of *mnʿ* is attested in CIH 291/3 and 573/5 ("to withhold, hold back") and in CIH 611/7 ("to prevent").

Ll. 26-27: *mnd̲rm*, cf. Arabic *mund̲ir*=*nad̲îr* "spy" (cf. *LaAEL*, p. 2782 C and B); the verb *nd̲r* is attested, e.g., in CIH 546/6. Cf. also the masculine name *md̲rn* (CIH 541/90 and Murayġân/7; cf. *RyISA*, X p. 277), and *md̲rm* (*sic* in Wâdî Maʾsil 2/5-6 according to *l.c.*, p. 307), which *RycIHS* (p. 329) identifies with the above-mentioned *md̲rn*; this *md̲rn* belongs to the 6th century A.D.

L. 29: *ʾtm*, cf. commentary on Ja 575/5: *ʾttm*. – *bʿlw* equals *bʿly* (cf. commentary on Ja 550/2).

L. 32: *mlqḥt*, pl. of *mlqḥ* "bond, fetter, chain"; *CoRoC* (p. 173 B) refers to "aeth. *malqeḥ... vincula, catena, carcer" (cf. also *DiLLA*, col. 910); cf. *hlqḥ* in Ja 601/9. – *d̲yġrw*, also in lines 34-35; cf. commentary on Ja 576/4: *hġr*.

Ll. 32-35: account of an event which took place during the Ḥaḍr retreat; the temple involved is most probably the Maḥram Bilqîs itself.

643 bis – Grayish sandstone; photograph; cf. Chapter I, C. – MaMB 316.

Almost the entire line 1 and the beginning of each line are covered by the shadow from the stones standing above and to the right of the stone; and the photograph is not in focus. – The upper right corner is splintered off and damaged; the right edge is also damaged; line 10 is badly damaged in one place.

1 *[w...   ...]/wʾqwl/wʾšʿb/ ...*
.../mryb/wtqdmw/bʿm/ḥḍrmt/
wmṣrhw/...
2 *...t/ydʿʾl/mlk/ḥḍrmwt/wmṣrhw/whrg/bn/*
mṣr/mlk/ḥḍrmwt/ṯny/ʾlfn/ʾsdm/whrgw/whnqḏn/
ʾfrshmw/wkl/...
3 *.../wʾʾblhmw/wḥmrthmw/wkl/grḥ/bʿm/mlk/*
ḥḍrmwt/wmṣrhw/wydʿʾl/mlk/ḥḍrmwt/wḏsʾr/bn/
mṣrhw/fʾtww/b..
4 *tm/wṯbrm/wmlqḥtm/wḥmdy/nšʾkrb/wṯwbn/bny/grt/*
mqm/ʾlmqhw/bʿl/ʾwm/bḏt/hwšʿ/mrʾhmw/krbʾl/
byn/bškr/wsḥt
5 *wḥsm/mlk/ḥḍrmwt/wmṣrhw/bhwt/tqdmn/wnšʾkrb/*
bn/grt/fwzʾ/ḥmd/mqm/ʾlmqhw/bʿl/ʾwm/bḏt/
hwšʿ/ʾlmqhw/ʿbdhw
6 *nšʾkrb/bn/grt/wšʿbhmw/smhrm/bhwt/tqdmn/*
lmqḥm/wmhrgm/wmltm/wġnmt/ṣdqm/bn/šʿbn/
ḥḍrmt/wbhw/ḥmd
7 *y...   ...ʾlbbn/wʾlmqhw/bʿl/ʾwm/fl/yzʾ/hwšʿn/*
ʾdmhw/nšʾkrb/wṯwbn/bn/grt/bwfy/mrʾhmw/
krbʾl/byn/wlwfy/by
8 *tn/slḥn/wʾbʿlhw/wl/wfy/ʾdmhw/nšʾkrb/wṯwbn/bn/*
grt/wšʿbhmw/smhrm/wkl/qlhmw/wʾšʿbhmw/wl/
ḏt/ysʿdnhw/ʾlmqhw/rḍw/mr
9 *ʾhw/krbʾl/byn/mlk/sbʾ/wnʿmtm/ṣdqm/wbry/ʾʾḏnm/*
wmqymtm/wl/wḍʿ/ḍr/wšnʾ/mrʾhmw/mlk/sbʾ/wl/
wḍʿ/ḍr/wšnʾ/ʾdmhw/bny/grt/bʿṯtr/wh
10 *wbs/wʾlmqhw/wʾlʾlt/hgrn/mryb/wb/ʾly[hmw/ʿṯ]tr/*
ʿzzn/wḏt/ẓhrn/bʿly/ʿrn/knn/wrṯdw/hqnythmw/
ʿṯtr/šrqn/wʾlmqhw/bʿl/ʾw[m]

1 [and...   ...]and the rulers and the tribes...of... ...Mârib; and they attacked the king of Ḥaḍramawt and his expeditionary corps...
2 ...Yadaʿʾil, the king of Ḥaḍramawt, and his expeditionary corps; and two thousand soldiers were killed from the expeditionary corps of the king of Ḥaḍramawt; and they took away and carried away their horses and all...
3 ...and their camels and their asses and every carnivorous animal [that was] with the king of Ḥaḍramawt and his expeditionary corps; and as for Yadaʿʾil, the king of Ḥaḍramawt, and those of his expeditionary corps who remained, they went back in...
4 and ruin and chains; and Našaʾkarib and Ṯawbân, descendants of Garat, have praised the power of ʾIlumquhû, master of ʾAwwâm, because He has assisted their lord Karibʾil Bayyin in defeating and overthrowing
5 and cutting in pieces the king of Ḥaḍramawt and his expeditionary corps in that attack; and as for Našaʾkarib, descendant of Garat, he has continued to praise the power of ʾIlumquhû, master of ʾAwwâm, because ʾIlumquhû has assisted His worshipper
6 Našaʾkarib, descendant of Garat and their tribe Sumhurâm in that attack with regard to perfect profit and war trophy and riches and booty from the tribe Ḥaḍramawt; and because of that both of them have praised
7 ...their hearts; and as for ʾIlumquhû, master of ʾAwwâm, may He continue to assist His worshippers Našaʾkarib and Ṯawbân, descendants of Garat, with the safety of their lord Karibʾil Bayyin; and that He may protect the house
8 Salḥân and its masters; and that He may protect His worshippers Našaʾkarib and Ṯawbân, descendants of Garat, and their tribe Sumhurâm and all their rulers and their tribes; and that ʾIlumquhû may make him happy with the grace of his lord
9 Karibʾil Bayyin, king of Sabaʾ, and (with) perfect prosperity and (with) the strength of understanding and of power; and that He may humiliate the foe and the enemy of their lord, the king of Sabaʾ; and that He may humiliate the foe and enemy of His worshippers, the descendants of Garat. By ʿAttar and Haw-
10 bas and ʾIlumquhû and the deities of the city [of] Mârib and by [their] two deities [ʿAṯ]tar ʿAzîzân and Ḏât-Ẓahrân, the two masters of the citadel Kinân. And they have entrusted their offering to the care of ʿAṯtar Šarqân and of ʾIlumquhû, master of ʾAww[âm.]

L. 3: *ḥmrt* and *ḥmr* (e.g., RÉS 3943/2) are plural forms of *ḥmr* (cf. *CoRoC*, p. 150 A); cf. Arabic *ḥimâr*, pl. *ḥumurât* and *ḥumûr* respectively; cf. also *UlCSH*, p. 193, and the Western Semitic cognates in *JeHoDISO*, p. 91: *ḥmr*$_{III}$. – *grḥ*, cf. Arabic *ǧâriḥat*, plural *ǧawâriḥu* "carnivorous animal; hunting animal *or* bird".

L. 4: *ṯbr*: noun; cf. commentary on Ja 561 bis/23-24; cf. Arabic *ṯubûr* "loss, ruin".

L. 5: *ḥsm*: doubtful reading.

L. 6: for *l* introducing *mqḥ*, cf. *HöASG*, p. 149 β.

L. 8: *slḥn*: doubtful reading.

g – Ḏamarʿalay Ḏariḥ: Ja 644

644 – Grayish sandstone; photograph in Plate 15. – MaMB 274.

STONE: thickness: 54.1 cm. – *Front:* lower corners broken; the center of the left edge is splintered off;

54.8 cm. × 91.7. – INSCRIPTION: letter height: 2.5 cm.; space between the lines: 0.2 cm.; distance from line 1 to the upper edge: 0.8 cm. – SYMBOL, cf. Ja 603, but four inside lines instead of three; cf. Plate A.

1 *ʾwsʾl/ydʿ/ḏġymn/⟨.⟩qwl/šʿbn/ġymn/hqny/ʾlmqh*
2 **Sym-** *bʿl/ʾwm/ṣlmn/ḏḏhbn/ḥmdm/bḏt/hwfy/wmtʿn*
3 **bol** *ʾlmqh/mrʾhmw/yhqm/bn/ḏmrʿly/ḏrḥ/mlk/sbʾ*
4 *wḏrydn/bn/mnšʾ/wqblt/tnšʾw/wqtbln/lḥyʿṯt/bn/sm*
5 *hsmʿ/wšʿbhmw/šddm/wrbʾwm/bn/šms/wʾns/kwnw/kwn*
6 *hmw/bʿly/mrʾhmw/yhqm/bkn/bhʾw/wtṣnʿn/ʾbyt/mlkn/s*
7 *lḥn/bhgrn/mryb/wʾwsʾl/fḥmd/mqm/ʾlmqh/bʿl/ʾwm/b*
8 *ḏt/hbrrw/wtḏlln/lḥyʿṯt/wšʿbhmw/šddm/wrbʾwm/bn/š*
9 *ms/bn/bytn/slḥn/wḫdgw/ʾbyt/mlkn/ṣḥḥn/bwfym/w*
10 *bḏt/tškrw/wʿyr/hwʾ/ʾysn/lḥyʿṯt/wšʿbn/šddm/wrbʾ*
11 *wm/bn/šms/wʾns/kwnw/kwnhmw/bmnšʾ/tnšʾw/wʾlm[q]*
12 *h/bʿl/ʾwm/fl/yzʾn/šrḥ/wmtʿn/whwfyn/mrʾhmw/yh[q]*
13 *m/wʾbythmw/slḥn/bn/bʾstm/wnkym/wqblt/wmnš[ʾ]*
14 *swʾm/wʾwsʾl/fwzʾ/ḥmd/mqm/ʾlmqh/bʿl/ʾwm/b[ḏt]*
15 *sʿdhmw/tqdmn/šʿbn/ġymn/bʿm/šʿbn/šddm/bkn/wqhhmw*
16 *mrʾhmw/yhqm/lsbʾ/bn/hgrn/ṣnʿw/ḏbn/šʿbn/ġymn/lt.(.)*
17 *bn/ʾsd/wzʾw/sbʾ/bn/ʾrḍ/šddm/lqdmn/whgzn/lḥy*
18 *ʿṯt/bn/smhsmʿ/wtqdmw/ʾsd/qrbw/bn/šʿbn/ġymn/b*
19 *ʿm/hmt/⌜ʾ⌝sdn/bkwmnn/wyhrgwhmw/wstqḥn/bhmw/w*
20 *stnqḏnhmw/kl/ʾfrshmw/wrkbhmw/wbʿrhmw/wḥṣqhm*
21 *w/wbmw/hwt/brṯn/bkwmnn/fwzʾw/tqdmn/šʿbn/ġymn/b*
22 *ʿm/šlṯ/mʾn/ʾsdm/ḏtfrqw/bn/hgrn/mryb/bn/ʾsd/t*
23 *ṣnʿw/bʿm/lḥyʿṯt/bbytn/slḥn/wyhrgw/kl/hmt/ʾsdn*
24 *wkwn/kl/mhrg/lfyw/šʿbn/ġymn/bkly/tʾdmynhn/b*
25 *n/šʿbn/šddm/sdṯ/mʾn/ʾḥllm/wʾrbʿ/ʾfrsm/wʾlm*
26 *qh/bʿl/ʾwm/fl/yzʾn/sʿd/ʿbdhw/ʾwsʾl/ḏġymn/wšʿ*
27 *[b]hmw/ġymn/rḍw/mrʾhmw/yhqm/wbry/ʾʾḏnm/wmqymt*
28 *[m/]bʿṯtr/whwbs/wʾlmqh/wbḏt/ḥmym/wbḏt/b*
29 *[ʿd]⌞n⌟m/wbšms/mlkn/tnf/wbšymhmw/ḥgrm/qḥmm*
30 *[wrṯdw]/hqnyt/hmw/ʾlmqh/bʿl/ʾwm*

1 **Sym-** ʾAwsʾil Yaḏiʿ, he of [the tribe] Ġaymân, ruler of the tribe Ġaymân, has dedicated to ʾIlumquh,
2 **bol** master of ʾAwwâm, this statue which [is] in bronze, in praise because ʾIlumquh has protected and saved
3 their lord Yuhaqam, son of Ḏamarʿalay Ḏariḥ, king of Sabaʾ
4 and Raydân, from the expedition and fight [that] raised up and started Laḥayʿaṯat, son of Sum-
5 husamîʿ and their tribe Šadâdum and Rabbʾawwâm, son of Šams, and the men [who] were with
6 them against their lord Yuhaqam, when they entered and strengthened the houses of the king, Sa-
7 lḥân, in the city [of] Mârib; and so ʾAwsʾil has praised the power of ʾIlumquh, master of ʾAwwâm, becau-
8 se were liquidated and submitted Laḥayʿaṯat and their tribe Šadâdum and Rabbʾawwâm, son of Ša-
9 ms, from the house Salḥân and they left the houses of the king Ṣaḥaḥân in safety, and
10 because they have defeated and overwhelmed this opponent Laḥayʿaṯat and the tribe Šadâdum and Rabbʾa-
11 wwâm, son of Šams, and the men [who] were with them in the expedition [which] they raised up; and as for ʾIlum[q]uh,
12 master of ʾAwwâm, may He continue to keep healthy and save and protect their lord Yuha[q]am
13 and their houses Salḥân from misfortunes and suffering and fight and disastrous expediti[on];
14 and as for ʾAwsʾil, so he has continued to praise the power of ʾIlumquh, master of ʾAwwâm, be[cause]
15 He has made them happy [in that] the tribe Ġaymân attacked the tribe Šadâdum when commanded them
16 their lord Yuhaqam that some of the tribe Ġaymân would attack from the city [of] Ṣanʿâʾ in order to
17 ...the soldiers from the land of Šadâdum [who] continued to fight in order to attack and shave Laḥay-
18 ʿaṯat, son of Sumhusamîʿ; and the soldiers [who] were from the tribe Ġaymân have attacked
19 these soldiers in Kawmanân; and they took away and drew profit from them and
20 they took away from them all their horses and their beasts of burden and their camel herd and their prisoner keepers
21 in this very place, in Kawmanân; so the tribe Ġaymân did continue to attack
22 three hundred soldiers whom they drove out from the city [of] Mârib from the soldiers [who]
23 have strengthened Laḥayʿaṯat in the house Salḥân and they killed all those soldiers;
24 and has been all the war trophy [which] the tribe Ġaymân brought back, during all the two military enterprises, from

25 the tribe Šadâdum, six hundred animals and four horses; and as for ʾIlum-

26 quh, master of ʾAwwâm, may He continue to make happy His worshipper ʾAwsʾil, him of Ġaymân, and their

27 tribe Ġaymân with the grace of their lord Yuhaqam and (with) the strength of understanding and of power.

28 By ʿAṯtar and Hawbas and ʾIlumquh and by Ḏât-Ḥimyâm and by Ḏât-Ba-

29 [ʿdâ]num and by Šams of the king, Tanûf, and by their patron Ḥagarum Qaḥîmum.

30 [And they entrusted] their offering to [the care of] ʾIlumquh, master of ʾAwwâm.

L. 1: *ʾwsʾl*, e.g., RÉS 3902, No. 5, Qat, 3321/1, Min (cf. *JaAFEQ*, p. 194) and *ʾlʾws*, e.g., Ja 831/1. – *ʾqwl*: the plural, certain on the stone, may be explained by attraction to the preceding collective proper name *ġymn*.

L. 3: *yhqm*, e.g., RÉS 4846/1.

L. 4: *qblt* and *qtbl*, singular noun and 8th form of the verb *qbl* respectively; cf. *CoRoC*, p. 228 B: *qabālu* "kämpfen (einen Kampf *qabla*)" and *qablu* or *qabaltu* "Kampf" (cf. *BeBAG*, p. 242 A) and also Arabic *qabala*, 8th form "to start (something)"; cf. *tqbl*, 6th form in RÉS 4909/6, Ḥaḏr, and also *stqbl*, 10th form of the same verb in Ja 762/4.

Ll. 4-5: *smhsmʿ*, clan name in Ist 7630/8 (cf. *BeFSTI*, pp. 277-78).

L. 5: *rbʾwm*, e.g., CIH 457/1; cf. also *rbbʾwm* in Ja 698/1. – *šms*, e.g., CIH 665 (cf. *HöIAI*, p. 86).

Ll. 6-7: *ʾbyt/mlkn/slḥn*: the different buildings belonging to the royal residence called Salḥân; cf. commentary on Ja 559/10.

L. 8: *hbrr*, cf. commentary on Ja 575/3; the present text requires a derived meaning of Hebrew *brr*, such as "to liquidate, put aside". – *tḏll*, 5th form of *ḏll*; cf. Arabic *ḏalla*, 5th form: "to humble, abuse one's self; give in; submit"; cf. the 4th form *hḏll* in Ja 669/21-22.

L. 9: *ṣḥḥn*, cf. Arabic *ṣaḥn* and *ṣaḥnat* (cf. *WüR*, p. 135 A and B).

L. 10: *ʿyr*, cf. Mehri *awêr* "verwunden, verletzen" (cf. *JaMSSA*, p. 165 B) and Daṯînah *ʿwwr* "abîmer, détériorer" (cf. *LaGD*, p. 2340); connected with *tškr*, *ʿyr* could be translated "to overwhelm".

Ll. 16-17: *t.bn* or *t..bn*: a synonym of *ṭrd* (Ja 660/11) "to pursue" would fit the context.

L. 19: *kwmnn*; cp. the Arabic name of place *kamînân* (cf. *WüR*, p. 186 B). – *stqḥn*, cf. commentary on Ja 559/8; here, *b* equals *bn*.

L. 20: *stnqḏ* or *stqḏ* (e.g., Ja 665/39), 10th form of *nqḏ*; cf. Arabic *naqaḏa*, 10th form "to save, deliver someone from danger". – *bʿr*, e.g., Ja 535/5; cf. *CoRoC*, p. 116 B. – *ḥẓqhmw* equals *ḥṣqhmw* (e.g., Ja 577/15).

L. 22: *tfrqw/bn*, cf. RÉS 4193/11 "to escape from"; cf. Arabic *faraqa*, 5th form + *ʿan* "to leave (a place)" (cf. *DoSDA*, II, p. 259 B); here, *tfrq/bn* means "to drive out from".

L. 24: *bkly/tʾdmynhn*: the two *y* indicate the grammatical case; *tʾdm*, cf. Arabic *ʾadama* "to join, add; to be chief, head"; *tʾdm* refers to the expeditions headed by the tribe Ġaymân.

L. 30: *hqnyt/hmw*: the usual form is *hqnythmw*.

h – Rabbšamsum Nimrân: Ja 645

645 – Grayish sandstone. – MaMB 276 = NaNAG 9 with photograph.

STONE: thickness: 34.7 cm. – *Front:* upper corners broken; the center of the left edge is splintered off; 1.558 m. × 43.2 cm. – INSCRIPTION: same disposition of lines as in Ja 552; letter height: 5.1 cm. (top) and 3.9 (bottom); space between the lines: 0.9 cm.; distance from line 1 to the top: 1 cm.

1 **[Sym-]** *whbʾl/y.[. . ./bn/y]*
2 **[bol]** *hʿn/wqrḍn/hqny/ʾ⸢l⸣*
3 *[mq]h/ṯhwn/bʿl/ʾwm/ṣlmn*
4 *ḏḏhbn/ḥmdm/bḏt/hwf*
5 *y/ʿbdhw/whbʾl/bn/yhʿn*
6 *wqrḍn/bkl/ʾmlʾ/stmlʾ/b*
7 *ʿmhw/wlḏt/yzʾn/ʾlmqh/b*
8 *ʿl/ʾwm/hwfyn/ʿbdhw/whbʾ*
9 *l/bn/yhʿn/wqrḍn/bkl/ʾmlʾ*
10 *yzʾn/stmlʾn/bʿmhw/wlḏt/h*
11 *wfy/wmtʿn/ʾlmqh/bʿl/ʾwm/grb*
12 *ʿbdhw/whbʾl/bn/yhʿn/wqrḍ⸢n⸣*
13 *bn/ẖwm/wʿws/wmwtt/kwn/bʾ*
14 *rḍn/bẖrf/ḥywm/bn/ʾbkrb/bn*
15 *krb/ẖll/ṯkmtn/wlḏt/yzʾn/ʾ*
16 *lmqh/bʿl/ʾwm/hwfyn/grb/ʿbdh*
17 *w/whbʾl/bn/yhʿn/wqrḍn/bn/kl/b*
18 *ʾstm/wnkym/wnḍʿ/wšṣy/šnʾm/wmn*
19 *gwt/swʾm/wl/sʿdhmw/ʾlmqh/bʿl/ʾw*
20 *m/ḥẓy/wrḍw/mrʾhmw/rbšmsm/nmrn/m*
21 *lk/sbʾ/wḏrydn/wnʿmtm/wmngyt/ṣ*
22 *dqm/ḏyhrḍynhmw/wl/sʿdhmw/ʾlm*
23 *qh/bʿl/ʾwm/ʾṯmr/wʾfql/ṣdqm/ḏyh*
24 *rḍynhmw/bn/kl/ʾrḍthmw/wʾsrrh*
25 *mw/wmfnythmw/bmryb/wnšqm/wrḥ*

26 *btn/bʿṯtr/whbs/wʾlmqh/wbḏt/ḥ*
27 *mym/wbḏt/bʿdnm/wbšms/mlkn/tnf*

1 **[Sym-]** Wahabʾil Y. [... ...of Yu-]
2 **[bol]** hʿîn and Qarḍân, has dedicated to ʾIlu-
3 [mqu]h Ṯahwân, master of ʾAwwâm, this statue
4 which [is] in bronze, in praise because He has showered
5 upon His worshipper Wahabʾil, descendant of Yuhʿîn
6 and Qarḍân, all the favors [for which] he besought
7 Him and in order that may continue ʾIlumquh, mas-
8 ter of ʾAwwâm, to shower upon His worshipper Wahabʾil,
9 descendant of Yuhʿîn and Qarḍân, all the favors [for which]
10 he shall continue to beseech Him, and because
11 ʾIlumquh, master of ʾAwwâm, has protected and saved the person
12 of His worshipper Wahabʾil, descendant of Yuhʿîn and Qarḍân,
13 from the pest and pestilence(?) and epilepsy [that] happened in the
14 land during the year of Ḥayûm, son of ʾAbkarib, descendant of
15 the Leader H̲alil Ṯakmatân; and in order that may continue
16 ʾIlumquh, master of ʾAwwâm, to protect the person of His worshipper
17 Wahabʾil, descendant of Yuhʿîn and Qarḍân, from all
18 misfortunes and suffering and (from every) [act of] hostility and wickedness of [any] enemy and [from]
19 devastating storms; and that ʾIlumquh, master of ʾAwwâm, may make them happy
20 with the esteem and grace of their lord Rabbšamsum Nimrân,
21 king of Sabaʾ and Raydân, and [with] perfect prosperity and security;
22 which would please them; and that may make them happy ʾIlum-
23 quh, master of ʾAwwâm, with perfect fruits and harvests, which would
24 please them, from all their lands and their valleys
25 and their lands irrigated by canals in Mârib and Našqum and Ruḥâ-
26 batân. By ʿAṯtar and Hawbas and ʾIlumquh and by Ḏât-Ḥi-
27 myâm and by Ḏât-Baʿdânum and by Šams of the king, Tanûf.

NaNAG's transliteration and translation (II, pp. 36-37) do not mention the symbol. In the same transliteration: line 9 and 12: *yhʿn* instead of *yhʾn*; line 10: *bʿmhw* instead of *bʾmhw*; line 12, omit bracket; line 18: *nḍʿ* instead of *nḍʾ*; line 19: omit *ṯhwn* and one bracket either preceding or following *ṯhwn*; line 22: *ḏyhrḏyn* instead of *ḏhrḏyn*; line 26: *ʿṯtr* instead of *ʾṯtr*; line 27: *wbḏt* instead of *wb/ḏt*, omit bracket, and *tnf* instead of *tnwf*.

L. 1: *whbʾl*, cf. Ja 129, Qat, and commentary. – *y*.[...]: of the 2nd letter only the lower half, belonging to either ʾ, *k*, *s*, or *ṣ*, remains; cf., e.g., *yʾḏf* (e.g., Ja 616/1 mentioning *whbʾwm*, another personal name formed with *whb*), *yʾmn* (e.g., *nšʾkrb/yʾmn*, e.g., in Ja 608/1), *yskr* (e.g., *sʿdm/yskr* in Ja 822/3), etc.

Ll. 13-14: *bn/ẖwm—/kwn/bʾrḍn*, cf. *bn/ẖwm/[ḏ]kyn/bkl/ʾrḍn* in RÉS 4138/6-7, where *ẖwm* is translated "epidemic, pest". – *ʿws*, cf. *BeSI*, p. 19: "pestilence (or, famine?)"; note that the modern Yemeni *ʿws* means "slogatura" (cf. *RoVSAY*, p. 309). *ẖwm* and *ʿws* are considered as synonyms by *RyHE* (p. 235): "plague". – *mwtt*, cf. Arabic *mûtat* "madness, epilepsy".

L. 15: *ṯkmtn*, e.g., CIH 567/6 (not 576 as in *RyNP*, I, p. 320 A).

i – Yasrum Yuhanʿim and his son Šamir Yuharʿiš: Ja 646-648

646 – Yellowish, slightly grayish sandstone. – MaMB 243.

STONE: maximum thickness: 9 cm. (center) and 8 (both sides). – *Front:* covered with red paint; 40.2 cm. (left) and 40.8 (right) × 27.6. – *Left side:* perpendicular to the lateral edge, a masonry mark: *n*: 6 cm. × 3, distance to the lateral edge: 2 cm. – INSCRIPTION, same disposition of lines as in Ja 561 bis; letter height: from 2 cm. to 2.2; space between the lines: from 0.4 cm. to 0.6; distance from line 1 to the upper edge: 0.5 cm. – SYMBOL, cf. Ja 582, but the two extreme triangles are shorter and the two inside lines are replaced by four.

1 **Sym-** *šrḥsmd/bn/yṯʾr/wʾlfnm*
2 **bol** *mqtwy/mrʾyhw/ysrm/yhn*
3 *ʿm/wšmr/yhrʿš/mlky/sbʾ/wḏ*
4 *rydn/hqny/mrʾhw⟨/⟩ʾlmqhbʿlʾwm*
5 *ṣlmn/ḏḏhbn/lḏt/ẖmr/ʿbdhw*
6 *šrḥsmd/bn/yṯʾr/wʾlfnm/nqm/w*
7 *twśʿ⟨/⟩ḏhrghw/bʿbr/mrʾhw/š*
8 *mr/yhrʿš/wlyẓʾn/mrʾhw/ʾl*
9 *mqh/nqm/kl/yẖrgnhw/bʿbr/*
10 *mrʾhw/wlẖmrhw/mrʾhw/ʾlm*

11 *qhw/rḍw/wẖmrn/mrʾhw/šmr/w*
12 *wfy/grbhw*

1 **Sym-** Šaraḥsamad, son of Yaṯʾir and ʾAlfanum,
2 **bol** high official of his two lords YasrumY uhan-
3 ʿim and Šamir Yuharʿiš, the two kings of Sabaʾ and
4 Raydân, has dedicated to his lord ʾIlumquh, master of ʾAwwâm,
5 this statue which [is] in bronze, because He has vouchsafed to His worshipper
6 Šaraḥsamad, son of Yaṯʾir and ʾAlfanum, to take vengeance and
7 to defeat him who has incited him against his lord Ša-
8 mir Yuharʿiš; and that his lord ʾIlumquh may continue
9 to take vengeance on anyone who would incite him against
10 his lord; and that his lord ʾIlumquhû may vouchsafe to him
11 the grace and the gracious act of his lord Šamir and
12 [also] the safety of his person.

L. 1: *šrḥsmd*: the first element is very well known; for the second, cf. the Arabic names of a place *samadân* (cf. *WüR*, p. 120 A) and of a person *as-sammâd* (*l.c.*, p. 461); cf. also the Safaitic personal name *smdl* (cf. *LiSI*, p. 332 A). – *yṯʾr*, cf. the personal name *ṯʾrn* (e.g., in Ja 649/2). – *ʾlfnm*, cf. Arabic *ʾalafa* "to keep to, to become familiar with"; cf. also the Thamudic personal name *ʾlf* (e.g., *vdBrTTPS*, p. 33; Ph 160 a 1).

L. 7: *twśʿ*; for the form *wśʿ*, cf. A. F. L. Beeston, in *BSOAS*, 16 (1954), p. 392, note 1; *wśʿ*, is mentioned in RÉS 4646/1: juridical text, where the verb has the meaning of "to promulgate" and also in RÉS 4324/1, Qat, with the probable meaning of "to grant plenteously"; here, cf. Arabic *wasiʿa*, 5th form in the expression *tawassaʿa fî l-bilâdi* "parcourir et conquérir plusieurs pays" (cf. *DoSDA*, II, p. 803 B); here a meaning such as, e.g., "to defeat" is acceptable. – *ẖrg*, RÉS 2831/3, Min, "to strip" (cf. *JaSAI*, p. 509 A, No. 10, note 10); here, the 2nd form, cf. Arabic *ẖarraǧa* "faire sortir" (cf. *DoSDA*, I, p. 358 A) and *ẖaraǧat* "(military) expedition"; here, with the meaning of "to induce, persuade to rebellion".

L. 11: *ẖmrn*: e.g., RÉS 4646/14-15.

647 – Stone re-used in the western pavement; cf. Chapter I, B. – MaMB 265.

Front: upper left part badly damaged. – INSCRIPTION, letter height: from 2.2 cm. to 2.4; same disposition of lines as in Ja 552; space between the lines: from 0.3 cm. to 0.5. – SYMBOL, cf. Ja 559.

1 **Sym-** *[ʾsdm/...]ḥ[/w... .../m]*
2 **bol** *qt$^{[t}_{[yt}$/y]⌜s⌝rm[/yhnʿm/wbnh]*
3 *[w]/šmr/yhr[ʿ]š/ml[ky/sbʾ/wḏ]*
4 *rydn/hqnyw/m[rʾhmw/ʾlmq]*
5 *[h]/ṯhwn/bʿlʾwm/[ṣlmn/ḏḏh]*
6 *bn/ḏšfthw/lḥm⌝[dhw/... ...]*
7 *ʾlmqh[bʿl]ʾw[m/... ...]*
8 *bmsʾl[hw]/k[.......]ʿb[dy]*
9 *hmw/ʾlmqhbʿlʾ[wm/.. ...h]*
10 *w/wldm/wẖmrhw/tb[š]rtm/bm*
11 *sʾlhw/kbknmw/[... .../mr]*
12 *ʾhmw/ʾlmqh[bʿl]ʾwm/hqnytm*
13 *lsbʾ/bʿbrhw/ʾ..t...../ʾḥgk*
14 *m/ḏt/dwsm/wḍʿn/...hw...*
15 *rḍḥ/wstydʿn/wwfyn/[ṣlm]*
16 *hw/ḏšfthw/kyhwfyn/l[hw/wl]*
17 *ẖmrhmw/ʾwldm/hnʾm/ḥgn/[t]*
18 *bšrhmw/bmsʾlhw/wlẖmrhmw*
19 *ʾlmqhṯhwnbʿlʾwm/ḥẓy/wrḍ*
20 *w/ʾlbb/ʾmrʾhmw/ysrm/yhnʿm*
21 *wšmr/yhrʿš/mlky/sbʾ/wḏrydn*
22 *wḥẓy/nṣr/slḥn/wrydn/wḥṣy/w*
23 *rḍw/šʿbhmw/sbʾ/wḥmdm/bḏt/ẖ*
24 *mrhmw/ʾlmqhbʿlʾwm/stwfyn*
25 *⌜k⌝l/syt/hwsyw/ʾmrʾhmw/ʾmlkn*
26 *bkl/syt/hwsyhmw/bmgʾt/sbʿt*
27 *ẖryftm/wbkl/mqwlthmw/wsyt*
28 *hmw/bmrb/wṣnʿw/wbnšqm/wnšn*
29 *wbkl/mqblt/wmʿdhmw/bʾrḍt/ẖm*
30 *sn/bdʿtn/wsqyn/wlyzʾn/ʾlmqh*
31 *bʿlʾwm/hwfyn/grb/ʿbdhw/ʾsdm*
32 *bn/kl/bʾstm/wnkytm/wbn/ṭwʿ*
33 *[wš]ṣy/wnḍʿ/šnʾm/ḏbnhw/dʾw/wʾl/d*
34 *[ʿw/]wḏrḥq/wqrb/bʾlmqhṯhwnbʿl*
35 */ʾwm/*

1 **Sym-** [ʾAsdum...]ḥ [and... ...high]
2 **bol** offi[cials of Ya](s)rum [Yuhanʿim and his son]
3 Šamir Yuhar[ʿi]š, [the two] kin[gs of Sabaʾ and]
4 Raydân, have dedicated to [their] l[ord ʾIlumquh]
5 Ṯahwân, master of ʾAwwâm, [this statue which (is) in bron-]
6 ze, which he has promised Him in order to prai[se Him...]
7 ʾIlumquh, [master of] ʾAww[âm,...
8 through [His] oracle that...their [two] serva[nts]
9 ʾIlumquh, master of ʾA[wwâm...H]is...
10 a child and [because] He has vouchsafed to him an anno[unce]ment through
11 His oracle whenever... ...their

12 [lor]d ʾIlumquh, [master] of ʾAwwâm an offering
13 in order to fight for him... ...the laws
14 which [were] abused and lost... ...him (or his)
15 he was bruised and has proved his reliability and payed off [his debt by erecting] his [statue]
16 which he has promised Him so that He would protect [him..; and that He may]
17 vouchsafe to them pleasing children as He has
18 [an]nounced to them through His oracle; and that may vouchsafe to them
19 ʾIlumquh Ṯahwân, master of ʾAwwâm, the esteem and gra-
20 ce of the hearts of their lords Yasrum Yuhanʿim
21 and Šamir Yuharʿiš, the two kings of Sabaʾ and Raydân,
22 and the esteem of the support troop of Salḥân and Raydân and the esteem and
23 grace of their tribe Sabaʾ; and in praise because
24 ʾIlumquh, master of ʾAwwâm, has vouchsafed to them to give protection to
25 all the work [that] their lords the kings undertook
26 in all the work he undertook for them during seven
27 years and in all their resting places and their work
28 in Mârib and Ṣanʿâʾ and in Našqum and Našân
29 and in their every meeting place and convention place in the lands of the five
30 wonders and of the irrigation; and that may continue ʾIlumquh,
31 master of ʾAwwâm, to protect the person of His worshipper ʾAsdum
32 from all misfortunes and sufferings and from the constraint
33 [and wick]edness and hostility of [any] enemy, those who are known and [those who] are not
34 kn[own], and who is remote and near. By ʾIlumquh Ṯahwân, master of
35 ʾAwwâm.

Ll. 1-2: read *mqtt* (e.g., Ja 576/14) or *mqtyt* (e.g., Ja 577/7).

L. 2: on the basis of the length of the blank, a noun is required after *yhnʿm* and is *bn* "son" according to, e.g., Ja 651/5-7.

L. 6: *lḥmdhw* restored after CIH 357/10.

Ll. 6-11: many restorations are equally possible; all of them are quite hypothetical.

L. 8: two letters must be restored at the end of the line.

Ll. 13-14: *ʾḥgk*, plural of *ḥgk*; e.g., RÉS 3854/1, Qat, "law, edict".

L. 14: *dwsm*, *maṣdar*; cf. Arabic *dâsa* (o) "to trod, trample down; to abuse"; idem in Daṯînah (cf. *LaGD*, pp. 880-81), Ḥaḍr and Šẖauri (cf. *RhVDD*, p. 19 B); *dwsm* is name of a Qat man in RÉS 3856/1. – *ḍʿn*, *maṣdar*; for the nominal form, cf., e.g., *ẖmrn*; cf. Arabic *ḍâʿa* (i) "to be lost, perish"; idem in Daṯînah (cf. *LaGD*, p. 2181); cf. also in Ẓofâr *ḍâʿ* "verloren gehen" (cf. *RhVDD*, p. 35 B) and same meaning in Mehri *ḍôya* or *ḍôwia* (cf. *JaMSSA*, p. 175 A).

L. 15: *rḍḥ*, cf. commentary on Ja 575/5. – *wfy*, here as well as in Ja 729/11-12, with the original meaning of Arabic *wafâ* (i) "to be faithful to his promise, pay off (debts)".

L. 22: the reading of line 22 was later checked on the stone. For the expression *ḥẓy/nṣr/slḥn/wrydn*, cf. *rdʾ/nṣrhmw* (RÉS 5085/9); the restoration of *w* before *nṣr* would be gratuitous, and is superfluous.

L. 25: *syt* and *hwsy*: noun derived from the root *wsy* and the 4th form of the same root respectively; cf. Daṯînah *wssy* "faire" (cf. *LaGD*, p. 2922) and the 3rd Arabic form *āsâ* "assister... faire, exécuter" (cf. *DoSDA*, II, p. 807 B); *syt* and *hwsy* may be translated as "work" and "to undertake" respectively.

L. 26: *mgʾt*, from the root *gyʾ*; cf. Arabic *mağîʾ* "arrival, coming" and *muğâyaʾat* "the act of coinciding" (cf. *LaAEL*, p. 492 B); *bmgʾt* means "in the occurrence of", that is to say "during".

L. 27: *mqwlt*, cf. Arabic *maqîl* "place where one takes a siesta", and in Daṯînah *qyyl* "se mettre à l'abri pendant l'heure de la plus forte chaleur" (cf. *LaGD*, p. 2546).

L. 29: *mqblt*, for the ordinary meaning, cf. commentary on Ja 574/12; here, cf. Daṯînah *qabal* "rendez-vous" (place) (cf. *LaGD*, p. 2457). – *mʿd*; the ordinary meaning is "help" (e.g., RÉS 4370) (from the root *wʿd*); cf. also *BeNL*, IV, p. 145; here, cf. Daṯînah *mîʿâd* "rendez-vous" (cf. *LaGD*, p. 2928) from the same root *wʿd*.

L. 30: *bdʿt*, pl. of *bdʿ*, cf. Arabic *badaʿa* "to become superlative in one's kind" (cf. *LaAEL*, p. 166 B).

648 – Whitish limestone; photograph (cf. Plate 15) and latex squeeze. – MaMB 94.

STONE: maximum thickness: 10.2 cm. – *Front:* upper edge broken and badly damaged; lower left corner broken; 22.7 cm. × 16.9 (top) and 17.1 (bottom). – INSCRIPTION: same disposition of letters as in Ja 559; letter height: 1.5 cm.; space between the lines: 0.3 cm. – SYMBOL, cp. Ja 574, but the upper part of the lower triangle is much thinner and longer, and the three inside lines are replaced by only one design; cf. Plate A.

1 ⸢**Sym-**⸣ *⸢n⸣[... /w...]⸢n/wbn⸣*
2 **bol** *yh[mw/ʾbšmr/h]⸢qny⸣w/ʾ*
3 *lmqh/bʿ⸢l/⸣ʾwm/ṣlmn/ḏḏhb*
4 *n/lqbly/ḏt/ḫmrhw/ḥyw/*
5 *lhw/brwhw/ʾbšmr/wlḫ*
6 *mrhw/⸢ʾ⸣lmqh/ḥẓy/wrḍ*
7 *w/mrʾhmw/ysrm/yhnʿm/w*
8 *šmr/yhrʿš/ʾmlk/sbʾ/wḏr*
9 *ydn/wlhʾnnhmw/bn/nḍʿ/w*
10 *šṣy/šnʾm/bʾlmqh/b*
11 *ʿlʾwm*

1 ⸢**Sym-**⸣ N[... and ...]n and the[ir]
2 **bol** son [ʾAbšamar have] dedicated to
3 ʾIlumquh, master of ʾAwwâm, this statue which [is] in bronze,
4 because of this: He has vouchsafed to him to grant life
5 for him to his son ʾAbšamar; and that may vouch-
6 safe to him ʾIlumquh the esteem and grace
7 of their lord Yasrum Yuhanʿim and
8 Šamir Yuharʿiš, kings of Sabaʾ and Ray-
9 dân; and that He may assist them against the hostility and
10 wickedness of [any] enemy. By ʾIlumquh mas-
11 ter of ʾAwwâm.

L. 4: *ḥyw*, cf. *JaPDSM*, p. 178, and the Western Semitic cognates in *JeHoDISO*, p. 87: *ḥyy*.

L. 5: *ʾbšmr*, e.g., CIH 319/1.

L. 9: *bn*: the first letter is *b* and not *m* in spite of the curved left stroke, because the bottom of the letter is free of any curved horizontal stroke. – *nḍʿ*: the second letter is shaped like *m*, that is to say the right vertical stroke is straight and not curved.

j – Šamir Yuharʿiš: Ja 649-655

649 – Yellow, grayish sandstone inscription, re-used in a small wall (cf. p. 255, note 2); bottom missing; photograph in Plate 15. – MaMB 223.

STONE: thickness: 17.4 cm. – *Front:* covered with red paint; the center of the left edge is splintered off; 1.232 m. × 35.7 cm. – INSCRIPTION, same disposition of lines as in Ja 561 bis; letter height: from 3 cm. to 2.4; space between the lines: from 0.6 cm. to 0.4. – SYMBOL, cf. Ja 574.

1 **Sym-** *wfym/ʾḥbr/bn/ḥbb/whynn*
2 **bol** *wṯʾrn/ḏʿmd/wsʾryn/wḥwlm*
3 *ʾqwl/šʿbn/ṣrwḥ/wḫwln/ḫḍlm/w*
4 *hynn/mqtwy/šmr/yhrʿš/mlk/sbʾ*
5 *wḏrydn/hqny/mrʾhmw/ʾlmqhṯhw*
6 *nbʿlʾwm/ṣlmn/ḏḏhbn/ḥmdm/bḏ*
7 *t/hwfyhmw/bmlʾhw/bkl/sbʾt/sb*
8 *ʾw/wšwʿn/mrʾhmw/šmr/yhrʿš/mlk*
9 *sbʾ/wḏrydn/ʿdy/shrtn/lyt/wḫ*
10 *ywn/wḍdḫn/wtnʿm/wnbʿt/whrg/*
11 *bḏt/sbʾtn/ḫmst/ʾsdm/bḍʿm/[wʾḥ]*
12 *d/ʾḫḏm/mhrgt/ṣdqm/wḏfrʿm/b[qdm]*
13 *gyšn/wʾtw/hʾ/wšʿbhw/bmhrgtm/w*
14 *sbym/wġnmm/ḏʿsm/ḏhrḍyhmw/wḥmdm*
15 *bsbʾt/wzʾw/sbʾ⟨⟩/wšwʿn/mrʾhmw/š*
16 *mr/yhrʿš/mlk/sbʾ/wḏrydn/ʿdy/srn/ḏ*
17 *ḍmdm/wstbrw/bmsgthw/ʿly/šʿbn/ḥrt*
18 *whrg/bhw/ḫmst/ʾsdm/bḍʿm/wḏfrʿm/b*
19 *qdm/gyšn/wzḫn/bhw/ḫms/zḫnm/mḍyt*
20 *m/fḫḏyhw/wrglyhw/wfrshw/ndf/wzḫ*
21 *n/wḥḏr/ktḫdʿnn/rglhw/wymtn/frṣh*
22 *w/wmtʿhw/ʾlmqhṯhwnbʿlʾwm/wʾtw/⟨hʾ⟩/wš*
23 *ʿbhw/bmhrgtm/wsbym/wġnmm/ḏhrḍwh*
24 *mw/wḥmdm/sbʾw/wšwʿn/mrʾhmw/šmr/y*
25 *hrʾš/mlk/sbʾ/wḏrydn/srn/ḥrb/ʿdy*
26 *qrytnhn/wbnhw/fwqhhmw/mrʾhmw/šm*
27 *r/yhrʿš/mlk/sbʾ/wḏrydn/hwt/wsbʿy/wm*
28 *ʾt/ʾsdm/ḏqrb/bn/šʿbhmw/ṣrwḥ/wḫwl*
29 *n/wbʿmhmw/sṯ/ʾfrsm/ltqdm/wtwśʿn/ʾš*
30 *ʿb/ʿkm/wḏshrtm/wtwśʿw/wtqdmn/kl/ʾš*
31 *ʿb/wʿšr/ʿkm/wḏshrtm/bʿqbtn/ḏrgzg*
32 *zn/wthrgw/bʿmhmw/bn/šf/šrqm/ʿdy/mq*
33 *ṭt/šmsn/wlyl/lylm/ʿdy/šrq/kwkbn/*
34 *ḏṣbḥn/whsḥthmw/whgbʾn/whrg/b⸢n⸣*
35 *hmw/ḏfrʿm/bqdm/gyšn/ʾsm/bḍʿm/wṯn*
36 *y/ʾḫḏn/wkwn/mhrgt/hrgw/bʿqbtn*
37 *ḏrgzgzn/ʿšrm/wmʾt/ʾsdm/bḍʿm/ws*
38 *ṯt/wʾrbʿy/ʾsdm/ʾḫyḏtm/wʿšry/wʾr*
39 *bʿ/mʾtm/sbym/wsṯ/wʿšrm/wṯlṯ/mʾtm*
40 *rkbm/brḥlhn/wġnmw/wmly/gmlm/wbq*
41 *rm/wḍʾnm/šfqm/wlḏmḫr/hwt/ywmn/fšwʿw*

1 **Sym-** Wafîum ʾAḥbar, descendant of Ḥabib and Haynân
2 **bol** and Ṯaʾrân, he of ʿAmîd and Saʾriyân, and Ḥawlum,
3 rulers of the tribes Ṣirwâḥ and Ḫawlân Ḫaḍlum and
4 Haynân, high official of Šamir Yuharʿiš, king of Sabaʾ
5 and Raydân, has dedicated to their lord ʾIlumquh Ṯahwân,
6 master of ʾAwwâm, this statue which [is] in bronze, in praise becau-
7 se He has showered upon them His favor in all the encounters [in which] they
8 fought and assisted their lord Šamir Yuharʿiš, king

9 of Sabaʾ and Raydân, in Saharatân Liyyat and Ḫa-
10 ywân and Ḍadaḫân and Tanaᶜum and Nabᶜat; and he killed
11 in that military campaign five soldiers beheaded and on]e
12 prisoner: a perfect war trophy; and it [was] of great importance in [front of]
13 the troop; and he and his tribe came back with war trophies and
14 captives and booty, which was desired [and] which pleased them; and in praise
15 because of the military campaign [in which] they have continued to fight and to assist their lord Ša-
16 mir Yuharᶜiš, king of Sabaʾ and Raydân, in the valley of
17 Ḍamadum; and he reconnoitred with his bodyguards against the tribe Ḥârat;
18 and he killed there five soldiers beheaded and it [was] of great importance in
19 front of the troop; but he was wounded there by five wounds [which are] passed:
20 his two thighs and his two feet and his horse Nâdif; and he was wounded
21 and feared his foot being lost and his horse crippled;
22 but ʾIlumquh Ṯahwân, master of ʾAwwâm, saved him and he came back and his
23 tribe with war trophies and captives and booty, which pleased
24 them; and in praise [because] they have fought and assisted their lord Šamir Yu-
25 harᶜiš, king of Sabaʾ and Raydân, [in] the valley Ḥarîb near
26 Qaryatnahân; and from there, ordered them their lord Šamir
27 Yuharᶜiš, king of Sabaʾ and Raydân, [i.e.] him and seventy and
28 one hundred soldiers who were close from their two tribes Ṣirwâḥ and Ḫawlân
29 and along with them six horsemen in order to attack and defeat the tribes
30 of ᶜAkkum and of Saharatum; and they defeated and attacked all the tri-
31 bes and the groups of ᶜAkkum and of Saharatum on the hill-slope of Ragazgazân;
32 and they effected a carnage among them from the appearance of sunrise until the heat
33 of the sun and all night long till the rise of the star
34 of the morning; and he destroyed them and drove back and killed from
35 them, – it [was] of great importance in front of the troop –, one man beheaded and two
36 prisoners; and was the war trophy [which] they took on the hill-slope
37 of Ragazgazân: one hundred and ten soldiers beheaded and
38 forty-six soldiers [made] prisoners and twenty-four
39 hundred captives and three hundred and sixteen
40 riding camels with the[ir] saddles; and they plundered and enjoyed [taking away] camels and
41 bovines and sheep plentiful; and [in praise] because did occur that day so that they have helped

L. 1: *wfym*, e.g., Ja 388, Qat. – *ʾḫbr*, cf. the masculine Arabic personal name *ʾaḫbirrat* (cf. *VNIA*, p. 8 B); in RÉS 5062, read *ḥbr mls* "Ḥabir Malus" (instead of *ḥbrm/s*).

L. 2: *ṯʾrn*, e.g., RÉS 3080/1 and in Thamudic (cf. *vdBrIT*, p. 372: Jsa 233); cf. also Thamudic personal name *ṯʾrl* (cf. *l.c.*, p. 495: Moritz. 6); the noun *ṯʾr* is also attested in Safaitic (cf. *LiSI*, p. 346 B); for Ugaritic, cf. *GoUM*, p. 334 B, No. 1994. – *ᶜmd*, CIH 40/1; personal name in Ja 882 E, Qat (cf. *JaPEQL*, p. 213), and *ᶜmdn*, e.g., name of a man in RÉS 5098/1. – *ḥwlm*, cf. *ḥwln* in Ja 556.

L. 9: *lyt*, Min proper name in RÉS 3703/5.

Ll. 9-10: *ḫywn*, hypothetical restoration in CIH 131/3: [*ḫy*]*wn*, considered as certain by *RyNP*, I, p. 340 A; cf. the Arabic clan name *banû ḫaywân* (cf. *WüID*, 252/4).

L. 10: *ḍdḫn*, cf. Arabic place name *ḍadaḫ* (cf. *MüHG*, p. 71 B). – *tnᶜm*, feminine personal name, e.g., in RÉS 4540; cf. also name of a passage (e.g., RÉS 3022/1, not line 4, as in *RyNP*, I, p. 351 A); it is impossible to determine whether *tnᶜmm* in CIH 843/1 designates a man (*sic* in *RÉS*, VII, p. 214, in commentary on RÉS 4368) or a woman; same doubt about Ja 233, Qat, cf. the tribe name *tnᶜmm* in Ja 618/3. – *nbᶜt*, Qat personal name (RÉS 3902, No. 177/1); cf. also *nbᶜm* in Hamilton 6, Ḥaḍr (cf. *JaRIH*, p. 149).

L. 11: three characters are missing at the end; the first is undoubtedly the word divider.

Ll. 11-12: *ʾḥd* is restored on the basis of the parallel in ll. 35-36.

Ll. 12-13: *ḏfrᶜm/b*[*qdm*] *gyšn*, cf. lines 18-19 and 35; cf. commentary on Ja 615/18-19.

Ll. 16-17: *ᶜdy/srn/ḏḍmdm*, cf. *bsrn/ḏḍmdm* in CIH 407/20-21, also dated from Šamir Yuharᶜiš's reign.

L. 17: *stbrw*, 10th form of *brw* (cf. commentary on Ja 631/4); cf. Arabic *barā*(*i*), 10th form, "to explore". – *msgt*, cf. Arabic *siyâǧ* "enclosure" (cf. *LaAEL*, p. 1460 A) and Syriac *syôgtō* "enclosure, stronghold" (cf. *PaSmCSD*, p. 374 B) from the root *swǧ*; *msgt* could possibly mean "bodyguards".

L. 19: *ẕḫn*, verb and plural of *ẕḫnt*: *CIH*, I, pp. 131 B and 383, III, p. 325 A, *CoRoC*, p. 143 B and

BeSI, p. 21; here, as well as in CIH 82/7 and 334/15, the verb is passive, but active in Ja 687/7. – *mḏyt*, feminine of *mḏy*; cf. Arabic *maḍā(i)* "to pass, take place" and Soqoṭri *mṣ̱y* "to pass" (cf. *LeLS*, p. 248).

L. 20: *fhḏ*, e.g., RÉS 4782/2 and *JaIHI*, p. 105. – *ndf*, name of the horse; cf. Arabic *nadafa* "to move the forefeet with great agility and to run very fast (horse)".

L. 21: *ḥḏr*, e.g., CIH 546/6. – *tḫdᶜ*, 5th form of *ḫdᶜ* (cf. Ja 511/4 and commentary, and also, e.g., RÉS 4646/13); the abstract and participle *mḫdᶜ* in Ja 511/4 and Kawkab 1/11, respectively; cf. *RhKTB*, II, p. 24: "to miss, not to fulfil its purpose"; the 5th form may be translated "to be lost, useless, without any utility"; cf. also the 4th Qat form *sḫdᶜ*, e.g., in RÉS 3854/4. – *ymtn*, e.g., RÉS 3910/5, where this imperfect is derived from *mwt* "to die"; this interpretation cannot be accepted here, because the parallelism with *tḫdᶜ* requires the same tense in the following verb which also depends on the conjunction *k*. Cf. Arabic *ʾamata* "to be or become curved", and *ʾamt* "curvity, crookedness, distortion" (cf. *LaAEL*, pp. 94 C–95 A).

Ll. 22-24: *wʾtw/⟨hʾ/⟩wšᶜbhw/– –/wḥmdm*, cf. lines 13-14; the pronoun *hʾ* must be restored here.

L. 25: *ḥrb*, RÉS 3550/4, name of a city and of a wâdî between Wâdî Beiḥân and Mârib (cf., e.g., *WiHöBGS*, pp. 40-45); name of a valley (RÉS 4904/2), of a tomb (RÉS 4668/4); cf. also the personal name *ḥrbm*, e.g., in Ja 642/5, and *ḥrb*, both noun (e.g., Ja 575/3) and verb (e.g., Ja 574/4).

L. 26: *qrytnhn*, cf. *qrytm*, e.g., in Ja 634/4 and the family name *qrnhn* (RÉS 4649/2).

L. 27: *hwt* instead of *hʾ*.

Ll. 27-28: *mʾt*, cf. commentary on Ja 572/4 and Mehri *miyêt* (cf. *JaMSSA*, p. 212 A).

Ll. 31-32 and 37: *rgzgzn*: *qataltalân* form; cf. the Arabic names of a man *ar-râǧiz* (cf. *WüID*, 133/18) and of places *ar-raǧǧâz* and *ar-riǧâz* (cf. *WüR*, p. 99 A).

L. 32: *thrg*, 5th form of *hrg*. – *šf*, cf. Arabic *šafā(o)* "to appear (new moon)". – *šrq*, cf. Arabic *šarq* "sunrise" and *šarîq* "rising sun"; in line 33, cf. Arabic *šarq* "rise".

Ll. 32-33: *mqṭt*, cf. *CoRoC*, p. 231 A at *qyẓ*, and Arabic *qâẓa* "to be warm, hot (summer day)" and commentary on Ja 594//10: *qṣ*.

L. 33: *lyl/lylm*, cf. Arabic *layl layîl* "long night", i.e., "all night long".

Ll. 33-34: *kwkbn/ḏṣbḥn*, same construction as the very well-known *ṣlmn/ḏḏhbn*; this interpretation is preferable to that according to which *ḏṣbḥn* would be the proper name of the star.

Ll. 35-36: *ṯny/ʾḫdn*, CIH 407/26 and commentary in *JaASAB*, pp. 163-64.

L. 40: *brḥlhn/*(also Ja 665/39); for *rḥl*, cf. Arabic *raḥl* "saddle for a camel" (cf. *LaAEL*, p. 1053 C); for *-hn* (cf. also *bythn* in Ja 734/5, and *ᶜṭwfhn* in Ja 735/9), article form previously unknown in Sab but usual in Ḥaḍr (cf. *HöASG*, p. 113).

Ll. 40-41: *gmlm/wbqrm/wḏʾnm*, cf. *gmlm/wbqrm/wᶜnzm* (Ḥimâ/9) and *ʾʾblm/wʾṯwrm/wbqrm/wḏʾnm* (Ja 665/26-27). *bqr* (cf. *CoRoC*, p. 117 B), cf. Arabic *baqar*, collective noun, and pl. *buqûr* "bulls and cows"; in Ja 665/26, *bqr* means "cows"; in Ḥimâ/9, the translation of *bqr* as "boeufs" (as *RyISA*, X, p. 287) is inaccurate; *bqr* means "bovines" cf.; also the Western Semitic cognates in *JeHoDISO*, p. 41: *bqr*$_1$. – *ḏʾn*, e.g., Ist 7630/7; cf. *CoRoC*, p. 226 B.

L. 41: *mḫr*, cf. *CoRoC*, p. 177 A.

650 – Yellowish, slightly grayish sandstone. – MaMB 200.

STONE: thickness: 30.5 cm. (top) and 21 (bottom). – *Front*, covered with red paint; 1.258 m. (left) and 1.254 m. (right) × 39.7 cm. (top) and 40 (bottom). – INSCRIPTION: same disposition of lines as in Ja 552; letter height: from 2.7 cm. to 3; space between the lines: from 0.3 cm. to 0.4. – SYMBOL, cf. Ja 603.

Sym- *bhl/ʾsᶜd/bn/grt/wbdš/ʾqwl/šᶜb*
bol *n/ḏmry/hwtn/ʾrbᶜw/ḏsmhrm/mqtw*
y/mrʾhmw/šmr/yhrᶜš/mlk/sbʾ/wḏrydn/h
qnyw/ʾlmqhṯhwnbᶜlʾwm/ṣlmn/ḏḏhbn
bn/ᶜšr/yᶜšrnn/lʾlmqhw/ṯhwnbᶜlʾwm/
bn/qyẓn/w⟨⟩gnyn/ḥgn/kwqhhmw/ʾlmqhṯhw
nbᶜlʾwm/bmsʾlhw/wlwfy/mrʾhmw/šmr/yh
rᶜš/mlk/sbʾ/wḏrydn/wlwfy/wṣḥ/ᶜbdhw/bh
l/ʾsᶜd/bn/grt/wbdš/wldṯ/yḫmrnhmw/ʾlm
qhṯhwnbᶜlʾwm/ḥẓy/wrḍw/mrʾhmw/šmr/yh
rᶜš/mlk/sbʾ/wḏrydn/wldṯ/yzʾn/ḫmrhmw/ʾ
lmqhṯhwnbᶜlʾwm/frᶜ/ʾmrt/dṯʾ/wḫrf/ws
ᶜsᶜm/wmlym/mhrbḏm/ᶜdy/kl/ʾrḍhmw/wʾs
rrhmw/wmqyẓhmw/wmšmthmw/wtbqlthmw
wʾṯmr/wʾfql/ṣdqm/ḏyhrḍwnhmw/ᶜdy/kl
ʾrḍhmw/mšrqm/wᶜltm/wmšrᶜhmw/wlhwf
ynhmw/ʾlmqhṯhwnbᶜlʾwm/bʾmlʾ/y
stmlʾnn/bᶜmhw/bmsʾlhw/wḥmdm/b
ḏt/hwfy/wmtᶜn/ᶜbdhw/bhl/ʾsᶜd/bn/gr
t/wbdš/bkl/sbʾt/wḥryb/sbʾw/wšwᶜn

21 *mrʾhmw/šmr/yhrʿš/mlk/sbʾ/wd̲rydn/ʿdy/s*
22 *hrtn/bkl/hnt/sbʾt/wḥryb/wʾtww/bʾ*
23 *ḥllm/wsbym/wġnmm/wmltm/d̲hh̲ḍf/whr*
24 *ḍwn/ʾlbbhmw/wʾlbb/šʿbhmw/d̲mry/ʾr*
25 *bʿw/d̲smhrm/wlwzʾ/hwfynhmw/bkl/sbʾ*
26 *t/ysbʾnn/wšwʿn/mrʾhmw/šmr/yhrʿš/m*
27 *lk/sbʾ/wd̲rydn/wlwzʾ/h̲mrhmw/ʾlmqhw*
28 *ṯhwnbʿlʾwm/ʿbdhw/bhl/ʾsʿd/bn/grt*
29 *wbdš/bry/ʾʾd̲nhmw/wmqymthmw/wlh̲mr*
30 *hmw/ʾwldm/ʾd̲krm/hnʾm/wld̲t/ymtʿn*
31 *wh̲ryn/ʿbdhw/bhl/ʾsʿd/bn/grt/wbdš/b*
32 *n/bʾstm/wnkytm/wnḥtm/wḥlṣm/wn*
33 *kytm/wʾ..tm/wmyqẓ/wnḍʿ/wšṣy/wtṯʿ*
34 *t/šnʾm/d̲rḥq/wqrb/d̲bnhw/dʿw/wd̲bnhw*
35 *ʾl/dʿw/bʾlmqhṯhwnbʿlʾwm/*

1 **Sym-** Bahal ʾAsʿad, descendant of Garat and Badaš, rulers of the tribe
2 **bol** Ḏamrî Hawtân, the fourths of [the tribe] Sumhurâm, high official
3 of their lord Šamir Yuharʿiš, king of Sabaʾ and Raydân, have
4 dedicated to ʾIlumquh Ṯahwân, master of ʾAwwâm, this statue which [is] in bronze,
5 from the tithe [which] they shall offer to ʾIlumquhû Ṯahwân, master of ʾAwwâm,
6 from the fruits of summer and the garden-fruits, as ʾIlumquh Ṯahwân, master of ʾAwwâm, has ordered them
7 through His oracle, and for the safety of their lord Šamir Yuh-
8 arʿiš, king of Sabaʾ and Raydân, and for the safety and the health of His worshipper Bahal
9 ʾAsʿad, descendant of Garat and Badaš; and in order that may vouchsafe to them ʾIlum-
10 quh Ṯahwân, master of ʾAwwâm, the esteem and grace of their lord Šamir Yuh-
11 arʿiš, king of Sabaʾ and Raydân; and in order that may continue to vouchsafe to them,
12 ʾIlumquh Ṯahwân, master of ʾAwwâm, the optimum crop of cereals of spring and of autumn and of
13 summer and of winter, favorable in their every land and all their wâdî-side
14 valleys and their summer settlement and their arable fields and their plantations,
15 and [also] perfect fruits and harvests, which would please them, in their
16 every land on the east and higher lands and their ploughed field; and that may shower
17 upon them ʾIlumquh Ṯahwân, master of ʾAwwâm, the favors [for which]
18 they shall beseech Him through His oracle; and in praise be-
19 cause He has protected and saved his worshipper Bahal ʾAsʿad, descendant of Garat
20 and Badaš, in all the encounters and the battles [in which] they fought and assisted
21 their lord Šamir Yuharʿiš, king of Sabaʾ and Raydân, in
22 Saharatân: from all those encounters and battles, they came back with
23 animals and captives and booty and riches, which soothed and fav-
24 ored their hearts and the hearts of their tribe Ḏamrî, the
25 fourths of Sumhurâm; and that He may continue to protect them in all the encounters
26 [in which] they will fight and assist their lord Šamir Yuharʿiš,
27 king of Sabaʾ and Raydân; and that may continue to vouchsafe to them ʾIlumquhû
28 Ṯahwân, master of ʾAwwâm, to His worshipper Bahal ʾAsʿad, descendant of Garat
29 and Badaš, the strength of their understanding and of their power; and that He may vouchsafe
30 to them male, pleasing children; and that He may save
31 and preserve His worshipper Bahal ʾAsʿad, descendant of Garat and Badaš, from
32 misfortunes and sufferings and beating and plunder and suffer-
33 ings and...and sleeplessness and [from] the hostility and wickedness and fear
34 of [any] enemy, who is remote and near, those who are known and those who
35 are not known. By ʾIlumquh Ṯahwân, master of ʾAwwâm.

L. 1: *bhl*, e.g., Ja 528/1 and commentary. – *bdš*, RÉS 2636/1, Ḥaḍr, and also the Arabic personal name *bâdâš* (cf. *SlGaVNPA*, p. 7 B).

L. 2: *hwtn*, cf. the Thamudic personal name *hwt* (cf. *vdBrTTPS*, e.g., p. 97: Ph 167 ao). – *ʾrbʿw* (also in lines 24-25), plural of *ʾrbʿ* (cf. *HöASG*, p. 104, §87; cf. also commentary on Ja 615/18-19); considered as noun.

L. 5: *bn/ʿšr/yʿšrnn*, CIH 342/5-6.

L. 6: *gny* (copy: *wwgnyn*) equals *gnw*; cf. commentary of Ja 574/6; *qyẓ* and *gny* indicate the fruits of summer and the garden-fruits, respectively.

L. 13: *mhrbḍ*, participle of the 4th form (*hrbḍ*) of *rbḍ*; cf. Arabic *rabaḍa*, 4th form "to manage, take care of the expenses of his own family"; here, related to each name of seasons with the meaning of "favorable", that is to say which provides the crops and the fruits expected during these periods of time; cp. *mrbḍn*, name of a temple dedicated to Taʾlab, e.g., in CIH 339/2-3; in Geukens 9/15, *mhšfq* replaces *mhrbḍ*.

L. 14: *tbqlt*, plural of *tbql*, e.g., RÉS 4995/1.

L. 16: *mšrʿ*, RÉS 4514/1; cf. *RoVSAY*, p. 313: "*šarīʿ* e *mašraʿ* tipi di 'aratro' a Ṣanʿāʾ e nel Yemen settentrionale".

L. 20: *ḥryb*, cf. commentary on Ja 574/4.

L. 23: *hẖdf*, 4th form of *ẖdf*; cf., with the metathesis of the last two consonants, Arabic *ẖafḍ* "tranquillity; quietness; quietude" (cf. *LaAEL*, p. 773 C); *hẖdf* may be translated "to render tranquil, soothe".

L. 32: *nḥt*, cf. Arabic *naḥt*, *masdar* of *naḥata* "to beat, strike...with a staff, *or* a stick" (cf. *LaAEL*, p. 2773 B). – *ḥlṣ*, cf. Syriac *ḥlôṣō* "pillage, abduction".

L. 33: *ʾ..tm*, ?

651 – White, slightly yellowish alabaster; upper left corner broken; photograph in Plate 16. – MaMB 108.

STONE: maximum thickness: 20.2 cm. (top) and 20 (bottom). *Front:* central part of the left edge damaged; 1.23 m. (right) and 1.245 (left) × 28 cm. (top) and 28.3 (bottom). – INSCRIPTION: same disposition of lines as in Ja 552; the signs of the left half of line 42 and all of lines 44, 46, 48, 50, 52, 54, and 56 are painted in red. – SYMBOL cf. Ja 603.

1 **Symbol** *ʿ⌜bd⌝ʿ[m/.../ḏmḏrḥm/...*
2 *wṯfyn/wm[...*
3 *d/ʾbʿl/bytn/šb[...*
4 *m/ʾqwl/šʿbynhn/mhʾnfm/wẓh⌜r⌝*
5 *mqtwy/šmr/yhrʿš/mlk/sbʾ⟨/⟩wḏr*
6 *ydn/bn/ysrm/yhnʿm/mlk/sbʾ/w*
7 *ḏrydn/hqny/lmrʾhmw/ʾlmqh*
8 *ṯhwnbʿlʾwm/ṣlmn/ḏḏhbn/ḥ*
9 *mdm/bḏt/hʿn/wmtʿn/grb/ʿb*
10 *dhw/ʿbdʿm/ḏmḏrḥm/wgrybt/*
11 *šʿbhw/wnẓrhw/wʾsdm/ḏhʾs*
12 *y/bʿmhw/bn/wdqt/wmḥqr/by*
13 *tnhn/byt/hmdn/wbtʿ/bkn*
14 *ẖtnw/bhmy/bytnhn/bkn/wq⟨h⟩*
15 *hw/mrʾhw/šmr/yhrʿš/mlk/s*
16 *bʾ/wḏrydn/lnẓr/wtnṣfn/(b)*
17 *hgrn/mrb/lḥḍr/ʾbhy/wḏnm*
18 *ḏnmn/bywm/tsʿm/ʿhdtn/w*
19 *bywm/šhrm/wywm/ṯnym/ḏnm*
20 *m/ḏʿsm/wwdqy/hmy/btnhn*
21 *ḏhmdn/wbtʿ/bn/hwt/ḏnmn/w*
22 *ḥmd/ʿbdʿm/ḏmḏrḥm/ẖyl/w*
23 *mqm/ʾlmqhṯhwnbʿlʾwm/b*
24 *ḏt/mtʿ/wẖlwn/ʿbdhw/ʿbdʿ*
25 *m/ḏmḏrḥm/wkl/ʾsdhw/wʾ*
26 *l/ḏfqdw/bn/ʾšrʿhmw/kbr*
27 *rḥlm/wwzʾw/ʾsyhw/ln/brṯ*
28 *w/mḥqr/bytnhn/bkn/wqhh*
29 *w/mrʾhmw/mlkn/lsbʾ/wqt*
30 *dmn/ẖms/sbʾ/lhʿn/wlbrʾ*
31 *ʾgnʾ/wmḥfdt/hgrn/mrb/w*
32 *lšym/lhw/mḍrfn/swn/ṭm*
33 *ḥnyn/ḏyḥmynhw/bn/ḏʿbn/*
34 *whgbʾ/ʿbdʿm/ḏmḏrḥm/tʾ*
35 *mntm/lẖyl/wmqm/mrʾhmw*
36 *ʾlmqhbʿlʾwm/kkhlw/whk*
37 *mln/bkl/ḏwqhhmw/mrʾhm*
38 *w/šmr/yhrʿš/mlk/sbʾ/wḏry*
39 *dn/wlẖmrhmw/ʾlmqh/ṣḥ/ww*
40 *fy/grb/mrʾhmw/šmr/yhrʿš/m*
41 *lk/sbʾ/wḏrydn/wlwzʾ/ʾl*
42 *mqh/hʿnn/wmtʿn/ʿbdhw/ʿ*
43 *bdʿm/ḏmḏrḥm/bn/kl/ḏbʾs*
44 *wlẖmrhw/ʾlmqh/ḥẓy/wrḍw*
45 *mrʾhmw/šmr/yhrʿš/mlk/s*
46 *bʾ/wḏrydn/wlẖmrhw/ʾlm*
47 *qh/bry/ʾʾḏn/wmqymtm/wn*
48 *ʾd/qyẓm/wṣrbm/ʿdy/kl/ʾ*
49 *rḍhmw/wlhʿnn/wmtʿn/wẖ*
50 *ryn/ʾlmqh/ʿbdhw/ʿbdʿm/ḏm*
51 *ḏrḥm/bn/bʾstm/wnkytm/wġ*
52 *ym/wnḍʿ/wšṣy/wtṯʿt/wšm*
53 *t/wšfʿ/whfʿ/wṭwʿ/kl/šnʾm*
54 *ḏrḥq/wqrb/ḏbnhw/ġrbw/w*
55 *ḏbnhw/ʾl/ġrbw/bʾlmqhṯhw*
56 *nbʿlʾwm*

1 **Symbol** ʿAbdʿ[amm,..., he of Maḏraḥum,...
2 and Ṯafyân, and M[...
3 d, masters of the house Šab[...
4 m, rulers of the two tribes Muhʾanifum and Ẓuhâr,
5 high official of Šamir Yuharʿiš, king of Sabaʾ and Ray-
6 dân, son of Yasrum Yuhanʿim, king of Sabaʾ and
7 Raydân, has dedicated to their lord ʾIlumquh
8 Ṯahwân, master of ʾAwwâm, this statue which [is] in bronze, in
9 praise because He has helped and saved the person of His
10 worshipper ʿAbdʿamm, him of Maḏraḥum, and the persons
11 of his tribe and of his subordinates and [the] soldiers whom he took away
12 with him both from the familiars and the low people of the
13 two houses, the two houses of Hamdân and Bataʿ, when

14 they allied these two houses by marriage when has ordered
15 him his lord Šamir Yuharʿiš, king of
16 Sabaʾ and Raydân, to protect and preserve
17 the city [of] Mârib until [the month] ʾAbhay arrives and falls
18 the rain during the period of the ninth [consecutive] rain and
19 during the period of [the] new moon and during the period of[the] second rain,
20 which was desired; and became allied these two houses [of]
21 Hamdân and Bataʿ from this rain on; and
22 ʿAbdʿamm, he of Madrahum, has praised the strength and
23 the power of ʾIlumquh Ṯahwân, master of ʾAwwâm, be-
24 cause He has saved and acted graciously toward His worshipper ʿAbdʿamm,
25 him of Maḏraḥum, and (toward) all his soldiers and those
26 who were not lost from their brave men of the Leader of
27 Raḥlum; and his messengers continued until they located
28 the low people of the two houses, when ordered him
29 their lord, the king, to fight and to take
30 command of the army of Sabaʾ in order to assist in building
31 the walls and the towers of the city [of] Mârib, and
32 (in order) to assure for him [the king] the construction [which was] made without cement, toward the Ṯam-
33 ḥânite, which he must protect against the waves;
34 and ʿAbdʿamm, he of Maḏraḥum, has given proofs of confidence
35 to the strength and power of their lord
36 ʾIlumquh, master of ʾAwwâm, for they have been able to act
37 perfectly in all that has ordered them their lord
38 Šamir Yuharʿiš, king of Sabaʾ and Ray-
39 dân; and that ʾIlumquh may vouchsafe to them the health and the sa-
40 fety of the person of their lord Šamir Yuharʿiš,
41 king of Sabaʾ and Raydân; and that may continue ʾIl-
42 umquh to protect and save His worshipper
43 ʿAbdʿamm, him of Maḏraḥum, from all that would harm;
44 and that ʾIlumquh may vouchsafe to him the esteem and grace
45 of their lord Šamir Yuharʿiš, king of Sa-
46 baʾ and Raydân; and that may vouchsafe to him ʾIlum-
47 quh the strength of understanding and of power and [also] the magni-
48 ficence of the fruits of summer and of autumn in their
49 every ground; and that may assist and save and pre-
50 serve ʾIlumquh His worshipper ʿAbdʿamm, him of Maḏ-
51 raḥum, from misfortunes and sufferings and per-
52 dition and (from) the hostility and wickedness and fear and abu-
53 se and invasion and advantage and constraint of every enemy,
54 who is remote and near, those who come from abroad and
55 those who do not come from abroad. By ʾIlumquh Ṯahwân,
56 master of ʾAwwâm.

The clan name *mḏrḥm* must be restored either in line 1 or in line 2.

L. 2: *ṯfyn*, e.g., CIH 41/1.
L.3: *šb...*: the possibilities of restoration are numerous.
L. 4: *šʿbynhn*: the *y* is the vowel of the declension of the noun. – *ẓhr*, cf. the name of the Qat sun goddess *ḏt/ẓhrn* (cf. *JaP*, pp. 107-08), and *ẓhrm*, family name (Ja 548/2) and name of a reservoir (Ja 511/2); cf. the historical commentary on Ja 576/6.
Ll. 5-6: *sbʾwḏrydn*: without word divider.
L. 7: *hqny/lmrʾhmw/ʾlmqh*: the use of the preposition after the verb *hqny* is also attested both in RÉS 4230/1-2 and JE 4/2 (cf. A. Jamme, in *BiO*, 14 [1957], p. 78); note that, in these three texts, the name of the deity is separated from the verb by some noun(s).
Ll. 11-12: *hʾsy*, 4th form of *ʾsy* "to take away".
L. 12: *wdqt* (CIH 396/9, where the immediate context is missing), plural of *wdq*; the form *ʾwdq* is also attested, e.g., in RÉS 3821/6; the verb *wdq* in Ja 619/7 means "to happen, occur"; here, as well as for the verb in dual *wdqy* in line 20, cf. Arabic *wadaqa* "to be accustomed to someone and become familiar with him"; *wdq*, present participle of the 1st form, "familiar". – *mḥqr*, cf. Arabic *muḥaqqar* "contemned, despised, mean", from the verb *ḥaqara* "to be contemptible, despicable" (cf. *LaAEL*, p. 611 C); *mḥqr* may be translated "low people".
L. 14: *ḫtn*, cf. commentary on Ja 570/4: *mḫtn*. – *hmy* (also in line 20): dual masc. demonstrative adjective (cf. commentary on Ja 576/10: *hmw*).
Ll. 14-15: *wqhw*: one *h* has been omitted by haplography and must be restored at the end of line 14.
L. 16: *tnṣf*, cf. commentary on Ja 564/11-12. – *ġ*

instead of *b* at the end of the line is certain on the stone.

L. 17: *ḥḏr*, cf. the 4th form *hḥḏr* in RÉS 4176/1; here, "to be present, arrive". – *ᵓbhy*, cf. name of a month, e.g., in RÉS 2726/10.

Ll. 17-18: *ḏnm/ḏnmn*, cf. Ethiopic *zănĕm* and *zĕnam* "to rain" and "rain", respectively.

L. 18: *ᶜhdt*, cf. *CoRoC*, p. 203 B; here, cf. Arabic *ᶜahdat* or *ᶜihdat*, plural *ᶜihâd* "rain at the beginning of the spring; rains following immediately after another one".

L. 19: *šhr*, e.g., RÉS 3688/6, Qat. – *ywm* equals *bywm* (lines 18 and 19).

Ll. 25-26: *ᵓl/ḏ*, cf. *HöASG*, p. 50, §43 and Arabic *ᵓallaḏ*.

L. 26: *fqd*, Ja 525/4 and commentary; cf. also *tfqd*, 5th form in Ja 665/48-49. – *ᵓšrᶜ*, plural of *šrᶜ*; the ordinary meaning of *šrᶜ* (cf. *CoRoC*, p. 253 A and also commentary on Ja 555/4) does not fit the present context; here, cf. Arabic *šarîᶜ* "brave, courageous", and *šarâᶜat* "courage, bravery". – *kbr(/?)rḥlm*: since it is divided into two parts by its location at the end of a line and at the beginning of the following, it is quite impossible to know whether it should be written as one or two words; cp., e.g., *kbrḫll* (e.g., Ja 613/11) or *kbr/ḫll* (e.g., Ja 696/2).

Ll. 26-27: *brṯ*: the verb is known in Sab RÉS 4624/1 with the meaning "to level", that is to say "to make room for"; here, the verb has the meaning "to locate", which is also directly connected with the basic meaning of the noun (cf. commentary on Ja 559/9).

L. 29: *mlkn*: the upper half of *k* is engraved on top of that of *ᵓ*.

L. 30: *lhᶜn/wlbrᵓ*, as well as *khlw/whkmln* (lines 36-37) obvious case of coordination of two verbs instead of dependance.

L. 32: *mḏrf*, plural *mḏrft* (e.g., CIH 540/29); cf. *CIH* (II, p. 272 B): probably construction without cement. – *swn*, preposition indicating the direction (cf. *HöASG*, p. 155).

Ll. 32-33: *ṭmḥnyn*: *ṭmḥn* with *nisba* ending; *ṭmḥn* is known as the name of a wâdî near Mârib in CIH 540/9, of some kind of lodging-house (cf. *JaISAR*, p. 121) in CIH 343/17 and RÉS 4006, and also of an unknown building in RÉS 4648/4. Here, the noun most probably refers to some building in connection with Wâdî Ṭamḥân.

L. 33: *ḏḥmynhw*: same meaning as in Ja 863/4, Qat; cf. the 5th form *ḥtmy* "to give protection"; e.g., in RÉS 4775/2 and NaNN 74/9-10. – *ḏᶜb*, cf. Arabic *ḏaᶜaba*, 7th form "It (*water*)... flowed in a continuous stream" (cf. *LaAEL*, p. 965 C) and *dawâᶜib*, plural of *dâᶜibat* (feminine of *dâᶜib*) "waves, which are rushing down one after the other".

Ll. 34-35: *hgbᵓ/tᵓmntm/lḫyl*, cp. *hṯb/lhw/–/tᵓmnm* (Ja 555/4, and commentary); here, *tᵓmn*, plural *tᵓmnt*, means "proof of confidence".

Ll. 36-37: *khlw/whkmln*, cf. the remark on *hᶜn/wbrᵓ* (line 30); for *khl*, cf. commentary on Ja 559/12; for *hkml*, 4th form of *kml*, cf. Arabic *kamala*, 4th form "to achieve, make something perfect and complete".

L. 43: *bn/kl/ḏbᵓs*: the ordinary formula is *bn/kl/ bᵓs(t)m*.

Ll. 51-52: *ġym*: at first sight, the *m* might either belong to the root or be the mimation. In the first hypothesis, cf. Arabic *ġaym* "thirst". The existence of the root *ẓmᵓ* (e.g., Ja 750/6) is, in my opinion, an indication to prefer the second hypothesis. Cf. Arabic *ġayy* "state of perdition" (cf. *LaAEL*, p. 2305 B) from the root *ġawā* (i) "to lose one's way"; this interpretation fits the context better.

L. 53: *šfᶜ*, cf. Syriac *šifᶜō* "abundance of water... rushing stream... flood", from *šfaᶜ* "to pour forth, overflow... abound" (cf. *PaSmCSD*, pp. 592 A and 591 B respectively). – *hfᶜ*, probably *maṣdar* of the 4th form of *nfᶜ* "to be useful, advantageous to someone" and *nafᶜ* "profit, gain"; *hfᶜ* might be translated "advantage".

L. 54: *ġrb*, e.g., RÉS 3341/3, Min; here, cf. Arabic *ġaraba* "to come from a foreign country" and its derived noun *ġurub* "foreigner".

652 – Grayish sandstone inscription, broken on top; photograph in Plate 16. – MaMB 161.

STONE: 16 cm. (top) and 21 (bottom). – *Front:* 22.8 cm. × 60.9 (right), 64.5 (center), and 60 (left). INSCRIPTION, same disposition of lines as in Ja 559; below line 24, two horizontal lines indicate the space for another line of the text which was never engraved; letter height: from 2.4 cm. to 2.5; space between the lines: from 0.1 cm. to 0.3.

1 **[Sym-** *šrḥbᵓl/.... /wᵓḫy]*
2 **[bol** *hw/mrṯdm/ḏḥẓrm/ᶜ]*
3 *⌜mrt/mqt⌝wyy/mrᵓhmy/šmr*
4 *yhrᶜš/mlk/sbᵓ/wḏrydn*
5 *bn/ysrm/yhnᶜm/mlk/s⌞b⌟*

6 *ʾ/wḏrydn/hqnyy/mrʾh⌉*
7 *mw/ʾlmqhbʿlʾwm/ṣlm⌈n⌉*
8 *ḏḏhbn/lwfy/mrʾhmy*
9 *šmr/yhrʿš/mlk/sbʾ/w*
10 *ḏrydn/wlwfy/ʿbdyhw/š*
11 *rḥbʾl/wʾḫyhw/mrṯdm*
12 *ḏḥẓrm/wlsʿdhmy/ʾlm*
13 *qh/ḥẓy/wrḍw/mrʾhmy*
14 *šmr/yhrʿš/mlk/sbʾ/wḏ*
15 *rydn/wlḫmrhmy/ʾlmq*
16 *hbʿlʾwm/sʿdhmy/ʾʾrḫ*
17 *wmngwt/ṣdqm/bḍrm/w*
18 *slmm/wlmtʿnhmy/ʾlm*
19 *qh/bn/ṭwʿ/wšmt/wšṣy*
20 *šnʾhmy/wlnqm/wwqm/ʾ*
21 *lmqh/kl/ḏ yḫrgnhmy/ʿ*
22 *br/mrʾhmy/whqny/ḏt*
23 *n/bywm/wqhhw/mrʾhw/š*
24 *mr/mlk/sbʾ/wḏrydn/lh⌉*
25 *wḍʿ/wšrḥ/bbytn/slḥn*

1 [**Sym-** Šaraḥbiʾil....and his bro-]
2 [**bol** ther Marṯadum, he of Ḥaẓrum]
3 [ʿA]mrat, the two high officials of the lord of them both Šamir
4 Yuharʿiš, king of Sabaʾ and Raydân,
5 son of Yasrum Yuhanʿim, king of Sabaʾ
6 and Raydân, have dedicated to their lord
7 ʾIlumquh, master of ʾAwwâm, this statue
8 which [is] in bronze, for the safety of the lord of them both
9 Šamir Yuharʿiš, king of Sabaʾ and
10 Raydân, and for the safety of His two worshippers Ša-
11 raḥbiʾil and his brother Marṯadum,
12 him of Ḥaẓrum; and that may make both of them happy ʾIlum-
13 quh with the esteem and grace of the lord of them both,
14 Šamir Yuharʿiš, king of Sabaʾ and
15 Raydân; and that may vouchsafe to both of them ʾIlumquh,
16 master of ʾAwwâm, to make both of them happy with undertakings
17 and security perfect in war and
18 peace; and that ʾIlumquh may save both of them
19 from the constraint and abuse and wickedness
20 of the enemy of both of them; and that may take vengeance and degrade
21 ʾIlumquh anyone who would incite both of them
22 against the lord of both of them; and he [Šaraḥbiʾil] has dedicated this
23 at the time when has commanded him his lord Ša-
24 mir, king of Sabaʾ and Raydân, to
25 bring favor and success in the house Salḥân.

L. 1: *šrḥbʾl*, e.g., Ja 489 C.

L. 2: *ḥẓrm*, e.g., Ja 391, Qat. – [.]*mrt*: many guesses are equally possible; *ʿmrt* is a well known family name; e.g., RÉS 3966/4-5 and Ja 348/1, Qat (cf. commentary).

Ll. 6-7: *hmw* (only once as in contrast to *hmy*: eight times) refers both to the subjects of the inscription and the king Šamir.

L. 20: *wqm*, cf. Arabic *waqama* "to treat someone with violence and hardness, debase, degrade".

L. 22: *hqny* has the same subject as that of *hw* in *wqhhw* (line 23).

Ll. 22-23: *ḏtn*: one would expect *hqnyt*; *ḏtn* obviously refers to the preceding understood noun; new singular demonstrative feminine pronoun.

Ll. 24-25: *hwḍʿ*, 4th form of *wḍʿ*; cf. Arabic *waḍaʿa*, 4th form "to be in agreement with someone about something"; here, *hwḍʿ* may be translated "to favor".

The usual final invocation does not exist and should have been engraved between the two horizontal lines traced below line 25 (cf. above).

653 – Yellowish, slightly grayish sandstone; cf. Chapter I, A. – MaMB 220.

STONE: thickness: 27.3 cm. (top) and 24.2 (bottom); *Front:* upper left and lower right corners broken; 39.2 cm. (only 30.5 on top) × 1.16 m. (only 97 cm. on the left side). – INSCRIPTION: same disposition of lines as in Ja 552; letter height: from 4.2 cm. to 3.2; space between the lines: from 0.7 cm. to 0.4. – SYMBOL, cf. Ja 565.

1 **Sym-** *šʿbn/sbʾ/khln/hqnyw[/ʾlmqh]*
2 **bol** *ṯhwnbʿlʾwm/ṣlmnhn/ḏd[hbn]*
3 *ḥmdm/bḏt/hwfyhmw/bʾmlʾ/whw[kl]*
4 *t/stwklw/bʿm/mrʾhmw/ʾlmqhbʿl*
5 *ʾwm/lqbly/ḏḫḫbt/brq/ḫrf/ḏhrf*
6 *tbʿkrb/bn/wddʾl/bn/ḥẓfrm*
7 *ṯlṯn/wtbšrw/bʿm/ʾlmqh/kyḫmrn*
8 *hmw/sqym/mlym/lmrb/wʾsrrhw/w*
9 *ʾklʾhw/bywm/ʾrbʿm/ḏfqhy/wrḫ/*
10 *ḏmlyt/ḏm(nḏ)/ḫrfn/wbmw/hwt⟨/⟩ywm*
11 *n/ḏbhw/stmlʾw/bʿm/ʾlmqh/fḫmrhm*
12 *w/ḏnmm/wsqym/ḏhrḍw/ʾdmhw/ʿd*
13 *y/ywm/ʿšrm/ḏʿšrnhn/bmw/hwt/wr*
14 *ḫn/ḏmlyt/wlwzʾ/ʾlmqhṯhwnbʿl*
15 *ʾwm/ḫmr/whwfyn/ʾdmhw/šʿbn/sb*
16 *ʾ/khln/bklʾmlʾ/whwkl/yzʾnn/*
17 *stmlʾn/wstwkln/bʿmhw/wlḫmrh*
18 *mw/ʾlmqhṯhwnbʿlʾwm/ḥẓy/wrḍ*

19 *w/mrʾhmw/šmr/yhrʿš/mlk/sb*
20 *ʾ/wḏrydn/bn/ysrm/yhnʿm/mlk/s*
21 *bʾ/wḏrydn/bʾlmqhṯhwnbʿlʾwm*

1 **Sym-** The tribe Sabaʾ Kahilân, [they] have dedicated to [ʾIlumquh]
2 **bol** Ṯahwân, master of ʾAwwâm, these two statues which [are] in br[onze],
3 in praise because He has showered upon them the favors and the recommen[dation]s
4 [for which] they have showed their confidence in their lord ʾIlumquh, master of
5 ʾAwwâm, because of this: has deceived the lightning season of the autumn of the year
6 of Tabaʿkarib, son of Waddʾil, descendant of Ḥazfarum,
7 the third; and they have begged of ʾIlumquh that He may vouchsafe to
8 them agreeable irrigation for Mârib and its wâdî-side valleys and
9 its young herbage grounds on the fourth day of Faqḥay and (during)the month of
10 Mulayat which [is] in autumn; and in this very day,
11 some of it [the tribe] have besought ʾIlumquh; so He has vouchsafed to them
12 rain and irrigation, which pleased His worshippers, on
13 the tenth day of the twenty in this very month
14 of Mulayat; and that may continue ʾIlumquh Ṯahwân, master
15 of ʾAwwâm, to vouchsafe to and shower upon His worshippers, the tribe Sabaʾ
16 Kahilân, all the favors and recommendation [for which] they shall continue
17 to beseech and show their confidence in Him; and that may vouchsafe to
18 them ʾIlumquh Ṯahwân, master of ʾAwwâm, the esteem and grace
19 of their lord Šamir Yuharʿiš, king of Sabaʾ
20 and Raydân, son of Yasrum Yuhanʿim, king of Sabaʾ and Raydân. By ʾIlumquh Ṯahwân, master of
21 ʾAwwâm.

L. 1: *hqnyw*: agreement *ad sensum.*

L. 5: *hḫbt*, 3rd feminine (the 3rd masculine, *hḫb*, is attested in Ja 735/5) person of the 4th form of *ḫbb*; cf. Arabic *ḫabba* "to be *or* become deceitful"; the 4th form may be translated "to deceive".

L. 6: *ḥzfrm*, e.g., Ja 540 A/4.

L. 8: *mly*: adjective: "bringing joy, agreeable".

L. 9: *ʾklʾ*, cf. *BeSI*, p. 5; here, place where the young herbage grows up. – *ḏfqḥy*, cp. Qat *ḏfqḥw* in RÉS 3854/3; the final *y*, instead of *w*, must be restored in RÉS 3154 (=Ist 7519)/2.

L. 10: *m(nḏ)* (but *mḏn* in my copy) preposition of time; cf. Arabic *miḏ* or *muḏ* and *minḏu* or *munḏu* (used only in matter of time) "in, during, from the beginning of" (cf. *LaAEL*, pp. 2699 A and 2738 A).

654 – Intact inscription; whitish sandstone; photograph in Plate 16. – MaMB 31.

STONE: almost constant thickness: 16 cm. – *Front:* upper and lower edges slightly damaged; 22.2 cm. (top) and 21.7 (bottom) × 46.5 (left) and 42.6 (right). – INSCRIPTION: same disposition of lines as in Ja 561 bis; letter height: 2.5 cm.; space between the lines: 0.3 cm.; distance from line 1 to the top: 0.5 cm. (left) and 1 (right), and from line 16 to the bottom: 2.5 cm. (right) and 3.3 (left). – SYMBOL: the curve is awkward; for the upper and lower inside lines, cp. the second (from the top) one in Ja 616, and the upper one in Ja 569 respectively; cf. Plate A.

1 **Sym-** *ʾbkrb/wḥywʿṯtr/w*
2 **bol** *ʿbdʿṯtr/wbnyhmw/w*
3 *hbʾwm/bnw/ʿqbm/hqnyw*
4 *mrʾhmw/ʾlmqhw/bʿl/ʾwm*
5 *ṣlmm/ḏḏhbm/ḥmdm/bḏt*
6 *ḫmrhmw/ʾlmqhw/wldm/ḏ*
7 *krm/wlwzʾ/ʾlmqhw/ḫ*
8 *mrhmw/ʾdmhw/ʾwldm/ʾ*
9 *ḏkrm/hnʾm/wlḫmrhw/wf*
10 *y/grbthmw/wlḫmrhmw/ḥ*
11 *ẓy/wrḍw/mrʾhmw/šmr/y*
12 *hrʿš/mlk/sbʾ/wḏrydn/wl*
13 *ḫmrhmw/ʾṯmrm/wʾfqlm*
14 *hnʾm/wlḫrynhmw/wmtʿn*
15 *hmw/bn/nḍʿ/wšṣy/wtṯʿt*
16 *šnʾm/bʾlmqhwbʿlʾwm*

1 **Sym-** ʾAbkarib and Ḥayûʿaṯtar and
2 **bol** ʿAbdʿaṯtar and their son Wa-
3 habʾawwâm, descendants of ʿAqbum, have dedicated to
4 their lord ʾIlumquhû, master of ʾAwwâm,
5 a statue which [is] in bronze, in praise because
6 ʾIlumquhû has vouchsafed to them a male
7 child; and that ʾIlumquhû may continue to
8 vouchsafe to them, His worshippers, male, pleasing
9 children; and that He may vouchsafe to him the safe-
10 ty of their persons; and that He may vouchsafe to them the
11 esteem and grace of their lord Šamir Yu-
12 harʿiš, king of Sabaʾ and Raydân; and that He
13 may vouchsafe to them pleasing fruits and

14 harvests; and that He may preserve them and save
15 them from the hostility and wickedness and fear
16 of [any] enemy. By ʾIlumquhû, master of ʾAwwâm.

L. 2: *ᶜbdᶜṯtr*, e.g., RÉS 4138/10.
L. 3: *ᶜqbm*, cp. *ᶜqbn*, e.g., in Ja 603/3.
L. 6: *ẖ* of *ẖmr* is normal, but dextrograde in *ẖmr* in lines 7-8, 9, 10, and 13, and also in *ẖry* in line 14.

655 – Yellowish, slightly grayish sandstone plaque. – MaMB 253.

PLAQUE: thickness: 8 cm. (top) and 6.5 (bottom). – *Front:* the center of the upper edge is widely splintered off; 61.5 cm. (left) and 61.7 (right) × 26. – INSCRIPTION: same disposition of lines as in Ja 552; letter height: from 2.1 cm. to 2.4; space between the lines: 0.2 cm. and 0.3.

1 *šrḥw⌜d⌝[m/bn/. . ./]wršdm*
2 *wẓᶜ/šᶜbn/mʾḏn/hqny/m*
3 *rʾhw/ʾlmqhṯhwnbᶜ*
4 *lʾwm⟨/⟩ḏn/ṣlmn/ḏḏhbm/ḥm*
5 *dm/bḏt/stwkl/bᶜmhw*
6 *lẖmrhw/ḥyw/lhw/wdd*
7 *m/bn/ʾṯthw/ẖlḥlk/w*
8 *ẖmrhw/mrʾhw/ʾlmqh*
9 *ḥyw⟨/⟩lhw/ġlmm/ḏystm*
10 *yn/mrsᶜm/wlwzʾ/ʾlmq*
11 *h/ẖmr/ᶜbdhw/šrḥwdm⟨/⟩ʾw*
12 *ldm/ʾḏkrm/hnʾm/ḏkwkbt*
13 *wmngt/ṣdqm/wḥẓy/wrḍw*
14 *mrʾhmw/šmr/yhrᶜš/mlk/*
15 *sbʾ/wḏrydn/bn/ysrm/yhnᶜ*
16 *m/mlk⟨⟩/sbʾ/wḏrydn/wnʾd/*
17 *qyẓ/wṣrb/⟨b⟩mlk/mʾyltn/wẖy*
18 *tmtn/wrḍw/šᶜbhmw/bʾlm*
19 *qhṯhwnbᶜlʾwm/wšym.hmw*
20 *wdm/bᶜlsmᶜnwšᶜbm*

1 Šaraḥwadd[um, son of. . .] and Rašidum,
2 chief of the tribe Muʾḏin, has dedicated to his
3 lord ʾIlumquh Ṯahwân, mas-
4 ter of ʾAwwâm, this statue which [is] in bronze, in
5 praise because he has shown his confidence in Him
6 so that He would vouchsafe to him to grant life for him to Waddum,
7 the son of his wife Ḫalḥalak; and
8 his lord ʾIlumquh has vouchsafed to him
9 to grant life for him to a youth who was to be benamed
10 Marasᶜamm; and that ʾIlumquh may continue
11 to vouchsafe to His worshipper Šaraḥwaddum male,
12 pleasing, numerous children,
13 and [also] perfect security and the esteem and grace
14 of their lord Šamir Yuharᶜiš, king
15 of Sabaʾ and Raydân, son of Yasrum Yuhanᶜim,
16 king of Sabaʾ and Raydân, and [also] the magnificence of
17 the fruits of summer and of autumn ⟨in⟩ the property of the luxuriant gardens and of
18 the sown fields, and [also] the grace of their tribe. By ʾIlum-
19 quh Ṯahwân, master of ʾAwwâm, and their patron
20 Waddum, master of Samᶜân and Šaᶜbum.

L. 1: *šrḥwdm*, cf. *šrḥwd* in RÉS 2999/1, Min, and Van Lessen 10/1, Qat. – Six letters are missing; *wʾẖ(y)hw* or *wbn(y)hw* is excluded by the following *w*.
L. 2: *wẓᶜ*, cf. Arabic *wâziᶜ* "chief, officer".
Ll. 6-7: *wddm*, e.g., RÉS 4596/1, and the family name *wdm* (RÉS 4852/4, Ḥaḍr).
L. 7: *ʾṯthw*, e.g., CIH 289/22. – *ẖlḥlk*: the two elements of this female name are previously attested in South Arabian.
Ll. 9-10: *ystmyn*, 3rd person masculine of the 8th form of *smy*: RÉS 3960/3; the 3rd person feminine, *tstmy*, is attested in RÉS 4233/10; for the 2nd form *smy*, cf. Ja 705/4.
L. 10: *mrsᶜm*: the 1st element is known as a personal name, e.g., in Thamudic (cf. *vdBrIT*, pp. 416-17; Doughty 16/6).
L. 11: after *šrḥwdm*, there is a space for a word divider which was not engraved. However, the lateral edges of that word divider are indicated by two lightly traced strokes which are slightly aslant to the left.
L. 12: *ḏkwkbt*, cf. *ʾly/kwkbt* in Ja 567/23.
L. 16: *mlk*, but *mlky* in my copy.
L. 17: *ṣrb/mlk* in my copy: the preposition *b* "in" is most probably missing by haplography: *ṣrb/bmlk*; the hypothesis of *bkl* instead of *mlk* is contradicted by the fact that, as in parallel expressions, *mʾylt* and *ẖytmt* should be determined by the personal pronoun (here, *hmw*). – *mʾylt*, plural of *mʾyl*; cf. Arabic *maʾlat*, plural *miʾâl* "luxuriant garden, *or* meadow".
Ll. 17-18: *ẖytmt*, plural of *ẖytm*; cf. Arabic *ẖitâm* "first watering of seed-produce, *or* of a sown field" (cf. *LaAEL*, p. 703 A).
L. 20: *wdm/bᶜlsmᶜnwšᶜbm*, cf. *JaP*, p. 76. For *smᶜn*, cf. the name of a man *smᶜm* in RÉS 5094/1, and the name of the lunar god *smᶜ* (cf. *JaP*, pp. 70-71, *JaDME*, pp. 5-6 and *JaRSAP*, p. 261). For *šᶜbm*, e.g., Ja 512/3, RÉS 4991 C and family name

in Ja 834/2; in RÉS 4610 B I, read *šʿbm* instead of "A droite, symbole divin: serpent (cf. *R.E.S.*, 4589 B)" (cf. *RÉS*, VII, p. 273); the last text referred to by *RÉS* shows a design entirely different from that in RÉS 4610 B II; besides, the two letters written above the 1st *d* of *wddʾl* are not mentioned by *RÉS*, and are the 2nd part of *šʿbm*; cf. also *šʿbntw* in RÉS 4909/1-2, Ḥaḍr.

3 – PERIOD *mlk/sbʾ/wḏrydn/wḥḍrm(w)t/wymnt:* Ja 656–671

a – Šamir Yuharʿiš: Ja 656-662

656 – Yellowish sandstone; photograph in Plate 16. – MaMB 135.

FRONT: left corners broken; covered with red paint; 1.195 m. × 35 cm. (top) and 30.5 (bottom). – INSCRIPTION, same disposition of lines as in Ja 552; letter height as well as distance between the lines: 0.7 cm. – SYMBOL: more regular than that in Ja 621, and two inside lines instead of one; cf. Plate A. – FLOWER: at the end of line 27; cf. the one in Ja 618; cf. Plate A.

1 **Sym-** *zydqwmm/ydrʾ/wbnyhw/rbʿt/*[. .]
2 **bol** *hr/wknnt/ybdr/wbnyhmw/tyml*
3 *t/ʾsʿd/wwfym/ʾẓrf/wwhblt/wyḥ*
4 *md/wʾbkrb/bnw/ʿṯkln/ʿṣyt/wḏrs*
5 *mm/hqnyw/mrʾhmw/ʾlmqh⟨w⟩bʿlʾwm/ṣ*
6 *lmn/ḏḏhbn/ḥmdm/bḏt/ẖmrhmw/ʾtw*
7 *bnhw/bwfym/wmhrgm/wġnmm/ḏh*
8 *rḍwhmw/bkn/šwʿw/mrʾhmw/šmr⟨/⟩y*
9 *hrʿš/mlk/sbʾ/wḏrydn/wḥḍrmt*
10 *wymnt/bn/ysrm/yhnʿm/mlk/sbʾ/w*
11 *ḏrydn/bḏr/hštʾ/bʿbr⟨/⟩mrʾhmw/šrḥ*
12 *ʾl/wrbšmsm/mlky/ḥḍrmwt/wwzʾw*
13 *ḥmd/ẖyl/wmqm/mrʾhmw/ʾlmqhw/bḏt/ʾ*
14 *tww/bnhw/bwfym/wmhrgm/wġnmm/ḏh*
15 *rḍwhmw/bkn/sbʾw/b(ʿ)m/šʿbhmw/s*
16 ⌊*bʾ*⌋*/khln/ʿdy/srrn/wrʾ/khwfyw/*
17 *mrʾhmw/ʾlmqhwbʿlʾwm/kl/ʾšr/g*
18 *bʾ/bʿlyhmw/bn/ʾrḍthmw/bn⟨/⟩rḥb*
19 *tn/wlwzʾ/ʾlmqhw/ẖmrhmw/ḥẓy/w*
20 *rḍw/mrʾhmw/šmr/yhrʿš/mlk/sbʾ*
21 *wḏrydn/wḥḍrmt/wymnt/bn/ysrm⟨/⟩y*
22 *hnʿm/mlk/sbʾ/wḏrydn/wlẖmrhm*[*w*]
23 *ʾlmqhwbʿlʾwm/wfy/grybthmw/w*
24 *ʾṯmrhmw/wʾfqlhmw/hnʾm/bn/ʾr*
25 *ḍthmw/bmrb/wrḥbtn/wlẖrynhmw*
26 *mrʾhmw/ʾlmqhwbʿlʾwm/bn/nḍʿ*
27 *wšsy/šnʾm/bʾlmqhwbʿlʾwm* **Flower**

1 **Sym-** Zaydqawwamum Yadraʾ and his two sons Rabîʿat. .
2 **bol** har and Kinnat Yabdar and their sons Taymalat
3 ʾAsʿad and Wafîum ʾAẓraf and Wahablat and Yuḥ-
4 mid and ʾAbkarib, descendants of ʿAṯkalân ʿUṣayyat and of Ras-
5 mum, have dedicated to their lord ʾIlumquh⟨û⟩, master of ʾAwwâm, this
6 statue which [is] in bronze, in praise because He has vouchsafed to them to come back
7 from there in safety and (with) war trophy and booty which
8 pleased them, when they assisted their lord Samir Yu-
9 harʿiš, king of Sabaʾ and Raydân and Ḥaḍramawt
10 and Yamnat, son of Yasrum Yuhanʿim, king of Sabaʾ and
11 Raydân, in the war [which] initiated against their lord, Šaraḥ-
12 ʾil and Rabbšamsum, the two kings of Ḥaḍramawt; and they have continued
13 to praise the strength and the power of their lord ʾIlumquhû, because they
14 have come back from there in safety and (with) war trophy and booty which
15 pleased them, when they fought with their tribe Sa-
16 baʾ Kahilân in Sarîrân; but now they have given
17 to their lord ʾIlumquhû, master of ʾAwwâm, all the tithe [that]
18 came to them from their lands, from Ruḥâbatân; and may ʾIlumquhû continue to vouchsafe to
19 tân; and may ʾIlumquhû continue to vouchsafe to them the esteem and
20 grace of their lord Šamir Yuharʿiš, king of Sabaʾ
21 and Raydân and Ḥaḍramawt and Yamnat, son of Yasrum Yu-
22 hanʿim, king of Sabaʾ and Raydân; and that may vouchsafe to the[m]
23 ʾIlumquhû, master of ʾAwwâm, the safety of their persons and
24 of their fruits and of their harvests, [both of them] pleasing, from their
25 lands in Mârib and Ruḥâbatân; and that may preserve them
26 their lord ʾIlumquhû, master of ʾAwwâm, from the hostility
27 and wickedness of [any] enemy. By ʾIlumquhû, master of ʾAwwâm. **Flower**

L. 1: *ydrʾ*, also second personal name, e.g., in RÉS 4855/1, Ḥaḍr.

L. 2: *knnt*, Ist 7613; full writing of *knt*, very well known personal name in Arabic *(al-)kinânat* (e.g., *WüID*, 18/9), Safaitic (e.g., *CIS*, p. 79 B: CIS 533) and Thamudic (cf. *vdBrTTPS*, p. 123: Philby 178 s 1/2) and perfect parallel of Greek *Χεννᾶτος*. – *ybdr*, cf. the personal name *bdrm* (Ja 194/1, Qat, and also Thamudic Philby 166 u 9, cf. *vdBrTTPS*, p. 80), the family name *bdrn* (RÉS 2864) and the feminine name *bdr* (cf. *MlHLM*, p. 23: Gl 1282/3, Min, and also in Safaitic, cf. *LiSI*, p. 302 A).

Ll. 2-3: *tymlt*, RÉS 3761, Min, and also *t(y)mm* in RÉS 4871/3, Ḥaḍr, and *tymm*, Qat, family name in Ja 486 (cf. *JaAFEQ*, p. 192); *tymm* is not attested in RÉS 5076/2-3 (cf. commentary on Ja 555/2; *ḥmʿṯt*). RÉS 3281 mentions *ḥmyn/ḏyfʿn* and *tymlt/ḏrdʿ*, who are attested in RÉS 3279/2 and 3280/1-2 respectively; therefore, *ḥm* in RÉS 3279/1 (note that the left part of *m* is unfinished; cf. *JaSaMA*, pl. CXXVI, No. 162) is a first attempt of the engraver, as already pointed out by the editors of the text (cf. *l.c.*, p. 345). Line 1 of RÉS 3279 is consequently to be suppressed. RÉS 3279, 3280, and 3281 belong to the same palaeographic type; for the drawing of these last two graffiti, cf. *l.c.*, pl. CXXV, Nos. 133 and 132 respectively. Another example of such an attempt which is left uncorrected is Ja 119: *ʿq* above and slightly to the left of the beginning of line 3: *ʿqrbm* (cf. *JaIRHY*, p. 191 A, commentary on Ja 119/1, and plate on p. 197, bottom).

L. 3: *ʾẓrf*, cp. the personal names, in Safaitic *(h)ẓrf* (cf. *LiSI*, p. 319 B, under *ẓrf*) and in Thamudic *ẓrf* (cf. *vdBrIT*, p. 263: HU 613, and commentary). – *whblt*, e.g., RÉS 4018/3 and Geukens 10/1-2 and 11.

Ll. 4-5: *rsmm*, cp. the family name *rsm*[...] in CIH 468 and the tribe name *yrsm*, e.g., in CIH 24/4; *rsm* is also a Thamudic personal name (cf. *vdBrTTPS*, p. 157: Philby 209 r 5).

L. 5: *ʾlmqh*: *sic* on the stone, but *ʾlmqhw* everywhere else (lines 13, 17, 19, 23, 26, and 27); the final *w*, as well as the word divider in lines 8, 11, 18, and 21, have probably been forgotten and may thus be restored.

L. 6: *ẖmrhmw*: *ẖ* was engraved instead of *h*; the upper central vertical stroke of *ẖ* was only partially erased.

Ll. 6-8: *ʾtw/——/ḏhrḏwhmw*: this pericope refers to lines 13-15 and mentions a fact posterior to the events recorded in lines 8-12.

L. 15: *bʿm*: *w* instead of ʿ is certain on the stone.

L. 16: *ʿdy/srrn*, CIH 397/9-10 and *CIH* (II, p. 57 B): city; here, Ḥaḍr country.

657 – Yellowish, slightly grayish sandstone; photograph in Plate 17. – MaMB 216.

STONE: thickness: 8 cm. (lateral sides) and 10 (bottom). – *Front:* the upper edge is widely splintered off; covered with red paint; 30.3 cm. (top) and 30 (bottom) × 42 (right) and 41 (left). – INSCRIPTION, same disposition of lines as in Ja 552; letter height: from 2.4 cm. to 1.8; space between the lines: from 0.4 cm. to 0.6. – SYMBOL, cf. Ja 656; cf. Plate A.

1 **Sym-** *lfʿ⌜ṯt/⌝[yšʿ/bn]⌜/mrḥbm/h⌝qny*
2 **bol** *mrʾhmw/ʾlmqhṯhwnbʿlʾ*
3 *wm/ṯlṯtn/ʾṣlmn/ʾly/ḏhbn/ḏš*
4 *fthw/ḥmd/bḏẖmrhw/ḏtnḍʿ/bʿmh*
5 *w/wrʾ/kẖmr/ʾlmqhbʿlʾwm/ʿbdhw/l*
6 *fʿṯt/yšʿ/bn/mrḥbm/hwfyn/lhw/ḏtn*
7 *ḍʿ/bʿmhw/wrʾ/khwfy/lmrʾhw/ʾl*
8 *mqh/ḏt/hqnytn/ḥgn/kšfthw/wʾl*
9 *mqhbʿlʾwm/lyzʾn/ẖmr/ʿbdhw/lfʿ*
10 *ṯt/yšʿ/ẖmrhw/ḏydʿn/bʿmhw/wʾṯm*
11 *r/ṣdqm/hnʾm/bn/kl/ʾrḍthmw/wlẖm*
12 *rhmw/ḥṣy/wrḍw/mrʾhmw/šmr/yhrʿ*
13 *š/mlk/sbʾ/wḏrydn/wḥḍrmt/wy*
14 *mnt/bʾlmqhṯhwnbʿlʾwmwḥrw*
15 *nm*

1 **Sym-** Laffʿaṯat [Yašwaʿ, descendant of (the clan)] (Marḥa)bum, has dedicated
2 **bol** to their lord ʾIlumquh Ṯahwân, master of
3 ʾAwwâm, these three statues which [are] in bronze, which he
4 promised to him in praise because He has vouchsafed to him what he implored from Him;
5 but now ʾIlumquh, master of ʾAwwâm, has vouchsafed to His worshipper
6 Laffʿaṯat Yašwaʿ, descendant of Marḥabum, to grant him what he
7 implored from Him; but now, he has given to his lord ʾIl-
8 umquh this offering as he has promised to Him; and as for ʾIl-
9 umquh, master of ʾAwwâm, may He continue to vouchsafe to His worshipper Laffʿa-
10 ṯat Yašwaʿ, to vouchsafe to him what he shall implore from Him, and [also] perfect,
11 pleasing fruits from all their lands; and that He may vouch-
12 safe the esteem and grace of their lord Šamir Yuharʿiš,
13 king of Sabaʾ and Raydân and Ḥaḍramawt and
14 Yamnat. By ʾIlumquh Ṯahwân, master of ʾAwwâm and Ḥirwâ-
15 num.

L. 1: *lfʿṯt*, for the first element, cf., e.g., the following Thamudic personal names *lf* (cf. *vdBrIT*, e.g., p. 145: HU 285, and *vdBrTTPS*, p. 142: Philby 196 4) and *lff* (cf. *vdBrIT*, p. 480: HuIR 137). – *yšʿ*, RÉS 3087/26. – *mrḥbm*, clan name, e.g., in RÉS 4963/1-2.

Ll. 3-4: *ḏšfthw/ḥmd/bḏ* equals *ḏšfthw/ḥmdm/bḏt* in Ja 658/5-6.

L. 4: *ḏtnḏʿ*: there is an oblique stroke inside ʿ.

Ll. 9-10: *ḫmr/‒‒‒/ḫmrhw*: the second verb *ḫmr* in line 10 is superfluous.

L. 10: *ḏyḏʿn*, from the verb *wḏʿ*; cf. Arabic *waḍaʿa* "to place, set, put"; here, same meaning as that of *tnḏʿ* in lines 4 and 6-7.

658 – Yellowish, slightly grayish sandstone; upper part = MaMB 244; bottom (photograph in Plate 17) = MaMB 182 = Ja 659.

UPPER PART: thickness. 12.8 cm. (top) and 19.6 (bottom); *front:* covered with red paint; upper left corner broken, left edge damaged; 19.5 cm. (top) and 21.6 (bottom) × 45.7 (right) and 50.5 (left). – BOTTOM: maximum thickness: 18.5 cm.; *front:* covered with red paint, 36.5 cm. (left) and 42 (right) × 21. – INSCRIPTION: same disposition of lines as in Ja 552; letter height: from 1.4 cm. to 2.5 (upper part) and from 2 to 2.3 (lower part); space between the lines: from 0.4 cm. to 0.5. – SYMBOL, cf. Ja 656.

Sym-bol

1 *ʾbšmr/ʾwlṭ/wrfʾ/ʾš[wʿ]*
2 *bnw/ḏḥfnm/wḏḏnm/ʾ[q]*
3 *wl/šʿbn/ʾyfʿ/hqny[y/m]*
4 *rʾhmw/ʾlmqhṯhwnbʿlʾw[m]*
5 *ṣlmm/ḏḏhbn/ḏšfthw/ḥmd*
6 *m/bḏt/hwfy/ʿbdyhw/ʾbšmr*
7 *wrfʾ/bn/kl/sbʾtm/wḏbʾ*
8 *t/šwʿy/mrʾhmw/šmr/yhrʿš*
9 *mlk/sbʾ/wḏrydn/wḥḏrmwt/w*
10 *ymnt/ʿdy/ʾrḏ/ḫwln/ʾlddn*
11 *wwqhhw/mrʾhw/šmr/yhrʿš/lr*
12 *tʿ/šrḥtm/bhgrn/ṣʿdtm/wl*
13 *gʾmn/ʿšr/ḫwln/ʾldd⟨n⟩/bʿd/ḥr*
14 *bt/mlkn/⟨. .⟩wbʿdnhw/ḏbʾw/b*
15 *ʿly/ʿšr/śnḥn/bsrn/dfʾ/w*
16 *ḫmrhmw/mrʾhmw/ʾlmqh/ḥ*
17 *mdm/wmhrgtm/wʾḫ ydt/ws*
18 *bym/wmltm/wġnmm/ḏʿsm*
19 *wbkn/sbʾw/wḏbʾ/bʿm/ʾq*
20 *w⌜l/wqh⌝ ⌞l/wqh⌟/mrʾhmw/šmr/yhrʿš/l*
21 *ḏbʾ/sh⌜rtn/wḥ⌝ ⌞rtn/wḥ⌟rbw/ʿšr/n*
22 *šdʾl/bsrn/ʿtwd/bšʾ⌜mt/⌝w*
23 *ḥmdw/ḫ yl/wmqm/ʾlmqhṯhw*
24 *nbʿlʾwm/bḏḫmr/ʿbdyhw*
25 *ʾbšmr/wrfʾ/bnw/ḥfnm/w*
26 *ḏnm/ʾḫllm/wʾḫ ydtm/ws*
27 *bym/wġnmm/ḏʿsm/wlwzʾ/ḫ*
28 *mrhmw/ʾlmqhṯhwnbʿlʾwm*
29 *ʾwldm/hnʾm/wbry/ʾʾḏnm*
30 *wmqymt/wḥẓy/wrḏw/mrʾh*
31 *mw/šmr/yhrʿš/mlk/sbʾ/wḏr*
32 *ydn/wḥḏrmwt/wymnt/wʿsm*
33 *ʾṯmrm/wʾbrq/ṣdqm/ḏyhrḏy*
34 *nhmw/bʾlmqhṯhwnbʿlʾwm*

Sym-bol

1 ʾAbšamar ʾAwlaṭ and Rafaʾ ʾAš[waʿ,]
2 descendants of [the two families] Ḥufnum and Ḏanam, [ru-]
3 lers of the tribe ʾAyfaʿ, have dedicated to their
4 [l]ord ʾIlumquh Ṯahwân, master of ʾAww[âm,]
5 a statue which [is] in bronze, which he [ʾAbšamar] has promised to Him in praise
6 because He has protected His two worshippers ʾAbšamar
7 and Rafaʾ from all the encounters and engagements
8 [in which] both of them assisted their lord Šamir Yuharʿiš,
9 king of Sabaʾ and Raydân and Ḥaḍramawt and
10 Yamnat, in the territory of Ḫawlân ʾIldôdân;
11 and his lord Šamir Yuharʿiš commanded him to es-
12 tablish a squadron in the city [of] Ṣadatum and to
13 cut off the groups of Ḫawlân ʾIldôd⟨ân⟩ after the battle
14 of the king; and after that, they waged war
15 against the groups of Śunḥân in the valley Dafaʾ; and
16 their lord ʾIlumquh vouchsafed to them
17 praise and war trophies and prisoners and cap-
18 tives and riches and booty, which was desired;
19 and when they fought and waged war along with the ru-
20 lers [whom] their lord Šamir Yuharʿiš ordered to
21 wage war against Saharatân and Ḥâratân; and they fought the groups of Na-
22 šadʾil in the wâdî-side valley ʿItwad in the north; and
23 they have praised the strength and the power of ʾIlumquh Ṯahwân,
24 master of ʾAwwâm, because He has vouchsafed to His two worshippers
25 ʾAbšamar and Rafaʾ, descendants of [the two families] Ḥufnum and
26 Ḏanam, animals and prisoners and cap-
27 tives and booty, which was desired; and that may continue to vouch-

28 safe to them ʾIlumquh Ṯahwân, master of ʾAwwâm,
29 pleasing children and the strength of understanding
30 and of power and [also] the esteem and grace of their lord
31 Šamir Yuharʿiš, king of Sabaʾ and
32 Raydân and Ḥaḍramawt and Yamnat, and [also] desirable,
33 perfect fruits and lightning seasons, which would please
34 them. By ʾIlumquh Ṯahwân, master of ʾAwwâm.

L. 1: *ʾbšmr: šmr* also enters in the composition of the name of a man *šmrẖls* in RÉS 4831/3-4 (instead of *šmr*[.). – *rfʾ*, cf., e.g., *rfʾm* (e.g., Ja 721/7) and *rfʾn* (e.g., RÉS 5095/2). – *ʾš*[]: two letters are missing; *ʾšwʿ* is a very common 2nd personal name.

L. 2: *bnw/ḏhfnm/wḏḏnm* = *bnw/ḫfnm/wḏnm* in lines 25-26; *ḫfnm* is ordinarily a personal name, e.g., Ja 144/1, Qat, and commentary; *ḏnm*, cf. *ḏnmm*, masculine personal and clan name in RÉS 4057/1 and Geukens 10/2 respectively; cf. also Thamudic personal name *ḏnwm* (cf. *vdBrIT*, p. 260; HU 600). For *ḏnnm* in RÉS 2734 R, cf. commentary on Ja 612/1.

L. 3: *ʾyfʿ* is better known as personal name (e.g., Ja 664/13) and especially as the name of a temple dedicated to Wadd (cf. *JaP*, p. 76). – *hqny*[*y*]: the dual is restored on the basis both of *ʿbdy* (lines 6 and 24) and of *šwʿy* (line 8).

L. 7: *sbʾtm*: the mimation excludes the relation of this noun with the verb *šwʿy* (line 8); this relation would however be expected.

L. 10: *ʾldn*, cf. *ddʾl*, e.g., in Ja 584/4.

Ll. 11-12: *rtʿ*, cf. commentary on Ja 576/7.

L. 12: *šrḥt*, e.g., NaNN 72+73+71/1; cf. *CoRoC*, p. 252 B: "squadron", but *BeSI*, p. 43: "property". – *ṣʿdtm*, cf. *ṣʿdt*, personal name, e.g., both in Thamudic (cf. *vdBrTTPS*, p. 107: Ph 170 f 2) and Safaitic (cf. *LiSI*, p. 332 B) and also place name in Arabic (cf. *GoAT*, p. 735 and *WüR*, p. 136 A); cf. also *ṣʿd*, name of a person, e.g., both in Thamudic (cf., e.g., *vdBrIT*, p. 345: Doughty 45) and Safaitic (cf. *LiSI*, p. 340 A) and of a place in Arabic (cf. *WüR*, p. 136 A); cf. also the Arabic name of a man *ʾabû ṣ-ṣʿdy* (cf. *GoAT*, p. 285).

L. 13: *gʾm*, cf. Syriac *gam* or *gôm* "to cut off" (cf. *PaSmCSD*, pp. 71 B and 64 B respectively).

L. 14: *mlkn/* is followed on the stone by two signs: first, a *w* the central vertical stroke of which takes the whole letter height, and secondly a word divider (my field book). – *bʿdn*, cf. *HöASG*, p. 146.

L. 15: *śnḫn*, name of a tribe; RÉS 4919+CIH 537/3; cf. also *śnḫ*, name of a tribe, temple or place connected with ʿAṯtar in RÉS 4673/3. – *dfʾ*, cf. *dafâ*, Arabic name of a place (cf. *WüR*, p. 90 A).

Ll. 16-17: *ḥmd* means here as well as in many other places, not simply "praise" but "reason for praise".

Ll. 21-22: *nšdʾl*, name of a man in Safaitic (cf. *LiSI*, p. 330 A).

L. 23: *ʿtwd*, cf. commentary on Ja 742/13.

L. 32: *ʿsm*, cf. *BeSI*, pp. 42-43.

659 = MaMB 182 = bottom of Ja 658.

660 – Yellowish, slightly grayish sandstone; broken on top; photograph in Plate 17. – MaMB 156.

STONE: thickness: 16.5 cm. (top) and 12.2 (bottom). – *Front:* 45.1 cm. (right), 52.2 (center) and 46 (left) × 31 (top) and 31.3 (bottom). – INSCRIPTION, same disposition of lines as in Ja 552; letter height: from 2 cm. to 2.3; space between the lines: from 0.3 cm. to 0.5; distance from line 20 to the bottom: 1.8 cm. (right) and 1 (left); the text is incomplete and continued on another stone.

1 **[Sym-** *whbʾwm*]⸢*/m*⸣[. . .
2 **[bol** . . */wḥ*]⸤*ḍrmwt/w*⸢*kdt*⸢[*/w*]⸢*mḏḥ*⸢[*gm*]
3 [*wbh*]⸢*lm/*⸣*wḥdʾn/wrḍwm/wʾẓlm/wʾ*⸢*m*⸣
4 ⸢*rm/mqtwy/šmr/yhrʿš/mlk/sbʾ/wḏry*
5 *dn/wḥḍrmwt/wymnt/hqnyw/mrʾhmw*
6 *ʾlmqhṯhwnbʿlʾwm/ṣlmn/ḏḏhbn*
7 *ḏšfthw/ḥmdm/bḏt/ẖmr/whwfyn/ʿ*
8 *bdhw/whbʾwm/bʾmlʾ/stmlʾ/bʿ*
9 *mhw/bkn/wqhhw/mrʾhmw/šmr/yhr*
10 *ʿš/mlk/sbʾ/wḏrydn/wḥḍrmwt/wymn*
11 *t/lṭrd/whwkbn/bʾṯr/ḥrṯn/bn/kʿ*
12 *bm/wswdm/bn/ʿmrm/grynhn/wʾsdhmw*
13 *nẖʿn/wgrm/bkn/tfrqw/bn/ḏẖzfn/bh*
14 *grn/mrb/wbʿmhmw/yʿmr/wzʿ/šʿbn/sbʾ*
15 *wʾẖḏhmw/hmt/ʾsdn/ḥrṯn/bn/kʿbm/w*
16 *s(w)dm/bn/ʿmrm/wʾsdhmy/ḏbn/grm/wnẖʿn*
17 *bfrṭn/wʾwlhmw/bʾqrnm/bʿbr/mrʾhm*
18 *w/šmr/yhrʿš/mlk/sbʾ/wḏrydn/wḥḍrmwt/w*
19 *ymnt/ʿdy/bytn/slḥn/whgrn/mrb/wḥmdm*
20 ⸤*bḏt/ẖmr/ʿbdyhw/hwfyn/mlʾ/stmlʾw/bʿmhw*

1 **[Sym-** Wahabʾawwâm] M[. . . . . .]
2 **[bol** Ḥa](ḍ)ramawt and Kindat [and] Maḏḥi-[gum]
3 [and Bahi]lum and Ḥadaʾân and Raḍwum and ʾAẓlum and ʾAm-

4 rum, high official of Šamir Yuharᶜiš, king of Sabaʾ and Ray-
5 dân and Ḥaḍramawt and Yamnat, have dedicated to their lord
6 ʾIlumquh Ṯahwân, master of ʾAwwâm, this statue which [is] in bronze,
7 which he promised to Him in praise because He has vouchsafed to and showered upon
8 His worshipper Wahabʾawwâm the favors [for which] he besought
9 Him when had ordered him their lord Šamir Yuhar-
10 ᶜiš, king of Sabaʾ and Raydân and Ḥaḍramawt and Yamnat,
11 to pursue and follow closely the trail of Ḥariṯân, son of Kaᶜ-
12 bum and Sûdum, son of ᶜAmrum, the two deputies, and their soldiers
13 Nuḫᶜân and Garam when they left (deserted) (the tribe) Ḫazfân in
14 the city [of] Mârib and with them Yaᶜmur, chief of the tribe Sabaʾ;
15 and he captured them, those soldiers: Ḥariṯân, son of Kaᶜbum, and
16 S(û)dum, son of ᶜAmrum and the soldiers of them both, among them Garam and Nuḫᶜân,
17 by outrunning [them]; and he brought them back as rebels to their lord
18 Šamir Yuharᶜiš, king of Sabaʾ and Raydân and Ḥaḍramawt and
19 Yamnat, to the house Salḥân and the city [of] Mârib; and in praise
20 because He has vouchsafed to His two worshippers to shower the favor [for which] they besought Him.

L. 3: *bhlm* is restored on the basis of Ja 665/3. – *ḥdʾn*, cf. the Arabic names of a place *ḥaddâʾu* (cf. *WüR*, p. 67 A) and of men *ḥadâʾu* (cf. *GoAT*, p. 125) and *miḥdâ* (cf. *HeBN*, p. 18 A). – *rḍwm*, cp. *rḍwn* (cf. commentary on Ja 166/1, Qat).

Ll. 3-4: *ʾmrm*: personal name in Ja (348/1), Qat (cf. *JaDME*, p. 20) and family name in Ja 832; cf. *ʾmr*, name of a Qat temple, e.g., in Ja 868/3 (cf. also commentary in *JaSQI*, p. 46).

L. 11: *ṭrd*, cf. Arabic *ṭarada* "to drive away, banish" (cf. *LaAEL*, p. 1838 B); here, with the obvious meaning "to pursue". CIH 547/3-4: – –/*ʾl*/ *hwfyhw*/*mṭrdhw*/*bḏmwṣbm*/– –, is translated by *CIH* (II, p. 311) and *BeSI* (p. 51) "– –, quia non solverant ei oblationem ejus in (mense) Dhû Mauṣib – –" and "– –, because they did not duly pay him his mtrd in the (month) ḏMWṢBm, – –", respectively. First of all, the interpretation of *hwfy* in *hwfyhw* in "solvere" or "to pay duly" is not justified and should have been explained; note that *hwfy* in *hwfyhmw* (line 8) is translated by *CIH* (*l.c.*) and *BeSI* (*l.c.*) "concedere" and "to protect", respectively. Besides, *hwfy* in *hwfyhw* is singular, and not plural, as suggested in the two preceding translations; note here again that *CIH* (*l.c.*) and *BeSI* (*l.c.*) translate *hwfy* in *hwfyhmw* (line 8) as a singular, and not as a plural: "concessit" and "he did – protect", respectively. With regards to *mṭrd*, *CIH* (*l.c.*, p. 310 A) does not attempt to justify in any way his conjecture of interpreting this noun as an offering. *BeSI* proposes two interpretations of *mṭrd* and finds the second "more attractive" (p. 52), namely "wild animals due to the god as an offering or sacrifice at fixed seasons" (p. 51) or "equivalent to the *ṣyd*/ or ritual hunt" (p. 52). The Semitic root *ṭrd* (see the study of J. C. Greenfield, "Lexicographical Notes I," in *Hebrew Union College Annual*, 29 [1958], pp. 210-12) does not support any of the two preceding interpretations of *mṭrd*; furthermore, for the so-called ritual hunt, cf. *JaIHI* and *JaPSAP*, p. 198; contrast *LuYFS*, p. 11, note 9. The prefix *m*- indicates primarily a place name (cf. *HöASG*, p. 97, §84, γ); and *mṭrd* may be related to Arabic *ṭarîdat* which means not only "stolen camels which are driven away together" but also (as already proposed by Fr. Praetorius; cf. *CIH*, II, p. 310 A), "camel caravan." I thus would interpret *mṭrd* as a "place for a camel caravan", which evidently implies a resting place in the most general meaning of the expression, and to translate the above-quoted South-Arabian expression as follows: "– –, because he did not take care of [protect] his [the god's] camel caravan (resting) place in [the month] of Mawṣibum, – –". – *hwkb*/*bʾṯr*; for *bʾṯr*, cf. commentary on Ja 575/4; the expression *hwkb*/*bʾṯr* may be translated "to follow closely the trail of". – *ḥrṯn*, cp. *ḥrṯm* in RÉS 4158/5 and *ḥrṯt* in RÉS 4145/1; cf. also the Arabic names of men *ḥâriṯ* (cf. *SlGaVNPA*, p. 24 B), *al-ḥâriṯ*, *ḥurṯân*, *ḥâriṯat*, *ḥurayṯ*, *al-ḥurayṯ*, *al-ḥuwayriṯ*, *am-muḥtariṯ*, (cf. *WüID*, 242/16, 107/14, 268/18, 236/1, 248/1, 60/12 and 118/5 respectively), and of a clan *banû ḥurṯân* (cf. *WüID*, 118/1).

Ll. 11-12: *kᶜbm*, cf. the Arabic names of a woman *kᶜb* (cf. *LiEHA*, p. 87 B), of a clan *kᶜb* (cf. *WüR*, p. 256 B) and of places *kaᶜb* (cf. *MüHG*, p. 96 A), *al-kaᶜabât* (cf. *l.c.*, and *WüR*, p. 185 B), *al-kaᶜbat* (cf. *GoAT*, p. 763 and *WüR*, *l.c.*) and *kᶜbt* (cf. *MüHG*, p. 96 A and *WüR*, *l.c.*); cf. the

Thamudic personal names *kᶜb* and *kᶜbn* (cf., e.g., *vdBrIT*, p. 191: HU 370, and *vdBrTTPN*, p. 142: Ph 373 b, respectively).

L. 12: *swdm*: the reading is certain; however *sᶜdm* is not less certain on line 16; it is rather difficult to determine which of those two forms is correct or better; *swdm* is mentioned first and the proper names of the text are not usual; I prefer thus *swdm* rather than *sᶜdm*; cf. commentary on Ja 563/16 and also the Safaitic personal name *swd*, *swdm*, *ᵓswd* and *sdy* (cf. *LiSI*, pp. 330 B, 330-31, 299 B and 330 B respectively), the Thamudic personal name *swdt* (cf. *vdBrTTPS*, p. 158: Ph 209 u), and in Arabic the names of places *as-sûd*, *as-suwad*, *as-sawd*, *as-sawdâᵓu*, *as-sûdân*, *sûdân* and *as-sûdat* (cf. *MüHG*, p. 62 A), *al-ᵓaswad* and *al-ᵓaswidat* (cf. *l.c.*, pp. 5 B-6 A), of a man *sûdân*, *sawâd* (e.g., *WüR*, p. 463), *su(w)wîd*, *suwayyid* and *ᵓusîwid* (cf. *HeBN*, p. 31 A), *al-ᵓaswad* (cf. *GoAT*, pp. 39-41), *ᵓaswad* (cf. *MüHG*, p. 131 B) and *ᵓaswid* (cf. *HeBN*, *l.c.*), of women *sawdat* (cf. *WüR*, p. 463) and *Sûde* (cf. *HeBN*, *l.c.*). – *ᶜmrm*, also personal name, e.g., in RÉS 4855/1, Ḥaḍr, and family name, e.g., in Ja 864/2, Qat; cf. also *ᶜmr*, first personal name in Ja 882 B/1, Qat (cf. *JaPEQL*, p. 212). – *grynhn*, cf. Arabic *ǧarîy* "a commissioned agent, a factor, a deputy" (cf. *LaAEL*, p. 416 A).

L. 13: *nẖᶜn*, cf. *nẖᶜ*, name of a man in Thamudic (cf. *vdBrIT*, p. 403: Jsa 149) and of a place in Arabic (cf. *MüHG*, p. 113 B: *naẖaᶜ*); cf. also in Arabic *ᵓn-naẖᶜ*, name of a man (cf. *GoAT*, p. 590) and of a clan (cf. *WüR*, p. 260 A) and also *ᵓn-nẖᶜy*, name of a man (cf. *l.c.*, p. 742 and *GoAT*, p. 591). – *grm*, e.g., RÉS 3788, Min; cf. also in Min *grmt* (RÉS 3735/2) and *grmnhy* (e.g., RÉS 3740). – *tfrqw/bn*, cf. commentary on Ja 644/22; here, *tfrq/bn* means "to desert"; the phrase mentions the desertion of two deputies, members of the tribe Ḫazfân, who fled with some of their soldiers and a chief of the tribe of Sabaᵓ. – *ẖzfn*, cf. the Safaitic masculine name *ẖzf* (cf. *LiSI*, p. 317 A) and the Arabic place name *al-ẖzf* (cf. *WüR*, p. 80 C).

L. 14: *yᶜmr*, e.g., CIH 529/1-2; in RÉS 5057/1 and 5069, the reading of *ṯᶜmm* is certain, *RÉS* reads *yᶜmr* and *ᶜmr* respectively. – *wzᶜ*, e.g., RÉS 2895 A/4, Min; cf. Arabic *wâziᶜ* "chief, officer" (see mention by *BeNL*, IV, p. 139).

L. 15: *ᵓḫdhmw*: obvious case of an expletive pronoun.

L. 16: *s(w)dm*: ᶜ instead of *w* is certain on the stone (cf. commentary on line 12).

L. 17: *frṭ*, cf. Arabic *faraṭa* "to precede, outrun", and *faraṭ* "race in which one outruns everybody".

661 – Yellowish, slightly grayish sandstone; badly damaged on top; photograph in Plate 18. – MaMB 242.

STONE: thickness: 31 cm. – *Front:* covered with red paint; 79.3 cm. × 28.5. – INSCRIPTION: same disposition of lines as in Ja 552; letter height: from 2.2 cm. to 2.8; space between the lines: from 0.5 cm. to 0.6; line 1 is missing.

1 [*ᵓsᶜd/... /wᵓsdm/... /wsᶜdm/... / bnw/ḏṯt/...*

2 *[.]⌈/⌉ᶜ⌈ṯlm/⌉.⌈t⌉[... ...]⌈tklm/⌉[mqt]*

3 *wt/šmr/yhrᶜš/mlk⌈/⌉[sbᵓ/wḏrydn/wḥḍrmwt/wymnt/bn/ ysrm/y]hnᶜm/mlk/sbᵓ⌈/⌉[wḏrydn/hq]⌈nyw⌉*

4 *mrᵓhmw/ᵓlmqhṯhwn⌈b⌉[ᶜlᵓwm/... ./ḥm]⌈d⌉m/bḏt/ẖmr/whᶜn/w⌈m⌉[tᶜ]⌈n/⌉ᵓdm*

5 *hw/ᵓsᶜd/wᵓsdm/wsᶜ⌈dm⌉/bn/⌈mrḍ⌉[/wḍll]⌈/mrḍw⌉/ w⌈ḍll⌉[n]⌈/⌉bhgrn/ṯt/wlẖmrhmw/ᵓlmqhṯhw*

6 *nbᶜlᵓwm/ᵓdmhw/ᵓsᶜd/wᵓsdm/wsᶜd⌈m/b⌉nw/ḏṯt/ḥẓy/ wrḍw/mrᵓhmw/šmr/yhrᶜš/mlk/sbᵓ/w*

7 *ḏrydn/wḥḍrmwt/wymnt/wbry/ᵓᵓḏnm/wmq ymtm/ wfrᶜ/ᵓmyrt/dṯᵓ/wẖrf/wsᶜsᶜm/wmlym*

8 *wᵓṯmr/ṣdqm/hnᵓm/bn/kl/ᵓrḍthmw/wᵓsrrhmw/wlhᶜn/ wmtᶜn/ᵓlmqhṯhwnbᶜlᵓwm/ᵓdm*

9 *hw/ᵓsᶜd/wᵓsdm/wsᶜdm/bn/nḍᶜ/wšṣy/wtṯᶜt/šnᵓm/ ḏbnhw/dᶜw/wḏbnhw/ᵓl/dᶜw/bᵓlmqhbᶜlᵓwm*

1 [ᵓAsᶜad...and ᵓAsdum.... and Saᶜdum..., descendants of Ṯât...]

2 [...] ᶜAṯlum... ...Tukalum, [high offici]als

3 of Šamir Yuharᶜiš, king of [Sabaᵓ and Raydân and Ḥaḍramawt and Yamnat, son of Yasrum Yu]hanᶜim, king of Sabaᵓ [and Raydân], have [de]dicated

4 to their lord ᵓIlumquh Ṯahwân, m[aster of ᵓAwwâm, ...in pr]aise because He has vouchsafed to and protected and sa[ved] His

5 worshippers ᵓAsᶜad and ᵓAsdum and Saᶜdum from the disease [and the state of perishing] they suffered and lay near death in the city [of] Ṯât; and that may vouchsafe to them ᵓIlumquh Ṯahwân,

6 master of ᵓAwwâm, to His worshippers ᵓAsᶜad and ᵓAsdum and Saᶜdum, descendants of [the tribe] Ṯât, the esteem and grace of their lord Šamir Yuharᶜiš, king of Sabaᵓ and

7 Raydân and Ḥaḍramawt and Yamnat, and [also] the strength of understanding and of power, and the optimum crop of the cereals of spring and of autumn and of summer and of winter,

8 and [also] perfect, pleasing fruits from all their lands and their wâdî-side valleys; and that ʾIlumquh Ṯahwân, master of ʾAwwâm, may protect and save His worshippers

9 ʾAsʿad and ʾAsdum and Saʿdum from the hostility and wickedness and spying of [any] enemy, those who are known and those who are not known. By ʾIlumquh Ṯahwân, master of ʾAwwâm.

Ll. 1-2: there is no way of knowing whether there was a symbol at the beginning of the text or not.

L. 2: *ʿṯlm*; tribe name; cf. the personal name *ʿṯl* in Thamudic (cf. *vdBrTTPN*, p. 118: Ph 358 ab) and in Liḥyanite (cf. *JaSaMA*, p. 492, No. 231) and the Thamudic personal name *ʿṯ(w)l* (cf. *vdBrTTPN*, p. 89: Ph 331 d). – *tklm*, name of a tribe; cf. Arabic *takila* and *takula* "to entrust his business to an agent" and *tukalat* and *tukalân* "who entrusts his business to an agent".

L. 5: *ḍll*, e.g., CIH 539/6; for the verb *ḍll*, cf. Arabic *ḍull* "state of perishing" and *ḍalla* "to err, stray, go astray" (cf. *LaAEL*, pp. 1797 C and 1796 B, respectively). *ṯt*, name of a city and of the tribe living in that city (line 6). The city Ṯât (cf. *SpAGA*, p. 311, No. 444) is located in the territory of Radâʿ (cf. *MüHG*, 102/9) on the eastern boundary of Bilâd ʿAns (cf. *l.c.*, 92/17), thus approximately 100 km. southeast of Ṣanʿâʾ. *FoSA* (p. 145, note 3, with reference to D. H. Müller, in *Sitz. Kön. Pr. Ak. der Wiss. zu Berlin*, 1886, p. 842) states that the name of the city *ṯt* is attested in CIH 937/4. However, the sign after *t* of *ṯt* is not a word divider, but seems to be the right vertical half of *ẖ*; one could thus suggest the 8th form of a verb (cf. *CIH*, III, p. 268 B) such as *ṯẖn*; cf. Arabic *ṯaẖuna* "to be, become big, gross, coarse" and 8th form "to be weakened by wounds". Cf. also the personal Thamudic name *ṯt* (cf. *vdBrIT*, pp. 130-31: HU 238/1).

662 – Yellowish limestone inscription, broken into three parts; top = MaMB 98 (latex squeeze); both center (MaMB 91) and bottom (MaMB 96) = Ja 663; three photographs in Plates 17-18.

Front: covered with red paint. – INSCRIPTION: same disposition of letters as in Ja 552; letter height: 2 cm., but 2.1 (lines 2, 4 and 5) and 2.3 (line 10); space between the lines: from 0.4 cm. to 0.5, but 0.7 between lines 9 and 10.

MaMB 98 (lines 1-10a): *stone:* maximum thickness: 11.5 cm.; *front:* upper part and upper half of the right edge damaged; 22.8 cm. (left) and 21.5 (right) × 19.4 (top) and 19.6 (bottom).

MaMB 91 (lines 10b-15a): *stone:* almost constant thickness: 12 cm.; *front:* right edge damaged; 19.4 cm. × 10.4 (left) and 14 (right).

MaMB 96 (lines 15b-23): *stone:* thickness: 12 cm. (top) and 11.6 (bottom); *front:* 30.3 cm. (right) and 32 (left) × 19.4 (top) and 19.2 (bottom).

1 [**Sym-** *yʿmr/ʾšwʿ/w...*
2 [**bol**⸣ *⸢h⸣w/dm[./..]r/bnw/t(k)*
3 *[l]m/ʾnmrm/wẓʿy/šʿbn*
4 *[s]bʾ/hqnyw/mrʾhmw/ʾl*
5 *mqhṯhwnbʿlʾwm/ṣlm*
6 *n/ḏḏhbn/ḥmdm/bḏ⸤t⸥*
7 *hwfy/lʿbdhw/yʿmr/ʾšwʿ*
8 *⸤b⸥mlʾ/stmlʾ/bʿmhw/bh*
9 *[grn]⸤/šbwt/bkn/wqhhw*
10a *⸤r/yhrʿš⸥*
10b *mrʾhmw/šm⸢r/y⸣ / ⸢š/⸣[m]*
11 *lk/sbʾ/wḏrydn/wḥḍ*
12 *⸤rmwt/wymnt/lqrn/wnẓr*
13 *bhgrn/šbwt/bʿm/šʿbh*
14 *mw/sbʾ/wlw⸤zʾ/ʾlmqh/h⸥w*
15a *⸤fyn/⸥*
15b *⸢fyn/⸣lʿb⸢d⸣hw/yʿmr/ʾšwʿ/b*
16 *kl/ʾmlʾ/ystmlʾn/bʿmh*
17 *w/bkl/ʾbrṯ/yqhn/mrʾhm*
18 *w/šmr/yhrʿš/wlwzʾ/⟨⟩*
19 *ʾlmqhṯhwnbʿlʾwm/sʿdh*
20 *mw/ḥẓy/wrḍw/mrʾhmw/šm*
21 *r/yhrʿš/mlk/sbʾ/wḏry*
22 *dn/wḥḍrmwt/wymnt/b*
23 *ʾlmqhṯhwnbʿlʾwm*

1 [**Sym-** Yaʿmur ʾAšwaʿ and...] his [...
2 (**bol**) Dam[. ..]r, descendants of Tu(ka-)
3 [l](um) ʾAnmarum, the two chiefs of the tribe
4 [Sa]baʾ, have dedicated to their lord ʾIl-
5 umquh Ṯahwân, master of ʾAwwâm, this statue
6 which [is] in bronze, in praise because
7 He has showered upon His worshipper Yaʿmur ʾAšwaʿ
8 the favor [for which] he besought Him in the c[i-]
9 [ty (of)] Šabwat, when ordered him
10 their lord Šamir Yuharʿiš,
11 king of Sabaʾ and Raydân and Ḥaḍ-
12 ramawt and Yamnat, to head for and protect
13 the city [of] Šabwat with their tribe
14 Sabaʾ; and that ʾIlumquh may continue to shower
15 upon His worshipper Yaʿmur ʾAšwaʿ

16 all the favors [for which] he shall beseech Him
17 in all the campaigns [which] shall order their lord
18 Šamir Yuharʿiš; and that may continue
19 ʾIlumquh Ṯahwân, master of ʾAwwâm, to make them
20 happy with the esteem and grace of their lord Šamir
21 Yuharʿiš, king of Sabaʾ and Ray-
22 dân and Ḥaḍramawt and Yamnat. By
23 ʾIlumquh Ṯahwân, master of ʾAwwâm.

As far as palaeography and phraseology are concerned, Ja 781 could easily be the upper left corner of Ja 662; however, the two are engraved on different kinds of stone.

L. 1 is missing. – The very last letters are probably *bn(y)* or *ʾẖ(y)*.
L. 2: *dm.*: restoration, e.g., of *dmṯ*, *dmm*, *dmn*, *dmk*, etc. is equally possible. –]*r*: many restorations are possible.
L. 12: *qrn*, not the ordinary meaning of "to attack", but of "to head for, proceed to"; cf. Arabic *qarana*, 3rd form.
L. 18: *wlwzʾ/wlwz*[ʾ]: this dittography is obvious on the stone.

663 = MaMB 91 + 96 = center and bottom of Ja 662.

b – Yasrum Yuhanʿim

1° – WITH ṮAʾRÂN ʾAYFAʿ: Ja 664

664 – Grayish sandstone; partial photograph; cf. Chapter I, C. – MaMB 293.

STONE: thickness: 25.5 cm. – *Front:* upper left corner broken; very porous; 32.8 cm. × 85.8. – INSCRIPTION, same disposition of lines as in Ja 558; letter height: 2.8 cm.; space between the lines: 0.7 cm.; distance between line 1 and the upper edge: 0.8 cm. – SYMBOL, cf. Ja 644.

1 **Sym-** *ʾlʾmr/ynhb/*[. . .
2 **bol** *m/bnw/ḏsḥr/*[*hqnyw/mrʾ*]
3 *hmw/ʾlmqhwṯhwnb*[*ʿlʾwm/ṣ*]
4 *lmn/ḏḏhbn/ḥmdm/bḏš*[*fthw*]
5 *lẖmrhw/wldm/ḏkrm/wrʾ/*
6 *kẖmr/ʿbdhw/ʾlʾmr/ḏsḥr/w*
7 *ld/lhw/bnhw/brlm/wrʾ/kh*
8 *wfy/lmrʾhmw/hqnythw/ḏ*
9 *šfthw/wlzʾn/ʾlmqh/ẖmr*
10 *hw/ʾwldm/ʾḏkrm/wlẖmrh*
11 *w/wfy/grybthmw/wlẖmr*
12 *hmw/ḥẓy/wrḍw/mrʾyhmw/ysr*
13 *m/yhnʿm/wṯʾrn/ʾyfʿ/ʾmlk*
14 *sbʾ/wḏrydn/wḥḍrmt/wymn*
15 *t/wlẖmrhmw/ʾṯmrm/wʾfqlm/*
16 *bn/ʾrḍthmw/bn/mrb/wnšqm/w*
17 *nšn/wlmtʿnhmw/bn/mtʿ/wšṣy/w*
18 *tṯʿt/šnʾm/wbn/ġlyt/mrʾm/bʾ*
19 *lmqhṯwnbʿlʾwm/wbʿṯtr/wsḥ*
20 *r/wb/mḍḥhmw/ysrn/wšmsyhmw*
21 */bʿlty/ʾwṯnm*

1 **Sym-** ʾIlʾamar Yanhub [. . .
2 **bol** m, descendants of Saḥar, [have dedicated to] their [lord]
3 ʾIlumquhû Ṯahwân, ma[ster of ʾAwwâm], this [sta-]
4 tue which [is] in bronze, in praise because of this: he had pro[mised to Him]
5 that He would vouchsafe to him a male child; and so
6 now He has vouchsafed to His worshipper ʾIlʾamar, him of Saḥar, [that] there be
7 born to him his son, Barlum; and now, he has
8 given to their lord his offering which
9 he has promised to Him; and that ʾIlumquh may continue to vouchsafe to
10 him male children; and that He may vouchsafe to him
11 the safety of their persons; and that He may vouchsafe to
12 them the esteem and grace of their two lords Yasrum
13 Yuhanʿim and Ṯaʾrân ʾAyfaʿ, kings of
14 Sabaʾ and Raydân and Ḥaḍramawt and Yamnat;
15 and that He may vouchsafe to them fruits and harvests
16 from their lands from Mârib and Našqum and
17 Našân; and that He may save them from the artifice(?) and wickedness
18 and spying of [any] enemy and from the injustice of a lord. By ʾI-
19 lumquh Ṯawân, master of ʾAwwâm, and by ʿAṯtar and Saḥar
20 and by their god of irrigation Yasrân and their two sun-goddesses,
21 the two mistresses of the boundaries.

The text contains two haplographies: *wl⟨y⟩zʾn* (line 9) and *hṯ⟨h⟩wn* (line 19).

L. 1: *ʾlʾmr*, CIH 980/3.
L. 4: *ḥmdm/bḏš*[*fthw*] is difficult. On the one hand, *ḏ* belongs to the expression *ḥmdm/bḏ*, but *šft* is ordinarily (e.g., lines 8-9) preceded by *ḏ*; and if *hw* of *š*[*fthw*] refers – as it does – to the deity, the verb itself remains without any direct object. On the other hand, the context requires *lqbl(y)/ḏ(t)* instead of *ḥmdm/bḏ*.

Ll. 6-7: *wld*, cf. the Western Semitic cognates in *JeHoDISO*, p. 107: *yld*$_{1}$.

Ll. 8-9: *hqnythw/ḏšfthw*: *ḏt* instead of *ḏ* would grammatically be right; here, the agreement is *ad sensum*, that is to say with the masculine *ṣlm*.

L. 9: *lzʾn* instead of *lyzʾn* is also attested in Ja 700/16 and 752/13.

L. 17: *mtʿ*, cf. Arabic *matâʿat*, *maṣdar* of *matuʿa* "to be cunning, crafty"; the noun *mtʿ* may be translated "artifice, trick, ruse".

L. 18: *ġlyt*, RÉS 4011/12.

L. 19: *ṯwn*, instead of *ṯhwn*, is also attested in Ja 736/4-5.

L. 20: *mḏḥ*, here, common noun indicating the deity of irrigation; cf. *JaP*, pp. 125-27 and *JaRSAP*, pp. 271-72 (cf. also *MoNTA*, p. 353: *nḏḥ* "irriguer"), contrary to the opinion suggested by *vdBrDSAMW* (pp. 183-86 and 187 where the general conclusion, which is repeated by *vdBrHT*, p. 85, must be discarded) and *vdBrHT* (p. 102). – *ysrn*, new name of a deity of irrigation.

Ll. 20-21: *šmsyhmw/bʿlty/ʾwṯnm*, cf. *JaP*, pp. 102-03 and *JaRSAP*, p. 266.

2° – WITH HIS SON ḎARAʾʾAMAR ʾAYMAN: Ja 665

665 – Grayish sandstone; partial photograph; cf. Chapter I, C. – MaMB 290.

STONE: thickness: 35 cm. (top) and 21 (bottom). – *Front:* covered with red paint, upper left corner damaged before engraving; 1.564 m. × 41.9 cm. (top) and 41 (bottom). – INSCRIPTION: letter height: 2.5 cm. and 2.6; space between the lines: 0.5 cm. and 0.6; distance from line 1 to the upper edge: 1.2 cm. (right) and 1 (left). – SYMBOL, cf. Ja 587.

1 **Sym-** *sʿdtʾlb/ytlf/bn/gdnm/kbr*
2 **bol** *ʾʿrb/mlk/sbʾ/wkdt/wmḏḥgm/wḥr*
3 *mm/wbhlm/wzydʾl/wkl/ʾʿrb/sbʾ/wḥmy*
4 *rm/wḥḍrmt/wymnt/hqny/mrʾhw/ʾlm*
5 *qhbʿlʾwm/ṣlmm/ḏḏhbm/ḥmdm/bḏt/ẖm*
6 *rhw/mrʾhmw/ʾlmqhbʿlʾwm/bkn/wqhh*
7 *mw/mrʾhmw/ysrm/yhnʿm/wbnyhw/ḏr*
8 *ʾʾmr/ʾymn/mlky/sbʾ/wḏrydn/wḥ*
9 *ḍrmwt/wymnt/lsbʾ/wqdmn/mrʾyhmw/ysr*
10 *m/wbnyhw/ḏrʾʾmr/mlky/sbʾ/wḏrydn*
11 *wḥḍrmt/wymnt/ʿdy/ʾrḍ/ḥḍrmt/ww*
12 *q⟨h⟩hmw/mrʾhmw/ysrm/lsbʾ/wqdmnhmw/wtm*
13 *hrthw/ʾʿrb/mlk/sbʾ/wkdt/wʾbʿl/nš*
14 *qm/wnšn/wsbʾw/bʿly/ʿbrn⟨/⟩wtgʿr/wʾt*
15 *tmn/kl/gyšhmw/ẖmsy/wsbʿ/mʾtm/ʾsdm*
16 *rkbm/wsbʿy/ʾfrsm/wrqyw/bn/mfgrtn*
17 *wḏkww/ṯlṯy/rkbm/wʾrbʿ/ʾfrsm/mqdmtm*
18 *wtwrdw/hmw/ʾsdn/mqdmtn/bʿm/sbʿy/ʾs*
19 *dm/rkbm/bn/ḥḍrmt/ḏḏkw/mlk/ḥḍrm*
20 *t/lʾḥḏ/lhw/ʾḥḏm/bn/msbʾ/hgrnhn*
21 *wmrb/wqdmhmw/mqdmthmw/wḏbn/gyšhmw*
22 *bʾrk/whrghmw/wʾśrhmw/klhmw/wm*
23 *tʿ/bn/hmt/ʾḥḍrn/ʾsm/rkbm/wṯlṯt*
24 *rglm/wbnhw/fhwṣlw/gyšhmw/whġrw/ʿdy*
25 *dhr/wrẖyt/wlfyw/mhrgtm/wʾẖyḏtm*
26 *wsbym/wʾʾblm/wʾṯwrm/wbqrm/wḏʾn*
27 *m/ḏhšfq/gyšhmw/wbnhw/fqflw/wḥ*
28 *rbw/bsfl/ʾʿynn/ẖrṣm/wbnhw/flhmw*
29 *bllyn/wqdmhmw/mṣr/ḥḍrmwt/bẖms/mʾ*
30 *tm/wṯlṯt/ʾʾlfm/ʾsdm/rkbm/wẖms*
31 *wʿšry/wmʾt/ʾfrsm/wʾswdyhmw/rbʿt*
32 *bn/wʾlm/wḏhlm/wʾlyn/wʾfṣy/bn/gmn*
33 *nḥl/rkbn/wʾqwl/wʾkbrt/ḥḍrmwt/w*
34 *sbṯhmw/whrgw/bnhmw/ẖmsy/wṯmn/mʾ*
35 *tm/bḏʿm/wʾẖḏw/bnhmw/ʾfṣy/nḥln/w*
36 *gšm/nḥl/ʾfrsn/wsbʿy/wʾrbʿ/mʾtm/ʾs*
37 *dm/nḥl/ʾqwlm/wmrʾs/ḥḍrmwt/whqḏw/bn/ʾfr*
38 *shmw/ẖms/wʾrbʿy/ʾfrsm/wʾblw/ṯlṯy/ʾfrs*
39 *m/wstqḏw/ṯty/mʾtn/wʾlfm/rkbm/brḥlhn/w*
40 *bʿdnhw/fṣrẖ/lhmw/khʿn/bʿly/ḥrbthmw/b*
41 *n/gyš/bśʾm/whʿn/ḏgdnm/wbʿmhw/ẖms/wṯlṯ*
42 *y/ʾfrsm/bn/gyšhmw/wsbṯhmw/wstqḏw/k*
43 *l/rwthmw/wrkbhmw/wḏmtʿ/bnhmw/ʿm/b*
44 *śʾm/kl/gwdm/frsm/wnqt/wʾtw/kl/gyšhm*
45 *w/bwfym/wḥmdm/wmhrgtm/wʾẖyḏtm/wnq*
46 *yḏm/ʾfrsm/wrkbm/wġnmm/wḥmdw/ẖyl/wm*
47 *qm/mrʾhmw/ʾlmqhbʿlʾwm/wlwzʾ/ẖmrhmw*
48 *ʾlmqh/ʾtw/hmw/wgyšhmw/bwfym/wʾl/tf*
49 *qd/bn/gyšhmw/ġyr/⌜ʾ⌝sm/bn/ẖrgt/bʾlmqh*

1 **Sym-** Saʿadtaʾlab Yatlaf, descendant of Gadanum, leader
2 **bol** of the Arabs of the king of Sabaʾ and of Kindat and of Maḏḥigum and of Ḥarimum
3 mum and of Bahilum and of Zaydʾil and of all the Arabs of Sabaʾ and of Ḥimya-
4 rum and of Ḥaḍramawt and of Yamnat, has dedicated to his lord ʾIlum-
5 quh, master of ʾAwwâm, this statue which [is] in bronze, in praise because has vouch-
6 safed to him their lord ʾIlumquh, master of ʾAwwâm, when ordered
7 them their lord Yasrum Yuhanʿim and his son Ḏara-

8 ʾʾamar ʾAyman, the two kings of Sabaʾ and Raydân and Ḥa-
9 ḍramawt and Yamnat, to fight [for] and to precede their two lords Yasrum
10 and his son Ḏaraʾʾamar, the two kings of Sabaʾ and Raydân
11 and Ḥaḍramawt and Yamnat, in the land of Ḥaḍramawt and
12 their lord Yasrum has ordered them to fight [for] and to precede them and his trained
13 corps (?): the Arabs of the king of Sabaʾ and of Kindat and the masters of Naš-
14 qum and Našân; and they fought against ʿAbrân; and banded together and mus-
15 tered all their troop: seven hundred fifty soldiers
16 cameleers and seventy horsemen; and they went up from the low grounds;
17 and thirty cameleers and four horsemen were detached as vanguard;
18 and these soldiers [composing] the vanguard, came together along with seventy sol-
19 diers, cameleers, from Ḥaḍramawt whom has detached the king of Ḥaḍramawt
20 in order to capture for himself a prisoner from the military campaign of the two cities
21 and Mârib; and their vanguard and some of their troop preceded them
22 to ʾArak; and he took them away and he fettered them, all of them, and he
23 saved from those dwellings one cameleer and three
24 foot-soldiers; and from there their troop assembled and made a raid on
25 Duhr and Raḫîyat and they brought back war trophies and prisoners
26 and captives and camels and bulls and cows and sheep,
27 that enriched their troop; and from there they came back and
28 fought in the lower country of the springs Ḫurṣum; and from there they feasted
29 during the night; and the expeditionary corps of Ḥaḍramawt preceded them with five hundred
30 and three thousand cameleers and five
31 and twenty and one hundred horsemen and their two commanding officers Rabîʿat,
32 son of Waʾilum and him of [the two families] Hillum and ʾAlayân, and ʾAfṣay, son of Gammân,
33 the commissioner of the camelry, and the rulers and the leaders of Ḥaḍramawt and
34 their executioners; and they killed among them eight hundred and fifty
35 beheaded and they captured among them ʾAfṣay, the commissioner, and
36 Gašum, the commissioner of the cavalry, and [also] four hundred and seventy sol-
37 diers, commissioners of the rulers and of the chiefs of Ḥaḍramawt; and they took away of their horsemen,
38 forty-five horsemen and they took possession of thirty horses
39 and they saved one thousand and two hundred riding camels with the[ir] saddles; and
40 after that, he [the king] called them to lend assistance in their battle
41 against the troop of Baśaʾum and [also] to lend assistance to [the tribe] Gadanum, and with him thirty-five
42 horsemen from their troop and their executioners; and they saved all
43 their water-carrier beasts and their beasts of burden and what was saved through them from Ba-
44 śaʾum: all excellent mare[s] and she-camel[s]; and all their troop came back
45 in safety and (with) praise and war trophies and prisoners and captured
46 horses and beasts of burden and small cattle; and they have praised the strength and the po-
47 wer of their lord ʾIlumquh, master of ʾAwwâm; and that may continue to vouchsafe to them
48 ʾIlumquh [that] themselves and their troop [would] come back in safety and [that] there would not
49 be sought [in vain] among their troop even one man from [any] expedition. By ʾIlumquh.

L. 1: *sʿdtʾlb*, e.g., RÉS 4031/2 and commentary on Ja 570/15. – *ytlf*, cp. the Arabic place names *talfum* (cf. *MüHG*, p. 20 A) and *talfîtâ* (cf. *WüR*, p. 50 A).

L. 3: *bhlm*, e.g., RÉS 2726/20 and *bhl*, e.g., in Ja 650/1. – *zydʾl*, cf. commentary on Ja 401/4-5 in *JaSIBS*, p. 34 A.

Ll. 11-12: *wqhmw* instead of *wqhhmw* is certain on the stone.

Ll. 12-13: *tmhrt*, cf. Arabic *mahara*, 5th form "to be *or* become skilled, expert, skilful"; *tmhrt* could possibly be translated as "trained corps (?)"; for *mhrt* in CIH 492/3, cf. commentary on Ja 752/9-10.

L. 14: *ʿbrn*, name of a city; e.g., CIH 540/7.

L. 16: *rqyw*, cf. *rqy* in both Arabic and Daṯînah "to ascend, go up, walk up". – *mfgrtn*: although this word could also be a proper name, I suggest interpreting it as a plural noun, which indicates the low parts of the country from where the soldiers came; cf. Arabic *mafǧar* and *mafǧarat*, pl. *mafâǧiru* "place through which water flows from a watering-trough, low ground into which valleys pour their water" (cf. *LaAEL*, p. 2342 A). For the place name, cf. the Arabic names of a man *fâğir* (cf. *HeBN*, p. 44 A), of a woman *fiğrîyah* (cf. *l.c.*) and of a place *al-fuğayrat* (cf. *WüR*, p. 163 A).

L. 18: *twrdw*, 5th form of *wrd*; cf. Arabic *wrd*, 5th form "to arrive little by little in a place".

L. 20: *msb*ʾ, cf. commentary on Ja 560/8.

L. 22: *ʾrk*, name of a place; cf. the clan name *dʾrkm* in Bombay 44/3 and 4 (cf. *RyISA*, VIII, p. 123). – *ʿsrhmw*, cf. *StSESA*, p. 524; here, with the meaning of "to enchain, fetter"; *whrghmw*/*wʾśrhmw*, cf. Muraygân/6: *whrgw*/*wʾśrw* (cf. *RyISA*, X, pp. 277-78, who erroneously translates the two verbs as passive forms).

L. 25: *dhr*: *dhr*/*ḏrn* is the name of a house in Ist 7630/3 (cf. *BeFSTI*, p. 277).

L. 26: *bqr*, being preceded by *ʾṯwr*, must be related to Arabic *baqar*, *buqur*, or *baqâr*, pl. of *baqarat* "cow"; cf. *bqr* "bovines", e.g., in Ja 649/40-41.

L. 27: *qflw*, e.g., Murayġân/8 (cf. *RyISA*, *l.c.*) and Arabic as well as Daṯînah "to come back from a trip".

L. 28: *ʾʿyn*, pl. of *ʿyn* "eye, spring". – *ẖrṣm*, cf. the Arabic names of a man *al-ẖiriṣî* (cf. *SlGaVNPA*, p. 32 B), *al-ẖurṣ* (cf. *WüID*, 298/10), and of a clan *banû ẖarûṣ* (cf. *l.c.*, 298/7), and also the Safaitic masculine personal name *ẖrṣt* (cf. *LiSI*, p. 318). – *lhmw*, cf. Arabic *lahima* "to swallow" (cf. also in Daṯînah, in *LaGD*, p. 2649) and its derived adjectives *lahim*, *luham*, and *liham* "gluttonous, greedy"; *lhm* may be translated "to feast".

L. 31: *ʾswdyhmw*: construct dual (cf. the two following personal names) of *ʾswd*, cf. *JaISAR*, p. 111, commentary on Ja 513/5, where *ʾswd* seems to be a superlative adjective.

L. 32: *wʾlm*, masculine personal name, e.g., in RÉS 4536/1 and 4852/3, Ḥaḏr. – *hlm*, family name, cf. the masculine personal names *hl* in Thamudic (cf. e.g., *vdBrTTPN*, p. 19: Ph 265 c 1) and *hll* in both Safaitic (cf. *LiSI*, p. 309 B) and in Thamudic (cf., e.g., *vdBrIT*, p. 135: HU 255/2); for some Arabic parallels, cf. *HeBN*, p. 52 B. – *ʾlyn*, cf. the Thamudic masculine personal name *ʾly* (cf., e.g., *vdBrIT*, pp. 61-62: HU 56/2) and the Arabic place names *ʾalyat*, *ʾulyat*, *ʾalîyat* (cf. *WüR*, p. 18 C). – *ʾfṣy* is also an Arabic masculine personal name (cf. *LöHSM*, p. 56 B and *MüHG*, p. 132 B); cf. also *ʾfṣym*, name of a Min man in RÉS 3768/3. – *gmn*: cf. *gm* in RÉS 3363/1, Min, in Thamudic (cf., e.g., *vdBrTTPS*, p. 62: Ph 163 j 1), in Safaitic (cf. *LiSI*, p. 305 A) and in Arabic (cf. *WüR*, p. 60 C: place name); cf. also the masculine personal name *gmm* in Ja 834/1, in Thamudic (cf. *vdBrIT*, p. 158: HU 333 A) and Safaitic (cf. *LiSI*, *l.c.*).

L. 33: *nḫl* (cf. *CoRoC*, p. 185 B), pl. *ʾnḫl*, Ist 7627/13; cf. p. 325, note 124. Here, *nâḫil* may be translated "commissioner" (cf. *BeSI*, p. 43), and is singular (lines 33, 35, and 37) and collective noun (line 37); *nḫl*/*rkbn* and *nḫl*/*ʾfrsn* (line 36) very probably were the commanding officers of the camelry and the cavalry respectively; but it is rather difficult to determine what the function was of *nḫl*/*ʾqwlm*/*wmrʾs*/*ḥḏrmwt* (line 37), since they were very numerous: 470 of them were captured. Note that there is also question of *ʾfrs* in CIH 350/11 as well as in *nḫl*/*ʾfrsn*.

L. 34: *sbṭ*: for the verb *sbṭ*, cf. commentary on Ja 578/6; also noun in CIH 380/6 with the meaning of "stroke with a whip" (cf. also Condé 16/4); here, collective noun with the meaning of "executioners"; cf. Ethiopic *zăbăṭi* "verberans, percussor, verberator" (cf. *DiLLA*, col. 1051).

L. 36: *gšm*, personal name; cf., e.g., *gšm*, third personal name in RÉS 3902, No. 71/1-2, ʾAwsânite, and *gšmm*, name of a house in RÉS 3964/2, Qat.

L. 38: *ʾbl*, cf. Arabic *ʾabala*, 2nd form "to take for himself, get, gain *or* acquire camels as permanent property" (cf. *LaAEL*, p. 8 A).

L. 39: *stqd* identical (assimilation of *n*) with *stnqḏ* in Ja 644/20.

L. 40: *ṣrḫ*, cf. Arabic *ṣaraḫa* "to call (out), cry (out)".

L. 41: *bśʾm*, cf. the Arabic place names *basâ* and *bussâʾu* (cf. *WüR*, p. 35 A) and the *nisba* masculine personal name *bśʾyn* in RÉS 2633/3.

L. 43: *rwt*, cf. RÉS 4123/1 "report"; here, cf. Arabic *râwiyat* "camel, mule, ass, *then* any beast upon which water is drawn" (cf. *LaAEL*, p. 1196 B). – *bnhmw*, for *bn* indicating the instrument, cf. *HöASG*, p. 141 ϵ.

Ll. 44-46: *kl*/*gwdm*/*frsm*/*wnqt* (line 44) and *nqyḏm*/*ʾfrsm*/*wrkbm*/*wġnmm* (lines 45-46), cf. *JaSASA*, p. 179 and *JaSAAA*, pp. 265-66. *gwd*: Arabic *ğawâd* is basically and primarily an adjective "liberal, generous, excellent" (cf. *LaAEL*, p. 482 B, *Muḥîṭ al-Muḥîṭ*, I, p. 313 B, and *Lisân*, III, p. 135 A), quality which may of course be found in animals, such as a horse, and is then translated as "fleet, swift, excellent" (cf. *LaAEL*, *l.c.*, *Muḥît al-Muḥît*, *l.c.*, and *al-Munğid*, p. 104 B). Similarly for *nqyḏ*, Arabic *naqaḏ* and *naqîḏ*, pl. *naqâʾiḏ*, are basically and primarily adjectives applicable either to men or horses (cf. e.g., *LaAEL*, p. 2837 B). For *nqt*, cf. Arabic *nâqat* (unity) and *nâq* (collect.) "she-camel".

Ll. 48-49: *tfqd*, 6th form of *fqd*; cf. Arabic *faqada*, 5th form "to seek, search carefully for"; cf. commentary on Ja 651/26.

L. 49: *ġyr*, e.g., Ja 525/2; the purpose of *ġyr* here is, as sometimes in classical Arabic, to double the negation; *ʾl...ġyr/ʾsm* means "not...even one man". – *ḫrgt*, cf. Arabic *ḫarağat* "(military) expedition"; for the meaning of "rebellion", cf. Ja 712/7.

c – Karibʾil (Watar) Yuhanᶜim: Ja 666 and 667

666 – Yellowish sandstone; photograph in Plate 18. – MaMB 140.

STONE: thickness: 24.8 cm. (top) and 12.8 (bottom). – *Front:* covered with red paint; upper right corner broken; left edge slightly damaged; 81.8 cm. (right) and 82 (left) × 33.5 (top) and 33.3 (bottom). – INSCRIPTION: letter height: 2.5 cm. (top) and 2.8 (bottom); space between the lines: between 0.5 cm. and 0.7. – SYMBOL, cf. Ja 582.

1 **Sym-** *ʾbkrb/ʾyhr/wᶜbdᶜṯtr/ʾšw*
2 **bol** *ᶜ/wbnyhmy/whbʾwm/ʾsᶜd/b*
3 *nw/ḏᶜḍdn/ʾqwl/šᶜbn/ᶜḍdn/hqnyw*
4 *mrʾhmw⟨/⟩ʾlmqhbᶜlʾwm/frsm/wrkb*
5 *hw/kly/ḏhbm/ḏšfthw/ḥmdm/bḏ⌉*
6 *t/hwfy/ʾlmqh/bn/mḥr/kwn/bʾr*
7 *ḍn/wlwẓʾ/mrʾhmw/ʾlmqh/šwf/wm⌋*
8 *tᶜn/ʾdmhw/ʾbkrb/wᶜbdᶜṯtr/ww*
9 *hbʾwm/bny/ḏᶜḍdn/bn/bʾst*
10 *wnkytm/wʾʾrẖ/swʾm/wnḍᶜ/wšṣ⌋*
11 *y/šnʾm/wlsᶜdhmw/bry/ʾʾḏn⌈m⌉*
12 *wmqymtm/wḥẓy/wrḍw/⟨⟩mrʾ⌊h⌉*
13 *mw/krbʾl/yhnᶜm/mlk/sbʾ/wḏ⌉*
14 *rydn/wḥḍrmt/wymnt/wlẖmrh*
15 *mw/ʾṯmrm/wʾfqlm/nʾdm/wfrᶜ*
16 *ʾmyrt⟨⟩/dṯʾ/wẖrf/bʾlmqhw*
17 *ṯhwnb(ᶜ)lʾwm*

1 **Sym-** ʾAbkarib ʾAyhar and ᶜAbdᶜaṯtar ʾAšwaᶜ
2 **bol** and their son Wahabʾawwâm ʾAsᶜad, descendants
3 of (the tribe) ᶜUḍdân, rulers of the tribe ᶜUḍdân, have dedicated
4 to their lord ʾIlumquh, master of ʾAwwâm, a horse and his saddle,
5 all of both of them in bronze, which he had promised to Him, in praise becau-
6 se ʾIlumquh has granted His protection against the land-surveyor [who] was in the coun-
7 try; and that their lord ʾIlumquh may continue to take care of and to
8 save His worshippers ʾAbkarib and ᶜAbdᶜaṯtar and Wa-
9 habʾawwâm, descendants of ᶜUḍdân, from misfortunes
10 and sufferings and disastrous calamities and [also] (from) the hostility and wicked-
11 ness of [any] enemy; and may He make them happy with the strength of understanding
12 and of power, and (with) the esteem and grace of their lord
13 Karibʾil Yuhanᶜim, king of Sabaʾ and
14 Raydân and Ḥaḍramawt and Yamnat; and may He vouchsafe to
15 them magnificent fruits and harvests and the optimum crop of
16 cereals of spring and of autumn. By ʾIlumquhû
17 Ṯahwân, master of ʾAwwâm.

L. 1: *ʾyhr*, name of a family in RÉS 4630, and of a man in RÉS 3964/1, Qat.

L. 3: *ᶜḍdn*, cf. e.g., the Arabic names of places *ᶜaḍudân*, *al-ᶜaḍadîyat* (cf. *WüR*, p. 152 B), and of men *al-ᶜaḍud* (cf., e.g., *LöHSM*, p. 74 B and *MüHG*, p. 80 A), *ᶜaḍad* (cf. *WüR*, p. 555) and *ḏû ᶜuḍdân* (cf. *LöHSM*, p. 66 B).

L. 4: no word divider between *mrʾhmw* and *ʾlmqh*.

L. 6: *mḥr*, cf. Syriac "*maḥḥōr*...fully written *maḥḥōr ʾarᶜô* a land-surveyor, geometrician" (cf. *PaSmCSD*, p. 265 B).

Ll. 12-13: *ʾmrʾhmw* instead of *mrʾhmw*; the first ʾ is certain on the stone.

Ll. 15-16: *frᶜ ʾmyrtm/dṯʾ/wẖrf*: *sic* on the stone. Because of the mimation of *ʾmyrt*, *dṯʾ/wẖrf* might be interpreted as a temporal noun-clause. However, this *m* in *ʾmyrtm* is doubtless another engraving mistake because the expression *frᶜ/ʾm(y)rt/dṯʾ/wẖrf* is attested thrice in the present collection of texts, viz. Ja 623/14-15, 650/12, and 661/7; see also *lʾmrt/dṯʾ/wẖrf* in Ja 615/18.

L. 17: *bwl* instead of *bᶜl* is certain on the stone.

667 – Yellowish sandstone inscription, broken into two parts; upper part = MaMB 15 = Ja 826; lower part = MaMB 86; two photographs in Plate 19.

INSCRIPTION: same disposition of lines as in Ja 552. MaMB 15: stone: thickness: 7 cm. *Front:* upper right corner broken; the center of the left edge is splintered off; 24 cm. × 18. *Inscription:* A/1-11a: letter height: from 1.6 cm. to 1.8; space between the lines: 0.5 cm. – *Symbol:* the upper two thirds are missing; for the rest, cf., e.g., Ja 657; there probably were four triangle-shaped inside incisions; cf. Plate A.

MaMB 86: stone: thickness: 7 cm. (top) and 8 (bottom). *Front:* 22.8 cm. (right) and 20.1 (left) × 18. *Inscription:* A/11b-18; letter height: from 1.6 cm. (line 13) to 2 (lines 11b et 15); space between the lines: from 0.3 cm. to 0.5. For TEXT B, cf. infra.

TEXT A:

1 ⸢**Sym-**⸣ *[r]⸤bbm/⸣[..]⸢ẖ⸣r/bn/ẖl*
2 **bol** *⸢f⸣n/ʾnm⸢r⸣m/wḥywm/h*
3 *qny/mrʾhmw/ʾlmqhṯhwn*
4 *bʿlʾwm/ṣlmn/ḏḏh⸣⸤bn⸥*
5 *ḥmdm/bḏt/ẖmr/w⸣[fy]*
6 *n/ʿbdhw/rbbm/bn⸣[/ẖlf]*
7 *n/ʾnmrm/wḏḥywm⸢/b⸣n*
8 *ḥbl/wqsdt/kwn/bhgr*
9 *n/ẓfr/bqdmy/ḏn/ywmn*
10 *wlwzʾ/ʾlmqh/ẖmr/w*
11a *⸤dh⸥[w]⸤/rbbm/bn⸥*
11b *mtʿn/ʿ⸢bdhw/rbbm/bn⸣*
12 *ẖlfn/bn/bʾstm/wnk*
13 *ytm/wṭwʿ/wšṣy/šnʾ*
14 *m/wlyẖmrnhw/ʾlmqhw*
15 *ḥẓy/wrḍw/mrʾhmw/k*
16 *rbʾl/wtr/yhnʿm/mlk*
17 *sbʾ/wḏrydn/wḥḍrmt*
18 *wymnt/bʾlmqhw*

1 ⸢**Sym-**⸣ [Ra]bîbum [..]ẖr, descendant of [the two families] H̱al-
2 **bol** fân ʾAnmarum and Ḥayûm, has
3 dedicated to their lord ʾIlumquh Ṯahwân,
4 master of ʾAwwâm, this statue which [is] in bronze,
5 in praise because He has vouchsafed to pr[otect]
6 His worshipper Rabîbum, descendant of [the two families] [H̱alf]ân
7 ʾAnmarum and Ḥayûm from
8 the revolt and the rebellion [which] occurred in the city [of]
9 Ẓafâr previous to this day;
10 and that ʾIlumquh may continue to vouchsafe to and
11 save His worshipper Rabîbum, descendant of
12 H̱alfân, from misfortunes and suffer-
13 ings and (from) the constraint and the wickedness of [any] enemy;
14 and that ʾIlumquhû may vouchsafe to him
15 the esteem and grace of their lord Ka-
16 ribʾil Watar Yuhanʿim, king of
17 Sabaʾ and Raydân and Ḥaḍramawt
18 and Yamnat. By ʾIlumquhû.

L. 1: *rbbm*, e.g., RÉS 3996 and Geukens 1/16. – [..]*ẖr*: two letters are missing; a *ʾaqtal* or *yaqtal* form from a verb such as *ḏẖr*, *mẖr*, etc., would fit.

Ll. 1-2: *ẖlfn*, name of a man in CIH 67/14; cf. *bny/ḏẖlfn/ʾnmrm* in Ja 506 A/2 and *bn ḏẖlfn*, e.g., in RÉS 4757/1-2; cf. also the name of a man *ẖlfm* in RÉS 4347/2.

L. 2: *ḥywm*, also family name in RÉS 4484.

L. 10: *ʾlmqh* as in line 3, but *ʾlmqhw* in lines 14 and 18.

L. 15: *k* is engraved on top of *l*, the upper part of which is still very clear; cf. text B.

TEXT B: on MaMB 86: remnant of a former text which is almost completely erased (cf. also commentary on A/15); at 0.6 cm. from the bottom, one line: 16.9 cm. × 1.5.

...]ʾsrrhw/bmrb/wnšn/..[...

...] his wâdî-side valleys in Mârib and Našân..]...

d – Ḏamarʿalay Yuhabirr and his son Ṯaʾrân Yuhanʿim: Ja 668

668 – Yellowish sandstone inscription, broken on top: photograph in Plate 19. – MaMB 236.

STONE: maximum thickness: 18 cm. – *Front:* upper half badly damaged; 72 cm. × 34.1 (bottom) and 33.5 (top). – INSCRIPTION: same disposition of lines as in Ja 552; letter height: from 2 cm. to 2.6; space between the lines: from 0.6 cm. to 0.8.

1 *...]šbm/w[...*
2 *...]ḥḍ[.....]rr/ʿ[...*
3 *...]r/bʿbr/mrʾ[hmw/ḏmr]ʿl[y/y]*
4 *[hbr/w]⸤bnyhw/ṯʾrn/yhnʿm/mlky/sb*
5 *ʾ/wḏrydn/wḥḍrmwt/wymnt/wḥ(m)[dw]*
6 *ẖyl/wmqm/mrʾhmw/ʾlmqh/[bḏ]t*
7 *mtʿ/whwfyn/ʾdmhw/šʿbn/sbʾ/k*
8 *hln/wbḏt/ẖmrhmw/mhrgtm/wʾẖ*
9 *yḏtm/wsbym/ḏʿsm/whrḍw/ʾdmh*
10 *w/šʿbn/sbʾ/khln/wbn/kl/hgr*
11 *srrn/ḏhsbʿw/wlwzʾ/ẖmr/ʾlmq*
12 *h/ʾdmhw/šʿbn/sbʾ/khln/hḥm*
13 *dn/whyhrn/ʾhnmw/yqhnnhmw/ʾm*
14 *rʾhmw/ʾml(k)/sbʾ/wbnw/ḏrydn/[w]*

15 *lẖmrhmw/ḥẓy/wrḍw/mrʾhmw/ḏm*
16 *rʿly/yhbr/wbnyhw/ṯʾrn/yhnʿm*
17 *mlky/sbʾ/wḏrydn/wḥḍrmwt/w*
18 *ymnt/wlyhʿnnhmw/wmtʿnhmw*
19 *bn/nḍʿ/wšṣy/šnʾm/bʾlmqhṯhwn*
20 *bʿlʾwm*

1 ...]šbum and [...
2 [... ...] Ḥaḍ[..... .]râr ʿ[... ...]
3 [... ...]r, for [their] lord [Ḏamar]ʿal[ay Yu-]
4 [habirr and] his son Ṯaʾrân Yuhanʿim, the two kings of Sabaʾ
5 and Raydân and Ḥaḍramawt and Yamnat; and [they have] p(rai)[sed]
6 the strength and the power of their lord ʾIlumquh [becau]se
7 He has saved and protected His worshippers, the tribe Sabaʾ Ka-
8 hilân, and because He has vouchsafed to them war trophies and pri-
9 soners and captives, which was desired and [which] pleased His worshippers,
10 the tribe Sabaʾ Kahilân, and from every city of
11 Sarîrân which they have pillaged; and that ʾIlumquh may continue to vouchsafe to
12 His worshippers, the tribe Sabaʾ Kahilân, to behave themselves in a
13 praiseworthy way and to exalt whatever will order them their
14 lords, the kings of Sabaʾ and the descendants of Raydân; and
15 that He may vouchsafe to them the esteem and grace of their lord Ḏamar-
16 ʿalay Yuhabirr and his son Ṯaʾrân Yuhanʿim,
17 the two kings of Sabaʾ and Raydân and Ḥaḍramawt and
18 Yamnat; and that He may help them and save them
19 from the hostility and wickedness of [any] enemy. By ʾIlumquh Ṯahwân,
20 master of ʾAwwâm.

Cf. the beginning of the commentary on Ja 792.

The exact number of the missing lines at the beginning of the text is unknown; as in Ja 653, the authors of the text are *šʿbn/sbʾ/khln* "the tribe Sabaʾ Kahilân", this expression must be restored at the beginning of the first missing line.

L. 3: *mrʾ[hmw* is restored on the basis of line 15.

Ll. 3-4: *yhbr*, cf. also the name of a man *yhbrr* in RÉS 4787/2.

L. 10: *bn* introduces a nominal proposition which, as well as *ḏʿsm...khln*, depends on the series *mhrgtm...wsbym*.

L. 11: *srrn*, cf. commentary on Ja 656/16.

Ll. 12-13: *hḥmd*, 4th form of *ḥmd*; cf. Arabic *ḥmd*, 4th form "to behave one's self in a praiseworthy way".

L. 13: *hyhrn*, infinitive as is also *hḥmdn*; cf. commentary on Ja 564/7: *yhr*.

L. 14: *ʾmln* instead of *ʾlmk* is certain on the stone.

e – Ṯaʾrân Yuhanʿim and his son Malikkarib Yuhaʾmin: Ja 669-671

669 – Yellowish sandstone; photograph in Plate 19. – MaMB 183.

STONE: maximum thickness: 16.5 cm. (top), 11.5 (center), and 13 (bottom). – *Front*, covered with red paint. – INSCRIPTION, same disposition of lines as in Ja 552; letter height: from 2 cm. to 2.4, but 1.5 on line 29; space between the lines: 0.4 cm. – SYMBOL, cf. Ja 561.

1 **Sym-** *rbtnf/yẓfr/wzydm*
2 **bol** *ʾwlṭ/wʾsʿd/ʾkf/w*
3 *bnyhmw/ʿbdʾwm/bnw/ʿbl*
4 *m/wqtrn/ʾtwn/hqnyw/m*
5 *rʾhmw⟨/⟩ʾlmqhbʿlʾwm*
6 *ṣlmn/wmśdm/ṣrfm/wmd*
7 *lthmy/ʿsym/wṣlmm/ḏ*
8 *ḏhbm/lqbly/ḏwld/lh*
9 *mw/bnm/ḏkrm/wšftw/ʾl*
10 *mqhw/kmhnmw/yldn/lh*
11 *mw/bnm/wyḥywn/fyhqny*
12 *nn/ṣlmm/wmśdm/ṣrfm/w*
13 *ṣlmm/ḏḏhbn/wyhślnn*
14 *ṯny/ṯwrn/bklwnm/wlh*
15 *wfrnn/ʾṯthmw/wbnhmw*
16 *ʿdy/mḥrmn/wlḥmdnn/mq*
17 *m/ʾlmqhw/wlwzʾ/ẖmrhmw*
18 *wldm/wlqbly/ḏʿdw/yḥmd/ʿd*
19 *y/ʾrḍhmw/wtsbṭ/bʿm/ʾwl*
20 *dhmw/wmyt/byd/bnhmw/wḏm*
21 *r/bʿmhmw/mrʾhmw/ʾsʿd/whḏ*
22 *ll/mʿbrn/wšftw/kmhnmw/y*
23 *mtʿn/ʾẖhmw/bn/hyt/ʾrẖn/f*
24 *⸤y⸥hqnynn/wyhślnn/ṯwrn/bkl*
25 *⸢wn/wrʾ/kmtʿhmw/bn/hyt/ʾ*
26 *rẖn/wlẖmrnhmw/ḥẓy/wrḍ*
27 *w/mrʾhmw/ṯʾrn/yhnʿm/wbn*
28 *yhw/mlkkrb/mlky/sbʾ/wḏr*
29 *⸤ydn/⸥wḥḍrmwt/wymnt⟨/⟩bʾlmqh*

1 **Sym-** Rabbtanûf Yaẓfur and Zaydum
2 **bol** ʾAwlaṭ and ʾAsʿad ʾAkaf and
3 their son ʿAbdʾawwâm, descendants of [the two tribes] ʿAblum

4 and Qatrân ʾAwtân, have dedicated to their
5 lord ʾIlumquh, master of ʾAwwâm,
6 this statue and an inscription which [is] in brass, and
7 the weight of them both [is] one *ʿasay*, and a statue in
8 bronze because of this: there was born to them
9 a male son and they have promised to ʾIl-
10 umquhû that if there should be born to
11 them a son and [if he should] live, they would then dedicate
12 a statue and an inscription in brass and
13 a statue which [would be] in bronze, and they would drive
14 two bulls to Kalwânum and they would
15 increase [the number of] their wives and their sons
16 in the temple and they would praise the power
17 of ʾIlumquhû; and that He may continue to vouchsafe to them
18 children; and [also] because of this: Yaḥmad entered
19 their land and had an affray with their children
20 and he was left dying through the hand of their sons, and condemned
21 them publicly their lord ʾAsʿad and he [the latter] rejected
22 the[ir] explanation; and they have promised [that] would
23 He save their brother from this calamity, they
24 would dedicate and drive the two bulls to Kal-
25 [wâ]n; and now He has saved them from this ca-
26 lamity; and that He may vouchsafe to them the esteem and gra-
27 ce of their lord Ṯaʾrân Yuhanʿim and of his
28 son Malikkarib, the two kings of Sabaʾ and
29 Raydân and Ḥaḍramawt and Yamnat. By ʾIlumquh.

L. 1: *rbtnf*, same nominal formation as that, e.g., of *rbšmsm* (e.g., RÉS 3621); for the second element, "the sublime", which characterizes the sun goddess in her highest splendor (cf. *JaP*, p. 106 and *JaRSAP*, p. 267). – *yẓfr*, cp. *ẓfr*, name of a city (e.g., Ja 631/20) and the Arabic masculine personal name *ẓâfir* (cf. *HeBN*, p. 37 B). – *zydm*, e.g., RÉS 2676/1.

L. 2: *ʾkf*: *RyNP* (I, p. 37 A) relates Safaitic *ʾkf* to Arabic *ʾukâf* "pack-saddle of a mule", and the second proper name *ʾkyf* to Arabic *kâfa* (i) "to cut (off)" (cf. *l.c.*, p. 114 A); the first parallel does not suit as the name of a man; and *ʾkyf* being the *scriptio plena* of *ʾkf*, there is no reason for looking for another root; cf. Arabic *wakifa* "to have a defect, a vice" and *wakaf* "defect, vice".

L. 3: *ʿbdʾwm*: the two parts of this theophorous name are well known.

L. 4: *qtrn*, cf. the Arabic masculine personal name *qtyrt* (cf. *GoAT*, p. 461). – *ʾwtn*, name of a sanctuary dedicated to Qaynân (cf. commentary on Ja 550/1) in CIH 560/5.

L. 6: *mśd* for *mśnd* (e.g., Ja 852/8, Qat) which equals *msnd* (e.g., Kawkab 1/2), contrary to *BePESA*, pp. 18 and 26 (where "Philby 444" is printed instead of "Philby 158"); cf. *CoRoC*, p. 255 B and *BeSI*, p. 11. – *ṣrfm* is apparently related to both *ṣlm* and *mśd*.

L. 7: *ʿsym*, cp. Arabic *ʿusûm* "small quantity"; this parallel seems better than the etymology from *ʿsy*; measure of weight.

Ll. 8-12 and 22-26, cf. *JaPDSM*, p. 176.

L. 14: *klwnm* but *klwn* on lines 24-25; name of a place; the restoration of [*k*]*lwn* instead of *lwn* in RÉS 3309 (BM 125167)/3, Min, is gratuitous.

Ll. 14-15: *hwfr*: RÉS 4767/4=RÉS 3687 bis where *RÉS* translates it as "produire comme fruit" (cf. VII, p. 355 and VI, p. 264 respectively); the latter refers to RÉS 2865/3 which has *hwfd* and not *hwfr*; 4th form of *wfr* (e.g., RÉS 4325/3); cf. Arabic *wafara*, 4th form "to increase".

L. 19: *tsbṭ*, 5th form of *sbṭ*; *tsbṭ/bʿm* may be translated "to have an affray with, to quarrel with".

L. 20: *myt*=*mwt*. – *byd*, RÉS 3610/1, Min; cf. also the preposition *bydn* (CIH 518/3).

Ll. 20-21: *ḏmr*, cf. *CoRoC*, p. 129 A, *RhGO*, p. 49 and *BeNL*, II, pp. 265-66; *ḏmr/bʿm* may be translated "to condemn publicly".

Ll. 21-22: *hḏll*, 4th form of *ḏll*; cf. Arabic *ḏalla*, 4th form "to lower, abase; render contemptible, despicable" (cf. *LaAEL*, p. 973 A); *hḏll* may be translated "to despise, contemn, reject"; the 5th form is attested in Ja 644/8.

L. 22: *mʿbr*, cf. Arabic *muʿabbar* "explanation"; for the ordinary meaning of *mʿbr*, cf. *CoRoC*, p. 201.

670 – Grayish sandstone; partial photograph; cf. Chapter I, C. – MaMB 292.

STONE: thickness: 18.2 cm. – *Front:* covered with red paint; the bottom of the right edge is splintered off; 22.4 cm. × 1.035 m. – INSCRIPTION: same disposition of lines as in Ja 552; letter height: from 2.4 cm. to 2.1; space between the lines: from 0.5 cm. to 0.7; distance from line 1 to the upper edge: 0.5 cm. – SYMBOL, cf. Ja 582.

1 **Sym-** *šrḥᶜṯt/⌜ᵓš⌝wᶜ/wbn⟨⟩*
2 **bol** *hw/mrṯdm/bny/sẖym*
3 *m/ᵓbᶜl/bytn/rymn/ᵓ*
4 *qwl/šᶜbn/yrsm/ḏsmᶜy/ḏ*
5 *ṯlṯn/ḏhgrm⟨/⟩hqnyw/mrᵓh*
6 *mw/ᵓlmqhbᶜlᵓwm/ṣl*
7 *mm/ḏḏhbm/ḏšfthw/ᶜ*
8 *bdhw/šrḥᶜṯt/ᵓšwᶜ/b*
9 *ḏt/mtᶜ/ᶜbdhw/bn/ḍllm*
10 *ḏḍll/bẓfr/whᵓwl/b*
11 *nhw/ksdm/bᶜntm/w*
12 *ḥmd/ẖyl/wmqm/mrᵓh*
13 *w/ᵓlmqhbᶜlᵓwm/bḏt*
14 *hᶜn/ᶜbdhw/bhwt/mrḍn*
15 *wlyzᵓn/ᵓlmqhw/šrḥ*
16 *grb/ᶜbdhw/bn/kl/mr*
17 *ḍm/wnkytm/wbᵓsm*
18 *wlymtᶜn/ᶜbdyhw/š*
19 *rḥᶜṯt/wmrṯdm/bny/s*
20 *ẖymm/wlẖmrnhmw/ḥ*
21 *ẓy/wrḍw/mrᵓyhmw/ṯᵓrn*
22 *yhnᶜm/wbnyhw/mlkkr*
23 *b/yhᵓmn/mlky/sbᵓ/wḏ*
24 *rydn/wḥḍrmwt/wymn*
25 *t/wlẖmrhmw/ᵓṯmrm/w*
26 *ᵓfqlm/sqym/wbrm/wš*
27 *ᶜrm/ᶜdy/ᵓrḍhmw/wᵓsr*
28 *rhmw/wlẖmrhmw/hgbᵓn*
29 *lhmw/ᵓġylhmw/ᶜdy*
30 *ᵓsrrhmw/bᵓlmqhb*
31 *ᶜlᵓwm*

1 **Sym-** Šaraḥᶜaṯat ᵓAšwaᶜ and his
2 **bol** son Marṯadum, descendants of [the tribe] Suẖaymum,
3 masters of the house Raymân, ru-
4 lers of the tribe Yarsum of [the tribe] Samᶜay,
5 the third of [the tribe] Hagarum, have dedicated to their
6 lord ᵓIlumquh, master of ᵓAwwâm, a
7 statue which [is] in bronze, which had promised to Him
8 His worshipper Šaraḥᶜaṯat ᵓAšwaᶜ be-
9 cause He has saved His worshipper from [the] grave illness
10 in which he was dying in Ẓafâr and was brought back his
11 son Kasdum thanks to [His] aid; and
12 he has praised the strength and the power of his lord
13 ᵓIlumquh, master of ᵓAwwâm, because
14 He has protected His worshipper in this disease;
15 and that ᵓIlumquhû may continue to keep
16 the body of His worshipper healthy from all disease
17 and sufferings and misfortune;
18 and that He may save His two worshippers Ša-
19 raḥᶜaṯat and Marṯadum, descendants of Su-
20 ẖaymum; and that He may vouchsafe to them the es-
21 teem and grace of their two lords Ṯaᵓrân
22 Yuhanᶜim and his son Malikkarib
23 Yuhaᵓmin, the two kings of Sabaᵓ and
24 Raydân and Ḥaḍramawt and Yamnat;
25 and that He may vouchsafe to them fruits and
26 harvests watered and wheat and
27 barley in their land and their wâdî-side
28 valleys; and that He may vouchsafe to them to drive back
29 for them their streams in
30 their wâdî-side valleys. By ᵓIlumquh, mas-
31 ter of ᵓAwwâm.

L. 1: *bn* is followed by a word divider which is certain on the stone (cf. my notebook).

L. 2: *šrḥᶜṯt*, e.g., RÉS 4150/5; cp. *šrḥṯt*, e.g., in Ja 603/2.

L. 5: the word divider before *hqnyw* is missing on the stone (cf. my notebook).

L. 10: *hᵓwl*, 4th form of *ᵓwl* "to bring back"; here, in passive form.

L. 11: *ksdm cf.* the Arabic place names *al-kasâd* (cf. *MüHG*, p. 96 A) and *kasâdun* (cf. *WüR*, p. 185 A); for *ksdyn*, cf. *StSESA*, p. 539 and *BePESA*, p. 24.

L. 26: *sqy*: adjective; cf. Arabic *saqîy* "watered (tree, etc.)". – *br*, cf. Arabic *burr* "wheat".

Ll. 26-27: *šᶜr*, cf. *CoRoC*, p. 251 A and *BePESA*, p. 2.

671 – Grayish sandstone; re-cut at the bottom; photograph; cf. Chapter I, C. – MaMB 294.

STONE: thickness: 23.5 cm. – *Front:* covered with red paint; upper right corner badly broken; 27 cm. × 76.6. – INSCRIPTION: same disposition of lines as in Ja 552; letter height: from 2.4 cm. to 2.7; space between the lines: 0.5 cm. and 0.6.

1 [**Sym-** *.../w]bny[hw/..]*
2 [**bol** *.../]ᵓsᵓr/bnw/⌜s⌝[ẖy]*
3 *[mm/ᵓbᶜl/byt]n/rymn/ᵓqwl/šᶜb*
4 *[n/y]rsm/⌜ḏ⌝smᶜy/ṯlṯn/ḏhg*
5 *[rm/ḏ]ẖwln/gddtn/hqnyw/m*
6 *[rᵓ]hmw/ᵓlmqhw/ṯhwn/bᶜl/ᵓwm*
7 */ṣlmm/ḏḏhbm/bkn/wqhhw/mrᵓ*
8 *hmw/ṯᵓrn/yhnᶜm/wbnhw/mlkk*
9 *rb/yᵓmn/mlky/sbᵓ/wḏrydn/wḥ*
10 *ḍrmt/wymnt/lqtdmn/ẖmsn/bᶜrbn*

11 *bkn/ṯbrt/ʿrmn/bḥbbḍ/wrḥbm*
12 */wṯbr/kl/mḍrfn/ḏbynn/ḥbbḍ/w*
13 *rḥbm/wṯbr/bn/ʿrmn/sbʿy/šwḥ*
14 *ṭm/wḥmdw/ẖyl/mrʾhmw/ʾlmqh*
15 *wṯhwn/bʿl/ʾwm/bḏt/ẖmrhmw/*
16 *hmlʾhmw/bʾmrhw/kyʾfqn/l[h]*
17 *mw/ḏʿbn/ʿdy/hšqrw/nklhmw/wḥ*
18 *md⟨w⟩/mrʾhmw/ʾlmqhwṯhwn/bʿl*
19 *ʾwm/bḏt/hwfy/lhmw/bmlʾ/st*
20 *mlʾw/bʿmhw/wlwzʾ/ẖmrhmw/ḥ*
21 *ẓy/wrḍw/mrʾyhmw/ṯʾrn/yhnʿm*
22 */wbnyhw/mlkkrb/yʾmn/mlky/*
23 *sbʾ/wḏrydn/wḥḍrmt/wymnt/whʿ*
24 *nw/hwt/mṯbrn/lqbly/ṯlṯt/ʾwrẖm*
25 *bḏsbʾ/wʾlʾlt/wʾbhy*[. .]

1 [**Sym-** . . . and his] son[(s?) . . .
2 [**bol** . . .] ʾAsʾar, descendants of [the tribe] Su[ẖay-]
3 [mum, master of] the [house] Raymân, rulers of [the] tribe
4 [Ya]rsum of the tribe Samʿay, the third of [the tribe] Haga-
5 [rum of] Ḫawlân Gaddatân, have dedicated to
6 their l[ord] ʾIlumquhû Ṯahwân, master of ʾAwwâm,
7 a statue which [is] in bronze, when ordered him their
8 lord Ṯaʾrân Yuhanʿim, and his son Malikka-
9 rib Yuʾmin, the two kings of Sabaʾ and Raydân and Ḥa-
10 ḍramawt and Yamnat, to take command of the army [composed] of Arabs,
11 when the dam was crushed in Ḥabâbiḍ and Raḥbum,
12 and [when] was ruined all the construction without cement which separated Ḥabâbiḍ and
13 Raḥbum, and [when] seventy *šawaḥiṭ* of the dam were ruined;
14 and they praised the strength of their lord ʾIlumquhû
15 Ṯahwân, master of ʾAwwâm, because He has vouchsafed to them
16 to favor them with His order that He would reverse for
17 [t]hem the waves till they have covered their artistic work; and they have
18 praised their lord ʾIlumquhû Ṯahwân, master
19 of ʾAwwâm, because He has showered upon them the favor [for which] they
20 besought Him; and that He may continue to vouchsafe to them the es-
21 teem and grace of their two kings Ṯaʾrân Yuhanʿim
22 and his son Malikkarib Yuʾmin, the two kings
23 of Sabaʾ and Raydân and Ḥaḍramawt and Yamnat; and they repair-
24 ed this ruin by means of three months [of work]
25 in which Sabaʾ and the deities and the ancestors . .

L. 2: *ʾsʾr*, also second personal masculine name in RÉS 4891/1, Ḥaḍr, for RÉS 4875/1, Ḥaḍr, cf. commentary on Ja 563/1.

L. 5: *gddtn*, cf. *gdt*, masculine personal name in CIH 710/3-4 and 719 (= Mars VII [and not VI, as mentioned by *RyNP*, I, p. 58 A where this name is considered, as by *CIH*, as feminine] but presently Mars No. 5308; cf. *JaASAB*, p. 176); cf. also the Arabic names of places *ǧudad*, *ǧadûd*, and *ǧadîdât* (cf. *MüHG*, p. 24 B), *ʾaǧdâd* (cf. *WüR*, p. 5 B) and *al-ǧudd*, *ǧudâd*, and *ǧidâd* (cf. *l.c.*, p. 56 B-C), of clans *ǧudayd* (cf. *l.c.*, p. 241 A), *banû ǧudayd* (cf. *MüHG*, p. 136 A), and of men (*al-*)*ǧadd* (cf. *SaIS*, p. 38 B), *ǧadad* (cf. *LöHSM*, p. 59 A) and *ḏû l-ǧddyn* (cf. *l.c.*, p. 64 B); cf. also the masculine personal Safaitic name *gdʾl* (cf. *LiSI*, p. 304 A).

L. 10: *qtdmn/ẖmsn/bʿrbn*, cf. *tqdm/šrḥtm bn/ʿrbn* in CIH 350/8-9.

L. 11: *ʿrm*, e.g., Ja 547/4 and commentary, and *RoVSAY*, p. 309. – *ḥbbḍ*: CIH 622/2 and RÉS 3943/5 (*ḥbḍḍ*): name of a reservoir of the dam; cf. references in the commentary on Ja 555/4 and especially *JaPSAP*, p. 160. – *rḥbm*, CIH 623/2; name of another reservoir; personal name in RÉS 4752, in yellowish sandstone; constant thickness from 6 cm. to 6.5; front (maximum) 22 cm. × 7.8 (left) and 5.3 (right), a genuine inscription, contrary to *RÉS*, VII, p. 348, who points out its doubtfulness; *n* is dextrograde (cf. *RÉS*, *l.c.*) but also the ʾ; cf. also *rḥbn*, the name of an incense burner sanctuary in RÉS 4198/2 and the 2nd masculine personal name *yrḥb*, e.g., Ja 716/1.

L. 12: *ḏbynn*: here as well as in RÉS 3954/2, *bynn* is the infinitive with *-n* ending (cf. *HöASG*, pp. 61-62) of the 2nd form of *byn*, cf. Arabic *bâna* (i), 2nd form "to separate, disjoin"; for the 1st form, cf. Ja 619/8.

Ll. 13-14: *šwḥṭ*, plural of *šwḥṭt*, cf. Ja 539/1-2; note that *RoVSAY* (p. 312) refers *šwḥṭ* to modern Yemeni *šayz* (pl.: *ʾašyâz*), a measure unit of about 20 cm. in length (cf. *RoAS*, p. 153: "pollice, della punta dell'indice alla punta del pollice distesi").

L. 15: *ṯhwn/bʿl*: the top of the word divider is connected with the following *b* by a small horizontal line (cf. my notebook).

L. 16: *ʾmr*, cf. *CoRoC*, pp. 106-07: "jussum, oraculum"; the translation of this word as "oraculum" (cf. also *RÉS*, in RÉS 4998/3) is gratuitous for the divinity had other means to make known her order or command, e.g., dreams, games, etc.; cf. also commentary on Ja 576/13; *bʾmrhw*, cp. *bʾmrh* in RÉS 4839 A (cf. *JaPSAP*, pp. 108-09) which reads as follows: *mslm***l***ḥyw/ḏḥšg***l***ḏstḥṯy/ ḏʾr***l***tʿ/ḏḥnm/b***l***ʾmrh* "Altar for libations of Ḥayû, him of [the family] Ḥašag, which Ḏû-ʾArtaʿ, he of [the family] Ḥanum, has hurriedly made upon his [Ḥayû's] order"; and B: **Monogram** *mrḍ***l***/ ḥyw***l***whl* "**Monogram** Ḥayû was sick and rejoiced greatly." A: the verb *ḥṯy*, whose 10th form is attested here, may be related to Arabic *ḥaṯṯ* "to hasten, hurry." B: the three parts are engraved on the front of the altar, to the right, on the left-hand side of the bucranium, and on the front of the altar, to the left, respectively. The monogram may be read "Wadd ʾAb" (not "ʾAb Wadd"), for both *w* and *d* are located in the upper part of the monogram. The verb *hl* (cf. Arabic *halla* "to rejoice greatly") alludes to the recovery of Ḥayû, which was a cause of great joy. This part of the text gives the reason for the offering. – *yʾfq*, cf., with ʾ = *w*, Arabic *wafiqa*, 2nd form "to accommodate, adapt, dispose, direct to the right course" (cf. *LaAEL*, p. 3057 A); the parallel with post-biblical Hebrew *ʾăfaq* "to turn, reverse...to overthrow" (cf. *JaDT*, p. 105 A) supposes a very unusual as well as quite unnecessary fact.

L. 17: *hšqr*: the tense of this verb is explained by the fact that the text was engraved after the realization of the order given by the god.

Ll. 23-24: *hʿn* "to give help" with the meaning "to repair".

L. 24: *mṯbr*, cf. *CoRoC*, p. 258 B; in CIH 334/12, *mṯbr* is not a passive participle (cf. *l.c.*); in *RyET* (p. 44, commentary on Fakhry 71/9), read "17" instead of "10" after RÉS 4190; cf. also commentary on Ja 561 bis/23-24: *ṯbr*. – *lqbly*: "on account of" means here "by the means of".

L. 25: *ʾbhy*[..] (cp. RÉS 2771/1, Min): *y* may be interpreted as the case ending (cf., e.g., *š́ʿbynhn* and *š́ʿbnhn*) on the basis of *ʾbhhw* in Ja 557.

— C —

INSCRIPTIONS WITHOUT ROYAL NAME: Ja 672–838 and 851

1 – STONE: Ja 672-830 and 851

a – Boustrophedon: Ja 672-682

672 – Yellowish sandstone plaque; photograph in Plate 20. – MaMB 92.

PLAQUE: constant thickness: 6.5 cm. – *Front:* the upper edge is slightly splintered off; the right lower side is badly damaged; covered with red paint; 44.5 cm. (top) and 45 (bottom) × 17.8 (right) and 17.5 (left). – INSCRIPTION (B): same disposition of lines as in Ja 552; line 1: 46.2 cm. ×6; distance to the upper edge: 1.4 cm., and to the right: 0.9 cm. and 1.9; space between the lines: 1.5 cm.; line 2: 42.5 cm. × 5.8; distance to the right edge: 1.6 cm.

B [A]

1 ← *ḥb/ytʾlk/hqmlʾ/ynqh* **I**[...

2 → *tnhn/wkl/wldhw/bʿ⌈ṯ⌉***I**[*tr/wb/hwbs/wb/ʾlmqh*]

1 ...] has dedicated to ʾIlumquh the two kinds of pure

2 objects and all his children. By ʿAṯ[tar and by Hawbas and by ʾIlumquh.]

The singular *hqny* suggests that A/1 had most probably the same length as B/1; the restoration of A/2 contains 18 signs as in B/2; however B/1 has 19 signs.

L. 1: *klʾty*, cf. commentary on Ja 557: *klʾy*.

Ll. 1-2: *bḥt*, cf. *CoRoC*, p. 112 and recently in RÉS 4921/2; cf. also *bḥtn*, name of a Qat clan in Ja 865/2-3. *GhNQI* (p. 2) translates *bḥt* as "phallus" with reference to the root *bwḥ*: "most probably the original sense of *bwḥ* is either *ḏkr*, *frǧ*, or *ǧimâʿ*; but I prefer here the first" (p. 3). The reason for the preference remains unexplained; and what is presented as "the original sense" of *bwḥ* is but a derived, secondary meaning, the first being "*ẓuhûr aš-šayʾin*" (cf. *Lisân*, II, p. 412; cf. also *Muḥîṭ al-Muḥîṭ*, p. 14 A) "the appearance of the thing" or "it...became apparent, *or* manifest" (cf. *LaAEL*, p. 273 B).

673 – Right part of a yellowish sandstone inscription; photograph (cf. Plate 20) and latex squeeze. – MaMB 113.

STONE: almost constant thickness: 6.3 cm. – *Front:* 20.4 cm. (top), 21 (center), and 19.4 (bottom) × 15.1 (right) and 14.5 (left). – INSCRIPTION: same disposition of lines as in Ja 552; letter height: 4.4 cm., 4.2, and 4.3; distance to the upper edge; 0.7 cm., and to the right edge: 2.8 cm., 1.6, and 1.6. – SYMBOL, cf. Ja 558, but in reverse position; furthermore, the upper and lower edge are convex; close to the extremities, a small horizontal line, and in the center, two parallel oblique lines: 4.4 cm. × 0.6; cf. Plate C, Fig. 2.

1 ← .../*n*]*b/nwtqm/nbʾḏ* **Symbol**

2 → ...]⌊*wb/mrʾhw/yṯʿ*

3 ← ...]⌊ʾ⌋/*bw/rtw/rmʾ*

1 **Symbol** Ḏaʾbân, the high official, so[n of...

2 ...] and by his lord Yaṯaʿ-

3 ʾamar Watar and by ʾ[...

L. 1: *d̲ʾbn*, clan name, e.g., in RÉS 4257 B, Qat (cf. *JaSAA*, p. 154 A); cf. also the name of a man *d̲ʾyb[n]* in Ja 196/1, Qat, and of a clan *d̲ʾbm* in Ja 868/2, Qat. – *mqtw*, *scriptio defectiva* of *mqtwy*.
L. 2: *yt̲ʿʾmr/wtr*, Ja 557.

674 – Yellowish sandstone; broken on the left side; two photographs in Plates 20-21. – MaMB 100.

FRONT: upper left corner broken; 16.4 cm. (top) and 16.1 (bottom) × 20.6 (right) and 18.1 (left). – INSCRIPTION (B): same disposition of lines as in Ja 552; line 1: 14.4 cm. × 5.5; distance to the upper edge: 1.7 cm, and to the right: 2.1; space between the lines: 0.8 cm.; line 2: not engraved but simply traced; 3.2 cm. × 5.2; distance to the right edge: 12.3 cm.; at 1.1 cm. below line 2; another horizontal line.

.../]*qfšmʿ*/	←	1	ʿAmmšafaq[...
...]*n*/	→	2	...]*n*.

ʿmšfq, e.g., RÉS 2891/1.

RIGHT SIDE: 17 cm. (top) and 20 (bottom). – MARK (A): the letter *f*: 15.7 cm. × 9.2; distance to the upper edge: 3.5 cm., and to the left: 5.5 cm., 4, and 6.8.

675 – Sandstone; broken on both lateral sides; photograph in Plate 20. – MaMB 22.

STONE: maximum thickness: 19.6 cm. – *Front:* maximum length: 17 cm., and width: 22.7 cm. – INSCRIPTION: same disposition of lines as in Ja 552. Line 1: letter height: 5.4 cm.; distance to the upper edge: 3.3 cm. (left) and 3.7 (right); space between the lines: 0.9 cm. Line 2; letter height: 5.7 cm.; at 0.9 cm. below line 2, another horizontal line.

1 ← .../*y*]⌞*n*⌝*bw*/*ysʿ*⌜/⌝[...
2 → ...*y*]*bynnn*[...

1 ...] has acquired and built[...
2 ...that they] separate[...

Ja 675 and 676 could at first sight belong to the same original as far as the texts are concerned: 675 in the center, a small fragment missing and then 676. This hypothesis must be discarded because of the letter height, the spacing between the lines, and surface of the front.

L. 1: *ʿsy*/*wbny*, e.g., Ja 540 A/1.

676 – Upper left corner of a reddish sandstone plaque with a yellowish stain on the right; photograph in Plate 21. – MaMB 68.

PLAQUE: thickness: 11.1 cm. – *Front:* maximum length: 9.4 cm., and width: 10.5 cm. – INSCRIPTION: line 1: 8.2 cm. × 5.2; space between the lines: 0.7 cm.

1 ← *qf*/⌞*y*⌝[*nbw*/*ysʿ*/...
2 → ⌞*ḥ*/*k*⌟[...

1 ...]has acquired and bui]lt the open-
2 ing of *k*[...

For the impossibility of connecting Ja 675 and 676, cf. beginning of the commentary on Ja 675.

Ll. 1-2: *fqḥ*: e.g., Ja 526/4 and commentary in *JaISAR*, p. 122; cf. also *BeSI*, p. 70.

677 – Fragment of a white alabaster plaque with blackish stain in the upper part; photograph in Plate 21. – MaMB 79.

PLAQUE: thickness: 3 cm. – *Front:* 6.2 cm. (length) × 11. – INSCRIPTION: same disposition of lines as in Ja 552; letter height: 3.4 cm.; space between the lines: 0.8 cm.

→	...]*h*⌝*mm*⌜/⌝[...	1	...]hmum[...
←	...]/*mlb*[...	2	...]blum[...

The possible restorations of the two proper names are too numerous. For the first, e.g., [*g*]*hmm*, [*n*]*hmm*, [*ṣ*]*hmm*, [*r*]*hmm*, etc.; for the second, e.g., [*g*]*blm*, [*n*]*blm*, [ʿ]*blm*, [*q*]*blm*, etc.

678 – Fragment of a white alabaster plaque; photograph in Plate 21. – MaMB 119.

PLAQUE: constant thickness: 5 cm. – *Front:* length: 10.3 cm.; and diagonal width: 12.4 cm. – INSCRIPTION: same disposition of lines as in Ja 552; letter height: 4.3 cm.; space between the lines: 0.5 cm.

←	...]⌜ʾ*r*/*br*⌝[...	1	...]rab Raʾ[...
→	...]⌞*d*/*klw*⌟[...	2	...].terrace[...
←	...]⌜ʿ*k*/*r*⌟[...	3	...].Kaʿ[...

L. 1: ...]*rb* and *rʾ*[...: too many restorations are possible; however one thinks of *rʾ*[*b*... or *rʾ*[*s*... for the second, as well as ...*k*]*rb* for the first.
L. 2: *klw*, e.g., RÉS 3943/6, and *RoVSAY*, p. 306.

679 – Right part of an inscription; grayish sandstone; photograph in Plate 22. – MaMB 129.

STONE: thickness: 25 cm. (top) and 21.2 (bottom). – *Front:* covered with red paint; 26 cm. (right) × 11.2 (above line 3). – INSCRIPTION, same disposition of lines as in Ja 552; letter height: 6.8 cm., 7, and 6.6; distance to the upper edge: 3.2 cm., and to the right: 5.2 cm., 5.1, and 5.2; a vertical line is engraved to the right of the text.

1 ← *.../qd]⌞ṣlʾ/*
2 → *..ʾlmqh/bʿl]/ḥr/*
3 ← *...]⌞nb/n/⌟*

1 ʾIlṣa[diq...
2 ...ʾIlumquh, master of] Ḥirw-
3 ân from (?) [...

L. 1: *ʾlṣdq*, e.g., Ja 404/1, Min.
Ll. 2-3, cf. Ja 629/45-46.

680 – Fragment of a slightly yellowish alabaster plaque; photograph in Plate 22. – MaMB 144.

PLAQUE: constant thickness: 7.7 cm. – *Front:* length (in the center of line 3): 18.2 cm.; width (vertically on *m* in line 3): 30.1 cm.; diagonal length: 37.2 cm. – INSCRIPTION: letter height: 7.3 cm.; space between the lines: 1.1 cm.

1 ← ...].[...
2 → ...]⌜*mʿʿʿ*/[...
3 ← ...]⌜*ʾ/wmh*.[...
4 → ...*ʾ*]⌞*l*⌟*fm/qn*⌝[*yhmw*/...
5 ← ...]⌞*bʾ*/⌟[...

1 ...].[...
2 ...] hundred and thirty [...
3 ...] their .[...
4 ...thou]sand [as their] sla[ves...
5 ...]ʾAb[...

L. 3: the letter preceding *hmw* is either *y*, *ṣ*, or *ṯ*; *bny*?, *ʾnṯ*?

681 – "Found near center of mausoleum, near surface level, about a meter or a little more above the floor" (F. P. Albright); copy by the same. – MaMB 303.

STONE: broken on top and on the right side. – *Front:* 30 cm. × 19.

1 ←...*lm(s)h/nr(b)*[*d*...
2 →.../*hmẓʾ/smh*[...
3 ←...*bqḏ/mdq/m*[...

1 ...Da](b)rân Ha(s)mal...
2 ...] let arrive Sumhu[...
3 ...]. commander of the tribe of Qab[...

L. 1: copy: */rn/hn/ml*. One might think of *kbrn*, family name, e.g., in Ja 881 A/1-2 and second family name in Ja 881 B/2-3, both Qat (cf. *JaPEQL*, pp. 208-09 and 209, respectively); cf. also the masculine personal name *kbrm*, e.g., in Ja 626/2. The reading *dbrn* is preferred because of Ja 682/1. – *hsml*, cf. the Thamudic masculine names: *hsmyl* (cf. *vdBrIT*, p. 267: Jsa 400) and *sml* (cf. *vdBrTTPN*, p. 135: Ph 367 r/1); cf. also the Arabic name *ʾabû sammâl* (cf. *SaIS*, p. 105 A). The text being boustrophedon, the difference between *l* and *g* is quite clear on the stone; there is thus no reason to think that the last proper name should be read *h(s)m(g)* (cf. *ʾsmg* in RÉS 3800, Min).
L. 2: *hmẓʾ*, 4th form of *mẓʾ* (e.g., Ja 576/6).
L. 3: *qdm* could possibly be a preposition (cf. commentary on Ja 575/3) "in front of", or a verb the form of which (cf. commentary on Ja 576/5) is unknown, or the noun "commander" (cf. Ja 547/2) or "front (of a building)" (cf. *CoRoC*, p. 229 B). The parallel text Ja 547/2-3: *ʾqdm/–/šʿb/ḏhmdn*, provides some basis for the preference of the adopted interpretation over an alternative. – *qb*[..., cf., e.g., the Min clan *qbl* (e.g., RÉS 3737/2); *ḏqb*[*ḏm* seems excluded since one would expect *ršw*, *qyn*, etc., instead or *qdm* before the name of the stellar god (cf. *JaP*, p. 93).

682 – "Painted on the outside wall of tomb *a* of South Tombs. The letters, in red paint on limestone, were not always distinct" (F. P. Albright); copy by the same; cf. *AlEMY*, p. 238 B. – MaMB 315.

qf/ysʿ/nrbd/nb/ʿmsklh ← 1
ḥ/ṯʿd(n/ʿ)sm(y)/gwlm/(b)šhr → 2

1 Halaksamîʿ, son of Dabrân, has acquired the open-
2 ing of the canalization (ʿA)sm(î) as property. (By) Šahar.

L. 2: copy: *ṯʿd/nwsmʿ/gwlm/yšhr*. *ṯʿd*: several etymologies have been proposed; cf. *RÉS*, V, p. 157, *CoRoC*, p. 261 A and *BeSI*, p. 70; this noun is ordinarily translated "irrigated field" or some synonymous expression (e.g., RÉS 3112/3). Cf. however modern Yemeni *sâᶜadah*, pl. *sawâᶜid* "piccolo argine nei campi" (cf. *RoVSAY*, p. 313). Cf. also *mṯᶜd* (e.g., RÉS 4815/2) "cultivated plot" (cf. *RoVSAY*, *l.c.*, and A. F. L. Beeston in *JRAS*, 1948, p. 179) although Daṯînah *masᶜad* means "*retaining* wall of the sôm, *the earth* embankment, in order to avoid the washing away by water" (cf. *LaGD*, p. 1933). The family name *ṯṯᶜd* (RÉS 4962/3) belongs to the same root. – *ᶜsmy*, cf., e.g., *ᶜsmym*, name of the anterior part of a building in Ja 411/3, and the place name *ᶜsmt* in Ja 550/1, and the name of a Qat person *ᶜsmm* in Ja 221. – *gwl*, cf. *CoRoC*, pp. 121-22 and especially *BeSI*, p. 68; cf. RÉS 4231/3. – *šhr*, cf. *šhrn*, epithet of the Min lunar god (cf. *JaP*, p. 75, *JaRSAP*, p. 263 and CIH 30/3) and the Qat name of the same deity *rbᶜ/šhr* (cf. *JaP*, p. 85 and *JaRSAP*, p. 264). The parallel RÉS 4231/1-3 excludes the interpretation of *b* as an equivalent of *bn*, a preposition indicating the origin and introducing the name of the person from whom the opening of the canalization would have been acquired. Cf. also the names of a man *šhrm* (e.g., RÉS 4891/1, Ḥaḏr) and *šhrn* (e.g., Khalidy-Condé 9 B/2, instead of *šhr*(ᵓ)).

b – Ordinary lettering: Ja 683-828 and 851

1° – COMPLETE AND BROKEN INSCRIPTIONS: Ja 683-761 AND 851

683 – Yellowish, slightly grayish sandstone; fragmentary on top; two photographs in Plate 22. – MaMB 47.

FRONT: upper edge broken; covered with red paint; length: 20.9 cm., and maximum width: 17 cm. – INSCRIPTION: lines 1-5; same disposition of lines as in Ja 559, plus short vertical lines delimitating the location of each sign; there are many small vertical lines between the lines; line 2: 20.1 cm. × 3.2; line 3: 19.8 cm. × 3; line 4: 19.2 cm. × 3; line 5: 19.7 cm. × 3.1; space between the lines: 0.4 cm., 0.4, 0.4, and 0.3.
LEFT SIDE: upper corners broken; covered with red paint; 13.6 cm. × 17.8. – INSCRIPTION: lines 6-9; a vertical stroke is traced in the center of the space separating the first letter of each line and the right edge; line 1: 8.5 cm. × 3.2; line 2: 10.1 cm. × 2.7; line 3: 11.2 cm. × 3; line 4: 3.4 cm. × 2.7; distance between the lines: 0.4 cm., 0.3, and 0.4; distance from line 6 to the upper edge: 0.6 cm.

1 . . .]⌜*sqrn*/⌝ᶜ⌜*bd*/⌝
2 *ḏᶜqbn/hqny/ᵓlm*⌜*qh/b*⌝ᶜ⌜*l*/⌝
3 *ᵓwm/ṣlmnhn/lwfyhmw/w*
4 *wfy/bnyhw/rbbm/wzyd*
5 *m/wrṯdhmy/ᵓlmqhw/bᶜṯt*
6 *r/wb/hw*⌜*bs*/⌝[*wb/ᵓ*]
7 *lmqh/wb/ḏt*⌟[/*ḥ*]
8 *mym/wb/ḏt/b*⌝ᶜ⌟
9 *dnm*

1 . . .of] Saqrân, servant of
2 [the tribe] ᶜAqbân, has dedicated to ᵓIlumquh, master of
3 ᵓAwwâm, these two statues for their safety and
4 the safety of his two sons Rabîbum and Zayd-
5 um and he entrusted both of them to the care of ᵓIlumquhû. By ᶜAṯt-
6 ar and by Hawbas [and by ᵓI-]
7 lumquh and by Ḏât-[Ḥi-]
8 myâm and by Ḏât-Baᶜ-
9 dânum.

The original first line is missing.

L. 1: *sqrn*, also family name, e.g., in RÉS 3998; cf. commentary on Ja 588/1.
L. 2: the worker engraved *hqny* at the beginning of the line; he then erased it by making a rectangular hole where he finally engraved *ḏᶜqbn*.
L. 4: *rbbm*: e.g., Ja 547/1 and Ist 7626/4 (instead of *rbb* as in *BeFSTI*, p. 271, the two following corrections should also be made on p. 272: *bn* instead of *b* at the end of line 6, and ⌞*wb/kl*⌟ instead of ⌜*w*⌝*gbl* at the beginning of line 7).

684 – White limestone inscription, broken on the upper corners; photograph in Plate 23. – MaMB 48.

STONE: thickness: 10.6 cm. – *Front:* damaged on the right, left and lower edges; 15 cm. × 20. – INSCRIPTION: same disposition of lines as in Ja 559; letter height: 1 cm.; space between the lines: 0.2 cm.; another horizontal line is engraved at 0.2 cm. below line 13. – SYMBOL: badly damaged. – FLOWER: at the end of line 13; cf. Ja 587; but six petals instead of eight; cf. Plate B.

1 (**Sym-**) ⌜*ynᶜm/b*⌟[*n/smln/ᶜbd/n*]
2 (**bol**) *mrn/ᵓwk*⌜*n*/⌝[*wᵓẖyhw/gḥ*]
3 *ḍm/ᵓḥṣn/bny/kbrẖ*⌝[*ll/wkbr*]
4 *ᵓqynm/wḏsẖymm/hqn*⌜*y*/⌝[ᵓ]

5 *lmqhṯhwnbᶜlʾwm/ḏn/ṣlm⸣*
6 *n/ḏdhbn/ḏšfthw/lẖmr/ᶜb⸥d⸥*
7 *hw/ynᶜm/bn/slmn/ḥẓy/wr*
8 *ḍw/mrʾyhw/nmrn/ʾwkn/w*
9 *⸢ʾẖyhw/gḥḍm/ʾḥṣn/bny/k⸥*
10 *[br]ẖll/wkbrʾqynm/wḏsẖymm/w⸣*
11 *lhᶜnn/wmtᶜn/ᶜbdhw/ynᶜm*
12 *bn/slmn/bn/nḍᶜ/wšṣy/šnʾ⸣*
13 *[m]/bʾlmqhṯhwnbᶜlʾwm* **Flower**

1 (**Sym-**) Yunᶜim, s[on of Salmân, servant of Ni-]
2 (**bol**) mrân ʾAwkân [and his brother Gaḥ-]
3 ḍum ʾAḥṣân, descendants of the Leader of H̱a[lil and of the Leader of]
4 ʾAqyânum and of [the tribe] Suẖaymum, has dedicated to [ʾI-]
5 lumquh Ṯahwân, master of ʾAwwâm, this statue
6 which [is] in bronze, which he had promised to Him because He has vouchsafed to His worship-
7 per Yunᶜim, son of Salmân, the esteem and gra-
8 ce of his two lords Nimrân ʾAwkân and
9 his brother Gaḥḍum ʾAḥṣân, descendants of the Lea[der of]
10 H̱alil and of the Leader of ʾAqyânum and of [the tribe] Suẖaymum; and
11 [because] He has protected and saved His worshipper Yunᶜim,
12 son of Salmân, from the hostility and wickedness of [any] enemy.
13 By ʾIlumquh Ṯahwân, master of ʾAwwâm. **Flower**

L. 1: *slmn*; also in line 7; also masculine personal name, e.g., in RÉS 4869/1, Ḥaḍr; this text may be read as follows:

1 *slmn[/]b(n)[/]ḥḏnm/(ḏ)ḍddm*
2 *(b)n/mrṯd(ʾ)[l]n/ ʾsdyn*

1 Salmân, so(n of) Ḥuḏunum, (he of) Ḍadidum,
2 (so)n of Marṯad(ʾi)(l)ân, the ʾAsadite.

Ll. 1-2 and 8: the name *nmrn/ʾwkn* was intentionally erased; this name and that of his brother *gḥḍm/ʾḥṣn* are also mentioned in Ja 594/4-5 where they are also introduced by *mrʾy*.

Ll. 4 and 10: *ḏsẖymm*: first text mentioning *sẖymm* introduced by *ḏ*; cf. note in *JaPEHA*, p. 28.

685 – Lower part of a yellowish sandstone inscription; re-cut on the right side; photograph in Plate 23. – MaMB 57.

STONE: thickness: 12.8 cm. – *Front:* both upper and left edges and end of line 6 damaged; 19.4 cm. × 13.4 (left) and 12.4 (right). – INSCRIPTION: same disposition of lines as in Ja 559; letter height: 1.9 cm.; space between the lines: 0.4 cm.; length of line 6: 9.4 cm.; distance from line 6 to the left edge: 9.5 cm., and to the bottom: 1.2 cm.; of line 1 only the lower part of several letters remains.

1 ...
2 *⸢hm⸢/⸣[wḥmd/ẖ]⸢y⸣l/wmqm/ʾlmqh/bᶜlʾwm*
3 *⸢bḏt/m⸢t⸣ᶜ⸢hw/b⸢n⸣/ywm/ḥrbt/bm*
4 *[.]lwn/wʾlmqh/wlyzʾn/mtᶜn/ᶜ*
5 *[b]dhw/ḏrᶜt/bn/nḍᶜ/wšṣy/šnʾm/b*
6 *⸤ʾlmqhbᶜlʾwm*

1 ...
2 *hm*; [and he has praised the str]ength and the power of ʾIlumquh, master of ʾAwwâm,
3 because He has saved him from the period of the battle in Ma-
4 [.]lwân; and as for ʾIlumquh, and may He continue to save
5 His wo[rsh]ipper Ḏirᶜat from the hostility and wickedness of [any] enemy. By
6 ʾIlumquh, master of ʾAwwâm.

Ja 685 and 723 cannot belong to the same original. Cf. also the beginning of the commentary on Ja 792.

L. 2: there is no space for *w* after *hm*.

Ll. 3-4: *m.lwn*. cp. *mẖlym*, name of a temple dedicated to Taʾlab, e.g., in Gl 1142/2 (cf. *JaITDL*, pp. 182-83).

L. 5: *ḏrᶜt* is known in Thamudic (cf., e.g., *vdBrIT*, p. 383: Jsa 43); cf. also the Arabic names of men *ḏirâᶜ* (cf., e.g., *GeKH*, p. 4 B), *ḏarâᶜ* (cf. *WüR*, p. 425), *bû-ḏurâᶜ* (cf. *SlGaVNPA*, p. 18 B), and *ʾibn ʾabî ḏirâᶜ* (cf. *SaIS*, p. 74 A) and of places *ḏirâᶜân* (cf. *WüR*, p. 96 A) and *ḏarwaᶜân* (cf. *MüHG*, p. 46 B); *ḏrᶜt* must be restored at the beginning of the missing text which contained a dedication to *ʾlmqh(/)bᶜlʾwm*.

686 – White limestone inscription, broken at the bottom; photograph in Plate 23. – MaMB 63.

STONE: almost constant thickness: 8.4 cm. – *Front:* length: 12.9 cm., and maximum width: 15.4 cm. – INSCRIPTION: same disposition of lines as in Ja 559; letter height: between 1.3 cm. and 1.6; space between the lines: from 0.2 cm. to 0.3: – SYMBOL: upper right corner and right edge of the frame damaged; cp. Ja 569; 2.2 cm. × 3.2; cf. Plate A.

1 **Sym-** *ḥmlt/wnᶜmsᶜd*
2 **bol** *ḏty/gbʾt/hqn[y]*
3 *tw/ʾlmqhbᶜlʾwm/ṣ*

4 *lmtn/ḥmdm/lḏt/ẖmrh*
5 *w/wldm/hyt/mrʾtn/nʿm*
6 *sʿd/wlẖmrhmw/šwft/g*
7 *rybthmw/wlwzʾ/ʾlmqh*
8 *[mtʿnhmw/bn/n]⌊ḏ⌋[ʿ]⌊/⌋w⌊šṣ⌋y/š*
9 *[nʾm/bʾlmqhbʿlʾwm]*

1 **Sym-** Ḥamlat and Naʿamsaʿad
2 **bol** both (women) of Gabaʾat, have dedi[cat-]
3 ed to ʾIlumquh, master of ʾAwwâm, this
4 female statue in praise because He has vouchsafed to
5 her a child, to this lady Naʿam-
6 saʿad; and that He may vouchsafe to them the care of their
7 persons; and that ʾIlumquh may continue
8 [to save them from the hos]tili[ty] and wickedness of [any] e-
9 [nemy. By ʾIlumquh, master of ʾAwwâm.]

L. 1: *ḥmlt*, very well-known personal name in Arabic (cf., e.g., *GoAT*, p. 151: man), in Thamudic (cf., e.g., *vdBrIT*, p. 404; Jsa 153+154/1: woman) and in Safaitic (cf., e.g., *LiSI*, p. 315 B); cf. also the Arabic names of men *ḥml* and *ḥmyl* (cf. *GoAT*, pp. 151 and 155 respectively). – *nʿmsʿd*, same nominal formation as that, e.g., of *nʿmgd*, also a feminine personal name (CIH 330/1).

Ll. 4-5: *hw* refers to *hyt/mrʾtn/nʿmsʿd.*

L. 6: *šwft*, CIH 43/6.

L. 8: one may restore *mtʿnhmw*; the letters of the line are closer to each other than the signs of the other lines.

687 – Left part of a whitish limestone inscription; left corners broken; photograph in Plate 23. – MaMB 64.

STONE: constant thickness: 7.5 cm. – *Front:* lower part badly damaged; covered with red paint; 24.5 cm. × 8.7. – INSCRIPTION: same disposition of lines as in Ja 559; letter height: 1.3 cm.; space between the lines: 0.3 cm.

1 **[Sym-** *whbš]⌈msm/bn/lqẓn/[.]*
2 **[bol** *...]/hqny/ʾlmqhṯ*
3 *[hwnbʿlʾ]wm/ṣlmn/ḏdh*
4 *[bn/ḥmd]⌊m/lqbly/ḏt/b*
5 *.../w]hbšms/bn/lq*
6 *[ẓn/ẖyl/w]mqm/ʾlmqhb(ʿ)*
7 *[lʾwm/bn]/zẖnt/zẖnhw*
8 *...]yn/bśn/byt/ḥ*
9 *...]hʿn/wmtʿn/b*
10 *...]b/ʿbdhw/whb*
11 *[šms(m)/bn/]bʾstm/wnkyt*
12 *[m/wnḍʿ/w]šṣy/šnʾm/bʾ*
13 *[lmqhṯ]⌊hwnbʿ[lʾw]⌊m*

1 **[Sym-** Wahabša]msum, son of Laqẓân.
2 **[bol** ...] has dedicated to ʾIlumquh Ṯa-
3 [hwân, master of ʾA]wwâm, this statue which [is] in bron-
4 [ze, in praise] because of this:
5 ...Wa]habšams, son of Laq-
6 [ẓân, the strength and] the power of ʾIlumquh, ma(s-)
7 [ter of ʾAwwâm, because of] the wound [which] wounded him
8 ...]. in the law of the house of Ḥa-
9 ...] protect and save
10 ...] His worshipper Wahab-
11 [šams(um) from] misfortunes and sufferings
12 [and (from) the hostility and] wickedness of [any] enemy. By ʾI-
13 [lumquh Ṯa]hwân, maste[r of ʾAwwâ]m.

L. 1: *whbšmsm*, obviously identical to *whbšms* in line 5; e.g., CIH 178/1 (cf. *MoMiSI*, p. 119); same nominal formation, e.g., as *whbḏsmwy* (cf. *RyHE*, p. 230), *whbʿṯt* (Ja 701 A/7) and *whbṯwn* (Ja 726/4). – *lqẓn*, 3rd masculine personal name in CIH 661/1, but 2nd in RÉS 4200, where *–llqẓn* is to be read instead of *–bqẓn.*

Ll. 4-6: the meaning of this phrase might be the following: *whbšms(m)* failed to thank the god for the aid received from Him when he was wounded.

L. 6: *b(ʿ)*: *bq* was first engraved, but the worker tried to correct his mistake by re-engraving ʿ deeper in the stone.

L. 7: *zẖnt/zẖnhw*, cf. commentary on Ja 649/19.

L. 8: *bśn* "in (according, under) the law", as in RÉS 3912/3.

688 – Limestone base of a statue; photograph in Plate 24. – MaMB 69.

STONE: thickness: 6.1 cm. – *Front:* lower left corner broken; upper left corner and right edge damaged; covered with red paint; 12.3 cm. × 9. – INSCRIPTION: same disposition of lines as in Ja 552; letter height: 1.6 cm. (line 1), 1.7 (line 2), 1.9 (line 3), and 2 (line 4); space between the lines: 0.2 cm., 0.25, and 0.2; distance from line 1 to the upper edge: 0.4 cm.

1 *⌈ʾ⌉lqdm/gr⌉(b)[n/hq]*
2 *ny/ʾlmqh/⌈lb⌉[nh]*
3 *⌊w/ʾlšrḥ/ẓlmn/*
4 *⌊ḏdhbn/*

1 ʾIlqadam Gar(b)[ân] has [de-]
2 [di]cated to ʾIlumquh for [h]is s[on],
3 ʾIlšaraḥ, this statue
4 which [is] in bronze.

L. 1: *ʾlqdm*, e.g., Ja 169/1, Qat. – *gr(b)[n]*: the lower extremity of the two vertical strokes of *b* are still visible; for *grbn*, cf., e.g., RÉS 4578.

L. 3: *ẓlm* (cf. *StSESA*, pp. 517-18) instead of the usual form *ṣlm*, cf. *CoRoC*, p. 161 A.

689 – Yellowish, slightly grayish sandstone; photograph in Plate 24. – MaMB 89.

STONE: maximum thickness: 16.9 cm. – *Top*: six pairs of holes according to the number of dedicated statues. – *Front:* upper edge slightly damaged; 64.8 cm. (top) and 64.3 (bottom) × 28.1 (right) and 26.1 (left). – INSCRIPTION: same disposition of lines as in Ja 559; at 0.9 cm. below line 5, another horizontal line; letter height: 4.5 cm.; space between the lines: 0.6 cm.; distance from line 1 to the upper edge; 1.2 cm. – SYMBOL, cf. Ja 603, but five inside incisions instead of three; cf. Plate A.

1 **Sym-** *sʿdʾwm/bn/ʾgylm/ʾdm/bn/ḥlḥlm/hqny*
2 **bol** *ʾlmqh/bʿl/ʾwm/ʾrbʿtn/ʾṣlmn/wṣl*
3 *mtnhn/lwfy/bnyhw/whbʾwm/wḏrḥn/wyšf/*
4 *wrbʾwm/wʾsmwm/wʿlym/bnw/ʾgylm/wl/wfyhw*
5 *wwfy/ʾbʿl/bythmw/bʿṯtr/wʾlmqh/wḏtḥmym*

1 **Sym-** Saʿadʾawwâm, son of ʾUgaylum, servants of [the clan] Ḥalḥalum, has dedicated
2 **bol** to ʾIlumquh, master of ʾAwwâm, these four statues and these two
3 female statues for the safety of his children Wahabʾawwâm and Ḏarḥân and Yašûf
4 and Rabbʾawwâm and ʾAsmawum and ʿAlayum, descendants of ʾUgaylum, and that He may protect him
5 and protect the masters of their house. By ʿAṯtar and ʾIlumquh and Ḏât-Ḥimyâm.

L. 1: *ʾgylm*, cf. the family name *ʾgln* (RÉS 3566/30, Qat). – *ʾdm*, refers to the two preceding names and not to the clan name which follows; idem in Ja 696/1-2, 697/1, 726/1 as well as in RÉS 4229/1-2 (contrary to *RÉS*, VII, p. 154); idem also with regard to *ʾmh* in Ja 731/2.

L. 3: *bnyhw*, cf. Ja 742/9 and commentary on lines 7-8. – *yšf*, CIH 88/1; cf. also the name of a man *yšfʾl* (e.g., RÉS 4884/1, Ḥaḍr).

L. 4: *ʾsmwm*, from the root *smw*. – *ʿlym*, e.g., Ja 155/1, Qat, and commentary, and Ja 882 Q, Qat (cf. *JaPEQL*, p. 216).

690 – White limestone; photograph in Plate 24. – MaMB 97.

STONE: thickness: 7.7 cm. (top) and 6.8 (bottom). – *Front:* covered with slightly brownish paint; 16 cm. (top) and 15.8 (bottom) × 24.4 (right) and 24.5 (left). – INSCRIPTION: same disposition of lines as in Ja 559; letter height: 1.5 cm, but 1.6 on line 13; distance from line 1 to the top and space between the lines: 0.3 cm. – SYMBOL: 2 cm. × 3; for the upper, central and lower part, cf. the same part in Ja 591, 621 and 583, respectively; cf. Plate A. – FLOWER on each side of line 13; 2.2 cm. × 1.7 for the one on the right and 2 × 1.7 for the other one. For the left one, cf. Ja 618; but here, the petals in oblique position have their stalk toward the periphery. The right one is awkward and has nine petals. Cf. Plate B.

1 **Sym-** *yḥmd/mqtwy/sʿdʾwm/ʾs*
2 **bol** *ʿ⸢d/⸣wʾẖyhw/ʾḥmd/bny*
3 */zbnr/hqny/ʾlmqh/ṯhwn/b*
4 *ʿlʾwm/ṣlmn/wṣlmtn/ḏḏhb*
5 *n/ḥmdm/bḏt/ẖmrhw/ʾlmq*
6 *h</>ḥyw/lhw/bnyhw/ʾbkrb/wḥ*
7 *qbḥmd/wl/wzʾ/ʾlmqh/ṯhw*
8 *n/bʿlʾw⸢m/⸣sʿd/ʿbdhw/yḥ*
9 *md/ʾwldm/wnʿmtm/wmngt*
10 *ṣdqm/wḥẓy/wrḍw/šʿbhm*
11 *w/sbʾ/wʾmrʾhmw/bny/*
12 *zbnr/bʾlmqhw/ṯhwn*
13 **Flower***bʿlʾwm***Flower**

1 **Sym-** Yaḥmad, high official of Saʿadʾawwâm ʾAs-
2 **bol** ʿad, and his brother ʾAḥmad, descendants of
3 Zabnâr, has dedicated to ʾIlumquh Ṯahwân, mas-
4 ter of ʾAwwâm, this statue and this female statue which [are] in bronze,
5 in praise because ʾIlumquh has vouchsafed to him
6 to grant life for him to his two children ʾAbkarib and Ḥa-
7 qabḥamad; and that may continue ʾIlumquh Ṯahwân,
8 master of ʾAwwâm, to make happy His worshipper Yaḥ-
9 mad with children and prosperity and security
10 perfect and (with) the esteem and grace of their tribe
11 Sabaʾ and of their lords, the descendants of
12 [the clan] Zabnâr. By ʾIlumquhû Ṯahwân,
13 **Flower** master of ʾAwwâm. **Flower**

L. 3: *zbnr*, e.g., CIH 541/19.

Ll. 6-7: *ḥqbḥmd*: for the first element, cf. the Qat personal names *ʾbḥqb* (e.g., Ja 138/1: woman) and *ḥqbm* (Ja 293/1).

691 – Yellowish sandstone inscription, fragmentary on the right side; photograph in Plate 24. – MaMB 99.

STONE: thickness: 12.6 cm. (top) and 11.8 (bottom). – *Front:* covered with red paint; right edge badly damaged; 24.5 cm. (right) and 24 (left) × 14.8 (top), 14.1 (bottom) and 13.3 on line 7 (minimum width). – INSCRIPTION: same disposition of lines as in Ja 552; letter height (irregular): 2.3 cm. on line 1 and 1.1 on line 13; space between the lines: between 0.4 cm. and 0.5; distance from line 1 to the upper edge: 1 cm.

1 *⌞hrymm/bn/šrḥṯ⌜t/⌝[w]*
2 *[z]ʿy/dwmn/yʾzm/ḏġym*
3 *[n/]hqnyw/ʾlmqhw/bʿl*
4 *[ʾw]m/ṣlmn/ḏḏhbm/ḥmdm*
5 *[bḏ]t/hwfyhw/bʾmlʾ/stm*
6 *[lʾ]⌞/⌟bʿmhw/wlḫmrhw/ʾlmq*
7 *[hw]⌜ṯ⌝hwn/bʿl/ʾwm/ḥẓy/wr*
8 *[ḍw]⌞/⌟ʾmrʾhmw/bny/ḏġymn/wl*
9 *[sʿ]⌜d⌝hmw/ʾṯmrm/šfqm/〈bn/〉dʿtm*
10 *[ws]qym/ḏyrḍwnhmw/wlḫry*
11 *[nhm]w/bn/nḍʿ/wšṣy/šnʾm/ḏrḥq*
12 *[wqrb/w]⌜ḏ⌟bnhw/dʿw/wḏbnhw/ʾl*
13 *[dʿw]/bʾlmqhw/bʿl/ʾwm*

1 Huraymum, son of Šaraḥṯat, [the]
2 two [chie]fs of Dawamân Yaʾzim, him of [the tribe] Ġaym[ân,]
3 have dedicated to ʾIlumquhû, master of
4 [ʾAww]âm, this statue which [is] in bronze, in praise
5 [becau]se He has showered upon him the favors [for which] he be-
6 [sought] Him; and that may vouchsafe to him, ʾIlumq[uh]û
7 Ṯahwân, master of ʾAwwâm, the esteem and gra-
8 [ce of] their lords, the descendants of Ġaymân: and that
9 He may [make] them happy with plentiful fruits 〈from〉 *daʿat-*
10 [and *sa*]*qay*-palms, which would please them; and that He may preser-
11 [ve th]em from the hostility and wickedness of [any] enemy, who is remote
12 [or near, and] those who are known and those who [are] not
13 [known.] By ʾIlumquhû, master of ʾAwwâm.

L. 1: *hrymm*, *qutaylum* form; cp. *hrwm*, name of a deity (cf. *JaP*, p. 140 and *JaRSAP*, p. 274) and *hrmm*, name of a city (e.g., RÉS 3459 bis/3).

L. 2: *yʾzm*, also second personal name, e.g., in Ja 500 C and NaNN 28/2.

L. 4: *bḏt* is more frequently used than *lḏt*.

L. 9: something is missing before *dʿtm*; either *w* or *bn* "from"; the second hypothesis seems more probable for its omission may be explained by the haplography of the word divider after *šfqm* and the left vertical stroke of *b*.

L. 10: *ḏyrḍwnhmw*, cf. Ja 586/7-8.

692 – Yellowish sandstone; photograph in Plate 25. – MaMB 110.

STONE: thickness: 6.2 cm. – *Front:* covered with red paint; upper edge damaged; 11.7 cm. (top) and 11.4 (bottom) × 18.8 (right) and 18.7 (left). – INSCRIPTION: same disposition of lines as in Ja 623; letter height: 1.2 cm.; space between the lines: 0.3 cm.; distance from line 1 to the upper edge: 0.4 cm. – SYMBOL: upper right corner of the frame damaged; cf. Ja 582; but here, there is only one long central line; cf. Plate A.

1 **⌜Sym-** *⌜lʿšm/brl⌝⌜m/b⌜n⌝*
2 **bol** *ḥgnn/hqny/ʾl*
3 *mqh⌞/⌟bʿl/ʾwm/ṣlmn*
4 *ḏḏhb⌉n/wʾlmqh/ly*
5 *ḫmrnhw/šrḥ/grbh*
6 *w/wlwfy/bklhw/ʾly*
7 *ḥgnn/wlḫmrhw/ḥẓy*
8 *wrḍw/mrʾhw/mrṯdʾ*
9 *sʾy/bn/ḏrnḥ/wṣdqʾ*
10 *l/wlsʿdhw/krbtm/wʾ*
11 *ṯmrm/wʾfqlm/nʾdm*
12 *bʾlmqhbʿlʾwm*

1 **Sym-** Liʿašam Barlum, descendant of [the clan]
2 **bol** Ḥaganân, has dedicated to ʾIl-
3 umquh, master of ʾAwwâm, this statue
4 which [is] in bronze; and as for ʾIlumquh, may
5 He vouchsafe to him to keep his body healthy,
6 and that He may protect His devotees, those of
7 Ḥaganân; and that He may vouchsafe to him the esteem
8 and grace of his lord Marṯadʾa-
9 sʾay, son of Ḏarnaḥ and Ṣadiqʾil;
10 and that He may make them happy with blessings and
11 fruits and harvests magnificent.
12 By ʾIlumquh, master of ʾAwwâm.

L. 1: *lʿšm*; composed of *l* and *ʿšm*; cf. Arabic *ʿašima* "to become dry, lean, dried"; same nominal formation as that, e.g., of *lʿzzm* (e.g., Ja 631/26); cf. also *ʿšm*, name of an Arabic clan (cf. *WüR*, p. 252 A: *ʿišm*) and of a Thamudic man (cf. *vdBrIT*, p. 247: HU 480/3), and the Thamudic *nisba ʿšmy* (cf. *vdBrTTPS*, p. 70: Ph 165 u 13) and masculine personal name *ʿšmn* (cf. *vdBrTTPN*, p. 34: Ph 271 z 2).

L. 2: *ḥgnn*, cf. Arabic *ḥağana* "to attach one's self strongly to someone, to follow closely" and the Arabic names of men *al-ḥağn*, *al-ḥuğanî* (cf. *SaIS*, p. 52 A), *al-ḥağin* (cf. *SlGaVNPA*, p. 22 B), *muḥayğîn* (cf. *HeBN*, p. 17 B), *miḥğan*, *ʾabû miḥğan* (cf. *WüID*, 127/10 and 185/4 respectively), and of tribes *banû ḥğnt* (cf. *MüHG*, p. 138 B) and *banû ʾaḥğan* (cf. *WüID*, 288/13).

L. 6: *bkl*: the center of the 1st letter is damaged; cf. Arabic *bukkila bihi* "he surrendered to him body and soul"; *bkl* might be understood as a collective noun designating the "devotees". The expression *bkl/bhgrn/ṣrwḥ* (CIH 601/13), with the preposition *b* introducing *hgrn/ṣrwḥ*, suggests understanding *bkl/tmnʿ* (Van Lessen 9/1, Qat) as *b+kl/tmnʿ*, and not *bkl*[one noun]*/tmnʿ*, as proposed by *GhNQI* (pp. 419-20), who translates *bkl* as "residents", which is ordinarily rendered by *ḥwr* (e.g., Ja 727/3).

Ll. 8-9: *mrṯdʾsʾy*, same nominal formation as that, e.g., of *mrṯdʾln* (e.g., RÉS 4069/1-2 and 4869/2, Ḥaḏr; cf. commentary on Ja 684/1).

Ll. 9-10: *ṣdqʾl*, e.g., Gl 1128+1129/4-5 (cf. *HöDSP*, p. 39); same nominal formation as that, e.g., of *ṣdqʾmn* (e.g., Ja 871/2, Qat).

693 – Yellowish sandstone inscription, fragmentary and broken into three parts; photograph in Plate 25. – MaMB 111.

STONE: maximum thickness: 10.2 cm. – *Front:* lateral edges damaged; 46.3 cm. × 23.5. – INSCRIPTION: same disposition of lines as in Ja 552; letter height: 2.3 cm. in the first lines and 2 in the last; space between the lines and distance from line 1 to the upper edge: 0.3 cm.

1 **[Sym-** *rbʿ]t/⌈ḏkr⌉(n)[/wbnhw/rbʾ]*
2 **[bol** *wm/b]nw/ʿmm⌈/ʾsbʾyn/⌉*
3 *. . .]⌊/⌋ḏrfdn/hqnyy*
4 *[ʾlmqh]⌈ṯh⌉[w]⌈n/b⌉[ʿ]lʾwm⌋⌊/⌋ṣlmn*
5 *hn/ʾḥd/ṣrfm/wʾḥd/ḏhbm⌉*
6 *lqbly/ḏšfthw/kmʿnmw/yḥ*
7 *[y]wn/lhw/bnhw/rbʾwm/wrʾ*
8 *⌊h̲⌋mr/ʾlmqhṯhwn/bʿlʾwm/ʿb*
9 *⌈dhw/rbʿt/bn/ʿmm/ḥyw/bnhw/r*
10 *⌈bʾwm/wlwzʾ/ʾlmqhṯhwn/bʿ*
11 *⌈lʾwm/h̲mr/ʿbdhw/rbʿt/hwfyn*
12 *hw/bkl/ʾmlʾ/ystmlʾn/bʿmh*
13 *w/wlh̲rynhmw/bn/nḍʿ/wšṣy/šn*
14 *ʾm/bʾlmqhṯhwnbʿlʾwm*

1 **[Sym-** Rabîʿ]at Ḏakr(ân) [and his son Rabbʾa-]
2 **[bol** wwâm, des]cendants of ʿAmmum, Sabaeans,
3 . . .,] of [the clan] Rafadân, have dedicated to
4 [ʾIlumquh] Ṯah[w]ân, ma[s]ter of ʾAwwâm, these two sta-
5 tues, one in brass and one in bronze,
6 because of this: he had made a promise to Him in the hope that He would
7 grant life for him to his son Rabbʾawwâm; and so now,
8 ʾIlumquh Ṯahwân, master of ʾAwwâm, has vouchsafed to His
9 worshipper Rabîʿat, descendant of ʿAmmum, the life of his son
10 Rabbʾawwâm; and that may continue ʾIlumquh Ṯahwân, mas-
11 ter of ʾAwwâm, to vouchsafe to His worshipper Rabîʿat to shower upon
12 him all the favors [for which] he shall beseech Him;
13 and that He may preserve them from the hostility and wickedness of [any] ene-
14 my. By ʾIlumquh Ṯahwân, master of ʾAwwâm.

L. 2: *ʾsbʾy*, pl. of *sbʾy* (Ja 741/2), the feminine of which is *sbʾyt* (Ja 706/1). – *ʿmm*, name, e.g., of the Qat lunar god (cf. *JaP*, p. 78 and *JaRSAP*, p. 263) and of a Min clan (e.g., RÉS 2774/5); cf. also the 2nd Min personal name *ʿmmm* (e.g., RÉS 3799/2) and the Qat personal name *ʿmymm* (Ja 329/1); for the personal name *ʿmm* in Fakhry 51, cf. *JaDME*, p. 17.

L. 3: *rfdn*, cf. the personal name *rfdm* (cf. *RyGSAS*, p. 559) and the clan name *mrfdm*, e.g., in RÉS 4788/4; *rfd* is also known as the name of a man both in Liḥyanite (cf. *JaSaMA*, p. 486, No. 208) and in Safaitic (cf., e.g., *LiSI*, p. 343 B); cf. also the masculine personal name *rfdm* in Thamudic (cf. *vdBrTTPS*, p. 102: Ph 168 r 1) and in Arabic, the names of places *ar-rufayd* (cf. *MüHG*, p. 52 B) and *ar-rafdat* (cf. *WüR*, p. 101 C) and of men *rfd* and *rfydt* (cf. *GoAT*, p. 196), *rufaydat* (cf. *SaIS*, p. 78 B), *rifâdah* (cf. *HeBN*, p. 26 A), and *bin-rafdat* (cf. *SlGaVNPA*, p. 43 B).

Ll. 6-7: *kmʿnmw/ – – /bnhw*, cf. *JaPDSM*, p. 179.

694 – Yellowish, slightly grayish sandstone; photograph (cf. Plate 25) and latex squeeze. – MaMB 114.

STONE: maximum thickness: 5.8 cm. – *Front:* covered with red paint; slightly damaged; 9.9 cm. (top) and 10.3 (bottom) × 20.8 (right) and 20.9 (left). – INSCRIPTION: same disposition of lines as in Ja 552; letter height: 1.5 cm.; space between the lines: 0.4 cm.; distance from line 1 to the upper edge: 0.4 cm. (left) and 0.3 (right). – SYMBOL: 2.2 cm. × 3.5; the inside incisions (cp. Ja 656) remain unfinished; cf. Plate A.

1 **Sym-** *ʾlhʿn/ʿb*
2 **bol** *d/mlkn/h*
3 *qny/ʾlmqh/b*
4 *ʿl/ʾwm/ṣlmtm*
5 *ḏhbm/lqbly*
6 *ḏt/mtʿ/bth*
7 *w/hnʾm/wlw*
8 *ẓʾ/hʿnhmw*

1 **Sym-** ʾIlhaʿan, ser-
2 **bol** vant of the king, has
3 dedicated to ʾIlumquh, mas-
4 ter of ʾAwwâm, a female statue
5 in bronze, because of
6 this: He has saved his daughter
7 Haniʾum; and that He may continue to protect them.
8 tinue to protect them.

L. 5-6: *lqbly/ḏt* has exactly the same meaning as *ḥmdm/bḏ(t)*.

L. 7: *hnʾm*: name of a man, e.g., in RÉS 3553/1 (cf. *JaPSAP*, pp. 36, 46-47, 65, 102-03, 105, and 106) and Ja 351/1, Qat; cf. also the personal names *thnʾm* (RÉS 4942) and *hnʾt* (Ja 280, Qat and commentary), and the Arabic personal name *al-hanâwi* (cf. *SlGaVNPA*, p. 25 B).

695 – Yellow, slightly grayish sandstone; fragmentary at the bottom and broken into two parts; photograph in Plate 25. – MaMB 116.

STONE: maximum thickness: 14.3 cm. – *Front:* damaged on the left edge and broken on top; 42.5 cm. × 33.9 (right) and 15 (left); the lower fragment contains lines 11 and 12 and also the lower half of line 10. – INSCRIPTION: same disposition of lines as in Ja 552; letter height: 2.9 cm.; space between the lines: 0.6 cm. – SYMBOL: some variant of Ja 616; 4.7 cm. (top) and 4.9 (bottom) × 6.3; cf. Plate A.

1 **Sym-** *ʾbš⸢m⸣[r/ʾw]⸢l⸣ṭ/bn/ġ⸢y⸣[m]*
2 **bol** *n/ʾbʿl/bytnhn/ḏrḥ[n]*
3 *wyḥḍr/ʾqwl/šʿbn/ġymn/hqn*
4 *yw/mrʾhmw/ʾlmqhwṯhwnbʿlʾw[m]*
5 *ṯwrm/ḏḏhbm/ḥmdm/bḏ⸤t/h⸥[ʿnn]*
6 *wmtʿn/ʿbdhw/ʾb⸤š⸥[mr/ʾwlṭ/bn]*
7 *ġymn/bn/ʾ[...*
8 *ẓfr/wḥm⸤d⸥[/ẖyl/wmqm/mrʾhw]*
9 *ʾlmqh[wṯhwnbʿlʾwm... .../h]*
10 *rdʾ[n/...*
11 *ġym[n/...*
12 *⸤bʿl⸥[...*

1 **Sym-** ʾAbšam[ar ʾAw]laṭ, descendant of Ġay-[m-]
2 **bol** ân, masters of the two houses Ḏarḥ[ân]
3 and Yaḥḍur, rulers of the tribe Ġaymân, have dedi-
4 cated to their lord ʾIlumquhû Ṯahwân, master of ʾAww[âm,]
5 a bull which [is] in bronze, in praise because He has as[sisted]
6 and saved His worshipper ʾAbš[amar ʾAwlaṭ, descendant of]
7 Ġaymân from .[...
8 Ẓafâr; and he has praised [the strength and the power of his lord]
9 ʾIlumquh[û Ṯahwân, master of ʾAwwâm,...
10 assisted [...
11 Ġaym[ân...
12 master [...

L. 3: *yḥḍr*, proper name (e.g., RÉS 4001) and name of a tower (e.g., RÉS 4329/2, Qat).

Ll. 7-8: the name *ẓfr* could be preceded by *bhgrn* or *b*.

L. 12: *bʿl* belongs to the final invocation *bʾlmqhwṯhwnbʿlʾwm* or *ʾbʿl* followed by the name of a tribe.

696 – Yellowish, slightly grayish sandstone; photograph in Plate 26. – MaMB 218.

STONE: thickness: 53.5 cm. – *Top:* two rectangular holes the length of which is perpendicular to the front; 17.5 cm. × 8 and 2.6 (depth). – *Front:* 28.5 cm. (top) and 28.1 (bottom) × 19.4; the upper edge is splintered off. – INSCRIPTION: same disposition of lines as in Ja 552; letter height: 4.3 cm.; space between the lines: 0.8 cm.

1 *ʿlhn/b[n]/ʿ⸢l⸣hn/ʾ*
2 *dm/kbr/ẖll/hq*
3 *ny/ṯrnhn/wmqṭrn*

1 ʿAlhân, descen[dant of (the family)] ʿAlhân, ser-
2 vants of the Leader of H̱alil, has de-
3 dicated these two bulls and this incense burner.

Cf. Ja 697.

Ll. 1-2: for *ʾdm*, cf. commentary on Ja 689/1.
L. 3: *mqṭr*, e.g., *CoRoC*, p. 231 A.

697 – Yellowish sandstone block, badly damaged on top and re-used as masonry stone; photograph in Plate 26. – MaMB 130.

STONE: thickness: 54 cm. – *Front:* lower corners broken; lateral edges damaged; 26.5 cm. (bottom) and 29.1 (center of line 2) × 15.7. – INSCRIPTION: same disposition of lines as in Ja 552; letter height: 4.5 cm.; space between the lines: between 0.9 cm. and 1.1.

1 *[ʿlh]⌈n/bn⌉[/]⌈ʿlhn⌉*
2 *⌈ʾd⌉m/k⌈br/ẖll/hq*
3 *ny/ṯrnhn/wmqṭrn*

1 [ʿAlh]ân, descendant of [the family] ʿAlhân,
2 servants of the Leader of H̱alil, has de-
3 dicated these two bulls and this incense burner.

Same contents as in Ja 696, but two different texts; cf. end of line 1. For commentary, cf. Ja 696.

698 – Yellowish sandstone; photograph (cf. Plate 26) and latex squeeze. – MaMB 131 = Geukens 11.

STONE: maximum thickness: 10.9 cm. – *Front:* covered with red paint; upper part of the right edge slightly damaged: 10.2 cm. (top) and 9.9 (bottom) × 28.4 (right) and 28.3 (left). – INSCRIPTION: same disposition of lines as in Ja 552; letter height: 2 cm.; space between the lines: 0.5 cm.; several letters are filled up with cement. – *Symbol:* a variant of Ja 616 and 656; cf. Plate A. – FLOWER at the end of line 11; cf. Ja 684; cf. Plate B; the flower is not mentioned by *RyISA*, XV, pp. 107-08.

1 **Sym-** *rbbʾwm*
2 **bol** *fyšnyn/ḏ*
3 *ṣrfn/hqny*
4 *ʾlmqh/ṯh*
5 *wnbʿlʾwm*
6 *ṣlmn/ḏdh*
7 *bn/lwfy/g*
8 *rbhw/ḥgn*
9 *šft/ʾbhw*
10 *bʾlmqhb*
11 *ʿlʾwm* **Flower**

1 **Sym-** Rabîbʾawwâm,
2 **bol** the Fayšanite, he of [the family]
3 Ṣarfân, has dedicated to
4 ʾIlumquh Ṯah-
5 wân, master of ʾAwwâm,
6 this statue which [is] in bron-
7 ze, for the safety of his
8 person, as
9 his father had promised.
10 By ʾIlumquh, mas-
11 ter of ʾAwwâm. **Flower**

L. 1: *rbbʾwm*, cf. *rbʾwm*, e.g., in Ja 644/5; same nominal formation as that, e.g., of *rbbʾl* (e.g., Ja 619/1).
L. 2: *ṣrfn*, also family name in CIH 530/1.
Ll. 8-9: *ḥgn šft/ʾbhw*: *RyISA* (XV, p. 108, where *šfṯ* must be corrected in *šft*) translates the expression as follows: "comme il [le dieu] avait ordonné à son père" with the following explanation: "Si le père avait fait la promesse, le texte porterait *ḥgn/šfthw*, comme dans RES 4636,5...; voir aussi Ry 542,5." The second example mentioned by *RyISA* is irrelevant for *ḥgn* does not exist in the text, but the very common expression *ḏšfthw*. Besides, the usual construction is *ḥgn/šfthw* immediately following the object of the dedication; cf., e.g., Ja 715/4-5, 717/3-5, and 750/3-4. RÉS 4636 is not an exception because the object of dedication is included in the verb itself; if the object existed, it would be written between *mrʾhmw/bʿl/ḥrnm* and *ḥgn/šfthw*, thus immediately before the latter expression. Furthermore, the reason presented by *RyISA* is disproved by Ja 641/7-8: *ḥgn/šftw/ʾlmqh*. Finally, when the subject of *šft* is a deity, this verb means "to grant" and not "ordonner" (cf. commentary on Ja 570/2); and if *RyISA*'s translation were correct, the verb *wqh* (not *šft*) would be expected according to the usual pattern.

699 – Yellowish, slightly grayish sandstone; photograph in Plate 26. MaMB 136 (copied a second time as MaMB 160).

STONE: maximum thickness: 16 cm. – *Front:* covered with red paint; 32 cm. (right) and 31.7 (left) × 22.5 (top) and 22.7 (bottom); upper left corner broken; the space below the upper left corner is splintered off; left side slightly damaged. – INSCRIPTION: same disposition of lines as in Ja 552; letter height: between 2.2 cm. and 2.4; space between the lines: between 0.4 cm. and 0.6; distance from line 1 to the upper edge: 0.9 cm. (right) and 1 (left). – SYMBOL, cf. Ja 654.

1 **Sym-** *smḏrḥ/ḏgmʿn/hqny*
2 **bol** *mrʾhw/ʾlmqhw/[ṯ]*
3 *hwn/bʿlʾwm/ṣlm/ḏ*
4 *ḏhbm/ḥmdm/bḏt/hʿn/w*
5 *mtʿn/grbhw/bn/mrḍ/mr*
6 *ḍ/wlwzʾ/ʾlmqhw/hʿnn*
7 *wmtʿn/ʿbdhw/smḏrḥ/ḏgm*
8 *ʿn/bn/nḍʿ/wšṣy/šnʾm/ḏr⌋*
9 *ḥq/wqrb/bʾlmw/bʿlʾwm⌋*

1 **Sym-** Sumḏariḥ, he of [the family] Gumʿân, has dedicated to
2 **bol** his lord ʾIlumquhû [Ṯa]h-
3 wân, master of ʾAwwâm, a statue which [is] in
4 bronze, in praise because He has protected and
5 saved his person from the disease from which he had been
6 suffering; and that ʾIlumquhû may continue to protect
7 and save His worshipper Sumḏariḥ, him of Gum-
8 ʿân, from the hostility and wickedness of [any] enemy, who is remote
9 and near. By ʾIlumû, master of ʾAwwâm.

L. 1: *smḏrḥ*, *scriptio defectiva* of *smhḏrḥ*; same nominal formation as that, e.g., of *smhʾmr* (e.g., Ja 550/1). – *gmʿn*, cf. the Arabic masculine personal names *ǧimʿân* and *ǧumayʿân* (cf. *HeBN*, p. 16 B); cf. also the masculine personal name *hgmʿ* in Thamudic (e.g., *JaSaMA*, p. 567, No. 320) and the following Arabic proper names: of a woman *ǧmʿt* (cf. *GoAT*, p. 107), of places *al-ǧmʿ* (cf., e.g., *l.c.*, p. 690), *ǧumâʿ* and *ǧumâʿat* (cf. *MüHG*, p. 26 B), of a man *ʾibn ǧumîʿ* (cf. *WüR*, p. 367), *ʾabû ǧmʿt* (cf. *SaIS*, p. 42 A), *ǧâmiʿ* (cf. *HeBN*, *l.c.*), *ǧmʿ Gumʿa* (cf. *LiEHA*, p. 83 B), and of a person *al-ǧimûʿay* (cf. *SlGaVNPA*, p. 17 B).

L. 9: *ʾlmw* instead of *ʾlmqhw* is certain on the stone.

700 – Yellowish sandstone inscription, broken into two parts; large block (photograph in Plate 27) = MaMB 139, and upper right corner = MaMB 142 = Ja 814.

STONE: constant thickness: 13 cm. – *Front:* covered with red paint. – *Large block:* 36.2 cm. (left) and 24.6 (right) × 11.5 (top) and 24.8 (bottom); in the center of the front a plate was nailed in 4 different places as shown by 4 small holes. – *Right corner:* maximum thickness: 12 cm.; height of the right edge: 11.5 cm.; maximum length (center of line 3): 7.8 cm. – INSCRIPTION: same disposition of lines as in Ja 552; at 0.4 cm. from the right edge a deeply engraved vertical line; letter height: 1.5 cm.; space between the lines: 0.3 cm. – SYMBOL, cf. Ja 692; but here, the inside incision is divided by three small perpendicular ones (e.g., Ja 554), and its extremities do not reach either the top or the bottom of the frame; cf. Plate A. – FLOWER: at each end of line 17; cp. with Ja 684; but here the 6 petals are elliptical and their diameter is about two thirds of that of the bud; 1.2 cm. × 1.2; cf. Plate B.

1 **Sym-** *ʿ⌈b⌉[ydm/w]* / *⌊sʿdm/bny/ḥywm/mq*
2 **bol** *twy⌈y⌉* / *⌈/ns⌉rm/ʾḥṣn/bn/mqrm/*
3 *hqnyw/ʾ⌊lm⌋* / *⌈mq⌊hbʿlʾwm/⌊ṯ⌋ny/ṣlmn/ṣrf*
4 *m/w⌊ṣl⌋* / *⌈lm⌉m/ḏhbm* **P** *ḥmdm/bḏt/ḫm*
l
5 *r⌊h⌋* / *⌈hw/ʾlmqhbʿl* **a** *ʾwm/ʿbdhw/sʿ*
q
u
6 *dm/ḫlyn/whẓ* **e** *mn/nfs/ʿbdh*
7 *w/sʿdm/lqbly/ḏstwšʿthw/ʾṯtn/b*
8 *rlt/nšnytn/ʾmt/bn/mqrm/lʾwln*
9 *lhw/bnhw/ʿmn/ʾshw/rbslm/wbhʾ*
10 *lʿbr/rbslm/sʿdm/ḥgn/stwšʿ/wsb*
11 *bynhmy/lḫmm/bʿly/hwt/wldn/wys*
12 *bṭ/sʿdm/rbslm/bqḍbm/wḫrṭ/rbsl*
13 *m/šzb/sʿdm/bn/ḥqwyhw/wtʿṣrw/b*
14 *ynhmy/bšzbn/wtlf/rbslm/bn/yd*
15 *yhw/bytn/sbt/yd/sʿdm/bʿlm/rbsl*
16 *m/wʾlmqhbʿlʾwm/lzʾn/hʿn/wrfʾ/whʿ*
17 **Flower** *n/ʿbdhw/sʿdm* **Flower**

1 **Sym-** ʿUba[ydum and] Saʿadum, the two sons of Ḥayûm, the two high
2 **bol** officials of Nasrum ʾAḥṣân, descendant of [the family] Maqrum,
3 have dedicated to ʾIlumquh, master of ʾAwwâm, these two statues in brass
4 and one statue in bronze, in praise because has vouch-
5 safed to him ʾIlumquh, master of ʾAwwâm, to His worshipper Saʿa-
6 dum to act pleasingly for and to inflame with zeal the person of His worshipper
7 Saʿadum, because of this: had requested His assistance the wife Bar-
8 lat, the Našânite, maidservant of the servants of [the family] Maqrum, in order to restore

9 to her her son by her husband Rabbsalam; and Saʿadum
10 went to(ward) Rabbsalam as he had been requested; and [there were] reproaches
11 between them both, fitting concerning this child, and so that Saʿadum
12 whipped Rabbsalam with a rod; and Rabbsalam took
13 the branch of Saʿadum away from his two buttocks; and they wrestled
14 over the branch between the two of them; and Rabbsalam perished by his [Saʿadum's] two
15 hands [in] the house; [but] the hand of Saʿadum was pierced as a mark of Rabbsalam;
16 and as for ʾIlumquh, master of ʾAwwâm, may He continue to help and heal and pro-
17 **Flower** tect His worshipper Saʿadum. **Flower**

L. 1: *ʿb*[. . : according to the repartition of the signs on the stone, 5 letters compose this personal name; I suggest *ʿbydm* (e.g., RÉS 3902, No. 81/1 Qat; cf. also the form *ʿbyd* in *RyGSAS*, p. 559) rather than *ʿbdʿm* (e.g., Ja 651/1) as fitting better *sʿdm*.

L. 2: *nsrm*, name of a family (Ist 7630/1) and of a deity (cf. *JaP*, p. 130 and *JaRSAP*, p. 273). – *ʾḥṣn*, e.g., CIH 106/1; in RÉS 4712=Ja 495/1, read *ʾḥḏn* instead of *ʾḥṣn* (cf. *JaIMS*, pp. 329-31).

L. 6: *hẓmn*, 4th form of *ẓmm*; cf. Syriac *ṭem*, Aphʿel *ʾaṭem* "to inflame with zeal".

Ll. 7-8: *brlt*, cf. commentary on Ja 567/2: *brlm*.

L. 8: *nšnyt*: feminine of the *nisba* derived from the name of the city *nšn*. – *ʾmt*, e.g., RÉS 4273/1, Qat.

L. 9: *bnhw* "her son", also in AshM 1957-17/4-5 where the stereotyped formula of the whole context leaves no doubt about the interpretation of the personal pronoun *hw* in *bnhw*. – *rbslm*, same nominal formation as that, e.g., of *rbʾwm* (e.g., Ja 644/5).

L. 10: *sb*, pl. of *sbt*; cf. Arabic *sabbat* "insult, matter of blame, reproach"; from the root *sbb*, cf. line 15.

L. 11: *lẖm*, participle adjective from *lẖm*; cf. Syriac *lḥem* "to suit with, fit, agree".

L. 12: *qḏb*, cf. Arabic *qaḏîb*, pl. *quḏub* "rod, stick". – *ẖrṭ*, cf. Arabic *ẖaraṭa* "to strip off the bark" and Syriac *ḥraṭ* "to scrape, scratch"; the context proves that Rabbsalam's action was not completely successful; *ẖrṭ* is also verb in NaNN 74/11 and is considered by *BeNL* (IV, p. 146) as "a near-synonym of *ʿqwt*" and translated as "to commit...sacrilege" (cf. *l.c.*, p. 147); such a translation is of course vague enough to cover all possible kinds of fault committed in a temple; J. Ryckmans (cf. *Le Muséon*, 69 [1956], pp. 92-93) does not attempt any interpretation of *ẖrṭ* and simply transliterates it (cf. *l.c.*, p. 94); the etymology of the root *ẖrṭ*, alludes, in the case of NaNN 74/11, to a fault related to physical nudity.

L. 13: *šzb*, cf. Arabic *šazîb* "rough branch". – *ḥqwy*, construct dual of *ḥqw*; cf. *ḥaqw* "waist" in Arabic and *ḥaqû* in Daṯînah (cf. *LaGD*, p. 465) "waist, buttock". – *tʿṣr*: 6th form of *ʿṣr*; cf. Arabic *ʿaṣara* "to press, squeeze as to force out"; the whole expression *tʿṣrw/bynhmy* indicates that they fought back and forth against each other.

L. 14: *tlf*, cf. commentary on Ja 567/27: *tlft*.

L. 15: *sbt*, feminine of *sb*, cf. Arabic *sabba* "to pierce". – *ʿlm*, cf. *CoRoC*, p. 207.

L. 16: *lzʾn* instead of *lyzʾn*, cf. Ja 664/9. – *rfʾ*, cf. *CoRoC*, p. 243 B, and also RÉS 4829/2-3: the infinitive *rfʾn* (cf. commentary on Ja 601/17-18).

701 – Yellowish sandstone block, re-cut on top; photograph in Plate 27. – MaMB 143.

STONE: thickness: 7 cm. (bottom) and from there increasing to 9 cm. at a point 6.3 cm. from the top; the last 6.3 cm. present a protuberance of 11.9 cm. – *Front:* upper edge damaged; 35 cm. × 22.7 (top) and 22.4 (bottom). – INSCRIPTION A: same disposition of lines as in Ja 552; letter height: 2.3 cm. (top) and 2.2 (bottom); space between the lines: 0.3 cm.

1 **[Sym-** . . . . . .]
2 **[bol]** ⌜*ḥbbt/hqny/ʾlmq*⌝
3 *hbʿlʾwm/ḏn/ṣlmn/ḥmd*
4 *m/bḏ/hwfyhmw/bkl/ʾm*
5 *lʾ/ystmlʾn/bʿmhw/w*
6 *lwzʾ/hwfyhw/whwfyn*
7 *grybt/bnyhw/whbʿṯt*
8 *wrbṯwn/bʾlmqhbʿlʾwm*

1 **[Sym-** . . . . . .]
2 **[bol]** Ḥabbat, has dedicated to ʾIlumquh,
3 master of ʾAwwâm, this statue in praise
4 because He has showered upon them all the fa-
5 vors [for which] they would have besought Him; and
6 that He may protect him and protect
7 the persons of his two sons Wahabʿaṯat
8 and Rabbṯawân. By ʾIlumquh, master of ʾAwwâm.

L. 2: the top part of each sign is damaged. – *ḥbbt*: here family name, but feminine personal name in Ja 509 (cf. commentary in *JaISAR*, pp. 106-07); cf. also the family name *ḥbb*, e.g., in Ja 617/7.

L. 7: *whbᶜṯt*, also masculine name in RÉS 3915/1.

L. 8: *rbṯwn*, same nominal formation as that, e.g., of *rbᵓwm* (e.g., Ja 644/5).

INSCRIPTION B: on the lower part of the front, several letters are engraved which do not belong to the present text: on the left side, *h* or *s* (2.1 cm. × 1) lying on its side; on the right side, *h* (2.1 cm. × 0.8); in the right corner, *hlḥm* (5.3 cm. × 2); *ḥ* is without lower vertical line and *m* is lying on its left side; immediately below and perpendicular to *hb* of *ᵓlmqhbᶜl* (line 8), *ḏ/b*; several other letters are partly engraved. For *hlḥm*, cf. Arabic *laḥama* "to consolidate, harden"; cf. also the Arabic names of men *ᵓabû l-laḥâm* (cf. *GeKH*, p. 10 B) and *ᵓabû l-laḥm* (cf. *WüR*, p. 626) and of a place *liḥâm* (cf. *GoAT*, p. 767), and the two Thamudic personal names *ylḥm* (cf. *vdBrTTPS*, p. 151: Ph 207 a 3/2; the commentary refers to the root *lḥḥ*) and *lḥm* (cf. *vdBrTTPN*, p. 88: Ph 330 e); in CIH 793, *ghmm* (cf. *CIH*) is certain instead of *lḥmm* (cf. *RyNP*, I, pp. 120 B+396 A) because of the difference already pointed out by *CIH* in the position of the upper left stroke in the first letter of this proper name and in the *l* of *ᶜzᵓl* in relation to the vertical stroke.

702 – Slightly grayish sandstone; photograph. – MaMB 145.

STONE: thickness: 16.1 cm. (top) and 10.6 (bottom). – *Front:* 58 cm. (right) and 58.9 (left) × 22.7 (top) and 23.3 (bottom). – INSCRIPTION: very poor engraving; lines 1-17 (on the front): letter height: 2.9 cm. (top) and 2.1 (bottom); space between the lines: from 0.5 cm. to 0.3. – SYMBOL, cp. Ja 630; but here, the center of the left lateral line shows a strong convex protuberance, and there is no inside design or ornament; cf. Plate A. – RIGHT SIDE: inscription: lines 18-21: letter height: 3 cm. (top) and 3.4 (bottom); space between the lines: from 0.6 cm. to 0.4.

FRONT:

1 **Symbol** *knmw/ṯwbᵓ*
2 *l/ḏᵓᶜzz/l*
3 */nḥ(b)rn/wl(/ḏ)r*
4 *n⟨/⟩kl/ršym/ḏᵓ*
5 *l/yšrḥn/ṣythw*
6 *bkn/yᶜdwn/ḏmqm*
7 *tn/bbt/ᵓlmqh*
8 *(b)ᵓwm/hẖṭᵓ/wś*
9 *b⟨/⟩ᵓl/śnyw/śyq/bw*
10 *sṭ/mḥrm/gnztn/w*
11 *nqm/ᶜbdhw/ṯwbᵓ*
12 *l/bmrb/ᵓ(ḍ)rshw/wṯn*
13 *hw/tᵓhrn/ᵓḍrsh*
14 *w/wṯnyhw/ᶜln/ḏś*
15 *f/ḏwkb/whᵓ/fl/śy*
16 *f/ḥwlm/mykbt/bhw*
17 *wᵓl⟨m⟩qh/lhᶜn/ᶜbdh*

RIGHT SIDE:

18 *w/bn/kl/bᵓ*
19 *stm/bᵓl*
20 *mqh/bᶜl*
21 *ᵓwm*

1 **Symbol** That may increase Ṯawbᵓil,
2 he of [the family]ᵓAᶜzaz, in order that
3 he may be joyful and [in order] that he may distribute
4 every gift which would
5 make his good fame flourish,
6 when will come Ḏû-Maqâm-
7 tân into the temple of ᵓIlumquh
8 (into) ᵓAwwâm. He[=Ṯawbᵓil] has seduced [others] into acting wrongfully and
9 has occasioned [that] the beasts did not draw water in the
10 middle of the sacred precinct of the dead; so
11 He took vengeance on His worshipper Ṯawbᵓil
12 in Mârib [with regard to] his molar teeth and his
13 incisor teeth [by] inflaming his molar teeth
14 and his incisor teeth . . .
15 . . . ; and as for himself, may he
16 . . .
17 and as forᵓ Ilu⟨m⟩quh, may He protect His worshipper
18 from all mis-
19 fortunes. By ᵓIl-
20 umquh, master of
21 ᵓAwwâm.

L. 1: *k*, cf. *HöASG*, p. 167. – *nmw*, cf. Arabic *namā* (o, i) "to increase".

Ll. 1-2: *ṯwbᵓl*, e.g., RÉS 3081 and Ja 867/1; clan name in RÉS 4219/2, Qat; same nominal formation as that, e.g., of *ṯwbsy[n]* (RÉS 4875/1-2, Ḥaḍr; cf. commentary on Ja 563/1).

L. 2: *ᵓᶜzz* (plural form of *ᶜzz*), family name, cf. commentary on Ja 559/18.

L. 3: *nḥ(b)rn*, 7th form of *ḥbr*; cf. Arabic *ḥabara* "to

make something beautiful, to embellish it; to make someone happy, joyful, glad" (cf. *LaAEL*, p. 498 B); cf. the verb *ḥbr* "to seduce, deceive" in Ja 635/35.

Ll. 3-4: copy: *wlḏ/rnkl* which I read as follows *wl(/ḏ)rn⟨/⟩kl*; for the verb *ḏrr*, cf. the commentary on Ja 735/13: *ḏr*.

L. 4: *ršy*, plural *ršyt* (Ja 718/9), cf. *JaIHI*, pp. 106-07 with regard to RÉS 4782/3.

Ll. 4-5: *ḏʾl*, for the negative meaning of that expression, cf., e.g., Ja 572/16; here, however, the preceding meaning must be discarded because line 5 with a negative meaning would make no sense at all, on the contrary, the affirmative meaning is expected (cf. the erroneous generalization presented by *RycSD*, p. 339 and foll.); *ḏʾl* here has the same meaning as *ʾl/ḏ* in Ja 651/25-26.

L. 5: *ṣyt*, cf. Arabic *ṣît*, *ṣawt*, *ṣât*, and *ṣîtat* "(good) fame, (good) reputation" (cf. *LaAEL*, p. 1743 A).

L. 6: *bkn/yʿdwn*: *bkn* ordinarily introduces either the perfect or infinitive (cf. *HöASG*, pp. 163-64).

Ll. 6-7: *ḏmqmtn*, cf. the Thamudic personal name *mqmt* (cf. *vdBrIT*, p. 322: HU 623).

Ll. 8-9: *śb*, cf. Arabic *sabba* "to make, cause, occasion".

L. 9: *śny*, cf. Arabic *sanā* (i, o) "to water, irrigate" and "to turn round about the well" (cf. *LaAEL*, p. 1448 B-C), and *sanā* (i) both in Daṯînah (cf. *LaGD*, p. 1991) and in modern Ḥaḏr (cf. *LaH*, p. 613) "élever, tirer *l'outre* en haut": here, with the meaning of "to draw water". – *śyq*, cf. Arabic *sayyiqat*, plural *sayâʾiqu* "beasts driven by someone".

L. 10: *gnzt*, plural of *gnz*, cf. Arabic *ǧinâzat* and *ǧanâzat*, plural *ǧanâʾizu* "dead person; bier" (cf. *LaAEL*, p. 470 A-B); hence, *mḥrm* here does not have the ordinary meaning of "temple", but that of "sacred place" (cf. Arabic *muḥarram*); *mḥrm/gnztn* means "the cemetery".

Ll. 12 and 13: *ʾḍrs*, plural of *ḍrs*, cf. Arabic *ḍirs*, plural *ʾaḍrâs* "the teeth, except the central incisors,..the molar teeth..next behind the canine teeth" (cf. *LaAEL*, p. 1785 C); in line 12: copy has *ʾḏrs* instead of *ʾḍrs*.

Ll. 12 and 14: *ṯn* and *ṯny* (*scriptio plena*), cf. Arabic *ṯanîyat*, plural *ṯanâyâ* "incisor".

L. 13: *tʾhrn*, 2nd form (*taʾhîr*; cf. *HöASG*, p. 61) of *ʾhr*, cf. Arabic *ʾawar* or *āra*, 2nd form "to inflame".

703 – Yellowish sandstone. – MaMB 148.

STONE: thickness: 30 cm. (upper right corner), 30.5 (both lower right and the upper left corners) and 20.5 (lower left corner). – *Front:* upper left corner broken; both upper and lower edges slightly damaged; 1.365 m. (top) and 1.38 (bottom) × 1.385 (center). – INSCRIPTION: same disposition of lines as in Ja 559; letter height: from 3.6 cm. to 4; space between the lines: from 0.7 cm. to 0.9. – SYMBOL, cf. Ja 561.

1 **Sym-** *ʾsʿd/hzd/ḏṣryhw/ṣdqʾl/wbnyhw/šrḥʾwm/ ʾsʾr/ḏṣryhw/smhkrb/w⸢ʾ⸣[lrm/r]*
2 **bol** *ym/ḏṣryhw/ʾbʾmr/ḏḏbyn/wršwn/wršw/ ʾlmqh/b⟨ʾ⟩wm/hqnyw/mr*
3 *ʾhmw/ʾlmqh/ṯhwn/bʿl/ʾwm/ṣlmn/ḏṣrfn/wẖmst/ ʾṣlmm/ḏhbm/ḥmdm/b*
4 *ḏt/ẖmr/wṯwbn/ʾdmhw/bny/ḏḏbyn/wršwn/ʾwldm/ ʾḏkrm/wbntm/ḏhrḍhmw/w*
5 *ḥmdw/mqm/mrʾhmw/ʾlmqh/wlwzʾ/ẖmrhmw/ ʾwldm/ʾḏkrm/hnʾm/ḏkwkbt/ṣdq*
6 *m/wlẖmrhmw/ʾṯmrm/wʾfqlm/hnʾm/bnkl/ʾrḍthmw/ wmfnthmw/wrṯdw/ʾlmqh*
7 *kl/wldhmw/wʾrḍthmw/bn/kl/bʾstm/wqlmtm/ wlẖmrhmw/ḥẓy/wrḍw/ʾm*
8 *rʾhmw/ʾmlk/sbʾ/wḏrydn/wrḍw/šʿbhmw/sbʾ/ wlẖmrhmw/ḥyw/grybtm/wb*
9 *ry/ʾʾḏnm/wmqymtm/wlmtʿn/ʾdmhw/ʾsʿd/wbnyhw/ šrḥʾwm/wʾlrm/wkl*
10 *wldhmw/bny/ḏḏbyn/wršwn/bn/kl/bʾstm/wnkytm/ wbn/nḍʿ/wšṣy/*
11 *wtṯʿt/šnʾm/ḏbnhw/dʿw/wḏbnhw/ʾl/dʿw/wrṯdw/ ʾlmqh/ṯhwn/bʿl/*
12 *ʾwm/hqnythmw/bn/mʾẖrm/wmśwrm/wdśśm/ bʾlmqh/ṯhwn/bʿl/ʾwm*

1 **Sym-** ʾAsʿad Hazid, he of Ṣarayhû Ṣadiqʾil, and his two sons Šaraḥʾawwâm ʾAsʾar, he of Ṣarayhû Sumhukarib and (ʾI)l[râm]
2 **bol** [Ri]yyâm, he of Ṣarayhû ʾAbʾamar, of [the two families] Ḏû-Bayyin and Rašwân, and priest of ʾIlumquh in ʾAwwâm, have dedicated to their
3 lord ʾIlumquh Ṯahwân, master of ʾAwwâm, this statue which [is] in brass and five statues in bronze, in praise be-
4 cause He has vouchsafed to and bestowed upon His worshippers, the descendants of [the two families] Ḏû-Bayyin and Rašwân, male children and daughters, which pleased them; and
5 they praised the power of their lord ʾIlumquh; and that He may continue to vouchsafe to them male, pleasing, numerous, perfect children;

6 and that He may vouchsafe to them pleasing fruits and harvests in all their lands and their land irrigated by canals; and they entrusted to the care of ʾIlumquh

7 all their children and their lands against all misfortunes and insect-pests; and that He may vouchsafe to them the esteem and grace of their

8 lords, the kings of Sabaʾ and Raydân, and [also] the grace of their tribe Sabaʾ; and that He may vouchsafe to them the life of [their] persons and the

9 strength of understanding and of power; and that He may save His worshippers ʾAsʿad and his two sons Šaraḥʾawwâm and ʾIlrâm and all

10 their children, the descendants of [the two families] Ḏû-Bayyin and Rašwân, from all misfortunes and sufferings and from the hostility and wickedness

11 and spying of [any] enemy, those who are known and those who are not known; and they entrusted to the care of ʾIlumquh Ṯahwân, master of

12 ʾAwwâm, their offering against [any] destroyer, depredator and receiver. By ʾIlumquh Ṯahwân, master of ʾAwwâm.

L. 1: *hzd*, cf. the second personal name *yzd*, e.g., in Ja 615/16. – *šrḥʾwm*, same nominal formation as that, e.g., of *šrḥʾl* (e.g., Ja 555/1). – *ʾlrm*, restored on the basis of line 9.

Ll. 1-2: *rym*: very well-known 2nd personal name (e.g., RÉS 2771/2, Min); at the end of line 1, there is place for only one letter after *ʾlrm/*.

L. 2: *b⟨ʾ⟩wm*: my copy has *bwm*.

L. 4: *ṯwbn*: infinitive of the 2nd form (e.g., Ist 7630/3); cf. *CoRoC*, p. 259 A. – Note the *scriptio defectiva hrḍ* instead of *hrḍw* or *hrḍy*.

L. 12: *mʾẖr*: participle of the 2nd form of *ʾẖr*; cf. *CoRoC*, pp. 102-03. – *mśwr*, participle of the 3rd form of *śwr*; cf. Arabic *sâra*, 1st and 3rd forms "to assail, attack, rush upon (from a man)"; cf. *sawrat* "violence (of a cruel man)"; here, with the meaning of "depredator"; the meaning of *mśwr* in RÉS 4326/4 and 4781/1 is still uncertain (cf. *BeNL*, III, pp. 129-30). – *dśś*, cf. Arabic *dassa* "to hide; plot, hatch", and *dasîs*, pl. *dasus* "spy, secret agent"; in modern Ḥaḍrami *dss* means "to give secretly" (cf. *LaH*, p. 573) and also in Daṯînah (cf. *LaGD*, pp. 773-76); on the basis of the context, *dśś* may be translated "receiver (of stolen goods)".

704 – Grayish sandstone; photograph (cf. Plate 27); latex squeeze. – MaMB 151.

STONE: thickness: 12 cm. – *Front:* covered with red paint; upper edge slightly damaged; 42.2 cm. (top) and 41.7 (bottom) × 33 (right) and 32.8 (left). – INSCRIPTION: same disposition of lines as in Ja 552; letter height: 3.1 cm.; space between the lines: 0.4 cm. – SYMBOL, cf. Ja 603.

1 **Sym-** *šrḥʾl/ʾzbr/wnmrm/ʾzʾd/bnw/ydm/ʾ*
2 **bol** *ḥšdn/ʾdm/bn/hmdn/hqnyw/ʾlmqhw*
3 *ṯhwn/bʿl/ʾwm/ṣlmn/ḥgn/ḏt/stwklhw*
4 *lsʿdhmw/ʾwldm/ʾḏkrwm/hnʾn/wlsʿdhm*
5 *w/ʾlmqh/nʿmtm/wwfym/wfrʿ/dṯʾ/wẖrf*
6 *wʾṯmr/ṣdqm/ʿdy/ʾrḍhmw/wmšymthmw/w*
7 *l/ẖrynhmw/ʾlmqh/bn/nḍʿ/wšṣy/šnʾ*
8 *m/wl/sʿdhmw/ʾlmqh/rḍw/wḥẓy/ʾmrʾ*
9 *hmw/bny/hmdn/wšʿbhmw/ḥšdm/bʾlmqh*

1 **Sym-** Šaraḥʾil ʾAzbar and Nimrum ʾAzʾad, the two sons of Yadum, the

2 **bol** Ḥâšidites, servants of the descendants [the tribe] Hamdân, have dedicated to ʾIlumquhû

3 Ṯahwân, master of ʾAwwâm, this statue by which he has shown his confidence in Him

4 in order that He may make them happy with male, pleasing children; and that ʾIlumquh may

5 make them happy with prosperity and safety and (with) the optimum crop of spring and of autumn

6 and (with) perfect fruits in their land and their arable fields; and

7 that ʾIlumquh may preserve them from the hostility and wickedness of [any] enemy;

8 and that ʾIlumquh may make them happy with the grace and esteem of their

9 lords, the descendants of Hamdâm and of their tribe Ḥâšidum. By ʾIlumquh.

L. 1: *ʾzbr*, cf. Arabic *ʾazbar* "noxious, malevolent"; cf., e.g., also the Arabic names of places *ʾaz-zabîr* and *ʾaz-zabîratân* (cf. *WüR*, p. 109 A), of a woman *zabrâʾ* (cf. *SaIS*, p. 81 A) and of men (*ʾibn* and *ʾabû*) *ʾaz-zubayr* (cf., e.g., *GoAT*, pp. 202-04), *zbyr*, (*ʾaz-*)*zbyr*, *al-ʾaz-zbyr*, *ʾibn ʾaz-zbyr* and *ʾaz-zabîr* (cf. *SaIS*, pp. 81 B-82 B), and the *nisba ʾaz-zbyry* (cf. *SaIS*, p. 82 B). – *nmrm*, e.g., Qat Ja 220/1 and (348/1) (cf. *JaDME*, p. 20), RÉS 4854 B/1 and 4901/1, Ḥaḍr and BM 103059/2, Qat (cf. *JaPSAP*, pp. 99-101 and 102); cf. also *nmrn* (e.g., Ja 594/4).

Ll. 1-2: *bnw/ydm/ʾḥšdn*, cp. *bnw/zʾdm/ʾḥšdn* in CIH 605 bis/2; cf. also *yḥmd/ʾḥšd* in Ja 713/2; cf. also the singular *ḥ[š]dy[n]* in Weigall 1 (cf. commentary on Ja 616/25; *ḥrmm*), and the plural *ʾḥšdn* in Ja 881 I (cf. *JaPEQL*, p. 210).

705 – Yellowish sandstone with many grayish stains; photograph in Plate 27. – MaMB 155.

STONE: constant thickness: 15 cm.; except for the bottom, all the sides are polished. – *Top:* the bronze right foot of a statue is still attached to the stone. – *Front:* upper edge badly damaged; lower right corner broken; 37.6 cm. × 28.2 (left) and 26.4 (right.) – INSCRIPTION: same disposition of lines as in Ja 552; letter height: from 2.8 cm. to 3; space between the lines: from 0.4 cm. to 0.5; distance from line 1 to the upper edge: 0.5 cm.

1 *ʾlw(hb)[....]⌈m⌉/wʾwsʿṯt⌈/⌉bn*
2 *w/ʿblm⌈/h⌉qnyw/ʾlmqh/bʿ*
3 *l/ʾwm/ṣlmn/ḏḏhbn/lwf*
4 *y/bnhmw/ḍbʿn/ḏsmy/ʾlmq*
5 *h/ʾwsʾl/bn/ʿblm/wl/wśf*
6 *hmw/ʾlmqh/wbnhmw/ʾw*
7 *sʾl/ʾwldm/wqnym/bʿṯtr*
8 *w b / ʾ l m q h*

1 ʾIlwa(hab) [.....]m and ʾAwsʿaṯat, descen-
2 dants of [the clan] ʿAblum, have dedicated to ʾIlumquh, mas-
3 ter of ʾAwwâm, this statue which [is] in bronze, for the safe-
4 ty of their son Ḍabiʿân whom ʾIlumquh has named
5 ʾAwsʾil, descendant of ʿAblum; and that ʾIlumquh may add
6 to them and to their son ʾAw-
7 sʾil children and slaves. By ʿAṯtar
8 and by ʾIlumquh.

L. 1: the 1st four letters of *ʾlwhb*'s 2nd name are missing.

L. 4: *ḍbʿn*, also name of a man, e.g., in Ja 136/1, Qat, and commentary; cf. the Qat names of women *ḍb*[ʿ]*m* in Ja 488 (cf. *JaAFEQ*, p. 193), *ḍbʿ* in Ja 256/1, and also the name of a citadel *ḏḍbʿnn* in Gl 1142/8 (cf. *JaITDL*, p. 185). – *smy*, cf. *CoRoC*, p. 197 B; here, the 2nd form "to give a name to someone"; the 1st form is attested, e.g., in RÉS 4324/3-4, Qat; for the 8th form *stmy*, cf. Ja 655/9-10 and commentary. The form *smw* is found in RÉS 5045 which reads as follows: *yfʿtmt/smw*[/]*mʾyr/* "Yafaʿtummat is called Muʾayyir."

706 – Slightly grayish sandstone; photograph in Plate 28. – MaMB 158.

STONE: maximum thickness: 7.2 cm. – *Front:* the lower right corner is splintered off; 19.2 cm. (top) and 19.6 (bottom) × 30.8 (right) and 30.6 (left). – INSCRIPTION: same disposition of lines as in Ja 552; letter height: from 1.7 cm. to 2.2; space between the lines: from 0.3 cm. to 0.5; distance from line 1 to the upper edge: 0.8 cm. (right) and 0.9 (left).

1 *ʾmtʾlmqh/sbʾytn/bt*
2 *ḫdqm/hqnyt/ʾlmqhṯh*
3 *wnbʿlʾwm/ṣlmtn/ḏt*
4 *ḏhbn/ḏšftt/mrʾhmw*
5 *ʾlmqh/lhʿnn/ʾmthw/*
6 *nḍrt/bn/mrḍ/mrḍt⌋*
7 *ʿynhw/wrʾ/khʿnhw*
8 *wlwzʾ/hʿnn/wmtʿn*
9 *grybthmw/bn/bʾstm*
10 *wnkytm/wṭwʿ/šnʾ*
11 *⌊m/b⌋ʾlmqhwbʿlʾwm*

1 ʾAmatʾilumquh, the Sabaean woman, daughter of
2 Ḫadaqum, has dedicated to ʾIlumquh Ṯah-
3 wân, master of ʾAwwâm, this female statue which [is] in
4 bronze, which she had promised to their lord
5 ʾIlumquh in order that He may protect His maid-servant
6 Naḍrat from the disease which suffered
7 her eye; but now He has protected her;
8 and that He may continue to protect and save
9 their persons from misfortunes
10 and sufferings and [from] the constraint of [any] enemy.
11 By ʾIlumquhû, master of ʾAwwâm.

L. 1: *ʾmtʾlmqh*, same nominal formation as that, e.g., of *ʾmtʿm* (RÉS 4704/1, Qat); for *ʾmt* in Fakhry 3/9; cf. *JaDME*, p. 15.

L. 2: *ḫdqm*, cf. *ḫdqn* in RÉS 2880.

L. 6: *nḍrt*, also feminine personal name in Ja 402/2, Ḥaḍr (cf. commentary in *JaIHB*, p. 162); cf. also the masculine personal names *ʾnḍr* (RÉS 4994/2) and *mnḍr*, instead of *mnwr* (RÉS 4594 A/2: *Munawwir*, and 4623A/3: *Munawir*).

707 – Yellowish, slightly grayish sandstone; photograph in Plate 28. – MaMB 159.

STONE: constant thickness: 11.5 cm. (top) and 11.4 (bottom). – *Front:* upper and lower edges broken; right edge slightly damaged; 25.3 cm. (top) and 23.9 (bottom) × 30.3. – INSCRIPTION: same disposition of lines as in Ja 552; letter height: 2.5 cm.; space between the lines: 0.5 cm. – SYMBOL: very awkward; cp. (?) Ja 637; cf. Plate A.

1 **[Sym-** ...]⌈*krb*/⌉*w*⌈*bnyhm*⌉*w*
2 **bol** *yḥmᵓl/wsᶜdᵓwm/wm*
3 *ᶜdkrb/bny/ḏbydn/wwh*
4 *bm/ᵓᵓbyn/ᵓdm/ḏnzḥt*
5 ⌊*h*⌋*qnyw/ᵓlmqhṯhwn/bᶜlᵓwm*
6 [*ṣ*]*lmnhn/ḏ yḏhbn/ḏšfthw*⌉
7 ⌈*lwfyhmw/wlsᶜdhmw/nᶜm*⌊*t*⌉
8 *m/wmngwt/ṣdqm/wrḍw/*[ᵓ]
9 *mrᵓhmw/bᵓlmqhṯhwn*⌉

1 **[Sym-** ...]karib and their sons
2 **bol** Yaḥamᵓil and Saᶜadᵓawwâm and Ma-
3 ᶜadkarib, descendants of [the two families] Baydân and Waha-
4 bum, the ᵓAbites, servants of [the tribe] Nazḥat,
5 have dedicated to ᵓIlumquh Ṯahwân, master of ᵓAwwâm,
6 these two [st]atues, both in bronze, which he had promised to Him
7 for their safety and in order that He may make them happy with prosperi[ty]
8 and security perfect and (with) the grace of
9 their lord[s]. By ᵓIlumquh Ṯahwân.

L. 2: *yḥmᵓl*, e.g., RÉS 4957/1, Qat.

L. 3: *bydn*, cf. the Arabic place names *baydân* (cf. *WüR*, p. 44 C), *bayd*, *baydat* (cf. *l.c.*) and also *al-baydâᵓu* (cf. *l.c.* and *MüHG*, p. 17 B); all the preceding parallels seem to confirm *RÉS*'s etymology of the masculine personal name *bydᵓl* (RÉS 4907/1), contrary to E. Littmann (cf. *ZDMG*, 101 [1951], p. 377), who proposes the following interpretation, *b*+*yd*+*ᵓl*, "In the hand of god". The restoration [ᶜ]*bydᵓl* suggested by *RÉS* in RÉS 4907/1 is unnecessary.

L. 4: *ᵓᵓbyn: nisba* plural. – *nzḥt*, Hamilton 4/3; cf. *JaRIH*, pp. 147-48.

708 – Yellowish, slightly grayish sandstone; photograph in Plate 28. – MaMB 162.

STONE: thickness: left side: 6.7 cm. (top) and 6.4 (bottom); right side: 5.8 cm. (top) and 5.6 (bottom). – *Front:* covered with red paint; slightly damaged; 22.4 cm. (top) and 21.8 (bottom) × 35.1 (right) and 34.6 (left). – INSCRIPTION: same disposition of lines as in Ja 552; letter height: from 2.5 cm. to 2.9; space between the lines: from 0.3 cm. to 0.5; distance between line 1 and the upper edge: 0.8 cm. (right) and 0.6 (left).

1 *hwfᶜṯt/yzkn/bn/mfyš*
2 *mqtwy/šfᶜṯt/ᵓšwᶜ/wbnyh⟨⟩w*
3 *zydm/ᵓymn/bn/hmdn/wḏf*
4 *yš/wsᵓrn/hqnyw/ᵓlmq/bᶜlᵓ*
5 *wm/mṯkḥm/wbᶜlyhw/ṣlmm*
6 *ḏḏhbm/ḥmdm/bḏt/mtᶜhw*
7 *bn/nḏᶜ/wšṣy/šnᵓm/wbḏt*
8 *ẖmrhw/ᵓtw/bwfym/wmhrg*
9 *m/bn/ḏbᵓt/hbᶜyn/wlwz*
10 *ᵓ/ẖmrhw/ᵓᵓrẖ/ṣdqm*

1 Hawfᶜaṯat Yazkân, son of Mufayaš,
2 high official of Šûfᶜaṯat ᵓAšwaᶜ, and his son
3 Zaydum ᵓAyman, descendants of Hamdân and of Fa-
4 yš and of Suᵓrân, have dedicated to ᵓIlumq, master of ᵓA-
5 wwâm, a stone tablet(?) and on top of it a statue
6 which [is] in bronze, in praise because He has saved him
7 from the hostility and wickedness of [any] enemy and because
8 He has vouchsafed to him to come back in safety and (with) war trophy
9 from the engagements he had instigated; and that He may continue
10 to vouchsafe to him perfect undertakings.

L. 1: *yzkn*, cf. the Arabic name of place *zakân* (cf. *WüR*, p. 110 B). – *mfyš*, cf. *fyš* in lines 3-4.

L. 2: in *bnyhw*, a word divider is engraved after *h*; the right curve of *w* coincides with a small portion of the word divider.

Ll. 3-4: *fyš*, 2nd personal name, e.g., Ja 403, Min; cf. also the very well-known tribe name *fyšn* (e.g., Ja 558/7) and *tfš* (RÉS 3946/6).

L. 5: *mṯkḥm*: *kḥ* are engraved on top of *ḥm* which have been slightly erased (the worker had first forgotten *ṯ*); cf. *CoRoC*, p. 260 A and *BeSI*, p. 40; no etymology has been proposed so far; nevertheless the translation as "stone tablet?" has been accepted. – *bᶜly*, cf. *HöASG*, p. 158.

L. 9: *hbᶜy*, 4th form of *bᶜy*; cf. Arabic *baᶜā* in commentary on Ja 578/10; the contents of the present text would indicate that *baᶜā* should be taken in the sense "to bring misfortune upon someone", and to translate *hbᶜy* as "to provoke, instigate".

709 – Grayish sandstone plaque; photograph in Plate 28. – MaMB 164.

PLAQUE: constant thickness: 6.4 cm. (right) and 5.2 (left). – *Front:* covered with red paint; 11.3 cm. (top) and 11.2 (bottom) × 16.5 (right) and 16.6 (left). – INSCRIPTION: same disposition of lines as in Ja 559; other horizontal lines in the lower part; letter height: 1.3 cm. in line 1 and 1.5 in the others; space between the lines: from 0.2 to 0.3

cm.; distance from line 1 to the upper edge: 0.3 cm. – SYMBOL: probably belongs to the same general type as that of Ja 616; cf. Plate A. – FLOWER: on both ends of line 7; cf. Ja 591, but here, the tracing is regular, and the space between the petals is divided into two almost equal parts by a straight line; cf. Plate B.

1 **Sym-** *ʿbdm/bn/hrmm*
2 **bol** *hqny/ʾlmqhṯ*
3 *hwnbʿlʾwm/ṣlmn*
4 *ḏḏhbn/ḏšfthw/l*
5 *wfy/grbhw/ww*
6 *fy/bʿrhw/bʾ*
7 **Flower** *lmqhbʿlʾwm* **Flower**

1 **Sym-** ʿAbdum, descendant of [the tribe] Haramum,
2 **bol** has dedicated to ʾIlumquh Ṯa-
3 hwân, master of ʾAwwâm, this statue
4 which [is] in bronze, which he had promised to Him for
5 the safety of his person and the sa-
6 fety of his camel herd. By ʾI-
7 **Flower** lumquh, master of ʾAwwâm. **Flower**

L. 1: *ʿbdm*, e.g., RÉS 3902, No. 48, Qat; cf. also *ʿbydm*, e.g., in Ist 7628/1. – *hrmm*, name of a city (e.g., RÉS 3945/17); cf. also the personal name *hrymm* in Ja 691/1.

710 – Yellowish, slightly grayish sandstone block, re-cut on the left side to be re-used in a wall; photograph in Plate 29. – MaMB 165.

STONE: constant thickness: 9.5 cm. – *Front:* 10 cm. (top) and 11 (bottom) × 21.2. – INSCRIPTION: same disposition of lines as in Ja 559; letter height: 1.6 cm.; space between the lines: 0.4 cm.; distance from line 1 to the upper edge: 0.9 cm. – SYMBOL, cp. Ja 591; but only the two extreme ornaments are engraved; cf. Plate B.

1 **Sym-** *šfʿṯt/mqtwy/[...*
2 **bol** *hqny/ʾlmqhṯh⌋[wnbʿl]*
3 *ʾwm/ḏn/ṣlmn/lḏ[t/hʾw]*
4 *l/grbhw/bn/shrtn/[bʾlmqh]*

1 **Sym-** Šûfʿaṯat, high official of [...
2 **bol** has dedicated to ʾIlumquh Ṯah[wân, master of]
3 ʾAwwâm, this statue becau[se He has brought]
4 [ba]ck his person from Saharatân. [By ʾIlumquh.]

The first three letters of lines 1 and 2, the first six signs of line 3 and the first one of line 4 have been intentionally erased but not enough to render impossible their reading which is certain.

L. 3: after *lḏt*, three signs are missing; a verb like "to bring back" would be suitable; e.g., *hʾwl* (Ja 670/10).

711 – Grayish sandstone; photograph in Plate 29. – MaMB 168.

STONE: maximum thickness: 10.7 cm., very frequently 10 cm. – *Front:* edges damaged; lower left corner broken; 19.4 cm. (top) and 19.8 (bottom) × 17 (right) and 17.8 (left). – INSCRIPTION: same disposition of lines as in Ja 552; letter height: from 1.5 cm. to 1.7; space between the lines: 0.3 cm.; distance from line 13 to the lower edge: 2 cm. (right) and 2.5 (left). – SYMBOL, same general type as that of Ja 698; cf. Plate B.

1 **Sym-** *šwf⌈ʾl/bn/⌉wśl/ʿb⌈d/kb⌋*
2 **bol** *rẖll/hqny/ʾlmqhṯhwn*
3 *⌊bʿlʾwm/ṣlmn/ḏḏhbm/ḥgn/w*
4 *⌈qhhw/bmsʾlhw/lhʿnnhw/bn/ḥ⌉*
5 *lẓ/ḥqwnhn/wḥlẓ/ymrnhw/dr⌋*
6 *⌊m/b⌋ẖrfm/wlẖmrhw/ʾlmqhbʿl*
7 *⌈ʾwm/ʿbdhw/šwfʾl/ḥẓy/wrḍ⌋*
8 *w/mrʾyhmw/[nmrn/ʾwkn/]wʾẖy*
9 *hw/gḥḍm/ʾḥṣn/ʾkbrw/ẖll⌈/⌉[w]*
10 *ʾqynm/wḏsẖymm/wlẖmrhw/ʾl*
11 *mqh/nʿmtm/ʾhnmw/ygzn/wlh*
12 *ʿnnhw/ʾlmqhbʿlʾwm/bn/nḍʿ*
13 *wšṣy/šnʾm/bʾlmqhbʿlʾwm*

1 **Sym-** Šûfʾil, son of Waśal, servant of the Leader
2 **bol** of H̱alil, has dedicated to ʾIlumquh Ṯahwân,
3 master of ʾAwwâm, this statue which [is] in bronze, as He has
4 ordered him through His oracle in order to protect him from the op-
5 pression of the [= his] two buttocks and (from) the oppression [that] occurs to him once
6 a year; and that may vouchsafe to him ʾIlumquh, master
7 of ʾAwwâm, to His worshipper Šûfʾil the esteem and gra-
8 ce of their two lords [Nimrân ʾAwkân] and his bro-
9 ther Gaḥḍum ʾAḥṣân, Leaders of H̱alil [and]
10 ʾAqyânum and of (the tribe) Suẖaymum; and that may vouchsafe to him ʾIl-
11 umquh prosperity [in] whatever he shall undertake; and that
12 ʾIlumquh, master of ʾAwwâm, may protect him from the hostility

13 and wickedness of [any] enemy. By ʾIlumquh, master of ʾAwwâm.

L. 1: *šwfʾl*, cf., e.g., the names of a house *yšfʾl* (RÉS 3972/1) and of a man *šwfm* (e.g., RÉS 4033/1); in RÉS 4892/1, Ḥaḍr, */ḥšyfm* must be read instead of [ʾ]*šyfm* or *šyfm* suggested by *BePC* (p. 330) and *RÉS* (VII, p. 407) respectively. The latter considers initial *h* as a divine symbol. But such divine symbol at the beginning of a small graffito is very rare and the form *hšyfm* is quite normal (cf., e.g., *hkrbm*, e.g., Ja 578/9). Furthermore, a vertical stroke engraved at the right of this initial *h* is not mentioned by A. F. L. Beeston and is interpreted by G. Ryckmans as the divine symbol *ḏ*; but this symbol requires not only one vertical stroke, but two, as well as two small horizontal strokes. Cf. also the personal name *šwf*, e.g., in RÉS 4186 (Ḥaḍr) B/1. RÉS 4186 A (vertical) reads as follows: (line 1)*mš*(line 2) *ʾ šḥrt* "(line 1) Maš(line 2)aʾ Šaḥrat"; and B (horizontal): boustrophedon: (line 1) ← *šwf* (line 2) → *ʾlʿṯ* "(line 1) Šûf(line 2) ʾIlʿaṯ." – *wšl*, feminine personal name, e.g., in RÉS 4489; cf. also the feminine personal name *wšlm* (RÉS 4364, where the family name reads *ḏr* "Ḏarr", instead of *br*) and *ʿmwšl* (e.g., Ja 387, Qat) and *rʾbšl* (Ja 507 C).

L. 5: *ymrnhw*, imperfect of the verb *mrr*; cf. Arabic *marra* "to happen, occur to someone" and in Daṯînah *mrr* means "to bind, fasten" (cf. *LaGD*, p. 2683).

L. 8: the personal name has been intentionally erased, but is restored on the basis, e.g., of Ja 684/8-9.

L. 9: *ʾkbrw*, pl. of *kbr*; cf. *CoRoC*, p. 166 B.

L. 11: *ygzn*, cf. *CoRoC*, p. 122 A and Arabic *ǧâza*, 2nd form "to carry out (e.g., a plan)".

712 – Yellowish sandstone block, re-cut at the bottom in order to be re-used in a wall; photograph in Plate 29. – MaMB 169.

STONE: thickness: left side: 4.7 cm. (bottom) and 4.9 (top); right side: maximum: 7 cm.; the right side is beveled to the inside. – *Front:* covered with red paint; 23.3 cm. (top) and 23.2 (bottom) × 31.7 (right) and 30.9 (left). – INSCRIPTION: same disposition of lines as in Ja 552; letter height: 1.8 cm.; space between the lines: 0.2 cm.; distance from line 1 to the upper edge: from 0.3 cm. to 0.5.

1 *[wf]dm/wʿqrbn/wʾmgd/wʾbkrb/w*
2 *⌈b⌉nyhmw/ʾšms/wʾbšmr/wmrṯdʾ*
3 *wm/wyfrʿ/ʾtnʿn/bnw/brqm/ʾdm*
4 *ḏkbsyn/hqnyw/ʾlmqhw/ṣlmm*
5 *ḏḏhbm/ḥmdm/bḏṯ/hʿn/wmtʿn*
6 *ʾlmqhw/ʿbdhw/wfdm/bn/ʾʾ*
7 *rẖ/wẖrgt/ẖrghw/ḏbn/šʿbhw*
8 *tnʿmm/bʿbr/mrʾhmw/mlkn*
9 *wrʾ/khʿn/wmtʿn/ʾlmqhw*
10 *ʿbdhw/wfdm/bn/hntʾʾrẖ*
11 *n/wlwzʾ/ʾlmqh/mtʿn/ʿbd*
12 *hw/wfdm/bn⟨/n⟩ḏʿ/wšṣy/šnʾ*
13 *m/wlsʿdhmw/bryʾʾḏnm/wmqm*
14 *tm/wl/sʿdhmw/ḥẓy/mrʾhmw/ḏ*

1 [Wâfi]dum and ʿAqrabân and ʾAmgad and ʾAbkarib and
2 their sons ʾAšmus and ʾAbšamar and Marṯadʾa-
3 wwâm and Yafraʿ, the Tanaʿites, descendants of Barqum, servants of
4 [the family] Kabsiyân, have dedicated to ʾIlumquhû, a statue
5 which [is] in bronze, in praise because has protected and saved
6 ʾIlumquhû His worshipper Wâfidum from the cala-
7 mities and (from) the rebellion [to which] tried to induce him some of his tribe
8 Tanaʿamum against their lord the king;
9 but now ʾIlumquhû has protected and saved
10 His worshipper Wâfidum from those calamities;
11 and that ʾIlumquh may continue to save His wor-
12 shipper Wâfidum from the hostility and wickedness of [any] enemy;
13 and that He may make them happy with the strength of understanding and of pow-
14 er; and that He may make them happy with the esteem of their lord Ḏ[.]

For the beginning, cf. Ja 719/1-2.

L. 1: *wfdm*, Van Lessen 9/4, Qat, and 2nd masculine personal name in RÉS 3087/22. – *ʿqrbn*, also masculine personal name, e.g., in RÉS 4338/1; cf. also the Qat personal name *ʿqrb* (Ja 158), the family names *ʿqrbtm* (RÉS 4198 bis/2) and *ʿqrbm* (e.g., RÉS 4648/1), which is also masculine personal name in Ja 121/1, Qat. – *ʾmgd*, cf. the name of a man *mgdm* (Khalidy-Condé 9 B/1), and also the Arabic names of men *ʿabd al-maǧîd* (cf. *SlGaVNPA*, p. 2 A), *maǧdîy* (cf. *SaIS*, p. 205 A), *mâǧid* (cf. *HeBN*, p. 48 A), of clans *banû maǧîd, banû muǧayd* (cf. *MüHG*, 193 A), *banû maǧîd* (cf. *WüID*, 296/16), of women *maǧd* (cf. *SaIS*, *l.c.*), *maǧdâ* (cf. *HeBN*, *l.c.*), *mâǧidat* (cf. *WüR*, p. 628), and of places *mâǧid* (cf. *l.c.*, p. 192 C), *maǧduwân*, *maǧdûn*, and *al-muǧdiyat* (cf., *l.c.*, p. 195 A); cf. also the Safaitic name of a man *mgd* (cf. *LiSI*, p. 323 A).

L. 2: *ʾšms*, the name of a man in CIH 287/7 (cf. *NaNN*, p. 73); cf. also the Arabic place names *ʾašmus* (cf. *WüR*, p. 14 A) and *ʾašmas* (cf. *MüHG*, p. 6 A); there is no reason to suppose that a letter such as *b* is missing between ʾ and *š*; in RÉS 3552/8, Qat, read *ʾbšmsmm* instead of *ʾbšbm* printed by *RÉS*; *RyNP*'s (I, p. 217 B) restoration in *ʾbšmsm* is gratuitous.

Ll. 2-3: *mrṯdʾwm*, same nominal formation as that, e.g., of *mrṯdʾl* (e.g., Ja 544/2).

L. 3: *yfrʿ*, e.g., CIH 79/7-8. – *brqm* is masculine personal name, e.g., in RÉS 4585 A; cf. also *brqn* in CIH 350/10.

L. 4: *kbsyn*, family name in CIH 581/3 as well as in Proche-Orient 1/1 (cf. *RyISA*, XI, pp. 100-01 and *JaDME*, p. 9); cf. also the family name *kbsym*, e.g., in Ja 618/2.

L. 12: *bnḏʿ* is certain on the stone; haplography of *n* and consequently omission of the word divider.

713 – Yellowish sandstone block, re-used in a wall; photograph in Plate 29. – MaMB 170.

STONE: constant thickness: 10.8 cm. – *Front:* left edge slightly damaged; 22.3 cm. × 42.2 (right), 42.6 (center) and 41.8 (left). – INSCRIPTION: same disposition of lines as in Ja 552; many letters, especially in the upper part are filled with cement (line 1 and the upper half of line 2 were completely filled with cement); letter height: from 2.1 cm. to 2.8; space between the lines: from 0.2 cm. to 0.4. – SYMBOL: the direction of the curve is opposite to the usual one; cf. also Ja 673; cf. Plate B.

1 ⌈**Symbol**⌉ *ʾbkrb/ʾrzn/wbnyhw*
2 *yḥmd/ʾḥšd/bnw/qbʿ*
3 *n/mqtwyy/šfʿṯt/ʾšwʿ*
4 *wbnyhw/zydm/ʾymn/bn*
5 *hmdn/hqnyw/mrʾhmw/ʾlmqh*
6 *mṯkḥm/wbʿlyhw/ṯwrm/w*
7 *ṯny/ṣlmn/ḏḏhbm/ḥmdm*
8 *bḏt/ṣdq/ʾlmq/ʿbdhw/ʾ⌋*
9 *bkrb/bʾmlʾ/stmlʾ/bʿm⌉*
10 *hw/ḥmdm/bḏt/ẖmrhw/hrg*
11 *wsby/wġnm/bsbʾt/sbʾ*
12 *bʿm/mrʾhmw/šfʿṯt/ʾšwʿ*
13 *bn/hmdn/wlwzʾ/ʾlmqhw/ẖm*
14 *r/ʿbdhw/ʾbkrb/hrg/wsby/w*
15 *ġnm/wḥẓy/ʾmrʾhw/bny/h*
16 *mdn/wšʿbhw/ḥšdm/bʾlm*
17 *[q]⌊hbʿlʾ⌋[w]⌊m⌋*

1 **Symbol** ʾAbkarib ʾArzan and his son
2 Yaḥmad ʾAḥšad, descendants of [the family] Qabaʿ-
3 ân, the two officials of Šûfʿaṯat ʾAšwaʿ
4 and of his son Zaydum ʾAyman, descendants of [the tribe]
5 Hamdân, have dedicated to their lord ʾIlumquh
6 a stone tablet (?) and on top of it a bull and
7 these two statues which [are] in bronze, in praise
8 because ʾIlumq has bestowed upon His worshipper ʾAb-
9 karib the favors [for which] he besought
10 Him in praise because He has vouchsafed to him to kill
11 and capture and plunder in the encounter [which] he fought
12 with their lord Šûfʿaṯat ʾAšwaʿ,
13 descendant of Hamdân; and that ʾIlumquhû may continue to vouchsa-
14 fe to His worshipper ʾAbkarib to kill and capture and
15 plunder and [also] the esteem of his lords, the descendants of Ham-
16 dân and of his tribe Ḥâšidum. By ʾIlum-
17 [q]uh, master of ʾA[wwâ]m.

L. 1: *ʾrzn*, 2nd masculine personal name, e.g., in RÉS 4400/1.

Ll. 2-3: *qbʿn*, cf. Arabic *qabbaʿ* "timid" and the Arabic names of places *qbʿt* and *qbʿyn* (cf. *WüR*, p. 169 C) and of men *al-qabâʿ* (cf. *GoAT*, p. 459) and *al-qubâʿ* (cf. *WüID*, 94/19).

714 – Yellowish sandstone; photograph in Plate 30. – MaMB 172.

STONE: maximum thickness: 10.5 cm. – *Front:* hammered and not polished; upper corners broken; 15.2 cm. (top) and 14.9 (bottom) × 18.1 (right) and 16 (left). – INSCRIPTION: same disposition of lines as in Ja 552; but irregular tracing; letter height: 5.5 cm. (maximum) and 2.8 (minimum).

hqnyt⌈ʾ⌉w	1	The offering of Wa-
hbʾwm	2	habʾawwâm,
ḏyhʿn	3	him of [the family] Yuhʿin.

For the formula, cp. Ja 749.

715 – Yellowish, slightly grayish sandstone block, broken on top; photograph in Plate 30. – MaMB 173.

STONE: thickness: 9.7 cm. (top) and 10.2 (bottom). – *Front:* 20.6 cm. (top) and 20.5 (bottom) × 17 (right), 18.3 (center) and 16.8 (left). – INSCRIPTION: same disposition of lines as in Ja 552; letter height: 2.3 cm. (top), 1.9 (bottom), and 1.5 (on line 12); space between the lines: from 0.3 cm. to 0.6. – SYMBOL, cf. lower half of Ja 589; cf. Plate B.

1 **[Sym-** *ᶜ]⌜bd/khl⌝[h/wḥbybm/wz]*
2 **bol** *ᶜy/⌜r⌝kbtn/wbny⌜hm⌝w⌜/ᶜ⌝*
3 *mrᵓl/hqnyw/mrᵓhmw/ᵓlm*
4 *qhṯhwnbᶜlᵓwm/ṣlmnhn*
5 *ḏḏhbn/ḥgn/šfthw/wḥmd*
6 *m/bḏt/hwfyhmw/wbḏt/yz*
7 *ᵓn/ᵓlmqhw/hwfyn/ᵓdmhw*
8 *ᶜbd/khlh/wḥbybm/wbnyh*
9 *mw/(ᶜ)mrᵓl/wlhᶜnnhmw/wm*
10 *tᶜnhmw/bn/bᵓstm/wnkytm*
11 *wšṣy/šnᵓm/bᵓlmqhṯhwnbᶜ*
12 *lᵓwm*

1 **[Sym-** ᶜA](bd Kahl)[ah and Ḥubaybum,] the two [chie]fs
2 **bol** of equitation and their son ᶜA-
3 marᵓil, have dedicated to their lord ᵓIlum-
4 quh Ṯahwân, master of ᵓAwwâm, these two statues
5 which [are] in bronze, as he had promised Him and in praise
6 because He has protected them and in order that may
7 continue ᵓIlumquhû to protect His worshippers
8 ᶜAbd Kahlah and Ḥubaybum and their son
9 (ᶜA)marᵓil; and that He may assist them and sa-
10 ve them from misfortunes and sufferings
11 and (from) the wickedness of [any] enemy. By ᵓIlumquh Ṯahwân, mas-
12 ter of ᵓAwwâm.

L. 1: *ᶜbd*, e.g., RÉS 2773/2, Min; cf. also *ᶜbdm* (e.g., Ja 709/1), *ᶜbdt* (e.g., RÉS 3732/1, Min) and *ᶜbydm* (e.g., RÉS 3902, No. 81/1, Qat). – *khlh*, cf. the name of the Min god *khln* (cf. *JaP*, p. 143 and *JaRSAP*, p. 274), the personal name *khlm* (e.g., RÉS 3902, No. 112, Qat) and the name of a valley *khln* (Ja 735/1); cf. also the commentary on Safaitic *khl* in *LiSI*, p. 320 B and the commentary on Ja 616/24-25. – *ḥbybm*, *qutaylum* form of *ḥbb*; cf. the Arabic names of men *ḥibîb*, *ḥibayyib* (cf. *HeBN*, p. 17 A), *bû ḥabîb* (cf. *SlGaVNPA*, p. 22 A), of a woman *ḥibayyibat* (cf. *HeBN*, *l.c.*), and of a person *al-ḥabîb* and *al-ḥabîbat* (cf. *SlGaVNPA*, *l.c.*); cf. also the name of clans *ḥbb* (e.g., Ja 649/1) and *ḥbbt* (e.g., Ja 701 A/2); the correction of *hbybm* (RÉS 4133/5) to *ḥbybm* suggested by *RyNP* (II, p. 57 B) is gratuitous; for *h* is clear on the photograph and the root *hbb* is attested in Semitic languages.

L. 2: *rkbt*, cf. Arabic *rikbat* "equitation, riding".
Ll. 2-3: *ᶜmrᵓl* same nominal formation as that, e.g., of *ᶜmrlt* (Ja 721/1).
L. 9: *w* instead of *ᶜ* in *ᶜmrᵓl* is certain on the stone.

716 – Orange colored sandstone with many grayish stains; photograph in Plate 30. – MaMB 174.

STONE: almost constant thickness: 9 cm. – *Front:* broken at the bottom; the upper edge is splintered off in two places; 40.8 cm. (top) and 40 (bottom) × 27 (right), 27.8 (left), and 32.6 (center). – INSCRIPTION: same disposition of the lines as in Ja 552; letter height: from 2.1 cm. to 2.2; space between the lines: 0.5 cm.; distance from line 1 to the upper edge: 1 cm. – SYMBOL, cf. Ja 639.

1 **Sym-** *nwf⌜m/⌝[ᵓ]⌜ḏ⌝rḥ/wbnyhw/yrm/⌜yrḥb⌝/wnšᵓkrb/ᵓ*
2 **bol** *rśl/bnw/ḏhmdn/wḏġymn/ᵓbᶜl/bytnn/hrn/w*
3 *ḏrḥn/ᵓqwl/šᶜbnn/ḥšdm/wġymn/hqnyw/ᵓlmqhṯhw*
4 *nbᶜlᵓwm/ṯny/ṣlmn/ḏṣrfm/ḥmdm/bḏt/ṣdq/whwf*
5 *yn/ᶜbdhw/nwfm/bṣry/wtbšr/stmlᵓ/bᶜmhw/lwfy/gryb*
6 *t/ᶜbdyhw/yrm/wnšᵓkrb/bny/ḏhmdn/wḏġymn/bkn/hr*
7 *bbhmy/šᶜbn⌞/⌟sfln/wšfthmw/ᵓlmqhṯhwn/kyᶜthdn/b*
8 *rwyhw/yrm/wnšᵓkrb/bwfym/ᶜdy/bythmw/byt/bny/h*
9 *mdn/whṯbw/lẖyl/wmqm/ᵓlmqhṯhwnbᶜlᵓwm/tᵓmnm/b*
10 *⌞ḏt/ṣdq/whwfynhmw/bhwt/mlᵓn/wlwzᵓ/ᵓlmqh/šr*
11 *[ḥ]⌞/⌟wšwf/wrtṯdn/grybt/ᶜbdyhw/yrm/wnš⌞ᵓkrb/bny⌟[/ḏh]*
12 *[mdn/w]⌞ḏġ⌟ymn/bn/b[ᵓ]⌞stm⌟/[w]⌞nky⌟[tm/. . .*
13 *. . . h]w/⌞ᵓlm⌟[qh. . .*

1 **Sym-** Nawfum [ᵓA]ḏraḥ and his two sons Yarum Yarḥib and Našaᵓkarib ᵓAr-
2 **bol** śal, descendants of [the tribe] Hamdân and of [the tribe] Ġaymân, masters of the two houses Hirrân and
3 Ḏarḥân, rulers of the two tribes Ḥâšidum and Ġaymân, have dedicated to ᵓIlumquh Ṯahwân,
4 master of ᵓAwwâm, these two statues which [are] in brass in praise because He has bestowed upon and assist-
5 ed His worshipper Nawfum with the counsel and the announcements [for which] he besought Him for the safety of the persons
6 of His two worshippers Yarum and Našaᵓkarib, descendants of Hamdân and of Ġaymân, when seized
7 upon them the tribe Saflân; and ᵓIlumquh Ṯahwân has granted to them both to take care of
8 his two children, Yarum and Našaᵓkarib, in safety in their house, the house of the descendants of Ham-

9 dân; and they presented to the strength and the power of ʾIlumquh Ṯahwân, master of ʾAwwâm, a testimony of confidence because

10 He has bestowed upon [them] and protected them by this favor; and that ʾIlumquh may keep

11 heal[thy] and take care of and preserve the persons of His two worshippers Yarum and Našaʾkarib, descendants of [Ham-]

12 [dân and] of Ġaymân, from mis[for]tunes [and] suffering[s...

13 ...hi]m ʾIlum[quh...

L. 1: *yrm/yrḫb*, also in CIH 352/1-2: in both inscriptions, *yrm/yrḫb* and his relatives belong to the tribe Hamdân; the high official of *yrm/yrḫb* in CIH 352 speaks of *šʿbhmw/ḥšdm* "their tribe Ḥâšidum" (line 14), and *yrm/yrḫb* and his relatives in the present text are rulers of the same tribe. The preceding features common to the two texts apparently suggest the identification of the two *yrm/yrḫb*. The difference between *bnw/ḏhmdn/wḏġymn* (here, line 2) and *bny/btʿ/whmdn* (CIH 352/2-3) does not seem to be inexplicable: the authors of the present text are rulers of the two tribes Ḥâšidum and Ġaymân (line 3), and the names of the three brothers in CIH 352 are followed by the mention of their origin. There is thus no formal opposition between the two expressions. For the dating of CIH 352, cf. *JaASAB*, p. 169, commentary on CIH 352/1-2. In CIH 963+962+978/3, the 2nd letter of the 2nd personal name is more probably *k* and not *r*, and the 4th letter is missing; nevertheless, *RycSD* (p. 346) transcribes it as *yrḫb*. Note that *RycSD* (p. 344) mentions this text as "CIH 962 (+963+978)". The order of the first two fragments must be reversed; CIH 962 is to be placed to the left of CIH 963, while CIH 978 finds its place under the two preceding fragments.

Ll. 2 and 3: *bytnn* and *šʿbnn*: *-nn*, ending of the dual absolute (cf. also *JaIAM*, p. 273, commentary on Ja 541/8: *ʾdbnn*), cf. commentary on Ja 552/3: *ẖẖnhn*.

Ll. 6-7: *hrbb*, 4th form of *rbb*, the 1st form of which is attested in Gl 1143/1 (cf. *HöTPK*, pp. 32-35); the 4th form may be translated "to seize upon"; the restoration of *r*[*bb*] in RÉS 4145/1 is not more probable than that of *r*[*gl*], *r*[*kb*], etc.

L. 7: *sfln*, also tribe name in CIH 353/10; cf. also the Qat family name *sflyn* (e.g., Ja 311). – *ʿthd*, 8th form of *ʿhd*; cf., e.g., RÉS 3306 A/9, Min "to take care of".

717 – Yellowish sandstone; broken into two parts; main block = MaMB 175; splinter (upper left corner) = MaMB 120 = Ja 805; two photographs in Plate 31.

MaMB 175: maximum thickness: 10 cm.; *front:* upper left corner broken; 30.2 cm. (right) and 25.8 (left) × 17.5 (top) and 17.8 (bottom). – MaMB 120: maximum thickness: 9.2 cm.; *front:* 9.5 cm. × 2.3; *text:* 8.4 cm. × 1.6; distance from the letters to the upper edge: 0.3 cm. – INSCRIPTION: same disposition of lines as in Ja 623; letter height: from 1.6 cm. to 1.8; space between the lines: from 0.2 cm. to 0.5. – SYMBOL, cf. Ja 692, plus a small straight line perpendicular to the inside incision, and located at the center of the symbol; cf. Plate B.

1 **Sym-** *mb⸢šmt⸣/l⸤/ṣr⸥w⸤ḥy⸥tn*
2 **bol** *hqnyt/⸢ʾlmqhṯ⸣[h]*
3 *wnbʿlʾwm/ṣlmn/ḏḏ*
4 *hbn/ḥgn/šftthw/ʾ*
5 *mthw/mbšmt/kmʿn*
6 *mw/yẖmrnhw/ḥyw/lh*
7 *w/wldm/thqnynhw/wr*
8 *ʾ/ẖmrhw/ḥyw/bnyhw*
9 *ṯwbʾl/wʿmrm/wlwfy*
10 *grybthmw/wlhʿnnhm*
11 *w/bn/bʾstm/wnkyt*
12 *m/bʾlmqbʿlʾwm*

1 **Sym-** Mubšamat, the Ṣirwâḥite woman,
2 **bol** has dedicated to ʾIlumquh Ṯa[h-]
3 wân, master of ʾAwwâm, this statue which [is] in
4 bronze, as had promised to Him His
5 maidservant Mubšamat if [=whenever]
6 He would vouchsafe to her to grant life for
7 her to children [which are] her offering; but
8 now He has vouchsafed to her the life of her two sons
9 Ṯawbʾil and ʿAmrum; and that He may protect
10 their persons; and that He may assist them
11 from misfortunes and sufferings.
12 By ʾIlumq, master of ʾAwwâm.

L. 1: *mbšmt*, cf. the personal name *bšmt* (RÉS 2632 B) and the name of the Sab god *bšmm* (cf. *JaP*, p. 140 and *JaRSAP*, p. 274).

Ll. 4-6, cf. *JaPDSM*, p. 179.

L. 7: *thqnyn*, noun derived from the 4th form *hqny* with the prefix *t* and the affix *n*; it means "the object of dedication".

718 – Upper part of a white alabaster plaque; cut into two parts; left part = MaMB 176; right part = MaMB 56 = Ja 785 (latex squeeze); two photographs in Plate 31.

PLAQUE: constant thickness: from 8.7 cm. to 8.9. – INSCRIPTION: same disposition of lines as in Ja 552; but in line 1, a 4th horizontal line is traced above the 3rd one; the signs of the even number lines and the symbol are painted in red; letter height: from 1.9 cm. to 2.2; space between the lines: from 0.3 cm. to 0.4; distance from line 1 to the upper edge; 0.5 cm. – SYMBOL: almost entirely destroyed; shaped as, e.g., in Ja 758.

MaMB 176: *front:* the four edges are badly damaged; width: 22.4 cm., and height: 23.6. – MaMB 56: upper left corner broken; upper right corner and left side badly damaged; *front:* 18.7 cm. × 10. – SPLINTER: missing; center part of lines 1-4.

1 ⌈**Sym-**⌉ *whbᵓwm/y⌉⌈ᵓḏf/⌉* | *[wᵓẖyhw/ydm]* | *⌈/ydrm/⌉[w]⌈bny⌉(h)[w/ḥm]*
2 ⌊**bol**⌋ *ᶜṯt/ᵓzᵓd/wᵓb⌈krb⌉* | *[/ᵓ]* | *⌊sᶜd/w⌈sẖ⌉ymm/yzᵓn/bnw⌈/⌉[s]*
3 *[ẖymm]⌊/ᵓb⌋ᶜl/bytn/rymn* | *[/ᵓ]* | *[q]⌊wl/šᶜbn/yrsm/ḏsmᶜy⌋[/ṯ]*
4 *[lṯn/ḏhgr]⌊m/hq⌋nyw/ᵓl* | *[mq]* | *[h]⌊ṯhwnbᶜlᵓwm/ṣlmn⌊/⌋[ḏḏ]*
5 *[hbn/....../wṣlm]t/⌋[....../ḏ* | *b]⌊h⌋⌊w/ḥmdw/ẖyl/wmqm/[ᵓl]*
6 *[mqh...* ... | */ᵓl]⌊mqh/hwt/wldn/s⌈ẖ⌉[ym]*
7 *[m/...* .. | *...]⌊ᵓ/wldn/sẖymm/ln/[...*
8 ... | *...]⌊/tfl⌋w/bᶜm/ᵓlmqh/[...*
9 | *...]⌊r⌋š⌊yt⌋[...*

1 **Sym-** Wahabᵓawwâm Yaᵓḏif [and his brother Yadum] Yadrim [and] hi[s] sons [Ḥamm-]
2 **bol** ᶜaṯat ᵓAzᵓad and ᵓAbkarib [ᵓA]sᶜad and Suẖaymum Yazᵓân, descendants of
3 [Suẖaymum,] masters of the house Raymân, [ru]ler[s] of the tribe Yarsum of Samᶜay,
4 [third of Hagar]um, have dedicated to ᵓIl[umquh] Ṯahwân, master of ᵓAwwâm, this statue [which (is) in]
5 [bronze,... ...and a] female [statue...by] which they have praised the strength and the power of [ᵓIl-]
6 [umquh... ᵓIl]umquh this child Suẖ[aymum]
7 ...]. this child Suẖaymum, until [...
8 ...]he turned to ᵓIlumquh [...
9 ...] the gifts [...

The text has the same authors as Ja 616 which served as basis for restoring the beginning; besides, the repartition of the signs on the stones does not allow us to restore *mqtt/nšᵓkrb* before the formula of dedication; this inscription is thus prior to Ja 616, that is to say anterior to the appointment as *mqtwy* mentioned in the latter text. The preceding conclusion is confirmed by the fact that *sẖymm/yzᵓn* is mentioned as *wld* "child".

719 – Left part of a yellowish, slightly grayish sandstone inscription; photograph in Plate 31. – MaMB 177.

STONE: maximum thickness: 8 cm. – *Front:* lower third of the left edge broken; 26.6 cm. × 13.1 (top), 12.5 (center) and 7.5 (bottom). – INSCRIPTION: same disposition of lines as in Ja 559; letter height; from 1.1 cm. to 1.2; space between the lines: from 0.2 cm. to 0.3.

1 [**Sym-** *wfd]m/wbnyhw/ᵓbšmr/w[.]*
2 [**bol** *..../w]⌊mrṯdᵓwm/bnw/wd*
3 *...]/hqnyw/ᵓlmqhṯhwnbᶜ*
4 *[lᵓwm/ṣlmm]/ḥmdm/bḏt/hwfy/ᶜbdh*
5 *[w/wfdm/]⌈bkl/ᵓmlᵓ/stmlᵓ/bᶜm*
6 *[hw/wlwzᵓ/]ᵓlmqh/hwfyn/lhw/gr*
7 *[ybt/bny]⌊h⌋w/wᵓmhmw/ᵓbḥmd/ḏt/w*
8 *[d.../wlẖm/]rhmw/ᵓlmqh/ḥẓy/ᵓmrᵓ*
9 *[hmw/......]/wšᶜbhmw/ḥmln/wlẖ*
10 *[mrhmw/ᵓlmq]h/bry/ᵓᵓḏnm/wmqy*
11 *[mtm/wlḏt/]⌈nᶜmt/wtnᶜmn/wlẖrynh*
12 *[mw/ᵓlmqh]/bn/nḍᶜ/wšṣy/wtṯᶜ⌊t/⌋[w]*
13 *[ṭwᶜ/šnᵓm/w]lẖmrhmw/ᵓlmqh/nᵓd/[d]*
14 *[ṯᵓ/wqyẓ/]wṣrb/ᶜdy/kl/ᵓrḍhm[w/w]*
15 *[ᵓsrrhmw]⌊/⌋wlwzᵓ/ᵓlmqh/wḍ[ᶜ/ḍr]*
16 *[hmw/wlwzᵓ]/hwfyn/grybth⌋[mw/...*
17 *[.../w...hm]w/bᵓlmqhb⌋ᶜ⌊l⌋[ᵓwm]*

1 [**Sym-** Wâfid]um and his sons ᵓAbšamar and..
2 [**bol** ...and] Marṯadᵓawwâm, descendants of Wad-
3 ...,]have dedicated to ᵓIlumquh Ṯahwân, mas-
4 [ter of ᵓAwwâm, a statue] in praise because He has showered upon H[is] worshipper
5 [Wâfidum] all the favors [for which] he besought
6 [Him; and that] ᵓIlumquh [may continue to] protect for him the per-

7 [sons of h]is [sons] and their mother ʾAbḥamad, her of Wa-
8 [d...; and that] ʾIlumquh [may vouchsa]fe to them the esteem of [their] lords,
9 [......] and of their tribe Ḥumlân; and that
10 [ʾIlumqu]h may vouch[safe to them] the strength of understanding and of po-
11 [wer; and that it may] have been pleasant and be pleasant; and that
12 [ʾIlumquh] may preserve t[hem] from the hostility and wickedness and spying [and]
13 [constraint of (any) enemy; and] that ʾIlumquh may vouchsafe to them the magnificence of [the fruits of]
14 [spring and of summer] and of autumn in thei[r] every land [and] all
15 [their wâdî-side valleys]; and that ʾIlumquh may continue to humi[liate their]
16 [foe; and that He may continue to] protect t[heir] persons [...
17 ... and thei]r [...]. By ʾIlumquh, master of [ʾAwwâm.]

For the beginning, cf. Ja 712/1-3.

L. 7: *ʾbḥmd*, e.g., CIH 255/2.
L. 8: three letters are missing at the beginning.

720 – Yellowish, slightly grayish sandstone; edges scarcely shaped out; photograph in Plate 32. – MaMB 180.

Front: 44 cm. (left), 59.5 (center) and 56.5 (right). – INSCRIPTION: defaced (especially in the lower half) and irregular cursive writing; mean letter height: 4.8 cm. (line 1) and 1.1 (line 18).

1 *ʾgrm/wšrḥ*
2 *m/ḏy/ḏbyn/hqnyw*
3 *mrʾhmy/ʾlmqhw/*
4 *bʿl/ʾwm/ṣlmn/ḏ*
5 *ṣrfm/tḏrm/lqbly/ḏh*
6 *ẖṭʾw/bmrʾhmw/ʾlmq*
7 *hw/bʿl/ʾwm/kʾl/ṣb*
8 *nw/wṯb/bmḥrmn/wys*
9 *tṣyn/bn/ḏfrʾn/wbn/bṣ*
10 *ln/wsʾr/ẖṭyʾn/ẖmrhmw*
11 *wtsn/nkr/ʿbdhw/ʾgrm*
12 *sṯt/ʾwrẖm/mrḍm/fšʾ*
13 *m/ḏʾl/mn/šʿr/kmhn/hʾ*
14 *ḥlẓhw/wbnw/ḏḏbyn/lḥḏrnn*
15 *bn/hẖṭʾn/bʾlmqh/wlmšw/m*
16 *ʿrbtm/bn/ḏḏbyn/wzʾk/šh*
17 *n/lʿbdhw/ʾgrm/bʿdn*
18 *ʾk/bn/nfshw/bʾl*
19 *mqh/bʿlʾwm*

1 ʾAgarum and Šarḥum,
2 both men of [the tribe] Ḏû-Bayyin, have dedicated to
3 the lord of them both ʾIlumquhû,
4 master of ʾAwwâm, this statue which [is] in
5 blown brass, because of this: they
6 have seduced [others] into acting wrongfully against their lord ʾIlumqu-
7 hû, master of ʾAwwâm, for they did not abstain
8 from sitting down in the temple as he [ʾAgarum] was
9 protecting himself against the stinking herbs and against the
10 onions; and the fines remained: He has vouchsafed to them
11 and decreed that His worshipper ʾAgarum be afflicted
12 [by] six months disease [and] then buy
13 what [was] missing from [the] barley, so he [ʾAgarum] would
14 shake off his oppression, and the descendants of Ḏû-Bayyin be afraid
15 of seducing [others] into acting wrongfully against ʾIlumquh; and were cast
16 [the] dice among Ḏû-Bayyin; and the mark went straight
17 toward His worshipper ʾAgarum [and so]
18 unhappiness was removed from his person. By ʾIl-
19 umquh, master of ʾAwwâm.

L. 1: *ʾgrm*, RÉS 4649/1.
L. 5: *tḏr*, *maṣdar* of the 6th form (*taḏârr*) of *ḏrr*; cf. the 4th form *hḏr* (Ja 575/4, and commentary) and participle *ḏr* (Ja 735/13); here, cf. especially *ḏarat* [from *ḏarâ*, *o* and *i*] *ar-rîḥu* "comme le traduit bien Lane" [cf. *LaAEL*, p. 964 A] "*the wind raised it* or *made it to fly and dispersed it*, ce qui est aussi le sens de *ḏrr*; ce sens est encore courant en Arabie" (cf. *LaGD*, p. 929); I propose translating *ṣrfn/tḏrm* as "brass [obtained as a result of] being sprinkled = blown" or "blown brass".
Ll. 7-8: *ṣbn*, cf. Arabic *ṣabana* "to put away, remove, put aside"; here, with the derived meaning of "to abstain from".
L. 8: *wṯb*, cf. *CoRoC*, p. 142 A: "to sit down, be seated".
Ll. 8-9: *ystṣyn*, 10th form of *ṣyn*; cf. Arabic *ṣâna* (o) "to protect, maintain"; in the 5th form in modern Ḥaḍr "to get unto shelter, under cover" (cf. *LaH*, p. 636).
L. 9: *ḏfrʾ*, cf. Arabic *ḏafira*, "to have, emit a pungent, *or* strong odour or smell" (cf. *LaAEL*, p. 967 A) and the adjective *ʾaḏfaru*, feminine *ḏafrāʾu*, "that which emits a strong odour," and

*ḏafrā*ʾ, "a certain herb, of foul odour, which camels etc. scarcely ever eat,...a certain green herb...the odour of which is like that of a slight wind from the anus: it makes the breath of camels to stink" (cf. *LaAEL*, *l.c.*, A-B).

Ll. 9-10: *bṣl*, cf. Arabic *baṣal* "onion"; cf. also in Soqoṭri (cf. *LeLS*, p. 93).

Ll. 10-11: *ḫṭy*ʾ, cf. Arabic *ḫaṭîʾat*, plural *ḫaṭâyâ* "error, sin; fine, penalty" and Nabataean *ḥṭyʾh* "amende" (cf. *JeHoDISO*, p. 86); the meaning "fine, penalty" is required by lines 11-13.

L. 11: *tsn*=*tśn* (for equivalence *s*=*ś*, cf. commentary on *mśd* in Ja 669/6), 5th form of *sn*; for *śn*, cf. *JaIAA*, pp. 319-20; in RÉS 2962/4, *tśnn* means "obligations (what have been imposed upon someone)" and not "limites (enclos?)" as proposed by *RÉS*, V, p. 262.

Ll. 11-13: *nkr*...*fšʾm*: double phrase mentioning two consecutive punishments pointed out as divine decree (*tsn*). For *nkr*, passive of the 1st form; in RÉS 4646/17 as well as in CIH 81/6 (cf. *BeSI*, pp. 19-20), *nkr* is active of the 3rd form (cf. Arabic *nâkara* "he contended with him in fight"; cf. *LaAEL*, p. 2849 B); for RÉS 5094/4 "change" (cf. also *JaPEHA*, p. 198), cf. *JaFSR*, pp. 15-16. For *šʾm*, cf. *CoRoC*, p. 246, *StSESA*, p. 530, and *RhGO*, pp. 22-23.

L. 13: *mn* instead of usual *bn* (cf. *HöASG*, p. 154), e.g., in CIH 547/10; for *m*=*mn* in CIH 160/7 and RÉS 5055 according to *RyISA* (X, p. 309), cf. *JaPDSM*, pp. 174-76. – *h*ʾ refers to ʾAgarum.

Ll. 13-14: *kmhn* and *lḥḏrnn* introduce the two effects of the imposed punishment and relate to ʾAgarum and the tribe Ḏû-Bayyin respectively. For *mhn*, cf. Arabic *mahana* "to shake off, pull about".

L. 14: *ḥlẓ* alludes to the weakness pointed out in lines 8-10.

L. 15: *lmš*, cf. Arabic *lamaša* "to play".

Ll. 15-16: *mʿrb*, plural *mʿrbt*, cf. *CoRoC*, p. 212 B "square stone" (cf. also *LaGD*, p. 2278, for Daṯînah *taʿârîb* with the same meaning). I proposed translating *lmšw*/*mʿrbtm* as "[the] dice were cast".

L. 16: *zʾk*, cf. Arabic *zaʾaka* and *zâka* (o, i) "to walk proudly" and *zaʾak*, *zaʾakânân*, *zawk*, and *zawakân* "proud gait"; here, with the derived meaning of "to go straight, unhesitatingly".

Ll. 16-17: *šhn* (*šh*+*n*), cf. Arabic *šiyat*, plural *šiyât* (from *šâha*, i) "sign, mark"; *šh* alludes to a die.

L. 18: ʾ*k*, cf. Arabic ʾ*awkat* "anger; evil, unhappiness".

721 – Upper part of a yellowish sandstone block, broken into two parts; photograph in Plate 32. – MaMB 185.

STONE: thickness: 5.1 cm. (top) and 5.7 (bottom); almost the entire line 6 is divided into two unequal parts by the fracture of the stone. – *Front:* length: 14.5 cm, and maximum width: 17.5. – INSCRIPTION: same disposition of lines as in Ja 559; letter height: from 1.5 cm. to 1.6; space between the lines: 0.2 cm. – SYMBOL, cf. Ja 639.

1 **Sym-** *ʿmrlt*/*ḏt*/*šrḥm*/ʾ
2 **bol** *mt*/*bn*/ʾ*nwyn*/*hqny*
3 *t*/ʾ*lmqh*/*bʿl*ʾ*wm*/*ḏn*/*ṣl*
4 *mn*/*ḏs*ʾ*lhw*/*bṣdġhw*/*lqb*
5 [*l*]*y*/*ḏstydʿthw*/*lwldm*/*wr*
6 ⌊ʾ/*ẖ*⌋*mrhw*/*wldm*/*bʿd*/*ḏstk*
7 [*n*/ʾ]⌊*l*⌋*mqh*/*bn*/*rf*ʾ*m*/*bn*/*hkrb*
8 [*m*/...[⌊*t*⌋⌊*thw*/*msḥm*/*tldm*
9 ...].⌊/⌋ʾ*lmq*⌊*h*/*ks*ʾ*lh*⌋
10 [*w*/...

1 **Sym-** ʿAmarlat, she of Šarḥum,
2 **bol** maidservant of [the family] ʾAnwayân, has dedicat-
3 ed to ʾIlumquh, master of ʾAwwâm, this sta-
4 tue which He has requested from her through His manifestation be[ca]use
5 of this: she had confided in Him in [hope for having] a child; and now
6 He has vouchsafed to her a child after [ʾI]lumquh
7 was petitioned by Rafaʾum, son of Hakrab[um], to realize
8 ...] his [...] Mâsihum a birth
9 ...] ʾIlumquh, in order that He would request from h[er]
10 [...

L. 1: *ʿmrlt*, same nominal formation as that, e.g., of *ʿmr*ʾ*l* (Ja 715/2-3).

L. 2: ʾ*nwyn*, also family name, e.g., in RÉS 4134/2; cf. ʾ*nwym*, name of a woman, e.g., in RÉS 4398.

L. 4: *s*ʾ*l*, cf. Arabic *saʾala* "to question, ask"; cf. also *CoRoC*, p. 192 A, *BeSI*, p. 16 and *StSESA*, pp. 522-23. – *ṣdġ*: RÉS 4151/6; cf. Arabic *ṣadaʿa* "to split, manifest, bring to light".

L. 6: *bʿd*/*ḏ*, e.g., CIH 314+954/17.

Ll. 6-7: *stk*[.]: according to the disposition of the letters in lines 3-6, only four signs precede *mqh* at the beginning of the present line; I propose reading *stkn*, 10th form of *kwn* (cf. *hkn*, 4th form of the same verb).

L. 7: *rf*ʾ*m*, second personal name in RÉS 4650/1.

L. 8: [. . .]*tthw*: five signs are missing at the beginning of the present line. – *msḥm*, cf. the feminine personal Thamudic name *msḥt* (cf. *vdBrIT*, p. 431: Jsa 198) and the Arabic names of places *mâsûḥ*, *masîḥat*, and *al-masḥâ'u* (cf. *WüR*, pp. 193 B, 204 C and A), of a clan *banû musîḥ* (cf. *MüHG*, p. 165 A) and of a man *al-masîḥ* (cf. *GoAT*, p. 551); cf. also *msḥ*, title of the 2nd Person in the Christian Trinity (cf. *JaCD*, p. 72 and *JaRSAP*, p. 276), attested in Arabic as *al-masîḥ bin maryam* (cf. e.g., *SaIS*, p. 221 A). One could also derive *msḥm* from the root *sḥm*; cf. *sḥm* in Ja 550/1. – *tld*, cf. Arabic *tawallud* "birth".

722 – Top and bottom parts of a yellowish sandstone inscription; photograph in Plate 32. – MaMB 186.

STONES: thickness: from 8.7 cm. (top) to 8.4 (bottom). – UPPER FRAGMENT: front: upper right corner broken; lateral edges and lower part damaged; length: 23.4 cm. and maximum width: 17.9. – LOWER PART: front: lower edge badly damaged; length: 23.3 cm., and width: 28 cm. (right) and 25.7 (left). – INSCRIPTION: lines 1-6 and a-e on stones A and B respectively; same disposition of lines as in Ja 552; letter height: between 2.7 cm. and 2.9; space between the lines: from 0.4 cm. to 0.5. – SYMBOL, cf. the lower part of Ja 700.

1 **[Sym-** . . . .]⌈*t*⌉/*wkᶜbb*/*wṯwbṯw*⌈*n*⌉
2 ⌈**bol**⌉ *wddsmy*/*bnt*/*klwdd*/*ᵓl*⌈*t*⌋
3 ⌊*šwqm*/*ᵓmh*/*ᵓlt*/*nᶜmbrl*/*hqn*[*y*]
4 ⌈*t*⌉[*w*]⌈/⌉⌊*ᵓ*⌋[*l*]*m*[*q*]⌊*h*/*ṯhwn*/*bᶜlᵓwm*/*ṣ*
5 ⌊*lm*⌊*n*⌋/*w*⌈*ṣlm*⌉*tn*/*ḏy*⌊/*ḏhbn*/⌋*ḥ*
6 [*mdm*/*b*]⌈*ḏ*/. .⌊*bl*⌋[. . .
a *ᶜmhn*/*ᵓ*⌈*lmqh*/⌉[ ](/*bᵓ*)*ẖ*⌉
b *msm*/*wlyẖmrn*/*ᵓlmqh*/*ṯhwn*
c *bᶜl*/*ᵓwm*/*ᵓmhhw*/*hwn*/*lhn*
d *lbhw*/*bᵓlmqh*/*ṯhwn*/*bᶜlᵓ*
e *wm*/*wṯwrbᶜlm*/*wḏt*/*ḥmym*

1 **[Sym-** . . . .t and Kaᶜbab and Ṯawbṯawân
2 **bol** and Dôdsumay, daughters of Kallwadd, they of
3 Šawqum, maidservants of them of Naᶜambaral, have dedi-
4 cated to ᵓIlumquh Ṯahwân, master of ᵓAwwâm,
5 this statue and this female statue, both in bronze, in
6 [praise be]cause [. . .
a to wrong ᵓIlumquh [. . .] (in) (army, ar-
b mies); and that may vouchsafe ᵓIlumquh Ṯahwân,
c master of ᵓAwwâm, to His maidservants to soothe for them [women]
d His heart. By ᵓIlumquh Ṯahwân, master of ᵓA-
e wwâm and Ṯawr Baᶜalum and Ḏât-Ḥimyâm.

Cf. preliminary note in commentary on Ja 786. – Both lateral sides have been cut again. The last (left) fourth of the final *t* in line 2 is missing and the distance between the bottom of the right stroke of that letter and the edge of the stone almost equals two thirds of the space between the lower part of the two strokes in the other *t*'s; besides, the last letter in lines 1, 3, and 4 is much too close to the edge. On the other hand, the right half of the first letters in lines 3 and 5 is missing. The restoration in lines 3-4 is based on the preceding consideration. – The exact number of missing lines is unknown.

L. 1: *kᶜbb*, *qatlal* form; cf. the Arabic name of a man *kᶜb* (cf. e.g., *GeKH*, p. 10 A) and *al-kᶜbyy* (cf., e.g., *SaIS*, p. 196 B); cf. also commentary on Ja 660/11-12; cf. also the Min noun *kᶜb* in RÉS 3401/4. In the commentary of the preceding text, *RÉS* (VI, p. 147) writes "Il faut lire vraisemblablement *kᶜbhw* au lieu de *šᶜbn* dans *C.I.S.*, IV, 522, d'après une révision que nous avons faite sur l'original". The letter *š* is perfectly clear on the original (actually BM 102457) as well as in the photograph reproduced by *CIH*; and *šᶜbhw* (not *šᶜbn*) is attested in CIH 522/4, 6. – *ṯwbṯwn*, CIH 963+962+978/3.

L. 2: *ddsmy*, same nominal formation as that, e.g., of *ddᵓl* (Ja 584/4), *ddḥmd* (Ja 731/1-2) *ddnmr* (Ja 291, Qat, and commentary) and *ddkrb* (RÉS 4579/1). – *klwdd*, for the 1st element, cf., e.g., *kly* (RÉS 3767, Min). – *ᵓlt*, e.g., Ja 544/2.

L. 3: *šwqm*, cp. the name of a woman (cf. also *NaNN*, p. 135 B) *šwqwd* "Šawiqwadd" in NaNN 56/1; cf. also in Arabic *šawq*, the name of a place (cf. *WüR*, p. 133 A), of a man *šâyiq* and *šuwayyiq* (cf. *HeBN*, p. 34 A) and of a woman *šuwayqah* (cf. *l.c.*); cf. also the Thamudic personal name *šwqn* (cf. *vdBrIT*, p. 285: Jsa 477). – *nᶜmbrl*, also, e.g., in Ja 741/3.

Ll. 5-6: *ḥ*[*mdm*/*b*]*ḏ*: five signs are missing at the beginning of line 6.

L. 6: to the left of what remains of *ḏ*, are the upper parts of four vertical strokes immediately preceding the top part of *bl* and most probably forming two pairs.

L. a: *ᶜmhn*, cf. Arabic *ᶜamaha*, 2nd form "to wrong someone" (cf. *LaAEL*, p. 2160 B). – Seven signs are missing after *ᵓlmqh*; then comes the extreme bottom of what could be a word divider, the bottom of two pairs of vertical strokes (*bʾ*?) and finally almost all the lower part of *ẖ*.

L. c: *hwn*, cf. Arabic *hâna* "to be light, easy", 2nd form "to render light, easy" and Hebrew *hwn* "to regard as easy"; here, the 2nd form the meaning of which is probably "to appease, soothe".

723 – Upper part of a yellowish sandstone inscription; photograph in Plate 32. – MaMB 187.

STONE: maximum thickness: 14.7 cm. – *Front:* length: 20.3 cm., and maximum width: 7.3. – INSCRIPTION: same disposition of lines as in Ja 552; letter height: 1.4 cm., 1.4, and 1.5; space between the lines: 0.3 cm.; distance from line 1 to the upper edge: 0.8 cm. – SYMBOL: the exterior lines are very slightly curved; the bottom is concave, and the inside design is a broken line; cf. Plate B.

1 **Sym-** *ḏrʿt/nḥyn/bn/ẖnʿm/ʿbd/mlk/sb*
2 **bol** *ʾ/hqny/ʾlmqh/ṯhwn/bʿlʾwm/ḏn*
3 *ṯwrn/ḏḏhbn/ḥmdm/bḏt/mtʿ/ʾlmqh*
4 *[bʿ]⸤lʾwm/⸥[ʿ]⸤bdh⸥[w/ḏrʿt]⸤/bn/ḥrmn/ḥrm⸥*

1 **Sym-** Ḏirʿat Naḥiyân, son of H̱âniʿum, servant of the king of Sabaʾ,
2 **bol** has dedicated to ʾIlumquh Ṯahwân, master of ʾAwwâm, this
3 bull which [is] in bronze, in praise because has saved ʾIlumquh,
4 [mast]er of ʾAwwâm, H[is wor]shipper [Ḏirʿat] from the interdict he incurred

Cf. the beginning of the commentary on Ja 685.

L. 1: *nḥyn*, family name in RÉS 5105; cf. also the verb *nḥ* in RÉS 4612/2 (*RÉS* does not mention it) (cf. commentary on Ja 585/1: *hʿll*). – *ẖnʿm*, cf. the first personal name *ẖnʿ* in Ja 882 K, Qat (cf. *JaPEQL*, p. 214) and also the Arabic *nisba al-ẖunâʿî* and clan name *ẖunâʿat* (cf. *WüR*, pp. 418 and 244 B respectively) and the Thamudic personal name *ẖnʿlt* (cf. *vdBrIT*, p. 401: Jsa 134).

L. 2: *ṯ* of *ṯhwn* is engraved on top of a *r*.

L. 4: *bn/ḥrmn/ḥrm*, cp. *bn/ḥrmn/ḥḥrm* in RÉS 4233/5 (cf. *JaSAI*, p. 507 B, No. 5); this expression may be followed either by the name of a place introduced by *b* "in" or by a phrase introduced by *bkn* "when" (cf. RÉS 4233/5); for the Western Semitic cognates of *ḥrm*, cf. *JeHoDISO*, p. 96: *ḥrm*I, II.

724 – Grayish sandstone plaque; two photographs in Plate 33. – MaMB 190.

PLAQUE: thickness: 7.3 cm. (right) and 7.9 (left). – *Top:* perpendicular to the upper edge of the front but upside down, a masonry mark *m*: 3 cm. × 1.1. – *Front:* 25.6 cm. × 4.3 (right) and 4.8 (left). – INSCRIPTION: same disposition of lines as in Ja 552; 19.6 cm. × 1.7; distance to the right edge: 1 cm., and to the upper edge: 0.3 cm.

hllḥmq⟨/⟩whlḥmq⟨/⟩wgrb⸤th(m)[w]
Hillâlḥamaq⟨and⟩Hilalḥamaq⟨and⟩th(ei)[r]
persons.

hllḥmq and *hlḥmq*, same nominal formation as those, e.g., of *hlʾly*, a name of the Sab lunar god (cf. *JaP*, p. 70 and *JaRSAP*, p. 261) and the Qat personal name *hlʿmd* (RÉS 3902, No. 40, Qat) respectively; for the 2nd element, cf. in Arabic the adjective *ḥamiq* "stupid" and the place name *al-ḥamqatân* (cf., e.g., *GoAT*, p. 697), and the Thamudic personal name *ḥmq* (cf. *vdBrTTPN*, p. 41: Ph 275 ai). – *grbth(m)[w]*: the lower left stroke of *t* is not engraved; after *t*, the letter *n* was first engraved and later corrected to *h*; this combination at first sight gives *s*; after *h* there is a vertical stroke traced but not engraved; is it the beginning of *m*? In any event, the plural is required. – Under the *h* of *grbth(m)[w]* and just on the edge of the stone, either *h* or *s* depending on the position of the stone when the letter was engraved.

725 – Upper part of a grayish sandstone inscription; photograph in Plate 33. – MaMB 196.

STONE: constant thickness: 15 cm. – *Front:* upper edge damaged; length: 26.6 cm., and width: 27.5. – INSCRIPTION: a great deal of the center has been intentionally erased; the letter height diminishes progressively from 3.5 cm. in line 1 to 2.3 in line 7; space between the lines: 0.3 cm. – SYMBOL: very awkward; for the two inside designs, cp. the central part of Ja 690; cf. Plate B.

1 ⸢**Symbol**⸣ *rbṯw⸤n/wṣdq⸣n/ʾdm/qr*
2 . . .]*w*[. . .
3 *ʾr*[. . . . . .*ẖm*]⸢*r*/⸣*rbṯ*
4 *wn*[/. . . . . .*w*]⸢*qh*⸣⸢*hw/bm*
5 *sʾlhw*[/. . .]⸢/⸣(ʾ)⸤*ṣlmm/bḥm*
6 ⸤*d/mqm/ʾlmqh/bḏt/hʿn/wmtʿn/ʾl*
7 ⸤*mqh/ʿbdhw/rbṯwn/bn/zẖn/wʾ*⸤*ṯ*⸥
8 [*ʾr*]⸤*/twṯbh*⸥*w/wṯʾr*⸤*hw/whbm/*⸥[. .]

1 **Symbol** Rabbṯawân and Ṣadiqân, servants of [the family] Qar-
2 ...
3 ʾr [... ...has vouchsa]fed to Rabbṯa-
4 wân [... ...has or]dered to him through His
5 oracle [... ...] statues in prai-
6 se of the power of ʾIlumquh because ʾIlumquh has assisted and saved
7 His worshipper Rabbṯawân from the wounds and the re-
8 [prisal]s [which] Wahbum had inflicted upon him and [by which] he took vengeance on him..

L. 1: *ṣdqn*, e.g., Ja 859/1, 1st personal name in Ja 881 E/1, Qat (cf. *JaPEQL*, p. 209), name of a tower in RÉS 4648/2; cf. also the name of a clan *ṣdqyn* (RÉS 5085/5) and the personal name *ṣdqm* (e.g., Ja 852/3 and 882 S/1, Qat; cf. *JaPEQL*, p. 216). In RÉS 5035 A, Ḥaḍr, read *ṣdq* instead of *ṣdqn*; the letter *n* belongs to another graffito, B, which begins immediately to the left of A and which reads *rnm* "Ranam".

Ll. 1-2: *qr*[...: several restorations are equally possible; e.g., *qrʿmtn* (e.g., RÉS 4033/2 a), *qrḍn* (e.g., Ja 581/10).

Ll. 7-8: *wʾ*(.)[..]: the letter following ʾ and which is the last of line 7, is either *y* or *ṯ*, but certainly not *ṣ*. According to the first hypothesis, one could refer to Arabic *waqʿ* "blow, knock"; but the second is certainly much better because of the verb *ṯʾr* on line 8. I propose reading *ṯʾr* "retaliation" in plural *ʾṯʾr* "reprisals".

L. 8: *twṯb*, 5th form of *wṯb*, cf. Arabic *waṯaba*, 5th form "to encroach upon someone's property"; here, with the meaning of "to inflict". – *ṯʾr*, cf. *CoRoC*, p. 258 A.

726 – Yellowish, slightly grayish sandstone; photograph in Plate 33. – MaMB 214.

STONE: constant thickness: 8.1 cm. – *Front:* covered with red paint; center of the upper edge badly damaged; 21.6 cm. (top) and 21.3 (bottom) × 17.2. – INSCRIPTION: same disposition of lines as in Ja 623; letter height: from 2.5 cm. to 2.9; space between the lines: from 0.3 cm. to 0.5. – SYMBOL: possibly an awkward imitation of Ja 698; cf. Plate B.

1 **Symbol** *ṯwb⌜m/ḥmẓ/yšr/⌝ʾdm/b*
2 *n/ʿṯkln/hqny/ʾ⌝lmqh/bʿl*
3 *ʾwm/ṣlmn/ḏstwklhw/lwf*
4 *y/bnhw/whbṯwn/bn/yšr/w*
5 *l/sʿdhw/wldm/wmngt/ṣdqm*

1 **Symbol** Ṯawbum, skinner of [the clan] Yašur, servants of the descen-
2 dants of [the tribe] ʿAṯkalân, has dedicated to ʾIlumquh, master of
3 ʾAwwâm, this statue by which he has showed his confidence in Him for the safe-
4 ty of his son Wahabṯawân, descendant of Yašur; and
5 that He may make him happy with a perfect child and security.

L. 1: *ṯwbm*, e.g., Ja 284/1, Qat, and RÉS 4867/4, Ḥaḍr; cf. also *ṯwbn* (e.g., Ja 604/2) and Qat *ṯwybm*, e.g., in Ja 119/1. – *ḥmẓ*: of the 1st letter, the lower vertical stroke and the lower extremity of the upper half remain; the lower half of *m* as well as the extremity of the left oblique stroke of *ẓ* are certain on the stone; cf. Arabic *ḥamaṭa* "to peel, skin, bark"; here, active participle which may be translated "skinner". – *yšr*, also clan name in RÉS 4678/5 (cf. commentary on Ja 552/4); also very well-known Min 2nd name of a man (e.g., RÉS 2813/1); cf. also the Qat name of a man *yšrm* in Ja 852/1, and *yšrn*, 1st family name in Ja 881 B/2, Qat (cf. *JaPEQL*, p. 209). – *ʾdm*, cf. commentary on Ja 689/1.

L. 4: *whbṯwn*, also name of a man in CIH 102/3.

727 – Yellowish, slightly grayish sandstone; photograph in Plate 34. – MaMB 215.

STONE: almost constant thickness: 6.5 cm. – *Front:* center of the upper edge and upper part of the left edge slightly damaged; 32.8 cm. (right) and 32 (left) × 29.8 (top) and 30.3 (bottom). – INSCRIPTION: same disposition of lines as in Ja 559; letter height: maximum 3.3 cm., ordinarily 2.8, but 1.8 in line 10; space between the lines inconsistent, but sometimes 0.2 cm.; *n* is always dextrograde. – SYMBOL, cp. the frame of Ja 707, but in reverse position; cf. Plate B.

1 **Sym-** *sʿdʾwm/ḏʿf*
2 **bol** *m⟨/⟩wbnyh/slmm/bn*
3 *w⟨/⟩ʿfm/ʾmrn/ḥwr/h*
4 *grn/nšqm/wsʿdʾ*
5 *wm/frṯd/mrʾhw*
6 *ʾlmqhw/bʿlʾw*
7 *m/bnhw/slmm/lḥ⟨y⟩w*
8 *grbthmw/whqnyw⟨/⟩ṣ*
9 *lmm/ḏdhbm/wlsʿdnh*
10 *wl⟨d⟩m/wfqlm*

1 **Sym-** Saᶜadᵓawwâm, he of [the family] ᶜAwfum,
2 **bol** and his son Salmum, descendants
3 of [the clan] ᶜAwfum ᵓAmrân, resident of the
4 city [of] Našqum; as for Saᶜadᵓa-
5 wwâm, he entrusted to the care of his lord
6 ᵓIlumquhû, master of ᵓAwwâm,
7 his son Salmum for the life of
8 their persons; and they have dedicated a sta-
9 tue which [is] in bronze; and that He may make him happy
10 with child and harvest.

Ll. 1-2: *ᶜfm* (CIH 361/3: *d̲ᶜfm*), *scriptio defectiva* of *ᶜwfm* (e.g., Ja 576/2; cf. commentary); cf. also the Qat personal name *ᶜwyfm* (Ja 208/1 and commentary), and the Sab clan name *ᶜfn* (cf. *RyGSAS*, p. 562); cf. also the Arabic personal name *ᵓâfîyat* (cf. *SlGaVNPA*, p. 3 B).

L. 2: *slmm*, e.g., RÉS 3547/2; cf. also the Min personal names *slm* (e.g., RÉS 3365) and *slymm* (e.g., RÉS 3063).

L. 3: *ᵓmrn*, cp. the family name *ᵓmrm* (e.g., Ja 660/3-4) and the *nisba* *ᵓmryn* (RÉS 4153/2). – *ḥwr*, e.g., RÉS 4694/1, Ḥaḍr (cf. also *HöBAI*, p. 64) and verb, e.g., in Ja 516/6-7.

Ll. 9-10: *lsᶜdnh wl⟨d⟩m*: the presence of the form *h* (in *bnyh*, line 2) instead of *hw* (in *mrᵓhw*, line 5, and *bnhw*, line 7) makes unnecessary the hypothesis of the haplography of *w* at the beginning of line 10: *lsᶜdnh w⟨/w⟩l⟨d⟩n*.

728 – Yellowish, slightly grayish sandstone; photograph in Plate 34. – MaMB 217.

STONE: constant thickness: 20.3 cm. – *Front:* center of the upper edge largely splintered off; left edge damaged; 32.7 cm. (right) and 32.3 (left) × 22.9. – INSCRIPTION: same disposition of lines as in Ja 552; many small vertical strokes; letter height: from 2.7 cm. to 3.3; space between the lines: from 0.3 cm. to 0.6. – SYMBOL, cf. Ja 603, but the two extremities are horizontal; cf. Plate B.

1 **Sym-** [... .../]⌜*d̲ry*⌝
2 **bol** ⌜*śn/hqny*⌝*w*⌜/ᵓ⌝*lmqhw*⌝
3 *t̲hwn/bᶜl/ᵓwm/ṣlmn/l*⌝
4 *wfy/bnhmw/whbm/wl*
5 *wfyhmw/wl/wzᵓ/ᵓlm*
6 *qh/sᶜdhmw/ᵓwldm/ᵓ*⌝
7 *d̲krwm/hnᵓn/bᶜt̲tr/w*⌟
8 *ᵓlmqh/wbd̲t/ḥmym*⌟

1 **Sym-** ...,] he of [the family] Ray-
2 **bol** śân, have dedicated to ᵓIlumquhû
3 T̲ahwân, master of ᵓAwwâm, this statue for
4 the safety of their son Wahbum and for
5 their own safety; and that may continue ᵓIlum-
6 quh to make them happy with male,
7 pleasing children. By ᶜAt̲tar and
8 ᵓIlumquh and by D̲ât-Ḥimyâm.

Ll. 1-2: *ryśn*, cf. the 1st name of a man *ryś* in RÉS 4934, Qat: *-/bḥt(n)*, and 4953, Qat: *-/ṣlfᶜn* "-Ṣalfaᶜân" (instead of *-/ṣ/fᶜn* or *-/(d̲y)fᶜn* suggested by *RÉS*, VII, p. 447); *ryś* is also the name of a Qat woman in Ja 292/1. Cf. also the Arabic names of a person *raysânat* (cf. *GoAT*, p. 200) and of places *ar-rayyisat*, *raysût* (cf. *MüHG*, p. 55 A) and *raysûn* (cf. *WüR*, p. 107 B). The verb *ryś* is attested, e.g., in RÉS 3910/1.

729 – Yellowish, slightly grayish sandstone block, broken into two parts; photograph in Plate 34. – MaMB 225.

RIGHT SIDE: long vertical hollow. – *Front:* 58.6 cm. (right) and 58.4 (left) × 13.7 (bottom) and 14.7 (top). – INSCRIPTION: same disposition of lines as in Ja 559; two other vertical lines below line 15; letter height: from 2.3 cm. to 3.3; space between the lines: from 1 cm. to 0.5. – SYMBOL: covers line 1 and the last upper fourth of line 2; cp. Ja 690; but here, no inside incision; cf. Plate B.

1 **Symbol** *sᶜdm/šb*
2 *ᶜn/wbnyh*
3 *w/ᶜmrn/hq*
4 *ny/mrᵓh*
5 *mw/ᵓlmqh*
6 *w/bᶜl/ᵓwm*
7 */ṣlmm/d̲d*
8 *hbm/d̲šft*
9 ⌞*h*⌟[*w/k*]⌞*hmy/yld*
10 ⌜*n/lh*⌝*w/d̲krm/*
11 *wh̲mrhmw/ww*
12 *fyw/mrᵓhmw/*
13 *ᵓlmqhw/bᶜ*
14 *l/ᵓwm/d̲šft*
15 *hw/*

1 **Symbol** Saᶜadum Šab-
2 ᶜân and his son
3 ᶜAmrân, has de-
4 dicated to their
5 lord ᵓIlumquhû,
6 master of ᵓAwwâm,
7 a statue which [is] in
8 bronze, which he has promised

9 to Hi[m i]f there would ever be born
10 to him a male child;
11 and He vouchsafed [that] to them; and they
12 paid off to their lord
13 ʾIlumquhû, master
14 of ʾAwwâm, what he had promised
15 to Him.

L. 1: *šbʿn*, also personal name, e.g., in RÉS 2787, Min, family name in Ja 748/2, and name of a sanctuary dedicated to ʾIlumquh (cf. *JaP*, p. 66) and the names of men *šbʿ* (e.g., CIH 52/1) and *šbʿt* (RÉS 4926/1-2).

L. 3: *ʿmrn*, e.g., CIH 722/3; cf. also the names of men *ʿmrm* (e.g., Ja 660/12) and *ʿmrt* (e.g., RÉS 3271/1, Min).

Ll. 9-10: *[k]hmy/yldn/lhw/ḏkrm*, cf. *kmhnmw/yldn/lhw/bnm* in Ja 669/10-11; for *[k]hmy*, cf. Ja 567/10-11.

Ll. 11-12: *wfy*, cf. commentary on Ja 647/15.

730 – Yellowish, slightly grayish sandstone; photograph in Plate 34. – MaMB 226.

STONE: thickness: 12.9 cm. (top) and 11.5 (bottom). – *Front:* upper right corner broken; covered with red paint. – INSCRIPTION: same disposition of lines as in Ja 552; letter height: from 1.8 cm. to 2.1; space between the lines: from 0.2 cm. to 0.4.

1 [**Sym-** *.../w...]hw/rbšms*
2 [**bol** *m/]⌈bnw/ʾ⌉wskrb/ḥwrw/hgr*
3 *[n/.]⌈z⌉rtm/ʾdm/bn/sẖymm/hqnyw*
4 *ʾlmqhṯhwnbʿlʾwm/ṣlmn/ḏṣly*
5 *fʿm/lsʿdhmw/nʿmtm/wwfy/gr*
6 *ybthmw/wl/sʿdhmw/ʾṯmrm/nʾd*
7 *m/ʿdy/ʾʿnbhmw/wʿbrthmw/wl/ṭʿ*
8 *⌊mn/lhmw/ʾfql/yfqlnn/ʿdy/byth*
9 *mw/wlsʿdhmw/ḥẓy/wrḍw/ʾmrʾhm*
10 *w/wšʿbhmw/wl/ẖrynhmw/bn/nḍʿ/w*
11 *šṣy/šnʾm/bʾlmqhṯhwnbʿlʾwm*

1 [**Sym-** ...and] his [...] Rabbšams-
2 [**bol** um,] descendants of ʾAwskarib, residents of [the] city [of]
3 [.]zratum, servants of the descendants [the tribe] Suẖaymum, have dedicated to
4 ʾIlumquh Ṯahwân, master of ʾAwwâm, this statue in solid
5 clay in order that He may make them happy with prosperity and the safety of their
6 persons and that He may make them happy with magnificent fruits
7 in their vineyards and their river-side fields and that He may give
8 them the taste of the harvests [that] they shall gather in their house
9 and that He may make them happy with the esteem and grace of their lords
10 and of their tribe and that He may protect them against the hostility and
11 wickedness of [any] enemy. By ʾIlumquh Ṯahwân, master of ʾAwwâm.

Ll. 1-2: *rbšms[m]*, more frequently used than *rbšms*, is certain because the width of the symbol ordinarily equals that of four signs; two signs are thus missing at the beginning of line 2 and *m/* fits the blank perfectly.

L. 1: between *w* and *hw*, one may restore either *bn* "son of" or *ʾẖ(y)* "brother of".

L. 2: *ʾwskrb*: the two elements of this proper name are very well known.

L. 3: *[.]zrtm*, cf. the Arabic names of places *buzrat* and *ḥazrat* (cf. *WüR*, pp. 34 C and 69 C respectively), etc. and also the Min family name *ḥzrn* (RÉS 3761/2).

L. 4: *ṣly*, cf. Arabic *ṣalā* (i) "to roast" (cf. Hebrew noun *ṣâlî* "roast") and *ṣallat* "dry ground"; I propose translating *ṣly* as "clay".

L. 5: *fʿm*, cf. Arabic *faʿm* "full"; here, with the meaning of "solid".

Ll. 7-8: the root *ṭʿm* means "taste (of the food)" (cf. *KoBaLVTL*, p. 355 A, *LaGD*, p. 2208, *JeHoDISO*, p. 102: *ṭʿm₁*); here, 2nd form with the meaning "to give to taste"; *l/ṭʿmn/lhmw/ʾfql* "that He may give them to taste the harvests".

731 – Yellowish, slightly grayish sandstone; photograph in Plate 35. – MaMB 228.

STONE: constant thickness: 14.3 cm. – *Front:* corners broken; the upper part of the left edge and the lower half of the right edge are splintered off; length: 16.1 cm., and width: 22.2. – INSCRIPTION: same disposition of lines as in Ja 552; letter height: from 2.7 cm. to 2.3; space between the lines: 0.6 cm. and 0.5. – SYMBOL: cp. Ja 582; cf. Plate B.

1 **Sym-** *nʿmt/ḏt/d⌈ḏḥm⌉*
2 **bol** *d/ʾmh/bn/ẖḏwt⌋*
3 *hqnyt/ʾlmqh/bʿl/⌉[ʾ]*
4 *wm/ṣlmtn/ḥmdm/bḏ⌉*
5 *[t/]mtʿ/whʿnn/bnthw*
6 *[r]bbtgwbn/bn/kl/ʾ*
7 *⌊mrḍ⌋/mrḍt/b⌊ʾlm⌊qh⌉*

1 **Sym-** Naʿamat, she of Dôdḥam-
2 **bol** ad, maidservants of the descendants of Ḥaḏwat,
3 has dedicated to ʾIlumquh, master of [ʾA-]
4 wwâm, this female statue in praise becau-
5 [se] He has saved and protected her daughter
6 [Ra]bîbatgawbân from all the di-
7 seases she was suffering. By ʾIlumquh.

L. 1: *nʿmt*, also name of a woman, e.g., in RÉS 3924, but of a man in RÉS 4854 B/4, Ḥaḍr; cf. also the proper names *nʿm* (e.g., Ja 869/1, Qat: woman), and *hnʿmt* (e.g., Ja 868/1, Qat: family); the gender of *nʿmt* in Ja 246/1, Qat (cf. commentary on this text and also on Ja 152) is unknown; in RÉS 5057/1, read *ṯʿmm* instead of *nʿmm*.

Ll. 1-2: *ddḥmd*, same formation as that, e.g., of *ddsmy* (Ja 722/2).

L. 2: the plural *ʾmh* refers to the two feminine personal names which precede, and not to the clan name which follows; cf. also *ʾdm*, e.g., in Ja 689/1.

L. 6: *rbbtgwbn*, the 1st element is also the name of a woman, e.g., in CIH 179/2; for the 2nd part, cf., e.g., the Arabic name *ǧawbân* (cf., e.g., *GoAT*, p. 691: place and *LöHSM*, p. 60 B: man); cf. also the Arabic names of places *ǧawbat*, *ǧûbat* (cf. *WüR*, p. 62 B), *ǧawb* (cf. *MüHG*, p. 27 B), and *ǧawbânân* (cf. *GoAT*, p. 691) and of men *ǧawb* (cf., e.g., *MüHG*, p. 137 B), *al-ǧuwâbî* (cf. *SlGaVNPA*, p. 18 A) and *ǧwbyn* (cf. *GoAT*, p. 110); cf. also the Min noun *gwb* (RÉS 2980 bis/4) "interstice".

732 – Left part of a yellowish, slightly grayish sandstone inscription; photograph in Plate 35. – MaMB 229.

STONE: maximum thickness: 11 cm. – *Front:* 7.8 cm. (top), 10 (bottom), and 13.8 (top of line 9). – INSCRIPTION: same disposition of lines as in Ja 559; letter height: from 2.1 cm. to 2.5; space between the lines: from 0.3 cm. to 0.5.

1 *. . .]ḏʾlm/h⸢q⸣*
2 *[ny/ʾlmqh]⸢bʿlʾwm/ṣ*
3 *[lmn/ḏhbn/]⸢lwfy/bnh*
4 *[w/. . /wl]⸤sʿdhmw/ʾlm*
5 *[qh/nʿmt/w]⸢mngt/ṣd⸤qm⸥*
6 *[wlẖmrhmw]/ʾlmqh/wfy*
7 *[grybthm]w/wlwzʾ/ʾlm*
8 *[qh/hʿnh]mw/bn/bʾstm*
9 *[wlsʿdhw/]⸤ʾ⸥lmqh/ḥẓy</>m*
10 *[rʾyhw/kr]⸤b⸥(ʿ)ṯt/wyhʿ*
11 *[n/. . . . . ./]bʾlmqh*

1 . . .,] he of [the family] ʾIlum, has dedi-
2 [cated to ʾIlumquh,] master of ʾAwwâm, [this] sta-
3 [tue in bronze] for the safety of hi[s] son
4 . . ., and that] ʾIlum[quh] may make them happy
5 [with] perfect [prosperity and] security;
6 [and that] ʾIlumquh [may vouchsafe to them] the safety
7 [of thei]r [persons;] and that ʾIlum[quh] may con-
8 tinue [to assist t]hem from misfortunes;
9 [and that] ʾIlumquh [may make him happy] with the esteem of
10 [his two] l[ords Kari]bʿaṯat and Yuhʿi-
11 [n. . . . . .] By ʾIlumquh.

L. 1: *ʾlm*, also family name, e.g., in RÉS 3553/1, Qat; *ʾlm* is especially known as the name of a temple dedicated to the Ḥaḍr lunar god in Šabwat and Sumhurâm (cf. *JaIHB*, pp. 159, 162-65, and *JaNA*); in RÉS 4595 B, read *klmn* instead of *ʾlmn*; cf. also the personal name *tbʿʾlm* in RÉS 4616.

Ll. 2-3: *ṣlmn*: the 1st letter was engraved as ʾ; the worker then engraved a circle on top of the lower vertical stroke of the characteristic part of ʾ, part of which was not erased.

733 – Yellowish, slightly grayish sandstone; photograph in Plate 35. – MaMB 230.

STONE: almost constant thickness: 10 cm. – *Front:* upper left and right edges damaged; 37.5 cm. (top) and 37 (bottom) × 76.5 (right) and 73 (left). INSCRIPTION: same disposition of lines as in Ja 552; letter height: from 2.8 cm. to 3; space between the lines: from 0.4 cm. to 0.5. – SYMBOL, cp. Ja 589; cf. Plate B.

1 **Sym-** *sʿdm/ʾrym/wbnyhw/hʿ⸢n⸣*
2 **bol** *wṯwbn/wšrḥʾwm/bnw/ḏḥy*
3 *wm/hqnyw/mrʾhmw/ʾlmqhwṯhwn*
4 *ṯwrbʿlmbʿlʾwm/ʾrbʿtn/ʾṣl*
5 *mn/ḏhbm/ḥmdm/bḏt/ẖmr/ʿbdhw/sʿ*
6 *dm/ʾrym/ḏḥywm/ʾwldm/ʾḏkrm/hn*
7 *ʾm/wlwzʾ/ẖmrhmw/mrʾhmw/ʾlmq*
8 *hw/ḥṣy/wrḍw/ʾmrʾhmw/ʾmlkn/*
9 *wlmtʿnhmw/mrʾhmw/ʾlmqw/bn/šṣ*
10 *⸢y/⸣šnʾm/wlẖmrnhmw/mrʾhmw/ʾlm*
11 *qhw/ʾṯmrm/wʾfqlm/wlẖmrnhmw*

12 */mrʾhmw/ʾlmqhw/nʿmtm/wʾʾr*
13 *ẖ/ṣdqm/wḥyw/grybthmw/wbr*
14 *y⌊/⌋⌊mqymtm/bʾlmqhwbʿlʾwm*

1 **Sym-** Saʿdum ʾAryam and his sons Haʿin
2 **bol** and Ṯawbân and Šaraḥʾawwâm, descendants of Ḥay-
3 ûm, have dedicated to their lord ʾIlumquhû Ṯahwân
4 Ṯawr Baʿalum, master of ʾAwwâm, these four statu-
5 es in bronze in praise because He has vouchsafed to His worshipper Saʿ-
6 dum ʾAryam, him of Ḥayûm, male, pleasing children;
7 and that their lord ʾIlumquhû may continue to vouchsafe to them
8 the esteem and grace of their lords the kings;
9 and that their lord ʾIlumqû may save them from the wicked-
10 ness of [any] enemy; and that their lord ʾIlumquhû may vouchsafe to
11 them fruits and harvests; and that may vouchsafe to them
12 their lord ʾIlumquhû prosperity and under-
13 takings perfect and [also] the life of their persons and the strength
14 of power. By ʾIlumquhû, master of ʾAwwâm.

L. 1: *hʿn*, also name of a man in RÉS 5095/1; cf. also the name of a man *hʿnm* (e.g., RÉS 4574/1).
L. 4: the top of the word divider before *ʾrbʿtn* looks like the incomplete appendage of *l*.

734 – Lower part of a yellowish, slightly grayish sandstone inscription; broken on the left; photograph in Plate 35. – MaMB 233.

STONE: constant thickness: 24.8 cm. – *Front:* maximum length (center of line 3): 32 cm., and width: 31 (right). – INSCRIPTION: letter height: from 3 cm. to 3.3; space between the lines: 0.5 cm.

1 *.../b]*
2 *⌜rṯ/hšʾmhm⌝[w]⌜/wḥmdm/bḏt/⌝[...*
3 *y/ʾlmqhw/bqlm/wyhʿn/bny/[...*
4 *ḏḥḏnn/wʾmhhw/ʾlt/škrt.[...*
5 *bythn/wḏqnyy/bn/hwt/[brṯn/... /w]*
6 *l/sʿdhmw/ʾlmqh/nʿmtm/[wmngt/ṣdqm]*
7 *wl/ẖrynhmw/bn/šsy/šnʾm/bʿṯ⌊ṯ⌋[r/whw]*
8 *bs/wʾlmqh/wbḏt/ḥmym/wbḏ[t/bʿdnm]*

1 ...pla-]
2 ce [which] He caused them to buy, and in praise because [...
3 ʾIlumquhû Baqilum and Yuhʿin, descendants (or sons) [of...
4 of [the clan] Ḥaḏnân and his maidservants, those of [the family] Šakrat [...
5 the two houses and what they both have acquired from this [place... ; and]
6 that ʾIlumquh may make them happy with [perfect] prosperity [and security;]
7 and may He preserve them from the wickedness of [any] enemy. By ʿAṯta[r and Haw-]
8 bas and ʾIlumquh and by Ḏât-Ḥimyâm and by Ḏâ[t-Baʿdânum.]

L. 1: *hšʾm*, 4th form of *šʾm*.
L. 4: *ḥḏnn*, also clan name in CIH 410/2; cf. also the personal name *ḥḏn* (e.g., RÉS 3735, Min), the 2nd name of a man *ʾḥḏn* (Ja 495/1; cf. commentary on Ja 700/2), and the name of a city *ḥḏnm* (RÉS 3945/11; cf. *WiHöBGS*, p. 64). The root *ḥḏn* is also attested in the name of a man *m(ḥ)ḏnm* in RÉS 4898/2, Ḥaḏr (instead of *m...* in *BePC*, p. 332, and *RÉS*, VII, p. 409). – *škrt*, name of a man in Liḥyanite (cf. *JaSaMA*, p. 523, No. 345/1) and of a woman in Thamudic (cf. *vdBrIT*, p. 447: Jsa 642); cf. also *škr*, name of a man in RÉS 4264/1, Min, in Liḥyanite (cf. *JaSaMA*, p. 469, No. 136) and in Safaitic (cf. *LiSI*, p. 345 A), the Sab personal name *škrʾl* (cf. *RyGSAS*, p. 559), the Qat name of a man *škrm* (Ja 343 A/1), and also the Arabic names of places *šakr*, *šakar* (cf. *WüR*, p. 131 A), of clans *škr* (cf. *WüR*, p. 248 B), *banû šâkir* (cf. *WüID*, 257/17), of men *šikur* (cf. *HeBN*, p. 33 A), *šākir* (cf. *LiEHA*, p. 85 A), (*ʾibn*) *škr*, *šakrân* (cf. *WüR*, p. 472), *bû-šakûr*, *bû-šikârat* (cf. *SlGaVNPA*, p. 12), *yaškur* (cf. *WüID*,2 5/3), and of persons *šâkir*, *šakîr*, and *miškûr* (cf. *SlGaVNPA*, pp. 12 A and 36 A respectively).

735 – Two yellowish, slightly grayish pieces of sandstone; top (photograph in Plate 36) = MaMB 234; bottom = MaMB 288 = Ja 754.

TOP: *stone:* maximum thickness (upper right corner): 28.2 cm.; *front*, covered with red paint, right half of the upper right edge splintered off, upper part of the left edge and left end of the lower edge damaged, 70 cm. × 34.3 (right) and 34 (left). – BOTTOM: *stone:* thickness: 25.5 cm. (right) and 16.5 (left); *front*, covered with red paint; upper right corner broken; 70.7 cm. × 32.7. – INSCRIPTION: same disposition of lines as in Ja 559; letter height:

from 2.7 cm. to 2.5; space between the lines: from 0.7 cm. to 0.5; *n* is always dextrograde (cf. Ja 727); lines 1-10 = MaMB 234, and lines 11-19 = MaMB 288. – SYMBOL, cp. Ja 589, but the two curved inside incisions are replaced by twelve oblique ones; cf. Plate B.

1 **Sym-**⌝ *[šʿbn/sbʾ/khln/]ʿd⟨/⟩hgrn/mrb/wʾsrrhw/ khln/ʾsd*⌟

2 **bol** *ʾḏ⌜hbn/hq⌝nyw/mrʾhmw/ʾlmqhbʿlʾwm/ ṣlmnhn/ḏ yḏhbm/ḥ*

3 *mdm/bḏt/ẖmr/wtbšrn/ʾdmhw/šʿbn/sbʾ/ khln/kyẖmrn/w*

4 *sqy/brq/ẖrf/bwrẖ/ḏʾbhy/ḏẖrf/tbʿkrb/bn/wddʾl/bn/ kbr/ẖ*

5 *ll/tsʿn/lqbly/ḏhẖb/sqy/wḏnm/ʾrḍn/mrb/wʾsrrhw/ wʾklʾhw*

6 *ṯlṯ/ʾbrqm/bqdmy/ḏt/brq/wybsw/ʾmṭrn/whmḥlt/kl/ ʾsrr/w*

7 *ʾklʾ/mrb/wmwt/ḏbn/ʾʿmdn/bn/ṣmʾm/wybs/ḏbn/ʾbʾrn/ wsbʾ*

8 *w/kl/šʿbn/sbʾ/wbnt/mrb/bʿbr/ʾlmqh/ʿdy/mḥrmn/ ḏʾwm/wsf*

9 *ḥw/rqthmw/wtʿrbn/lmrʾhmw/ʾlmqh/wʾnṯn/ʿṭwfhn/ wstml*

10 *ʾw/wtbšrn/bʿm/mrʾhmw/ʾlmqh/lẖmrhmw/sqy/ whġṯn/mrb⟨/⟩w*

---

11 *[ʾm]⌞ṭrn/wʾsrrn/[w.. ..hmw]/ʾlmqhw/ʾmrm/ frʿm/kysqynhmw/wsʾr⟨/⟩b*

12 *[n/]⌜hwt/ywmn/tʾtww/bn/mn/mḥrmn/ḏʾwm/ḏnm/ wmẓʾ/ḏʿbn/bl*

13 *[l]yn/wmlʾw/ʾmṭrn/wsqyw/kl/ʾsrrn/ḏrm/wwzʾw/ hrʿln*

14 *[n]/wsqy/kl/ʾnẖln/wʾrḍtn/šfqm/ʾsyṭm/ʿsmm/wbʿdnh*

15 *w/fhfsw/mnfstn/wḏnm/kl/ʾklʾn/wḥmdw/ʾdmhw/šʿb*

16 *n/sbʾ/khln/ẖyl/wmqm/mrʾhmw/ʾlmqhbʿlʾwm/bḏt/ ẖm()r*

17 */whwfyn/h(y)t/brqn/ḥgn/tbšr/ʾdmhw/wlwzʾ/ ʾlmqhbʿlʾwm*

18 */ʾdmhw/šʿbn/sbʾ/khln/hwfyn/lhmw/kl/ʾmlʾ/wtbšr/ yzʾnn*

19 *stmlʾn/wtbšrn/bʿmhw/bʾlmqhbʿlʾwm*

1 **Sym-** [The tribe Sabaʾ Kahilân] in the city [of] Mârib and its valleys Kahilân, those of

2 **bol** the irrigated lands, have dedicated to their lord ʾIlumquh, master of ʾAwwâm, these two statues, both in bronze, in

3 praise because He has vouchsafed and predicted to His worshippers, the tribe Sabaʾ Kahilân that He would vouchsafe and

4 irrigate the lightning season of autumn in the month of ʾAbhay of the year of Tabaʿkarib, son of Waddʾil, descendant of the Leader of Ḫa-

5 lil, the 9th, because of this: has deceived the irrigation and the rain of the land [of] Mârib and of its valleys and of its pastures [during the]

6 three lightning seasons before this lightning season; and the irrigated fields have dried up; and all the wâdî-side valleys became barren as well as

7 the pastures of Mârib, and some part of the naturally watered fields have died from drought; and some of the wells have dried up; and have contended

8 the whole tribe Sabaʾ and the daughters of Mârib against ʾIlumquh in the temple, the one of ʾAwwâm, and they have

9 displayed their sorcery and they have given pledges of submission to their lord ʾIlumquh and [also] loving wives; and they have besought

10 and begged of their lord ʾIlumquh that He would vouchsafe to them to irrigate and water with rain Mârib and

11 the [irrigated] field[s] and the wâdî-side valleys [; and... ...them] ʾIlumquhû optimum cereals so that they could irrigate them; and [the] rest fr[om]

12 this very day they withdrew from the temple, the one of ʾAwwâm, [because of the] rain; and the waves came during the

13 n[i]ght and filled the irrigated fields and irrigated all the wâdî-side valleys, spreading far and wide; and they continued to move forward

14 and to irrigate all the palm groves and the grounds [with] plentiful, desired water ponds; and after that,

15 [the water from] the distributors and [the water from the] rain have covered all the pastures; and have praised His worshippers, the tribe

16 Sabaʾ Kahilân, the strength and the power of their lord ʾIlumquh, master of ʾAwwâm, because He has vouchsafed

17 and granted this lightning season as He announced to His worshippers; and that ʾIlumquh, master of ʾAwwâm, may continue,

18 [as far as] His worshippers, the tribe Sabaʾ Kahilân [are concerned], to bestow upon them all the favors and announcements [for which] they shall continue to

19 beseech and beg of Him. By ʾIlumquh, master of ʾAwwâm.

L. 2: *ḏhb*, plural *ʾḏhb*, cf. *CoRoC*, p. 128 B, *RoVSAY*, p. 303 and *JaDME*, p. 10; *LuYFS* (p. 13, note 21) alludes to *PiPISA*'s opinion on *ḏhb*, but fails to mention that A. F. L. Beeston had already rejected it in *BiO*, 16 (1959), p. 79 B.

L. 5: *hẖb*, cf. commentary on Ja 653/5.

L. 6: *ybs*, verb; cf. the noun, e.g., in Ja 576/2. – *mṭr*, cf. RÉS 2952/3, Min, and commentary; cf. also Soqoṭri *méṭere* "vallée" (cf. *LeLS*, p. 242);

in *RyET* (p. 43, commentary on Fakhry 71/8), read *mṭîra* and 56 B instead of *mṭîr* and 57 respectively. – *hmḥlt*, 4th form of *mḥl*; cf. Arabic *maḥala*, 4th form "to be sterile, barren (a dried field)"; for the feminine ending, compare Arabic: verb preceding a subject which does not refer to men.

L. 7: *ṣmʾ*, cf. Hebrew *ṣâmâʾ* "thirst"; cf. also the verb *ẓmʾ* (Ja 750/6) and its derived Qat adjective *mẓmʾt* (RÉS 3858/11), plural of *mẓmʾ*, cf. Arabic *maẓmaʾîy* "watered [only] by rain"; another example of the equivalence of *ṣ* and *ẓ* (cf. also *ḥṣy* and *ḥẓy*).

Ll. 8-9: *sfḥ*, cf. modern Ḥaḍr *sfḥ* "to throw, pour (out), shed" (cf. *LaH*, p. 608); here with the derived meaning of "to display".

L. 9: *rqt*, cf. Arabic *ruqyat* "sorcery, witchcraft, magic", from the root *rqy*. – *ʿṭwf* (cf. *ʿṭf* in RÉS 3956/3), cf. Arabic *ʿaṭûf* "(A woman) loving to her husband, affectionate to her child(ren)" (cf. *LaAEL*, p. 2081 C).

L. 10: *hġṯ*, 4th form of *ġyṯ* (not *ġwṯ* which is mentioned by *CoRoC*, p. 215 B); cf. Arabic *ġâṯa* (i) "to water with rain; fall upon (rain)" (cf. *LaAEL*, p. 2314 A-B).

L. 11: [*ʾm*][*ṯrn*: of *ṯ*, the left rectangle remains; cf. lines 6 and 13 where this noun is also mentioned, however not immediately, with *ʾsrr*. – ..*hmw*] refers to the subjects of the inscription and was preceded by a verb such as "to grant, give". – *frʿm*, cf. commentary on Ja 615/18-19.

Ll. 11-12: *sʾr*, e.g., RÉS 2894/5, Min; cf. also the verb, e.g., in Ja 575/6.

L. 12: *tʾtw*, 5th form of *ʾtw* (e.g., Ja 550/2); may be translated "to withdraw, draw back, go away". – *bn/mn*: double preposition of removal.

Ll. 12-13: *bl*[*l*]*yn*, e.g., Ja 619/9.

L. 13: *ḏrm* has nothing to do with the following Qat names, *ḏrmm* (e.g., Ja 140/1) and *ḏrmt* (e.g., Ja 123); for the interpretation of *t* ending in Qat personal names, cf. *JaDME*, pp. 12-15; in the two texts where the genus of *ḏrmt* is mentioned, the name is feminine: Ja 319 and Blaymires 3/1, where *BeOSA* (p. 21) writes that *ḏrmt* "should no doubt be related etymologically to Hebrew *zerem* 'heavy rain'"; however, Arabic *ḏarama* "to give birth once (a woman which is being confined)" is more suitable than "heavy rain". In the present text, *ḏrm* is the mimated active participle (*ḏârr*) of the 1st form of *ḏrr*, the 4th form of which, *hḏr*, is mentioned in Ja 575/4 (cf. commentary). – *hrʿl*, 4th form of *rʿl*, cf. Arabic *raʿala*, 1st and 4th forms "to pierce, give a strong blow"; the Hebrew hophal means "to be shaken"; here, *hrʿl* may be translated "to move"; cf. the noun *rʿlt* in the very fragmentary text RÉS 4760 A/2.

L. 14: *ʾsyṭ*, plural of *syṭ*; cf. Arabic *sawṭ*, plural *ʾaswâṭ* "a place where water collects and stagnates" (cf. *LaAEL*, p. 1467 B) and "water pond". – *ʿsmm*, mimated adjective; cf. commentary on Ja 574/9: *ḏʿsm*.

L. 15: *hfsw*, plural of the 4th form of *nfs*; here *hfs* apparently has the same meaning as *tanaffasa*, 5th form of Arabic *nafusa*, "to increase, sprinkle" (cf. *LaAEL*, pp. 2826 C-2827 A) and means "to cover (water)". – *mnfst*, plural of *mnfs* (RÉS 3309/2, Min); here, *mnfst* and *ḏnm* do not refer to distributors and rain directly, but to the water itself.

L. 17: *h*(*y*)*t* (cf. commentary on Ja 585/7): *hwt* in my notebook.

736 – Yellowish, slightly grayish sandstone; photograph. – MaMB 239.

STONE: thickness: 18.2 cm. (top) and 10 (bottom). – *Front:* lateral edges slightly damaged; 25.3 cm. × 74.1. – INSCRIPTION: same disposition of lines as in Ja 552; letter height: from 2.4 cm. to 2.9; space between the lines: from 0.5 cm. to 0.6. – SYMBOL, cf. Ja 559; the photograph cannot be used satisfactorily as the basis for a drawing.

1 **Sym-** *šrḥm/ʾzʾd/wbny*
2 **bol** *hw/krbʿṯt/wʾbkr*
3 *b/bnw/ḏḥḍnn/bqlm/hq*
4 *nyw/mrʾhmw/ʾlmqhw/ṯw*
5 *n/bʿl/ʾwm/ṣlmm/ḏḏhbm*
6 */ḏšfthw/kmʿnmw/kyẖm*
7 *rnhw/bnn/ʾḏkrm/hnʾm*
8 */wrʾ/kẖmrhw/ʾlmqhw/*
9 *bnyhw/krbʿṯt/wʾbkrb*
10 */whwfy/lmrʾhmw/ḏšfth*
11 *w/wyẓʾn/hwfyn/ʾṣlmm/*
12 *kmʿ⌈h⌉nmw/yẖmrnhw/ʾḏkr*
13 *m/hnʾn/wyẖmrhmw/ḥyw*
14 */grbthmw/wḥẓy/ʾmrʾh*
15 *mw/ʾmlkn/wʾṯmrm/wʾfq*
16 *lm/hnʾm/wymtʿnhmw/b*
17 *n/ṭwʿ/wnḍʿ/wšṣy/šnʾ*
18 *m/bʾlmqhw/bʿl/ʾwm*

1 **Sym-** Šarḥum ʾAzʾad and his two
2 **bol** sons Karibʿaṯat and ʾAbkar-
3 ib, descendants of Ḥaḍrân Baqilum, have

4 dedicated to their lord ʾIlumquhû Ṯaw-
5 ân, master of ʾAwwâm, a statue which [is] in bronze,
6 which he had promised to Him in the hope that He would some day
7 vouchsafe to him male, pleasing sons;
8 and now ʾIlumquhû has vouchsafed to him
9 his two sons Karibʿaṯat and ʾAbkarib;
10 and he has offered to their lord what he has promised to
11 him; and he will continue to offer statues
12 whenever He will vouchsafe to him pleasing
13 males; and that He may vouchsafe to them the life
14 of their persons and the esteem of their lords,
15 the kings, and [also] pleasing fruits and
16 harvests; and that He may save them from
17 the constraint and hostility and wickedness of [any] enemy.
18 By ʾIlumquhû, master of ʾAwwâm.

Ll. 4-5: *ṯwn* instead of *ṯhwn* is certain on the stone and already attested in Ja 664/19.

Ll. 6-7, cf. *JaPDSM*, p. 179.

L. 7: *bnn* is certain on the stone; cf. Arabic *ʾibn*, plural *banûn* "son".

Ll. 11-13, cf. *JaPDSM*, pp. 176-77.

737 – Bottom of a yellowish, slightly grayish sandstone inscription; photograph in Plate 36. – MaMB 240.

STONE: thickness: 19.7 cm. (top) and 20.5 (bottom). – *Front:* a thin splinter has scaled off over a large area; left corners broken; 54.6 cm. (right) × 40.7 (top). – INSCRIPTION: same disposition of lines as in Ja 561 bis; letter height: 4.5 cm.; space between the lines: 0.5 cm.

1 *⌜mhn⌜k⌝rb/rz⌜ḥ⌝ym/ʾwldm/ʾḏk*
2 *rm/hnʾm/wl/wśy/bny/gdnm*
3 *wl/wśyhmw/wl/hʿnnhmw/bn*
4 *nḍʿ/wšṣy/šnʾm/rhqm/wqrb*
5 *m/bʿṯtr/whwbs/wʾlmqhw*
6 *wbḏt/ḥmym/wbḏt/bʿdnm*

1 Mâhinkarib Razḥayum male, pleasing
2 children; and that He may comfort the descendants of Gadanum;
3 and that He may comfort them; and that He may preserve them from
4 the hostility and wickedness of [any] enemy, remote and near.
5 By ʿAṯtar and Hawbas and ʾIlumquhû
6 and by Ḏât-Ḥimyâm and by Ḏât-Baʿdânum.

The last missing line was probably ended by *ʿbdhw* "His worshipper" preceded by the name of the god *ʾlmqh(w)*; the verb was, e.g., *ẖmr*, *(w)śf*, etc.

L. 1: *mhnkrb*, cf. Arabic *mahnat* "service, ministration" and *mahîn* "contemptible, abject" (cf. *LaAEL*, p. 3025 C); cf. also the Arabic place name *mahnûn* (cf. *MüHG*, p. 110 B). – *rzḥym*, cf. the proper names *rzḥ* (CIH 24/5) and *rzḥn* (e.g., RÉS 4020); cf. also the Arabic names of a man *rizâḥ* (cf., e.g., *GoAT*, p. 193), of clans, *razâḥ* (cf. *WüR*, p. 245 B), *banû rizâḥ* (cf. *SaIS*, p. 77 B) and of a place *râziḥ* (cf. *MüHG*, p. 49 B).

L. 2: *wśy*, cf. Arabic *wâsā*, 3rd form of **wsy*, "to console, comfort".

738 – Yellowish, slightly grayish sandstone. – MaMB 247.

STONE: almost constant thickness: 11.6 cm. – *Front:* 21.4 cm. (top) and 20.8 (bottom) × 32.7 (right) and 32.4 (left). – INSCRIPTION: same disposition of lines as in Ja 561 bis; letter height: 2.1 cm. and 2.2; space between the lines: 0.3 cm. and 0.4; distance between line 1 and the upper edge: 0.8 cm. (right) and 0.7 (left). – SYMBOL, cf. Ja 690.

1 **Sym-** *yḥmd/wʾẖyhw/mḥmd*
2 **bol** *m/wbnyhw/ḥywʿṯtr*
3 *bnw/gldn/ʾḥmln/hqnyw*
4 *ʾlmqhṯhwnbʿlʾwm/ṣlm*
5 *m/ḏḏhbm/ḏšfthw/ḥmd*
6 *m/bḏt/ẖmrhmw/ʾlmqh/wl*
7 *dm/ḏkrm/lhmw/wlwzʾ/ẖm*
8 *rhmw/ʾwldm/ʾḏkrm/hnʾm/b*
9 *n/ʾṯthmw/bnt/ḏt/gldn/wʾ*
10 *ṯmrm/wʾfqlm/ṣdqm/hnʾm*
11 *wlwfy/grybthmw/bʾlm*
12 *qh*

1 **Sym-** Yaḥmad and his brother Maḥmûd-
2 **bol** um and his son Ḥayûʿaṯtar,
3 descendants of Gildân, the Ḥumlânites, have dedicated to
4 ʾIlumquh Ṯahwân, master of ʾAwwâm, a statue
5 which [is] in bronze, which he had promised to Him in praise
6 because ʾIlumquh has vouchsafed to them a male
7 child of their own; and that He may continue to vouchsa-
8 fe to them male, pleasing children from
9 their wives, daughters of [the house] Gildân, and [also]
10 perfect, pleasing fruits and harvests;
11 and that He may protect their persons. By ʾIlum-
12 quh.

Ll. 1-2: *mḥmdm*, e.g., CIH 353/1 (see infra) (not *mḥmmdm* as in *CIH*, and even less *mḥmmd* as in

RyISA, XVI, p. 115) and Ootacamund[1]; cf. also *mḥmd* (CIH 420/1; *RyISA*, *l.c.*, erroneously states that "CIH 420 porte *mḥmdm*").

L. 3: *gldn*, cf. the Arabic names of a place *ǧldyt* (cf. *WüR*, p. 60 A), of men *ǧald* (cf. *LöHSM*, p. 59 B), *ʾabû l-ǧald* (cf., e.g., *SaIS*, p. 41 B), *ǧilîdî*, *ǧilûdî* (cf. *SlGaVNPA*, p. 17), *ʾabû ǧldt*, *al-ǧlwdy* (cf. *GoAT*, p. 106), *ʾabû* and *ibn al-muǧâlid* (cf. *GoAT*, p. 498) and *muǧâlid* (cf., e.g., *WüR*, p. 633), and of persons *ǧillâd* and *miǧâlid* (cf. *SlGaVNPA*, pp. 17 A and 36 B respectively); the preceding name of a man *al-ǧlwdy* as well as the place name *ǧalûd* (cf. *WüR*, p. 60 B), both derived from the root *ǧld*, must be compared with the Min family name *glwd* (RÉS 3752), which *RyNP* (I, p. 222 bis A) derives from the root *ǧlw* and interprets as *gl* + *wd* "splendor of Wadd".

739 – Yellowish, slightly grayish sandstone. – MaMB 248.

STONE: almost constant thickness: 15.5 cm. – *Front:* upper edge badly damaged; the upper right edge is largely splintered off; two large holes in the upper and lower part. – INSCRIPTION: same disposition of lines as in Ja 552; letter height: 1.1 cm. and 1.3; space between the lines: 0.3 cm. and 0.4; personal names on lines 2 and 13 intentionally erased. – FLOWER, at the beginning of line 20; cf. Ja 690, but here, there is no frame; another flower was engraved at the end of line 20.

1 **[Sym-]** *s˺ʿd[šmsm/ . . . . . . /mq]*
2 *twy⌊/⌋[nmrn/ʾwkn]/wʾẖ yhw/*
[bol] *˹g˺[ḥ]˹ḍ˺[m/ʾḥ]*
3 *ṣn/bny/kbrẖll/wkbrʾqynm/wḏ*
4 *[sẖ]ymm/hqny/ʾlmqhbʿlʾwm/ṣlmn/ḏḏ*
5 *[h]bn/ḏbhw/ḥmd/ẖyl/wmqm/ʾlmqhb*
6 *ʿlʾwm/bḏt/hwfy/ʿbdhw/sʿdšm*
7 *sm/bkl/ʾmlʾ/stmlʾ/wtbšrn/bʿ*
8 *mhw/wrʾ/khwfy/ʿbdhw/sʿdšms˹m˺*
9 *bn/kl/sbʾt/sbʾ/wġzw/bʿm/ʾʿrbn*
10 *⟨b⟩ʾrḍ/mḍḥyn/wrdmn/wqtbn/wbḏt/ẖmr*
11 *hw/mhrgm/wġnmm/ḏhrḍw/lbhw/wl*
12 *wzʾ/ʾlmqh/sʿd/[ʿbdhw/sʿdš]ms*
13 *m/ḥẓy/wrḍw/mr(ʾ)[yhmw/nmrn/ʾwk]*
14 *n/wʾẖ yhw/gḥḍm/[ʾḥṣn/w]˹r˺ḍw/šʿb*
15 *hmw/bklm/wlwzʾ/ʾlm˹qh/˺hwfyn/ʿ*
16 *bdhw/sʿdšmsm/bkl/ʾmlʾ/ystm*
17 *lʾn/wtbšrn/bʿmhw/wlhʿnnhw/bn/b*
18 *ʾstm/wnkytm/wtlf[tm/wnḍʿ]/wšṣ⌋*
19 *y/šnʾm/wmhbʾsm/[ḏbnhw/dʿw/wḏʾl/d]*
20 **Flower***ʿw/bʾlmq[hbʿlʾwm***Flower**]

1 **[Sym-]** Saʿad[šamsum . . . . . . , high]
2 official of [Nimrân ʾAwkân] and his
[bol] brother Ga[ḥ]ḍ[um ʾAḥ-]
3 ṣân, descendants of the Leader of Ḫalil and of the Leader of ʾAqyânum and of
4 [Suḫ]aymum, has dedicated to ʾIlumquh, master of ʾAwwâm, this statue which [is] in bron-
5 ze, by which he has praised the strength and the power of ʾIlumquh,
6 master of ʾAwwâm, because He has bestowed upon His worshipper Saʿadšam-
7 sum all the favors [for which] he besought and begged of
8 Him; and now He has protected His worshipper Saʿadšamsum
9 in all the encounters [in which] he fought and made raids against the Arabs
10 ⟨in⟩ the land of Muḍḥayân and Radmân and Qatabân, and [also] because He has vouchsafed
11 to him war trophy and booty which pleased his heart; and that
12 ʾIlumquh may continue to make happy [His worshipper Saʿadša]ms-
13 um with the esteem and grace of [their two] lor(d)[s Nimrân ʾAwk-]
14 ân and his brother Gaḥḍum [ʾAḥṣân and (with)] the grace of their
15 tribe Bakîlum; and that ʾIlumquh may continue to shower upon His wor-
16 shipper Saʿadšamsum all the favors [for which] he shall beseech
17 and beg of Him; and that He may preserve him from mis-
18 fortunes and sufferings and ruin [and (from) the hostility] and wickedness
19 of [any] enemy and evil-doer, [those who are known and those who are not]
20 **Flower** [kn]own. By ʾIlumq[uh, master of ʾAwwâm. **Flower**].

L. 2 is restored on the basis, e.g., of Ja 594/4-5.

L. 4: *[sẖ]ymm*, cf. Ja 758/3.

L. 9: *ġzw*, cf. commentary on Ja 577/14.

Ll. 9-10: the preposition introducing *ʾrḍ* (line 10) is missing; *ʿdy* is normally used in similar contexts; nevertheless, *b* seems preferable because of the probable haplography of *b* in *ʾʿrbn* (end of line 9).

L. 18: seven signs are missing.

L. 19: *mhbʾs*: participle of the 4th form of *bʾs*; e.g., RÉS 4653/4; cf. *CoRoC*, p. 111 A; in RÉS

[1] Cf. *RyISA*, XVI, p. 114; in *l.c.*, pp. 116-18, correct the Bombay numbers as follows: Ry 577, 578, 579, 580, and 581 are Bombay 122, 118, 116, 115, and 117 respectively.

4829/4 (cf. commentary on Ja 601/17-18), *mhbˀs* indicates the mistreatment inflicted by a malefactor. After *mhbˀs*, 12 signs are certainly missing; the most used formula, *ḏbnhw/dᶜw/wḏbnhw/ˀl(/)dᶜw* (e.g., Ja 614/19-20) is too long; the shorter one, *ḏbnhw/dᶜw/wḏˀl/dᶜw* (Ja 619/20-21), fits the blank perfectly.

740 – Grayish sandstone inscription; upper left corner broken, especially on the front. – MaMB 249.

STONE: constant thickness: 6.5 cm. – *Right side:* masonry mark (B): *w///ṣ*: 10.2 cm. × 4.6. – *Front:* 17.6 cm. × 24.8. – INSCRIPTION (A): same disposition of lines as in Ja 552; letter height: from 1.3 cm. to 1.5; space between the lines: from 0.2 cm. to 0.3; the number of signs in lines 1-8 is much greater than in lines 9-14 and especially in lines 12-14. – SYMBOL, cf. Ja 603.

A: 1 **Sym-** *rbˀwm/ˀṣdq/bn/[... .../wbnyhw]*
2 **bol** *sᶜdˀwm/wrbnsrm/ˀs[bˀyn/bnw/ḥz]*
3 *frm/ḏrfdn/hqnyw/ˀlmqh/ṯhwn/bᶜ⌜l/⌝[ˀwm/ṣl]*
4 *mnhn/ḏḏhbn/ḥmdm/bḏt/ẖmrhw/ˀlm*
5 *qh/ˀwldm/ˀḏkrm/ḥgn/kstydᶜhw/wḥm*
6 *dm/bḏt/hwfy/ᶜbdhw/rbˀwm/bkl/sbˀ*
7 *t/sbˀ/wšwᶜn/šᶜbhmw/sbˀ/ᶜdy/ˀrḍ*
8 *ḥmyrm/wlwzˀ/ˀlmqhw/ṯhwn/bᶜl/ˀwm*
9 *hwfyn/grb/ᶜbdhw/rbˀwm/wb*
10 *nyhw/sᶜdˀwm/wrbnsrm/wl*
11 *wzˀ/ˀlmqh/sᶜdhmw/wldm*
12 *wᶜḏrm/wḥẓy/wrḍw/ˀmrˀh*
13 *mw/bnw/ḥzfrm/wšᶜbhmw/s*
14 *bˀ/bˀlmqhṯhwnbᶜlˀwm*

A: 1 **Sym-** Rabbˀawwâm ˀAṣdiq, son of [... ..., and his two sons]
2 **bol** Saᶜadˀawwâm and Rabbnasrum, [the] Sa[baean]s, [descendants of Ḥaz-]
3 farum of Rafdân, have dedicated to ˀIlumquh Ṯahwân, master of [ˀAwwâm,] these two
4 [stat]ues which [are] in bronze, in praise because ˀIlumquh has vouchsafed to
5 him male children as he had confided in Him; and in prai-
6 se because He has protected His worshipper Rabbˀawwâm in all the encounters
7 [in which] he fought and assisted their tribe Sabaˀ in the land
8 of Ḥimyarum; and that ˀIlumquhû Ṯahwân, master of ˀAwwâm, may continue
9 to protect the person of His worshipper Rabbˀawwâm and of his
10 two sons Saᶜadˀawwâm and Rabbnasrum; and that
11 ˀIlumquh may continue to make them happy with a child
12 and a settler and [also] with the esteem and grace of their
13 lords the descendants of Ḥazfarum and of their tribe Sa-
14 baˀ. By ˀIlumquh Ṯahwân, master of ˀAwwâm.

741 – Yellowish, slightly grayish sandstone inscription; upper right corner broken. – MaMB 251.

STONE: almost constant thickness: 13.7 cm. (top) and 13 (bottom). – *Front:* red paint faded away: 17.2 cm. × 32.2. – INSCRIPTION: same disposition of lines as in Ja 559: letter height: from 1.9 cm. to 2.7; space between the lines: 0.3 cm. and 0.5.

1 **[Sym-** *hyṯᶜ]/bn/klb/ḏk*
2 **[bol]** *rm/sbˀyn/ᶜbd/ḏ*
3 *t/nᶜmbrl/wḥbt/hq*
4 *ny/ˀlmqhṯhwnbᶜlˀwm*
5 *ṣlmnhn/ḏḏhbn/ḏšft*
6 *hw/ᶜbdhw/hyṯᶜ/bkn*
7 *tˀwl/bwfym/bn/š*
8 *bwt/wbn/bḥrn/wl*
9 *wzˀ/ˀlmqh/hwf*
10 *yn/ᶜbdhw/hyṯᶜ/b*
11 *ˀlmqh/bᶜl/ˀwm*

1 **[Sym-** Hayṯaᶜ,] son of Kalb Ḏak-
2 **[bol]** rum, the Sabaean, servant of [the families]
3 Naᶜambaral and Ḥabbat, has dedi-
4 cated to ˀIlumquh Ṯahwân, master of ˀAwwâm,
5 these two statues which [are] in bronze, which had promised
6 to Him His worshipper Hayṯaᶜ when
7 he came back in safety from Ša-
8 bwat and from the sea; and that
9 ˀIlumquh may continue to protect
10 His worshipper Hayṯaᶜ. By
11 ˀIlumquh, master of ˀAwwâm.

Cf. Ja 756.

L. 1: *hyṯᶜ*, cf. the family names *yhyṯᶜ* (RÉS 4950/2 and Blaymires 3/2, Qat) and *myṯᶜm* (Ja 556).

L. 2: *sbˀy*, singular here as well as in CIH 84/3; cf. commentary on Ja 693/2: *ˀsbˀy*.

Ll. 2-3: *ᶜbd/ḏt*, cf. *JaPEHA*, pp. 29-30.

L. 3: *nᶜmbrl/wḥbt*, also in RÉS 4938/9, where *RÉS* erroneously reads *nᶜmbrg* and interprets *ḥbt* as a feminine verbal form.

742 – Lower part of a yellowish sandstone inscription. – MaMB 252.

STONE: maximum thickness: 11.8 cm. – *Front:* the last 0.7 cm. of both the left and right edges as well as the last 2.5 cm. of the lower edge are polished; 31.4 cm. (right) and 27 (left) × 19.9. – INSCRIPTION: cursive lettering; irregular letters; the *b* is small and ordinarily equals the height of the lower half of ʾ; mean letter height: 2.7 cm.

1 **[Sym-** ...
2 **[bol** *ḏt/*
3 *[../hqnyt/ʾ*
4 *[lmqhṯhwnbʿ]*
5 *lʾwm/[wḥrw]*
6 *nm/ʾrbʿt/ʾ*
7 *ṣlmm/wṣlm*
8 *tn/ḏšftt*
9 *lbnyhw/ʾbk*
10 *rb/wsʿdʾw⟨m⟩*
11 *wzy⟨d⟩m/wtb*
12 *ʿm/wkhlʿl*
13 *wʾbʿtd/*

1 **[Sym-** ...
2 **[bol** she of (the family)
3 [.., has dedicated to ʾI-]
4 [lumquh Ṯahwân, mas-]
5 ter of ʾAwwâm [and Ḥirwâ-]
6 num four
7 statues and two female sta-
8 tues, which she had promised
9 for her children ʾAbka-
10 rib and Saʿadʾawwâ⟨m⟩
11 and Zay⟨d⟩um and Taba-
12 ʿum and Kahilʿal
13 and ʾAbʿatad.

Ll. 7-8: *ṣlmtn: -n*, ending of the absolute dual (cf. commentary on Ja 649/35-36: *ʾḫdn*); six statues for six children the last two being girls because of *ṣlmtn* (cf. also Ja 689/3); the plural masculine *bny*, as in classical Arabic, designate boys as well as girls; cf. also *ʾly* and *bʿly*, masculine nouns in construct dual qualifying the stellar god ʿAṯtar and the sun goddess Ḏât-Ẓahrân, e.g., in Ja 559/18-19.

L. 10: the last letter is missing.

L. 11: the 3rd letter of *zydm* is missing.

Ll. 11-12: *tbʿm*, e.g., CIH 287/9; cf. also the Qat personal name *tbʿt* in Ja 137 (cf. commentary in *JaPEHA*, p. 40).

L 12: *khlʿl*, cf. *khln*, name of a valley in Ja 735/1 (cf. commentary) and the proper names *khlh* (Ja 715/8), *khlm* (e.g., Ja 634/5) and *khl* (e.g., RÉS 3766, Min).

L. 13: *ʾbʿtd*: for the 2nd element, cf. the Arabic place names *ʿatdân* (cf. *MüHG*, p. 76 A), *al-ʿattâbîyûn*, *ʿattûd*, *ʿitwad*, and *al-ʿutayd* (cf. *WüR*, p. 147 C) and *ʿatyad* (cf. *l.c.*, p. 148 A).

743 – Yellowish, slightly grayish sandstone. – MaMB 255.

STONE: thickness: 11 cm. (top) and 9.2 (bottom). – *Front:* edges badly cut; 40.2 cm. (right) and 39.8 (left) × 35.1 (top) and 35.4 (bottom). – INSCRIPTION: cursive lettering; mean letter height: 4.8 cm., 5.2, 4.9, 4.5, 3.7, 3.5, 2.7, and 2.4. – SYMBOL, cf. Ja 559.

1 **Symbol** *mgdḥlk/ḏt/mrḥbm/*
2 *hqnyt/mrʾhw/ʾlm*
3 *qh/bʿl/ʾwm/ṯny/ṣl*
4 *mn/ḥmdm/bḏt/ḫmrhw*
5 *ʾwldm/ʾḏkrm/wbntm/ḏ*
6 *lhmw/šftt/ḏt/hqnyt/w*
7 *lḫmrhw/ʾlmqh⟨/⟩rḏw/lbh*
8 *w⟨/⟩bʾlmqh*

1 **Symbol** Magadḥalak, she of Marḥabum,
2 has dedicated to her lord ʾIlum-
3 quh, master of ʾAwwâm, these two sta-
4 tues in praise because He has vouchsafed to her
5 male children and daughters
6 for whom she had promised this offering; and
7 that ʾIlumquh may vouchsafe to her the grace of His heart.
8 By ʾIlumquh.

L. 1: *mgdḥlk*: same nominal formation as that, e.g., of *mgdʿl* (CIH 544/8) and *ʾbḥlk* (Ja 751/1).

Ll. 7-8: *hwbʾ*: haplography of the word divider and the right vertical of *b*.

744 – Yellowish, slightly grayish sandstone block; the four sides are polished. – MaMB 257.

STONE: constant thickness: 26.8 cm. – *Front:* covered with red paint; upper right corner badly broken; lower right corner badly damaged; 30.8 cm. × 32. – INSCRIPTION: letter height: from 3.8 cm. to 4.2; space between the lines: from 0.6 cm. to 0.7. – SYMBOL, cf. Ja 558, but only two small horizontal lines, one in each vertical part of the design.

1 **Sym-** *krbʿṯt/⌈bn/⌉[ʿṯkl]*
2 **bol** *n/hqny/ʾlmqh/⌈b⌉[ʿl/ʾ]*
3 *wm/ṣlmn/ḏḏhbn/lwfy⌈/b⌉*
4 *nhw/rbšms/bn/ʿṯkl*
5 *n/wl/wfyhmw/*

1 **Sym-** Karibʿaṯat, descendant of [(the clan) ʿAṯkalâ]n,
2 **bol** has dedicated to ʾIlumquh, ma[ster of ʾA-]
3 wwâm, this statue which [is] in bronze, for the safety of his
4 son Rabbšams, descendant of ʿAṯkalân,
5 and for their safety.

745 – Stone re-used in the western pavement; broken on top; cf. Chapter I, B. – MaMB 261.

INSCRIPTION: letter height: from 2 cm. to 2.2; space between the lines: 0.5 cm. and 0.6. – SYMBOL, cf. Ja 587.

1 **Sym-** *ʾlġz/ʾywkn/wbnyhw*
2 **bol** *ʿlym/ʾtlwt/ʾfrs/mlk*
3 *n/hqnyw/mrʾhmw/ʾlmqhṯh*
4 *wnbʿlʾwm/frsn/wrkbhw*
5 *ḏḏhbn/hqnyt/šftw/lnqd*
6 *mm/ḥmdm/bḏt/stwfy/frs*
7 *mlkn/gdn/bkn/rkbhw/ʿdy*
8 *shrtn/wḥmdm/bḏt/mtʿ/fr*
9 *snhn/dynrm/wẓbym/bkn/r*
10 *kby/bn/srn/bryn/yrtʿnn*
11 *ʿdy/ẖbtn/bl[t/]šʿrhmw/wḥ*
12 *mdm/bḏt/mtʿ[/whʿ]⌈n⌉/ʿbdh⟨⟩w/ʾ*
13 *lġz/bn/d[qt/btʾ]wln/ʾbl*
14 *⌊h⌋[w/...*

1 **Sym-** ʾAlġaz ʾAywakân and his son
2 **bol** ʿAlayum, equerries of the horses of the king,
3 have dedicated to their lord ʾIlumquh Ṯah-
4 wân, master of ʾAwwâm, this horse and its saddle,
5 which [are] in bronze, an offering [which] they had promised befo-
6 re, in praise because He has given protection to the horse
7 of the king, Gâdin when he rode it in
8 Saharatân, and in praise because He has saved the
9 two horses Daynrâm and Ẓabayum when they
10 were ridden from the valley [of] Baryân in order to determine
11 in Ḫabtân the rent of their barley; and in
12 praise because He has saved [and protec]ted His worshipper ʾAl-
13 ġâz from [a fall at the re]turn of hi[s] ca-
14 mel[...

L. 1: *ʾlġz*, cf. Arabic *laġaza* "to distort" and its derived nouns *luġaz* "a winding, *or* tortuous, excavation *or* burrow" and *ʾalġâz* "winding, *or* tortuous, roads *or* ways" (cf. *LaAEL*, p. 2664 C). One might also think of the noun *ʾil* with either *ġzz* "to choose someone for oneself" or *ġwz* "to go straight toward someone". – *ʾywkn*, cp. the name of a country *ʾykm* (RÉS 3945/15) and the Arabic place names *ʾayk*, *ʾîk*, and *al-ʾaykat* (cf. *WüR*, p. 23 A).

L. 2: *ʾtlwt*: broken plural form *ʾqtlt*, of *tly* (Ja 584/1).

Ll. 5-6: *lnqdmm*: adverbial sentence composed of the conjunction *ln* introducing the *maṣdar* of the 1st form of *qdm*.

L. 7: *gdn*: name of the horse; name of a man in RÉS 2975 A/7, Min; cf. also the clan name *gdnm* (e.g., Ja 565/3). – *rkb*, cf. Ja 513/9-10 and commentary in *JaISAR*, p. 111.

L. 9: *dynrm*: for the 1st element, cf. the Arabic names of a place *dayn* (cf. *MüHG*, p. 45 A) and of a woman *daynat* (cf. *GoAT*, p. 182) and the Nabataean personal names *dyn*, *dynw*, and *dyny* (cf. *JaSaMA*, p. 206, No. 282, p. 226, No. 357 and, e.g., p. 198, No. 249 respectively).

L. 10: *bryn*, cf. *bry*[], name of a temple dedicated to the sun goddess (cf. *JaP*, p. 101).

L. 11: *ẖbtn*, cf. the Arabic names of places *ẖabt*, *al-ẖabtân* (cf. *MüHG*, p. 36 A) and the Thamudic name of a man *ẖbbt* (cf. *HaLiSTI*, p. 52 B).

L. 12: three signs are missing after *mtʿ*. – On the stone *ʿbdhmw* instead of *ʿbdhw*.

L. 14: several very short parts of letters are still visible.

746 – Stone re-used in the western pavement; cf. Chapter I, B. – MaMB 264.

Front: right part badly damaged; lower half worn out. – INSCRIPTION: letter height: from 3.4 cm. to 3.7; space between the lines: from 0.5 cm. to 0.7. – SYMBOL, cf. Ja 559.

1 **Sym-** *rbb⌋[ʾl/....]ym/wbnhw/yfʿ/bny/kbs*
2 **bol⌋** *[ym/ʾqwl/sʿ]bn/tnʿmm/wtnʿmt/⌊h⌋qny*
3 *[w/ʾlmqhwbʿl]ʾwm/⌈ṣ⌉[lm./ḥm]⌊d⌋m[/]bḏt/hw*
4 *[fy/ʿbdhw/r]⌊bbʾl/kl/st[......]ḥ[.]hw*
5 *.../]ʿdy/⌊m⌋[šymt]hmw/byfd/[w]ḥ[m]*
6 *[dw/ẖyl/wmq]m/ʾlm[q]hw/bḏt/hwfyhm[w]*
7 *[bkl/ʾmlʾ/]stmlʾ[w/bʿmhw/w]l[w]zʾ/ʾ[l]*
8 *[mqhw/ẖmr/]b[n]y[/kbsym/]frʿ/ḏ⌈h⌉b[h]*
9 *[mw/... ...]m/n[. .]l[.]*
10 *...]b[..]*

11 *...]ʾhbhmw/*
12 *...]l[... .../rḍw/w]⌜ḥẓ⌝y/mrʾh*
13 *[mw/... ...]bn/wh*
14 *.../mrʾ]h⌜m⌝w/ʾl*
15 *[mqhwbʿlʾwm/ ...ʾdmhw/]rb*
16 *[bʾl/wbnyhw/yfʿ/bʾlmqhwbʿlʾw]m*

1 **Sym-** Rabîb[ʾil....]ym and his son Yafaʿ, descendants of [the clan] Kabsa-
2 **bol** [yum, rulers of] the two [tri]bes Tanʿamum and Tanʿamat, ha[ve] dedicated
3 [to ʾIlumquhû, master of] ʾAwwâm, [this *or* a] st[atue in prai]se because He has show-
4 [ered upon His worshipper Ra]bîbʾil all ..[... ...] his [..].[.]
5 ...] in their ara[ble fields] in Yafad, [and they have] pr[ais-]
6 [ed the strength and the po]wer of ʾIlum[qu]hû because He has showered upon the[m]
7 [all the favors (for which) they] besought [Him, and] that may [con]tinue ʾI[l-]
8 [umquhû to vouchsafe] to the des[cend]ants of [Kabsayum] the optimum crop of [their] irrigated
9 land [...
10 [...
11 ...] their equipment [...
12 ...].[... ...the grace and] esteem of th[eir] lord
13 [...
14 ...] their [lord] ʾIl-
15 [umquhû, master of ʾAwwâm,... ...His worshippers] Rab-
16 [îbʾil and his son Yafaʿ. By ʾIlumquhû, master of ʾAwwâ]m.

L. 1: *rbbʾl* is restored on the basis of line 4. – [....]*ym*: the first four letters are missing.

L. 2: restoration based on Ja 627 and 628.

L. 3: *ṣ*[] may be restored either as *ṣ*[*lmm*] or *ṣ*[*lmn*].

L. 4: *st*[......]*ḥ*[.]*hw*: six signs are missing between *st* and *ḥ* and only one between *ḥ* and *hw*; the context suggests a verb such as *stwkl*, *stydʿ*, or *stmlʾ*, the latter being attested on line 7 and ordinarily followed by *bʿm* introducing the name of the deity or the personal pronoun referring to this name; []*ḥ*[.]*hw* probably is the subject of the verb *st*[]; cf. a similar case in Ja 629/21.

L. 5: nine signs are missing at the beginning, and the expression *rbbʾl/wyfʿ* is composed of ten. – *m*[....]*hmw*: four letters are missing; one might think of *mfnyt* (Ja 645/25), but *mšymt* is much more frequently mentioned in the present collection, e.g., Ja 562/13-14. – *yfd*, e.g., 2nd personal name or family name in RÉS 5084; cf. also *ḏyfd*, e.g., name of a palm-grove in RÉS 4781/2.

L. 11: *ʾhbhmw*: the entire context being missing, it is not possible to attempt a definitive interpretation of *ʾhb*; however compare Arabic *ʾuhbat*, plural *ʾuhab* "apparatus, equipment", which seems more suitable in the context than *ʾihâb*, plural *ʾahab*, *ʾuhub*, and *āhibat* "skin *or* hide not yet tanned".

L. 13: []*bn/wh*[] could possibly be interpreted as mentioning first the term introducing a family name (in association with the personal name missing at the beginning of the same line) and secondly the beginning of this family name; they also could possibly be the end and the beginning of two verbs.

747 – Stone re-used in the western pavement; cf. Chapter I, B. – MaMB 268.

Front: left edge and upper part of the right edge badly damaged; upper edge broken; upper corners widely rounded. – INSCRIPTION: same disposition of lines as in Ja 552; letter height: from 3.8 cm. (top) to 4.5 (bottom); space between the lines: 0.7 cm.

1 **[Symbol** *...]r⌜y⌝mn/⌜y⌝rdf/wbnhw/bnw/⌜y⌝*
2 *[hfrʿ]/ʾġymn/hqn[y]w/ʾlmqh/ṯh[wn]*
3 *[bʿlʾ]wm/ṣlmnhn/wṣlmtn/ʾly/[...*
4 *../]⌞ḥ⌟mdm/bḏt/hwfy/ʾlm⌞qh/⌟[ʿbdh]*
5 *[w/.../r]ymn/bn/[yh]frʿ/bn[...*
6 *...]/bʿm/ʾlmqh/wḥmd[m/bḏt]*
7 *[ḥmrh]mw/ʾlmqh/wfy/m[rʾyhmw/.]*
8 *.../]ʾgrm/wrbbḥgrm[/...*
9 *.../b]⌞n⌟y/yhfrʿ/wl/wẓ⌟[ʾ/ʾlmqh/sʿ]*
10 *[d/ʾdmhw]/⌜b⌝ny/yhfrʿ/ʾwldm/[ʾḏ]*
11 *[k]rm/hnʾ⌝n/wl/sʿdhmw/[ʾlmqh/nʿ]*
12 *mtm/wwfym/wmn⌜g⌝t/ṣdq⌜m⌝[/wḥ]*
13 *ẓy/wrḍw/ʾm[rʾ]h[m]w/ʾ[mlk/sb]*
14 *ʾ/wbny/ḏġymn/wl/sʿdhm[w/ʾl]*
15 *mqh/ʾṯmr/wʾfql/ṣ[dqm/wsqym/w]*
16 *dʿtm/šfqm/bn/kl/ʾrḍ⌜h⌝[mw/wl/g?]*
17 *yr/ʾlmqh/kl/šnʾh⌞m⌟[w/...*
18 *bʿlyhmw/bšṣy/swʾm/[wl/hwf](yh)*
19 *mw/bn/nḍʿ/wšṣy/šnʾm/bʾlmqh*
20 *ṯhwn/wbšymhmw/ḥgrm/qḥmm*

1 **[Symbol** ...]raymân Yardaf and his son, descendants of Yu-
2 [hfaraʿ,] the Ġaymânites, have dedi[cated to] ʾIlumquh Ṯah[wân,]

3 [master of ʾA]wwâm, these two statues and this female statue, these [...
4 ...] in praise because ʾIlumquh has helped [His worshipper]
5 [...r]aymân of [Yuh]faraᶜ from [...
6 ...] from ʾIlumquh; and in praise [because]
7 ʾIlumquh [has vouchsafed to th]em the safety of [their two] l[ords]
8 ...] ʾAgarum and Rabîbḥagarum [...
9 ..., des]cendants of Yuhfaraᶜ; and that [ʾIlumquh] may conti[nue to make happy]
10 His two worshippers,] the descendants of Yuhfaraᶜ, [with] children [ma-]
11 [le,] pleasing; and that [ʾIlumquh] may make them happy [with pros-]
12 perity and safety and security perfect, [and with the es-]
13 teem and grace of th[ei]r l[or]ds, the [king]s [of Saba]ʾ
14 and of the descendants of Ġaymân; and that may make the[m] happy [ʾIl-]
15 umquh with per[fect] fruits and harvests [and (with) *saqay-* and]
16 *daᶜat*-palms plentiful from t[heir] every land, [and that]
17 ʾIlumquh [may pros]trate thei[r] every enemy [...
18 against them in vicious wickedness; [and that He may pro](tect)
19 [t]hem from the hostility and wickedness of [any] enemy. By ʾIlumquh
20 Ṯahwân and by their patron Ḥagarum Qaḥamum.

L. 1: [...]*rymn*: judging from lines 7, 11, and 14-15, the name of the deity mentioned in the body of the text is *ʾlmqh* without any qualification or title, contrary to both the beginning (lines 2-3) and the end (lines 19-20) of the inscription; this fact justifies the restoration of *ᶜbdhw* mostly at the end of line 4 rather than at the beginning of the following line. Consequently, three letters are still missing between *w*/ and *rymn* at the beginning of line 5; the 1st personal name of the dedicator is thus composed of seven letters and, at the beginning of line 1 and to the left of the full personal name, there is still space for a small symbol as wide as two letters. As far as the 1st personal name is concerned, one could suggest *ᶜbdrymn* (CIH 536/1), *rṯdrymn* (CIH 102/2), etc. – *yrdf*, also 2nd masculine personal name in CIH 349/2.

Ll. 1-2: *yhfrᶜ*: here as well as in line 5, this proper name is restored on the basis of lines 9 and 10; also family name, e.g., in CIH 36, 37/8, and Khalidy-Condé 8/3.

L. 6: *bᶜm*: the preceding context being missing, the meaning of *bᶜm* is uncertain.

L. 15: *wsqym*/*w* fits the blank perfectly; cf., e.g., Ja 615/9-10 where *sqy* precedes *dᶜt*.

Ll. 16-17: [.]*yr*: the conjunction *l* is separated from the following verb in lines 9, 11, and 25; only one letter is thus to be restored at the end of line 16; a verb such as *gyr* (cf. Arabic *ǧâra* [o], 2nd form "to prostrate, thrown down, oppress") fits the context.

748 – Yellowish sandstone block with many traces of bronze; cf. *AlEMY*, p. 227 B and note 34, p. 230 A and Pl. 162 (plan): O-8. – MaMB 272.

STONE: thickness: 37.9 cm. – *Front:* badly damaged; 1.995 × 43.1 cm. – INSCRIPTION: same disposition of lines as in Ja 552; another vertical line at 1.2 cm. and 1.5 to the right of the text, and at 1.6 and 1.7 to its left; another horizontal line at 1.2 cm. above and below the inscription; line 1: 11 cm. × 4.8; line 2: 11.5 cm. × 5.1; space between the lines: 0.9 cm.

ᶜblm 1 ᶜAblum of [the family]
šbᶜn 2 Šabᶜân.

749 – Grayish sandstone. – MaMB 280.

STONE: thickness: 9.3 cm. (top) and 10 (bottom). – *Front:* covered with red paint; upper edge slightly damaged; 19.3 cm. × 13.1. – INSCRIPTION: same disposition of lines as in Ja 552; letter height: from 1.4 cm. to 1.5; space between the lines: 0.3 cm.; distance from line 1 to the upper edge: 0.6 cm. – SYMBOL, cf. Ja 559.

1 **Sym-** *hqnyt*/*ʾbkr*
2 **bol** *b*/*ʾṣḥḥ*/*bn*/*m*
3 *ḥfdm*/*mqtwy*/*mlkn*

1 **Sym-** The offering of ʾAbkar-
2 **bol** ib ʾAṣḥaḥ, son of Ma-
3 ḥfadum, high official of the king.

Cp. Ja 714.

Ll. 2-3: *mḥfdm*, cf. the family name *mḥfdn*, e.g., in RÉS 4636/4.

750 – Grayish sandstone. – MaMB 282.

STONE: the lower left corner has been cut again so that the edges of the stone are at right angle; a thin section has also been cut away from the right side; these two facts as well as the presence of cement in many letters (cf. below) prove that the stone was re-used in a masonry work; thickness: 18 cm. (maximum) and 4.5 (minimum). – *Front:* 25.3 cm. (top), 24.7 (above the hollow at the lower left corner) and 18.4 (bottom). – INSCRIPTION: the first three and the last two lines as well as the entire left edge are filled with cement; letter height: from 2.1 cm. to 2.3; space between the lines: 0.3 cm.; distance from line 1 to the upper edge: 0.7 cm.; the first two signs are missing from line 3 down to the bottom. – SYMBOL, cf. Ja 559.

1 ⸢**Sym-** *frwly/myḥyn/wbnyhw/ᶜbd*
2 ⸢**bol** *ᵓbs/wᵓlsᶜd/wᵓṯthw/wdᶜ*
3 *[tn]/hqnyw/ᵓlmqh/bᶜlᵓwm/ṯwrn*
4 *[ḏd]hbn/ḥgn/šfthw/lqbly/ḏsbᵓ/ᶜ*
5 *[dy]/ᵓrḍ/ḥḍrmt/bltn/ᵓḏnhw/ᶜ[dy]*
6 *[hb]ᶜyw/bmsbᵓn/wẓmᵓw/wšm/lᵓlm*
7 *[qh]/zᵓdᵓm/bhbtn/lgrmy/mwm/ḏ*
8 *[ys]tqynn/wyfᶜ/ẖyl/ᵓlmqh/wwkb*
9 *[w/]qll/mwm/ḏšrḥ/ᵓfshmw/ᶜdy/m*
10 *[ẓᵓ]w/msbᵓn/wmwn/wlḏhᶜnhmw/ᵓ*
11 *[lm]qh/bn/ftḥm/ḏkyn/bnhmw/b*
12 *[ᶜm]/hdym/ḏkd/ᵓfshmw/whᶜnhm*
13 *[w/]ᵓlmqh/wlhᶜnnhmw/ᵓlmqh/bn/l*
14 *[ẖb]n/ḏyknn/bynhw/wbyn/ᵓṯthw*
15 *[wl]hᶜnnhmw/ᵓlmqh/bn/hwt/lẖ*
16 *[bn]</>bᶜm/ᵓṯthw/wlhᶜnnhmw/bn/nḍᶜ/w⌊š⌋*
17 *[ṣy]/šnᵓm/ḏrḥq/wqrb/bᵓlmqh[/bᶜlᵓwm]*

1 **Sym-** Farrwalî Mayḥayân and his two sons ᶜAbd-
2 **bol** ᵓabas and ᵓIlsaᶜad and his wife Wadaᶜ-
3 [tân] have dedicated to ᵓIlumquh, master of ᵓAwwâm, this bull
4 [which (is) in br]onze, as he had promised to Him because of this: he was fighting
5 i[n] the land of Ḥaḍramawt, reward for his understanding, u[ntil]
6 they [acted] corruptly during the military campaign; and they became thirsty and he gave to ᵓIlum-
7 [quh some] provisions as a gift for two full-sized skins of water [by] which
8 they [could sla]ke their thirst; and the strength of ᵓIlumquh raised; and [they] received
9 a small quantity of water, which kept them healthy until they
10 [fi]nished the military campaign and [exhausted] the water; and [also] because has protected them ᵓI-
11 [lum]quh from the edict which existed against them be-
12 [cause of] Hudayum who grieved them; and did protect the[m]
13 ᵓIlumquh; and that ᵓIlumquh may protect them against the
14 con[tentions] which may happen between him and between his wife;
15 [and that] ᵓIlumquh [may] protect them against these conten[tions]
16 with his wife; and that He may protect them against the hostility and wic-
17 [kedness of (any) enemy, who is remote and near. By ᵓIlumquh, [master of ᵓAwwâm.]

L. 1: *frwly*: the two elements of this personal name are known; for the 1st, cf., e.g., the Thamudic name *fr* (cf. *vdBrIT*, pp. 416-17: Doughty 16/11: woman) and the Arabic names of a place *farrîrat* and of a clan *farîr* (cf. *WüR*, pp. 165 A and 254 B, respectively); for the 2nd element, cf. *wly*, name of a man in Thamudic (cf., e.g., *vdBrIT*, pp. 435-36: Jsa 18) and in Safaitic (cf. *LiSI*, p. 311 B). – *myḥyn*, compare the Arabic place name *mayḥân* (cf. *MüHG*, p. 111 B).

Ll. 1-2: *ᶜbdᵓbs*: for the 2nd element, cf., e.g., the proper name *āl ᵓabî ᵓbs* in Arabic (cf. *SaIS*, p. 3 A); same nominal formation as, e.g., *ᶜbdḥmd* (cf. *RyGSAS*, p. 559), and Thamudic *ᵓbssᶜd* (cf. *vdBrIT*, p. 88: HU 123) and *ᵓbᵓs* (cf. *HaLiSTI*, p. 10, No. 12).

L. 2: *ᵓlsᶜd*, e.g., Ja 870/1-2, Qat.

Ll. 2-3: *wdᶜ[tn]*: the personal name *wdᶜt* (e.g., Ja 353/1, Qat: woman; also common in Arabic) makes possible the restoration of *wdᶜ*[..] as *wdᶜ[tn]* (cf., e.g., *wdftn* in Ja 574/6) more probable than that of *wdᶜᵓl*, *wdᶜᵓb*, *wdᶜwd*, etc., none of the latter being known in South Arabian.

L. 5: *bltn*, cf. commentary on Ja 560/8-9. – *ᵓḏn* means here the understanding, cleverness of Farrwalî in the art of fighting.

Ll. 5-6: *ᶜ[....]ᶜyw*: two letters are missing at the end of line 5 as well as at the beginning of line 6. If the restoration of *ᶜ*[..] as *ᶜ[dy]* at the end of line 5 is accepted, the beginning of line 6 mentions the plural of one of the derived forms (4th to 8th) of the verb [.]*ᶜy*. Roots suitable for the restoration of this verb are but very few, and the meaning of most of them does not fit the context; e.g., either 6th or 8th form of *dᶜy*. The 5th form of *fᶜy* with its meaning "to become like the viper in evil" (cf. *LaAEL*, p. 2421 B) is very rarely used; although it suggests evil acts, this verb is not indicated by any details mentioned in the present inscription. On the contrary, *hbᶜy* "to provoke, instigate to crime, act corruptly" (cf. Ja 708/9 and commentary) fits the context perfectly: a *fth* (line 11) requires a judiciary action which is not taken unless a serious misdeed had been previously committed. Furthermore, the fear of slaps pointed out in lines 13-14 implies the existence of some others in the past. However, the mention of this fear after the story which ended with a judgment is preceded by an incidental phrase, *dkd/ʾfshmw* which evidently suggests that a quarrel between the husband and wife occurred after and because of the serious misdeed and its punishment.

L. 6: *ẓmʾ*, cf. *CoRoC*, p. 161 A, Ugaritic *ǵmʾ* (cf. *GoUM*, p. 310 B, No. 1485), and the noun *ṣmʾ* in Ja 735/7 (cf. commentary). – *šm*, cf. *CoRoC*, pp. 248-49.

L. 7: *zʾdʾ*, cf. post-biblical Hebrew *zewâdâʾ* "outfit for travelling, provision" (cf. *JaDT*, p. 384 A) and also *zâd* "provisions for travelling" in Arabic (cf. *LaAEL*, p. 1267 C), Ḥaḍrami (cf. *LaH*, p. 600) and Ẓofâr (cf. *RhVDD*, p. 24 B) as well as in Daṯînah *zuwwâd, zuwwâdat* (cf. *LaGD*, p. 1874) and Ḥaḍrami *zuwâd, zawâd* (cf. *LaH*, *l.c.*) with the same meaning; Farrwalî made thus to the god a present from his travel provisions. – *hbt*, cf. Arabic *hibat* "gift, present"; for the form *whbt*, cf. *CoRoC*, p. 135 B. – *grmy*: construct dual of *grm*; cf. Arabic *ǧirm, ǧurum*, and *ǧurûm* "body; bag". Daṯînah *ǧarm*, plural *ǧirâm* "pelisse en peau de mouton" (cf. *LaGD*, p. 279), and modern Yemeni "*ǧärm* pl. *ǧrūm* pelli bovine rozzamente conciate e usate come pellicce da viandanti e pastori" (cf. *RoVSAY*, p. 302). *grm* here seems to indicate a full body-size skin bag and not only a small bag because the water granted by the god allowed Farrwalî and his family to stay with the army at least a certain time (lines 9-10). Further, the special request for water addressed by Farrwalî to his god suggests that he and his family were deprived of the right of using water brought to the army; it probably was one of the punishments imposed on them, and the beginning of line 8 clearly indicates that they had no water. – *mw*, cf. *CoRoC*, p. 175 B; there is no reason for considering *mwy* as the plural of *mw* (cf., e.g., *RÉS* in RÉS 4774/2); *mwy* is the *scriptio plena*.

L. 8: [*ys*]*tqynn*: 8th form of *sqy*; cf. Arabic *saqā*, 8th form "to become satisfied with drinking of water", that is to say "to have one's thirst slaked with water" or "to slake one's thirst with water".

L. 9: *qll*, cf. Arabic *qill* "small quantity"; *qll* is a noun here, but an adjective (cf. Arabic *qalîl* "rare, infrequent") in *mwm/qllm* (CIH 547/10). – *ʾfs*, contracted form of *ʾnfs* (cf., e.g., *CoRoC*, p. 189 A).

Ll. 9-10: *m*[..]*w* could possibly be restored as *m*[*ẓʾ*]*w*; cf. Arabic *maḍā* "to pass (away); to execute, perform, accomplish" (cf. *LaAEL*, p. 3021 B). *msbʾn/wmwn* could be either subjects or direct objects of *m*[*ẓʾ*]*w*. In the first hypothesis, the phrase may be translated "until the military campaign and the water passed away", that is to say "until the end of both the military campaign and the water"; however, we do not know whether they stayed until the end of this campaign; it would be a strange coincidence that both the campaign and the water given to Farrwalî's family came to an end at exactly the same time. It seems more reasonable to admit that Farrwalî's family left the campaign when they ran out of water; this interpretation is possible thanks to the 2nd hypothesis on the grammatical case of *msbʾn/wmwn* according to which the sentence may be translated "until they finished the military campaign and the water". For the ordinary meaning of *mẓʾ*, cf. Ja 576/5-6 and commentary. In RÉS 3884 bis/7-8, *mẓʾ ʿl* must be related to Syriac *mṭô ʿall* "to happen, befall, attain, come upon" (cf. *PaSmCSD*, p. 266 A).

L. 11: *fth*, cf. *CoRoC*, p. 221 A and the verb in Ja 643/20; *fthm/dkyn*, cp. *ʾywnm/dkwn* in RÉS 4230/9 (cf. *JaASAB*, pp. 187-88).

Ll. 11-12: *bnhmw/b*[..]*/hdym*: the hypothesis of *bn scriptio defectiva* of *byn* seems to be excluded by the *scriptio plena* attested twice in line 14; *bʿm* indicates the origin of the edict, Hudaym's action. *hdym* is also name of a man in CIH 96/1; cf. also the family name *mhdmm* (e.g., Ja 581/1). The hypothesis of interpreting *hdym* as a noun (cf. Arabic *hady* "way, course, method, mode, *or* manner, of acting, *or* conduct, *or* proceeding"; see *LaAEL*, p. 3042 B) must be discarded for there would be a contradiction between lines 10-11 and line 12.

L. 12: *dkd*: *d*+*kd*, cf. Arabic *kadda* "to fatigue, weary, jade"; the context suggests a derived meaning such as "to grieve, afflict"; *d* introducing *kd* is related to *fth* (line 11) as well as *d* preceding *kyn*.

Ll. 13-14: *l*[..]*n* is partially restored on the basis

of *lḫ* (end of line 15); cf. Arabic *laḫaba* "to slap"; *lḫb* here and in lines 15-16 is a collective noun with the meaning "slaps, contentions".

Ll. 15-16: *lḫ*[. .]: preceded by *hwt*, *lḫ*[*b*] should have the article; but no letter can be restored at the end of line 15 and there are only two signs missing at the beginning of line 16. Yet three signs, *bn/*, are needed. I suggest accepting the hypothesis of the haplography of the word divider and the right vertical stroke of *b* (cf. Ja 743/8) rather than the simple omission of *n*.

L. 16: *bʿm*: its meaning is given by line 14.

L. 17, end: the restoration of */bʿl/ʾwm* is justified by the fact that the stone has been cut after being engraved in order to be re-used in masonry work; cf. line 3.

751 – Grayish sandstone. – MaMB 283.

STONE: thickness: 16.2 cm. (bottom) and 17 (top). – *Front:* both upper right and lower left corners broken; width: 20.6 cm. – INSCRIPTION: many letters damaged; letter height: from 2.3 cm. to 2.5; space between the lines: from 0.2 cm. to 0.3; distance from line 1 to the upper edge: 0.8 cm. – SYMBOL, cf. Ja 559. – ORNAMENTS: for the flower on each side of line 13, cf. Ja 690; between each lateral side and the flower, an ornament inside a rectangular frame and composed of one central element of the not-framed design in Ja 581; the top of this element is facing the flower as in Ja 581; cf. Plate B.

1 **Sym-** *ʾbḥlk/ḏt/ḏbyn/h*
2 **bol** *q[nyt/]ʾlmqhṯhwnb*
3 *ʿlʾwm/ṣlmtn/ḏt/ḏhbn*
4 *ḏt/bhw/ḥmdt/ḫyl/wmq*
5 *m/ʾlmqh/bḏt/šrḥ/wmtʿn*
6 *grbhw/bhry/hryt/bḫr*
7 *f/smhkrb/bn/ʾbkrb/b[k]*
8 *n/ḥmdt/bn/ḫbṭn/kwn/b*
9 *hwt/ḫrfn/wʾlmqhṯhwnb*
10 *ʿlʾwm/fl/yzʾn/šrḥ/wm*
11 *tʿn/grb/ʾmthw/ʾbḥlk*
12 *ḏt/ḏbyn/bʾlmqhṯhwnbʿ*
13 **Des. Fl.***lʾwm***Fl. Des.**

1 **Sym-** ʾAbḥalak, she of [the family] Ḏû-Bayyin, has
2 **bol** de[dicated to] ʾIlumquh Ṯahwân, mas-
3 ter of ʾAwwâm, this female statue which [is] in bronze,
4 by which she has praised the strength and the pow-
5 er of ʾIlumquh because He has kept healthy and saved
6 her person from the severe cold she was suffering in the year
7 of Sumhukarib, son of ʾAbkarib, w[h]en
8 she gave praise in connection with the bad cold in the head [that] occurred in
9 that year; and as for ʾIlumquh Ṯahwân, mas-
10 ter of ʾAwwâm, may He continue to keep healthy and sa-
11 ve the person of His maidservant ʾAbḥalak,
12 her of Ḏû-Bayyin. By ʾIlumquh Ṯahwân, mas-
13 **Des. Fl.** ter of ʾAwwâm. **Fl. Des.**

L. 1: *ʾbḥlk*, also name of a woman in RÉS 4938/8.

L. 6: *bhry/hryt*, cf. Arabic *haraʾa* "to be very cold (wind), to give pain (cold)", passive form *huriʾa* "to suffer very much from the cold; perish from cold", and also the adjective *mahrûʾ* "which was suffering very much from the cold".

L. 8: *ḫbṭ*, cf. Arabic *ḫabṭ* "bad cold in the head".

752 – Grayish sandstone. – MaMB 284.

STONE: constant thickness: 13 cm. – *Front:* 16 cm. (top) and 17.7 (bottom) × 70.5. – INSCRIPTION: letter height: from 2 cm. to 2.5; space between the lines: from 0.5 cm. to 0.7; distance from line 1 to the upper edge: 0.3 cm. – SYMBOL, cf. Ja 639.

1 **Sym-** *ʿbdmlk/ʾw*
2 **bol** *md/wsʿdʾw*
3 *m/wšrḥʾwm*
4 *ʾzʾd/bnw/ḥḍ*
5 *nn/hqnyw/mrʾ*
6 *hmw/ʾlmqhw/bʿ*
7 *lʾwm/frsm/ḏt*
8 *ḏhbm/ḏt/šfth*
9 *w/lgrm/mhrth*
10 *mw/kwldt/mh*
11 *rtm/ʾṯym/whfy*
12 *lhmw/mlʾhw/w*
13 *lzʾn/mrʾhmw*
14 *ʾlmqhw/hfynh*
15 *mw/wbʿrhmw*

1 **Sym-** ʿAbdmalik ʾAw-
2 **bol** mad and Saʿadʾawwâm
3 and Šaraḥʾawwâm
4 ʾAzʾad, descendants of Ḥaḍ-
5 nân, have dedicated to their
6 lord ʾIlumquhû, mas-
7 ter of ʾAwwâm, a mare which [is] in
8 bronze, which he had promised to
9 Him for the body of their filly

10 in order that may be brought forth a firm-fleshed
11 filly; and He did grant
12 to them His favor; and
13 that may continue their lord
14 ʾIlumquhû to protect
15 them and their camel herd.

Note the omission of the first radical of the two verbs *wfy* (in the 4th form *hfy*, lines 11 and 14) and *wẓʾ* (line 13).

Ll. 1-2: *ʾwmd*, *ʾaqtal* form from *wmd*; cf. Arabic *wamida* "to become irritated with someone".

Ll. 4-5: *ḥḏnn*, e.g., CIH 410/2.

L. 9: *grm*, cf. commentary on Ja 750/7.

Ll. 9-10: *mhrthmw*; also *mhrtm* in line 11. The use of *grm*, instead of *grb*, which is referred to in relation to human beings, suggests that *mhrt* is not a human being (cf. Arabic *mahîrat* "a free [married] woman"; cf. *LaAEL*, p. 2740 B). I propose to relate *mhrt* to *muhrat* "filly" (cf. *l.c.*). This interpretation may also be applied in CIH 110, 111, and 492/3; in the latter inscription, *CIH* (II, p. 194) translates *mhrt* as "opes" (cf. also *CoRoC*, p. 175 B). The first of the three just referred to reads as follows: (1) *rʾshw/ymw*(2)*lḏqẓnhqny*(3)*ḏt/ẓhrnmhrt*[*h*](4)*w* "Raʾshû Yamûl, he of [the family] Qayẓân, has dedicated to Ḏât-Ẓahrân, [h]is filly"; and the second: (1)*hʿn/whwfn/wlḥyn*(2)*wḥywm*⌞/*w*⌟*mr*⌜*b*⌝*ḍn/bnw/ḥnn* (3)*hqnyw*(*ḏ*)*t/ẓhrn/mhrthmw/* "Haʿn and Hawfân and Laḥayân and Ḥaywum and Marbiḍân, descendants of Ḥanan, have dedicated to (Ḏ)ât-Ẓahrân, their filly". The root *mhr* is also found in its present participle *mhr*, pl. *ʾmhr* (RÉS 4877/3) "specialized worker".

L. 10: *kwldt*: the verb *wld* is also passive in the present collection.

L. 11: *ʾṯym*: the three following roots must be discarded: *ʾṯm* which indicates the idea of unlawfulness or transgression, *ʾṯw* which means "to report something to the authority" and *wṯy* which applies to an injury to a member of the body; cf. Arabic *waṯîm* "who has firm flesh".

753 – Two large slabs of grayish sandstone; front covered with red paint; photograph; cf. Chapter I, C. – MaMB 285, 286, and 287.

STONE A (on the right): thickness: 39.8 cm. – *Front:* upper left corner broken; right edge splintered off in two places; lower part damaged; 1.552 m. × 48 cm.; a small rim (height: 0.3 cm., located at 30.5 cm. from the top) divides the text into two parts.

STONE B (on the left): thickness: 35.5 cm. – *Front:* upper part broken; lower part badly damaged; 1.535 m. × 48 cm.; a rim (cf. stone A) is located at 29.6 cm. from the top.

INSCRIPTIONS: same disposition of lines as in Ja 552. – *I:* letter height: from 2.6 cm. to 2.8; space between the lines: from 0.3 cm. to 0.5; distance from line 1 to the top (on stone A) 0.4 cm.; engraved on the upper part of the two stones; MaMB 285; *symbol*, cf. Ja 728, but the lower end of the lower incision is triangular. *II* and *III:* letter height: from 5.5 cm. to 5.6; space between the lines: 0.5 cm. *Particularities of II:* engraved on the lower part of stone A; distance from line 19 to the bottom: 6 cm., MaMB 286; *and of III:* engraved on the lower part of stone B, distance from line 19 to the bottom: 6.5 cm., MaMB 287.

STONE A STONE B

I

1 **S** *sʿdšmsm/ʾsrʿ[/wbnhw/mrṯdm/bny/g***|***rt/ʾqwl/šʿbn/]⌜ḏ⌝[mry/hq]n(y)[w/ʾlmqhw/ṯ]*
2 **y m** *hwn/bʿl/ʾwm/ṣlmnhn/ḥngn/wqhhmw***|***[b]msʾlhw/lsʿdhmw/ʾlmqhw/n[ʿm]t[m/w]*
3 **b o** *wfym/wmngt/ṣdqm/ḏyhrḍyn/ʾlb***|***[bhmw]/wlsʿd/ʾlmqhw/ʾdmhw/bny/grt/rḍ*
4 **l** *w/wḥẓy/ʾmrʾhmw/ʾmlk/sbʾ/wl***|***[wzʾ/]ʾlmqhw/ṣdqhmw/whwfynhmw/bkl*
5 *ʾmlʾ/ystmlʾnn/bʿmhw/wl/ẖrynhmw/ʾl***|***[mqhw]/bn/bʾstm/wnkym/wbn/kl/nḍʿ/wš*
6 *ṣy/šnʾm/ḏrḥq/wqrb/wkwnt/ḏt/hqnyt***|***[n/lḏ]t/nʿmt/wtnʿmn/lsʿdšmsm/wbnhw/m*
7 *rṯdm/bny/grt/wqlhmw/wšʿbhmw/smh***|***[rm/]bʿṯtr/whbs/wʾlmqhw/wḏt/ḥmy*
8 *m/wḏt/bʿdnm/wb/šms/mlkn/tnf/w⌝***|***[b]ʾlyhmw/ʿṯtr/ʿzzm/wḏt/ẓhrn*
9 *bʿly/ʿrn/knn/wrṯdw/hqnythmw***|***[ʿ]ṯtr/šrqn/wʾlmqhw/bʿl/ʾwm*

II

1 *hw/lsʿdhmw/ʾlmqhw/nʿmtm*
2 *wwfym/wmngt/ṣdqm/ḏyhrḍw*
3 *n/ʾlbbhmw/wlsʿd/ʾlmqhw/ʾd*
4 *mhw/bny/grt/rḍw/wḥẓy/ʾmrʾh*
5 *mw/ʾmlk/sbʾ/wlwzʾ/ʾlmqhw*
6 *[ṣ]dqhmw/whwfynhmw/bkl/ʾm*
7 *lʾ/ystmlʾnn/bʿmhw/wlẖryn*
8 *hmw/ʾlmqhw/bn/bʾstm/wnk*
9 *ym/wbn/kl/nḍʿ/wšṣy/šnʾm*
10 *ḏrḥq/wqrb/wkwnt/ḏt/hqny*
11 *tn/lḏt/nʿmt/wtnʿmn/lsʿdš*
12 *msm/wbnhw/mrṯdm/bny/grt*
13 *wqlhmw/wšʿbhmw/smhrm/bʿ*
14 *ṯtr/whwbs/wʾlmqhw/wbḏt*
15 *ḥmym/wbḏt/bʿdnm/wb/šms*
16 *⌜m⌝lkn/tnf/wbʾlyhmw/ʿṯtr/ʿ*
17 *zzm/wḏt/ẓhrn/bʿly/ʿrn/kn*
18 *n/wrṯdw/hqnythmw/ʿṯtr*
19 *šrqn/wʾlmqhw/bʿl/ʾwm*

III

1 *lsʿdhmw/ʾlmqhw/nʿmtm/ww*
2 *fym/wmngt/ṣdqm/ḏyhrḍwn/ʾ*
3 *lbbhmw/wlsʿd/ʾlmqhw/ʾdmh*
4 *w/bny/grt/rḍw/wḥẓy/ʾmrʾh*
5 *mw/ʾmlk/sbʾ/wlwzʾ/ʾlmqhw*
6 *ṣdqhmw/whwfynhmw/bkl/ʾml*
7 *ʾ/ystmlʾnn/bʿmhw/wlẖryn*
8 *hmw/ʾlmqhw/bn/bʾstm/wnk*
9 *ym/wbn/kl/nḍʿ/wšṣy/šnʾm*
10 *ḏrḥq/wqrb/wkwnt/ḏt/hq[n]yt*
11 *n/lḏt/nʿmt/wtnʿmn/ls[ʿ]dš*
12 *msm/wbnhw/mrṯdm/bny/grt*
13 *[wq]lhmw/wšʿbhmw/sm[h]rm/bʿ*
14 *[ṯt]r/whwbs/wʾlmqhw/wb⌜ḏ⌝[t]*
15 *[ḥ]mym/wbḏt/b[ʿ]dn[m]/wb/šm[s]*
16 *[ml]kn/t⌊n⌋[f]/wb⌜ʾ⌝lyhmw/ʿṯt[r]*
17 *[ʿzzm/wḏt/]ẓhrn/bʿly/ʿrn*
18 *[knn/wrṯ]dw/hqnythmw/ʿṯtr*
19 *[šrqn/wʾ]lmqhw/bʿl/⌊ʾ⌋wm*

Translation of text I.

1 Saʿadšamsum ʾAsraʿ [and his son Marṯadum, descendants of Garat, rulers of the tribe]
S Ḍa[mrî, have de]di(cat)[ed to ʾIlumquhû, Ṯa-]
2 **y** hwân, master of ʾAwwâm, these two statues as He had ordered them through His oracle in
m order that ʾIlumquhû may make them happy with pr[osperi]ty [and]
3 **b** safety and security perfect which would please [their] hearts, and in order that ʾIlumquhû
o may make His worshippers, the descendants of Garat, happy with the gra-
4 **l** ce and esteem of their lords, the kings of Sabaʾ; and that ʾIlumquhû may [continue] to bestow upon them and to grant them all the
5 favors [for which] they shall beseech Him, and that ʾIl[umquhû] may preserve them from misfortunes and suffering and from every [act of] hostility and wick-
6 edness of [any] enemy, who is remote and near; and this offering was [presented in order] that it may have been pleasant and be pleasant for Saʿadšamsum and for his son Mar-
7 ṯadum, descendants of Garat, and for their ruler and their tribe Sumhu[râm]. By ʿAṯtar and Hawbas and ʾIlumquhû and Ḏât-Ḥimy-
8 âm and Ḏât-Baʿdânum and by Šams of the king, Tanûf, and [by] their two deities ʿAṯtar ʿAzîzum and Ḏât-Ẓahrân,
9 the two masters of the hill-town Kanin; and they entrusted their offering to the care of [ʿA]ṯtar Šarqân and of ʾIlumquhû, master of ʾAwwâm.

Commentary on text I. – Cf. Ja 606, 607, and 568. – L. 2: *ḥngn*: noteworthy that four *n*'s are found in only eight signs (*nhn/ḥngn*); the engraving of *ḥ* being very close to that of *h* as far as both the distance and resemblance between the two letters are concerned, may suggest and explain the dittography of *n* following *ḥ* (*hn/ḥn*). Further, *ḥgn* is very frequently used in contrast to the unique case of *ḥngn*; the hypothesis of a mistake is thus very probable and would at first sight be accepted; however, Arabic *ḥinǧ* means "root, origin (where one comes from)"; *ḥngn* may in my opinion be preserved for it makes sense by pointing out the origin of the preceding act, that is to say the reason why the offering was presented to the deity.

Text II = I/2b to end, with the following differences: *ḏyhrḍwn* (lines 2-3), *lẖrynhmw* (lines 7-8), *hwbs* (line 14), *bḏt ḥmym* (lines 14-15), and *bḏt/bʿdnm* (lines 15) instead of *ḏyhrḍyn*, *l/ẖrynhmw*, *hbs*, *ḏt/ḥmym*, and *ḏt/bʿdnm* in text I, lines 3, 5, 7, 7-8, and 8, respectively.

Text III: identical with II, except the first three signs of II/1 are missing in III.

Engraving of I, II, and III. – Each stone originally had the complete text, II on the first and III on the second; however, most of the upper part of the front of either one was not entirely occupied by the three presently missing lines. Above these lines there still was a large space but we do not know whether it was with or without inscription(s); the first hypothesis is far the most probable. In any case, a thin section, the thickness of which was 0.3 cm., was later on taken off (cf. the rim) and text I was engraved there.

754 = MaMB 288 = lines 11-19 of Ja 735.

755 – Grayish sandstone. – MaMB 296.

STONE: thickness: 12.4 cm. – *Front:* upper right corner damaged; a plaque was attached in the center right below the upper edge by four dowel pins, the lower ends of which are still in the stone; 15.7 cm. × 12.7. – INSCRIPTION: letter height: from 1.7 cm. to 1.4; space between the lines: 0.3 cm.; distance from line 1 to the upper edge: 0.4 cm. – SYMBOL, cf. Ja 574.

1	**Sym-**	*rd*	**P** **l**	*myn/ḏ[ṣ]*
2	**bol**	*rf*	**a**	*n/hqny*
3	*ʾlmqh*		**q** **u**	*ṯhwnbʿ*
4	*lʾwm/ṭ*		**e**	*fn/ḏṣr*

5 *fn/wṣlmn/ḏḏhbn/hqnyt*
6 *šfthw/lwfyhw/wwfy/ʾw[l]*
7 *dhw/bʾlmqh*

1	**Sym-**	Rad-	**P** **l**	miyân, he of [the family Ṣa-]
2	**bol**	rf-	**a**	ân, has dedicated to
3	ʾIlumquh		**q**	Ṯahwân, mas-
4	ter of ʾAwwâm, this		**u** **e**	plaque which [is] in brass,

5 and this statue which [is] in bronze, an offering [which]
6 he had promised to Him for his own safety and the safety of his
7 ch[il]dren. By ʾIlumquh.

L. 1: *rdmyn*, cf. *rdmyt* in BM 132171/1.
L. 4: *ṭf* (CIH 529/4) indicates the plaque which was fastened on the front of the stone; for the etymology, cf. *CIH*, II, p. 245 B, followed by *StSESA*, p. 539 and *CoRoC*, p. 159 B; cf. also *JeHoDISO*, p. 103: *ṭf*.

756 – Grayish sandstone. – MaMB 297.

STONE: constant thickness: 12.3 cm. – *Front:* upper right and lower left corners broken; 17.3 cm. × 33.2. – INSCRIPTION: same disposition of lines as in Ja 552; letter height: 2 cm.; space between the lines: from 0.4 cm. to 0.6; distance from line 1 to the upper edge: 0.5 cm. – SYMBOL, cf. bottom of Ja 728.

1 [**Sym-** *hyṯʿ*]*/bn/klb/ḏk*
2 **bol** *rm/sbʾyn/ʿbd/ḏ*
3 *t/nʿmbrl/wḥbt/hq*
4 *ny/ʾlmqhṯhwnbʿlʾwm*
5 *ṣlmnhn/ḏḏhbn/ḏšft*
6 *hw/ʿbdhw/hyṯʿ/bkn*
7 *tʾwl/bwfym/bn/š*
8 *bwt/wbn/bḥrn/wl*
9 *wzʾ/ʾlmqh/hwf*
10 *yn/ʿbdhw/hyṯʿ/b*
11 *ʾlmqh/bʿlʾwm*

For the translation, cf. Ja 741, text identical with the present one even as far as the composition of the lines is concerned; yet they are engraved on two different stones: (a) 741 is a yellowish sandstone covered with red paint, and 756 a grayish one with no trace of paint; (b) in 741 the upper right corner only is broken, in 756 both the upper right and lower left corners are broken; (c) in 741, the entire symbol is missing, in 756 the lower half of it is still existing; (d) in 741 two horizontal lines frame the letters, in 756 there are three horizontal lines; (e) the thickness of the stone, the letter height as well as the space between the lines are different in 741 and 756. – The text mentions the offering of two statues; each engraved stone supported one statue.

757 – Slightly bluish alabaster plaque. – MaMB 298.

PLAQUE: constant thickness: 14.3 cm.; re-used after being engraved as shown by seven small bronze ties and a hole for the eighth one, all of them visible in front of the plate. – *Front:* 47 cm. × 27.4 (right) and 23 (left). – INSCRIPTION: same disposition of lines as in Ja 559; letter height: 3.4 cm.; space between the lines: 0.8 cm. and 0.7; distance from line 1 to the upper edge: 1.6 cm. – SYMBOL: composed of three parallel lines (cf. Ja 552) making two curves convex with respect to the text and ended on both extremities by one horizontal line (cf., e.g., Ja 552); two sets of two horizontal lines: one in the center of the symbol and the other in the center of the upper part (cf. Ja 552); cf. Plate B.

1 **Sym-** *ʾlsʿd/mḏyn/hqny/ʾlmqh/bʿl/ʾwm/*
2 **bol** *šlṯtn/ʾṣlmn/ʾly/ḏhbn/lwfyhw/ww*
3 *fy/bnyhw/msylm/wswsm/whwfʿṯt/b*
4 *ny/mḏyn/wl/wśfhw/ʾlmqhw/ʾwldm*
5 *ʾḏkrwm/hnʾn/bʿṯtr/wʾlmqh*

1 **Sym-** ʾIlsaʿad Maḏayân has dedicated to ʾIlumquh, master of ʾAwwâm,
2 **bol** these three statues which [are] in bronze, for his own safety and the sa-

3 fety of his sons Musaylum and Sawsum and Hawfʿatat, des-
4 cendants of Maḏayân; and that ʾIlumquhû may add to him male,
5 pleasing children. By ʿAṯtar and ʾIlumquh.

Ll. 1 and 4: *mḏyn*, also family name in CIH 567/2; cf. also *mḏy*, name of people in RÉS 3022/3 Min.

L. 3: *msylm: qutaylum* form of *msl*; cf. the personal name *msyl* (cf. *RyGSAS*, p. 560) and also the name of a man *mslm* (related to the root *slm* by *RyNP*, I, p. 150 B) in RÉS 3833, Min.

757 bis – Grayish sandstone. – MaMB 299.

STONE: constant thickness: 7.5 cm. – *Front:* upper right corner broken; 18.2 cm. (top) and 16.8 (bottom) × 23.5. – INSCRIPTION: letter height: from 2.5 cm. to 2.7; space between the lines: 0.7 cm.; distance from line 1 to the upper edge: 0.8 cm. – SYMBOL, cf. Ja 603.

1 **Sym-** *rṯdm/bn/ẖ*
2 **bol** *ḏwm/mqtwy/*
3 *bn/yhʿn/hqny/*
4 *ʾlmqhw/bʿl/ʾ*
5 *wm/ṣlmn*

1 **Sym-** Raṯadum, son of Ḫa-
2 **bol** ḏwum, high official of
3 the descendants of Yuhʿîn, has dedicated to
4 ʾIlumquhû, master of ʾA-
5 wwâm, this statue.

Ll. 1-2: *ẖḏwm*, cf. *ẖḏwt*, e.g., in Ja 731/2.

758 – Grayish sandstone. – MaMB 300.

STONE: constant thickness: 13.8 cm. – *Front:* 32.7 cm. × 40.4. – INSCRIPTION: same disposition of lines as in Ja 552; letter height: 1.3 cm.; space between the lines: 0.2 cm.; distance from line 1 to the upper edge: 0.6 cm. – SYMBOL, cf. Ja 589, but only one horizontal line in the center.

1 **Sym-** *sẖmn/ʾwḥm/bn/krbn/mqtwy/nm*
2 **bol** *rn/ʾwkn/wʾẖyhw/gḥḏm/ʾḥṣn*
3 *bny/kbrẖll/wkbrʾqynm/wḏsẖymm*
4 *hqnyʾlmqhṯhwnbʿlʾwm/ḏn/ṣlmn/ḏ*
5 *ḏhbn/ḥmdm/bḏt/hwfy/ʿbdhw/sẖmn*
6 *bn/krbn/bʾmlʾ/wtbšrt/stmlʾ/wtb*
7 *šrhw/ʾlmqh/bkn/sbʾw/wḍbʾ/wġz*
8 *w/ʿdy/ʾrḍ/rdmn/wmḏḥym/wsrn/ʾ*
9 *ẖr/ḏqtbn/bʿm/ʾʿrbn/wrʾ/kḥm*
10 *d/ẖyl/wmqm/ʾlmqhṯhwnbʿlʾw*
11 *m/bḏt/hwfy/ʿbdhw/sẖmn/bmlʾ*
12 *wtbšr/tbšrhw/wʾtw/bwfym/w*
13 *mhrgm/wsbym/wmltm/wġnmm/wlwz*
14 *ʾ/ʾlmqhṯhwnbʿlʾwm/ẖmr/ʿbdhw*
15 *sẖmn/bn/krbn/ḥẓy/wrḍw/mrʾyhm*
16 *w/nmrn/ʾwkn/wʾẖyhw/gḥḏm/ʾḥ*
17 *ṣn/bny/kbrẖll/wkbrʾqynm/wḏs*
18 *ẖymm/wlhʿn/wẖryn/ʿbdhw/sẖmn*
19 *bn/krbn/bn/nḍʿ/wšsy/šnʾm/ḏbnh*
20 *w/dʿw/wḏʾl/dʿw/bʾlmqhṯhwn*
21 *bʿlʾwm*

1 **Sym-** Saḫmân ʾAwḥum, son of Karbân, high official of Nim-
2 **bol** rân ʾAwkân and his brother Gaḥḏum ʾAḥṣân,
3 descendants of the Leader of Ḫalîl and of the Leader of ʾAqyânum and of Suḫaymum,
4 has dedicated to ʾIlumquh Ṯahwân, master of ʾAwwâm, this statue which [is] in
5 bronze, in praise because He has showered upon His worshipper Saḫmân,
6 son of Karbân, the favors and the announcement [for which] he besought and
7 begged of Him, ʾIlumquh, when they were fighting and making war and raids
8 in the land of Radmân and Muḏḥayum and [in] the wâdî-side valley [of] ʾA-
9 ḫar of Qatabân against the Arabs; and now he has prais-
10 ed the strength and the power of ʾIlumquh Ṯahwân, master of ʾAwwâm,
11 because He has showered upon His worshipper Saḫmân the favor
12 and the announcements [for which] he begged of Him and [because] he has come back in safety and
13 (with) war trophy and captives and riches and booty; and that may continue
14 ʾIlumquh Ṯahwân, master of ʾAwwâm, to vouchsafe to His worshipper
15 Saḫmân, son of Karbân, the esteem and grace of their two lords
16 Nimrân ʾAwkân and his brother Gaḥḏum ʾAḥ-
17 ṣân, descendants of the Leader of Ḫalîl and of the Leader of ʾAqyânum, and of Su-
18 ḫaymum; and that He may protect and preserve His worshipper Saḫmân,
19 son of Karbân, from the hostility and wickedness of [any] enemy, those
20 who are known or those who are not known. By ʾIlumquh Ṯahwân,
21 master of ʾAwwâm.

L. 1: *ʾwḥm*, cf. the name of man *ʾyḥ* both in Liḥyanite (cf. *JaSaMA*, p. 461, No. 101) and in

Thamudic (cf. *vdBrTTPN*, p. 54: Ph 279 aq) rather than ᵓ*aqtal* form derived from the root *wḥm*, cf. Arabic *waḥama* "to get ready for something" and its derived noun *waḥam* "desire" and adjective *waḥîm* "burning, hot (day)".

Ll. 8-9: *srn*/ᵓ*ẖr*, cf. *srhw*/ᵓ*ẖr* in RÉS 4100/5; cf. also RÉS 4689/2.

759 – "Statue base found on pavement in front of bench outside the outer hall structure. At 018 on my chart. That is, outside the door near the alabaster table which is on the mezzanine" (F. P. Albright); copy of the text by James Rubright. – MaMB 305.

Front: length: 32 cm., and width: 22; side: depth: 26 cm.

1 *hqnyt/bn/*
2 *yḥm*ᵓ*l/lbnh*
3 *mw/s*ᶜ*dm*

1 The offering of the descendants
2 of Yaḥamᵓil for their son
3 Saᶜadum.

Cf. formula, e.g., in Ja 749.

760 – Small sandstone block; photograph; cf. Chapter I, D. – MaMB 310.

Front: upper edge badly damaged. – INSCRIPTION: upper half of the symbol and of all the signs is destroyed. – SYMBOL, cf. lower half of Ja 556.

⌜**Symbol** *hqnyt/bn/sẖymm*⌝

Symbol The offering of the descendants of Suẖaymum.

Same formula as in Ja 759/1-2.

761 – Block of sandstone located on the left of Ja 760; photograph; cf. Chapter I, D, and *AlEMY*, p. 295 B. – MaMB 311.

Front: upper edge badly broken. – INSCRIPTION: the 1st line almost completely destroyed as is the center of line 2. – SYMBOL: only the lower extremity remains.

1 [**Sym-** . . . . . ./*hqnyw*/ᵓ*lmq*]*h*
2 ⌜**bol**⌝ *ṯ*⌜*h*⌝[*wn*]/*b*ᶜ*l*/ᵓ*w*⌜*m*/*ṣlmn*/⌝[. . .
. . .*h*]ᶜ⌜*n*⌝/*bytn*
3 *slḥn/w*ᵓ*b*ᶜ*lhw/wlḏt/n*ᶜ*mt/wtn*ᶜ*mn/lhmw/*ᶜ*m/mlk/*
ᵓ*lmqh/b*ᶜ*ṯtr*
4 *whbs/w*ᵓ*lmqh/wbḏt/ḥmym/wbḏt/b*ᶜ*dnm/wbšms/*
mlkn/tnf

1 [**Sym-** . . . . . .have dedicated to ᵓIlum-
qu]h
2 **bol** Ṯah[wân], master of ᵓAwwâm, this statue
. . . . . .He has] protected the house
3 Salḥân and its masters; and that it may have been pleasant and be pleasant for them with the property of ᵓIlumquh. By ᶜAṯtar
4 and Hawbas and ᵓIlumquh and by Ḏât-Ḥimyâm and by Ḏât-Baᶜdânum and by Šams of the king, Tanûf.

L. 2: [.]ᶜ*n*: *h*ᶜ*n* is more probable than *mt*ᶜ*n*.

851 – See addendum, pp. 251-52.

2° – SMALL FRAGMENTS: Ja 762-828

762 – Fragment of white alabaster, broken on each side; photograph in Plate 36. – MaMB 20.

STONE: constant thickness: 6.5 cm. – *Front:* maximum length: 17 cm., and width: 11. – INSCRIPTION: same disposition of lines as in Ja 552; letter height: 2.7 cm.; space between the lines: 0.4 cm.

1 . . ./*ml*]⌜*k*/*sb*ᵓ⌝[. . .
2 . . ./]*ṭybn*/*ḏmd*⌞*l*⌟[*thw*/. . .
3 . . .]⌞/⌟⌞*bms*ᵓ*lhw*⌜/⌝[. . .
4 . . ./*bw*]*rẖ*/*stqbl*/*b*⌟[ᶜ*mhw*/. . .
5 . . ./*bn*/]⌞*ḥ*⌟*lẓ*/*ḥl*⌞*ẓ*/⌟[. . .
6 . . ./*w*]⌞*kl*⌟[/]⌞*b*⌟[ᶜ*rhw*/. . .

1 . . .kin]g of Sabaᵓ [. . .
2 . . .] good [. . .,] the weight of which [(is). . .
3 . . .] through His oracle [. . .
4 . . .during] (the month) he was calling (on) [Him.
5 . . .from] the oppression he was suffering [. . .
6 . . .and] all [his camel] h[erd. . .

L. 2: *ṭyb* is either a noun designating some kind of incense or more probably an adjective which was preceded by a noun such as *ṯwr* "bull", *ṣlm* "statue"; etc.

L. 4: *stqbl*, 10th form of *qbl* (cf. commentary on Ja 644/4); cf. Arabic *qabala* 10th form "to call on a person; be in front of someone".

L. 6: *b*[. . .] is restored as *b*ᶜ*rhw* on the basis, e.g., of Ja 709/6.

763 – Splinter from the left side of a slightly yellowish sandstone inscription;

left edge damaged; photograph in Plate 36. – MaMB 27.

Front: covered with brownish paint; length; 10.5 cm., and width: 24.5 cm. – INSCRIPTION: same disposition of lines as in Ja 559.

1 *...]⌈n/⌉ʾl*
2 *...]⌈ht/ʾm*
3 *.../]⌊wlʿzm/w*
4 *.../ʾlm]⌊q⌋h/ʿbd*
5 *[hw/... /bn/ ...]zʾt⌋*

1 ...
2 ...
3 ...] and for the undertaking and
4 ...ʾIlum]quh [His] worshipper
5 ...from...] the constraint of

Cf. the beginning of the commentary on Ja 775 and 792.

Ll. 1-2: ...]*n/ʾl*[... could possibly be the end and the beginning of a personal name, or /*b*]*n/ʾl*[.. either "so]n of ʾIl[..." or "o]f ʾIl[...", or *ʾṣlm*]*n/ʾl*[*y*/... "statue]s i[n...", etc.

L. 2: ...]*ht* could possibly be restored as *q*]*ht* (e.g., Ja 565/6) "obedience; authority".

Ll. 2-3: *ʾm*[...] could possibly be restored as *ʾm*[*hw* or *ʾm*[*hmw* "his" or "their mother", *ʾm*[*rʾ*.. "lords", *ʾm*[*t*... or *ʾm*[*h*... "maid-servant(s)", etc.

L. 3: *ʿzm*, cf. Arabic *ʿazama* "to undertake" and its derived noun *ʿazm* "undertaking"; *ʿzm* here is either noun or infinitive; the root *ʿzm* is also attested in *ʿzmm*, 2nd personal name in Altounyan 1 B; for the 1st personal name of the latter text, cf. commentary on Ja 563/19-20: *ṯwr/bʿlm*.

L. 5: *bn* "from" is to be restored somewhere between [*hw*] and *zʾt*.

764 – Lower part of a sandstone inscription, damaged on both lateral sides; photograph in Plate 37. – MaMB 28.

Front: covered with reddish paint; 15.2 cm. × 9.4. – INSCRIPTION: same disposition of lines as in Ja 559; letter height: 2 cm.; space between the lines: 0.5 cm.

1 *.../ḥmdm/bḏt]*
2 *[ẖmr/ʾlmqh/ʾ]m*
3 *⌈th/ḥ⌉yw⌈t/⌉wld⌊m⌋*
4 *[w]⌊hwfyhw/ʾlmqh⌊/⌋*
5 *[ḥ]⌊yw/bnth/ʾẖtʾ⌋[l]*

1 [... ...in praise because]
2 [ʾIlumquh has vouchsafed to] His
3 [mai]dservant Ḥaywat a child,
4 [and because] ʾIlumquh has granted to her
5 the [li]fe of her daughter ʾUẖatʾi[l.]

L. 3: the signs are wider in line 3 than in lines 4 and 5. – *ḥywt*, cf. Ja 174/1, Qat, and commentary; see the form *ḥyyt* in *RyGSAS*, p. 559.

L. 5: *ʾẖtʾ*[*l*], a feminine personal name with the meaning "sister of ʾI(l)"; cf. *ʾẖtʾmh* (CIH 389/1) and *ʾẖyyt* (e.g., Ja 265/1 and also commentary on Ja 271, Qat). *ʾẖthw* in RÉS 4017 and 4084/6 and 9 is not a feminine personal name (cf. *RyNP*, I, p. 391 A and *RÉS*, VII, p. 75) but a noun with the personal pronoun, "her sister".

765 – Left part of an inscription of whitish sandstone; photograph in Plate 37. – MaMB 29.

STONE: maximum length: 8.3 cm.; width: 16.5 cm.; left side and a small part of the upper edge are preserved; thus no line is missing on the top. – INSCRIPTION: same disposition of lines as in Ja 552; letter height: 1.3 cm.; space between the lines: 0.2 cm.; at 0.2 cm. below line 7, another finely traced horizontal line.

1 *.../hqny/]⌊ʾlmqh/ṯ*
2 *[hwn/bʿl/ʾwm/]⌊ṣlmn/ḏdh*
3 *[bn/ḥmdm/bḏt/]mtʿhw/b⌈n⌉*
4 *.../]wlwzʾ/⌊ʾ⌋l*
5 *[mqh/bʿl/ʾw]⌊m⌉/mtʿn⌋⌊/⌋ʿ⌊bdh⌋*
6 *[w/... ...]m/wlsʿ⌈dh⌉w⌈/⌊ḥ⌉*
7 *[ẓy/wrḍw/šʿ]bhw*

1 ...has dedicated to] ʾIlumquh Ṯa-
2 [hwân, master of ʾAwwâm,] this statue which [is] in bron-
3 [ze, in praise because] He has saved him from
4 ...;] and that may continue ʾIl-
5 [umquh, master of ʾAww]âm to save His worshipper
6 ...].; and that He may make him happy with the es-
7 [teem and grace of] his [tri]be.

766 – Fragment (right part) of inscription of yellowish sandstone with a reddish stain; the right side is most probably original; photograph in Plate 37. – MaMB 30.

STONE: maximum thickness: 6.8 cm. – *Front:* maximum length: 7.8 cm., and width: 12.7. –

INSCRIPTION: same disposition of lines as in Ja 559; letter height: 1.6 cm.; space between the lines: 0.2 cm.; the 1st letter of each line is certain. – SYMBOL; almost entirely obliterated; shaped, e.g., as in Ja 733.

1 ⸢**Sym-**⸣ [...
2 ⸤**bol** [...
3 [... *hqnyw*/... .../*ᵓlmq*]
4 *h*⸢*b*⸣[*ᶜlᵓwm*/...
5 *mrᵓ*⸥*h*⸢*m*⸣*w*/*wh*[*b*... .../*mlk*/*sbᵓ*]
6 *wḏrydn*/*ᶜdy*⸢/⸣[... ...*hm*]
7 *w*/*ᵓlmqh*/*ṯ*[*br*...
8 ⸤*n*/*bwfym*/*wmh*⸥[*rgm*/...

1 **Sym-**
2 **bol**
3 [...have dedicated to...ᵓIlumqu]h,
4 m[aster of ᵓAwwâm,...
5 their lord Waha[b... , king of Sabaᵓ]
6 and Raydân in [... ...thei]r [...
7 ᵓIlumquh to cr[ush...
8 .in safety and (with) war [trophy...

The present text and Ja 780 do not belong to the same original because of the different palaeography in *m* and *q*. Cf. also the beginning of the commentary on Ja 792.

L. 3: *hqnyw* must be restored somewhere in the line.
L. 5: *wh*[*b*...: both the name of the king and the relationship between *wh*[*b*... and the king himself remain unknown.
L. 6: *ᵓrḍ* might be restored after *ᶜdy*.
L. 8: *n*, ending of the proper name of a city, country, etc. – *mhrg* is used in more inscriptions than *mhrgt*.

767 – Upper right corner of an inscription in whitish sandstone, broken into four fragments; photograph in Plate 37. – MaMB 32.

Front: 10.8 cm. × 14. – INSCRIPTION: same disposition of lines as in Ja 559; letter height: 1.4 cm.; space between the lines: 0.3 cm.; the entire line 1 is missing; the right edge is certain. – SYMBOL, only the lower left corner remains.

1 [**Sym-**] *ᶜm*⸢*rf*⸣[*ᵓ*/...
2 ⸤⸢**bol**⸣ *wrbᶜt*/*wsmh*⸣[...
3 [./*w*]*ḏrḥᵓ*⸤*l*/*w*⸤*yd*⸥*m*/[... .../*bnw*]
4 *b*⸢*ymm*/*ᵓ*⸤*ġym*[*n*... .../*hqn*]
5 *yw*/*ᵓ*⸣[*lmqh*/...
6 ⸤*ḏš*⸢*f*⸣*t*/*ᶜ*⸢*mrfᵓ*/⸢*bkn*/[...
7 ⸤*ᵓbl*⸣⸢*h*⸣[*w*]⸤/⸥[...

1 [**Sym-**] ᶜAmmrafa[ᵓ and...
2 **bol** and Rabîᶜat and Sumhu[...
3 [.and] Ḏaraḥᵓil and Yadum[..., descendants of]
4 Bayamum, the Ġaym[ânite]s, [...] have [dedicat-]
5 ed to ᵓI[lumquh...
6 that ᶜAmmrafaᵓ had promised when [...
7 hi[s] camel [...

Ll. 1 and 6: *ᶜmrfᵓ*, same nominal formation as that, e.g., of *ᵓlrfᵓ* (CIH 451/1); cf. also *rfᵓm* and *rfᵓn* in Qat Ja 346/2 and 327/2, both family names.
L. 3: *ḏrḥᵓl*, e.g., Ja 506 A/1 and monogram D.
L. 4: *bymm*, cf. *bym* in CIH 897/1-2. – *ᵓġym*[*n*, cf. *fyšny* in Ja 747/2.
L. 7: after *ᵓblh*[*w*]/ upper extremities of four signs are still visible.

768 – Fragment of a slightly yellowish and pinkish alabaster plaque with a lateral brim; facsimile in Plate P. – MaMB 33.

PLAQUE: constant thickness: 4.8 cm. – *Front:* 15 cm. × 21.5; lateral brim: width: 2.5 cm., and thickness: 0.5 cm. – INSCRIPTION: cursive writing; on the brim and parallel to its length; line 1: 6.4 cm. × 1, distance to the top of the brim: 0.4 cm.; line 2: 2.8 cm. × 0.4, engraved at 0.6 cm. below and on the right of line 1.

1 *ᵓbkrb*/*bn*/*brt*⸤*n*⸥
2 *bqyn*

1 ᵓAbkarib, son of Barratân
2 Baqîyân.

L. 1: *brtn*, family name in RÉS 3902, No. 27, Qat.
L. 2: *bqyn*, cf. in Arabic the adjective *bâqin* "who remains, survives" and the names of men *bqy* (cf. *WüR*, p. 345), *baqîyat* (cf. *SaIS*, p. 26 B) and *ᶜabd al-bâqî* (cf. *SlGaVNPA*, p. 1 B).

769 – Fragment of yellowish sandstone slightly speckled with grayish lines; broken on the left; upper right corner broken. – MaMB 34.

STONE: constant thickness: 7.7 cm. – *Front:* 12 cm. × 10.5. – INSCRIPTION: same disposition of lines as in Ja 559; 10 cm. × 7; distance to the right and lower edges: 1.7 cm. and 1.8 respectively.

⸢*hwf*⸣*ᶜ*⸢*ṯt*   Hawfᶜaṯat.

There is no possibility of considering Ja 769 as the end of Ja 565/1.

770 – Upper left corner of an inscription; slightly yellowish sandstone. – MaMB 35.

STONE: thickness: 8.6 cm. – *Front:* 10.3 cm. × 7.2. – INSCRIPTION: 6.3 cm. × 3.8; distance to the upper edge: 1.7 cm.

1 . . .]⌊*ʾb*⌋*ḥy*
2 [*l*/. . .

1 . . .] ʾAbḥay-
2 [l. . .

ʾbḥy[, cf. *ʾbḥl* (cf. *JaDME*, p. 17); one might also think, e.g., of *ʾbḥyw*.

771 – Fragment of slightly yellowish sandstone. – MaMB 36.

STONE: thickness: 8.2 cm. – *Front:* (maximum) 11 cm. × 4.2. – INSCRIPTION: 10 cm. × 4.3.

. . .*b*]⌈*n*⌉⌈*y*/⌊*sqr*⌋[*n*/. . .

. . ., des]cendants of Saqr[ân,. . .

772 – Upper left corner of an inscription; whitish, slightly brownish sandstone; two photographs in Plate 38. – MaMB 37.

FRONT: right part and bottom missing; 10.2 cm. × 5. – LEFT SIDE: left part and bottom missing; 10.1 cm. × 7.7. – INSCRIPTION: same disposition of lines as in Ja 552; letter height: 2 cm.; space between the lines: 0.5 cm.

	Front	*Left*
1	. . .]⌈/*hl*⌉*t*⌋	⌈*n*⌉/*ʾlt*/⌊*ʾl*⌉[. . .
2	./*bʿl*]/*ʾw*	*m*/*ṣlmn*/[. . .
3	. ./*b*]⌈*kn*/*sb*⌉	*ʾ*/*bʿm*/*r*⌋[. . .
4	. . ./]⌊*šʾmt*⌋	*wrm*⌊*n*/*w*⌋.[. . .

1 . . .] Hillatân, those of ʾIl[. . .
2 . . .master of] ʾAwwâm, this statue [. . .
3 . . ., w]hen he fought against R[. . .
4 . . .] north and Râmân and [. . .

L. 1: *hltn*, cf. the names of a woman *hllt* (e.g., Ja 314, Qat) and of a family *hllm* and *hlm* (e.g., Ja 642/2 and 665/32 respectively). – *ʾl*[. . .; in RÉS 4596/2, read *ʾln* instead of *kln*.

L. 2: *ṣlmn* was probably followed by *ḏḏhbn*.

L. 3: *r*[. . . could possibly be restored as *rmn* (cf. line 4).

L. 4: *rmn*, name of a wâdî-side valley in RÉS 4085/4; cf. also the personal name *qmrrmn* (cf. *RyGSAS*, p. 559).

773 – Upper left corner of a yellowish-sandstone plaque; top partially preserved; photograph in Plate 38. – MaMB 38.

PLAQUE: thickness: 5.5 cm. – *Front:* 8.8 cm. × 5.6. – INSCRIPTION: same disposition of lines as in Ja 552; 7.2 cm. × 4.3.

. . .]⌈/⌉⌈*ḥy*⌋*w* 1 . . .Ḥayû-
[. . . 2 [. . .

774 – Upper left corner of an inscription in white, slightly yellowish alabaster; photograph in Plate 38. – MaMB 39.

STONE: maximum thickness: 12.5 cm. – *Front:* 6.3 cm. × 5.1. – INSCRIPTION: letter height: 2 cm.; length of lines 1 and 2: 4.7 cm. and 4.5 respectively; space between the lines: 0.5 cm.

1 . . ./*ḏ*]⌊*m*⌋*ḏrḥm*/
2 . . .]⌊*n*⌋/*ḏ*⌋*ʿmy*
3 { [*ṯʿ* / [*dm* } /. . .

1 . . ., he of] Maḏraḥum,
2 . . .]ân, he of [the clan] { ʿAmmya- / ʿUmay- }
3 { [ṯaʿ / [dum } ,. . .

L. 2: *ʿmy*. . . could possibly be completed as *ʿmydm* (e.g., Ja 355/1-2, Qat), *ʿmyṯʿ* (e.g., Ja 555/2).

It would be tempting to attribute this fragment to Ja 651, because of *ʿbdʿm*/*ḏmḏrḥm* (e.g., line 10), and also because the letter *d* (beginning of line 3) would complete perfectly the missing part in the present fragment. However, the lettering of the two texts Ja 651 and 774 is not identical; for instance the top of the upper central vertical stroke of *ḥ* is shaped as an upside-down triangle and square respectively; and the opening of the central curve of *r* is much wider in the first than in the second.

775 – Fragment from the upper left corner of an inscription; yellowish sandstone; photograph in Plate 39. – MaMB 40.

STONE: maximum thickness: 3.8 cm. – *Front:* covered with reddish paint; 9.6 cm. × 5.1. – INSCRIPTION: same disposition of lines as in Ja 559; 9.6 cm. × 3.3.

...]⌜⌞*qr/bn/ḏ*⌝⌟	1	...]qar, son of Ḏ-
...	2	...

Ja 775 does not belong to the same original as that of Ja 763 especially because the top part of *b* is slightly curved in the former but flattened in the latter. – Nor is the present text to be joined to Ja 734, the central part of *n* of Ja 734 being more oblique than that shown in Ja 775 while the central curvature of *r* of Ja 775 is greater than that of Ja 734. – The present text and Ja 811 could at first sight belong to the same original; however, the character of the *r* is different in each case; the width of *n* is smaller (in the latter) but larger (in the former) than that of the other letters; finally, the upper part of *b* is horizontal in Ja 775 but concave in line 1 of Ja 811; with regard to *b* or *ḍ* (line 2 of the 2nd), the upper extremities of both lateral strokes are much less curved than those in Ja 775. The letter preceding *r* is *q*, and neither *w* or ʿ, for the line of the breaking of the stone above the center of the letter is straight; this fact suggests that it follows the line of a depression existing previously, that is to say the vertical stroke of *q*. Too many restorations are equally possible; e.g., *w*]*qr* (cf. *wqrn* in CIH 431+438/1), *s*]*qr* (cf. *sqrn*, e.g., in Ja 683/1), etc.

776 – Fragment of yellowish alabaster; photograph in Plate 39. – MaMB 41.

STONE: maximum thickness: 7.1 cm. – *Front:* 7.8 cm. × 3.3. – INSCRIPTION: same disposition of lines as in Ja 559; line 1: 6.2 cm. × 1.6; space between the lines: 0.2 cm.; line 2: 6.8 cm. × 1.1.

1 ...]⌜⌞*ʾl/mḏy*⌜*n*⌝[...
2 ...]⌞*yṯ*⌟ʿ⌞*n/hq*⌟[*ny*...

1 ...]ʾil Maḏayân [...
2 ...] Yaṯiʿân, dedi[cated to...

L. 2: *yṯʿn*: the lower part of each letter is missing; also family name, e.g., in Ja 298/2, Qat; cf. also *yṯʿm* (e.g., Gl 1128+1129/12) and *yṯʿt* (e.g., Ja 148/1, Qat). – *hq*[*ny* is the minimal restoration; both the number of the verb and its genus are unknown.

777 – Fragment of pink sandstone speckled with white stains; right side preserved; photograph in Plate 39. – MaMB 43.

STONE: maximum thickness: 2.6 cm. – *Front:* 7.2 cm. × 6.2. – INSCRIPTION: same disposition of lines as in Ja 552, but to the right of the beginning of line 3, two vertical strokes; their cutting indicates that they are not part of any letter; line 2: 4.7 cm. × 2.5; space between the lines: 0.5 cm.; line 2: 6.8 cm. × 3.2.

1 ...*hgr*]
2 [*h*]*mw*⌜*/mr*⌝⌞*b*⌝⌟[/... .../*h*]
3 ⌜⌞*q*⌝⌞*ny*⌟⌞*t*</>⌞*ḥ*⌟[*grm/qḥmm*/...

1 ...t]heir [city]
2 Mârib [... ...] has [de-]
3 dicated to Ḥa[garum Qaḥamum...

778 – Fragment of slightly yellowish sandstone; right side partly preserved; photograph in Plate 40. – MaMB 45.

STONE: maximum thickness: 4.6 cm. – *Front:* 7 cm. × 2.8. – INSCRIPTION: same disposition of lines as in Ja 561 bis; 5 cm. × 2.2; a vertical line is at 0.1 cm. to the right of the 1st letter.

[...	1	...
⌜*thm*⌟⌞*w*⌟[...	2	their [...

Ja 778 and 781 cannot be reunited because of the difference in the stones and in the disposition of the lines.

..]*t* could belong to *b*(*n*)*t*, *b*(*y*)*t*, *grybt*, etc.

779 = MaMB 49 = upper right corner of Ja 641.

780 – Fragment of the left side of an inscription; yellowish sandstone; photograph in Plate 40. – MaMB 50.

FRONT: 11.9 cm. × 8.1; space between the lines: 0.8 cm. – LEFT SIDE: 9.1 cm. – INSCRIPTION: same disposition of lines as in Ja 552.

1 ...].⌜*m/hq*⌝
2 [*ny*()/*ʾlmqh/ṯhwn*]⌜⌞*/b*⌝ʿ*l*⌟
3 [*ʾwm*/..

1 ...].um dedi-
2 [cated to ʾIlumquh Ṯahwân,] master of
3 [ʾAwwâm,..

Cf. the beginning of the commentary on Ja 766 and 792.

L. 1: the letter preceding *m* could be *g*, *h*, *ḥ*, *y*, *l*, etc.
Ll. 1-2: for *hqny*, cf. remark on Ja 776/2.

781 – Upper left part of an inscription; yellowish, slightly brownish sandstone; photograph in Plate 40. – MaMB 51.

FRONT: covered with red paint; 7.3 cm. × 2.7; INSCRIPTION: 6.7 cm. × 2.1; distance to the upper edge: 0.3 cm. – LEFT SIDE: 10.6 cm. × 3.7. – TOP: fragmentary ellipsis the great axis of which is perpendicular to the front; great and small axis: 6.4 cm. and at least 4 respectively.

..]⸤*r*⸥⸢*f*⸣/*w*⸤*b*⸥*n*	1	..]raf and [.] son(s?)
[..	2	[..

Cf. the beginning of the commentary on Ja 662 and 778.

L. 1: ..]*rf* belongs to a personal name either derived from or having the 2nd element composed of a root such as *ḫrf*, *ṣrf*, etc.
Ll. 1-2: *bn* could be read *bn*, *bnw* or *bny*, followed by either *hw* or *hmw*.

782 – Fragment of yellowish sandstone; upper edge preserved; photograph in Plate 40. – MaMB 52.

STONE: maximum thickness: 2.2 cm. – *Front:* 6.3 cm. × 4.8. – INSCRIPTION: same disposition of lines as in Ja 552; letter height: 1.8 cm.; space between the lines: 0.4 cm.; distance from line 1 to the upper edge: 0.7 cm.

1 .../ʾ]⸤*lmqhṯh*⸣[*wnbʿlʾwm*/...
2 ...]*m*/ʾ*lm*⸥⸤*qh*⸥[...

1 ...ʾI]lumquh Ṯah[wân, master of ʾAwwâm,...
2 ...]. ʾIlumquh [...

This text does not belong to Ja 803 because of palaeographic differences, viz. both lateral lines (but only the outside one in the upper part of *h*) are curved strongly in Ja 782 and slightly in Ja 803. Nor can it be joined to Ja 804 because the letters are more slender in that text. The difference in color of the stone as well as that of the front renders impossible the reunion of Ja 782 with Ja 813. Finally, palaeographically Ja 782 is completely different from Ja 839.

783 – Fragment of the left side of an inscription; yellowish sandstone; photograph in Plate 40. – MaMB 53.

STONE: maximum thickness: 3.4 cm.; the top is certain. – *Front:* covered with red paint; 2.9 cm. × 11.1. – INSCRIPTION: same disposition of lines as in Ja 552; letter height: 2.3 cm.; space between the lines: 0.4 cm.

1 ...]*ḥw*
2 [*hqnytw*/ʾ*l*]⸤*mq*⸢*h*⸣
3 [*bʿlʾwm*/*ṣlm*]⸤*tn*
4 [*d̲t*/*d̲hbn*/*d̲*]⸤*t*/*š*
5 [*ftthw*/...

1 ...]ḥû,
2 [have dedicated to ʾIl]umquh,
3 [master of ʾAwwâm,] this female [statue]
4 [which (is) in bronze, wh]ich [she had] pro-
5 [mised to Him,...

This inscription cannot possibly be the end of Ja 812/3-6 even if one were to suggest that the top of the former had been re-cut. – Cf. also the beginning of the commentary on Ja 792. – The remains of line 4 exclude the restoration of *ṣlm* before *ṣlmt* (line 3) but justify that of *d̲t*/*d̲hbn* (line 4); and -*n* in *ṣlmtn* is the article and not the dual ending because of *t* in *d̲t*. The restored lines 3 and 4 have precisely 12 signs; I restore thus *hqnytw* in line 2 so that this line would also have the same number of signs. The preceding interpretation of the remains of the stone suggests that *ḥw* is the ending of a proper name.

784 – Alabaster plaque, broken on the right side; photograph in Plate 41. – MaMB 55.

PLAQUE: thickness: between 5.8 cm. (almost constantly) and 6.4 (maximum). – *Front:* 22.2 cm. × 13.2. – INSCRIPTION: same disposition of lines as in Ja 552; letter height: 3.4 cm., 3.5, and 3.5; space between the lines: 0.6 cm.; distance from line 1 to the upper edge: 0.9 cm., and to the left: 1.5 cm.; from line 2 to the left edge: 1 cm.; and from line 3 to the lower edge: 0.7 cm. – BOTTOM: damaged, but certain.

1 ...].⸢/*y*⸣⸢*ḥm*ʾ*l*/ʾ*d*⸢*m*/*m*⸣*lk*
2 [*n*/*hqnyw*/ʾ*lm*]⸢*q*⸣⸢*h*/*bʿl*/ʾ*wm*/*ṣlmn*/⸤*l*⸥
3 [*wfy*/*bnhmw*/]⸤*rb*ʾ⸥*l*/*wl*/*wśfhmw*/*ġlmm*⸣

1 . . .]. Yaḥamʾil, servants of [the] king
2 [have dedicated to ʾIlum]quh, master of ʾAwwâm, this statue for
3 [the safety of their son] Rabbʾil, and that He may add to them a youth.

L. 1: to the right of the 1st word divider remains the lower half of a vertical stroke belonging to ʾ, *b*, *ḏ*, etc.

L. 3: *rbʾl* may be complete; the restoration offers the same number of signs as in line 2; nevertheless a name such, e.g., as [*k*]*rbʾl* is also possible. – For the 2nd half of the line, cp. Ja 757/4, 2nd half.

785 = MaMB 56 = right part of Ja 718.

786 – Fragment from the left of an inscription; yellowish sandstone; photograph in Plate 41. – MaMB 58.

STONE: thickness: 2.9 cm. – *Front:* 14 cm. × 6.8. – INSCRIPTION: same disposition of lines as in Ja 552; letter height: 2.8 cm.; space between the lines: 0.6 cm., 0.5, 0.6, and 0.5.

1 . .
2 . . .]⸢*hʿnn*
3 . . . *ʾmh*]⸢*hw*/*wd*
4 . . . /]⸢⸤*ʾẖthn*
5 *t*/. . /*bn*]⸤/*bʾst*⸥

1 . .
2 . . .] protect
3 . . .] His [maidservants] Wadd-
4 . . .] their sister
5 . . . from] misfortunes

This text does not belong to Ja 722 because of the difference in the palaeography of *d* and *w*. – Cf. also the beginning of the commentary on Ja 792.

L. 3: the plural *ʾmh* instead of the singular *ʾmt* is suggested by *hn* (line 4).

Ll. 3-4: *wd*[. . ., name of a woman; could be restored as *wd*[*dʾl*], *wd*[*dm*], etc.

L. 4: *ʾẖthn*, for *ʾẖthw* in RÉS 4017 and 4084/6, cf. commentary on Ja 764/5: *ʾẖtʾl*.

787 – Right part of a white alabaster plaque; right corners damaged; photograph in Plate 41. – MaMB 61.

PLAQUE: thickness: 8.8 cm. (lower part) and 6.4 (upper part). – *Front:* maximum length: 21.5 cm.; the upper part on which line 1 is engraved is a raised margin with a width and depth of 2.7 cm. and 1.7 respectively; width of the lower part: 12.2 cm. – INSCRIPTION: letter height: 2.5 cm. (line 1), 3.4 (line 2), 3.5 (line 3), and 3.6 (line 4); space between the lines: 0.4 cm. between lines 1-2 and 3-4, but 0.5 between lines 2-3; line 1 reaches the lower edge of the brim. – SYMBOL: the outside design may be compared with that, e.g., of Ja 552; the inside incisions are a simplification of, e.g., those of Ja 554; cf. Plate B.

1 **Sym-** *kryb*⸣⸢*m*/.⸣[. . .
2 **bol** *hqn*⸢*y*/⸣*ʾl*⸢*mq*⸣[*h*. . ./*lwfy*/*bn*]
3 *hw*/*lḥyʿṯt*/*wl*/*w*⸢*fyh*⸣[*mw*/. . .
4 ʾ ʿ *t* *b* *n*

1 **Sym-** Kuraybum. [. . .
2 **bol** has dedicated to ʾIlumq[uh. . . for the safety of] his [son]
3 Laḥayʿaṯat and for t[heir own] safety [. . .
4 the ʿAtabites.

L. 1: the 1st letter of the 2nd personal name is *b*, *g*, *d*, *ḏ*, *ẖ*, etc.

788 – Upper right corner of an inscription; yellowish, slightly grayish sandstone; photograph in Plate 42. – MaMB 62.

STONE: thickness: 14.5 cm. – *Front:* 18.5 cm. × 6.7. – INSCRIPTION: same disposition of lines as in Ja 552; several lines cross the text; letter height: 2.5 cm. (lines 1 and 3); 2.1 (line 2), and 2.7 (line 4); space between the lines: 0.4 cm., 0.5, 0.7, and 0.6. – SYMBOL: the outside design is shaped as, e.g., in Ja 692; the bottom and top lines are curved inwards; in the upper part, two parallel incisions whose lower extremities make a rather sharp curve; in the center, there are two small, almost vertical lines (cf. Ja 550); at the bottom, two other parallel incisions whose upper extremities end with a strongly concave line; cf. Plate B.

1 **Sym-**⸣ [*whbʾwm*/*yʾḏf*/*wʾẖyhw*/*ydm*/*ydrm*/ *wbnyhw*/*ḥ*]
2 **bol** *mʿ*⸣⸥[*ṯt*/*ʾzʾd*/*wʾbkrb*/*ʾsʿd*/*wsẖymm*/*yzʾn*/ *bnw*/*sẖ*]
3 *ymm*/*ʾbʿ*⸣⸥[*l*/*bytn*/*rymn*/*hqnyw*/*ʾlmqhṯhwnbʿlʾwm*/*ṣlm*]
4 *nhn*/⸤*y*⸥[. . . . . . /*wldm*/*ḏk*]
5 *rm*/*w*⸥[. . . . . . *ẖm*]
6 ⸤*rh*⸥[*mw*/. . .

1 **Sym-** [Wahabʾawwâm Yaʾḏif and his brother Yadum Yadrim and his sons Ḥa-]
2 **bol** mmʿa[ṯat ʾAzʾad and ʾAbkarib ʾAsʿad and Suḫaymum Yazʾân, descendants of Suḫa-]
3 ymum, maste[r]s [of the house Raymân, have dedicated to ʾIlumquh Ṯahwân, master of ʾAwwâm,] these two [statues]
4 ...a child ma-]
5 le and [... ...vouch-]
6 safe to t[hem...

This inscription is restored on the basis of Ja 616 (cf. Ja 718), but the appointment of the persons as rulers of the tribe Yarsum recorded in the text cannot be restored; thus the chronological order is Ja 788, 718, and 616.

789 – Fragmentary upper left corner of an inscription; gray, yellowish sandstone; photograph in Plate 42. – MaMB 65.

STONE: maximum thickness: 8.8 cm. – *Front:* 9.5 cm. × 16. – INSCRIPTION: same disposition of lines as in Ja 552; letter height: 5.5 cm.; space between the lines: 0.9 cm.

1 .../*ʾlmq*]⌜*h*⌝*wb*⌟(ʿ)
2 [*lʾwm*/... ...]*rt*/ʾ⌟

1 ...ʾIlumq]uhû, ma(s-)
2 [ter of ʾAwwâm... ...]rat.

L. 1: ʿ is still visible although badly damaged.
L. 2: ...]*rt* might be restored *grt*, *ḥrt*, *krt* (Ja 400 B/2-3), etc. – ʾ is most probably the sign of the plural of a word such as *wld*, etc.; the bottom of the word divider and the lower right extremity of ʾ are connected by a fully engraved stroke similar, e.g., to the top of *b*.

790 – Fragment of an inscription; upper left corner; yellow, slightly grayish sandstone; photograph in Plate 42. – MaMB 71.

STONE: thickness: 16.1 cm. – *Top:* rest of an elliptical hollow: 8.1 cm. × 4.9 and 2.4 (depth). – *Front:* length: 7 cm., and width: 6.8. – INSCRIPTION: same disposition of lines as in Ja 552; letter height 2.2 cm.; space between the lines: 0.5 cm.; distance from line 1 to the upper edge: 0.4 cm.

1 .../]⌞⌜*hq*⌝*nyw*
2 [*ʾlmqhṯhwn*]*bʿlʾwm*
3 [*ṣlmn*/*ḏhbn*]⌞/*bḏt*/*h*⌟
4 [*wfy*...

1 ...]have dedicated to
2 [ʾIlumquh Ṯahwân,] master of ʾAwwâm,
3 [this statue in bronze,] because He has bes-
4 [towed upon...

Ja 790 does not belong to Ja 594 because its lettering is more regular than that of the latter.

Ll. 3-4: *h*[...: *hwfy* is used in such contexts more frequently, e.g., than *hwšʿ*.

791 – Fragment of an inscription; grayish sandstone; photograph in Plate 42. – MaMB 72.

STONE: maximum thickness: 14.1 cm. – *Front:* covered with red paint; diagonal length: 12.1 cm. (left) and 14.8 (right); length of the right edge: 4.7 cm. – INSCRIPTION: same disposition of lines as in Ja 552.

1 .../*sb*]⌜ʾ/⌝*wḏr*⌞*y*⌟[*dn*/...
2 ...]⌜/*m*⌝⌜*lk*/*s*⌞*b*ʾ/⌟[...
3 ⌜*kr*⌝*b*/*w*ʾ⌟⌞*ṣb*⌟[...
4 ʿ*dy*/⌞*kl*⌟[/...
5 ⌞*t*⌝⌟[...

1 ...Saba]ʾ and Ray[dân...
2 ...] king of Sabaʾ [...
3 karib and ʾAṣb[...
4 in all [...
5 ...

Palaeographically Ja 791 could belong to Ja 595; but the color of the stone is different in each case, and the red paint covers the front of the 1st and not that of the 2nd; furthermore, the letter height in the 1st is certainly at least 3 cm. but only 1.7 cm. and 1.8 in the 2nd. – The preceding remarks are also true with regard to the present text and Ja 597, with the following exception: the upper part of *k* is more curved in the 2nd text than in the 1st. – Cf. also the beginning of the commentary on Ja 625.

L. 3: the letter following ʾ is *ṣ* and neither *y* nor *ṯ*, because the upper right corner of the lower half of *ṣ* is still preserved on the stone. The following letter is either *b* or *ḍ*; the personal name could be ʾ*ṣbḥ* (cf. the Arabic names of men ʾ*aṣbaḥ* and *al-*ʾ*aṣâbiḥ*; cf. *LöHSM*, p. 56 B), ʾ*ṣbġ* (cf. the Arabic name of a man *al-*ʾ*ṣbġ*; cf. *SaIS*, p. 14 A), etc.

792 – Upper right corner of an inscription; yellowish sandstone; photograph in Plate 42. – MaMB 73.

STONE: maximum thickness: 12.3 cm. – *Front:* covered with red paint; diagonal length: 8.5 cm.; width: 5. – INSCRIPTION: same disposition of lines as in Ja 561 bis. – SYMBOL, cp. Ja 707; cf. Plate B.

⌜**Sym-**	*h*⌝[. . .	1	**Sym-**	Ha[. . .
bol	*ḏ*⌝[. . .	2	**bol**	.[. . .
.		3	.	

The letter height (about 3 cm.) and the palaeography of *ḏ* (the central lines are leaning to the right) exclude the re-union of the present text, e.g., with Ja 597 and 766. – It is palaeographically impossible to re-unite the present text with Ja 638, 685, and 815. – The restoration of *š^{c}bn/sbʾ/khln* at the beginning of line 1 in Ja 668 excludes the possibility of re-uniting this text with the present inscription. – Ja 792 does not belong to Ja 786 because of the difference in palaeography of *h*: the lower vertical stroke is much higher in the latter than in the 1st. – The preceding remark is also valid with regard to the present text and Ja 783. – The *h* is thicker here than in Ja 763 and 780.

L. 2: *ḏ* may belong to a proper name or introduce a family name.

L. 3: at the beginning, the upper part of a circle which belongs to one of the four following letters: *y*, *ẓ*, *ṣ*, or *ṯ*.

793 – Fragment of an inscription; yellowish sandstone; photograph in Plate 43. – MaMB 75.

STONE: maximum thickness: 9.5 cm.; the top side is ascertained. – *Front:* diagonal length: 11.8 cm.; width at the second letter: 3.5 cm.

. . .]⌞*n*⌟*l^c*[. . .   . . .]Nil^{c}a[. . .

The lower end of the second letter is rounded; the letter is thus complete. To the left of the vertical stroke of *l* and at the same distance as that between *l* and the upper vertical stroke of *n*, there is a damaged circle, without any trace of a vertical stroke in its center, whose diameter equals the width of the center of the first letter. The name is derived from the root *l^c*[.].

794=MaMB 76=fragment of Ja 810.

795 – Fragment of white limestone, broken on both lateral sides and at the bottom; top partly preserved; photograph. – MaMB 77.

STONE: maximum thickness: 6.2 cm. – *Front:* covered with red paint; diagonal length: 10.3 cm.; width on the letter *ṯ*: 3 cm. – INSCRIPTION: same disposition of lines as in Ja 552; letter height: 1.7 cm.; space between the lines: 0.6 cm.; distance from line 1 to the upper edge: 0.4 cm.

1 . . .]⌜⌞*śl/ḏ*⌜ʾ*ws*⌝[. . .
2 . . .]⌞*rb*⌟*^{c}ṯt/ṣ*⌝[. . .

1 . . .]śal, he of [the family] ʾAws[. . .
2 . . .] Rabb^{c}aṯat Ṣ[. . .

It is palaeographically impossible to re-unite Ja 795 with Ja 798.

L. 1: . . .]*śl*, cf., e.g., *wśl* in Ja 711/1.

L. 2: *rb^{c}ṯt*, also attested, e.g., in Ja 812/2; if its beginning is fragmentary, cf., e.g., *krb^{c}ṯt*. – *ẖ*[. . . most probably beginning of the 2nd personal name.

796 – Upper left corner of an inscription; yellowish sandstone; photograph in Plate 43. – MaMB 80.

STONE: thickness: 4.7 cm. – *Front:* 10.8 cm. × 8.3. – INSCRIPTION: same disposition of lines as in Ja 552; letter height: 3.7 cm.; space between the lines: 0.6 cm.; distance from line 1 to the upper edge: 1.6 cm.

1 . . .]⌞*lt*⌟*n/ḏqy*
2 . . .](*w*)⌞*hb*ʾ⌟
3 [{*wm*/. . . | *l*/. . .}

1 . . .]latân, he of [the family] Qay-
2 . . .] (Wa)hab{ʾa- | ʾi-}
3 [{wwâm | l}. . .

L. 1:]*ltn* could possibly be restored as *hltn* (Ja 772/1), *zltn* (Ja 557), etc.

Ll. 1-2: *qy*[could be read *qyḥn* (RÉS 4875/1, Ḥaḍr; cf. commentary on Ja 563/1), *qytm*, personal name in Ja 882 T, Qat (cf. *JaPEQL*, pp. 216-17), etc.

Ll. 2-3: the letter preceding *b* is either *h* or *ẖ*; on the left of the latter, a right triangle, the base of which is contiguous to the upper right stroke of the preceding letter, and the length of which equals the length of *n/* in line 1, is free of any letter remains; the missing letter is thus either *w* or ᶜ.

797 – Fragment (left part) of a block of whitish alabaster; two photographs in Plate 43. – MaMB 81.

Front: broken on the right, bottom and top; 11.5 cm. × 6.5. – LEFT SIDE: broken on top and bottom; 9.8 cm. × 5.5 (right) and 6.1 (left). – INSCRIPTION: same disposition of lines as in Ja 552; the text begins on the front (part A) and is continued (part B) on the left side. A: letter height: 2.4 cm., and space between the lines: 0.3 cm. B: letter height: 2.5 cm., and space between the lines: 0.4 cm.

A

1 *.../ʾlmq]⸢h⸣w⸢/ṯh⸣w⸢n/b⸣ᶜ⸢l⸣*
2 *[ʾwm/... ../ṣl]⸤mtn⸥/ḥgn⸤/⸥w⸤qh⸥*
3 *[hw/...* ..

1 ...ʾIlumqu]hû Ṯahwân, master of
2 [ʾAwwâm... ...] this female [sta]tue, as He had ordered
3 [her... ..

B

...]⸢tḥ⸣rm	1	...]Taḥarram-
⸢n/⸣wbthw	2	ân and her daughter
⸤hn⸥ʾ⸤ṯwn/.	3	Haniʾṯawân.

B. – Ll. 1-2: *tḥrmn*, same nominal formation as that, e.g., of *tḥywm* (Ja 232, Qat).
L. 3: *hnʾṯwn*, also name of a woman in CIH 581/1-2. – The last remaining letter is either *h* or *ẖ*.

798 – Fragment of the upper part of a white limestone plaque; photograph in Plate 44. – MaMB 84.

PLAQUE: almost constant thickness: 8 cm. – *Front:* covered with red paint; maximum length: 5.7 cm.; width: 8.7 cm. – INSCRIPTION: same disposition of lines as in Ja 552; letter height: 1.8 cm.; space between the lines: 0.3 cm.

...]⸤bn/ḏby[n/...	1	...], descendants of Ḏû-Bayy[in...
...]⸢hmw/b⸥[...	2	...]their[...
...]kl⸥[/...	3	...]all[...
...]⸤h⸥[...	4	...

Cf. the beginning of the commentary on Ja 795.

799 – Bottom of an inscription broken into two parts; yellowish sandstone; top fragment = MaMB 121 = Ja 806; main block = MaMB 93; two photographs in Plate 44.

FRONT: covered with red paint. – INSCRIPTION: same disposition of lines as in Ja 561 bis; letter height: 1.4 cm. and 1.3; space between the lines: from 0.25 cm. to 0.3; at 0.3 cm. below line 7 there is another horizontal line finely traced. – MaMB 121: maximum thickness: 4.2 cm.; front: 7.2 cm. × 5 (right). – MaMB 93: almost constant thickness: 8.8 cm.

1 *...hm]*
2 *w/w⸢ld⸣[m/... .../w]*
3 *lsᶜdhm⸢w/⸣[.../ḏyhrḍwnh]*
4 *mw/wlsᶜdh⸢m⸣[w/ḥẓy/wrḍw]*
5 *⸤mrʾhmw/⸥ | ⸢hmw/d⸣wmn/yʾzm/ḏġym⸢n/w⸣*
6 *l⸢s⸣ᶜdhmw/ᶜdy/ʾrḍhmw/ʾṯmr*
7 *ṣdqm/bʾlmqhṯhwnbᶜlʾwm*

1 ...to the]m
2 [a] child [... ..., and]
3 that He may make them happy [... ..., which would please t]hem
4 and that He may make the[m] happy [with the esteem and grace of]
5 their lord Dawamân Yaʾzum, him of Ġaymân, and
6 that He may make them happy in their land with fruits
7 perfect. By ʾIlumquh Ṯahwân, master of ʾAwwâm.

Cf. commentary on Ja 807.

Ll. 3-4: *ḏyhrḍwnhmw* was probably preceded by a noun such as *ʾṯmr*, *ʾfql*, etc.; instead of the preceding verb one could possibly think of *ʾlbb*.
Ll. 4-5: *mrʾhmw*: *mrʾ* could also have originally been in plural form *ʾmrʾ*; if so the end of line 4 would be *wrḍw/ʾ*.
L. 5, cf. Ja 691/2-3.

800 – Fragment, broken on the right; yellowish sandstone; photograph in Plate 44. – MaMB 101.

STONE: maximum thickness: 25.8 cm. – *Front:* upper right corner broken; 19 cm. (top), 21.3 (center), and 20.5 (bottom) × 17 (right), 23.6 (center), and 25.7 (left). – INSCRIPTION: 13.6 cm. × 6.5.

...]⸢r⸣⸢m/yᶜd ...]rum Yaᶜud.

. . .]*rm* could be restored, e.g., as *kbrm* (Ja 626/2), *dbrn* (Ja 682/1), etc. – *y*ᶜ*d*, cf. RÉS 3963/3, Qat: name of a house.

801 – Upper part of a statue base; yellowish sandstone; photograph in Plate 45. – MaMB 102.

STONE: maximum thickness: 9.2 cm. – *Front:* covered with red paint; 10.2 cm. × 4. – INSCRIPTION: same disposition of lines as in Ja 552; length: 9.5 cm.

. . .]⌊*yf*ᶜ/*yḥm*⌋[. . . . . .]yafaᶜ Yaḥam[. . .

Ja 801 does not belong to Ja 809 because the horizontal part of the ornamental triangle is wider in the latter than in the former.

Too many restorations are equally possible for each of these two names.

802 – Left corner of a reddish sandstone plaque; two photographs in Plate 45. – MaMB 103.

TOP: diagonally broken; remains of the lower left corner of a hollow, probably with a concave bottom. – FRONT: 7.1 cm. (right) and 7.2 (left) × 4.6 (top) and 6.3 (bottom); part A of the text. – LEFT SIDE: 7.2 cm. (right) and 7.3 (left) × 4.5 (top) and 5.6 (bottom); part B of the inscription. – INSCRIPTION: same disposition of lines as in Ja 683.

A B

. . ./*b*]⌊*n*/*yl*⌋*śq*⌋[. . . . . .s]on of Yâśaq[. . .

yśq, for the verb *wśq*, cf. commentary on Ja 557: *hwśq*.

803 – Right part of an inscription; yellowish sandstone; photograph in Plate 45. – MaMB 104.

STONE: maximum thickness: 3.6 cm. – *Front:* lightly covered with red paint; 16.6 cm. × 5.6. – INSCRIPTION: same disposition of lines as in Ja 559; letter height: 1.8 cm.; space between the lines: 0.4 cm. – SYMBOL. The outside design: for the lower and upper parts, cf. the corresponding parts, e.g., in Ja 612 and 729 respectively. The inside design: a small incision perpendicular to the outside lines is located in the center (cf. Ja 690); in the upper part of the lower half of the symbol there is another incision the length of which equals the half of the right part of the symbol; cf. Plate B.

1 **Sym-**⌝ [. . .
2 **bol** [. . ./*hqny*()/ʾ*lmqhṯh*]
3 *wnb*ᶜ⌝[*l*ʾ*wm*/. . .
4 *lwfyh*⌋[{*w* / *mw*}/. . . . . ./ʾ*lm*]
5 *qh*/*b*ᶜ*l*[/ʾ*wm*/. . . . . ./*wl*]
6 *h*ᶜ*nn*⌊*h*⌋[{*w* / *mw*}. . . . . ./*bn*/*nḍ*ᶜ]
7 *wšṣ*⌋[*y*/*šn*ʾ*m*/*b*ʾ*lmqhṯhwnb*ᶜ*l*ʾ*wm*]

1 **Sym-** [. . .
2 **bol** [. . .dedicated to ʾIlumquh Ṯah-]
3 wân, mast[er of ʾAwwâm, . . .
4 for the safety of (him) (her) (th)[em . . .ʾIlum-]
5 quh, master of [ʾAwwâm, ..., and that may]
6 protect (him) (her) (th)[em. . . . . .from the hostility]
7 and wicked[ness of (any) enemy. By ʾIlumquh Ṯahwan, master of ʾAwwâm.]

Cf. commentary on Ja 782.

Ll. 4 and 6: it is not possible to determine whether the form of the personal pronoun *h* should be maintained or completed as *hw* or *hmw*.

804 – Two fragments from the lower left corner of an inscription; yellowish sandstone; photograph in Plate 45. – MaMB 118.

STONE: maximum thickness: 2.5 cm. – *Front:* covered with red paint; length: 5.9 cm., and width: 8.3 cm. – INSCRIPTION: same disposition of lines as in Ja 559; letter height: 1.7 cm.; space between the lines: 0.3 cm. – FLOWER at the end of line 4; cf. Ja 597.

1 . . .].⌜*sfl*⌝[. . .
2 . . ./*wlẖ*]*mrhn*/*rḍw*
3 [*wḥẓy*/. . . . . ./*wlmt*ᶜ*hn*/]⌊*bn*/*ṭw*ᶜ/*š*
4 [*n*ʾ*m*/. . . . ./*b*ʾ*lmqhṯhwnb*ᶜ]⌊*l*⌋ʾ*wm* **Flower**

1 . . .] lower country[. . .
2 . . .; and that He may vou]chsafe to them [women] the grace
3 [and esteem of. . . . . ., and that He may save them] from the constraint of [any] e-
4 [nemy. . . . . .By ʾIlumquh Ṯahwân, mas]ter of ʾAwwâm. **Flower**

Cf. the beginning of the commentary on Ja 569 and 782.

The stone is broken under line 3 but obliquely so that the lower fifth of /*š* belongs to the bottom fragment.

L. 1: above the space between *n* and the following word divider on line 2, the lower extremity of *f*; to its right and left, the lower extremity of three and one vertical strokes respectively; on the left of the latter, which is just above the top of *r* on line 2, the bottom of the line contains the remains of no lettering as far as the last third of *ḏ* where the stone is broken; those remains suggest the reading of *.sfl*.

L. 3: *ṭwʿ* is more frequently connected with *mtʿ* than with *ẖry* "to preserve"; *ḥʿn* (e.g., Ja 651/49) and *hwfy/grb* (Ja 647/31) are also sometimes connected with *ṭwʿ*.

805 = MaMB 120 = upper left corner of Ja 717.

806 = MaMB 121 = upper right corner of Ja 799.

807 – Fragment from the left edge of an inscription; yellowish sandstone; photograph in Plate 46. – MaMB 122.

STONE: maximum thickness: 2.5 cm. – *Front:* lightly covered with red paint; 7.4 cm. (left) × 5 (center). – INSCRIPTION: same disposition of lines as in Ja 561 bis; letter height: 1.3 cm. (lines 1 and 2) and 1.4 (lines 3 and 4); space between the lines: 0.2 cm., 0.3, and 0.3.

1 *...hw]⌈t/⌉⌈mrḍn*
2 *...]⌈/⌉bn/nḍʿ*
3 *[wšṣy/šnʾm/... .../wlsʿ]⌊d⌋hw/ʾlm*
4 *[qh... .../ḥẓy/wrḍw]⌊/m⌋rʾy[h]*
5 *[w/...*

1 ...th]is disease,
2 ...] from the hostility
3 [and wickedness of (any) enemy.. ..; and that may make] him [hap]py ʾIlum-
4 [quh.. .., with the esteem and grace of] [his] two lords
5 [...

It is impossible to re-unite the present text with Ja 597 or 599; nor does the present text belong to Ja 799, since the letters are much closer together in the former than in the latter.

808 = MaMB 123 = center of lines 9-11 of Ja 816.

809 – Three fragments from an inscription; yellowish sandstone; two photographs in Plate 46. – MaMB 124 + 105 + 67.

STONE: maximum thickness: 5.6 cm., 6.9, and 12.1 respectively. – *Front:* covered with red paint; length of the upper edge: 7 cm., 5.7, and 7.1 respectively; diagonal length: 13 cm., 13.1, and 13.3 respectively; width: 4 cm. (on ʾ), 3.9 (on *r*), and 4.5 respectively. No. 67 fits very well on the left of No. 105, but a fragment is missing between No. 124 and No. 105. – INSCRIPTION: same disposition of lines as in Ja 552. – SYMBOL: only a small part of the upper left corner remains.

124 105 67
[**Symbol**⌋⌊*sʿdʾ*⌋*w*⌈*m/w*⌉[... ...]⌊*/wrbʾ*⌉*l*⌊*wm/wb*⌉.
[...

(**Symbol**) Saʿadʾawwâm and ... ...and Rabbʾawwâm and B. [...

Cf. the beginning of the commentary on Ja 801.

No. 124: on the right of *s* there is a very small corner making a right angle which does not belong to any letter; it is the remainder of a symbol.
No. 67: the space on the left of *b* is too badly damaged to ascertain any reading.

810 – Two fragments of a white alabaster plaque with black stains; major fragment = MaMB 125; small fragment = MaMB 76 = Ja 794; two photographs in Plates 46-47.

INSCRIPTION: same disposition of lines as in Ja 559; letter height: 1.6 cm. and 1.7; space between the lines: 0.3 cm.

MaMB 125: thickness: 5.8 cm.; *front:* length: 5.4 cm. and 6.3 in the center of lines 2 and 3, respectively; maximum width: 6.2 cm.; part A of the text.

MaMB 76: thickness: 6.1 cm.; *back:* length: 9.3 cm.; *front:* 6 cm. × 2.5; *inscription:* part B; distance to the lower edge: 0.4 cm.; possibly the last line.

A

1 *....../ʾl]mqh/⌈b⌉ʿ⌈l⌉[/ʾwm/...*
2 *...]⌊l⌋wfy/bnhw⌈/lḥ⌉[...*
3 *...]⌊/⌋ʾlmqh/lwfyhw⌈/⌉[w...*

1 ...ʾIl]umquh, master of [ʾAwwâm,...
2 ...] for the safety of his son(s?) Laḥ[...
3 ...] ʾIlumquh for his own safety [and...

B

.../wlwś]⸢fh⸣w/ʾlmqh/ʾ⸥⸤w⸣[ldm/...

...; and that] ʾIlumquh [may a]dd to him ch[ild]ren [...

A. – L. 2: *bn* is singular, dual, or plural. – *lḥ*[..., cf., e.g., *lḥym* (e.g., Ja 871/1, Qat), *lḥyʿṯt* (e.g., Ja 556), *lḥyd* (CIH 804 and *JaDME*, p. 21), etc.

B. – In similar contexts (e.g., Ja 784/3), *wśf* is more frequently used than *ś(w)f* "to take care of".

811 – Upper right corner of an inscription; yellowish sandstone; photograph in Plate 47. – MaMB 127.

STONE: constant thickness: 28.3 cm. – *Front:* covered with red paint; 13.7 cm. × 6.2. – INSCRIPTION: same disposition of lines as in Ja 559; letter height: 3.3 cm.; space between the lines: 0.6 cm.; distance from line 1 to the upper edge; 0.7 cm. – SYMBOL: 3.7 cm. (top) and 3.9 (bottom) × 4.9 (left) and 5.1 (right); depth: 0.6 cm.; cf. Ja 603 with the upper extremity of Ja 728.

1 **Sym-** *rzn/⸤y⸥.[...*
2 **⸤bol⸥** *.[...*

1 **Sym-** Razîn Ya.[...
2 **bol** .[...

Cf. the beginning of the commentary on Ja 775.

L. 1: *rzn*, cf. CIH 378/6. – *y*.[...: the reading *ṯ* instead of *y* is not probable; the lower circle of *ṯ* would have left some trace.

Ll. 1-2: the letter following *y* and the 1st letter of line 2 are either *b* or *ḏ*.

812 – Right part of a yellowish sandstone plaque, re-cut at the bottom; photograph in Plate 47. – MaMB 132.

STONE: constant thickness: 2.8 cm. (top) and 2.5 (bottom). – *Front:* upper edge damaged; 13.6 cm. (right) and 15.9 (left) × 6 (top) and 7 (bottom). – INSCRIPTION: same disposition of lines as in Ja 559; letter height: 1.6 cm.; no space between the lines.

1 *yšf/rz[n/... .../wbn]*
2 *yhw/rbʿṯ[t/w...*
3 *n/ʾdm/ml⸣[kn/... ../ḥw]*
4 *rw/hgrn[/... .../h]*
5 *qnyw/ʾlm⸢q[h... ...bʿl]*
6 *ʾwm/ṣlm[...*
7 *ḥmdm/bḏt/ḫ⸣[mr/.. ../ʾbr]*
8 *whw/rbʿṯt/w[...*
9 *[ʿ]⸤bdhw/rbʿṯt⸥/...*

1 Yašûf Raz[în... ...and] his
2 [son]s Rabbʿaṯ[at and...
3 ân, servants of [the] kin[g,... ..., resi-]
4 dents of the city [... ...], ha-
5 ve [de]dicated to ʾIlumqu[h..., master of]
6 ʾAwwâm [.] statue [...
7 in praise because He has vou[chsafed... ...to] his
8 [so]n[s] Rabbʿaṯat and [...
9 His [wo]rshipper Rabbʿaṯat [...

Cf. the beginning of the commentary on Ja 783.

L. 1: *rz*[..., cf., e.g., *rzn* in Ja 811/1.

Ll. 1-2 and 7: *bnyhw* is also mentioned with *brw* in Ja 716/1 and 7-8 respectively; *bny* is plural and not dual because of lines 7-8 where the dual form of *brw* cannot be restored.

813 – Lower left corner fragment; yellowish, slightly grayish sandstone; photograph in Plate 47. – MaMB 141.

STONE: maximum thickness: 14.9 cm. – *Front:* covered with red paint; 5.5 cm. × 12.2. – INSCRIPTION: same disposition of lines as in Ja 552; letter height: 1.8 cm., 1.7, and 1.8; space between the lines: 0.3 cm.

1 *...]⸢ʿm/bn*
2 *...]⸢ṯwʿ/wš*
3 *[ṣy /šnʾm /bʾlmqh]⸢bʿlʾwm*

1 ...]ʿum from
2 ...] the constraint and wick-
3 [edness of (any) enemy By ʾIlumquh], master of ʾAwwâm.

Cf. the beginning of the commentary on Ja 569, 595, 600, and 782.

L. 1:]ʿ*m*, ending of a proper name. – *bn*: introducing a proper name (either of a person of a clan) or preposition "from"; according to the 1st hypothesis, the preposition *bn* "from" must be restored in line 2.

L. 2, cf. Ja 804/3.

814 = MaMB 142 = upper right corner of Ja 700.

815 – Left part of an inscription; yellowish sandstone; photograph in Plate 48. – MaMB 166.

STONE: thickness: 9.5 cm. (top) and 11 (bottom). – *Front:* covered with red paint; 12 cm. (top) × 12.9 (center of line 3) and 11.6 (bottom). – INSCRIPTION: same disposition of lines as in Ja 561 bis; letter height: 1.7 cm. and 1.9; space between the lines: from 0.4 cm. to 0.5; distance from lines 9 to the bottom: 10 cm.; a vertical line is traced at 0.6 cm. from the left edge.

1 *.../]⌜bn⌝w/⌜ʾḥgrm⌝*
2 *[hqnyw/... ʾlm]⌜qh⌝⌜bʿlʾwm/ṣlmn*
3 *.../]⌞ḏḏhbn/ḏšfthw/ḥ*
4 *[mdm/bḏt/... /]⌜grybt/bnyhmw/d*
5 *[wsm/wrbʿ... /]bnw/ḏʾḥgrm/w*
6 *[lwzʾ/... /wḫr]⌞yn/wmtʿn/grybt*
7 *.../bny]⌞hmw/dwsm/wrbʿ*
8 *.../wlḫryn]⌜h⌝mw/bn/bʾstm*
9 *[wnkytm/... /bʾl]⌞m⌟qhbʿlʾwm*

1 ...,] descendants of [the family] ʾAḥgarum,
2 [have dedicated to...ʾIlum]quh, master of ʾAwwâm, this statue
3 ...,] in bronze, which he had promised to Him, in
4 [praise because...] the persons of their sons Da-
5 [wsum and Rabîʿ... ,] descendants of ʾAḥgarum; and
6 [that He may continue to...and pre]serve and save the persons of
7 ..]their [sons] Dawsum and Rabîʿ
8 ..; and that He may preserve] them from misfortunes
9 [and sufferings... By ʾIl]umquh, master of ʾAwwâm.

Cf. the beginning of the commentary on Ja 792.

L. 1: *ʾḥgrm*, cf. the proper name *ḥgrw* (Ja 550/1) and the name of the deity *ḥgrm* (e.g., Ja 564/30 and commentary).

L. 2: *ʾlmqh* might be preceded by *mrʾhmw* and followed by *ṯhwn*.

L. 7: *rbʿ*, e.g., RÉS 4856/2, Ḥaḍr; possibly incomplete, cf., e.g., *rbʿt* (e.g., Ja 693/1), *rbʿṯt* (e.g., Ja 795/2), etc.

816 – Yellowish sandstone inscription, badly broken and damaged; large block = MaMB 191; small fragment (center of lines 9-11) = MaMB 123 = Ja 808; two photographs in Plate 48.

LARGE BLOCK: thickness: 7.4 cm. (bottom) and 13.9 (top); upper right corner and right part of the upper edge splintered off; broken on the left. – SMALL FRAGMENT: a splinter; maximum thickness: 3.4 cm.; front: length: 7.2 cm. (center of 2nd line), and maximum width: 5.4. – INSCRIPTION: same disposition of lines as in Ja 552; letter height: from 2 cm. to 2.3; space between the lines: between 0.2 cm and 0.3.

1 **[Sym-]** *ʾ⌟b⌝⌜ʾmr/⌝bn/⌜ṣ⌝[... .../qd]*
2 **[bol]** *m/kbr/ʾḥśr⌜n/⌝w⌜ʾq⌝(y)[nm/...*
3 *wʾdhwn/hqny/ʾ⌟⌞lmqh/⌟[ṣlmn/...*
4 *ḏstwklhw/ʾbʾ⌟[mr/...*
5 *tnḍʿ⌞hw/lmlk⌟[...*
6 *ḥẓrn[...*
7 *l/lʾ[bʾmr/... ...hw]*
8 *fyn/gr(y)bt⌟[... .../ʾlm]*
9 *qh⟨/⟩bny[... .../]⌜wʾmlk⌟[... .../ḏq]*
10 *nyw/w[... ...]hgr/bn[y... .../wṭ]*
11 *[w]ʿ/šn[ʾm/... .../b]⌞ʾ⌟⌞lmqh/⌟...*

1 **[Sym-]** ʾAbʾamar, son of Ṣ[... ..., command-]
2 **[bol]** er of the Leader of ʾAḥśarân and ʾAq(yâ)-[num...
3 and ʾAdhawân, has dedicated to ʾIlumquh, [this statue...
4 by which ʾAbʾa[mar] showed his confidence in Him, [...
5 he has implored Him for the property of [...
6 Haẓrân [...
7 .to ʾA[bʾamar... ... bes]tow
8 upon the persons of [... ...ʾIlum-]
9 quh the descendants of [... ...] and the properties of [.. ..what] they have
10 [pos]sessed and [... ...] the city of the descend[ants of .. ..and the cons-]
11 [tr]aint of [any] ene[my... ...By] ʾIlumquh[...

L. 1: *ʾbʾmr*: the remains in both lines 1 and 4 make certain the reading of this personal name. There was thus a symbol at the beginning of line 1 and probably also of line 2.

L. 2: */k* is engraved on top of *kb*; the worker had thus first omitted the word divider. – *ʾḥśrn*, cf. *ḥśrn* in CIH 733. – *ʾq(y)*[..: on the left of *q* one can see the lower extremity of a vertical stroke; its distance to *q* excludes a letter such as *b*, *d*, *l*, etc., and suggests *h*, *ḥ*, or *y*; I propose restoring *ʾq(y)[nm*.

L. 3: *ʾdhwn*, *ʾqtln* form; cf. the Thamudic epithet of ʾIlâh, *dhwn* (Jsa 409), related by *JaSaMA* (p. 584) to the root *dhn*; this opinion is hesitatingly followed by *vdBrIT* (p. 268); cf. also the Arabic clan names *bnw dhy* (cf. *MüHG*, p. 142 B) and *dahy* (cf. *WüR*, p. 244 B).

L. 5: *mlk* (cf. *ʾmlk* in line 9) was followed either by *hw* or *bny/*...

L. 6: *ḥẓrn*, cf. the Arabic personal name *ḏû ḥazurân* (cf. *LöHSM*, p. 64 B), and the name of the country *ḥẓrm* in CIH 462/9, and also the verb *ḥẓr* in RÉS 4176/2; cf. also the Arabic names of a man *ʾabû al-ḥaẓâʾir* (cf. *WüR*, p. 400) and of a place *al-ḥaẓîrat* (cf. *l.c.*, p. 72 A), *ḥaẓâʾir* and *ḥaẓîrat* (cf. *MüHG*, p. 35 A).

L. 7: *lʾ*[..: the context suggests *lʾ*[*bʾmr*] rather than *lʾ*[*lmqh*].

Ll. 9-10: *ḏq*]*nyw*, e.g., Ja 489 A/7 and the singular in Ja 844/5-6.

L. 11: the space on the left of the last word divider is free of any letter remains; according to the width of the letters, remains of at least either *w* or ʿ should be visible; *ʾlmqh/* is thus the end of the line and of the text.

817 – Fragment of the upper part of an inscription; yellowish, slightly grayish sandstone; photograph in Plate 48. – MaMB 194.

STONE: thickness: about 4.8 cm. – *Front:* length: 25.4 cm. (upper edge) and 25.9 (top of line 2). – INSCRIPTION: same disposition of lines as in Ja 559; letter height: 4.3 cm. (line 1) and 4.2 (lines 2 and 3); space between the lines: 0.6 cm.; distance from line 1 to the upper edge: 1.8 cm.

1 ...*ʾbʾ*]⌜*ns/wʾẖyhw/bny/ʿb*⌞*lm*⌝[...*hqnyw/*...*ʾlmqh*
2 ...*b*]⌞⌜*ʿl/ʾwm/ṣlmn/ḏḏhb*⌞*n/ḥ*⌝[*mdm/bḏt/*...
3 ...]⌞*/*⌟*whḥdṯ/mṯln*⌟⌞*/*⌟.[...
4 ...]⌞*/bn*⌟[*w*]⌞*/*⌟[*ʿblm/*...

1 ...ʾAbʾa]nas and his brother(s?), the descendants of ʿAblum, [...have dedicated to...ʾIlumquh
2 ...m]aster of ʾAwwâm, this statue which (is) in bronze, in [praise because...
3 ...] and renewed this image.[...
4 ...,] the descend[ants of ʿAblum,...

The original length of the lines is unknown; there is thus no way of knowing where to restore *hqnyw* and *ʾlmqh*.

L. 1: ..]*ns* may be restored, e.g., *ʾbʾns* (e.g., Ja 852/1, Qat).

L. 3: after the last word divider, the upper circle of *y*, *ẓ*, *ṣ*, or *ṯ*.

818 – Grayish sandstone inscription, broken on both sides and re-cut at the bottom; photograph in Plate 49. – MaMB 197.

STONE: thickness: 14 cm. – *Front:* right edge badly damaged. – INSCRIPTION: same disposition of lines as in Ja 552; letter height: from 2.8 cm. to 3; no space between the lines.

1 .../*hqny*()*/ʾl*]
2 [*mqhw/bʿ*]⌜*l/ʾwm/mṯln/ḏḏhb*⌝[*n*]
3 [*ḥgn/ḏt/*]*w*⌞⌜*q*⌝*hhmw/ʾlmqhw/b*⌜*m*⌝
4 [*sʾlhw*]⌞*/*⌟*lwfy/bnhmy/ʾḥḏr/*[*w*]
5 [*lśfhm*]*w/ʾlmqh/ʾwl*⌞*dm*⌟*/*⌞*ʾḏ*⌝[*k*]
6 [*rwm*]⌞*/hnʾm/ʾly/ywfyh*⌟[*mw/*.]

1 ...dedicated to ʾIl-]
2 [umquhû, mast]er of ʾAwwâm, this image which [is] in bronze,
3 [as] ʾIlumquhû had ordered them through [His]
4 or[acle] for the safety of the son of both of them ʾAḥḏar; [and]
5 [may]ʾIlumquh [add to the]m children ma-
6 [le,] pleasing, whom He would protect [...

L. 1: this line in the preceding restoration could be the original one.

The *m* in lines 2-4 and 5-6 are dextrograde and senestrograde respectively.

L. 3: the restoration *ḥgn/ḏt* instead of *ḥgn* is suggested by the number of signs, 23 in both lines 2 and 4.

L. 4: *ʾḥḏr*, cf. the family name *ḥḏʾr*; e.g., RÉS 2774/1, Min, and *ḥḏr* in RÉS 2827 B/8, Min; cf. also the Arabic names of a man *ḥadrân* (cf. *HeBN*, p. 18 A), *ʾabû maḥdûrat* (cf. *WüID*, 83/8), and of a place *al-ḥidriyat* (cf. *WüR*, p. 67 C).

L. 6: at least one letter is missing at the end of the line.

819 – Two units of frieze in yellowish, slightly grayish sandstone; two photographs in Plate 49. – MaMB 235 (right part) + MaMB 17 = Ja 827 (left part).

MaMB 235. – STONE: maximum thickness: 18 cm. – *Front:* upper register: 34.5 cm. (top) and 34.1 (bottom) × 14.2; lower register: 32.2 cm. × 9.7; width of the rectangular panels: 4.4 cm. (right; broken at the bottom), 11.7 (center; broken at the bottom), and 11.9 (left; complete but both lower corners are broken); distance between the panels:

2.7 cm. and 2; depth of the spacing: 1.7 cm. and 1.4. – INSCRIPTION: 33.3 cm. × 10.1; distance to the right edge: 0.6 cm., and to the upper one: 2.1 (right) and 1.9 (left), engraved on the upper register.

MaMB 17. – FRONT: 23 cm. (top) and 30 (bottom) × 22.5 (right) and 23 (left). Upper register: length at the bottom: 27 cm.; height: 14.2 cm.; lower register: width of each panel: 10.7 cm.; distance between the two panels: 2.3 cm.; length of the remaining space at the left of the left panel: 1.5 cm.; depth of the first spacing: 1.7 cm. – INSCRIPTION: 24 cm. × 10.2; distance to the upper edge: 2 cm.; engraved on the upper register.

819 827
*. . . /]***l***wb/krbʾ***l***l/wb/s***l***[mh. . .*

. . .]and by Karibʾil and by Su[mhu. . .

820 – Lower part of an inscription; yellowish, slightly grayish sandstone; photograph in Plate 49. – MaMB 241.

STONE: thickness: 21 cm. (top) and 22 (bottom). – *Front:* 33.4 cm. × 23.2 (right) and 19.8 (left). – INSCRIPTION: same disposition of lines as in Ja 552; letter height: 4.1 cm.; space between the lines: 0.7 cm.

1 *. . . /wlsʿdhmw/n]*
2 *ʿ⌈mtm/wmngt/ṣdqm/[wlwfy/gryb]*
3 *thmw/bʾlmqh/ṯhwn/wṯwr/bʿlm*
4 *bʿly/ʾwm/wḥrwnm/wbḏt/ḥmym*

1 . . ; and that He may make them happy with pros-]
2 perity and security perfect; [and that He may protect] their
3 [person]s. By ʾIlumquh Ṯahwân and Ṯawr Baʿalum,
4 the two masters of ʾAwwâm and Ḥirwânum and by Ḏât-Ḥimyâm.

Ll. 2-3: for the restoration, cf. Ja 738/11, where this request also precedes the final invocation.

821 – Lower part of an inscription; yellowish, slightly grayish sandstone. – MaMB 256.

STONE: maximum thickness: 21.7 cm.; height: 42.5 cm. – *Front:* upper and both lateral edges badly damaged; 39.7 cm. × 16.5. – INSCRIPTIONS. A: same disposition of lines as in Ja 552; letter height: 3 cm. and 2.8; space between the lines: 0.4 cm. and 0.6; the number of signs increases from line to line. B: on the left side; 16.5 cm. × 6.5; distance to the lower edge: 5 cm.

A: 1 . . .
2 *[ṣlm]nhn/lwfyhw/wwfy/ʾ[n]*
3 *ẖl/wtbqlt/ṣyḥ/wbqln/[ʿd]*
4 *[y/s]flm/wʾrḍ/bn/ḥzfrm/bʿṯ[t]*
5 *[r]/whbs/wʾlmqh/wḏt/ḥmym/wḏt*
6 *[bʿdnm/. . .*

1 . . .
2 these two [statues] for his own safety and the safety of the [pa]lm-
3 groves and of the plantations [which] he has leveled and sowed [in]
4 lower country and [in] the land of the descendants of Ḥazfarum. By ʿAṯ-
5 [tar] and Hawbas and ʾIlumquh and Ḏât-Ḥimyâm and Ḏât-
6 [Baʿdânum. . .

L. 1: tiny extremities of letters remain but not enough to suggest any reading.

L. 3: *tbqlt/–/.bqln*, cp. *bqlw/tbqlt/ʾrḍhmw/–* (RÉS 4636/6), which is translated by *RyHE* (p. 233) as follows: "they parcelled out their ground – with a view to the cultivation of the agricultural products". *bql* (cf. also *RoVSAY*, p. 301) and *tbql* simply mean "to sow" and "plantation", and the meaning of the above-mentioned expression reads "they sowed the plantations of their land". – *ṣyḥ*, cf., e.g., Ja 527/2: *ṣyḥw*; cf. also the 4th form *hṣyḥ* (e.g., RÉS 4069/5) and the nouns *ṣyḥ* (RÉS 4085/2) and *mṣyḥ* (RÉS 4176/4; cf. *BeSI*, p. 79).

B: *. . .]⌈.zr/f⌉[. . .* . . .].zar F[. . .

Immediately to the right of *z*, the lower half of a vertical stroke.

822 – Yellowish, slightly grayish sandstone. – MaMB 258.

STONE: thickness: 28.3 cm. (top) and 18.7 (bottom). – *Front:* six spots are splintered off; 24.6.cm. × 90.1. – INSCRIPTION: partial copy that I never had time to complete. – SYMBOL, cf. Ja 559.

1 **Sym-** *ʾsʿd/yzd/wʾẖyhw/smhyf*
2 **bol** *ʿ/yhḥmd/wbnyhmy/ʾsdm*
3 *yʿf/wsʿdm/yskr/. . .*

1 **Sym-** ʾAsʿad Yazid and his brother Sumhuyaf-
2 **bol** aʿ Yuhaḥmid and the two sons of them both ʾAsdum
3 Yaʿûf and Saʿadum Yaskar..

Same persons as in Ja 615; here the two sons have a second personal name.

L. 3: *yʿf*: the root *ʿwf* seems to be more frequently used than *ʿff*. – *yskr*, NaNN 51/1; cf. also *yhskr* (CIH 350/13), and *tskr* (Ja 487/1, Qat; cf. *JaAFEQ*, p. 193).

823 – Two "fragments found in the mausoleum; in fill which was much disturbed" (F. P. Albright); copy by the same. – MaMB 308.

A: 46 cm. × 9; letter height: 7 cm.

...](*h*)*w*/*bʾlmqh*/*wb*/(*h*)[*bs*/*wb*/...

..] (hi)s [..] By ʾIlumquh and by (Ha)[wbas and by..

Copy: twice *y* instead of *h*.

B: 28 cm.

...](/)*yṯʿʾl*/⸢*ḏmt*⸣[...

..] Yaṯaʿʾil, he of Mat[..

Copy: *n* instead of the 1st word divider; the latter might not have been copied; in that case, read the beginning as follows: ..]*n*⟨/⟩, and translate ".., s]on of."

824 – "On cover slab to one of the burial compartments in the mausoleum" (F. P. Albright); copy by the same; cf. *AlEMY*, p. 237 B. – MaMB 309.

...*yṯʿ*](ʾ)*mr*/*byn*/*bn*/*ykrbmlk*/*wtr*

...Yaṯaʿ](ʾa)mar Bayyin, son of Yakrubmalik Watar.

Copy: a vertical stroke on the right of *mr*. Cf. Ja 550 and 555. – There is actually no way of knowing whether Ja 824 and 825 belong to the same original.

825 – "On cover slab to one of the burial compartments in the mausoleum" (F. P. Albright); copy by the same; cf. *AlEMY*, p. 237 B. – MaMB 312.

...]*smhʿly*/*y*[*nf*/...

...] Sumhuʿalay Ya[nûf...

Cf. end of the commentary on Ja 824.

826 = MaMB 15 = upper half of Ja 667.

827 = MaMB 17 = left part of Ja 819.

828 – Right part of an inscription; yellowish sandstone; upper edge and upper half of the left edge broken; photograph in Plate 50. – MaMB 18.

STONE: thickness: 11.5 cm. – *Front:* 24 cm. × 12.5. – INSCRIPTION: same disposition of lines as in Ja 552; letter height: 1.8 cm.; space between the lines: 0.2 cm.; distance from line 8 to the bottom: 11 cm.

1 [**Sym-** ..
2 [**bol** ...*gd*]⸢*šfq*/*ẖ*.[...
3 [*hqny*]⸤*t*⸣/*ʾlmqṯhw*[*nbʿlʾ*]
4 [*wm*/]⸤*ṣ*⸣*lmtn*/*ḏt*/[*ḏhbn*/*ḥ*]
5 [*mdm*]/*bḏt*/*ẖmrhw*/[*ʾlmqh*/*wl*]
6 [*dm*/]⸤*wstwfyn*/*lh*[*w*/*bntm*/*ḏt*]
7 ⸤*y*⸣⸢*stmyn*/*gdšfq*[... .../*bʿ*]
8 *l*/*ʾmh*/*mlkn*/*bʾ*[*lmqh*...]

1 [**Sym-** ..
2 [**bol** ...Gadd]šafaq H̱a.[...
3 she [has dedicated] to ʾIlumq Ṯahw[ân, master of ʾA-]
4 [wwâm,] this female statue which (is) [in bronze, in]
5 [praise] because [ʾIlumquh] has vouchsafed to her [a]
6 [child] and has given protection for h[er to a daughter, which]
7 was to be named Gaddšafaq, [.. .., mast]er
8 of the maidservants of the king. By ʾI[lumquh...

L. 3: *hqnyt*: the author is probably Gaddšafaq's mother. – the letter *ṯ* is engraved on top of the upper right vertical stroke of the *h*.
Ll. 6-7, cf. Ja 655/9-10.
Ll. 7-8: Gaddšafaq's contemplated job was to be connected in some way with the man in charge of the maidservants of the king.

c – Texts in relief: Ja 829 and 830

829 – Fragment of a slightly yellowish alabaster plaque; broken on both sides; photograph in Plate 50. – MaMB 54.

PLAQUE: maximum thickness: 1.4 cm. – *Front:* 2.9 cm. (top) and 2.6 (bottom) × 1.7. – INSCRIPTION: in relief; letter height: 1.2 cm.; height of the upper margin: 0.2 cm.; depth of the hollow: 0.1 cm.

...]⌜*šms*⌞/⌟[... ...]šams[...

šms is either complete (e.g., Ja 644/5) or the end of a theophorous name (e.g., *rbšms*, e.g., in Ja 744/4).

830 – Upper right corner of a slightly yellowish alabaster plaque; photograph in Plate 50. – MaMB 83.

PLAQUE: maximum thickness: 6.6 cm. – *Front:* length: 10.3 cm., and width: 7.5 cm. – INSCRIPTION: in relief of 0.3 cm.

⌞/*kr*⌟[*b*... Kar[ib...

The first vertical stroke belongs to the frame.

2 – BRONZE: Ja 831 and 832

831 – Bronze plaque fastened with two rivets in the pavement of the trough located west of the main door; cf. *AlETM*, p. 31 and note 4, and Fig. 3, where the exact location of the plaque may be seen on the oblique slab put as cover to protect the plaque itself; cf. also *AlEMY*, pp. 228-29, 230 A, 231 B, and pl. 166 (photograph of the location) and pl. 162 (plan): E-8; photograph in Plate 51. – MaMB 147 (formerly Ja 828; cf. *AlEMY*).

PLAQUE: 1.113 m. × 25.5 cm.; thickness: 0.6 cm. – *Top:* height of the lateral edge: 9.5 cm.; in the upper corners, there are protuberances the width of which is 3 cm. at the bottom and 3.5 on top; their length is 4 cm. – INSCRIPTION: boustrophedon; covered with hardened sand. – SYMBOL: in relief; facing the three lines of the text; cf. Plate C, Fig. 2.

1 ← **S** */nb/myrhms/dbᶜ/bd̲md̲/brkᵓšn/nb/swᵓlᵓ*
y *ᶜmḥ/whnb/hqmlᵓ/ynqh/lᵓᶜdy*
2 → **m** *t̲t/wkl/wldhw/ywm/hwfyhw/ᵓlmqh/bkl/*
b *ᵓdbᵓ/wmwṣtt/hyᶜ/bᶜm/mrᵓhw/sm*
3 ← **o** */bw/mymḥtd̲/bw/hqmlᵓ/bw/rtt̲ᶜb/myrh*
l *lᵓᶜdy/nb/myrhms/whᵓrm/bw/ndᶜbtd̲*

1 **S** ᵓIlᵓaws, son of Našaᵓkarib, he of [the family]-Mad̲ab, servant of Sumhuriyyâm, son of Yadaᶜ
y ᵓil, has dedicated to ᵓIlumquh his son Ḥammᶜa-
2 **m** t̲at and all his children, when ᵓIlumquh saved him in all the engagements and affrays [which]
b he has built up with his lord Sum-
3 **o** huriyyâm. By ᶜAt̲tar and by ᵓIlumquh and by D̲ât-Ḥimyâm and by D̲ât-Baᶜdân and by his
l lord Sumhuriyyâm, son of Yadaᶜᵓil.

L. 1: *ᵓlᵓws*, e.g., Gl 1128+1129/5. – *md̲b*, family name; cf. name of a house in RÉS 4834/1, Min (cf. *JaPSAP*, pp. 30 and 65-72), of a hall in RÉS 3535/1, Min, of a place in RÉS 3945/15, etc.; cf. also *md̲bm*, name of a temple dedicated to the Ḥaḍr moon god Sîn, cf. CaTh 4/4. – *smhrym*, e.g., RÉS 3103.

Ll. 1-2: *ḥmᶜt̲t*, e.g., RÉS 3303/1.

L. 2: *mwṣt*, pl. *mwṣtt*, e.g., CIH 338/5; cf. *CoRoC*, p. 139 B and *BeSI*, p. 38. On the basis of the Hebrew parallel *yṣt* (cf. *CIH*, I, p. 395 A and *KoBaLVTL*, p. 397 A), *mwṣt* of the present text may be translated "affray".

832 – Bronze plaque attached to the floor at the northern end of the platform facing the entrance door; for its exact location, cf. *AlETM*, pp. 29-30, Fig. 4, and plan in Fig. 2, *AlEMY*, pp. 226 and 230 A, and pl. 172 (photograph of the location) and pl. 162 (plan): H – J – 10; photograph in Plate 51. – MaMB 302 (previously 313; cf. *AlETM*, p. 29, note 3).

PLAQUE: 2.30 m. × 89 cm.; thickness: 2.5 cm.; the last 53 cm. on the right are covered by a large slab; the plaque is composed of two panels: the last 20 cm. from the edge which faces the entrance door are 19 cm. higher than the rest; the part connecting these two panels is vertical. – INSCRIPTION: in relief and along the above-mentioned edge. – DESIGN: small, running ostrich also in relief, facing the text and having the same height as that of the letters; cf. Plate C, Fig. 2.

[sm]hwtr/d̲ᵓmrm/ᵓḫ/ydᶜᵓl/wyt̲ᶜᵓmr/hqny/ᵓlmqh/bythw/ mšrᶜm/bᵓlmqhg **Ostrich**

[Sum]huwatar, he of [the family] ᵓAmrum, brother of Yadaᶜᵓil and of Yat̲aᶜᵓamar,
has dedicated to ᵓIlumquh his house Mašraᶜum. By ᵓIlumquh. G. **Ostrich.**

[sm]hwtr, e.g., RÉS 3943/1 and 3566/26, Qat. – *mšrᶜm*, cf. the family name *mšrᶜn* (Ja 547/1) and the noun *mšrᶜ*, e.g., RÉS 3167/3; cf. the Arabic names of men *mišriᶜ* (cf. *HeBN*, p. 32 A), *marsûᶜ* (cf. *WüID*, 239/2), *bin širᶜat* (cf. *SlGaVNPA*, p. 13 A)

*šâri*ᶜ and *šir*ᶜ*ân*, of a woman *šar*ᶜ*â* (cf. *HeBN*, *l.c.*), of a clan *šar*ᶜ and of a place *šâri*ᶜ (cf. *WüR*, pp. 248 A and 126 B respectively). – *b*ʾ*lmqh* is followed by the letter *g* which is probably the initial of the name of the worker who cast the plaque. This sign is also attested in Qatif 1/5 (cf. commentary on Ja 552/1). F. V. Winnett interprets this letter as "3"; therefore *g*/ would mean "30" and indicate "the age of the decease" (cf. *The Geographical Journal*, 107 [1946], p. 44). Such an interpretation requires that the natives of the Persian Gulf country had their own figures, different from those used in South Arabia, although they have the same alphabet in common. Furthermore, the vertical stroke on the left of *g* is normally interpreted as a word divider (cf. that after *d*ʾ*l* on line 4). The same letter *g* is also attested at the end of RÉS 4845 bis: –/*yd*ᶜᶜ*b*/*g*; note that neither *BePC* (p. 313) nor *RÉS* (p. 389) mention it, and the latter even considers the word divider after *yd*ᶜᶜ*b* as missing.

3 – POTTERY: Ja 833-838

833 – Fragment of a large, slightly yellowish jar; photograph in Plate 51. – MaMB 42.

SHERD: thickness on and below the brim: 2.5 cm. and 1.6 respectively. – *Front:* 6.9 cm. × 5.2. – INSCRIPTION: end of a text in a cartouche; 5.2 cm. × 2.5; distance to the lower edge: 2 cm. (right) and 1.3 (left).

. . .]*wġfr*/ . . .]and Ġafâr.

ġfr, cf. *ġfrt* (RÉS 3902, No. 18, Qat, cf. *JaPEHA*, pp. 55-56) and [*ġ*]*frm* (Ja 159 A/1, Qat); cf. also the Arabic names of a man *ġafâr*, *al-ġafârî* (cf. *SaIS*, p. 182 B), *al-ġufûr* (cf. *LöHSM*, p. 76 A), ᶜ*abd al-ġaffâr*, ᶜ*abd al-ġafûr* (cf. *SlGaVNPA*, p. 2 A), of a clan (*banû*) *ġifâr* (cf. *WüR*, p. 254 A and *SaIS*, p. 182 B), and of a place *al-ġafâ*ʾ*ir* (cf. *MüHG*, p. 85 B), *ġufr*, *ġifârat*, *al-ġaffâritayn* and *al-ġaffârîyat* (cf. *WüR*, p. 160 B).

834 – Fragment of dark-brown pot; photograph in Plate 51. – MaMB 44.

POT: constant thickness: 0.9 cm. – *Front:* 7.4 cm. × 5.2. – INSCRIPTION: line 1: 3.2 cm. × 1.8, space between the lines: 0.1 cm.; line 2: 4.6 cm. × 1.2 and 1.8 (last letter).

gmm/ 1 Gamâm [of the family]
*š*ᶜ*bm* 2 Šaᶜabum.

L. 1: *gmm*, cf. commentary on Ja 665/32: *gmn*.
L. 2: *š*ᶜ*bm*: the ᶜ is a lozenge.

The text may be incomplete on the left.

835 – Two fragments of a large reddish jar; photograph in Plate 52. – MaMB 74.

A: thickness of the brim: 3.5 cm., of the collar: 1.2 cm., and of the side: 1.1; length of the brim: 7.5 cm.; *front:* length: 7.8 cm., and width: 7.4; *inscription:* on top of the brim; 6.7 cm. × 3.6. – B: length of the brim: 7.7 cm., and width: 3.7; *front:* 22.1 cm. × 11.2; *inscription:* 17 cm. × 3.7.

B A
. . .]⌈*š*ᶜ*m*/*hqnyw*⌋**/**/ʾ*lm*[*qh*. . .

. . .]šaᶜam have dedicated to ʾIlum[quh. . .

The ᶜ, *w* and the circle of *y* are lozenges (cf. Ja 834/2). – . . .]*š*ᶜ*m*: person or family name; either from the root .]*š*ᶜ (cf., e.g., *yš*ᶜ) or Qat name ᶜ*m* preceded by a verbal form ending with *š*.

836 – Sherd; photograph in Plate 52. – MaMB 78.

SHERD: constant thickness: 1.5 cm. – *Back:* reddish color and polished. – FRONT: rough; reddish grey color; 12.2 cm. × 5.2. – INSCRIPTION: complete; on the front: 4.8 cm. × 2.

qḥdm Qâḥidum.

qḥdm, cf. the Arabic adjectives *qâḥid* and *qaḥḥâd* "solitary", and the name of a man ʾ*ibn al-quḥâdîyat* (cf. *WüR*, p. 614).

837 – Fragment of a reddish bowl; photograph in Plate 52. – MaMB 106.

SHERD; thickness: 0.6 cm. – *Front:* polished; 9.1 cm. × 5.2. – INSCRIPTION: double-line tracing with small perpendicular strokes; 2.1 cm. × 1.6.

dh Dîh

The normal position of the sherd is with the large opening on top; *h* is senestrograde; cf. the Thamudic personal name *dyh* (cf. *vdBrTTPN*, p. 9; Ph 248 a/2). There is absolutely no reason to think either that the pot to which the sherd belongs was engraved upside down or that the text is dextrograde.

838 – "On lip of vessel – amphora or pithos; found in sub-floor chamber of mausoleum, which was very much disturbed" (F. P. Albright); copy by the same. – MaMB 304.

Diameter of lip: 15 cm., and of neck: 3 cm. (in) and 7 (out). – INSCRIPTION: in circle.

k(*l*)*b*⌜/⌝*d̲byt*⌜*n*⌝(*h*)*n*

Ka(l)b, he of [the family] Baytna(h)ân.

bytn(*h*)*n*: same nominal formation as that, e.g., of *ʾrbʿnhn* (Ja 556 and commentary).

Copy: the vessel is broken in two places: one where the top of the word divider after the personal name is missing; the other where the upper third of the 1st *n* is missing as well as the upper two thirds of what I read *h*; and *k*/*b* instead of *k*(*l*)*b*.

— D —

INSCRIPTIONS FROM THE IMMEDIATE VICINITY

Ja 839–847

839 – Lower part of an inscription, found between the wall and the columns; yellowish sandstone; top badly damaged; photograph in Plate 53. – MaMB 1.

STONE: maximum thickness: 6 cm. – *Front:* maximum 13 cm. × 11.

1 *. . .]n/[. . .*
2 *. . ./wlwz]⌈ʾ/⌉ʾlmqh/ẖ⌈mr/ʿbdh⌉w*
3 *. . ./]⌊wwfym/wmngt/ṣdqm*
4 *. . ./wġn]⌊m⌉m/wlẖry(n)hmw/bn/n*
5 *[ḍʿ/šṣy/. . .   . . ./šn]⌊ʾm/bʾlmqh/bʿl/ʾwm*

1 . . .
2 . . .; and that] ʾIlumquh [may conti]nue to vouchsafe to His worshipper
3 . . .] and perfect safety and security
4 . . .and boot]y; and that He may preserve them from the hos-
5 [tility and wickedness. . .of (any) ene]my. By ʾIlumquh, master of ʾAwwâm.

Cf. the beginning of the commentary on Ja 569 and 782.

L. 3: *n* is engraved on top of *g*.

L. 4: the worker engraved first *ẖryhmw/*, and then *hmw* on top of *mw/* without erasing a single stroke; he finally forgot to correct the first *h* in *ẖryhmw*.

840 – Yellowish limestone found about 20 m. north of the columns; upper edge badly damaged; lower part of the left edge splintered off; edges slightly damaged; photograph in Plate 53. – MaMB 7.

STONE: thickness: 13.7 cm. (top) and 12.7 (bottom). – *Front:* maximum height: 23.7 cm.; length: 16.5; several places are splintered off, especially the lower third of the left edge and below the symbol. – INSCRIPTION: same disposition of lines as in Ja 559. – SYMBOL, cf. Ja 603.

1 ⌈**Sym-**⌉ *⌈rb⌉[. . ./mqtw]⌈y⌉/k*
2 **bol** *rbʿṯ⌈t/ynf⌉[ṯ/]⌈bn⌉/ṣʿqn*
3 *[w]zbnr/wẖymm/hq⌈ny⌉/ʾlm*
4 *qhṯhwnbʿlʾwm/ṣlmn/ḏd*
5 *hbn/ḏšfthw/lqbly/ḥl*
6 *⌈ẓ⌉/ḥlẓ/rglyhw/wlwzʾ/ʾ*
7 *lmqh/hʿnnhw/bn/ḥlẓ/*
8 *⌊rglyhw/wlsʿdhw/ḥẓ⌊y/⌋[w]*
9 *⌊rḍw/mrʾhw/krbʿṯt/[yn]*
10 *fṯ/bʾlmqh/bʿlʾw[m]*

1 **Sym-** Rabb[. . ., high offi]cial of Ka-
2 **bol** ribʿaṯat Yanfa[ṯ], descendant of Ṣaʿiqân
3 [and] Zabnar and Ḫaymum, has dedicated to ʾIlum-
4 quh Ṯahwân, master of ʾAwwâm, this statue which [is] in
5 bronze, which he had promised to Him because of the lan-
6 guor his two feet were suffering; and that may continue ʾI-
7 lumquh to protect him from the languor

8 of his two feet, and that He may make him happy with the esteem [and]
9 grace of his lord Karibᶜaṯat [Yan-]
10 faṯ. By ᵓIlumquh, master of ᵓAwwâ[m.]

L. 3: *ḫymm*, cf. the Arabic place names *ḫaym*, *ḫîm*, *(al-)ḫaymât* (cf. *MüHG*, p. 42 A and *WüR*, p. 85 B), *ḫiyam*, *ḫaymâᵓ*, *(al-)ḫaymat* (cf. *WüR*, *l.c.*).

Ll. 2 and 9-10: the 2nd personal name of *krbᶜṯt* is [..]*fṯ* (cf. lines 9-10); on line 2, *ṯt*/ is followed by the lower two thirds of two vertical strokes; being too far from each other they cannot belong to the same letter; they would suit a reading such as *yd*, *yl*, *yn*, etc. On the other hand, only two roots are practically suitable, *faṯṯa* "to empty" and *nafaṯa* "to blow". The first must be discarded for the personal name would be *yhfṯ* and *yh* cannot be read in line 2. The verb *ᵓafṯay* "to be exhausted" would also give *yhfṯ*, but the *scriptio plena* would be expected. The form *ynfṯ* perfectly suits the letter remains on line 2. Cf. the Arabic names of a man *nufâṯat* and of a clan *banû nufâṯat* (cf. *SaIS*, p. 239 A).

841 – Blue stone found about 200 m. northeast of Maḥram Bilqîs; probably broken on both upper and right corners; photograph in Plate 53. – MaMB 13.

STONE: thickness: 32 cm. – *Front:* maximum 82 cm. × 54. – INSCRIPTION: line 1: 70 cm. × 8; distance to the right edge: 2 cm.; to the upper one: between 5 cm. and 7; and to line 2: 1.5 cm. Line 2: 32.5 cm. × 8; distance to the right edge: 1 cm. – SYMBOL: at 2.6 cm. (top) and 1 (bottom) from the last letter; 8 cm. × 1.3; normally curved design whose lower extremity is identical with that of Ja 673; five inside incisions: two horizontal ones in both the upper and lower parts and another perpendicular to the frame, in the center; the upper extremity is a curved duplicate of that of Ja 555; cf. Plate B.

1 *yrᵓb/wmtᶜm/bn/ḥmᶜṯt/rṯd/*
2 *ᵓlmqh/qnym/* **Symbol**

1 Yarᵓab and Mataᶜum, descendants of [the family] Ḥammᶜaṯat, has entrusted to the care of
2 ᵓIlumquh one slave. **Symbol**

L. 1: after *yrᵓb/*, *w* inside another *b* (haplography). – *mtᶜm*, e.g., RÉS 3522/1, Qat; cf. also the name of a man *mtᶜt* (RÉS 4867/1, Ḥaḍr); cf. the Arabic name of a man *al-ᵓamtâᶜî* (cf. *SlGaVNPA*, p. 33 A).

842 – Yellowish sandstone; left and lower corners slightly damaged; found about 100 m. northeast of the columns; photograph in Plate 54. – MaMB 14.

STONE: maximum thickness: 27 cm. – *Front:* strongly concave, contrary to the back which is strongly convex; 70.4 cm. (top) and 67 (bottom) × 37 (left) and 27 (right). – INSCRIPTION: letter height: from 9.5 cm. to 11; distance between the lines: from 0.5 cm. to 1.5; stroke width: 0.8 cm.; diameter of *w*, ᶜ, and the circle of *y*: 6 cm. to 6.5, 5.5, and from 4.5 to 5.5 respectively; a vertical line on the right of the first two lines, and at 7.8 cm. and 7 from the right side of the stone, at the top and the bottom respectively. – SYMBOL: 21 cm. × 7.5; cf. infra; cf. Plate B.

1 ← *kdsᵓ/nb/mrhy* **Sym-**
2 → *rb/ᶜsy/wbny* **bol**
3 ← *whtwnf/lkw*

1 **Sym-** Yahram, son of ᵓAsadka-
2 **bol** rib, has acquired and built
3 and achieved his canal.

Ll. 1-2: *yhrm/bn/ᵓsdkrb*, also in CIH 654 (Mars 5311; cf. *JaASAB*, pp. 178-79); both texts are boustrophedon and have the verb *bny* in common (incidentally, the *n* of this verb in CIH 654 was first engraved as senestrograde; the worker then erased almost completely the two vertical strokes and engraved two others in the right places). A vertical line at the right of the first three lines in Ja 842, but of the first two in CIH 654; the symbol has single-line incising in the latter, but double-line incising in the first. Finally, CIH 654 was engraved by an amateur, contrary to the case of Ja 842. The difference in engravers explains the points of discordance between the two inscriptions, which have the same person as author.

L. 3: *kl*, cp. *kll*, e.g., in Ja 542 A/2 and commentary in *JaIAM*, pp. 274-75; here, the text referred to as "Jamme 849" is the present one, the number of which was changed after the publication of *JaIAM*; cf. also *JeHoDISO*, p. 121: kly_{I}. The verb *kl* is also attested in RÉS 4905/2: *b(n)y/kl/–* "has built [and] achieved–"; cf. the same asyndeton of verbs, e.g., in Ja 538/2: *–/qwm/bny/–* "has erected [and] built –", and RÉS 4912/2 (cf. *JaSAI*, p. 512, No. 21): *–/šqr/ṣll/–* "– roofed [and] paved –". – *kl/fnwthw*, cf. RÉS 4552/1-2, where *blḥ* and *kl* are personal name and verb respectively: the text is complete at the right (cf. *GrKFG*, p. 91); the translation of RÉS 4552 reads as follows: "Balaḥ achieved his canal." For *fnwt* (e.g., Ja 541/4-5), pl. *fnw*, cf. *CoRoC*, p. 218 B, *BeSI*, p. 59 and *RoVSAY*, p. 310.

843 – Block, found about 50 m. to the south of the columns; sandstone; photograph in Plate 54. – MaMB 16.

STONE: maximum thickness (center): 22.4 cm. – *Front:* 30.5 cm. (top) and 29.5 (bottom) × 15.3 (right) and 12 (left); central hole: 15.5 cm. × 3 × 10 (depth), and three others: small, diameter: 1 cm. – INSCRIPTION: line 1: 23.5 cm. × 3.8 (minimum) and 4.8 (maximum); distance to the right and upper edges: 3.7 cm. and 2 (from *ṯ*) respectively; space between the lines: 0.5 cm. Line 2: 8 cm. × 4.5; distance to the left and lower edges: 4.2 cm. and 1 respectively.

1 *krbᶜṯt/hrw*
2 *ḥʾl*

1 Karibᶜaṯat [of the family] Harwa-
2 ḥʾil.

Ll. 1-2: *hrwḥʾl*, composed of the 4th form of *rwḥ* and *ʾl*; for the 1st element, cf. the Arabic name of a man *rawâḥat* (cf. *WüID*, 169/5).

844 – Inscribed stone found about 30 m. northeast of the columns; yellowish sandstone; photograph in Plate 54. – MaMB 19.

STONE: almost constant thickness: 14 cm. – *Front:* badly damaged; 25.5 cm. × 20. – INSCRIPTION: most of the reading is very difficult; the decipherment is nevertheless certain; letter height: 3.5 cm.; space between the lines: 0.4 cm. – SYMBOL: damaged; cf. probably Ja 567.

1 **Sym-** *lḥyᶜṯt/ḏnfʾn*
2 **bol** *hqny/ʾlmqh/*
3 *ṯhwn/bᶜl/ʾwm/ṣl*
4 *mn/ḏḏhbn/lwfy/*
5 *qnyhw/ᶜṯt/ḏqn*
6 *y/bᶜṯtr/wʾlmqh*

1 **Sym-** Laḥayᶜaṯat, he of [the family] Nafaʾân,
2 **bol** has dedicated to ʾIlumquh
3 Ṯahwân, master of ʾAwwâm, this sta-
4 tue which [is] in bronze, for the safety of
5 his slave ᶜAṯat whom he has possessed.
6 By ᶜAṯtar and ʾIlumquh.

Almost all the signs are more or less damaged; the use of half brackets is thus practically superfluous.

Ll. 5-6: *ḏqny*, cf. Ja 816/9-10.

845 – Upper left corner of a block; greenish alabaster; found about 20 m. northeast of the columns. – MaMB 23.

STONE: maximum thickness: 21.1 cm. – *Front:* extremity of the upper left corner broken; 47.6 cm. × 35.5. – INSCRIPTION: letter height: 11 cm.; distance to the top: 3.7 cm.

1 . . /ʾ]*lmqh/ḥmᶜ*⸢/⸣
2 [*ṯt*/. .

1 . . ʾI]lumquh Ḥammᶜa
2 [ṯat. .

846 – Inscription broken on the left side; sandstone; found about 150 m. to the north of the columns; photograph in Plate 54. – MaMB 24=RÉS 3955.

STONE: thickness: 53 cm. – *Front:* maximum length: 43.8 cm.; width: 24 cm. – INSCRIPTION: boustrophedon; same disposition of lines as in Ja 683; vertical lines indicate the location of each letter; letter height: 6 cm.; space between the lines: 0.8 cm.; distance from line 1 to the top: 1.4 cm. (left) and 2.4 (right).

1 . . . /*nb*]⸢/⸣*tṯᶜfw*⸢*h/n*⸣*b/mwyḥ* ←
2 [ᶜ*sy/wbny/r*]⸤⸢*b*⸣ᶜ/*ẓllm/ḥwln/ḏby* →
3 . . . /*nrḥbm/*ᶜ]⸢*brw/nytḥt/lwḥ/nn* ←

1 Ḥayûm, son of Hawfᶜaṯat, [descendant of (the family)...
2 [has acquired and built] the [fou]rth of [the] rooms, the one part on the cupo-
3 la, the other part of the substructure, and the fourth of [the foundation..

Ll. 1-2: N. Rhodokanakis' restoration is all the more hypothetical since the parallel text, RÉS 3954, mentions the family name, which could also be expected here.

L. 2: *ẓllm*: proper name in *RÉS*; however, RÉS 3954, referred to by *RÉS*, suggests that this proper name should be preceded by the noun indicating the nature of building; here, *ẓllm* is noun; cf. CIH 371/4 (*CIH*, II, p. 19, III, p. 354 A and

BeSI, p. 117; *RyNP*, I, p. 341 B: proper name); for the interpretation of *ẓll*, pl. *ẓlt*, cf. *CIH*, III, p. 354 A and *CoRoC*, p. 160 B.

Ll. 2 and 3: *ḥwln* and *ḥwl*: prepositions according to *RÉS* (VII, p. 9) and *BeSI*, p. 110; the reference to *LaGD*, p. 523, mentioning the equivalence of Daṯînah *ḥâl* and Arabic *baʿḏ*, as well as the different treatment of *ḥwln*+*ḏ* and *ḥwl*+noun indicate that *ḥwl* is noun here; *ḥwl* is verb in RÉS 4917/2, Ḥaḏr.

Ll. 2-3: *byn* and *mbḫr*, RÉS 3954, commentary on line 2; cf. also *mbḫrn*, name of a palm-grove in RÉS 4815/2 and 8.

847 – Whitish sandstone fragment; broken on the right corner; in the east wall of the building located about 200 m. to the north of the columns; photograph in Plate 55. – MaMB 25.

STONE: maximum thickness: 16.5 cm. – *Front:* covered with red paint; maximum length: 28 cm., and width: 28.5 cm. – INSCRIPTION: same disposition of lines as in Ja 552; letter height: 5 cm., 5, 4.8, 4.5, and 4.8; space between the lines: 0.8 cm.

1 ...]*n*/*b*
2 ...]⌜*s*⌝*fl*/*w*
3 .../*ḥ*]⌜*gn*/*khw*
4 [*fy*... ...]./*hwt*/*by*
5 [*tn*... /*ml*]⌜*k*/*sbʾ*/*lʾd*
6 [*mhw*...

1 ...
2 ...] the lower country of .
3 ...] as He has grant-
4 [ed... ...].this hou-
5 [se... ...ki]ng of Sabaʾ to [his] ser-
6 [vants...

Line 6 was engraved on a second stone.

Appendix

1 – UNINSCRIBED VOTIVE LIBATION ALTAR: Ja 848.

848 – Votive libation altar in yellowish sandstone; slightly damaged; three photographs in Plate 55. – MaMB 46=MB m 8 [field book].

TOP: length of the bucranium: 1.9 cm.; central cavity: 6.1 cm. × 2.7; plaque: 7.2 × 3.8; thickness of the plaque: 1.8 cm. (front) and 2 (back). – BUCRANIUM: height: 2.3 cm. (front) and 2 (neck); length: 1.8 (bottom); width: 1.8 cm. (top) and 1 (bottom).

2 – FRAGMENTS OF CEMENT: Ja 849 AND 850.

These two fragments of cement show (in reverse) parts of original bronze texts.

849 – Left side of a cement block; photograph in Plate 55. – MaMB 59.

BLOCK: thickness: 6.8 cm. – *Front:* 7 cm. × 6. – LETTERS: height: 2.6 cm.; space between the lines: 0.6 cm.; boustrophedon.

→ *lhyʿ*[*tt*/... 1 Laḥayʿa[ṯat...
← .*n*/*h*[*qny*.. 2 ..[has] de[dicated to...

850 – Right side of a cement block; three photographs in Plate 55. – MaMB 70.

BLOCK: maximum thickness: 2.6 cm. – *Front:* 4.7 cm. (length) × 6.5.

→ ...].*r* 1
→ ...]*h* 2

L. 1: the letter preceding *r* is either *b*, *ḏ*, etc.

Addendum

[Due to editorial misunderstanding, Ja 851 was placed here, following Ja 850, rather than after Ja 761 (p. 228) as the author intended.]

851 – Standing stone somewhat on the left of Ja 561; left part covered by another stone; partial photograph; cf. Chapter I, C. – MaMB 317.

SYMBOL: for the outside line, cp. Ja 690, and for the inside incision, cf. Ja 692; but here, without any triangle on either extremity; cf. Plate B.

1 **Sym-** *šʿbn*/*sb*⌉[*ʾ*/*khln*/... .../*hqnyw*/ (*mrʾhmw*/)*ʾlmqh*(/*ṯhwn*)/*bʿl*]
2 **bol** *ʾwm*/*ṯlṯtn*/*ʾ*[...*n*/... .../*ḥmdm*/ *bḏt*/*ḥmrhmw*/*ʾlmqh*(/*ṯhwn*)/*b*]
3 *ʿlʾwm*/*hwfyn*/*wt*[...
4 *ḏt*/*brqn*/*sbʿt*/*ḫrft*[...
5 *ʾsrrhmw*/*ysrn*/*whbšm*⌉[...
6 *wḏytlwnhw*/*ʾḏbḥm*/*w*[...
7 *sqym*/*mhḏrm*/*mhšfq*/*ʾ*[...

1 **Sym-** The tribe Saba[ʾ Kahilân... ...have dedicated to (their lord) ʾIlumquh (Ṯahwân), master of]
2 **bol** ʾAwwâm, [these] three [...]s...in praise because has vouchsafed to them ʾIlumquh (Ṯahwân), mas-]
3 ter of ʾAwwâm to shower upon and to .[...
4 this lightning season seven years [...
5 their wâdî-side valleys Yasrân and Habšam [...
6 and of which they took care for Him [as] sacrifices [...
7 an extensive, plentiful irrigation [...

In the present collection, Ja 653 and 735 also are dedicatory inscriptions to the god ʾIlumquh by the tribe Sabaʾ Kahilân, and deal with favors concerning rain.

L. 2: ʾ...: e.g., *ʾṣlmn* (Ja 567/4) and *ʾṯwrm* (Ja 581/4). – *ḥmdm/bḏt/ẖmrhmw* is more probable than *lwzʾ*, because of the place of the expression in the whole inscription.

L. 5: *hbšm*, proper name derived from the root *bšm*, as also is *bšmm*, name of a minor Sab god (contrary to *JaP*, p. 140, note 765, end).

L. 6: *ḏytlwnhw*, cf. commentary on Ja 584/1.

L. 7: *mhḏr* and *mhšfq*, cf. commentary on Ja 575/4.

Part II

Historical Studies

Chapter I

THREE GROUPS OF INSCRIBED STONES RE-USED IN THE ENTRANCE HALL

The information given in this preliminary chapter has been partly published in *JaAPCR*. However, since the publication of that monograph, some additional photographs have become available; these new photographs, as well as the one I already had, have been subjected to study under greater magnification, which has made possible the identification of several stones. I am thus able to supplement considerably the notes published in *JaAPCR*, and thereby to shed definitive light on the relative chronology of these three groups.

All the inscriptions in and from the entrance hall of Maḥram Bilqîs have not been recorded, and the three groups described below are not the only ones from those excavations. Other groups may, in fact, be seen on the photographs published by *AlEMY*: one in the right part of No. 171 (p. 256), and another one in the left part of Nos. 174 and 175 (p. 258).

Finally, a fourth group is to be studied in connection with the three mentioned above.

A - GROUP A: WESTERN ROW OF 14 STANDING STONES (cf. *JaAPCR*, pp. 7-8)

The most complete photograph published of this western row of fourteen standing inscribed stones, as they were before the fall of the piers, [1] is to be found in *PhQS*, p. 281, bottom.

This row of stones was located immediately in front of piers W1-5 [2]; it was not continuous however. Stones Nos. 1 and 2 were south and north of pier W1 respectively, [3] thus leaving free the passage between piers W1 and SW5 (east of the preceding); this passage would otherwise have been partly blocked. Stones Nos. 13 and 14 were also south and north of pier W5 respectively. Stones Nos. 4, 8, and 11 were exactly in front of piers W2, W3, and W4 respectively.

The seven stones described in *JaAPCR* (pp. 7-8) are respectively from left to right (i.e., from south to north), Nos. 3, 4, 5, 7, 8, and 9, No. 6 being the support of Nos. 5 and 7.

South of stone No. 3, were Nos. 1 = Ja 609,
2 = 629.

North of stone No. 9, were Nos. 10 = Ja 628,
11 = 631,
12 = 653,
13 = 559,
14 = 560.

[1] For a general view after the fall of the piers, cf. *AlEMY*, p. 260, Nos. 168 and 178. For the purpose of facilitating the location of the piers, I suggest the following systematization. The western and eastern colonnade are represented by W and E respectively, counting from the south. The southern colonnade is divided into two parts by the doorway (cf. *AlEMY*, p. 225 B and No. 172): one on the west and the other on the east, thus SW and SE; in each case, I start counting from the doorway.

[2] Pier W2 is "the second pier" in *AlEMY*, p. 228 A, third paragraph, where mention is made of a secondary wall built up with "more ancient blocks, including at least six that were inscribed". I remember only one inscription that was copied as MaMB 223=Ja 649. This inscribed stone is lying on its right side, with its upper side against the western wall of the entrance hall, and was re-used as lintel in the northern side of a small passage or opening in the secondary wall, at the foot of the entrance hall wall; this small opening is about 80 cm. high and about 65 cm. wide.

[3] When discovered, these two stones were leaning against each other.

The fourteen texts are thus Ja 559, 560, 561 bis, 601, 602, 604, 609, 610, 627, 628, 629, 631, 641, and 653.

B – GROUP B: WESTERN GROUP OF 11 RECUMBENT STONES (cf. *JaAPCR*, p. 16)

From my study of the photograph of *PhQS*, p. 281, bottom, already mentioned above, and another photograph taken at about the same time, and with the help of the comparative approximation of the measurements of the stones themselves, these eleven inscribed stones re-used in the pavement occupy a rectangle the western side of which borders upon the bottom of the stones Nos. 2 (right part), 3, 4, 6, and 8 of group A; its southern side is about 50 cm. north from the southwestern colonnade and occupies the distance from stone No. 2 of group A to the northwestern edge of pier SW3.

The respective location of these stones is reconstructed as follows:

2
1 7 9 11
3 4

5 6 8 10

The eleven texts are Ja 563 (No. 11), 565 (No. 8), 578 (No. 5), 586 (No. 4), 618 (No. 1), 630 (No. 9), 642 (No. 2), 647 (No. 7), 745 (No. 3), 746 (No. 6), and 747 (No. 10).

C – GROUP C: EASTERN ROW OF 19 STANDING STONES

This group of nineteen inscribed stones is standing in front of piers E1-7; the group described in *JaAPCR* (p. 8) is almost at the center of the whole row.

An almost general view of the row may be seen in photograph No. 174 in *AlEMY* (p. 258), partly also in No. 175 (p. 258); the identification of most of the other inscribed stones is based on other, still unpublished photographs.

To the left (north) of the group described in *JaAPCR* (*l.c.*), was a row of six inscribed stones, Nos. 1, 2, 3, 4, and 5 from north to south, No. 6 being standing in front of the center of No. 5. Apart from No. 5 which has been partly deciphered as Ja 851 from the original of the photograph No. 177 in *AlEMY* (p. 259, extreme left), none of the others has been deciphered or photographed close enough to allow any decipherment. All that I can see, is a very large symbol in the upper right corner of stone No. 4.

To the right (south) of the group described in *JaAPCR* (*l.c.*), was another row of eight inscribed stones listed from left to right as follows: Ja 664, 670, 567, 665, 607, 753 (I, II, and III),[4] and 606.

Besides the five texts undeciphered, the present row contains the following texts: Ja 561, 564, 567, 568, 606, 607, 643 bis, 664, 665, 670, 671, 753, and 851.

D – RELATIVE CHRONOLOGY OF THESE THREE GROUPS

The identity of the kings mentioned in the three groups makes it clear that the additions to the primitive structure of the entrance hall were made first in the western part and later in the eastern one.

The following scheme illustrates the situation. In each column, the top and the bottom are occupied by the earliest and the latest royal names, respectively. (See the scheme on page 257.)

The additions and modifications made in the western part of the entrance hall were thus performed after the sole reign of Šamir Yuhar^{c}iš, and therefore after the dynasty of Yasrum Yuhan^{c}im, because none of this dynasty would, I think, have removed from its original place an offering made during the reign of another member of the same dynasty. Consequently, the period of about the middle of the 4th century A.D. could possibly be suggested for these additions and modifications.

Because of Ja 670 and 671, the additions to the eastern part may be dated of the end of the 5th or the early beginning of the 6th century A.D. An eventual postponement of that period would of course depend on the contents of the first six stones of group C.

E – GROUP Ja 760 and 761

The group Ja 760 and 761 is suggested by *AlEMY* (p. 232 B) as probably being re-used. The group is reproduced in photograph No. 180 (p. 261) of *AlEMY*, Ja 760 being on the left.

[4] For Ja 753 which is engraved on two stones, cf. *JaAPCR*, p. 5.

Group A	Group B	Group C
Našaʾkarib Yuhaʾmin, King of Sabaʾ (Ja 559 and 560)		
	Karibʾil Watar Yuhanʿim, King of Sabaʾ (Ja 563)	
		ʾIlšaraḥ Yaḥḍub, King of Sabaʾ and Raydân (Ja 567 and 568)
	to	
to		
	Yasrum Yuhanʿim's Coregency with his son Šamar Yuharʿiš; Kings of Sabaʾ and Raydân (Ja 647)	
		to
Šamir Yuharʿiš's Sole Reign; King of Sabaʾ and Raydân (Ja 653)		
		Ṯaʾrân Yuhanʿim's Coregency with his son Malikkarib Yuhaʾmin; Kings of Sabaʾ and Raydân and Ḥaḍramawt and Yamnat (Ja 670 and 671)

The wall in which these two inscribed stones are inserted, is very small indeed, and the four stones which compose it, match each other perfectly in the wall. Further, the present condition of the two stones makes it clear that neither the upper side nor the two lateral sides of either of them have been re-cut. These two reasons compel me to believe that the two stones now under study are *in situ.* Furthermore, Ja 760 is a dedicatory text from the Suẖaymite clan, it is therefore possible that both Ja 760 and 761 were engraved by Suẖaymites, and thus that "the small room with a bench along three walls and a stone table in the center", to which these two inscribed stones belong, may very well be considered as the religious meeting place for Suẖaymites.

Chapter II

RESEARCH ON THE MURAL INSCRIPTIONS Ja 550–557

The study of the mural inscriptions Ja 550-557 includes several questions common either to all or at least to some of them, such as the location of the inscriptions, the genealogy of the family mentioned in Ja 552-555, the relative chronology of the texts, and the genealogical research on the Sab rulers attested in them. Some of these questions need only be pointed out; others require more research in order to receive some plausible, even if partial explanation; others finally are only mentioned, for their solution must be attempted in a general study of Sab rulers.

A - METHODOLOGICAL NOTE

The most important question relating to the mural inscriptions is doubtless the genealogical tree of the Sab rulers attested in them. The solutions presented here are but an attempted beginning toward a more complete solution to the very difficult problem raised by the chronology of Sab rulers, which obviously enough is out of the question here. Such a general study involves much further research toward a sound solution to the various problems, and may be classified under three major headings, viz. palaeography, detailed study of the contents of the texts, and finally explicative hypotheses suggested in the line of the material already known. Many examples of these three major fields of research are given in *JaPSAP*.

Palaeography must be based on facsimiles made as accurately as possible. However, the making of such drawings of letters is very far from being as easy as it at first sight looks, as plainly demonstrated by *JaPSAP*, especially pp. 57-106. The making of these facsimiles is often made even much more arduous and its result inaccurate because of the defect of the photographic material, as is, for instance the case, for Khalidy-Condé 1.

Nothing should be spared to get the best possible material from which the drawing is to be made, namely a good squeeze when the original is not available. The study of the lettering characteristics must then take every single one of them into consideration so that the development of the various types through the different letterings may be pointed out, and the influence of one type upon another recognized and described. These requirements are necessary if palaeography is to be used as a valid source of information.

The classification of the Sab rulers involved in the texts is based on sound hypotheses. I wish to point out here and to discuss two ideas which, in my opinion, do not meet with such a requirement.

With regard to the *mukarribs*, I consider as unsound the hypothesis, which is presented as a certainty, according to which those rulers "ont exercé synchroniquement le pouvoir, sans que leur règne fût toutefois, au sens strict, simultané ou partagé".[1] A reality such as synchronical, yet not strictly simultaneous or divided reigns is quite abnormal. On the one hand, synchronism necessarily implies simultaneousness; otherwise, there simply cannot be any synchronism. On the other hand, synchronism of reigns in the same country also implies necessarily some kind of division or subordination of power. Such obvious difficulties should have been removed, if possible, when the

[1] Cf. *RyISA*, XVII, p.163, with reference to *PiPISA*, p. 117.

theory was presented for the first time. No explanation has, however, been presented; the theory is simply repeated all over again. That explanation is all the more needed as the theory necessarily involves practical difficulties. How, for instance, could one man have been administrator for three (Ja 550) or four (Ja 555) rulers synchronally, or another one servant of five rulers (Ja 557) also synchronally, if those rulers are to be understood according to that theory?

Having to explain two pairs of father and son, determined by the expression *ʾmlk/qtbn* "kings of Qatabân" in BM 132529 (Van Lessen 1)/7, *GhNQI* writes: "I think that the title 'king' in such a case meant primarily that the person thus designated was of princely descent, the title being used publicly to apply to those members of the ruling or reigning family who...had some public duties delegated to them.... The relation of these 'kings' to the sovereign would be a family matter".[2] The preceding opinion amounts to the actual denial of the only definitive, assured epigraphic proof that a person actually reigned, that is to say his name is qualified by the noun *mlk* "king"; it is also the denial of another, correlative epigraphic fact (cf., e.g., Ja 551 and 558): a prince, even the king's own son, is *never* presented in the texts as *mlk*. The repudiation of epigraphic facts such as the two preceding ones would make impossible any scientific epigraphic study, and open the road to arbitrary conjectures, as illustrated by the attitude of the preceding author who considers as princes the four persons designated formally as *ʾmlk/qtbn* "kings of Qatabân", but understands as a probable king the person listed in line 1 of the same text, and who is not indicated as *mlk/qtbn*.

The groups of rulers mentioned below are listed chronologically. However, unless otherwise pointed out, they do not follow each other immediately. They are listed here because their names are found in the texts published in the present collection from Maḥram Bilqîs.

B – EARLY *Mukarribs* (cf. Plate C)

Among the texts discovered during the excavations, four of them mention the names of some early *mukarribs*.

1 – *Ja 819*: The two rulers attested in this inscription, namely Karibʾil and Sum[hu...], are palaeographically much earlier than the following group.

[2] P. 10, with reference to *RycIMAM*, p. 238, who deals with an entirely different matter, the coregents.

2 – *Ja 831, 832, and 673*: Ja 832 introduces Yadaʿʾil and Yaṯaʿʾamar as brothers of [Sum]huwatar, the author of the bronze plaque facing the entrance door. The palaeography of Ja 831 justifies the identification of Yadaʿʾil of Ja 832 with the father of Sumhuriyyâm who was the master of the author of the other bronze plaque in the entrance hall. The proportion height-incising is 1/10 and the height-width 1/2.5 in both texts. Thus, the following scheme may be presented:

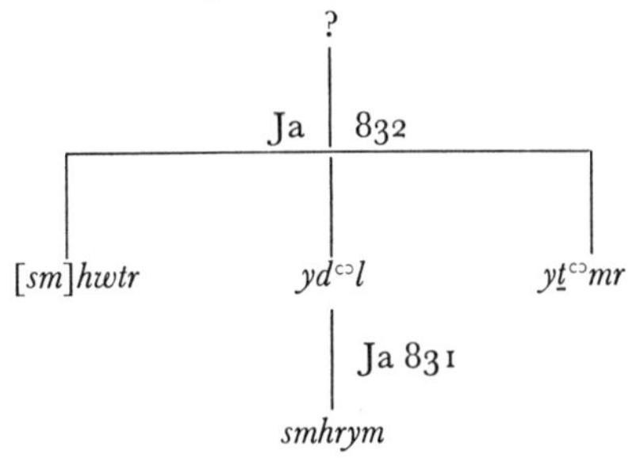

The two rulers Yaṯaʿʾamar Watar and ʾ[...], the latter being unknown before, both attested in Ja 673, are posterior to the preceding group and also to the lettering types found, e.g., in CIH 496, 493, and RÉS 4700 respectively.

C – THE MURAL INSCRIPTIONS

The eight mural inscriptions Ja 550-557 are engraved on the outside of the enclosure wall of ʾAwwâm. Their study brings up several questions which will be discussed below.

1 – *Location of* Ja 550-557[3] (cf. Plate C, Fig. 1)

The relative location of the eight mural inscriptions to each other and to the western door, the measurements between each of them, and the length of each text are given in the following scheme where the stippling represents one uninscribed masonry course, and the solid line one inscribed line of the text, that is to say one masonry course, with the exception of Ja 552 and 553 (see page 260).

2 – *Genealogy of the authors of* Ja 552-555

a – The identity of the authors in Ja 552 and 553 may be accepted on the basis of the identity of the palaeography which suggests also the identity of the workman. Ja 553, however, is anterior to Ja 552 because of their respective location, and also because of the absence of any title for the author of

[3] *AlEMY*'s statement (pp. 222 A and 231 A; cf. also pp. 293-94) according to which Ja 550 is "on the north side of the wall" is to be understood in relation with Ja 551. For the location of Ja 552 and 553, cf. *l.c.*, pp. 220 A and 222.

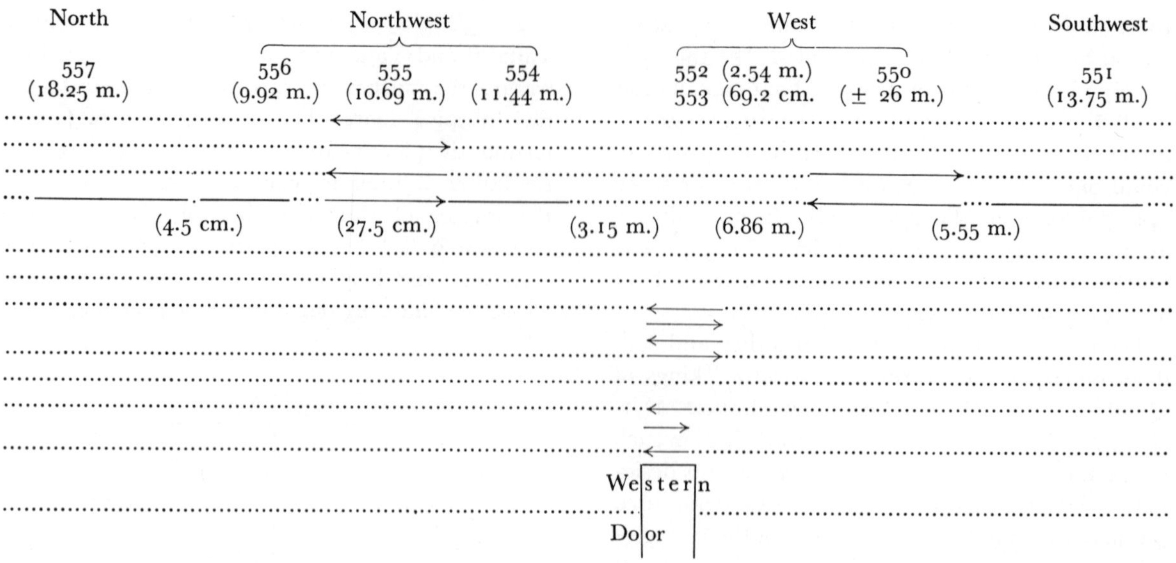

Ja 553. This absence of title cannot indeed be explained by the location of the text, since there is ample space for a fourth line in the lower half of the second stone. Finally, there is no way of judging the period of time which separates the engraving of Ja 552 from that of Ja 553.

b – The author of Ja 555 seems to be identified as a son of the writer of Ja 552 because each one is *qyn* for some rulers and lives in the house called Yahar. The following genealogical tree in which the family names are printed in capital letters, may thus be presented:

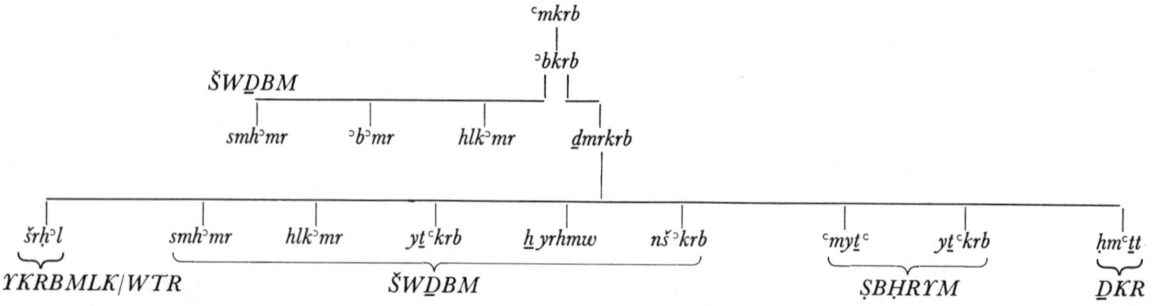

From the point of view of onomastics, it is worth mentioning that two names, ᶜ*mkrb* and ᶜ*myṯ*ᶜ have ᶜ*m* as a component, six names have the component *krb* and five others ᵓ*mr*; while two half-brothers are called *yṯ*ᶜ*krb*, *smh*ᵓ*mr*, and *hlk*ᵓ*mr* are the names of two pairs of brothers, the persons of the first pair being uncles of those of the second. The last two remarks give a very strong invitation not to identify too quickly persons bearing the same name.

The division of Ḏamarkarib's children into four groups most probably implies an equal number of Ḏamarkarib's wives. However, the major question is the interpretation of *bn/ykrbmlk/wtr* which follows Šaraḥᵓil's name, the first listed child of Ḏamarkarib, compared with *bn/šwḏbm*, *bn/ṣbḥrym*, and *bn/ḏkr*. The perfect structural similarity of the four expressions as well as the value of the family name in the last three suggest that *ykrbmlk/wtr* would be interpreted as the family headed by Yakrubmalik Watar I of my genealogical tree (see p. 264) rather than the ruler himself. Šaraḥᵓil's mother was a lady belonging to the ruling family, but not necessarily a daughter of the ruler. Furthermore, the mention of Šaraḥᵓil in the first place does not require that his mother be the woman Ḏamarkarib first married, she probably became Ḏamarkarib's first-rank or preferred wife because of her origin or at least her relationship with the ruler's family.

Since Ḏamarkarib, author of Ja 555, is not listed among ᵓAbkarib's sons in Ja 552/2, it seems necessary to conclude that he was not yet born when his father engraved Ja 552. In order, then, to give him time to grow up as well as to get the social position and to accomplish all the deeds listed in his text, a period of about 45-50 years should be allowed between the engraving of the two texts.

c – The first author of Ja 554 does not seem to be identified with the author of Ja 555, although each one calls himself *ḏmrkrb/bn/ʾbkrb/bn/šwḏbm*. The two persons are moving in different spheres of activity, and their success is also very unequal. The author of Ja 554 is a sworn man of the administrator of the temple, while his homonym is an administrator for the rulers themselves. Further, the first one refers to the dedicatory inscription of *ḏmrkrb/bn/šwḏbm* who obviously is different from himself; otherwise, he would have used another expression.

All the preceding considerations are apparently confirmed by palaeography. The difference in style between Ja 552 and 555 is such that some links, such as Fakhry 69, are necessary to make the transition.

3 – *Comparative study of* Ja 550, 552, 555, *and* 557

The comparative study of this group of texts requires a thorough analysis of their contents in order to attempt a genealogy of the rulers mentioned in them, and also to visualize the possible relation between the different groups of rulers.

a – SEPARATE ANALYSIS OF THE TEXTS

1°. *Ja 550*: This inscription is a short autobiography written by Tabaʿkarib apparently after his retirement from public life, which coincides with the beginning of Karibʾil Watar's reign. All events recorded by the text were performed during the reigns of the rulers mentioned at the beginning of the inscription and Karibʾil Watar's name appears in the final invocation.[4] Furthermore, the mention of two generations of Sab rulers, unusual as it may be,[5] does not support the opinion according to which Tabaʿkarib might allude to the fact that his ancestors had been *qyn* of the preceding rulers,[5] since those two facts have no relation whatever to each other, and Tabaʿkarib obviously speaks of himself and his career without dealing with that of his ancestors. Furthermore, according to his own testimony, Tabaʿkarib "stayed in the hostilities...for five years during the war of Qatabân". This reference to the length of Tabaʿkarib's military service obviously does not allude to the total length of the war itself[6]; on the contrary, it suggests a longer duration for the Sab-Qat war. Tabaʿkarib's five-year military activity covers the end of Yakrubmalik Watar II's reign and the beginning of that of Yaṯaʿʾamar Bayyin II; the first ruler sent him to war and the second granted him a testimony of confidence after the end of that particular war. Ja 550 deals thus with the last five years of a war.

2°. *Ja 552*: This text does not provide any historical fact that could be of some help in reconstructing the genealogical tree of the Sab rulers. Worthy of mention, however, is the fact that these two rulers are referred to in the final invocation only by their first names contrary to both Ja 550 and 555.

3°. *Ja 555*: The main historical facts alluded to in this text are that the author was appointed as administrator of Mârib, and especially that he waged war in Qatabân with Sumhuʿalay Yanûf II.

4°. *Ja 557*: Very important here is the mention of a king of Mârib; unfortunately, only the initial letter of his name remains on the stone.

b – COMMON STUDY

Besides the preceding details, the four texts have several features which may be compared and which are presented in the following scheme, namely the profession of the authors, the rulers with whom they were connected, and the rulers mentioned in the final invocation.

Ja 552	Ja 555	Ja 557	Ja 550
qyn/ydʿʾl/byn *sm[ʿly/* *]ynf*	*qyn/yṯʿʾmr* *ykrbmlk* *smhʿly* *ydʿʾl* *ykrbmlk*	*ʿbd/ydʿʾl/* *byn* *smhʿly/* *ynf* *yṯʿʾmr/* *wtr* *ykrbmlk/* *ḏrḥ* *smhʿly/* *ynf*	*qyn/ydʿʾl/* *byn* *ykrbmlk/* *wtr* *yṯʿʾmr/* *byn*
b ydʿʾl *smhʿly*	*b ykrbmlk/* *wtr* *yṯʿʾmr/* *byn*		*b ydʿʾl/byn* *ykrbmlk/* *wtr* *yṯʿʾmr/* *byn* *krbʾl/* *wtr*

[4] The text was thus not engraved during Yaṯaʿʾamar Bayyin's reign, as stated by *RycIMAM*, p. 156, where the text is referred to as CIH 374 instead of CIH 375.

[5] Cf. *RycIMAM*, *l.c.*

[6] Contrary to *PiPISA*, e.g., p. 174.

A simple glance at the preceding scheme shows a confusing number of identical names of rulers; several considerations need be pointed out before any attempt is made to reconstruct their genealogical tree.

1° – The series of personal names, such as those mentioned above, are composed of pairs of names listed according to the normal genealogical order, father-son, unless the contrary is indicated by the context itself, as is the case in Ja 555 where the order is reversed. When the preceding relationship is not to be applied in the texts, mention is normally made either explicitly or implicitly (by comparing the text involved with others belonging to the same period) of what relationship is to be understood in each case. The preceding interpretation seems all the more suitable in that its rejection (which cannot be accepted unless based on a reason as strong as the above-mentioned epigraphic fact), would lead to a complete deadlock with regard to the understanding of these lists. The principle of genealogical order, however, does not necessarily have to be applied in direct, consecutive line as in father-son-grandson-great grandson, because to serve as administrator for four rulers listed according to the consecutive genealogical order, although not impossible, is doubtless more than unusual. It is for this reason that until more information is available, I consider the two middle names as those of the sons of the first listed one, and the fourth name as that of the son of the third.

2° – The study of those lists of names gives the strong impression that the second elements *byn* and *wtr* were alternatively borne every other generation.

3° – The first series in Ja 555 mentions the names according to an inverse genealogical order, namely son-father, contrary to all the other series, including those mentioned in the final invocations. It is indeed quite normal and natural that the two youngest members of the dynasty would have been the last two to be alive at the time of the engraving of the text which, like Ja 550, is a short autobiography. On the contrary, if the normal genealogical order is maintained, the two remaining rulers, attested in the final invocation, would be the two oldest ones. Further, the first person mentioned in this invocation is naturally the father of the second, and not vice versa.

4° – The list of five names in both Ja 555 and 557 has in common a rather surprising feature, namely the perfect homonymity of the second and the fifth names: *ykrbmlk* in Ja 555 and *smhᶜly/ynf* in Ja 557. Do these two identical names refer to only one person or to two different ones? If the first hypothesis is true, what could be the reason for such a repetition? A clue to the solution for that problem is given in Ja 555, where the second name of the first series is the first in the final invocation, that is to say the leader of the dynasty at the time of the engraving of the text. It is, however, rather difficult to determine why it should be the second name listed, since the apparent reason for inverting the normal genealogical order in Ja 555 was to have *ykrbmlk/wtr* in second place.

5° – The lack of photographs prevents the use, here, of Ja 824 and 825, two texts from the mausoleum, which attest *yṯᶜ*](ᵓ)*mr/byn/bn/ykrbmlk/wtr* and]*smhᶜly/y*[*nf* respectively, and does not allow us to consider Ja 824 as confirming *RhSLG*'s (II, p. 17) restoration of *yṯᶜᵓmr* at the beginning of CIH 966 (Gl 508)/1: ...*b*]*yn*/[*bn*]/*ykrbmlk/wtr*. Although the restoration of *bn* is justified, that of *yṯᶜᵓmr* is simply hypothetical; in my genealogical scheme, I prefer to retain *ydᶜᵓl* than *yṯᶜᵓmr*.

6° – A very important question is the connection of any of the texts now under study with RÉS 3858, a Qat text which refers to a war between the Qat king Yadaᶜᵓab Yagul son of Ḏamarᶜalay, against *ydᶜᵓl/byn/wsmhᶜly/ynf/wyṯᶜᵓmr/wtr/wᵓmlk/sbᵓ/wᵓšᶜbhmw/wᵓmlk/rᶜnn/wrᶜnn*.

The war alluded to in the Qat text is not the one referred to in Ja 550, for the two rulers Yakrubmalik Watar II and his son Yaṯaᶜᵓamar Bayyin II, mentioned in the second text, are not listed in the first.

The three Sab rulers mentioned in the Qat inscription have exactly the *same names* and are *listed according to the same order* as the first three in the series of names in Ja 557; such a double common feature can hardly be a casual coincidence.

Another very important question is whether the rulers Yadaᶜᵓil Bayyin II, Sumhuᶜalay Yanûf II, and Yaṯaᶜᵓamar Watar in both RÉS 3858 and Ja 557 were *mukarribs* or kings? According to some authors,[7] they would be kings; and according to some others, *mukarribs*. This is the opinion of *RycIMAM* (e.g., p. 59) according to whom *ᵓmlk/sbᵓ* would refer to the first Sab kings (e.g., p. 76). However, the same author considers (e.g., pp. 278-

[7] E.g., *AlCAS*, p. 8 and also *JaAIVC*, pp. 37-38, an opinion which after further study, I can no longer maintain.

79) Yada°°il Bayyin listed in RÉS 3858 as king, as well as Yakrubmalik Watar and Yaṯa°°amar Bayyin who are not mentioned in that text. So also is *PiPISA*'s (e.g., p. 174) opinion which can be summarized as follows: the three rulers listed were *mukarribs*, and *ᵓmlk/sbᵓ* refers to kings who are individually known as *mlk/sbᵓ* and who belong to the same period as that of the three *mukarribs*.

However, RÉS 3858 is considered by the above-mentioned author as belonging to type C4 of her palaeographic classification in both the official list of the texts referred to C4 (p. 168) and the general list of the texts (p. 303). And yet, for some unexplained reason, the same text is ascribed to "C3-4" (p. 173) or doubtfully to "C3-C4" (p. 174). Since the war alluded to in the text belongs to the past, it is ascribed to C2 (e.g., p. 174). One might ask the reason for excluding C1. At any rate, according to the same author (*l.c.*), "les rois de Sabaᵓ qui y sont mentionnés avec les *mukarribs* s'identifient tout naturellement aux collatéraux de ceux-ci, qui porteront le titre de roi à cette même période C2" and in note 4, reference is made to pp. 186-87 and to the general scheme on p. 339. In these two places, three names are mentioned as belonging to C2: the king Sumhuᶜalay Ḏariḥ, Karibᵓil Bayyin, son of Sumhuᶜalay, and ᵓIlšaraḥ, the brother of the same Karibᵓil Bayyin; for these three persons (see below). Three remarks suffice here: the same Karibᵓil Bayyin son of Sumhuᶜalay is considered as *mukarrib* by the same author in p. 324; there is no proof whatever that ᵓIlšaraḥ ever became king; finally, the king Sumhuᶜalay Ḏariḥ is not known to have had any part in that particular war. There would, therefore, be only one king by whom *PiPISA* could hypothetically explain the mention of *ᵓmlk/sbᵓ* "the kings of Sabaᵓ".

The expression *ᵓmlk/sbᵓ* must be interpreted in an entirely different way.

a – The mention of a king of Mârib at the end of Ja 557 simply proves a reality which has long been suspected, namely the existence of local or provincial kings ruling some parts of Sabaᵓ under the authority of the *mukarribs*. These kings no doubt had to lend assistance to their masters in case of war. These local kings could not have been referred to by the Qat author of RÉS 3858 otherwise than as *ᵓmlk/sbᵓ*, that is to say Sab kings; furthermore, the ruler of the Qat author was himself king.

b – The very expression *ᵓmlk/sbᵓ* was not strictly a title which characterized the rulers of the following historical period, not even in the Sab texts, since *ᵓmlk/sbᵓ* is also found in inscriptions related to the periods of *mlk/sbᵓ/wḏrydn* and *mlk/sbᵓ/wḏrydn/wḥḍrmwt/wymnt*. It is thus unsound to give that expression when mentioned in a *Qat* text a specific connotation which does not even exist in *Sab* inscriptions, and thereby to infer that the persons alluded to by *ᵓmlk/sbᵓ* are some of those who are known individually as having borne the official title of *mlk/sbᵓ* in Mârib (see below).

c – The antithetic value given by both *RycIMAM* and *PiPISA* to the conjunction *w* which introduces the expression itself, and on which they base the contrast between *mukarribs* and kings, is overstated. Why should there be more antithesis between the three names of the *mukarribs* and *ᵓmlk/sbᵓ* than between *qtbn* and *wld/ᶜm* in the section *qtbn/wwld/ᶜm* mentioned in the same line of the same text? The expression *wld/ᶜm* includes not only the kingdom of Qatabân but also other allied Qat groups. The same remark is also valid in the case of the expression *ᵓmlk/sbᵓ/wᵓšᶜbhmw*, where Sabaᵓ includes not only the *ᵓšᶜb* but also other elements. Therefore, the expression *ᵓmlk/sbᵓ*, in my opinion, refers to the three *mukarribs* as well as to local or provincial kings who were reigning at that time under the authority of the three *mukarribs*, and who waged war alongside their masters.

On the basis of the preceding considerations, I propose the following genealogical scheme, until the complete study of the *mukarrib* period is made, and the photograph of Ja 557 is available. The three following considerations need especially to be kept in mind when reading the scheme.

a – The time which separates the engraving of Ja 552 from that of Ja 555 is too great to permit us to identify the homonymous rulers mentioned in them.

b – The characteristics common to both Ja 555 and 557 suggest that they should both be considered as belonging to the same general period, and therefore we must identify the homonymous rulers mentioned in them. However, the respective location of the two texts makes it certain that Ja 555 is anterior.

c – If Ja 555 and 557 belong to the same general period, the homonymous rulers common then to Ja 557 and 550 cannot be identified as being the same persons.

yd⁽ᵒ⁾l/byn I

Ja | 552

smh⁽ᶜ⁾ly/ynf I   *yd⁽ᵒ⁾l/byn II*

yt⁽ᶜ⁾mr/wtr   *smh⁽ᶜ⁾ly/ynf II*   *ykrbmlk/wtr I*

ykrbmlk/drh   Ja 555   *yt⁽ᶜ⁾mr/byn I*

Ja 557; cf. RÉS 3858

?

yd⁽ᵒ⁾l/byn III

ykrbmlk/wtr II   yt⁽ᶜ⁾mr/byn II } Ja 550

krb⁽ᵒ⁾l/wtr

4 – Ja 551 *and* 558

The author of the first text, ʾIlšaraḥ, son of the king Sumhuᶜalay Ḍariḥ, mentions a certain Karibʾil as *ʾhhw* "his brother". The second text is written by several persons who mention in the final invocation their two lords, Yadaᶜʾil son of the king Karibʾil Bayyin, and Yadaᶜʾil's *ʾh* "cousin" or "ally", namely ʾIlšaraḥ, son of Sumhuᶜalay Ḍariḥ. This information has already been dealt with in *JaPSAP*, pp. 162-63, where the distinction between Karibʾil and Karibʾil Bayyin is pointed out; the situation may be summarized as follows:

krb⁽ᵒ⁾l/byn   *smh⁽ᶜ⁾ly/drh*

                                    Ja | 551

Ja | 558

yd⁽ᵒ⁾l   *ʾlšrh*   *krb⁽ᵒ⁾l*

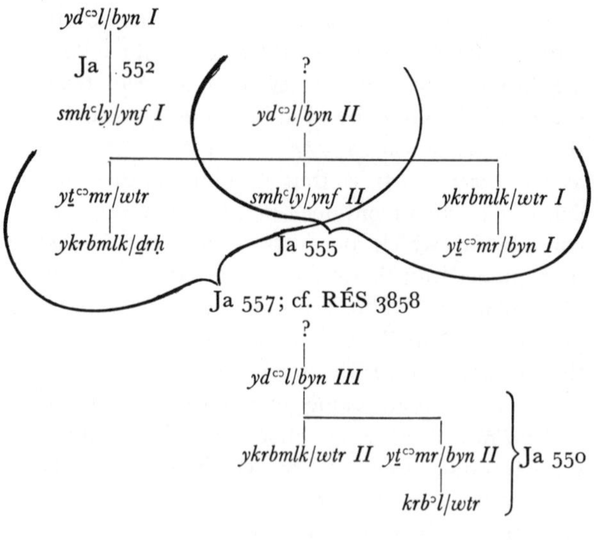

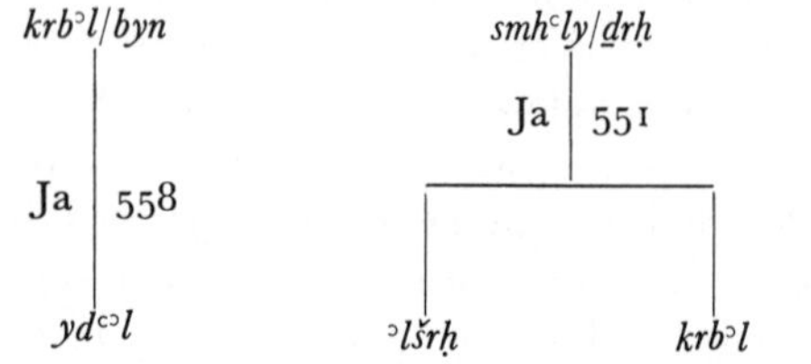

It is noteworthy that Sumhuᶜalay Ḍariḥ is presented as king in Ja 551, but not in Ja 558 which was engraved during Karibʾil Bayyin's reign; Ja 558 is thus anterior to Ja 551 and posterior to Ja 550.

The preceding case of Karibʾil and Karibʾil Bayyin is another indication that one should not too quickly identify persons bearing the same name.

The possible relation between the information presented by Ja 551 and 558 and that contained in Ja 550, is to be solved inside the frame of a general study of that period.

5 – *Palaeographical Note* (cf. Plate D)

Palaeographically, the study of the mural inscriptions Ja 552 (and 553), 555, 554, 550, and

551 shows different style developments of the lettering. In Ja 552, 555, and 551, a progressive reduction is attested both in the proportion height-incising (1/32 in Ja 552, 1/40 in Ja 555, and 1/66 in Ja 551) and in the proportion height-width (1/3.55 in Ja 552, less than 1/6 in Ja 555, and mostly 1/6.666 in Ja 551). On the contrary, in both Ja 554 and 550, the two proportions are preserved: 1/20 as height-incising and mostly 1/5 as height-width. The variation of the shape of the letters will be treated more thoroughly in a general study of palaeography.

D – SYMBOLS AND DESIGN
(cf. Plate C, Fig. 2)

Each inscription of the above-mentioned collection except Ja 553, bears either symbol(s) or a design. The symbols are not new and their interpretation has already been discussed by *GrGST*. Although the ostrich is already known from rock inscriptions (e.g., Philby-Qarya 24 a) as well as from a relief on the wall of a house at Hajar bin Humeid, this bird is for the first time found in unquestionable connection with a text and furthermore with an inscription recording the offering of a house to the moon deity ʾIlumquh. It should be remembered that the beginning of Ja 832 could not have been recorded, as pointed out in the introduction of the text. Some symbol doubtless introduces the inscription, but it is impossible at the present time to imagine what actually occupies the first 53 cm. which are covered by a slab. In any event, the ostrich was connected with the lunar god ʾIlumquh, as was the eagle. [8]

1 – *Texts belonging to the early* mukarribs

Ja 673: The symbol is composed of two undulating (from right to left) parallel lines, the lower extremities of which are united to each other by a line shaped in the form of a reversed basket handle; further, the two upper extremities are united to each other by a semi-circle. Furthermore, a horizontal line is located close to each end of the symbol, and a pair of oblique lines decorates the center. The rectangle in which the symbol fits, and which will be called in the following paragraphs the rectangle of the symbol, is a little

[8] Cf. *GrGST*, p. 75.

smaller than half of its height (60 × 24; thus 1/2.5); the proportion height-width and height-incising are between 1/6 and 1/5 (11; thus 1/5.454) and 1/40 (1.5) respectively.

Ja 831: The symbol is in relief and is composed of an undulated (from left to right) block; its lower extremity is horizontal but its top is hollowed out in such a way that the edges form convex lines. Three longitudinal hollows decorate the inside of the symbol; the width of each one is more than five times smaller than the width of the symbol (10.5 × 2); they are located between four thick transversal strips, where the bronze is thicker than on both sides of each hollow as well as above the last upper strip; in the drawing, the longitudinal edges of the strips are indicated by thin white lines. The proportion height-width is 1/5.714 (60 × 10.5); the rectangle of the symbol is somewhat narrower than half of its height (60 × 27; thus 1/2.222).

Ja 832: The image of a highly stylized, running ostrich, which does not appear clearly on the photographs, is reproduced after the drawing in my field book.

2 – *Mural Inscriptions and* Ja 558

Ja 550 (beginning of line 2)[9]: The distances between the three elements of the symbol are also reproduced to scale. – The body of the right element is composed of two strongly undulated (from left to right), parallel lines the lower extremities of which remain free while their tops end in two imbricate semi-circles; the common lateral side of the latter runs down between and parallel to the two body lines, to the upper inside ornament, namely two small lines, perpendicular to the body lines.[10] Two other pairs of small parallel lines are located a little higher than the lower third and almost at the bottom respectively. The rectangle of the right element is 1/3 higher than it is wide (60 × 45), and the proportion height-width is closer to 1/9 than to 1/8 (60 × 7; thus, 1/8.571). – The rectangle of the central element is four times higher than wide (60 × 16); the proportion between the height of the element and that of its upper part is almost between 1/3 and 1/2 (60 × 24; thus, 1/2.5); there are only two curves in the lower part. – The rectangle of the left element is also (cf. the rectangle of the central element) four times higher than its width (32 × 8); these figures show that the surface of the triangle of the left element is four times smaller than that of the triangle of the central element. The distance between each horizontal line and the corresponding extremity of the element seems to be 1/10 smaller than 1/3 of the element height. – The incising is constant; the proportion height (right element)-incising is 1/40 (60 × 1.5).

Ja 551[11]: The double symbol at the end[12] is reproduced after the drawing in my field book. – The rectangle of the right element measures 28.5 cm. × 9.5 (thus, 1/3). The proportion between the height of the element and that of its upper part is 1/3 (60 × 20); this part is thus much dumpier than in Ja 550. There are four curves in the lower part. – The rectangle of the left element is 16 cm. × 3.5 (thus, almost exactly between 1/4 and 1/5); 1 cm. separates the two rectangles from each other. – The incising is constant; the proportion height (right element)-incising is 1/40 (60 × 1.5).

Ja 552 (cp. CIH 393[13]): The symbol is composed of two undulated (from left to right), parallel lines (cf. Ja 550, right element) both extremities of which are joined together by horizontal lines. The inside of the body shows two pairs of small lines, perpendicular to the body lines and located at the two curves, practically at 1/3 and 2/3 of the length of the symbol. Further, the inside is divided longitudinally into two equal parts by another undulated line which is parallel to the two body lines. The height and the width of the symbol are 23 cm. and 2.1 cm. respectively (thus, 1/10.952). According to the drawing in my field book, the height of the rectangle should be twice as high as its base (60 × 30), and the proportion height-incising 1/60 (60 × 1).

Ja 554: The symbol is composed of three undulated, parallel lines the two extremities of which are, as well as in Ja 552, united to each other by horizontal lines. The inside presents three small lines: two horizontal ones, each one located at the end of the vertical parts, and the oblique one is perpendicular to the center of the symbol. The rectangle of the latter is 23.5 cm. × 13 (thus, 1/1.808), and the width of the symbol measures 4.5 cm. (thus, 1/5.222); finally, the proportion height-incising is 1/40 (60 × 1.5).

[9] Cf. *l.c.*, Fig. 22 a and 34 c. For the single symbol at the beginning of line 1, cf. *l.c.*, p. 11 and Fig. 15 b.

[10] Cp. with the lower part of Gl 717; cf. *l.c.*, p. 16, Fig. 27 m.

[11] For the single symbol at the beginning of the text, cf. *l.c.*, p. 13 and Fig. 22 b.

[12] Cf. *l.c.*, p. 19 and Fig. 34 d.

[13] Cf. *l.c.*, p. 9, Fig. 8 a.

Ja 555: The symbol is composed of two undulated (from left to right), parallel lines (cf. Ja 550, right element); their lower extremities are joined together by a horizontal line (cf., e.g., Ja 554) and their upper extremities by two convex lines forming a sharp-pointed angle (cf. top of Ja 831). The inside shows three small straight lines located in the upper, central and lower part respectively, and parallel to the body lines. The rectangle of the symbol measures 21.5 cm. × 8 (thus, 1/3.062) and its width 4 cm. (thus, 1/5.375).

Ja 556: The symbol is identical with that of Ja 554; only measurements differ; here, 26 cm × 3.5 (thus, 1/7.428).

Ja 557: The shape of this symbol is identical with that of Ja 554 with the following differences. The upper inside straight line is located a little above the upper curve. However, the major difference is the design of the upper extremity which presents two imbricated, reversed semi-circles (cf. Ja 550, right element) the bases of which rest on a horizontal line. The rectangle of the symbol is 22.5 cm. × 9.5 (thus, 1/2.368), and the width of the latter 4 cm. (thus, 1/5.625).

Ja 558: My field book unfortunately gives no measurement at all except that the symbol is facing the beginning of the first two lines; its total height is thus 8.7 cm. (two letter heights and one space between the lines). According to my drawing in my field book, the symbol should cover a square, its width be 1/4.5 of its height, and the tracing be 1/5.6 of the width. The body is composed of two undulated (from left to right), parallel lines the lower extremities of which are joined together by a horizontal line (cf., e.g., Ja 555). The inside shows three small straight lines: one horizontal, located on top of the lower vertical part of the symbol, and two oblique ones, each located on a curve; a fourth small line has disappeared with the damaging of the stone and was located at the bottom of the upper vertical part of the symbol.[14]

Appendices

I – *The Meaning of the Two Expressions* ʾmlkn "*the kings*" *and* ʾmlk/sbʾ "*the kings of Sabaʾ*"

In the study of the interpretation of RÉS 3858 in relation to Ja 557, the expression *ʾmlk/sbʾ* was discussed, though not fully, in order not to interrupt the normal coherence of the presentation. The object of this appendix is to justify the interpretation of *ʾmlk/sbʾ* proposed above, and at the same time to discuss the opinion set forth in *RycIMAM*.

According to *RycIMAM*, the meaning of the two expressions *ʾmlkn* and *ʾmlk/sbʾ* changed over a period of time. During the period of *mlk/sbʾ*, both expressions would have been used "pour désigner d'une façon générale la dynastie" (p. 115). During the following historical period, *mlk/sbʾ/wḏrydn*, *ʾmlkn* would "faire allusion au pouvoir royal en général" (p. 174)[15], but *ʾmlk/sbʾ* "ne peut servir qu'à désigner d'une façon impersonnelle les titulaires successifs de la fonction royale" (p. 174). Finally, in the period of *mlk/sbʾ/wḏrydn/wḥḍrmwt/wymnt*, *ʾmlkn* has the same meaning as in the second period (p. 227).

In these explanations, "dynastie" and "pouvoir royal", although different in meaning, are apparently considered as synonymous. The reason for giving a different meaning to the two expressions during the period of *mlk/sbʾ/wḏrydn* is not explained; and I do not know what it could be. Furthermore, if an abstract concept was intended, it seems surprising that the Sabaeans did not use nouns with a form which would normally be interpreted as abstract,[16] such as *mlkn* (cp. *ḫmrn* from *ḫmr*) or *mlkt* (cp. *hqnyt* from *hqny*). And, if *mlkn*, e.g., in the expression *ʿbd/mlkn* indicates "la monarchie",[17] why do the texts not use the same singular form which, as a matter of fact, in case of only one king, would doubtless be fitting instead of the plural form? The preceding question is all the more relevant in that the singular form *mlk* in *mlk/sbʾ* in RÉS 4336/3 refers to ʾIlšaraḥ Yaḥḍub during his first coregency. It should also be emphasized that the two expressions are often introduced by *ʾmrʾh(m)w* "their *or* his lords"; e.g., *ʾmrʾhmw/ʾmlkn* (e.g., RÉS 2695/3), *ʾmrʾhw/ʾmlk/sbʾ* (e.g., CIH 365/12-13) and *ʾmrʾhmw/ʾmlk/sbʾ* (e.g., CIH 315/19). In all the texts mentioning *mrʾ*, this noun always refers to a person, either divine or human. There is no reason for making an exception in the case of

[14] Cf. *l.c.*, p. 11, Fig. 14 c or p. 16, Fig. 27 h.

[15] On the same page, the author points out that the expression *ʾmlk/sbʾ* is mentioned in "inscriptions où par ailleurs un ou deux rois de Saba et ḏû-Raydân sont mentionnés avec leur titre" with reference to note 14 where five texts are referred to. Yet, there is no royal name in CIH 315, RÉS 3912 and 4137; there is no royal title in CIH 315 and RÉS 4137; the royal title in RÉS 3912 is restored in its essential part: *mlk]/sbʾ/wḏrydn*; finally, CIH 315 belongs to the period of *mlk/sbʾ* and not to that of *mlk/sbʾ/wḏrydn*.

[16] Cf. *HöASG*, p. 98, ϵ.

[17] Cf. *RycIMAM*, p. 35.

the two expressions now under study, and of the formula *ᶜbd/mlkn*. Note also that, under the title "*ʾmlkn* '*les rois*'",[18] the same author lists texts which have *ʾmlkm* and not *ʾmlkn*; e.g., CIH 609/7 and RÉS 4771/1: *kl/ʾlʾltm/wʾmlkm/wʾqwlm/wʾšᶜbm*, where none of the nouns are abstract, not even *šᶜb* which is a collective noun.

In Ja 576 and 577, a text engraved by the two royal brothers ʾIlšaraḥ Yaḥḍub and Yaʾzil Bayyin, there is a definitive contrast between *mlknhn* and *ʾmlk/sbʾ*.[19] The most striking use of *mlknhn* is in the expression *ʾlmqh/wmlknhn* (Ja 576/2 and 3) "ʾIlumquh and the two kings", the main god and the two kings who had the highest human authority. Since the dual is used in this case, it means that the text makes the number of the noun agree with the number of the intended persons; and that excludes the interpretation of *ʾmlk/sbʾ* or *ʾmlkn* as abstract nouns with the meaning of "royal power" or something similar. The same conclusion is to be drawn from the other expression *lmky/sb*[ʾ/...] "for the two kings of Saba[ʾ...]", mentioned in line 5 of NaNN 15.[20]

Finally, the existence of local or provincial kings is not taken into consideration by the opposite opinion which only reckons with "titulaires successifs de la fonction royale", and adds the final touch to my interpretation according to which both *ʾmlkn* and *ʾmlk/sbʾ* refer to the persons of the main king (or kings, in case of coregency; in Mârib) and of those subordinate kings.

II – *Connection with some texts from the Persian Gulf Region*

Several inscriptions related to the *mukarrib* period have in common with some inscriptions from the Persian Gulf region two features which, although pointed out in their commentary, need to be presented together here.

1 – The family name *šwḏbm* in Ja 552/1, 553/2, 554, and 555/1, 2 may be compared with *šwḏb* in RÉS 4685/6-7 and probably ᶜAin Jawan 1/4, and also with *šḏb* in Qatif 1/5, as indicated in the commentary on Ja 552/1.

2 – Ja 832 ends with the letter *g* which is also found at the end of Qatif 1/5.

It is very difficult to evaluate the impact of these two features on the historical relations between Sabaʾ and the region of the Persian Gulf, and also on the dating of the texts belonging to the latter. However, their presence along with the palaeographic characteristics of these texts clearly indicate, in my opinion, for the latter a much earlier date than that ascribed to them; e.g., Qatif 1 is dated "from the fifth or sixth century A.D."[21]; I would suggest tentatively the 4th century B.C.

[18] Cf. p. 174.

[19] The expression *ʾmlk/sbʾ* is found in Ja 576/11 and 577/3, 4, 6, 8, 9 (thrice), 10, and 14. This fact renders inaccurate *RycIMAM*'s statement (*l.c.*) according to which that expression was found only in texts written by persons other than king(s). Note that *RyISA* (XIII, pp. 160-61) fails to make the remark in relation to Ja 576/11.

[20] Cf. p. 115, where the text is related to the period of *mlk/sbʾ*. If the choice of late type characters in the transcription (cf. *NaNN*, p. 20) has some value – and it does, since the characters used in that publication show several different letter types –, NaNN 15 belongs to the period of *mlk/sbʾ/wḏrydn* or to that of *mlk/sbʾ/wḏrydn/wḥḍrm(w)t/wymnt*; and the period of *mlk/sbʾ* is excluded. The same author adds that *mlky/sbʾ* "se trouve aussi dans CIH 550, 4". This text is not reliable.

[21] Cf. *The Geographical Journal*, 107 (1946), p. 44.

Chapter III

THE FAMILY OF ḎAMARʿALAY ḎARIḤ

Bo 4; CIH 433, 573; Fakhry 9, 28; Gl 756; Ja 559, 560, 561, 853 A-F, 854, and 855.

The family of Ḏamarʿalay Ḏariḥ gave Sabaʾ one king who immediately preceded the Hamdânid dynasty initiated by Wahabʾil Yaḥûz.

A – THE FATHER, ḎAMARʿALAY ḎARIḤ

Ḏamarʿalay Ḏariḥ, whose father's name is still unknown, is not yet attested as having been king, and therefore cannot at the present time be considered as king.[1] His dynastic name is a strong indication that he could have been king, but does not by any means prove it.

CIH 729, which presents a text identical with that of CIH 791/1-3, is to be related to Ḏamarʿalay Ḏariḥ, king of Sabaʾ and Raydân, and not to the present person, as stated by *RycIMAM*.[2] Furthermore, disregarding *GrKFG*'s information according to which Gl 587 (cf. RÉS 3389) is CIH 979,[3] which mentions a *mukarrib*, *RycIMAM*[4] still connects RÉS 3389 with the present person.

Bo 4 seems to be related to the present person. According to its publisher,[5] this inscription is composed of three fragments, A 677, 678, and 679, for the following accurate description of which I am greatly indebted to M. Höfner (letter of July 19, 1958):

A 677

n/bn/ḏmrʿly/ḏrḥ/hḥdṯ
n/lšmshw/bʿ l t / ġ

A 679		A 677	A 678
	⌜t⌟	*r⌟⌞tn/ʾṣlmn/hq⌞n⌟*	*⌜n⌝yt/šmshm*
	w/tnf/lwf⌜yh⌝	*⌞yh⌟w/wwf⌟*	*⌞fy/mlkhmw*
	bʿṯtr/wb/⌞š⌟	*⌞m⌟*	*shmw/tnf*

Note that A 679 still has the right lower corner of the letter *t* of *rtn* in A 677/3.

BoAGI's proposed text reads as follows:

1 [................../ʿ*bd/nšʾkr*]
2 [*b/yhʾm*]*n/bn/ḏmrʿly/ḏrḥ/hḥdṯ*
3 [*whgbʾ*]*n/lšmshw/tnf/bʿlt/ġ*
4 [*ḍrn/ʿš*]*rtn/ʾṣlmn/hqnyt/šmshm*
5 *w/tnf/lwfyhw/wwfy/mlkhmw*
6 *bʿṯtr/wb/šmshmw/tnf*

First of all, *RycIMAM*'s interpretation (p. 104, note 6): "il faut lire...: [*nšʾkrb yhʾmn mlk sb*](?) *bn ḏmrʿly*", is contradicted by the decipherment of both *BoAGI* and M. Höfner, which I checked on the squeeze itself; the letter preceding */bn/ḏmrʿly* is *n* and not ʾ. The main question, however, is whether *BoAGI*'s restoration of one line above that containing *n/bn/ḏmrʿly/ḏrḥ/hḥdṯ*, is justified on the basis of E. Glaser's squeezes. Here again, I am very much indebted to M. Höfner for checking carefully the edges of the squeezes and especially

[1] Contrary to *RycIMAM*, e.g., p. 337, No. 15 in his list of kings. The same author also relates to the present person both RÉS 3903 (e.g., p. 104, note 6) and 3994 (p. 109). The first text, which is an extract from Ist 7632 (cf. *BeFSTI*, p. 282) mentions *ḏmrʿly/byn* (not *ḏrḥ*), and the second *smhʿly* (not *ḏmrʿly*)/*ḏrḥ*.

[2] Cf. pp. 103 and note 3, 118 and note 1.
[3] Cf. p. 78.
[4] Cf. p. 281, and list of royal names on p. 337.
[5] Cf. *BoAGI*, pp. 436-37.

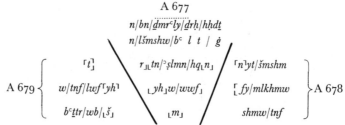

that on top of A 677. Her accurate description reads as follows (letter of November 16, 1958):

> An den *Seiten* scheint der Stein glatt und gerade abgeschnitten; jedenfalls ist kein unregelmässiger Bruch zu erkennen. *Oben* endet A 677 knapp über den oberen Enden der Buchstaben von Z. 1. Auch hier ist kein unregelmässiger Bruch zu sehen. Ob die obere Kante nachträglich gerade abgemeisselt wurde oder ob sie das ursprüngliche obere Ende des Steines, bzw. des beschriebenen Feldes darstellt, lässt sich auf Grund des Abklatsches allein schwerlich sicher aussagen. Jedenfalls schliesst der Befund des Abklatsches die Ergänzung einer Zeile über der jetzigen Zeile 1 von A 677 nicht aus.

The top of A 677 could, of course, have been cut again; in that case, the top edge would naturally present no sign of irregular breaking. This hypothesis is at the present time supported by no evidence at all and is thus, in my opinion, much less probable than the interpretation which considers the text intact on the top as it is on the lateral and lower edges. But then, the author of the inscription would be a (half-) brother of Našaʾkarib Yuhaʾmin, and his name was composed of either five or six letters, the last one being *n* (cf. a similar case at the beginning of Ja 551). The translation of the inscription would then read as follows:

1 [.....(.)]n, son of Ḏamarʿalay Ḏariḥ, has renewed
2 [and restored] for his Šams Tanûf, mistress of Ġa-
3 [ḏarân,] these [te]n statues, offering to their Šams
4 Tanûf, for his safety and the safety of their king.
5 By ʿAṯtar and by their Šams Tanûf.

B – THE ḲING NAŠAʾKARIB YUHAʾMIN (cf. Plate E)

The present collection contains three inscriptions engraved by some of Našaʾkarib Yuhaʾmin's people: Ja 559 and 561 show an identical text and were written by *bnw/grt* "the descendants of Garat"; Ja 560 was engraved by some ʾA[y]nawumites. Further, the inscriptions published previously and mentioning the present king, were written by himself. Furthermore, I copied some other texts in the fortress (*nâṣerah*) and the city of Mârib.

1 – *Inscriptions not belonging to the present collection*

a – *The first group* is composed of Fakhry 9[6] and 28[7] which were discovered in Ṣirwâḥ, and which present an identical text; the translation of this unique text reads as follows:

1 **Sym-** Našaʾkarib Yuhaʾmin, king of Sabaʾ,
2 **bol** son of Ḏamarʿalay Ḏariḥ, has dedicated to
3 ʾIlumquh, master of the ibexes of Ṣirwâḥ, six
4 statues which [are] of bronze, for his own safety and the safety
5 of the house Salḥân and of their property; and that He may make happy.

b – *The second group* contains all other texts, some of which were found at Mârib and others of which may have been found there. The most elaborate of these is CIH 573, which needs several remarks; and special attention is given to Ja 855.

1° – *The study of* CIH 573 deals first with the relation between CIH 573, Gl 756 and 757, and then with six other copies of the same text.

(a) – CIH 573 = Os 31 = BM 125034 (its right part is Gl 757 = RÉS 3855) and Gl 756.

It seems necessary to stress that RÉS 3855 is Gl 757, and not 756,[8] as stated twice by *RhKTB*[9] and corroborated by *RÉS*' reproduction of *RhKTB*'s note (p. 66: "Gl. 757 1-6 aus Mârib mit dem vollständigen Namen: *nšʾkrb/yhʾmn/*(Filiation abgebrochen) und mit dem Titel *mlk/sbʿ*[/]") in RÉS 3855 as follows: *nšʾkrb/yhʾmn/.../mlk/sbʾ*. Further, according to *RhKTB*'s (*l.c.*) explicit testimony, Gl 757 "ist der rechter Teil von Os. 31". Os 31 being CIH 573[10] = BM 125034, the three points of suspension and one word divider introduced by *RÉS* between *nšʾkrb/yhʾmn* and *mlk/sbʾ* must be omitted, and both *RyET*[11] and *RycIMAM* (p. 104, note 6) erroneously refer to CIH 573 and RÉS 3855 as to two different texts. Furthermore, *RycIMAM* interchanges identity of contents and identity of engraved stones when he writes that "Gl. 757, ainsi que 756" (p. 121, note 6) are "deux exemplaires" (p. 121) of CIH 573, and that Gl "756, 757 = CIH 573" (p. 352 A), Gl 756 and 757

[6] Line 6 in *RyET*'s (p. 10) transliteration and translation must be put between brackets since the stone has only 5 lines.

[7] The parentheses including *h* and *w* (line 4) and *w* (line 5) as well as the brackets including *l* (line 5) in *RyET*'s transliteration (*l.c.*) indicate that the publisher based his decipherment exclusively on Fakhry's copy (cf. *FaAJY*, I, p. 48, Fig. 17, bottom) without using the latter's photograph where these four letters are perfectly clear (*l.c.*, III, Pl. XVI).

[8] As stated by *RycIMAM*, p. 121, note 6.

[9] Cf. II, p. 12, note 1, and p. 66.

[10] Cf., e.g., *CIH*, II, p. 365.

[11] Cf. p. 10, commentary on Fakhry 9/1.

apparently have the same contents,[12] but are two different stones.[13] The translation of CIH 573 may be presented as follows:

1 Našaʾkarib Yuhaʾmin, king of Sabaʾ, son of Ḏamarʿalay Ḏariḥ, has.
2 dedicated to his Šams Tanûf, mistress of Ġaḍarân, these twenty-four
3 statues for their safety and the safety of the house Salḥân and of its masters
4 and of their property; and that She [Šams] may make them happy with the strength of understanding and of power; and that
5 She may humiliate and crush and hold back and put aside their every foe and their enemy.
6 [By ʿAṯ]tar and ʾIlumquh and by their Šams Tanûf, mistress of Ġaḍarân.

(b) – *Six other copies*: Ja 853 A-F.

Besides CIH 573 and Gl 756, I presently know six other copies of the same text, namely Ja 853 A (MaN 2), B (MaN 3), C (MaN 4), D (MaN 5), E (MaN 20), and F (MaV 12+7); the first five were copied in the *nâṣerah* of Mârib and the sixth in the city itself.

I first have to describe the location of Ja 853 (A, B, C, and D) and 854. These five inscribed stones are re-used side by side in the same masonry course (at 1.37 m. above the pavement level of the door) of the outside of the eastern wall of a salient in the enclosure wall of the *nâṣerah*; this salient is located at about 2 m. south of the northern entrance door of the same *nâṣerah*. Starting from the conjunction of the salient with the enclosure wall, i.e., from left to right if one faces the eastern wall of the salient, the inscriptions were copied in the following order: Ja 853 D, C, B, A and 854.

Ja 853 A – STONE: *Front:* 51 cm. (top) and 52 (bottom) × 27. – INSCRIPTION:

1 *(n)šʾkrb/yhʾmn/mlk/sbʾ/bn/ḏmrʿly/ḏrḥ/hq*
2 *[n]y/šmshw/tnf/bʿlt/ġḍrn/ʾrbʿtn/wʿšr(nhn/)*
3 *[ʾ]ṣlmn/lwfyhmw/wwfy/bytn/slḥn/wʾbʿlhw/*
4 *wmlkhmw/wl/sʿdhmw/bry/ʾʾḏnm/wmqymtm/w*
5 *[l]/wḍʿ/wṯbr/wmnʿ/wʾẖrn/kl/ḍrhmw/wšnʾhmw/*
6 *[b]ʿṯtr/wʾlmqh/wbšmshmw/tnf/bʿlt/gḍrn*

Fa 853 B – STONE: *Front:* 53.5 cm. (top) and 53 (bottom) × 29 (right) and 29.5 (left). – INSCRIPTION:

1 *nšʾkrb/yhʾmn/mlk/sbʾ/bn/ḏmrʿly/ḏrḥ/hqn*
2 *y/šmshw/tnf/bʿlt/ġḍrn/ʾrbʿtn/wʿšrnhn/*
3 *ʾṣlmn/lwfyhmw/wwfy/bytn/slḥn/wʾbʿlhw*
4 *[w]mlkhmw/wl/sʿdhmw/bry/ʾʾḏnm/wmqymtm/wl*
5 *[w]ḍʿ/wṯbr/wmnʿ/wʾẖrn/kl/ḍrhmw/wšnʾhmw/*
6 *[b]ʿṯtr/wʾlmqh/wbšmshmw/tnf/bʿlt/ġḍrn*

Ja 853 C – STONE: *Front:* 51 cm. × 28.5 (right) and 27.5 (left). – INSCRIPTION:

1 *nšʾkrb/yhʾmn/mlk/sbʾ/bn/ḏmrʿly/ḏrḥ/h*
2 *[q]ny/šmshw/tnf/bʿlt/ġḍrn/ʾrbʿtn/wʿšrnhn*
3 *ʾṣlmn/lwfyhmw/wwfy/bytn/slḥn/wʾbʿlhw*
4 *wmlkhmw/wl/sʿdhmw/bry/ʾʾḏnm/wmqymtm/wl*
5 *wḍʿ/wṯbr/wmnʿ/wʾẖrn/kl/ḍrhmw/wšnʾhmw*
6 *[bʿ]ṯtr/wʾlmqh/wbšmshmw/tnf/bʿlt/ġḍrn*

Ja 853 D – STONE: *Front:* 60.5 cm. (top) and 59.5 (bottom) × 30.2 (right) and 31.5 (left). – INSCRIPTION:

1 *nšʾkrb/yhʾmn/mlk/sbʾ/bn/ḏmrʿly/ḏrḥ/hqny/šmshw*
2 *tnf/bʿlt/ġḍrn/ʾrbʿtn/wʿšrnhn/ʾṣlmn/lwfyhmw/ww*
3 *fy/bytn/slḥn/wʾbʿlhw/wmlkhmw/wl/sʿdhmw/bry*
4 *ʾʾḏnm/wmqymtm/wl/wḍʿ/wṯbr/wmnʿ/wʾẖrn/kl/ḍrhm*
5 *w/wšnʾhmw/bʿṯtr/wʾlmqh/wbšmshmw/tnf/bʿlt/ġḍrn*

Ja 853 E – STONE: found inside the fortress; thickness: 29.7 cm. (right) and 19.7 (left). – *Front:* slightly damaged; 52.5 cm. (top) and 52 (bottom) × 36.8 (left) and 37.3 (right). – INSCRIPTION:

1 *nšʾkrb/yhʾmn/mlk/sbʾ/bn/ḏmrʿly/ḏrḥ*
2 *hqny/šmshw/tnf/bʿlt/ġḍrn/ʾrbʿtn*
3 *wʿšrnhn/ʾṣlmn/lwfyhmw/wwfy/bytn/slḥ*
4 *n/wʾbʿlhw/wmlkhmw/wl/sʿdhmw/bry/ʾʾḏnm*
5 *wmqymtm/wl/wḍʿ/wṯbr/wmnʿ/wʾẖrn/kl/ḍrhmw/wš*
6 *nʾhmw/bʿṯtr/wʾlmqh/wbšmshmw/tnf/bʿlt/ġḍrn*

Ja 853 F: broken into two almost equal parts: MaV 7 and 12; re-used in the exterior side of the wall of a house belonging to as-Saif Muḥammed al-Ǧazâr. MaV 12: in the eastern side on the eastern edge of the wall; upside down; right part of the text. – MaV 7: in the western side; at 1.58 m. above the ground level; lying on its right side; edges badly damaged; cut again on top, so line 1 is almost entirely missing; about 31 cm. × 29; photograph in Plate 56. – INSCRIPTION: letter height: 4.3 cm.; space between the lines: 0.6 cm.

1 *nšʾkrb/yhʾmn/mlk⌈/s⌉bʾ|⌈/bn⌉[ḏmrʿly/ḏrḥ/hqny]*
2 *šmshw/tnf/bʿlt/ġḍr|n/ʾrbʿtn/wʿšrnhn*
3 *ʾṣlmn/lwfyhmw/wwf|y/bytn/slḥn/wʾbʿlhw*
4 *wmlkhmw/wl/sʿdhmw|⌊bry/ʾʾḏnm/wmqymtm/wl*
5 *wḍʿ/wṯbr/wmnʿ/wʾẖrn|⌈/⌉kl/ḍrhmw/wšnʾhmw*
6 *bʿṯtr/wʾlmqh/wbšmsh⌉|mw/tnf/bʿlt/ġḍrn*

[12] Cf. E. Glaser, *Skizze der Geschichte Arabiens*, Munich, 1889, p. 84.
[13] Cf. *RhKTB*, II, p. 66.

The repartition of the text on the different stones is sometimes almost identical (cp., e.g., CIH 573 and Ja 853 A: end of lines 2 and 3, and lines 4-5) and sometimes extremely different (cp., e.g., CIH 573 and Ja 853 D: six and five lines respectively).

2° – *Another text* from the city of Mârib is Ja 855 (MaV 39), already known as Fakhry 67.[14] The stone has been re-used, at 1 m. above the ground level, in the outside of the southern wall of a house belonging to Šerîf Muḥammed Sirḥân.

STONE: *Front:* maximum measurements: 34.5 cm. × 31; broken on the left, partly broken at the bottom and damaged on the right. – INSCRIPTION: letter height: 4.5 cm.; space between the lines: 0.5 cm.; distance from the text to both the upper and lower edges of the stone: 7 cm.; photograph in Plate 56.

1 *nšʾkrb/yhʾmn/*[. . .
2 *d̲mrʿly/d̲rḥ/hqny/d̲*[. . .
3 *sfly/sdt̲tn/ʾṣlm*⌉[. . .
4 *lwfyhmw/wwfy/mlkhmw/b*⌉[. . .

The restoration of this inscription must reckon with the three following facts: the length of line 1 is certain because of the title of the king, line 3 is a perfect parallel of Fakhry 9/3-4 and 28/3-4: *sdt̲tn/ʾṣlmn/ʾly/d̲hbn*, and finally the number of characters is different in each line as shown by the following scheme:

length of line 1:	9.5 cm., and number of signs:	13
2:	10.0	17
3:	10.5	15
4:	10.8	21

The restoration of *mlk/sbʾ/bn* in line 1 and of *n/ʾly/d̲hbn* in line 3 would give a length of 17 cm. Taking both this length and the number of characters in lines 2 and 3 into consideration, the restoration of lines 2 and 4 would require 11 and 14 characters respectively. Further, *sfly* whose reading is certain in line 3, is a proper name (cp. the names of a tribe *sfln*, e.g., in Ja 716/1, and of a person *sflyn* in RÉS 3566/26, Qat). Furthermore, the god *d̲sm(w)y* is not attested in *nšʾkrb/yhʾmn*'s inscriptions; on the contrary, the sun goddess connected with *ġd̲rn* is the object of the offering in CIH 573. The restoration of *t/ġd̲rn/bʿlt* in line 2 supplies the exact number of signs required by the length of the line. Finally, the god *ʿt̲tr* is mentioned in the first place of the final invocation of CIH 573, although this text contains an offering to the sun goddess. I thus suggest restoring *ʿt̲tr/wbd̲t/ġd̲rn* in line 4, as giving the perfect number of characters, 14, as pointed out above.

The text would thus read and be translated as follows:

1 *nšʾkrb/yhʾmn/*[*mlk/sbʾ/bn*]
2 *d̲mrʿly/d̲rḥ/hqny/d̲*[*t/ġd̲rn/bʿlt*]
3 *sfly/sdt̲tn/ʾṣlm*⌉[*n/ʾly/d̲hbn*]
4 *lwfyhmw/wwfy/mlkhmw/b*⌉[*ʿt̲tr/wbd̲t/ġd̲rn*]

1 Našaʾkarib Yuhaʾmin, [king of Sabaʾ, son of]
2 D̲amarʿalay D̲ariḥ, has dedicated to D̲[ât-Ġaḍarân, mistress of]
3 Saflî, [these] six statues, [which (are) in bronze,]
4 for their own safety and the safety of their property. By [ʿAt̲tar and by D̲ât-Ġaḍarân.]

3° – *The last two texts* written by Našaʾkarib Yuhaʾmin, CIH 433 and Ja 854, belong to the same group. The last inscription comes from the city of Mârib; the first one may also be assumed as being found in the same general area because of the lexicographical feature identical with the first, namely *hḥdt̲/whgbʾn*.

CIH 433:

1 **Sym-** *nšʾkrb/yhʾmn/mlk/sbʾ*
2 **bol** *bn/d̲mrʿly/d̲rḥ/hḥdt̲/w*
3 *hgbʾn/ʾṣlm/whqny/ʿt̲tr/d̲d̲b*
4 [*n*/. . .

1 **Sym-** Našaʾkarib Yuhaʾmin, king of Sabaʾ,
2 **bol** son of D̲amarʿalay D̲ariḥ, has renewed and
3 restored [some] statues, and has dedicated to ʿAt̲tar, Him of D̲abâ[n,]
4 . . .

The word *ʾṣlm* is interpreted either as a plural noun (cf. H. Derenbourg in *CIH*, II, p. 124 B) or as a proper name by *CIH* (II, p. 124), and *RyNP* (I, p. 363 A), who nevertheless raises the question: "Subst., pl. de *ṣlm*?." *CIH* is also followed by *RycIMAM* (p. 121). However, all the inscriptions engraved by *nšʾkrb/yhʾmn* suggest interpreting *ʾṣlm* as a plural noun, and especially the two inscriptions belonging to the group of CIH 433.

Ja 854 (MaN 1): the location of the stone is described above. – STONE: upper right edge broken; 47.5 cm. × 28 (right) and 29 (left).

1 *nšʾ*(*krb/yhʾ*)*mn/mlk/sbʾ/b*
2 *n/d̲mrʿly/d̲rḥ/hḥdt̲/whgb*
3 *ʾn/ʾrbʿtn/ʾṣlmn/hqnyt*
4 *šmshmw/tnf/bʿlt/ġd̲rn*
5 *lwfyhmw/wwfy/m*(*l*)*khmw*

[14] Cf. *FaAJY*, I, p. 106, Fig. 51, and *RyET*, p. 39.

1 Naša᾽(karib Yuha᾽)min, king of Saba᾽, son
2 of Ḏamarᶜalay Ḏariḥ, has renewed and restored
3 these four statues, offering to
4 their Šams Tanûf, mistress of Ġaḏarân,
5 for their own safety and the safety of their pro(per)ty.

2 – *Interpretation of the texts*

The analysis of the texts already published leads to a picture of the king's origin and reign which is somewhat different from that presented by *RycIMAM*.

The first question to be dealt with is that of the king's name. *RycIMAM* (p. 291) simply states that "nom et épithète sont hamdanides... Ce nom s'explique, croyons-nous, comme une concession – qui s'avéra insuffisante et inutile – faite par la dynastie traditionnelle à l'influence déjà menaçante des Hamdanides". Yet, the king's name is not necessarily Hamdânid because it was borne by a Bakîlite king. The first element, *nš᾽krb*, is well known in texts written by persons who did not belong to the tribe *hmdn*, but to the clans or tribes *sẖmn* (CIH 24/3), *ġḍbm* (CIH 286/3), *ᶜr*[] (CIH 594), *kbr/ẖll* (CIH 601/19), *nzḥtn* (RÉS 3951/7), etc.; this element is even the name of a Ḥaḍramî (RÉS 2641) and also of a Sabaean from Mârib (Ja 555/2). The second element, *yh᾽mn*, is known as Hamdânid (CIH 187/1-2) but also belongs to the name of a person from the tribe *ᶜmrt* (RÉS 3966/3) as well as of a Sabaean from Mârib (CIH 519/1). Furthermore, a Bataᶜite influence would normally involve the imposition of some religious practice rather than that of some names. It is thus rather difficult to agree with the so-called Hamdânid origin of the king's name.

The history of Naša᾽karib Yuha᾽min's origin and activities is presented by *RycIMAM* (p. 121) as follows:

> Il résulte de la comparaison de ces inscriptions, que Naša᾽karib Yuha᾽min a dédié à quatre divinités différentes plusieurs séries de statues pour la sauvegarde de Salḥîn. Si l'on tient compte de la rareté des dédicaces royales de ce genre, on ne manquera pas de s'étonner de la diversité des dédicaces du seul roi Naša᾽karib et du nombre des statues offertes. Le palais de Salḥîn, pour la protection duquel trois de ces offrandes sont expressément dédiées [reference to note 7: "CIH 573; Fakhry 9; 28."] était la résidence royale de Mârib. A notre avis le nombre de dédicaces et la diversité des dieux auxquels elles étaient adressées, indiquent que Salḥîn, et par conséquent la capitale, étaient gravement menacés. Nous mettons ces dédicaces en relation avec le soulèvement des Hamdanides, qui renversèrent la dynastie dont Naša᾽karib était le dernier représentant.

Several points of the preceding statement are not accurate and the general interpretation misconstructed.

1 – The safety of *bytn/slḥn* "the house Salḥân" is never either the first or the only aim of Naša᾽karib Yuha᾽min's offerings.

2 – Only two series of statues were dedicated by the king in connection with Salḥân, and neither "plusieurs séries de textes" nor "trois de ces offrandes". The latter expression implies the interchange of different inscriptions and different copies of one text since the note refers to CIH 573, Fakhry 9 and 28. Further, Gl 756 and 757 should also have been referred to because of the mention of Fakhry 28, and Fakhry 9 and 28 being two copies of the same text, that is to say they refer to only one offering, the mention of Fakhry 28 is superfluous and leads the reader into confusion.

3 – The first purpose of the two offerings mentioning Salḥân is *lwfyhw* (Fakhry 9/4) and *lwfyhmw* (CIH 573/3), *hw* and *hmw* refer respectively to the king and both to the preceding and his father. This fact, connected with the mention of the royal fortress and of their possessions, is better explained if these two offerings are understood as having been presented to the deities at the beginning or at least during the first part of the king's reign. It seems quite natural that a king, at the beginning of his reign, would entrust his personal safety, and also the safety of his royal palace and of their possessions to the care of the deities by presenting them with a very special offering. Furthermore, the texts do not contain the slightest clue alluding to any danger or threat against the person of the king, his power or his fortress. Even the rather long formula composing the last request in CIH 573/4-5, *wl wḍᶜ/wṯbr/wmnᶜ/w᾽ẖrn/kl/ḍrhmw/wšn᾽hmw*, which is the only data of the texts that could eventually be understood in that way, does not actually reflect any such critical condition. The following example proves it in a rather clear way: Ja 567/1-25 does not allude in any way to any kind of fighting or war, yet its last request (lines 26-28) is even more elaborate than the above-mentioned one of CIH 573/4-5.

And, the serious threat against Salḥân pointed out by *RycIMAM* is but the result of his connecting CIH 289 with CIH 287. But, this connection does not exist, as it is mentioned in the study of Naṣrum Yuhaᵓmin (see below).

4 – The deity mentioned in Ja 855 is not obviously different from one of those known by the other texts. According to my restoration of this text, only three deities would thus have received offerings from Našaᵓkarib Yuhaᵓmin, *ᵓlmqh* (Fakhry 9), *šms* (CIH 573 and Ja 855), and *ᶜṯtr* (CIH 433), that is to say the three most important South-Arabian deities.

5 – The number of statues offered by Našaᵓkarib Yuhaᵓmin as well as the multiplicity of copies of one text (e.g., 8 copies of CIH 573) are not at all unusual if compared with the offering of 30 statues made by the two Sab kings ᶜAlhân Nahfân and his son Šaᶜirum ᵓAwtar, and known by sixteen copies (cf. CIH 308).

6 – There is at the present no basis supporting the assertion that Našaᵓkarib Yuhaᵓmin is the last member of the traditional dynasty, nor that his father actually reigned.

The comparative study of all the material known up to the present time suggests that the king Našaᵓkarib Yuhaᵓmin originates from the tribal groups Garat of the tribe Sumhurâm where the cult of the sun goddess was in special favor, and also that he does not have any apparent relation to the so-called traditional dynasty.

a – The *bnw/grt*, as well as Našaᵓkarib Yuhaᵓmin himself (cf. Fakhry 9 and 28), made copies of one inscription; cf. Ja 559 and 561.

b – The final invocation of Ja 559 (and 561) and 560 also mention the king's favored deities: *ᵓlmqh* (Fakhry 9), *ᶜṯtr* (CIH 433) and *šms/tnf* (CIH 573), and lists *ᶜṯtr* in the first place in spite of the fact that the offerings are made to *ᵓlmqh*.

c – Besides the preceding features, the text of Ja 559 and 561 presents the two following peculiarities: the beginning of the final invocation lists *ᶜṯtr/šrqn* which is immediately followed by *ᶜṯtr/ḏdbn*, the latter being the same as that under which the king made an offering to the stellar god (CIH 433). The same final invocation mentions the sun goddess once more than the stellar god: *ḏt/ḥmym*, *ḏt/bᶜdnm*, *šms/mlkn/tnf* and *ḏt/ẓhrn* for the first, and *ᶜṯtr/šrqn*, *ᶜṯtr/ḏdbn* and *ᶜṯtr/ᶜzzm* for the second. The preceding favor for the sun goddess is confirmed by the two following facts: the sun goddess is also mentioned once more than the lunar god in the final invocation of Ja 560 (*ḏt/ḥmym*, *ḏt/bᶜdnm*, and *šms/mlkn/tnf* for the first, and *ᵓlmqh* and *ᵓlmqh/ḏgblm* for the second), and the sun goddess is the deity which receives the most important offerings made by the king: 24 statues (CIH 573), 4 statues (Ja 854), and probably 6 statues (Ja 855); contrast the 6 statues dedicated to *ᵓlmqh* (Fakhry 9) and "statues" to *ᶜṯtr* (CIH 433). The diversity of deities honored by the king as well as his preference for the sun goddess are obviously enough completely in the line of Ja 559-561.

Another question is the formula associating *ᶜṯtr* with *šms*, namely *ᵓlyhmw/ᶜṯtr/ᶜzzm/wḏt/ẓhrn/bᶜly/*... (e.g., Ja 559/18-19), which must be connected with the Qat expression *ḏt/ḥmym/ᶜṯtr/yġl* (Ja 122/2[15]), although the first expressly maintains the difference between the two deities and the second does not stress it. It is noteworthy that the identity of the denominations of the solar goddess is perfect, *ḏt/ḥmym* corresponding to *ḏt/ẓhrn* (cf. *JaP*, p. 107). However, two inversions exist in the two formulas: *ᶜṯtr* is listed first in the Sab expression but second in the Qat one, and the Sab text uses the Qat name and the Qat inscription the Sab appellation (*l.c.*, p. 111). The texts do not contain any clue leading to one explanation of these obvious, apparently intended inversions rather than another. Furthermore, the two adjectives of *ᶜṯtr*, *ᶜzzm*, and *yġl*, although related to different roots, point out the same characteristic, viz. strength. The association of *ᶜṯtr* and *šms* is beautifully illustrated by the two lionesses and their infant riders (from Timnaᶜ), in which I recognize the "symbols of the summer and winter sun-goddess and...the star-god" respectively.[16] The artistic interpretation of these statues has been presented by B. Segall.[17] As for the religious connotation of these two groups from Timnaᶜ, one should keep in mind that influence in artistic representations does not necessarily involve or imply influence in religious ideas or concepts. Since South-Arabian epigraphical material does not contain any information which would suggest that the second influence did actually take place, it is safer to stay within the limits given by the various data gathered from the epigraphical material until further light is shed on some foreign influence in South-Arabian religious ideas.

[15] Cf. *JaIRHY*, pp. 189-90 and 191-92.

[16] Cf. *l.c.*, p. 193 B; cf. also the end of commentary on Ja 550/2.

[17] Cf. "The Lion-Riders from Timnaᶜ", in *BoAlADSA*, pp. 155-64.

3 – *Palaeography*

A complete palaeographic study of the seventeen above-mentioned inscribed stones is unfortunately not possible at this time since the photographs of ten of them (Bo 4; Gl 756; Ja 559, 560, 853 A-E, and 854) are not available.[17a] The seven photographs (CIH 433, 573; Fakhry 9, 28; Ja 561, 853 F and 855) which I have at hand are very important because the two groups of inscriptions written by the king himself as well as the Mârib group engraved by some of his people are represented, and especially because two copies of two different texts are known by photographs. This has led me to take advantage of this limited photographic material and to draw a set of letters common to them.

The letter types used in the seven inscribed stones actually belong to one general, unique pattern, which will be dealt with in the general survey of South-Arabian palaeography. This unique lettering is best shown in the following letters: *h*, *ḥ*, *n*, ᵓ, *s*, *b*, *ḏ*, *ṣ*, *y*, *ṯ*, *w*, *r*, *d*, *m*, *t*, and even *f*, although each set is slightly different from any other one and major discrepancies are attested in *l*, chiefly in *k* and ᶜ and very specially in *š*. In other words, each lettering style constitutes a subdivision of one general type and may be considered as a variant of the latter.

The preceding general evidence is all the more important as Fakhry 9, 28 and CIH 573, Ja 853 F are different copies of the same texts. Striking stylistic differences exist nevertheless in Fakhry 9 and Fakhry 28: viz. the way the appendage of *k* is connected with the lower half of the letter; the ellipses of *ṣ*, *y*, *ṯ*, ᶜ, *q*, and *w* in Fakhry 9 contrast with the perfectly regular circles of *ṣ* and second ᶜ in Fakhry 28; the left strokes of *r* and the upper half of *k* are less curved in Fakhry 9 than in Fakhry 28; the central part of *š* in Fakhry 9 is a broken line of which the width of the center is 1 1/2 as large as the letter width and becomes progressively thinner and thinner toward both extremities; in Fakhry 28, on the contrary, the central part is a well formed curve with a constant width, and a tiny, short horizontal stroke is added to the left side of its center; the size of the lozenge of *f* in Fakhry 9 is reduced (more in height than in width) so that the four angles could be engraved as point shaped; the reduction of the width of the lozenge in Fakhry 28 is identical with that in Fakhry 9, but that of the height is almost twice as much as that in Fakhry 9; such a strong reduction allowed the engraver to trace the outside edges of the lozenge as almost perfect, flat ellipses.

The most obvious stylistic discrepancies between CIH 573 and Ja 853 F may be presented as follows: the letters of Ja 853 F are generally larger than those of CIH 573, that is specially noticeable in *k*, *r*, *š*, *t*, and *f*, and consequently the curves in the first three above-mentioned letters are stronger in Ja 853 F than in CIH 573; the connection between the upper part of *k* and its lower half is much thicker in Ja 853 F than in CIH 573; the left extremity of the appendage of *l* is a straight line in CIH 573 (also in Fakhry 9 and 28) but a concave line in Ja 853 F; and finally the *w* in Ja 853 F is much larger (and thus its ellipse is more flattened) than in CIH 573. Note that *f* in CIH 573 is identical with that in Fakhry 28, and that the reduction of the lozenge of *f* in Ja 853 F is almost identical with that in Fakhry 9, if the difference of the letter width is not taken into consideration.

[17a] The photographs of Bo 4 and the partial photograph of Ja 559 became available to me long after the redaction of the present chapter.

4 – *Relative chronology of the texts*

The only information leading to some relative chronology is the variation, already pointed out above, in the wording of the first aim of Našaᵓkarib Yuhaᵓmin's offerings. This variation is even more important because it coincides with the different origin of the texts. On the one hand, the text from Ṣirwâḥ mentions Salḥân and gives as first purpose of the king's offerings, *lwfyhw* "for his own safety" (Fakhry 9/4 and 28/4) and, on the other, the texts from Mârib, either with the mention of Salḥân (CIH 573 and copies) or without it (Ja 854 and 855), indicates *lwfyhmw* "for their safety" (CIH 573/3 and copies, Ja 854/5 and 855/4), that is to say for the safety of both the king and his father as the first petition in connection with the offerings of statues. This variation at first sight suggests that the king stayed in Mârib while his father was still living, but after the latter's death, moved to Ṣirwâḥ, at least temporarily.

My relative chronology suggested by the preceding remark may be presented as follows:

1° – the texts from Mârib:
- *first*, the offering of 24 statues (CIH 573 and 8 copies)
- *second*, Ja 559-561;

2° – the inscription from Ṣirwâḥ (Fakhry 9 and 28).

The preceding relative chronology entails the assumption of an archaizing tendency in some engravers of Ṣirwâḥ, shown by the protracted use of the circle in *ṣ* and second ᶜ (Fakhry 28). Mârib seems to be more progressive in developing styles than Ṣirwâḥ; e.g., the central part of *š* in CIH 433 might be understood as a further development of the joined central parts of the same letter in Fakhry 9 and 28. On the other hand, the engraver of Ja 561 probably belonged to some old school where developments were accepted at a slower pace; e.g., the very slightly progressive form of *f* compared with all the other forms. Note that *š* in Ja 561 is very close to that in CIH 573. The presence of several variants of one general type is an obvious fact, and both archaizing and more or less progressive tendencies are not less obvious; it would be thus venturesome to attempt placing both CIH 433 and Ja 855 in the above-mentioned scheme of relative chronology.

5 – *Symbols*

Only three symbols are in reasonably good condition, although neither one is intact (Fakhry 9, 28 and Ja 561); the one in CIH 433 is too damaged to be drawn. The common features of these three symbols are the following: the usual (e.g., Ja 550), undulated (from left to right) body is in relief (Ja 831); however, the two curves in Fakhry 28 are quite regular and the lower one in the two others is angular; three elongated holes are located in the center of the body and parallel to the lateral edges of the latter (Ja 831), their width is 1/7 and 1/3 of that of the body in Fakhry 9 and Fakhry 28, Ja 561 respectively. However, on both extremities of the symbol in Ja 561, the central hole is widened progressively, yet more sharply than the lateral edges of the body itself. The bottom of the symbol in Fakhry 9 may be compared with that in Ja 673, but in reverse; that in Fakhry 28 may be compared with that of the top in Ja 831 with the following difference: in Fakhry 28, the center penetrates the bottom of the adjoining central hole, making a triangle-shaped notch in it; in Ja 831, the center does not reach the central hole. The lateral edges of the extremities of the symbol in Fakhry 9 are made of straight lines; those in Fakhry 28 and Ja 561 form respectively slightly and strongly concave cups. The bottom line of these extremities is strongly concave in Fakhry 9, a triangle-shaped line in Fakhry 28 and coincides with the horizontal line of the frame in Ja 561.

6 – *Number of copies and number of dedicated statues*

A question to be dealt with here is the relation between the number of the copies of the same offering and the number of statues mentioned in the offering itself.

Concerning CIH 308, *GlAAA* (p. 41) suggests that the text was engraved on 30 different stones, and is followed by *RycIMAM* (p. 120) who comments as follows: "une par statue consacrée" (*l.c.*) and "on possède par exemple en deux exemplaires (*a* et *b*) l'inscription CIH 342, qui mentionne l'offrande de deux statues" (*l.c.*, note 4). Ja 559 and 561 could also be referred to, for the text of each of them mentions the offering of two statues. However, a mathematic relation such as that alluded to above, does not actually exist; each case is to be studied separately. One should take into consideration first the possibility that the offered statues were or were not attached to the inscribed stones[18] and secondly the size of the statues and of the inscribed stones. For instance, the 6 statues mentioned in Ja 869 were attached on the inscribed block; and since the length of the top is 64.8 cm., the width of the shoulders of each statue must have been about 8 cm., which is the size of most of the small statues of the Kaiky Muncherjee collection. With regard to the kings ᶜAlhân Nahfân and his son Šaᶜirum ᵓAwtar, it is possible to indicate whether they offered life sized or double sized statues[19] or only smaller sized statues.[20] The size of the stones bearing the copies of CIH 308 definitively excludes the first two possibilities. The height of these stones was less than 80 cm.,[21] and their width ranges from 38 cm. (e.g., Berlin 2670[22]) to 46.6 cm. (e.g., Ist 7515), including 42 cm. (e.g., Sem 2) and 46 (e.g., Berlin 2669[22]

[18] E.g., Ja 576 whose remaining parts of the top do not show any kind of hole or tenon which could have secured the feet of the statues.

[19] Cf., e.g., C. Ansaldi, *Il Yemen nella storia e nella leggenda*, Rome, 1933, Fig. 12 (only the head) and 13 respectively.

[20] E.g., the statue of Maᶜadkarib whose width across the shoulders is 27 cm.; cf. F. P. Albright, "Catalogue of Objects Found in Mârib Excavations", in *BoAlADSA*, p. 269 B.

[21] E.g., Sem 1 still has parts of both the top and bottom, and its height is 75.5 cm.

[22] 40 cm. and 58 in Berlin 2670 and 2669 respectively, according to *MoHIA*, p. 12.

and Sem 1 [23]). Stones of that size did not support statues of normal size, and even less double sized ones, for there would be too great a disproportion between height of the stone and that of the human figures; and the width of the statues across shoulders would be much too large in relation to that of most of the stones. Then the hypothesis of normal-size statues remains. The proportion between the width of the statues and their height is roughly speaking between 1/3 and 1/3.5; the probable size of the statues attached to the different copies of CIH 308 could thus have been approximately 75 cm. × 24, that is to say smaller than Maᶜad-karib's statue (93 cm. × 27). Such dimensions would have made possible two statues on each larger stone (e.g., Ist 7515), but only one on smaller ones (e.g., Berlin 2670).

With regard to Fakhry 9 and 28, there is no information now available as to the presence or absence either of holes or tenons on the top part of the stones. The text of Fakhry 9 and 28 is very close to that of CIH 573 and its copies; its original text was thus very probably composed of 8 lines. The height of each stone is 39 cm. or about 39 cm.,[24] which would indicate an original height of about 63 cm. (39 cm.: 5 lines = 7.8 cm. × 3 = 23.4 cm. + 39 = 62.4 cm.). Further, the length of both inscribed stones is about 57.5 cm.[25] Granted that the height of the statue(s) attached on top of the stones was 60-65 cm., the latter's width would have been 18-19 cm. Three of such statues could thus easily have been attached on top of each stone.

As to CIH 573 and copies, it will remain impossible for a long time to know whether the top of the inscribed stones have holes or not; the top of CIH 573 is broken off and my six copies are re-used in walls. However, the size of these stones is even smaller than that of the copies of CIH 308, since the front of the largest one, Ja 853 D where the text is composed of 5 lines instead of 6, has only 60.5 cm. × 31.5. In their case, the exclusion of either normal or double sized statues is even more obvious than in CIH 308. Since the height of most of the stones is less than 30 cm., except Ja 853 E with 36.8 cm. and CIH 573 with 38-39 cm.,[26] it seems reasonable to think of statues having approximately the same height; their width would thus be about 9 cm. Three of such small statues, about 30 cm. × 9, could easily have been attached on top of each inscribed stone.

It is noteworthy that in both cases of Fakhry 9, 28 and CIH 573, 8 copies, the proposed number of statues attached on each stone suggests that the two texts were engraved in 2 and 8 copies respectively; and it happens that those 10 inscribed stones are known.

[23] *RhIGC* states "81 cm Höhe und 48 cm Breite" (p. 69).

[24] Cf. *FaAJY*, I, p. 48.

[25] The length of Fakhry 9 and 28 is respectively "57.5" and "52" (cf. *FaAJY*, *l.c.*). A. Fakhry apparently took the measurements of the length on the highest possible level where the lateral edges are preserved, and those of the height on the right side of the stone, because "57.5 × 39" in Fakhry 9 has about the same proportion (1/1.5) as that (1/1.482) of the same dimensions taken on the photograph, 12.6 cm. × 8.5 (cf. *l.c.*, III, pl. XVII A). As for Fakhry 28, the proportion between the same measurements, "52 × 39", is 1/1.333, but 1/1.467 between those on the photograph, 15.8 cm. × 10.7 (cf. *l.c.*, pl. XVI). The multiplication of the present height, 39 cm., by 1/1.467 gives 57.21 cm. as the probable length of the stone; such a dimension is close enough to that of the other stone, 57.5 cm., to suggest that the two stones actually had either about or exactly the same length; note that both height and width are already identical in both stones, "39 × 45" (cf. *l.c.*, I, p. 48). A. Fakhry may have misread his tape measure; the short lines indicating 2 and 7 are equally distant from the longer ones which indicate 0 and 5. The length of Fakhry 28 may safely be considered at least as approximately, if not exactly, identical to that of Fakhry 9, namely 57.5 cm.

[26] The present height of CIH 573 is 33.5 cm. (*CIH*, II, p. 365: 33 cm.), but the top part is missing to such an extent that 1/7 of the actual height is certainly missing.

Chapter IV

THE HAMDÂNID DYNASTY OF WAHAB'IL YAḤÛZ

BM 104395; CIH 1, 195, 244, 287, 315, 326, 333, 360, 517; Gl 1197 (RÉS 3564), 1228, 1320, 1364; Ja 561 bis, 562, 563, 564; NaNN 7; RÉS 3992, 4130, 4994, and 4995

INTRODUCTION

As an introduction to the dynasty of Wahab'il Yaḥûz, it seems necessary to present the study of the personality of the Hamdânid Naṣrum Yuha'min, who very probably lived during the beginning of the lifetime of Wahab'il Yaḥûz. It is also advisable to sketch the religious situation before and during the dynasty of Wahab'il Yaḥûz.

1 – *The Hamdânid chief Naṣrum Yuha'min*: CIH 287; NaNN 7; RÉS 4994 and 4995

Naṣrum Yuha'min and his activities have been last studied by *RycIMAM* and *BePSC*; certain remarks, however, must be added to what is said in these two publications.

The Hamdânid chief is mentioned alone in only one text, NaNN 7[1] where he offers a statue to his favored god Ta'lab. Three other inscriptions actually either mention or did mention Naṣrum Yuha'min along with Ṣadiq [Yahub], who are described as *bny/hmdn* (CIH 287 2/2, 11, and 15) or introduced by *'mr'hmw* in RÉS 4994/3, a text written by five Dedânides, Barig Yaḥmad and his four sons, at the occasion of the purchase and the building of their house Watrân, or *mr'yhmw* in RÉS 4995/2; this text was engraved either by the same persons as RÉS 4994, or some of them or some of their relatives; for it also refers to the house [Wa]trân, to which the mention of their plantation is added.

Further, Naṣrum Yuha'min is never presented as king[3] and should therefore not be listed among the Sab kings – not even as a possible one.[4] But more should be said about CIH 287 and 289.

The value of CIH 287 has been considerably overstated. According to *RycIMAM*,[5] this text presents Naṣrum Yuha'min as a powerful leader having many *mqtt* "military chiefs" under his command, and thus "suggère l'existence d'une coalition qui aurait eu Naṣr Yuha'min pour chef" (p. 288). Besides, CIH 289, which likely belongs to the same period as that of CIH 287, mentions military activities and probably the return of armies to Mârib and Salḥân (*l.c.*). Furthermore, from Naṣrum Yuha'min on, there is a radical change: new royal names, and Hamdânid expressions are used, and "la suprematie subite aussi bien que totale accordée au culte de Ta'lab Riyyâm" (p. 289). This fact, connected with the threat against Naša'karib Yuha'min, seems to lead to the conclusion that Naša'karib Yuha'min "fut le dernier roi de la dynastie traditionnelle; que celle-ci fut renversée par une coalition militaire hamdanide, dirigée vraisemblablement par Naṣr Yuha'min, et qu'elle fut remplacée par une dynastie hamdanide" (*l.c.*). Finally, he might have been king; if not, he at least played an important role in the foundation of the new dynasty (p. 112).

In his discussion of *RycIMAM*'s theory, *BePSC*

[1] *RycIMAM* (p. 112, note 38) also refers to NaNN 30; but this text is RÉS 4995, which is rightly listed by him in the same note as mentioning the two leaders. In that note, and also p. 140, note 11, pp. 352 B and 357 B, he refers both to NaNN 30 and RÉS 4995 separately, as if they were two different texts.

[2] CIH 287 is NaNN 58, and not 57 (as *RycIMAM*, p. 112, note 38, and p. 352 B).

[3] Cf. also *RycIMAM*, p. 112, and *BePSC*, p. 54.

[4] Cf. also *BePSC*, contrary to *RycIMAM*. Naṣrum Yuha'min's case cannot be compared with that of Ḏamar'alay Ḏariḥ, dealt with in the preceding chapter, for his name does not belong to the royal onomastics.

[5] Cf. pp. 112 and 287.

(p. 54) rightly discards Naṣrum Yuhaʾmin from the list of the Sab kings since no text ever presents him as such, and emphasizes that *mqtwy* is not necessarily a military person and also that all the *mqtt* mentioned in the text are at the service not simply of Naṣrum Yuhaʾmin (as repeatedly stressed by *RycIMAM*) but of both Naṣrum Yuhaʾmin and Ṣadiq [Yahub], the two Hamdânids (*l.c.*, note 6 which ends as follows: Ṣadiq [Yahub] "would thus also have to be regarded as a possible king!"). Further, "CIH 287 is simply a record of a tribal assembly (*mᶜšrt*) of the Hamdanid clans under their paramount chief". He then discards the use of CIH 289 by referring to the commentary of *tḥrb* in RÉS 3512. *BePSC* concludes as follows: "*Nṣr Yhʾmn* was in fact simply an important Hamdanid chieftain living probably during the reign of *Nšʾkrb Yhʾmn* or *Whbʾl Yḥz* or both. There are thus no grounds for inserting an extra reign between *Nšʾkrb Yhʾmn* and *Whbʾl Yḥz*" (p. 54).

It is first of all difficult to understand why CIH 287 is ascribed only to Naṣrum Yuhaʾmin. *BePSC*, it is true, stresses the point in his note 6, but seems to have forgotten it when he presents his own view on the whole text since he refers only to Naṣrum Yuhaʾmin. The text does not allude to a "coalition militaire" and an assembly of the Hamdânid clans, nor presents Naṣrum Yuhaʾmin as a "paramount chief"; both Naṣrum Yuhaʾmin and Ṣadiq [Yahub] call themselves *bny/hmdn*, which cannot possibly be translated as "(paramount) chiefs of Hamdân", and the noun *mᶜšrt* is not in the text. The inscription only deals with the construction of some buildings by Naṣrum Yuhaʾmin and Ṣadiq [Yahub] and several persons attached to their service. In CIH 289, *RycIMAM* rightly considers *tḥrb* as referring to military operations; unfortunately, the text belongs to the period of the coregency of ᶜAlhân Nahfân and his son Šaᶜirum ʾAwtar. There is thus so far no information which would lead one to accept both Naṣrum Yuhaʾmin and Ṣadiq [Yahub] as military leaders or as intervening in politics; there is thus no ground for the opinion according to which Naṣrum Yuhaʾmin would have played a major role in the change of dynasty. Finally, Naṣrum Yuhaʾmin and Ṣadiq [Yahub] could have lived at the time of Wahabʾil Yaḥûz; but they certainly were his senior by a good number of years, and they probably died shortly after the beginning of the reign of Wahabʾil Yaḥûz.

[6] Cf. *HöSEG*, p. 47.
[7] Cf. *l.c.*, p. 48.

One of the *mqtt* mentioned in CIH 287, is ʾAwsalat son of ʾAᶜyân (lines 9-10); and according to *GlAAA* (p. 63), ʾAwsalat Rafšân's father is ʾAᶜyân in Gl 1218, a dedicatory text to Taʾlab,[6] and the same person is *bn/hmdn* in Gl 1320, which is another dedicatory inscription to Taʾlab.[7] Furthermore, Barig Yuharḥib, a son of the preceding ʾAwsalat Rafšân, is also mentioned in a dedicatory text to the same Taʾlab (CIH 313/7), where the lords of the authors are described as "the descendants of ʾAᶜyân" (line 5). The addition of the second element *rfšn* to ʾAwsalat's name could be connected with his appointment as *qwl* "ruler" of the tribe *smᶜy/ṯlṯn/ḏḥšdm*,[8] which happened during the reign of Wahabʾil Yaḥûz. Gl 1218 is most probably to be connected with the latter's reign because of the presence of the second element of his name. But when did the promotion of ʾAwsalat son of ʾAᶜyân from the service of Naṣrum Yuhaʾmin and of Ṣadiq [Yahub] to the leadership of the tribe *smᶜy/ṯlṯn/ḏḥšdm* take place? A promotion of that kind ordinarily represents a reward for loyal service; it happened only a few years after Wahabʾil Yaḥûz came to the throne. But then, why did ʾAwsalat quit his two masters? Probably they had already died.

Furthermore, in all the texts connected with Našaʾkarib Yuhaʾmin, Naṣrum Yuhaʾmin, Ṣadiq [Yahub] and Wahabʾil Yaḥûz, there is no evidence of any relation between the first and all the others; the contrast between the information on Našaʾkarib Yuhaʾmin and the clearly expressed relations between Naṣrum Yuhaʾmin and Wahabʾil Yaḥûz on the one hand and the dynasty of Wahabʾil Yaḥûz and that of Yarum ʾAyman on the other, rather suggests a gap between Našaʾkarib Yuhaʾmin and Wahabʾil Yaḥûz. In any event, it is an error to consider Naṣrum Yuhaʾmin as belonging to the dynasty of Wahabʾil Yaḥûz as *RycIMAM* does when he writes that "la dynastie hamdanide de Naṣr Yuhaʾmin [9] ne s'est pas prolongée au-delà des fils de Wahabʾil Yaḥûz" (p. 290). Incidentally, one should note that here Naṣrum Yuhaʾmin is considered as a true king.

2 – *The religious situation before and during the dynasty of Wahabʾil Yaḥûz*

The study of the religious attitudes of the different dynasties is very interesting. In his interpre-

[8] *GlAAA* (*l.c.*) does not say whether ʾAwsalat Rafšân in Gl 1218 was already ruler of the tribe *smᶜy/ṯlṯn/ḏḥšdm*, or not.
[9] Cf. also *RycYA*, end of note 3 on p. 134.

tation of that situation, *RycIMAM* does not seem to have viewed the facts in their true light, and the new texts from Mârib actually suggest a solution entirely different from that proposed by him.

In order fully to understand the facts, one should keep in mind that the final invocation of a good number of the dedicatory inscriptions engraved during the reigns of the first kings of Saba', even in Mârib, the stronghold of 'Ilumquh (e.g., Ja 550, 551, 552, and 555), mention the three principal deities according to a standard formula in which the stellar god comes first, the moon god in the second place and the sun goddess in the third, the last two deities being ordinarily listed under two different denominations. However, the final invocation of some other inscriptions only have the name of the deity to which the offering is made (e.g., Ja 556).

An important change occurs with Naša'karib Yuha'min. As already pointed out above, the diversity of deities to which the king made his offerings, as well as the number of statues dedicated are to be connected with the religious habits of the clan to which he belonged and which most probably was Garat, a part of Sumhurâm. This clan seems to have had as favored deities *ᶜṯtr* and very especially *šms/tnf/bᶜlt/ġḏrn*. The cult of these two deities was of such importance that Naša'karib Yuha'min, even when he lived in Mârib, continued to offer to them and not to 'Ilumquh either as *bᶜl/'wm* or as *bᶜl/br'n*. Furthermore, he also continued to use the old scheme of the final invocations by listing ᶜAṯtar first, then 'Ilumquh and thirdly the sun goddess under her favored appellation used in his clan. The only one exception yet known, Ja 885 – if my restoration is correct – may be explained by lack of space in the engraving. However, Naša'karib Yuha'min did offer to 'Ilumquh in Ṣirwâḥ (Fakhry 9 and 28). The reason for such an inconsistency is not apparent. Nevertheless, the contrast between the religious activity of Naša'karib Yuha'min and that of the preceding kings is certainly at least as obvious as that between 'Ilšaraḥ Yaḥḏub and Naṣrum Yuha'-min; yet, *RycIMAM* (p. 291) considers that contrast precisely as the basis of the following conclusion: "il résulte clairement que ces rois et leur lignée ne se rattachent pas à la dynastie...de Naṣr Yuha'min". This author should thus have no difficulty in rejecting his assumption according to which "Naša'karib Yuha'min, fils de Ḏamarᶜalay Ḏariḥ, doit être considéré comme appartenant à l'ancienne dynastie sabéenne" (*l.c.*).

A second important change occurs with the accession of the dynasty of Wahab'il Yaḥûz, but here again, the situation is somewhat different from that described by *RycIMAM* (p. 289). The royal names are entirely new. It is also true that a Hamdânid expression comes into use. But, here again, it should be stressed that the Hamdânid expression *bmq(y)m(t)* is new from a literary or stylist standpoint but not ideologically, for it is the Hamdânid form of the Mârib formula *bšft/wmᶜd* (e.g., RÉS 4370). Finally, there is no question of "la suprématie subite aussi bien que totale accordée au culte de Ta'lab Riyyâm" (*l.c.*). The fact that the tribe Hamdân had as very favored god Ta'lab, is to be concluded from the study of the texts engraved by Hamdânids. But, the texts prove that as soon as the Hamdânids leave their own territory, they adopt the local deity of their new country. This reflects a profound difference in religious attitudes between the dynasty of Naša'karib Yuha'min and that of Wahab'il Yaḥûz. All the inscriptions related to the dynasty of Wahab'il Yaḥûz and discovered in Mârib (namely Ja 561 bis for Wahab'il Yaḥûz's reign; CIH 517 and Ja 562 for 'Anmarum Yuha'min's reign; and Ja 563 and 564 for Karib'il Watar Yuhanᶜim's reign) mention offerings to 'Ilumquh, but not even one to Ta'lab. The contrast between Naša'karib Yuha'min and the people of the dynasty of Wahab'il Yaḥûz is thus that the first remains loyal to his own deities even in Mârib, and that the second give up their clan god to adopt 'Ilumquh. They, however, agree in maintaining in the final invocation the old structure of the formula, which starts with the mention of the stellar god followed by that of the lunar god and the sun goddess. This scheme, however, is far from rigid; as a matter of fact, its constitutive elements keep growing in number, and this progressive increase of deities mentioned in the final invocations is accompanied by a progressive decrease in the importance of Ta'lab and finally by the total absence of any reference to Ta'lab during the reign of Karib'il Watar Yuhanᶜim.

The shortest final invocation (Ja 561 bis/24) replaces the mention of the sun goddess – which was the favored deity of Naša'karib Yuha'min – by that of Ta'lab, and is composed of only three names. In Ja 562/17-19, ᶜAṯtar is followed by the two usual names of the lunar god and then the two usual appellations of the sun goddess; then comes the mention of *šms mlkn/tnf* and finally that of Ta'lab. Both in Ja 563 and 564, all reference to Ta'lab has disappeared; in the first text (lines 18-21), the mention of ʾIlumquh is more elaborate than before; and in the second (lines 27-32), the mention both of ʿAṯtar and ʾIlumquh is more elaborate than in the preceding, whereafter comes the mention of the god *ḥgrm/qḥmm* followed by that of *šmsyhmw/bʿlty/nhd*[.

The preceding remarks also disprove *HöTPK*'s statement (p. 29) according to which "Taʾlab... wird zur Zeit der Hamdaniden...geradezu die beherrschende Göttergestalt im sabäischen Reich und tritt mehr oder weniger an die Stelle des Reichsgottes ʾAlmaqah, des sabäischen Mondgottes".[10]

A – THE KING WAHABʾIL YAḤÛZ: CIH 315, 333, 360; BM 104395; Gl 1228, 1320, 1364; Ja 561 bis; RÉS 4130

It is well known that the dynasty of Wahabʾil Yaḥûz was shortlived; it is composed only of its founder and his two sons, ʾAnmarum Yuhaʾmin and Karibʾil Watar Yuhanʿim.

As far as can presently be determined, the authors of the texts related to Wahabʾil Yaḥûz belong to the important tribe Hamdân where the god Taʾlab was held in special favor.

A member of the clan Saqrân offers four statues to the god Taʾlab (CIH 360); BM 104395[11] deals with a royal edict in favor of the Bataʿites; the unpublished Gl 1364[12] and RÉS 4130 also mention a royal ordinance; the authors of CIH 315, 333, and Ja 561 bis call themselves Hamdânids; the unpublished Gl 1320 and 1228 mention offerings to Taʾlab,[13] the first being written by ʾAwsalat Rafšân of Hamdân,[14] and the second alluding to Wahabʾil Yaḥûz's war against Ḏamarʿalay of Raydân.[15]

It should be pointed out, however, that the name of the king's father is never mentioned in any presently known text. Both BM 104395 and RÉS 4130 are very fragmentary, it is true, but the filiation of the king could easily have been mentioned in BM 104395/1, 3 or 4 and RÉS 4130/3. The king was thus probably of such humble extraction that his father was almost, if not completely, unknown; compare Yarum ʾAyman's father, who never reigned; nevertheless he was *qwl* "ruler" of the tribe *smʿy/tltn/ḏḥšdm* according to Gl 1320.[16] Furthermore, the king was certainly a usurper; otherwise his father's name would have been mentioned along with his royal title; contrast with *ʾnmrm/yhʾmn/mlk/sbʾ/bn/whbʾl/yḥz/mlk/sbʾ* (Ja 562/5-6.)

In spite of the fact that Gl 1228, 1320, and 1364 are not published yet, it is possible to determine a few points in the relative chronology of the historical texts which mention Wahabʾil Yaḥûz.

1 – The authors of Gl 1320 are *ʾwslt/rfšn/bn/hmdn* and one of his companions, according to *GlAAA* (p. 63; and "mit einem anderen Genossen"); those of Ja 561 bis are precisely two of the sons of the same ʾAwsalat Rafšân and the son of ʾAwsalat Rafšân's first mentioned son. One generation separates thus Gl 1320 from Ja 561 bis.

2 – Ja 561 bis is posterior to Gl 1228. Lines 8-10 of the first text refer to wars between *bny/ḏrydn* and "the kings of Sabaʾ", that is to say the Sab king of Mârib and his subordinate, local or provincial kings.[17] These military activities of Wahabʾil Yaḥûz are referred to by Gl 1228, whose authors remain unknown to us and which gives us more details on the two opponents: "Als Anhänger des sabäischen Königs...erscheinen Haufʾâm, Makhṭarân, Sukhaim, D̲û Khaulân, ferner die Benû Bataʾ u.s.w., während Saʾdšems und Marthad zu D̲û Raidân hielten."[18] Ja 561 bis also mentions military campaigns against Arabs on the border of Ḥâšidum and some lands of the tribe of the Sab king (lines 10-14). This fighting is not alluded to by *GlAAA* in his summary of Gl 1228. Ja 561 bis is thus posterior to Gl 1228.

3 – CIH 315 precedes Ja 561 bis by several years – and thus belongs to the reign of Wahabʾil

[10] Cf. *JaITDL*, p. 183, which disproves also *vdBrDSAMW*'s affirmation (p. 186 B): "les rois de Saba n'adoraient que les trois grandes divinités astrales qui, à notre avis, composaient la triade exclusive de la religion de l'état". The preceding relative proposition revives D. Nielsen's inaccurate opinion on the exclusiveness of the South-Arabian triad; see my paper "D. Nielsen et le panthéon sud-arabe préislamique (synthèse et critique)", in *RB*, 55 (1938), pp. 227-44.

[11] Cf. *RyISA*, XI, pp. 107-08 and pl. II. The inscription is engraved on yellowish limestone; maximum thickness: 9 cm.; front: 51 cm. × 29. *HöSEG*'s description (p. 49) of Gl 1364 does not permit one to accept the hypothesis, timidly suggested by *RyISA* (*l.c.*, pp. 108-09), according to which BM 104395 and Gl 1364 could be the same inscription.

[12] Cf. *RhKTB*, II, p. 69 and *HöSEG*, p. 49.

[13] Cf. *HöSEG*, pp. 48 and 47 respectively.

[14] Cf. *GlAAA*, p. 63.

[15] Cf. *l.c.*, p. 67.

[16] Cf. *l.c.*, p. 63.

[17] Cf. chapter II, appendix.

[18] Cf. *GlAAA*, p. 67. Although he does not give any reference, *RycIMAM* (p. 299) must have had in mind the above-mentioned quotation from *GlAAA* when he writes that "Wahabʾil Yaḥûz...a comme allié la tribu de Marṯad; celle de Ḫawlân est avec son adversaire". It is just the contrary. Further, Marṯad[um?] is not necessarily a tribe name.

Yaḥûz – because Yarum ᵓAyman only mentions his brother Barig Yuharḥib in the first text. In the second, however, he also mentions his son ᶜAlhân who was no longer a child at the time of the engraving of the text, but was at least a young man; otherwise he could not have been *qwl* "ruler" of a tribe. This relative chronology is very important since it proves that the peace brought about by Yarum ᵓAyman between "the kings of Sabaᵓ and Raydân and Ḥaḍramawt and Qatabân" (CIH 315/6) and especially between "the kings of Sabaᵓ and the descendants of Raydân" (CIH 315/8-9) was of very short duration; Ja 561 bis alludes to ALL the military campaigns against "the descendants of Raydân" (lines 8-10) without any allusion to the previous peace. Ja 561 bis then goes on to relate military campaigns "against some of the lands of the Arabs" (line 12).

4 – The question of the relative chronology of Gl 1228 and CIH 315 is now to be studied. Since no photograph of any of these two texts has been published, we must limit ourselves to the study of their respective contents. They represent two different stages of the hostilities between Wahabᵓil Yaḥûz and *d̲rydn*, and it seems reasonable to admit that Gl 1228 precedes CIH 315. In the first text, *d̲rydn* did not have very powerful allies.[19] The second text, on the contrary, testifies that *d̲rydn* had won to her cause both Ḥaḍramawt and Qatabân. That *d̲rydn* was the instigator of all trouble is also suggested by CIH 315/9-10 where only the two main opponents, *ᵓmlk/sbᵓ* and *bny/d̲rydn*, are formally mentioned as the two who took pleasure in the peace, both Ḥaḍramawt and Qatabân being listed under the anonymous expression *wsᵓr/ᵓmlkn* (line 9) "and the other kings".[20] As is well known, the main object of CIH 315 is to report Yarum ᵓAyman's successful efforts toward peace between the two parties. Furthermore, by referring to *d̲rydn* as the only opponent of Wahabᵓil Yaḥûz, Ja 561 bis seems to stress that both Ḥaḍramawt and Qatabân did not intervene with full strength and full power but rather partially, that is to say, in a manner that could be compared with that of Saᶜadšams[um?] and Marṯad[um?] in the first phase of the war.

There is other information which is valuable for the reconstruction of the whole period. The principal author of Ja 561 bis, which mentions the king Wahabᵓil Yaḥûz, became king in association with Wahabᵓil Yaḥûz's son, Taribᵓil Watar Yuhanᶜim; thus, the reign of ᵓAnmarum Yuhaᵓmin was relatively short, regardless of the length of that of Wahabᵓil Yaḥûz.

B – THE KING ᵓANMARUM YUHAᵓMIN: CIH 195, 244; Gl 1197 (RÉS 3564); Ja 562; RÉS 3992

As has been pointed out by *RycIMAM* (p. 110, note 22), the second element of the royal name is *yhᵓmn* and not *yhnᶜm*.[20a]

Ja 562 is the only complete text yet known which mentions the king ᵓAnmarum Yuhaᵓmin, and also the first recording an offering to *ᵓlmqhw/bᶜl/ᵓwm*. RÉS 3992[21] is almost complete, and refers to the offering of a statue to the god Taᵓlab because a royal decree had favorably ended a strife in which the author of the text was engaged. Both CIH 195 and 244 are very fragmentary dedicatory inscriptions to Taᵓlab, and the unpublished Gl 1197 (extract in RÉS 3564[22]), which mentions the construction of some buildings, is also fragmentary.[23]

Ja 562 is written by *bn/btᶜ* represented by Suẖmân Yuhaṣbiḥ. It should be remembered that, according to *RhKTB* (II, p. 69), Gl 1228 and 1364 testify to the close relations maintained by the king's father with *bnw/btᶜ*. Such a policy was wise. The *bnw/btᶜ* were very powerful and seem to have been especially gifted by nature to become chiefs; the family of Yarum ᵓAyman and Suẖmân Yuhaṣbiḥ and his clan became respectively "rulers of the tribe Samᶜay, third of Ḥumlân" and "rulers of the tribe Samᶜay, third of Ḥâšidum".

[19] Only Saᶜadšams[um?] and Marṯad[um?], according to *GlAAA*.

[20] According to *RycCSAPS* (p. 206 A), "le texte *CIH* 315 relate qu'un certain Yarīm ᵓAyman...négocia la paix entre les *rois de Saba et de Qatabān*". Since the last expression is underlined in the text, one would normally think that it is the translation of *ᵓmk/sbᵓ/wqtbn*, some part of the inscription. The two passages mentioning the contracted peace read, however, as follows: *ᵓmlk/sbᵓ/wd̲rydn/wḥḍrmwt/wqtbn* (line 6) and *ᵓmlk/sbᵓ/wbny/d̲rydn/wsᵓr/ᵓmlkn* (lines 9-10), that is to say "the kings of Sabaᵓ and Raydân and Ḥaḍramawt and Qatabân" and "the kings of Sabaᵓ and the descendants of Raydân and the other kings" respectively.

[20a] *WiHöBGS* (p. 18) still retains *yhnᶜm*, in spite of *MoMiSI* (e.g., p. 141) and *RhKTB*'s (II, p. 66) explicit affirmation, which is confirmed – if necessary – by Ja 562/5 and 10.

[21] Cf. *BeNL*, VI, pp. 313-16.

[22] It is rather difficult to understand *RÉS*'s (VI, p. 212) reference both to CIH 10 and 258 in his commentary on RÉS 3564.

[23] *HöSEG* writes: "Wohl allseits abgebrochen" (p. 47).

C – THE KING KARIBʾIL WATAR YUHANʿIM: CIH 1, 326, 517; Ja 563 and 564

The only two texts published before the present collection and belonging to the reign of this king are the short CIH 1 [24] which commemorates some carpentry work, and CIH 326 which informs us of the punishment of the two tribes Gušamum and Šadâdum.

The two dedicatory inscriptions, Ja 563 and 564, are much longer than the preceding ones and are of varying importance. The contents of the first show nothing unusual: a statue was offered to ʾIlumquh at the god's request for the safety of two persons and their child.

Of much greater interest is Ja 564. Here, lines 11-12 directly allude to the fact that two persons had authority in Mârib, and were acting under the direct control of the king (lines 10 and 11). The residence of these two governors, we are further informed (lines 2 and 7), was Salḥân and last, but not least, lines 4-27 allude to some kind of major trouble which involved the capital of Mârib. The study of Ja 564 itself and the comparative study both of Ja 562 and 564 make it possible to gain a fair understanding of the events themselves. The central section of Ja 564 (lines 4-27) is composed of two divisions. The first contains three parts, each one being a summary of several events of the past and is introduced by a formula of praise.

a – *ḥmd/ʾnmrm/– –/bd̲t* (lines 3-4) introduces the first part (lines 4-7) presented as follows: the security in Mârib was restored after some major disturbance during which both the army and the rulers had a chance to prove their reliability to their king. b – *wḥmdm/bd̲t* (lines 7-8) opens the description of the second part (lines 7-13) which describes how the god ʾIlumquh gave protection both to ʾAnmarum of Ġaymân, master of Salḥân and ruler of the tribe Ġaymân, and to his associate (called "brother" in line 12) Rat̲adum of Muʾd̲inum, both governors of Mârib, when they run into protracted difficulties ("*bmlʾ/ḫ̲mst/ʾwrḫ̲n* "during five full months"; lines 12-13) because of an edict which they had issued by order of the king. c – *wḥmdm/bd̲t* (line 13) introduces the third part (lines 13-15): the god ʾIlumquh secured the success of all security measures taken by the king *bkl/hmt/ʾwrḫ̲n* "during all these months" (lines 14-15). Finally, the second division (lines 15-27) of the central section contains five petitions addressed to the god ʾIlumquh (lines 15-26) and one wish (lines 26-27).

The first division is the only one which I shall discuss here. It is at first sight obvious that the facts alluded to in its second and third parts belong to the same series of events. In order to understand the situation, one should keep in mind that Ja 562 discreetly, but clearly, alludes to military activities led by the king ʾAnmarum Yuhaʾmin against the tribe Ġaymân. But the author of Ja 564 is a very high official and belongs to the same tribe Ġaymân, and he and his associate in the government of the city of Mârib had, at the request of the king, to issue an edict for the protection of their own authority in the city. It does not seem impossible that the resentment of the population of Mârib against Ġaymân, based on events unknown to us which had compelled the king ʾAnmarum Yuhaʾmin to re-establish order and peace by force, also fell upon ʾAnmarum of Ġaymân because of his relationship with that tribe. This resentment most probably materialized in some kind of riot, and since ʾAnmarum of Ġaymân was completely exonerated before the king, the latter ordered the two governors of Mârib to promulgate an edict aimed at protecting their own authority. However, the rioting did not cease immediately, but, on the contrary, lasted for five months during which the king repeatedly had to order his two representatives to take certain security measures which finally succeeded in reestablishing order. The positive intervention of the king in ordering the two governors to promulgate the first edict as well as to take security measures also suggests that the governors might have informed the king of their willingness to step down in order to assure the tranquillity of Mârib.

The contents of the first part of the first division can easily be understood in the perspective of these events, that is to say, that neither the rulers nor the army joined the rioters but remained faithful to their king and his two officials. The rejoining of this first part with the two following ones seems to be confirmed by the mention of *ʾsbʾn*, preceding that of *ʾqwln/wḫ̲msn*. By *ʾsbʾn* the text alludes to the fighting men belonging to *ḫ̲msn* "the army," a number of whom may very well have taken part in the military activities conducted by the king ʾAnmarum Yuhaʾmin against Ġaymân. These *ʾsbʾn* had suffered a number of casualties during these military activities. The *ʾsbʾn* could have

[24] Cf. *BeSI*, pp. 1-4.

been the first to join the rioters in order to force the resignation or removal of ʾAnmarum of Ġaymân. Yet they stayed faithful to their king and his appointed governors.

The last question to be dealt with here is the period of CIH 517=BM 125114.[25] *CIH* (II, p. 230) restores *krbʾl/wtr/yhnʿm* (line 3) on the basis of CIH 1/5. This opinion has been commonly accepted; e.g., *RycIMAM* first mentions the fact of the restoration[26] and later simply states the filiation.[27] This restoration of Wahabʾil Watar Yuhanʿim's name might have been suggested by the similarity of the two proper names *tfḏ* (CIH 1/4) and *yfḏ* (CIH 517/2). They designate, however, two different buildings, and the two texts were written by different persons. There is thus so far no reason to prefer the restoration of Karibʾil Watar Yuhanʿim's name to that of ʾAnmarum Yuhaʾmin. Since the photographic documentation presently available is very fragmentary, there is, unfortunately, little hope of solving this question on the basis of palaeography.

Though they belong to the reign of ʾAnmarum Yuhaʾmin, there are no photographs of CIH 195, 244 and Ja 562, while that of Gl 1197 is still unpublished. Concerning Karibʾil Watar Yuhanʿim, Ja 563 is not known by any photograph, but CIH 326 and Ja 564 fortunately are. The squeeze of CIH 1, which also belongs to the latter king and is reproduced by *CIH*, pl. II, is not reliable because the stylistic characteristics are not adequately preserved; nevertheless it is not very difficult to see that its style belongs to the period of Wahabʾil Yaḥûz's sons; e.g., *d* and *ś* correspond to the same letters in CIH 326; *w* to *w* in Gl 1197 and especially CIH 517; *ḥ* to *ḥ* in Ja 564, *f* and *m* to the same letters in Gl 1197 and CIH 326; and *r* to *r* in CIH 326 and Ja 564.

The photograph of Gl 1197, which is in relief as is CIH 517, did not allow the drawing of the bevelling lines as I did for CIH 517.

The comparison between the four sets of letters (cf. Plate O) shows that the incising of Ja 564 differs from that of CIH 326 (both of which belong to the reign of Karibʾil Watar Yuhanʿim) especially in the following points: its letters are heavier; absence of pointed appendage at the center of the top part of the lower half of *h* and *ẖ*, and of the center of the left of the central curve of *ś*; the upper extremity of *k* as well as the four extremities of *t* are horizontal and do not make a curved oblique line; the length of the central curve of *ś* is shorter than the letter height; the central curve of *r* is larger and more rounded; the triangle of *d* is higher and shorter. It is thus obvious that the two texts Ja 564 and CIH 326 show two different stylistic techniques.

The comparison of CIH 517 with the three other inscriptions indicates that CIH 517 and Ja 564 belong to the same general style, and Gl 1197 and CIH 326 to another one. The first style may be described as follows: thick and heavy letters; very rounded *r*; short triangle of *d*; massive *m* and *ś*, and almost perfect lozenge-shaped *f*. The second type may be characterized as follows: narrower letters; smaller *w*; flattened central part of *r*; elongated triangle of *d*; slender central part of *m*; appendage on the left center of the central line which becomes a broken line; and finally pointed lozenge of *f*.

Notwithstanding the preceding remarks, CIH 326 and Ja 564 have in common the fact that the circles of *ṣ*, *y*, *ṯ*, ʿ, and *q* are perfectly circular, contrasting with the ellipsis of *w*. On the contrary, in Gl 1197, the top of *y*, the center of *q* and both ʿ and *w* are elliptical. CIH 517 is similar to Gl 1197, in that the top of *y* and both extremities of *ṯ* are elliptical, and ʿ and *w* as well; only the center of *q* is a perfect circle. All this manifests a mixture of stylistic characteristics such as to preclude any clear division or grouping of these inscriptions.

The only information leading to the solution of the problem is the fact that CIH 517/4 does not list Taʾlab and does not allow for its restoration, because the mention of this god should be found between *ḏt/bʿ]dnm* and *wrṯ[dw*. CIH 517 should thus be ascribed to the period of Ja 563 and 564 with which it has in common the absence of Taʾlab in the final invocation; furthermore, as far as the scheme of the final invocation[28] is concerned, Ja 563 is the closest to CIH 517.

[25] In the text proposed by *CIH*, read *sbʾ/* instead of *sbʾ* (line 3), and *rṯd]* instead of *rṯ* (line 4); further, there is no trace of a fifth line.

[26] Cf. pp. 105, note 12, and 140, note 12.

[27] Cf. pp. 144, note 2, and 313. On p. 350 A, the reference to p. 142, note 25, should be suppressed; the text referred to there is CIH 519.

[28] *CIH*'s restoration of *wb/ʾlmqh/wb/hwbs* is disproved by the final invocation of the Mârib texts belonging to the dynasty of Wahabʾil Yaḥûz: *hbs*, always written in *scriptio defectiva*, always precedes *ʾlmqh*, and both *hbs* and *ʾlmqh* are never introduced by *b*.

Chapter V

THE BATAᶜITE-HAMDÂNID DYNASTY OF YARUM ʾAYMAN

(cf. map on Plate F)

CIH 2, 155, 289, 296, 305, 308, 308 bis, 312, 313, 315, 326, 328, 333, 334, 401, 408, 693; Fakhry 55, 71, 75, 102; Geukens 1; Gl 1228, 1371; Kensdale 3 (RÉS 3194); NaNN 19, 26, 43, 48, 72+73+71; Ja 565, 631, 632, 633, 634, 635, 636, 637, 638, 639, 640, 641, 741, 756; RÉS 4149, 4152, 4155, 4190, 4216, 4842.

The Bataᶜite-Hamdânid dynasty of Yarum ʾAyman formed the subject of a special study by *RycYA* (and also by *RycCSAPS*), in which the genealogical tree of that family as well as its relations with both the Hamdânid dynasty of Wahabʾil Yaḥûz and the Bakîlite dynasty of Fariᶜum Yanhub are presented.

A – ORIGIN OF THE FAMILY OF YARUM ʾAYMAN

The origin of Yarum ʾAyman's family is commonly referred to as being Ḥâšidite-Hamdânid. This opinion seems to be confirmed by the frequent title borne by those persons, *ʾqwl/šᶜbn/smᶜy/ṯlṯn/ḏḥšdm* (e.g., CIH 315/2), as well as by the expression *wšᶜbhmw/ḥšdm* (CIH 333/21) which refers to the authors of the text, their two chiefs Barig Yuharḥib and ᶜAlhân, his associate. The tribe Ḥâšidum may have been the native tribe of ᶜAlhân, as it is of the authors of CIH 333, but certainly not of Barig Yuharḥib. For both ᶜAlhân Nahfân and Šaᶜirum ʾAwtar are called *bn/btᶜ/whmdn* respectively in CIH 2/12 and NaNN 26/4 [1]; this origin is confirmed by CIH 305. However, most of the time, their origin is stated simply as follows: *bn/hmdn* (e.g., ʾAwsalat Rafšân in Gl 1228, and the same, his two sons and his grandson in Ja 561 bis). Since Ḥâšidum is the tribe which they commanded, and not the tribe of their origin, it seems quite normal to speak of the Bataᶜite-Hamdânid family of Yarum ʾAyman.

B – THE GENEALOGICAL TREE OF THE FAMILY OF YARUM ʾAYMAN: CIH 305, 308, 313, 315, 326, 333; Fakhry 71; Gl 1228; Kensdale 3 (RÉS 3194); Ja 641

The genealogical tree of the family of Yarum ʾAyman has previously been drawn. Several questions, however, need be studied more deeply and many remarks are necessary. The genealogical tree may be presented as follows; each relationship is mentioned with the reference to one text which offers an unquestionable proof of it.

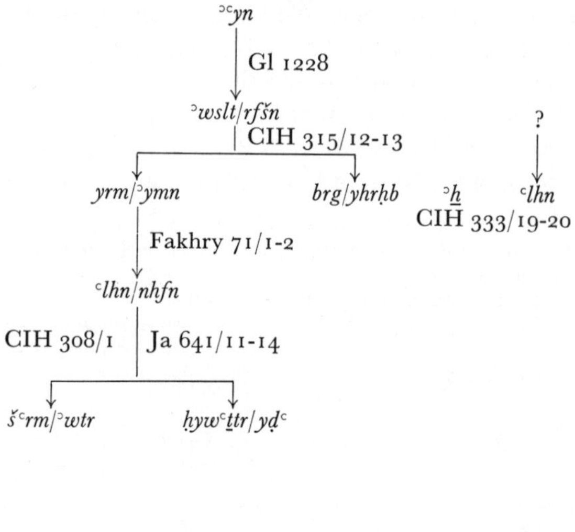

[1] The restoration *b[n/btᶜ/whmdn]* in NaNN 43/2 is no more probable than *b[n/ᶜlhn/nhfn]*. – For the location of the clan of Bataᶜ, cf. *HaAF*, p. 238.

The person of ʿAwsalat Rafšân has been discussed in the study on Naṣrum Yuhaʾmin above;
the relationship between Šaʿirum ʾAwtar and
Ḥayûʿattar Yaḍiʿ as brothers is formally attested
in Ja 641/11-14.

It remains very doubtful whether ʿAlhân was or
was not the brother of Barig Yuharḥib, as suggested, e.g., by *RycIMAM²*; neither CIH 313 nor 326
is of any help, for the fact that these two persons
are mentioned together in no wise demonstrates
any blood relationship.   The beginning of CIH 326
is missing so that there is no way of knowing
whether Barig Yuharḥib and ʿAlhân were presented
as brothers or not.   However, Yarum ʾAyman does
not present Barig Yuharḥib as his brother in CIH
315/1, it is true, but the two of them are formally
mentioned as *bny/ʾwslt/rfšn* in line 13 of the same
text.

Why did Barig Yuharḥib not act similarly in
CIH 326/2? In any case, he does not.   Thus,
there remains only CIH 333.   *CIH*'s decipherment
of lines 19-21 reads as follows:

19 |*wrdw*|*whẓy*|*mrʾ*[*hmw*|*b*]
20   *rg*|*yhrḥb*|*wʾḫyhw*|ʿ*lhn*|*bny*|*h*[*md*]
21   *n*|*wšʿbhmw*|*ḥšdm*| . . .

But, the right third of the circle of *y* immediately
on the left of *mrʾ* (line 19) is still on the stone; and
the vertical stroke of that letter is located slightly
on the right of *y* of *bny* in line 20.   The lower fourth
of *m* and the lower extremity of the vertical stroke
of *d* of *hmdn* are still visible on the stone.   The text
reads thus as follows:

19   . . .|*wrḍw*|*whẓy*|*mrʾy*¹[*hmw*|*b*]
20   ⌊*r*⌋*g*|*yhrḥb*|*wʾḫyhw*|ʿ*lhn*|*bny*|*h*⌈*md*⌉
21   ⌊*n*⌋|*wšʿbhmw*|*ḥšdm*| . . .

It is very well known that ʾḫ does not necessarily
mean "brother" but can simply mean "associate,
ally".   We may cite two examples, which are all
the more important as they come from texts
belonging to the period of ʾAwsalat Rafšân's sons:
ʾAnmarum of Ġaymân calls Raṭadum of Muʾdinum
ʾḫhw "his associate" in the governorship of Mârib
(Ja 564/12); the king Yarum ʾAyman is presented
with ʾḫyhw "his associate" the king Karibʾil Watar
Yuhanʿim (Ja 565/12).   Further, the blood relationship between Barig Yuharḥib and ʿAlhân is
not, however, indicated by the fact that they were
rulers of the same tribe Ḥâšidum.   Furthermore,
no text ever mentions this ʿAlhân as brother either

of Yarum ʾAyman or Barig Yuharḥib, not even the
musnad of CIH 305.   Until further information is
available, it would seem safer to consider ʿAlhân
simply as Barig Yuharḥib's associate.

The two *musnad* of CIH 305 and Kensdale 3
mention persons which may be considered as identical with those listed in the above mentioned
genealogical tree.   Surprisingly enough, Kensdale
3 reproduces a part of the beginning of CIH 305
with the transposition of *bnw*/*hmdn*.   Since the
blood relationship between ʾAwsalat Rafšân,
Yarum ʾAyman, Barig Yuharḥib, and ʿAlhân
Nahfân is beyond any doubt, the information
given by those two *musnad* cannot be understood as
it reads.   CIH 305 could be the result of the con-
flation of two texts; in any event, if so understood,
the information is perfectly normal and adequate:

$$\text{ʿ}lhn/nhfn/ \ldots \qquad\qquad hywʿttr/yḍʿ/$$
$$\searrow \qquad\qquad \nearrow$$
$$wbnyhw/$$
$$\nearrow \qquad\qquad \searrow$$
$$\text{ʾ}wslt/rfšn/ \qquad\qquad yrm/\text{ʾ}ymn/wbrg/yhrḥb$$

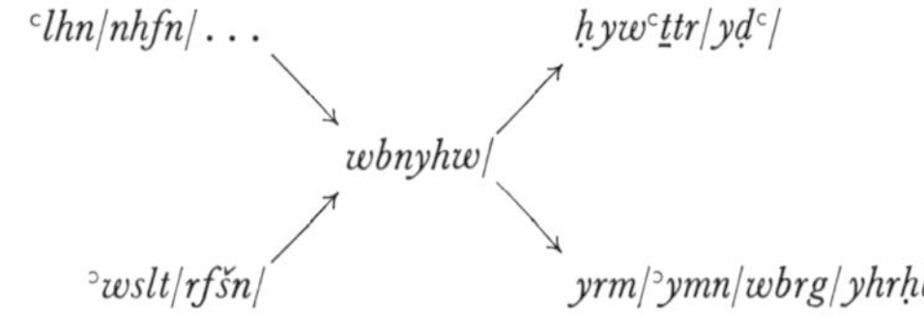

It is also surprising that both ʿAlhân Nahfân
(CIH 305) and ʾAwsalat Rafšân (Kensdale 3)
mention Ḥayûʿattar Yaḍiʿ in the first place, even
before Barig Yuharḥib, and do not mention
Šaʿirum ʾAwtar.   Even if CIH 305 is understood
according to the above-mentioned suggestion, the
absence of Šaʿirum ʾAwtar is no less surprising.
Any attempt to explain such a statement seems
hopeless until an inscription turns up with some
clue to the probable answer.   Finally, the city of
Ḥadaqân mentioned in CIH 305 is located 27 km.
north-northeast of Ṣanʿâʾ.³

C – THE FAMILY OF YARUM ʾAYMAN PRIOR TO HIS REIGN

The family of Yarum ʾAyman apparently
emerges from obscurity when ʾAwsalat became a
mqtwy of Naṣrum Yuhaʾmin (CIH 287).   However,
it is not until the appointment of ʾAwsalat Rafšân and another man as "rulers of the tribe
Samʿay"⁴ during Wahabʾil Yaḥûz's reign that
this family gained some prominence.   Later, but
under the same king, his son Yarum ʾAyman and
both the brother of the latter, Barig Yuharḥib, and
his son, ʿAlhân, held the same office (Ja 561 bis),

---

² E.g., p. 111, with reference to CIH 313/7, 326/2, and
333/20.

³ Cf. *WiHöBGS*, p. 17 and note 3, and *WeCGC*, p. 129 and
maps.

⁴ Cf. *GlAAA*, p. 63.

after ᵓAwsalat Rafšân's death or retirement. Three generations were thus contemporary with Wahabᵓil Yaḥûz.

Two facts seem of a very special importance for the understanding of the life of Yarum ᵓAyman. On the one hand, Yarum ᵓAyman and his relatives were chiefs in the early battles (line 9), but they only joined in (line 11) the later ones. On the other hand, Yarum ᵓAyman does not mention the name of his king in CIH 315, but does in Ja 561 bis. It does not seem unreasonable to conjecture that because of certain actions on the part of Yarum ᵓAyman – of which the engraving of CIH 315 might be symptomatic – he came to be suspected by the king as being inordinately ambitious. It is then easy to understand why Wahabᵓil Yaḥûz kept Yarum ᵓAyman as commanding officer of his troops in the campaigns, if granted that the reopening of the military activities started very shortly after the peace negotiations; the popularity of Yarum ᵓAyman among the soldiers and the people was much too high, and a break between the king and Yarum ᵓAyman could have endangered the success of the war. But later on, when the emergency had passed, the king did not call on him when he had to send military expeditions against the Arabs. Such an initiative suggests that Yarum ᵓAyman had to some extent fallen from the king's favor.

Concerning Barig Yuharḥib, *RycIMAM* (p. 294) sees in the variation between CIH 315/1 (authors: Yarum ᵓAyman and Barig Yuharḥib) and 333/19-20 (mention of Barig Yuharḥib and ᶜAlhân) the indirect proof that the second text was engraved after the beginning of the reign of Yarum ᵓAyman. Such an opinion cannot be reconciled with the evidence offered by CIH 326 whose authors are Barig Yuharḥib and ᶜAlhân and which dates from the reign of Karibᵓil Watar Yuhanᶜim; the latter did certainly precede the accession of Yarum ᵓAyman to the throne. The fact that one text mentioning Barig Yuharḥib does not allude to Yarum ᵓAyman does not prove, however, that the latter was no longer *qwl* "ruler" of the tribe Samᶜay, but already king, but simply confirms what was already understood, namely that they had some personal independence in their common office and had sometimes to deal personally with some parts of the tribe.

The relative chronology of the three texts related to Barig Yuharḥib must reckon with the following facts:

a – CIH 326 belongs to the reign of Karibᵓil Watar Yuhanᶜim, and Barig Yuharḥib mentions his associate ᶜAlhân.

b – It seems more plausible to admit that the association of Barig Yuharḥib with one person (cf. the dual *mrᵓy[hmw]* in CIH 333/19) is prior to that with two or more (cf. the plural *ᵓmrᵓhmw* in CIH 313/7).

c – Yarum ᵓAyman and Barig Yuharḥib in CIH 315 do not mention the name of their king. CIH 333[5] mentioning Barig Yuharḥib and ᶜAlhân could also be related to the same reign, that is to say that of Wahabᵓil Yaḥûz, because the authors of the text could have followed Yarum ᵓAyman and his relatives in their bold attitude toward their king.

d – The restoration of *ᶜlhn/bny/hmd* at the end of CIH 313/7 is purely hypothetical since there is no way of knowing whether ᶜAlhân was still alive when all the events related in the text occurred, and thus whether ᶜAlhân's name is to be restored or not. Even granted that ᶜAlhân's name must be restored, Barig Yuharḥib now has at least two associates (cf. the plural *ᵓmrᵓhmw* in line 7). Since the association of Barig Yuharḥib with one person probably precedes that with at least two persons, CIH 313 is then posterior to CIH 326. Then, the absence of any royal name must be taken into consideration and could very probably suggest that CIH 313 is related to the end of the sole reign of Karibᵓil Watar Yuhanᶜim, that is to say during the period in which the star of Karibᵓil Watar Yuhanᶜim was declining and that of Yarum ᵓAyman was rising. Finally, it should be noted that no one text mentioning a member of the family of Yarum ᵓAyman is yet known which is also related to the reign of ᵓAnmarum Yuhaᵓmin; this too might be interpreted as an indication of the brevity of his reign.

D – THE REIGN OF YARUM ᵓAYMAN

1 – *Coregency with Karibᵓil Watar*: Ja 565 *and* RÉS 4190

The accession of Yarum ᵓAyman to the throne seems to be the result of two series of events.

[5] *RycIMAM* (p. 141, note 22) simply states that CIH 333 belongs to the period of Karibᵓil Watar Yuhanᶜim and Yarum ᵓAyman. This opinion is but a logical consequence of his erroneous interpretation according to which the absence of Yarum ᵓAyman's name in the text proves that the latter was already reigning (see above). Furthermore, the same author claims that *rḍw/wḥẓy* (line 19) is followed by *mrᵓ* "au pluriel"; yet, *CIH*'s reading *mrᵓ* (singular) should be corrected to *mrᵓy* (dual).

Yarum ᵓAyman had on several occasions given proof of his outstanding qualities both as military chief and as diplomat. However, Ja 561 bis sheds a very interesting light on the activity of Yarum ᵓAyman: outstanding as it may have been, his performance as peace maker was soon forgotten after the war started again. It is thus difficult to admit that the influence derived from that particular event could adequately explain the accession of Yarum ᵓAyman to the throne[6]; and, there is no way of knowing whether Karibᵓil Watar Yuhanᶜim had any posterity or not.[7]

Further, the absence of any royal name in CIH 315 seems to allude to the fact that, conscious of his own personality, Yarum ᵓAyman had some further goal in mind. The partial humiliation which was imposed upon him by Wahabᵓil Yaḥûz had no effect in quelling his ambition or soothing his relations with the reigning family. Although there is no conclusive evidence, the following hypothesis seems very attractive: Yarum ᵓAyman would have in some way taken advantage of the psychological situation resulting from the riot mentioned in Ja 564. This text clearly specifies that peace was reestablished; nevertheless, the riot lasted five months, and such protraction could not but weaken the king's popularity and leave some residue of resentment against him. Whatever the events might have been that secured the crown for Yarum ᵓAyman, it is difficult to agree with J. Ryckmans's statement: "Karibᵓil Watar...appelle au pouvoir Yarîm ᵓAymân" (p. 297; idem p. 299) or Yarum ᵓAyman is "appelé à partager le trône avec Karibᵓil Watar" (p. 110).[8] Such an interpretation assumes that Yarum ᵓAyman was second in authority, and that the initiative of the coregency came from Karibᵓil Watar Yuhanᶜim. Yet, the two texts belonging to that period, RÉS 4190[9] and Ja 565, whose authors belong to the tribes Suḫaymum and Gadanum respectively, mention Yarum ᵓAyman in the first place and Karibᵓil Watar in the second. Besides, the partial humiliation imposed upon Yarum ᵓAyman by Wahabᵓil Yaḥûz does not suggest that that latter's son would have invited Yarum ᵓAyman to associate him in his kingship. That Karibᵓil Watar Yuhanᶜim had only the second place seems to be confirmed by the fact that the two texts related to that period of their coregency and which are written by individuals, give the official name of the kings, but they do not mention the third element of Karibᵓil Watar Yuhanᶜim's name, contrary to all the texts related to his sole reign: CIH 1/5, 326/4; Ja 563/9 and 564/10. I can see no reason for which the king would so alter his "official name" (i.e., that which was usually used in official documents and records); further it would seem probable that he would hardly approve such an abbreviation of his name or consider it a sign of honor or respect. I should conclude, therefore, that the initiative in this was not that of Karibᵓil Watar Yuhanᶜim but rather that of Yarum ᵓAyman.

Two other details may be gathered from the two dedicatory inscriptions RÉS 4190 and Ja 565. The authors of the second text are already mentioned along with their father as authors of CIH 1, which was written during the reign of Karibᵓil Watar Yuhanᶜim. In these two texts, the names of the two kings are introduced by the same *mrᵓyhmw* (RÉS 4190/13 and Ja 565/11) and followed by the same *mlky/sbᵓ* (RÉS 4190/14 and Ja 565/12); however, in Ja 565/12, the name of Karibᵓil Watar is preceded by *wᵓḫyhw*. This again brings up the question of the relationship between the two families. It has already been pointed out that the name of neither the father nor tribe of Wahabᵓil Yaḥûz is known, and that ᵓAᶜyân is known to be the father of ᵓAwsalat Rafšân. In all probability, the only relationship between the two families is that they both belonged to the large tribe Hamdân. Thus, the noun *ᵓḫ* once more means an "associate".

The preceding study shows that no one particular historical event is yet given by the texts concerning the coregency of Karibᵓil Watar Yuhanᶜim and Yarum ᵓAyman.

[6] As *RycIMAM*, p. 293 and *RycYA*, p. 133.

[7] As *RycIMAM*, *l.c.*

[8] Idem in *RycYA*, p. 133, and *RycCSAPS*, p. 206 A.

[9] RÉS 4190 (cf. *HöSSE*, p. 8): whitish limestone; maximum thickness: 10.5 cm.; ordinary width of the lateral faces: from 6 cm. to 7; the top is still visible; letter height: from 38 mm. to 40. – Line 1: the letter before *d/w* (certain, but top damaged) is ᵓ (cf., e.g., *ᵓḏᵓd*, *ᵓzᵓd*, etc.); the *w* is followed by four (neither two [cf. *HöSSE*] nor three [*RÉS*]) letters; the lower half of the first two is rectangular (thus ᵓ, *s*, or *k*); however, the second one is either ᵓ or *s* since the lower extremity of a vertical stroke is visible immediately above the center of the rectangle. – Line 2: *n/b* in *rfšn/b* is visible on the stone, as well as the lower extremity of the following *n*. – Line 3: only the lower extremity of the vertical stroke of *y* is still visible. – Line 4: the first *š* is certain although the upper right angle is damaged. – Line 5: ⌜*hmw* instead of [*h*]*mw*. – Line 11: the lower extremity of the second *r* is still visible. – Line 13: the *n* of *ᵓymn* is intact. – Line 14: the initial *w* is visible; read *sbᵓ/* instead of *sbᵓ*. – Line 15: the first *l* is certain; its upper appendage is clear; the top part of the second *m* of *rymm* is still on the stone. – Line 16: the *ḍ* is certain although a great deal of its lower half is gone. – Line 17: the first *w* is certain on the stone.

2 – *Sole reign:* CIH 312 *and* 328

Our information concerning the sole reign of Yarum ʾAyman is unfortunately no richer. The only text mentioning the king's name is CIH 328, which is a part of the last three lines of a dedicatory inscription to Taʾlab. This text needs to be restudied.

According to *CIH*, the text reads as follows:

1 *w*]*l*/*sʿdhw*/*rḍw*/*mrʾhmw*/*y*[*rm*/*ʾymn*/*bn*/*ʿlhn*/*nhf*]
2 *n*/*mlk*/*sbʾ*/*wl*/*wḏʿ*/*wṯbr*[/*wḏrʿn*/*kl*/*ḏrhmw*/*wšn*]
3 *ʾhmw*/*btʾlb*/*rymm*

CIH also suggests another restoration at the end of line 1: *ʾwslt*/*rfš* instead of *ʿlhn*/*nhf*; the text would thus read as follows: . . .*mrʾhmw*/*y*[*rm*/*ʾymn*/*bn*/*ʾwslt*/*rfš*]*n*/*mlk*/*sbʾ*/. . . Concerning the second restoration, J. Ryckmans remarks that "la restoration certaine de CIH 328, mutilée, où il donne le nom de son père et son titre",[10] and "cette lecture est justifiée tant au point de vue de la titulature que du nombre de lettres qui doivent combler la lacune".[11] However, a careful study of the photograph published by *CIH* (p. XXXIV) and *MoHIA* (Pl. V, No. 2690) necessitates the rejection of both restorations.

1 – The photograph reproduced by *CIH* is fragmentary; its left side has been cut as shown by its comparison with that published by *MoHIA*.

2 – The left side of the stone had a raised margin (cf., e.g., RÉS 3403) which, according to *MoHIA*'s photograph, has been mostly leveled. The significance of this is obvious: the text cannot possibly be restored on the left; /*y* and *ṯbr* end respectively lines 1 and 2.

3 – It is also certain that almost the entire shape of the letter *m* may be seen on the right of *n* of line 2. The beginning of line 2 reads thus as follows: [*rm*/*ʾy*]⌊*m*⌋*n*. There is thus no possible mention of any relative of the king in the petition starting with [*w*]*l*/*sʿdhw*. The first reading, then, proposed by *MoHIA* (p. 36), *kl*/*šnʾhmw*, after *ṯbr*, fits the blank perfectly. The text thus reads as follows:

1 . . ./*w*]*l*/*sʿdhw*/*rḍw*/*mrʾhmw*/*y*
2 [*rm*/*ʾy*]⌊*m*⌋*n*/*mlk*/*sbʾ*/*wl*/*wḏʿ*/*wṯbr*
3 [*kl*/*šn*]*ʾhmw*/*btʾlb*/*rymm*

1 . . . and] that He make him happy with the grace of their lord Ya-
2 rum ʾAy]man, king of Sabaʾ; and that he may humiliate and crush
3 their [every ene]my. By Taʾlab Riyyâm.

E – THE CAREER OF ʿALHÂN NAHFÂN

The career of ʿAlhân Nahfân is far more interesting and important than that of his father Yarum ʾAyman, at least insofar as can be deduced from the information contained in the published inscriptions.

1 – *Before becoming king:* CIH 2, 296, 305, *and* 312

Four texts are known to be related to ʿAlhân Nahfân prior to his becoming a king,[12] namely CIH 2, 296, 305, and 312.

The first question is the reading of CIH 296. The stone is broken off on both lateral sides[13]; there is thus absolutely no reason either for putting all restorations on the right side alone[14] or for restoring something on the left of line 1 and nothing on the left of line 2.[15] Further, the lower extremity of a vertical stroke is still visible on the right of the second *n* of line 1; and the distance between the two of them is almost identical with that between *n* of *nhfn* and the following word divider and much too short to allow the restoration of *y*. It is also gratuitous to admit that *gnʾ* is the last word of line 2,[16] instead of being followed either by the common name designating the building or its proper name.[17] The presence of an addition after *gnʾ* is also suggested by the fact that the letters of *gnʾ* are stretched; that is to say the number of letters in line 2 was less than that in line 1. On the basis of the parallel Ja 561 bis, I propose restoring CIH 296 as follows:

1 [*ʿlhn*/*n*]*hfn*/*bn*⌈/⌉[*yrm*/*ʾymn*/*bn*]
2 [*btʿ*/*whm*]*dn*/*gnʾ*[/. . .

1 [ʿAlhân Na]hfân, son of Yarum [ʾAyman, of
2 Bataʿ and Ham]dân, has built the enclosure wall of [. . .

According to the preceding remarks, CIH 296 (as well as CIH 305) would mention the name of

[10] Cf. *RycIMAM*, p. 294.
[11] Cf. *RycYA*, pp. 145-46.
[12] This fact is considered by *RycIMAM* first as likely (p. 110 for CIH 2, 296, and pp. 103 and 294 for CIH 312) and then certain (p. 131 for CIH 2; p. 119 for CIH 296, and p. 110 for CIH 312). However, on pp. 131-32, the same author clearly relates CIH 312 to the reign of ʿAlhân Nahfân.
[13] Cf. *MoHIA*, p. 40, contrary to *CIH* (I, p. 313): "a dextera fracta".
[14] As *CIH* whose reading is simply accepted by *RycIMAM*, p. 119.
[15] As *MoHIA*.
[16] As *MoHIA* followed by *CIH*.
[17] As *RycIMAM*, p. 119.

Yarum ᵓAyman without the royal title, and CIH 312 with it. CIH 312 obviously dates from the reign of Yarum ᵓAyman and most probably when he was reigning alone. The period of CIH 2 and 296 is very probably the reign of Karibᵓil Watar Yuhanᶜim rather than that of ᵓAnmarum Yuhaᵓmin. The reign of Wahabᵓil Yaḥûz is excluded because the same ᶜAlhân was only a youth at the time of Ja 561 bis, which was engraved late in the reign of Wahabᵓil Yaḥûz and CIH 2/10-11 mentions *kl/msbᵓ/sbᵓw/lšwᶜn/mrᵓhmw/ᶜlhn/nhfn* "every military campaign [which] they [the authors] fought in order to assist their lord ᶜAlhân Nahfân". Such a phrase alludes to the fact that ᶜAlhân Nahfân had been the commanding officer of at least a group of soldiers during several military campaigns. It would thus seem reasonable to suggest that several years had passed between Ja 561 bis and CIH 2; further, since the reign of ᵓAnmarum Yuhaᵓmin must have been rather brief, the reign of Karibᵓil Watar Yuhanᶜim seems to be a very plausible period for the engraving of both CIH 2 and 296. CIH 326, which belongs to the reign of Karibᵓil Watar Yuhanᶜim, alludes to military campaigns against the two tribes Gušamum and Šadâdum.[18] Furthermore, the absence of any royal name both in CIH 2 and 296 could belong to the end of the sole reign of Karibᵓil Watar Yuhanᶜim, that is to say when tension was rising between the king and Yarum ᵓAyman. An important question related to CIH 312 is the reading and the interpretation of the proper name in line 6. *CIH* reads *ẓfr* and considers it as the name of the Ḥimyarite capital of Ẓafâr.[19] Such an opinion[20] is difficult to accept, because it is historical anachronism to consider Ẓafâr as a Sab city during Yarum ᵓAyman's sole reign. The reading of *ẓfr*, again, is far from being certain. The lower half of the left side of the letter is badly damaged, it is true; however, the lower half of the letter presents three small vertical strokes, like *ṣ* of *ṣlm* (line 3). One could thus read *ṣfr*, which could be related to Ṣâfir, a market in Hamdân and belonging to the tribe Qudam,[21] northwest of ᶜAmrân.[22] Ṣâfir was thus on the border of Hamdân, and so a good and easy prey for enemies.

2 – *Sole Reign:* Fakhry 71 *and* NaNN 26

The only inscription connected with the reign of ᶜAlhân Nahfân without any allusion to an heir is Fakhry 71[23] from Mârib, which relates an offering made to *ᶜṯtršrqn* by the king himself[24] because the stellar god had sent rain.

The second text belonging to the same period of the reign of ᶜAlhân Nahfân mentions an heir, Šaᶜirum ᵓAwtar who most probably played some role already in the kingdom alongside the king, his father. This text, NaNN 26, commemorates the building of some constructions related to a house. However, some remarks must be made on the published form of this text. First of all, ᵓ of *ᵓwtr* is restored and should thus be placed between brackets.[25] Further, the name of *ᵓlmqh* is not to be found in the text; it is thus rather difficult to understand why *RycIMAM* (p. 301) simply states that this inscription "est adressée à ᵓAlmaqah". Furthermore, the comparison of NaNN 26 with RÉS 4994, which is not suggested either by *NaNN* (pp. 43-44) or J. Ryckmans, is very helpful. These two texts have in common their origin (the city of Nâᶜiṭ) and *bythmw/wtrn/bmqm/šymhmw . . . ᵓmrᵓhmw* (NaNN 26/2-3 and RÉS 4994/2-3); they thus deal with the same house and use the same literary formula, very well known in Hamdânid texts. NaNN 26/3-4 restored on the basis of RÉS 4994/2-3, reads as follows:

2 *–/bmqm/šymhmw*
3 *[tᵓlb/rymm/wbmqymt/]ᵓmrᵓhmw/ᶜlhn/nhfn/mlk/sbᵓ/ bn/yrm*
4 *[ᵓymn/wbnyhw/šᶜrm/ᵓ]wtr/bn/btᶜ/whmdn/wrṯdw/ bythmw/ᶜṯtr*

2 – with the power of their patron
3 [Taᵓlab Riyyâmum, and with the power of] their lords ᶜAlhân Nahfân, king of Sabaᵓ, son of Yarum

[18] Cf. *HaAF*, pp. 304 and 366. For *šddm*, cf. p. 321, note 95.

[19] Some 170 km. northwest of ᶜAden and about 175 km. southwest of Mârib.

[20] Followed by *RyNP*, I, p. 341 B. *RycIMAM* does not consider the problem.

[21] B. beit Qudam is located about 25-30 km. west-northwest of ᶜAmrân. *WeCGC* (p. 134 and maps) mentions the town of Qudam about 32 km. west-northwest of ᶜAmrân.

[22] Cf. *MüHG*, 113/16.

[23] In my catalogue, Fakhry 71 = MaN 26, which is in yellowish sandstone (cf. *FaAJY*, I, p. 107: "granite"); maximum thickness: 34.2 cm.; front: 98 cm. × 29.4. In *RyET*, p. 42, line 15 of the transcription of the text and p. 87 B, correct *fdḥn* to *fdḥm*. Since A. Fakhry's journey to Mârib, the stone has been damaged: *n/nhfn* (line 1), *r* (line 2) and the first *l* in line 19 had disappeared when I copied the inscription.

[24] *RycIMAM* (p. 121) writes, in connection with CIH 312, that here "c'est à Aṯtar Šarqân que ce même roi offre". Such a statement is confusing, because ᶜAlhân Nahfân was not yet king in CIH 312.

[25] Contrary to *RycIMAM*, p. 103, note 4, and *RycYA*, pp. 139 and 144.

4 [ʾAyman, and his son Šaʿirum ʾA]wtar, of Bataʿ and Hamdân. And they have entrusted their house to ʿAṯtar's care.

The following conclusions may be drawn from the preceding reading where each restored part is composed of 15 characters and 3 word dividers: the word introducing *ʾmrʾhmw/ʿlhn/...* is *bmqymt* and not *bmqm*[26]; the insertion of *mlk/sbʾ*[27] after *yrm/ʾymn* is impossible because of lack of space; and in oblique cases as here, *bn* in *bnyhw* (line 4) is usually written in *scriptio plena*.[28]

The contents of Fakhry 71 could very well be considered as giving the major characteristics of the first part of ʿAlhân Nahfân's reign: the king took very seriously the internal welfare of his kingdom; by doing so, he was building up the strength without which the texts belonging to the following coregency cannot be accounted for.

3 – *Coregency with his son, Šaʿirum ʾAwtar*

Before beginning the study of the historical events during the coregency of ʿAlhân Nahfân and Šaʿirum ʾAwtar, it is absolutely necessary to establish our documentation.

a – REMARKS ON SOME TEXTS:
CIH 155, 289, 308, 401; NaNN 72+73+71; RÉS 4216

Several inscriptions related to the coregency of ʿAlhân Nahfân and his son Šaʿirum ʾAwtar need comment before they can be properly utilized.

CIH 155 – Here, there is some question regarding the identity of the author(s) of the text. *CIH*'s final opinion (III, p. 334 A) is that the text was written by *ʿlhn/nhfn/mlk/sbʾ/wbnyhw*. In his study of the text, *RycIMAM* (p. 114) proposes restoring *mrʾ* instead of *mlk* in line 3 (note that *CIH* had already rejected the restoration of *mlk* in III, *l.c.*) because "nous ne connaissons pas d'autre exemple certain de l'emploi du mot *mlk* avec un suffixe". Yet, this parallel does exist in NaNN 71/1, a text which is considered by the same author (p. 132) as belonging to the period of CIH 155. Then, because of the restoration of *mrʾ*, the same author rejects the opinion according to which ʿAlhân Nahfân is the author of the text (pp. 121-22[29]); this opinion, however, came to be doubted on p. 290, note 37. It is very strange that the proper name *ḥmln* (line 5) apparently remained unnoticed, especially because this clan name is found at the end of a very characteristic phrase: *[w]l/ṯbr/.../wḍrʿn/k[l/.../]ḥmln*. The second blank in such a phrase formulating a petition necessarily begins with *ḍr* or *šnʾ* or both (or something of that kind) followed either by the name(s) of the author(s) accompanied by his (or their) tribe name (*X bn Y* or *X ḏY*) or by the preceding information followed by *wšʿbh(m)w/–* (cf., e.g., Ja 564/24-26: *wlnḍʿ/wṯbr/.../kl/ḍr/wšnʾ/ʾnmrm/wbny/ḏġymn/wšʿbhmw/ġymn*). Thus, the text was written not by the king, but by at least two (cf. *hmw* in *hwšʿhmw* in line 1) persons related to the tribe Ḥumlân,[30] and who may have been descendants of the author of Ja 562.

CIH 289 – The most important question raised by this very fragmentary text is that of the period to which it belongs. Contrary to *RycIMAM*,[31] who dates it from the period of Naṣrum Yuhaʾmin, the text must doubtless be connected with NaNN 19. Both have in common the mention of a woman called *qlkhl/ḏt/hmdn* (NaNN 19/8 and CIH 289/9) and that of *ġlmm* (NaNN 19/8-9 and CIH 289/8)[32] and of *bmw(/)hwt* (NaNN 19/7 and CIH 289/8 and 11). The information concerning *ġlmm* clarifies the relative chronology of the two texts: NaNN 19 is posterior to CIH 289 because the first speaks of *ġlm[m/]ṯnym* "a second youth" and the second only of *ġlmm* "a youth".

CIH 308 – On the basis of my study of Sem 1, confirmed by my squeeze, the beginning of the text reads as follows:

1 *[ʿ]⌈l⌉hn/nhfn/wbnyhw/šʿrm/ʾwtr/mlky⌉⌈/sbʾ⌉[/bny/yr]*
2 *⌊m/ʾymn/mlk/sbʾ/hqnyw/šymhmw/tʾlb/rymm[/bʿl/t]*
3 *⌊rʿt/–*

1 [ʿA]lhân Nahfân and his son Šaʿirum ʾAwtar, the two kings of Sabaʾ, [the two descendants of Yar-]
2 um ʾAyman, king of Sabaʾ, have dedicated to their patron Taʾlab Riyyâmum, [master of Tu-]
3 rʿat, –

Line 1: ʿ of *ʿlhn* is missing.[33] – *y* of *mlky* is complete on the stone; only the edges of the upper left

[26] As *RycIMAM*, p. 140 and note 13.
[27] As *RycYA*, pp. 139 and 144.
[28] Cf. also *l.c.*, p. 144; contrast *bnhw* in *l.c.*, p. 139.
[29] Cf. also *l.c.*, p. 136, note 7.
[30] About 60 km. northwest of Ṣanʿâʾ (cf. *HaAF*, p. 376).
[31] Followed by *BePSC*; cf. the study on Naṣrum Yuhaʾmin.
[32] These two parallels have been pointed out by *NaNN*, p. 28.
[33] Cf. also *CIH*, I, pp. 324-25; contrary to *RycYA*, p. 144.

side are damaged. – Line 2: the initial *m* is not restored[34]; its very characteristic left angles are still on the stone. – Lines 2-3: no letter is missing at the beginning of line 3[35]; *t* of *trᶜt* must be restored at the end of line 2. Further, the end of line 3 cannot be taken into consideration for the restoration of lines 1 and 2 because the width of *hwf* is more stretched than that of the preceding letters on the same line. There are thus 34 letters in lines 1 and 2, and 33 in line 3; and there are 8, 9, and 6 word dividers respectively in lines 1, 2, and 3.

To begin with, then, we must note that the text was written by both ᶜAlhân Nahfân and his son Šaᶜirum ʾAwtar,[36] and clearly enough not by ᶜAlhân Nahfân.[37]

Line 8: *tšᶜw*. The equation Hebrew *šᶜh*=*šᶜw* in *tšᶜw* is accepted by *StSESA*[38] and very recently by *LeESAC*[39] and is mentioned by *BeSI* (p. 29). *BePESA* (p. 16) questions it but does not decide between the opinions presented by E. Glaser (*ašᶜâ bi* "to take care of") and N. Rhodokanakis (*šᶜy* "to scatter"), and adds: "the former translates it 'arrangement'...; the latter 'irrigation'". Both E. Glaser and N. Rhodokanakis refer to the same Arabic root *šᶜw* whose 4th form *ʾašᶜâ* has two meanings, the first being selected by E. Glaser and the second by N. Rhodokanakis, who translates *tšᶜw* as "zerstreuen=disperse, scatter" and not as "irrigation". In the context, which deals with all kinds of improvements, the second meaning is most fitting, and *tšᶜw* may be translated "to spread, extend, expand".

CIH 401=Ist 7473: whitish limestone; maximum thickness: 11.5 cm.; front: maximum: 27.5 cm. × 31.8. The most recent study of that text was published by *RycYA* (p. 421[40]), who reads the beginning of the text as follows:

1 [*ᶜlhn wbnyhw šᶜrm mlky*] *sbʾ bny yrm ʾymn mlk sbʾ*
2 [*hqnyy ʾlmqh bᶜl brʾn d̲*]*n ṣlmn ḥgn wqh bmsʾlhw l-*

1 – Assuming J. Ryckmans' implied opinion that no line is missing on top and also that the left side has not been cut again, *RycYA*'s restoration is disproved by CIH 308, another text written by the same authors and where the second element of each royal name is formally indicated. CIH 693 also gives the second element of the second royal name and the full name of the father must be restored at the beginning of line 1.[41] *RycIMAM* (p. 106) simply states the absence of the second element of each royal name, but fails to mention and to explain the obvious variance of his restoration with the two above-mentioned parallel texts. *RycYA* (*l.c.*) is all the more convinced of the impossibility of any other restoration so that he claims that his reading "comble exactement l'espace de 18 lettres que devait comporter la lacune, comme en fait foi la restitution indiscutable de la ligne 2 dans le *Corpus*".[42] Yet, *CIH*'s restoration must be discarded because it renders impossible the presence of the two full names. As a matter of fact, the use of the expression of CIH 314+954/5, 21, and 29 would provide exactly for the 26 letters required by the restoration of the two full names. No further explanation is given for the employment of the hyphen following the final *l* in line 2; it cannot be justified because *sbʾ* being assumed as the last word of line 1, the letter *l* must also be considered as the final letter of line 2. Finally, the form *hqnyw* must be preferred to *hqnyy* in view of the perfect parallel in CIH 308/2. The beginning of the text would thus read as follows:

1 [*ᶜlhn/nhfn/wbnyhw/šᶜrm/ʾwtr/mlky*]/*sbʾ/bny/yrm/ʾymn/mlk/sbʾ*
2 [*hqnyw/ʾlmqhbᶜlmsktwytwbrʾn/d̲*]*n/ṣlmn/ḥgn/wqh/bmsʾlhw/l*

2 – J. Ryckmans' tacit assumption described above does not reckon with the two following facts. On the one hand, the left side of the stone (as well as the right one) is missing, as it is shown by *CIH* whose restoration is portioned out on both sides of the remaining text. The cut on the left side is also proved by the fact that both the upper corner of the left extremity of the appendage of the last *l* in line 2 of the remaining text, and the lower left

[34] Cf. also *CIH*, *l.c.*, contrary to *RycYA*, *l.c.*

[35] Contrary to *CIH*, *l.c.*, and also to *RycYA*, *l.c.*, who accepts evidently *CIH*'s restoration since he mentions the presence of 34 characters in line 3, which is exactly what *CIH* has.

[36] Cf. also *RycIMAM*, e.g., p. 106.

[37] As *l.c.*, p. 251.

[38] Cf. p. 537: *tšᶜw* "'to look after'(?)".

[39] P. 54: *tšᶜw* "'be observed'".

[40] Cf. also *RycIMAM*, p. 106 connected with p. 222, note 6; and also pp. 120 and 301.

[41] Cf. *RycIMAM*, pp. 106 and 222, note 6, and *RycYA*, p. 142.

[42] *RycYA* had already written (p. 135): "la restitution certaine, dans le *Corpus*, de la ligne 2 de CIH 401 atteste que la partie manquante de l'inscription avait exactement la même largeur que la moitié connue, soit l'espace de 18 lettres". The remaining part either of line 1 or line 2 has 19 (not 18) letters.

corner of the last *t* (in *ʾsy/b⌜lt⌝* "the two men of the rent") in line 7 of the same text are missing because they have been cut again. On the other hand, the top is missing. Although this fact does not necessarily mean that a part of the original text is missing,[43] the location of ...]*/wkrbʿṯt/ḥnnyn/ʾsy/b⌜lt⌝*[/... in the remaining text seems to suggest that these two rent collectors were the authors of the inscription. In this hypothesis, one line is certainly missing. Then, the beginning of the original text could hypothetically be restored as follows:

0 [.../*wkrbʿṯt/ḥnnyn*/...
.../*ʾsy/bl*]
1 [*t/ʿlhn/nhfn/wbnyhw/šʿrm/ʾwtr/mlky*]/*sbʾ/bny/yrm/ʾymn/mlk/sbʾ*[/*h*]
2 [*qnyw/ʾlmqhbʿlmsktwyṯwbrʾn/ḏ*]*n/ṣlmn/ḥgn/wqh/bmsʾlhw/l*[.]

0 [...and Karibʿaṯat the Ḥanânite, ..., the two men of the rent]
1 [of ʿAlhân Nahfân and his son Šaʿirum ʾAwtar, the two kings of] Sabaʾ, the two descendants of Yarum ʾAyman, king of Sabaʾ, [have]
2 [dedicated to ʾIlumquh, master of Maskat and Yaṯaw Baraʾân, th]is statue, as He has ordered through His oracle to [.]

or also

0 .../*wkrbʿṯt/ḥnnyn/ʾsy/blt/ʿlhn/nhfn/w*]
1 [*bnyhw/šʿrm/ʾwtr/mlky*]/*sbʾ/bny/yrm/ʾymn/mlk/sbʾ*[/*h*]
2 [*qnyw/ʾlmqh/bʿl/brʾn/ḏ*]*n/ṣlmn/ḥgn/wqh/bmsʾlhw/l*[.]

0 [...and Karibʿaṯat the Ḥanânite, the two men of the rent of ʿAlhân Nahfân and]
1 [his son Šaʿirum ʾAwtar, the two kings of] Sabaʾ, the two descendants of Yarum ʾAyman, king of Sabaʾ, [have]
2 [dedicated to ʾIlumquh, master of Baraʾân, th]is statue as He has ordered through His oracle to [.]

The two preceding readings would need some adjustment in case of a symbol preceding either the first or the first two lines of the text; the first restoration would be more probable if the origins of the two rent collectors were mentioned.

NaNN 72+73+71 – *RycIMAM* (p. 132, note 13) considers as a "possibilité réelle" the connection of NaNN 71 "à la droite" of NaNN 72+73, and sees it as follows:

line 1: *bywm h/ʿlyhmw*
line 2: *ʾšʿbn/ḏḥym/wqtbn*
line 3: *wbʿdn ḏt b/rḍ wnwyn ḏrydn*

He finally proposes translating this fragment of line 3 as follows: "et ensuite ḏû-Raydân fit défaut et se sépara de" and admits as "probable que l'inscription émane de Raydanites, contre lesquels ʿAlhân avait levé les armées de ses alliés" (p. 132). The wording of the last phrase is rather strange: it seems quite unusual for a king to have "levé les armées de ses allies"! Besides, */ḏḥym*,[44] the proper name before */wqtbn* (line 2) must be corrected and restored to read *mḏḥym*[45]; and since "Radmân and Muḏḥayum are very well known as old allies of Qatabân",[46] it is certainly possible that *rdmn* actually preceded *mḏḥym/wqtbn*; and CIH 334 indicates that it did. In any event, at least one letter is missing at the beginning of NaNN 72+73/3. Consequently, the above-mentioned connections in lines 1 and 2 do not stand, and one would have to read *h/.ʿlyhmw* (line 1) and *ʾšʿbn/.ḏḥym* (line 2); further, the difficulty would be even greater if *rdmn* had to be restored before *mḏḥym*. Furthermore, it is rather difficult to justify the translation of *brḍ* as "faire défaut" as well as that of *nwy* (without any preposition) as "se séparer de" (cf. Arabic *nawâ*+*ʿan*). The connection of NaNN 71, not on the right, but on the left of NaNN 72+73 gives a plausible meaning to the text: Sabaʾ had as ally Raydân against the coalition of Muḏḥayum, Qatabân, Ḥabašat, and Ḥaḍramawt. Finally, *RycIMAM* ascribes the text to the period of CIH 155, that is to say to the sole reign of ʿAlhân Nahfân (e.g., p. 132); later, however, he seems to doubt this opinion (p. 294, note 11). The remark previously made about CIH 155 is true here also.

RÉS 4216 – Lines 3-4 of this fragmentary inscription are deciphered and restored by *MoMiASI* (p. 46) as follows:

3 [*wl/sʿdh*]*mw/ḥ*[*ẓ*]*y/wrḍw/mrʾy*[*hmw/*]
4 [*ʾlšrḥ/yḥḍb/wb*]*nyhw/*[*wtrm*/...

The restoration of a word divider at the end of line 3, as suggested above, is superfluous. – Since the letter *n* in *b*]*nyhw* is given as certain by the editors of the text, the restoration of *ʾlšrḥ/yḥḍb* and of *wtrm* is quite unlikely since in the only two texts (see below) mentioning these two persons, the

[43] As suggested by M. Hartmann, followed by *CIH*.
[44] Cf. *RycIMAM*, p. 132: "ḏû-Ḥaym".
[45] Noteworthy is that *NaNN* himself includes *ḏ* of *ḏḥym* in the restoration of the text in his transcription in Hebrew characters (p. 93).
[46] Cf. *JaDCR*, p. 29, and Geukens 1/6.

name of the first is introduced by the singular noun *mrᵓ* (not the dual construct *mrᵓy*) and is followed by his royal title. For some unstated reason, *RycIMAM* maintains the name of *ᵓlšrḥ/yḥḍb* at the beginning of line 4. The rest of his interpretation is difficult. On the one hand, his reading (p. 169, note 5) supposes the following restoration in line 4: [*ᵓlšrḥ/yḥḍb/wᵓ*](*ḫ*)*yhw*/[*yᵓzl/byn*/. . . ; and this restoration becomes certain on p. 195 and note 27. On the other hand, that is to say later on in his work (pp. 204 and note 2, and 295 and note 18), the same author still considers RÉS 4216 as related to *ᵓlšrḥ/yḥḍb* and his son *wtrm*. *RycIMAM*'s correction of *n* of *b*]*nyhw* to *ḫ* of *ᵓ*](*ḫ*)*yhw* in his first two mentions of the text, based only on the restoration proposed by *MoMiASI*, of *ᵓlšrḥ/yḥḍb* at the beginning of line 4, remains unjustified, for the editors of the text consider the letter *n* of *b*]*nyhw* as certain. The photograph of the text has not been published; this fact prevents us from knowing both the palaeography and the repartition of the letters of the text. It must be strongly emphasized that there is no reason whatsoever for correcting *MoMiASI*'s reading of *n* to that of *ḫ*. Further, the restoration of the name of *ᶜlhn/nhfn* and that of his son *šᶜrm* fits the text very well; NaNN 19/14-16 is very close to RÉS 4216/2-4, both from ideological and lexicographical viewpoints. Until the photograph of the text is published, I suggest reading the end of the inscription as follows:

3 [*wl/sᶜdh*]*mw/ḥ*[*ẓ*]*y/wrḏw/mrᵓy*[*hmw*]
4 [*ᶜlhn/nhfn/wb*]*nyhw*/[*šᶜrm/mlky*]
5 [*sbᵓ*/. . .

Finally, *RyISA* (XIV, pp. 371-72) simply refers to the interpretation of *MoMiASI* without noting that of *RycIMAM* and without making any comment.

b – RECONSTRUCTION OF HISTORICAL EVENTS: CIH 155, 289, 308, 308 bis, 401, 693; NaNN 19, 72+73+71; RÉS 4216

The first question to be studied is the period of CIH 155. J. Ryckmans has connected this inscription with the sole reign of ᶜAlhân Nahfân.[47] To my knowledge the only evidence for this is the singular pronoun *hw* in *ᵓḫhw* (line 3); although this obviously refers to only one person, it nevertheless does not exclude the existence of the coregency. Furthermore, no Sab royal name is given in the text. There appears thus no compelling reason to ascribe this text to the sole reign of ᶜAlhân Nahfân in preference to the period of his coregency with his son. On the contrary, CIH 155 and 308 both mention the Ḥaḍr king Yadaᶜᵓab Ġaylân; it seems thus normal to ascribe both texts to the same period.

The second preliminary question is the relation between CIH 308, 401, and 693 on the one hand, and on the other NaNN 19 with regard to the filiation of ᶜAlhân Nahfân. *RycYA* (p. 146) sees in the presence (first group of texts) and the absence (second group) of the filiation of ᶜAlhân Nahfân a suggestion of the anteriority of the first group. We should be inclined to follow this suggestion if the four texts had the same authors; however, those of the first group are the two kings, while those of the second are particular individuals. The relative chronology should thus be searched for somewhere else.

Finally, CIH 401, 693, and RÉS 4216 are very fragmentary, and what is left does not contain any historical information. Further, there is no photograph of either CIH 693 and RÉS 4216; and the stylistic characteristics of CIH 401 should be studied in the frame of the palaeographic study of that period.

Our information on the reign of ᶜAlhân Nahfân is, obviously enough, very fragmentary. The two texts known to belong to that period point out a peaceful atmosphere which certainly did not exclude small military expeditions here and there, as well as a rather intensive activity in foreign policy and the strengthening of military power.

The first document in date, related to the coregency of ᶜAlhân Nahfân and his son Šaᶜirum ᵓAwtar, CIH 155, sheds an unexpected light on the activity of Sabaᵓ. The text relates a joint expedition composed of the Sab army and that of the Ḥaḍr king Yadaᶜᵓab Ġaylân,[48] against Ḥimyar who, in an attempt to expand outside its territory (cf. *ᶜtym/bn/ᵓrḍ/ḥmyrm*, in line 2) had launched an expedition and was laying siege to the city of ᶜArmân.[49] The alliance referred to between Sabaᵓ and Ḥaḍramawt cannot be explained *a priori* by the geographical position of Qatabân, and even less as a possible result of the occupation of Qatabân

[47] Cf. *RycIMAM*, e.g., p. 132, *RycYA*, e.g., p. 138, and *RycCSAPS*, p. 206 A.

[48] The text from Wâdî Beiḥân mentioned by *AlCAS* (p. 10), is WB 1-3.

[49] CIH 155/2: *mṣnᶜtn/ḏtᶜrmn*, compare with the expression *ṣlmtn/ḏt/ḏhbn* (e.g., Ja 584/8).

by one of the two allies.[50] It should be remembered that alliances primarily aimed at developing trade and business; and that is even more understandable between Saba᾿ and Ḥaḏramawt. The only consequence known to us, of this alliance, is a joint campaign against the expansionist policy of Ḥimyar[51] westward, that is to say toward the Red Sea, since the city of ᶜArmân belonged to the tribe of Ḏubḥân located in the southwestern end of the peninsula.[52] Such a location is agreeable with a close connection between CIH 155 and 307.

CIH 308 refers to the offering by the two Sab kings of 30 statues[53] for the following reasons: several works (ornamental gardens) had been successfully completed in a place which most probably was one of their summer residences; an alliance had been concluded with Gadarat, king of Ḥabašat, and finally minor wars had been successfully ended, including the submission of Ḫawlân (southwest of Ṣirwâḥ), which received help from Raydân, and also of some rebels from ᵓAšᶜûb (west of Laḥej). The Ḥabašat of South Arabia was located north of Ḏubḥân,[54] and was left untouched during the preceding military events. It was Gadarat, king of Ḥabašat across the Red Sea (cf. CIH 308/17: *nblw/.../bbḥrm*) who sought an alliance with Saba᾿. Probably the growing strength of Ḥimyar, which was a threat to South-Arabian Ḥabašat, led Gadarat to seek an alliance with some insular power and more precisely with Saba᾿ which, because of its alliance with Ḥaḏramawt, was the strongest one, and also because Saba᾿ was the closest of the two to Ḥabašat. The alliance was concluded (CIH 308/11-14), and the two powers are listed as being on the Sab side, Salḥân and ᶜAlhân, and on the Ḥabašite side, Zararân and Gadarat, the first name of each group being the palace of the ruler. In this context I cannot justify the contention that "ce texte fait allusion à un conflit qui mettait aux prises tous les territoires de quelque importance en Arabie du Sud, et même l'Abyssinie".[55] Finally, the cities of *qyhrn* (line 7) and *lqṭ* (line 8) remain unidentified. The second place name has hardly anything to do with "Heit Laqait",[56] 25 km. east-southeast of Beiḥân al-Qaṣâb. The clan name of *ḥqln* also remains unidentified.

CIH 308 bis is interesting, in comparison with CIH 308, for certain omissions and additions. The alliance with Ḥaḏramawt is not mentioned, but the importance of its omission should not be overstated[57] since it evidently played no important role in the events described in CIH 308. This omission does not seem more important than, e.g., the omission of *wmṣr/ᵓḥbšn* (CIH 308/12) or the addition of *wslmw/wsmᶜn/qhtm* (CIH 308/25) in CIH 308 bis. The general contents of the texts were given, but some freedom with regard to the definitive wording, either including (e.g., *ḏrm* in CIH 308/13) or omitting (e.g., *wkl/msqyhmw*, in CIH 308/5) some details, was apparently left to the discretion of the engravers. These additions and omissions suggest that more than one engraver was hired; besides, why would the two kings have hired only one worker who could not have completed the job in less than several weeks? Furthermore, all the copies of CIH 308 could also have been engraved before the copies of CIH 308 bis were begun; thus, the additions and omissions pointed out above would not be of any importance from a historical point of view. The alliance between Saba᾿ and the Ḥaḏr king Yadaᶜᵓab Ġaylân ceased to exist before the engraving of NaNN 19 (very probably because of the death of Yadaᶜᵓab Ġaylân),[58] it is true; but no information now available places this event between the engraving of CIH 308 and that of CIH 308 bis.

The military expeditions against the western highland continued, as attested by the very fragmentary text CIH 289, which is earlier than NaNN 19 but related to it. The author of these two texts was very much concerned about having male posterity of his own, since he speaks of it in both texts. His only son born of his wife (CIH

[50] As *RycCSAPS*, p. 206 A. Further study of the Qat kingdom is needed to determine its precise relationship to this alliance.

[51] It is rather difficult to understand *RycIMAM*'s remark (p. 299), pointed out in connection with CIH 155, according to which Ḥimyar "fut vraisemblablement à un moment donné sous la dépendance de ḏû-Raydân".

[52] Cf. *WiDME*, sketch map on p. 324; cf. also *WiHöBGS*, p. 48, note 4.

[53] For the relation between the number of dedicated statues and the number of copies of the text, cf. pp. 275 B-276.

[54] Cf. *WiHöBGS*, map facing p. 64.

[55] As *RycCSAPS*, p. 206 A. The same author goes on to state that "du fait que Qatabān n'est pas mentionné parmi les belligérants, il semble que ce royaume avait alors cessé d'exister". Such a conclusion is unfounded since there is no reason why Qatabân should have been mentioned. Further, Ja 629 is proof that the Qat kingdom did not disappear at that time, and even less at an earlier period (cf. pp. 341 B-343)

[56] Cf. *WiHöBGS*, p. 51: "Āl Laqaiṭ".

[57] Cf. *RycIMAM*, p. 133, and *RycYA*, p. 147.

[58] *RycYA* (p. 147) sees in the alliance with Gadarat, king of Ḥabašat, a probable reason explaining the termination of the alliance with Yadaᶜᵓab Ġaylân of Ḥaḏramawt. This opinion is a consequence of the hypothesis according to which this end came before the engraving of CIH 308 bis and after that of CIH 308.

289/22) *qlkhl/ḏt/hmdn*,[59] evidently died[60]; the story of this loss was almost certainly given in CIH 289 (at least line 8). One purpose of his second offering (NaNN 19) was *wbmw/hwt/ḫr[fn/wl]dt/qlkhl/ḏt/hmdn/ġlm[m/]ṯnym/ḥgrm* (lines 7-9) "and in this ye[ar] [that] Qâlkahil, she of Hamdân, [gave] birth to [a] second, consecrated[61] youth". The author of CIH 289, which probably was a dedicatory inscription to ᶜAṯtar (cf. line 24), was a governor of Mârib, since he and his associates returned (cf. the plural of *tʾwlw* and [ᶜ]*dww*) to Mârib and Salḥân, the latter being both the royal palace and the residence of the governors. They had taken part in a military expedition[62] in the territory of Ḥimyar (line 16) and of other cities(?), whose names are very doubtful,[63] and also in the territory of *ḏrydn* (line 17). The rest of the text contains the usual petitions to the deity.

Several months (or only weeks?) after the engraving of CIH 289, NaNN 19 was chiseled in the stone, and contains an offering to the Hamdânid god Taʾlab Riyyâm. The atmosphere of this text is as peaceful as that of the inscriptions related to the sole reign of ᶜAlhân Nahfân. The author begs his favored deity for favorable weather and abundant fruits, for the birth of a second boy, for an alliance between his king ᶜAlhân Nahfân and Yadaᶜʾil, king of Ḥadramawt, for the favor and grace of his two kings, and finally for protection against the hostility of any enemy. The fact that a governor of Mârib was so anxious to see an alliance concluded with the new Ḥaḍr ruler suggests in no way that such was likely.[64] Even had Yadaᶜʾil of Ḥaḍramawt desired this alliance, there is a strong probability that he did not have a chance to realize his plan, since the first major military campaign of the sole reign of Šaᶜirum ʾAwtar is already directed against ʾIlᶜazz, king of Ḥaḍramawt.

It is here, some time after NaNN 19, that I should like to place NaNN 72 + 73 + 71, as a consequence of CIH 155 and an introduction to CIH 334. The Sab intervention in the southwest no doubt greatly disturbed the peace of all the population of Qatabân[65] and of its long standing allies, because they had to fear being crushed between the giant Sab tongs, which were extending themselves at that time. Too, Gadarat of Ḥabašat tried to save the insular Ḥabašat from being swallowed by Sabaʾ, by making peace with it. The petition addressed to the deity for an alliance with Yadaᶜʾil of Ḥaḍramawt, mentioned in NaNN 19, could easily reflect the fear of the governor of Mârib that the intrigues of Muḏḥayum and Qatabân would be successful. They apparently were successful; and NaNN 72 + 73 + 71 would be the witness of a tremendous coalition of Muḏḥayum, Qatabân, Ḥabašat, and Ḥaḍramawt against Sabaʾ and its ally Raydân. The text, being very fragmentary, does not give any information about the side taken by Ḥimyar, which later was to be the ally of Šaᶜirum ʾAwtar. This coalition, however, did not overpower Sabaʾ; on the contrary, it is probably immediately after and as a consequence of it, that Šaᶜirum ʾAwtar will lead his four major military expeditions.

F – THE REIGN OF ŠAᶜIRUM ʾAWTAR

Some time after the coalition mentioned in NaNN 72 + 73 + 71 was crushed, ᶜAlhân Nahfân disappeared from the historical arena, and his son Šaᶜirum ʾAwtar became sole ruler; later, he shares his power with his brother Ḥayûᶜaṯtar Yaḍiᶜ. Before entering upon the study of Šaᶜirum ᶜAwtar's reign, two preliminary questions need some attention.

1 – *Sole Reign*

a – PRELIMINARY QUESTIONS

The testimony of the unpublished Gl 1371 raises difficulties; too, the significance of *ḏrydn* in the new royal title needs some explanation.

[59] This title does not justify *RycIMAM*'s suggestion according to which the lady was "peut-être de la famille royale" (p. 143).

[60] Cf. also *NaNN*, p. 28.

[61] Without any etymological attempt, *NaNN* considers *ḥgr* as equivalent to Arabic *mâniᶜ* "defender of" or *ᶜâṣib* "bound to" the heritage of his ancestors (p. 28; in his translation on p. 30, the *y* is to be corrected to *b*), that is to say a faithful member of his clan. However, the first meaning of *ḥgr* is "to prevent, hinder, withhold, interdict". Even before his birth, the boy was probably consecrated to the deity, and thus was already, in a sense segregated from the rest of his family.

[62] Line 16: *rt*... is restored by *CIH* as *rt*[*klm*]; a restoration involving *rtḍḥ* (cf., e.g., Ja 575/5) is also possible and equally probable.

[63] The first of them would be *mrymtm* according to *CIH*, III, p. 341 B. Is it the Qat city located at the conflux of Wâdî Jaba al-ᶜAlay and Wâdî Beiḥân, 8 km. south of Beiḥân al-Qaṣâb, or some city connected with Jebel Maryama, near Ẓafâr (cf. *WiHöBGS*, p. 48)? The mention of *ḏrydn* in line 17 renders the second hypothesis almost certain.

[64] As *RycIMAM*, p. 134.

[65] According to *RycCSAPS* (p. 206 A), Qatabân is mentioned in this inscription "au titre, semble-t-il, de simple tribu, non de royaume indépendant". A. F. L. Beeston rightly doubts the correctness of this remark (cf. *BiO*, 9 [1952], p. 216 A). Cf. p. 294, note 55.

1° – Gl 1371.

In all the texts dealt with above in relation to Yarum ᵓAyman's dynasty, the royal title is *mlk/sbᵓ* from the beginning to the coregency of ᶜAlhân Nahfân with his son Šaᶜirum ᵓAwtar; but from the beginning of the latter's sole reign, the title is *mlk/sbᵓ/wḏrydn*. According to K. Mlaker,[66] who confirms *GlAAA*'s testimony (e.g., p. 34), both ᶜAlhân Nahfân and Šaᶜirum ᵓAwtar bear the new title: *mlk/sbᵓ/wḏrydn* in Gl 1371, a dedicatory inscription to the god Taᵓlab,[67] found in Ḏaibân,[68] which is located about 16 km. northeast of Ṣanᶜâᵓ.[69] The difficulty resulting from ᶜAlhân Nahfân's title in this text cannot be solved by doubting the testimony of the two above-mentioned authors.[70] Can *wḏrydn* in that title be considered as a mistake of the workman? The royal titles are always so accurately and carefully given in the texts that such a mistake is extremely difficult to accept. Further, it must be strongly emphasized that in no inscription yet known from Šaᶜirum ᵓAwtar's sole reign does he bear the title *mlk/sbᵓ*, but on the contrary all evidence points to his taking the title *mlk/sbᵓ/wḏrydn* from the very outset of his reign. This must be considered in the light of the contrasting situation presented by Šamir Yuharᶜiš who bore two titles. Only two hypotheses are possible: either Šaᶜirum ᵓAwtar proclaimed the new title when he began his sole reign (and if he did so, it could only be as a consequence of events brought about by his father and himself during the preceding coregency) or he already had it at the very end of the coregency. As a consequence of Gl 1371, the following hypothetical reconstruction of events, which includes the two above-mentioned hypotheses, could be offered. A certain number of events were planned or used by the two coregents ᶜAlhân Nahfân and his son Šaᶜirum ᵓAwtar which led to a political situation rendering possible, or even requiring, the change of the title *mlk/sbᵓ* into that of *mlk/sbᵓ/wḏrydn*. The change itself would actually have occurred at the very end of the coregency; but the new title was not officially proclaimed until after ᶜAlhân Nahfân's death which followed immediately the *effective* change. Gl 1371 would simply allude to the fact that ᶜAlhân Nahfân actually was *mlk/sbᵓ/wḏrydn*; but all the other texts would follow the custom of using the *officially* known title.

2° – *The meaning of* ḏrydn *in the title* mlk/sbᵓ/wḏrydn

My opinion on the meaning of *ḏrydn* in the expression *mlk/sbᵓ/wḏrydn* has already been expressed in 1952, in *JaPEHA*, p. 21, note 13.[71]

Since *RycPRSA* (p. 81, note 18) still refers to *RycIMAM*, pp. 160-62, I feel justified in coming back to *RycIMAM*.

The first remark to be made is that the beginning of note 18 (which has no reference to *JaPEHA*), "Raydān étant un nom de localité" contradicts the discussion in *RycIMAM* (pp. 161-62) which rejects such an idea. Note 18 goes on by stating that "le nom de la tribu et du territoire qui en dérivent sont toujours précédés de *ḏ-*: on dira donc *bny hmdn*, mais *bny ḏrydn*, de même pour le nom de la province du ḏū-Sahart, issu du nom d'une ville (CIH 314, 14)". This argumentation seemingly does not reckon with the information given in *JaPEHA* (p. 29) and especially *bnw/ḏhmdn* (Ja 716/2) = *bny/ḏhmdn* (Ja 716/6 and [11-12]). The situation is not different for the country of *shrtm* (Ja 635/21-22) = *shrtn* (e.g., Ja 575/4), and the tribe *ḏshrtm* (e.g., Ja 574/3-4) = *shrtn* (e.g., Ja 616/18).

Much more important than the preceding remarks are the three following considerations.

1 – The proper name *rydn* is attested in a Qat text[72] and even in a text which belongs to the period of some Sab *mukarribs*: RÉS 3858, line 12 mentions *nḫlm/brydn/ḏhmrr* "one palm-grove in Raydân of Ḥamrâr". Besides, *ḏrydn* is also mentioned in the Qat inscription RÉS 4336/3: *šmr/ḏrydn* "Šamir, he of Raydân".

[66] Cf. *AAWW, Ph.-hist.Kl.*, 11-22 [1938], p. 78.

[67] Cf. *HöSEG*, p. 50.

[68] Cf. *l.c.*, p. 29.

[69] Cf. *MüHG*, 82/11, 22 and 109/26, and *FoSA*, p. 114, note 5.

[70] As does *RycIMAM*, pp. 106, note 16, and 165, note 14.

[71] E. Ullendorff remarks that "*ḏ* merely fulfils the function which the construct state does in the first case. This is amply proved by the repeated use of this particle at the beginning of Aksum inscription No. 8" (cf. *Orientalia*, 23 [1954], p. 325). Such a remark might lead the reader to think that the problem of South-Arabian *ḏ* was misunderstood, and that no attention was given to expressions such as *mlk/sbᵓ/wḏrydn/wḥḍrm(w)t/wymnt*. Besides, the beginning of Aksum 8 does not have a single *ḏ* (cf. E. Littmann, *Deutsche Aksum-Expedition*. Bd. IV, Berlin, 1913, p. 18), which is only to be found "in vokalisierter äthiopischer Schrift" (cf. *l.c.*, p. 19) of the text by E. Littmann. – The particle *ḏ* would have to be translated as "lord of" according to *RÉS* (VII, p. 505; practically identical with *RyCS*, p. 242, note 4) because of the parallel between *mlk/sbᵓ/wḏrydn* and *ᵓmlkn/ᵓbᶜl/rdn*. This opinion, already rejected by *RycIMAM*, p. 159, is also disproved by the use of *ḏ* (cf. *JaPEHA*, pp. 19 sq.).

[72] *RycIMAM* (p. 160) affirms that "Ḏû-Raydân n'est mentionné que dans des documents sabéens, d'où il ressort, semble-t-il, que cette région n'était pas directement en contact avec Qatabân".

2 – If "le territoire et la population de d̲û-Raydân tiraient leur nom de la forteresse Raydân à Ẓafâr",[73] that is to say "*d̲ū-Raydân*..., la population et le territoire entourant un toponyme du nom de *Raydân*", then *d̲rydn*, country and population, is to be identified with Ḥimyar, as the classical authors do, as well as *WiHöBGS*: "*Ḥimyar* ...mit der Hauptstadt *Ẓafár* und der Burg *Raydān*"[74] and *RycPRSA*: "le royaume himyarite de d̲ū-Raydān" (p. 77), "Ḥimyar-d̲ū-Raydān" (p. 85) and "Šāmir de d̲ū-Raydān, c'est-à-dire, à notre avis, un roi himyarite du sud".[75] Yet, *d̲rydn* and *ḥmyrm* are allied against the two royal brothers ʾIlšaraḥ Yaḥḍub and Yaʾzil Bayyin; and the *ʾrydn* "the Raydânites" are still distinguished from *ʾḥmrn* "the Ḥimyarites" more than three centuries later at the time of CIH 353, during the coregency of the two sons of Yasrum Yuhanʿim, as they already were only a few years before the addition of *d̲rydn* to the title, that is to say during ʿAlhân Nahfân's coregency with his son, in CIH 289; and it is in relation to this text that *RycIMAM* (p. 130) speaks of Ḥimyar and Raydân as "ces deux tribus, étroitement liées entre elles".

3 – The title *mlk/sbʾ/wd̲rydn* was assumed, at least officially, by Šaʿirum ʾAwtar; and it is precisely during the latter's reign that Liʿazzum Yuhnaf Yuhaṣdiq is mentioned, the first provincial king of Ẓafâr known up to the present time. It seems, however, rather amazing that the name of the fortress Raydân is not mentioned in the record of the siege and the battle of Ẓafâr. On the contrary, the citadel is called *ʿr ʾln* "the citadel of the god". It seems quite natural that the provincial king of Ẓafâr would have entrenched himself in Raydân, if the latter had already been built.

I therefore maintain my interpretation according to which *d̲rydn* in the Sab royal title refers to the Qat tribe and country connected with the famous J. Raydân, south of Wâdî Beiḥân. It should be recalled that *GlAAA* (p. 116) already suggested that it is possible "Reidân, im ḳatabanischen Gebiet zu suchen", and also that *WiHöBGS* (p. 48) alludes to the possibility that Ḥimyar took as name for their fortress that of the Qat one.

[73] Cf. *l.c.*, p. 161.

[74] Cf. p. 69; cf. also pp. 33 and 19, note 2: "*Raydān* war die Burg der *Ḥimyar* in *Ẓafár*".

[75] P. 91. Note that *WiHöBGS* (p. 34) already wrote about the same Šamir of Raydân: "Als *Herr von Raydān* in Ẓafár und als letzter Führer der *Ḥimyar* tritt *Shammar* auf".

[76] The identification of *d̲ġylm* with Hajar bin Ḥumeid, suggested by *WiHöBGS* (p. 47), is controversial (cf. already A. Jamme, in *Le Muséon*, 66 [1953], p. 181). The guard tower named Ḥuṣn el-Ḫuḍeirî is located in the western part of Wâdî Beiḥân, and Hajar bin Ḥumeid in the eastern one. In my opinion, the city of D̲û-Ġaylum would better be sought in the western part of Wâdî Beiḥân, at the eastern end of Wâdî Mablaqah.

[77] Cf. commentary on Ja 574/6. In such cases, however, the use of *hgrnhn* is more common; e.g., Ja 576/8, 14; etc. Note also that *RhIG* (pp. 56 and 59) and *WiHöBGS* (e.g., p. 38) suggest *hgrn*, which is considered as singular.

b – REMARKS ON FIVE TEXTS:
CIH 334; Fakhry 75, 102;
Geukens 1; RÉS 4842

A few remarks need to be made about the publication of five inscriptions.

CIH 334 is very important because of the historical events recorded in it. Two expressions need to be studied again: *bḫrf/d̲t/ġ[r]bm*, and *ʿdy/hgrn[hn/m]wt/wṣwʾrn* (*CIH*; lines 5-6 and 17-18, respectively).

As regards the first expression, *CIH*'s commentary (I, p. 380 A) contains some words to the effect of justifying his reading. However, *RhIG* (pp. 55-56) simply transliterates *d̲t/ġ*... .*m*, and makes no comment on the restoration of the proper name. The location of *d̲t/ġ* at the end of line 5, compared with the last letters of lines 3-4 and 6-7 – the name *ḥḍrmt* is not necessarily to be restored in *scriptio plena* (as *CIH* and *RhIG*) – requires the restoration of only one letter. Furthermore, the reading of the first letter of line 6 as *b* is disproved by the two following facts. The supposed right vertical stroke of *b* is a concave line whose extremities are at a lower level than that of both ends of the following vertical stroke. Further, the space between the supposed *b* and the following *m* is at least twice as wide as the space between any *b* and its following letter; it is thus much too wide. The preceding objection disappears if one reads the letter *l*. Then, the name of *d̲t/ġ[y]⌜l⌝m* in CIH 344/5-6 could be compared with the name of the Qat city of D̲û-Ġaylum[76] whose walls were built by the Ḥaḍr king Yadaʿʾab Ġaylân, the former ally of both ʿAlhân Nahfân and Šaʿirum ʾAwtar.

With regard to the second expression, two questions need to be discussed, namely the decipherment of the text, and the location of the town *ṣwʾrn*. As far as the reading of the text is concerned, it should be stressed that *CIH*'s restoration of *hgrn* to *hgrn[hn]* is not justified "quum duo oppida nominentur" (p. 381 A), since the singular *hgrn* introduces the names of two cities in Ja 629/27.[77] Therefore, if one sign must be restored at the end of line 17, it has to be a word divider, and a word divider is superfluous in such a place, as also is the one restored by *CIH* at the end of line 12. The space between *hgrn* and the border of the stone, which shows no trace of any character, is even smaller than that at the end of lines 14 and 16; yet, the restoration of any letter in these two places is positively excluded. There is thus no reason whatsoever for restoring a sign at the end of line 17. On the other hand, the comparison of the beginning of lines 16-20 indicates that two characters only are missing at the beginning of line 18; this fact positively excludes the restoration of the last part of the dual ending *hgrn[hn]*. Some authors do not attempt to read the first proper name.[78] *GlAAA* (p. 109) suggests *šbwt*; however, the remaining part of the letter preceding *w* points, according to him, more to the letter *m*, and he finally (p. 110) retains the reading *mwt*. This interpretation is accepted by *CIH*, although M. Hartmann had already considered the restoration of *šbwt* as "kaum zu zweifeln",[79] apparently because "das alte Sabota liegt ja für den gegen *ḥaḏramaut* Ziehenden so recht auf dem Wege". *RyNP* (I, p. 347 A) follows *CIH* and identifies *mwt* with the same name in CIH 429/2, that is to say a city about 100 km. south of Ṣanᶜâ᾿, and about 40 km. northwest of Ẓafâr. This identification does not fit the third military campaign of Šaᶜirum ᾿Awtar, and must be disregarded. *RycIMAM* avoids the question, but suggests that the sack of Šabwat occurred during the campaign mentioned in CIH 334 because of Fakhry 75 and 102 (pp. 185 and 300). According to *WiHöBGS* (p. 113, note 4), these two texts of Fakhry confirm the restoration of *šbwt* (cf. also pp. 38 and 124), which was already secured by the identification of *ṣw᾿rn*. However, a close study of the good photograph of the text printed by *CIH* shows that the letter preceding *wt* is *s* the centre of which is damaged, and the top of the upper vertical stroke, which is in the vertical axis of the two lower strokes, is destroyed. The letter on the right of *swt* is very much damaged, it is true, but appears to be *r*. I read thus *(r)swt*, which is the present Rîsût (20 km. southwest of Ṣalâlah in Ẓafâr), identified with Κωσευδη πόλις of Ptolemaeus by *SpAGA* (pp. 94-95).

MüHG (88/15-17) is very important for the identification and the localization of the town *ṣw᾿rn*. This author lists indeed five towns called Qašâqiš, Ṣuwarân, Sidbat, al-ᶜAǧlânîyat, and Manwab (for the latter, cf. Ja 629/30). The last three towns are located east of Wâdî al-ᶜAin–Wâdî al-Kasr; the first two were therefore also in the same general area; this fact would of course exclude the identification of *ṣw᾿rn* with Sûr,[80] located on Wâdî Sûr and about 20 km. east of Haynan (presently Hênin, about 35 km. southwest of Šibâm). *WiHöBGS* (p. 124) identifies *ṣw᾿rn* with present al-ᶜÂdîya (about 5 km. southwest of Hênin, but still east of Wâdî al-ᶜAin–Wâdî al-Kasr), because "ein solcher Name deutet immer auf antike Ruinen". However, Qašâqiš and Ṣuwarân of *MüHG* could very well be al-ᶜÂdîya and al-Manṣûra[81] (about 2 km. east of Hênin), respectively.

I thus read the text as follows: *ᶜdy/hgrn (r)swt/ wṣw᾿rn* "to the two cities of (Rî)sût and Ṣawa᾿rân", the two extreme points of the Sab conquest of Ḥaḍramawt, al-Manṣûra(?) in the northeast and (Rî)sût in the far southeast, corresponding to the two major phases of the campaign, the first of which includes Šabwat, located between Mârib and Ṣawa᾿rân, and the second Qana᾿, which defended the Wâdî Ḥaḍramawt on the south, as well as the coastal route eastward to Ẓafâr.

Fakhry 75,[82] MaN 21 in my field book, is in yellowish limestone. Maximum thickness: 18 cm.; *front:* 89.5 cm. × 25; text in relief. Line 1: read *bn(y)/gdnm* instead of *bn(y/g)dnm*; line 2: *wzbnr* is neither translated nor listed among the proper names by *RyET*; lines 3-4: read *m]lk* instead of *[ml]k*.

Fakhry 102[83] is MaN 25 in my field book. The height of the stone seen by A. Fakhry was 43 cm.[84]; the stone was cut again on top (present height: 33 cm.; with only 12 lines of text) and re-used in a pavement located at the center of the court of the *nâṣerah* and reserved for prayers. Line 1: the first six letters, corresponding to *[y] ᾿lmqh* in line 2, are missing; the obvious restoration is *rṯdm bn*; read *⌜m⌝ᶜ⌜n⌝* instead of *m.n*; thus *[rṯdm/bn]⌜/m⌝ᶜ⌜n⌝/᾿dm/ mlkn*; cp. RÉS 4229/1-3: *᾿lršd/bn/šl᾿l/᾿dm/ḏ᾿nwyn*. Line 3: *ġnmh* is certain instead of *ġnmm* (cf. commen-

[78] Cf., e.g., *MoHIA*, p. 9, and *RhIG*, p. 56.

[79] Cf. *ZA*, 10 (1895), p. 158; opinion mentioned by *RhIG*, p. 59, note 1.

[80] Cf. *CIH*, I, p. 381 A.

[81] Note that the two proper names *ṣw᾿rn* and al-Manṣûra have in common the three letters *ṣwr*.

[82] Cf. *RyET*, pp. 49-50.

[83] Cf. *l.c.*, pp. 62-64.

[84] Cf. I, p. 116; not "34" as in *RyET*, p. 62.

tary on Ja 561 bis/8). Lines 7-11: cf. commentary on Ja 560/8-9. Line 13: read *bʾlmqhb*⌋ᶜ⌊*l*⌋[ʾ*wm*] instead of *bʾlmqhbᶜlʾwm.*

The photographic reproduction of Geukens 1 [85] does not permit verification of the reading of several important terms; it is only recently that I was able to apply to this photograph the same process applied before to the photograph of Ja 576 [86]; and it is my conviction that the careful study of the original negative would provide more data. – The reading of ⌊*qdm*⌋*y* (line 3) [87] is disproved by the photographic reproduction; the third letter is *h* and its lower vertical stroke being in the vertical axis of the two upper ones cannot belong to the letter *m*. Nevertheless, *RyISA* (p. 302) excludes *h* because "le *h* est rectangulaire" affirming that "le trait horizontal supérieur se distingue assez nettement". However, this letter is no more rectangular than the other letter *h*'s; and either the bottom or the top of *m* is formed with an oblique concave (not horizontal) stroke. The study of *RyISA*'s decipherment is furthermore facilitated by comparing *qdmy* in line 22 with the beginning of line 4: the third letter is entirely different in each case; it is also obvious that the diameter of the first letter of line 3 is much larger than the circle of all the letter *q*'s, including that of *qdmy* in line 22. The dual in line 3 [88] is thus highly questionable; as a matter of fact, the subject of the text seems to be *ʾsdm*/*ʾsᶜd* and not *rbbm*/*ʾẖṯr* and *ʾsdm*/*ʾsᶜd*.[89] This fact perfectly explains the singular of the verb *sbʾ* (line 4),[90] and is confirmed by the mention of *ʾsdm*/*ʾsᶜd* alone in line 13; further the expression *ʾẖhw*/*rbbm*/*ʾẖṯr* is explicable only on the hypothesis that *ʾsdm*/*ʾsᶜd* is the sole author of the text. The expression *rbbm*/*ʾẖṯr*/*wʾsdm*/*ʾsᶜd* (line 16) may be explained as follows: the two persons were associated in some function (therefore, *ʾsdm*/*ʾsᶜd* calls *rbbm*/*ʾẖṯr* his brother); but *rbbm*/*ʾẖṯr* occupied the higher rank (thus, *rbbm*/*ʾẖṯr* comes first when both are mentioned); both took part in a military campaign which is recorded by the second in rank, namely *ʾsdm*/*ʾsᶜd*. Consequently, the hypothesis of one missing line at the beginning of the text is superfluous. As regards that hypothesis, *RyISA* (*l.c.*) writes that "l'inscription nous paraît avoir été mutilée dans sa partie supérieure, bien que la photographie ne décèle pas cette mutilation, à part peut-être vers la gauche, où pourraient apparaître quelques traces de lettres". Yet, the only place where some remains of writing could eventually be found, is located above /*ʾs* (line 1), that is to say in the right part of the original; and no traces of writing are to be seen there. – At the beginning of line 4, *RyISA* (pp. 298 and 299) reads ⌊*q*⌋[*n*]⌈ʾ⌉, and explains that "Le *q* et la partie supérieure du ʾ apparaissent sur la photographie" (p. 302). Therefore, the half brackets in *q* are not justified, and those in ʾ should be placed at the bottom (not the top) of that letter. The photographic reproduction shows the following features: more than the lower half of the first letter is damaged; the upper third of the location of the second letter is not damaged at all, and presents no trace of a vertical stroke (the restoration of *n* is thus excluded, and that either of *w* or ᶜ necessary); the upper part of the third character (read as ʾ by *RyISA*) belongs to a word divider; there follow two half vertical strokes (letter *b*), and two complete vertical strokes (letter *ḏ*). The preceding decipherment is confirmed by applying here the length (6 mm.) of /*bḏt*/ (lines 13 and 19), and also by comparing the location of the first three signs in lines 3-5. The name of the city mentioned at the beginning of line 4 is composed of only two letters. Were the reading of the first letter as *q* more probable than as *n*, *s*, or *f*, one could suggest reading ⌊*q*⌋[ᶜ]; *MüHG* (183/23) mentions a place named al-Qâᶜ in Jauf, located, according to E. Glaser,[91] about 6.5 km. west-southwest of ᶜAmrân, and southwest of Jebel Qâᶜ. – In line 8, read *lfẖrhmw* instead of *lmẖrhmw*.[92] – In lines 19-21, *RyISA* (pp. 298 and 299) reads –/⌈*b*⌉*ḏt*/*wkb*/*ʾẖhw*/*rbbm*/*ʾẖ*(20)*ṭr*/*bn*/*sʾrn*/ᶜ. . . *hmw*/*wmṣnᶜhmw*/*w* . . . (21) . . . . . /*bn*/*ʾgyš*/*wʾṣḥb*/ *ʾḥbšn*/–, and comments as follows (p. 307): "ᶜ. . . *hmw*; il s'agit d'un ouvrage militaire, en relation avec *mṣnᶜ*" and "*w*. . ., probablement un verbe tel que «et il échappa à»?'' With regards to ᶜ. . .*hmw*, the first letter could also be *w*, and the fourth letter seems to be *r*; the term preceding *hmw* could very well be a verb with *rbbm*/*ʾẖṯr* as subject. At the beginning of line 21, seven signs (not merely 5) could precede /*bn*/*ʾgyš*/– if compared with the beginning of line 20; and the second seems to be *b*. – For the interpretation of lines 27-28, cf. commentary on Ja 550/2; for remarks on lines 10-11, cf. commentary on Ja 574/9.

[85] Cf. *RyISA*, XII, pl. I, between pp. 306 and 307.
[86] Cf. *JaDCR*, pp. 26-27.
[87] Cf. *RyISA*, XII, pp. 298, 299, 301, and 302.
[88] Cf. *l.c.*, pp. 301, 302, and 307.
[89] As in *l.c.*
[90] *L.c.* (p. 303) considers the king as the subject of the verb.
[91] Cf. *WeCGC*, p. 132, and maps.
[92] As *RyISA*, *l.c.*, pp. 298, 299, and 304.

RÉS 4842.[93] – The letter *d* of *ḫmdm* cannot be read at the beginning of line 1 (there is no space for it), but must be restored at the end of the preceding line. The first letter of line 3 must be restored as *w*, thus *sbʾ*[*w*] in plural (cf. *hmw* in line 8); therefore, the dedicatory verb is *hqnyw* instead of *hqny*.

c – TEXTS WITHOUT HISTORICAL REFERENCE: Fakhry 55; Ja 638, 639; NaNN 48; RÉS 4149, 4152, and 4155

Several inscriptions contain no historical information, and these are mentioned here.

In Fakhry 55, the Ḫalfânites proclaim their agreement with two ordinances dealing with employment; the first one was given by *ʿṯtr/šrqn* and *ʿṯtr/bʿl/bḥr/ḥṭybm*, and the other by *ʾlmqh/bʿlʾwm*. RÉS 4155 is a dedicatory text written by some individuals belonging to the same Ḫalfânites; however, the fragmentary condition of the text does not inform us of the deity to whom the offering was given or the nature of the two things offered (possibly, two statues). RÉS 4152 refers to an offering made by individuals to *ʿṯtr/bʿl/bḥrḥtbm* (cf. Fakhry 55). RÉS 4149[94] mentions the record of the offering of at least a statue to the sun goddess ʿUzzayin, probably because of some successful military event. Finally, three very fragmentary texts should be mentioned, namely Ja 638, 639, and NaNN 48[95]; the latter deals with the building of a house.

d – RECONSTRUCTION OF HISTORICAL EVENTS

The historical events of the reign of Šaʿirum ʾAwtar may be divided into five major military campaigns, the relative chronology of which is partially given by the inscriptions themselves. The expedition against the south of Mârib (Geukens 1) presupposed the conquest of Ḥaḍramawt (CIH 334) and may be explained as a retaliation campaign because of the activities of Radmân during the Ḥaḍr war. This campaign was most probably contemporaneous with the expedition against Ḥabašat (Ja 631). Then, after subjugating the southwest and the south, and after liberating Ẓafâr from the Ḥabašite occupation, Šaʿirum ʾAwtar was free to subdue the northwest (Ja 635). Finally, he had to go back to east Ḥaḍramawt to help his vanquished ally in local affairs (Ja 640).

1° – *First campaign*: ʾIlʿazz, king of Ḥaḍramawt and Ẓafâr; CIH 334; Ja 632, 636, 637, 741, 756; Fakhry 75 and 102

The war against ʾIlʿazz, king of Ḥaḍramawt, is composed of two major phases: the attack and pursuit of the Ḥaḍr army, which developed into the conquest of Ḥaḍramawt and of the far east Ḥaḍr province of Ẓafâr.

The Sab king Šaʿirum ʾAwtar and his *ḫmsy* "two armies", a Sab one, and a Ḥimyarite one, attack (*tqd*[*m*] *bʿm*; lines 3-4) and defeat ʾIlʿazz, king of Ḥaḍramawt, and his *mṣyrt* "expeditionary forces". This last information indicates that these Ḥaḍr soldiers were outside their own territory. The identification of *ḏt/ġ*[*y*]⌈*l*⌉*m* with the city of *ḏġylm* located in Qatabân perfectly explains the use of the noun *mṣyrt* and indicates that the battle took place in the Wâdî Beiḥân. During the *first phase* of the campaign, a secondary engagement took place most probably either when Šaʿirum ʾAwtar's armies were already in place, waiting for the battle, or immediately after the beginning of the battle. This secondary development is mentioned because of the role played by the author of CIH 334. He had under his command 200 men from the tribe Ḥumlân and was charged with the protection of *ḥrt/mlkn/wḫmsnhn* (line 7). These *ḥrt* were definitively not the Mârib dam and its canals,[96] since that vitally important irrigation system undoubtedly had a permanent guard. The expression itself suggests that these *ḥrt* were a part of the armies because the guard along with their commanding officer moves eastward as soon as the armies begin to pursue ʾIlʿazz. In the present text, *ḥrt* is the *scriptio defectiva* of *ḥyrt* "encampments, camps".[97] They were attacked and invaded by Radmânites, but fortunately not destroyed. The aggressors were driven back, but the author of the text was wounded in the fighting. The intervention of the tribe Radmân which attacked the rear of both the Sab and Ḥimyarite armies confirms the abovementioned interpretation of NaNN 72 + 73 + 71, as well as the isolation of Sabaʾ which was a cause of concern to the governor of Mârib, and incited him to pray for an alliance with Ḥaḍramawt (NaNN 19).

[93] Cf. also commentary on Ja 559/4 and *JaASAB*, p. 160, commentary on CIH 407/15.

[94] There is some difficulty in *RycIMAM*'s notes, since he relates this text to ʾIlšaraḥ Yaḥḍub and Yaʾzil Bayyin (p. 196, note 30).

[95] In *NaNN*'s transcription in Hebrew letters (p. 64), read *b*]*rʾ* instead of *b*]*rʾw*.

[96] As *WiHöBGS*, p. 38.

[97] Cf. commentary on Ja 576/12.

The second phase of the expedition against Ḥaḍramawt is told in two short lines: the author of the text went with his king fighting *ʿdy/hgrn (r)swt/wṣwʾrn* (lines 17-18). This is indeed a brief record for an expedition which carried the Sab conquest to its greatest extent in taking the cities of Rîsût (in the southeast; if my reading of the beginning of line 18 is correct), and Ṣawaʾrân (in the east; about 115 km. east of Šabwat). Such an expedition starting from Mârib through Wâdî Beiḥân obviously includes the invasion of both Šabwat and Qanaʾ. It is precisely from the booty brought back from these two cities that the authors of Ja 632 offer to ʾIlumquh four statues and a bull, all in bronze. A very interesting piece of information is found in Ja 741/6-8 and 756/6-8, which are related to the second phase of the Ḥaḍr campaign: the Sab Hayṯaʿ offers two statues in bronze, which he promised when "he came back in safety from Šabwat and from the sea". This clearly suggests that at least a part of the coastal expedition was conducted by sea, and thus makes almost certain the understanding according to which the far east Ḥaḍr colony was attacked by sea and not by land; and the location of the Ḥaḍr settlement in Ẓafâr perfectly fits this information. The four dedicatory inscriptions, Ja 636, 637, Fakhry 102 and 75, also refer to the booty brought back from Šabwat, and from which offerings were made for the god ʾIlumquh (the first three texts) and for the deity of irrigation Munḍiḥ.[98]

The Ḥaḍr king ʾIlʿazz did not die during the campaign; on the contrary, as will be noted later, he apparently made the best of the new situation imposed upon him, and collaborated with his Sab conqueror.

2° – *Second campaign:* south of Mârib; Geukens 1 (text from Raydat, about 50 km. northwest of Ṣanʿâʾ)

The intervention of the tribe Radmân against Šaʿirum ʾAwtar at the beginning of the first phase of the Ḥaḍr campaign was proof of the aggressiveness of that tribe, which thus had to be punished; such an example might easily be followed by others. Probably to make sure that the tribes south of Mârib would remain quiet, especially in the eventuality of a war, Šaʿirum ʾAwtar decided to take action.

Geukens 1, which relates this campaign, needs further study. According to the editor of the text,[99] the campaign started *bnhyt/hgrn* (line 5), that is to say from Qanaʾ (line 4); however, the military activity, in which Sab troops fought against the tribes of Qatabân, Radmân, Muḏḥayum, and ʾAwsân (line 6), covered the land "entre Redaʿ et la mer" (p. 305), that is to say "jusqu'à Ḥurmatum et jusqu'aux embarcations du port (1.9)" (p. 304); furthermore, the Ḥabašites invaded Ḥaḍramawt after Šaʿirum ʾAwtarʾs campaign in that country (p. 302).

The reading of *q[n]ʾ* in line 4 is excluded, as indicated above, by the epigraphical study of that part of the photograph; it is also excluded on grounds of content. The text clearly indicates that the military expedition went from northwest to southeast, not only because of the expressions *(b)rydn*[100]*/ʿdy/hgrn/qn[ʾ]* (line 8) and *bʾrḍ [..]ʿ/ʿdy/bḥrn* (lines 11-12) but also because of the geographical position of the four tribes, Qatabân, Radmân, Muḏḥayum, and ʾAwsân, which were scattered from northwest to southeast. Since Qatabân is listed first among the four tribes attacked by Šaʿirum ʾAwtar, and Raydân is the starting point of the military expedition, it seems logical on the one hand to locate Raydân in Qatabân, and on the other to see in [..]ʿ a Qatabanian city, and not *[rd]ʿ*,[101] which was connected with Radmân, the second tribe in the list. Further, *ḥrmtm* can hardly be the ending point of the military expedition.[102] Why would the text give the number of the vessels in the harbor, 47? The city of *ḥrmtm* in connection with the tribe Bakîlum is also attested in Ja 578/8 and 34, where there is no question of a harbor. It was probably in fact located in the vicinity of Jebel ʾItwat.[103]

The reconstruction of the events related in Geukens 1 may be presented as follows. ʾAsadum ʾAsʿad, along with the Sab army which was residing

[98] Cf. commentary on Ja 664/20.

[99] Cf. *RyISA*, XII, pp. 297-308. In lines 15-16 and 31 of the text, the proper name *tl.m* is restored by J. Ryckmans as *tl[q]m*; cf. pp. 298, 299, 300, and 306-07 where the commentary does not refer to CIH 40/2, 3 and 4: *tlfm*. This form is also much more common in Arabic (cf. *MüHG*, II, p. 20, and *HaAI*, p. 25) than *tlṯm* (cf. *HaAI*, *l.c.*) and even more than *tlqm* (only a few manuscripts).

[100] *RyISA* reads *[m]rydn* (p. 298), *[m]rydn* (p. 299) and *mrydn* (p. 304), where he writes, "La préposition *m* pour *mn*, cf. Ry 510, 4: *mhnsbʾtn*, «au sujet de ces campagnes»; voir les autres références dans le commentaire de ce passage". For *mhn*, demonstrative pronoun in Wâdî Maʾsil 2/4, and also for the texts referred to, cf. *JaPDSM*, pp. 175-76.

[101] As suggested by J. Ryckmans, in *RyISA*, *l.c.*, p. 305.

[102] As *RyISA*, *l.c.*, p. 304.

[103] Cf. *HaAI*, p. 66; for Jebel ʾItwat, cf. *WiHöBGS*. p. 18.

in the district of the town of al-Qâᶜ (?),[104] and also along with his associate Rabîbum ᵓAẖṯar, went "from this city" (*bnhyt/hgrn*; line 5) to fight with their king against the tribes Qatabân, Radmân, Muḏḥayum, and ᵓAwsân, setting out from the Qatabanian city of [..]ᶜ. A contingent from the tribe Bakîlum, to which both ᵓAsadum ᵓAsᶜad and Rabîbum ᵓAẖṯar belonged, also took part in the fighting as well as in the rest of the expedition until all of them reached Qanaᵓ on the sea. The Bakîlite fighters joined ᵓAsadum ᵓAsᶜad, Rabîbum ᵓAẖṯar and their companions (*lfẖrhmw*; line 8) in order to head back home together until they arrived (*ymẓw*; line 8) in the city of Ḥurmatum, bringing back a great quantity of booty packed in 47 trunks,[105] and which had been given to them as a reward for their collaboration. Then, Rabîbum ᵓAẖṯar, of higher rank than his associate ᵓAsadum ᵓAsᶜad, was received[106] in ?.[107] The country of ᵓAsadum ᵓAsᶜad had to suffer from the Ḥabašites *bk⌜n⌝[/s]bᵓw/bᶜly/ḥḏrmt/bqdmy/ḏt/hqnytn* "when they fought against Ḥaḍramawt, prior to the present offering" (lines 21-22). The plural subject of *sbᵓw*, as well as the plural pronoun *hmw* in *mṣnᶜhmw*, refer to the author of the text and his companions, who also took part in Šaᶜirum ᵓAwtar's campaign against Ḥaḍramawt. The preceding information indicates another complication during the Ḥaḍr campaign. As is already known, the tribe Radmân attacked the camps of the Sab king and of his two armies; on their side, the Ḥabašites attacked northwards. The latter will be the object of the next military campaign of Šaᶜirum ᵓAwtar.

3° – *Third campaign:* The Ḥabašites; Ja 631, 633; NaNN 43

The Ḥabašite attack against the north of Sabaᵓ, perpetrated during the Sab campaign against Ḥaḍramawt, was more than a local expedition from southwestern Arabian Ḥabašat, but was a consequence of an invasion from African Ḥabašites[108]; all those attacks are mentioned in line 7: *bn/ḏbḥrm/wybsm* "by sea and land". Obviously enough, the Sab king had to take action against the Ḥabašite threat. The action taken by Šaᶜirum ᵓAwtar is divided into three phases, the first two of which are recounted by Qaṭbân ᵓAwkân who, along with his tribe Sumhurâm Yuhawlid, took part in them; the last one is to be assumed from Ja 633.

The first phase (lines 11-16) refers to an expedition in the land of Gadarat, king of Ḥabašat and of ᵓAksûman (line 13), also called Neguš (line 15). Qaṭbân ᵓAwkân and his tribe came back with "all their train" (line 14) after completing to their king's satisfaction all the military duties imposed upon them by Šaᶜirum ᵓAwtar (lines 14-16).

The second phase (lines 16-36) is an expedition which expanded from Naᶜiḍ to Ẓafâr against "Baygat, the child of the Neguš, and the expeditionary forces of the Ḥabašites" (line 21), because these Ḥabašites had occupied Ẓafâr as well as the neighboring country (lines 21-22). Through some artifice executed during the night, Qaṭbân ᵓAwkân and his tribe Sumhurâm Yuhawlid infiltrated in Ẓafâr, and more precisely in Qatr Waᶜd, which probably was a quarter of the city (lines 22-24). This first success had two major consequences. The Ḥabašites concentrated their troops in the citadel, in the center of the city (lines 24-25), and the Sab made connection with Liᶜazzum Yuhnaf Yuhaṣdiq, the provincial king of Sabaᵓ and Raydân (lines 25-27). The effect of this reunion of Sab and Ḥimyarite forces was the defeat of the Ḥabašites and their withdrawal from the center of the city (lines 27-28). Then, the night following the third day after this first success, a part of each of the two forces took the hamlets of the Ḥabašites by surprise and beheaded 400 soldiers (lines 28-31). Three days later, a hemming-in attack of Qaṭbân ᵓAwkân and his tribe scattered the Ḥabašites in Maᶜâfirum (lines 31-33) (region about 150 km. northwest of ᶜAden[109]). The latter gathered together again in their encampments (line 34) but famished, the second day, they withdrew from the country of Ẓafâr into Maᶜâhiratân, probably the main city of Maᶜâhir. The record of this double campaign against the Ḥabašites is immediately followed by the petition to ᵓIlumquh to secure the author of the text and his companions the esteem and the grace of their lord Lahayᶜaṯat Yarẖam, the provincial king of Sabaᵓ and Raydân (lines 36-38).

The preceding record of the Sab expedition

[104] Cf. remarks on p. 299 B. Whatever the name of that city may be, this town was located in the northwest.

[105] The nouns *śdq* and *flk* (line 9) probably indicate trunks and chests of different form or size. *RyISA* (*l.c.*, pp. 300 and 304-05) considers them as small boats, as a consequence of his assumption of *ḥrmtm* as a city harbor.

[106] For the verb *wkb*, cf. commentary on Ja 567/11.

[107] The connection between lines 20 and 21 is unknown; cf. above, p. 299 B.

[108] Cf. *WiHöBGS*, p. 119, note 3.

[109] Cf. A. Grohmann, in *RhAST*, I, p. 120 and map.

against Ḥabašat and the Ḥabašites involves several questions which need to be studied.

1 – The expression *wld/ngšyn* "the child of the king of Ethiopia", qualifying Baygat, the commanding officer of the Ḥabašite expeditionary forces, indicates the relationship son-father, because of the other expression *ᶜqb/ngšyn* (Ja 577/10) "the representative of the king of Ethiopia".

2 – A very important question is whether Šaᶜirum ᵓAwtar actually invaded African Ḥabašat or not. It seems rather strange at first sight that such an important expedition is described so briefly and without any details, contrasting with the well-described second expedition which apparently was sent only to liberate Ẓafâr from the Ḥabašite occupation, and not to destroy the Ḥabašite power. As a matter of fact, the description of the second expedition seems to be the main purpose of the text because of the major role played by the author of the text and his tribe; therefore, the first expedition could be summarized. Further, the expression *ᶜdy/ᵓrḍ/ḥbšt*, connected with the full title of Gadarat, "king of Ḥabašat and of ᵓAksûman", indicates African Ḥabašat, especially if compared with *mṣr/ᵓḥbšn* "the expeditionary force of the Ḥabašites" under the command of Baygat, which was operating in South Arabia. The next question connected with such an expedition abroad is where the Sab troops embarked. The solution of that question depends on the relative chronology of the two phases of Šaᶜirum ᵓAwtar's action against Ḥabašat. There is not the slightest reason to doubt the relative chronology given by Ja 631, and all the more since the second phase aimed only at the liberation of Ẓafâr. Further, *bkn/sbᵓw/whᶜnn/–/bn/hgrn/nᶜḍ ᶜdy/hgrn/ẓfr* (lines 18-20) might suggest that some of Baygat's force went as far north as Naᶜiḍ, but this city may also be understood as the starting point of the Sab troops. In any event, the presence of Baygat's expeditionary force in the southwest suggests al-Ḥudaydat as the harbor for the embarkation of the Sab troops, and that Naᶜiḍ could have been the point where the Sab armies separated in two directions: one part going to Ḥabašat through al-Ḥudaydat against Gadarat, and the other to Ẓafâr against Baygat.

3 – The questions related to the mention of the two Sab kings listed in lines 26 and 37, as contemporaries of Šaᶜirum ᵓAwtar, are of such importance that they will be treated separately in the last part of the present chapter.

[110] Cf. *SpAGA*, pp. 250 and 274.

4 – NaNN 43 refers probably to the second phase of the expedition against the Ḥabašites, because of the mention both of the city of Ẓafâr and of the king Šaᶜirum ᵓAwtar.

The third phase of the campaign is to be assumed from Ja 633. ᵓAbkarib ᵓAḥras offers his god ᵓIlumquh a statue in bronze at the request of the god because of the help received in connection with a physical oppression after his return from *lḥgm* (line 6), where he had been in charge of the Ḥimyarites "between the two armies" (line 8). The mention of the place *lḥgm*, which is Laḥej (about 35 km. northwest of ᶜAden; known because of its dam and its Qat population[110]), connected with that of the Ḥimyarites, excludes any relation of the text with Šaᶜirum ᵓAwtar's first two campaigns, but suggests that the second phase of the third was followed by a third one, farther south. However, what is referred to by the expression *ḏkwnw/byn/ḫmsnhn* is not clear. One could think of the following interpretation: the two armies (probably one Sab, and one Ḥimyarite, exactly as in the first campaign) were separated from each other, and ᵓAbkarib ᵓAḥras was put in command of the Ḥimyarite population living between the two armies in order to coordinate and supervise their collaboration with both armies especially with regard to food and water supply.

4° – *Fourth campaign:* northwest of Mârib; Ja 634 and 635

The beginning of Ja 635 alludes to attacks against the king Šaᶜirum ᵓAwtar "from south and from north and from sea and land" (lines 12-13); such an expression is a summary of all the preceding events and therefore suggests that the campaign northwest of Mârib was the last one.

This campaign is divided into four phases; in the first three, Šaᶜirum ᵓAwtar is the leader and is accompanied by the author of the text; in the last one, the latter is in command, apparently without the presence of his king.

In the *first phase* (lines 16-23), Šaᶜirum ᵓAwtar is fighting in Saharatum, a district located southwest of Jîzân,[111] against the two tribes ᵓAšᶜarân and Baḥrum. The first tribe was, in antiquity, scattered along the west coast from Jîzân down to Bâb el-Mandeb,[112] but was apparently restricted to the district of Maᶜâfir at the time of Hamdânî.[113] Baḥrum is mentioned by *MüHG* (114/20-21)

[111] Cf. *JaASAB*, p. 161, commentary on CIH 407/18-19.
[112] Cf. *SpAGA*, p. 63.
[113] Cf. *MüHG*, 53/25-54/1.

as a part of the tribe Rabî^c^at. The location of Baḥrum and also of the fraction of ʾAšʿarân attacked by Šaʿirum ʾAwtar is to be sought east of Jîzân, since they are closely connected in a campaign mentioning Najrân and Qaḥṭân.

In the *second phase* (lines 23-25) of his military campaign, Šaʿirum ʾAwtar went eastward in the district of Najrân against the Ḥabašite forces and their collaborators.

In the *third phase* (lines 25-28), the Sab king came back westward against the city of Qaryatum of Kahilum, and battled twice against Rabîʿat of ʾIlṯawrum, king of Kindat and of Qaḥṭân, and also against the masters of the city of Qaryatum. Qaḥṭân is a country northeast of Jîzân.[114] Kahilum might have survived in Kahal, the name of one of the two peaks of the Jabalain ridge, west of the two ʾAkwat cones, located about 15 km. northwest of Ṣabyâ.[115] The city of Qaryatum, located somewhere in that country, was plundered by Sabaeans since a statue is offered to ʾIlumquh from the booty from that city (Ja 634 and 641).

The *fourth phase* (lines 28-39) is headed by the author of the text, ʾAbkarib ʾAḥras, who was put in command (probably as a reward for his performance during the preceding phase) of some of Ḫawlân Ḫaḍlum, Najrân and Bedouin Arabs[116] in order to punish the seductors of Jaw[.]um and Qaryatum; and ʾAbkarib ʾAḥras fought them at the border of the country of ʾIlsaʿad Magûzat Mawnahân of Ṯimâl. The Ṯimala range and well described by *PhAHL* (pp. 26, 31, and 109), located about 350 km. northwest of ʾUḫdûd, could be too far in the north. Note, however, that the tribe Ḫawlân occupies a territory about 110 km. northeast of Jîzân and 130 northwest of ʾUḫdûd.

5° – *Fifth campaign:* East Ḥaḍramawt; Ja 640; and mention of his brother Ḥayûʿaṯtar Yaḍiʿ

The only one text yet known, related to Šaʿirum ʾAwtar's sole reign with the mention of his brother Ḥayûʿaṯtar Yaḍiʿ, is the dedicatory inscription Ja 640. In spite of its fragmentary condition, this text is very valuable because of the mention of the city of ʾ*wsrn*,[117] which is "*Αὔσαρα*... Ghaytza",[118] presently the coastal town of Ġayẓat, about 220 km. southwest of Rîsût.[119] The king Šaʿirum ʾAwtar had to go back to the Saʾkalite country to aid the Ḥaḍr king ʾIlʿazz against the Ḥaḍr tribes. Although the text remains silent concerning the course of this rebellion, one might easily assume that some of the Ḥaḍr tribes resented the collaboration of their own king with the Sab invader who had defeated him possibly only a few months previously. Did this Sab expedition occur before the selection of Ḥayûʿaṯtar Yaḍiʿ as future coregent or not? Both hypotheses are equally possible. On the one hand, the text was, obviously enough, written after the return to Mârib of the authors of Ja 640, and the new appointment could have preceded the engraving of the text; according to this hypothesis, Ḥayûʿaṯtar Yaḍiʿ had to be mentioned in the final invocation. On the other hand, if the king's brother was already selected at the time of the campaign, it is no less obvious that the king alone was the leader and especially in military affairs; in this hypothesis, Ḥayûʿaṯtar Yaḍiʿ did not need to be mentioned in relation to the campaign.

2 – *Coregency with his brother Ḥayûʿaṯtar Yaḍiʿ:* CIH 408; Ja 641; RÉS 4842

After a certain period of time and because of reasons still unknown to us, the king Šaʿirum ʾAwtar associated his brother Ḥayûʿaṯtar Yaḍiʿ in the kingship. The most important text related to this coregency is Ja 641, because lines 12-14 present the two royal persons as actually being brothers, and not merely as allies (*wʾḫyhw*), since they are given as *bny/ʿlhn/nhfn* "the two sons of ʿAlhân Nahfân". The main fact recorded in the text is the offering of a statue from the booty taken back from Qaryatum, a city which had been raided during the fourth expedition of Šaʿirum ʾAwtar. This text is another example of a protracted delay before making an offering after an expedition.

The dedicatory text RÉS 4842 refers to all the expeditions which the author, Rabîʿat, made with his king Šaʿirum ʾAwtar. It is not possible to determine which expeditions are alluded to in the text.

[114] Cf. map of Qizan, and also map by W. Thesiger.

[115] Cf. *PhAHL*, p. 651, and map of Qizan.

[116] Cf. *WiHöBGS*, p. 119, end of note 3.

[117] According to my field book, the upper extremity of ʾ is missing; the letter *ṣ* could thus at first sight be restored. However, the reading of *ṣwʾrn* (CIH 334/18), although very attractive because of the events recorded in CIH 334, is excluded by the third letter which is *s* according to my field book.

[118] Cf. *SpAGA*, p. 93.

[119] Cf. map of Bahr as-Safi.

The third text related to this coregency is CIH 408, which records an offering made as a consequence of several favors received, the first of them being that its authors were granted the esteem of their two kings.

After the above-described coregency, the Bataᶜ-ite-Hamdânid dynasty of Yarum ᵓAyman vanished for reasons still unknown to us.

G – ḤAḌRAMI DYNASTIC SYNCHRONISMS

The Ḥaḍr synchronisms mentioned in the texts dealing with Yarum ᵓAyman's dynasty may be summarized as follows.

The two Sab kings ᶜAlhân Nahfân and his son Šaᶜirum ᵓAwtar are allied with the Ḥaḍr king Yadaᶜᵓab Ġaylân (CIH 155); the latter, however, soon disappears, since a governor of Mârib begs his god for an alliance with the new Ḥaḍr king Yadaᶜᵓil (NaNN 19). These two Ḥaḍr kings may be identified with Yadaᶜᵓab Ġaylân[120] and his son Yadaᶜᵓil[121] Bayyin, known from RÉS 4698/1-2, where their father and grandfather respectively is mentioned as ᵓUmaynum. Then, Šaᶜirum ᵓAwtar during his sole reign fought and defeated the Ḥaḍr king ᵓIlᶜazz (CIH 334), and during his coregency with his brother Ḥayûᶜaṯtar Yaḍiᶜ, had to go back to Ḥaḍramawt in order to help ᵓIlᶜazz in local affairs (Ja 640). This Ḥaḍr king ᵓIlᶜazz is not to be identified with ᵓIlᶜazz[122] or ᵓIlᶜa<u>dd</u>[123] Yaluṭ son of ᶜAmmḏaḫar, because the latter is explicitly mentioned by two Ḥimyarites as the contemporary and ally of Ṯaᵓrân Yaᶜûb Yuhanᶜim, king of Sabaᵓ and Raydân[124] (RÉS 4909/5-6).

H – RELATION BETWEEN THE DYNASTY OF YARUM ᵓAYMAN AND THAT OF FARIᶜUM YANHUB

The question of the relation between Yarum ᵓAyman's and Fariᶜum Yanhub's dynasties was raised by CIH 398. The importance of this dedicatory inscription comes from the mention both of the king Šaᶜirum ᵓAwtar in connection with the record of some *past* event, and of the two kings ᵓIlšaraḥ Yaḥḍub and his brother Yaᵓzil Bayyin in the prayer for the *future* addressed to the deity. This double feature has been variously understood.

Already in 1895, *GlAAA* (p. 83) published what may be called the common opinion which was accepted, e.g., by *HoGSA* (pp. 90-91). *GlAAA* writes: "Aber die Gleichzeitigkeit der Söhne des Fâriᵓ Janhab mit den Söhnen des ᵓAlhân Nahfân, also auch die Gleichzeitigkeit ᵓAlhâns und Fâriᵓs selbst gehen unzweideutig aus dieser Inschrift hervor. ᵓAlhân Nahfân und Fâriᵓ Janhab waren somit Gegenkönige oder Rivalen".

However, one year earlier than F. Hommel's acceptance of the preceding opinion, *RhASI* (p. 468) had suggested another interpretation of that information, according to which the period of the two royal brothers (to which the text belongs) actually followed the reign of Šaᶜirum ᵓAwtar. There is thus no longer any contemporaneity. However, the author does not explain how he solves several obvious difficulties.

N. Rhodokanakis's interpretation is considered as "pas plausible" by *RycIMAM* (p. 297), who holds, though with varying degrees of confidence,[125] that the three kings mentioned are contemporaneous. Almost at the same time, but independently, *WiHöBGS* affirm the same contemporaneity, but without entering into discussion of the problem.[126] A year later, *BePSC* (p. 53) disturbs the whole historical perspective by stating "the existence of two parallel lines of kings, reigning simultaneously", on the one hand Yarum ᵓAyman's dynasty and, on the other, both Wahabᵓil Yaḥûz's and Fariᶜum Yanhub's dynasties. It is not easy to determine exactly how this author reconstructs the simultaneous kings' lines in the question now under study because he also states (p. 52) that it was ᵓIlšaraḥ Yaḥḍub who inaugurated the new royal title *mlk/sbᵓ/w<u>d</u>rydn*, when he acceded to the throne.

Finally, J. Pirenne only refers to *RycIMAM*'s

[120] Two other kings bearing the name of Yadaᶜᵓab Ġaylân are known. One is son of Ġaylân (WB 1-3 alluded to by *AlCAS*, p. 10, and also M 508, an inscription discovered at Ḥôr Rôrî by F. P. Albright); the other is son of Yadaᶜᵓil Bayyin (RÉS 4915) and brother of Rabbšams (RÉS 4916).

[121] Yadaᶜᵓil is a name frequently attested in Ḥaḍr dynasties. At the present time, all the Ḥaḍr kings who have had *ydᶜᵓl* as first name, have *byn* as second: the son of Sumhuya[faᶜ] in RÉS 3869, the son of Rabbšams (e.g., RÉS 4871), and the father of Yadaᶜᵓab Ġaylân (RÉS 4915).

[122] In all Sab inscriptions: CIH 334/4, Ja 640/4, and RÉS 3958/8.

[123] In all Ḥaḍr texts: e.g., RÉS 4852/5.

[124] Cf. p. 384 A.

[125] The opinion, first introduced by the following restriction "si, comme nous le pensons" (p. 298), becomes certain on p. 302 (cf. also p. 155). Later, the same author states that "ces deux rois [ᵓIlšaraḥ Yaḥḍub and Šaᶜirum ᵓAwtar] peuvent donc être considérés comme contemporains" (cf. *RycCSAPS*, p. 208 A).

[126] Cf. pp. 20, note 1, 33 and 38.

opinion and declares it to be definitely certain.[127] One must note that, according to all the preceding authors, the three kings mentioned would be reigning *at the same time in Mârib*.

Since the problem of CIH 398 must be studied in the light of another text that was unknown to the preceding authors, the discussion of *RycIMAM*'s (pp. 298-99) argumentation against N. Rhodokanakis may safely be omitted. The comparative study of both CIH 398 and Ja 631 is best indicated by presenting their common features in the following scheme:

CIH 398	Ja 631
authors:	
several Ṣirwâḥites[128] who call themselves ᵓ*dm/mlk*[*n*] "servants of [the] king".	some Garatites of the tribe Sumhurâm Yuhawlid.
PAST *event:*	
with the double mention of the king Šaᶜirum ᵓAwtar, who is introduced by *mr*ᵓ*hm*[*w*] (lines 7-8) and [*mr*ᵓ]*hw* (line 9).	with several mentions of the king Šaᶜirum ᵓAwtar, who is introduced every time by *mr*ᵓ*hmw* (lines 6, 10, 12, and 14).
	with the preceding king, they rescued Liᶜazzum Yuhnaf Yuhaṣdiq, king of Sabaᵓ and Raydân (lines 26-27) who was besieged in the city of Ẓafâr. This king is *not* introduced by *mr*ᵓ*hmw*.
PETITION TO THE GOD *for ḥẓy/wrḍw*	
*mr*ᵓ*yhmw* ᵓIlšaraḥ Yaḥḍub and his brother Yaᵓzil Bayyin, the two kings of Sabaᵓ and Raydân (lines 14-16).	*mr*ᵓ*hmw* Laḥayᶜaṯat Yarḫam, king of Sabaᵓ and Raydân (lines 37-38).

There cannot be any doubt about the fact that Liᶜazzum Yuhnaf Yuhaṣdiq mentioned in Ja 631, was the provincial king of Ẓafâr where he was besieged by the Ḥabašites and later rescued by Šaᶜirum ᵓAwtar and his troops. The authors of the text are not the subjects of that provincial king; the latter is thus not introduced by the title *mr*ᵓ*hmw* "their lord". They were rather subjects of the other provincial king, Laḥayᶜaṯat Yarḫam, whose kingdom most probably was located at the northern border of that of Ẓafâr because the Garatites and the tribe Sumhurâm Yuhawlid were called to join the Sab army from Mârib. On the basis of that parallel then the two brothers ᵓIlšaraḥ Yaḥḍub and Yaᵓzil Bayyin of CIH 398 were also provincial kings in Ṣirwâḥ. This information solves the problem of the relationship between Yarum ᵓAyman's dynasty and that of Fariᶜum Yanhub in a most satisfactory way.

There is thus contemporaneity between the main king in Mârib and the other kings, but also subordination of the latter to the former, and no equality and independence.

Characteristic of the above described historical situation is the identity of royal title borne by all the kings, whether main or provincial. The true explanation of such a historical feature remains unknown. It is, however, not impossible that it might be explained as a concession granted by the main king in Mârib in order to secure strong ties between himself and his provincial subordinates. It is nevertheless certain that, in case of a provincial kingdom composed of several adjacent districts and different tribal elements, the above-mentioned feature was the simplest way of solving the question of the title which, otherwise, would have had to list the different tribes included in the recently formed kingdom, as in the case of the rulers of the southern part of the Sab kingdom toward the end of Yasrum Yuhanᶜim's dynasty.

Fariᶜum Yanhub founded a provincial dynasty in a country located west of Mârib, and was succeeded by his two sons who, after the disappearance of the two coregents Šaᶜirum ᵓAwtar and his brother Ḥayûᶜaṯtar Yadiᶜ, succeed in mounting the throne in Mârib, thus leaving their provincial kingdom for the kingship of Sabaᵓ as a whole.

I – SOME EPONYMS FROM THE CLAN FAḌḤUM

The continuity of the administration through the change of dynasty seems to be indicated by comparing Fakhry 71 with Ja 610, on the basis of the

[127] Cf. *PiPISA*, p. 44, and *PiIRC* (p. 180): "M. J. Ryckmans a en effet bien établi...".

[128] Not at all, either "un personnage" or "un 'ᵓ*dm* du roi'", as stated by *RycIMAM*, pp. 192 and 296, respectively.

results arrived at in the preceding section of the present chapter.

Fakhry 71 was engraved during the fourth year of the eponym Maʿadkarib, son of [Su]mhukarib (lines 14-15), and during ʿAlhân Nahfân's sole reign. The eponym ʾAbkarib in Ja 633/14, which belongs to Šaʿirum ʾAwtar's sole reign, is the son of [...]adkarib (line 17); the latter may thus be identified with the above-mentioned Maʿadkarib. Further, the eponym Našaʾkarib in Ja 610/6, which dates to Našaʾkarib Yu(ha)ʾmin Yuharḥib, is the son of Maʿadkarib, and could very well be a youngest son of Maʿadkarib in Fakhry 71.

The preceding information may be presented in the following scheme:

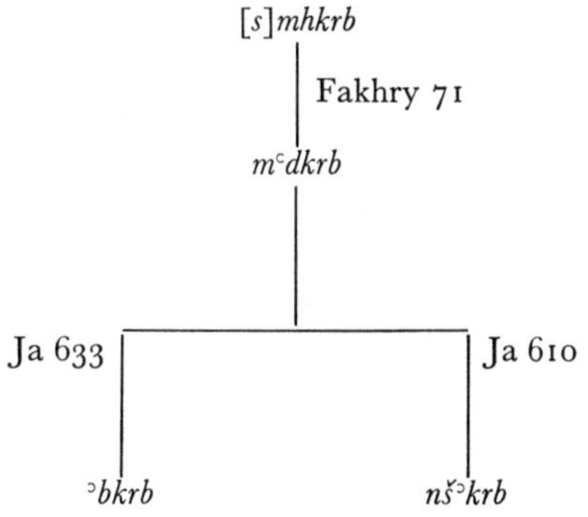

Chapter VI

THE T̲ANIATITE-HAMDÂNID DYNASTY OF FARIᶜUM YANHUB

(cf. map on Plate G)

CIH 10, 24, 69, 135, 140, 141, 145, 172+241, 257, 258, 299, 314+954, 398, 429; Fakhry 3, 76, 95+94, 123; Geukens 4, 6, 9; HC 12; Ist 7627, 7628; Ja 115, 566, 567, 568, 569, 570, 571, 572, 574, 575, 576, 577, 578, 579, 580, 581, 582, 583, 584, 585, 586, 587, 588, 589, 590, 591, 592, 594, 595, 597, 598, 599, 600, 601, 602, 603, 604, 605, 606, 607, 608, 609, 610, 611, 612, 613, 614, 615, 616, 617, 618, 619, 620, 621, 623, 624, 625, 626, 627, 628, 629, 630, 684, 711, 718, 739, 753, 758, 877; NaNAG 5, 8; NaNN 24, 59; RÉS 314, 2695, 3563, 3929, 3968, 3990, 4134, 4136, 4139, 4150, 4191, 4215, 4233, 4336, 4646, 4729, and 4962

A – CAREER OF FARIᶜUM YANHUB

The dynasty founded by Fariᶜum Yanhub is undoubtedly the most illustrious among South-Arabian dynasties, not only because of the number of its members, but especially because of the glorious ᵓIlšaraḥ Yaḥḍub whose reign is known through so many important inscriptions.

1 – *Origin of Fariᶜum Yanhub's Family*

The dynasty initiated by Fariᶜum Yanhub is referred to as being Bakîlite[1] or Mart̲adite[2] because of the identification of ᵓIlšaraḥ Yaḥḍub of the clan Mart̲adum of the tribe Bakîlum with ᵓIlšaraḥ Yaḥḍub, son of Fariᶜum Yanhub.[3] The preceding statement involves three different questions intimately connected with one another, namely the origin of ᵓIlšaraḥ Yaḥḍub I, his relationship to ᵓIlšaraḥ Yaḥḍub II, and finally Fariᶜum Yanhub's origin.

As regards the origin of ᵓIlšaraḥ Yaḥḍub I, it is necessary to stress that – as has already been pointed out in relation to the family of Yarum ᵓAyman – the clan which a person commanded was not necessarily his clan of origin. ᵓIlšaraḥ Yaḥḍub I is not presented as a Mart̲adite but as *kbr/ᵓqynm* (CIH 140/2) and *k*(*b*)[*r/ᵓqy*]*nm/wbn/mrt̲*(*d*)[*m*] (CIH 141/1-2),[4] that is to say as "Leader of ᵓAqyânum and of (the clan) Mart̲a(d)[um]." Were the clan which ᵓIlšaraḥ Yaḥḍub I commanded that of his origin, it would be illogical to call him a Mart̲adite, since he is mentioned twice as *kbr/ᵓqynm* and only once – and in second place – as leader of the clan Mart̲adum.

On the other hand, no one text related to ᵓIlšaraḥ Yaḥḍub I (CIH 135, 140, 141, and 145) ever mentions any relationship with a royal family[5]; the deity honored in CIH 140 is Rummân and that of Ilšaraḥ Yaḥḍub II after becoming king is ᵓIlumquh.[6] These two remarks could at first sight be understood as disproving the identification of the two ᵓIlšaraḥ Yaḥḍub's; as a matter of fact, the first can easily be explained by epigraphical material, and the second is irrelevant.

Up to the present time, only one text is beyond any doubt related to Fariᶜum Yanhub's reign,

[1] E.g., *BePSC*, p. 53 and *BeFSTI*, p. 276.
[2] Cf. *RhKTB*, II, p. 75, note 5.
[3] E.g., *RycIMAM*, p. 295.
[4] Cf. *RhKTB*, II, p. 71, note 3.
[5] Cf. *HaAF*, p. 282, note 2.
[6] Cf. *HaAF*, p. 231.

Ja 566, where the royal title already includes the names of the two sons of the king. It is therefore very plausible that Fariᶜum Yanhub became king when he was advanced in years – that is to say, he had a short reign – and that, shortly after his coronation, he took to himself as aids his two sons. But then, ᵓIlšaraḥ Yaḥḍub could have been *kbr* "leader" before his father became king; and in this case, ᵓIlšaraḥ Yaḥḍub could not possibly have mentioned his relationship with any royal family.

The objection taken from the difference of deities is entirely irrelevant, for the author of CIH 140, and thus the worshipper of Rummân, is not ᵓIlšaraḥ Yaḥḍub,[7] but his *mqtwy* "military official". Why should a servant have the same preferred deity as his master?

Finally, the name of ᵓIlšaraḥ Yaḥḍub is so unique that two persons bearing it and mentioned in texts which belong to the same palaeographical style, should be identified; and such an identification need not be based on a fragile argumentation such as follows: once king, ᵓIlšaraḥ Yaḥḍub had very friendly relations with the clan Marṯadum.[8] These ties could indeed have had an entirely different origin.

Ja 566 also provides another common point with the texts discovered in Šibâm ᵓAqyân, and in doing so, sheds a very interesting light on the origin of Fariᶜum Yanhub's family. The main author of the text is *rgly/mlkn* "the orderly of the king", and belongs to the clan Ṯaniat (lines 3-4). Since it is natural to believe that the king would preferably select his orderly from his own clan of origin, it seems logical to speak of the Ṯaniatite-Hamdânid dynasty of Fariᶜum Yanhub. Furthermore, the clan Ṯaniat apparently inhabited the country of Šibâm ᵓAqyân (CIH 144); the country of Kawkabân (northwest of Ṣanᶜâᵓ) [9] was thus a part of Fariᶜum Yanhub's kingdom. With regard to the clan Ṯaniat, it is not impossible that it originated from the country surrounding the present Ṯaniya Ridge, the southern end of which is about 55 km. northwest of Šabwat,[10] and that a part of it moved into the country of Šibâm ᵓAqyân some time before Fariᶜum Yanhub became king. This hypothesis seems all the more attractive in that the god Rummân, whose name is the epithet of the north-Semitic god Hadad,[11] is hardly to be expected in the Hamdânid pantheon; his introduction is reasonably explained by the moving-in of a foreign clan.

2 – *Reign of the Provincial King Fariᶜum Yanhub:* Ja 566; CIH 299; NaNN 59

Several details concerning Fariᶜum Yanhub's reign are related in the preceding inquiry about the origin of his family; a few more should be mentioned here.

The very fragmentary inscription CIH 299 could easily be related to Fariᶜum Yanhub's reign; as a matter of fact, there is no reason against the preceding hypothesis.[12] Unfortunately, this text only alludes to fightings and wars. This inscription is certainly anterior to Ja 566, because it does not mention any name of a presumptive heir. The first and only text which is undoubtedly related to Fariᶜum Yanhub's reign is Ja 566. Although very short and containing no historical information concerning military operations and alliances, the text dates from the last period of Fariᶜum Yanhub's reign (cf. the singular nouns *mrᵓ* in line 8, and *mlk* in line 10), for the royal title includes the names of his two sons ᵓIlšaraḥ Yaḥḍub and Yaᵓzil, the first being the heir presumptive and the second a simple partaker in some royal duties.[13] This last detail is very important, because it indicates that Fariᶜum Yanhub himself had already decided upon the coregency of his two sons.

Finally, the very fragmentary text NaNN 59 (from Nâᶜiṭ) which refers to the remodeling of a house, could also be related to Fariᶜum Yanhub's reign. However, *NaNN* (pp. 76 and 77) restores *bny* before */frᶜ]m/ynhb/mlk/sbᵓ/–* (line 3), and *RycIMAM* (p. 105, note 8) goes so far as to present the preceding restoration as certain. Yet no reason is given in support of such a restoration. The only clue that could lead to a solution is the mention of the clan names *sᵓ]rn/wmḫylm* (line 1). Individuals belonging to that clan are also attested in Ja 572 (period of ᵓIlšaraḥ Yaḥḍub alone). CIH 314+954, Ja 578, RÉS 4139 (the three to the coregency of ᵓIlšaraḥ Yaḥḍub and his brother), Ja 632 (Šaᶜirum ᵓAwtar's reign), and finally

[7] As, e.g., *CIH*, I, p. 206.

[8] Cf. *RhKTB*, *l.c.*, note 4.

[9] It is possibly on the basis of this information that *PiIRC* writes: that this dynasty is "issue de la région de Ṣanᶜā, comme j'aurai l'occasion de le montrer ailleurs" (p. 168). Her study is still unpublished.

[10] Cf. *PhSD*, especially pp. 363-67, and map.

[11] Cf. *JaP*, pp. 143-44, and *JaRSAP*, p. 274.

[12] *RycIMAM* (p. 105, note 8) presents without any supporting remarks his opinion according to which CIH 299 is doubtfully related to ᵓIlšaraḥ Yaḥḍub and Yaᵓzil Bayyin.

[13] Cf. *JaPSAP*, p. 171.

CIH 282, which does not contain any royal name, but has in common with NaNN 59 the name of the divinity Samîʿ. The ascription of NaNN 59 to Fariʿum Yanhub's reign is thus possible, and there is no reason for imposing the restoration of the name of the two royal brothers.

The research on CIH 398 and Ja 631 led to the discovery of three provincial kingdoms at the time of Šaʿirum ʾAwtar's sole reign: one around Ẓafâr, the other immediately north of the preceding, and the third one west of Mârib, that of the two sons of Fariʿum Yanhub. The information gathered up to the present indicates that Fariʿum Yanhub's provincial kingdom extended west of Mârib, including the countries of Ṣirwâḥ and Ṣanʿâʾ, as well as the area south of Ṣirwâḥ. Because of his title *mlk/sbʾ*, Fariʿum Yanhub began to reign during ʿAlhân Nahfân's sole reign or even during the latter's coregency with his son Šaʿirum ʾAwtar.

It now remains to elucidate an objection against the above-proposed location of Fariʿum Yanhub's kingdom, namely the preference given to CIH 144 rather than to Ja 566. It seems more plausible to admit that an ordinary person engraved an inscription in the very place where his clan was dwelling, rather than to locate the site of a clan on the basis of an inscription written by a member of that clan, who was "the orderly of the king", because the second inscription could easily have been engraved during a trip made by his king to the capital city of Mârib.

B – CAREER OF ʾILŠARAḤ YAḤḎUB[14]

The career of ʾIlšaraḥ Yaḥḏub may be divided into two major periods: before becoming king, and his reign.

1 – *Before becoming provincial king:*
CIH 135, 140, 141, 145; RÉS 314

CIH 135, 140, 141, and 145, all of them found in the city of Šibâm ʾAqyân, are apparently related to the same period of ʾIlšaraḥ Yaḥḏub's career, when he was *kbr/ʾqynm* (CIH 140/2) */wbn/mrṯ(d)[m]* (CIH 141/1-2) in that city.[15]

CIH 135[16] only mentions an incomplete name; CIH 141 only states ʾIlšaraḥ Yaḥḏub's title as Leader of ʾAqyânum and of the clan Marṯadum. – CIH 145, which is not referred to by *RycIMAM* (p. 348), alludes to the building of some construction by some Yarumites, who speak of *ʾmrʾhmw*[17]*/ʾlšrḥ/yḥḏb[/* (line 4) "their lords ʾIlšaraḥ Yaḥḏub ..."; the missing part had the mention either of the clan Yarum[18] or the tribe to which the clan belonged. Another inscription to be referred to here is CIH 140[19] whose importance is considerably reduced because of the bad condition of the copy, which renders both the reading and the interpretation of a great part of the text uncertain.[20] A military official of ʾIlšaraḥ Yaḥḏub[21] offers to his god Rummân a statue because he was granted by Him war trophies and captives when he and his companions assisted their lord ʾIlšaraḥ Yaḥḏub in a battle that took place in the southern part of Ḫawlân,[22] a district lying west of Mârib.

The main question is who was fighting against whom? The answer to that question requires a discussion of E. Glaser's copy of the involved passage, which reads as follows:

line 4: *–/ṣdqmʾ..r....hmyrḏ/wr.m...*
line 5: *bn/ḥḏrmnlbhlf...../rḏ/.wln/–*

A few remarks are needed for the accurate understanding of the preceding transliteration. The ʾ after *ṣdqm*, and both the stippling of the circle at the bottom of *y* and the letter *ḏ* in *hmyrḏ*, are written much lighter than the rest of the copy; the bottom horizontal line of *ḏ* in *hmyrḏ* is missing; the space after ʾ..*r*, if compared with line 3, equals that of four characters and a half; in *r.m*, which may be followed by three signs, the point corresponds to a vertical stippling in E. Glaser's copy; between *hlf* and */rḏ*, if compared with line 3, at least five signs

[14] In spite of *MoMiSI*'s (p. 18, note 1) study of E. Glaser's squeeze, according to whom CIH 147/1 reads as follows: *y]šrḥʾl/ʾ[s]rʿ[/...]*, *RycIMAM* (p. 169 and note 4) still claims that this reference mentions *ʾlšrḥ/yḥḏb* with his title of *kbr/ʾqynm*. Yet, neither *yḥḏb* nor *kbr/ʾqynm* can possibly be read in this text. Note also that neither *MoMiSI* nor *RycIMAM* alludes to *CIH*'s correction (III, p. 333 A) of his first decipherment (I, p. 210).

[15] Cf. *WiHöBGS*, p. 18.

[16] *RycIMAM* (pp. 168 and note 1, 175 and note 2) simply relates the text to ʾIlšaraḥ Yaḥḏub's reign.

[17] *CIH* gratuitously introduces a word divider between ʾ and *mrʾhmw*.

[18] The lack of space disproves *CIH*'s restoration of *s* between *y* and *rm* in *yrm* (line 2).

[19] *RycIMAM* repeatedly refers CIH 140 to the period when ʾIlšaraḥ Yaḥḏub was not king (pp. 169, 185, 199-200, 295, and 300); yet, the same author dates the same text from the period of the kings of Sabaʾ and Raydân (p. 145 and note 13).

[20] Cf. also *HaAF*, p. 376.

[21] *HaAF* (p. 449) rightly remarks that the Hamdânid chiefs Naṣrum Yuhaʾmin and Ṣadiq [Yahub] also had *mqtt*.

[22] Cf. *l.c.*, p. 362.

may be restored; the vertical stroke in */rḏ* may belong to the right edge of ᵓ; finally, after *rḏ/*, E. Glaser's copy shows two upper vertical strokes which belong either to *h* or *ẖ*.

CIH restores the text as follows[23]:

line 4: *–/ṣdqm/b[d]r[/byn/]ḥmyrm/wr[d]m[n/w]*
line 5: *b[y]n/ḥḍrmt/bẖlf[/b]ᵓrḍ/ẖwln/–*

Therefore, *CIH* (I, p. 204 A) interprets the text as follows: ᵓIlšaraḥ Yaḥḍub supported by Ḥimyar and the latter's ally, the tribe of Radmân, fought against Ḥaḍramawt. *RycIMAM*'s interpretation of the military situation is rather difficult. He first (p. 185) repeats *CIH*'s opinion, but later, he affirms that "un chef militaire de ᵓIlšaraḥ. . . est en lutte contre Ḥimyar et sans doute aussi contre le Ḥaḍramawt (CIH 140)" (p. 300); on the other hand, "les opérations se déroulèrent en terre de H̲awlân" (p. 185), affirmation which apparently is identified with the following "les opérations commencées contre H̲awlân" (*l.c.*). The restorations of the text in support of *RycIMAM*'s second and fourth opinions are still unpublished.

Several remarks should be made regarding *CIH*'s restoration of the text. The blank in line 4 (between *r* and *hmyrd*) and that in line 5 (between *hlf* and */rd*), which is *wider* than the preceding, are surprisingly enough restored with five (*/byn/*) and six (*/. . ./b*) signs respectively. Further, the first word in E. Glaser's copy of line 5 is *bn*, which *CIH* gratuitously corrects to *b[y]n*, apparently because of the restored *byn* in line 4. Finally, an expression such as *bẖlf[/b]ᵓrḍ/ẖwln* is quite unusual; *ẖlf* was certainly followed by the name of a city since the name of the country follows immediately; the name of the city was composed probably of only three letters.

The restoration of the text such as presented below is no less probable or less hypothetical than any other attempt:

line 4: *–/ṣdqm(/b)[ᶜb]r[/mṣr/](ḥ)m(y)r(m)/ wr.m[. . .]*
line 5: *bn/ḥḍrm(t/)b(ẖ)lf[/. . ./b](ᵓ)rḍ/(ẖ)wln/–*

The translation reads as follows:

line 4: – perfect, (a)[gai]nst [the expeditionary force of] (Ḥi]m(ya)r(um) and of R.m[. . .]ites
line 5: from Ḥaḍram(awt), in the (co)untry of [. . ., in] the (l)and of (H̲a)wlân, –

[23] Cf. I, p. 205, with corrections in III, p. 332 B.

[24] *RycIMAM* (pp. 168 and note 1, 200 and note 5) refers RÉS 314 to the reign of ᵓIlšaraḥ Yaḥḍub without specifying what period; nor does he mention any particular reason for his choice.

According to the preceding restoration, CIH 140 would allude to a clash between ᵓIlšaraḥ Yaḥḍub and an expedition composed of Ḥimyarites and of R.m[. . .]ites from Ḥaḍramawt. In any event, on the basis of the preceding discussion of the text, one may consider as certain the fact that ᵓIlšaraḥ Yaḥḍub defeated an expedition involving some Ḥaḍr soldiers, in a battle which took place in the country of a southern H̲awlânite city. The role played by Ḥimyar remains uncertain, but was very probably hostile to Sabaᵓ; the clash was in all probability the result of the invasion of H̲awlân by Southerners.

Furthermore, the absence of any name of *mlk/sbᵓ* coupled with the fact that the clash took place in the southern part of H̲awlân, suggests that the military operation was local and not a part of a regular war, and also that H̲awlân and Kawkabân belonged to the same political division, that is to say, to Fariᶜum Yanhub's kingdom. But, where did the Ḥaḍr soldiers come from? This question is insoluble, since their allies – if any – remain unknown.

Finally, RÉS 314, which was found in the country of Yâfiᶜ (about 150 km. north of ᶜAden; thus about 90 km. south of H̲awlân), could very well allude to events which were consequent to those mentioned in CIH 140.[24]

2 – *His Reign*

The relative chronology of the different periods in ᵓIlšaraḥ Yaḥḍub's reign, such as presented below, is entirely new.

The main division is based on my interpretation of CIH 398, that is to say ᵓIlšaraḥ Yaḥḍub's reign as provincial king and, later, as main king in Mârib. The second part of his reign was reconstructed as follows by *RycIMAM* (pp. 295-96). ᵓIlšaraḥ Yaḥḍub started as sole ruler and later associated his son Watarum as heir presumptive; the latter's death is followed by the coregency of the king with his brother Yaᵓzil Bayyin,[25] to which Našaᵓkarib Yu(ha)ᵓmin Yuharḥib immediately succeeds.

The reconstruction of ᵓIlšaraḥ Yaḥḍub's reign in Mârib depends on the two following facts which are the two extreme links in the chain of events.

[25] This coregency is also considered by *BePSC* as the last chapter in the life of the two royal brothers, for he states that Yaᵓzil Bayyin "disappears from the scene at the same time as his brother" (p. 55).

On the one hand, the king of Saba᾽, Fariᶜum Yanhub, already associated as aids his two sons ᾽Ilšaraḥ Yaḥḍub and Ya᾽zil, according to Ja 566. On the other hand, the king Watarum Yuha᾽min (Ja 601-607) is obviously enough the same person as Watarum (RÉS 3990/7 and 4150/8), for he is presented as son of ᾽Ilšaraḥ Yaḥḍub in all the texts. Furthermore, Naša᾽karib Yu(ha)᾽min Yuharḥib is never mentioned in any inscription related to ᾽Ilšaraḥ Yaḥḍub's reign. The only logical reconstruction of the dynasty is to place the coregency of ᾽Ilšaraḥ Yaḥḍub with his brother Ya᾽zil Bayyin before ᾽Ilšaraḥ Yaḥḍub's sole reign; this relative chronology is demanded by the mention of Šaᶜirum ᾽Awtar in CIH 398. ᾽Ilšaraḥ Yaḥḍub's sole reign is composed of two periods, that is to say without and, later, with his son Watarum as heir presumptive. Then follows ᾽Ilšaraḥ Yaḥḍub's second coregency, now with his son Watarum Yuha᾽min. Finally, Watarum Yuha᾽min became sole king.

Before beginning the description of the royal career of the great ᾽Ilšaraḥ Yaḥḍub, a preliminary note must be inserted regarding three inscriptions.

PRELIMINARY NOTE

Texts of unknown period:

CIH 257; RÉS 4136 and 4215

The period to which belong the three very fragmentary inscriptions CIH 257, RÉS 4136 and 4215 cannot be determined; they have also in common the fact that the length of their lines cannot be guessed.

CIH 257 alludes to the building of some construction and is characterized by the mention of the god Ta᾽lab. Line 4 only contains .../*s*]*b*᾽/*wḏrydn*/*bny*[/... *CIH* (I, p. 277 B) rightly declares that he does not know who the two kings alluded to in the text were; however, *RycIMAM* affirms repeatedly, but without offering any evidence in support of his contention,[26] that these two kings are ᾽Ilšaraḥ Yaḥḍub and his brother. There is, however, no evidence to support the restoration of the names of these two persons rather than those of Saᶜadšamsum ᾽Asraᶜ and his son Marṯadum Yuhaḥmid whose names are also followed by *mlky*/*sb*᾽/*wḏrydn*/*bny*/– (e.g., Ja 626/10-11). It is noteworthy that the god Ta᾽lab is also mentioned in Ja 601/20, a text related to the reign of Watarum Yuha᾽min, the immediate predecessor of the coregency of Saᶜadšamsum ᾽Asraᶜ with his son. Unfortunately, the lack of a photograph of CIH 257 makes it impossible to determine to which of the two coregencies the inscription belongs.

RÉS 4136 does not belong to Fariᶜum Yanhub's reign,[27] for the remains of line 4 are such that *mr*᾽*h*(*m*)*w* cannot possibly fill the blank in lines 2-3; furthermore, no clue exists that would indicate whether the text belongs to ᾽Ilšaraḥ Yaḥḍub's coregency with his brother or his son or to his sole reign.

RÉS 4215 which, like RÉS 4136, is a dedicatory text, mentions some illness which doubtless occasioned the offering. The text belongs to ᾽Ilšaraḥ Yaḥḍub's coregency with either his brother Ya᾽zil Bayyin or his son Watarum[28]; the first hypothesis is more probable than the second, because of the greatest number of inscriptions related to the first coregency.

a – COREGENCY OF ᾽ILSARAḤ YAḤḌUB WITH HIS BROTHER YA᾽ZIL BAYYIN AS PROVINCIAL KINGS

᾽Ilšaraḥ Yaḥḍub's coregency with his brother Ya᾽zil Bayyin as provincial kings is, in my opinion, clearly attested in CIH 398. The most difficult problem in relation to this coregency is to determine the texts which belong to it. There is, as far as I see, no internal evidence in the non-historical texts whereby one might determine the question. Such a situation is not surprising and no one should be disturbed because the contemporaneity of the main dynasty in Mârib with other provincial kings, although clearly indicated, is only casually indicated; even the same royal title is borne by subordinate kings and by the main ones as well. The complete palaeographic study of the two dynasties of Yarum ᾽Ayman and of Fariᶜum Yanhub should reveal some clue as to the solution of the question.

1° – CIH 398

CIH 398, discovered in Ṣirwâḥ by E. Glaser, is a dedicatory text to ᾽Ilumquh, master of the ibexes of Ṣirwâḥ. The most important element of the part related to the past is the record (lines 4-10[29]) of both the clearing of the first author by ᶜAbdᶜaṯtar and his companion and his reinstatement by the main king Šaᶜirum ᾽Awtar. The main feature of

[26] Cf. pp. 140, note 15, 173 and note 11, 193 and note 5, and 301.

[27] As *RycIMAM*, pp. 110-11.

[28] Cf. *MoMiASI*, p. 46. *RycIMAM* (p. 168, note 1, and p. 301) mentions the text in connection with ᾽Ilšaraḥ Yaḥḍub alone. Yet, *mr*᾽*y* in *mr*᾽*yhmw* (line 3) is a dual.

[29] For my translation of that part of the text, cf. *JaFSR*, p. 14.

the part related to the future is the petition to the god for the esteem and grace of the two provincial kings, the two royal brothers ʾIlšaraḥ Yaḥḍub and Yaʾzil Bayyin.

2° – *Texts without Historical Information*, and of Unknown Period: CIH 172+241; Ja 582, 583, 584, 587, 588, 591, 592, 595, 597, 598, 600; NaNN 24; RÉS 2695, 3929, 4134, 4139, and 4962

The eighteen following inscriptions are related to the coregency of ʾIlšaraḥ Yaḥḍub and his brother, and contain no historical information. It is not possible, given the present state of knowledge, to determine to which period of the coregency they belong. They may be divided into three groups: two decrees (RÉS 2695 and 4134), one commemoration of building (CIH 172+241), and fifteen dedicatory inscriptions (Ja 582, 583, 584, 587, 588, 591, 592, 595, 597, 598, 600; NaNN 24; RÉS 3929, 4139, and 4962).

In RÉS 2695,[30] the two kings, who mention both the name and the title of their father, graciously grant and sign the renewal of some titles of possession in favor of the descendants of the Leader of ʾAqyânum and their tribe Bakîlum. In RÉS 4134, the two kings[31] give some grounds in usufruct to certain warriors belonging to the clan of ʾAnwiyân.[32] CIH 172+241 alludes to the building, by some Bataᶜites, of the incense sanctuary (*mśwd*) of their house Ġaylân[33]; the title of the two kings does not mention the name of their father and his royal title.[34] *MoMiSI* (p. 60) rightly connects the two fragments CIH 172 and 241; however, his interpretation according to which CIH 241 and 172 are respectively the right and left parts of the original, needs some discussion.[35] This opinion is attractive because the two monograms are at the same level, that is to say, take the height of the three upper lines. However, several objections may be presented against this interpretation. First of all, it looks very suspicious that the original would have been cut precisely between the two central monograms, as if the workers had done their very best to save them. In addition to this, it is quite unusual to find the two monograms at the center of an inscription; they usually are located on both sides of the text (e.g., Fakhry 72). By considering the left side of CIH 172 as complete, *MoMiSI* does not reckon with *CIH*'s statement (I, p. 229) according to which "lapis...a sinistra mutilatus". Furthermore, according to *MoMiSI*'s restoration, the inscribed rectangle of CIH 241 would present 40, 42, 39, and 34 signs in lines 1-4 respectively; such a disproportion of letters is disproved by E. Glaser's copies of the inscribed rectangle of CIH 172 (18, 17, 19, and 18 signs respectively) and of CIH 241 (18 [15+3 missing], 19, 19, and 21 characters). Finally, the name of the tribe would rather be expected after *wšᶜbhmw*. I thus suggest reversing the order of the two fragments and considering CIH 172 and 241 respectively as the right and the left parts of the original, which thus would read as follows:

CIH 172 — CIH 241

1 *...]nm/wbnyhw/šrḥm* **m**
2 **m** *yhḥ[m]d/bnw/btᶜ/ʾbᶜl[/wklm/brʾw/whš]qrn/mśwd/bythmw/ġyl* **o n o g**
o n o *n/b[ᶜ]ṯtr/whbs/wbʾl[mqh/w..../wmnḍ]ḥhmw/bᶜl/wklm/wbšmsh* **r a m**
3 **g r a**
4 **m** *mw/bᶜ[l]t/myfᶜ/brdʾ/w[mqm/mrʾyhmw/ʾ]lšrḥ/yḥḍb/wyʾzl/byn/m[lk]*
5 *y/sbʾ/wḏrydn/wšᶜbhmw[/wklm/...*

[30] According to *RycIMAM*, the text is "sans filiation" (p. 166 and note 18; although he affirms the contrary on p. 105 and note 8); it bears "la signature du roi" (p. 192 and note 3; although he rightly mentions "la signature des deux rois" on p. 180), and finally it "confirme subsidiairement" (p. 180); the preceding interpretation of the text is not accurate.

[31] Cf. also *RycIMAM*, pp. 105, note 8; 173 and note 12; cf. also p. 117 and note 3.

[32] *RycIMAM* erroneously considers that the land concession is given "par un roi à une tribu énchange de prestations militaires" (p. 179).

[33] *RycIMAM* erroneously again affirms that the text alludes to "la construction...d'une maison avec *mśwd*" (p. 196 and note 16).

[34] *RycIMAM* affirms that the filiation of the two kings is mentioned in the text (pp. 166-67, and note 21). This opinion is an echo of *CIH*'s restoration (I, p. 269) of CIH 241/5; yet, this restoration, proposed before the reunion of the two fragments CIH 172 and 241, was affirmed by *MoMISI*, but is impossible because of that very reunion.

[35] According to this opinion, the text is to be referred to as CIH 241+172. Since he refers to the lines of *MoMiSI*'s interpretation, *RycIMAM* rightly mentions CIH 241+172 (pp. 140, note 5; 193, note 7; and 194, note 16); nevertheless, the same author refers to the text as CIH 172+241 (pp. 167, note 21; 173, note 11, and also in the list of the inscriptions on pp. 348 B and 349 A).

1 ...]num **M**
o
and his son Šarḥum **n**
2 **M** Yuhaḥ[mi]d, descendants of Bataᶜ, masters of **o**
o [Wakilum, have built and co]vered the **g**
n incense sanctuary of their house Ġayl- **r**
3 **o** ân. By [ᶜA]ṯtar and Hawbas and by ᵓIlu[m- **a**
g quh and....and] their [Munḍi]ḥ, master **m**
r of Wakilum, and by their
4 **a** Šams, mis[tr]ess of Mayfaᶜ, with the help and
m [power of their two lords ᵓI]lšaraḥ Yaḥḍub and
Yaᵓzil Bayyin, the two k[ing]s
5 of Sabaᵓ and Raydân and their tribe [Wakilum...

The photographs of the two fragments would obviously enough solve this question. One could object that the two monograms are not at the same level. However, RÉS 4198 shows that the two side monograms were not necessarily at the same level as they are, e.g., in Fakhry 72 and CIH 40.

Among the fifteen dedicatory inscriptions, five are written by high officials of the two kings (Ja 582, 583, 584, 591 and RÉS 3929), and four groups of texts may be determined according as they only contain petitions (Ja 582, 591, 595, 598 and RÉS 3929) or mention the occasion for the offering: recovery from an illness (Ja 583 and RÉS 4139), protection granted to a herd of camels (Ja 600), favors received (Ja 584, 587, 592, 597; NaNN 24 and RÉS 4962) and the birth of a male child (Ja 588).

Several inscriptions contain only petitions addressed to the deity. A high official of the two kings requests protection for himself, and the esteem and grace of his kings as well (Ja 582). The last request is also presented to the deity by the treasurer of the royal rent who is also praying for fruits, sons and preservation from any enemy (Ja 591); this high official belonged to the house *rḍwn*; according to *MüHG* (66/19 and 124/22), the Riḍwânites lived in the region of Ḫaywân. Another high official of the two kings makes an offering at the request of his god, and asks for the protection of his two kings, their esteem and grace for himself and also for aid concerning his person, his crops and against any enemy (RÉS 3929 [36]). The two inscriptions, Ja 595 and 598, are very fragmentary; what is left of Ja 595 contains only the petition of the dedicator for the esteem and grace of his two kings; Ja 598 mentions only a petition for grandchild[ren] and protection against any enemy.

Two dedicatory texts are directly connected with some kind of physical pain. The deity itself orders a high official of the two kings to offer a statue when he was suffering in his foot (Ja 583). In the fragmentary text RÉS 4139,[37] two brothers,[38] who may be high officials of the two kings,[39] make an offering because of the protection granted probably during an illness that occurred in Ṣanᶜâᵓ. These two texts also mention the usual petitions.

The author of Ja 600 offers a statue for protection granted to the herd of camels belonging to his two kings. In Ja 588, an individual and his son offer two statues because the father was granted a male child previously announced by the god. These two texts also contain the usual petitions.

Seven offerings of statue(s) are made after receiving favors. An equerry of the royal horses and his son were saved probably from danger incurred during battles (Ja 584); a Faḍlumite was protected during all the battles in which he was involved (Ja 587); some Ḥaḏᵓabumites were granted by their two kings the house of the descendants of Ḥaḏᵓabum (Ja 592); a certain ᵓAbfan(ad) received favors (unknown because of the fragmentary condition of the text) during the battles which he fought for his two kings (Ja 597). The unknown author of NaNN 24 (from Nâᶜiṭ), which is a dedicatory inscription to the sun goddess, probably received favors the nature of which remains unknown because of the fragmentary condition of the text.[40] In RÉS 4962,[41] two Taṯaᶜidites offer a

[36] In *RycIMAM*, p. 195, note 27, note that the whole expression *ḥẓy/wrḍw* is a restoration of the text.

[37] *RycIMAM* relates the text to the period of ᵓIlšaraḥ Yaḥḍub and his brother (e.g., p. 166 and note 19) and also to the time of *šᶜrm/ᵓwtr* (p. 183 and note 4).

[38] For the first one, a name such as *sᶜd[wdm]* would fit *MoMiHI*'s drawing (pl. VII, line 4). The name of the second is restored by *MoMiHI* (p. 29) as *ᵓ[lsᶜd]*. However, no explanation is presented; the distance between /ᵓ and /ᵓzᵓd is 19 mm. on the drawing however, and the length of *lsᶜd* would at least be 20.5 mm.

[39] This possibility is considered as a certainty by *RycIMAM* (pp. 145 and note 13, 200 and note 6).

[40] According to *RycIMAM* (pp. 182-83 and note 3), the text would allude to certain campaigns of the two kings. This interpretation is probably based on the translation of *brṯ* (line 2) as "military campaign". Yet, the noun *brṯ* has other meanings (cf. commentary on Ja 559/9); since the following noun may be restored as *ṣ[dǧ]* "manifestation" (Ja 721/4), *brṯ* here could thus mean "proclamation". Furthermore, the verb *hwšᶜ* (line 6) is not always connected with military campaigns; cf., e.g., Ja 642/12-13, where the verb is connected with a petition for pleasing, male children.

[41] *RycIMAM* (p. 191) notes that "dans RES...4962, 18-21 [read 17-23], les dédicants implorent l'aide de ᵓAlmaqah pour les campagnes militaires ou les expéditions que leurs seigneurs les rois leur ordonneront d'accomplir". *BeNL* (V, p. 109) rightly points out that *brṯ* here means "place" and not "military expedition", the dedicators request the deity to continue to come to their assistance according to all their petitions, in every place, near or far, in peace or war, in all that their two kings will impose upon them.

statue in thanksgiving for the assistance granted to them by the deity in all that they requested. With the exception of Ja 684 and NaNN 24, all the other texts contain the usual petitions.

b – SAME COREGENCY OF THE TWO ROYAL BROTHERS AS MAIN KINGS

The reasons for the disappearance of both Šaᶜirum ᵓAwtar and his brother Ḥayûᶜaṯtar Yaḏiᶜ whose coregency ended the dynasty of Yarum ᵓAyman, remain unknown. However, since the two royal brothers ᵓIlšaraḥ Yaḥḍub and Yaᵓzil Bayyin succeeded them by moving from their provincial capital to the main capital of Mârib, the question may be raised as to whether the first pair of brothers died from natural causes or not. At any rate, the following military campaigns exceed, in my opinion, the realm of provincial kings and seem to be reasonably ascribed to the coregency of the two brothers as main kings.

1° – *Beginning of* the Political Life of the two brothers Nimrân ᵓAwkân and Gaḥḍum ᵓAḥṣân

Because of the identity of Nimrân mentioned in CIH 429/6 (see below) with the first of the two brothers Nimrân ᵓAwkân and Gaḥḍum ᵓAḥṣân, Ja 594, 684, 711, 739, and 758 must be related to the coregency of ᵓIlšaraḥ Yaḥḍub and his brother Yaᵓzil Bayyin, during which the first two brothers achieved notoriety and power. It is, however, very possible that the beginning of their notoriety belongs to the coregency of the two royal brothers as provincial kings.

Ja 594, the last 13 lines of a dedicatory inscription, starts with the names of the two kings who were involved in a petition of the two dedicators, who almost certainly were asking for their esteem and grace; then several more petitions follow: esteem and grace of their two clan chiefs, safety for themselves, their mother, their wives and children, birth of male children, good weather and finally protection against any enemy. The names of the two clan chiefs, Nimrân ᵓAwkân and his brother Gaḥḍum ᵓAḥṣân mentioned in lines 4-5 of that inscription, are also found in Ja 684/1-3, 8-9, 711/8-9, 739/2-3, 13-14, and 758/1-2, 16-17. These four texts must thus be related to the reign of ᵓIlšaraḥ Yaḥḍub, although they do not mention any royal name, and more precisely to the coregency of ᵓIlšaraḥ Yaḥḍub and his brother; this opinion fits well the new relative chronology of the two periods in the reign of ᵓIlšaraḥ Yaḥḍub. The five inscriptions mentioning the two clan chiefs provide enough information to sketch their life. Ja 594 refers to the first step of their political life: the contrast between their title in this inscription and that in the four other texts indicates that, at the time of Ja 594, they were not yet clan leaders, although they already have people at their service; their father is called Saᶜ(d)[um] (Ja 594/5). They then became *bny/kbrḫll/wkbrᵓqynm/wḏsẖymm* (Ja 684/3-4, 9-10, 739/3-4 and 758/3 and 17-18), that is to say they became members of those groups from which the leaders are chosen. Finally, they became *ᵓkbrw/ḫll/[w]ᵓqynm/wḏsẖymm* (Ja 711/9-10).

In Ja 684, a servant of the two chiefs promised and offered a statue because the god granted him the esteem and grace of his two chiefs and also because he was protected against any enemy. In Ja 711, the god himself ordered another of his worshippers to offer a statue for the protection against an ailment which the latter used to have every year in his buttocks. In Ja 739 and 758, a high military official makes an offering in thanksgiving for favors received during some raids (see below).

2° – *Reconstruction of* historical events

The new historical information found in the 14 texts of the present collection written either by the two royal kings ᵓIlšaraḥ Yaḥḍub and his brother Yaᵓzil Bayyin (Ja 574, 575, and 576-577) or related to them, sheds an entirely new light on the military activities of these two kings.

Granted that the events recorded in Ja 576 and 577 are related according to their relative chronology, the five following events are in successive order: the campaign against Malikum, king of Kindat (Ja 576/2-3), the campaign against the Ḥabašites and their allies in the west (Ja 576/3), the war against Šamir of Raydân and his allies (Ja 576/3-577/6, 585 and CIH 314+954), the expedition against Ṣaḥbum, son of Gayšum (Ja 577/6-8) and finally the campaigns against Najrân (Ja 577/8-14, and 599/2). These last campaigns were probably followed by the campaign against Ḥimyar and Ḥaḍramawt (Ja 115). However, the problems of relative chronology of the other historical events mentioned in the texts remain unsolved; in most of the cases, we are left without the slightest clue. The plan suggested below is but an attempt to present a historical reconstruction of the military campaigns.

(a) CAMPAIGN against the South: Ja 739 and 758

The two inscriptions Ja 739 and 758 have several features in common: each author is a military official, Saᶜadšamsum and Saḫmân ᵓAwḥum respectively, of the two clan chiefs Nimrân ᵓAwkân and his brother Gaḥḏum ᵓAḥṣân, and they refer to battles and raids *bᶜm/ᵓᶜrbn* "against the Arabs" in the territories of the tribes Radmân, Muḏḥayum, and Qatabân. Muḏḥayum is not to be identified[42] with Maḏḥigum (Hamdânî: *maḏḥiǧ*); this tribe was, as well as Radmân,[43] a part of Maḏḥigum which was located east of Radâᶜ.[44] This location fits *mḏḥgm* in connection with Ḥaḍramawt (Ja 660/2-3) and with Sabaᵓ (Ja 665/2). The difference of commanding officers, and the two following differences, *mḏḥyn/wrdmn* in Ja 739/10 and *rdmn/wmḏḥym* in Ja 758/8, *qtbn* in Ja 739/10 and more precisely *srn/ᵓḫr/dqtbn* in Ja 758/8-9, seem to indicate that two different groups took part in the same campaign, although the existence of two separate campaigns is not ruled out. The location of ᵓAqyânum and Suḫaymum where the two chiefs were in command, suggests that the starting point of the campaign was somewhere north of Ṣanᶜâᵓ. The location of the valley ᵓAḫar in Qatabân is unknown.

(b) FIRST CAMPAIGNS against the Ḥabašites in the West: Ja 574, 575, and 590/5

Ja 574 and 575, written by the two royal brothers themselves, refer to two campaigns against the Ḥabašites established in the west and their local allies. It seems reasonable to admit that the two Sab kings first attacked the enemies which were closest to them, before adventuring further westward.

(1) Because of its fragmentary condition, Ja 575/2-8 does not give a very clear picture of the *first campaign*. The first step taken by the Sab army was to attack the Ḥabašites and the Saharatites whose bands were scattered in the vicinity of the citadel Waḥadat.[45] Although of unknown location, this fortress was probably somewhere in the vicinity of Wâdî Mawr, closer to the sea than to the highland, for those bands fled to the sea. They nevertheless were pursued by the Sabaeans, who later attacked them along with the ᶜAkkites (between Wâdî Mawr, some 95 km. north of al-Ḥudaydat, and Wâdî Sahâm, some 10 km. south of the latter city); all of them were either killed or captured. After that, the Sabaeans went back eastward to fight the rest of their enemies and those whom they had called for help; the battle took place in ᶜAynum and Huᶜân. The identification of the first with al-ᶜAin (some 40 km. northwest of Ṣanᶜâᵓ and about 10 km. southwest of ᶜAmrân[46]), and of the second with Huwâᶜ (about 35 km. northwest of ᶜAmrân[47]), suggests that the tribe Bakîlum, mentioned in line 3, had also taken part with the Ḥabašites. The above-mentioned campaign against Saharatân may also be referred to in Ja 590/5, if headed by ᵓIlšaraḥ Yaḥḍub alone.

(2) The *second campaign*, recorded in Ja 574, was also directed against a coalition of Ḥabašites and Saharatites, who had settled in the valley of Sahâm, that is to say that of Wâdî Sahâm. After that, ᵓIlšaraḥ Yaḥḍub and his army turned northward and went against the Ḥabašites in the valley of Śurdad; Wâdî Surdad being about 40 km. north of al-Ḥudaydat.[48] The battle took place in the plain of Wadfatân and Wadîfân as well as in the fields of Laqaḥ[49]; the location of these three places is unknown. There, the Sabaeans fought 25 campings of ᵓAksûmites, Gumdânites, ᶜAkkites, and Saharatites. The first two groups are called after their native cities, namely ᵓAksûman and Gumdân, and the last two after their tribes, ᶜAkkum and the northern Saharatum. After completing their mission, ᵓIlšaraḥ Yaḥḍub and his army went back to Ṣanᶜâᵓ where messengers reached them from the city of Gumdân, bringing firm pledges and peace-offerings as well. The peace, which followed these campaigns, is possibly referred to in Ja 576/3.

(c) CAMPAIGNS against Karibᵓil of Raydân and Ḥimyar: Ja 578, 580/8-9, 581, 586, and 589

Ja 578 and 589 deal entirely with military activities against Karibᵓil of Raydân, and Ja 586/7-9 as well; Ja 581 also belongs to the same period. A common link between these texts is the expression

[42] As, e.g., *WiHöBGS*, pp. 59 and 83.
[43] Cf. *MüHG*, 55/13.
[44] According to *MüHG*, *l.c.*; cf. also *FoSA*, p. 139, note 2.
[45] Wâdî Waḥadat is in Ḥimyar (cf. *MüHG*, 89/17) and more precisely west of Qaᶜṭabat (cf. *FoSA*, p. 137, note 10), which is located some 125 km. north-northwest of ᶜAden and 170 km. northeast of al-Muḫâ.

[46] Cf. *WeCĠC*, p. 119 and map.
[47] Cf. *l.c.*, p. 128 and map.
[48] Cf. *JaASAB*, p. 156, commentary on CIH 407/2.
[49] Laqâḥ, mentioned by *MüHG* (94/8) as being located east of Radâᶜ (in the Sarw Madḥiǧ, thus some 180 km. east of al-Ḥudaydat), is not suitable here.

ʾšʿb/wmṣyrt/ḥmyrm, which is mentioned in connection with Karibʾil of Raydân (Ja 589/10; a longer expression in Ja 578/7, and a shorter one in Ja 586/9) or not (Ja 581/7). Note that this expression is not mentioned in connection with Šamir of Raydân (Ja 576 and 577). The striking characteristic is that Karibʾil of Raydân and his ally Ḥimyar (*kl/mṣr/wʾšʿb/wḫms/ḥmyrm* in Ja 578/7, and *ʾšʿb/wmṣyrt/ḥmyrm* in Ja 589/10) are mentioned as *wldʿm* "children of ʿAmm"; this expression is commonly used to indicate the Qatabanians.[50] The use of such an expression would be inexplicable were not one member at least of the coalition a true Qatabanian; therefore, *rydn* in *ḏrydn* indicates Karibʾil as a Qatabanian and is not at all connected with Ẓafâr, the capital of Ḥimyar. It is no less obvious that each campaign against Karibʾil of Raydân (Ja 578/5-9 and 15-24) is immediately followed by an invasion of the Ḥimyarite country. Taking Ja 578 as the basis of a reconstruction of historical events, I would present the following picture of the military operations: each of the two campaigns against Karibʾil of Raydân (Ja 578/5-13 and 15-24, which are referred to in Ja 586/7-9 and 589) is continued by a campaign against Ḥimyar (Ja 578/13-15 and 24-30, referred to in Ja 581 and 586/3-7); the second campaign against Ḥimyar is followed by a third one (Ja 586/10-24). Finally, in none of these four texts, is Karibʾil of Raydân mentioned as fighting along with one of the ordinary allies of Qatabân, for instance Radmân and Muḏḥayum, as in the case of Šamir of Raydân. The coalition led by Karibʾil was thus smaller than that headed by Šamir. Karibʾil's coalition seems to have preceded that of Šamir; Karibʾil probably thought that he could achieve his aim only with Ḥimyar as an ally. His failure did not put an end to the plans of the Qat leaders but rather incited Šamir to increase the number of his allies before resuming the struggle which ended in the defeat of Karibʾil. The two authors of Ja 578, two brothers, rulers of the tribe Bakîlum and high military officials of the two royal kings, took part in the first two campaigns.

(1) *First campaign:* Ja 578/5-13 and 13-15.

ʾIlšaraḥ Yaḥḏub led the first phase of the first campaign against Karibʾil of Raydân (Ja 578/5-13), who had as an ally Ḥimyar which sent strong forces, *kl/mṣr* "the whole expeditionary force", *ʾšʿb* "the tribal contingents" and *ḫms* "the regular army". The starting point of the Sab army was the country of Ḥurmatum, which is a place in the vicinity of J. ʾItwat, southeast of Raydat.[51] Karibʾil of Raydân was defeated in a series of battles which are extended from the citadel ʾAsʾay and Qarnnahân to ʿArwaštân, Ẓalmân, and Hakrabum; the locations of the first, second and fifth places are unknown. ʿArwaštân may be identified with al-ʿArûš on the country of Radâʿ,[52] and which is located[53] between ʿAyal Saʿîd and Banû Ẓubyân[54]; E. Glaser also mentions Bilâd al-ʿArûš some 95 km. southwest of Mârib and about 70 km. southeast of Ṣanʿâʾ,[55] as well as J. ʿArûš almost halfway between Ṣirwâḥ and Ḏamâr.[56] With regard to Ẓalmân, *FoSA*[57] mentions the city of Ẓalma, 3 hours west of Saḥûl, which is in Ḥimyar[58]; Wâdî Suḥûl is north of ʾIbb, between the two cities of Meširk (west) and Meḫader (east), and in the territory of the Banû Merġamir. This phase of the campaign was immediately followed by an attack upon the land of Ḥimyar (lines 13-15).

(2) *Second campaign:* Ja 578/15-24 and 24-30.

After the preceding expedition in the territory of Ḥimyar, the two Sab kings went back against Karibʾil who apparently was left alone by his Ḥimyarite ally. Karibʾil was defeated in the valley of ʾAẓwar; he then retreated to the cities Yaklaʾ and ʾAbwân; the location of the latter is unknown. ʾAẓwar was, according to Ja 576/4, a Ḥimyarite town at the border of Qašamum. As regards Yaklaʾ,[59] a city of that name, Yaklâ (*ykly*), is known as being located north of Ḏamâr,[60] and which E. Glaser locates about 6 hours south of Zirâġa[61]; it seems, however, preferable to think of Yaklâ, northeast of Radâʿ,[62] connected with J. Yaklâ.[63] Karibʾil was forced to give pledges of submission, and the two Sab kings gained control

[50] Cf. *JaDCR*, pp. 28-29.
[51] Cf. *HaAI*, p. 66 and *MüHG*, 109/26.
[52] Cf. *MüHG*, 102/9.
[53] Cf. E. Glaser, in *FoSA*, p. 166, note 4.
[54] According to E. Glaser, Banû Ẓubyân were located some 30 km. northeast of Bilâd al-ʿArûš (cf. *MüRhGRM*, p. 175 A and plate 1).
[55] Cf. *MüRhGRM*, pp. 175 A, 185 A, and plate 1.
[56] Cf. *l.c.*, pl. 3.
[57] P. 97, note 6. The location given to Ẓalmum (RÉS 3945/3) by *WiHöBGS* (p. 29, note 3, and map facing p. 64) fits Ẓalmân perfectly.
[58] Cf. *MüHG*, 68/4.
[59] *HaAI* mentions the great ruins of a city Yaklâ (p. 103), which was an accursed place (p. 119).
[60] Cf. *MüHG*, 80/20.
[61] Cf. *FoSA*, p. 182, note 4.
[62] Cf. *MüHG*, 94/9.
[63] Cf. *MüRhGRM*, plate 3.

of his land. However, the two kings had to invade the land of Ḥimyar again (lines 24-30), because Karib'il had intrenched himself in Hakirum; they besieged the city until they plundered it and received the submission of Karib'il. *MüHG* (80/17 and 104/5)[64] mentions the city Hakir[65] in the vicinity of Ḏamâr, south-southwest of J. Isbîl, and between Yarîm and Radâᶜ.[66] The campaign *ᶜdy/'rḏ/ḥmyrm* in Ja 580/8-9 is headed by the two Sab kings; it could thus be identified with either (Ja 578/15 and 25: *ᶜdy/'rḏ/ḥmyrm*) of the operations in the territory of Ḥimyar mentioned during the second Sab campaign against Karib'il of Raydân and Ḥimyar.

(3) *Third campaign* against Ḥimyar and attack on Qašamum: Ja 586/10-24.

The campaigns against Ḥimyar, led by the two Sab kings, are placed here because they are described after allusion is made (lines 7-9) to the campaign against Karib'il of Raydân. The account of these campaigns, preceded by a short summary (lines 10-15), opens with the description of raids in the country of Sâriᶜân (lines 15-19). *MüHG* (94/15) refers to Sâriᶜ as being located in the territory of Banû Šubrumat, which puts it near Waᶜlân.[67] These raids are followed by an attack against the tribe Qašamum (lines 20-23), during which 'Ilza'ad of Rabḥum was killed. This person was probably the chief of some clan, but in any event a trouble-maker. The location of the tribe Qašamum may be identified on the basis of the following information, viz. that Qašamum is on the border of Ḥimyar (Ja 576/4) and contiguous to Muḏḥayum (RÉS 4196/1). Taking the location of Sâriᶜân into consideration and also the fact that neither Radmân nor Muḏḥayum is mentioned, the location of the tribe Qašamum would seem to be south of Radmân and west of Muḏḥayum.

(d) CAMPAIGN against Malikum, king of Kindat: Ja 576/2-3

Ja 576, written by the two Sab kings, is continued by Ja 577. This long record of military campaigns starts with a short summary (lines 1-2) pointing out the defeat of all enemies north and south, on land and on sea (also in Ja 585/11-14).

Malikum, king of Kindat, had given assistance to Mara'laqas, king of Ḫiṣâṣatân; the two Sab kings captured him, and the leaders of Kindat, as well as Malikum, were detained in the city Marab until Mara'laqas and the sons of Malikum and of the chiefs and the leaders of Kindat were given over to the Sabaeans; they also paid tribute.

The city *mrb* (also in Ja 572/7) is not Mârib, for the latter is mentioned in line 3 as *mryb*, as well as in Ja 577/17. In his commentary on Wâdî Ma'sil 1/7: *ḥḏrmwt/wsb'/[w]bny/mrb*, where *RyISA*[68] interprets *mrb* as Mârib, W. Caskel[69] rightly refers to the Marabites who inhabited the country of ᶜAden.[70] This obviously excludes the interpretation of Kindat as referring to the kingdom of al-Ḥîra or to that located about 150 km. northwest of Najrân and some 150 km. northeast of Jîzân (cf. Ja 635/26-27); it would of course be inconceivable that the two Sab kings would have brought Malikum and his chiefs all the way down (about 550 km.); they would obviously have stopped in Ṣanᶜâ'. Malikum was the king of a small kingdom located somewhere in the far south of the Arabian peninsula. Its location in the west would be hard to agree with because that part of the country was controlled by Ḥimyar, with which the two Sab kings were constantly fighting. Furthermore, it is almost probably contiguous to the country of the Marabites. Therefore, I would tentatively locate this tiny kingdom of Kindat south of Qašamum. This location, although hypothetical, fits Ja 660/2 and 665/2, which mention *ḥ]ḏrmwt/wkdt[/]wmḏḥ[gm* and *sb'/wkdt/wmḏḥgm* respectively. The location of the kingdom of *ḫṣṣtn* is no less hypothetical. The Arabic noun *ḫiṣâṣ* or *ḫuṣâṣ*, "reservoirs, tanks, basins",[71] reminds one of ᶜAden[72] and its natural crevices in the rock into which rainwaters gathered and collected and whose efficiency was greatly improved by the building of tanks.[73] The kingdom of Ḫiṣâṣatân could have been called after this very characteristic of ᶜAden; a natural, isolated fortress such as ᶜAden would be a very well selected place for an independent kingdom. Furthermore, the

[64] Cf. also *HaAI*, p. 137, and *HaAF*, p. 326.

[65] Hakar is also a mount near ᶜAryeb, in the vicinity of Mukéras, and is known in the rock inscriptions from that country as a city whose name was *hkrm*.

[66] Cf. *FoSA*, p. 103, note 10; cf. also *WiHöBGS*, p. 61, note 3.

[67] Cf. *FoSA*, p. 150, note 2.

[68] X, pp. 304 and 306.

[69] *Entdeckungen in Arabien*, Cologne, 1954, p. 9.

[70] Cf. *MüHG*, 53/13, 14, and 124/19.

[71] Cf. *DoSDA*, I, p. 375 B.

[72] Cf. *WiHöBGS*, pp. 88-89.

[73] Cf. H. T. Norris and F. W. Penhey, *An Archaeological and Historical Survey of the Aden Tanks*, Aden, 1955. Richard LeBaron Bowen, Jr., suggests that the tanks of ᶜAden "were probably built sometime before the start of the Christian era" (cf. "Archaeological Survey of Beiḥân", in *BoAlADSA*, p. 8 A).

preceding interpretation fits very well the information concerning the Marabites given in the same context.

(e) OTHER CAMPAIGNS against the Ḥabašites and their Western allies: Ja 576/3

The two campaigns mentioned in Ja 575 and 574 were followed by some kind of treaty and peace to which possibly reference is made in Ja 576/3; we are not informed, however, how the Ḥabašites achieved their revolt; the Ḥabašites and the Saharatites had increased their fighting power by the addition of two new allies, Šamir of Raydân and the Ḥimyarite tribes. The new anti-Sab coalition was crushed by ʾIlšaraḥ Yaḥḍub, but no location is indicated. However, the two new partners of the coalition do not seem to have been hurt too badly since they reappear in the lengthy campaigns which follow.

(f) CAMPAIGNS against Šamir of Raydân and his allies: Ja 576/3-577/6, 585 and CIH 314+954

The military activities against Šamir of Raydân undoubtedly lasted a long time; those recorded in Ja 576/3-577/6, which apparently were conducted by ʾIlšaraḥ Yaḥḍub alone, may be divided into three phases: the first in Ja 576/3-11, the second (cf. *drm/ṯntm* "a second time" in line 11) in Ja 576/11-577/3, and finally the third one, in Ja 577/3-6, which is characterized by the intervention of the Ḥabašites, whose main forces remained in the south and were headed by Garmat, son of the Ḥabašite king ᶜAḏbah, while another contingent, smaller than the preceding, went to settle in the district of Najrân and which was under the command of Sabqalum, the representative of the same Ḥabašite king. ʾIlšaraḥ Yaḥḍub apparently scattered his reserves in three different places: somewhere between Mârib and Ṣanᶜâʾ (Ja 576/4 and 577/2: *ᶜdy/byn/hgrnhn*), Ṣanᶜâʾ (Ja 576/10, 11 and 577/3) and Naᶜiḍ (Ja 576/8, 10 and 577/2), a city located 33 km. southeast of Ṣanᶜâʾ, east of the military road to Taᶜizz, in Bilâd ar-Rûs.[74]

(1) *First phase:* Ja 576/3-11, 579/7-8, and 590/7-11

The Sab army headed by ʾIlšaraḥ Yaḥḍub left Mârib for Ṣanᶜâʾ to fight Šamir of Raydân and his allies, Ḥimyar, Radmân, and Muḏḥayum. This first series of operations is composed of four campaigns separated from each other by returns to one of the three above-mentioned bases of operation.

(a) In Ḥimyarite country: Ja 576/4. During this first operation, ʾIlšaraḥ Yaḥḍub went deep into the Ḥimyarite country, destroying and plundering the centers of two clans and two cities[75]; the area of the clan Šamatân,[76] the town Dalâl, east of ʾIbb,[77] the district of the clan Yahar,[78] and the city ʾAẓwar, at the border, in the territory of Qašamum. Then, the Sab army went back to its camp between Mârib and Ṣanᶜâʾ, with plenty of captives and booty.

(b) Northern Ḥimyar: Ja 576/4-7 and 590/7-11. While ʾIlšaraḥ Yaḥḍub was in his reserve camp (lines 4-5), Šamir of Raydân tried to consolidate his position by sending Ḥimyarite soldiers in the country of the city of Baʾsân, which is Bûsân,[79] some 65 km. southeast of Ṣanᶜâʾ, to protect the border. ʾIlšaraḥ Yaḥḍub immediately attacked, defeated the Ḥimyarite force and plundered Baʾsân. After that (lines 5-6), the Sab army invaded the plain of Dargaᶜan; there was no battle for the expeditionary force of Raydân had withdrawn.

The Sabaeans then (line 6) proceeded against the land of Muhaʾnifum which they raided. From there (lines 6-7), through the pass of Yalrân, the Sab army went to besiege the city Taᶜramân; the city was seized and its inhabitants captured, after which (line 7), the Sab army went back to its reserve camp at Naᶜiḍ. The tribe Muhaʾnifum is mentioned along with Bakîlum in CIH 40/1-2, and is also attested in the country of Mârib according to Ja 555/3; this double information cannot of course be taken into consideration. The same tribe is also mentioned along with the tribe Ẓuhâr in Ja 651/4. E. Glaser locates Ẓuhâr, which is referred to by

[74] Cf. *MoMiHI*, p. 26, commentary on RÉS 4138/8.

[75] *RyISA* (XIII, pp. 156 and 156-57) suggests that the two proper names introduced by *hgrn* "the city" are the main towns of the "agglomérations de Ḏû-Šamatim [however, "Šamatum" on p. 147] et de Yahar" because of "Voir l. 13: *bytn/rʾs* et *hgrn/rʾsw*" (p. 156) and "*bytn/rʾs*, cf. l. 4: *byt/ḏšmtm* et *byt/yhr*" (p. 162). Yet, the parallel to be valid should have *byt/rʾs* and not *bytN/rʾs*.

[76] *MüHG* (68/20, 72/8, and 106/12) mentions a place called Šumm in the territory of Ḥaḍûr, and E. Glaser refers to Šammat, two hours southwest of Kawkabân, west of Wâdî al-ʾAhǧur (cf. *FoSA*, p. 175, note 4).

[77] According to E. Glaser. Dalâl is referred to by *MüHG*, 75/22 and 100/22.

[78] A place called Yahar (or Yahr) belonged to the Banû Šuᶜayb in the time of Hamdânî (cf. *MüHG*, 89/5 and 8) and is located south of J. Ṯamar (cf. *FoSA*, p. 136, note 6), some 120 km. northeast of ᶜAden.

[79] J. Ryckmans (cf. *RyISA*, *l.c.*, p. 157) also refers to the town Bûsân mentioned by E. Glaser as being located 3 or 4 hours east of Zirâǧa. *MüRhGRM* (plate 1) locates the town almost on Wâdî Manqaḍa.

MüHG (103/22), southeast of J. Bara^c,[80] which is about 45-55 km. east of al-Ḫudaydat. The present campaign may thus have taken place in the northern Ḥimyarite country, and might be tentatively described as follows.

After capturing the city of Ba$^\circ$sân, the Sab army proceeded eastward and invaded the plain of Darga^{c}an (possibly the plain along Wâdî Rima^c). After a raid against the tribe Muha$^\circ$nifum (possibly north of J. Rima^c), they went through the pass of Yalrân (probably northeast of the present town Ziyarat), and attacked the city of Ta^{c}ramân (probably located somewhere east of the present city Menâẖa).

Ja 590/7-11 has three points in common with Ja 576/5-6: $^\circ$Ilšaraḥ Yaḥḍub is alone, he is fighting in the country of Ḥimyar, and *mṣr/ḏrydn* "the expeditionary force of Raydân" is mentioned. The action described in Ja 590/7-11 may very well be a part of the military operation related in Ja 576/4-7, which would have taken place after the invasion of the plain of Darga^{c}an and before the attack against the land of Muha$^\circ$nifum. $^\circ$Ilšaraḥ Yaḥḍub would have pursued the expeditionary force of Raydân which had withdrawn before his army, and would have defeated it in the area of Raymatum, a city in Ma^{c}âfir,[81] which E. Glaser locates west of al-Muḏayẖirat, west of $^\circ$Ibb,[82] and therefore about 75 km. southwest of Ḏamâr and some 170 km. northwest of ^{c}Aden.

The description of the campaign against Ḥimyar in Ja 579/7-8 is characterized by two facts: $^\circ$Ilšaraḥ Yaḥḍub alone is given as the leader and the passage mentions the expression *$^\circ$rḍ/ḥmyrm*. This campaign may thus very well be one of the two above-mentioned campaigns in Ḥimyar, either Ja 576/4 or 590/8. Ja 579/7 mentions a campaign against *ḏshrtm*, conducted by $^\circ$Ilšaraḥ Yaḥḍub alone. These two characteristics belong to some campaigns against the west (Ja 574/3-4, 6, and 8) and against Šamir of Raydân (Ja 576/3, 577/3 and 5). Ja 579/7 would seem to allude to an operation conducted during the first phase (Ja 576/3) of the war against Šamir, because of the plausible connection of Ja 579/7-8 with either Ja 576/4 or 590/8.

[80] Cf. *FoSA*, p. 169, note 1.

[81] Cf. *MüHG*, 68/4, and *HaAI*, p. 25.

[82] Cf. *FoSA*, p. 65, note 3.

[83] A town called Maḏraḥ is located by E. Glaser (cf. *WeCGC*, p. 135, and map) about 70 km. northwest of Ṣan^{c}â$^\circ$; cf. also *MüHG*, 69/6: Maḏraḥ or Maḏrağ belongs to Qudam (cf. also *FoSA*, p. 73, note 8).

[84] *ḍfw* may be identified with Ḍâff, a city at the northern border of Ğahrân (cf. *FoSA*, p. 187 and note 4).

(c) Eastern Qašamum: Ja 576/7-8. The king $^\circ$Ilšaraḥ Yaḥḍub made a raid in the eastern part of the area occupied by the tribe Qašamum, and plundered the city $^\circ$Ayḍamum, whose location is unknown, before going back to his reserve camp in Na^{c}iḍ.

(d) Second campaign against Muha$^\circ$nifum: Ja 576/8-11. The king $^\circ$Ilšaraḥ Yaḥḍub went back again waging war in the land of the tribe Muha$^\circ$nifum and seized the two towns of ^{c}Aṯay and ^{c}Aṯay, whose location is unknown. From there, he went against the unknown city of the clan Maḏraḥum[83]; he met there this clan and the tribe Muha$^\circ$nifum, which fled to Ḍâffaw.[84] From there, the Sabaeans returned to the district of the city of Yakla$^\circ$, where they encountered some of the Raydânite chiefs and the expeditionary force of Ḥimyar. The Sabaeans attacked their enemies, and pursued them from Marḥiḍân, of unknown location, to Yakla$^\circ$. They then returned to their camp of operation in Na^{c}iḍ. The Ḥimyarites took advantage of the withdrawal of the Sab forces to incite Yakla$^\circ$ to some kind of revenge and proposed to the leaders of that city an expedition in the valley of Nagrarum, whose location is unknown.[85] The Sab king must have had an inkling of the Ḥimyarite plan, for he immediately was on his way to meet the planned expedition. Such a move, however, became unnecessary, since the leaders of Yakla$^\circ$ turned down the Ḥimyarite plan. $^\circ$Ilšaraḥ Yaḥḍub went thus back home, first to Na^{c}iḍ, and then to Ṣan^{c}â$^\circ$.

(2) *Second phase:* Ja 576/11-577/3, 585, 599/1 and CIH 314+954.

Šamir of Raydân was not yet ready to give up his ambitions. Convinced by now that he would not be successful with only his Arabian allies, he decided to send messengers to ^{c}Aḏbah, the king of $^\circ$Aksûman and to ask him for help. $^\circ$Ilšaraḥ Yaḥḍub, however, got wind of the departure of those envoys. Immediately then, he decided to take action by sending envoys to Ḥabašat (Ja 577/6) and also by attacking Šamir and his allies of the hinterland, Ḥimyar, Radmân and Muḍḥayum, and the

[85] Nagrarum cannot possibly be identified with Neğr, a Hamdânid town (cf. *MüHG*, 107/10) located by E. Glaser 2 km. south of ^{c}Amrân (cf. *WeCGC*, p. 136, and map), J. Neğre is located by the same about 75 km. west-northwest of Ṣan^{c}â$^\circ$ (cf. *l.c.*, p. 126 and map). Nagrarum was located somewhere south of Na^{c}iḍ, since $^\circ$Ilšaraḥ Yaḥḍub returned to the latter and then to Ṣan^{c}â$^\circ$. Were Nagrarum north of Ṣan^{c}â$^\circ$, $^\circ$Ilšaraḥ Yaḥḍub's move toward Na^{c}iḍ and then to Ṣan^{c}â$^\circ$ would make no sense at all.

Ḥabašites of the hinterland as well (Ja 585/5-6), in order to reduce their fighting power and to disrupt their plan. This second phase of the conflict is composed of a series of operations, with their apparent climax ʾIlšaraḥ Yaḥḍub's victory against the allied forces which were concentrated between Hirrân and Ḏamâr.

(a) FIRST OPERATION: Ja 576/11-12

Leaving Ṣanᶜâʾ, the Sab army suddenly attacked the country of Ḥarûr, ᶜArṣum and Dargaᶜan. Both the city and mount Ḥarîr, occupied by the population al-ʾAᶜḍûd, are in Sarw Ḥimyar,[86] and J. Ḥarîr is about 105 km. north-northwest of ᶜAden and 10 km. northeast of aḍ-Ḍâlaᶜ. ᶜArṣum may be "ᶜ.râṣim", a wâdî in Bilâd ar-Rakb,[87] and which could be identified with Wâdî Dami,[88] Bilâd ar-Rakb being located north and east of Mauzaᶜ.[89] The Sab army went as far as the two cities of Qarîb and Qarîs, leveled the wells of these two towns and occupied the latter city. If Qarîb is unknown,[90] Qarîs may be identified with Qarîs, located in Ǧahrân,[91] and about 10-15 km. northeast of Ḏamâr.

(b) SECOND OPERATION: Ja 576/12-13

After capturing the town Qarîs, ʾIlšaraḥ Yaḥḍub did not rest under the shade of his laurels, but pushing northward he attacked the country of Yahbašir, Muqraʾum, and Šadâdum. The location of the first is unknown. Muqraʾum may be identified with Muqrâ (*mqry*),[92] a country inhabited by a Ḥimyarite population bearing the same name, one day journey south of Ṣanᶜâʾ,[93] and more precisely west of the southern end of the route from Ṣanᶜâʾ to Maᶜbar.[94] Šadâdum is the Banû Šaddâd, southeast of Ġaymân, on the road to Mârib,[95] inhabitants of Bilâd aš-Šidâdî in the Wâdî Malâḥâ, which was bordered on the west by Wâdî Ġarbah.[96] The Sab army also captured the clan Raʾs and its city of the same name as well as the clan Sanfarum, and the rebels placed among them by Raydân as well. The clan Sanfarum was probably composed of descendants of emigrants from the small island Ṣanâfir, south of Aqaba.[97] The location of these two clans as well as the city of the first is unknown; they probably were on the border of Sabaʾ.

(c) THIRD OPERATION: Ja 576/13-14

Šamir of Raydân had sent rebels not only to reinforce the clans Raʾs and Sanfarum, but also to the city of Ẓalm, whose location is unknown. ʾIlšaraḥ Yaḥḍub attacked the city with considerable force and destroyed it.

(d) FOURTH OPERATION: Ja 576/14-16 and 599/1

The main forces of Šamir and his allies, Ḥimyar, Radmân, and Muḏḥayum, were concentrated between the two cities of Hirrân and Ḏamâr. Hirrân, which is also mentioned in Ja 599/1, obviously is the city of that name located in the vicinity of Ḏamâr,[98] immediately north of the latter,[99] and E. Glaser specifies that the ruins of Hirrân are a half hour from Ḏamâr, on the way to Ṣanᶜâʾ[100]; J. Hirrân is northwest of Ḏamâr.[101] ʾIlšaraḥ Yaḥḍub crushed the coalition, and his defeated enemies fled to Ḏamâr.

(e) FOLLOWING OPERATIONS AND EVENTS: Ja 577/1-3, 585 and CIH 314+954

The beginning of Ja 577 presents the record of the last mentioned phase of Šamir's fight, but the narrative story of the events that occurred between Ja 576/16 and 577/1 is missing. Since Ja 577 has been recut on its left side, it is possible that Ja 576 also was recut on its lower side. If so, there is no clue as to the extent of the missing part. The hypothesis of an intermediate missing stone, although not to be ruled out, does not seem likely.

Inasmuch as it is allowed by Ja 585 and CIH 314 +954, which have in common among other points the expression *bn hgrn/śwm/wshrtn* (as already pointed out in the commentary on Ja 585/4-5), the reconstruction of historical events may be presented as follows. The call for the help of Ḥabašat

[86] Cf. *MüHG*, 89/23; cf. also *HaAI*, p. 89, and *FoSA*, p. 138, note 3.

[87] Cf. *MüHG*, 75/15.

[88] Cf. *FoSA*, p. 91, note 11.

[89] Cf. *l.c.*, p. 44, note 2.

[90] *MüHG* (122/23) mentions a Wâdî Qarib, located east of Kinâna. Such a location is not suitable here; it is much too far in the north.

[91] Cf. *MüHG*, 111/15; also mentioned by J. Ryckmans, in *RyISA*, XIII, pp. 161-62.

[92] Cf. *MüHG*, e.g., 68/15.

[93] Cf. *SpAGA*, p. 244.

[94] Cf. *FoSA*, p. 69, note 5; also mentioned by J. Ryckmans, in *RyISA*, *l.c.*, p. 162.

[95] Cf. *WiHöBGS*, p. 22; according to *MüHG* (96/21-23), Banû Šaddâd also inhabited a few wâdîs in the area of the upper Wâdî Marẖa, about 60 km. east-southeast of Beiḥân al-Qaṣâb.

[96] Cf. *MüRhGRM*, pp. 185 and 187.

[97] In the commentary of CIH 537/1, note that the first letter of Ṣanâfir is *ṣâd* and not *sîn*.

[98] Cf. *MüHG*, 80/20.

[99] Cf. *FoSA*, p. 104, note 12.

[100] Cf. *MüRhGRM*, p. 54 B.

[101] Cf. *l.c.*, map, No. 2.

by Šamir and Ḥimyar (Ja 576/11 and CIH 314+954/17-18), evidently received a favorable answer, for Ja 585/5-6 refers to the sending of the Ġaymânite Hawfᶜatat ᵓAṣḥaḥ against the Ḥabašites. His expedition was, however, unsuccessful; he fell into the hands of his enemies, and during his two-year captivity in Śawum and Saharatân, he was subjected to the humiliation of having his body shaved (Ja 585/6-8). Śawum (as-Sawâ) was located in the country of Maᶜâfirum, about 130 km. northwest of ᶜAden.[102] In the meantime, however, another expedition more efficient than the preceding one must have succeeded, as did also the following operation which is referred to in Ja 577/1-3.

The Sab army, headed by ᵓIlšaraḥ Yaḥḍub, went to the city of Zaḫmum (of unknown location) where they defeated the expeditionary forces of Ḥimyar, Radmân, and Muḍḥayum, and then back to Taraznân (also of unknown location). Probably after another move, the description of which has disappeared along with the end of line 2, ᵓIlšaraḥ Yaḥḍub went back to Ṣanᶜâᵓ. After a certain period of time, during which the two Sab kings granted a favor to two of their military commanders, authors of CIH 314+954,[103] in Ṣanᶜâᵓ and Ruḥâbatân, a town located about 20 km. north-northeast of Ṣanᶜâᵓ,[104] and also during which the second expedition against the Ḥabašites developed successfully, the two Sab kings received the submission of Šamir and his Ḥabašite allies (CIH 314+954/13-16); and it seems plausible that Hawfᶜatat ᵓAṣḥaḥ came back from captivity (Ja 585/4-5) at this time. Furthermore, since Ja 585/14-16 mentions the defeat of the Ḥabašite royal prince Garmat after Šamir and his Ḥabašite allies had sent their submission to the two Sab kings, the hostilities had started again after the peace was broken; it is this, possibly, which is referred to in Ja 577/2 by the expression *hyf/hyfhmw/šmr/ḏrydn/wᵓšᶜb/ḥmyrm/wldᶜm* "the injustice [which] Šamir, he of Raydân, and the tribes of Ḥimyarum, the children of ᶜAmm, had committed against them", ᵓIlšaraḥ Yaḥḍub, his brother and their army. This re-opening of the hostilities may have been the consequence of Garmat's arrival, since he is not mentioned in relation to the first battles (Ja 585/3-6).

[102] Cf. *SpAGA*, pp. 75 and 183, and *WiHöBGS*, pp. 61, 69, and map facing p. 64.

[103] *PiIRC* misinterprets CIH 314+954, when she writes that the two Sab kings "avaient réussi à s'établir fermement à Ṣanᶜā et Raḥba (CIH 314+954)" (p. 169).

(3) *Third phase:* Ja 577/3-6 and 585/14-16

The envoys sent by Šamir to ᶜAḏbah, king of ᵓAksûman (Ja 576/11), succeeded in their mission; no less than Garmat son of the Ḥabašite king himself, headed the auxiliaries requested by Šamir, who also received some help from Saharatum. This Ḥabašite help was sent to Šamir in spite of a sworn peace between Sabaᵓ and Ḥabašat (line 2), and also in spite of the messengers sent by ᵓIlšaraḥ Yaḥḍub (line 6). This campaign is composed of three operations, which were three Sab victories; unfortunately, the names of locations of the first two clashes have disappeared along with the end of lines 3 and 4.

The first operation was the most important one, for ᵓIlšaraḥ Yaḥḍub had to fight the main part of the allied armies which had been congregated by Šamir. After cutting them to pieces, ᵓIlšaraḥ Yaḥḍub went to destroy five bedouin camps. The latter move was a preventive one, since the Sab king succeeded in outrunning the auxiliaries sent by Ḥabašat and Saharatum; he met them and destroyed them in the plain of ᵓAḥdaqân.[105] After defeating Garmat, ᵓIlšaraḥ Yaḥḍub and his soldiers went back to Ṣanᶜâᵓ.

(g) EXPEDITION against Ṣaḥbum, son of Gayšum: Ja 577/6-8

Šamir of Raydân was not the only thorn in the Sab crown; Ja 577/6-8 mentions another rebel, named Ṣaḥbum, son of Gayšum, who was apparently much less dangerous, for the two Sab royal brothers did not deem it necessary to command the expedition which was of rather small dimensions. Nawfum was put in charge of a small troop composed of Ḥâšidites and Ġaymânites; the city of Ġaymân is located 12 km. southeast of Ṣanᶜâᵓ.[106] The expedition was unusually successful; they brought back, among other things, the head of the rebel Ṣaḥbum. The mention of the tribe Ḫawlân Gaddum (line 8) follows that of Ṣaḥbum's defeat and beheading, and therefore may suggest that Ṣaḥbum was Ḫawlânite.

(h) CAMPAIGNS against Najrân: Ja 577/8-14, 579/8, and 599/2

The tribe Najrân had already been subjugated before; now, they rebelled because of and for the

[104] Cf. *MüHG*, 82/3, *RaWiVIS*, map 1 and *WiHöBGS*, p. 19.

[105] ᵓAḥdaqân has nothing to do with Ḥadaqân, located on Wâdî Ḫarîd, 27 km. north-northeast of Ṣanᶜâᵓ (cf. p. 285 B and note 3).

[106] Cf., e.g., *WiHöBGS*, p. 20.

Ḥabašites. ᵓIlšaraḥ Yaḥḏub began a campaign to punish them and to bring them back into submission. Unfortunately, all the names of places where events occurred are unknown.

(1) *First phase:* Ja 577/8-11. – The first phase of the campaign is characterized by the siege of the city Ẓarbân,[107] which defended itself successfully, being strengthened as it was by the double hope of help from Najrân and Ḥaḍramawt. Finally, after two months of unsuccessful siege, ᵓIlšaraḥ Yaḥḏub gave up, and went back to Ṣanᶜâᵓ (line 11). He, however, left some troops behind under the command of two officers, Nawfum, who had previously defeated and beheaded Ṣaḥbum, and another whose name started with K. In the meantime, the representative of the Ḥabašite king, Sabqalum (line 12), whose headquarters were in the city and the tribe Najrân, received reinforcements. The Sab army left behind by ᵓIlšaraḥ Yaḥḏub victoriously attacked the two valleys of Najrân; after that, they returned to Ṣanᶜâᵓ. ᵓIlšaraḥ Yaḥḏub's reason for returning to Ṣanᶜâᵓ was probably to rebuild his army, because he is now seen, after the return of the troops from Najrân, ready to strike again, and to start the second and decisive phase (lines 11-14) of the fighting.

(2) *Second phase:* Ja 577/11-14. ᵓIlšaraḥ Yaḥḏub personally headed a very successful raid in the valley Rakbatân,[108] where many of the enemy were killed, and the chiefs and freemen of Najrân captured; the latter were brought to Maslamân,[109] and the Ḥabašite representative could do nothing to help them. The mercenaries made their submission, and gave ᵓIlšaraḥ Yaḥḏub, as hostages, their sons and their daughters who were taken to the city of Ṣarbân and its two valleys, Najrân. The summary of the campaign against Najrân, although incomplete because of the missing end of line 14, is already impressive: 924 soldiers killed, 562 captives, 68 towns subjugated, 60,000 watered fields plundered, and 97 wells leveled. Finally, the mention of Najrân in Ja 579/8 and 599/2, preceded by the preposition *bn* "from", most probably alludes to booty taken away during the punitive campaign against that city and its tribe.

(i) CAMPAIGN against unknown enemies: Ja 115/2-6

Ja 115 is a dedicatory inscription written by Tabaᶜkarib. The fact that ᵓIlšaraḥ Yaḥḏub is mentioned alone in the first part of the text (line 3), but with his brother in the second (line 7), cannot suggest that the inscription "se place vraisemblablement peu après"[110] the beginning of the coregency, since during that coregency, sometimes ᵓIlšaraḥ Yaḥḏub alone, sometimes he and his brother, and sometimes neither of them commanded an expedition.

The story referred to in the first part of the text (lines 2-6) deals with the complete victory won by ᵓIlšaraḥ Yaḥḏub against some enemies who *tᵓtmw/wrtḏḥn* (line 5) "had gathered together and were slain" in the plain of *Ḥq*... As shown in the commentary on Ja 575/5, the preceding formula does not allude in any way to peace negotiations; besides, the text being fragmentary on the left side, the place name *ḥq* is incomplete,[111] leaving thus unknown the place where the battle occurred.

(j) CAMPAIGN against Ḥimyar and Ḥaḍramawt: Ja 115/7-13, and alliance with Ḥimyar: Ja 115/a-g

After Ḥaḍramawt had committed itself by promising help to the Ḥabašites during the Najrân campaign, it is quite natural that Sabaᵓ would decide to take action against its Ḥaḍr enemy. Nor is it difficult to understand that Ḥaḍramawt would have looked toward Ḥimyar, the old enemy of Sabaᵓ, to find an ally. Ja 115/7-13 tells us about an expedition headed by the two Sab kings in the country of Ḥimyar[112] and of Ḥaḍramawt.

[107] The town of Ṭarib, located on "the main route from Abha to Najrân," when passing "through the Tathlith oasis" (cf. *PhAHL*, p. 18), is much too distant from Najrân, about 200 km. northwest.

[108] The two following places are not suitable here: ar-Rakûbat, which belongs to the Banû Ḥakam (cf. *MüHG*, 120/2), who were located in Tihâmat, south of Jîzân; and ar-Rukbatân (cf. *MüHG*, 105/23), which, according to E. Glaser (cf. *FoSA*, p. 174, note 5), is located in J. Baraᶜ (south of Wâdî Sahâm).

[109] *PhAHL* (pp. 132 and 172) refers to a small town called Maslum, in the vicinity of Ḫamîs Mušayṭ, about 180 km. northwest of Najrân and some 150 km. northeast of Jîzân. Such a place is much too far north.

[110] Cf. *RycIMAM*, p. 187, and also p. 207.

[111] Ḥaql (cf. *MaTSAI*, pp. 3 and 4) or *ḥqb* (cf. G. Ryckmans, in *RB*, 36 [1927], p. 383) or Ḥuqqa (cf. *RÉS*, VI, p. 339) are no more probable, e.g., than al-Ḥaqlain (cf. *MüHG*, e.g., 68/16), al-Ḥaiq (cf. *l.c.*, e.g., 53/12), or Ḥâqir (cf. *l.c.*, 107/15).

[112] Dealing with RÉS 3884=Ja 115/1-13, *RycIMAM* refers to Fakhry 119 (p. 187), which mentions *bn/sbᵓt/(w)ḏr/ḥmyrm* (lines 6-8) "from the battle (and) the war of Ḥimyarum", and states that "certains indices permettent de supposer qu'il s'agissait de la même expédition" (*l.c.*). To specify these "indices", he simply refers to G. Ryckmans, "Inscriptions du Yémen relevées par M. Ahmed Fakhry", in *Le Muséon*, 61 (1948), p. 232. The latter simply states that "il est possible" that the two texts deal with the same campaign; this opinion is also presented by *RyET* (p. 69) in his commentary on Fakhry 119/7: "pourrait". No palaeographical support can be offered for this thesis, for Fakhry 119 is known only by a sketchy facsimile.

Unfortunately, no further details are given on that campaign, except that, afterward, Sabaʾ and Ḥimyar (Ja 115/d) must have jointly taken part in some action, which requires a previous treaty of peace and an alliance.

(k) FOURTH PHASE of the war against Šamir of Raydân, and alliance of Ḥaḍramawt with Sabaʾ: RÉS 4336, Qat[113]

Before discussing the relative chronology between RÉS 4336 and the other inscriptions mentioning ʾIlšaraḥ Yaḥḍub's campaigns against Šamir, several questions must first be dealt with.

(1) *Decipherment* and remarks on RÉS 4336/2-3.

The pericope important for the present question is lines 2-3 which read as follows: *–/ywmn/wbḏt/ʾrẖ/ mrʾs/bšmm/wmt⌉ʿs/bn/ʾqrḥm/qrḥ/bwsṭ/hgrn/ṯbyr/ʾr⌊ḍ/ y⌋ḥr/bywm/kwn/ḍr/byn/šmr/ḏrydn/wb⌊y⌋n/ʾbʾns/bn/ mʿhr/wb⌊ẖ⌋wl⌈m⌉/(w)mlk/sbʾ/wʾmlk/ḥḍrmwt/–*
"–, when and because his lord Bašamum had acted favorably and saved him [the author] from pustules [with which] he broke out in the center of the city [of] Ṯabîr in the land of Yaḥar, when there was war between Šamir, him of Raydân, and between ʾAbʾanas of Maʿâhir and of Baẖawlum and the king of Sabaʾ and the kings of Ḥaḍramawt, –". For *ʾrẖ*, cf. commentary on Ja 567/24. *HöKSI* (p. 32, note 6) relates *qrḥ* to Arabic *qarḥ* and translates it as "wound". However, "wound" and "to wound" are usually rendered by *ẓẖnt* (pl. *ẓẖn*) and *ẓẖn*; besides, the meaning of "wound" in Arabic *qrḥ* comes from *ǧrḥ*. Therefore, I suggest relating *qrḥ*, pl. *ʾqrḥ*, to Arabic *qarḥ* and *qurḥ* (nomen unitatis, *qarḥat*) "(purulent) pustules" and *qariḥ* "a man, or a man's skin *breaking out* with *qurûḥ*".[114] The preceding translation of *qrḥ* greatly affects the interpretation of the whole text. The sickness of ʾAbrataʿ of Ḥadlân[115] ʾIlšarr occurred in the city of Ṯabîr during a war; such a piece of information does not necessarily imply that that city was involved in the war, as suggested by *WiHöBGS* (p. 39; see infra); therefore, the location of the city of Ṯabîr and of the country where this city was built, may be determined independently from the location of the countries involved in the war and mentioned in line 3 of the text.[116] I suggest the possibility that the country of Yaḥar was located west of Yerîm[117]; and somewhere there was the city of Ṯabîr.[118]

The next question to be discussed is the title of ʾAbʾanas. *HöKSI* (p. 44) reads *ʾbʾns/bn/mʿhr[/ w]ḏhwl[n]*. The reading of *ḏ* is not possible on the stone. The letter in discussion is composed of two vertical strokes more apart from each other than in any *ḏ* of the inscription; and its top is closed by a horizontal stroke. A very slant scratch is located in the upper half of the letter, goes beyond the two vertical strokes and is almost five times as thick as any stroke in the text. The possibility of an error in engraving *b* instead of *ḏ* is excluded by the last letter of the tribal name, which is *m*, and not *n*, as always in *ẖwln*. The name *bẖwlm*, a *qatawlum* form, is the name of a country which may be related to Wâdî Baẖal[119] (or, Baẖâl?), a southern tributary of Wâdî Bana; the city of Baẖal (or, Baẖâl?) is located on the wâdî of the same name, 16 km. east of Qaʿṭabat (about 125 km. north-northwest of ʿAden). The well-known Qat tribe Maʿâhir[120] was probably located southwest of Radmân, a location which fits very well that of Baẖawlum southwest of Maʿâhir.

The opponents mentioned in line 3 are clearly

[113] Add the following information to *HöKSI*, pp. 43-44: Yellowish sandstone: top: 32 cm. × 23.7; right side: 21 cm. (top) and 23.5 (bottom) × 13.5; front: 31.6 cm. (top) and 32.2 (right) × max. 14.4; left side: 24 cm. × 14.2. In line 4 of *RÉS*' transliteration (cf. *RÉS*, VII, p. 197), read *mʾdbs/ʾbrtʿ* instead of *ʾbrtʿ/mʾdbs*. For the end of line 6, cf. commentary on Ja 577/14.

[114] Cf. *LaAEL*, p. 2510–11.

[115] Read *ḏhdln* instead of *ḏhd.n* (cf. *HöKSI*, p. 44).

[116] *WiHöBGS* (p. 39, and, e.g., map on p. 60) locates Yaḥar between Radmân and Ḫawlân, and the city of Ṯabîr east and about halfway between Radaʿ and Baynûn, after identifying Ṯabîn (of Wâdî Ṯabîn mentioned by *MüHG*, 109/14) with Ṯabîr and the present Ṣabúr; they, however, note that "die Namen Thabīr and Ṣabúr sind freilich sehr verschieden" (p. 39). The basic reason for seeking the location of Ṯabîr in that part of the country seems to be the following: "Das Gebiet, in dem wir die Stadt *Thabyir* suchen müssen, ist das alte Grenzgebiet, damals zwischen *Ḥadramaut* und *Sabaʾ*, genauer zwischen *Radmān – Khaulān* und *Dhū Raidān – Ḥimyar*" (*l.c.*). However, the name of the tribe Ḫawlân does not exist in the text; the city of Ṯabîr was not necessarily in the territories where the war was raging; it suffices that the city was in their vicinity.

[117] *MüHG* knows *yẖr*, a mountain (193/3) located in the south, a mountain pass (68/7) almost two hours north of Sumâra (cf. *FoSA*, p. 67, note 2), and also a town in the upper part of Wâdî Suḥûl, mentioned along with Yerîm (101/6).

[118] *MüHG* (126/21) mentions a mountain Ṯabîr, which was famous among the Arabs and celebrated in their poetry.

[119] According to E. Glaser (cf. *FoSA*, p. 138, note 4), Wâdî Baẖâl is the name of the upper part of Wâdî ʿUtabat (cf. *MüHG*, 89/17) which joins Wâdî Waḥadat (cf. *MüHG*, *l.c.*) immediately southeast of the town of Qaʿṭabat (cf. *FoSA*, p. 137, note 10).

[120] Cf. *WiHöBGS*, pp. 38-39. On the basis of RÉS 3958/1-2, read *–/bn/mʿhr/w(ḏh)*(line 2) *[wln]⌈/⌉qyl/rdmn/–* in CIH 658/1-2, and ...]⌈*/bn/m*⌉[ʿ]⌈*hr*⌉(line 2)*[wḏhwln/qy]l/rdmn/–* in RÉS 4100/1-2; further, in RÉS 4100/4, read *ḍfẖm* instead of *ḍfẖn*.

specified, since each of them is introduced by the preposition *byn* "between": on the one hand, Šamir and, on the other hand, a coalition composed of ʾAbʾanas of Maʿâhir and Baẖawlum, the king of Sabaʾ and the kings of Ḥaḍramawt.[121]

(2) *Question* of chronology

All the inscriptions which deal with Šamir's warfare and mention the name of his royal Sab opponent, are related to the coregency of ʾIlšaraḥ Yaḥḍub and his brother Yaʾzil Bayyin; RÉS 4336 must therefore be related to the same coregency.[122] The mention of *mlk/sbʾ* (line 3) perfectly fits the information already pointed out, namely that most of the fighting against this Šamir was conducted by ʾIlšaraḥ Yaḥḍub alone.

The war in which Sabaʾ and Ḥaḍramawt were allies against Šamir,[123] fits perfectly well the period which follows the events mentioned in Ja 115/7-13 and a-g. On the one hand, Ḥimyar as well as Ḥaḍramawt, which had committed itself against the two Sab kings during their campaign against Najrân, had been defeated; and afterward, Ḥimyar had joined Sabaʾ in some military action. Similarly here, Ḥaḍramawt, defeated, joined Sabaʾ in the latter's struggle against Šamir. On the other hand, it is not until the reign of Našaʾkarib Yu(ha)ʾmin Yuharḥib that we find a Sab expedition against Ḥaḍramawt; this leaves plenty of time for the historical fact indicated by the expression *ʾmlk/ḥḍrmwt* (line 3). Furthermore, RÉS 4336 presents Šamir as apparently fighting all alone, that is to say without any ally. Such a condition easily characterizes the end of a career. Šamir's former allies had met only with defeat, which did not please them at all. Subsequently, some of them became allies of their former Sab enemy; others doubtless hesitated to taste defeat again with such an unsuccessful partner as Šamir.

(l) UNCLASSIFIED EVENT: Ist 7627/7

Ist 7627[124] mentions the return of his author in safety from *ʾrḍ/ḥmyrm* (line 7). *RyISA*[125] states that this campaign belongs to the operation headed by ʾIlšaraḥ Yaḥḍub and mentioned in Ja 576/3. However, the text does not tell us who was the leader of the campaign, and campaigns against Ḥimyar, characterized by the expression *ʾrḍ/ḥmyrm*, were led by ʾIlšaraḥ Yaḥḍub alone (Ja 576/4 and 590/8, against Šamir of Raydân), by the two royal brothers (Ja 578/15 and 25, against Karibʾil of Raydân), or by a commanding officer, without the presence of either of the two kings (Ja 586/15, against Karibʾil of Raydân). There is thus no way of knowing whether the campaign of Ist 7627/7 is different from any of the already known campaigns, and if not, it is no more possible to determine to which of the known campaigns it is identical.

C – SOLE REIGN

After the death of his brother Yaʾzil Bayyin, ʾIlšaraḥ Yaḥḍub must have reigned alone for a certain period of time before associating his own son Watarum as heir presumptive.

[121] Cf. also *HöKSI*, p. 46; contrast, however, *WiHöBGS*: "*Shammar von Raydān* ist hier [SE 101 = RÉS 4336] auf seiten von *Sabaʾ* Heerführer gegen *Ḥadramaut*, während er zuvor der letzte *Herr von Raydān* und der Ḥimyaren gewesen war, der gegen *ʾIlsharaḥ Yaḥḍib* Krieg geführt hatte, sich dann aber... mit *ʾIlsharaḥ* versöhnt und sich diesem unterworfen hatte [CIH 314 = Gl. 424...]" (pp. 38-39). *RycIMAM*'s interpretation is bewildering: the tribe Ḫawlân, which is to be read Baẖawlum as indicated above, first is not mentioned (p. 113), then is considered as a partner either of the king of Sabaʾ (p. 184) or of Šamir (p. 300).

[122] The dating of this text from the general period of Yarum ʾAyman's dynasty is contrary to the epigraphical evidence. *RycIMAM* connects the text first with the beginning of Šaʿirum ʾAwtar's sole reign (p. 184), but then with the coregency of ʿAlhân Nahfân and his son Šaʿirum ʾAwtar (pp. 299-300; cf. also *RycCSAPS*, p. 206 A); finally *RycCSAPS* (p. 208 B) refers the text to the period which precedes this coregency.

[123] *RycCSAPS*'s (*l.c.*) affirmation according to which "*RÉS* 4336 fait allusion au même conflit, et à la même alliance" as those mentioned in CIH 308 (on which, see above) hardly seems likely. The main purpose of CIH 308 is to celebrate the alliance with the Ḥabašite king Gadarat, which was successfully attained as the alliance with the Ḥaḍr king Yadaʿʾab Ġaylân had been before. Šamir of Raydân is in no way involved. Even if one were to assume that Ḫawlân is mentioned in RÉS 4336/3 (which it is not) it is as an ally of Sabaʾ; Ḫawlân, on the contrary, apparently headed by ʿAmmʾanas son of Šanḥân, had been the enemy of Sabaʾ in CIH 308/18-19.

[124] Ist 7627 was published by *RyISA*, XV, pp. 118-19. The following remarks should be made. Yellowish limestone; maximum thickness: 8 cm.; front: 24 cm. × 18.5; letter height: from 1.6 cm. to 1.5; space between the lines: from 0.3 cm. to 0.2. Line 1: *k* of *rkbn* is complete; the last letter, *y*, is completely destroyed. Line 5: read *sbq* instead of *sbʿ*; the last noun is *ẖrf* and not either *ẖr*[*q*] (p. 118) or *ẖr*[*q*] (p. 119). Line 6: the first letter, ʾ, is complete; the plural *ʾqdmn* is erroneously translated (p. 119) by a singular. Lines 4-6 mean "because His Lord [the god] has vouchsafed to him to have the precedence in his preceding years". Line 9: the first letter, *r*, is complete. Lines 12-13: instead of *wl*/[*w.zʾ*]/*ẖmr*⌊*h*⌋[*w*/..]*w*⌊/ʾ⌋.⌈*ḥ*⌉... (p. 118) or *wl*/[*wzʾ*]/*ẖmr*[*h*][*w*/..]*w*[/ʾ]..[*ḥ*]... (p. 119), read *wl*/⌊*wzʾ*⌋/*ẖ*⌊*mrh*⌋[*w*/]*rḍ*⌊*w*⌋/ʾ*nḥl*⌋[... "and that He [the god] may continue to vouchsafe to him the grace of the commissioners...". In his commentary on lines 2-3 (p. 120), *RyISA* misapplies *JaSQI*'s opinion by failing to point out that this opinion deals only with "*ʾmr/wšmr* mentioned after the two Qatabanian divinities ʾAnbay and Ḥawkum in several Qatabanian texts". There is thus no question of Sab inscriptions, such as Ist 7627.

[125] Cf. *RyISA*, *l.c.*, p. 120.

1° – *Alone:* CIH 429; Fakhry 95+94, 123; Ja 567, 568, 569, 570, 571, 572, 594, 684, 711, 739, 758; NaNAG 5; RÉS 4646

Eleven inscriptions are related to the first period of ʾIlšaraḥ Yaḥḍub's sole reign, CIH 429, Fakhry 95+94, 123; Ja 567-572; NaNAG 5 and RÉS 4646; the palaeography of that period is well illustrated by the photographs of eight of these inscriptions (CIH 429; Ja 568-572; NaNAG 5 and RÉS 4646). Ten of those texts reflect a rather peaceful time, contrasting with the rather violent tone of the preceding coregency, which seems to survive in CIH 429.

RÉS 4646 contains an ordinance[126] given by the king in favor of some of his Suḫaymite servants and of their tribe Yarsum, and mentioning some prohibitions related to fields and harvest.[127] This ordinance is dated from the first month of Niswar, during the sixth year of the eponymate of Maʿadkarib, son of Tabaʿkarib, of the tribe Ḥazfarum.[128]

Fakhry 95+94, copied in the *nâṣerah* of Mârib, refers to the remodeling of some buildings, including an oratory, *lšymhw*[/... "for their patron..."; the deity was thus not ʾIlumquh. Besides, *RyET* (p. 60) reads line 2 as follows: *–/lwfy/mrʾhmw/ʾlšrḥ/yḥḏb/mlk/sbʾ/wḏrydn/wb[nhw/wtrm/...* The preceding passage means "for the safety of their lord ʾIlšaraḥ Yaḥḍub, king of Sabaʾ and Raydân, and of [his] s[on Watarum...". *RyET*'s decipherment is considered by *RycIMAM*[129] as agreeing with the original. Yet, the sign read as *b* after *wḏrydn/w* is, in A. Fakhry's copy,[130] much narrower than every one of the other *b*'s, and, what is more important, its upper part is composed of a concave line instead of a horizontal line as in all the other letter *b*'s. The reading of *b* is therefore highly questionable, and that of *l/* more plausible.

Fakhry 123, copied in Mârib, deals with plantations. The tribe Ḥammat (line 11), which is not identified by *RyET* (p. 75), could have lived in the territory of the same name, reported by *MüHG* (104/9) as being between Isbîl and Ḏamâr.

All the other inscriptions copied in Mârib are from the Maḥram Bilqîs and mention offerings of statues to ʾIlumquh. Ja 571 contains only petitions to the deity. Ja 567 and 572 allude to a special intervention of the lunar god who cured the physical oppression of the Saḥarite ʾAbʾamar ʾAṣdiq (Ja 567) and also saved the king himself from an illness he suffered in Mârib (Ja 572 and NaNAG 5[131]). Ja 568, 569, and 570 mention rather unusual facts. Is it not strange that the three Marbaʾanite men in Ja 569 offer a *female* statue to ʾIlumquh in order to be granted the esteem and grace of their king? The statue offered by two Garatites in Ja 568 was requested by the deity through the king because of the recommendations by which the latter bound himself to these two persons. Finally, a servant of the king offered a statue, which he had promised before, very probably in reparation for the damage incurred by the god because he did not collect the garden products for ʾIlumquh the eighth day. Among the petitions addressed to the deity, one is noteworthy: *wlšrḥ/ydhw/wlsnhw* (Ja 570/13) "and that He [the god] may give success to his hand and his tongue".

The last text to be referred to here is CIH 429 which contains the last thirteen lines of an offering made by *ʾlšrḥ/yḥḏb/mlk/sbʾ/wḏrydn* (lines 2-3 and 9-10 (without the mention of his filiation[132]) to the stellar god ʿAṯtar. The importance of this fragmentary text is undoubtedly overstated by *RycIMAM*,[133] concerning whose interpretation a few remarks might be made. *RycIMAM* summarizes the contents of the text as follows: "le roi ʾIlšaraḥ Yaḥḍub exprime sa reconnaissance envers ʿAṯtar Baḥr Ḥaṭab, pour la protection reçue lors d'opérations militaires contre un ennemi, et pour la protection de ses résidences de Salḥîn, Ġundân et Ṣirwâḥ, contre toutes les entreprises de l'ennemi".[134] The text speaks of *ʾbythmw* (line 10) "their [not "ses"] houses". Besides, *CIH* (pp. 115 and 117), followed by *RycIMAM*, accepts H. Derenbourg's restoration of the last proper name as [*ṣrw*]*ḥ*. Yet, this restoration must be discarded,

[126] *RycIMAM* (p. 179) considers this text as referring to a concession given previously or stated in another document. This opinion is but a consequence of the interpretation according to which the prohibitions concerned the servants of the king who are mentioned in the text. Such an interpretation is contradicted by the expression *ḏhmr* (line 4) "which He vouchsafed", that is to say something pleasant.

[127] *RhEASW* (p. 5) affirms that "der Sinn dieser Inschrift ist ein Akt der Übergabe von Ländereien". The meaning of the concession or ordinance is clear, and there is no question of cession of fields in the text.

[128] Cf. *BeESACD*, pp. 29-32.

[129] Cf. pp. 164, note 11, 169 and note 5, 204 and note 2, 295 and note 18.

[130] Cf. *FaAJY*, I, p. 114, Fig. 62.

[131] In the transliteration of NaNAG 5 by *NaNAG* (II, p. 22), suppress the word divider at the end of line 2; correct *šrḫ* and *grbl* (line 10) to *šrḥ* and *grb/*, *ṯhwn* (line 14) to *ṯhwn*, and *šsy wttʿyt* (line 20) to *šsy/wttʿt*.

[132] Cf. also *RycIMAM*, p. 164 and note 8; however, the same author expressly lists CIH 429 in the first place of the texts which contain the filiation of the king (p. 295 and note 16).

[133] Also repeated by *RycCSAPS*, p. 207.

[134] Cf. p. 176; cf. also p. 285.

for ᵓ*bythmw* is followed by names of three palaces: Salḥân (in Mârib), Ġundân (in Ṣanᶜâᵓ), and [...]ḥ; Ṣirwâh is the name of a city. Furthermore, the expression "contre toutes les entreprises de l'ennemi" does not reflect the text which reads as follows: *wṣtdqn/wnᶜm/lhw/bn/kl/bᵓst[m/wn]kytm* (lines 11-12) "and that He [the god] may do justice to him and please him against all evil [and su]fferings".

The most important part of *RycIMAM*'s opinion is his historical interpretation of the text.

According to this author, the king ᵓIlšaraḥ Yaḥḍub thanks his god because of "la victoire remportée sur un ennemi cruel, dont le nom n'est pas donné, et qui se trouvait 'en opposition avec les dieux et les hommes'" (p. 285), and "Eu égard à la rareté des dédicaces faites par les rois, et par conséquent à l'importance exceptionnelle de l'événement qui les occasionnait – importance que souligne d'autre part, dans le cas de CIH 429, le soin particulier avec lequel a été exécutée cette inscription – nous serions tenté de voir dans CIH 429 une allusion, qui n'a pas été relevée jusqu'ici, à l'invasion d'Aelius Gallus en Arabie. A Aelius Gallus, qui certainement ne ménageait pas les temples des dieux barbares d'Arabie du Sud, s'applique parfaitement la description de l'ennemi de ᵓIlšaraḥ. Le palais de Salḥîn, objectif de choix pour les soldats romains avides de butin, avait effectivement couru un grand danger" (p. 286).[135]

It must be emphasized that the inscriptions written by the kings themselves are certainly not as rare and unusual as it is pictured by *RycIMAM*; nor do the engraving of the text and its physical appearance show anything out of the ordinary, if compared with the other texts engraved by the same ᵓIlšaraḥ Yaḥḍub. Further, the remark about Aelius Gallus' attitude toward South-Arabian deities, put in a rather dramatic way, cannot possibly be considered as exclusive to him, because there is no reason why a similar attitude could not have been taken by a native. As a matter of fact, Ja 629 illustrates vividly that it really happened: the two coregents Saᶜadšamsum ᵓAsraᶜ and his son Marṯadum Yuhaḥmid, among other things, leveled and destroyed *mḥrmt/whyklt* "temples and palaces" (lines 28-29) in the country of Ḥalzawum, which is a South-Arabian city. Ja 643 follows the same line of thought: during their retreat, the Ḥaḍr army intended to plunder a temple which most probably is Maḥram Bilqîs. Furthermore, the affirmation concerning "un ennemi cruel, dont le nom n'est pas donné" is not correct. First of all, it should be pointed out that it is contrary to ᵓIlšaraḥ Yaḥḍub's habit to hide the names of his enemies, and an exception would be even more inexplicable in the case of the Roman invader since he would represent something extraordinary indeed. The passage involved reads as follows: *h]wt/ᵓysn/nmrn* (lines 5-6). *RycIMAM* agrees with H. Derenbourg's interpretation (followed by *CIH*) of *nmrn* as a noun; and *RyISA*[136] interprets *nmrn* similarly but does not make any allusion to *RycIMAM*'s theory. *GlAAA* (p. 108), however, had already considered this *nmrn* as a personal name, opinion accepted as doubtful by *RyNP* (II, p. 94 B). Yet, *GlAAA*'s interpretation must be accepted as certain on the basis of the following parallels:[136a]

RÉS 3992 (period of ᵓAnmarum Yuhaᵓmin, king of Sabaᵓ)/14: *–/ᵓysn/msᶜdm/–*;

Ja 577 (by ᵓIlšaraḥ Yaḥḍub and his brother)/7: *–/hwt/ᵓysn/ṣhbm/bn/gyšm/–* (cf. also line 6);

Ja 585 (same period; different authors)/14-15: *–/ᵓsn/grmt/wld/n[g]šyn/–* (cf. also line 15: *hᵓ/ᵓsn/grmt*);

Ja 644 (period of *yhqm/bn/ḏmrᶜly/ḏrḥ/mlk/sbᵓ/wḏrydn*)/10: *–/hwᵓ/ᵓysn/lḥyᶜṯt/–*

The preceding parallel texts show that ᵓ(*y*)*s* is always followed by a personal name; therefore, the enemy defeated by ᵓIlšaraḥ Yaḥḍub and referred to by CIH 429 is Nimrân, a kind of fanatic who had no respect whatsoever either for deities or men; CIH 429 thus does not allude at all to Aelius Gallus' expedition in South Arabia. It would of course be very interesting to know more about this fanatic Nimrân. I suggest identifying Nimrân of CIH 429 with Nimrân ᵓAwkân of Ja 594, 684, 711, 739, and 758. Only the first of these five texts mentions the names of ᵓIlšaraḥ Yaḥḍub and of his brother; and the last four do not contain any allusion to any king.[137] Further, Nimrân ᵓAwkân and his brother Gaḥḍum ᵓAḥṣân had at least two *mqtwy* (Ja 739 and 758) at their service.[138] It would not be very difficult to think that power had gone to Nimrân ᵓAwkân's head and led him to

[135] According to *BePSC* (p. 52), *RycIMAM* "convincingly suggests" that CIH 429 refers to Aelius Gallus. *WiHöBGS* (p. 34) allude to *RycIMAM*'s opinion.

[136] Cf. XIII, p. 162, commentary on Geukens 3/13.

[136a] Cf. commentary on Ja 577/6.

[137] Compare with Yarum ᵓAyman's attitude toward the king Wahabᵓil Yaḥûz.

[138] Compare with the Hamdânid chiefs Naṣrum Yuhaᵓmin and Ṣadiq [Yahub].

dream of more power, more authority, and finally of the throne itself. CIH 429 would then allude to his rebellion – and do it in such a way that Nimran ʾAwkân is pictured as a rebel who, in his despair of seeing victory, waged a desperate war in which neither man nor deity was spared. That CIH 429 refers only to Nimrân and not to both him and his brother, would not disprove the proposed identification. The consideration proposed below on the erasure of Nimrân ʾAwkân's name, indicates that Nimrân ʾAwkân alone rebelled against his king. Since the two brothers always are mentioned as acting closely together, and Gaḥḍum ʾAḥṣân in the second place, it would seem that the latter would, willingly or unwillingly, have followed his brother in his rebellion; the fact therefore that the brother is not mentioned in CIH 429 is better explained by the hypothesis according to which he had already died when Nimrân ʾAwkân decided to try his luck, to start his great adventure. That Nimrân ʾAwkân was, at a certain time, hated by some people, is clearly pointed out by the erasure of his name in Ja 711/8; his brother's name is still intact in the following line. The same phenomenon of hatred aimed at destroying Nimrân ʾAwkân's name is also attested in Ja 739/2 and 13, although more violence was used in the latter case. In line 13, the first act, in fact, was a blow that also destroyed parts of lines 12 and 14. If Nimrân ʾAwkân became a fanatic rebel such as the one described in CIH 429, it is no wonder that some persons decided to destroy even his memory by erasing his name. However, some texts escaped their hands.

The preceding identification of Nimrân (CIH 429) and Nimrân ʾAwkân (e.g., Ja 594) suits perfectly well the above-proposed relative chronology of ʾIlšaraḥ Yaḥḍub's coregency with his brother and his sole reign. It would of course be unthinkable that, after such a rebellion which amounted to total war, Nimrân ʾAwkân would still have enjoyed his post of leader of three clans.

2° – *With his son Watarum* as heir presumptive: RÉS 3990 and 4150.

Only two inscriptions, RÉS 3990 and 4150,[139] are related to the second period of ʾIlšaraḥ Yaḥḍub's sole reign, that is to say when he associated as heir presumptive, his son, Watarum. Unfortunately, these two dedicatory inscriptions do not give any political information. In RÉS 3990 (from al-Ġirâs), some Suhaymites offer five statues to the god Taʾlab for the welfare of their lords, themselves and of their house. In RÉS 4150[140] (from Mârib), two individuals make an offering to their god ʿAṯtar because of favors received from the deity.

d – COREGENCY WITH HIS SON Watarum Yuhaʾmin: Ist 7628[141]

Some remarks on the original are needed. The measurements of this whitish limestone slab are 84.5 cm. × 34.5[142]; maximum thickness: 11 cm. A monogram, not alluded to by *BeFSTI* and whose remains, the letter *š* (most probably from ʾIlšaraḥ Yaḥḍub), are still visible on the right of lines 1-2, extended the whole height of the stone. In line 4, *[mr]ʾyhmw* is absolutely certain instead of *[mr]ʾhmw*.[143] Finally, the expression "[and by]" restored by *BeFSTI* (p. 277) at the beginning of lines 3 and 4, must be transferred to the end of lines 2 and 3 respectively.

The very fragmentary text Ist 7628 deals with buildings. Because he did not notice the dual *[mr]ʾy*, the editor of the text does not mention or discuss the question raised by line 4 which reads as follows: *[mr]ʾyhmw/ʾlšrḥ/yḥḍb/mlk/s[bʾ*, which *BeFSTI* (pp. 276 and 277) correctly completes by adding to it */wḏrydn*. This formula is extremely important.

The expression *mrʾyh(m)w*, when followed by the name of a king, *normally* introduces the names of two kings, which are followed by a royal title *common* to the two of them[144]; therefore Ist 7628/4 did mention a coregency. Since ʾIlšaraḥ Yaḥḍub's coregency with his brother Yaʾzil Bayyin is constantly expressed by this unique formula, *ʾlšrḥ/yḥḍb/wʾḫ(y)hw/yʾzl/byn/mlky/sbʾ/wḏrydn*, – the men-

[139] *RycIMAM* also mentions Fakhry 95+94 (e.g., pp. 164, note 11 and 169, note 5) and RÉS 4216 (pp. 204, note 2 and 295, note 18). Fakhry 95+94 belongs to the first part of ʾIlšaraḥ Yaḥḍub's sole reign, and RÉS 4216 to the coregency of Saʿadšamsum ʾAsraʿ and Marṯadum Yuhaḥmid.

[140] In *RycIMAM*, p. 169, note 5, correct "4170, 7-8" to "4150, 7-8".

[141] Cf. *BeFSTI*, pp. 275-77 and pl. II A and B.

[142] The length of the two fragments put together is quite obviously much longer than the width; therefore, "84" should be read instead of "34" (as *BeFSTI*, p. 275), provided of course that "34 × 32 cm." (cf. *l.c.*) are not the measurements of the left part (cf. pl. II B), which is almost square.

[143] As *l.c.*, pp. 276 and 277, translation.

[144] E.g.: *mrʾyhmw/yrm/ʾymn/wʾḫyhw/krbʾl/wtr/mlky/sbʾ* (Ja 565/11-12) and *mrʾyhmw/ʾlšrḥ/yḥḍb/wʾḫyhw/yʾzl/byn/mlky/sbʾ/wḏrydn* (e.g., Ja 578/26-28). Sometimes, *mrʾ* in singular may replace the dual; e.g., *mrʾhmw/ysrm/yhnʿm/wšmr/yhrʿš/ʾmlk/sbʾ/wḏrydn* (Ja 648/7-9).

tion of their family relationship with Fariᶜum Yanhub is here of no importance – the great frequency of this formula excludes the *restoration* of any other one. ʾIlšaraḥ Yaḥḍub's coregency with his brother Yaʾzil Bayyin is excluded then from the present text, and there remains thus his coregency with another person. Since we know that ʾIlšaraḥ Yaḥḍub did have his son Watarum as heir presumptive and also that the latter reigned alone, the possibility of ʾIlšaraḥ Yaḥḍub's coregency with a person other than his son Watarum, although at first sight not to be discarded, is not suggested by any epigraphical or historical evidence. Therefore I assume that Ist 7628 belongs to ʾIlšaraḥ Yaḥḍub's coregency with his son Watarum, which is to be inserted between ʾIlšaraḥ Yaḥḍub's sole reign with his son Watarum as heir presumptive and the latter's reign. Then the formula of Ist 7628/4 may be completed on the basis of the parallel case in RÉS 4771/2, which mentions two coregents, father and son, each name being followed by the royal title in singular, and without any mention of the family relationship between the two persons; thus *[mr]ʾyhmw/ʾlšrḥ/yhḏb/mlk/s[bʾ/ wḏrydn/wwtrm/yhʾmn/mlk/sbʾ/wḏrydn]*.

C – REIGN OF WATARUM YUHAʾMIN: CIH 10, 258; Geukens 4; Ja 601-07 and 753

The most important question to be dealt with here is that of the identification of the present king Watarum Yuhaʾmin with the second king mentioned during the preceding coregency.

This identity is denied by *RycIMAM* (pp. 164, note 11, and 296) for the simple reason that ʾIlšaraḥ Yaḥḍub's sole reign, the coregency of the latter and his brother, and finally Našaʾkarib Yu(ha)ʾmin Yuharḥib's reign follow each other immediately; there is thus no room for Watarum Yuhaʾmin. However, as stated above, the relative chronology of the first two above-mentioned reigns must be inverted. The following expressions, *lšrḥ/yhḏb/mlk/sbʾ/wḏrydn/wbn(y)hw/wtrm* (RÉS 3990/5-7 and 4150/7-8) and *wtrm/yhʾmn/mlk/sbʾ/wḏrydn/bn/ʾlšrḥ/yhḏb/mlk/sbʾ/wḏrdyn* (Geukens 4/4-5; Ja 601/6-7, 602/6-7, 603/8-11, 604/4-5, 606/8-10, 607/8-10; idem in Ja 605/8-9, but *yhḏb* is missing) obviously allude to the same persons, as has been suggested by *MoMiSI*.[145] Further, the name of Yaʾzil Bayyin is never mentioned in Watarum Yuhaʾmin's title.

The immediate succession of Watarum Yuhaʾmin after ʾIlšaraḥ Yaḥḍub's second coregency is corroborated by Ja 568 and Ja 606, 607; the first text is dated from the latter's reign, and the two others from that of the former, all three of them being written by Saᶜadšamsum ʾAsraᶜ and his son Marṯadum ([Yuh]aḥmid). Too, Ja 573, I, II, III is closer to Ja 606, 607 than to Ja 568; e.g., the son is called *mrṯdm* in Ja 607/2 and [753 I/1 and 606/1-2], but *[mrṯdm/yh]ḥmd* in Ja 568/1-2; the offering is *ṣlmnhn* in Ja 606/4, 607/4 and 753 I/2, but *ṣlmn* in Ja 568/4; the expression *ḥ(n)gn/wqhhmw* in Ja (606/4-5), 607/4-5 and 753 I/2 equals *ḥgn/kwqh* in Ja 568/4; in the final invocation, the expression *bʾlyhmw* which introduces *ᶜṯtr/ᶜzzm/wḏt/ẓhrn* in Ja 606/21, 607/21 and 753 I/8, II/16, and III/16, is replaced by *b/ʾlyhmw* in Ja 568/24. Those features common to Ja 606, 607, and 753 do not vitiate others which are common to Ja 568 and 753, e.g., the insertion of *wb(/)šms/mlkn/tnf* after *ḏt/bᶜdnm* in the final invocation (Ja 568/23-24 and 753 I/8, II/15-16, and III/15-16).

The excavations at the entrance court of Maḥram Bilqîs are responsible for the only six inscriptions which give the king's full title. Prior to those excavations, the king's name was found in two very fragmentary texts, CIH 10 and 258.[146] Among the six texts from Maḥram Bilqîs, two are known by two copies, namely Ja 601 = 602 and 606 = 607. Only Ja 601 = 602 gives any historical information by alluding to two battles ordered by the king against Ḫawlân Gaddân "because of the offences they committed against" the king. The contents of the five others mention already known facts concerning the offering of statues, namely for the safety of the authors and of their sons (Geukens 4[147] and Ja 604), the building and repairing of several constructions (Ja 603), the safety of the author's son (Ja 605) and finally the order from the deity for the welfare of the authors (Ja 606 = 607) as well as in order for them to receive favors (Ja 753 I-III).

Appendix on CIH 951. – The lack of photography prevents us from solving the case of CIH

[145] Cf. p. 59; cf. also *RyISA*, XIV, pp. 371-72, who, however, does not refer to the contrary opinion of *RycIMAM*.

[146] *RycIMAM* (p. 118 and note 3) describes CIH 258 as follows: "un nom royal sans titre". Yet, the text is very fragmentary.

[147] In line 2 of the text, instead of *wwfy* (cf. *RyISA*, XIV, p. 370, in both transcriptions), read *wlwfy*; in line 3, *lᶜzz* is as possible and probable as *yᶜzz* (cf. *l.c.*), and instead of *ᶜhwfᶜṯt* (cf. *l.c.*, transcription in South-Arabian letters), read *whwfᶜṯt*; in line 4, read *sbʾ* instead of *sbn* (cf. *l.c.*).

951 which only contains, according to E. Glaser's copy,

m/y/
wḏr

CIH (III, p. 278) conjectures *[ysr]m/yh[nᶜm/mlk]*
[sbᵓ/]wḏr[ydn]

The fragmentary condition of the text makes this restoration highly questionable; the respective locations of *m* and *w* remain unknown. *CIH*'s restoration is improbable for the two lines would be too unequal in length and would begin at different levels. *RycIMAM* (p. 162, note 1) improves upon *CIH* by mentioning "[Yâsi]r Yu[hanᶜim] (ou [Karibᵓil Wata]r Yu[hanᶜim])". In each one of these two suggestions, the *r* does exist in E. Glaser's copy, and *h* is represented by the second word divider. The second suggestion must be definitively discarded because the second name of the king is *wtr* and not *wtrm*. The Sab king alluded to in CIH 951 could be one of the four following kings: *wtrM/YHᵓmn* (e.g., Ja 601), *mrṯdM/YHḥmd* known as second coregent with his father *sᶜdšmsm/ᵓsrᶜ* (e.g., Ja 626), *ysrM/YHnᶜm* known as first coregent in three different coregencies (e.g., Ja 646, 664, and 665) and *ysrM/YHṣdq* (e.g., RÉS 4775).

D – REIGN OF NAŠAᵓKARIB YU(HA)ᵓMIN YUHARḤIB

1 – *Introduction*

Before presenting the information mentioned in the texts engraved during the reign of Našaᵓkarib Yu(ha)ᵓmin Yuharḥib, two questions must be discussed here, namely his name and filiation.

a – THE ROYAL NAME

The royal name of the present king is *nšᵓkrb/yᵓmn/yhrḥb* in most of the inscriptions. However, the form *yhᵓmn* must be accepted as a different spelling, for it is attested four times, Ja 619/15, 620/14, and 623/8 and 12-13, which can be checked on photographs. The form *yrḥb* is attested only once, NaNAG 8/20-21 [148]; if this spelling is not a mistake in the engraving of the inscription, it could possibly have something to do with the actual pronunciation of the letter *h*.

b – THE KING'S FILIATION

Since the title of the king always mentions *bn/ᵓlšrḥ/yḥḍb/wyᵓzl/byn/mlky/sbᵓ/wḏrydn*, the question must be raised concerning the exact meaning of the second mentioned personal name, *yᵓzl/byn*. It seems quite obvious that the present king should be considered as the son of ᵓIlšaraḥ Yaḥḍub, since the latter's name always follows the noun *bn* "son of". However, the latest study on the question enlarges the problem considerably by questioning the king's filiation. *RycIMAM* indeed presents his opinion as follows: "Si Našaᵓkarib avait été fils de ᵓIlšaraḥ, non seulement celui-ci n'aurait eu aucune raison d'associer son frère à son pouvoir, mais encore Yaᵓzil ne serait pas nommé dans la filiation de Našaᵓkarib. Au contraire, si comme nous le pensons, Našaᵓkarib était fils de Yaᵓzil, la mention de ᵓIlšaraḥ dans sa filiation s'expliquerait aisément du fait qu'il était en quelque sorte le fils adoptif de ᵓIlšaraḥ, dont il recueillait la succession royale" (p. 296).[149] Two facts stated before, namely on the one hand, the association by Fariᶜum Yanhub to his royal duties, of his two sons, ᵓIlšaraḥ Yaḥḍub and Yaᵓzil and, on the other hand, the immediate succession of ᵓIlšaraḥ Yaḥḍub's second coregency by his son Watarum Yuhaᵓmin, disprove *RycIMAM*'s preceding argumentation. By associating his brother Yaᵓzil to his kingship, ᵓIlšaraḥ Yaḥḍub did nothing but to be faithful to his own father's will. Further, why should he have adopted Našaᵓkarib since he had a son of his own? As a matter of fact, *RycIMAM* does not even speak of a real adoption, but a very vague one indeed since it only consists of a mere succession in the king list. The hypothesis of Našaᵓkarib as Yaᵓzil's son does not seem to me very reasonable, because of the following reasons. What reason could Našaᵓkarib have had that his cousin Watarum did not have, to mention his uncle's name in his title, and especially why did he not mention his real father's name first, since there is no evidence that such a form of adoption existed, and that suggested by *RycIMAM* is so vague that it amounts to nothing? The mention of ᵓIlšaraḥ Yaḥḍub's name in the first place means, in my opinion, that the latter was the father of Našaᵓkarib. But then, why does he always mention his uncle's name in his title? The answer to that

[148] The publisher of the text (cf. *NaNAG*, II, pp. 35 and 36) does not restore the missing *h*, nor does he make any comment on it.

[149] *PiIRC* repeats *RycIMAM*'s ideas without referring to the latter: "on comprendrait... qu'il[Našaᵓkarib] ait été le fils de celui [Yaᵓzil Bayyin] qui avait abandonné son pouvoir à son frère [ᵓIlšaraḥ Yaḥḍub], et qu'il était ainsi fils de l'un par le sang et fils de l'autre pour le pouvoir royal" (p. 171).

question may be found in the drastic change in the policy followed by Watarum and Naša'karib. A policy of expansion doubtless characterizes the reign of the two brothers 'Ilšaraḥ Yaḥḍub and Ya'zil Bayyin, but was apparently abandoned by Watarum Yuha'min. All the texts belonging to Watarum's reign express peace and activities within the limits of his kingdom and not at all war and conquest; only Ja 601 = 602 alludes to a punitive expedition against Ḫawlân Gaddân. The first of these two remarks must also be made about the texts belonging to the reign of 'Ilšaraḥ and his son Watarum, as his heir presumptive, a good sign that the latter had already curbed his father's policy during his last years. Quite to the contrary, Naša'karib resumes the policy of 'Ilšaraḥ Yaḥḍub and Ya'zil Bayyin, as is shown by his military campaigns in Ḥaḍramawt and Saharatân. That is the way I should like to explain his royal title; besides indicating 'Ilšaraḥ Yaḥḍub as his real father, he also makes clear, by mentioning his uncle's name in the second place, that he intends to follow their policy which was abandoned by his oldest brother and predecessor on the throne, Watarum Yuha'min.

2 – *Family of Wahab'awwâm Ya'ḏif and his brother Yadum Yadrim:*
CIH 24, 314+954; Geukens 6; Ja 616, 718; NaNAG 8; RÉS 3968 and 4646

Although the study of the family of Wahab-'awwâm Ya'ḏif and of his brother Yadum Yadrim does not give any unquestionable confirmation of the above proposed historical reconstruction, because the first link is not absolutely certain, and no text dated from Watarum Yuha'min's reign is yet recorded as belonging to a member of that family, this study is important because of the discussion of the first link and the development of that family under several kings. This study is placed here, because the family of Wahab'awwâm Ya'ḏif reached its apogee during the reign of Naša'karib Yu(ha)'min Yuharḥib.

a – REMARKS ON SOME TEXTS:
CIH 24, 314+954; Geukens 6; NaNAG 8; RÉS 3968 and 4646

CIH 24 and *MoMiSI* (p. 22, note 1). This text is not alluded to by *RycIMAM*. All the other inscriptions related to the same persons, except CIH 314+954, suggest the correction of E. Glaser's copy of *s̲hmn*[150] to *s̲h*[*y*]*m*(*m*).[151] E. Glaser's copy of the second name of *whb'wm* is *ysbr* (line 1); and *MoMiSI*[152] does not justify his reading of it as *yskr*. In relation to CIH 24, *MoMiSI* also allude to CIH 889/1; however, his correction and restoration of the text is far-fetched.

CIH 314+954/2-3: *whb*[..]*m*/*y'ḏf*/*bn*/*gdnm*/*whḏwt*. Since *GlAAA* (p. 117) to *RhIG* (p. 50), including *CIH* (I, pp. 342 and 344), the two missing letters are restored as *'w*; and the reading of *whb'wm* is even considered certain by *RyNP* (II, p. 52 B). At first sight, however, one might think of *whb*[*ry*]*m* which, although possible,[153] is not yet attested, for CIH 196/1 and 263/1 are both very fragmentary and mention *whbry*[and *whbrym*[respectively. In neither case may *whbrym* be considered either complete or certain,[154] and the restoration *whbrymn*[155] is not supported because of *whbrymm* in RÉS 4578.[156]

Geukens 6 (cf. *RyISA*, XIV, pp. 372-75): it should be emphasized that the published photograph of the text (pl. III) is completely useless from a palaeographical point of view, and practically useless for checking the reading of many letters. – In line 1, instead of [*bn*/*s̲hym*]*m* proposed by *RyISA*, read [*w'ḫyhw*/*yd*]*m* on the basis of Ja 616/1. – Another question is *RyISA*'s reading of *lb'n* (lines 24 and 28), *lb'nhn* (line 31) and *nmrn* (lines 28 and 31). In his commentary on line 24, *RyISA* notes that "dans la lettre initiale de *lb'n*, le crochet est un trait oblique qui forme un angle aigu en rejoignant la hampe. La lecture *gb'n* nous paraît donc devoir être écartée" (p. 380). The letter *g* occurs seven times in *RyISA*'s decipherment of the text; none of them can be checked on the published photograph. The difference between *l* and *g* in the texts written during Naša'karib Yu(ha)'min Yuharḥib's reign, and more precisely in the texts belonging to the same authors as those of Geukens 6, namely Ja 616, 718 and NaNAG 8, is not at all whether the left appendage is or is not oblique, that appendage in all the *l*'s in Ja 718 being almost horizontal, but both in the slanting degree of the appendage and the height of its extreme

150 Cf. *Mittheilungen*, Prag, 1886, p. 56, and also *MoMiSI*, *l.c.*
151 Cf. already *CIH*, I, p. 38.
152 Cf. *l.c.*, followed by *RyNP*, I, p. 397 B.
153 Cf. *RyISA*, III, p. 186.
154 As *RyNP*, I, p. 225 A and II, p. 53 A, respectively.
155 As *MoMiSI*, p. 83.
156 Cf. also *RyNP*, I, p. 402 B.

left edge. Therefore, *RyISA*'s reason for discarding the reading of *g* and for stating that of *l*, does not touch the specific difference between the two letters, and cannot thus be considered valid. Until a clear, useful photograph of the text is published, the reading of *lbʾ* is in no way more probable than that of *gbʾ*.

NaNAG 8. – *NaNAG* (II, p. 33) confuses the left edge of the hollow containing the symbol with a word divider; thus, this sign located at the beginning of line 2 must be suppressed. Further, in *NaNAG*'s (pp. 33-34) transliteration of the text, correct *dsmʿy* (line 5) to *d̲smʿy*, *hmdm* (line 8) to *ḥmdm*, *t̲ʾhwn* (line 9) to *t̲hwn*, *w*.(16).*m* (lines 15-16) to *wy*(16)*dm*, *ḥmʾt̲t* (line 16) to *ḥmʿt̲t*, *hẓy* (line 19) to *ḥẓy*, *frʾm* (line 23) to *frʿm*, and *w*[*d̲*]*rḥq* (line 27) to *wrḥq*. In *RyISA*'s (XIV, p. 376) restoration of lines 1-2, the letter *w* of ʾ*h̲*]⌜*yhw*⌝ (line 1) has disappeared entirely on the stone; in line 2, what the author considers as the lower end of *f* is actually the lower part of *r*; thus instead of ..⌜*f*⌝., read ⌜*ydrm*⌝.

RÉS 3968. – On the basis of Geukens 6/1-5, Ja 616/1-4, 718/1-4 and NaNAG 8/1-6, the end of line 1 must be restored to read .../*bnw*/*sh̲ymm*/ ʾ*bʿl*/*bytn*/*rymn*/ʾ*qwl*/*šʿbn*/*yrsm*/*d̲smʿ*], instead of ...ʾ*qwl*/*šʿbn*/*smʿ*.[157] This text is not mentioned by *RyISA* (XIV, pp. 376-77), in his discussion of Geukens 6/1-4; and *RycIMAM* does not mention the problem.

RÉS 4646: Yellowish sandstone; maximum thickness: 10 cm.; thickness of the lateral faces: 7.5 cm.; letter height: from 1.8 cm. to 2.5; space between the lines: from 0.3 cm. to 0.6. *MiScASIH* (p. 17) reads *whbʾwm*/*wydmm*(/)*wḥmʿt̲*[*t*] in line 5, and *RhEASW* (p. 2) reads the end as follows: *wydmmwḥmʿt̲*[*t*]. In note 3, the latter points out that there is in *whbʾwm* the same mistake as that at the end of line 4, that is to say "statt eines ʾ ein Monstrum aus *s* oder ʾ zu sehen, mit Falschsetzung des Oberteiles" (cf. note 2). Both statements are not correct, since ʾ in both cases is clear and engraved properly. The detail that led N. Rhodokanakis into error is that the lower vertical stroke of the upper part of the letter hits the upper concave line of the lower half of the letter, not in its center, but in its right part. The same author continues: "im Text *wydmm*, hingegen im Photo nach dem *y* ein *wym*(?)*mm* oder ähnlich." On the other hand, *RÉS* (VII, p. 290) reads *wyddm*(/)*wḥmʿt̲*[*t*], and *RyISA* (XIV, p. 377) *wydmm*/*wḥmʿt̲t*. In these two readings, either (/) or / is erroneous, since there is no word divider on the stone; besides the last letter of *ḥmʿt̲*[*t*] is a restoration of the text. The worker actually engraved first *ymdm*; he then corrected the first *m* to *d* by erasing the upper left part of the letter and by engraving the central appendage of *d*; he also corrected the second *d* to *m*. However, he did not correct the second *m* which is to be corrected to a word divider. The text reads thus as follows: *wy*(*dm*/)*wḥmʿt̲*[*t*]. The preceding example of careless engraving is not too surprising, considering the engraving of *yḥd̲b* (line 2). The four letters are all distorted and obviously engraved on top of *sbʾ*. The right vertical stroke of *s* was enlarged and re-used in *y*; the left vertical stroke, the left half of the horizontal stroke and the upper vertical stroke of the same letter *s* were re-used in the engraving of the right edge of *ḥ*; the upper half of the right vertical stroke of *b* was re-used in the upper left vertical stroke of *ḥ*; the lower half of the same stroke of *b* is still on the stone; and the rest of the letter *b* disappeared in the engraving of *d̲*; the letter ʾ is almost entirely erased (both the oblique and horizontal strokes of the upper half are still visible) and replaced by *b*. Furthermore, in *RÉS*'s transcription, insert *w* before *mḥglt* (line 9), suppress *w* before *mḥglm* (line 10) and correct *t̲mrn* (line 18) to *ḥmrn*; correct]/*yrsm* to /]*yrsm*.

[157] Cf. *MoMiSI*, p. 22, followed by *RÉS*, VII, p. 22.

b – THE FAMILY TREE AND THE RELATIVE CHRONOLOGY OF THE TEXTS

The family tree of the persons mentioned in CIH 24, 314+954, Geukens 6, Ja 616 and 718, NaNAG 8, RÉS 3968 and 4646 may be presented as follows:

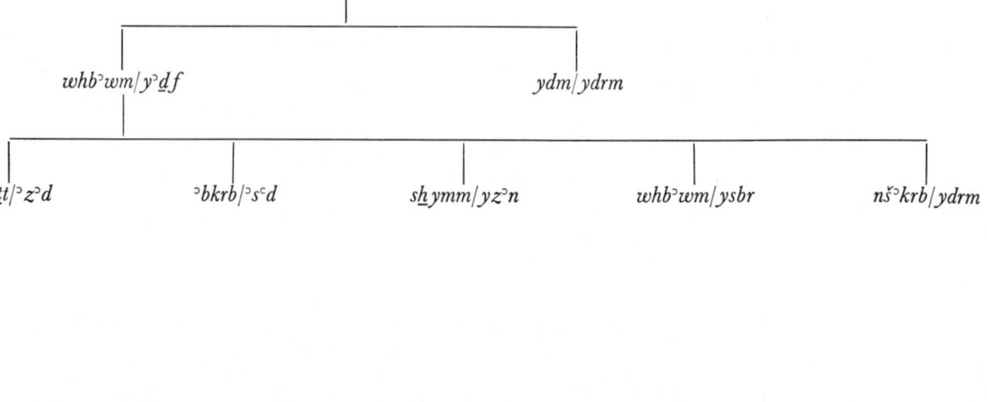

The case of CIH 314+954 is first to be discussed, namely the identity of *whb*[..]*m*/*yʾḏf*/*bn*/*gdnm*/*wẖḏwt*. Four facts, if considered together, suggest the restoration of *whb*[..]*m* to *whb*[ʾ*w*]*m* as almost certain, and support the identification (upon which *MoMiSI* [p. 22, note 1] does not decide) of that person with *whbʾwm*/*yʾḏf*, e.g., in CIH 24/3; no personal name yet attested fits the blank, except *whbʾwm* which is a very well known personal name; *yʾḏf* is attested, so far, only as a second name after *whbʾwm*; finally, CIH 314+954 and RÉS 4646, which mentions *whbʾwm* who undoubtedly is *whbʾwm*/*yʾḏf*, are both dated from the time of ʾIlšaraḥ Yaḥḍub. The only difficulty to the preceding identification is the difference of title: *bn*/*gdnm*/*wẖḏwt* in CIH 314+954/3, and *bn*(*w*)/*sẖymm*, e.g., in RÉS 4646/6. The preceding diversity is not a real difficulty because either the two families Gadanum and Ḫaḏwat were parts of the tribe Suẖaymum, or Wahabʾawwâm Yaʾḏif, as a consequence of circumstances unknown to us, became a member of a tribe other than that of his origin. It has already been pointed out, in connection with the kings Yarum ʾAyman and ʾIlšaraḥ Yaḥḍub, that the clan where a person has some charge, is not necessarily his clan of origin. The above-mentioned difference in title certainly does not rule out the proposed identification of the two Wahabʾawwâm Yaʾḏif's, which, in my view, is to be accepted because of the unusual second personal name *yʾḏf* mentioned in texts belonging to the same general period.

The relative chronology of the texts related to Wahabʾawwâm Yaʾḏif's family has been ascertained thanks to the evolution of the titles and also to the relationship between the different members of that family. The following scheme presents this relative chronology, mentioning the order of the inscriptions, the serial numbers of the texts, the royal names, the names of the members of Wahabʾawwâm Yaʾḏif's family and their titles, in five consecutive columns. The restorations of texts quoted in the following scheme are so firmly supported that they are not pointed out as such; however, they are still to be considered as restorations and not as found on the stones.

1	CIH 314+954	*ʾlšrḥ*/*yḥḍb* and his brother *yʾzl*/*byn*	*whbʾwm*/*yʾḏf*	*bn*/*gdnm*/*wẖḏwt*
2	RÉS 4646	*ʾlšrḥ*/*yḥḍb* alone	*whbʾwm*; *ydm*; *ḥmᶜṯt* and *ʾbkrb*	*bnw*/*sẖymm* *šᶜbn*/*yrsm*
3	Ja 718	(missing)	*whbʾwm*/*yʾḏf*, his brother *ydm*/*ydrm*, and his sons *ḥmᶜṯt*/*ʾzʾd*, *ʾbkrb*/*ʾsᶜd* and *sẖymm*/*yzʾn*	*bnw*/*sẖymm* *ʾbᶜl*/*bytn*/*rymn* *ʾqwl*/*šᶜbn*/*yrsm*/*ḏsmᶜv*/ *ṯlṯ*(*n*)/*ḏhgrm*
4	NaNAG 8	*nšʾkrb*/*yʾmn*/*yhrḥb*	same as in 3	
5	RÉS 3968	(missing)	*ydm*/*ydrm* and his brother...	
6	Geukens 6	same as in 4	same as in 3	same as in 3, PLUS the following: *mqtt*/*nšʾkrb*/*yʾmn*/ *yhrḥb*/*mlk*/–
7	Ja 616			
8	CIH 24	(missing)	*whbʾwm*/*ysbr* and his brothers *nšʾkrb*/*ydrm*, *ḥmᶜṯt*/*ʾzʾd* and *ʾbkrb*/*ʾsᶜd*, *bnw*/*whbʾwm*/*yʾḏf*	*bn*/*sẖymm* *ʾqwl*/*šᶜbn*/*yrsm*

Several questions must be discussed in relation to the information presented in the preceding scheme.

The continuous persistence of the title *bn*(*w*)/*sẖymm* in texts 2-8 would hardly admit the intrusion, somewhere along the list, of the title *bn*/*gdnm*/*wẖḏwt*, and suggests that the latter be dated from an earlier period. This conclusion perfectly fits the relative chronology, proposed above, where the reign of the two brothers ʾIlšaraḥ Yaḥḍub and Yaʾzil Bayyin precedes that of ʾIlšaraḥ Yaḥḍub alone.

The four persons mentioned in RÉS 4646/5-6 are obviously identical with the first four listed in NaNAG 8/1-3; they are even listed in the same order. However, if the person in CIH 314+

954/2-3 is identical with the first in RÉS 4646/5, and since RÉS 4646 is prior to NaNAG 8 and posterior to CIH 314+954, why are the same persons mentioned by their first personal names only? This feature of RÉS 4646 may be explained by the fact that the text is an ordinance given by the king in favor of some of his servants. Two good parallels, belonging to the same dynasty, are Fakhry 3 and 76. In these two royal decrees, the names of the beneficiaries are single and are introduced by the noun *ʾdm* "servants", exactly as in RÉS 4646/4-5.

The identity of persons and of their titles in Ja 718 and NaNAG 8 suggests that the first most probably belongs to the same period as the second, namely Našaʾkarib Yu(ha)ʾmin Yuharḥib's reign. Besides, NaNAG 8 seems to be posterior to Ja 718, because it does not make any special remark about either one of the three sons of Wahabʾawwâm Yaʾd̲if; on the contrary, Ja 718 speaks at least twice (lines 6 and 7) of *wldn/sh̲ymm* "this child Suh̲aymum".

The authors of RÉS 3968 are Yadum Yadrim *wʾh̲yh[w* "and hi[s] brother" or "and hi[s] two brothers" or "and hi[s] brothers"; in any hypothesis of interpretation, Wahabʾawwâm Yaʾd̲if may have been mentioned in the missing part of the text; the first author of CIH 24 also associated two of his oldest brothers. The title mentioned in RÉS 3968 suggests that this text belongs to the same period as that of Ja 718 and NaNAG 8. However, a definitive relative chronology does not seem possible at the present time. On the one hand, Wahabʾawwâm Yaʾd̲if, his brother and his sons, already known in Ja 718 and NaNAG 8, are still in charge in Ja 616 and Geukens 6, both posterior to RÉS 3968. On the other hand, Ja 718 is not necessarily the first text engraved after its authors were put in the two offices mentioned by their title; and Ja 718 and NaNAG 8 do not necessarily follow each other so closely that the engraving of some other text between is excluded. RÉS 3968 could thus possibly be anterior either to Ja 718 or only to NaNAG 8. However, since it has to be listed somewhere, I place it after NaNAG 8 because its principal author is Wahabʾawwâm Yaʾd̲if's younger brother.

Ja 616 and Geukens 6 have in common with the text of NaNAG 8 the same royal name and the same authors; the title of the latter has a fourth additional part, which make the first two texts posterior to the last one.

Finally, CIH 24 belongs to the second generation of Wahabʾawwâm Yaʾd̲if, since the authors of the text are his two youngest sons; they were never mentioned before and are listed here along with the first two of the three sons of Wahabʾawwâm Yaʾd̲if, already known. It looks as if "the child Suh̲aymum" did not live very long. The lost part of the text probably mentioned the royal name. Since the authors of the text are no longer *mqtt* of the king Našaʾkarib Yu(ha)ʾmin Yuharḥib, although the last two of them were *mqtt* before (Ja 616/4 and Geukens 6/1-6), it is quite probable that the present text was engraved during the reign of the successor of the preceding king, who did not renew or confer the same office on those four sons of Wahabʾawwâm Yaʾd̲if.

3 – *Texts related to the reign of Našaʾkarib Yu(ha)ʾmin Yuharḥib*

The inscriptions related to the reign of Našaʾkarib Yu(ha)ʾmin Yuharḥib are twenty-seven, one of which is known by two copies, namely Ja 608 = 609. Most of them are dedicatory inscriptions, and only three of them, Geukens 6, Ja 612 and 616, give any historical information. As usual, the study of all these texts begins with remarks concerning the publication of these inscriptions.

a – REMARKS ON SOME TEXTS:

CIH 69, Fakhry 76, RÉS 3563, 4191, 4233 and 4729

CIH 69 = Ist 7517: yellowish sandstone; maximum thickness: 17 cm.; *front:* maximum: 44.7 cm. × 24.5; letter height: from 4 cm. (line 1) to 2.5 (line 6); space between the lines: from 0.5 cm. to 0.4. The beginning of line 1 must be read as follows: *[nšʾkr]b/yʾmn/⌜yhr⌝[ḥb/mlk/s]⌜bʾ/⌝wd̲ryd⌝[n/* .... Read *d̲rḥ/* instead of *mrḥb* (line 2), and *]/ʾsdn* instead of */]ʾsdn* (line 3).

Fakhry 76 = MaN 14: long granite stone broken into two parts; the right edge is partly hidden (visible length: 2 m.); height: 33 cm. in the first 67 cm. from the left, and 47 cm. in the rest; a hollow (1.31 m. × 31 cm.; depth: 1 cm.) begins at 69.6 cm. from the left edge and ends at 6.1 cm. from the top. In *RyET* (pp. 50-51), suppress all brackets and parentheses in *nšʾ[k]rb* and *(h)wfyn(/)* *[w](b)ʿln* (line 1), *(w)wh(bʾ)w*, *bny[h]mw* and *ʾ(n)t̲n* (line 2), *ʾl(ġ)z* and *ʾmhth()mw* (line 3), all these signs in line 5 (save in *d*ᵓ(ᶜ)*drhn*, where *w* instead of ᶜ is certain on the stone; cf. also *FaAJY*, I, p. 111, Fig. 58) and instead of *wbnt[h]w* and ᵓ[*m*]*r*(ᵓ)*hn*, read *wbnt(h)w* and ᵓ[*m*]*r*ᵓ*hn* respectively, and all these signs in line 6. Further, read *zrb* instead of *zbr* (line 1), *s*[ᶜ]*dm* instead of *sdm* (line 3); *bnthn*/ *w*ᵓ*w*[*l*]*dhn*/*wd*ᵓᶜ*drhn*/*bny*/ and ᵓ*sdn*/ᵓ*slm*/[*w*] instead of *bnthn*(*w*ᵓ*w*(*l*)*d*(*hn*/*wd*ᵓᶜ*dr*(*hn*(/(ᵓ*l*)*y*[/] and ᵓ*slm*(/*kl*)*l*/ ....../*w* (line 4; for the second reading, cf. beginning of line 6); ᵓ*hy*, ᵓ*hthw* and ᵓ*wldhw* instead of ᶜ*hy*, *l*ᵓ*hth*(*w*) and (ᵓ)*wl*(*d*)[*h*]*n* (line 5) respectively; *wlmw* (RÉS 3959/3) instead of (ᶜ)*lm*[*n*] (line 7); and finally ᵓ*l*[/]*ṣtrw*, *lqbly*/*dt*, *wksdw*, and *wlmw* instead of ᵓ*mṣtrw*, *lqblydt*, *w.sdw*, and ᶜ*lmw* (line 8) respectively.

RÉS 3563/1: *nš*ᵓ*krb*/..*mn*/*yhrḥb*/--: E. Glaser correctly restores [*y*ᵓ]*mn*, since he mentions that only two letters are missing. *RÉS*'s commentary (VI, p. 211), "lire: [ᵓ*y*]*mn*", is erroneous, and *RhKTB* (II, p. 66) as well, when he writes: "NŠᵓKRB ᵓIMN".

RÉS 4191: yellow, grayish sandstone; constant thickness: 10.3 cm. In *RÉS* (VII, pp. 132-33), read [/*mlk*, *yhrḥb*[/ (line 3) and *l*ᵓ*ZL* (line 4) instead of /[*mlk*, *yhrḥb*/[and ᵓ*LL*, respectively. In *l.c.* (p. 132) and *HöSSE* (pp. 9-10), read ᵓ*lšrḥ* instead of ᵓ*lš*[*r*]*ḥ* (line 4); ᵓ*lm*⌜*q*⌝[*hthwnb*ᶜ*l*ᵓ*wm* (cf. lines 8-9) instead of ᵓ*lm*[*qh*/*b*ᶜ*l*/ᵓ*w*ᶜ*ln* (line 5); ᵓ[... instead of ᵓ(?)[... (line 6); *wh*⌝[... instead of *w*[... (line 8); at the end of line 8, restore .../*b*ᵓ*lm*]; in line 9, which is not recorded by *HöSSE* and *RÉS*, read ⌞*qhthwnb*ᶜ*l*ᵓ*wm*/⌟[....

RÉS 4233 (cf. *JaSAA*, p. 154 A and especially *JaSAI*, p. 507 B, No. 5 with revised translation). Limestone; thickness: 5.1 cm.; front: 30.5 cm. × 18.5. In *RÉS* (VII, pp. 159-60), the end of line 1 is to be read .../]*rwd*/*w*, and read *hq(n)y* instead of [*hqny* (line 2), *hmr*[/*whw*] (4) [*kn*]⌞*n*⌟ (cf. line 7) instead of *hm*[*r*/*w*.](4)../ (lines 3-4), *yṣ*[*bḥ* instead of *y*[*ṣbḥ* (line 4), *bkn*/[... instead of *b*(?)*kn*(?)... (line 5), *mr*ᵓ⌜*hm*⌝[*w* instead of *mr*ᵓ[*h*]*m*(?)[*w* (line 6), *ġ*[*l*](10)*mtn* "this girl" instead of *b*.(10)*z*(?)*tn* (lines 9-10) and *bkb*(11)(*g*)*n* instead of *bkl*(?)(11).*n* (lines 10-11); finally, the following letters are certain on the stone: the last *w* in line 11, the last *h* in line 13, the *k* of *mlk* and the last *w* in line 14, the *y* of *y*ᵓ*zl* in line 15, and the *w* of *wfy* in line 16.

RÉS 4729 = Ja 416.[158] The actual length of the text is unknown. However, if the full royal title must be restored, as suggested by the other texts belonging to the same king Našaᵓkarib Yu(ha)ᵓmin Yuharḥib, and preferring the more common form *y*ᵓ*mn* to *yh*ᵓ*mn*, line 4 would read as follows: ⌞*yhrḥb*⌟/*ml*⌞*k*/⌟[*sb*ᵓ/*wdrydn*/*bn*/ᵓ*lšrḥ*/*yḥdb*/*wy*ᵓ*zl*/*byn*/ *mlky*/*sb*ᵓ/*wdrydn*, and thus have 49 letters and 11 word dividers. Line 3 containing only the signs such as in *JaAMNR* (p. 27) cannot thus be complete,[159] for it only has 42 letters and 8 word dividers. Furthermore, since *bklm* appears in the monogram of RÉS 4729 and is mentioned in Ja 562/2 in a title which has *n*/*dhmln* in common with RÉS 4729/2, and also on the basis of the fact that the tribal name *bt*ᶜ occurs in CIH 187/2 and where the title (lines 2-3) is partly identical with that of Ja 562/1-3, I suggest that RÉS 4729/1 be read *m*⌝*rtdm*⌜/ᵓ⌝*ry*(*m*)/*w*[... .../*bn* (or *bnw* or *bny*)/ *bt*ᶜ/ᵓ*b*ᶜ*l*/*bytn*/*wklm*/ᵓ*qwl*/*š*ᶜ*bn*/*sm*ᶜ*y*/*tlt*], that is to say 42 (or 43) letters and 12 word dividers, leaving the space of 7 (or 6) for the name of the second person, thus making it almost identical in length with line 4 as restored above. Finally, note that *d*[*hmln* in RÉS 4022 is not more probable than either *d*[*hšdm* or *d*[*hgrm*, and under *dhmln*, *RyNP* (I, p. 296 B) also refers to SE 8 = RÉS 4190/4 and 9, where *dhgrm* is certain.

b – Ja 877; SQUEEZE AND PHOTOGRAPH IN PLATE 56 – AM 205

STONE: whitish limestone; broken into two parts; splintered off largely at the left bottom of the text, at the beginning and in the center of line 1, at the upper left corner and also at the end of lines 13-14; several letters are more or less damaged; 66.9 cm. × 27.3 (line 5), 27.8 (line 15 and bottom); thickness maxima: 11 cm. – INSCRIPTION: many letters are aslant to the right; the letter height increases slightly; e.g., 2.1 cm. (lines 1-8), 2.3 (line 9), and 2.4 (lines 14-18). Same evolution in the spaces between the lines: 0.4 cm. (beginning), 0.5 (e.g., between lines 10 and 11), and 0.6 (e.g., between lines 17 and 18); distance from line 18 to the bottom: 19.1 cm. – SYMBOL: for the extremities, cf. Ja 656; for the inside incisions, cf. Ja 698; cf Plate B.

1 **Sym-** *nš*ᵓ*krb*[/*yh*]⌜ᵓ*m*⌝*n*/*yhr*⌜*ḥ*⌝[*b*/*m*]
2 **bol** *lk*/*s*⌟⌞*b*ᵓ/*wdrydn*/*bn*/ᵓ*l*[*šr*]
3 *ḥ*/*yḥdb*/*wy*ᵓ*zl*/*byn*/*mlky*/*sb*ᵓ⌝
4 *wdrydn*/*hqny*/ᵓ*lmqhthwnb*ᶜ*lms*
5 *ktwytwbr*ᵓ*n*/*dn*/*ṣlmn*/*ddhbn*/*h*
6 *gn*/*kwqhhmw*/*bms*ᵓ*lhw*/*s*ᵓ*lm*/*b*ᶜ
7 *ly*/*ṣrythmw*/*bkn*/*tṣryw*/*b*ᶜ*mh*

[158] Cf. *JaAMNR*, pp. 27-28 and pl. II.
[159] Contrary to *l.c.*, p. 28.

8 *w/bwrẖ/ḏhbs/ḏẖrf/smhkrb/b*
9 *n/ʾbkrb/bn/ḥḏmt/ṯlṯn/wrʾ⌋*
10 *kẖmrhmw/ʾlmqh/ṣrytm/wʾml*
11 *ʾ/ṣdqm/ḏhrḍwhmw/wlwzʾ/ʾ⌊l⌋*
12 *mqhbʿlmsktwyṯwbrʾn/ẖmrh*
13 *mw/ṣryt/wʾmlʾ/ṣdqm/wwfy*
14 *hmw/wwfy/bytn/slḥn/wʾbʿ*
15 *lhw/wwfy/mlkhmw/wẖmshmw*
16 *wlwḍʿ/⌊ḍ⌋rʿ/whms/whkm⌊s/⌋[k]*
17 *l/ḍrhmw/wšnʾ⌊h⌋mw/bʾ⌋[lmqhṯ]*
18 *hwnbʿlmsktwyṯwb⌋[rʾn]*

1 **Sym-** Našaʾkarib [Yuha]ʾmin Yuharḥi[b, k]ing
2 **bol** of Sabaʾ and Raydân, son of ʾIl[šara]ḥ
3 Yaḥḍub and of Yaʾzil Bayyin, the two kings of Sabaʾ
4 and Raydân, has dedicated to ʾIlumquh Ṯahwân, master of Mas-
5 kat and Yaṯaw Baraʾân, this statue which [is] in bronze,
6 as He has ordered them through His oracle, request
7 because of their advice when they asked for advice from
8 Him in the month of Hawbas, in the year of Sumhukarib, son
9 of ʾAbkarib, descendant of Ḥaḏmat, the third; but now,
10 ʾIlumquh has granted them advice and favors
11 perfect which pleased them. And that may continue ʾIl-
12 umquh, master of Maskat and Yaṯaw Baraʾân, to vouchsafe
13 to them perfect advice and favors, and to protect
14 them, and to protect the house of Salḥân and its
15 masters, and to protect their property and their army;
16 and that He may humiliate and humble and break down and wither
17 their [eve]ry foe and their [every] enemy. By ʾI[lumquh Ṯa-]
18 hwân, master of Maskat and Yaṯaw Ba[raʾân]

C – TEXTS WITHOUT HISTORICAL INFORMATION

Twenty-six inscriptions related to Našaʾkarib Yu(ha)ʾmin Yuharḥib's reign do not present any historical information: nine of these have the king himself as author.

1° – *Inscriptions* written by the king: CIH 69; Fakhry 3, 76; Ja 608, 609, 610, 611, 877; RÉS 3563.

Among the nine texts which have the king as author, three (CIH 69; Fakhry 3 and 76) mention a decree; five others (Ja 608, 609, 610, 611, and 877) are dedicatory inscriptions; the contents of the last one, RÉS 3563, cannot be determined with any certainty.

The three edicts issued by Našaʾkarib Yu(ha)ʾmin Yuharḥib almost certainly are of the same nature, namely the king grants certain persons and their descendants as property to others. That is the case of Fakhry 3 (from Ṣirwâḥ) and 76 (from Mârib) in favor of certain members of the tribes Ḥabîb and ʿAṯkalân ʿUṣayyat respectively; and is almost certainly also the case in CIH 69 (of unknown origin), in favor of a Ġaymânite and his two houses. The fact that the three known decrees deal with the same social question, suggests that Našaʾkarib Yu(ha)ʾmin Yuharḥib was faced with various problems of stabilizing the members of the tribes or of rewarding some of his faithful servants, as is possibly the case of CIH 69.

The five dedicatory inscriptions engraved by the king mention the offering of statues and allude to favors (Ja 608 and 609), favors and recommendations (Ja 611) and advice and favors (Ja 877) granted to him before, and also to protection given to all his *daʿat*-palms (Ja 610).

The last inscription written by the king, RÉS 3563, is known through some extracts, the full text being still unpublished. The presence of *mrʾs* (line 3) which is used in the texts presenting a clear context[160] with a personal meaning, "chiefs," and also of *m*]*qṭn* with the meaning of "the ordinary people", justifies the interpretation of *mśwd* as having also a personal meaning, "the great counsel", and disproves the interpretation of these three nouns as buildings.[161]

2° – *Texts* engraved by other persons: Geukens 9; Ja 613, 614, 615, 617, 618, 619, 620, 621, 623, 624, 625, 718; NaNAG 8; RÉS 4191, 4233, and 4729

As for the seventeen texts not engraved by the king himself and without any historical information,

[160] Cf. commentary on Ja 576/2.

[161] As *RÉS*, VI, p. 212, commentary, *RycIMAM*, pp. 176 and 181, note 17, and *RyISA*, X, p. 288. *RÉS* (*l.c.*) bases his interpretation of *mśwd*, accepted from E. Glaser, "d'après le contexte". Yet, the text as presently known does not have any verb, and the noun *mśwd* is followed by *mrʾs* and [*m*]*qṭn*. In his summary of the text, *RycIMAM* does not allude to the restoration of the third noun as *mḏqn* (p. 176), and points out that the translation of the three other nouns is not certain (*l.c.*, note 6). A few pages later (p. 181, note 17), the same author gratuitously affirms that the text deals with "la construction de" and goes on translating line 3, where he accepts the above-mentioned restoration of the text. He finally remarks that "la traduction de *mrʾs* et *mqṭ* [read *mqṭn*] est d'autre part conjecturale, à défaut de passages parallèles."

all of them, except RÉS 4729, mention the offering of bronze statue(s)[162] or a bull in bronze (Ja 621) to ʾIlumquh, master of ʾAwwâm; however, the mention of the offered object is missing in the dedicatory texts Geukens 9; Ja 623 and 625.

Some of the authors are persons in the service of the king: here, *mqtwy* "a high official" (Ja 613), *mqtwyy* "two high officials" (Ja 614, 615, and most probably Ja 617 and 624), *mqtt* "high officials" (restored in RÉS 4191/1 instead of *ʾdm* suggested by *HöSSE*, p. 9)[163]; there, two *ʿqbt/mlkn/bhgrn/nšqm* "representatives of the king in the city [of] Našqum" (Ja 619). The authors of the other inscriptions are either *ʾqwl* "rulers" of some tribe (Ja 618, 718 and NaNAG 8) or ordinary persons (Ja 620, 621, and 623); the quality of the authors of Geukens 9, Ja 625 and RÉS 4233 cannot be determined.

Beside the more usual occasions for an offering to ʾIlumquh, such as favors received in the past (Ja 614, 621, 623, 624; NaNAG 8 and RÉS 4191) and to be received in the future as well (Ja 621), some other occasions are more specific: the deliverance from a physical oppression (Ja 613), a gift as a tithe from some harvest (Ja 615), a gift from the produce of palm trees (Ja 617), the completion of a caravan station (Ja 618), recovery in a fall from a camel and also from aversion of food and disease which afflicted the author and all his cattle (Ja 619), recovery from diseases incurred as a consequence of ill treatment inflicted by the enemy (Ja 620), some unknown favor granted to the youngest son of the author (Ja 718), the request of the deity made known through His oracle (NaNAG 8), and probably "the judicial acquittal of a man who was falsely considered as a member of a conspiracy, although he had resisted the propaganda of ʾAwsum" (RÉS 4233).[164] Because some dedicatory inscriptions are either too fragmentary (Ja 625) or are only known through the lower part of the text (Ja 623 and Geukens 9), the reason for the offering remains unknown.

The petitions mentioned in all these dedicatory inscriptions are usual ones, e.g., the continuation of favors and the protection of the author (Ja 613), the humiliation of any kind of enemy (Ja 614), etc.

Finally, RÉS 4729 = Ja 416 commemorates the construction of a building of unknown nature. *RycIMAM*'s statement according to which this inscription "est adressée à Taʾlab" (p. 302), and the fact that this author fails to summarize the contents of the text, could easily indicate that *bny* (line 2) is interpreted by him as a noun, "son(s) of". Such an opinion, however, must be discarded, for the filiation always precedes a title of a length such as the one in the text. Furthermore, it is well known that, even in dedicatory inscriptions, the mention of a deity, among others, in the final invocation, does not necessarily suggest that that deity was the one who was the object of the offering.

The authors of Ja 617 have some estates in the region of *mšr/whynn/wʾṯʾbtm* (line 6). The list in *MüHG*, 105/10, indicates the identification of *mšr* with J. Masâr, about 55 km. west of Naʿiḍ. *MüHG*, 110/8, mentions the city of Haynân in the northern part of the Jauf, and this city is, according to E. Glaser,[165] located in Banû Jebr. The place name *ṣlyn* in Ja 618/11 may be identified with aṣ-Ṣulaiy[166] which is located east of J. Baraʿ and south of Wâdî Sahâm.[167] The clan Ḥalḥalum (Ja 619/2) lived in the region of the city of Ḥalḥalân which may be identified with the town of Ḥalḥal located about 100 km. north-northwest of Ṣanʿâʾ, on the Wâdî Ḥalḥal.[168] Since all the texts mentioning *ḥlḥlm* and *ḥlḥln* are Sab, it seems natural to exclude the possibility of any connection with Wâdî Ḥalḥal about 40 km. east of Wâdî Beiḥân.[169] Therefore, the authors of Ja 619 were the representatives of the king in Našqum (al-Beiḍâ), a town which was about 35 km. northeast of Ḥalḥalân.

3° – *Elements* of relative chronology between Ja 611, 613, 615, and 618.

The relative chronology of several events is made possible thanks to the mention of the eponymates during which they occur. However, in one case, this information is of no use, for the mention of a Faḍḥumite eponymate only occurs once, during Našaʾkarib's reign, that of the *second* year of Našaʾkarib, son of Maʿadkarib (Ja 610/6-7).

The other eponymates can be classified. First comes the *fourth* year of Waddʾil, son of ʾAbkarib of the clan of the Leader of Ḫalil (Ja 618/9-10), during which the rulers of Tanaʿamum and Tanaʿamatum successfully completed the caravan station

[162] The first object of dedication in RÉS 4191/5 is missing.
[163] Cf. already *RycIMAM*, pp. 198 and 199.
[164] Cf. *JaSAI*, p. 507 B. *RycIMAM* does not summarize the text.
[165] Cf. *FoSA*, p. 185, note 2.
[166] Cf. *MüHG*, 68/14.
[167] Cf. *FoSA*, p. 68, note 11.
[168] Cf. *WeCGC*, p. 129 and maps.
[169] Cf. *WiHöBGS*, pp. 51 and 52.

of Yafid (lines 7-8) as well as the enlargement of two places (lines 10-12). During the *sixth* year of the above-mentioned Waddʾil (Ja 613/10-11 and 615/12-13), a high official of the king was saved from a physical oppression which overwhelmed him in Mârib (Ja 613/7-9). The tithe from two date harvests, the first one during the same year (Ja 615/9-12) as the one mentioned just above, and the second later on, as indicated by the succession of dates in Ja 615/12-14, during the *third* year of Našaʾkarib, son of Maʿadkarib of the tribe Ḥaḏmat (Ja 615/13-14), was used by some rulers of the tribe Bakîlum to offer a bronze statue to their lunar god ʾIlumquh. Also during the *third* year of the same Našaʾkarib (Ja 611/8-9), the king received some favors and recommendations from his god ʾIlumquh (lines 6-7).

d – HISTORICAL TEXTS:
Geukens 6, Ja 612 and 616

Each one of the three historical texts related to the king Našaʾkarib Yu(ha)ʾmin Yuharḥib mentions offering a bronze statue to the lunar god ʾIlumquh Ṯahwân, master of ʾAwwâm.

The expedition in the land of Ḥaḍramawt, alluded to in Ja 612, was headed by the author of the text, and not by the king, and appears to have been a military campaign since the rulers and the army took part in it. No detail, however, is given about the expedition which may well have been of the same nature as that of Ja 640 during Šaʿirum ʾAwtar's reign, that is to say a campaign aimed at establishing peace and order. There is so far no information available as to the relative chronology of that campaign with regards to the other two.

It has already been pointed out that the two other texts, Geukens 6 and Ja 616, have the same authors; they also have in common the mention of Saharatân (Geukens 6/15 and Ja 616/18). Yet, the military campaigns mentioned in them are different, for the Sab soldiers are from the tribes of Suḫaymum and especially Yarsum in Geukens 6, but men from the tribes of Yarsum and Ḫawlân in Ja 616. Geukens 6 may be considered as anterior to Ja 616 because the expedition mentioned in the latter is presented as a consequence of a widespread rebellion connected with the refusal to pay taxes. This obligation of giving up these incomes may have been imposed as a result of the campaign briefly described in Geukens 6.

The authors of Geukens 6, five high military officers, report an expedition headed by the king himself in Saharatân. Before summarizing the campaign, the translation of two terms needs to be discussed, as well as the participation of the five authors in the expedition. The achievements of the two leading officers, Ḥammʿaṯat ʾAzʾad (cf. also commentary on Ja 613/11), and his brother ʾAbkarib ʾAsʿad, are recorded in the following passages: *ḫmrhw/ʾlmqh/hrg hwʾ/lbʾn*[170] (lines 23-24), and *ḫmrhw/ʾlmqh/hrg/lbʾn/wnmrn*[170] (lines 27-28), respectively; these two deeds are put together in the following phrase: *bkn/šwʿw/qylyhmw/ln/hrgy/lbʾnhn/wnmrn*[170] (lines 30-31). As is pointed out above, the reading of *gbʾ* "coward"[171] is at first sight as probable as that of *lbʾ* in the three preceding quotations; only a good, clear photograph will determine which reading, *gbʾ* or *lbʾ*, is right. If *lbʾ* is to be accepted, the interpretation both of *lbʾ* and *nmr* needs to be discussed. According to *RyISA*'s commentary (p. 379), these two terms are nouns, because of the dual form *lbʾnhn*, which is a summary of the two *lbʾn* (lines 24 and 28). Such an opinion is obvious. However, two questions remain intimately connected with each other: who is represented by *lbʾ* and *nmr*? and what is the meaning of these two nouns?

According to *RyISA*,[172] *lbʾ* "désigne l'ensemble

[170] *RyISA*'s translation reads respectively as follows: "ʾAlmaqah le gratifia du meurtre de ce 'lion'" (XIV, p. 375), "le gratifia ʾAlmaqah du meurtre du 'lion' et de la 'panthère'" (p. 376), and "lorsqu'ils ont escorté leurs deux préposés, lorsqu'ils tuèrent les deux 'lions' et la panthère" (cf. *l.c.*). The term *hrg* is a verb, and not a noun (cf. commentary on Ja 575/6); *hwʾ* an adjective and not a pronoun (cf. commentary on Ja 577/15); *ln* means "until" and not simply "when" (cf. commentary on Ja 584/7), and the noun "panthère" in the last passage should also be between inverted commas.

[171] The noun *gbʾ* may be related to Arabic *ǧabaʾa* "to restrain, refrain, turn back", and to its derived adjectives *ǧubbaʾ* and *ǧubbâʾ* "fearful, cowardly", and may be translated as "coward, poltroon". *RyISA* (cf. *l.c.*, p. 380) refers to the same Arabic verb, and suggests translating it as "adversaire". Obviously enough, this man was an enemy; but such a translation does not reflect the specific meaning of Arabic *ǧabaʾa*.

[172] *RyISA* publishes two minor statements which have nothing to do with the present context and which need to be corrected. He writes: "en sud-arabe le n.pr. *lbʾ* est un n.pr. de femme" (cf. *l.c.*, p. 379), without any reference. *RyNP* (II, p. 78 B) refers to I, p. 117 B. Both mention the same passage, CIH 961/1, as having *lbʾm* and *lbʾ* respectively; the proper name there is *lġbm* (see below). Besides, I, p. 117 B: *lbʾ*, also refers to RÉS 3902, No. 78, where *lbʾm* is a feminine personal name. The gender of *lbʾ* in RÉS 2888 and Ja 301/1, Qat, is unknown. In CIH 961 which is mentioned just above, the reading of *b* in *lbʾ* is quite impossible on the photograph. The second letter is obviously *ġ*: the small appendage is still complete, and along with the appendage of *l* determines exactly the letter height, 8 mm. Besides, the width of the lower part of that letter is 2.5 mm., and that of all

des adversaires avec lesquels se trouvent aux prises" the two leading officers separately (p. 379), and *lbʾ* and *nmr* mean "lion" and "panthère" metaphorically (p. 380).

The first opinion cannot be accepted, because lines 23-24 (*hrg hwʾ/lbʾn*), line 27 (*hrg/lbʾn*), and line 31 (*hrgy/lbʾnhn*) would mean the "massacre des deux groupes d'adversaires" (p. 379), that is to say that of "l'ensemble des adversaires"; and that is simply impossible. Besides, the masculine personal adjective *hwʾ* (cf. commentary on Ja 577/15), which introduces *lbʾ* in line 24, is used in connection with an individual person, not with a collective noun. Finally, if the author's interpretation is right, what would *nmr* allude to, since "l'ensemble des adversaires" is already indicated by *lbʾ*? The author does not mention the problem in his commentary on *lbʾ* and *nmr*.

The second opinion is as unacceptable[173] as the first. The frequently used noun *ʾsd*,[174] which is naturally connected with the same root as that of *ʾasad*, the most common Arabic noun for "lion" does not seem to have retained any metaphoric connection with the animal itself, and means "soldier". The noun *nmr* (e.g., CIH 329/2: plural: *ʾnmr*), which is to be related to the same root as that of the present *nmr*, means some kind of building. On the one hand, the nouns *ʾsd* "soldier", *lbʾ* and *nmr* suggest that the names of some large, wild animals were also used in military terminology, and the case of *ʾsd* indicates that these nouns are not used of men simply in a metaphorical sense but rather are quite specific terms in the military vocabulary. The preceding remark would favor reading *lbʾ* rather than *gbʾ*. On the other hand, the article affixed twice to *lbʾ* (lines 24 and 28) and also twice to *nmr* (lines 28 and 31) suggests that these individuals were known to a certain extent, at least by the charge they were appointed to. On the basis of the preceding remarks and of the context as well, I would suggest that the nouns *lbʾ* and *nmr* most probably indicate the commanding officer (the commander; the officer in charge of a military unit or group) and the second in command, respectively. The battles in those days were essentially and primarily hand-to-hand fights; and the great pride of a commanding officer was of course to kill the commanding officer of the opposing force. I would thus translate the three above-mentioned expressions as follows: "ʾIlumquh granted to him to kill this commanding officer", "ʾIlumquh granted to him to kill the commanding officer and the second in command" and "when they assisted their two rulers, until these killed the two commanding officers and the second in command", respectively.

The five high military officers went in campaign with two groups of soldiers, one from Suḫaymum, the tribe of their origin, and one from Yarsum, the tribe which they commanded.

Of the first group, nothing is said except that they won a victory and came back with much booty (lines 17-19). They apparently had nothing to do with the two leading officers' exploits which are recorded only in lines 22-31. Further, the fact that this group of soldiers is reported to have come back before the mention of the two leading officers must be understood as a literary device, as is the mention of the king's return in lines 16-17, and not as a suggestion that they, the Suḫaymites and the king, would have come back earlier and independently from the second group[175]; because the text formally states (lines 11-15) that all of them, Suḫaymites and Yarsumites, were fighting when the king was doing battle in Saharatân. The Suḫaymite group is mentioned by the five authors of the text, for these doubtless knew all those soldiers and probably had been in close contact with most of them, or at least with a part of them.

The second group of soldiers, the Yarsumites, most probably were divided into two units headed by Ḥammʿaṯat ʾAzʾad and ʾAbkarib ʾAsʿad respectively. They assisted these two until (lines 30-31) the first one killed, on the sixth day of the campaign, the commanding officer of the adversary

the *b*'s between 3.5 mm. and 4 mm. The third letter cannot possibly be ʾ, since the height of both vertical strokes is 7 and 6 mm. respectively, and the height of the lower vertical strokes of the three complete ʾ's is 5.5 mm.; there is thus no room at all for the diacritic upper part of ʾ. Cf. Arabic *laġaba* "to be fatigued, tired, wearied...in the greatest degree" and *lâġib* "fatigued, tired, wearied...in the utmost degree".– *RyISA* also writes that "en sud-arabe *lbʾn* est un n.pr. d'homme; cf. RES 4561, etc.". However, in the inscription referred to, the gender of *lbʾn* is unknown. Besides, *RyNP* (II, p. 78 B) also refers to "*lbʾn* 385", that is to say to I, p. 385, which only contains Ethiopic proper names.

[173] One could rightly quote A. F. L. Beeston saying that "a metaphor of this nature is entirely foreign to the style of the inscriptions, which are uniformly characterized by a rigidly prosaic and matter-of-fact phraseology" (cf. *BSOAS*, 16 [1954], p. 391).

[174] Cf. commentary on Ja 560/12.

[175] As suggested by *RyISA*, XIV, p. 380, commentary on Geukens 6/29-31: "Après le retour du roi, Ḥamʿaṯat et ʾAbkarib ont poursuivi la campagne avec les gens de Yarsum".

group (lines 22-24), and also until the second killed both the commanding officer and the second in command of the opposing group, later during the same month (lines 27-28). After that, all of them, military officers and Yarsumites, went back in safety (lines 31-32) and no doubt with much booty.

The activities of all five authors of Geukens 6 in the military campaign related in the text need to be studied because of the apparent contradiction between the two following facts. On the one hand, the plural verb *sb'w* (line 11), as well as *hqnyw* (line 8), *tbšrw* (line 11) and the personal pronoun *hmw* (line 10) obviously have as subjects at least the five authors of the text. All these five persons thus took part apparently in the military campaign. On the other hand, the detailed account of the deeds of the Yarsumites, Yarsum being the tribe of which they were in command, mentions only two persons out of the five, and in such a manner that only these two appear to have actually had an effective command. Thus, the question may be raised: were Wahab'awwâm Ya'd̲if and his brother Yadum Yadrim too aged and his son Suh̲aymum Yaz'ân too young to take any active part in the battles? Or were Ḥamm-ᶜat̲at 'Az'ad and his brother 'Abkarib 'Asᶜad chosen as actual commanding officers because of their special ability and strength, along with the fact that they apparently were Wahab'awwâm Ya'd̲if's two oldest sons? Possibly. However, that the Yarsumites composed two fighting units or groups does not seem to bear relation to the fact that the effective commanding officers were two, because of Ja 616 where the same two persons also are in command and there seems to have been only one fighting unit. At any rate, the three other high military officers apparently did not take any active part in the battles; they merely went along with the two commanding officers, the father and the uncle possibly as advisers and the brother as a member of the family.

The five authors of Geukens 6 also relate in Ja 616 a campaign ordered by the king, but headed by the same two commanding officers as in Geukens 6. These two are assigned the duty (lines 9-17) of protecting and fixing the groups and tribes of H̲awlân Gaddum, and also of making sure that they brought back to Ṣanᶜâ' a certain number of persons. However, certain groups of Daw'at and the group of Rad̲h̲atân of Ḥârat rebel apparently in connection with payment of taxes (lines 17-26) and were defeated (lines 27-31) in the country of the three wâdîs Bi'rân, H̲ulab, and Tadḫân (lines 26-27) by the two commanding officers.

The tribe Daw'at probably lived in the hilly country between Saharatân on the west and Ṣuḥârum and Ḥârat on the east, and Ḥârat probably between Ṣaᶜdat and Najrân.[176] In the present text, however, Daw'at seems to control some other groups which previously were independent, such as Ḥakam (*ḥkmm*; line 24) which lived north of ᶜAkkum in Tihâmat and whose principal place was al-H̲aṣûf on Wâdî H̲ulab.[177] The location of all the other groups mentioned in lines 24-26 remains unknown. On the contrary, the location of the wâdî mentioned in second place is beyond any doubt: Wâdî H̲ulab flows into the Red Sea 35 km. south of Jîzân[178] and originates near al-Qufâᶜat and al-Bâr[179]; these two places are thus in the area located about 30-40 km. northwest of Ṣaᶜdat. The mine al-Qufâᶜat was the western border of H̲awlân,[180] and is located by E. Glaser in ᶜIzzlet al-Ašᶜûb.[181] The al-Bâr referred to above, which is mentioned twice by *MüHG* (69/25 and 73/12) in intimate connection with H̲ulab,[182] may be related to Wâdî *b'rn* of the present text. The Wâdî *tdḫn* may be related to Wâdî Tindâḫat and to the city of the same name which was located north of ancient Juraš.[183] The city of Tindâḫat on the wâdî of the same name is located 14 km. east of H̲amîs Mušayṭ, thus 160 km. northeast of Jîzân.

E – COREGENCY OF SAᶜADŠAMSUM 'ASRAᶜ AND HIS SON MART̲ADUM YUHAḤMID[184]

1 – *Introduction*

The American excavations in the entrance court of Maḥram Bilqîs are also responsible for ascer-

[176] Cf. *JaASAB*, p. 161, commentary on CIH 407/19.
[177] Cf. *FoSA*, p. 28, note 4.
[178] Cf., e.g., *JaASAB*, *l.c.*
[179] Cf. *MüHG*, 73/12.
[180] Cf. *l.c.*, 67/11.
[181] Cf. *FoSA*, p. 62, note 5.
[182] Note that in *MüHG* (69/25) as well as in Ja 616/27, *h̲lb* is immediately preceded by al-Bâr and *b'rn* respectively.
[183] Cf. *MüHG*, 119/4. *MüHG* (118/14) refers to another city whose name, almost identical with the preceding, is *ta*(or *i*)*nda*(or *i*)*ḫat* (118/14, and II, p. 20 A; cf. also II, p. 121, remarks on 118/14). Since this author puts the two cities in close relation with the city of Juraš, the question might be raised on the identification of the two names. The location of the above-mentioned Tindâḫat fits al-Idrîsî's location of Juraš (cf. *FoSA*, p. 77, note 3): 4 days to Bîšâ and H̲aywân, and 6 days to Najrân.
[184] Cf. also appendix on CIH 951, in the study of Watarum Yuha'min (cf. pp. 329 B-330 A).

taining both the second name of the first coregent and the blood relationship of these two persons to each other; they were already known before as *bny/ʾlšrḥ/yḥ(ḍ)b/mlk/sbʾ/wḏrydn* (HC 12/3; see below).

The preceding pair of father and son supplies the most convincing proof that great caution is required identifying persons with homonymous names. The case also involves the authors of Ja 568, 606, 607, and 753. The unicity of the mention of the two names *sʿdšmsm/ʾsrʿ* and *mrṯdm/yhḥmd*[185] together in both instances is even underlined not only by the existence of the same blood relationship in both pairs of persons, but also by their general contemporaneity; the persons of Ja 568, etc., are attested during ʾIlšaraḥ Yaḥḍub's sole reign and that of his immediate successor and son, Watarum Yuhaʾmin. The difficulty based on the Garatite origin of the authors of Ja 568, etc., could easily be set aside by the hypothesis of their having become members of the family of ʾIlšaraḥ Yaḥḍub, by some kind of adoption. Why would ʾIlšaraḥ Yaḥḍub have "adopted" a mature man such as Saʿadšamsum, since the latter already had a son old enough to be the ruler of a tribe at the time of his sole reign? And if the son Marṯadum Yuhaḥmid alone was adopted, his father would have had no right to count himself among the *bny* "children" of the late king.

2 – *Texts without historical information:* HC 12; Ja 626, 627, 628, and 630

Among the five texts which do not contain any historical information are four dedicatory inscriptions (Ja 626, 627, 628, and 630). The other text, HC 12,[186] from Wâdî Ḍahr (northwest of Ṣanʿâʾ), commemorates the building of several irrigation works. The place name *qḥfn* (line 2), which is not identified by *RyISA* (*l.c.*), may refer to al-Quḥf which may be located north-northeast of Bilâd al-ʿArûš.[187]

The four dedicatory inscriptions, from Maḥram Bilqîs, mention the offering of one statue to ʾIlumquh for favors received and to be received (Ja 630) in relation to some irrigation works and crops (Ja 627 and 628), or simply to receive some favors (Ja 626); the offering was sometimes (Ja 626 and 630) ordered by the god through His oracle. It seems rather difficult to propose any relative chronology between Ja 627 and 628, which have in common not only the authors but also the mention of the water-barrier of Yafid, which obviously must have been of an unusual importance. The anteriority of either one can easily be explained and justified.

3 – *Campaign against the Southeast:* Ja 629

a – SUMMARY OF THE CAMPAIGN

The great importance of Ja 629, the only historical text known as belonging to the coregents Saʿadšamsum ʾAsraʿ and his son Marṯadum Yuhaḥmid, cannot be surmised, because of the

[185] Gl 1228 (cf. Chapter V) being still unpublished, it is not possible at present to know whether "Saʾdšems und Marthad" (cf. *GlAAA*, p. 67) are another pair of homonymous father and son.

[186] Cf. *RyISA*, VIII (1949), p. 86, and one facsimile on p. 101. The first letter of the first part of the clan name, which is read as dubious *ʿtbn*, seems to be *q* (not *ʿ*). H. Clark's copy is right with regard to the second name of the first king: *ʾsrʿ* (*RyISA* accepted *ʾsrw*, and also *RycIMAM*, e.g., p. 338). Since we know the exact title of these two coregents, 12 letters are missing in lines 2-3 as presently known. Finally, *RyISA* (p. 87) writes: "*yḥb*, d'après les trois copies, ce qui exclut la lecture *yḥḍb*", and this opinion is accepted by *RycIMAM* (e.g., p. 170, note 20: "Yaḥubb"). Yet, it is obvious that, on the facsimile, it would be very easy to restore one letter after *m* of *mlk*, the right and left vertical strokes of which being the left vertical stroke of *b* and the word divider respectively.

[187] Cf. *MüHG*: "al-Quḥf" (80/21 and 109/2) and "al-Qaḥf" (109/14).

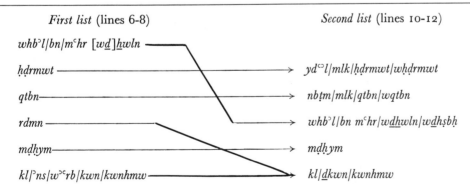

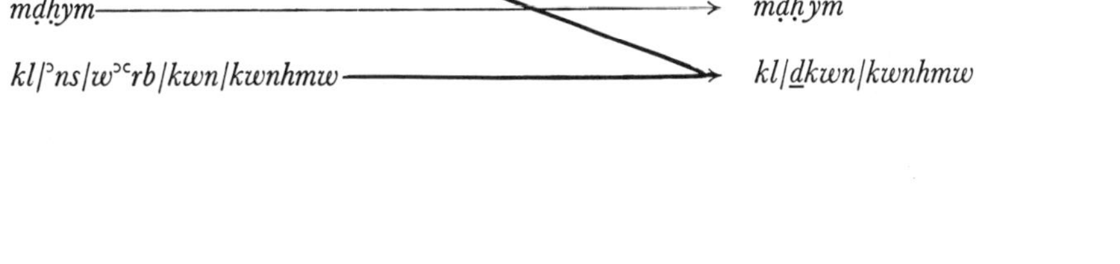

dynastic synchronisms between these two Sab kings and their contemporary kings Yada^cʾil in Ḥaḍramawt and Nabaṭum in Qatabân (lines 10-11). These dynastic synchronisms are mentioned in connection with a war between the two Sab kings and a southern coalition which was composed of Wahabʾil of Maʿâhir and Ḫawlân, and also of Ḥaḍramawt, Qatabân, Radmân, Muḍhayum, and some unspecified allies (*ʾns*) and Bedouin (*ʾʿrb*).

Before describing the military operations mentioned in the text, it is very important to compare the two lists of the enemies of Sabaʾ. As is shown in the scheme above, these two lists, although identical as far as their contents are concerned, differ in their literary structure.

The most striking feature shown by this tabular scheme is that the second and the third member of the second list clearly gives the actual meaning of *ḥḍrmwt* and *qtbn* mentioned in the first list. Such a fact cannot but demand great caution before concluding, from the mere mention of *qtbn* in an inscription, the disappearance of the Qat kingdom. The first list suggests that the instigator of the whole coalition was Wahabʾil; he is the only one person listed and is mentioned in the first place. In the second list, which is given in connection with military activities, the order of the Sab enemies is slightly different from that in the first, and may very well list the partners according to their respective military strength: Yadaʿʾil and Ḥaḍramawt, Nabaṭum and Qatabân, Wahabʾil, Muḍḥayum, and the rest.

The military campaign recorded in the text may be divided into five phases.

First Phase. – The origin and the beginning of the war remain unknown to us; it seems, however, that the coalition first met with some success since the Garfumite Ḏarḥân ʾAšwaʿ, the second dedicator of the text and son of the first, was caught in Radmân (line 6), probably in the country of Waʿlân,[188] the chief city of Radmân and located about 90 km. southwest of Timnaʿ[189] and southwest of as-Suwâdîyat.[190]

Second Phase (lines 8-21). – The preceding interpretation is suggested by the fact that the move made by the two Sab kings, mentioned in the text immediately after the record of Ḏarḥân's liberation, and thus very probably the move that liberated him, was against the area of that city (lines 8-10). The preceding information seems to suggest that Ḏarḥân, head of a military unit which was composed of Fayšânites and Yuhbiʿilites, was operating separately from the main army, was then trapped by his enemies and finally rescued by the two kings themselves. At any rate, the Sab army attacked and crushed the coalition (lines 13-15). During that time, Ḏarḥân and his group successfully attacked several tribes (lines 17-21).

Third Phase (lines 24-29). – After that, Ḏarḥân and his unit fought along with their two kings in the country of Ḫalzawum and Mašraqîtân (lines 25-27), two cities whose location remains unknown. However, the first of these two towns, for a reason unknown to us, did not fare well, and was besieged. The two Sab kings plundered the valleys in these two countries and leveled and destroyed temples, palaces, wells, and irrigation works in the first one (lines 27-29).

Fourth Phase (lines 29-30). – The two Sab kings pillaged and humiliated the city of Manwabum, every city and fortress of the tribe ʾAwsân and the city of Šayʿân as well. A very important clue to the location of the two cities just mentioned is that they apparently are, according to lines 30-31, separated from each other by the tribe ʾAwsân.[191] Manwabum is Manwab mentioned by *MüHG* (88/17 and 101/4) as a town belonging to Banû Baddâ and in connection with Ṣuwarân (Ṣuwaʾrân, presently al-Manṣûra?); the Wâdî Menwab[192] flows into Wâdî Ḥaḍramawt west of al-Ḫauṭa, which lies about 20 km. southwest of Šibâm. Šayʿân is located by *WiHöBGS*[193] about 80 km. south of Timnaʿ.

Fifth Phase (lines 31-36). – In spite of the success met with by the two Sab kings, it seems that the end of the campaign was much less brilliant, since reinforcements reached the country of Timnaʿ, and Ḏarḥân ʾAšwaʿ and his companion Rabbšamsum Yuʿirr were in danger. But, thanks to the protection and the help of their god, they and their two kings successfully fought their way back home (also lines 21-23).

The last historical section of the text (lines 36-41)

188 Cf. *MüHG*, 94/15.

189 Cf. *JaDCR*, p. 29.

190 Cf. *FoSA*, p. 150, note 3.

191 This fact excludes the hypothesis of *mnwbm* and *šyʿn* being identified with Manwab and Šayʿân (in Maʿâfir), as indicated by *MüHG* (68/6), both of which are located northwest of Maḫâdir and west of Yerîm respectively (cf. *FoSA*, p. 66, who reads the name of the first city as Manwaz), thus approximately halfway between Ḏamâr and ʾIbb.

192 Cf. *MüHG*, 86/23, and *WiHöBGS*, p. 132.

193 P. 58, and map facing p. 63.

clearly indicates that the first author of the text, Marṯadum Y..., father of Ḏarḥân ᵓAšwaᶜ, did not take part in the military campaign, but stayed in Ṣanᶜâᵓ where he had to carry out some edict; five other rulers had to do the same thing in Ruḥâbatân, a city which is, as already noted above,[194] located about 20 km. north-northeast of Ṣanᶜâᵓ.

b – DYNASTIC SYNCHRONISMS

The Ḥaḍr king mentioned as partner in the coalition against the two Sab kings is called Yadaᶜ-ᵓil. Yadaᶜᵓil Bayyin, son of Yadaᶜᵓab Ġaylân, (RÉS 4698/1-2) is excluded because he belongs to an earlier period, that of the coregency of ᶜAlhân Nahfân and his son Šaᶜirum ᵓAwtar. It is not possible at the present time to determine whether this Yadaᶜᵓil is already attested in Ḥaḍr texts (at least three different persons named Yadaᶜᵓil are presently known) or not.

[194] Cf. p. 322 A.

[195] Cf. *JaAGM*, p. 300.

[196] Cf. *JaAGM*, *l.c.*, note 5, and *JaPSAP*, p. 170.

[197] As W. F. Albright (cf. *JAOS*, 73 [1953], p. 37 A). The identification of this king with Šahar Hilâl son of Ḏaraᵓkarib (RÉS 3854/1), suggested by *AlCAS* (p. 9; followed by *Ryc-CSAPS*, p. 206 B) is disproved by palaeography.

As far as Qatabân is concerned, Ja 629 gives two details of great importance; this information is much more valuable and accurate than that mentioned about Ḥaḍramawt. The Qat king, who took part in the coalition against Sabaᵓ, is called Nabaṭum,[195] that is to say Nabaṭum Yuhanᶜim, son of Šahar Hilâl, mentioned along with his son Marṯadum as his coregent in H 2-c.[196] This Šahar Hilâl may be identified with Šahar Hilâl Yuhaqbiḍ,[197] who is attested in the two following unpublished texts from Timnaᶜ itself, TS p and TTI-100. Palaeographically these two texts belong to Timnaᶜ; but H 2-c is a late development of the Mablaqah type,[198] which is only attested in RÉS 3534[199] and 3550.[200] Such an influence is easily explained by the geographic location of Hajar bin Ḥumeid on the eastern bank of Wâdî Beiḥân, facing the eastern end of Wâdî Mablaqah.[201] The second piece of historical information of considerable importance is the mention, in line 34 of Ja 629, of the Qat capital, Timnaᶜ.

[198] Cf. *JaPSAP*, p. 36.

[199] Cf. *l.c.*, pp. 30-31, 36, 99-101, 102, 167-69, and 190.

[200] Cf. *l.c.*, pp. 31, 33, 36, 167-69, and 190.

[201] Another influence of the Mablaqah style has already been pointed out by *JaPSAP* (p. 36) in RÉS 4330, which is engraved on J. Šeqîr.

Chapter VII

THE DYNASTY OF ḎAMARᶜALAY BAYYIN, KING OF SABAᵓ AND RAYDÂN

CIH 143, 373, 609, 729, 750, 791; Geukens 12; Ja 642, 643, 643 bis, 644, 878, 879; RÉS 3895, 3959, 4132, 4391, 4767, and 4771

Ja 644 is related to the king Ḏamarᶜalay Ḏariḥ, and Ja 642-643 bis to the latter's son and successor, Karibᵓil Bayyin; the whole dynasty to which these kings belong, needs therefore to be studied in order to put these two texts in their historical context.

The fragmentary text RÉS 4767, which deals with matters related to sacrifice, may be related to the present dynasty.[1] However, unless its palaeography is known, it remains impossible to decide whether Ḏamarᶜalay, the name of the father's unmentioned king, is to be completed either as *byn* or as *ḏrḥ*.

A – THE KING ḎAMARᶜALAY BAYYIN: cf. CIH 373

It has been suggested that Ḏamarᶜalay Bayyin may never have reigned because his name is not followed by the royal title in CIH 373, and is otherwise not yet attested as king.[2] The second reason must be handled with great caution, as pointed out by the example of his great-grandson who was totally unknown before the American excavations in Maḥram Bilqîs; yet, three texts discovered during these excavations give both his name and his royal title. The validity of the first reason cannot be accepted, because of the perfect parallel between the two following royal titles which are all the more interesting in that they belong to the same family and are separated from each other by only one generation:

krbᵓl/wtr/yhnᶜm/ *mlk/sbᵓ/wḏrydn/*
bn/ḏmrᶜly/byn/(CIH 373) and

ḏmrᶜly/ḏrḥ/ *mlk/sbᵓ/wḏrydn/*
bn krbᵓl/wtr (Geukens 12/1-2).

Furthermore, it is also worth while to point out the difference between the name of *ḏmrᶜly/byn* on the one hand and on the other *hlkᵓmr* and *yhqm*, these two being without any second personal name and belonging to royal princes, the grandson and the great-grandson of Ḏamarᶜalay Bayyin respectively.

B – THE KING KARIBᵓIL WATAR YUHANᶜIM

The most striking feature of this king is that, up to the present time, he is never mentioned in a text without one of his two sons. His reign may be divided into two sections, namely his sole reign and his coregency with his son Ḏamarᶜalay Ḏariḥ.

1 – *Remarks on some texts:* CIH 609; RÉS 3895 and 4132

CIH 609. – The decipherment of line 7 is difficult: it is given either as *–/ᶜmn/kl/ᵓlᵓltm/wᵓmlkm/wᵓ[ml]ktm/wᵓ[šᶜb]m/wsbᵓ/–*,[3] or as *–/ᶜmn/kl/ᵓlᵓltm/wᵓ[ml]km/wᵓ*... ± 15 letters .../*wsbᵓ/–*.[4] The photographs are not yet published; we are thus unable to know exactly what is on the squeezes. Nevertheless, one may suspect some dittography in the first decipherment, if it is compared with the second. Furthermore, this line should doubtless be compared with a striking parallel mentioned in RÉS 4771 which belongs to the coregency of Karibᵓil

[1] *RycIMAM* does not relate the text to any dynasty.
[2] Cf. *RycIMAM*, p. 163; cf. also *RycCSAPS*, p. 207 B, and *BePSC*, p. 55, note 3.

[3] Cf. *CIH*, II, p. 36, from *RhGO*, p. 27.
[4] Cf. *RhIMG*, p. 52.

Watar Yuhanʿim with his son Ḏamarʿalay Ḏariḥ. We read in line 1: *–/ʿmn/kl/ʾlʾltm/w(ʾ)mlkm/wʾqwlm/ wʾšʿbm/–*; *qwlm/wʾšʿbm* easily cover the ± 15 letters indicated as missing by N. Rhodokanakis's second decipherment.

RÉS 3895 – The royal title should be completed by the addition of *bn/ḏmrʿly/byn*. It remains however unknown whether the whole expression or only a part of it should be restored in line 1 or in lines 1-2.

RÉS 4132. – Line 1 should be partially completed on the basis of RÉS 4771/1; thus *.../ʿmn/kl/ʾlʾltm/ wʾmlkm/wʾqwlm/wʾšʿbm/wkl/ʾnsm/b]ht̲m/wqṭnm/...*

Appendix: The spurious Ja 879 = KM, my No. 122; squeeze and photograph; cf. *AlbM*, I, ph. 44 A, No. 10.[5]

STONE: whitish alabaster plaque with pinkish-brown striations; thickness: from 3.8 cm. to 4.8. – *Front:* 23.4 cm. × 17.4 (left side); top damaged. – INSCRIPTION: very irregular in height (ordinarily about 1.5 cm.) and type; for instance, some *r*'s (e.g., in *wtr* line 1) are shaped like *š* (thus; late period), some others (e.g., in *krbʾl*, line 1) are composed of two small straight lines making a wide angle; the *r* of *rydn* (line 2) is dextrograde; spurious copy of CIH 373.

1 **Symbol** *srḥbʾl/wtr/yhnʿm/mlky/*
2 *sbʾ/wḏrydn/bn/ḏmrʿlʿ/by*
3 *n/whlkʾmr/bn/krbʾl/hḥdt̲*
4 *ytlt/nkl/gwbn/gʾlmqh/*
5 *gwy/bytn/slḥn/wh/rnmryb*

The mistakes are obvious and gross: *srḥbʾl* instead of *krbʾl*; *mlky* instead of *mlk*; *ḏmrʿlʿ* instead of *ḏmrʿly*; *tlt* instead of */zlt*; *gʾlmqh* instead of *lʾlmqh*; *gwy* instead of *lwfy*, and *h/rn* instead of *hgrn*.

2 – *Sole Reign:*
CIH 373, 609, 750; RÉS 3895 and 3959

All the texts related to Karibʾil Watar Yuhanʿim's sole reign mention his son Halakʾamar. Two texts, CIH 373 and RÉS 3895, have the king himself as author. In the first, he and his son Halakʾamar made some repairs on the wall of Maḥram Bilqîs; the contents of the decree mentioned in the second inscription and thus the role of the royal prince remain unknown due to the fragmentary condition of the text, which was copied somewhere in Yemen.

Two other texts contain decrees. The first one, CIH 609,[6] deals with a lease for the tribe Maʿîn in Qarnâwû, Yat̲il, and Šuʿûbum, and is ratified by the royal prince Halakʾamar.[7] The second decree, RÉS 3959, comes from Mârib; the contents of the first part remain unknown, and the second part alludes to the purchase of some land by the descendants of Ḥufnum.[8] The last text to be referred to here is the fragmentary CIH 750 from al-Baiḍâ (Našqum), which apparently has only the beginning of the original: *hlkʾmr/bn/*,[9] which must be completed by *[krbʾl/wtr/mlk/sbʾ/wḏrydn]*.

3 – *Coregency with his son Ḏamarʿalay Ḏariḥ*[10]*:*
RÉS 4132 and 4771

The only two texts which indicate the coregency of Karibʾil Watar Yuhanʿim with his son Ḏamarʿalay Ḏariḥ, are two decrees, RÉS 4132 and 4771.[11] Their very fragmentary condition does not allow us to know their exact nature, but the second is given in favor of a clan.

The peculiarity of the title of the two coregents is, in the texts such as known to us at the present time, not only that each name is followed by the full title (RÉS 4771/2),[12] but especially that their family

[5] Cf. A. Jamme, *Les albums photographiques de la Collection Kaiky Muncherjee (Aden)*, Rome, 1955, pp. 57 and 33.

[6] From Šuʿûb (cf. *HöSEG*, p. 33), near Ṣanʿâʾ (cf. *RhIMG*, p. 49).

[7] Cf. also *RycIMAM*, p. 202 and note 7. This author also affirms erroneously that this decree was "revêtu de la signature du roi" (p. 192 and note 3).

[8] *RycIMAM*'s treatment of the text is difficult. He states that the noun *mlkn* "the king" may precede the king's name, thus Halakʾamar (p. 167, note 24); this opinion is confirmed on p. 175 by his interpretation of CIH 750. Yet, he also affirms that Halakʾamar's reign is uncertain (p. 164), and the royal list (p. 338) mentions Halakʾamar between parentheses. Basing his whole interpretation on G. Ryckmans' translation which he partially reproduces (pp. 163 and 191), "sur l'ordre (?) du roi (?) Halakʾamar" he concludes that "la restitution de *mlkn* est très douteuse" (p. 204, note 5). Yet, *mlkn* is not restored at all. If *mlkn* means "the king" here, the preceding part of the text, which E. Glaser could not decipher satisfactorily, could be either a verb with *mlkn* and *hlkʾmr* as subject and direct complement respectively, or a verb followed by the preposition *l* introducing *mlkn*, in which case *hlkʾmr* would be the subject of the verb.

[9] *RycIMAM* erroneously writes: "un roi est mentionné par...le nom seulement" (p. 175) and "Halakʾamar...est certes mentionné...même seul" (p. 204). Yet, the text is fragmentary.

[10] This coregency is also accepted by *RycIMAM*, e.g., p. 164, note 11.

[11] In the commentary on line 1 (as *RÉS*, VII, p. 358), RÉS 3646 is to be corrected to RÉS 3436.

[12] *RycIMAM* mentions as parallels CIH 365/16-18, 407/30-32, and 620/1-3 (pp. 220-21 and 221, note 3). The second parallel is not valid, since this text belongs to the sole reign of Šamir Yuharʿiš.

relationship is not indicated.[13] Further, the length of the original of RÉS 4132 was considerable (cf. the proposed restoration of line 1); the present line 4 could thus easily be the repetition of a fuller expression, identical with RÉS 4771/2; therefore, the title in dual is not necessarily to be restored after the present line 4, as stated by *RycIMAM* (p. 205).

C – THE SOLE REIGN OF ḎAMARᶜALAY ḎARIḤ: CIH 143, 729, 791; Geukens 12; Ja 644, 878; RÉS 4391

1 – *Remarks on* Geukens 12[14]

Although the original photograph of the inscription is not very good, it is doubtless good enough to provide a decipherment more complete than that proposed by the editor. For instance, the last third of line 1 is certainly more damaged and less clear than the same section of line 2; yet, the decipherment of the first is presented as complete and certain, and that of the second is partial and partly erroneous. The preceding remark is true provided, of course, that the decipherment of the end of line 1 was not partly borrowed, e.g., from CIH 791. At any rate, the last letter of the verb which follows *wtr*/, is *r*, and certainly not ᵓ (from *gn*ᵓ) or *y* (from *bny*), as suggested by *RyISA*, p. 110. The end of line 2 is not "mutilée" (*l.c.*, p. 111), but, instead of ᵓ.*š*., as *l.c.*, p. 109, which is interpreted as "ᵓ⌜ᶜ⌝⌞ ⌟*šr*(?)" (*l.c.*, p. 111), read *n*/*wšg*, *n* being the last letter of the preceding word, which is a place name, and *šg*, which is to be completed, at the beginning of line 2, by ᶜ; thus *šg*ᶜ, Šiǧâᶜ, the name of the pass where the text is engraved.

2 – Ja 878 = AM 200, Qat

STONE: grayish and bluish sandstone, broken into two parts and fragmentary on the right and at the bottom; although very damaged, both the top and the left edge are certain. – *Front:* height maxima: 27.9 cm.; length: maxima (center of line 3): 31 cm. INSCRIPTION: letter height: 3.5 cm., 3.3, 3.1, 3, 3, and 3 respectively (only about the upper third of line 7 remains); length of the lines: 24.5 cm., 28.5, 30, 30.5, 26, 21, and 13 respectively; spaces between the lines: 0.7 cm., 0.7, 0.5, 0.6, 0.6, and 0.6 respectively; distance from line 1 to the top: 2.5 cm.; slender and beautiful lettering.

1 . . . /*ḏ*]*hṣbḥ*/*wḫrf*/*wḍrn*/*wgmlm*⌜/⌝ (*b*?)]*nw*]
2 . . . /*sqn*]⌜*y*⌝/ᵓ*ls*/*wmr*ᵓ*s*/ᶜ*m*/*ḏẓrm*/*b*ᶜ*l*/*šy*[.]
3 . . . /]*šb*ᶜ*n*/*ḥg*/*tkrbs*/*wlḏt*/*hwfy*/ᶜ*m*/*ḍr*
4 [*n*/. . . . . . /]*kl*/*sb*ᵓ*t*/*sb*ᵓ/*ḍrn*/*b*ᶜ*m*/*mr*ᵓ*hmw*/⌞*yḥl*⌟
5 . . . /*ḏ*]*mr*ᶜ*ly*/*ḏrḥ*/*mlk*/*sb*ᵓ/*wḏry*⌞*dn*⌟[/. .]
6 . . . /*wr*]⌞*ṯ*⌟*d*/*ḍ*⌟*rn*/*mqms*/*w*ᵓ*ḏns*/*w*(*bns*)[/ . . . . . .]
7 . . . /*b*]⌞*n*/*msf*ᵓ*ym*/*wms*⌟[*nkrm*/ *bn*/*brṯs*]

1 . . .he of] Haṣbaḥ, and Ḫarf and Ḍarân and Gamlum, (des)[cendants ? of]
2 . . .ha]s [dedic]ated to his god and his lord ᶜAmm, Him of Ẓarum, master of Šay.
3 . . .]Šabᶜân, according to what he has attributed to Him, and because ᶜAmm has bestowed upon Ḍar-
4 [ân. . . . . .]all fighting [which] Ḍarân fought along with their lord Yuḥal-
5 . . .Ḏa]marᶜalay Ḏariḥ, king of Sabaᵓ and Raydân. .
6 . . .and] Ḍarân has [ent]rusted his power, and his understanding and (his son)[. . .
7 . . .f[rom [anyone who would] remove or dis[place from its place].

This Qat inscription shows a strong Sab influence by including the verbal form *Hwfy* and the personal pronoun in *mr*ᵓ*HMW*. The author's local chief was Yuḥal[. . ., and his king Ḏamarᶜalay Ḏariḥ.

Line 1: *hṣbḥ*, clan name, e.g., in RÉS 3878/18, Qat. – *ḫrf*: personal name as, e.g., in RÉS 3194 bis/2, Sab; cf. also name of tower in RÉS 2775/1, Ḥaḍr. – *ḍrn*: personal name, possibly also in RÉS 4169/2, Sab.; cf. also Arabic *Ḍârân* in *LöHSM*, p. 73 A. – *gmlm*, personal name; cf. commentary on Ja 560/2: *gmyln*.

Line 2: *ḏẓrm*, cf. *ẓrm* and *ẓrn*, personal names in CIH 37/5 and 304/1 respectively. In CIH 304/1, *RyNP* (I, p. 111) corrects *ẓrn* to *ẓr* on the basis of CIH 37/5 and *CIH* (I, p. 318) to *ẓrn*; such corrections do not seem justified. Cf. also *ẓr*, second clan name in RÉS 3566/32, Qat.

[13] In CIH 365/16-18, the first coregent is mentioned as *bn* "son" of the second, both names being introduced by *mr*ᵓ*yhmw* "their two lords". In CIH 620/1-3, *bny* (rather than *bnw* as in *CIH*, III, p. 54), restored at the beginning of line 3, indicates that the first two are at least descendants (son and grandson) of the third mentioned king.

[14] Cf. *RyISA*, XV (1957), p. 109 and pl. II; cf. also *JaPSAP*, p. 198.

Lines 2-3: *šy*.[: proper name, most probably of a temple; to the left of *y*, remains the lower extremity of a vertical stroke; thus *w* or ᶜ are excluded.

Line 3: *šbᶜn*, name of a clan (RÉS 3566/31, Qat) and also of a terrace (RÉS 3856/2, Qat). This proper name is also known as designating two temples dedicated to ᵓIlumquh: one is located in Našqum (Sab RÉS 3959/4 and 4188/4; cf. also Khalidy-Condé 5/2), and the other in Mârib (Fakhry 120). The restoration *ᵓlmqh/bᶜl/šb*]*ᶜn* in RÉS 4169/1, Sab, is purely hypothetical.

Line 7: the end is restored on the basis of RÉS 3856/6, Qat, and, e.g., Ja 350/4, Qat. The space left at the end of line 7 is too small to allow the restoration *ᵓbrṯsm*; the plural form of both noun and pronoun does not exactly fit in the case of only one offering. Furthermore, the contents of line 7 are a characteristic end of a Qat dedicatory text; there is therefore no reason to suppose an eighth line. The mention of the offering which was described at the beginning of line 3, was repeated at the beginning of line 7.

3 – *The Reign:*
CIH 143, 729, 791; Geukens 12;
Ja 644, 878; RÉS 4391

It should be stressed that in the only text in which the king's full title and filiation are mentioned, Geukens 12/1-2, the name of his father has lost its third element; *krbᵓl/wtr* is indeed *immediately* followed by a verb.

Ḏamarᶜalay Ḏariḥ is already known through CIH 791 and RÉS 4391. CIH 729 must also be referred to him,[15] and not to Ḏamarᶜalay Ḏariḥ king of Sabaᵓ, as stated by *RycIMAM*,[16] who was probably led into error by the royal title printed in *CIH*, *mlk/s*[*bᵓ*. Since the text is fragmentary, nothing prevents us from adding */wḏrydn*; this addition is based on the fact that CIH 729 comes from the dam near Mârib, exactly as RÉS 4771 which belongs to the present king.

The two fragmentary texts CIH 791 and RÉS 4391 tell us nothing about the activities of the king; the location, however, of CIH 729, namely the dam near Mârib, implies that some repairs were made on the dam during his reign. Geukens 12 mentions a royal hunting party, which was particularly successful, at the occasion of some action in relation to the acropolises of three places, the last one being Šiğâᶜ where the text is engraved.

Ja 644, the only historical text thus far known, has as author a Ġaymânite, ruler of his tribe which apparently was under the command of the king's son, Yuhaqam; the latter is already attested in the fragmentary text CIH 143 (from Šibâm), which was engraved by some Bakîlites. The text is all the more interesting in that it deals with the temporary occupation of the royal houses Salḥân in Mârib by an expedition of Šadâdites (lines 10-11), against whom ᵓIlšaraḥ Yaḥḏub had already directed an attack, under the leadership of Laḥayᶜaṯat and Rabbᵓawwâm. The usurpers were liquidated and defeated (lines 8-10). The ripost came from the faithful tribe Ġaymân; the city of Ġaymân is located 12 km. southeast of Ṣanᶜâᵓ,[17] the Šadâdites were located southeast of Ġaymân, on the road to Mârib.[18]

The fighting did not, however, stop with the liberation of Salḥân; on the contrary, after escaping from Mârib, Laḥayᶜaṯat continued the revolt and Yuhaqam ordered a group of Ġaymânites (lines 15-16) to put an end to the disorder. The clash occurred in the place called Kawmanân (lines 19 and 21), which is the Bilâd Kawmân located, according to *MüHG*, 104/8 (cf. also 80/18, etc.), north of Jebel Isbîl, therefore about 95 km. southeast of Ṣanᶜâᵓ and about 30 km. northwest of Radâᶜ.[19] The Ġaymânite victory was complete and crowned by plentiful booty.

It would of course be very interesting to know when this important event, the capture of Salḥân, happened. Unfortunately, there is not the slightest clue. Finally, it should be emphasized that, in spite of the seriousness of the situation and of the revolt which temporarily deprived the king of using the palace Salḥân in Mârib, the king is not mentioned at all. One may suggest that he was away at that time; and one thinks of course of the hunting party recorded in Geukens 12. The preceding suggestion seems all the more attractive in that Geukens 12 does not mention Yuhaqam.

Finally, the Qat text Ja 878 alludes to fighting which involved the Sab king Ḏamarᶜalay Ḏariḥ; however, there is no way of knowing which engagements are referred to in that inscription.

[15] Cf. already *CIH*, III, p. 147 A.
[16] Cf. above, p. 268 B and note 2.
[17] Cf. *WiHöBGS*, p. 20.
[18] Cf. above, p. 321 A and note 95.
[19] Cf. also *FoSA*, p. 104, note 1, *MüRhGRM*, p. 54 B and map 3, and *WiHöBGS*, p. 40.

D – THE KING KARIBʾIL BAYYIN: Ja 642, 643, and 643 bis

The existence and filiation of this Karibʾil Bayyin, who was totally unknown before the American excavations at the Maḥram Bilqîs, are ascertained by Ja 642, 643, and 643 bis; e.g., *krbʾl/byn/mlk/sbʾ/wḏrydn/bn/ḏmrʿly/ḏrḥ* in Ja 643/35-36.

Ja 642 records only the offering by some Hilalumites of one statue because the first dedicator was cured of a disease with which he came back to Mârib.

Ja 643 and 643 bis are the two parts of the same inscription which was written by two Garatites, Našaʾkarib and Ṯawbân. Ja 643 is most interesting and exceedingly valuable. Although both lateral sides are badly broken in the upper quarter of the stone, thus depriving us of valuable information, the rest of the text makes it clear that the kingdom of Sabaʾ, although still independent, had recognized the suzerainty of Ḥaḍramawt at least in the southern part of its country. There was once again peace after certain military activities still unknown to us; however, things had not been too favorable for Sabaʾ. The Ḥaḍr king Yadaʿʾil had promised security to Mârib (line 9) and even promised to take from the personal guard of the other Ḥaḍr king, Yaʿkirân, warriors and rulers who were to be put at the disposal of the Sab king, Karibʾil Bayyin. However, the situation soon deteriorated when Karibʾil Bayyin decided to send the Garatite Našaʾkarib, along with 300 Sumhurâmite soldiers, to Ḥanan, a city which was located somewhere not very far from Mârib.[20] The rescript appointing Našaʾkarib to Ḥanan could not have any effect unless the latter was invested by Yadaʿʾil. Feeling that this new appointment would reinforce the Sab position in Ḥanan where most probably he himself was, Yadaʿʾil refuses to invest Našaʾkarib; military activities started all over again, but now in the former Min country. First, Yadaʿʾil moves his army into the country of Yaṯil, a city near present Berâqiš[21] (some 85 km. northwest of Mârib), and reaches the gates of the city which open for him; he settles down there at least for a short while. He then penetrated into the district of the two cities of Našqum (al-Baiḍâ) and Našân (as-Saudâ) (a few km. apart, and about 25 km. northwest of Yaṯil); he indeed planned to attack the two cities and their system of fortifications. Karibʾil Bayyin immediately ordered the Garatite Našaʾkarib to take command of both the expeditionary corps and the cavalry of the Sab army and to go and lend assistance to the two cities which were in danger. Yadaʿʾil, hearing of this sudden help coming from Karibʾil Bayyin, retreated to Yaṯil. Karibʾil Bayyin and his soldiers from Mârib and also the Garatite Našaʾkarib with his soldiers from Našqum attacked Yadaʿʾil who was defeated and subsequently retreated to Ḥanan. However, before reaching there, he decided to plunder *mḥrmn*, "*the* temple", which most probably is the present Maḥram Bilqîs. The Garatite Našaʾkarib with his soldiers from Našqum protected the temple, and Yadaʿʾil went on his way to Ḥanan. However, Karibʾil Bayyin, the Garatite Našaʾkarib (Ja 643/35-36), along with new recruits from Mârib (Ja 643 bis/1) decided against the last Ḥaḍr move (Ja 643/35) and actually attacked Yadaʿʾil and his army (Ja 643 bis/1-2). 2000 Ḥaḍr soldiers were killed and the Sab soldiers took away from the Ḥaḍr army all kinds of animals. The Ḥaḍr defeat was complete (Ja 643 bis/4-5) and the booty enormous (Ja 643 bis/6).

Such a complete victory doubtless ended, at least temporarily, the suzerainty of the Ḥaḍr king Yadaʿʾil over some of the southern part of the Sab kingdom. However, there are no other records from Karibʾil Bayyin's reign.

[20] *MüHG* (79/22) mentions a town *ḥnnt*, immediately after Mauzaʿ, in the lower part of the country of the Banû Maǧîd, that is to say in the extreme southwest of the Arabian peninsula. This location does not fit here. From the fact that Geukens 10, written by two Ḥananites, comes from the American excavations in Mahram Bilqîs near Mârib, and also that the city Ḥanan is mentioned in RÉS 3943/4, in a series of constructions, between Raydân and the dam near Mârib, one may safely assume that the Sab city Ḥanan was located not far from Mârib.

[21] Cf. *WiHöBGS*, pp. 14 and 32.

Chapter VIII

THE KING RABBŠAMSUM NIMRÂN, KING OF SABAʾ AND RAYDÂN

CIH 164; Geukens 10; Ja 496, 645; RÉS 4138

The king Rabbšamsum Nimrân is presently known by five inscriptions, CIH 164; Geukens 10; Ja 496, 645 and RÉS 4138. Before summarizing the contents of the texts and discussing the relative chronology of this reign, I must make some remarks on the reading of the inscriptions.

A – EPIGRAPHICAL REMARKS

CIH 164 – E. Glaser's copy of lines 6-7 reads as follows:*–/mrʾhmw/r⌜b⌝šmsm/nmrn//*(7)*⌞t/⌟w⌞š⌟ʿbhmw/–*; and *CIH* (I, p. 225) interprets this copy by writing *–/mrʾhmw/rbšmsm/nmrn/b[n/...* (7) *ʿṯ]t/wšʿbhmw/–*. The restoration of *ʿṯ* at the beginning of line 7 cannot be accepted because the beginning of line 7 is exactly at the same level as that of lines 4-6; and here, there is no letter missing, even in *CIH*'s transcription of the text. The length of the lines is further ascertained by lines 4 and 5, which have 28 and 29 letters respectively. In E. Glaser's copy of line 6, there are already 26 letters; the first *ʾ* in *[bʾm]lʾ* (as *CIH*) is not necessary at all. Two or three letters may thus be restored at the end of line 6; and *CIH* suggests the restoration of at least five: "*b[n/...*". Finally, the interpretation of the last two vertical strokes in E. Glaser's copy as *b*, although at first sight justified by E. Glaser's copy of *r//šmsm* instead of *rbšmsm*, creates a problem since the following proper name, that of the king's father, would be composed of only one or two letters. The solution of the problem of the end of line 6 does not seem possible until the whole text is better known.

Geukens 10 (cf. *RyISA*, XV, pp. 104-05 and pl. I). – A better photographic reproduction is needed to check the interpretation of the remains of line 13, as proposed by *RyISA*, and also to check the lower half of the left side of the text. In line 1, read *[mr]⌜ṯdm⌝* instead of *[mr]⌜ṯ⌝[d]⌜m⌝*, proposed by *RyISA*.

Ja 496 (cf. *JaIMS*, pp. 332-34 and *JaPSAP*, pp. 12-13). – I rechecked C. Ansaldi's photographic plate, and I cannot but maintain that, at the end of line 3, "l'espace libre ne permet la restitution que de trois lettres et non de quatre...; nous croyons pouvoir lire *mlk* sous réserve d'une meilleure photographie" (cf. *JaIMS*, p. 333).

RÉS 4138 – Photographs even better than the two published by *MoMiHI* (plates D and E) are needed to ascertain the accurate reading of the text. I mention here a few corrections. Correct *š[ʿb]hmw* (line 1; the second bracket is omitted by *RÉS*) to *hwšʿnhmw* "assisted them"; *[/wḍby]ʾ* (line 4) to */w[ʾb]rṯ* "and the military expeditions"; *ʿbdhw[/* (line 6) to *ʿbdhw/r*; *ẖwm.* (line 6) to *ẖwm/*; *wḏr[ydn]* (line 8) to *wḏr[y]dn*; *bwfym[/]* (line 8) to *bwfym*; *mnlyt* (line 9) to *mngyt;* and *sʿd[hmw* (line 12) to *sʿdh[mw*. In line 11, omit the last word divider.

B – SUMMARY OF THE TEXTS

CIH 164, Geukens 10, Ja 645, and RÉS 4138 are dedicatory inscriptions, the first to Taʾlab Riyyâm, and the others to the moon god ʾIlumquh. Only the last one alludes to the military campaigns and operations which the dedicators fought upon the order of their king; the text also mentions the city Naʿiḍ which is located, as pointed out above, 32 km. southeast of Ṣanʿâʾ. Ja 496 is the only text commemorating some constructions made to a house, by certain rulers of the tribe Sahimân.

The filiation of the king is not yet found in any text, since he is referred to ordinarily by the expression including his name and his royal title. Note, however, that, until a better photograph is produced of Ja 496, the king's name is simply *rbšmsm* followed by his title *mlk* [*sbʾ*/*wḏrydn*]. A case similar to the preceding is that of *ʾlšrḥ*/*mlk*/*sbʾ*/*wḏrdyn* in Ja 568/11-12; see also *yʾzl* instead of *yʾzl*/*byn* in Ja 620/15.

C – RELATIVE CHRONOLOGY

There is presently no historical clue as to the position of Rabbšamsum Nimrân's reign in the period of *mlk*/*sbʾ*/*wḏrydn* from Karibʾil Bayyin to Yasrum Yuhanʿim.

RycIMAM suggests that Rabbšamsum Nimrân's reign should be placed toward the end of the period of *mlk*/*sbʾ*/*wḏrydn* (p. 338), that is to say about the first quarter of the 3rd century A.D. (p. 316) because "suivant la transcription de Nami 70, le *w* [est] en deux cercles séparés" (*l.c.*).[1] This argument is without foundation as shown by the facsimile of the text,[2] and also because of the following statement: "les *w* sont déjà des ellipses".[3]

[1] *RyISA* (XV [1957], p. 107) deals with the texts mentioning *rbšmsm*/*nmrn*, but does not refer to both the text NaNAG 9 (published in 1955, =Ja 645) and the article *JaIMS* (published in 1954). The last omission enables him to refer to *RycIMAM*'s above-mentioned opinion.

[2] Cf. *JaIMS*, p. 332.

[3] Cf. *l.c.*, p. 334.

Chapter IX

THE DYNASTY OF YASRUM YUHAN^{c}IM, KING OF SABA$^{\supset}$ AND RAYDÂN

(cf. map on Plate H)

CIH 46, 353, 407, 430, 431 +438, 448, 628, 948; Gl 1594 (cf. RÉS 3866); Ja 646, 647, 648, 649, 650, 651, 652, 653, 654, 655, 656, 657, 658, 660, 661, 662, 664, 665; RÉS 3910, 4196, 4230, 4790, and 4938

A – INTRODUCTION

When compared with recent studies on the dynasty of Yasrum Yuhan^{c}im, the following presentation of that period acknowledges three new coregencies. The first one is demanded by a thorough study of CIH 353, which leads to the conclusion that this text belongs to the coregency of Malik[um. . . .] with his brother Šamir Yuhar^{c}iš; this coregency must be placed after the coregency of Yasrum Yuhan^{c}im with his son Šamir Yuhar^{c}iš, which, on the basis of the inscriptions known at the present time, opens Yasrum Yuhan^{c}im's dynasty. The two other coregencies are to be placed after Šamir Yuhar^{c}iš's sole reign, which, as is already known, is divided into two parts on the basis of the development of his royal title. In each case, the first coregent is the elderly Yasrum Yuhan^{c}im himself, who associates to his royal power first his third son called Ḏara$^{\supset\supset}$amar $^{\supset}$Ayman (Ja 665), and after, a stranger to his own family, whose name is Ṯa$^{\supset}$rân $^{\supset}$Ayfa^{c} (Ja 664). Note that the present collection of texts adds eighteen new inscriptions to the fourteen already known.

B – PALAEOGRAPHY OF THE TEXTS

(cf. Plates I-L)

The palaeographic study of the texts involved in Yasrum Yuhan^{c}im's dynasty is needed because palaeography has been used to solve the problem of CIH 353 and 448, and also because this study shows a good example of archaizing tendency. Unfortunately, the letter type of both Ja 664 and 665 remains unknown. This gap is most unfortunate, for it would be interesting to see whether the tendency shown by most of the texts related to Šamir Yuhar^{c}iš's reign continued through the two following coregencies. Another remark of great importance is that all the texts known by photograph are cut in the stone, and that none of the others is reported as being in relief.[1]

1 – *Some Preliminary Remarks*

CIH 46 – In the photograph printed by *CIH*, of a retouched squeeze, the two features which could characterize the lettering, are *b* and *w*.

According to the retouched squeeze, a horizontal stroke is located between the two vertical strokes and at about the third fifth from the bottom of the letter *b*. This horizontal stroke seems highly questionable. The copy shows it in only four cases (*bšr*, *š^{c}b*, *bwrẖn*, and *bẖrfym*) and places it at different levels, namely at 3 mm., 4.5, 2.5, and 4.25 from the top of the letter. In the last case, another horizontal stroke, but not retouched, may be seen at

[1] Contrary to *RycIMAM* (p. 313): "certaines inscriptions de Šamir Yuhar^{c}iš, et notamment CIH 448, sont en relief". The case of CIH 448 is not doubtful, because of the difference in the drawing where hatching fills up the space in the rectangle, which remains unoccupied by the monogram in relief; but there is no hatching between the letters of the text itself. The presence of the monogram could possibly have misled *RycIMAM*. For monograms in relief with a text cut in the stone and not in relief, see, for instance, CIH 40.

3.75 mm. from the top of the letter. In six other instances, there is no horizontal stroke to be seen: *brd*ʾ and *bnh* (line 5), first *b* in *bś*ʿ*b*, *bn*, *mbḥn*, and ʾ*bḥḏ* (line 6). Furthermore, the retouched copy shows two oblique strokes in *b* of *b*ʿ*l* (line 5), exactly as in *ḏ*. Finally, the retouched copy indicates an oblique stroke in the last letter of ʾ*bḥḏ* (line 6); but, the original horizontal stroke is still visible and is located further down in the letter. Until a better reproduction is available, the preceding remarks would seem to justify my considering the horizontal stroke in some *b*'s as the work of the retoucher who could easily have understood a scratch in the stone as a part of the letter, as he indeed did in *b*ʿ*l* (line 5).

A close look at the different occurrences of *w* shows that one type only is used.

Gl 1594 (cf. RÉS 3866) – The paper squeeze was apparently not pounded regularly on the stone which would explain the incomplete and misformed picture of several letters.

CIH 448 – An approximate reconstruction of the lettering is not possible on the basis of the facsimile published by *CIH* (II, p. 147); the letters in my plate are those of *CIH*'s facsimile reproduced photostatically.

RÉS 4196 – The facsimile is, as in CIH 46, made from a retouched photograph.

RÉS 3910 – The width of the only *ẖ* (in *wrẖm*, line 4) is too small and the center of the letter abnormal; the engraver had to make the best of *w* engraved previously by mistake.

2 – *General Description*

Two main letterings are attested in the first group of texts. The first type (CIH 46 and RÉS 4196), which could be called progressive, presents slender letters, two overlapping circles for *w*, and *d* with a plain triangle. The second type (Ja 648 and RÉS 4938), which is strongly archaizing, shows thick, heavy letters, elliptical *w* and hollow *d*. Gl 1594 combines the heavy type (not as heavy as that in the second type, but with wider letters) and the hollow *d* of the second type, with the two overlapping circles of *w* from the first one. The facsimile of CIH 448 is so vague that it cannot be studied.[2] It is noteworthy that, except *w* of the second main type, all the other letters composed of circular parts, show perfect circles.

CIH 353 presents a mixture of elements taken from the first main type (namely the curving of the upper part of the vertical strokes in *b* and *l*, and *d* with a plain triangle) and also from the second (the elliptical *w*); it also attests two other major influences: the widening of the central curve of *r* and the splitting of *t* into two vertical parts. According to *RycIMAM* (p. 313), the lettering of the present text "diffère à peine de CIH 315" [Read 314].[3] The lettering of CIH 314 belongs to the beautiful classical period from which the heavy, archaizing type of CIH 353 is inspired.

During Šamir Yuharʿiš's reign, the first main type disappears as such. As a matter of fact, the first phase of his reign is characterized by three main types contrasting with only one main type during the second period.

The types used during the first phase of Šamir Yuharʿiš's reign may be presented as follows:

a – Elliptical circles; plain *d*, compact *m* and *š* and slanting extremities in *t* along with a heavy lettering in Ja 649, 654, and CIH 407. However, the opening of *r* is in these three texts, normal, wide and very narrow (compare with that in the second main group of the first period) respectively. Further, the circle of *ẓ* is perfect in CIH 407, and the center of *t* in Ja 654 is made of a short vertical stroke.

b – Large, perfect circles with elliptical *w*, normally open *r*, open *d*, rather stretched *m* and *š*, and slanting extremities in *t* along with a heavy lettering in Ja 652 and RÉS 3910, and with a half heavy lettering in Ja 651. However, *r* is widely open, *d* is plain and the extremities of *t* are horizontal (compare the same feature in the first main type of the first period) in Ja 652; ʿ is elliptical, *w* is composed of two overlapping circles and *t* is very large in RÉS 3910; finally, the base of the upper half of *h*, *ḥ*, and *ẖ* is composed of broken lines in Ja 651.

c – RÉS 4230 constitutes in itself a special type with slender tracing (yet most of the letters are wide); very small, perfect circles; three forms of *w* (wide, perfect circle; wide ellipse, and two overlapping circles); slanting, narrowly open *r*; the three forms of *m*, the horizontal stroke inside the second upper third of *b*; the opening of the two extremities

[2] Contrast M. Lidzbarski (cf. *Ephemeris für semitische Epigraphik*, II, 1908, p. 93) who sees so great a similarity of type between CIH 46 and 448 that they could have been engraved by the same workman.

[3] *RycIMAM* (*l.c.*) goes on to state that this very strong similarity between the two letterings is the reason why *MoMiSI* (p. 220) identifies the two Šamir's mentioned in them. *MoMiSI*'s argumentation does not allude to palaeography.

of *ḍ*, the two head-by-head overlapping triangles as center of *ḍ*, the very archaizing three vertical strokes in the lower half of *ṣ*, and the two strokes, vertical and horizontal, composing *t*.

The lettering attested during the second period of Šamir Yuharᶜiš's reign may be characterized as follows: horizontally stretched *w*; horizontal ends of the extremities of *t*, and absence of any overlapping circles for *w*. This lettering is developed in three types: the heavy, the extra heavy, and the half heavy ones.

In the first one (Ja 656 and 657), *d* is open, the two central strokes of *d̲* are slanting to the left, and the ellipses are more flattened than in the third one.

In the second one (CIH 430, 431 + 438, 948, and Ja 662), except Ja 662, the ellipses are much wider than in the third one, and give the lettering a clumsy appearance; and the *d* is open. Besides, the two central strokes of *d̲* slant to the right. Note the awkward left half of *t* in CIH 948.

In the third one (Ja 658, 660, and 661), the ellipses are of normal size; the two central strokes of *d̲* slant to the right (as in the second one); *d* is closed; *r* is widely open, although almost entirely closed in Ja 658.

C – COREGENCY OF YASRUM YUHANᶜIM WITH HIS SON ŠAMIR YUHARᶜIŠ:
CIH 46, 448; Gl 1594 (cf. RÉS 3866); Ja 646, 647, 648; RÉS 4196 and 4938

As already noted, the inscriptions known up to the present time show that Yasrum Yuhanᶜim's dynasty opens with the latter's coregency with his son Šamir Yuharᶜiš. Before taking up the description of this coregency, a few remarks are needed on some inscriptions, and especially CIH 448 and Gl 1594 need to be studied at length in order to determine whether or not they belong to the present coregency. In connection with Yasrum Yuhanᶜim, reference also should be made to the appendix on CIH 951 in the study on Watarum Yuhaᵓmin, son of ᵓIlšaraḥ Yaḥḍub.

1 – *Remarks on some texts:*
CIH 46, 448; Gl 1594; RÉS 4196 and 4938

a – CIH 46

After studying the photograph of the squeeze printed by *CIH*, I feel certain that line 4 could partly be read and deciphered. On the basis of the present documentation, the beginning of that line may tentatively be read as follows:

. . *w/grb/ᶜbdhmw/ᶜt̲*. . .
. . . the person of their servant (or, worshipper) ᶜAt̲. . .   .

CIH (I, p. 78) read lines 5-6 as follows:

(5) – –*/mrᵓyhmw/ysrm/yhnᶜm/wbnh*[*w*]/
(6) *mlkhm*]*w*[/]*šmr*[*/yhrᶜš*]*/wbrdᵓ*/– –

RycIMAM states that "on ne peut tirer aucune donnée précise de l'emploi de la formule" (p. 207) after using it in many different ways: as the proof that "seul Šamir est qualifié du titre 'le roi', alors que les deux souverains règnent ensemble" (p. 165), as the confirmation of a restored title (p. 167), as a proof that "le mot *mlkn* 'le roi' pouvait précéder le nom d'un roi, sans aucun titre" (cf. *l.c.*)[4] and finally as a foundation on which to base the highly improbable conclusion that "CIH 46, qui pourrait dater du règne de Šamir: la construction mentionnée dans cette inscription, commencée sous l'égide des deux souverains, se serait achevée alors que seul le fils régnait encore" (pp. 167-68). Incidentally, this last theory contradicts the one presented on p. 165 (see above). *RycIMAM* failed to take note of the corrections presented by *CIH* himself[5]: "L. 34 [of *CIH*, I, p. 78] (v. 6), dele *mlkhmw* et post *yhrᶜš* adde *mlky/sbᵓ/wd̲rydn*."
CIH's definitive reading of the text is thus

(5) – –*ysrm/yhnᶜm/wbnh*[*w*]/
(6) *šmr*[*/yhrᶜš/mlky/sbᵓ/wd̲rydn*]*/wbrdᵓ*/– –.

According to Langer, again the beginning of line 6 reads as follows[6]: ". . . . . . *wšmr*. . . . . . *h*(?)*wbrd*", which is followed by the part visible on line 6 of the photograph: ᵓ/*šᶜbyhmw*/– –.

The dubious *h* is doubtless an error for *n/* which belongs to *rydn*. Furthermore, *w* introducing *šmr* may be at first sight interpreted as the last element,

[4] The same author points out "l'emploi du mot *mlk* 'roi' avec un suffixe" (p. 114; with the remark that it is restored); he then mentions "leu[r roi]" (p. 165), "*mlk*[*hmw*] 'leur roi,'" (p. 173) and "leur [roi]" (p. 207); and finally he drops any allusion to the personal pronoun, "le mot *mlkn* 'le roi' pouvait précéder le nom d'un roi" (p. 167; the expression "*mlkn* 'le roi'" comes from his commentary on p. 165, where the "titre 'le roi'" is discussed).
[5] Cf. III, p. 320, lines 2-3, right column.
[6] Cf. *CIH*, I, p. 77.

which is restored by *CIH*, of the personal pronoun affixed to *bn*. At any rate, there is no difficulty on the photograph itself; I read the end of line 5 as follows: – –/*wbnhw*/*šmr*. My decipherment of lines 5-6 is thus – –/*ysrm*/*yhnᶜm*/*wbnhw*/*šmr*[/*yhrᶜš*/ *mlky*/*sbʾ*/*wḏryd*](*n*/)*wbrdʾ*/– –. Note that I do not indicate the beginning of line 6, for I really do not know where to put it because of the two following reasons. First, the beginning of line 6 would be "..... *šmr*", according to S. Langer[7]; yet, *šmr* is legible at the end of line 5 of the squeeze. Secondly, the end of line 6 is – –/*ʾbḥḏ*/*bᶜṯt*[; and the number of signs which followed *ᶜṯt*[, remains unknown.

Three remarks need to be made on the date itself. – Although *ḫrfyn*[8] might stand for *ḫryfn*,[9] I prefer *CIH*'s (*l.c.*, p. 78 B) interpretation according to which *y* indicates the genitive, as it so often happens with *bn–bny*, than to see in *ḫrfy* "a noun of secondary derivation from *ḫrf*, with a meaning something like 'date'",[10] because other parallels do not suggest another meaning than "year". *RÉS*' interpretation in RÉS 4966/3, which considers *ḫrfy* as a dual form, is further improbable since other parallels refer to one year only. – *CIH*'s correction (III, p. 320 B) of *ṯmny* (I, pp. 76, 77, and 78) in *ṯmnyy* is certain; the circle of the second *y* is visible but was not touched by the tracing which extends all the way to the top of the vertical stroke. Further, there is enough space between the second *y* and the following *w* to insert a word divider. – *CIH* (I, *l.c.*) reproduces *ḫrfm* which is clearly attested on the photograph. However, this letter, *m*, must be suppressed and considered as a dittography of the first letter of the following word, *mbḥḏ*.[11]

b – CIH 448

The difficulty in ascribing this half fragmentary text to some period of Yasrum Yuhanᶜim's dynasty comes, as is well known, from the presence, on the left edge of the remaining part, of a monogram interpreted as that of Šamir Yuharᶜiš. The whole question depends primarily on the solution to the problem of the possibility of another – and if any, of whom? – monogram on the right edge of the original stone.

Without apparent discussion of the preceding fact, *GlAAA*[12] and G. Ryckmans[13] simply relate the text to Šamir Yuharᶜiš's sole reign; and, according to H. St. J. B. Philby,[14] "it is clear that the son [namely Šamir Yuharᶜiš] was on the throne alone" at the time of the present text. However, the absence of the right missing half of the stone precisely raises the problem of another monogram, and thus of another name; therefore, using thus only the left half without any consideration of the right, one cannot legitimately draw any conclusion, certain[15] or even probable,[16] concerning the text's relationship to the sole reign of Šamir Yuharᶜiš.

Some other scholars, like M. Lidzbarski,[17] who is followed by *MoMiSI* (p. 180), practically leave the problem unsolved in view of the possibility of Yasrum Yuhanᶜim's monogram on the missing right part. Finally, *PiIRC* relates the text to the coregency of Yasrum Yuhanᶜim with his son Šamir Yuharᶜiš because "en nous fondant sur l'examen paléographique, nous constatons que l'inscription CIH 448 est d'une graphie haute et mince attestée par les inscriptions du père de Šāmir, mais que les inscriptions du règne de celui-ci seul sont d'un style tout différent. Nous en concluons que le monogramme du père pouvait se trouver à l'autre extrémité, brisée, de l'inscription et que ce texte relève de la corégence des deux rois et non du règne de Šāmir seul" (p. 166, note 5). A simple glance at the chart of letterings shows that the preceding statement on palaeography is incorrect, because the palaeographic evidence presented by both Gl 1594 and RÉS 4938 is misunderstood.

There remain thus two sources of information, namely the monogram on the left and the contents of the remaining text.

The monogram on the left edge had almost certainly its counterpart in a monogram on the right edge of the inscription,[18] as may be deduced from

[7] Cf. *l.c.*, p. 77 B.
[8] Cf. *l.c.*, pp. 76, 77, and 78.
[9] Cf. also *BeESACD*, note 89.
[10] Cf. *l.c.*, p. 34.
[11] The same idea is suggested by *BeESACD* (note 90) as a possibility.
[12] Pp. 31-32; cf. also *GlSGGA*, pp. 510 and 542; followed by *HoGSA*, p. 96.
[13] Cf. *RÉS*, VII, p. 442. A few years earlier (cf. *RyCS*, p. 240), the same author held this opinion only as "possible".
[14] Cf. *The Background of Islam* (Alexandria, 1947), p. 110.
[15] Cf. *RycIMAM*, pp. 168, note 2, 176, and 313; and *BePSC*, p. 41.
[16] Cf. *RycIMAM*, pp. 205, note 10, and 304.
[17] Cf. *l.c.*, II, p. 97. His statement was misunderstood by *HaAF*, p. 157.
[18] Ja 542 with four monograms (B on the left, and C, D, and E on the right) is an obvious exception due to the desire to make use of the hole located to the right of C. The engraver could, as a matter of fact, have added a fifth one, just above the hole.

parallel cases such as CIH 40, 648; Fakhry 72,[19] RÉS 4196 and 4198.

With regard to the study of the text itself, M. Lidzbarski is the only one who paid any attention to the inscription; and he indeed made two interesting remarks. According to him, the authors of the text could have been either some *ʾqwl* "rulers" or the reigning king with his sons (p. 97). The preceding remark is doubtless based on the mention of *h̲mys* (line 5) "armies", and also on the context in which this noun is inserted. The author then gives more precision to his thought by adding that "letzteres ist deshalb warscheinlicher, weil zwischen der Nennung der Götter und des Kriegsvolkes in Z.5 nicht auch die Herrscher genannt wird" (*l.c.*). This interpretation explains the restoration of *hmw* at the beginning of line 6, thus *h̲mys[hmw]* "[their] armies".[20] However, the restoration of *mlk/sbʾ* instead of *hmw* is at first sight also possible; the authors then would have been some high ranking persons in the service of the king, some chief (or, chiefs) and some of his relatives.

The expression *h̲ms/mlk/sbʾ* is ordinarily found in phrases having as subject a king (e.g., Ja 629/10), but not always (e.g., Geukens 1/3, where the subjects are two persons mentioned as *(b)n/(ʾ)s* (line 1) "(fr)om the (per)sons" of the king himself). Further, it hardly seems likely that the kings would formally commemorate their having completed some kind of construction *bʾh̲yl/wmqymt/h̲mys[hmw* "with the strength and the power of [their] armies".[21] On the contrary, the whole expression with the restoration of *mlk/sbʾ* sounds quite natural if expressed by some high ranking servants of the king, such as chieftains.

After pointing out that the authors of the text were most probably not the king(s), and since a monogram is to be restored on the right edge of the stone, it remains to study the identity of the person whose monogram is missing and also the contents of the text in order to ascertain the name of that person.

At first sight, one might think that the missing monogram was made of the letters of the name of the first author of the text. The first author of an inscription can easily have his own name in one monogram which is usually located on the right of the text,[22] and the name of his tribe in the other (e.g., Fakhry 72). However, no author would ever have put himself (or, any other person, either individual or collective), at the same level as that of his king by devoting a monogram to his own name and another one to his king's name. The monogram on the right of the present text doubtless contained a royal name, as the other does, and more precisely the name of the first coregent.

Only one question needs to be answered, namely that of the identity of the first coregent.

At first sight, two possibilities stand, either *ysrm/yhnʿm* or *mlk[m/. . . .]* (cf. CIH 353). The choice of one of these two persons depends, at least at the present time, on a further study of the contents of the text. The literary parallel between CIH 46 and the present text is very striking.

Besides the common fact of relating the building of some constructions, these two texts contain some expressions whose basic similarity should be noted, because the difference in other expressions, contrasting with the above-mentioned similarity, is, in my opinion, the key to the interpretation of the problem under study now. Here follows the first group of expressions which are mentioned in line 5 of each text:

CIH 46	CIH 448
–/brdʾ/wmqm/mrʾhmw/ʿt̲tršrqn	*bmqm/mrʾhmw/ʿt̲tršrqn*
/wʾlyhmw/– – →	→ */wʾšmshmw*
/wʾšmshmw →	→ */wʾlʾlthmw*

The two preceding pericopes doubtless derive from a unique formula which is not, however, reproduced entirely "ad litteram".[23] They immediately precede the following expressions in lines 5-6:

CIH 46	CIH 448
/wbrdʾ/mrʾyhmw/ysrm/yhnʿm/wbnhw/ *šmr[/yhrʿš/mlky/sbʾ/wd̲ryd](n/)–*	*/wbʾh̲yl/wmqymt/h̲mys[/mlk/sbʾ/. . .*

[19] For the study of the monograms of Fakhry 72, cf. *JaJEQH*, p. 132, notes 1 and 4.

[20] This restoration is adopted by *CIH* and also by *BeSI* (p. 115), but is disregarded by *BeNL*, IV, p. 140, note 5, where *h̲yl* is to be corrected as *ʾh̲yl*.

[21] The expression *b(h̲)yl/ʾdmhmw/. . .* in RÉS 4775/4 belongs to the final invocation.

[22] In Ja 542, the monogram of the author, A, is exceptionally on the left. This fact may be accounted for by the use of the hole on the right of the text: if the worker wanted to make use of that hole, the monogram of the tribe was doubtless much more fitting for a triple repetition than that of the author. Note that the text and the monogram A could not have been engraved on the right of the three monograms because they would have been in the way of the persons using the rough stairs leading to the platform (cf. *JaIAM*, pp. 274-75).

[23] Gl 1594 cannot be used here, since its complete text is still unpublished.

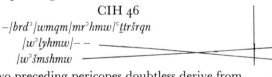

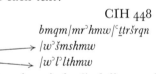

It is necessary to stress that the description of CIH 46 does not allude in the least to any monogram. The presence of a monogram, even very damaged, would have been easily detected because of the sharp contrast between it and the text.

The difference between these two formulas, contrasting with the unicity of the formula found in the first group of expressions, may be explained as follows. If the authors of CIH 448 had previously decided upon engraving the names of their two kings in two monograms, it became unnecessary to repeat them in the text, but it sufficed to allude to them by the expression *mlk/sbˀ*; in other words, the royal title in CIH 46/5-6 has as counterpart in CIH 448/5-6, the mention of [*mlk/sbˀ*] and its precise commentary and explanation in the two monograms.

c – Gl 1594 = A 492; EXTRACT IN RÉS 3866

Before beginning the main question related to Gl 1594, it is necessary to determine the value of the text introduced as RÉS 3866 by *RÉS*, and which reads as follows: *ysrm/yhnᶜm/mlk/sbˀ/wḏrydn.*[24]

RÉS introduces RÉS 3860-3868 with the reference to *RhKTB*, II, followed by the note: "Textes de Rhodokanakis, extraits de diverses copies inédites de Glaser". According to the reference to the page of *RhKTB*, the above-quoted text is to be found on p. 66, where *RhKTB* only states that "*yhnᶜm* Beiname, 1. des ISRᵐ von S[abaˀ] ḏ[ū] R[aidan] in ... Gl ... 1594". This, however, is not sufficient to justify the formula reproduced as RÉS 3866, which is formally expressed in the following statement of *RyCS* about Gl 1594: "Yasirum Yuhanᶜim y est mentionné seul, avec le titre de 'roi de Saba et Ḏû-Raydân" (p. 240).

The most important question to be dealt with here is the relation of Gl 1594 with Yasrum Yuhanᶜim's family, that is to say the title mentioned in that inscription.

On the one hand, K. Mlaker states that the two well-known kings "ISRᵐ IHNᶜM und ŠMR IHRᶜŠ, die, ebenfalls als gemeinsame Regenten, ... Gl 1594₆ₛ. (unveröffentlicht) aus dem Jahre 389 'von den Jahren des MBḤḌ, Sohn des ˀBḤḌ an' datieren".[25] Such a statement confirms *RhKTB*'s affirmation but does not support the text such as introduced as RÉS 3866.[26]

On the other hand, *HöSEG* (p. 56) alludes to only one king mentioned in the text. The solutions to that problem are varied. *RÉS* admits the coregency with reference to K. Mlaker's statement, but fails to allude to *HöSEG*'s affirmation.[27] According to *RycIMAM*, "tout deviendrait clair en effet si l'on supposait que dans Gl. 1594 Šâmir régnait seul. Dans sa titulature, le nom de Yâsir Yuhanᶜim devait être mentionné ... seul Šâmir peut être considéré comme 'le souverain' sous le règne duquel celle-ci fut rédigée".[28] According to *BePSC* (p. 41), the text belongs "apparently to the sole reign of Šmr Yhrᶜš". According to M. Höfner's letter (June 9, 1959), Gl 1594/3-4 read as follows: (3)– –/*mrˀhmw/ysrm*/[... (4) ...]*bˀ/wḏrydn*/– –, and, although its contents cannot be questioned, the date itself is also fragmentary. Note the singular *mrˀ* (neither *ˀmrˀ* nor *mrˀy*), which at first sight may be interpreted as introducing the name of only one king. *RhKTB*'s affirmation then and especially that of K. Mlaker must be explained. *GlAAA*, speaking of Šamir Yuharᶜiš, states that "nun haben wir von demselben König, als er noch dem kürzeren Titel von 'Saba und ḏû Raidân' führte, eine vom Jahre 281 n. Chr. datirte Inschrift (Glaser 379 [= CIH 448], während sein Vater Jâsir Yuhanˀim inschriftlich für die Jahre 270 und 274 bezeugt ist" (pp. 31-32), alluding to CIH 46 and Gl 1594 respectively. Since Glaser could easily have transcribed the royal names without indicating exactly the restored elements in them, and because he does not allude to Šamir Yuharᶜiš's name in CIH 46, his testimony proves only that, in his own opinion, Šamir Yuharᶜiš was reigning alone in CIH 448,[29] and also that Yasrum Yuhanᶜim was king (without bringing up the question of a coregent in CIH 46 and Gl 1594). Both *RhKTB* and K. Mlaker doubtless base their information on E. Glaser's documentation which obviously goes beyond the squeeze of Gl 1594 as it is known now.

[24] Cf. *RÉS*, VI, p. 325.

[25] Cf. *WZKM*, 40 (1933), p. 224. *RycIMAM* misunderstands this statement when he writes that "K. Mlaker... signale que Gl 1594, 6, mentionne Yâsir et Šâmir; il en conclut que les deux rois régnaient ensemble à cette époque" (p. 305). According to K. Mlaker's text, Gl 1594 mentions the names of the two kings, and Gl 1594/6-7 the date.

[26] Although printed in August 1955 (cf. *RÉS*, VI, p. 321), RÉS 3866 does not refer to K. Mlaker's statement, nor does *RycIMAM* allude to the difficulty created by that statement compared with RÉS 3866.

[27] Cf. *RÉS*, VII, pp. 441 and 442. The author refers, it is true, to *HöSSE*, pp. 25-26, where the author does not touch the question of Gl 1594. There was, of course, no problem for *HoGSA* coming from *HöSEG*'s statement.

[28] P. 304; cf. also p. 163, note 5; on p. 175, the same author refers to the present text (in note 1) as stating that "un roi est mentionné par son nom et son titre".

[29] The same conclusion is drawn by *HaAF*, pp. 157-58.

There are only two possible explanations: either the squeeze only covers a part of the original text which was copied in its entirety by E. Glaser, or the latter's copy was partially completed by the restoration of the missing part.[30]

The first hypothesis is, in my opinion, to be rejected. E. Glaser did not, in so far as we know, make partial squeezes of the texts he saw. Again, in K. Mlaker's statement quoted above, the last element of the date is put between quotation marks, which would normally indicate the translation of the text. If true, this quotation would prove that that precise element of date actually was in Gl 1594 as known to K. Mlaker, and therefore that the latter had at hand the contents of the original text. The quotation marks used by K. Mlaker are justified but unfortunately do not prove the point, because the element of date in its entirety, mentioned in connection with CIH 46/6 and Gl 1594/6-7, is formally attested in the first of these two texts.

The second hypothesis explains the whole situation in a very easy, almost obvious way, and is confirmed by *RhKTB*'s reasoning concerning Yuharᶜiš's name.

It is of course very tempting to use CIH 46 and RÉS 4196, both related to the coregency of Yasrum Yuhanᶜim and Šamir Yuharᶜiš, in order to restore Gl 1594, since the name of Yasrum is attested there and especially since the fragmentary date had to be completed on the basis of the first. However, *RhKTB*'s approach seems suggestive. In his study of *yhrᶜš* (*l.c.*), which is separated by only 8 lines of text from that of *yhnᶜm* where he formally refers to Gl 1594, instead of referring also to Gl 1594, *RhKTB* only refers to "Glaser, Abess. 128 ff.; Hartmann, Arab. Frage, 155" (*l.c.*). Yet, *GlAAA*, pp. 128-29, deals only with CIH 353, and *HaAF*, p. 155, does not deal with any text; on the contrary, *HaAF* and *GlAAA* refer to Gl 1594, on p. 156 and pp. 31-32 respectively (cf. above). That *RhKTB* does not refer to Gl 1594 in connection with *yhrᶜš*, and that he twice avoids referring to the exact page which either mentions or alludes to Gl 1594, cannot be considered as a mere accident, but rather indicates that he did not wish to connect Gl 1594 with *yhrᶜš*, for were *šmr/yhrᶜš* positively attested in Gl 1594, there would not have been any reason for hiding the fact. One may object that *yhnᶜm* is not attested in the squeeze either, and *RhKTB* mentions it with reference to the text. He could have done it safely, for *ysrm* is known as *ysrm/yhnᶜm*.

[30] The hypothesis according to which Gl 1594 would be completed by another text, must be excluded, since this other text would have another number. Gl 1593, referred to by *HöSEG* (*l.c.*), cannot be taken into consideration because, according to M. Höfner's letter, the legible part of it does not mention any royal name.

It is preferable to retain *šmr/yhrᶜš*'s name rather than that of his brother *mlk*[*m*/....], which is found in CIH 353 and has exactly the same number of characters, because the present text fits very well the period defined by CIH 46 and 448 which attest Šamir Yuharᶜiš's name.

d – RÉS 4196

In *RÉS*' transcription (VII, p. 138), correct *mdyḥm* (line 1) to *mdḥym*; *brwʾ* (line 2) to *brʾw*; and *bnhmw* (line 3) to *bnhw*; and insert a word divider between *bn* and *nbṭ* (line 4). Note that the end of line 5 is published by *RycPCH*, p. 23, note 76.

e – RÉS 4938

To the information given about the stone in *RÉS* (*l.c.*, p. 439), add that the original is a yellowish limestone slab with a thickness of 12 cm. (top) and 13 (bottom). The height of the stone is 80 cm. In the text, the letter *m* in the name of the moon god (line 4) does not exist on the stone; thus [*m*] instead of (*m*); for *nᶜmbrl* instead of *nᶜmbrg* (line 9) and the interpretation of *wḥbt* (line 9) as a family name and not as a verb, cf., e.g., Ja 741/3 and commentary; finally, suppress the word divider before *bᶜl* (line 17).

2 – *The coregency itself*

Even a simple glance at the contents of the eight texts which are known at the present time as related to the coregency of Yasrum Yuhanᶜim and his son Šamir Yuharᶜiš, suggests two remarks. First, the four texts from Maḥram Bilqîs (Ja 646, 647, 648, and RÉS 4938) have no date; and the four others have one. Secondly, except the date included in some of the texts, the contents of the inscriptions give almost no historical information on the coregency itself. The first remark is of great importance in the understanding of the origin of the dates mentioned in the texts.

a – CONTENTS OF THE INSCRIPTIONS

A fact worthy of mention is that the four texts from Maḥram Bilqîs are dedicatory inscriptions, and the four others allude to the building of some constructions.

In the texts from Maḥram Bilqîs, the offering of a statue[31] to the moon god is connected with a great variety of circumstances.

In Ja 646, a high official of the two coregents was able to take vengeance and to defeat the person who incited him against the second coregent. In Ja 647, the offering is connected with a child and some events, including various work in four different cities. In Ja 648, the statue is dedicated in gratitude for the god's having granted life to the author's son. Finally, in RÉS 4938, the statue is ordered by the god himself who had been requested to save the life of the first dedicator's wife.

The four other texts are typical inscriptions relating to the construction of some buildings; only RÉS 4196 is complete and tells us that the tribe rulers built two tanks. CIH 448, whose right part is missing, commemorates the building of some constructions and in particular on the walls, glacis(?) and towers of the city. Only the end of CIH 46 is known; but the text certainly dealt with the building of some constructions.[32] What is preserved from Gl 1594 also belonged to a text similar to CIH 46.

b – THE ERAS

The remark made above, concerning the presence of a date in the texts found outside Mârib, is very important, because this fact gives a clue to the solution of a much-debated question, viz. that of the relation between the Sab era, the era of *mbḥḏ/bn/ʾbḥḏ* and the era of *nbṭ*; the last two being mentioned in CIH 46, Gl 1594, CIH 448, and in RÉS 4196 respectively. The *crux* of this problem lies in the relation between the Sab and the *mbḥḏ/bn/ʾbḥḏ* eras.

Let us summarize the recent developments relative to this question.

In 1943, *RyCS* (pp. 238-39) considered the two eras to be one and the same by interpreting the date mentioned in RÉS 3958 which he wrongly ascribes to the *mbḥḏ* era, on the basis of CIH 621 which belongs to the Sab era.

A few years later, *RycIMAM* (pp. 305-12) concluded on the basis of the three following arguments that there were two different dating systems.[33]

a – The *mbḥḏ* era is known in only three texts related to the coregency of Yasrum Yuhanᶜim and Šamir Yuharᶜiš, in which the *nbṭ* era, obviously different from the Sab era, is also attested (p. 305);

b – The Sab era contains only numerals, to which the *mbḥḏ* system adds some specification (p. 305); further, the latter and the *nbṭ* era are "deux computs analogues" for they are specified by "une expression similaire: *bn ḫrf mbḥḏ* et *bn ḫryf nbṭ*" (p. 306).

c – The identity of the *mbḥḏ* era with the Sab system would entail a gap (unaccounted for in the texts) of at least 40 years between the end of Šamir Yuharᶜiš's reign (at the latest about A.D. 295) and the Abyssinian occupation. Therefore, the end of Šamir Yuharᶜiš's reign is to be placed just before this Abyssinian occupation. This conclusion is confirmed by the an-Nemârah epitaph (A.D. 328) of ʾImruʾl-qays, which would be unexplicable, had Šamir Yuharᶜiš's reign ended more than 30 years earlier (pp. 306-11).

The author states his conclusions as follows:

a – The end of the coregency of Yasrum Yuhanᶜim with Šamir Yuharᶜiš may be dated about A.D. 320, and occurred between 385 and 389 of the *mbḥḏ* era which therefore started between 69 and 65 B.C. (pp. 311-12);

b – The *nbṭ* era would have begun during the last decade B.C. (p. 312).

Since the relation between the *mbḥḏ* era and the Sabaean will be dealt with later, only three remarks are needed here. Contrary to *RycIMAM*'s opinion, both Gl 1594 and CIH 448 belong to the coregency of Yasrum Yuhanᶜim and Šamir Yuharᶜiš. – The dates of CIH 46 and RÉS 4196, the only texts ascribed by the author to the preceding coregency, are 385 *mbḥḏ* and 316 *nbṭ*. Since this year 316 *nbṭ* is, in his opinion, anterior to 389 *mbḥḏ*, there are about 70 years difference between the two systems. Therefore, if *mbḥḏ* system started between 69 and 65 B.C., the *nbṭ* era should have started during the first decade A.D., and not the last decade B.C. – The identification of Šamir mentioned in the an-Nemârah epitaph with Šamir Yuharᶜiš is accepted here as a hypothesis

[31] The mention of the offering disappeared from Ja 647; the restoration proposed in the edition of the text is based on parallel texts.

[32] *RycIMAM* (p. 194, and note 14) speaks of "fortifications". This information comes from *CIH*'s reading in I, p. 78, which *CIH* himself rejects in III, p. 320 A (last line), by correcting *mqḏrt* in S. Langer's copy to *mbqrt* "tombs".

[33] This solution is acknowledged by *WiHöBGS*, p. 116, note 4.

because of the uncertain situation of the vicinity of Najrân such as indicated by Ja 649/10.

It is interesting to see that *WiHöBGS* also place Šamir Yuharᶜiš's sole reign at the beginning of the 4th century (p. 133),[34] since CIH 353 is dated "um 300 n. Chr." (p. 20), and the intervention of ᵓImruᵓl-qays "etwa um diese Zeit" as Šamir Yuharᶜiš's victory in Ḥaḍramawt (p. 11).

A. F. L. Beeston[35] considers RÉS 3958 and 4197 bis as mentioning a date referring to the Ḥaḍr era and further he suggests that "in the third century A.D. two rival systems were competing against each other in Saba, but later one of them fell into disuse, so that it was no longer necessary to specify that the dating referred to the other one, which had by then become generally accepted...it was the *nbṭ* era which fell out of use; the later Sabaean era is thus to be regarded as identical with the *mbḫḏ* era".[36] He furthermore understands *RycIMAM*'s interpretation of the an-Nemârah epitaph as "a misapprehension of the implications of"[37] this inscription. In his opinion, ᵓImruᵓl-qays's attack on Najrân, which can be dated about A.D. 310, occurred "in a period of confusion and Himyaritic weakness which supervened shortly after his [Šamir Yuharᶜiš's] death".[38] He then suggests dating Šamir Yuharᶜiš's sole reign "roughly A.D. 280-300".[38]

W. F. Albright recently[39] accepted *RycIMAM*'s opinion on the Sab era and the *mbḫḏ* system, and holds the *nbṭ* era for late Qat, which may be dated A.D. 5 and which most probably began with the reign of the Qat king Nabaṭum Yuhanᶜim. As already pointed out above, *nbṭ* of the *nbṭ* era cannot be identified with *nbṭm*,[40] the first name of a Qat king who belongs to the middle of the first century A.D.

The possibility of the Sab system's being "an abbreviation of a fuller formula", that of the *mbḫḏ* system, was suggested by W. F. Albright in 1953,[41] because all the texts mentioning the latter are anterior to the inscriptions attesting the other. The idea of an abbreviated formula, although not adequately supported,[42] is fully endorsed by J. Pirenne,[43] but considered only as a strong possibility by *RycPCH* (p. 23).

The study of the three dating systems needs to be based on two facts to which sufficient consideration has hitherto not been given, namely the area in which the texts were found, and the period to which they belong. Such an approach was made, with partial success, for RÉS 3958 and 4197 bis. W. F. Albright rightly pointed out[44] that these two texts are related to Qatabân. As proof of his interpretation according to which the dates of these two texts belong to the Ḥaḍr dialect and era,[45] A. F. L. Beeston says "as can be seen from the -s suffix and the HAD dual-ending *hy* in the decad numeral *ᵓrbᶜhy*".[46] Yet, neither of these two features is specifically Ḥaḍr; as is very well known, the dual-ending *hy* exists also in Min,[47] and the *-s* suffix is also Qat.[48]

These two texts, RÉS 3958 and 4197 bis, as well as RÉS 4196, which mentions the *nbṭ* era, must be subjected to yet further investigation. The first author of RÉS 4196 was the ruler of two well-known *Qat* tribes: Qašamum and Muḏḫayum; the writer of RÉS 3958[49] was the ruler of two tribes, the first being another well-known *Qat* tribe, Radmân; these three tribes were located in the same general area, south of Timnaᶜ. Further, the dates mentioned in these three texts have three features in common, contrasting with all the dates belonging to the *mbḫḏ* era, namely the absence of *ḏ* introducing the name of the month, the absence of *ḫrf* before the numeral when the month is mentioned,[50] and finally the noun *ḫryftm*[51] immediately

[34] This suggestion postpones by about 30-20 years the beginning of Šamir Yuharᶜiš's sole reign such as accepted by *HöSSE* (p. 26): about A.D. 270-280. On the basis of this evaluation, *HöSSE* concluded that the latest possible date for the beginning of the *nbṭ* era was 46-36 B.C.

[35] Cf. *BePSC*, pp. 37-42 and *BeESACD*, pp. 35-38.

[36] Cf. *BeESACD*, p. 36; cf. already *BePSC*, p. 41.

[37] Cf. *BePSC*, *l.c.*

[38] Cf. *l.c.*, p. 42.

[39] Cf. "Zur Chronologie des vorislamischen Arabien", in *Von Ugarit nach Qumran. Festschrift für Otto Eissfeldt*, Berlin, 1958, p. 6.

[40] Cf. already *RycPCH*, p. 23, note 76.

[41] Cf. *JAOS*, 73 (1953), p. 37 B, note 4. This possibility led the author to identify the two Sab and *mbḫḏ* eras, an opinion which he abandoned in 1958, as pointed out above.

[42] Cf. also *BeESACD*, p. 36.

[43] Cf. *Le Muséon*, 69 (1956), p. 166.

[44] Cf. *JAOS*, *l.c.*, notes 4 and 5.

[45] Cf. *BePSC*, p. 37, note 1, and *BeESACD*, pp. 15 and 35; this opinion is accepted by *RycPCH*, p. 23.

[46] Cf. *BeESACD*, p. 15.

[47] Cf. *HöASG*, p. 133: "Im Min. sind die Formen *ᵓrbᶜhj*=40 und *ṯmnhj*=80 überliefert".

[48] Cf. also *RÉS*, VII, p. 14, commentary on l. 14 of the text.

[49] The Sab origin of the author explains the use of the Sab dialect in the text.

[50] "The *mbḫḏ* era texts differ by introducing the word 'year' before the numeral...instead of immediately after", so *BeESACD*, p. 36, This statement is not exactly true nor complete.

[51] Also in RÉS 3958/14, instead of *ḫryfm* as in *RhSLG*, III, p. 4; *RÉS*, VII, p. 12; and *BeESACD*, p. 35.

following the numeral. These three differences contradict the parallelism of expression between the *mbḥḏ* and the *nbṭ* systems, such as stated by *RycIMAM* (p. 306) on the single basis of "une expression similaire" (see above).

The preceding remarks suggest, in my opinion, on the one hand that we should refer the three dates of RÉS 3958, 4196, and 4197 bis to *Qat* populations in south Wâdî Beiḥân, and more precisely the *nbṭ* era to the tribes Qašamum and Muḏhayum, and the other to at least the tribe Radmân, and on the other hand to relate them both to a unique, and basic *Qat* formula [52] which, apart from the additional specification concerning the *nbṭ* era, was adapted differently to two cases, namely with (RÉS 3958 and 4196) or without (RÉS 4197 bis) the mention of the month.

The fact that the Radmânite era instead of the official Qat era is mentioned in a text engraved in the heart of Wâdî Beiḥân, is sufficiently explained by the fact that, at the time of the engraving, the Qat kingdom as such had disappeared. Again, with regard to RÉS 4196 which mentions Šamir Yuharᶜiš's name, it seems rather easy to understand that the Sab official era was not obligatory for those who were not Sab, and especially for rulers of non-Sab tribes, such as Qašamum and Muḏhayum.

The texts mentioning the *mbḥḏ* system come from the west and south of Ṣanᶜâʾ.

CIH 46 was found in Yakâr, a city located east of Ḏâff on the road from Ḏamâr to Ṣanᶜâʾ.[53] Bûsâm, which gave Gl 1594,[54] was most probably located west of Ṣanᶜâʾ and south of Kawkabân.[55] CIH 448 was discovered in Ḥaqîr, a city not very far east of Yerîm,[56] and about 70-80 km. south of Yakâr. This city and Bûsâm are approximately the same distance from Ṣanᶜâʾ.

The location of these three cities has nothing to do with the two tribes Qašamum and Muḏhayum mentioned in connection with the *nbṭ* era. This geographical difference, together with the dialectal difference, does not support *BeESACD*'s (p. 36) opinion quoted above, that the *nbṭ* and *mbḥḏ* eras were "two rival systems", and that the *nbṭ* system "fell out of use". Those two systems were simply in use in different parts of the country, as well as the two Qat systems used by different tribes.

Finally, the approximate date for the beginning of the *mbḥḏ* era in no way supports the identification of that system with the Sab one. Two considerations are, in my opinion, basic to the solution of the problem: the relative chronology of Yasrum Yuhanᶜim's dynasty, and the interpretation of the an-Nemârah epitaph.

a – The length of Yasrum Yuhanᶜim's dynasty is to be evaluated on the basis of three facts.

First, this dynasty appears under the form of the coregency of Yasrum Yuhanᶜim with Šamir Yuharᶜiš; therefore, the first coregent was about 40 years of age at the beginning of that coregency, so that the second coregent, his own son, could be about 20 years of age.

Secondly, this coregency lasted about 15 years, since the period of 11 years is already ascertained by CIH 46 and 448.

Thirdly, the same Yasrum Yuhanᶜim returned to power during two consecutive coregencies – and that after another coregency and Šamir Yuharᶜiš's sole reign. These two periods cannot be stretched too far; otherwise, Yasrum Yuhanᶜim would be too old when he came back to power. It seems reasonable to allow about 5 years for the coregency and 10 for Šamir Yuharᶜiš's sole reign. In this case, Yasrum Yuhanᶜim would have been 70 years of age when he started his coregency with his son Ḏaraʾʾamar ʾAyman.

According to the preceding evaluation of the facts, 30 years would be allowed to the three following periods:

Yasrum Yuhanᶜim and Šamir Yuharᶜiš:	about 15 years;
Malik[um...] and Šamir Yuharᶜiš:	about 5 years;
Šamir Yuharᶜiš alone:	about 10 years.

b – With regard to the an-Nemârah epitaph of the king ʾImruʾl-qays (300-328),[57] an accurate translation of the phrase which mentions "Najrân, the city of Šamir", is still to be desired.[58] The

[52] *BeESACD* (p. 36) already notes "that the formula of R.4196 is similar to that used in" RÉS 3958 and 4197 bis.

[53] Cf. *MüHG*, 111/14: "Yakârâ", and *FoSA*, p. 187, note 6.

[54] Cf. *HöSEG*, p. 35.

[55] On the basis of the location of the places where Gl 1591-1592 and 1597-1598 come from, Gl 1593-1596 being from Bûsâm.

[56] Cf. *CIH*, II, p. 147.

[57] Cf. R. Dussaud, *La pénétration des Arabes en Syrie avant l'Islam*, Paris, 1955, p. 65.

[58] For instance: "qui apporta le succès(?) au siège de Nadjrān, ville de Shammar" (cf. *Répertoire chronologique d'épigraphie arabe*, Le Caire, I [1931], p. 2) or "er drang vor mit Erfolg zur Belagerung von Nagrān, der Stadt des Shammar" (cf. *WiHöBGS*, p. 11). However, *ḥbǧ* interpreted as a *maṣdar*, could also be read *ḥibǧ* which would allude to the oasis itself as a meeting place for all the tribes connected with Najrân. R. Dussaud translates the same phrase as follows: "qui alla frapper Nedjrân, ville de Shamir" (*l.c.*, p. 64). This translation is based on the reading of *ḥrb* instead of *ḥbǧ*, and does not render *bzǧy* which immediately follows *wǧʾ* "et

mention of "siege" or "stroke" cannot be accepted unless ᵓImruᵓl-qays actually succeeded in his enterprise. But, then, why did the engraver use such a complicated phrase, compared with the simplicity of the other expressions of parallel contents (verbs *mlk* [twice] and *hrb*), to state the simple fact that his late king took possession of Najrân? The text probably alludes only to the fact that ᵓImruᵓl-qays went to bring order among the tribes connected with Najrân, and did succeed in his undertaking. Such an event could easily have taken place at the end of Šamir Yuharᶜiš's sole reign; so it would be explained why Šamir Yuharᶜiš did not bring order himself. *BePSC*'s remark according to which the great conqueror Šamir Yuharᶜiš could not easily "have allowed encroachments on his northern border" (p. 42) does not exactly fit into the picture such as presented by the texts which make it plain that both Yasrum Yuhanᶜim and Šamir Yuharᶜiš did have to cope with a lot of trouble in the far north of their kingdom, due to the restless condition of the tribes. Furthermore, Šamir Yuharᶜiš's disappearance from the political scene was not followed by a lacuna in the dynasty but by two coregencies headed by his own father. These two consecutive coregencies, which do not appear to be "a period of political confusion and weakness", as stated by *BePSC* (p. 42), compel us to reconsider the implications of the an-Nemârah epitaph.

According to the opinions contrary to *RycIMAM*'s interpretation, only two possible explanations exist for solving the questions raised by the data which we have for the period of ᵓImruᵓl-qays: either "shortly after"[59] the sole reign of Šamir Yuharᶜiš or some years later.

In the first hypothesis, ᵓImruᵓl-qays's operation doubtless occurred during the coregency of Yasrum Yuhanᶜim with his son Ḏaraᵓᵓamar ᵓAyman; and according to the second, either at the end of that coregency or during the following coregency, that of Yasrum Yuhanᶜim and Ṯaᵓrân ᵓAyfaᶜ. In any case, the name of Yasrum Yuhanᶜim had undoubtedly replaced that of Šamir Yuharᶜiš in official documents and private conversations immediately after the beginning of the above-mentioned first coregency; why then would the engraver have mentioned Šamir Yuharᶜiš instead of the first coregent at the time of the intervention? In such historical circumstances, what could an expression like *njrn mdynt šmr* mean besides referring to *šmr* either as to the founder or the builder of the city? But, Šamir Yuharᶜiš neither founded the city, nor built it, nor re-built it, nor made it his capital city. Besides, the subjects of the late ᵓImruᵓl-qays were no doubt much more acquainted with the name of the city itself, because of its commercial importance, than with that of a Sab king; in other words, the mention of *šmr* can hardly be explained as a detail intended to help the North-Arabs to locate Najrân. However, if the second hypothesis implies a greater number of years than that understood above, ᵓImruᵓl-qays' intervention could have occurred after the last coregency of Yasrum Yuhanᶜim. Then, if there was a king in Mârib, my objection pointed out above is still valid: why not mention the reigning king? But, if there was no king but "a period of political confusion", what is the glory of robbing a dead man or a headless country of one of his or its possessions? That Šamir Yuharᶜiš was actually reigning at the time of ᵓImruᵓl-qays' intervention seems to me the only possible interpretation of the contents of the an-Nemârah inscription; however, it does not imply that Šamir Yuharᶜiš was still reigning when the epitaph was engraved. I shall now attempt a reconstruction of the relative chronology involved in the matter. The account of ᵓImruᵓl-qays' intervention in the Najrân area is mentioned third in a list of six events, and could therefore have occurred about the middle of the king's reign; about A.D. 315. The best time for that intervention seems to be the very end of Šamir Yuharᶜiš's sole reign: the difficult situation in the northern part of his kingdom most probably got worse as a consequence of his campaign in Ḥaḍramawt, which kept his soldiers busy in the southeast; and the northern tribes took full advantage of it. This hypothesis would also explain, as pointed out above, why Šamir Yuharᶜiš did not himself re-establish peace in the northern border of his kingdom.

According to this hypothesis, the relative chronology of the beginning of Yasrum Yuhanᶜim's dynasty could be presented as follows:

Yasrum Yuhanᶜim and Šamir Yuharᶜiš:	about A.D. 285-300;
Malik[um. . . .] and Šamir Yuharᶜiš:	about A.D. 300-305;
Šamir Yuharᶜiš's sole reign:	about A.D. 305-315

Note that the length of 15 years given tentatively to the first coregency has nothing to do with Ja 647/26-27 where mention is made of "seven years", since the relative chronology of the text remains

il alla". The reading of *ḥrb* is apparently disproved by the fact that the tracing of two letters read as *rb* does not at all resemble that of *rb* which appears twice in the text (in *ᶜrb*, line 1; and *hrb*, line 2).

[59] Cf. *BePSC*, *l.c.*

unknown; besides, the contrast between lines 18-23 and 23-30, with regard to the royal names, suggests that the expression *ʾmrʾhmw/ʾmlkn* (line 25) includes more names than the two mentioned in lines 20-21. Note also that my date for Šamir Yuharʿiš's sole reign is precisely between that of *BePSC* and that of *RycIMAM*, and practically coincides with that which *WiHöBGS* had in mind when dating CIH 353 about A.D. 300.

With regard to the *mbḥḍ* era, the year 389 occurs toward the end of the first half of the period between 385 and 396; and if the same relation is conveyed to ± A.D. 285-300, the period of the first coregency of the dynasty, 389 of *mbḥḍ* era coincides with ± A.D. 292. The *mbḥḍ* era would then have started about 97 B.C., and it cannot thus be identified with the Sab era. Concerning the *nbṭ* system, since it remains unknown whether 316 of this era is anterior to 385 of the *mbḥḍ* era or posterior to 396 of the same system or somewhere between these two dates, we have to reckon with all these three possibilities and accept a middle solution which suggests that there could have been a displacing of ± 73 years between the two eras; therefore, the *nbṭ* era could have begun ± 24 B.C.

The preceding research combined with that devoted to Ṯaʾrân Yarkub's dynasty, the results of which are anticipated here in order to make the study of the different eras complete, may be summarized as follows.

The eras attested up to the present time come from Sabaʾ and Qatabân.

In Sabaʾ, the texts mentioning the *mbḥḍ* era were discovered to the west and south of Ṣanʿâʾ, precisely the country where a provincial kingdom was established from which the names of three provincial kings are already known. The origin of that era may thus be connected with the foundation of that provincial kingdom, about 97 B.C.

Also in Sabaʾ, the Sab era is in use and started roughly about 110 B.C. This era is only found in monotheistic texts; however, the circumstances which led monotheistic circles to start a new era, remain unknown.

In Qatabân, the formula used for the era is basically unique, but is adapted differently according as it includes or omits the mention of the month, and its use is peculiar to the tribes Qašamum and Muḏḥayum because of the addition of *bn/nbṭ/wḏhrf*.[60]

[60] The *nbṭ* era "pourrait être d'origine nabatéenne", according to *RycPCH*, p. 24, note 80. This hypothesis is not given any support. The proper name *nbṭm* means "Nabataeans" in Philby-Tritton 103/3 and 135 a/2 (cf. *JaDN*, pp. 165-71), it is true. However, *nbṭ* and *nbṭm* are well known as South-Arabian personal names, and the root *nbṭ* enters frequently in the composition of personal names; in all these cases, it would be very temerarious to see any connection with the name of the Nabataeans, apart from the identity of the root *nbṭ*. Cf. similar case in *BiO*, 12 (1960), pp. 263-64.

D – COREGENCY OF MALIK[UM....] WITH HIS BROTHER ŠAMIR YUHARʿIŠ: CIH 353

The rejection of this Malik[um....] by most of the studies of Yasrum Yuhanʿim's dynasty, makes it necessary to discuss at length the only text connected with him, namely CIH 353 and more precisely lines 6-7.

1 – *Study of* CIH 353

As is well known, the right part, which may be evaluated as a third of the original, is missing. Besides some few remarks on lines 1, 13, and 17, the study is devoted to lines 6-7 which may doubtless be called *crux interpretum*.

Line 1: the workman most probably engraved first *mḥmmdm*[61]; he then wrote *d* over the third *m*, and, without complete success, he tried to erase the letter *d* of the first engraving. He subsequently engraved another *m* on top of the right part of the last *m* of the first engraving because the letter was too far away from the letter *d* of the correction; thus *mḥmdm*.[62]

Lines 6-7:

– –*/wmwrhmw/bhw/mlk*

(7) [... .../*wšm*]*r/yhrʿš/mlky/sbʾ/wḏrydn/*– –

Note first of all that *r* of *šmr* is visible on the stone.[63] The crucial problem raised by the preceding pericope is the interpretation of *mlk*[....[64]

In their publication of the text, J. and H. Derenbourg consider *mlk* to be a noun and suggest the

[61] Cf. *CIH*, I, pp. 430 and 433.

[62] Cf. also *CIH*, III, p. 351 B and commentary on Ja 738/1-2.

[63] Since J. and H. Derenbourg (cf. *JA*, 1883, II, pp. 269, 271, and 273), followed by *CIH*, *RyCS* (p. 240, note 3) and *RycIMAM* (p. 167), this letter has always been considered as missing. The word divider after [*šm*]*r* is rightly indicated by *CIH* (pp. 430 and 431, and also by J. and H. Derenbourg, *l.c.*, pp. 269 and 270) but pointed out as missing by the same *CIH*, p. 433.

[64] In connection with the expression "mot *mlk* 'roi' avec un suffixe" (p. 114), *RycIMAM* refers to it as being restored in CIH 353/6-7 (note 18). Some suffix has been suggested as restoration of *mlk*[..., but the word *mlk* is clear on the stone.

restoration of "*mlk*[*yhmw* 'leurs deux rois'" (p. 273); however, they translate it "le roi" (p. 270).[65]

The opposite opinion with *mlk* as the beginning of a personal name, probably *mlkkrb*, was suggested very soon after, by J. H. Mordtmann.[66]

A few years later, Derenbourg's basic interpretation was given renewed life by *GlAAA*'s statement: "Die Inschrift gehört der Zeit der beiden Könige Jâsir Juhanʾim und Šamar Juharʾiš" (p. 128). It would of course be very interesting to know how *GlAAA* restores *mlk*[.... Unfortunately, he does not touch that question, not even when, a few lines further down (pp. 128-29), he gives a free translation of lines 6-7 by putting Yasrum Yuhanʿim's name between brackets and by introducing "[Jâsir Juhanʾim und] Šamar Juharʾiš" by "der Könige" (p. 128). Indeed, this last expression would correspond to *ʾmlkn*, which is contrary to the text.

Without referring to *GlAAA*'s opinion, *CIH* accepts J. M. Mordtmann's suggestion of *mlk*[*krb*],[67] but he also considers the reading of *mlkškr* as possible. *CIH* is cautiously followed by *MoMiSI*, p. 181: "mit Wahrscheinlichkeit...Malikī[karib]".

GlAAA's opinion on the restoration of Yasrum Yuhanʿim's name is accepted by several authors, such as *HaAF* (p. 370, note a), *RhKTB* (II, p. 74), *HoGSA* (p. 96) and *WiHöBGS* (p. 20); however, no detail is given as to the restoration of *mlk*[...

In the meantime, J. M. Mordtmann's suggestion of *mlk*[*krb*] is developed by *RyNP* (I, p. 233 B), where the royal name is no longer accepted as half restored, but is presented as fully attested on the stone. A few years later, *RyCS* (p. 240) accepts *GlAAA*'s interpretation and devotes note 3 to the justification of his new opinion.

After quoting *CIH*'s restoration of lines 6-7, and after mentioning *MoMiSI*'s (not *RyNP*'s) acceptance of that restoration, he states that "cette lecture...nous paraît inadmissible", saying:

> Ce Malikkarib, dont aucune autre inscription ne fait mention, serait cité ici avant Šâmir; il serait donc, ou le père, ou le frère aîné de ce dernier. La première hypothèse est exclue, le père de Šâmir étant Yasirum. La seconde hypothèse ne paraît pas plus admissible, puisqu'elle impliquerait l'association de Malikkarib et non de Šâmir au règne de Yasirum du vivant de celui-ci [Here, reference to *GlAAA*, p. 128] Aussi lisons-nous *mlk*[*n ysrm yhnʿm wbnhw šmr*] *yhrʿš*, etc.; nous restituons le premier mot *mlk*[*n*] d'après RÉS 3910, 1.

The preceding argumentation needs some clarification.

1 – The study of the true impact of RÉS 3910/1 is given here first, for it immediately clarifies in what line the solution to the problem of the interpretation of *mlk* is to be found. RÉS 3910/1 indicates that no tautology was felt in the expression (not yet attested before Yasrum Yuhanʿim's period), *MLKN*/*royal name*/*MLK*/*sbʾ*/*wd̲rydn*.[68] Besides, the noun *mlkn* introduces a single royal name, and not two as would be the case in CIH 353; and the two cases presently known where a noun in singular introduces two royal names as an apposition, have *mrʾ* (Ja 648/7 and 665/7), and not *mlk*. Furthermore, the authorship of RÉS 3910 and CIH 353 should also be pointed out.[69] The author of the first is the king himself, whose personal name is introduced by *mlkn* (line 1). However, the authors of the second text are not the two kings, but certain high ranking individuals, most probably chiefs (see below). The preceding remark is very important because the expression composed of *mlkn* followed by a royal name, without being introduced itself by *mrʾ*+personal suffix (e.g., *mlkn*/*ʾlšrḥ* in Ja 576/4 and *mlkn*/*ʾlšrḥ*/*yḥḍb*, e.g., in Ja 576/4 and 577/1) is found only in inscriptions written by the king or kings, which is precisely the case of RÉS 3910. But, even in those inscriptions, if the above-mentioned expression is found in phrases having as subjects persons different from the king or kings, this expression is introduced by *mrʾ*+personal suffix[70] (e.g., *mrʾhmw*/*mlkn*/

[65] This translation is accepted by J. Halévy, in *JA*, 1884, p. 105.

[66] Cf. *CIH*, *l.c.*, pp. 431-32.

[67] Cf. *l.c.*, and p. 433.

[68] The same understanding was kept by the following generations, as attested by some texts related to ʾAbraha; e.g., – –/*MLKN*/*ʾbrh*/*MLK*/*sbʾ*/– – in Ja 546/2.

[69] *RyCS* does not discuss the question of the authorship of CIH 353; nor does he allude to the author of RÉS 3910, who is mentioned in the text.

[70] RÉS 3992, which belongs to the period of *mlk*/*sbʾ*, is written by an individual who refers to *mlkn*/*ʾnmrm* (line 10), and this expression is not introduced by *mrʾ*+personal pronoun. Some could think of an evolution in the use of *mlkn*+royal name by comparing RÉS 3992/10 with the above-mentioned expression used during the period of *mlk*/*sbʾ*/*wd̲rydn*. However, the study of the text shows that the author could not easily have used *mrʾ* before *mlkn*/*ʾnmrm*. He could not have written *mrʾhmw*, because *hmw* would only have referred to the subjects of the phrase, namely the author's legal opponents (cf. *BeNL*, VI, p. 316), and not to the author himself. Yet, *ʾnmrm* was the king of them all. The only pronoun allowable here, that of the first person plural, is never attested in the inscriptions.

ʾlšrḥ/yḥḏb in Ja 577/13). Both the interpretation of *mlk* as a noun and its restoration as *mlk[n]* or any other form, are therefore most unlikely. The last and only alternative then is to consider *mlk[*... as the beginning of a royal name (cf. below).

An objection must be brought up here. Since the authors of CIH 353 are not the two kings, the names of the two coregents should have been introduced by the noun *mrʾ* + personal pronoun, *mrʾhmw* rather than *mrʾyhmw* because of the best parallel Ja 665/6-8, where both the verb *wqh* and the noun *mrʾ* are in the singular, since the verb *mwr* in CIH 353/6 is also singular. The necessity just mentioned above comes from the rule[71] according to which the personal name of the ruler (either king or chief) of the author,[72] if mentioned in the story related in the text,[73] is normally introduced by *mrʾ* + personal pronoun. The reason why *mrʾhmw* was not engraved could eventually be found in the grammatical wording of the phrase: the introduction of *mrʾhmw* would have created the immediate succession of three personal pronouns, including two *hmw* referring to two different groups of persons: *mwrHMW/bHW/mrʾHMW*, unless one prefers the hypothesis of haplography between the two following terms: *MwRHMW* and *MRʾHMW*.

A final remark concerns the mention of *mlky/sbʾ/wḏrydn* (line 7) after *šm]r/yhrʿš*. The insertion of that expression is well justified by the fact that lines 6-7 contain not only the first, but the only mention of the two royal names.

2 – The incidental note about Malikkarib's being otherwise unknown, although stating a true epigraphic fact, is to be handled with great caution, since the names of all South-Arabian rulers are not yet known to us. This remark, already emphasized a few years ago,[74] is all the more fitting in the present case since Ja 664 and 665 mention the names of two previously unknown kings who belong to the same historical period. Khalidy-Condé 8/4-5 too, published recently by *RyISA* (XVII, p. 172) mentions another *mlk/sbʾ/wḏrydn* who was entirely unknown before, namely Ḏamarʿalay Watar Yu[....

3 – The father of Šamir Yuharʿiš is doubtless Yasrum Yuhanʿim. However, a coregency of Malik[... and Šamir Yuharʿiš cannot necessarily imply that Malik[... was either the father or the eldest brother of Šamir Yuharʿiš, nor that Malik[... should have been mentioned with Yasrum Yuhanʿim in a previous coregency. As a matter of fact, nothing prevents us from thinking that Malik[... was a younger brother of Šamir Yuharʿiš, and that he succeeded in getting the first place instead of his brother, in other words, that he supplanted Šamir Yuharʿiš. A similar case occurs in Šaraḥbiʾil Yakûf's dynasty, in which Maʿadkarib Yanʿam supplanted his elder brother Laḥayʿat Yanûf.[75]

RyCS' arguments are unable to justify his interpretation of *mlk[*... as a noun, and his restoration of *mlk[n]* "the king", is disproved by the inscriptions. Finally, the length of his restoration at the beginning of line 7 is unacceptable (see below).

Finally, *RycIMAM* (p. 167) repeats *RyCS*' argumentation, but then goes on to make several statements which should be studied.

1 – With reference to G. Ryckmans' note 3, the author states (note 27) that he "restitue *mlk[n ysrm yhnʿm wbnhw šmr] yhrʿš*, suivant RES 4196, 3-4 et 4938, 12-14". As *RyCS* explicitly states, he refers only to RÉS 3910/1 in connection with *bnhw*; further, he does not even allude to RÉS 4938 in his study of Yasrum Yuhanʿim's dynasty (pp. 240-41). What *RycIMAM* had in mind is the insertion of *bnhw* in G. Ryckmans reading; but, *bnhw* does not exist in RÉS 4938/12-14.

2 – The author then affirms that "cette restitution [which includes *bnhw*] dépasserait les dimensions de la lacune, qu'on peut fixer à 14 lettres" (*l.c.*), "c'est pourquoi il faut lire *mlk[n ysrm yhnʿm wšmr] yhrʿš*" (p. 167). The preceding evaluation of the average number of missing letters is seemingly

[71] There is obviously no question here of the *mukarrib*'s period.

[72] It is of course necessary that the author of the text be the subject of the ruler at the time of the narrated event. That the author is not a subject of the king is the whole question. Therefore, *mrʾ* + personal pronoun is not to be found before the name of the following persons: a foreign king as such ("as such" excludes of course the case of an alliance which would give a foreign king authority over some Sabaeans), a king mentioned in the genealogy, a king ruling outside the territory where the author of the text lives. An example of the third case is to be found in Ja 631/26-27, where the name of the provincial king of Ẓafâr is not introduced by *mrʾhmw*, simply because this king had no authority over the authors of the text nor over the Sab forces. Such was not the case of Hamdân, which depended on the authority of the kings who ruled in Mârib.

[73] If mentioned in the title of the author, the ruler's name is introduced by either a word such as *mqtwy* (for king or chief) or an expression such as *bn/ʾs* (only attested for a king). The preceding case is not an exception, but rather another application to a context entirely different from a grammatical point of view, of the same basic rule; the name of the ruler is to be preceded by some element which indicates either the dependence of the inferior or the authority (cf. *mrʾ*) of the ruler.

[74] Cf. *BASOR*, No. 137, February, 1955, p. 38.

[75] Cf. *JaDSY*, p. 19.

based on *CIH*'s restorations which fill up completely lines 3, 4, 5, 6, 18, and 19 with 15, 13, 14, 13, 13, and 14 letters respectively. *CIH* explains "numerum litterarum a nobis conjectum" (p. 431 A) by pointing out that "tertiam partem cujusque versus, olim circiter octo et quadraginta litteras tenentis, a dextera abruptam esse" (p. 429). A look at the photograph shows that the arrangement of the signs is far from similar in every line; it seems thus necessary to check *CIH*'s affirmations. Now follow four columns of figures concerning lines 2-9[76]; in each column, the two figures give the number of letters and word dividers respectively.

Column A describes the left half of the original stone. The location of right edge is obtained by projecting from the central point between the two feet located on the upper side of the stone.[77]
Column B, being the double of A, represents thus the whole original stone.
Column C deals with the whole remaining stone known at the present time.
Column D, being the result of the subtraction of C from B, indicates the right missing part, thus the number of letters and word dividers to be restored.

	A	B	C	D
Line 2	21½+4	43+8	27+5	16+3
3	19+5	38+10	25+6	13+4
4	20+5	40+10	27+7	13+3
5	19+5	38+10	25½+6	12 or 13+4
6	22+5	44+10	30+6	14+4
7	20+5	40+10	28+7	12+3
8	20+4	40+8	27½+6	12 or 13+2
9	22+5	44+10	30+7	14+3

Remark on A, line 7: by mentioning the number of letters as 20, I accept *CIH*'s reading of two letters after *ḥ*. The restoration of the second one, although possible on the basis of lines 9, 10, and 11, cannot be checked.

Some conclusions may be drawn from the preceding figures:

1 – The irregular disposition of the letters attested in the left remaining part (cf. column C) must be taken into consideration in any attempt at restoration in the right missing part, and cannot be based on any average number of letters which is 12-13 in lines 3-9, and even if line 2 is counted too, it would be 13 and not 14 letters, as stated by *RycIMAM*.

2 – The average number of letters suggested by *CIH*, "about 48", is obviously much too high, and "octo et" can all the more safely be omitted from *CIH*'s statement that the number of letters in lines 3-6, which *CIH* restores completely, is 40, 39, 39, and 42 respectively. Furthermore, the restoration of 15 letters, as presented by *CIH*, in line 3, includes too many letters. I thus suggest restoring *ṯf* (CIH 529/4) instead of *mśnd*.[78]

3 – The number of letters to be restored at the beginning of line 7 does not allow restoration of *mlk*[*n*, *nhn*, *hmw* or anything of that kind], which is already disproved by epigraphic material, followed by *ysrm*/*yhnᶜm* and even less with *bnhw* following the latter's name.

3 – *RycIMAM*'s most important statement reads as follows (p. 167): "Dans CIH 353, la forme *mlkn* au singulier peut provenir du souci des dédicants de spécifier qu'à l'époque des évènements relatés dans l'inscription, seul le premier des deux souverains portait le titre royal".

First of all, *mlkn* in the singular is not attested at all. But, were *mlkn* in the singular even certain, the suggested interpretation of the fact would have to be discarded for two reasons. On the one hand, the royal title in the dual *mlkY*/*sbʾ*/– is formally attested and given to the two kings precisely during the narration of the events, and not at all, for instance, in the final invocation. On the other hand, a noun in the singular introducing two names in apposition must be interpreted somewhat like the following fact which is very common in the inscriptions, namely a verb in the singular with a subject in plural. The act or activity depicted by

[76] Consideration is given to the place of damaged or destroyed letters; line 1 was left aside because of the correction at the end of the line; finally, the width and the height of a monogram, if any, being unknown, were not taken into consideration.

[77] The left edge of the stone is not quite perpendicular. The difference between the present left edge and the fictitious perpendicular line projected from the top of the left edge to the bottom is very slight and can safely be ignored with regard of the first 10 lines. However, that difference should be reckoned with in the restoration of the last lines; in other words, there the right half of the original stone contains one or two letters more than the other half.

[78] These two nouns have in common the fact that they were used to indicate a bronze plaque. The noun *mśnd* also refers to an inscription engraved either on the rock (RÉS 2633) or on a slab (e.g., Khalidy-Condé 3/1).

the verb is attributed to the first of the subjects as its main, principal author. Similarly, in the so-called case of *mlkn* "the king", the act referred to in the phrase is to be understood as ordered or carried out by a king, the first of the two coregents. Ja 665/6-12 illustrates the idea: the order was given (lines 6-9) by the first of the two coregents; that explains the singular of both the verb *wqh* and the noun *mrʾ*. The origin of that order is clearly expressed in the third part (lines 11-12) where the name of the second coregent is not mentioned any more. Yet, the two coregents take part in the expedition according to the second part of the text (lines 9-11). The coregents almost certainly divided among themselves the duties of royal power; and the first coregent, because he was the first, doubtless reserved for himself the most important tasks, such as foreign relations and wars. How such a division of the work, which was unavoidable, did work out and to what extent this division of the royal power was complete, remain to be known. It seems normal however that, in case of any really important decision, the coregent who was not in charge of the field involved was duly consulted; but the final decision would normally remain up to the coregent responsible for that particular field and was attributed to him. In a like manner the very frequently attested fact of a singular verb with a plurality of subjects should be understood: the act described by the verb is set to the account of the first of the subjects as the responsible agent. In texts such as Ja 648, allusion could be found to that division of royal duties among the coregents themselves. In this text, the dedicator begs his moon god ʾIlumquh to grant him "the esteem and grace of their lord Yasrum Yuhanʿim and Šamir Yuharʿiš, kings of Sabaʾ and Raydân". The singular *mrʾ* can easily be explained by the fact that, because of his job or for any other reason, the author of the text was involved in one of the spheres of action reserved to the first coregent. However, since the author does not mention what kind of activity was his, it seems possible to infer that he was one of the ordinary people of Mârib, and that these were the special lot of the first coregent.

On the basis of the argumentation presented above and until information on the right missing part of the original stone is available, I think that *mlk*[... must be considered as the first part of a royal name.

The restoration of *ʾḫyhw* before *šm* is highly improbable since there would be space left for only 4 letters, which should cover both the ending of the first element and the whole second element of the royal name. A first element such as *mlk*, although possible because of *šmr*, does not seem very probable; *mlkm* (compare with *ysrm*) would be better; but then, there would be only three letters left for the second element; such an element is not attested in Yasrum Yuhanʿim's dynasty and is rather rare. The restoration of *ʾḫhw* would leave space for 5 letters; then *mlk*[./....]'s full name would have exactly the same number of letters as that of *ṯʾrn/ʾyfʿ*, another king belonging to the same dynasty. However, if the king's first nominal element is composed of two normal roots, such as *mlkkrb*, even the restoration of *ʾḫhw* becomes impossible. According to this hypothesis, the name of *mlk*[*krb/yhʾmn*] could tentatively be suggested, because the name of *ḏrʾʾmr/ʾymn* is already common to the dynasties of Yasrum Yuhanʿim and Damarʿalay Yuhabirr II.

Personally, I prefer the second hypothesis, namely *mlk*[*m/..../wʾḫhw/šm*]*r*, because it fits the blank perfectly well and also because it is rather difficult to suggest, without any clue in the texts, that a stranger would step in Yasrum Yuhanʿim's dynasty and supplant his three sons.

Lines 13 and 17: *CIH* (pp. 430 and 431) has [...]*w/ʿšry* and *wl/sʿdhmw* respectively; these readings are correct instead of *w/*]*ʿšry* and *wlsʿdhmw* on p. 433.

2 – *The coregency itself*

The description of the coregency of Malik[um ....] with Šamir Yuharʿiš involves at least the mention, if not the solution, of several questions which have to be dealt with here.

Since the texts related to Yasrum Yuhanʿim's dynasty do not present any clue, any information either on the personal relations between the members of that dynasty or on historical as well as social facts which could be connected with those relations, it is not possible at the present time to suggest any plausible explanation of the seeming setback of Šamir Yuharʿiš in his rise to sole kingship. Was the present coregency the result of an exclusively family dispute or of anything else? Whatever the reason may be, it doubtless was an unprecedented, strong pressure that imposed such a condition upon such an ambitious man as Šamir Yuharʿiš.

The only suitable period to place this coregency

is before Šamir Yuhar^c^iš's sole reign which sees the lengthening of the royal title due to his successful campaign against Ḥaḍramawt. Without any evidence, this coregency cannot reasonably be inserted during the first part of Šamir Yuhar^c^iš's sole reign: and the second part of this reign is in any event excluded because of the royal title.

The length of this coregency must have been rather short if we take into consideration primarily both the age of Yasrum Yuhan^c^im and the length of his coregency with Šamir Yuhar^c^iš and a duration of about 10 years for the latter's sole reign. Another reason suggests the same conclusion: such an ambitious man as Šamir Yuhar^c^iš certainly did not at all like to see one of his brothers get the best of him for the first place in a coregency, and he doubtless could hardly wait to get the whole power exclusively for himself in order to realize the plans of conquest which probably had already been in his head for some time. As a consequence of all these considerations, I suggested only about 5 years for that coregency.

CIH 353 is a dedicatory inscription to the god Ta^ɔ^lab by some Maš^c^arânites, the subjects of Yasrum and Barig of Bata^c^ and Hamdân,[79] in connection with military activities against Ḥimyarite rebels. The first events occurred in a place which remains unknown,[80] and they were not favorable to the rebels, for they strengthened themselves in the city of Ḍahr, northwest of Ṣan^c^â^ɔ^,[81] where they were trapped and killed by the two Sab kings.

The contents of lines 9-14 are difficult to understand because the right part is missing. However, the Maš^c^arânites, because they are the authors of the text, as well as their Bata^c^ite-Hamdânid chiefs, did not take part in the Ḥimyarite rebellion,[82] for, in all the texts known up to the present time, the authors are always on the side of the Sab rulers. Furthermore, the elements mentioned in line 10 among whom are listed the Raydânids, most probably entered into the struggle after the Ḥimyarite defeat at Ḍahr, which seemingly was not as complete as stated in the text and was not the last event in the military activities.

E – SOLE REIGN OF ŠAMIR YUHAR^c^IŠ: CIH 407, 430, 431 + 438, 628, 948; Ja 649, 650, 651, 652, 653, 654, 655, 656, 657, 658, 660, 661, 662; RÉS 3910, 4230, and 4790

After Malik[um....] had disappeared from the political scene because of a reason unknown to us but which most probably was not entirely foreign to Šamir Yuhar^c^iš's ambition, the latter took over as sole ruler in Mârib. His reign is divided, as is well known, into two parts on the basis of the lengthening of his royal title as a consequence of his military conquests.

A phenomenon which may indicate some change in Šamir Yuhar^c^iš's attitude toward his father is that, among the 12 texts related to the first part of his reign, 8 mention his father and 4 do not. This situation is reversed in the second part of his sole reign: among the 9 texts related to that period, only 3 mention the filiation but 5 do not; CIH 948 is too fragmentary to be mentioned here. Does this new situation have something to do with the pride, the glory of having conquered Ḥaḍramawt and Yamnat?

1 – *First part of the reign*

The first part of Šamir Yuhar^c^iš's sole reign is characterized by the title identical to that used in the two preceding coregencies: *mlk/sb^ɔ^/wḏrydn*, and is illustrated by 12 inscriptions, 3 of which contain historical information.

a – NON-HISTORICAL TEXTS: CIH 628; Ja 651, 652, 653, 654, 655; RÉS 3910, 4230, and 4790

1° – *Remarks on some texts:* CIH 628; RÉS 3910 and 4790

CIH 628 – Line 4 in J. Arnaud's copy must be transferred to the end of line 3; this point, though already mentioned by F. Fresnel[83] and E. Glaser,[84] is disregarded by *CIH* (III, p. 65). Later, the text

[79] The clan of Maš^c^arân was ruled by two Bata^c^ite-Hamdânids; this fact does not imply that the clan itself was a part of Hamdân, as asserted by *RycIMAM*, p. 189: "les dédicants hamdanides".

[80] *RycIMAM* (*l.c.*) speaks of "une attaque...contre [Mâ]rib" on the basis of a *restoration* accepted by *CIH* (p. 433).

[81] Cf. *CIH*, p. 431 B, and *WiHöBGS*, p. 20. Wâdi Ḍahr flows about 18 km. west of Ṣan^c^â^ɔ^ and about 13 km. north of that city into Wâdî Ḫârid, which, at that place, is also called Seil Šu^c^ûb (cf. *WeCGC*, p. 140 and maps).

[82] Cf. also *RhKTB*, II, p. 74 (followed by *CIH*, III, p. 351 B). Contrary, e.g., to *RycIMAM*: "les dédicants hamdanides de l'inscription, qui avaient sans doute partie liée avec les rebelles ḥimyarites" (p. 189) et "une révolte, soutenue par des Hamdanides" (p. 190).

[83] Cf. *JA*, 1845, II, p. 188.

[84] Cf. *OLZ*, 9 (1906), p. 139.

was republished by *HöIGT* (p. 9) where the same fact is stated again. Yet, *RycIMAM*[85] still alludes to line 4 when referring to the royal title which includes the filiation.

RÉS 3910 – STONE: yellowish sandstone; thickness maxima: 9.8 cm.; left edge largely re-cut. *Front:* 88.8 cm. (top) and 88.9 (bottom) × 20.8 (left) and 22.8 (right) upper right corner splintered off.

TEXT – The whole inscription was first published after decipherment made from the original by *RyISA*.[86] Four years later, and on the basis of a copy made by E. Glaser and a verification on the original by "G. Furlani-Florenz", the text was republished by *RhEA* (pp. 172-81), whose reading and translation are reproduced in RÉS 3910. In this reproduction, read [*kn*/] instead of (*kn*/) (line 1), *fʾw* instead of *fʿw* (line 3), and in the copy of *RhEA*'s translation, insert a comma before "seinen" (line 2) and "und" after "Magd" (line 3), read "kauft" instead of "Kauft" (line 3), "Stück" instead of "Stuck" (line 3), "Termiete" instead of "Termiese" (line 5), and "Ma[gd" instead of "Magd" (line 7).

The study of the original made possible for me the completion of the decipherment of the text.

Line 1, beginning: read ⌜*š*⌝⌞*k*⌟*wqh* instead of *wqh*[87] or "......*wqh*"[88]; the upper half and most of the left edge of the lower half of *k* are still on the stone; the letter *š* is more damaged, but the bottom is still on the stone. *šk*=*škn*.[89] The expression *škwqh* was preceded by a symbol.

Lines 1-2: the upper half of *ḏrydn*/*bn*/*ysrm*/*yh*, which occupies the end of line 1, has disappeared with the re-cutting of the stone; besides, *nʿm*/*ml*, which is restored at the end of the line 1 by both *RyISA* (p. 166) and *RhEA* (p. 172), must be restored at the beginning of line 2, for the width of those six signs perfectly equals that of *mnn*/*ws* (line 3), the left vertical stroke of *k* of *mlk* being just above the upper left extremity of *t* of *stqdn*.

Line 3: *RyISA* (*l.c.*) and *RhEA* (p. 173, note 1) remark that *l* is missing in *ʾblm* (cf. *RyISA*, p. 165) or *ʾb*[*l*]*m* (cf. *RhEA*, p. 173). In fact, the workman first engraved *ʾlm*. He did not, however, notice his mistake until it was too late to add any other letter. He then corrected *ʾlm* to *ʾbl*.

Line 5: instead of *wbʾn* (cf. *RyISA*, *l.c.*, and *RhEA*, *l.c.*), read *wbkn*. The workman first engraved *wbʾn*, but the correction of *ʾ* to *k* is beyond any doubt on the stone.

Line 7: instead of *ẓmrm* (cf. *RyISA*, p. 165)[90] or *ṭmrm* (cf. *RhEA*, p. 173), read *ḍmrm*; cf. Arabic *dayn ḍimâr* "debt of which the payment is not hoped for" and *ḍimâr* "debt of which the payment is deferred."[91]

Lines 8-9: very fragmentary; engraved on top of the left hand side; continuation and end of the text:

line 8: ⌜*t*/⌝.[the letter *t* belongs to *ʾm* at the end of line 7;

line 9: ?*k*/*ʾ*⌝[

RÉS 4790.

Line 1: the beginning could be read (*ʾl*)*šmr*(/*y*)*gr* on the basis of the information given by *HöIGT* (p. 27, note 1): "drei kurze senkrechte Striche, deren erste zwei unten durch einen waagrechten Strich verbunden sind; zwischen *r*.*g* an Stelle des Punktes ebenfalls zwei kurze senkrechte Striche".

Line 10: *šmr*'s name could have been preceded by *bmrʾhmw* (cf. *HöIGT*, *l.c.*, note 4: according to E. Glaser: "Z. 10: '7 Buchstaben'", and *hmw* in lines 2, 9, and 12). However, E. Glaser's evaluation of missing letters cannot be pressed, for he notes "6 [Buchstaben] fehlend" (cf. *l.c.*) in line 11; yet, the restoration requires 7 letters and 3 word dividers: /*mlk*/*sbʾ*/*w*.

Line 12: in *m*....*hmw*/*wbʿ*..., the letters *m* and *ʿ* could be the initials of *m*(*n*)*ḏḥ*(*y* or *t*) and *ʿṯtr* respectively.

CIH 407 and RÉS 4230: some remarks are to be found in *JaASAB*, pp. 151-67 and 185-89 respectively.

2° – *Contents of the non-historical texts*

The non-historical texts present an overwhelming majority of dedicatory inscriptions, 7 texts out of 9.

The dedicatory inscriptions from Maḥram Bilqîs refer of course to the moon god ʾIlumquh, and mention the offering of one or two (Ja 653) statues.

In Ja 651, a high official made his offering when

[85] Cf. pp. 165, note 13, and 193, note 1.

[86] Cf. I, p. 165; cf. also *CoRoC*, No. 43, pp. 52-53.

[87] Cf. *RyISA*, *l.c.*

[88] Cf. *RhEA*, p. 172, who notes that *kn* "so" is a restoration suggested by E. Glaser (cf. *l.c.*, note 3) and translates the beginning as follows: "[So] hat befohlen".

[89] Cf. *HöASG*, p. 173.

[90] This *ẓmrm* is probably a slip for *ṭmrm*, since in his commentary on p. 168, the same author writes that the noun starts with "un *ṭ* ou un *ḍ*". However, the noun remains without commentary (*l.c.*) or translation (p. 169).

[91] Cf. *LaAEL*, p. 1803 C.

requested by the king to ally the two tribes Bata^c and Hamdân, to assist in the building of walls and towers at Mârib and also some other construction against the waves. In Ja 652, two high officials make an offering for the safety of their king and also for their own safety; among the requests presented to the deity, there is one begging the god to take vengeance against anyone who would incite them against their king. The tribe Saba' Kahilân makes an offering after receiving rain and irrigation for Mârib, its valleys and pasturages (Ja 653). The birth of a male child is the reason for some ᶜAqbumites' offering (Ja 654). The god granted the son of the chieftain of the tribe Mu'd̲in to live; so the father offers to his god (Ja 655). RÉS 4790 also comes from Mârib; but it is so fragmentary that the contents are almost gone. RÉS 4230, which does not come from Mârib, mentions the offering to the stellar god ᶜAt̲tar Šarqân, of the incense burner bearing the text, and also of fruits, when the dedicator was appointed representative of the king in the tribe T̲a'rân of Salyat and ᶜAmrân. The first city is located by *MüHG* (100/4 and 12) in the country of as-Saḥûl bin Sawâdat, and the second is about 42 km. northwest of Ṣanᶜâ' and 18 km. northeast of Kawkabân.[92]

The fragmentary text CIH 628 refers to the construction of some unknown buildings. E. Glaser identified the author of the text with a chief mentioned in CIH 353/11,[93] and rightly considers CIH 628 as posterior to the other, for its author is now mentioned with his son.[94]

Finally, RÉS 3910 contains an ordinance from the king himself in favor of "the tribe Saba', masters of the city [of] Mârib and its wâdî-side valleys"[95] and deals with purchases and payments[96] for slaves, camels, bulls and cattle.

b – MILITARY CAMPAIGN IN THE NORTH AND NORTHWEST: CIH 407, Ja 649 and 650

The two dedicatory inscriptions from Maḥram Bilqîs, CIH 407 which has already been discussed in *JaASAB*, and Ja 649, appear to deal with only one full-scale military campaign headed by the king Šamir Yuharᶜiš against the northwestern part of present Yemen. The third dedicatory text, discovered in the same place, makes only a vague allusion to the same campaign in Saharatân. Note that the principal author of each text is a high military officer of the king.

The relation of the military events leads to the following picture. After fighting five battles, the group A (Ja 649) joined group B (CIH 407) for the important battle in the valley of Ḍamad, but the pursuit was handled by group B alone. In the meantime, group A fought three other engagements. Three phases may thus be considered such as described in the two texts.

1° – *First Phase:* Ja 649/6-14

Ja 649/6-14 mention the names of five locations (lines 9-10) where fighting took place: Saharatân Liyyat, H̲aywân, Ḍadah̲ân, Tanaᶜum, and Nabᶜat.

Saharatân Liyyat is doubtless the part of Saharatân immediately west of Daw'at, which is watered by Wâdî Liyyat,[97] a northern tributary of Wâdî Taᶜaššar 55 km. southeast of Jîzân; the latter flows into the Red Sea 50 km. southeast of Jîzân.

The next place is H̲aywân[98] which is located on the Wâdî H̲abaš[99] and in the most important region of Ḥâšid,[100] and is the second relay station from Ṣaᶜdat to Ṣanᶜâ'[101]; the city is located about 190 km. southeast of Jîzân and some 90 km. southeast of Ṣaᶜdat,[102] thus about 105[103] north of Ṣanᶜâ'.

The third place is Ḍadah̲ân. Wâdî Ḍadah̲[104] runs almost parallel to Wâdî 'Amlaḥ[105] and south of it,[106] and about 35 km. south-southeast of 'Uh̲dûd; *FoSA* (p. 121, note 2) alludes to E. Glaser mentioning a city bearing the same name north of the wâdî.[107]

[92] Cf. *JaASAB*, pp. 186-87.
[93] Cf. *Skizze der Geschichte Arabiens*, Munich, 1889, p. 85.
[94] Cf. *GlAAA*, p. 130.
[95] *RycIMAM* (p. 177) speaks of "un édit...destiné à la tribu de Ṣirwâḥ, qui possède le territoire de la ville de Mârib". I do not know the source of the mention of Ṣirwâḥ, since the text of line 2 (partly translated above) was already known since *GlAAA*, p. 50.
[96] *RycIMAM* (*l.c.*) speaks of "vente" instead of payments; that is a remnant from *RyISA*, I, pp. 165 and 168. Note that *RyISA*, p. 166 (commentary) has the right idea of payment, which becomes sale elsewhere.
[97] Cf. *MüHG*, e.g., 73/16, and *PhAHL*, e.g., pp. 611-14 and 641-43: W. Liya. There is some confusion in *FoSA*'s transcription of this proper name: "Lija" (p. 86), "Līja" (p. 51), and "Lijja" (p. 306 A).
[98] Cf. *MüHG*, 66/18, *FoSA*, p. 61, note 1, and C. Rommel, *Abulfedea Arabiae descriptio*, p. 52.
[99] Cf. *MüHG*, 82/18.
[100] Cf. *l.c.*, 112/15.
[101] Cf. *SpAGA*, p. 179.
[102] Cf. *WiHöBGS*, map facing p. 64, and *WiGGF*, map on pp. 72-73.
[103] *RyNP* (I, p. 340 A): about 120 km.
[104] Cf. *MüHG*, e.g., 83/26.
[105] Cf., e.g., *l.c.*, 83/26 and 168/3.
[106] Not north, as indicated in *MüRhGRM*, maps Nos. 2 and 3.
[107] Cf. also *WiGGF*, maps between pp. 72-73: "Ḍadakh".

For the fifth place *nbᶜt*, I venture to refer to Nabᶜa described by *PhAHL* (p. 329)[108] as a "ridge...furthest out towards the plain", which belongs to "a mass of hills" between Wâdî Ḥabawnat and its northern tributary Wâdî Ṯâr. The location of this ridge raises the question as to whether *nbᶜt*, which may very well survive in Nabᶜa, is not the ancient name of present Majonna,[109] 25 km. northwest of Biʾr Salwâ and 63 km. northwest of ʾUẖdûd. If my identification of *nbᶜt* is correct, the fourth place, *tnᶜm*[110] would be located somewhere between Ḍadaẖân and Nabᶜat.

The preceding information on the five names where battles occurred clearly shows the circling movement of group A, who afterward proceeded to the valley of Wâdî Ḍamad where, jointly with group B, they fought the great battle.

2° – *Second Phase:* CIH 407/19-21 = Ja 649/14-17, and CIH 407/21-24

The second phase of the campaign is composed of two acts. In the first, the two groups A and B – the latter had apparently come through the hinterland and not along the coast – battle the enemy forces which most probably consisted mainly of Saharatites who were reinforced by fighting groups from their allied tribes Dawʾat, Ṣuḥârum, and Ḥârat. The location of these tribes may be stated as follows[111]: Dawʾat on the east of northern Saharatân, Ṣuḥârum on the south of Ṣaᶜdat, and Ḥârat between Ṣaᶜdat and Najrân.

The main shock took place in the valley of Ḍamad, city on the wâdî of the same name, 35 km. north of Jîzân. The enemy forces were defeated and they retreated northward. After this victory, group A apparently parted from group B, and the latter started to pursue the enemy; that is the second act of the second phase.

Even if the enemy forces did not engage their whole manpower in the Ḍamad battle, they nevertheless were unable to defend themselves in Jebel ᶜAkwat pass. Defeated again, they sought refuge in fleeing toward and into the Red Sea by following the natural exit, namely Wâdî Naẖlân and Wâdî Ṣabyâ. The Sab group, however, went after the fugitive soldiers who subsequently were killed during the last battle which took place on the Red Sea.

3° – *Third Phase:* Ja 649/17-41

The third phase of the campaign is composed of two expeditions, which are preceded by a kind of private raid.

This show of personal strength on the part of the dedicator (lines 17-24) was apparently due to his own initiative, for he does not mention the name of his king in connection with it, as he does in the two subsequent expeditions. However, the price of success was high: the author received five wounds and his horse was also wounded; he even feared that his foot might be lost and his horse crippled.

Some weeks later, after convalescing, he took part in the two campaigns, the first in the wâdî-side valley Ḥarîb near Qaryatnahân (lines 24-26), and the second in the hill-slope of Ragazgazân, against ᶜAkkum and Saharatum (lines 26-41). The location of these three geographic names remains unknown to me. However, the hill-slope Ragazgazân is most probably to be sought in the vicinity of Wâdî Mawr, because the Sab group B fought and completely destroyed all the tribes and groups of ᶜAkkum and Saharatum; and ᶜAkkum lived between Wâdî Mawr in the north and Wâdî Sahâm in the south. Therefore, Qaryatnahân would be somewhere between Ḍamad and Wâdî Mawr.

Such an expedition suggests a few considerations. It is to be noted that Najrân is not mentioned in Ja 649; yet, that a Sab army group had to operate in the immediate vicinity of that city, in the south and very probably in the north as well, makes it clear that the situation was very far from being peaceful. Besides, the battles in the far northwest, and the two others related in Ja 649/24-41, which almost certainly occurred in the northern part of Tihâmat, did not lead to the annexation of those parts to the Sab kingdom, since the name of Tihâmat is not incorporated into the Sab royal title until much later.

[108] Other possibilities do not fit into the campaign: "Nubâᶜ" (cf. *MüHG*, 109/14), a village south of Jebel Kanin (cf. *FoSA*, p. 183, note 5), or "Wâdî Nebaᶜ", east-southeast of Wâdî Taᶜaššar (cf. *MüRhGRM*, map No. 2), or Wâdî Nebᶜa which originates in Bilâd Ḥadâ, southeast of Ṣanᶜâʾ (cf. *l.c.*, p. 186 A and map No. 1).

[109] *Sic* on the map; but *PhAHL* mentions it as Majanna and writes (p. 333): "It is certainly difficult to get away from the conclusion that it dates far back beyond modern times; the inscriptions and the pictures were sufficient evidence of that".

[110] Tanâᶜim, city located 14 km. east-northeast of Ṣanᶜâʾ (e.g., *MüHG*, 90/19) and at-Tanᶜîm, between Mekka and Madînat (cf. *FoSA*, p. 54, note 8) do not fit here.

[111] Cf. *JaASAB*, p. 161, commentary on CIH 407/19.

2 – *Second part of the reign:*
CIH 430, 431 + 438, 948;
Ja 656, 657, 658, 660, 661, and 662

The American excavations in Mârib were favored by the discovery of the first three complete texts belonging to the second part of Šamir Yuharᶜiš's reign, Ja 656, 657, and 658, and all the more because Ja 656 and 658 are, as shown below, of primary historical importance. Ja 660, 661, and 662 are almost complete and the very small fragment missing in each of them does not, fortunately, affect the interpretation of the story related by them.

a – REMARKS ON CIH 430 AND 431

CIH 430 – The restoration of *rḏw* at the end of the line 7[112] is no more probable than that of *ḥẓy* (cf. Ja 578/35-36). In any event, the text is *ḥmdm/bḏt/ ẖmr/ᶜ[bdhw/krbᶜṯt/rḏw* or *ḥẓy*] and not *ḥmdm bḏt ẖmrhmw rḏw*, as stated by *RycIMAM* (p. 213); further, there is no need to restore a word divider at the end of the line. – The filiation restored by *CIH* (*l.c.*) in lines 9-10, [*bn/ysrm/yhnᶜm/mlk/sbᵓ*(10) *wḏrydn*], is contradicted by the remains on the stone. The beginning of line 9, ⌊*ḥḏrmt/*⌋[*w*]⌊*ymnt*⌋ equals *mrᵓhmw/šmr/y* (line 8) in length, and the word divider after *ymnt* is a little to the right of the axis of the upper right vertical stroke of *h* of *yhnᶜm*. In line with the space between ᶜ and *š* of *yhrᶜš*, one can see the top part of the letter *m*. There is, of course, no possibility of restoring *bn/ysr* between ⌊*ymnt/*⌋ and ⌊*m*⌋ in line 9.

CIH 431 – Yellowish limestone with a brownish stain in the centre of the front; thickness maxima: 4.7 cm. *Front:* 29.5 cm. × maximum 14.2. – Line 7: in *ḏrydn*, the *r* is engraved on top of a *w*. – Line 11: below *r* of line 10, the top part of *m* is preceded by either *w* or ᶜ which is completely gone and which is preceded by a letter having a circle on top: either, *y*, *ṯ*, *ṣ* or *ẓ*.

b – NON-HISTORICAL TEXTS:
CIH 430; Ja 657 and 661

Although the three dedicatory texts dealt with here are obviously posterior to the campaign against Ḥaḍramawt, there is no way of determining their relative chronology either to each other or to the time of engraving Ja 656, which relates the war against Ḥaḍramawt, for the simple reason that the length of time between the facts alluded to in the texts and their engraving on the stones cannot be judged.

Two dedicatory texts come from Maḥram Bilqîs and evidently refer to ᵓIlumquh. In Ja 657, a Marḥabite offers a statue which he had promised because of favors received from the moon god. In Ja 661, three Ṯâtites, who had a special relationship with Šamir Yuharᶜiš, because the latter's name precedes the verb [*hq*]*nyw* (line 3), make an offering because the god saved them from a disease. The last text, the upper right part of which alone remains, CIH 430, refers to the stellar god ᶜAṯtar.

c – HISTORICAL TEXTS:
CIH 431 + 438, 948; Ja 656, 658, 660, and 662

From a purely historical point of view, Ja 656 and 658 are exceedingly important, for they are the very first texts dealing explicitly with the war against Ḥaḍramawt[113] and against the northern part of the Sab kingdom respectively. The events related in Ja 656, and also those in Ja 662, because the latter is the last phase of the Ḥaḍr conquest as far as Šabwat is concerned, are obviously anterior to those mentioned in Ja 658. Those in CIH 948 may have been instigated by Ḥaḍramawt in order to take full advantage of the situation related in Ja 658.

1° – *Campaign* against Ḥaḍramawt: CIH 431 + 438; Ja 656 and 662

The dedicatory text, Ja 656, is the first inscription which states exactly who was the head of the Ḥaḍr kingdom during the war; as far as the last point is concerned, it is of course necessary to keep in mind that Ja 656 is Sab. Besides, this text gives but a very partial account of the war, which was doubtless not limited to only one battle.

During Šamir Yuharᶜiš's reign, Ḥaḍramawt was headed by two kings, Šaraḥᵓil and Rabbšamsum; and it is they who are said to have initiated the war. The reasons which led the two kingdoms into war, are, as usual, not mentioned. The authors of the text, who lived in Ruḥâbatân, a city about 20 km. north-northeast of Ṣanᶜâᵓ, as has been pointed out above, mention only one battle which took place in *srrn* which may be identified[114] with Wâdî Sarr,

[112] Cf. *CIH*, II, p. 19.
[113] Cf. *WiHöBGS*, pp. 116-18.
[114] Identifications with any wâdî either north or south of Ṣanᶜâᵓ (e.g., as-Sirr or as-Sarîr) are excluded, and also with Wâdî Sirr which flows into the Red Sea 21 km. southeast of the mouth of Wâdî ᶜItwad.

a northwestern tributary of Wâdî Ḥaḍramawt which flows into it about 7 km. west of Šibâm.[115] This identification necessarily implies that the battle referred to was one of the last battles, if not the last one, fought between the Sab and Ḥaḍr forces in Wâdî Ḥaḍramawt. It also implies the capture of the two most important northern cities of Ḥaḍramawt, namely Šabwat and Šibâm.

This identification is confirmed by Ja 662 in which two chiefs of the tribe Sabaᵓ offer a statue for a favor obtained in Šabwat where the first chief had been ordered to go in order to protect the city with the tribe Sabaᵓ; that simply means the occupation of the Ḥaḍr capital by the tribe Sabaᵓ, immediately before the Sab army itself withdrew westward.

CIH 431+438,[116] two fragments of the end of a dedicatory text to the stellar god ᶜAṯtar, mentions the same tribe Sabaᵓ and the city of Šibâm. Because of the missing part, it remains impossible to determine even conjecturally either the actual event involved (possibly the same as for Šabwat), or the exact period of the event (before or after the campaign against the northwest).

The two Ḥaḍr kings Šaraḥᵓil and Rabbšamsum are not attested in Ḥaḍr sources; and this Šaraḥᵓil was only known through CIH 948/2. This Rabbšamsum is not to be identified with Rabbšams whose name is never attested with a final *m*, son of Yadaᶜᵓil Bayyin (RÉS 4914/1-2) and father of Yadaᶜᵓil Bayyin (e.g., RÉS 4871/4-5).

2° – *The administration* of Southern Sabaᵓ according to Ja 660

The dedicatory text deals with a case of desertion. A high official of the king offers a statue in connection with a mission imposed upon him by his king which he had successfully conducted. He was ordered indeed to pursue two deputies who deserted Mârib, along with two soldiers and the chief of the tribe Sabaᵓ all of whom he brought back to Salḥân.

The main importance of the text lies in the title of the author, which can at least partially be restored on the basis of Ja 665, and which suggests that the high official of the king was a *kbr* "leader" of the eight districts listed in lines 2-4.

The list containing the eight tribal groups is characterized by two facts. First, the groups are mentioned according to their size and respective importance: the names of the three more important groups, *ḥḍrmwt*, *kdt*, and *mḏḥgm*, precede those of the smaller ones, *bhlm*, *ḥdᵓn*, *rḍwm*, *ᵓẓlm*, and *ᵓmrm*, which had remained unknown up to the present time in South-Arabian material. Secondly, the last three groups, which are not identified, should be located south of Mârib, as are the first five, for it is quite natural to admit that the territories put under the command of Wahabᵓawwâm formed one block and were not scattered over the Sab kingdom, in which case his task would have been impossible to fulfil.

Both Ḥaḍramawt and Maḏḥigum point to the southeast of Mârib. Kindat has already before been tentatively located southwest of the preceding group; such an opinion certainly fits the present list. The group *bhlm* can be identified with Bahîl which *MüHG* (100/6) mentions in the country of as-Saḥûl bin Sawâdat, thus somewhere about 25 km. north of Taᶜizz. The group *ḥdᵓn* can be identified with al-Ḥadâ which is mentioned by *MüRhGRM* (map No. 3), northeast of Ḏamâr. All the territories put under Wahabᵓawwam's command were thus most probably the whole south of Mârib; therefore, the deserters' plan to escape involved a southern itinerary, and not a northern one.

3° – *Campaign* against the Northwest: Ja 658

After returning from his conquest of Wâdî Ḥaḍramawt, the king Šamir Yuharᶜiš had to set out on another campaign, this time against the north and the northwest.

The first move (lines 6-14) was to do battle in the land of the tribe Ḫawlân ᵓIldôdân and to isolate these groups by establishing a garrison in the city *ṣᶜdtm*, the well known Ṣaᶜdat.[117] These groups thus lived north-northwest of that city. After that, the Sabaeans went to fight the groups of Śanḥân in the valley of Dafaᵓ (lines 14-18). *MüRhGRM* (map No. 2) mentions Sanḥân southeast of Janb, and *PhAHL* (e.g., pp. 364-67) still mentions Sanhan in the far northeast of Ṣabyâ. Wâdî Dafâᶜ – note the addition of ᶜ in the present Arabic transcription – fits the geographic location, as a southeastern tributary (about 110 km. northeast of Jîzân) of Wâdî Bayš and was thus the

[115] Cf. H. von Wissmann, map of Aden Protectorate, 1958, sheet 2; and *WiHöBGS*, p. 133 and map (end of the book): W. Sirr.

[116] *RycIMAM* usually refers to "CIH 438+431" (e.g., p. 165, note 13) instead of "CIH 431+438", which is mentioned once, on p. 283, note 10.

[117] Cf. *SpAGA*, Nos. 241 and 290; C. Rommel, *l.c.*, pp. 53-54, *FoSA*, pp. 9 and 61, note 3, and *WiHöBGS*, e.g., p. 12.

country of Šanḥân.[118] After that campaign which provided the Sabaeans with rich booty, they went again against Saharatân and Ḥâratân (lines 19-21), the country of the tribe Ḥârat, which was previously mentioned in the expedition headed by Šamir Yuharᶜiš before his conquest of Ḥaḍramawt. Finally, they went back northward to fight the groups of Našadʾil in the valley ᶜItwad,[119] which flows into the Red Sea 85 km. northwest of Jîzân; and 8 km. northeast of its mouth lay the small city ᶜItwad.[120]

4° – *Revolt* of Ḥaḍramawt: CIH 948

CIH 948, which was written by the king Šamir Yuharᶜiš himself,[121] indicates, although it is very fragmentary, that the king actually had a notable military success in Ḥaḍramawt against the Ḥaḍr king Šaraḥʾil.[122] The text does not seem to allude to the conquest of Wâdî Ḥaḍramawt but rather to a revolt of Ḥaḍramawt which took advantage of the removal of the Sab army – such is a fact since the tribe Sabaʾ was sent to watch Šabwat – and especially of the military campaign conducted by the Sab army in the far northwest.

The preceding hypothesis seems to be suggested by the fact that the second Ḥaḍr coregent is not mentioned in the text; some time must thus have elapsed since Ja 656. On the other hand, the absence of his name does not allude at all to the fact that the second Ḥaḍr coregent would have been killed during the campaign itself, for it would be rather difficult to understand that the mention of such an important event would have been omitted by the author of Ja 656.

A minor difficulty is pointed out by *CIH*,[123] namely the writing of *yrᶜš* instead of *yhrᶜš*.[124] It is to be remembered that the name of the king *nšʾkrb/yʾmn/yhrḥb* suffered even more different spellings than *šmr/yhrᶜš*, namely *yhʾmn* and *yrḥb*. The spelling of *yrᶜš* as well as that of *yrḥb* could very well be mistakes in engraving made possibly by the close proximity of the two *r*'s. However, as already pointed out concerning *nšʾkrb/yʾmn/yhrḥb*, the omission of *h* in *yh...* could easily have something to do with the pronunciation of *h*.

3 – SOME REFLECTIONS

On the basis of the reconstruction of historical events presented above, the lengthening of the Sab royal title was a consequence of the campaign alluded to in Ja 656, and not at all a consequence of CIH 948.[125]

The extent of the conquest of Ḥaḍramawt is not to be overestimated. The material available indicates that it was limited to the northwestern course of Wâdî Ḥaḍramawt. Even Ja 665, which is related to the following coregency, mentions only the northwest and the west of Šabwat; and the simple fact that a Sab expedition had to be sent there proves the precariousness of Šamir Yuharᶜiš's conquest, which was already indicated by Šaraḥʾil's revolt. It seems thus certain that Šamir Yuharᶜiš's fame has been overstated and that he cannot be compared with the great ʾIlšaraḥ Yaḥḍub. Of course, his glory comes from the fact that he is the one who first bore the lengthened royal title. But, that of course depends on the accurate meaning of *ymnt* mentioned in the new title. If this new title is understood in the light of the campaign recorded in Ja 656 – and this understanding seems confirmed by the meaning of the noun *ymnt* "south" compared with *šʾmt* "north" – *ymnt* seems to indicate the countries south of Sabaʾ,[126] a part of which had been previously occupied by Ḥaḍramawt (cf. RÉS 3958). As a result of his conquest of Wâdî Ḥaḍramawt, Ḥaḍramawt obviously lost control on the south of Sabaʾ. It is then easy to understand that, in order to record his occupation of both the south of Sabaʾ and Wâdî Ḥaḍramawt, Šamir Yuharᶜiš mentions them both in his royal title by adding to it *wḥḍrm(w)t/wymnt*.

[118] This *šnḥn* has nothing to do with Jebel Sinḥ about 150 km. northeast of ʾUhdûd (cf. J. Sanh in P. Lippens, *Expédition en Arabie centrale*, Paris, 1956, p. 154 and map).

[119] Cf. *MüHG*, e.g., 54/13; *SpAGA*, pp. 45, 54, 197; *FoSA*, especially p. 51, note 9.

[120] Cf. *MüRhGRM*, map No. 2.

[121] *RycIMAM* (p. 212) says that Šamir Yuharᶜiš perhaps wrote the text. In the expression *ḫmr/ᶜbdhw/–*, the personal name introduced by *ᶜbdhw* normally refers to the author himself.

[122] Cf. also *RycIMAM*, pp. 211 and 213, and *RÉS*, VII, p. 441. However, A. F. L. Beeston (in *BiO*, 9 [1952], p. 216 A) writes: "The remainder of the text of these lines... is nothing more than a plausible conjectured restoration." The South-Arabian material suggests that even a fragment like CIH 948 must be interpreted as referring to a victory of Šamir Yuharᶜiš against Šaraḥʾil, and more precisely the capture of Ḥaḍr towns and fortresses.

[123] Cf. III, p. 276 A.

[124] A. F. L. Beeston remarks that "some explanation of this discrepancy ought to be offered" (cf. *l.c.*). This author does not however make any suggestion.

[125] E.g., *RycIMAM*, pp. 211 and 213, and *RÉS*, *VII*, p. 441.

[126] Cf. *JaASAB*, pp. 153-54.

F – COREGENCY OF YASRUM YUHANᶜIM AND HIS SON ḌARAᵓᵓAMAR ᵓAYMAN: Ja 665

1 – *Preliminary questions*

Two important questions need to be dealt with here, namely the identity of the two coregents and their place in Yasrum Yuhanᶜim's dynasty.

It seems obvious that the identity of the present Yasrum Yuhanᶜim with Šamir Yuharᶜiš's father needs no proof; the names are identical, and there is nothing unreasonable in the father's return to power after the disappearance of his son from the political scene. Besides, the title of these two coregents refers to a period following Šamir Yuharᶜiš in Wâdî Ḥaḍramawt, and indeed they give even more reality to Šaraḥᵓil's revolt recorded in CIH 948, by pointing out that the first conquest of Wâdî Ḥaḍramawt was by no means definitive. It is also quite normal to visualize that Yasrum Yuhanᶜim's coregency with his own son precedes that with a stranger to his own family, Ṯaᵓrân ᵓAyfaᶜ, for it was natural for him to have tried to save his own dynasty by having recourse to Ṯaᵓrân only after exhausting all the possible candidates who belonged to his family. Finally, note that this son of Yasrum Yuhanᶜim bears the same name as that of another king belonging to a later period, namely one son of Malikkarib Yuhaᵓmin (cf. below).

2 – *Campaign in northwestern Ḥaḍramawt*

Ja 665 is the only text belonging to the coregency now under study and is quite valuable from three different aspects. Besides mentioning the second coregency of Yasrum Yuhanᶜim with another of his sons, the text gives, in the title of the author, important information on some parts of South Arabia which were integrated into the Sab kingdom, and also a detailed account on another expedition against northwestern Ḥaḍramawt.

a – THE TITLE OF THE AUTHOR

The author of the text presents himself as *kbr ᵓᶜrb/mlk/sbᵓ/wkdt/wmḏḥgm/wḫrmm/wbhlm/wzydᵓl/wkl/ᵓᶜrb/sbᵓ/wḥmyrm/wḥḍrmwt/wymnt* (lines 1-4).

The first question to be raised is to know whether *ᵓᶜrb* and *kl/ᵓᶜrb* are followed by only one definitive (*mlk/sbᵓ* and *sbᵓ*, respectively) or by six and four respectively. The second hypothesis would impose the accepting of an almost impossible administrative situation because of the splitting of each of the following eight tribal groups (*kdt, mḏḥgm, ḫrmm, bhlm, zydᵓl, ḥmyrm, ḥḍrmwt,* and *ymnt*) into two parts, namely the *ᵓᶜrb* and the non-*ᵓᶜrb*. Besides, there cannot be any doubt that the groups *ḫrmm, bhlm* and *zydᵓl*, never before mentioned in the texts, were rather small, and therefore, their division into two groups would doubtless have made impossible their administration, because the two groups were undoubtedly connected with each other. The first hypothesis which avoids the splitting of every tribal group into two parts, indicates that the whole south, southwest, and southeast of Sabaᵓ were put under the command of only one man, exactly like in Ja 660/2-4. Besides, Ḥimyar was no longer ruled by a *mlk/sbᵓ/wḏrydn*, but was apparently reduced to the common condition of all its neighbors. Furthermore, the opposition between *ᵓᶜrb/mlk/sbᵓ* and *ᵓᶜrb/sbᵓ* plainly indicates the difference between the property of the crown (or at least, privileges) and that of the Sab state itself. Another characteristic of the title, exactly as in Ja 660/2-4, is the repartition of the tribal groups into two groups according to their size and importance; the first series obviously contains the less important ones, (*kdt, mḏḥgm, ḫrmm, bhlm, zydᵓl*, and also the crown property), and the second the most important ones (*sbᵓ, ḥmyrm, ḥḍrmwt*, and *ymnt*).

Further, the names mentioned in the title shed further interesting light on the location of *ymnt*. On the one hand, it seems quite normal to admit that the territories put under the command of the author formed one block, as already mentioned. On the other hand, *mḏḥgm* and *ḥmyrm* point to the south of Sabaᵓ; it is thus there that we have to look for a possible location of the other tribal groups; and the suggested location of *kdt* certainly fits the present text. Besides, if *ḫrmm* is identified with *ḏû-ḫrym*,[127] this group could be located somewhere about 60-70 km. southwest of Beiḥân al-Qaṣâb. The location of *zydᵓl*, whose name does not sound more incongruous than that of *nšdᵓl* mentioned in Ja 658/21-22, remains unknown, although it apparently is somewhere in the southwest, possibly between Bahilum and Muhaᵓnifum.

Taking the preceding identifications into consideration, it seems obvious that the countries

[127] Cf. *MüHG*, 94/19.

covered by all the names besides *sbʾ*, *ḥḍrmwt*, and *ymnt* are located south, southeast, and southwest of the Sab kingdom. However, between the crescent formed by those groups and the original Sab kingdom, which is referred to as *sbʾ*, lies a large strip of territory whose center is Qatabân...and the only noun not accounted for above is precisely *ymnt*. Such a conclusion confirms my interpretation suggested above, that the location of *ymnt* is to be found south of Mârib. Besides, if the identification of *bhlm* with Bahîl is correct, Bahilum being mentioned by *MüHG* (100/6) among the Ḥimyarite tribes, the title would also indicate that the term *ḥmyrm* is taken as a general term which does not prevent the author from mentioning at least one of its groups. Therefore, it is also possible that *ymnt* is not restricted to the above-mentioned strip, but could also contain the whole south.

b – CAMPAIGN NORTHEAST AND EAST OF ŠABWAT

The leader of southern Sabaʾ was ordered by the first (cf. singular *wqh* and *mrʾ* in lines 6-7 and 11-12) of the two coregents Yasrum Yuhanᶜim to take part in a campaign against Ḥaḍramawt, which was conducted by the two coregents (cf., e.g., dual *mrʾy* in line 9).

They first fought against ᶜAbran (line 14) which is mentioned by *MüHG*,[128] as a place with wells; the city of Ḥuṣn al-ᶜAbr[129] is located about 2.5 km. west of Wâdî al-ᶜAbr which flows northwest-southeast, about 85 km. northwest of Šabwat and about 145 km. west-northwest of Šibâm.

Later, there was a clash with a Ḥaḍr vanguard along with a detachment of regular troops in ʾArak (line 22), of unknown location. This battle was followed by a successful raid against Duhr and Raẖîyat (line 25). The two Wâdîs Duhr and Raẖîyat, mentioned together by *MüHG*,[130] are parallel to each other, the bed of the first being about 20 km. west of that of the other; they flow southwest-northeast and their mouths in Wâdî Ḥaḍramawt are about 70 and 85 km. from Ḥuṣn al-ᶜAbr, respectively.

After this raid, the Sab army returned to the spring H̱urṣum (line 28), where a major battle took place, in which the Sab army successfully defeated the Ḥaḍr expeditionary force. H̱urṣ[131] is located about 12 km. southeast of al-ᶜAbr, about 2 km. west of Wâdî al-ᶜAbr, and about 78 km. northeast of Šabwat. Note that the verb *qflw* (line 27) "they came back" in order to reach H̱urṣum. How true, for the Sabaeans had gone far in the southeast and they had to go back northwards.

Finally, they were called by their king Yasrum Yuhanᶜim to fight against the troops of Baśaʾum (line 41) (of unknown location) and also to lend assistance to the tribe Gadanum (line 41).

G – COREGENCY OF YASRUM YUHANᶜIM WITH ṮAʾRÂN ʾAYFAᶜ: Ja 664

The introduction to the preceding coregency already solved most of the preliminary questions connected with the present coregency. One point needs to be emphasized. The contrast between the presence, on the one hand, in Ja 665, of *wbnyhw* mentioned twice (lines 7 and 10), that is to say each time that the names of the two coregents were listed, and, on the other hand, the omission of the same expression in Ja 664/13, suggests that Ṯaʾrân ʾAyfaᶜ was not Yasrum Yuhanᶜim's son, but was, as has been noted, an outsider to that family who was selected by Yasrum Yuhanᶜim after he had exhausted all possibilities within his own family.

Ja 664 unfortunately gives no historical information besides the fact that the authors of the text, certain Saḥarites, had property in Mârib, Našqum, and Našân. They offered a statue which had been promised in order to get a son and the god had answered their prayers.

[128] Cf. 84/22 and 85/18: al-ᶜAbr. Cf. also *WiHöBGS*, map at the end, *FoSA*, p. 126, note 4, cf. also *MüHG*, 188/21-23: a road from al-ᶜAbr leads to Jauf and Ṣaᶜdat, and another one to Najrân through the desert.

[129] Cf. also *SpAGA*, pp. 189 and 306.

[130] Cf. 84/24-25 and 88/17. Cf. also *FoSA*, p. 126, note 5; 127, note 1; *SpAGA*, pp. 189 and 306, and *WiHöBGS*, map at the end.

[131] "Qarn al Khurs" is a "little...hillock" (cf. *PhSD*, p. 68, and map).

Chapter X

THE REIGN OF KARIBᵓIL (WATAR) YUHANᶜIM
KING OF SABAᵓ, RAYDÂN, ḤAḌRAMAWT, AND YAMNAT

Ja 666 and 667

The main question in the study of the reign of this king, who previously was totally unknown, is (at least presently) that of his identity, for the only two texts related to this part of Sab history do not provide us with any specific historical information.

A – THE IDENTITY OF THE KING

Our position in regard to Karibᵓil (Watar) Yuhanᶜim is as it is regarding Rabbšamsum Nimrân, that is to say we know only their names and titles while the names of their fathers remain unknown and their reign isolated without any successor from their respective families.

The identification of this king with his homonym who is Ḏamarᶜalay Bayyin's son and the father of Ḏamarᶜalay Ḏariḥ is obviously to be discarded. The royal title is different in each case; it is also to be noted that the name of the king's father is not mentioned in either one of the two texts Ja 666 and 667, contrasting with CIH 373.

It should be noted that the king's name is *krbᵓl/yhnᶜm* in Ja 666/13, but *krbᵓl/wtr/yhnᶜm* in Ja 667/15-16. However, it should also be noted that the engraving of Ja 666 shows three mistakes: a word divider is missing after *mrᵓhmw* (line 4), the noun *mrᵓ* is in the plural form *ᵓmrᵓ* (line 12), and *w* replaces ᶜ in *bᶜl* (line 17). The absence of *wtr* in Ja 666 cannot therefore be pressed too far.

B – THE REIGN ITSELF

Ja 666 and 667 do not present very much historical information. The only significant point is an allusion to a revolt in the city of Ẓafâr in Ja 667 in which an individual offers a statue because his god protected him from being involved in that rebellion. In Ja 666, three rulers of the tribe ᶜUḍdân, which seems to be Ḥimyarite,[1] offer a horse and his saddle because their god granted to them protection against the land-surveyor.

[1] Cf. *LöHSM*, p. 49, No. 1198.

Chapter XI

THE DYNASTY OF ṮA᾿RÂN YARKUB, KING OF SABA᾿, RAYDÂN, ḤAḌRAMAWT, AND YAMNAT

Gl 389 (cf. RÉS 3383), 823; Ja 668, 669, 670, 671, 856; RÉS 3444, 3960, and 4716

The information presented by Ja 668-671 when confronted with several texts previously published, brings up several questions of major importance. Some of them, although not directly connected with the kings actually attested in Ja 668-671, need none the less be treated for the purpose of the complete description of the import of the present material.

The starting point is that the three kings of Ja 668-671 are homonymous with some of those attested in the dynasties of Yasrum Yuhaṣdiq and (Ḥaśan) Malikkarib Yuha᾿min. The study of so complex a question must begin with an analysis of the genealogy of the two above-mentioned dynasties in comparison with Ja 668-671, and thereafter to proceed with the presentation of the dynasties involved in the texts.

A – THE GENEALOGICAL TREES OF YASRUM YUHAṢDIQ AND OF (ḤAŚAN) MALIKKARIB YUHA᾿MIN, AND THEIR COMPARISON WITH Ja 668-671

The following schemes summarize the results of the previous studies of the dynasties of Yasrum Yuhaṣdiq and of (Ḥaśan) Malikkarib Yuha᾿min, and their comparison with the information offered by Ja 668-671.

GROUP A: *mlk/sb᾿/wḏrydn*

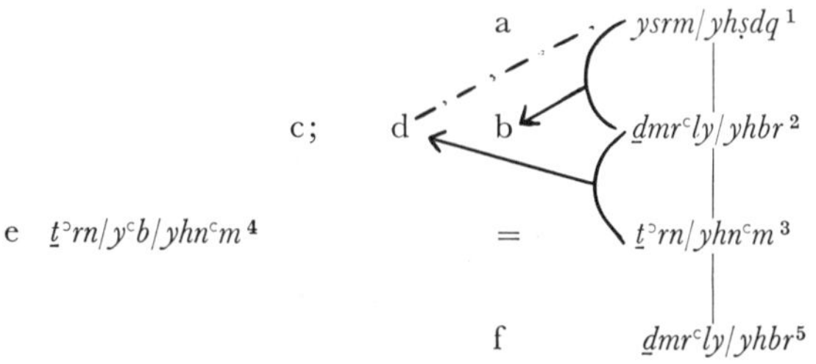

GROUP B: *mlk/– – –/wymnt* and *mlk/– – – – – –/wthmt*

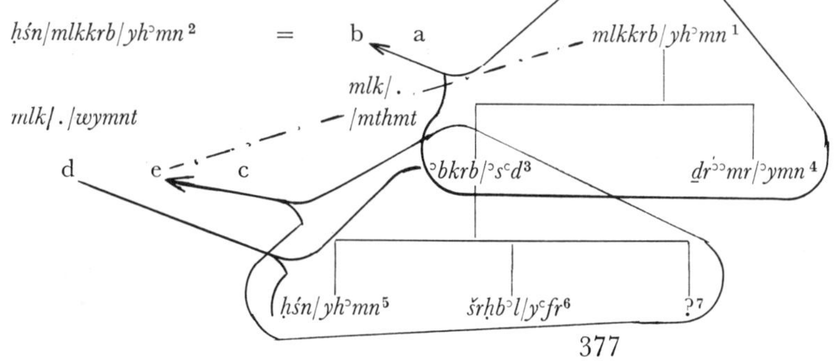

GROUP C: *mlk/– – –/wymnt*

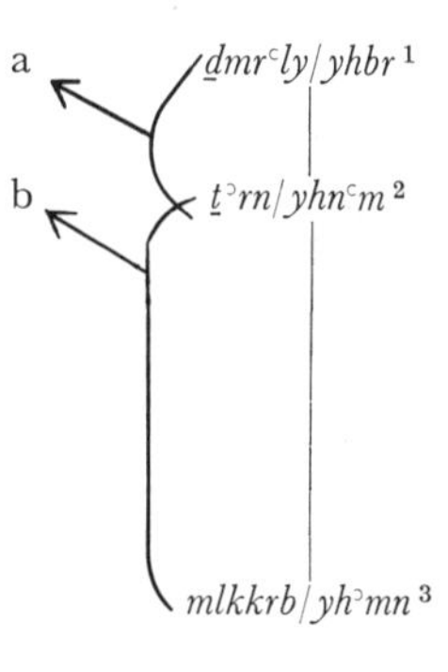

1 – *Explanatory Note*

Schemes A and B present the commonly accepted opinion on the genealogy of the dynasties of Yasrum Yuhaṣdiq and of (Ḥaśan) Malikkarib Yuhaʾmin respectively; scheme C indicates where Ja 668-671 could fit into them. Braces and closed curved lines indicate a coregency (either of two or more coregents), and they are distorted in such a way that their ending arrow points to the line of the first coregent.

The family relationship between the rulers, each one being numbered to facilitate the reference to them in the following study, is indicated, as usual, by the vertical line. The identification of two persons as being one and the same is indicated by the sign of equation. The lower-case letters, always written on the same line as that of the related royal name, represent references to the texts in the list which follows:

A a: CIH 41
b: CIH 365
c: CIH 457; RÉS 4708
d: RÉS 4775
e: CIH 569; RÉS 4716, 4909
f: RÉS 3960

B a: RÉS 3444; ? Gl 823: *mlk/./wymnt*
b: Gl 389 (cf. RÉS 3383): *mlk/./wymnt*
c: Philby 229
d: Wâdî Maʾsil 1: *mlk/./wthmt*
e: Fakhry 60: *mlk/./wthmt*

C a: Ja 668
b: Ja 669, 670, 671

If not associated with an arrow, the lower-case letter indicates that the corresponding text refers either to the sole reign of the king or to his isolated name. When a text also mentions the name of the first coregent's father, who is not coregent himself, a broken line joins the small lower-case letter to the name of the mentioned father. When the father's name is followed by his royal title, the latter is indicated at the center of this broken line.

2 – *Schemes A and B*

Scheme A is stated by *RÉS*, VII, p. 331, and *RycIMAM*, e.g., pp. 315 and 338. However, the first author does not refer to CIH 41 in connection with No. 1, or to RÉS 4716 in connection with No. 4; and he omits the last element of the names of Nos. 3 and 4 (also sometimes *RycIMAM*, e.g., p. 314) (cf. remark on CIH 569). The identity of No. 3 with No. 4 is also accepted by *WiHöBGS*, p. 113, note 3, pp. 114 and 144. Further, *RÉS* (*l.c.*) leaves unanswered the question of the person or persons actually reigning in CIH 365. Furthermore, the kings mentioned in RÉS 3960 are presented by *RycIMAM* as "Ḏamarʿalay Yuhabirr b. Ṯaʾrân Ya[ʿûb...]" (p. 168, note 1), thus A5 son of A3, but also as "Ḏamarʿalay Yuhabirr et... son fils Ṯaʾrân" (p. 179), thus A2 and his son A3.

Scheme B is stated by *RyCS*, pp. 241-43, *RycIMAM*, pp. 318 and 338-39, and also *WiHöBGS*, p. 120. However, *RyET* (p. 34) considers as subjects of Fakhry 60, Nos. 3, 6, 5, and 7, but *RycIMAM* (p. 222, note 9) Nos. 3, 5, 6, and 7.

The second part of scheme C is already alluded to by *SoSoIGCM*, p. 203.

3 – *Remarks on the Three Schemes*

Even before studying the texts themselves, a simple glance at the three schemes A, B, and C, shows that those genealogies have to be revised, because they cannot possibly stand together.

In scheme A, the identification of No. 3 with No. 4 creates a difficulty because the name of the first is always composed of only one element, contrasting with the three elements of the name of the second; and also because the family relationship of the first with No. 2 is always attested, contrasting with that of the second, which still remains unknown.

In scheme B, the identification of No. 1 with No. 2 is proposed only on the basis of the homonymity of their sons, mentioned as No. 3, but the following differences are not taken into account:

a – The *first* element of the name of No. 2 is not attested in any text written during his reign, but is mentioned in one text written under his immediate successors. This difficulty is not pointed out.

b – The difference in title between No. 1 and No. 2 remains without explanation.

c – The title of No. 1 based on *RyET*'s and *RycIMAM*'s restoration of Fakhry 60/1-2 contradicts *RycIMAM*'s statement (p. 215) according to which No. 3, not No. 1, is the one who inaugurated the new title; and the title of No. 1 is also formally disproved by the text itself which is republished as Ja 856 in *JaLSI*.

d – According to *RyCS* (*l.c.*), No. 6, who is attested in 564 of the Sab era (CIH 540), would be reigning *seventy-one* years after his father, No. 3, counting from 493 of the same era (Gl 389); and No. 6's surprising longevity would probably have to be stretched a little more because No. 3 was with his younger brother, coregent of their father, and also because Gl 389 cannot be proved to belong to the very end of the three coregencies involved.

Furthermore, schemes A and B must be somehow correlated because of scheme C; yet, 150 years separate A5 from B1, according to *RycIMAM*, who places the reign of A3=A4 between ±190-205[1] (thus, ±205-220 for the reign of A5, son of A3) and mentions B1 after the first Ethiopian occupation, thus after A.D. 370.

Finally, palaeography shows very clearly that some rearrangement of the texts is needed; e.g., RÉS 3960 belongs to the type of Ja 668, and not to that, e.g., of CIH 365; nor Gl 389 to the type of Wâdî Ma'sil 1 but, e.g., to RÉS 3960.

It is therefore necessary to revise all the texts involved and to reclassify the royal names on the basis of a sound chronology.

4 – *Epigraphical Remarks on the Texts Involved*

CIH 41/4 – The king's name is *ys*[*r*]*m*[/]*yhṣdq*; the *m*, formally attested in E. Glaser's copy (cf. *CIH*, I, p. 68) and accepted by *CIH* (*l.c.*, pp. 68, 69B, and 70), is confirmed by CIH 365/17 (cf. infra) and RÉS 4775/1; this letter is unduly suppressed by *CIH* (III, p. 319 B) on the basis of *CIH*'s reading of CIH 365/17, where the commentary (cf. II, p. 8 B) states that "in tit. 41 v. 4 apographon Langeri *ysm yhṣdq* praebet, sed non dubium quin *r*/ pro *m* legendum sit". The preceding remark, which should have been inserted in the commentary on CIH 41/4, goes against E. Glaser's copy where the empty space between *ys* and *m* is the obvious place to restore the letter *r*; but *m* cannot be suppressed.

CIH 365 – *CIH*'s restorations (II, p. 9) at the end of lines 2, 3, and 12 are confirmed by the reading of the photographs; although damaged, the letters are certain.

In line 14, instead of *bny*/..*lm* (p. 7) or the restoration *bny*/[*'s*]*lm* (pp. 8 B and 9), read *bny*/*bqlm*. The lateral extremities of the top of *b*, more than the lower third of the two vertical strokes of the same letter, as well as an almost complete *q*, are still on the stone.

Line 17: the first element of the king's name is *ysrm*, and not *ysr* as presented by *CIH*, II, pp. 7, 8 B, 9, and 10. In the photograph printed by *CIH*, the vertical stroke of *m* and the word divider after *ysrm* are in the axis of the right vertical stroke of *b* in *bʿṯtr* (line 18), and in that of the extreme right part of ʿ in the same *ʿṯtr*, respectively. Finally, about the upper third of the left part of *m* is still visible on the photograph.

CIH 457=Ist 7631 – STONE: whitish limestone; the four lateral sides are certain; thickness maxima: 9 cm.; front: 69.5 cm. × 40.

Line 5: the last letter of *sb'* is damaged.

Line 8: read *w'*[*f*]⌜*ql*⌝*hmw*.

Line 9: of the first letter after *kl*/, there remains the upper fourth of a letter such as either *b* or *ḥ* (*ẖ*, as suggested by *CIH*, II, pp. 160 A and 161, is obviously excluded). The following letter, although much more damaged, seems to be of the same type as that of the preceding one; I thus read ⌞*bd*⌟[*ʿm*] "territo[ry]".

Line 11: the right half of the first letter of *s*⌉[*b'* is still on the stone.

Lines 17-18: after *šms*/, read *m* (not *b* as suggested by *CIH*, *l.c.*, pp. 159, 160 B, and 161), thus *šms*/*m*(18)[*lkn*/*tn*]*f*, a common expression, instead of *b*[*ʿlt*/..]*f* (cf. *l.c.*, p. 161). The *m* of *m*[*lkn*] is the last letter of line 17, for it is exactly in the vertical axis of the first *m* of *ḥ*⌜*m*⌝(17)[*ym*].

Lines 18-19: instead of *w*(19)..*w* (cf. *l.c.*, p. 159, top) or *wb*......(19)..*w* (p. 159, bottom) or [*wb*/...(19)*hm*]*w* (p. 161, top) or [*et gentis*(?) (19)*ipso*]*rum* (p. 161, bottom), read *wb*[/*m*(19) *ḏḥh*]*mw* "and by [t]heir [divinities of irrigation]; for *mḏḥhmw*/*ysrn*, cf. also the final invocation of Ja 664 (line 20).

CIH 569 – *CIH* (cf. *l.c.*, pp. 353 and 354), followed by *RÉS* (VII, p. 331) and *RycIMAM* (p. 193 and note 5), considers the text as complete on the left, as shown by the drawing reproduced in *CIH*. An expression such as *bmqm*/*mr'hmw*/*ṯ'rn*/*yʿb* cannot be accepted, for the name of the king involved is *ṯ'rn*/*yʿb*/*yhnʿm* which would be amputated here without evidence, and the royal title should be mentioned after the king's name. Therefore, the original inscribed stone is broken off or was re-cut before being re-used; the drawing reproduced by *CIH* affords no support for one opinion over the other. Further, the engraving of one text on two or several stones placed side by side is not attested at such a late historical period; the hypothesis of such a case is thus to be considered unlikely here.

Gl 389 – See the remarks pointed out in *JaLSI*,

[1] This opinion is endorsed by *WiHöBGS*, pp. 113, note 3, pp. 114 and 144.

notes 11 and 20. In note 11, which deals with the reading *ḏrʾʾmr*, "the vertical stippling" is actually composed of two small vertical strokes separated from each other by a dot. The empty spaces between these three elements are precisely the right ends of the two oblique strokes of *ḏ*. This detail was only seen while studying E. Glaser's facsimile considerably enlarged.

RÉS 3960 = Vienna 1148 – BLUE LIMESTONE: broken on the left side and damaged on the other sides; thickness maxima: 11.5 cm. *Front:* 45 cm. × 20.7; covered with red paint; each line of the text is engraved between two finely traced horizontal lines, as in Ja 559. During my work in the *Kunsthistorisches Museum* in Vienna, I was told that this text had been previously designated as spurious by J. Ryckmans. The hypothesis that the top of the stone has been re-cut is not plausible, for the re-cutting very carefully would have avoided damaging line 1; such care would be rather unusual. The actual left side started thus with *ḏmrʿly/yhbr*, who is therefore the first subject of the text.[2]

The remains at the end of line 1 read as follows:

–/*ṯʾrn/y⌉r⌊kb⌋⌈/ml⌉k⌈/⌉[sbʾ/wḏrydn/* . . .

In line 2, the workman first engraved *hʾʾn* instead of *hʾmnn*; these letters have the same depth as that of all the other signs. However, it is not easy to determine why he gave the second ʾ such a distorted form: the two lower strokes are strongly aslant to the left, and the central oblique stroke of the upper half is twice as long as that of the first ʾ. The engraver made no apparent attempt to erase his mistake, but he simply engraved superficially three thin letters: *m* on top of the left half of the first ʾ (this is another mistake); then another *m* a little shorter than the ordinary letters to the left of the first ʾ whose right lower stroke is re-used, and finally *n* which uses the left lower stroke of the second original ʾ. – At the end of the line, the edge of the stone makes a slightly concave curve whose upper extremity projected to its lower one, is 8 mm. to the left of the latter. The whole right side of ʾ is still visible. One thinks immediately of ʾ⌋[*lmqh*.[3]

RÉS 4708 = Ja 491, cf. *JaIMS*, pp. 324-28: in the South-Arabic transcription of *ṯʾrn*, correct the printing slip *ẖ* to ʾ which is correctly indicated in the commentary (p. 324).

[2] Cf. also *RycIMAM*, p. 199, but without explanation with regard to the stone.

[3] Contrary to *RycIMAM* (p. 199): *mrʾhmw*, which introduces ʾ⌋[*lmqh*, "désignerait non le roi mais le chef de tribu... avec moins de vraisemblance...*mrʾhmw* désignerait une divinité."

RÉS 4716 – Additional note to Ja 499: *hqšbn* (line 1) is beyond any doubt in C. Ansaldi's photograph; *RyISA* (IV, p. 259) erroneously reads *hqšrn* in both transcription and commentary, but does not explain his putting *hqšbn* between parentheses in *RÉS*.

5 – *Palaeographical Notes* (cf. Plates M and N)

In my chart of facsimiles, CIH 569, Gl 389, Philby 229, and RÉS 4708 are photostatically reproduced. – The facsimile of both CIH 457 and RÉS 3960 are made from my own squeezes. – The ʾ in RÉS 4716 is much too damaged to be drawn. – For RÉS 4775, the only photograph available was of A 55b which contains about the second third of the text. – The drawing of RÉS 4909 was omitted because the palaeography of the text belongs to the Ḥaḍr type and not to the Sab one; further, palaeographic details cannot be studied from the reproduction of Philby's very small photograph. – The lettering of Wâdî Maʾsil 1 attests so much liberty, which most probably is partly due to the roughness of the rock itself, that even a long, arduous compilation of measurements gives no more than an approximate representation of the model itself; other examples of that kind are Ja 544-547. My drawing does not reproduce the type of *n* in which the oblique upper stroke is vertical and is placed a little to the right of the axis of the lower vertical stroke, because such a disposition of the strokes is most probably due to the roughness of the rock, unless it is an optical illusion caused by the angle of inclination of that part of the rock on the lens of the camera. – The original photographs of Ja 670 and 671 are much too small to allow accurate drawings. It is, however, possible to assert that the two texts are to be connected with Ja 669 and 668 respectively, and also that the extremities of *t* in Ja 671 are shaped like those in Ja 669.

B – PROPOSED NEW ARRANGEMENT OF DYNASTIC TREES

The royal titles, the palaeography and the information found in the texts themselves (e.g., the reading of RÉS 3960/1) suggest the following rearrangement of the dynastic trees.

Group d: *mlk/sbʾ/wḏrydn*

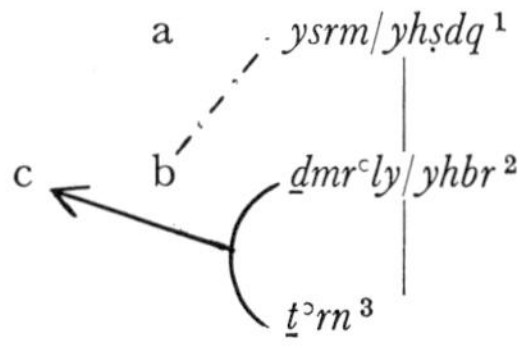

Group e: *mlk/sbʾ/wḏrydn*

a *ṯʾrn/yʿb/yhnʿm*

Group f: *mlk/– – –/wymnt*

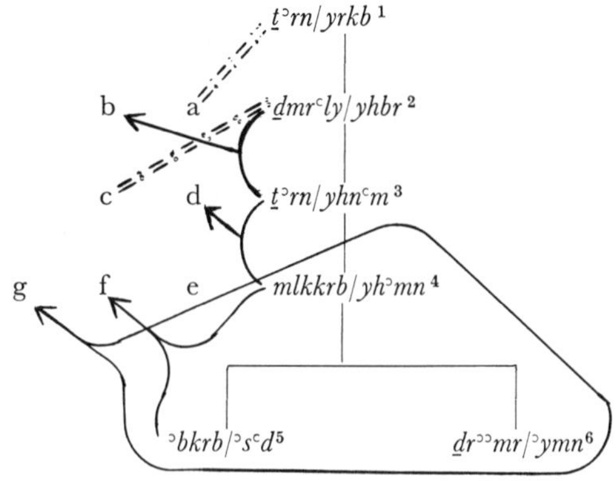

Group g: *mlk/– – –/wymnt* and *mlk/– – – – – –/wthmt*

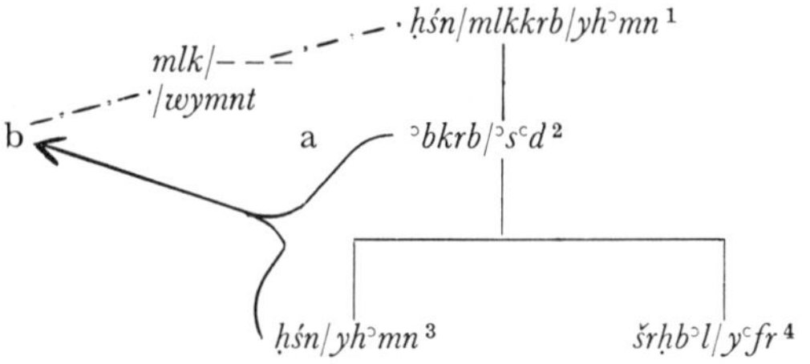

List of the texts:

D a: CIH 41
b: CIH 365
c: CIH 457; RÉS 4708 and 4775

E a: CIH 569; RÉS 4909

F a: RÉS 3960
b: Ja 668
c: RÉS 4716
d: Ja 669, 670, and 671
e: RÉS 3444
f: Ja 856
g: Gl 389 and 823

G a: Philby 229
b: Wâdî Maʾsil 1

The explanatory note given in connection with groups A-C is also valid here; the double broken line indicates that the text was engraved during the father's reign.

Group D contains the first three names of group A, and group E is A4. Group F is group C augmented by names taken from groups A and B. Group G is identical with group B from which two names were transferred to group F and another one was suppressed. The preceding comparison may be summarized as follows:

D1 = A1	E = A4	F3 = C2	F6 = B4	G3 = B5
D2 = A2	F1 = A3	F4 = C3 = B1	G1 = B2	G4 = B6
D3 = A3	F2 = A5 = C1	F5 = B3	G2 = B3	

C – THE DYNASTY OF YASRUM YUHAṢDIQ, KING OF SABAʾ AND RAYDÂN: CIH 41, 365, 457; RÉS 4708 and 4775

Yasrum Yuhaṣdiq's dynasty is composed of three kings in direct genealogical line and is divided into two main parts: Yasrum Yuhaṣdiq's sole reign and the reign of Ḏamarʿalay Yuhabirr I, the latter period being itself divided into two sections; namely the king's sole reign and his coregency with his son Ṯaʾrân.

1 – *The sole reign of Yasrum Yuhaṣdiq*: CIH 41

Yasrum Yuhaṣdiq's sole reign is presently known by only one text, CIH 41. A thorough comparison of this text with CIH 40[4] sheds an interesting light on the origin and the development of Yasrum Yuhaṣdiq's dynasty.

D. H. Müller[5] already connected the two texts and on the basis of the common mention of *ṯfym* and *mlykm*; he suggests that the king mentioned in CIH 40 probably was the father of Yasrum Yuhaṣdiq. *CIH* (*l.c.*) accepts the connection, but adds: "utrum Laʿaz ante Yâsir an Yâsir ante Laʿaz ordine sit collocandus, et quando uterque regnaverit, ignoramus". Finally, *RycIMAM* (p. 316) considers Yasrum Yuhaṣdiq as the immediate successor of the other king, and attributes such an opinion to *CIH*; however, he does not maintain any blood relationship between the two kings.

The comparison between the two texts as made by D. H. Müller remains incomplete as is that made

[4] The second element of the king's name in CIH 40/6 is [.]*nwfn*. In his translation of the text (I, p. 64) and his commentary (p. 67 B), *CIH* does not mention the empty space 4 mm. in width, left by the destroyed letter to the right of *nwfm*. The same omission is noted in *RycIMAM*, p. 164 (transliteration of the text) and p. 359 B. – For the two monograms of the text, cf. *JaJEQH*, p. 132, note 2, and p. 133, notes 1 and 2.

[5] Cf. *CIH*, I, p. 70.

by *RycIMAM* (*l.c.*), which needs to be revised, since the author writes that "les noms des mêmes personnages... reviennent dans CIH 41."

The comparison between the two texts is presented in the following points:

1 – They both deal with constructions, although those mentioned in CIH 40 are much greater and more important than those in CIH 41 [6] (two houses [7] and one incense shrine [8]).

2 – The names of the authors as well as their title show the posterity of CIH 41. The main authors of both texts belong to the same clan: *bn(w)/mḏrḥm*; they nevertheless are different and without any stated relationship. The secondary authors of CIH 40 are five in number; and only two of them, those pointed out by D. H. Müller, are repeated in CIH 41. Again, the authors of CIH 40 are rulers of two tribes: Muhaᵓnifum and Bukaylum; those of CIH 41 became priests of ᶜAṯtar in the temple ᶜAlam and remained rulers of the only tribe Muhaᵓnifum.

3 – The final invocations have in common *brdᵓ* – – *ᵓl(lt)hmw/ᶜṯtr/ḏg(w)ftm/bᶜl/ᶜlm* – –*w(ᵓ)šmshmw/wm(n)ḍḥ(t)* – – *brdᵓ* – – *wbᵓẖyl* – *šᶜb(y)hmw/mhᵓnfm*.

4 – The texts come from the same general area. CIH 40 was found in the village Maḏâb near Ḍûrân [9]; these two names are mentioned together by *MüHG* (68/15); the first place is located half a hour from the other, [10] that is to say about 50 km. northwest of Ḏamâr and 62 km. south-southwest of Ṣanᶜâᵓ. CIH 41 was seen in Ḍâff, [11] at the northern end of Jahrân, [12] and about 18 km. northeast of Ḍûrân and about 47 km. south-southwest of Ṣanᶜâᵓ.

The preceding comparative study should be completed by two additional remarks.

1 – It is necessary to stress the characteristics common to the three following expressions:

lᶜzzm/yhnf		Ja 631/26-27,
lᶜzm/[.]nwfn	*}/yhṣdq/mlk/sbᵓ/wḏrydn* in {	CIH 40/6,
ysrm		CIH 41/4.

They have in common the final element of the name followed by the same title, as well as the absence of any filiation, and the first two elements in the first two names are composed of the same components.

2 – The palaeographical connection of CIH 40 with CIH 46 and Gl 1594 (cf. RÉS 3866) is all the more indicated since CIH 46 was found in a city east of Ḍâff (cf. CIH 41) and Gl 1594 in Bûsâm, west of Ṣanᶜâᵓ, and also in that the two texts commemorate the building of some constructions, and finally that the final invocation of CIH 46 is worded in the same general pattern as is CIH 40 and 41.

All the preceding considerations suggest, in my opinion, viewing the situation as follows.

a – Liᶜazzum [.]anûfân Yuhaṣdiq precedes Yasrum Yuhaṣdiq very closely, because of the mention of the same two men in CIH 40 and 41. However, since the length of their reigns as well as the procedure in their appointment as kings remain unknown, their blood relationship – if any – and the proximity of their reigns remain open questions.

b – Liᶜazzum [.]anûfân Yuhaṣdiq and Yasrum Yuhaṣdiq (at least during the first part of his reign) most probably were provincial kings of the south and the west of Ṣanᶜâᵓ, as Liᶜazzum Yuhnaf Yuhaṣdiq was in Ẓafâr. Yasrum Yuhaṣdiq apparently succeeded in getting for himself the throne of Mârib, and in securing it for his own family. Therefore, since CIH 46 and Gl 1594 mention the *mbḥḍ* era, the origin of that era, which may have started about 97 B.C., may be connected with the foundation of that provincial kingdom inside the great Sab kingdom.

2 – *The reign of Ḏamarᶜalay Yuhabirr I:* CIH 365, 457; RÉS 4708 and 4775

The reign of Ḏamarᶜalay Yuhabirr I is divided into two parts: his sole reign (CIH 365) and his coregency with his son Ṯaᵓrân (CIH 457; RÉS 4708 and 4775).

a – SOLE REIGN: CIH 365

The existence of this sole reign is attested in CIH 365, [13] lines 16-18: *mrᵓYhmw/ḏmrᶜly/yhbr/mlk/*

[6] According to *RycIMAM* (*l.c.*), the texts deal with "une construction" and "une construction analogue" respectively.
[7] Not "deux forts", as in *RycIMAM*, p. 194 and note 15.
[8] "Autel à combustion", cf. *RycIMAM*, *l.c.*
[9] Cf. *CIH*, I, p. 63.
[10] Cf. *FoSA*, p. 69, note 3.
[11] Cf. *MüHG*, 111/14.
[12] Cf. *FoSA*, p. 187, note 4.

[13] Cf. already *JaDSY*, pp. 17-18. Contrary to *RycIMAM*: "on ne connaît pas d'inscription de l'époque où Ḏamarᶜalay Yuhabirr I régnait seul" (p. 205), because "il semble que.. Yâsir Yuhaṣdiq ait régné avec son fils Ḏamarᶜalay Yuhabirr I, d'après CIH 365" (*l.c.*). On p. 208, the same author writes: "Ḏamarᶜalay Bayyin et son père Karibᵓil, dans CIH 365, 16-17". A pair of kings such as those mentioned in the quotation is not attested.

sb³/wdrydn/bn/ysrm/yhṣdq/mlk/sb³/wdrydn. The same formula with *mr³hmw* instead of *mr³Yhmw*, would not raise any difficulty, and would indicate Ḏamar-ᶜalay Yuhabirr I's sole reign. The formula as it stands, does not, however, indicate a coregency because of the strong contrast with the three other texts related to a coregency headed by Ḏamarᶜalay Yuhabirr I which follow the common pattern: CIH 457/4-5; RÉS 4708/1 and 4775/1. However, the filiation of the first coregent is added immediately after the latter's name. The insertion of *y* between *mr³* and *hmw*, provided it is not a mistake in the engraving, could in no wise suggest that Yasrum Yuhaṣdiq was still living during the sole reign of his son.

CIH 365 comes from Mârib[14] and is a dedicatory text to ³Ilumquh for several favors and protection received from the god. Among other expeditions, the author alludes to one against the clan Ḥazfarum. Although all detail on this campaign remains unknown, the importance of the expedition cannot be minimized because of the importance of the clan, which had given in the past so many eponyms in the history of the Sab kingdom.[15]

b – COREGENCY WITH HIS SON ṮA³RÂN: CIH 457; RÉS 4708 and 4775

The three texts related to that coregency present three outstanding characteristics which may be listed as follows.

1 – In the royal identification formulas the son's name is always composed of only one element, *ṯ³rn* (CIH 457/5 and 11; RÉS 4708/1 and 4775/1). The latter cannot, therefore be identified with ...]*m/bn/ḏmrᶜly* in RÉS 4716/2; RÉS 4716 was engraved during the sole reign of ...]*m*'s father; why would the son have lost the second or the last two elements of his name after becoming coregent? And if he did not, why would only the first element be mentioned in the texts related to that coregency?

2 – In the same identification formulas the first coregent's filiation follows immediately the latter's name in only one text, RÉS 4775/1, and not in the two other inscriptions. Such a difference, which is all the more striking since both RÉS 4708 and 4775 have the two coregents as authors, could imply that Yasrum Yuhaṣdiq was still living at the time of RÉS 4775. There is, however, no indication mentioned in the texts so far as the relative chronology of CIH 457 and RÉS 4708 is concerned.

3 – The two coregents apparently maintained their preference for the stellar god ᶜAṯtar in spite of their presence in Mârib, according to RÉS 4775/3-4, where the final invocation basically refers to the same general pattern as that of CIH 40 and 41: *ᶜṯtr*, (³)*šms*, and *m(n)ḏḥ(t)*, *³lmqh* being mentioned because of the presence of the two coregents in Mârib. Their servants in CIH 457 have the same attitude.

The epigraphical material related to the coregency now under study does not contain much historical information.

In RÉS 4775, the two coregents mention the building, near Mârib, of a breakwater whose destruction had caused great damage.[16] In RÉS 4708=Ja 491, which was found in Naḫlat al-Ḥamrâ, which is the city Silâᶜ,[17] the same royal persons say that they inaugurated two gifts,[18] two bronze statues, from three of their courtiers, for the incense shrine[19] which belonged, according to M. Höfner,[20] to the royal palace[21] Ṣanᶜ. Finally, CIH 457,[22] whose origin remains unknown, is a dedicatory text to the stellar god mentioned as ᶜAṯtar and Saḥar, written by individuals not of the royal family. Its contents are very ordinary; but its final invocation (lines 16-19) has in common with that of CIH 40 and 46, the mention of *ᶜṯtr*, *šms*, and *mḏḥ*.

[14] Cf. *CIH*, II, p. 6.

[15] *RycIMAM* (p. 189) writes that the text deals with "une opération militaire... contre la tribu de Ḥazfar. Cette tribu n'ayant pas une importance prépondérante, l'expédition... ne constitutit sans doute qu'une opération de police sans grande envergure".

[16] The pericopa inserted between two series of names of deities, reads as follows (line 4): *wwy*(?)*l*(?)*y*(?)*wsmydᶜ* "und wehe dem SMIDᶜ!", Sumyadaᶜ being understood as having had some part in the destruction of the breakwater (cf. also *HöASG*, p. 175, and *RycIMAM*, p. 175). I suggest reading *ww(dm/)wsmydᶜ* "and Waddum and Sumyadaᶜ", the latter being a deified man (cf. other examples in *JaP*, pp. 144-45).

[17] Cf. *WiHöBGS*, p. 22; cf. also J. Ryckmans, in *BiO*, 12 (1955), p. 208 B.

[18] J. Ryckmans speaks of "l'inscription de donation" (cf. *l.c.*, without any reference to *JaIMS*, pp. 324-28, although *RycIMAM* (p. 177) had mentioned "deux concessions".

[19] "Autel à combustion" (cf. *RycIMAM*, *l.c.*), but "terrasse (? *mśwd*)" (cf. J. Ryckmans, *l.c.*).

[20] In a private letter dated on March 21, 1955.

[21] J. Ryckmans (cf. *l.c.*, note 2) also interprets *byt* as "palais", but he does not specify to whom it belonged.

[22] In *RycIMAM*, read "457, 9-10" instead of "457, 19" (p. 195, note 23), and "457, 10" instead of "457, 9-10" (*l.c.*, note 27).

D – THE PROVINCIAL KING ṮA'RÂN YAᶜÛB YUHANᶜIM, KING OF SABA' AND RAYDÂN: CIH 569 and RÉS 4909[23]

The king Ṯa'rân Yaᶜûb Yuhanᶜim was, in my opinion, a provincial king ruling to the south and southwest of Ṣanᶜâ'. CIH 569 was found in the city of Ḏamâr, and CIH 40, as already stated above, in the village Maḏâb, about 50 km. northwest of Ḏamâr. Again, like CIH 40, the text commemorates some building, and its final invocation, although very fragmentary, is worded on the basis of the same general formula: *br[d'/... ...wmn]ḏḥt/'bythmw/wbmqm/mr'hmw/....* Furthermore, the king is represented in official ceremonies in Ḥaḍramawt, not by Sabaeans, but by *ḥmyryynhn* (line 2) "two Ḥimyarites" who are the authors of RÉS 4909. Were he reigning in Mârib, why did he not send two Sabaeans instead of two Ḥimyarites as delegates for an official visit such as that described in the text? Finally, the king's filiation is not attested in RÉS 4909, exactly like all the other provincial kings, but contrasting to the filiation of the Ḥaḍr king. The text was composed as well as engraved by Ḥaḍramites; but the sketch of the contents was given by the two Ḥimyarites. If their king was known as using his filiation in his royal title, these two servants would doubtless have given the full title to the Ḥaḍr workmen.

RÉS 4909 alludes to an official delegation sent by Ṯa'rân Yaᶜûb Yuhanᶜim to his ally the Ḥaḍr king 'Ilᶜaḏḏ Yaluṭ, son of ᶜAmmḏahar. The occasion was "when he [the Ḥaḍr king] proceeded to the fortress 'Anwadum in order to sojourn and to give titles" (lines 3-4[24]). The purpose of the two Ḥimyarite delegates is described by *mt/slḥsmyn/mr'smyn/ṯ'rn/yᶜb/yhnᶜm mlk/sb'/wḏrydn/tqblm/hšyᶜ/'ḫs* (lines 4-7) "when their lord Ṯa'rân Yaᶜûb Yuhanᶜim, king of Saba' and Raydân, delegated them both to go south [and] to take care of the [Ḥimyarite] train for his brother [=ally]".[25]

E – THE DYNASTY OF ṮA'RÂN YARKUB, KING OF SABA', RAYDÂN, ḤAḌRAMAWT, AND YAMNAT: Gl 389, 823; Ja 668, 669, 670, 671, 856; RÉS 3444, 3960, and 4716

The dynasty of Ṯa'rân Yarkub is composed of six kings whose reigns are now to be studied.

1 – *The Sole Reign of Ṯa'rân Yarkub:* RÉS 3960

The only text related to Ṯa'rân Yarkub's sole reign is RÉS 3960. The inscription, about the left half of which is missing, was written by the king's son and commemorates the consecration of men and women, by a group headed by the author [Ḏama]rᶜalay Yuhabirr himself, to the moon god 'Ilumquh.

2 – *The Reign of Ḏamarᶜalay Yuhabirr II:* Ja 668 and RÉS 4716

The reign of Ḏamarᶜalay Yuhabirr II seems to be divided into two parts: his sole reign (RÉS 4716) and his coregency with his son Ṯa'rân Yuhanᶜim.

a – HIS SOLE REIGN: RÉS 4716

The very fragmentary text RÉS 4716 (=Ja 499), which commemorates some construction, mentions *...]m/bn/ḏmrᶜly/mlk/sb'/wḏr[ydn/....* At first sight, the first name could be restored as *krb'l/wtr/yhnᶜ]m* or *yhq]m* or *ṯ'rn/yhnᶜ]m*, and therefore *ḏmrᶜly* would be either *ḏmrᶜly/byn* or *ḏmrᶜly/ḏrḥ* or *ḏmrᶜly/yhbr II. RycIMAM* (p. 164, note 12) prefers a fourth restoration, that of *ṯ'rn/yᶜb/yhnᶜm* rather than that first mentioned above, because the engraving is in relief.[26] Such a reason is also valid against the second hypothesis. However, *RycIMAM*'s identification is not to be accepted because Ṯa'rân Yaᶜûb Yuhanᶜim is not to be identified with the son of either Ḏamarᶜalay Yuhabirr I or II.

I suggest the restoration *.../mr'hmw/ṯ'rn/yhnᶜ]m/bn/ḏmrᶜly/mlk/sb'/wḏr[ydn/wḥḏrmwt/wymnt/...*, because of the parallel of RÉS 3960, and also because of the identity of the son of Ḏamarᶜalay Yuhabirr II.

[23] RÉS 4716 (not 4176) is ascribed to Ṯa'rân Yaᶜûb Yuhanᶜim by *RycIMAM* (p. 193, note 1), but is not mentioned with the two texts related to the sole reign of the same king (p. 205, note 8).

[24] These lines are identical with RÉS 4852/6-7 which are translated in *JaSAI*, p. 513 B and corresponding notes.

[25] *BeAIP* (pp. 449-50) relates *slḥ* to *slḥ* "weapons" (CIH 548/1) compares *tqbl* with Arabic *qbl*, 6th form "to meet together", and gives the same meaning to both *hyšᶜ* and *šwᶜ*; his translation reads as follows (p. 449): "when their lord... had equipped them on an embassy(?) in order to accompany his ally". For the verb *slḥ*, cf. Ethiopic *sälăḥă=śäläḥă* (cf. *DiLLA*, col. 325 A) I *vim exercere,polestatem habere*, II *potestatem, facultatem...facere alicui*" (cf. *l.c.*, col. 233 A). For *tqbl*, cf. Arabic *qabala*, 5th form "to go south".

[26] P. 164, note 12, more cautiously on p. 192, note 6, and with certainty on p. 193, note 1.

b – HIS COREGENCY WITH HIS SON ṮA'RÂN YUHANᶜIM: Ja 668

The full name of each coregent, their blood relationship and their common royal title (*mlky*/...) are formally attested in lines 15-18, and also in lines 3-5 where, however, the first coregent's name is almost entirely restored (line 3).

The text, whose upper part is missing, is a dedicatory inscription to 'Ilumquh, by the tribe Saba' Kahilân, because of successes met with during military expeditions which the tribe made in different places whose names are either missing or very fragmentary (lines 1-3), and more precisely during the plundering of every city of the district of Sarîrân (lines 10-11), which is the country of Wâdî as-Sarîr that originates east of Dammâj and flows into Wâdî Maḏâb,[27] thus about 100 km. southeast of Ṣaᶜdat.

The expression introducing the names of the two coregents is *mr'hmw* (line 15), and not *mr'Yhmw*. This singular, to be explained the same way as *mlkn*, simply indicates, according to the context, either a special relation with or an order given by the first of the two actual coregents.

3 – *The coregency of Ṯa'rân Yuhanᶜim with his son Malikkarib Yuha'min:* Ja 669, 670, and 671

Ṯa'rân Yuhanᶜim's coregency with his son Malikkarib Yuha'min is attested by Ja 669, 670, and 671, three dedicatory inscriptions to 'Ilumquh.

Besides the repetition of *mr'hmw* (Ja 669/7 and 671/7-8; but *mr'yhmw* in Ja 671/21 and 670/21), the royal identification formulas show a certain fluctuation in the name of the second coregent:

mlkkrb	in Ja 669/28,
mlkkrb/y'mn	in Ja 671/9 and 22,
mlkkrb/yh'mn	in Ja 670/23.

The facts alluded to in the three dedicatory texts are, as usual, diversified. Among them, the most important one is related in Ja 671: the destruction of the dam between the two reservoirs Ḥabâbiḍ and Rabḥum, whose building is recorded in CIH 622, 623, and RÉS 3943, and their subsequent repair, which took three months of work, was accomplished by the army of the Arabs conducted by the main author of the text, a Suẖaymite, one of the rulers of the tribe Yarsum.

The question of the relation between Ja 670 and 671 must be studied. The authors of the two texts have approximately the same title, namely

bnw (or *y*)/*sẖymm*,
'bᶜl/bytn/rymn,
'qwl/šᶜbn/yrsm/ḏsmᶜy/ḏtlṯn/ḏhgrm;

to which only Ja 671/5 adds *ḏ]ẖwln/gddtn*. It is of course quite possible that the rulers of the tribe Yarsum could have changed during the coregency; it is however reasonable to consider the possibility that the authors of Ja 670 and 671 are identical; 'As'ar (Ja 671/2) would then be the second element of Marṯadum's name (Ja 670/2); this addition would suggest the posteriority of Ja 671.

The main author of Ja 670 had been dying in Ẓafâr, and was protected by his god. A son was born to the authors of Ja 669, and he lived, and the brother of the main author of the same text was left dying after a quarrel and was saved by his god.

4 – *The coregencies of Malikkarib Yuha'min with his sons:* Gl 389, 823; Ja 856; RÉS 3444

The four above-mentioned texts attest a single spelling of the second element *yh'mn*. Before describing the contents of Ja 856 and Gl 389 and the coregencies alluded to in them, one question needs be mentioned.

a – QUESTION OF THE SOLE REIGN OF MALIKKARIB YUHA'MIN: RÉS 3444[28]

According to E. Glaser,[29] RÉS 3444 = Gl 386 is a panel composed of five parts: the two monograms and the central symbol identical to and in the same order as, e.g., those of CIH 540/14-15, and between those three, the monograms of *mlkkrb* and of *yh'mn* from right to left respectively.[30] RÉS 3444 does not justify, in my opinion, the hypothesis of Malikkarib Yuha'min's sole reign, because it also fits very

[27] Cf. *FoSA*, p. 116, note 7. *WiHöBGS* (pp. 37 and 42) identify *srrn* with Hagar Ḥenû az-Zurîr, in Wâdî Ḥarîb.

[28] Cf. *JaDSY*, p. 16.

[29] Cf. *MVAG*, 1897, 6, p. 41.

[30] *RyISA*'s (IX, pp. 100-01) statement that *ḏr''mr/'ymn*'s monograms are also parts of RÉS 3444, comes from a confusion with CIH 724 = Gl 385. *RycIMAM*'s (p. 212, note 9) interpretation of the five parts of the panel is disproved by E. Glaser's description.

well the king during his coregencies with some of his sons.[31]

b – HIS COREGENCY WITH HIS SON ᵓABKARIB ᵓASᶜAD: Ja 856

The full study of Ja 856 (formerly Fakhry 60) is published in *JaLSI*. The two coregents commemorate the building of their domestic shrine Burayk.

c – HIS COREGENCY WITH HIS TWO SONS ᵓABKARIB ᵓASᶜAD AND ḎARAᵓᵓAMAR ᵓAYMAN: Gl 389 and 823

In Gl 389, the three coregents allude to the building of their palace with the power of the monotheistic god *mrᵓ/smy[n]* "The Lord of Heaven". One cannot but wonder why the kings called that palace Šawḥaṭân, an appellation so close to Šawḥaṭ,[32] which is the name of a temple dedicated to ᵓIlumquh and mentioned during the last three kings of Fariᶜum Yanhub's dynasty, Ja 618/33, 627/28-29, and 628/28.

The actual contents of Gl 823 still remain unknown. However, F. Hommel's statements combined with that of *WiHöBGS* (p. 120), do not leave any doubt concerning either the identity of the coregents or the relative chronology of the text with Gl 389.

HoGSA (p. 104) writes that "in diesem Jahr [A.D. 378] dem der ersten wieder datierten Inschrift (Gl 389 und 823) finden wir einen König Malkî-kariba Juhaᵓmin nebst seinen beiden Söhnen Abî-kariba Asᶜad und Wirᵓî-amara Aiman, wiederum mit dem gleichen längeren Titel, den wir schon bei Šammar trafen". *WiHöBGS* (*l.c.*) summarize the same information when writing that "um 378 erscheint... *Malkikarib Yuhaᵓmin*, mit dem gleichen Titel, den *Shammar Yuharᶜisch* führte (Gl. 389, 823)".

Since the year A.D. 378 is the equivalent, in these authors' systems, of the year 493 of the Sab era, which is attested in Gl 389/3, the mention of Gl 823 immediately after that of Gl 389 means, in my opinion, that both texts[33] contain the same date.[34] Furthermore, the three coregents as well as their order of precedence are attested identically in both Gl 389 and 823.[35]

d – GENERAL CONSIDERATIONS

Besides some reflections already pointed out in *JaLSI*, and which are summarized here to make the present study complete, some others need be mentioned.

1° – *Attempt of Chronology*

The only basis available at the present time, on which one might attempt to reconstruct a chronology, is the date given in Gl 389/4, the year 493 of the Sab era. Since the length of 55 years can safely be allowed to four generations of kings, Ṯaᵓrân Yarkub's dynasty could be assigned the period of ±440–455 of the Sab era, that is to say 70 years in the 4th century A.D. starting several years after the turn of the century.

2° – *Remarks on Religion*

Gl 389 attests that Malikkarib Yuhaᵓmin and his sons broke away from the traditional religion of their ancestors to adopt some form of monotheism; such a step would be better placed, in my opinion, at the beginning of the first coregency headed by this Malikkarib Yuhaᵓmin. Further, Gl 389 is the first text which mentions the Sab era; and since that mention is found only in monotheistic texts, as already noted, such a coincidence, which can hardly be accidental, suggests that this era is in some way related to the monotheistic movement.[36]

[31] The relation of RÉS 3444 with Ṯaᵓrân Yuhanᶜim's coregency with his son seems less probable, but cannot be positively excluded.

[32] It would be useless to argue on the possible identity of *šwḥṭn* and *šwḥṭ*, and then suggest the identification of the lunar god ᵓIlumquh, master of the first, with *mrᵓ/smy* (*sic* in *SoSoIGCM*'s decipherment). The reading of *mrᵓ/smy[n]* must be accepted; and Gl 389 commemorates the construction of a *new* building.

[33] Since F. Hommel himself says, according to *RycIMAM* (p. 212, note 7), that Gl 823 is apparently complete and is composed of one line and a half, with a date, "Inschrift" in F. Hommel's above-quoted statement refers to Gl 389 and not to both Gl 389 and 823, and does not support *RycIMAM*'s (*l.c.*) interpretation according to which F. Hommel would give the same text two numbers in E. Glaser's collection. Further, *RycPCH*'s (p. 22, note 74) new interpretation, according to which Gl 389 "serait partiellement représenté par Gl. 824", is not closer to F. Hommel's statement, apart from the fact that, the two texts having several features in common, the first is "partiellement représenté" by the second. – *SoSoIGCM*'s silence about Gl 823 in his publication of Gl 389 cannot be understood as a proof of the distinction of Gl 389 and 823, because his article is devoted exclusively to the publication of Gl 389 and especially his study of the expression *mrᵓ/smy*; finally, the author was not in a position to deal with other texts of E. Glaser's collection.

[34] Cf. also *RycPCH*, *l.c.*

[35] The expression "einen König" in F. Hommel's statement and *WiHöBGS*'s restriction to the only name of Malikkarib Yuhaᵓmin, simply indicate that these authors characterize a coregency by the first coregent.

[36] Cf. also the last hypothesis suggested by *RycPCH*, p. 24; the others remain unsupported.

The presence of the central symbol in Ja 856, Gl 389, and RÉS 3444 indicates that the authors of the texts indulged "in some syncretism in order to please their subjects, who remained faithful to their ancestors' religious way of life".[37]

F – BEGINNING OF THE DYNASTY OF ḤAŚAN MALIKKARIB YUHAʾMIN: CIH 540; Geukens 2; Philby 229; RÉS 5085; Wâdî Maʾsil 1

The following lines deal with the beginning of the dynasty of Ḥaśan Malikkarib Yuhaʾmin inasmuch as it is required by Philby 229 and Wâdî Maʾsil 1 which are mentioned in the genealogical scheme B.

Neither the sole reign of Ḥaśan Malikkarib Yuhaʾmin nor his coregency (e.g., with his son ʾAbkarib ʾAsʿad) is attested in the inscriptions. Yet, he was king in one way or another, and bore the same title as that inaugurated by Šamir Yuharʿiš, as is attested by Wâdî Maʾsil 1/3-4.

It also remains unknown whether ʾAbkarib ʾAsʿad reigned alone or not, before his coregency with his son Ḥaśan Yuhaʾmin. Philby 229, which cannot, obviously enough, be related palaeographically to Ja 856, does not prove the first alternative.

Wâdî Maʾsil 1 attests the coregency of ʾAbkarib ʾAsʿad with his son Ḥaśan Yuhaʾmin, and was engraved during a military campaign in the far north.

The main question regarding a possible connection between groups F and G, is the date of the present text. Several elements are fortunately at hand and are given here in chronological order:

Wâdî Maʾsil 1	ʾAbkarib ʾAsʿad and his son Ḥaśan Yuhaʾmin	?
Geukens 2	ʾAbkarib ʾAsʿad and ? ?]zaʾân and Šaraḥbiʾil Yaʿfur	543 of the Sab era
RÉS 5085	*ʾmlkn/ʾbʿl/rdn*	560 of the Sab era
CIH 540	Šaraḥbiʾil Yaʿfur	565 of the Sab era

In Geukens 2, *RyISA*'s (XII, p. 311) restoration of lines 2-3 as *ḥś[n/yhʾmn/bny/mlkkrb/yhʾmn/wbnyhmw/ʿmr/y]zʾn/wšrḥbʾl/yʿfr/– –*, is considered by its own author as presenting "un caractère insolite du fait que *bny/mlkkrb/yhʾmn* (dans Ry 509 [=Wâdî Maʾsil 1]: *bny/ḥśn/mlkkrb/yhʾmn*) s'insère ici entre les noms du premier et du deuxième fils de ʿAbkarib" (*sic*). The mention of the grandfather in such a place contradicts all identifications known up to the present time, and especially Wâdî Maʾsil 1/1-4: *ʾbkrb/ʾsʿd/wbnhw/ḥśn/yhʾmn/. . . bny/ḥśn/mlkkrb/yhʾmn.* Again, this pericope attests that ʾAbkarib ʾAsʿad's father is Ḥaśan Malikkarib Yuhaʾmin, and not Malikkarib Yuhaʾmin. Finally, it is a formal error to restore the text in such a way that *šrḥbʾl/yʿfr* becomes *bn* of *ḥśn/yhʾmn*, since he is his brother, and neither his son or grandson.

The only restoration which would fit all the epigraphical material would have to be based on the assumption that ʾAbkarib ʾAsʿad's name was followed by the names of five sons, namely *ḥś[n/yhʾmn*, [No. 2], [No. 3], [. . ./.]*zʾn* and *šrḥbʾl/yʿfr.* This solution immediately brings to memory the case of five incomplete monograms still attested in the very fragmentary upper side of RÉS 4106.[38]

The main problem raised by the expression *ʾmlkn/ʾbʿl/rdn* in line 8 of RÉS 5085[39] is its historical implication. *RÉS*[40] states that "la région de ʿAzzan faisant partie du territoire de Raydân, on comprend que les rois de Saba y étaient qualifiés du seul titre de 'souverains de Raydân'", with reference to *RyCS* (p. 242), who introduces the same statement, by the following phrase: "le pluriel *ʾmlkn* permet de supposer qu'il est fait allusion à trois souverains associés, comme l'étaient Malikkarib et ses deux fils ʾAbkarib et Ḏaraʾʾamar". On the other hand, *RyclMAM* suggests the hypothesis of ʾAbkarib ʾAsʿad's coregency either with his son Šaraḥbiʾil Yaʿfur (p. 213) or with his two sons ʿAmr and Šaraḥbiʾil Yaʿfur, because of the plural *ʾmlkn* (p. 319).

The text RÉS 5085 is engraved on a rock in Wâdî Raẖaylah, north of ʿAzzân, that is to say about 310 km. east of Ẓafâr, the Himyarite capital; but only about 195 km. east-southeast of Beiḥân al-Qaṣâb. That the kingdom of Ẓafâr would have

[37] Cf. *JaLSI*, p. 5 A.

[38] *MoMiASI* (p. 24) and *RÉS* (VII, p. 84) do not allude to those remains.

[39] Read line 1 as follows: */rgnm/yzd/wdwlym/yzd/* instead of *m.lym/yzd/w.w.ym/yz(?)d(?)/* in *RÉS*, *l.c.*, p. 502. For the use of *ʾmlkn/ʾbʿl/rdn* in the translation of *ḏrydn*, cf. above. Further, this expression is not attested in RÉS 4969/6, which is republished as Ja 876.

[40] Cf. *l.c.*, p. 505.

extended so far eastward, is improbable, in my opinion. Here again, *rdn* refers, in my opinion, to the provincial kingdom of Raydân in former Qatabân.

Returning to the relative chronology of Wâdî Maʾsil 1, another remark is needed. Geukens 2 is more probably to be related to an early date in the history of the successive coregencies, because of the number of coregents. I therefore suggest the following approximative relative chronology, the years being given according to the Sab era:

ʾAbkarib ʾAsʿad and Ḥaśan Yuhaʾmin	±535-540	Wâdî Maʾsil 1: ±537[41]
ʾAbkarib ʾAsʿad and his five sons	±540-550	Geukens 2: 543
Šaraḥbiʾil Yaʿfur's sole reign	±550-570	CIH 540: 565

The last question is that of the possible relation between group F and group G, since my suggested chronology ascribes ±495 of the Sab era for the end of the last coregency of group F and ±535 for the beginning of the first coregency of group G. Most probably two links, possibly even more than two, are still missing between the two groups which may very well be two branches of the same family.

[41] The date suggested by *RycIHS* (p. 327), "des environs du premier quart du 5e siècle de notre ère", seems to me too early.

Chapter XII

DATING OF THE RULERS MENTIONED IN THE PRECEDING STUDIES

The dating of the Sab rulers, both *mukarribs* and kings, who are mentioned in the preceding historical studies, is best presented in a separate chapter, for a general historical frame is provided by five synchronisms. Four of them, which are sufficiently well known as not to need any special comment, are given by foreign literatures, and the fifth one is Sab. They may be listed as follows:

a – The Assyrian synchronisms dated of 738, 714 and 685 B.C. mention Sabaeans, Yaṯaʿʾamar, and Karibʾil respectively[1];

b – Strabo and *Res gestae* state that Ilasaros defended Mariaba against the soldiers of Aelius Gallus in 24 B.C.;

c – The *Periplus* (about A.D. 70) alludes to Charibael king of Sabaeans and Homerites, and to Eleazos, king of the country of Sabbatha;

d – The an-Nemârah epitaph (A.D. 328) mentions Najrân, the city of Šamir; and

e – The Sab synchronism of Ja 619/11 with the name of the Qat king Nabaṭum.

Inside this frame, the relative chronology of Sab rulers is suggested in many instances by epigraphical data. This frame and the epigraphical ribs constitute a keel for palaeographical research, which can thenceforth be developed as a sound basis on which to attempt the fixing of the dates of those rulers of whom we have but scant knowledge.

A – EARLY *MUKARRIBS*

Karibʾil and Su[mhu...] in Ja 819:
about 8th-7th century B.C.
The group of Ja 831 and 832:
early 7th century B.C.

[1] The validity of these two synchronisms is also accepted very recently by A. Grohmann in his article "Arabia", in *Enciclopedia Universale dell'Arte*, Vol. I (1960), col. 480-81.

B – LAST *MUKARRIBS* AND EARLY KINGS OF THE MURAL INSCRIPTIONS

The dating of the mural inscriptions is centered on the historical interpretation of Ja 550. G. W. Van Beek has demonstrated[2] that this text lies between masonry types 1 (about 650 B.C.) and 2 (about 450 B.C.); the approximate dating of Ja 550 may therefore be suggested about 500 B.C. Further, the data on relative chronology offered by the study of these mural inscriptions suggests the following historical scheme, which illustrates well the palaeographic development of the script:

Ja 552 and 553	about 595 B.C.
Ja 555 (one generation later than Ja 552)	about 550 B.C.
Ja 554	about 545 B.C.
Ja 557	about 540 B.C.
Ja 550	about 500 B.C.
Ja 551 and 558	about 450 B.C.

C – THE FAMILIES OF ḎAMARʿALAY ḎARIḤ, WAHABʾIL YAḤÛZ, YARUM ʾAYMAN, FARIʿUM YANHUB, AND ḎAMARʿALAY BAYYIN

These five families, whose members known at present were kings with the exception of Ḏamarʿalay Ḏariḥ, Halakʾamar and Yuhaqam, followed each other on the Sab throne for about 170 years. Their absolute dating is centered on two synchronisms, viz. Ilasaros and Aelius Gallus in 24 B.C.,

[2] Cf. in *BoAlADSA*, p. 294.

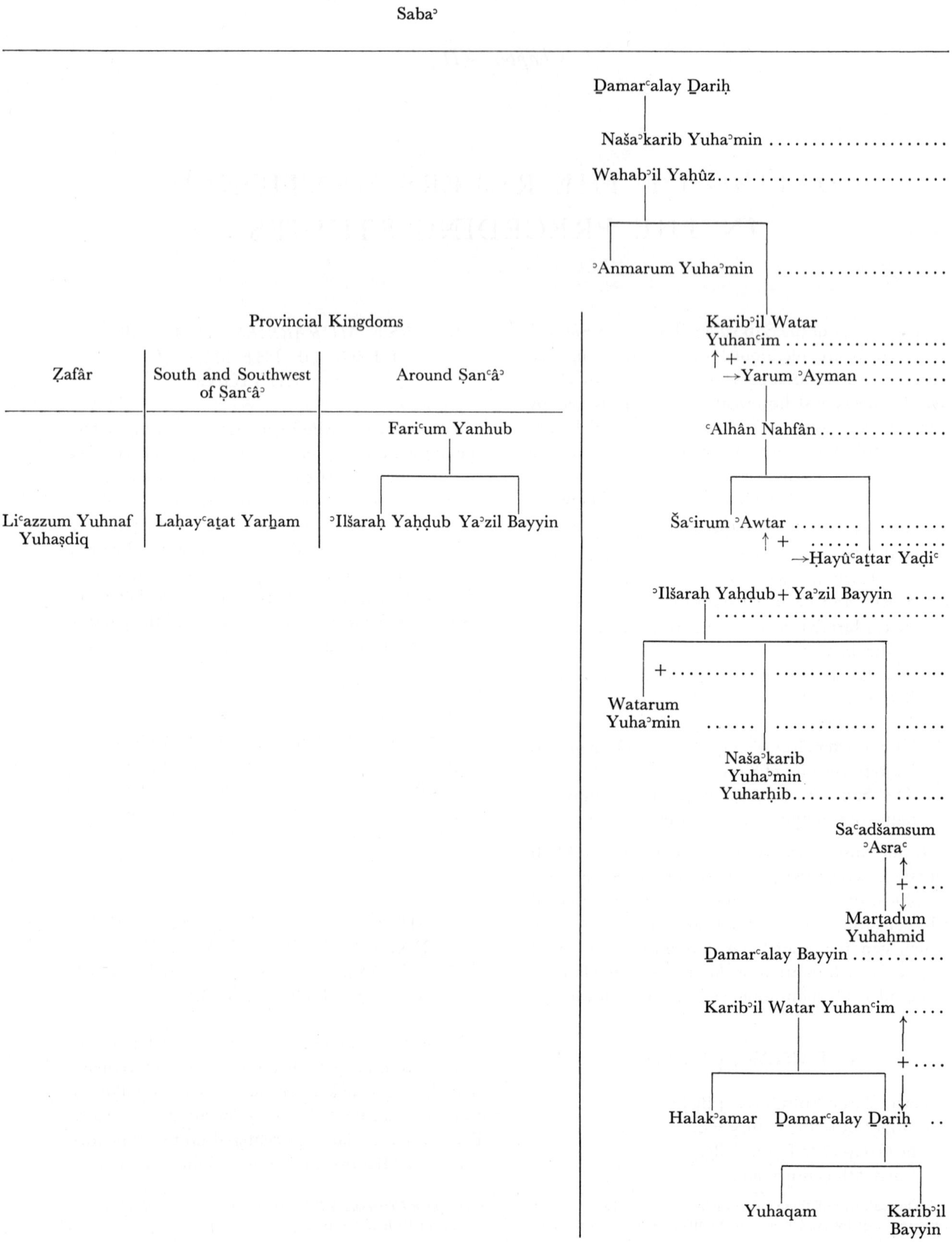
Sabaʾ
Ḏamarʿalay Ḏariḥ
Našaʾkarib Yuhaʾmin
Wahabʾil Yaḥûz
ʾAnmarum Yuhaʾmin
Provincial Kingdoms
Ẓafâr
South and Southwest of Ṣanʿâʾ
Around Ṣanʿâʾ
Fariʿum Yanhub
Liʿazzum Yuhnaf Yuhaṣdiq
Laḥayʿaṯat Yarḫam
ʾIlšaraḥ Yaḥḍub
Yaʾzil Bayyin
Karibʾil Watar Yuhanʿim
Yarum ʾAyman
ʿAlhân Nahfân
Šaʿirum ʾAwtar
Ḥayûʿaṯtar Yaḏiʿ
ʾIlšaraḥ Yaḥḍub + Yaʾzil Bayyin
Watarum Yuhaʾmin
Našaʾkarib Yuhaʾmin Yuharḥib
Saʿadšamsum ʾAsraʿ
Marṯadum Yuhaḥmid
Ḏamarʿalay Bayyin
Karibʾil Watar Yuhanʿim
Halakʾamar
Ḏamarʿalay Ḏariḥ
Yuhaqam
Karibʾil Bayyin

	Foreign synchronisms	Ḥaḍramawt	Qatabân	Dating of Sabaean rulers
				about 175-160 B.C.
				about 160-145 B.C.
				about 145-130 B.C.
				about 130-115 B.C.
				about 115-100 B.C.
				about 100-85 B.C.
		Yadaʿʾab Ġaylân		about 85-65 B.C.
				about 65-55 B.C.
		Yadaʿʾil Bayyin//ʾIlʿazz		about 55-50 B.C.
				about 50-30 B.C.
	Aelius Gallus' expedition: 24 B.C.			about 30-20 B.C.
				about 20-5 B.C.
				about 5 B.C.-A.D. 10
			Šahar Hilâl Yuhaqbiḍ	about A.D. 10-20
			Nabaṭum Yuhanʿim	about A.D. 20-30
			Marṯadum	about A.D. 30-45
	Periplus (about A.D. 70)	ʾIlʿazz		about A.D. 45-60
				about A.D. 60-65
				about A.D. 65-80
		Yadaʿʾil and Yaʿkirân		about A.D. 80-95

and the Qat king Nabaṭum and the coregency of Saʿadšamsum ʾAsraʿ and his son Marṯadum Yuhaḥmid. Using these two pieces of evidence as a starting point, and basing the relative chronology of the rulers of the five above-mentioned families on the studies of chapters III, IV, and V, I suggest the scheme shown on pages 390 and 391 which includes South-Arabian and foreign synchronisms, and which places the beginning of *mlk/sbʾ/wḏrydn* about 65 B.C.[3]

D – THE 2ND AND MOST OF THE 3RD CENTURIES A.D.

The 2nd and most of the 3rd centuries A.D offer only scattered kings, who may be presented as follows on the basis of palaeography.

	Sabaʾ	Ḥaḍramawt	
	Rabbšamsum Nimrân..	....	...about A.D. 120-140
Provincial kingdom south and southwest of Ṣanʿâʾ			
Liʿazzum [.]anûfân Yuhaṣdiq..	....	....	...about A.D. 170-180
Yasrum Yuhaṣdiq	....	....	...about A.D. 190-200
	Yasrum Yuhaṣdiq	....	...about A.D. 200-205
	Ḏamarʿalay Yuhabirr	....	...about A.D. 205-220
	↑ + ...	....	...about A.D. 220-230
	Ṯaʾrân		
Taʾrân Yaʿûb Yuhanʿim[4].....	....	.ʾIlʿaḏḏ Yaluṭ, son of ʿAmmḏaḫar	...about A.D. 265-275

[3] *BePSC* (p. 52) prefers to date it "*circa* 30 B.C.". Further, according to this author (p. 54), Našaʾkarib Yuhaʾmin "may plausibly be dated in the years around about 100 B.C.".

[4] According to *RycIMAM* (p. 216), this king would have reigned about A.D. 190-205.

E – THE END OF THE 3RD CENTURY AND ALMOST THE ENTIRE 4TH CENTURY A.D.

The end of the 3rd century and almost the entire 4th century present two dynastic families separated from each other by a sole reign; such a reconstruction is in perfect agreement with palaeographical development of the script.

Saba'	Ḥaḍramawt	
Yasrum Yuhanʿim		
Malik[um....]		...about A.D. 285-300
+		...about A.D. 300-305
Šamir Yuharʿiš ...	Šaraḫ'il and Rabbšamsum	...about A.D. 305-315
+		...about A.D. 315-320
Daraʾʾamar 'Ayman		
+		...about A.D. 320-325
Ṭaʾrân 'Ayfaʿ		
Karib'il (Watar) Yuhanʿim ..		...about A.D. 325-330
Ṭaʾrân Yarkub..........		...about A.D. 330-335
Damarʿalay Yuhabirr II ..		...about A.D. 335-340
+		...about A.D. 340-350
Ṭaʾrân Yuhanʿim		
+		...about A.D. 350-365
Malikkarib Yuha'min		
+		...about A.D. 365-375
+		...about A.D. 375-385
'Abkarib 'Asʿad Daraʾʾamar 'Ayman		

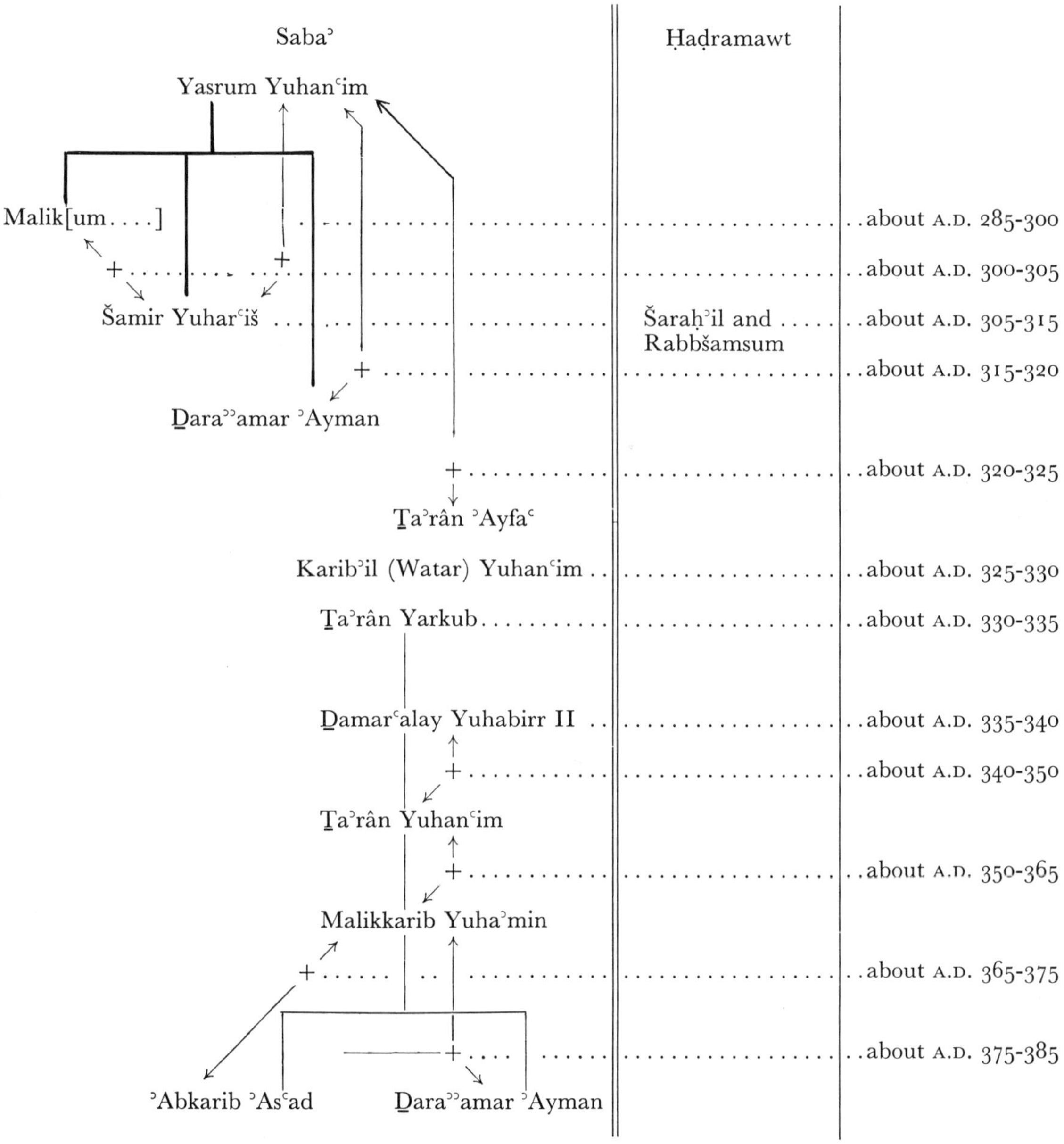

F – THE BEGINNING OF THE 5TH CENTURY A.D.

The last royal family mentioned in the preceding historical chapters began to hold the Sabaean throne about A.D. 415. The inscriptions treated in connection with the historical study of the beginning of this family suggest the following scheme.

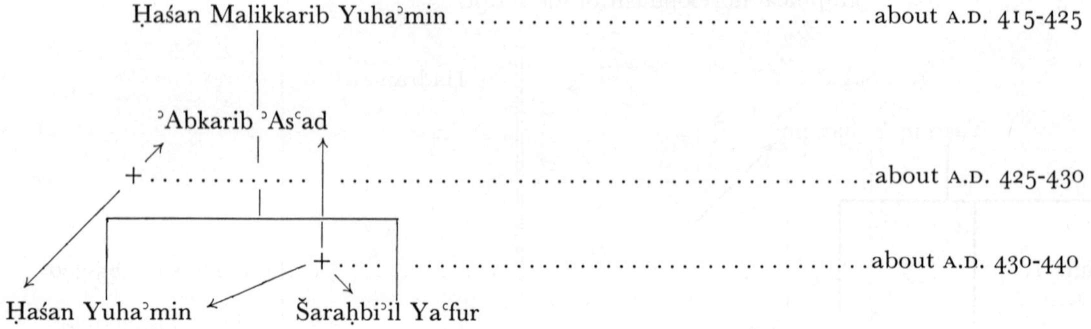

ABBREVIATIONS AND BIBLIOGRAPHICAL NOTE

Preliminary note: The following list contains abbreviations, most of them of publications which are used frequently in the present work. For the many other publications referred to in the text, see the list of authors.

A = Catalogue of E. Glaser squeezes (cf. *HöSEG*).
AlCAS = W. F. Albright, *The Chronology of Ancient South Arabia in the Light of the First Campaign of Excavation in Qataban* [Reprint from *BASOR*, No. 119], Baltimore, 1950.
AlEMY = F. P. Albright, "Excavations at Mârib in Yemen", in *BoAlADSA*, pp. 215-68.
AlETM = F. P. Albright, "The Excavation of the Temple of the Moon at Mârib (Yemen)", in *BASOR*, No. 128, December, 1952, pp. 25-38.
AM = Aden Museum.
AshM = Ashmolean Museum.
BeAIP = A. F. L. Beeston, "Appendix on the Inscriptions Discovered by Mr. Philby", in *PhSD*, pp. 441-56.
BeBAG = C. Bezold, *Babylonisch-assyrisches Glossar*, Heidelberg, 1926.
BeESACD = A. F. L. Beeston, *Epigraphic South Arabian Calendars and Dating*, London, 1956.
BeFSTI = A. F. L. Beeston, "Four Sabaean Texts in the Istanbul Archeological Museum", in *Le Muséon*, 65 (1952), pp. 271-83 and Plates I-III.
BeNL = A. F. L. Beeston, "Notes on Old South Arabian Lexicography", in *Le Muséon*, I in 63 (1950), pp. 53-57; II in *l.c.*, pp. 261-68; III in 64 (1951), pp. 127-32; IV in 65 (1952), pp. 139-47; V in 66 (1953), pp. 109-22; VI in 67 (1954), pp. 311-22.
BeOSA = A. F. L. Beeston, "Old South Arabian Antiquities", in *JRAS*, 1952, pp. 20-23 and Plates II-IV.
BePC = A. F. L. Beetson, "The Philby Collection of Old-South-Arabian Inscriptions", in *Le Muséon*, 51 (1938), pp. 311-33.
BePESA = A. F. L. Beeston, "Phonology of the Epigraphic South Arabian Unvoiced Sibilants", in *Transactions of the Philological Society*, 1951, pp. 1-26.
BePSC = A. F. L. Beeston, "Problems of Sabaean Chronology", in *BSOAS*, 16 (1954), pp. 37-56.
BeSI = A. F. L. Beeston, *Sabaean Inscriptions*, Oxford, 1937.
BeTMS = A. F. L. Beeston, "Two Middle Sabaean Votive Texts", in *BiO*, 16 (1959), p. 17.
BiSSS = M. Bittner, *Studien zur Šhauri-Sprache*, Vienna, I and II, 1916; III and IV, 1917.
BiVSS = M. Bittner, *Vorstudien zur Grammatik und zum Wörterbuche der Soqotri-Sprache*, Vienna, I 1913; II and III 1918.
BM = British Museum.
Bo = Botterweck.
BoAGI = G. J. Botterweck, "Altsüdarabische Glaser-Inschriften", in *Orientalia*, 19 (1950), pp. 435-44.
BoAlADSA = R. LeBaron Bowen, Jr., and F. P. Albright, *Archaeological Discoveries in South Arabia*, Baltimore, 1958.
BrDSL = J. Brun, *Dictionarium syriaco-latinum*, Beyrouth, 1911.
BrBeSIS = W. L. Brown and A. F. L. Beeston, "Sculptures and Inscriptions from Shabwa", in *JRAS*, 1954, pp. 43-62 and Plates XVIII-XXII.
vdBrDSAMW = A. van den Branden, "Les divinités sud-arabes *mnḏḥ* et *wrfw*", in *BiO*, 16 (1959). pp. 183-87.
vdBrHT = A. van den Branden, *Histoire de Thamoud*, Beyrouth, 1960.
vdBrIT = A. van den Branden, *Les inscriptions thamoudéennes*, Louvain, 1950.
vdBrTTPN = A. van den Branden, *Les textes thamoudéens de Philby*. Vol. II: *Inscriptions du Nord*, Louvain, 1956.
vdBrTTPS = A. van den Branden, *l.c.* Vol. I: *Inscriptions du Sud*, Louvain, 1956.
CaTh = Caton Thompson.
CIH = *Corpus Inscriptionum Semiticarum*. Pars Quarta: *Inscriptiones himyariticas et sabaeas continens*, 3 vol., Paris, 1889-1930; Plates: 3 vol., 1889-1932.
CIS = *L.c.* Pars Quinta: *Inscriptiones saracenicas continens*, Paris, 1950; Plates, 1951.
CoRoC = C. Conti Rossini, *Chrestomathia arabica meridionalis epigraphica edita et glossario instructa*, Rome, 1931.
DiLLA = A. Dillmann, *Lexicon linguae aethiopicae*.
DoSDA = R. Dozy, *Supplément aux dictionnaires arabes* (2 vol., 2nd ed.), Paris, 1927.
FaAJY = A. Fakhry, *An Archaeological Journey to Yemen (March-May*, 1947), Cairo, I, 1952; II=*RyET*; III, 1951.
FoSA = L. Forrer, *Südarabien nach al-Hamdānī*'s "*Beschreibung der arabischen Halbinsel*", Leipzig, 1942.
FrIAL = G. W. Freytag, *Lexicon arabico-latinum ex opere suo maiore in usum tironum excerptum*, 1837.
GeKH = R. Geyer, *Kitâb al-ḥamâsat*, Leiden, 1909.
GhNQI = M. A. Ghul, "New Qatabāni Inscriptions", in *BSOAS*, 22 (1959), pp. 1-22, Pl. I-IV and 419-38, Pl. I-III.
Gl = E. Glaser.
GlAAA = E. Glaser, *Die Abessinier in Arabien und Afrika*, Munich, 1895.
GlSGGA = E. Glaser, *Skizze der Geschichte und Geographie Arabiens*, II, Berlin, 1890.

GoAT = M. J. de Goeje, *Annales quos scripsit Abu Djafar Mohammed Ibn Djarir at-Tabari, Indices*, Leiden, 1901.
GoUM = C. H. Gordon, *Ugaritic Manual*, Vol. III, Rome, 1955.
GrGST = A. Grohmann, *Göttersymbole und Symboltiere auf südarabischen Denkmälern*, Vienna, 1914.
GrKFG = K. Grebenz, "Die Kleinen Fragmente aus Glasers Tagebuch XI (Mârib)", in *WZKM*, 42 (1935), pp. 67-92.
HaAF = M. Hartmann, *Die arabische Frage*, Leipzig, 1909.
HaAI = al-Hamdânî, *al-Iklīl*, edited...by N. A. Faris, Princeton, 1940.
HaLiSTI = G. L. Harding – E. Littmann, *Some Thamudic Inscriptions from the Hashemite Kingdom of Jordan*, Leiden, 1952.
Ḥaḍr = Ḥaḍrami.
HeBN = J. J. Hess, *Beduinennamen aus Zentral-arabien*, Heidelberg, 1922.
HoGSA = F. Hommel, "Geschichte Südarabiens im Umriss", in *Handbuch der altarabischen Altertumskunde*, Copenhagen, 1927, pp. 57-108.
HöASG = M. Höfner, *Altsüdarabische Grammatik*, Leipzig, 1943.
HöBAI = M. Höfner, "Die Beduinen in den vorislamischen arabischen Inschriften", in *L'antica società beduina*, Rome, 1959, pp. 53-68.
HöDSP = M. Höfner, "Drei sabäische Personenwidmungen", in *WZKM*, 51 (1948), pp. 38-42.
HöIAI = M. Höfner, "Zur Interpretation altsüdarabischer Inschriften II", in *WZKM*, 43 (1936), pp. 77-108.
HöIGT = M. Höfner, "Die Inschriften aus Glasers Tagebuch XI (Mārib)", in *WZKM*, 45 (1938), pp. 7-37.
HöKSI = M. Höfner, "Die ḳatabanischen und sabäischen Inschriften der südarabischen Expedition im Kunsthistorischen Museum in Wien (II)", in *WZKM*, 42 (1936), pp. 31-66.
HöSEG = M. Höfner, *Die Sammlung Eduard Glaser. Verzeichnis des Glaser-Nachlasses, sonstiger südarabischer Materialbestände und einer Sammlung anderer semitischer Inschriften*, Vienna, 1944.
HöSSE = M. Höfner, "Die sabäischen Inschriften der südarabischen Expedition im Kunsthistorischen Museum in Wien (I)", in *WZKM*, 40 (1933), pp. 1-36.
HöTPK = M. Höfner, "Taᵓlab als Patron der Kleinviehhirten. Die Inschriften Gl 1142, 11143", in *Serta Cantabrigiensia*, 1954, pp. 29-36.
HC = Hajar Koḥlân, Cemetery.
Ist = Istanbul.
Ja = A. Jamme.
JaAFEQ = A. Jamme, "Antiquités funéraires épigraphiques qatabanites", in *Cahiers de Byrsa*, 7 (1957), pp. 189-95 and four plates.
JaAGM = A. Jamme, "Aperçu général des inscriptions copiées à Mâreb (Yémen)", in *Académie Royale de Belgique. Bulletin de la Classe des Lettres et des Sciences Morales et Politiques*, 5e série, 38 (1952), pp. 289-306.
JaAIVC = A. Jamme, "An Archaic South-Arabian Inscription in Vertical Columns", in *BASOR*, No. 137, February, 1955, pp. 32-38.
JaAPCR = A. Jamme, *A propos d'une chronique récente*, Washington, 1959.
JaASAB = A. Jamme, "Les antiquités sud-arabes du Musée Borély à Marseille", in *Cahiers de Byrsa*, 8 (1958-1959), pp. 149-89 and 12 plates.
JaCD = A. Jamme, *Classification descriptive générale des inscriptions sud-arabes*, Tunis, 1948.
JaCRR = A. Jamme, *Le compte rendu de G. Ryckmans des* Annales d'Ethiopie, I, Washington, 1959.
JaDCR = A. Jamme, "On a Drastic Current Reduction of South-Arabian Chronology", in *BASOR*, No. 145, February, 1957, pp. 25-30.
JaDME = A. Jamme, *De la méthode en épigraphie*, Washington, 1955.
JaDN = A. Jamme, "Un désastre nabatéen devant Nagrân", in *Cahiers de Byrsa*, 6 (1956), pp. 165-71.
JaDSY = A. Jamme, *La dynastie de Šaraḥbiᵓil Yakûf et la documentation épigraphique sud-arabe*, Istanbul, 1961.
JaDT = M. Jastrow, *A Dictionary of the Targumim, the Talmud Babli and Yerushalmi, and the Midrashic Literature* (2 vol.), New York, 1950.
JaFSR = A. Jamme, *Le faux sabéen RÉS 4964*, Washington, 1956.
JaIAA = A. Jamme, "Inscriptions de al-ᶜAmâyid à Mâreb", in *Le Muséon*, 68 (1955), pp. 313-24 and Pl. II.
JaIAM = A. Jamme, "Inscriptions des alentours de Mâreb (Yémen)", in *Cahiers de Byrsa*, 5 (1955), pp. 265-81 and 2 plates.
JaIH = J.-A. Jaussen, "Inscriptions himyarites", in *RB*, 35 (1926), pp. 548-82 and Plates X-XIII.
JaIHB = A. Jamme, "Une inscription ḥaḍramoutique en bronze", in *Orientalia*, 22 (1953), pp. 158-65.
JaIHI = A. Jamme, "L'inscription ḥaḍramoutique Ingrams 1 et la chasse rituelle sub-arabe", in *Le Muséon*, 69 (1956), pp. 99-108.
JaIMS = A. Jamme, "Inscriptions du Musée de Ṣanᶜâᵓ d'après les photographies de M. C. Ansaldi", in *Le Muséon*, 67 (1954), pp. 323-38.
JaIMT = A. Jamme, "Les inscriptions minéennes TaAM 4 et 5", in *Cahiers de Byrsa*, 4 (1954), pp. 125-51.
JaIRHY = A. Jamme, "Inscriptions Related to the House Yafash in Timnaᶜ", in *BoAlADSA*, pp. 183-98.
JaIRM = A. Jamme, "Les inscriptions rupestres de la région de Mukérâs", in *Académie Royale de Belgique, Bulletin*..., 5e série, 37 (1951), pp. 307-20.
JaISAR = A. Jamme, "Inscriptions sud-arabes de la collection Ettore Rossi", in *RSO*, 30 (1955), pp. 103-30.
JaITDL = A. Jamme, "L'identification de Taᵓlab au dieu lunaire et les textes sabéens Gl 1142 et 1143", in *BiO*, 13 (1956), pp. 182-86.
JaJEQH = A. Jamme, "La jarre épigraphique qatabanite de Hağr bin Ḥumeid et son étude par Paulo Boneschi", in *RSO*, 34 (1959), pp. 127-36.
JaLSI = A. Jamme, "The Late Sabaean Inscription Ja 856", in *BiO*, 17 (1960), pp. 3-5 and Plate I.
JaMSSA = A. Jahn, *Die Mehri-Sprache in Südarabien*, Vienna, 1902.
JaNA = A. Jamme, "Notes additionnelles à l'inscription Jamme 402", in *Orientalia*, 23 (1954), p. 252.
JaP = A. Jamme, "Le panthéon sud-arabe préislamique d'après les sources épigraphiques", in *Le Muséon*, 60 (1947), pp. 57-147.

JaPDSM = A. Jamme, "Le pronom démonstratif sabéen *mhn* et les conjonctions composites *lqbl(y)/d̲(t)*, *kmhnmw* et *kmᶜnmw*", in *Cahiers de Byrsa*, 6 (1956), pp. 173-80.
JaPEHA = A. Jamme, *Pièces épigraphiques de Ḥeid bin ᶜAqîl, la nécropole de Timnaᶜ (Hagr Koḥlân)*, Louvain, 1952.
JaPEQL = A. Jamme, "Les pierres épigraphiques qatabanites Lyon 818 *bis* et *ter*", in *Cahiers de Byrsa*, 7 (1957), pp. 205-17 and 2 plates.
JaPSAP = A. Jamme, *La paléographie sud-arabe de J. Pirenne*, Washington, 1957.
JaQISA = A. Jamme, *Quatre inscriptions sud-arabes*, Washington, 1957.
JaRIH = A. Jamme, "Remarks on the South-Arabian Inscriptions Hamilton 3-13", in *JRAS*, 1956, pp. 146-56; illustrations in *l.c.*, 1958, pl. I.
JaRSAP = A. Jamme, "La religion sud-arabe pré-islamique", in *Histoire des religions* (Bloud et Gay), Paris, vol. 4 (1956), pp. 239-307.
JaSAA = A. Jamme, "South-Arabian Antiquities in the U.S.A.", in *BiO*, 12 (1955), pp. 152-54, and Plates II and III.
JaSAAA = A. Jamme, "The Syntax of South-Arabian Adjectives Again", in *JSS*, 4 (1959), pp. 264-67.
JaSAI = A. Jamme, "South-Arabian Inscriptions", in *Ancient Near Eastern Texts Relating to the Old Testament* (2nd ed.), Princeton, 1955, pp. 506-13.
JaSASA = A. Jamme, "Syntax of the Adjective in South Arabian", in *JSS*, 2 (1957), pp. 176-81.
JaSIBS = A. Jamme, "Sabaean Inscriptions on Two Bronze Statues from Mârib (Yemen)", in *JAOS*, 77, No. 1 (1957), pp. 32-36.
JaSQI = A. Jamme, "Some Qatabanian Inscriptions Dedicating 'Daughters of God'", in *BASOR*, No. 138, April, 1955, pp. 39-47.
JaSaMA = Jaussen et Savignac, *Mission archéologique en Arabie. II: El-ᶜEla, D'Hégra à Teima, Harrah de Tebouk*, Texte et Atlas, Paris, 1914.
JE = Journal d'entrée (Addis Ababa).
JeHoDISO = Ch.-F. Jean-J. Hoftijzer, *Dictionnaire des inscriptions sémitiques de l'Ouest*, (2 fasc.), Leiden, 1960.
JM = Jedda Museum.
KeHYNI = W. E. N. Kensdale, "Ḥaywᶜat̲tar Yadaᶜ and the Nāᶜiṭ Inscription", in *Le Muséon*, 66 (1953), pp. 371-72.
KoBaLVTL = L. Koehler et W. Baumgartner, *Lexicon in Veteris Testamenti Libros*, Leiden.
LaAEL = E. W. Lane, *Arabic-English Lexicon* (8 vol.).
LaGD = Landberg, *Glossaire dat̲înois* (3 vol.), Leiden, 1920, 1923, and 1942.
LaH = Landberg, *Ḥadramoût*, Leiden, 1901.
LeESAC = W. Leslau, *Ethiopic and South Arabic Contributions to the Hebrew Lexicon*, Los Angeles, 1958.
LeLS = W. Leslau, *Lexique soqoṭri (sudarabique moderne)*, Paris, 1938.
LiEHA = E. Littmann, "Eigennamen der heutigen Ägypter", in *Studi orientalistici in onore di Georgio Levi Della Vida*, Rome, 1956, vol. 2, pp. 81-93.
LiSI = E. Littmann, *Safaïtic Inscriptions*, Leiden, 1943.
LöHSM = O. Löfgren, *al-Hamdānī: Südarabisches Muštabih*, Uppsala, 1953.
LuYFS = A. G. Lundin, *Yadaᶜᵓil D̲ariḥ, fils de Sumhuᶜalay, mukarrib de Sabaᵓ*, Moscow, 1960.
M = Texts from Ḫôr Rôrî.
MaMB = Mârib, Maḥram Bilqîs.
MaN = Mârib, en-Nâṣerah.
MaPI = Mârib, Provenance Inconnue.
MaTSAI = D. S. Margoliouth, *Two South Arabian Inscriptions* [Reprint without date], London.
MaV = Mârib, Village.
Mars = Marseille.
MiScASIH = E. Mittwoch und H. Schlobies, "Altsüdarabische Inschriften im Hamburgischen Museum für Völkerkunde", in *Orientalia*, 5 (1936), pp. 1-34, 278-93, 349-57; 6 (1937), pp. 83-100, 222-33, 305-16; 7 (1938), pp. 95-99, 233-38 and 343-54.
Min = Minaean.
MlHLM = K. Mlaker, *Die Hierodulenlisten von Maᶜīn nebst Untersuchungen zur altsüdarabischen Rechtsgeschichte und Chronologie*, Leipzig, 1943.
MoHIA = [J. H. Mordtmann,] *Himjarische Inschriften und Alterthümer in den königlichen Museen zu Berlin*, Berlin, 1893.
MoMiASI = J. H. Mordtmann und E. Mittwoch, *Altsüdarabische Inschriften* [Reprint], Rome, 1933.
MoMiHI = J. H. Mordtmann und E. Mittwoch, *Himjarische Inschriften in den Staatlichen Museen zu Berlin*, Leipzig, 1932.
MoMiSI = J. H. Mordtmann und E. Mittwoch, *Sabäische Inschriften*, Hamburg, 1931.
MoNTA = Y. Moubarac, "Les noms, titres et attributs de Dieu dans le Coran et leurs correspondants en épigraphie sud-sémitique", in *Le Muséon*, 68 (1955), pp. 93-135 and 325-68.
MüHG = D. H. Müller, *al-Hamdânî's Geographie der arabischen Halbinsel*, Leiden. I [Arabic Text], 1884; II: *Noten und Indices*, 1891.
MüRhGRM = D. H. Müller und N. Rhodokanakis, *Eduard Glasers Reise nach Mârib*, Vienna, 1913.
NaNAG = Ḫ. Y. Nâmî, "Nuqûš ᶜarabîyat ǧunûbîyat", in *Maǧallat kullîyat al-ᵓadāb* (Cairo), 9 (1947), pp. 1-13, and Part 2, Fasc. 16 (1954), pp. 21-43.
NaNN = Ḫ. Y. Nâmî, *Našr nuqûš sâmîyat qadîmat min ǧanûb bilâd al-ᶜarab wašarḥuhâ*, Cairo, 1943.
Os = Osiander.
PaSmCSD = J. Payne Smith, *A Compendious Syriac Dictionary*, Oxford, 1903.
PhAHL = H. St. J. B. Philby, *Arabian Highlands*, Ithaca (N.Y.), 1952.
PhQS = W. Phillips, *Qataban and Sheba: Exploring the Ancient Kingdoms on the Biblical Spice Routes of Arabia*, New York, 1955.
PhSD = H. St. J. B. Philby, *Sheba's Daughters: Being a Record of Travel in Southern Arabia*, London, 1939.
PiIRC = J. Pirenne, "L'inscription 'Ryckmans 535' et la chronologie sud-arabe", in *Le Muséon*, 69 (1956), pp. 165-81.
PiPISA = J. Pirenne, *Paléographie des inscriptions sud-arabes. Contribution à la chronologie et à l'histoire de l'Arabie du Sud antique. I: Des origines jusqu'à l'époque himyarite*, Brussels, 1956.
Qat = Qatabanian.
RaWiVIS = C. Rathjens und H. von Wissmann, *Vorislamische Altertümer*, Hamburg, 1932.

RÉS = *Répertoire d'épigraphie sémitique*, Vol. 5-7, Paris, 1928-1950.
RhASI = N. Rhodokanakis, "Altsüdarabische Inschriften", in H. Gressmann, *Altorientalische Texte zum Alten Testament*, Berlin, 1926, pp. 463-71.
RhAST = N. Rhodokanakis, Altsabäische Texte, I, Vienna, 1927; II in *WZKM*, 39 (1932), pp. 173-226.
RhEA = N. Rhodokanakis, "Zur altsüdarabischen Epigraphik und Archäologie I", in *WZKM*, 38 (1931), pp. 167-82.
RhEASW = N. Rhodokanakis, "Eine altsüdarabische *Watf*-Inschrift", in *AAWW*, *Ph.-hist. Kl.*, 1-3 (1937), pp. 1-6.
RhGO = N. Rhodokanakis, *Der Grundsatz der Öffentlichkeit in den südarabischen Urkunden*, Vienna, 1915.
RhIAI = N. Rhodokanakis, "Zur Interpretation altsüdarabischer Inschriften I", in *WZKM*, 43 (1936), pp. 21-76.
RhIG = N. Rhodokanakis, "Die Inschriften Gl. 424 and 825", in *WZKM*, 47 (1940), pp. 50-60.
RhIGC = N. Rhodokanakis, "Die Inschrift Glaser 1076 a=CIH 308", in *AAWW*, *Ph.-hist. Kl.*, 11-22 (1938), pp. 69-75.
RhIMG = N. Rhodokanakis, "Die Inschriften Margoliouth I und Gl. 1548/49", in *l.c.*, 17-19 (1939), pp. 47-56.
RhKTB = N. Rhodokanakis, *Ḳatabanische Texte zur Bodenwirtschaft*, Vienna, I, 1919; II, 1922.
RhSLG = N. Rhodokanakis, *Studien zur Lexikographie und Grammatik des Altsüdarabischen*, Vienna, I, 1915; II, 1917; III, 1931.
RhVDD = N. Rhodokanakis, *Der vulgärarabische Dialekt im Ḍofâr* (*Ẓfâr*). II: *Einleitung, Glossar und Grammatik*, Vienna, 1911.
RoAS = E. Rossi, *L'arabo parlato a Ṣanᶜâʾ*, Rome, 1939.
RoVSAY = E. Rossi, "Vocaboli sud-arabici nelle odierne parlate arabe del Yemen", in *RSO*, 18 (1940), pp. 299-314.
Ry = G. Ryckmans.
RyCS = G. Ryckmans, "Chronologie sabéenne", in *CRAI*, 1943, pp. 236-46.
RyET = G. Ryckmans, *Epigraphical Texts* [in French; =*FaAJY*, II], Cairo, 1952.
RyGSAS = G. Ryckmans, "Graffites sabéens relevés en Arabie Saᶜudite", in *Scritti in onore di Giuseppe Furlani*, Rome, 1957, II, pp. 557-63.
RyHE = G. Ryckmans, "Heaven and Earth in the South Arabian Inscriptions", in *JSS*, 3 (1958), pp. 225-36.
RyISA = G. Ryckmans, "Inscriptions sud-arabes", in *Le Muséon*; I in 40 (1927), pp. 161-200; II in 45 (1932), pp. 285-313; III in 48 (1935), pp. 163-87; IV in 50 (1937), pp. 239-68; V in 52 (1939), pp. 51-112; VI in 52 (1939), pp. 297-319; VII in 55 (1942), pp. 125-30; VIII in 62 (1949), pp. 55-124; IX in 64 (1951), pp. 93-126; X in 66 (1953), pp. 267-317; XI in 67 (1954), pp. 99-119; XII in 68 (1955), pp. 297-312; XIII in 69 (1956), pp. 139-63; XIV in 69 (1956), pp. 369-89; XV in 70 (1957), pp. 97-117; XVI in 71 (1958), pp. 105-19; XVII in 72 (1959), pp. 159-76; XVIII in 73 (1960), pp. 5-25.
RyNP = G. Ryckmans, *Les noms propres sud-sémitiques* (3 vol.), Louvain, 1934-1935.
RycCSAPS = J. Ryckmans, "La chronologie sud-arabe du premier siècle avant notre ère", in *BiO*, 10 (1953), pp. 205-11.
RycIHS = J. Ryckmans, "Inscriptions historiques sabéennes de l'Arabie Centrale", in *Le Muséon*, 66 (1953), pp. 319-42.
RycIMAM = J. Ryckmans, *L'institution monarchique en Arabie Méridionale avant l'Islam* (*Maᶜîn et Saba*), Louvain, 1951.
RycPCH = J. Ryckmans, *La persécution des chrétiens himyarites au sixième siècle*, Istanbul, 1956.
RycPRSA = J. Ryckmans, "Petits royaumes sud-arabes d'après les auteurs classiques", in *Le Muséon*, 70 (1957), pp. 75-96.
RycSD = J. Ryckmans, "Le sens de *ḏʾl* en sud-arabe", in *Le Muséon*, 67 (1954), pp. 339-48.
RycYA = J. Ryckmans, "Yarîm ʾAymân II, roi de Saba?", in *Le Muséon*, 64 (1951), pp. 133-50.
SaIS = E. Sachau, *Ibn Saad*. IX: *Indices*. Part III: *Verzeichnis derjenigen Personen*, Leiden, 1940.
Sab = Sabaean.
Sem = Kunsthistorisches Museum in Vienna.
SlGaVNPA = M. G. de Slane and Ch. Gabeau, *Vocabulaire..des noms de personnes et de lieux...de l'Algérie*. I: *Noms de personnes*, Paris, 1868.
SoSoIGCM = J. M. Solá Solé, "La inscripción Gl. 389 y los comienzos del monoteísmo en Sudarabia", in *Le Muséon*, 72 (1959), pp. 197-206.
SpAGA = A. Sprenger, *Die alte Geographie Arabiens*, Berne, 1875.
StSESA = D. Stehle, "Sibilants and Emphatics in South Arabic", in *JAOS*, 60 (1940), pp. 507-43.
TaAM = M. Tawfiq, *Les monuments de Maᶜîn* (*Yemen*) [in Arabic], Cairo, 1951.
UlCSH = E. Ullendorff, "The Contribution of South Semitics to Hebrew Lexicography", in *Vetus Testamentum*, 6 (1956), pp. 190-98.
UlSLE = E. Ullendorff, "The Semitic Languages of Ethiopia and their Contribution to General Semitic Studies", in *Africa*, 1955, pp. 154-60.
VNIA = *Vocabulaire...des noms des indigènes... del'Algérie*, Alger, 1891
WB = Wâdî Beiḥân.
WeCGC = J. Werdecker, *A Contribution to the Geography and Cartography of North-West Yemen*, Cairo, 1939.
WiDME = H. von Wissmann, "De Mari Erythraeo", in *Die Lautensach-Festschrift. Stuttgarter geographische Studien*, Bd. 69 (1957), pp. 289-324.
WiGGF = H. von Wissmann, "Geographische Grundlagen und Frühzeit der Geschichte Südarabiens", in *Saeculum*, 4 (1953), pp. 61-114.
WiHöBGS = H. von Wissmann und M. Höfner, *Beiträge zur historischen Geographie des vorislamischen Südarabien*, Mainz, 1953.
WüID = F. Wüstenfeld, *Ibn Doreid's genealogisch-etymologisches Handbuch*, Göttingen, 1854.
WüR = F. Wüstenfeld, *Jacut's geographisches Wörterbuch*. VI: *Register*, Leipzig, 1870-71.

CONCORDANCES

I – Jamme 550-851, 853 A-F, 854-856 and 876-879

550=MaMB	3+4+5=CIH 375 =Fakhry 89, 92+91 +90, and 93
551	2 = CIH 374 = Fakhry (88)
551 bis=AM	207
552=MaMB	6
553	8
554	9
555	10
556	11
557	12
558	201
559	221
560	222
561	313
561 bis	204
562	279
563	269
564	314
565	266
566=MaPI	2
567=MaMB	291
568	295
569	188
570	227
571	189
572	85+Ja 573 and 593
573 (cf. 572)	133+134
574	153
575	224=Geukens 7
576	212=Geukens 3
577	219
578	263
579	281
580	184
581	254
582	163
583	167
584	246
585	137
586	262
587	149
588	152
589	179
590	181

591=MaMB	82+Ja 596
592	95
593 (cf. 572)	112
594	115
595	126
596 (cf. 591)	192
597	193
598	195
599	198
600	231
601	205
602	209=NaNAG 7
603	87
604	207
605	232
606	278
607	289
608	109
609	202
610	208
611	277+21=NaNAG 10
612	88
613	157
614	90
615	107
616	154+Ja 622
617	237
618	259
619	178
620	150
621	171
622 (cf. 616)	199
623	238
624	26
625	66
626	146
627	210=NaNAG 6
628	211
629	203
630	267
631	213
632	301
633	271
634	273
635	270
636	245

637=MaMB	60
638	128
639	117
640	250
641	206+Ja 779
642	260
643	275
643 bis	316
644	274
645	276=NaNAG 9
646	243
647	265
648	94
649	223
650	200
651	108
652	161
653	220
654	31
655	253
656	135
657	216
658	244+Ja 659
659 (cf. 658)	182
660	156
661	242
662	98+Ja 663
663 (cf. 662)	91+96
664	293
665	290
666	140
667	86+Ja 826
668	236
669	183
670	292
671	294
672	92
673	113
674	100
675	22
676	68
677	79
678	119
679	129
680	144
681	303

682=MaMB	315
683	47
684	48
685	57
686	63
687	64
688	69
689	89
690	97
691	99
692	110
693	111
694	114
695	116
696	218
697	130
698	131=Geukens 11
699	136
700	139+Ja 814
701 A, B	143
702	145
703	148
704	151
705	155
706	158
707	159
708	162
709	164
710	165
711	168
712	169
713	170
714	172
715	173
716	174
717	175+Ja 805
718	176+Ja 785
719	177
720	180
721	185
722	186
723	187
724	190
725	196
726	214
727	215
728	217
729	225
730	226
731	228
732	229
733	230
734	233
735	234+Ja 754
736	239
737	240
738	247
739	248
740	249
741	251
742	252
743	255

744=MaMB	257
745	261
746	264
747	268
748	272
749	280
750	282
751	283
752	284
753	285, 286, and 287
754 (cf. 735)	288
755	296
756	297
757	298
757 bis	299
758	300
759	305
760	310
761	311
762	20
763	27
764	28
765	29
766	30
767	32
768	33
769	34
770	35
771	36
772	37
773	38
774	39
775	40
776	41
777	43
778	45
779 (cf. 641)	49
780	50
781	51
782	52
783	53
784	55
785 (cf. 718)	56
786	58
787	61
788	62
789	65
790	71
791	72
792	73
793	75
794 (cf. 810)	76
795	77
796	80
797	81
798	84
799	93+Ja 806
800	101
801	102
802	103
803	104
804	118

805 (cf. 717) =MaMB	120
806 (cf. 799)	121
807	122
808 (cf. 816)	123
809	124+105+67
810	125+Ja 794
811	127
812	132
813	141
814 (cf. 700)	142
815	166
816	191+Ja 808
817	194
818	197
819	235+Ja 827
820	241
821	256
822	258
823	308
824	309
825	312
826 (cf. 667)	15
827 (cf. 819)	17
828	18
829	54
830	83
831	147
832	302
833	42
834	44
835	74
836	78
837	106
838	304
839	1
840	7
841	13
842	14
843	16
844	19
845	23
846	24=RÉS 3955
847	25
848	46
849	59
850	70
851	317

Second Part

853 A=MaN	2
853 B	3
853 C	4
853 D	5
853 E	20
853 F=MaV	12+7
854=MaN	1
855=MaV	39=Fakhry 67
877=AM	205

II – Other Collections and Ja

878	= AM 200
879	= KM my No. 122
AM 200	= Ja 878
205	877
207	551 bis

CIH 374	= Ja 551
375	550
Fakhry 67	855
(88)	551
89, 92+91+90, 93	550

Geukens 3	= Ja 576
7	575
11	698
KM my No. 122	879

MaMB

1	= Ja 839
2	551
3, 4, 5	550
6	552
7	840
8	553
9	554
10	555
11	556
12	557
13	841
14	842
15	826 (cf. 667)
16	843
17	827
18	828
19	844
20	762
21	cf. 611
22	675
23	845
24	846
25	847
26	624
27	763
28	764
29	765
30	766
31	654
32	767
33	768
34	769
35	770
36	771
37	772
38	773
39	774
40	775
41	776
42	833
43	777
44	834
45	778
46	848
47	683
48	684
49	779 (cf. 641)
50	780
51	781
52	782
53	783
54	= Ja 829
55	784
56	785 (cf. 718)
57	685
58	786
59	849
60	637
61	787
62	788
63	686
64	687
65	789
66	625
67	cf. 809
68	676
69	688
70	850
71	790
72	791
73	792
74	835
75	793
76	794 (cf. 810)
77	795
78	836
79	677
80	796
81	797
82	591
83	830
84	798
85	cf. 572
86	667
87	603
88	612
89	689
90	614
91	cf. 663 (cf. 662)
92	672
93	799
94	648
95	592
96	cf. 663 (cf. 662)
97	690
98	662
99	691
100	674
101	800
102	801
103	802
104	803
105	cf. 809
106	837
107	= Ja 615
108	651
109	608
110	692
111	693
112	593 (cf. 572)
113	673
114	694
115	594
116	695
117	639
118	804
119	678
120	805 (cf. 717)
121	806 (cf. 799)
122	807
123	808 (cf. 816)
124	cf. 809
125	810
126	595
127	811
128	638
129	679
130	697
131	698
132	812
133, 134	573 (cf. 572)
135	656
136	699
137	585
138	(cf. 161)
139	700
140	666
141	813
142	814 (cf. 700)
143	701 A, B
144	680
145	702
146	626
147	831
148	703
149	587
150	620
151	704
152	588
153	574
154	616
155	705
156	660
157	613
158	706
159	707

160=Ja	(cf. 136)
161	652
162	708
163	582
164	709
165	710
166	815
167	583
168	711
169	712
170	713
171	621
172	714
173	715
174	716
175	717
176	718
177	719
178	619
179	589
180	720
181	590
182	659 (cf. 658)
183	669
184	580
185	721
186	722
187	723
188	569
189	571
190	724
191	816
192	596 (cf. 591)
193	597
194	817
195	598
196	725
197	818
198	599
199	622 (cf. 616)
200	650
201	558
202	609
203	629
204	561 bis
205	601
206	641
207	604
208	610
209	602
210	627
211	628
212	576
213	631
214	726
215	727
216	657

217=Ja	728
218	696
219	577
220	653
221	559
222	560
223	649
224	575
225	729
226	730
227	570
228	731
229	732
230	733
231	600
232	605
233	734
234	735
235	cf. 819
236	668
237	617
238	623
239	736
240	737
241	820
242	661
243	646
244	658
245	636
246	584
247	738
248	739
249	740
250	640
251	741
252	742
253	655
254	581
255	743
256	821
257	744
258	822
259	618
260	642
261	745
262	586
263	578
264	746
265	647
266	565
267	630
268	747
269	563
270	635
271	633
272	748
273	634

274=Ja		644
275		643
276		645
277		cf. 611
278		606
279		562
280		749
281		579
282		750
283		751
284		752
285, 286, 287		753
288		754 (cf. 735)
289		607
290		665
291		567
292		670
293		694
294		671
295		568
296		755
297		756
298		757
299		757 bis
300		758
301		632
302		832
303		681
304		838
305		759
308		823
309		824
310		760
311		761
312		825
313		561
314		564
315		682
316		643 bis
317		851
MaN	1 = Ja	854
	2	853 A
	3	853 B
	4	853 C
	5	853 D
	20	853 E
MaPI	2	566
MaV	12+7	853 F
	39	855
NaNAG	6	627
	7	602
	9	645
	10	611
RÉS	3955	846

PROPER NAMES AND EPITHETS

Preliminary Note: 1 – The spurious Ja 880 is not listed in the following series of names. 2 – Regular use is made of the ditto mark; in secondary entries it represents the primary entry, otherwise the nearest preceding entry.

A – DEITIES

Preliminary Note: Unless the contrary is pointed out, the preposition *b* in the present list introduces a final invocation.

ʾ

ʾlw: *''zʿln*, cf. *ʿṯtr*.

ʾlmw: *b''/bʿlʾwm:* 699/9.

ʾlmq: 713/8; *''/bʿlʾwm:* 708/4-5; *''ṯhwnbʿlʾwm:* (828/3-4); *b''bʿlʾwm:* 717/12.

ʾlmqh: 550/1,2; 551; 552/2,4; 553/2; 554; 555/1,3,4; 556; 557; 558/4-5,5,6,7; 559/4,11,13,16; 560/5,16,17,20; 561/4,11,13,16; 561 bis/6,15,17,23,24; 563/5,7,14,17; 564/(4),15,18,19; 565/7-8,16; 567/10,12,22; 568/4,10-11,14, 18,20,22-23; 570/[7],10,15; 576/2,3,5,6,14; 577/5,6,7,8,18; 581/12-13,13-14,17-18; 583/8; 584/4; 585/18; 586/(9-10),11, 17,21; 588/10; 590/14,18,22; 592/7,8-9; 597/4; [598/5]; 599/8; 601/4,13,15,17,19; 602/4,12-13,15,17,19; 603/7,11,12; 604/3,6; 610/5,7-8; 617/5,13; 618/5,12,15,18,21,25,29,30-31; 619/6,10,14,19; 620/7,11,13; (625/2); 626/5,5-6,7,12,14,20; 629/13,21,22,31-32,37,41,43; 630/4,16,18,21; 632/8; 633/10, 12-13,17,20; 635/14, 16-17, 29,39,44; 636/8-9,17; 640/6,7, (9); 641/8; (643/3); 644/3,28; 645/26; 646/8-9; 648/6; 651/39,41-42,44,46-47,50; 652/12-13,18-19,20-21; 653/7,11; 655/8,10-11; 657/7-8; 658/16; 662/14; 664/9; 665/48; 666/6,7; 667 A/10; 668/6,11-12; 672/1,[2]; 683/6-7; 685/4; 686/7; 688/2; 689/5; 690/5-6; 692/4; 702/7,17; 703/2,5,6; 704/5,7,8; 705/4-5,6,8; 706/5; 711/10-11; 712/11; 713/5; 716/10,(13); 718/[5-6],(6),8; 719/6,8,(10),[12],13,15; 721/(7),9; 722/a; 725/6,6-7; 728/5-6,8; 732/(4-5),6,(7-8),9; 734/6,8; 735/8,9,10; 738/6; 739/12,15; 740 A/4-5,11; 741/9; 743/7; 747/4,6,7,[9],[11],(14-15),17; 750/8,(10-11),13,15; 751/5; 756/9; 757/5; 758/7; 761/3,4; (763/4); 764/[2],4; 766/7; (767/5); 782/2; (787/2); (807/3-4); 810 A/3,B; 816/3,(8-9); 818/5; 821 A/5; [828/5]; 831/1,2,3; 832; (835); 839/2; 840/6-7; 841/2; 844/6; (845); 853 A/6,B/6, C/6,D/5,E/6,F/6; 877/10;
b'' [adversative]: 720/15;
b'': 553/3; 556; 584/12; 599/10; 634/11; (640/10); 641/16; 665/49; 669/29; 704/9; [710/4]; 731/7; 732/11; 738/11-12; 743/8; 755/7; (816/11); 823 A; (828/8); 832;
l'': 570/8,9; (750/6-7).

ʾlmqh[]bʿlʾwm: 812/5-6; (813/3); (817/1-2).

ʾlmqhbʿlʾwm: 567/9; 569/4; (570/2); 572/7,11; 579/8-9; 580/(9-10),12; 583/5,(10-11); 585/16; 588/2,3-4; 589/13-14; 590/7,11; 599/9; 619/4; 621/3; 646/4; 647/(7,9,12),24,30-31; 651/36; 652/7,15-16; 653/4-5; 657/5,8-9; 665/4-5,6,47; 666/4; 669/5; 670/6,13; 686/3; (687/6-7); 700/3,5,16; 701 A/2-3; 711/6-7,12; (732/2); 735/2,16,17; 739/4,5-6; (766/3-4); (783/2-3); (815/2);
b'': 570/16; (583/15); 588/12-13; 591/11-12; 592/10; 661/9; 670/30-31; 685/5-6; [686/9]; 692/12; 698/10-11; 701 A/8; 709/6-7; 711/13; (713/16-17); (719/17); 735/19; (739/20); (815/9).

ʾlmqh/bʿlʾwm: (566/11); 584/2,7-8; (588/5-6); 618/32; 641/9-10; 685/2; 721/3; (723/3-4); 750/3;
b'': 566/12-13; 582/10; 619/21; 632/9; 633/21; 635/46; (638/5); 648/10-11; 720/18-19; (750/17); 756/10-11; (840/10).

ʾlmqh/bʿl/ʾwm: 558/2; 559/3,7,20; 561/3,7,20; 564/22,24-25, 32; 566/4; 568/(3-4),8-9,(27); 601/21; 602/21; 618/7-8; 626/24; 629/16-17,19,34-35; 630/6-7,9-10; 644/1-2,7,(11-12), 14,25-26,30; 645/7-8,11,15-16,19-20,22-23; 648/2-3; 683/2-3; 689/2; 692/2-3; 694/3-4; 705/2-3; 726/2-3; (731/3-4); 743/2-3; (744/2-3); 757/1; (765/4-5); (784/2); (803/4-5); (810 A/1);
b'': 702/19-21; 741/10-11; 839/5.

ʾlmqh/bʿl/ʾwm/wḥrwnm: *b'':* 629/45-46.

ʾlmqh/bʿl/ḥrn: (679/2-3).

ʾlmqhbʿlmsktwyṯwbrʾn: 877/11-12.

ʾlmqh/bʿl/mskt/wyṯw/brʾn: 564/29.

ʾlmqh/bʿl/mtbʿm/wrwẓn: 629/46.

ʾlmqh/bʿl/šwḥṭ: 618/33.

ʾlmqh/ḏgblm: 560/21.

ʾlmqhṯhwn: (599/5); 716/7; *b'':* 707/9.

ʾlmqh/ṯhwn: 635/42; *b'':* 747/19-20.

ʾlmqhṯhwnbʿlʾwm: 567/4,5,13-14,15; 571/1-2; (572/3-4); 574/2,12; [576/1]; 577/3,15,(16),17,19; 578/4,15-16,30, 33,35,40,43; 579/4,11-12; 580/3-4; 581/3-4,8-9; 585/2,9, 11-12,19-20; 586/2; 587/2,6,11-12; 589/5; 590/2-3; 591/4-5, (5-6); (592/1-2); 600/[1-2],9; 608/4-5,9; 609/4,9; 610/(3-4), 9-10; 611/4-5,10,16; 612/6,6-7,10-11, 12-13,15; 613/5-6,

11-12,17; 614/5,7,10,13-14,17-18; 615/8,15,22-23; 616/6,13, 28,31-32,34-35,38; 617/4,6,10; (618/3-4); 620/3; 623/[c, 1-2],9,14,18-19,21; (624/4); 647/19; 649/5-6,22; 650/4,6-7, 9-10,11-12,17; 651/7-8,23; 653/(1-2), 14-15,18; 655/3-4; 657/2-3; 658/(4),23-24,28; 660/6; 661/(4),5-6,8; 662/4-5,19; 667 A/3-4; 684/4-5; (687/2-3); 706/2-3; 709/2-3; (710/2-3); 711/2-3; 715/3-4; 716/3-4,9; (717/2-3); (718/4); (719/3-4); 730/4; 738/4; 741/4; 745/3-4; 751/2-3,9-10; 755/3-4; 756/4; 758/4,10-11,14; (761/1-2); (782/1); [788/3]; (790/2); (803/2-3); 840/3-4;

b'': 567/28; 572/16; 574/13; 581/19; 587/13; 590/25; (598/6); 608/14; 609/14; 610/18; 611/21-22; 612/20; 613/22; 614/20; 615/28-29; 616/40; 617/15; 623/24-25; 647/34-35; 650/35; 651/55-56; 653/21; 655/18-19; 658/34; 662/22-23; 668/19-20; 684/13; (687/12-13); 693/14; 715/11-12; 730/11; 740/14; 751/12-13; 758/20-21; 799/7; [803/7]; (804/4).

ʾlmqhṯhwn/bʿlʾwm: 693/(4),8,10-11; 707/5.

ʾlmqh/ṯhwnbʿlʾwm: 582/5; 698/4-5; (747/2-3).

ʾlmqh/ṯhwn/bʿlʾwm: 565/3-4; 632/2; (633/2-3); 637/2-3; (647/4-5); 690/3-4,7-8; (722/4); 723/2;

b'': 722/d-e.

ʾlmqh/ṯhwn/bʿl/ʾwm: (560/3-4); 561 bis/4-5; 563/(3-4), 11-12; (564/2-3); 603/3-4; 604/1; 626/3-4; 629/2; 630/2; 635/2-3; 641/3; 643/2; (645/2-3); 703/3,11,12; 722/b-c; [740 A/3]; (761/1-2); (765/1-2); (780/2-3); 844/2-3; (851/1-2,2-3);

ʾb'': 597/8; 703/12.

ʾlmqhṯhwnbʿlʾwmwḥrwnm: *b'':* 657/14-15.

lmqhṯhwnbʿlʾwm/wḥrwnm: (742/3-6).

ʾlmqhṯhwnbʿlmsktwyṯwbrʾn: 877/4-5; *b''*: (877/17-18).

ʾlmqh/ṯhwn/wṯwr/bʿlm/bʿly/ʾwm/wḥrwnm: 563/19-20; 564/28-29;

b'': 820/3-4.

ʾlmqhṯwnbʿlʾwm: *b'':* 664/18-19.

ʾlmqhw: 558/4; 562/15,(17-18); (605/11,12-13); 606/5,6,14, 20; 607/5,6,13,19; 627/3,6-7,9,12,14-15,19,21,24,27; 628/4, (9),13,16,20,22,23,26; 632/7; 634/5-6; 642/7,(10),12,14,15; 643 bis/5,8,10; 646/10-11; 654/6,7; 656/13,19; 667 A/14; 669/9-10,17; 670/15; 683/5; 699/6; 712/4,6,9; 713/13; 715/7; 733/7-8,10-11,12; 734/3; 735/11; 736/8; 737/5; (746/6, 7-8); 752/14; 753 I/2,3,4,(5),7,II/1,3,5,8,14,III/1,3,5,8,14; 757/4; 818/3;

b'': 667 A/18.

ʾlmqhwbʿlʾwm: 656/5,17,23,26; (746/3,14-15); (789/1-2);

b'': 654/16; 656/27; 706/11; 733/14; (746/16).

ʾlmqhw/bʿlʾwm: 727/6-7; 752/6-7.

ʾlmqhw/bʿl/ʾwm: 562/3,9,12,20-21; 606/24; (607/24); 627/30; 628/7,30; 629/24-25; (642/3-4); 643 bis/4,5,7,(10); 654/4; (691/3-4); 720/3-4,6-7; 729/5-6,13-14; 753 I/9, II/19, (III/19); 757 bis/4-5; (818/1-2);

b'': 691/13; 736/18.

ʾlmqhw/bʿl/šwḥṭ: *b'':* 627/28-29; 628/28.

ʾlmqhwṯhwnbʿlʾwm: 631/17; 650/27-28; (664/3); (695/4,9);

b'': 571/8; 631/42; 636/18-19; 666/16-17.

ʾlmqhwṯhwnṯwrbʿlmbʿlʾwm: 733/3-4.

ʾlmqhwṯhwn/bʿlʾwm: *b'':* 594/12-13.

ʾlmqhwṯhwn/bʿl/ʾwm: (594/6-7); 631/39-40; 671/14-15,18-19; (691/6-7).

ʾlmqhw/ṯhwnbʿlʾwm: 631/2; *l'':* 650/5.

ʾlmqhw/ṯhwn/bʿlʾwm: 631/36; *b'':* 690/12-13.

ʾlmqhw/ṯhwn/bʿl/ʾwm: 601/2-3; 602/3; 605/3; (606/3-4); 607/3-4; 627/2-3; 628/3; 634/2-3; 671/6; (699/2-3); 704/2-3; 728/2-3; 740 A/8; (753 I/1-2); (797 A/1-2).

ʾlmqhw/ṯwn/bʿl/ʾwm: 736/4-5.

ʾlmqw: 733/9.

b

bʿl: ''/*ʾwm:* (566/7-8); (772/2);

''/*ḥrnm:* 584/9.

bʿlm, cf. *ṯwr*.

ḏ

ḏ: ''*lf/ḏmr:* 584/3.

ḏtbʿdn: 552/4; 555/4; 831/3;

b'': 557.

ḏt/bʿdn(m): 550/2; 559/17; 561/17; 683/8-9; 753 I/8; (821 A/5-6);

b'': 551; 558/6; 560/20-21; 562/18; 563/21; 564/30; 565/16-17; 568/23; (577/19); 601/20; 602/20; 604/6; 606/20-21; 607/20: 618/34; 626/21; 627/27; 628/27; 629/46; 630/22; (644/28-29); 645/27; (734/8); 737/6; 753 II/15, (III/15); 761/4.

ḏtḥmym: 552/4; 555/4; 689/5; 831/3;

b'': 557.

ḏt/ḥmym: 550/2; 559/17; 561/16; (683/7-8); 722/e; 753 I/7-8; 821 A/5; (879/6-7);

b'': 551; 558/6; 560/20; (562/18); 563/20-21; 564/29-30; 565/16; 568/23; 577/19; 601/19-20; 602/19-20; 604/6; 606/20; 607/19-20; 618/33-34; (626/20-21); 627/27; 628/27; 629/46-47; (630/21); 644/28; 645/26-27; 728/8; 734/8; 737/6; 753 II/14-15, (III/14-15); 761/4; 820/4;

brbʿhmw/''/ʿṯtrygr: 618/35-36.

ḏt/ẓhrn, cf. *ʿṯtr*.

ḏt/ġdrn: 550/1,2;

b'': [855/4];

''/*bʿlt/sfly:* (855/2-3).

h

hbs: 560/20; 561/16; 562/17; 563/19; 564/28; 565/15-16; 568/22; 606/19-20; 645/26; 753 I/7; 761/4; 821 A/5; (823 A).

hwbs: 550/2; 551; 556; 558/6; 559/16; 577/19; 601/19; 602/19; 604/6; 607/19; 626/20; 627/26-27; 628/26; 629/45; 630/21; 643 bis/9-10; 644/28; [672/2]; 683/6; (734/7-8); 737/5; 753 II/14,III/14.

w

wdm: ''/*bʾlsmʿnwšʿbm:* 655/20.

z

zʿln, cf. *ʾlw*.

ḥ

ḥgrm: *''/qḥmm:* (598/7); 644/29; 747/20; (777/3); *''/qḥmm/bᶜl ᶜrnhn/tnᶜ/wlms:* 626/22-23; *''/qḥmm/bᶜl/ᶜrnhn/tnᶜ/wlms/wbytn/ᵓḥrm:* 564/30-31.

y

ygr, cf. *ᶜṯtr.*

ysrn: *mdḥhmw/'':* 664/20.

l

lmqh: *b''/ṯhwn/bᶜlᵓwm:* 579/13.

m

mdḥ: *''hmw*, cf. *ysrn.*

s

sḥr: 550/1; 664/19-20.

ᶜ

ᶜzzm, cf. *ᶜṯtr.*
ᶜzzn, cf. *ᶜṯtr.*
ᶜm: *wld'':* 576/16; 577/2; 578/7,18; 589/10.
ᶜṯtr: *b'':* 550/2; 551; 552/3; 555/4; 557; 558/5-6; 560/20; 561 bis/24; 562/17; 563/18; 565/15; 568/22; 577/19; 578/43; 601/19; 602/19; 603/12; 604/5; 606/19; 607/18-19; 618/32; 626/20; 627/26; 628/26; 629/45; 630/20; 643 bis/9; 644/28; 645/26; 664/19; (672/2); 683/5-6; 689/5; 705/7; 728/7; (734/7); 737/5; 753 I/7,II/13-14,(III/13-14); 757/5; 761/3; (821 A/4-5); 831/3; 844/6; 853 (A/6),B/6,C/6), D/5,E/6,F/6; (855/4);
''/ḏdbn: 559/16; 561/15-16;
''/ḏdbn/bᶜl/bḥr/ḥṭbm: *b'':* 564/27;
''ygr, cf. *ḏt/ḥmym;*
ᶜṯ[t]rwᵓlwzᶜlnbᶜlyᶜrnbyfᶜ: 578/43-44;
''(/)ᶜzzm/wḏt/ẓhrn/bᶜly/ᶜrn/knn: 559/18-19; 561/18-19; 568/24-26; 606/21-23; (607/21-22); 753 I/8-9,II/16-18,(III/16-18);
''ᶜzzn: 631/20; *''/wḏt/ẓhrn/bᶜly/ᶜrn/knn:* (643 bis/10);
''šrqn: 564/32; (568/26-27); 626/24; 627/30; 628/30;
''/šrqn: 559/20; 561/20; 562/20; 606/23-24; (607/23-24); 643 bis/10; 753 (I/9),II/18-19,(III/18-19); *b'':* 559/15-16; 561/15.

q

qḥmm, cf. *ḥgrm.*

r

rbᶜ: *''hmw*, cf. *ḏt/ḥmym.*

š

šhr: *b'':* (682/2).
šms: *''/mlkn/tnf:* 560/21; 561/17; 753 I/8,II/15-16,(III/15-16); *b'':* 559/17-18; 562/18-19; 563/21; 565/17; 568/24; 604/6; 626/21-22; 627/28; 628/27-28; 629/47; 630/22; 644/29; 645/27; 761/4.
''hw: *''/bᶜlt/ġḏrn:* 853 A/2,B/2,C/2,D/1-2,E/2,F/2;
''hmw: *''/bᶜlt/ṣyḥyn:* 629/47;
b''/bᶜlt/qyf/ršm: 627/29; 628/28-29;
''/tnf/bᶜlt/ġḏrn: 854/4; *b'':* 853 A/6,B/6,C/6,D/5,E/6,F/6;
''yhmw: *''/bᶜlty/ᵓwṯnn:* 664/20-21;
b''/bᶜlty/nhd[]ᵓm: 564/31-32;
b'' bᶜlty/qyf/ršm: 618/34-35.
šrqn, cf. *ᶜṯtr.*

t

tᵓlb: *''/rymm:* 561 bis/24; (598/6-7); 601/20; 602/20; *''/rymm/bᶜl/šṣrm:* 562/19-20.

tnf, cf. *šms.*

ṯ

ṯhwn, cf. *ᵓlmq, ᵓlmqh, ᵓlmqhw, lmqh.*
ṯwn, cf. *ᵓlmqh, ᵓlmqhw.*

ṯwr: *''bᶜlm:* 722/e; cf. also *ᵓlmqh, ᵓlmqhw.*

B – PERSONS

ʾ

whbʿṯt: 701 A/7.
whbšms: (687/5, 10-11?).
whbšmsm: (687/1,10-11?).
whbṯwn: 726/4.
wzʿn: 632/1.
wfdm: 712/(1),6,10,12; 719/(1),[5].
wfym: "/*ʾḥbr:* 649/1;
"/*ʾẓrf:* 656/3.

wśl: 711/1.
wtr, cf. *ykrbmlk*, *yṯʿʾmr*, *krbʾl*.
wtrm: "/*yhʾmn/mlk/sbʾ/wḏrydn:* 601/12,14-15; 602/11-12,14-15;
"/*yhʾmn/mlk/sbʾ/wḏrydn/bn/ʾlšrḥ/yḥḍb/mlk/sbʾ/wḏrydn:* 601/6-7; 602/6-7; 603/8-11; 604/4-5; (605/8-10) [note that *yḥḍb* is missing in 605/10]; 606/8-10; 607/8-10;
"/*mlk/sbʾ/wḏrydn:* 606/15-16; 607/14-15.

z

zydm: 683/4-5; 742/11;
" *ʾwlt:* 669/1-2;
"/*ʾymn:* 708/3; 713/4.

zydqwmm: "/*ydrʾ:* 656/1.
]*.zr:* "/*f*[: 821 B.

ḥ

]*ḥ*, cf. *ʾsdm*.
ḥbybm: 715/[1],8.
ḥwlm: 649/2.
ḥyw[*:* 773/1-2.
ḥywʾwm: (569/2-3).
ḥywm: 556; 614/1,8,11; 618/(1-2),13,20,25; 645/14; 700/1; 846/1.
ḥywʿṯtr: 569/3; 654/1; 738/2;
"/*ydʿ*, cf. *šʿrm*.

ḥywt [woman]*:* 764/3.
ḥmlt [woman]*:* 686/1.
ḥmʿṯt: 555/2; 831/1-2; (845/1-2);
"/*ʾzʾd:* 616/2,(7-8); (718/1-2); (788/1-2);
"/*ʾrśl:* 632/1.
ḥqbḥmd [woman]*:* 690/6-7.
ḥrbm: 642/(4-5),5; "/*ynhb:* (642/1).
ḥrṯn: 660/11,15.

ẖ

ẖ[, cf. *gdšfq*.
ẖdqm: 706/2.
ẖḏwm: 757 bis/1-2.
ẖyrhmw: 555/2.

ẖlḥlk: 655/7.
ẖnʿm: 723/1.
]*ẖr*, cf. *rbbm*.

ẓ

ẓbym: 586/19,23; "/*yrẓḥ:* 586/[1],11;
ḏ": 586/24.

ẓbnm: "/*ʾṯqf:* 637/1.

y

y[, cf. *mrṯdm*.
y.[, cf. *whbʾl*, *rzn*.
yʾḏf, cf. *whbʾwm*.
yʾzl, cf. *nšʾkrb*, *frʿm*;
"/*byn*, cf. *ʾlšrḥ*, *nšʾkrb;*
"/*byn/mlk/sbʾ/wḏrydn:* 575/8.
yʾzm, cf. *dwmn*.
yʾmn, cf. *mlkkrb*, *nšʾkrb*.
ybdr, cf. *knnt*.
ygʿr, cf. *ʾlrm*.
ydm: 704/1; 767/3;
"/*ydrm*: 616/1; (718/1); [788/1].
ydʿʾl: 552/4; 555/1; 558/6; 643/7; 831/1,3; 832;
"/*byn:* 550/1,2; 552/1; 557;
"/*mlk/ḥḍrmwt:* 629/10-11,14-15; (643/5-6); 643 bis/2,3.
ydrʾ, cf. *zydqwmm*.
ydrm, cf. *ydm*.
yhʾmn, cf. *ʾnmrm*, *wtrm*, *mlkkrb*, *nšʾkrb*.
yhbr, cf. *ḏmrʿly*.
yhḥmd, cf. *mrṯdm*, *smhyfʿ*.
yhnʿm, cf. *ysrm*, *krbʾl*, *ṯʾrn*.
yhnf, cf. *lʿzzm*.
yhʿn: 563/16; (732/10-11); 734/3;
"/*ʾẖtr:* 589/1;

"/[]*m:* 563/1-2.
yhṣbḥ, cf. *sḥmn*.
yhṣdq, cf. *lʿzzm*.
yhqm: 644/6,(12-13),16,27;
"/*bn/ḏmrʿly/ḏrḥ/mlk/sbʾ/wḏrydn:* 644/3-4.
yhrḥb, cf. *brg*, *nšʾkrb*.
yhrm: 842/1.
yhrʿš, cf. *šmr*.
yhšʿ, cf. *hwfʿṯt*.
yhtf, cf. *rṯdšmsm*.
yzʾn, cf. *hwfʿṯt*, *yḥmd*, *sẖymm*.
yzd: 620/1,8; cf. also *ʾḥmd*, *ʾsʿd*, *rbšmsm*.
yzkn, cf. *hwfʿṯt*.
yḥz, cf. *whbʾl*.
yḥm[, cf. *yfʿ*.
yḥmʾl: 707/2.
ḥmd: 656/3-4; 669/18; 690/1,8-9; 738/1;
"/*ʾḥšd:* 713/2;
"/*yzʾn:* 623/[a],(3),10-11.
yḥḍb, cf. *ʾlšrḥ*.
yẓfr, cf. *rbtnf*.
ykrbmlk: 555/1;
"/*ḏrḥ:* 557;
"/*wtr:* 550/1,2; 555/1,4; 824.

]ym, cf. *rbbʾl*.
ynhb, cf. *ʾlʾmr, ḥrbm, frʿm*.
ynʿm: 684/1,7,11; *lʾʾ:* (626/17);
 ''/ʾḏrḥ: 626/1.
ynf, cf. *smhʿly*.
ynfṯ, cf. *krbʿṯt*.
yskr, cf. *sʿdm*.
ysrm: 665/12;
 ''/yhnʿm, cf. *šmr*;
 ''/yhnʿm/wšmr/yhrʿš/ʾmlk/sbʾ/wḏrydn: 648/7-9;
 ''/yhnʿm/wšmr/yhrʿš/mlky/sbʾ/wḏrydn; 646/2-4; 647/20-21;
 ''/yhnʿm/wbnhw/šmr/yhrʿš/mlky/sbʾ/wḏrydn: (647/2-4);
 ''/yhnʿm/wṯʾrn/ʾyfʿ/ʾmlk sbʾ/wḏrydn/wḥḏrmt/wymnt: 664/12-15;
 ''/yhnʿm/wbnyhw/ḏrʾʾmr/ʾymn/mlky/sbʾ/wḏrydn/wḥḏrmwt/wymnt: 665/7-9;
 ''/wbnyhw/ḏrʾʾmr/mlky/sbʾ/wḏrydn wḥḏrmt/wymnt: 665/9-11.
yʿd, cf. *]rm*.
yʿkrn: ''/mlk/ḥḏrmwt: 643/11.
yʿmr: 660/14; *''/ʾšwʿ:* 662/[1],7,15.
yʿf, cf. *ʾsdm*.
yʿrr, cf. *rbšmsm*.
yġnm, cf. *ʾḥmd, ʿwfm*.
yfʿ: 746/1,[16].
]yfʿ: ''/yḥm[: 801.
yfrʿ: 712/3.
yṣbḥ: 585/8-9; *''/ʾšwʿ:* 585/1,3,18.
yṣḥm: 571/6.
yḏʿ, cf. *ʾwsʾl, ḥywʿṯtr*.
yqbl, cf. *ʾʿrqm*.
yrʾb: 841/1.
yrdf, cf. *]rymn*.
yrẓḥ, cf. *ẓbym*.
yrḥb, cf. *yrm*.
yrẖm, cf. *lḥyʿṯt*.
yrm: 629/41; 716/6,8,11;
 ''/ʾymn: 561 bis/1;
 ''/ʾymn/wʾẖyhw/krbʾl/wtr/mlky/sbʾ: 565/11-12.
 ''/yrḥb: 716/1.
yrʿd: 629/40.
yšʿ, cf. *lfʿṯt*.
yšf: 689/3; *''/rzn:* (812/1).
yśq[: 802.
ytd: ''/ʾbkʾ: 621/1.
ytlf, cf. *sʿdtʾlb*.
yṯʾr: 646/1,6.
yṯʿʾl: 823 B.
yṯʿʾmr: 555/1; 832;
 ''/byn: 550/1,2; 555/4; (824);
 ''/wtr: 557; 673/2-3.
yṯʿkrb: 555/2.

k

k[: 577/10.
kbrm: 626/2,18.
khlh, cf. *ʿbd*.
khlʿl [woman]: 742/12.
klb: 838; *''/ḏkrm:* 741/1-2; 756/1-2.
klbm: 563/2,6,16.
klbn: 582/1.
klwdd [woman]: 722/2.
knnt: ''/ybdr: 656/2.
ksdm: 670/11.
kʿbb [woman]: 722/1.
kʿbm: 660/11-12,15.
kr[b: 830.
]krb: 707/1; 791/2-3.
krbʾl: 551; 564/7,14; 819;
 ''/byn: 643/8,10,12,15,17,19,23,27; 643 bis/4,7;
 ''/byn/mlk/sbʾ: 558/6; 643 bis/9;
 ''/byn/mlk/sbʾ/wḏrydn: 643/(4), 30-31;
 ''/byn/mlk/sbʾ/wḏrydn/bn/ḏmrʿly/ḏrḥ: (642/8-9); 643/35-36;
 ''/ḏrydn: 578/6,8,17-18,19-20,22,26,28; (586/9); 589/9-10;
 ''/wtr: 550/2; cf. also *yrm*;
 ''/wtr/yhnʿm/mlk/sbʾ/bn/whbʾl/yḥz/mlk/sbʾ: 563/9-11; 564/5-6, 10-11,(17-18);
 ''/wtr/yhnʿm/mlk sbʾ/wḏrydn/wḥḏrmt wymnt: 667 A/15-18;
 ''/yhnʿm/mlk/sbʾ/wḏrydn/wḥḏrmt/wymnt: 666/13-14.
krbn: 758/1,6,15,19.
krbʿṯt: 567/(2-3),15,17; 578/35; (732/10); 736/2,9; 744/1; 843/1;
 ''/ʾsʿd: 578/[1],31,34;
 ''/ynfṯ: (840/1-2,9-10).
krybm: 787/1.

l

l[: 569/1.
lḥ[: 810 A/2.
lḥyʿṯt: 556; 569/1; 630/5,7-8,10,18-19; 644/4,8,10,17-18,23; 787/3; 844/1; (849/1);
 ''/ʾṣḥḥl: 630/1;
 ''/yrẖm/mlk/sbʾ/wḏrydn: 631/37-38.
lʿzzm: ''/yhnf/yhṣdq/mlk/sbʾ/wḏrydn: 631/26-27.
lʿšm: ''/brlm: 692/1.
lfʿṯt: ''/yšʿ: 657/(1),5-6,9-10.
lqẓn: 687/1,(5-6).
]ltn: 796/1.

m

]m: 664/1-2; cf. also *ʾlwhb, yhʿn*;
 ''/rkbn: 570/1.
]m.: 625/1.
]m[, cf. *whbʾwm*.
m[: 651/2.
mbšmt [woman]: 717/1,5.
mgdḥlk [woman]: 743/1.
mgzt, cf. *ʾlʾsd*.
mḏyn, cf. *]ʾl, ʾlsʿd*.
mḏkrm: 613/1,8,13-14.
mhnkrb: ''/rzḥym: 737/1.
mhqbm: 632/1.
mwnhn, cf. *ʾlʾsd*.
mḥmdm: 738/1-2.
mḥfdm: 749/2-3.
myḥyn, cf. *frwly*.
mlkkrb: ''/yʾmn and *''/yhʾmn*, cf. *ṯʾrn*.
mlkm: 576/2; *''/mlk/kdt:* 576/2.
msḥm [woman]: 721/8.
msylm: 757/3.
mʿdkrb: 588/1,5,6; 610/7; 611/9; 615/14; (633/17); 707/2-3.
mfyš: 708/1.

mqrm: 603/1.
mrʾlqs: 576/2; *''/bn/ʿwfm/mlk/ẖsṣtn:* 576/2.
mrsʿm: 655/10.
mrṯdʾwm: 712/2-3; 719/2.
mrṯdʾsʾy: 692/8-9.
mrṯdm: 568/8,10,(12),15; 569/2; 606/[1-2],12,17-18; 607/2, 11-12,17; 629/9,12-13,16,21-22,24,31,34,37,39,41,44; 652/[2],11; 670/2,19; 753 I/[1],6-7,II/12,III/12;
''/y[: 629/1;
''/yhḥmd: (568/1-2); cf. also *sʿdšmsm.*
mtʿm: 841/1.

n

]n: 648/1; 774/2; 812/2-3.
n[: 648/1.
nbṭkrb: 557.
nbṭm: *''/mlk/qtbn:* 629/11.
nhfn, cf. *ʿlhn.*
nwfm: 577/7,10; 716/5; *''/ʾḏrḥ:* (716/1).
nḥyn, cf. *ḏrʿt.*
nḥʿn: 660/13,16.
nlʿ[: 793.
nmrm: *''/ʾzʾd:* 704/1.
nmrn, cf. *rbšmsm;*
''/ʾwkn: 594/4; 684/(1-2),8; [711/8]; 739/[2],(13-14); 758/1-2, 16.
nsrm: *''/ʾḥṣn:* 700/2.
nʿmsʿd [woman]: 686/1,5-6.
nʿmt [woman]: 731/1.
nḏrt [woman]: 706/6.
nšʾy: 612/1,16.
nšʾkrb: 555/2; 559/(7-8),11-12; 561/8,11; 610/6; 611/8; 615/13; 625/3; 643/[1,3],12,14,23-24,28,32,36; 643 bis/4,5, 6,7,8; 716/6,8,11; 831/1;
lʾʾ: 643/16-17;
''/ʾršl: 716/1-2.
''/yʾmn/yhrḥb/mlk/sbʾ/wḏrydn: 608/10-11; 609/10-11; 611/17-19; 613/18-19; 614/15-16; 615/24-25; 616/16; 623/5-6;
''/yʾmn/yhrḥb/mlk/sbʾ/wḏrydn/bn/ʾlšrḥ/yḥḍb/wyʾzl/byn/mlky/sbʾ/wḏrydn: 608/1-4; (609/1-3); 610/(1-3),10-12; 611/(1-4), 11-14; 612/2-5,16-19; 613/2-5; 614/2-5; 615/5-8; 616/4-6, 10-12,35-37; 617/(2-3), 11-13; (618/26-29); 621/7-11; (624/1-4);
''/yhʾmn/yhrḥb/mlk/sbʾ/wḏrydn: 623/7-8,12-13;
''/yhʾmn/yhrḥb/mlk/sbʾ/wḏrydn/bn/ʾlšrḥ/yḥḍb/wyʾzl/byn/mlky/sbʾ/wḏrydn: 619/15-18;
''/yhʾmn/yhrḥb/mlk/sbʾ/wḏrydn/bn/ʾlšrḥ/yḥḍb/wyʾzl/byn/mlky/sbʾ wḏrydn: (877/1-4);
''/yhʾmn/yhrḥb/mlk/sbʾ/wḏrydn/bn/ʾlšrḥ/yḥḍb/wyʾzl: 620/13-15;
''/yhʾmn/mlk/sbʾ/bn/ḏmrʿly/ḏrḥ: 559/5-6; 560/(9-10),19-20; 561/5-6; 853 A/1,B/1,C/1,D/1,E/1,(F/1); (854/1-2); (855/1-2).
''/mlk/sbʾ: 560/15.

s

sbqlm: 577/12.
swdm: 660/12,(16); *lʾʾ:* 563/16;
''/ʾsʾr: (563/1).
swsm: 757/3.
sẖymm: 718/(6-7),7;
''/yzʾn: 616/2: 718/2; [788/2].
sẖmm: 562/9; 758/5,11,15,18; *lʾʾ:* 562/14;
''/ʾwḥm: 758/1;
''/yhṣbḥ: (562/1).
slmm: 727/2,7.
slmn: 684/[1],7,12.
smḏrḥ: 699/1,7.
s[mh: 819.
smh[: 681/2; 767/2.
smhʾmr: 550/1; 552/2; 554; 555/1.
smhwtr: (832).
smhyfʿ: 617/[1],7,10,13; 643/24,28,33;
''/yhḥmd: (615/(1-2),16-17; 822/1-2.
smhkrb: 567/7; 751/7; 877/8.
smhsmʿ: 644/4-5,18.
smhʿly: 552/4; 555/1,4;
''/ḏrḥ: 558/7;
''/ḏrḥ/mlk/sbʾ: 551;
''/ynf: (552/1-2); 555/4; 557; (825).
smhrym: 831/1,2-3,3.
sʿdʾwm: 590/[1],4,23; 603/2-3; 604/2; 689/1; 707/2; 727/1, 4-5; 740 A/2, 10; 742/10; 752/2-3; 809;
''/ʾsʿd: 690/1-2.
sʿdwdm: 605/1-2.
sʿdm: (594/5); 615/(2-3),17; 661/[1],5,6,9; 700/1,5-6,7,10, 12,13,15,17; 759/3;
''/ʾrym: 733/1,5-6;
''/yskr: 822/3;
''/šbʿn: 729/1-2.
sʿdšmsm: 566/2; 568/(7-8),9,12,(14); 606/11; 607/11; 739/(1),6-7,8,(12-13),16; *lʾʾ:* 606/17; 607/16; 753 I/6,II/11-12,(III/11-12);
''/ʾsrʿ: [568/1]; [606/1]; (607/1); 753 I/1;
''/ʾsrʿ/wbnhw/mrṯdm/yhḥmd/mlky/sbʾ/wḏrydn/bny/ʾlšrḥ/yḥḍb/mlk/sbʾ/wḏrydn: 626/9-12; 627/16-18; 628/17-19; (629/4-6); 630/12-15 (*bnyhw* instead of *bnhw*);
''/wmrṯdm: 629/9,29-30,35,38;
''/wmrṯdm/mlky/sbʾ: 629/14,22-23,26-27;
''/wmrṯdm/mlky/sbʾ/wḏrydn: 629/42.
sʿdtʾlb: *''/ytlf:* 665/1.
sʿdṯwn: 565/2,9; 584/1.

ʿ

ʿbd: *''/khlh:* 715/(1),8.
ʿbdʾbs: 750/1-2.
ʿbdʾwm: 669/3.
ʿbdm: 709/1.
ʿbdmlk: *''/ʾwmd:* 752/1-2.
ʿbdʿm: 651/(1),10,22,24-25,34,42-43,50.
ʿbdʿṯtr: 654/2; 666/8; *''/ʾšwʿ:* 666/1-2.
ʿbydm: (700/1).
ʿblm: 748/1.
ʿḏbh: *''/mlk/ʾksmn:* 576/11.
ʿwfm: *''/yġnm:* 613/1,7-8,13; cf. also *mrʾlqs.*
ʿkm: *''/ʾrym:* 614/1,7-8,11.
ʿlhn: (561 bis/2); 696/1; (697/1);
''/nhfn/mlk/sbʾ, cf. *šʿrm.*
ʿlym: 689/4; 745/2.
ʿlyn: 575/2.

]ʿm: 813/1.
ʿmyṯʿ: 555/2.
ʿmkrb: 552/1; 553/1.
ʿmrʾl: 715/2-3,9.
ʿmrlt [woman]: 721/1.
ʿmrm: 660/12,16; 717/9.
ʿmrn: 729/3.
ʿmrfʾ: 767/(1),6.
ʿmšfq: 674 B/1.
ʿqrbn: 712/1.
]ʿr: 642/2.
ʿrbm: 585/1,3,9,18.
ʿṯt: 844/5.

ġ

ġwṯm: 560/5,16,18; "/[]*r:* (560/1).
ġyln: 639/1.
ġfr: 833.

f

f[, cf.].*zr*.
frwly: "/*myḥyn:* 750/1.
frʿm: 603/1; "/*ynhb/wbnyhw/ʾlšrḥ yḥḍb/wyʾzl/mlk/sbʾ:* (566/8-10); cf. also *ʾlšrḥ/yḥḍb*.

ṣ

ṣ[*:* 816/1; cf. also *rbʿṯt*.
ṣdqʾl: 692/9-10.
ṣdqn: 725/1.
ṣḥbm: 577/6,7.

ḍ

ḍbʿn: 705/4.

q

qḥdm: 836.
qṯbn: "/*ʾwkn:* 631/1,3,11,17,18-19,22-23,25,31.
]*qr:* 775/1.
qšn: "/*ʾšwʿ:* 641/1.

r

]*r*, cf. also *dm*[, *ġwṯm*.
rʾ[, cf.]*rb*.
rʾbm: 632/1.
rb[*:* 840/1.
]*rb:* "/*rʾ*[*:* 678/1.
rbʾwm: 644/5,8,10-11; 689/4; 693/[1-2],7,9-10; 740 A/6,9; 809;
"/*ʾṣdq:* 740 A/1.
rbʾl: 620/1,5,8; 784/3.
rbbʾwm: 698/1.
rbbʾl: 619/6-7; (746/4,15-16);
"/*ʾšwʿ:* (619/1);
"/[]*ym:* (746/1).
rbbḫgrm: 747/8.
rbbm: 667 A/6,11; 683/4;
"/[]*ẖr:* 667 A/1.
rbbtgwbn [woman]: (731/6).
rbnsrm: 605/6; 740 A/2, 10.
rbslm: 700/9,10,12,12-13,14,15-16.
rbʿ[*:* 815/[5],(7-8).
rbʿt: 665/31; 693/9,11; 767/2;
"/*ḏkrn:* (693/1);
"/[]*hr:* 656/1-2;
"/*ḏʾlṯwrm/mlk/kdt/wqḥṭn:* 635/26-27.
rbʿṯt: 812/(2),8,9; "/*ṣ*[*:* 795/2.
rbšms: 744/4; "/*ʾḏʾd:* 566/1.
rbšmsm: 578/35; (730/1-2); cf. also *šrḥʾl*;
"/*yzd:* 578/1,31;
"/*yʿrr:* 629/32;
"/*nmrn/mlk/sbʾ/wḏrydn:* 645/20-21.
rbtnf: "/*yẓfr:* 669/1.
rbṯwn: 701 A/8; 725/1, 3-4,7.
rdmyn: 755/1.
rzḥym, cf. *mhnkrb*.
rzn: "/*y*.[*:* 811/1; cf. also *yšf*.
rḥʾl: (629/40).
rym, cf. *ʾlrm*.
]*rymn:* (747/5); "/*yrdf:* 747/1.
rkbn, cf.]*m*.
]*rm:* "/*yʿd:* 800.
]*rf:* 781.
rfʾ: 658/7,25; "/*ʾšwʿ:* (658/1).
rfʾm: 721/7.
rfšn, cf. *ʾwslt*.
ršdm: 613/1-2,8,14; 655/1.
rṯdʾlw: 618/13,20,25; "/*ʾzkn:* (618/1).
rṯdm: 564/12; 757 bis/1.
rṯdšmsm: "/*yhtf:* (591/1).
rṯdṯwn: 565/8; 566/3: "/*ʾzʾd:* 565/1.

š

š[*:* 557.
šbʿn, cf. *sʿdm*.
šwfʾl: 711/1,7.
šwqm [woman]: 722/3.
]*šms:* 829?.
šms: 644/5,8-9,11; 829?.
šmr: 646/11;
"/*ḏrydn:* 576/3,5,11,14,15,16,(16-a); 577/2,3,3-4,4;
"/*yhrʿš:* 646/7-8; 658/11,20; 662/18; cf. also *ysrm;*
"/*mlk/sbʾ/wḏrydn:* 652/23-24;

''/*yhrʿš/mlk/sbʾ/wḏrydn:* 649/4-5,8-9,15-16,24-25,26-27; 650/3, 7-8,10-11,21,26-27; 651/15-16,38-39,40-41,45-46; 652/9-10, 14-15; 654/11-12;
''/*yhrʿš/mlk/sbʾ/wḏrydn/bn/ysrm/yhnʿm/mlk/sbʾ/wḏrydn:* 651/5-7; 652/3-6; 653/19-21; 655/14-16;
''/*yhrʿš/mlk/sbʾ/wḏrydn/wḥḍrm(w)t/wymnt:* 657/12-14; 658/8-10, 31-32; 660/4-5,9-11,18-19; 661/6-7; 662/10-12,20-22;
''/*yhrʿš/mlk/sbʾ/wḏrydn/wḥḍrmt/wymnt/bn/ysrm/yhnʿm/mlk/sbʾ/wḏrydn:* 656/8-11,20-22; (661/3).
]*šʿm*(?)*:* 835.
šʿrm: 639/5;
''/*ʾwtr:* 639/3; ''/*mlk/sbʾ/wḏrydn:* 631/(6-7),7-8,10-11,12, 14-15; 632/5; 635/20-21,40-41; (640/3-4); 641/6-7;
''/*ʾwtr/mlk/sbʾ/wḏrydn/bn/ʿlhn/nhfn/mlk/sbʾ:* 633/18-20; 634/6-9; 635/6-8; 636/2-4,11-13; (637/6-8); (638/2-4);
''/*ʾwtr/wʾẖyhw/ḥywʿṯtr/yḍʿ/mlky/sbʾ/wḏrydn bny/ʿlhn/nhfn/mlk/sbʾ:* 641/12-14;
''/*ʾwtr/mlk/sbʾ/wḏrydn/wʾẖyhw/ḥywʿṯtr/yḍʿ:* (640/8-9).
šfʿṯt: 589/3; 710/1; ''*ʾšwʿ:* 708/2; 713/3,12.
šrḥʾwm: 703/9; 733/2;
'' *ʾzʾd:* 752/3-4;
''/*ʾsʾr:* 703/1.
šrḥʾl: 555/1; 558/[1],3;
''/*ʾzbr:* 704/1;
''/*wrbšmsm/mlky/ḥḍrmwt:* 656/11-12.
šrḥbʾl: 652/[1],10-11.
šrḥwdm: 655/(1),11.
šrḥm: 634/1; 720/1-2; 721/1;
''/*ʾzʾd:* 736/1.
šrḥsmd: 646/1,6.
šrḥʿṯt: 670/18-19; ''/*ʾšwʿ:* 670/1,8.
šrḥṯt: 603/2; 629/40; 691/1.

ś

]*śl:* 795/1.

t

]*t* [woman]*:* 722/1.
]*t*[*:* 558/2.
tbʿkrb: 550/1; 554; 653/6; 735/4.
tbʿm: 742/11-12.
tzʾd: ''/*ʾṯqf:* 605/1.
tḥrmn: 797 B/1-2.
tymlt: ''/*ʾsʿd:* 656/2-3.

ṯ

ṯʾrn: 649/2;
''/*ʾyfʿ*, cf. *ysrm;*
''/*yhnʿm*, cf. *ḏmrʿly;*
''/*yhnʿm/wbnyhw/mlkkrb/mlky/sbʾ/wḏrydn/wḥḍrmwt/wymnt:* 669/27-29;
'' *yhnʿm/wbnyhw/mlkkrb/yhʾmn/mlky/sbʾ/wḏrydn/wḥḍrmwt/wymnt:* 670/21-25;
''/*yhnʿm/wbnhw/mlkkrb/yʾmn/mlky/sbʾ/wḏrydn/wḥḍrmt/wymnt:* 671/8-10;
''/*yhnʿm wbnyhw/mlkkrb/yʾmn/mlky/sbʾ/wḏrydn/wḥḍrmt/wymnt:* 671/21-23.
ṯwbʾl: 702/1-2,11-12; 717/9.
ṯwbm: 726/1.
ṯwbn: 604/2; 643 bis/4,7,8; 733/2;
''/*ʾnṯ*[*:* 643/1.
ṯwbṯwn [woman]*:* 722/1.
ṯly: 579/1; 580/1,10,13.
ṯfyn: 651/2.

C – TRIBES (CLANS, GROUPS, AND FAMILIES) AND PLACES (COUNTRIES, BUILDINGS, AND ESTATES)

ʾ

ʾbʾmr, cf. *ṣryhw.*
ʾbʾs: 616/24.
ʾbwn: 578/20.
ʾbkrb, cf. *ṣryhw.*
ʾdhwn: 816/3.
ʾdfm: 614/2.
ʾḏnt: 560/3; *b*''*:* 550/1.
ʾhlny: 616/25.
ʾwm: 557; 575/7; 772/2; *b*''*:* 554; (702/8); 703/2; *ḏ*''*:* 735/8,12;
cf. also *ʾlmw, ʾlmq, ʾlmqh, ʾlmqhw, lmqh, bʿl.*
ʾwmm: 616/26.
ʾws[*: ḏ*''*:* 795/1.
ʾwskrb: 730/2.
ʾwsn: 629/31.
ʾwsrn: 640/2.
ʾwtn, cf. *qtrn.*
ʾẖgrm: 815/1; *ḏ*''*:* 815/5.
ʾḥdqm: ḏ''*:* 577/5.
ʾḥṭbn: 555/3.
ʾḥrm, cf. *ḥgrm.*
ʾḥśrn, cf. *kbr.*
ʾẖr: 758/8-9.
ʾẓwr: 576/4; *ḏ*''*:* 578/19.
ʾẓlm: 660/3.
ʾydʿn: 616/24.
ʾyfʿ: 658/3.
ʾyḏmm: 576/7.
ʾksmn: 574/7; cf. also *gdrt, grmt, ʿḏbh.*
ʾl[*:* 772/1.
ʾlddn, cf. *ẖwln.*
ʾlw: 615/5.
ʾlyn: 665/32.
ʾlm: ḏ''*:* 732/1.
ʾlṯwrm: ḏ'', cf. *rbʿt.*
ʾmrm: 660/3-4; *ḏ*''*:* 832.

w

w[...]bn: *ḏ*'': 643/3.
wd[: 719/2-3,7-8.
wddʾl, cf. *ṣryhw*.
wdyfn: 574/6.
wdftn: *ḏ*'': 574/6.
whbm: 707/3-4.
wḥdt: 575/4.
wklm: 562/2.
wʿd, cf. *qtr*.
wʿln: 629/10,43-44.
wġmm: 550/1.
wrq: 550/1.

z

zbnr: 690/3,12; 840/3.
zẖnm: 577/1.
zydʾl: 665/3.
zltn: *ḏ*'': 557.
zmn: 550/1.
[.]*zrtm:* 730/3.

ḥ

ḥ[: 687/8-9.
ḥbb: 649/1; *ḏ*'': 617/[1],7,10,13-14.
ḥbbḍ: 671/12; *b*'': 671/11.
ḥbbt: 701 A/2.
ḥbšt: 574/5; 576/3; 577/3,4,10; 585/16; 631/13; cf. also *gdrt*.
ḥbt: 741/3; 756/3.
ḥgnn: 692/2,7.
ḥgr: ''/*lmd:* 616/25.
ḥgrw: 550/1.
ḥdʾn: 660/3.
ḥdlnt: 616/24.
ḥḏʾbm: 592/[1],6.
ḥḏmt: 567/7; 611/9; 615/14; 877/9.
]*ḥw:* 783/1.
ḥwln: 556.
ḥzfrm: 653/6; 740 A/13; 821 A/4;
''/*ḏrfdn:* (740 A/2-3).
ḥṭbm, cf. *bḥr*.
ḥẓrm: *ḏ*'': 652/12;
ḏ''/*ʿmrt:* (652/2-3).
ḥẓrn: 816/6.
ḥywm: 667 A/2; *ḏ*'': 667 A/7; 733/2-3,6.
ḥkmm: 616/24.
ḥlzwm: 629/27,28.
ḥlḥlm: 619/2; 637/1-2; 689/1.
ḥmyrm: 576/3,4,5,9,11,15,16; 577/1,2; 578/7,15,25; 579/8; 580/9; 581/7; 586/6,9,15,17; 589/10; 590/8; 665/3-4; 740 A/8.
ḥmln: 562/15; 719/9; *ḏ*'', cf. *smʿy*.
ḥmʿṯt: 841/1.
ḥnn: 643/7,10,13,16,20,30,32,35.
ḥfnm: 658/25; *ḏ*'': 658/2.
ḥḏnn: 752/4-5; *ḏ*'': 734/4; *ḏ*''/*bqlm:* 736/3.
ḥḏrmwt: 577/9; 629/7,11; 643/6,10,15,21,26,29,31,34; 643 bis/2,3,5; (660/2); 665/29,33,37; cf. also *ḏmrʿly*, *ydʿʾl*, *ysrm*, *yʿkrn*, *šmr*, *šrḥʾl*, *ṯʾrn*.
ḥḏrmt: 612/10; 636/5; (640/5); 643/13,14,18,25; 643 bis/1,6; 665/4,11,19,19-20; 750/5; cf. also *ʾlʿz*, *ysrm*, *krbʾl*, *šmr*, *ṯʾrn*.
ḥrb: 649/25.
ḥrwnm, cf. *ʾlmqh*.
ḥrwr: 555/3; *ḏ*'': 576/12.
ḥrmm: 616/25; 665/2-3.
ḥrmtm: 578/8,34.
ḥrn, cf. *ʾlmqh*.
ḥrnm, cf. *bʿl*.
ḥrt: 616/26; 649/17.
ḥrtn: 658/21.
ḥšdm: 561 bis/7,12; 577/7,11; 704/9; 713/16; 716/3;
ḏ'', cf. *smʿy*.

ẖ

ẖbtn: 745/11.
ẖḏwt: 634/1; 731/2.
ẖwln: 601/8; 602/8; 616/19,23; 649/28-29;
ḏ'': 629/(7),12;
''/*ʾlddn:* 658/10,13;
''/*gddm:* 577/8; 616/12,14;
''/*gddn:* 601/5,10; 602/5,10;
ḏ''/*gddtn*, cf. *smʿy*;
''/*ẖḏlm:* 635/33; 649/3.
ẖzfn: *ḏ*'': (588/1-2); 660/13.
ẖywn: 649/9-10.
ẖymm: 840/3.
ẖlb: 616/27.
ẖll and ''/*ṯkmtn*, cf. *kbr*.
ẖlfn: 667 A/12; ''/*ʾnmrm:* 667 A/1-2, (6-7).
ẖṣṣtn, cf. *mrʾlqs*.
ẖḏlm, cf. *ẖwln*.
ẖrṣm: 665/28.

ṭ

ṭrydm: 576/16.

ẓ

ẓhr: 651/4.
ẓlm: 576/13-14.
ẓlmn: 578/9.
ẓfr: 631/20,22,23,35; 667 A/9; 695/8;
b'': 670/10.
ẓrbn: 577/8.

y

yʾzl: 557.
ybrn: 555/3.
yhbʿl: 629/2,18,44.
yhbšr: 576/13.
yhgl: 600/8.
yhdl: *b*'': 550/1.
yhwld, cf. *smhrm.*
yhʿn: 630/1,5,8,19; 645/(1-2),5,9,12,17; 757 bis/3;
ḏ'': 714/3.
yhfrʿ: 747/(1-2,5),9,10.
yhr: 552/3; 555/2; 576/4.
ywnm: (635/35-36).
yḥmʾl: 759/2; 784/1.
yḥmḏl: 633/2; [635/2].
yḥḏr: 695/3.
yklʾ: 576/9,10; 578/20.
ylrn: *ḏ*'': 576/6.
ymlʾṣḥl: 555/2.
ymnt: 665/4; cf. also *ḏmrʿly*, *ysrm*, *krbʾl*, *šmr*, *ṯʾrn.*
ysrn: 851/5; *b*'': 550/1; 555/3.
yʿd: *ḏ*'': 627/7-8.
yfd: *b*'': 746/5; *ḏ*'': 618/7,8,16; 627/11; 628/5,9,12.
yfʿ: *b*'', cf. *ʿṯtr.*
yqnʿm: 575/2.
yrsm: 616/22;
''/*ḏsmʿy*/*ṯlṯn*/*ḏhgrm:* 616/3-4; (718/3-4);
''/*ḏsmʿy*/*ṯlṯn*/*ḏhgrm*/*ḏhwln*/*gddtn:* (671/4-5);
''/*ḏsmʿy*/*ḏṯlṯn*/*ḏhgrm:* 670/4-5.
yšr: 726/1,4.
yṯw: ''/*brʾn*, cf. *ʾlmqh.*
yṯl: 619/9; 643/19,20,21,27,29.
yṯʿn: 776/2.

k

kbsym: 618/(2,13-14),20,(21-22),26; 627/[1],4,10,13,15,24-25
628/[1],11,14-15,24; 746/(1-2),[8].
kbsyn: *ḏ*'': 712/4.
kbr: ''ʾ*qynm:* 684/(3-4),10; 739/3; 758/3, 17;
ḏ''ʾ*qynm:* 615/3,11-12,17-18,21;
''*ẖll:* 613/11; 615/13; 618/10; (684/3,9-10); 711/1-2;
739/3; 758/3, 17;
''/*ẖll:* 696/2; 697/2; 735/4-5;
''/*ẖll*/*ṯkmtn:* 645/15;
''/ʾ*ḥśrn:* 816/2;
''*rḥlm:* 651/26-27;
ʾ''*w*[pl.]: ''/*ẖll:* 711/9.
kdt: 576/2; 660/2; 665/2,13; cf. also *mlkm*, *rbʿt.*
khlm: 616/24-25; cf. also *qrytm.*
khln: 735/1; cf. also *sbʾ.*
kwmnn: *b*'': 644/19,21.
klwn: *b*'': 669/24-25.
klwnm: *b*'': 669/14.
kmdm: 552/1.
knn, cf. *ʿṯtr.*
krbm: 590/2,23.
ktm: 550/1.

l

lḥgm: *ḏ*'': 633/6.
lyt, cf. *shrtn.*
lmd, cf. *ḥgr.*
lms, cf. *ḥgrm.*
lqḥ: 574/7,11-12.

m

]*m:* 586/1-2; 651/3-4; 780/1; 816/1-2.
m[.]*lwn:* *b*'': 685/3-4.
mʾḏn: 655/2.
mʾḏnm: *ḏ*'': 564/12.
mḏb: *ḏ*'': 831/1.
mḏyn: 757/4.
mḏḥgm: (660/2); 665/2.
mḏmrm: 550/1,2.
mḏrḥm: *ḏ*'': 576/8; 651/[1],10,22,25,34,43,50-51; (774/1).
mhʾnfm: 555/3; 576/6,8; 651/4.
mhdmm: 581/1,9-10.
mḥylm: 572/2; 578/2; 632/2.
mḥḏn: 550/1.
mṭrn: 550/1.
mydʿm: 560/3.
myṯʿm: 556; 604/1,3.
mnwbm: 629/30.
mskt, cf. *ʾlmqh.*
mslmn: *b*'': 577/12.
msqmm: *ḏ*'': 555/2.
mʿdkrb, cf. *ṣryhw.*
mʿdnm: 590/2,(23-24).
mʿhr: 629/6,12,15.
mʿhrtn: 631/36.
mʿfrm: 631/33.
mṣlynn: (618/11-12).
mḏḥym: 576/3,11,(15); 577/1; 629/7,12; 758/8.
mḏḥyn: 739/10.
mqldn: 555/2.
mqrʾm: 576/13.
mqrm: 700/2,8.
mrb (Marab): 576/2;
(Mârib): 572/7; 613/9; 651/17,31; 660/14,19; 664/16;
665/21; 735/1,5,7,8,10; 777/2;
b'': 647/28; 656/25; 667 B; 702/12;
l'': 653/8.
mrbʾn: 569/3-4.
mrḥbm: 657/1,6; 743/1.
mrḥḏn: 576/9.
mryb: 550/2; 555/3; 557; 560/11, (14-15); 564/(9-10),12;
576/3; 577/17; 629/23,36; 636/7; 642/6; 643/9,16,18,19-20,
27,31,33; 643 bis/1,10; 644/7,22;
b'': 645/25.
mšmn: *ḏ*: 555/3.
mšr: 617/6.
mšrʿm: 832.
mšrqytn: 629/27.
mt[: *ḏ*'': 823 B.
mtbʿm, cf. *ʾlmqh.*

n

nʾsm: *ḏ*'': 626/2,8,19.
nbʿt: 649/10.
ngrn: 577/8,9,(9-10),10,11,12,13,14; 579/8; 599/2; 635/23,34.
ngrrm: 576/10.
nhd[]*ʾm:* cf. *šmsy*.
nzḥt: *ḏ*'': 707/4.
nʿmbrl: 722/3; 741/3; 756/3.
nʿḍ: 576/7,8,10; 577/2; 631/19.
nfʾn: *ḏ*'': 844/1.
nšʾkrb, cf. *ṣryhw*.
nšdʾl: 658/21-22.
nšn: 643/22,25,26; 647/28; 664/17; 665/14; 667 B.
nšqm: 555/3; 577/17; 619/3,13; 643/22,25, 26,28,33; 645/25; 664/16; 665/13-14; 727/4;
b'': 647/28.

s

sʾryn: 617/[1],7-8,11,14; 649/2.
sʾrn: (572/2); 578/[1],34,[36]; 629/40-41; 632/2,4,6,9; 708/4.
sbʾ: 550/2; 561 bis/9-10,14; 565/7; 568/19-20,21; 574/11; 575/3; 576/11; 577/3,4,6,8,9,10,14,[17],18; 601/9; 602/9; 629/8,10; 643/12,23,24; 643 bis/9; 647/23; 651/30; 660/14; 662/(4),14; 665/2,3,13; 668/14; 690/11; 703/8; 723/1-2; 735/8; 740 A/7,13-14; (747/13-14); 753 I/4,II/5,III/5; 762/1; [766/5]; 791/1,2; 847/5;
bḏ'': 671/25;
l'': 623/9;
cf. also *ʾlšrḥ*, *ʾnmrm*, *ḏmrʿly*, *whbʾl*, *wtrm*, *yʾzl*, *yhqm*, *ysrm*, *yrm*, *krbʾl*, *lḥyʿṯt*, *lʿzzm*, *nšʾkrb*, *smhʿly*, *sʿdšmsm*, *ʿlhn*, *rbšmsm*, *šmr*, *šʿrm*, *ṯʾrn*;
''/*khln:* 653/1,15-16; 656/15-16; 668/7-8,10,12; 735/[1],3,16, 18; (851/1).
sbsm: 616/25.
shm: *ḏ*'': 574/4.
shrtm: 635/21-22;
ḏ'': 574/3-4,6,8; 575/5,7; 576/3; 577/3,5; 579/7; 649/30,31.
shrtn: 575/4; 585/5; 590/5; 616/18; 650/21-22; 658/21; 710/4; 745/8;
''/*lyt:* 649/9.
sḥm: 550/1.
sḥr: *ḏ*'': 567/3,15; 664/2,6.
sẖymm: 575/2; 601/1,15-16,18; 602/1,15,18; 616/3,8,32; 629/40; 670/2-3,19-20; (671/2-3); [718/2-3]; 730/3; 760; (788/2-3);
ḏ'': 684/4,10; 711/10; (739/3-4); 758/3,17-18.
slḥn: 559/10,14; (560/7); 561/10,14; 562/6-7; 564/[2],7; 575/8; 577/(16-17),19; 643 bis/8; 644/6-7,9,13,23; 647/22; 652/25; 660/19; 761/3; 853 A/3,B/3,C/3,D/3,E/3-4,F/3; 877/14.
smhkrb, cf. *ṣryhw*.
smhrm: 559/2; 561/2; 568/16,19; 606/13,19; 607/13,18; 643/[2],13; 643 bis/6,8; 753 (I/7),II/13,(III/13);
''/*yhwld:* 631/[1],4,18,19,23,25-26,32;
ḏ'', cf. *ḏmry*.
smʿy:
''/*šlṯn*/*ḏhgrm:* 601/2; 602/2;
''/*ṯlṯn*/*ḏḥmln:* 562/2-3;
''/*ṯlṯn*/*ḏḥšdm:* 561 bis/4;
ḏ''/*ḏṯlṯn*/*ḏhgrm*, cf. *yrsm*;
ḏ''/*ṯlṯn*/*ḏhgrm*, cf. *yrsm*;
ḏ''/*ṯlṯn*/*ḏhgrm*/*ḏẖwln*/*gddtn*, cf. *yrsm*.
smʿn, cf. *wdm*.
snfrm: *ḏ*'': 576/13.
sfly, cf. *ḏt*/*ġḍrn*.
sfln: 716/7.
sqrn: 683/1; (771).
srʿn: 586/16,20.
srrn: 656/16; 668/11.

ʿ

ʿblm: 558/[1],3,7; 585/3-4,19; 621/2; [633/1]; 635/1,17-18; 669/3-4; 705/2,5; 817/1,[4];
ḏ'': 585/1.
ʿbrn: 665/14.
ʿgntn: 555/2.
ʿynwm: *ḏ*'': (560/2).
ʿynm: *b*'': 575/6.
ʿkm: 574/7-8; 575/5,6,7; 649/30,31.
ʿlhn: 696/1; 697/1.
ʿlfqm: 629/23.
ʿmd: *ḏ*'': 649/2.
ʿmydm: *ḏ*'': (774/2-3)?
ʿmyṯʿ: *ḏ*'': (774/2-3)?
ʿmm: 693/2,9.
ʿmrt, cf. *ḥẓrm*.
ʿsmy: 682/2.
ʿsmt: 550/1.
ʿfm: *ḏ*'': 727/1-2; ''/*ʾmrn:* 727/3.
ʿṣyt, cf. *ʿṯkln*.
ʿḍdn: 666/3; *ḏ*'': 666/3,9.
ʿqbm: 654/3.
ʿqbn: *ḏ*'': 603/3,7; 683/2.
ʿrgn, cf. *gmyln*.
ʿrwštn: 578/9.
ʿrṣm: 576/12.
ʿtwd: 658/22.
ʿṯy: 576/8.
ʿṯkln: 563/(3),6,17; 726/2; 744/[1-2],4-5;
''/*ʿṣyt:* 589/4; 656/4.
ʿṯlm: 661/2.

ġ

ġ[*:* 639/2.
ġymn: 564/1,2,9,19,23,25-26,27; 577/7,11; 626/3,8,(19-20); 644/1,15,16,18,21,24,27; 695/(1-2),3,7,(11); 716/3;
ḏ'': 562/7; 564/8,(15-16),18,20,23,25,26; 577/7,10; 585/4, 7,8,10; 626/2,(18-19); (642/3,16); 644/1,26; 691/(2-3),8; 716/2,6,12; 747/14; 799/5.
ġmdm: 616/24.
ġndn: 577/17,19.
ġḍrn, cf. *šms*.

f

fyš: *ḏ*'' 708/3-4.
fyšn: 558/7; 629/18,44.
fḍḥm: 610/7; 633/17.
fḍlm: 587/1.

ṣ

ṣbḥrym: 555/2.
ṣdqʾl, cf. *ṣryhw*.
ṣwm: *ḏ*'': 555/2.
ṣḥḥn: 644/9.
ṣyḥyn, cf. *šms*.
ṣlyn: *b*'': 618/11.
ṣnʿw: 574/10; 575/3; 576/3,10,11; 577/3,6,11,17; 616/17; 629/38; 644/16; 647/28;
b'': 575/8.
ṣʿdtm: 658/12.
ṣʿqn: 641/2; 840/2.
ṣrbn: 577/13.
ṣrwḥ: 649/3,28.
ṣryhw:
ḏ''/*ʾbʾmr*: 703/2;
ḏ''/*ʾbkrb*: 589/1;
ḏ''/*wddʾl*: 589/3;
ḏ''/*mʿdkrb*: 567/1,2; 589/2;
ḏ''/*nšʾkrb*: 567/3;
ḏ''/*smhkrb*: 589/3-4; 703/1;
ḏ''/*ṣdqʾl*: 703/1.
ṣrfn: *ḏ*'': 698/2-3; (755/1-2).

ḍ

ḍdḫn: 649/10.
ḍmdm: *ḏ*'': 649/16-17.
ḍfw: 576/8,9.

q

qb[: *ḏ*'': 681/3.
qbʿn: 713/2-3.
qḥṭn, cf. *rbʿt*.
qy[: *ḏ*'': 796/1-2.
qnʾ: 632/3.
qsdm: 567/8.
qr[: 725/1-2.
qrb: 576/12.
qrytm: 635/28,36; 641/5;
''/*ḏt*/*khlm*: 634/4-5; 635/25-26.
qrytnhn: 649/26.
qrnnhn: 578/9.
qrs: 576/12.
qrḍn: 581/1,10; 645/2,6,9,12,17.
qšmm: 576/4,7; 586/20.
qtbn: 550/2; 555/5; 629/7,11; 739/10;
ḏ'': 758/9; cf. also *nbṭm*.
qtr: ''/*wʿd*: 631/24.
qtrn: ''/*ʾwtn*: 669/4.

r

r[: 772/3.
rʾs: 576/13.
rʾsw: 576/13.
rbḥm: *ḏ*'': 586/21.
rgzgzn: *ḏ*'': 649/31-32,37.
rglm: 634/1-2.
rdmn: 550/1; 576/3,11,15; 577/1; 629/6,7; 739/10; 758/8.
rwẓn, cf. *ʾlmqh*.
rḥbm: 671/11,13.
rḥbmm: 616/18.
rḥbtn: 645/25-26; 656/18-19,25;
b'': 626/38-39.
rḥlm, cf. *kbr*.
rḫyt: 665/25.
rydn: 647/22;
ḏ'': 561 bis/10; 575/3; 576/6,9,13,15,16; 590/10; 631/27,29; 668/14; 703/8; 766/6; (791/1); cf. also *ʾlšrḥ*, *ḏmrʿly*, *wtrm*, *yʾzl*, *yhqm*, *ysrm*, *krbʾl*, *lḥyʿṯt*, *lʿzzm*, *nšʾkrb*, *sʿdšmsm*, *rbšmsm*, *šmr*, *šʿrm*, *ṯʾrn*.
rydt: *ḏ*'', cf. *bklm*.
rymm, cf. *tʾlb*.
rymn: 616/3; 670/3; 671/3; 718/3; [788/3].
ryśn: *ḏ*'': 728/1-2.
rkbtn: 577/12.
rmdn: 555/2.
rmn: 772/4.
rmtm: *ḏ*'': 590/10-11.
rsmm: *ḏ*'': 656/4-5.
rfdn: *ḏ*'': 693/3; cf. also *ḥẓfrm*.
rḍwm: 660/3.
rḍwn: 591/1,10.
rḍḫtn: 616/26.
ršwn: 554; 703/2,4,10.
ršm, cf. *šms*, *šmsy*.
]*rt*: 789/2.

š

šb]: 651/3.
šbwt: 632/3; 636/1; 637/4-5; 662/9,13; 741/7-8; 756/7-8.
šbmm, cf. *bklm*.
šbʿn: 748/2.
šddm: 576/13; 644/5,8,10,15,17,25.
šwḏbm: (552/1); 553/2; 554; 555/1,2.
šwḥṭ, cf. *ʾlmqh*, *ʾlmqhw*.
šyʿn: 629/31.
škrt: 734/4.
šmtn: *ḏ*'': 576/4.
šʿbm: 834/2; cf. also *wdm*.
]*šʿm* (?): 835.
šfbm: 831/2.
šṣrm, cf. *tʾlb*.
šrwn: 555/2.

ś

śwm: 585/5,7,11.
śmkm: 578/2.
śnḫn: 658/15.
śrdd: 574/6.

t

tdḫn: 616/27.
tẓ'd: 605/2,5,13.
thrgb: 550/2.
tklm: 661/2; "/'*nmrm:* (662/2-3).
tmnᶜ: 629/34.
tnᶜ, cf. *ḫgrm.*
tnᶜm: 649/10.
tnᶜmm: 618/19; 627/8,23; 712/8;
"/*wtnᶜmt:* (627/1-2); (628/2); 746/2;
"/*wtnᶜmtm:* 618/3,22.
tnᶜmt, cf. *tnᶜmm.*
tnᶜmtm, cf. *tnᶜmm.*
tᶜrmn: 576/6.
trd: 550/1.
trẓnn: ḏ": 577/1.

ṯ

ṯkmtn, cf. *ḫll.*
ṯml: ḏ": 635/37.
ṯnt: 566/3-4.
ṯt: 661/5; ḏ": 661/[1],6.

D – ANIMALS

gdn [horse]: 745/7.
dynrm [horse]: 745/9.
wḥẓ [horse]: (577/1).
ẓbym [horse]: 745/9.
klbym [camel]: 619/8.
ndf [horse]: 649/20.

E – MONTHS

'bhy: 651/17; ḏ": 735/4.
'l'lt: ḏ": 642/6.
dnm: ḏ": 633/16.
hbs: ḏ": 877/8;
ḏ"/*wᶜṯtr:* 611/7-8.
mlyt: ḏ": 613/10; 653/10,14.
ᶜṯtr: ḏ": 567/6-7; cf. also *hbs.*
fqḥy: ḏ": 653/9.

F – FRAGMENTARY PROPER NAMES OF UNKNOWN VALUE

]*blm:* 677/2.
]*hmm:* 677/1.
]*ḫḏ*[: 668/2.
*k*ᶜ[: 678/3.
]*n:* 674 B/2.
ᶜ[: 668/2.
]*r:* 668/3.
]*rr:* 668/2.
]*šbm:* 668/1.
]*t*[: 661/2.

G – ELEMENTS ENTERING INTO THE COMPOSITION OF PROPER NAMES

A – *Roots*

'

'b: 'b'mr, 'b'ns, 'bwn, 'bḥyl, 'bḥlk, 'bḥmd, 'bkrb, 'bᶜtd, 'bfnd, 'bšmr.
'bh: 'bhy.
'bs: ᶜbd'bs.
'gl: 'gylm.
'gr: 'grm.
'df: 'dfm.
'ḏn: 'ḏnt, m'ḏn, m'ḏnm.
'ḏf: y'ḏf.
'hl: 'hlny.
'wḥ: 'wḥm.
'wm: 'wm.
'ws: 'ws[, 'ws'l, 'wskrb, 'wslt, 'wsn, 'wsᶜṯt, 'l'ws, ḏ'wsn.
'zl: y'zl.
'zm: y'zm.
'ẖw: 'ẖt'l.
'ẖr: 'ẖr.
'yk: 'ywkn.
'kf: 'kf.
'lb: t'lb.
'lw: 'lw, rṯd'lw.
'ly: 'lyn.
'lf: 'lfnm.
'mn: y'mn, yh'mn.

ʾmr: ʾbʾmr, ʾlʾmr, ʾmrm, ʾmrn, ḏrʾʾmr, hlkʾmr, yṯʿʾmr, smhʾmr.
ʾmt: ʾmtʾlmqh.
ʾnw: ʾnwyn.
ʾns: ʾbʾns.
ʾnf: mhʾnfm.
ʾsd: ʾlʾsd, ʾsdkrb, ʾsdm.
ʾrk: ʾrk.
ʾtb: ʾtb.

b

bʾs: ʾbʾs, bʾsn.
bʾr: bʾrn.
bdr: ybdr.
bdš: bdš.
bhl: bhl, bhlm.
bḥr: bḥr, bḥrm.
byg: bygt.
byd: bydn.
bym: bymm.
byn: byn, ḏbyn.
byt: bytnhn.
bkʾ: ʾbkʾ.
bkl: bklm.
bʿd: ḏt/bʿdn(m).
bʿl: bʿl, bʿlm, yhbʿl.
bqy: bqyn.
bql: bqlm, sbqlm.
brʾ: brʾm, brʾn.
brg: brg.
bry: bryn.
brl: brlm, brlt, nʿmbrl.
brq: brqm.
brt: brtn.
brr: ybrn, yhbr.
bšm: bšm, hbšm, mbšmt.
bšr: yhbšr.
bśʾ: bśʾm.
btʿ: btʿ.

g

gbʾ: gbʾt.
gbl: gblm.
gdd: gddm, gddn, gddtn, gdšfq.
gdl: gdlm, gdlt.
gdn: gdn, gdnm.
gdr: gdrt.
ghr: ghrn.
gwb: rbbtgwbn.
gwz: mgzt.
gwl: yhgl.
gwr: ygr.
gḥḏ: gḥḏm.
gyš: gyšm.
gld: gldn.
gmd: gmdn.
gml: gmyln.
gmm: gmm, gmn.
gmʿ: gmʿn.
gnʾ: gnʾn.
gʿn: drgʿn?
gʿr: ygʿr.
grb: grbn.
grm: grm, grmt.
grf: grfm.
grt: grt.
gšm: gšm.

d

dbr: drbn.
dhw: ʾdhwn.
dhr: dhr.
dwʾ: dwʾt.
dwd: ʾlddn, ddʾl, ddḥmd, ddsmy.
dwm: dwmn, ydm.
dws: dwsm.
dwr: drgʿn?
dḥy: tdḥn.
dyn: dynrm.
dll: dll.
dfʾ: dfʾ.
drʾ: ydrʾ.
drm: ydrm.
drs: drsm.
drʿ: drʿ.

ḏ

ḏʾb: ḏʾbn.
ḏʾd: ʾḏʾd.
ḏbn: ḏbn.
ḏhg: mḏḥgm.
ḏhr: ḏhrm.
ḏyḥ: ḏḥ.
ḏkr: ḏkr, ḏkrm, ḏkrn, mḏkrm.
ḏll: yḥmḏl.
ḏmr: ḏmr, ḏmry, ḏmrydʿ, ḏmrkrb, ḏmrʿly, mḏmrm.
ḏnm: ḏnm.
ḏrʾ: ḏrʾʾmr.
ḏrḥ: ʾḏrḥ, ḏrḥ, ḏrḥʾl, ḏrḥn, mḏrḥm, smḏrḥ.
ḏrʿ: ḏrʿt.

h

hgr: hgrm.
hdm: hdym, mhdmm.
hdl: yhdl.
hwf: hwfʾl, hwfʿṯt.
hyn: hynn.
hkr: hkrm.
hlk: hlkʾmr, hlksmʿ.
hll: hlḥmq. hllḥmq, hllm, hlm, hltn.
hmd: hmdn.
hnʾ: hnʾm, hnʾṯwn.
hrr: hrn.
htf: yhtf.

w

wʾl: wʾlm.
wdd: wddʾl, wddm, klwdd.
wdᶜ: wdᶜtn.
wdf: wdyfn, wdftn.
whb: ʾlwhb, wh[b, whbʾwm, whbʾl, whblt, whbm, whbᶜṯt, whbšms, whbšmsm, whbṯwn.
wzʾ: yzʾn.
wzᶜ: wzᶜn.
wḥd: wḥdt.
wḥẓ: wḥẓ?
wkl: wklm.
wkn: ʾwkn.
wld: yhwld.
wlṭ: ʾwlṭ.
wly: frwly.
wmd: ʾwmd.
wsr: ʾwsrn.
wᶜd: wᶜd.
wᶜl: wᶜln.
wġm: wġmm.
wfd: wfdm, yfd.
wfy: wfym.
wḍᶜ: yḍᶜ.
wrq: wrq.
wśl: wśl.
wtd: ytd.
wtn: ʾwtn, hwtn.
wtr: ʾwtr, wtr, wtrm, smhwtr.
wṯw: yṯw.
wṯl: yṯl.

z

zʾd: ʾzʾd, ʾlzʾd, tzʾd.
zbnr: zbnr.
zbr: ʾzbr.
zḫn: zḫnm.
zyd: hzd, zydʾl, zydm, zydqwmm, yzd.
zkn: ʾzkn, yzkn.
zlt: zltn.
zmn: zmn.
zᶜl: zᶜln.

ḥ

ḥbb: ḥbb, ḥbbt, ḥbybm, ḥbt.
ḥbḍ: ḥbbḍ.
ḥbr: ʾḥbr.
ḥbš: ḥbšt.
ḥgn: ḥgnn.
ḥgr: ʾḥgrm, ḥgr, ḥgrw, ḥgrm.
ḥdʾ: ḥdʾn.
ḥdl: ḥdlnt.
ḥdq: ʾḥdqm.
ḥḏb: ḥḏʾbm.
ḥḏm: ḥḏmt.
ḥḏr: ʾḥḏr.
ḥwz: yḥz.
ḥwl: ḥwlm, ḥwln.
ḥzfr: ḥzfrm.
ḥṭb: ʾḥṭbn, ḥṭbm.
ḥẓr: ḥẓrm, ḥẓrn.
ḥyw: hḥyᶜṯt, ḥyw[, ḥywʾwm, ḥywm, ḥywᶜṯtr, ḥywt.
ḥyl: ʾbḥyl, mḥylm.
ḥkm: ḥkmm.
ḥlz: ḥlzwm.
ḥlk: ʾbḥlk, ḫlḥlk, mgdḥlk.
ḥll: ḫlḥlm.
ḥmd: ʾbḥmd, ʾḥmd, ddḥmd, ḥqbḥmd, yhḥmd, yḥmd, mḥmdm.
ḥmy: ḏt(/)ḥmym.
ḥml: ḥmln.
ḥmm: ḥmlt, ḥmᶜṯt, yḥmʾl, yḥmḏl.
ḥmq: hlḥmq, hllḥmq.
ḥmr: ḥmyrm.
ḥfd: mḥfdm.
ḥnn: ḥnn.
ḥfn: ḥfnm.
ḥṣn: ʾḥṣn.
ḥḍb: yḥḍb.
ḥḍn: ḥḍnn.
ḥḍr: ḥḍrm(w)t, yḥḍr.
ḥqb: ḥqbḥmd.
ḥrb: ḥrb, ḥrbm.
ḥrm: ʾḥrm, ḥrmm, ḥrmtm, tḥrmn.
ḥrn: ḥr(w)nm, ḥrn.
ḥrs: ʾḥrs.
ḥrr: ḥrwr, ḥrt, ḥrtn.
ḥrṯ: ḥrṯn.
ḥšd: ʾḥšd, ḥšdm.
ḥśr: ʾḥśrn.

ḫ

ḫbt: ḫbtn.
ḫdq: ḫdqm.
ḫḏw: ḫḏwm, ḫḏwt.
ḫwl: ḫwln.
ḫzf: ḫzfn.
ḫṭr: ʾḫṭr.
(*ḫyw*): ḫywn.
ḫym: ḫymm.
ḫyr: ḫyrhmw.
ḫlb: ḫlb.
ḫll: ḫlḥlk, ḫll.
ḫlf: ḫlfn.
ḫnᶜ: ḫnᶜm.
ḫṣṣ: ḫṣṣtn.
ḫḍl: ḫḍlm.
ḫrṣ: ḫrṣm.

ṭ

ṭrd: ṭrydm.

ẓ

ẓby: ẓbym.
ẓbn: ẓbnm.
ẓhr: ḏt/ẓhrn, ẓhr.
ẓwr: ʾẓwr.
ẓlm: ʾẓlm, ẓlm, ẓlmn.
ẓfr: ẓfr, yẓfr.
ẓrb: ẓrbn.
ẓrf: ʾẓrf.

y

ybs: h(w)bs.
ydʿ: ʾydʿn, ḏmrydʿ, ydʿʾl, mydʿm.
yhr: ʾyhr, yhr.
ywn: ywnm.
ymn: ʾymn, ymnt.
ysr: ysrm, ysrn.
yfʿ: ʾyfʿ, yfʿ, smhyfʿ.
yḍm: ʾyḍmm.
yṯʿ: hyṯʿ, yṯʿʾl, yṯʿʾmr, yṯʿkrb, yṯʿn, myṯʿm, ʿmyṯʿ.

k

kbs: kbsym, kbsyn.
kbr: kbr, kbrm.
khl: khlh, khlm, khln, khlʿl.
klʾ: yklʾ.
klb: klb, klbym, klbm, klbn.
klw: klwn, klwnm.
kll: klwdd.
kmd: kmdm.
kmn: kwmnn.
knd: kdt.
knn: knn, knnt.
ksd: ksdm.
ksm: ʾksmn.
kʿb: kʿbb, kʿbm.
krb: ʾbkrb, ʾwskrb, ʾlkrb, ʾsdkrb, ḏmrkrb, hkrbm, ykrbmlk, yṯʿkrb,]krb, krb[, krbʾl, krbm, krbn, krbʿṯt, krybm, mhnkrb, mlkkrb, mʿdkrb, nbṭkrb, nšʾkrb, smhkrb, ʿmkrb, tbʿkrb.
ktm: ktm.

l

lwr: ylrn.
lḥg: lḥgm.
lḥy: lḥyʿṯt.
lḥm: hlḥm.
lyt: mlyt, lyt.
lmd: lmd.
lms: lms.
lġẓ: ʾlġẓ.
lff: lfʿṯt.
lqḥ: lqḥ.
lqẓ: lqẓn.
lqs: mrʾlqs.

m

mgd: ʾmgd, mgdḥlk.
mḏb: mḏb.
mḏy: mḏyn.
mhn: mhnkrb.
mw: mwnhn.
mwt: ḥḏrm(w)t.
mẖḏ: mẖḏn.
mṭr: mṭrn.
myḥ: myḥyn.
mlʾ: ymlʾṣḥl.
mlk: ykrbmlk, mlkkrb, mlkm, ʿbdmlk.
mnb: mnwbm.
mnʿ: tmnʿ.
msḥ: msḥm.
msk: mskt.
msl: msylm.
mʿd: mʿdkrb.
mrʾ: mrʾlqs.
mšr: mšr.
mtʿ: mtʿm.

n

nʾs: nʾsm.
nbṭ: nbṭkrb, nbṭm.
nbʿ: nbʿt.
nbr: ʾnbr.
ngr: ngrn, ngrrm.
ndf: ndf.
nhb: ynhb.
nhd: nhd[]ʾm.
nhf: nhfn.
nwf: yhnf, ynf, nwfm, tnf.
nzḥ: nzḥt.
nḥy: nḥyn.
nḥr: ʾnḥrm.
nẖʿ: nẖʿn.
nmr: ʾnmrm, nmrm, nmrn.
nsr: nsrm.
nʿm: yhnʿm, ynʿm, nʿmbrl, nʿmsʿd, nʿmt; tnʿmm, tnʿmt, tnʿmtm.
nʿḍ: nʿḍ.
nfʾ: nfʾn.
nfr: snfrm.
nfṯ: ynfṯ.
nḍḥ: mḍḥ.
nḍr: nḍrt.
nšʾ: nšʾy, nšʾkrb.
nšd: nšdʾl.
nšn: nšn.
nšq: nšqm.

s

sʾy: ʾsʾy, mrṯdʾsʾy.
sʾr: ʾsʾr, sʾryn, sʾrn.
sbʾ: sbʾ.
sbs: sbsm.
shm: shm.
shr: shrtm, shrtn.
swd: swdm.
sws: swsm.
sḥm: sḥm.
sḥr: sḥr.
sḫm: sḫymm, sḫmn.
skr: yskr.
slḥ: slḥn.
slm: ʾslm, mslmn, slmm, slmn, rbslm.
smd: šrḥsmd.
smw: ʾsmwm.
smy: ddsmy, smḏrh, s[mh, smh[, smhʾmr, smhwtr, smhyfʿ, smhkrb, smhsmʿ, smhʿly, smhrym, smhrm.
sml: hsml.
smʿ: hlksmʿ, smhsmʿ, smʿy, smʿn.
sʿd: ʾlsʿd, ʾsʿd, nʿmsʿd, sʿdʾwm, sʿdwdm, sʿdm, sʿdšmsm, sʿdtʾlb, sʿdṯwn.
sfl: sfly, sfln.
sqm: msqmm.
sqr: sqrn.
srʿ: ʾsrʿ, srʿn.
srr: srrn.

ʿ

ʿbd: ʿbd, ʿḃdʾbs, ʿbdʾwm, ʿbdm, ʿbdmlk, ʿbdʿm, ʿbdʿṯtr, ʿbydm.
ʿbl: ʿblm.
ʿbr: ʿbrn.
ʿgn: ʿgntn.
ʿdn: mʿdnm.
ʿḏb: ʿḏbh.
ʿhr: mʿhr, mʿhrtn.
ʿwd: yʿd.
ʿwn: ʾlhʿn, hʿn, yhʿn.
ʿwf: yʿf, ʿwfm, ʿfm.
ʿzz: ʾlʿz, ʾʿzz, lʿzzm, ʿzzm, ʿzzn.
ʿyn: ʿynwm, ʿynm.
ʿkk: ʿkm.
ʿkr: yʿkrn.
ʿlh: ʿlhn.
ʿly: ḏmrʿly, smhʿly, ʿlym, ʿlyn.
ʿll: hʿll, khlʿl.
ʿlf: ʿlfqm.
ʿmm: ʿm.
ʿmd: ʿmd, ʿmydm.
ʿmr: yʿmr, ʿmrʾl, ʿmrlt, ʿmrm, ʿmrn, ʿmrt.
ʿsm: ʿsmy, ʿsmt.
ʿfr: mʿfrm.
ʿṣt: ʿṣyt.
ʿḍd: ʿḍdn.
ʿqb: ʿqbm, ʿqbn.
ʿqrb: ʿqrbn.
ʿrb: ʿrbm.
ʿrg: ʿrgn.
ʿrm: tʿrmn.
ʿrṣ: ʿrṣm.
ʿrq: ʾʿrqm.
ʿrr: yʿrr.
ʿrš: ʿrwštn.
ʿšm: lʿšm.
ʿtd: ʾbʿtd, ʿtwd.
ʿṯr: ʿṯtr.
ʿṯy: ʿṯy.
ʿṯkl: ʿṯkln.
ʿṯl: ʿṯlm.

ġ

ġwṯ: ġwṯm.
ġyl: ġyln.
ġym: ġymn.
ġmd: ġmdm.
ġnd: ġndn.
ġnm: yġnm.
ġfr: ġfr.
ġḍr: ġḍrn, ḏt/ġḍrn.

f

fgr: mfgrtn.
fyš: mfyš, fyš, fyšn.
fnd: ʾbfnd.
fṣy: ʾfṣy.
fḍḥ: fḍḥm.
fḍl: fḍlm.
fqḥ: fqḥy.
frʿ: yhfrʿ, yfrʿ, frʿm.
frr: frwly.

ṣ

ṣbḥ: hṣbḥ, yhṣbḥ, yṣbḥ, ṣbḥrym.
ṣdq: ʾlṣdq, ʾṣdq, yhṣdq, ṣdqʾl, ṣdqn.
ṣwm: ṣwm.
ṣḥb: ṣḥbm.
ṣḥḥ: ʾṣḥḥ.
ṣḥl: ʾṣḥḥl, ymlʾṣḥl.
ṣḥm: yṣḥm.
ṣḥn: ṣḥḥn.
ṣyḥ: ṣyḥyn.
ṣly: mṣlynn, ṣlyn.
ṣnʿ: ṣnʿw.
ṣʿd: ṣʿdtm.
ṣʿq: ṣʿqn.
ṣrb: ṣrbn.
ṣrḥ: ṣrwḥ.
ṣry: ṣryhw.
ṣrf: ṣrfn.

ḍ

ḍbʿ: ḍbʿn.
ḍẖy: mḍẖym, mḍẖyn.
ḍmd: ḍmdm.
ḍfw: ḍfw.
(*ḍdẖ*)*:* ḍdẖn.

q

qbl: yqbl.
qbm: mhqbm.
qbʿ: qbʿn.
qdm: ʾlqdm.
qwh: ʾlmqh(w).
qwm: ḏmqmtn, zydqwmm, yhqm, ʿlfqm.
qḥd: qḥdm.
qḥṭ: qḥṭn.
qḥm: qḥmm.
qṭb: qṭbn.
qyn: ʾqynm.
qld: mqldn.
qnʾ: qnʾ.
qnʿ: yqnʿm.
qsd: qsdm.
qrʾ: mqrʾm.
qrb: qrb.
qrm: mqrm.
qrn: qrnnhn.
qrs: qrs.
qrḍ: qrḍn.
qrt: qrytm, qrytnhn.
qšw: qšn.
qšm: qšmm.
qtb: qtbn.
qtr: qtr, qtrn.

r

rʾb: yrʾb, rʾbm.
rʾs: rʾs, rʾsw.
rbʾ: mrbʾn.
rbb: rbʾwm, rbʾl, rbnsrm, rbslm, rbʿṯt, rbšms, rbšmsm, rbtnf, rbṯwn, rbbʾwm, rbbʾl, rbbḥgrm, rbbm, rbbtgwbn.
rbḥ: rbḥm.
rbʿ: ʾrbʿnhn, rbʿ, rbʿ[, rbʿt.
rgb: thrgb.
rgz: rgzgzn.
rgl: rglm.
rdm: rdmyn, rdmn.
rdf: yrdf.
rwḥ: hrwḥʾl.
rwẓ: rwẓn.
rwm: ʾlrm, dynrm; yhrm, yrm.
rzḥ: yrzḥ, rzḥym.
rzn: ʾrzn, rzn, trznn.
rḥb: yhrḥb, yrḥb, mrḥbm, rḥbm, rḥbmm, rḥbtn.
rḥḥ: rḥʾl.
rḥl: rḥlm.
rḥḍ: mrḥḍn.
rẖy: rẖyt.
rẖm: yrẖm.
ryb: mrb, mryb.
ryd: rydn, rydt.
rym: ʾrym, hrymm, hrmm, smhrym, smhrm, ṣbḥrym, rym, rymm, rymn;]rymn, rmn, rmtm.
ryś: ryśn.
rkb: rkbn, rkbtn.
rmd: rmdn.
rnḥ: ḏrnḥ.
rsm: yrsm, rsmm.
rsʿ: mrsʿm.
rʿd: yrʿd.
rʿš: yhrʿš.
rfʾ: ʿmrfʿ, rfʾ, rfʾm.
rfd: rfdn.
rfš: rfšn.
rḍw: rḍwm, rḍwn.
rḍḥ: rḍḥtn.
ršd: ršdm.
ršw: ršwn.
ršm: ršm.
rśl: ʾrśl.
rṯd: mrṯdʾwm, mrṯdʾsʾy, mrṯdm, rṯdʾlw, rṯdm, rṯdšmsm, rṯdṯwn.

š

šbw: šbwt.
šbm: šbmm.
šbʿ: šbʿn.
šdd: šddm.
šḏb: šwḏbm.
šhr: šhr.
šwʿ: ʾšwʿ, yhšʿ, yšʿ, šyʿn.
šwf: yšf, šwfʾl, šfʿṯt.
šwq: šwqm.
šwr: yšr.
šḥṭ: šwḥṭ.
šym: mšmn, šmtn.
škr: škrt.
šms: šms(y).
šmr: ʾbšmr, šmr.
šʿb: šʿbm.
šʿr: ʾšʿrn, šʿrm.
šfb: šfbm.
šfq: gdšfq, ʿmšfq.
šṣr: šṣrm.
šrw: šrwn.
šrḥ: ʾlšrḥ, šrḥʾwm, šrḥʾl, šrḥbʾl, šrḥwdm, šrḥm, šrḥsmd, šrḥʿṯt, šrḥṯt.
šrʿ: mšrʿm.
šrq: mšrqytn, šrqn.

ś

śwm: śwm.
śmk: śmkm.
śnḥ: śnḥn.
śrd: śrdd.

t

tbʿ: mtbʿm, tbʿkrb, tbʿm.
tym: tymlt.
tkl: tklm.
tlf: ytlf.
tnʿ: tnʿ, tnʿm.
trd: trd.

ṯ

ṯʾb: ʾṯʾbtm.
ṯʾr: yṯʾr, ṯʾrn.
ṯhy: ṯhwn.
ṯwb: ṯwbʾl, ṯwbm, ṯwbn, ṯwbṯwn.
ṯwr: ṯwr.
ṯkm: *ṯkmtn.*
ṯly: ṯly.
ṯml: ṯml.
ṯny: ṯnt, ṯt.
ṯfy: ṯfyn.
ṯqf: ʾṯqf.

B – *Names related to deities*

I – NAMES OF DEITIES

ʾl: ʾwsʾl, ʾẖtʾl,]ʾl, ʾlʾws, ʾlʾlt, ʾlʾmr, ʾlʾsd, ʾlddn, ʾlhʿn, ʾlwhb, ʾlzʾd, ʾlkrb, ʾlm, ʾlsʿd, ʾlʿz, ʾlʿṯt, ʾlṣdq, ʾlqdm, ʾlrm, ʾlšrḥ, ʾlṯwrm, ddʾl, ḏrḥʾl, hwfʾl, hrwḥʾl, wddʾl, whbʾl, zydʾl, ydʿʾl, yḥmʾl, yṯʿʾl, krbʾl, nšdʾl, ʿmrʾl, ṣdqʾl, rbʾl, rbbʾl, rḥʾl, šwfʾl, šrḥʾl, šrḥbʾl, ṯwbʾl, the various forms of ʾlmqh.
ʾlmqh: ʾmtʾlmqh.
h(w)bs: hbs.
wd(m): sʿdwdm; šrḥwdm.
ḥgrm: rbbḥgrm.
lt: ʾwslt, whblt, ḥmlt, ʿmrlt, tymlt.
nsrm: rbnsrm.
ʿm: ʿbdʿm; ʿmyṯʿ; ʿmkrb; ʿmm; ʿmrfʾ, ʿmšfq.
ʿṯtr: ḥywʿṯtr, ʿbdʿṯtr, ʿṯtr, ʿṯtrygr,
ʿṯt: ʾwsʿṯt, ʾlʿṯt, hwfʿṯt, hḥyʿṯt, whbʿṯt, ḥmʿṯt, krbʿṯt, lḥyʿṯt, lfʿṯt, ʿṯt, rbʿṯt, šfʿṯt, šrḥʿṯt;
ṯt: šrḥṯt.
šms: ʾšms, whbšms(m), sʿdšmsm, rbšms(m), rṯdšmsm,]šms, šms.
tʾlb: sʿdtʾlb.
ṯwr: ʾlṯwrm.

2 – EPITHETS OF DEITIES

tnf: rbtnf.
ṯwn: hnʾṯwn, whbṯwn, sʿdṯwn, rbṯwn, rṯdṯwn, ṯwbṯwn.

3 – NAME OF TEMPLE

ʾwm: ʾwwm, whbʾwm, ḥywʾwm, mrṯdʾwm, sʿdʾwm, ʿbdʾwm, rbʾwm, rbbʾwm, šrḥʾwm.

C – *Other elements*

I – AT THE BEGINNING

ḏ and *ḏt:* ḏbyn, ḏmqmtn, ḏrnḥ, ḏt(/)bʿdn(m), ḏt(/)ḥmym, ḏt/ẓhrn, ḏt/ġḏrn.
l [preposition]*:* lʿzzm, lʿšm.
s: sbqlm, snfrm.

2 – IN THE CENTER

b [preposition]*:* šrḥbʾl.
h [possess. pron.]*:* s[mh, smh[, smhʾmr, smhwtr, smhyfʿ, smhkrb, smhsmʿ, smhʿly, smhrym, smhrm.

3 – AT THE END

Preliminary note: Endings such as, e.g., *-y*, *-yn*, *-n*, *-t*, *-tn*, are very well known and are not listed here.

-h: khlh, ʿḏbh.
-hw: ṣryhw.
-hmw: ẖyrhmw.
-wm: ḥlzwm, ʿynwm.
-ym: rzḥym.
-nhn: ʾrbʿnhn, bytnhn, mwnhn, qrytnhn, qrnnhn.
-ny: ʾhlny.
-nm: ʾlfnm, klwnm.
-nn: mṣlynn.
-nt: ḥdlnt.
-mm: rḥbmm.

LIST OF PHOTOGRAPHS

Ja 550 (nine); 552; 566; 569; 570; 571; 572 (four); 574; 580; 582; 583; 585; 587; 588; 589; 590; 591 (two); 592; 594; 595; 597; 599; 600; 603; 605; 608; 611; 612; 613; 614; 615; 616; 617; 619; 620; 621; 623; 624; 625; 637; 638; 639; 641; 644; 648; 649; 651; 652; 654; 656; 657; 658; 660; 661; 662 (three); 666; 667 (two); 668; 669; 672; 673; 674 (two); 675; 676; 677; 678; 679; 680; 683 (two); 684; 685; 686; 687, 688; 689; 690; 691; 692; 693; 694; 695; 696; 697; 698; 699; 700; 701; 704; 705; 706; 707; 708; 709; 710; 711; 712; 713; 714; 715; 716; 717 (two); 718 (two); 719; 720; 721; 722; 723; 724 (two); 725; 726; 727; 728; 729; 730; 731; 732; 733; 734; 735; 737; 762; 763; 764; 765; 766; 767; 772 (two); 773; 774; 775; 776; 777; 778; 780; 781; 782; 783; 784; 786; 787; 788; 789; 790; 791; 792; 793; 796; 797 (two); 798; 799 (two); 800; 801; 802; 803; 804; 807; 809 (two); 810 (two); 811; 812; 813; 815; 816 (two); 817; 818; 819 (two); 820; 828; 829; 830; 831; 832; 833; 834; 835; 836; 837; 839; 840; 841; 842; 843; 844; 846; 847; 848; 849; 850; 853F; 855; 877.

LIST OF DRAWINGS AND FACSIMILES

Plate A: symbols of Ja 559, 566, 567, 569, 574, 582, 583, 585, 587, 589, 590, 591, 603, 612, 613, 614, 616, 619, 620, 621, 630, 637, 639, 644, 648, 654, 656, 657, 667, 686, 689, 690, 692, 694, 695, 698, 700, 702, 707, and 709.

Plate B: symbols of Ja 710, 711, 713, 715, 717, 723, 725, 726, 727, 728, 729, 731, 733, 735, 757, 851, 787, 788, 792, 803, 841, 842, 877, and 879, and designs of Ja 581, 587, 591, 597, 618, 684, 690, 698, 700, 709, and 751.

Plate C: Fig. 1: west half of ʾAwwâm; location of Ja 550-557.
Fig. 2: symbols of Ja 550, 551, 552, 554, 555, 557, 558, 673, and 831, and design of Ja 832.
Lettering of Ja 819, 832, 831, and 673.

Plate D: lettering of Ja 552, 553, Fakhry 69, Ja 555, 554, 550, and 551.

Plate E: lettering of Fakhry 9, 28, CIH 573, Ja 853 F, CIH 433, Ja 561, and 855, and symbols of Fakhry 9, 28 and Ja 561.

Plate F: map: the Bataʿite-Hamdânid dynasty of Yarum ʾAyman.

Plate G: map: the Ṯaniatite-Hamdânid dynasty of Fariʿum Yanhub.

Plate H: map: the dynasty of Yasrum Yuhanʿim.

Plate I: lettering of CIH 46 and Gl 1594; photostat of the copy of CIH 448; lettering of RÉS 4196, 4938, Ja 648, and CIH 353.

Plate J: lettering of Ja 652, 649, 651, 654, RÉS 3910, CIH 407, and RÉS 4230.

Plate K: lettering of Ja 656, 657, 658, and 660.

Plate L: lettering of Ja 661, 662, CIH 430, 431 + 438, and 948.

Plate M: lettering of CIH 365, 457, RÉS 4775; photostat of the copy of RÉS 4708, CIH 569, Gl 389, and Ph 229.

Plate N: lettering of RÉS 3960, 4716, Ja 856, Wâdî Maʾsil 1, Ja 668 and 669.

Photographs and Facsimiles

Ja 550, no. 1
–/ḏmrydʿ/bn/mḏmrm/hqny/–;
/ḏt/ġḍrn/wb/– –/wtr/wb/ (y) ṯ°mr/–.

Ja 550, no. 2
–/gnʾn/ln/ʾʾwdn/ – – /wmḥfdt/ḏn/mhyʿn/–;
–/yṯ°mr/byn/ – – /ḏt/ḥmym/–.

Ja 550, no. 3
–/šqrm/wkl/ – – /ḏmrydʿ/wsmhʾmr/–;
–/bslm/sbʾ/ – – /tʾmnm/bʿṯtr/–.

Ja 550, no. 4
–/ḏmrydʿ/wsmhʾmr/ – – /ʾnḫlhw/bʾḏnt/–;
/–ḫrfy/hrs/ – – /bslm/sbʾ/–.

Ja 550, no. 5
/–ʾnḫlhw/bʾḏnt/– – /wġmm/wʿsmt/–;
–/šʿbn/wkl/– – /hrs/bkbtn/–.

Ja 550, no. 6
–/wġmm/wʿsmt/–;
–/wʾšʿbn/ḫmst/– – /wkl/ʾrgl/–.

Ja 550, no. 7
–/wtr/wyʿqb/– – /qtbn/whwfy/–.

Ja 550, no. 8
–/wmḫḍn/byhdl/ywm/–;
–/wywm/hwṣthw/– – /wʾšʿbn/ḫmst/–.

Ja 550, no. 9
–/wmḫḏn/byhdl/ywm/hwfyhw/–;
Triple Symbol ḏt/tnbʾhw/– – /wtr/wyʿqb/–.

Ja 552

Ja 566

Ja 569

Ja 570

Ja 572, part = Ja 593

Ja 571

Ja 572, part = MaMB 85

Ja 572, part = Ja 573 B

Ja 572, part = Ja 573 A

Ja 574

Ja 580

Ja 582

Ja 583

Ja 585

Ja 587

Ja 588

Ja 589

Ja 590

PLATE 7

Ja 591, right part = MaMB 192

Ja 591, left part = MaMB 82

Ja 592

Ja 594

Ja 595

Ja 597

Ja 599

Ja 600

Ja 603, top

Ja 605

Ja 608

Ja 611, part = MaMB 21

Ja 612

Ja 613

Ja 614

Ja 615

Ja 616, top = MaMB 154

Ja 617

Ja 619

Ja 620

Ja 621

Ja 623

Ja 624

Ja 625

Ja 639

Ja 638

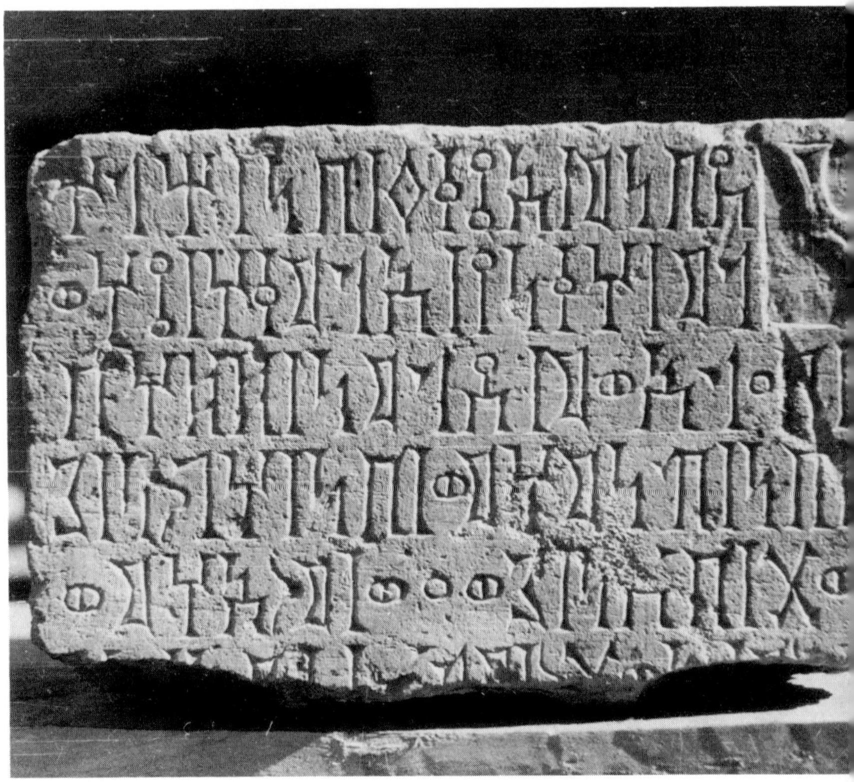

Ja 637

Ja 641, part = MaMB 49

Ja 644

Ja 648

Ja 649

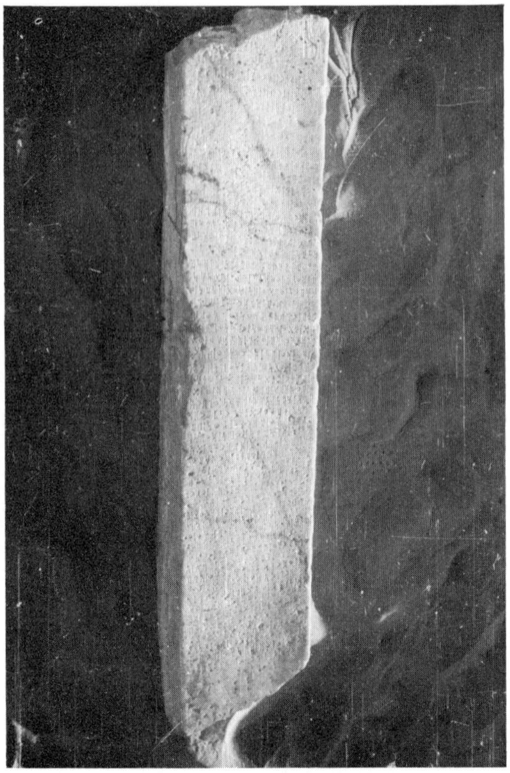

Ja 651

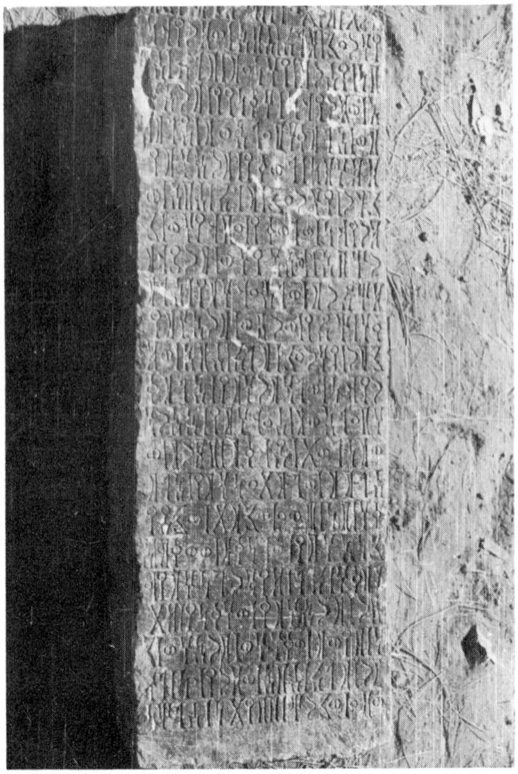

Ja 652

Ja 654

Ja 656

Ja 657

Ja 658, bottom = MaMB 182

Ja 660

Ja 662, top = MaMB 98

Ja 661

Ja 662, bottom = MaMB 96

Ja 662, center = MaMB 91

Ja 666

Ja 667, top = MaMB 15

Ja 667, bottom = MaMB 86

Ja 668

Ja 669

Ja 672

Ja 673

Ja 675

Ja 674, front

Ja 674, left side

Ja 677

Ja 676

Ja 678

Ja 679

Ja 680

Ja 683, left side

Ja 683, front

Ja 684

Ja 686

Ja 685

Ja 687

Ja 688

Ja 689

Ja 690

Ja 691

Ja 692

Ja 693

Ja 694

Ja 695

Ja 696

Ja 697

Ja 698

Ja 699

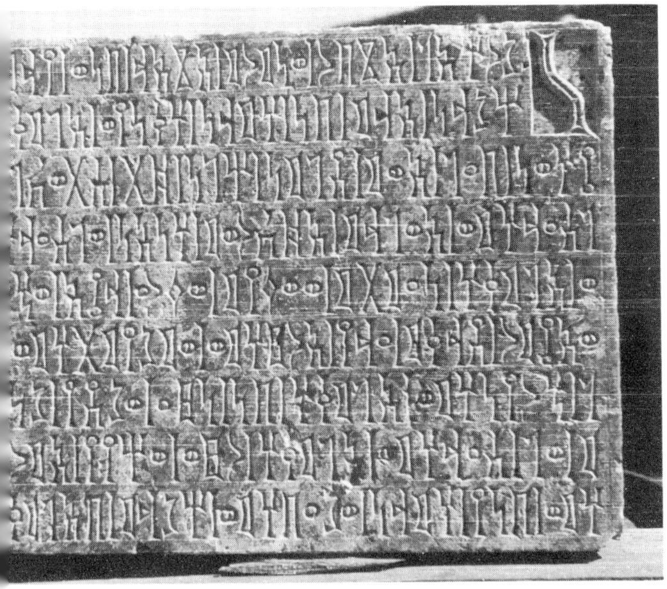

Ja 704

Ja 700, main part = MaMB 139

Ja 705

Ja 701

Ja 706

Ja 707

Ja 708

Ja 709

Ja 710

Ja 711

Ja 712

Ja 713

Ja 714

Ja 715

Ja 716

Ja 717, part = MaMB 120

Ja 718, right part = MaMB 56

Ja 717, main part = MaMB 175

Ja 718, left part = MaMB 176

Ja 719

Ja 720

Ja 721

Ja 722

Ja 723

Ja 724

Ja 724, top of the stone

Ja 726

Ja 725

Ja 727

Ja 729

Ja 728

Ja 730

Ja 731

Ja 732

Ja 733

Ja 734

Ja 737

Ja 735, top = MaMB 234

Ja 763

Ja 762

Ja 764

Ja 765

Ja 766

Ja 767

Ja 772, front

Ja 772, left

Ja 773

Ja 774

Ja 775

Ja 776

Ja 777

Ja 778

Ja 783

Ja 781

Ja 780

Ja 782

Ja 784

Ja 787

Ja 786

Ja 788

Ja 789

Ja 791

Ja 790

Ja 792

Ja 793

Ja 796

Ja 797 A

Ja 797 B

Ja 798

Ja 799, top = MaMB 121

Ja 799, bottom = MaMB 93

Ja 800

Ja 801

Ja 802

Ja 803

Ja 804

Ja 807

Ja 810 A = MaMB 125

Ja 809, left = MaMB 105 + 67

Ja 809, right = MaMB 124

Ja 810 B = MaMB 76

Ja 811

Ja 812

Ja 813

Ja 815

Ja 816, main part = MaMB 191

Ja 816, bottom = MaMB 123

Ja 817

Ja 818

Ja 819, left part = MaMB 17

Ja 819, right part = MaMB 235

Ja 820

Ja 828

Ja 829

Ja 830

Ja 831

Ja 832

Ja 833

Ja 834

Ja 835

Ja 836

Ja 837

Ja 839

Ja 840

Ja 841

Ja 842

Ja 843

Ja 844

Ja 846

Ja 847

Ja 848

Ja 849

Ja 850

Ja 853 F, right part = MaV 7

Ja 855

Ja 877 = AM 205

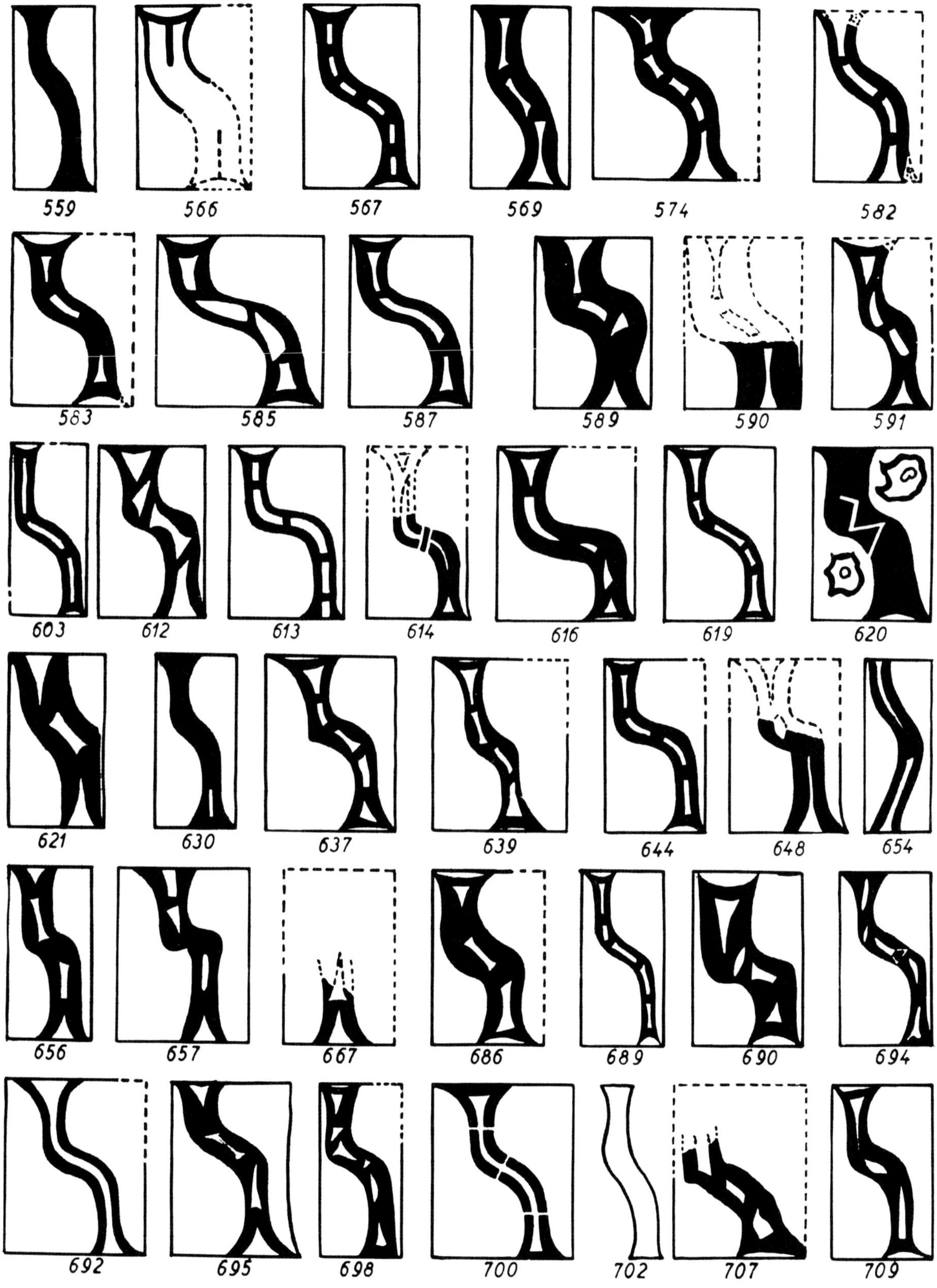
559
566
567
569
574
582
583
585
587
589
590
591
603
612
613
614
616
619
620
621
630
637
639
644
648
654
656
657
667
686
689
690
694
692
695
698
700
702
707
709

Plate A

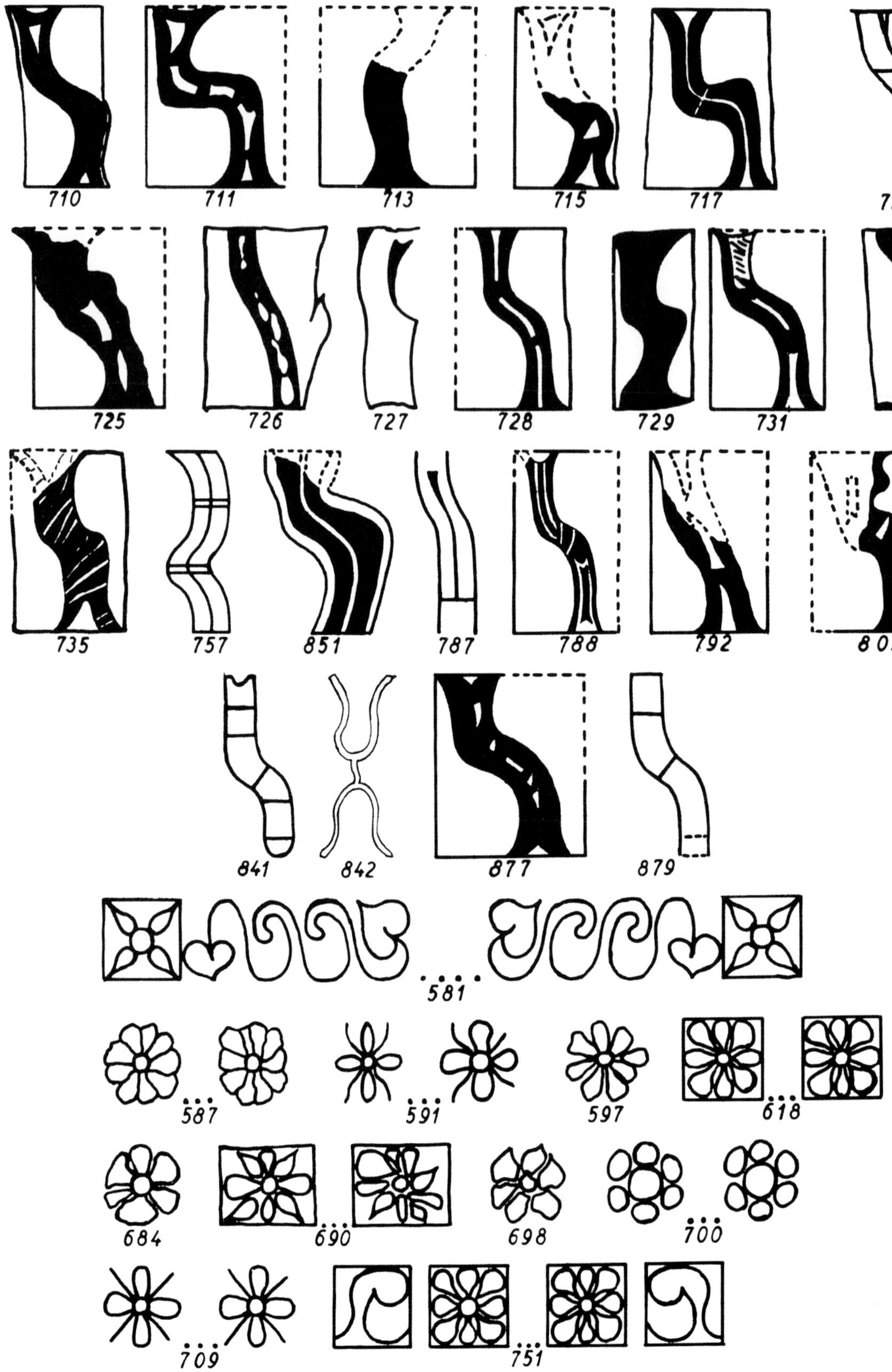
710 711 713 715 717 723
725 726 727 728 729 731 733
735 757 851 787 788 792 803
841 842 877 879
581
587 591 597 618
684 690 698 700
709 751

PLATE B

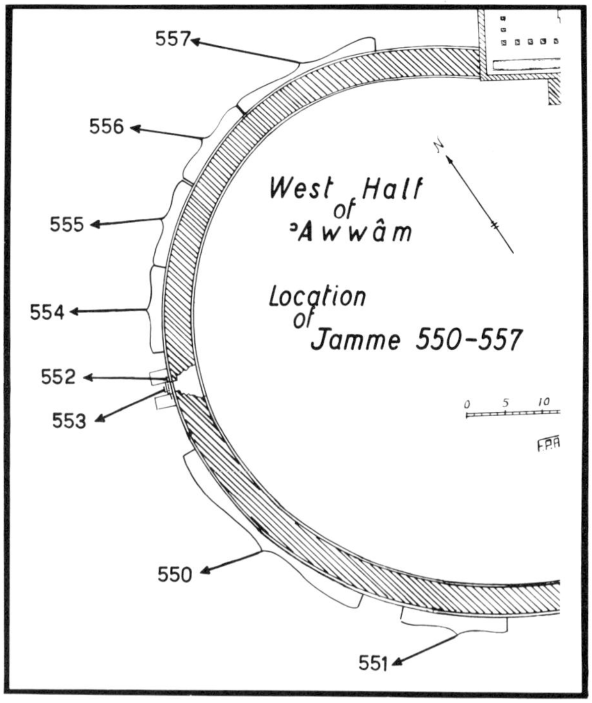

Fig. 1

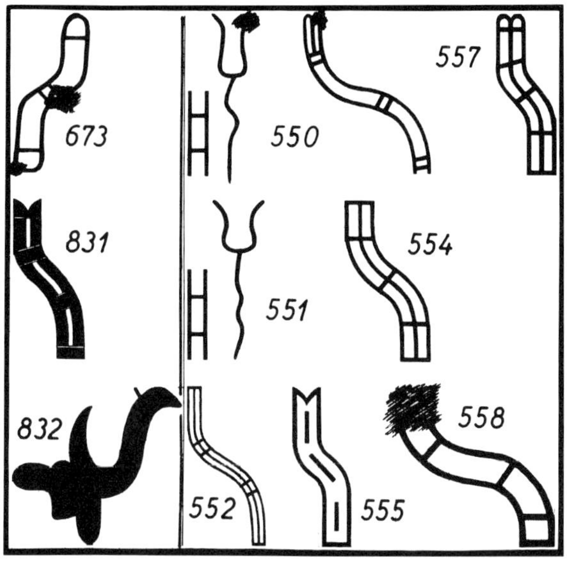

Fig. 2

Ja 819

Ja 832

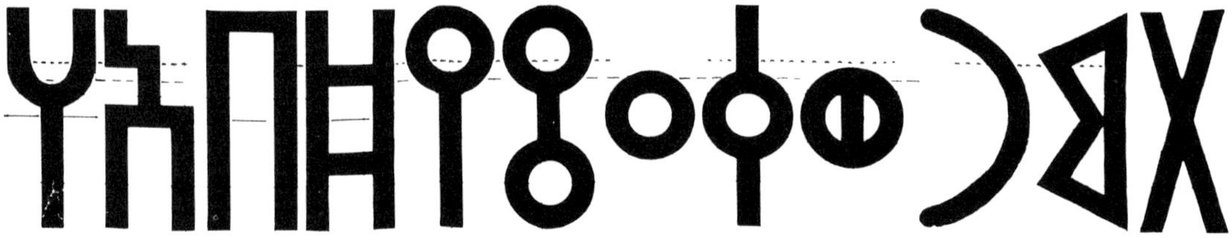

Ja 831

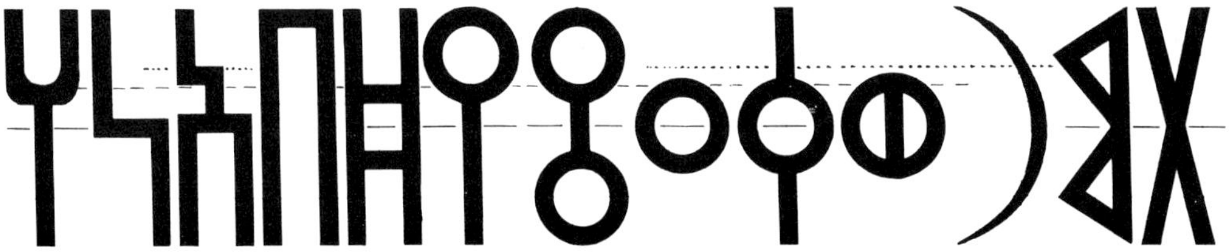

Ja 673

Plate C

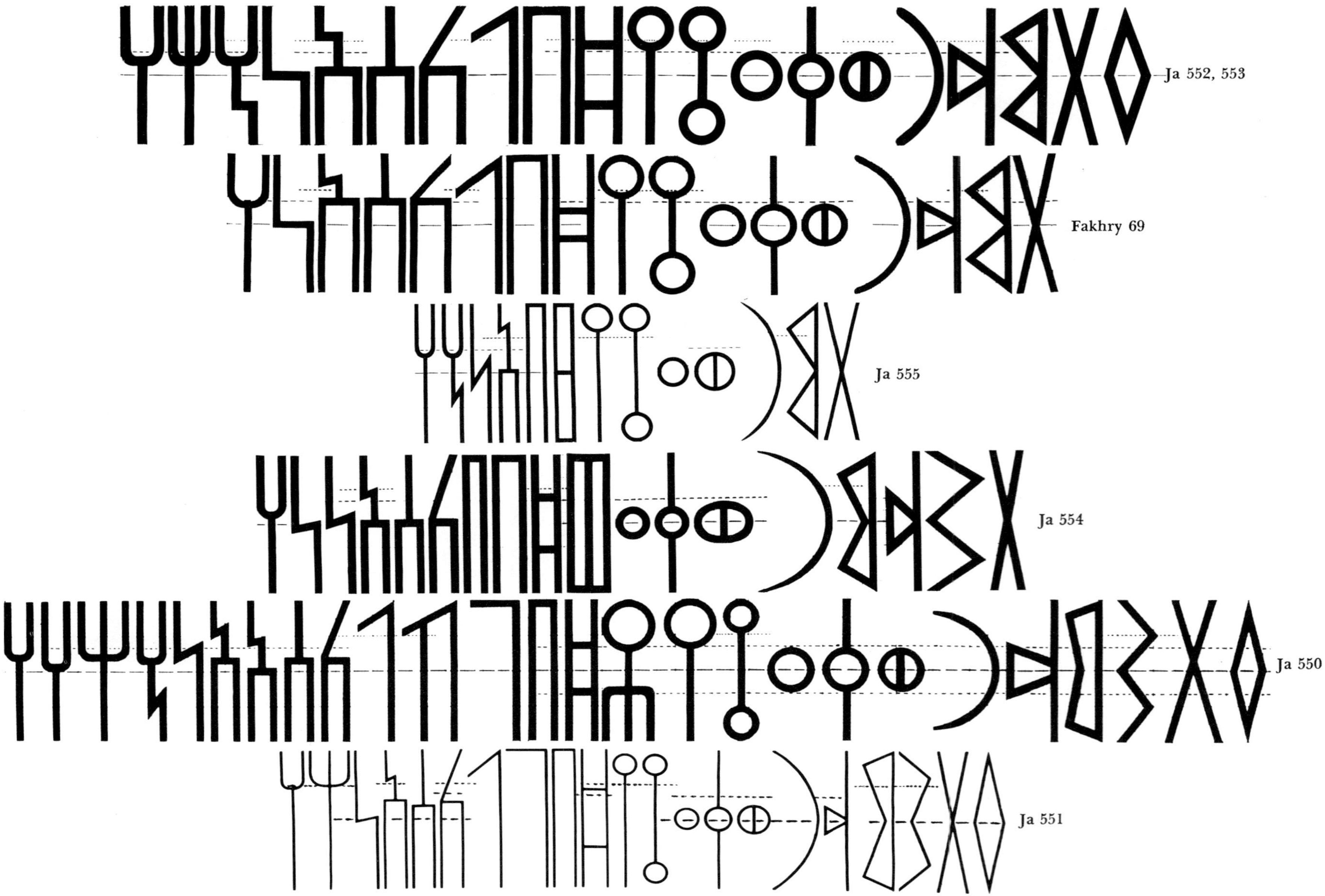

Plate D

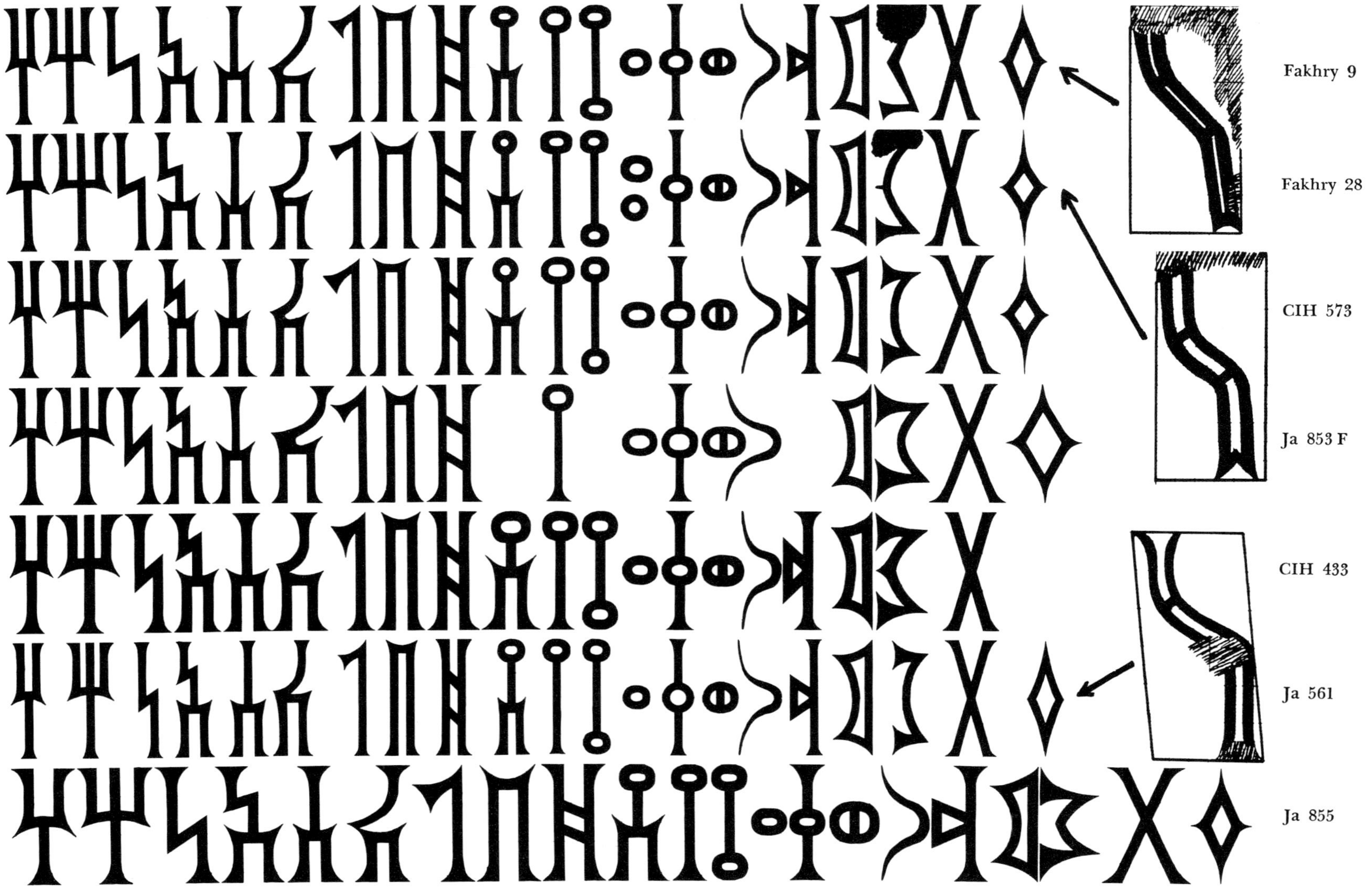

PLATE E

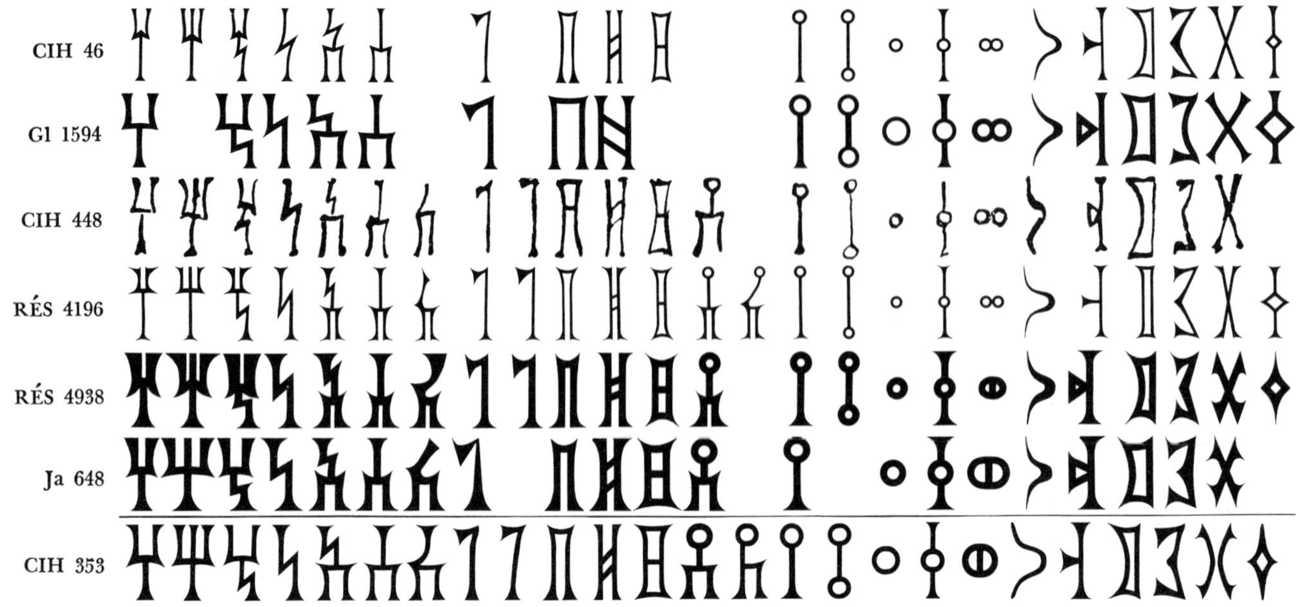

PLATE I

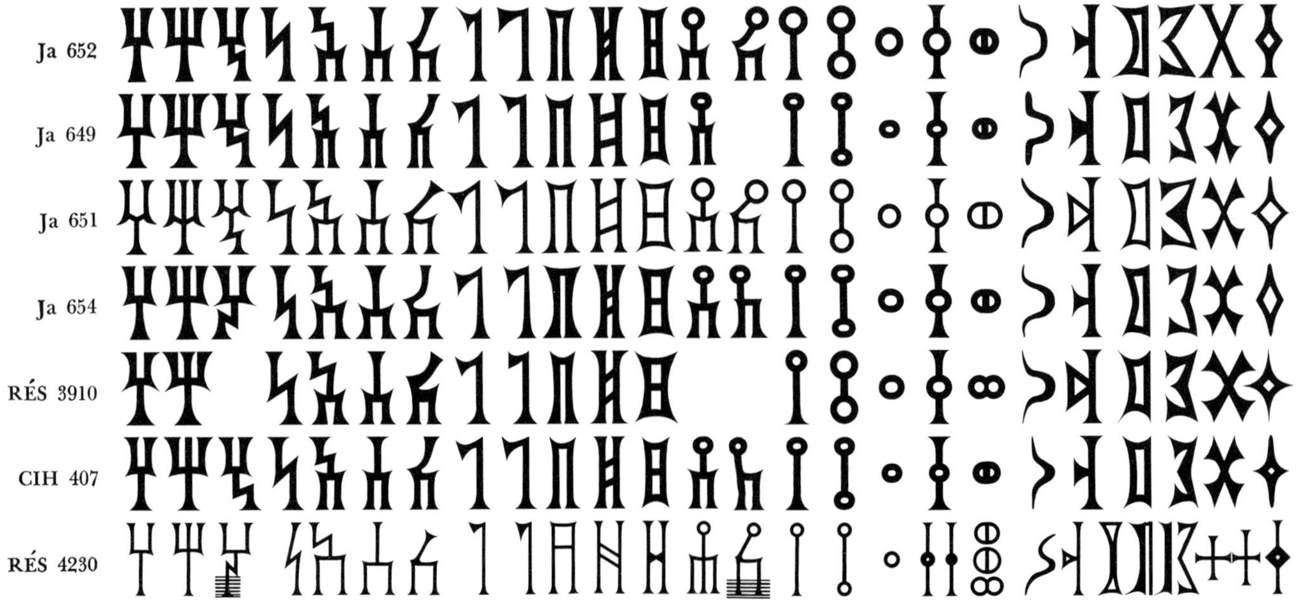

PLATE J

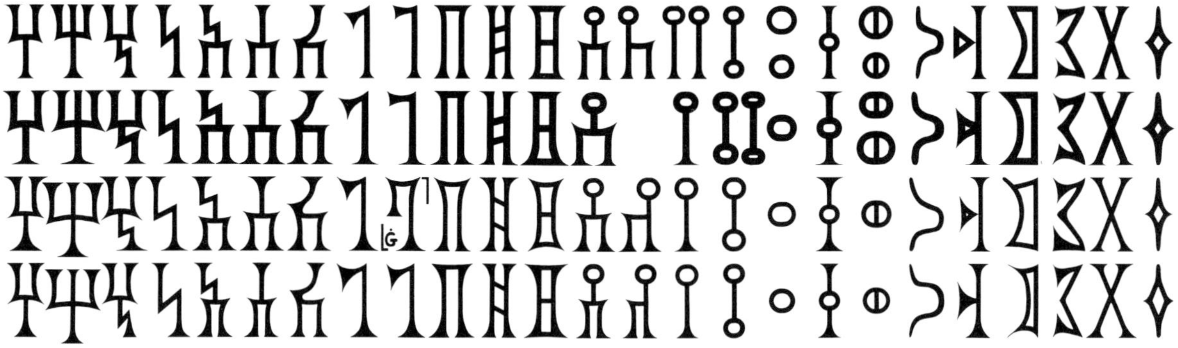

Ja 656
Ja 657
Ja 658
Ja 660

PLATE K

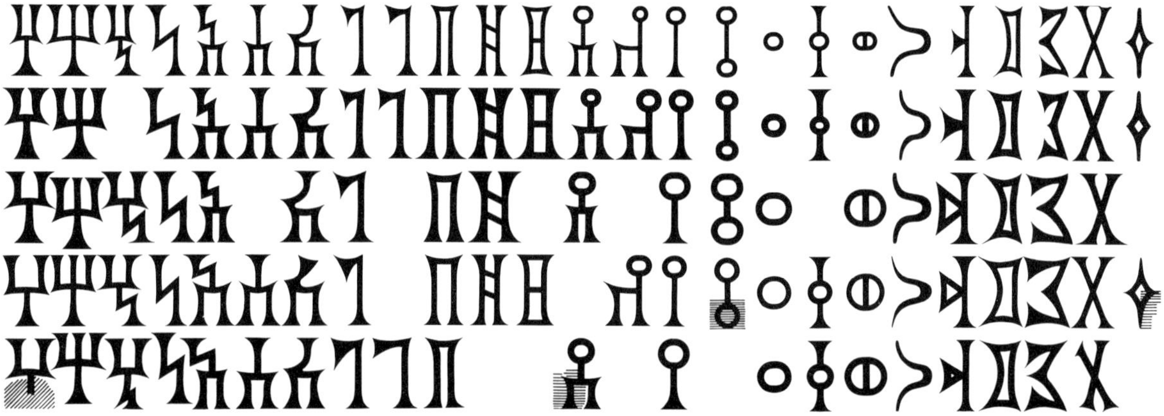

Ja 661
Ja 662
CIH 430
CIH 431 + 438
CIH 948

PLATE L

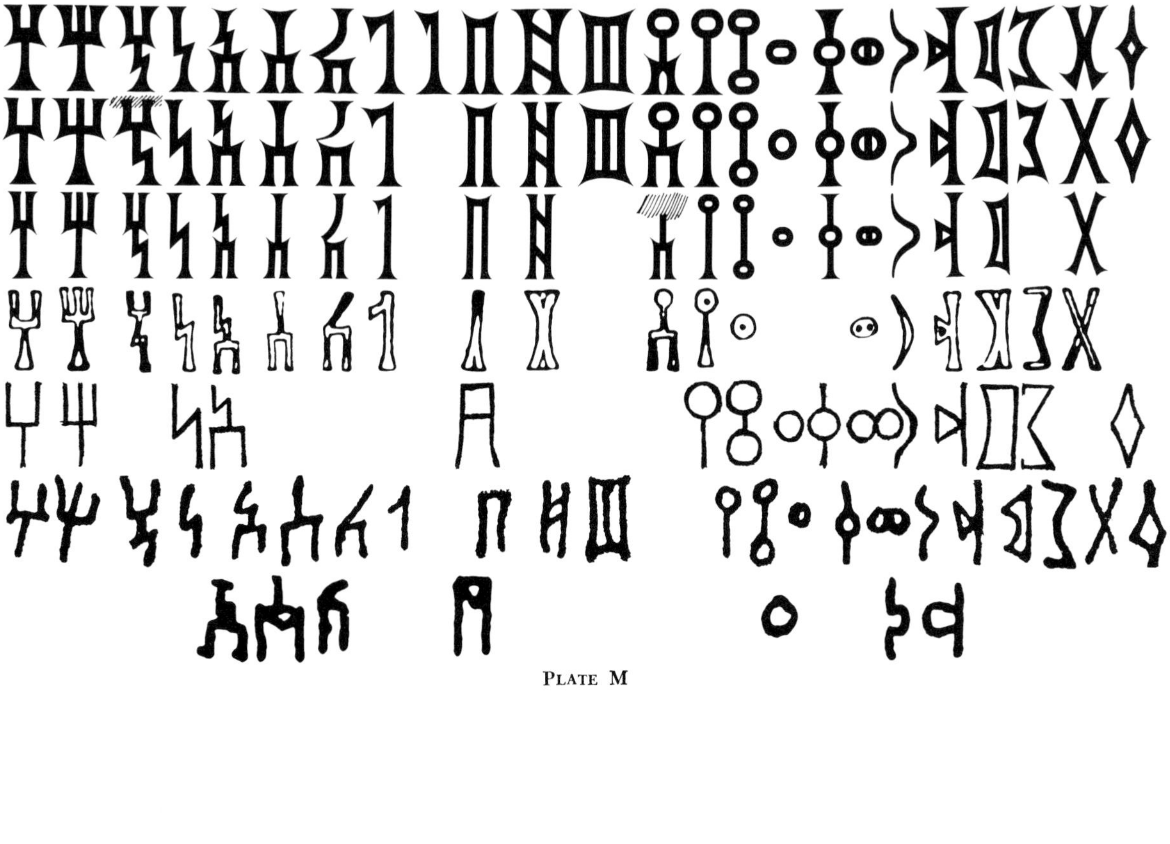

CIH 365
CIH 457
RÉS 4775
RÉS 4708
CIH 569
Gl 389
Ph 229

PLATE M

RÉS 3960
RÉS 4616
Ja 856
Wâdî Ma'sil 1
Ja 668
Ja 669

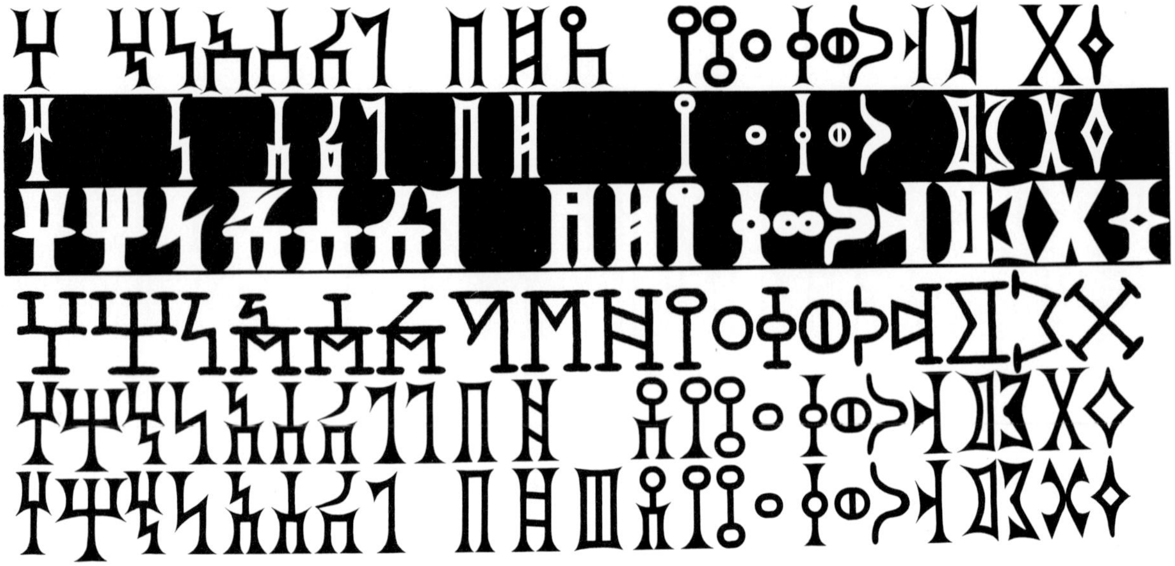

Plate N

CIH 326
CIH 517
Gl 1197
Ja 564

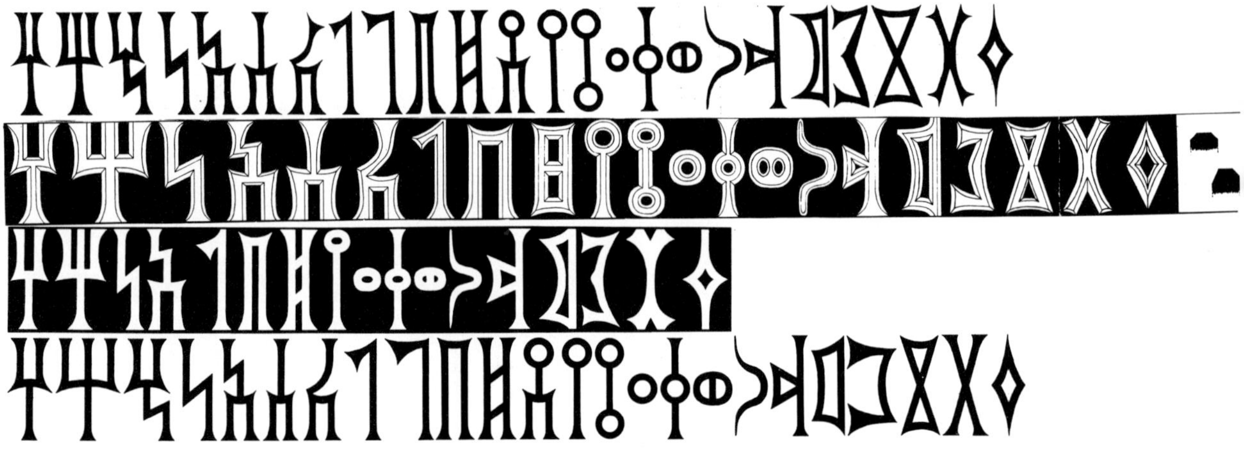

Plate O

Ja 768

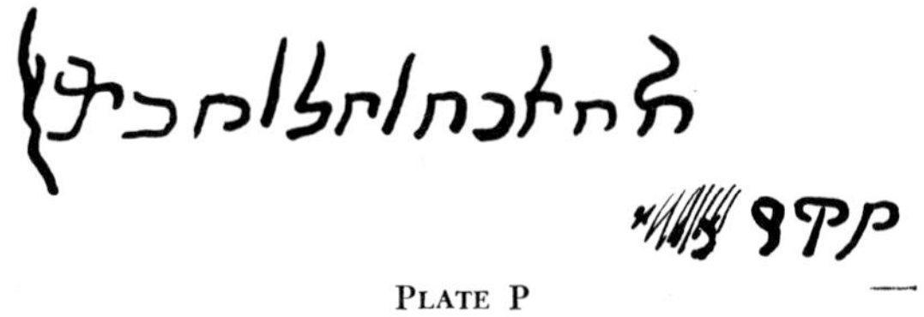

Plate P

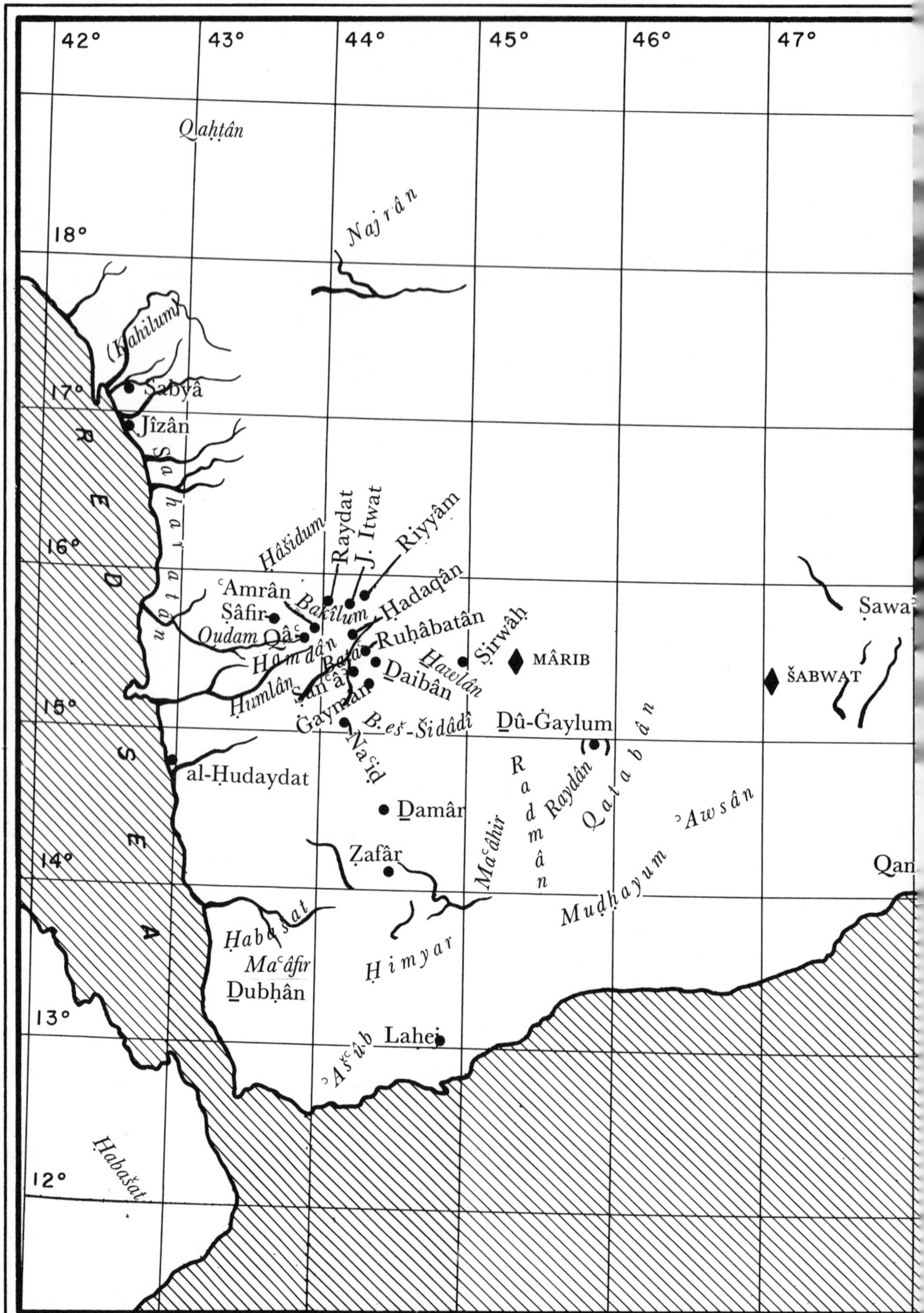
42°
43°
44°
45°
46°
47°
18°
17°
16°
15°
14°
13°
12°
Qaḥṭân
Najrân
(Kahilum)
Ṣabyâ
Jîzân
RED SEA
Saharatan
Ḥâšidum
Raydat
J. Itwat
Riyyâm
ʿAmrân
Bakîlum
Ḥadaqân
Ṣâfir
Oudam
Qâʿ
Ruḥâbatân
Hamdân
Ṣirwâḥ
MÂRIB
ŠABWAT
Ḥawlân
Ṣanʿâʾ
Ḍaibân
Humlân
Gaymân
B. eš-Šidâdî
Dû-Ġaylum
Naʿid
al-Ḥudaydat
Radmân
Raydân
Qatabân
Damâr
ʾAwsân
Maʿâhir
Ẓafâr
Mudḥayum
Ḥabašat
Maʿâfir
Ḍubḥân
Ḥimyar
Lahej
ʾAšʿûb
Ḥabašat

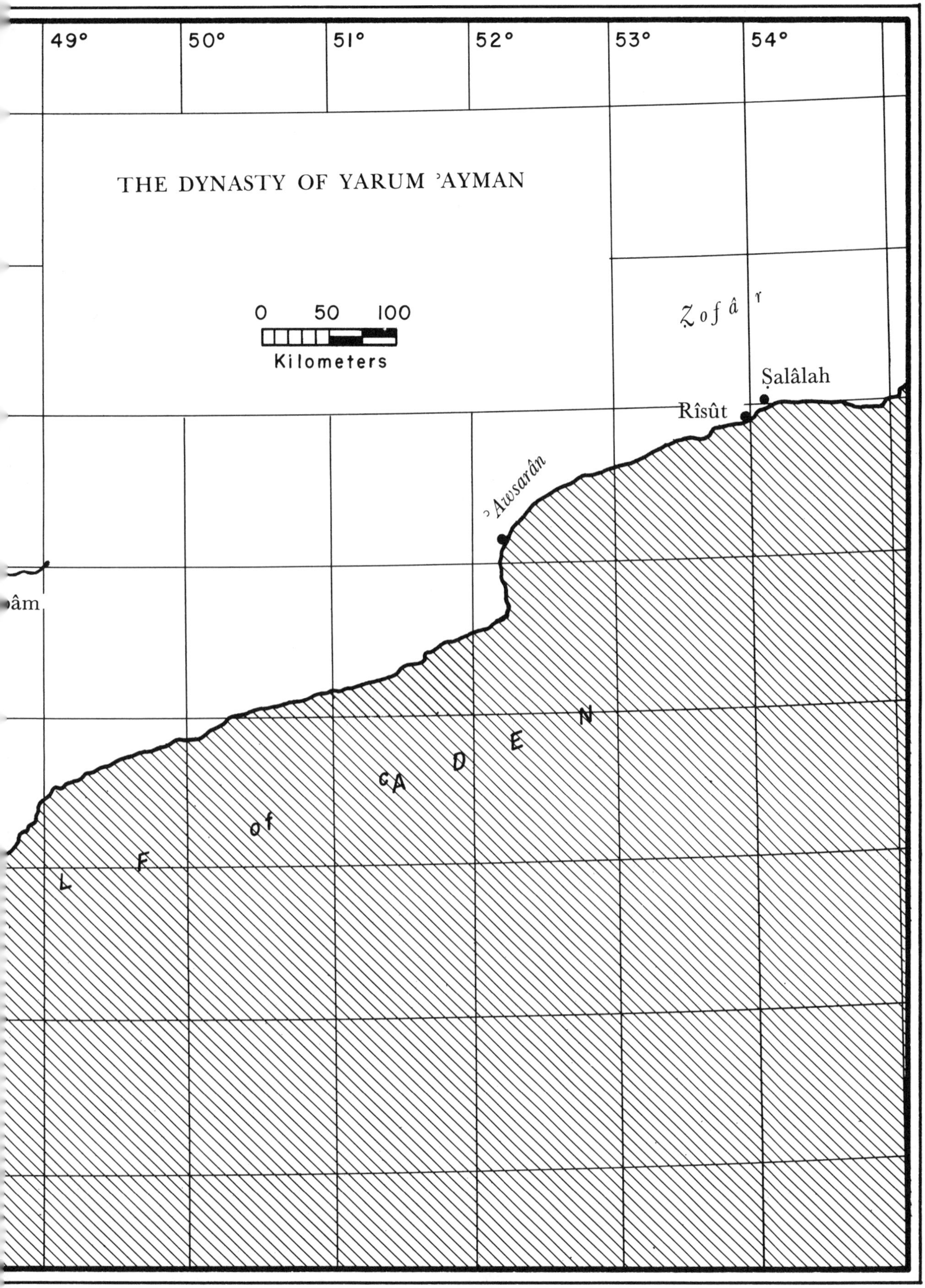

49°
50°
51°
52°
53°
54°
THE DYNASTY OF YARUM ʾAYMAN
0 50 100
Kilometers
Ẓofâr
Ṣalâlah
Rîsût
ʾAwsarân
âm
L F of ʿA D E N

PLATE F

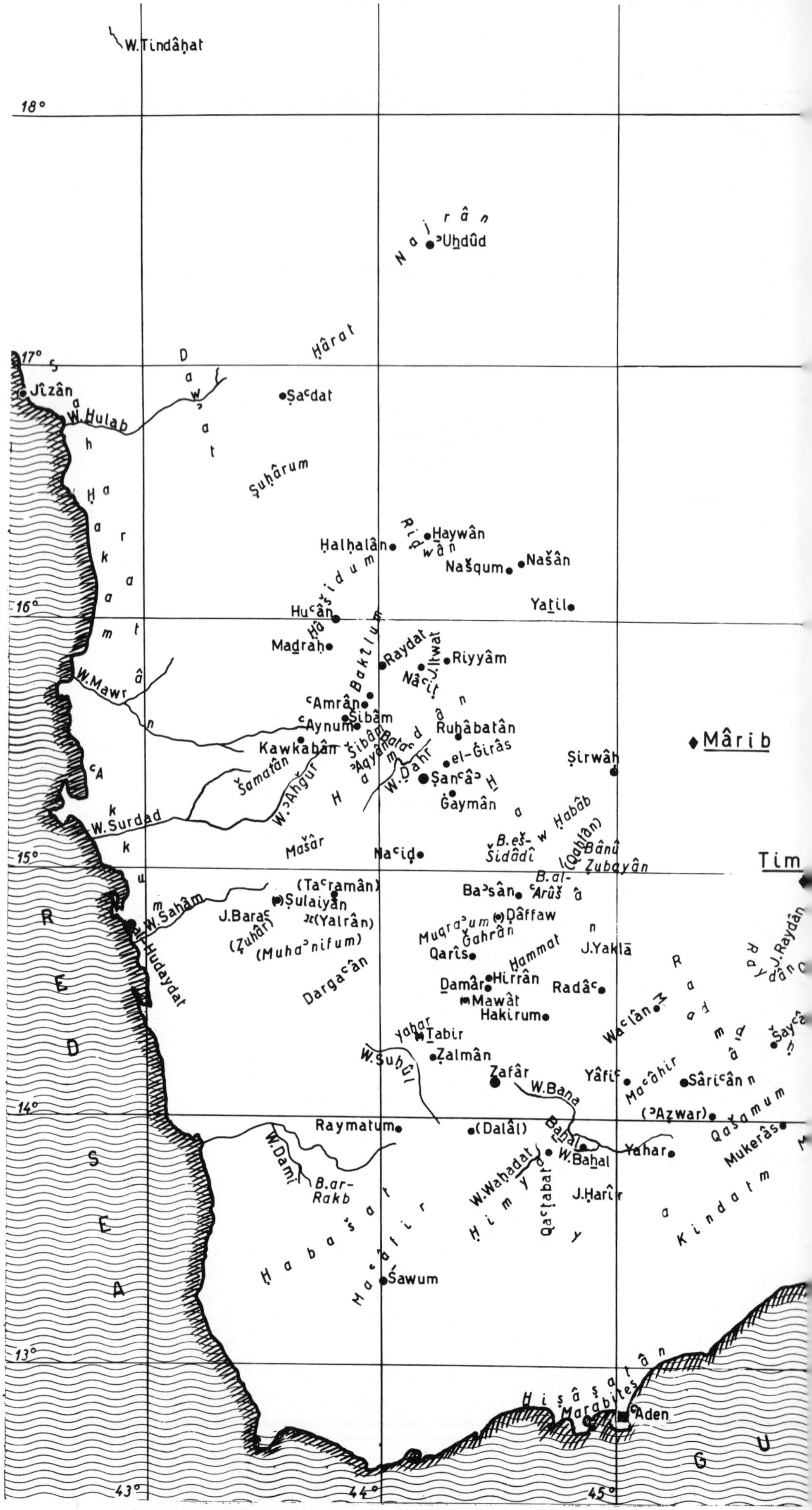

W.Tindâḥat
18°
17°
16°
15°
14°
13°
43°
44°
45°
ʾUḫdûd
Ḥârat
Jîzân
W.Ḫulab
Ṣaʿdat
Ṣuḥârum
Ḥalḥalân
Ḥaywân
Našqum
Našân
Yaṯil
Huʿân
Madraḥ
Raydat
Riyyâm
ʿAmrân
Sibâm
ʿAynum
Ruḥâbatân
Mârib
Kawkabân
el-Girâs
Ṣirwâḥ
Ṣanʿâʾ
Gaymân
W.Mawr
W.Surdad
W.Dahr
Mašâr
Naʿiḍ
(Taʿramân)
Ṣulaiyân
J.Baraʿ
(Yalrân)
(Ẓuhâr)
(Muhaʾnifum)
W.Sahâm
al-Hudaydat
Dargaʿân
Baʾsân
Ḍâffaw
Qarîs
J.Yaklâ
Damâr
Hirrân
Radâʿ
Mawât
Hakirum
Tabir
Zalmân
W.Suḥûl
Ẓafâr
W.Bana
Yâfiʿ
Sâriʿân
(ʾAzwar)
Raymatum
(Dalâl)
W.Baḥal
Yahar
Mukerâs
W.Wahadat
J.Ḥarîr
W.Dami
B.ar-Rakb
Ṣawum
Aden
Marabites
R E D S E A

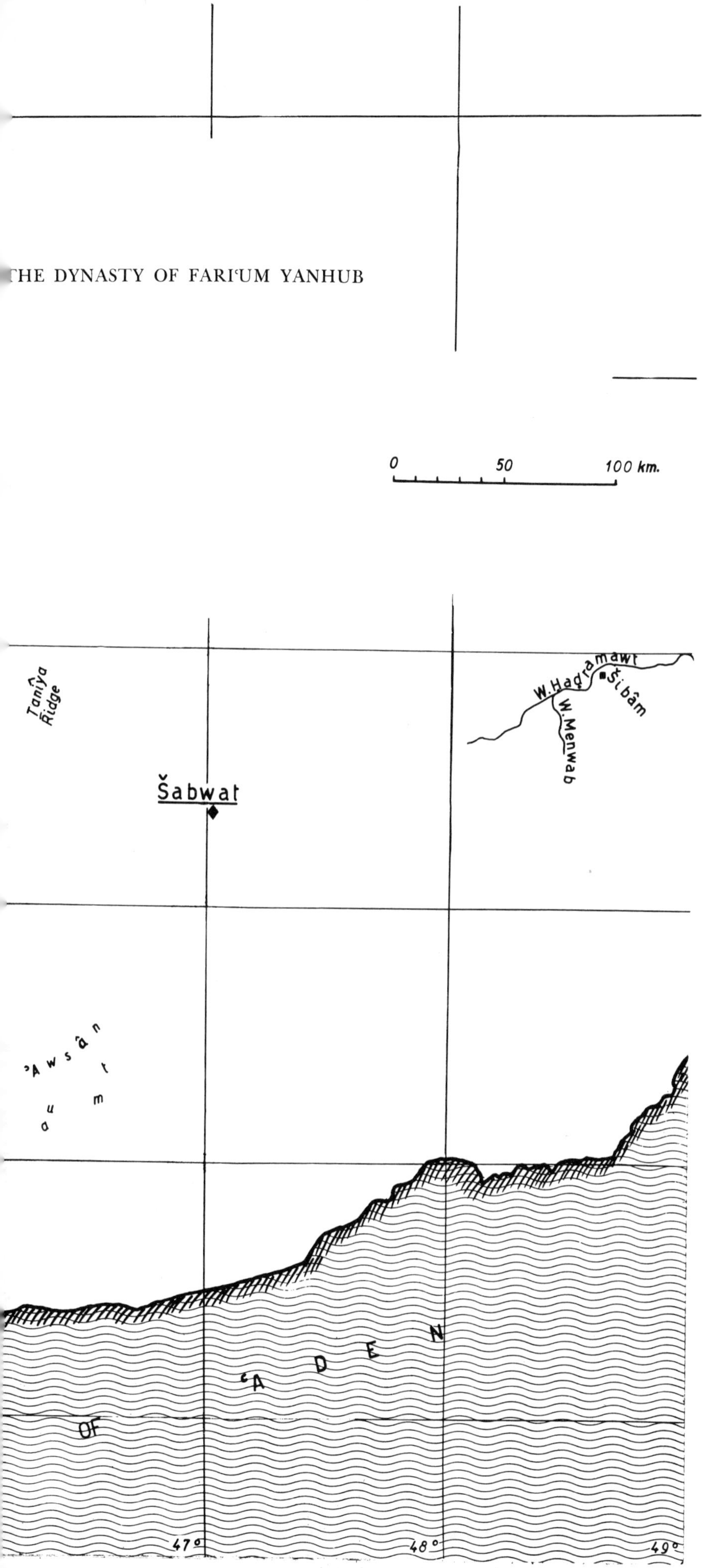
THE DYNASTY OF FARIʿUM YANHUB
0 50 100 km.
Ṭanîya Ridge
Šabwat
W. Haḍramawt
Šibâm
W. Menwab
ʾAwsân
ʿADEN
OF
47°
48°
49°

Plate G

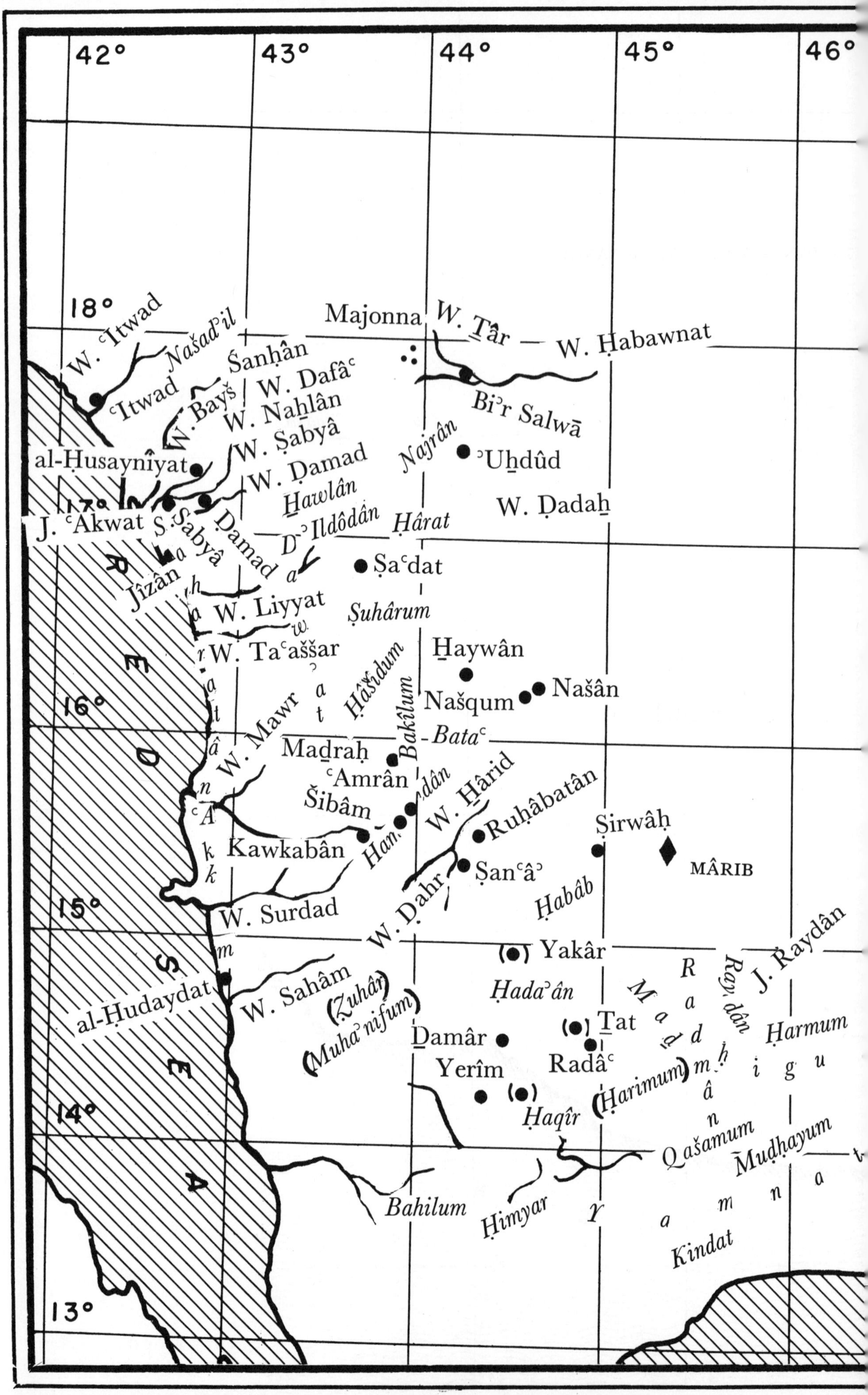
42°
43°
44°
45°
46°
18°
17°
16°
15°
14°
13°
W. ᶜItwad
ᶜItwad
Našadᵓil
Šanḥân
W. Bayš
W. Dafâᶜ
W. Naḫlân
W. Ṣabyâ
W. Ḍamad
Majonna
W. Ṯâr
W. Ḥabawnat
Biᵓr Salwā
Najrân
ᵓUḫdûd
W. Ḍadaḫ
al-Ḥusayniyat
Ḫawlân
J. ᶜAkwat
Ṣabyâ
Ḍamad
Dᵓ Ildôdân
Ḥârat
Jîzân
Ṣaᶜdat
W. Liyyat
Ṣuhârum
W. Taᶜaššar
Ḫaywân
Ḥâšidum
Bakîlum
Našqum
Našân
W. Mawr
Madraḥ
Bataᶜ
ᶜAmrân
Šibâm
Hamdân
W. Ḫârid
Ruḥâbatân
Ṣirwâḥ
Kawkabân
Ṣanᶜâᵓ
MÂRIB
Ḥabâb
W. Surdad
W. Ḍahr
Yakâr
al-Ḥudaydat
W. Sahâm
(Ẓuhâr)
(Muhaᵓnifum)
Ḥadaᵓân
Ṯat
Ḍamâr
Radâᶜ
Yerîm
(Ḥarimum)
Ḥaqîr
Maḍḥâm
Raydân
J. Raydân
Ḥarmum
Qašamum
Mudḥayum
Bahilum
Ḥimyar
Kindat
R E D S E A

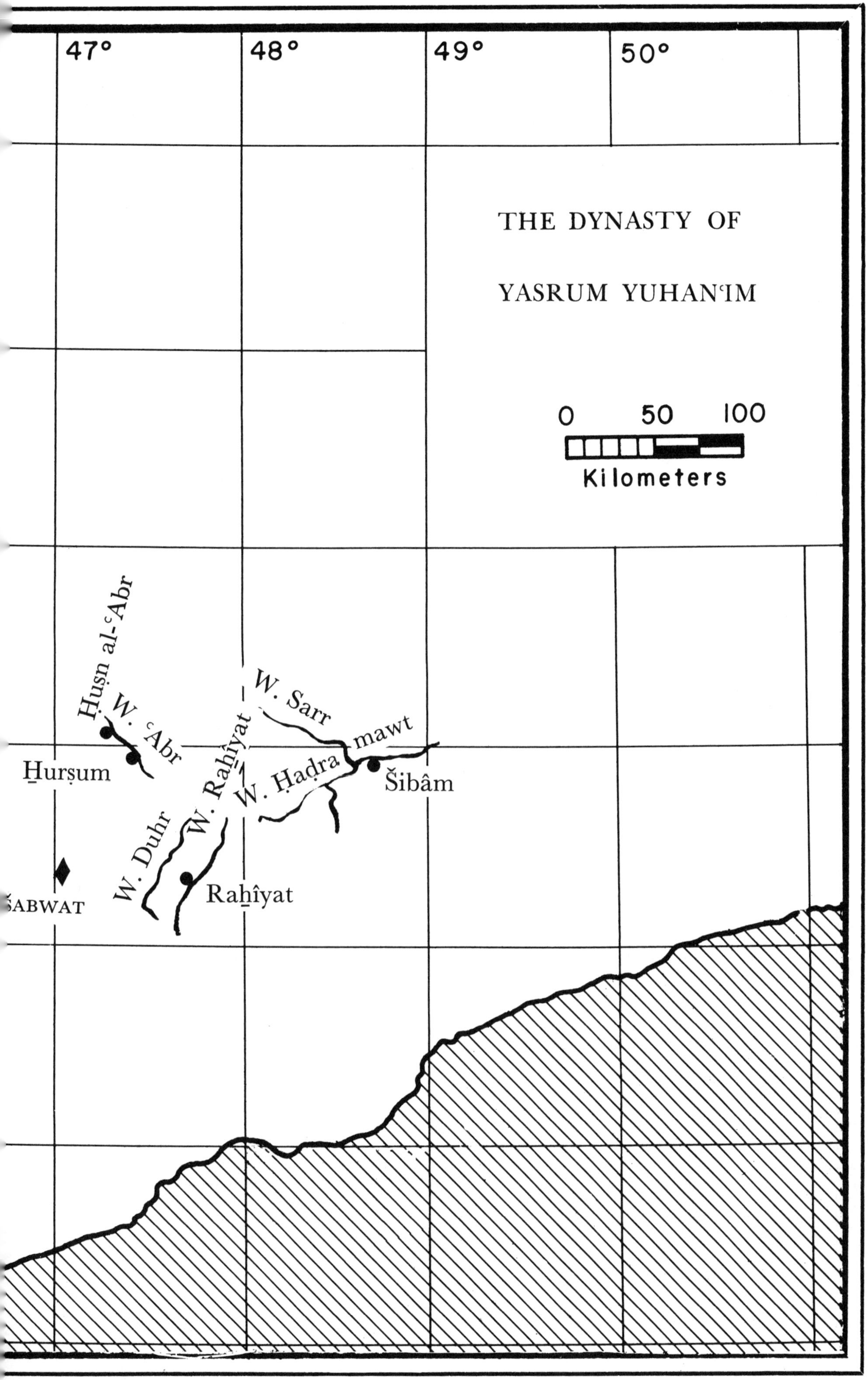
47°
48°
49°
50°
THE DYNASTY OF
YASRUM YUHANʿIM
0 50 100
Kilometers
Ḥuṣn al-ʿAbr
W. ʿAbr
Ḫurṣum
W. Sarr
W. Raḫîyat
W. Ḥaḍramawt
Šibâm
W. Duhr
Raḫîyat
ŠABWAT

GLOSSARY

With Special Glossary of Qat Ja 878 Appended

Explanatory Notes: (1) Primary entries are listed alphabetically according to the order ʾ, b, g, d, ḏ, h, w, z, ḥ, ẖ, ṭ, ẓ, y, k, l, m, n, s, ʿ, ġ, f, ṣ, ḍ, q, r, š, ś, t, ṯ. (2) Secondary entries, consisting of such items as plural forms of nouns, imperfect forms of verbs, and forms with various prefixes and/or suffixes, are set off from the preceding material by a period. Secondary entries are frequently not written out in full, but use is made of the ditto mark. (3) In addition to the use of the ditto mark in a secondary entry to indicate the repetition of the primary entry, it is also used to indicate a repetition of the nearest preceding entry, whether primary or secondary. Example: "*gbḏ* to plunder. *y*" [imperf.]; "*w* [pl.], (577/14)" would be read "*gbḏ* to plunder. *ygbḏ* [imperf.]; *ygbḏw* [pl.], (577/14)." Note that in the listing of additional secondary entries, the ditto refers back to the primary entry. (4) Each primary entry is followed immediately by the suggested translation (in Roman type to distinguish it from the entry, which is printed in italics); additional meanings are treated as secondary (or tertiary) entries. Identification of an entry or form according to part of speech, number, gender, etc. is given in brackets. (5) Homographs, including different words from the same root, are distinguished by a capital letter in parentheses after each of the separate entries, as *bt* (A). (6) Parentheses enclosing references to text or line(s) of an inscription indicate that the entry is fragmentary. Similarly, brackets or a question mark indicate that the entry is restored or doubtful respectively. (7) The conjunction *w*, the article *-n*, mimation and the spurious Ja 879 are not considered in this glossary. (8) The plural verb ending *-w* is not given an entry, nor is the dual ending of either nouns or verbs (the three equivalents of the latter, *-yn*, *-ynhn*, and *-ynn*, are very rare). The dual noun ending *-nhn*, although well known and well attested, has an entry to permit ready comparison of its use with that of its three equivalents, *-hn*, *-n*, and *-nn*.

ʾ

]ʾ [?], 680/3; 718/7.

ʾ[[?], 789/2-3; 851/7; [pl.], 695/7; 851/2.

ʾ. . *t* [noun], 647/13; 650/33.

ʾ*b* father; "*hw*, 550/2; 551; 698/9; "*hmy*, 585/4, 6-7, 8, 9, 11. ʾ*bh* [pl.], "*hw*, 557; "*y*, 671/25.

ʾ*bd* permanent dwelling. "*t* [pl.], *b*", 633/7.

ʾ*bh* [verb], cf. the 5th form *t*ʾ*bh*.

ʾ*by* ʾAbite [*nisba*]; ʾ" [pl.], 707/4.

ʾ*bl* (A) camel; "*hw*, 619/7,8; (745/13-14); (767/7); [pl.], (576/15). ʾ" [pl.], 665/26; "*hmw*, 643 bis/3.

ʾ*bl* (B) [2nd form] to take away; "*w* [pl.], 665/38.

ʾ*bq* alluvion, 594/10-11.

ʾ*gr* mercenaries [collect.], 577/10, 12.

ʾ*db* to engage, persuade. *y*" [imperf.], "*hmw*, 576/10.

ʾ*dm* servants; worshippers, 689/1; 696/1-2; 697/2; 704/2; 707/4; 712/3; 725/1; 726/1; 730/3; 784/1; 812/3. "*hw*, 559/15; 561/14; 561 bis/6; 562/7-8; 565/8; 567/14, 16; 568/18; 601/15,18; 602/15, 17-18; 606/11; 607/10-11; 615/15; 616/32; 617/7,10; 618/21; 620/7-8; 623/10; 626/8; 629/44; 642/10; 643/27-28; 643 bis/7, 8,9; 653/12,15; 654/8; 661/4-5,6,8-9; 666/8; 668/7, 9-10,12; 703/4,9; 715/7; 735/3,15,17,18; [746/15]; [747/10]; 753 I/3,II/3-4,III/3-4; *l*", (847/5-6). "*hmw*, 643/22. "*hmy*, 568/21-22; 629/9.

ʾ*ḏn* (A) ʾAḏnite; ʾ" [pl.], 621/2-3.

ʾ*ḏn* (B) understanding, 558/4; 559/13: 561/12; 612/14;

613/20; *ʾʾhw*, 750/5; *bʾʾ*, 557. *ʾʾʾ* [pl.], 568/17; 601/16; 602/16; 614/16; 615/25; 616/37; (621/11-12); 623/20; 629/43; 631/38; 643 bis/9; 644/27; 651/47; 658/29; 661/7; 666/11; 703/9; 712/13; 719/10; 853 A/4,B/4,C/4,D/4,E/4,F/4; *ʾʾhmw*, 650/29.

ʾḏn (C) to dismiss; *lʾʾ* [inf.], 643/16. Cf. also the 10th form *stʾḏn*.

ʾhb equipment [collect.]; *ʾʾhmw*, 746/11.

ʾhn; *ʾʾmw* whatever, 668/13; 711/11; *bʾʾmw*, 578/37; 623/7. *bʾʾmw* wherever, 623/5.

ʾhr [verb], cf. the 2nd form *tʾhr*.

ʾwd line, 551; 554; 556; 557. *ʾʾʾ* [pl.], 550/1; 555/1.

ʾwl [2nd form] to bring back; *ʾʾhmw*, 660/17; *ʾʾw* [pl.], 577/7; 616/14; *lʾʾn* [inf.], 700/8. Cf. also the 4th, 5th and 10th forms, *hʾwl*, *tʾwl*, and *stʾwl*.

ʾḥd one, 586/22; 609/5-6; (649/11-12); 693/5.

ʾẖ brother; cousin; ally, 832; *ʾʾhw*, 551; 558/6; 564/12; 575/8; 580/10; *ʾʾhmw*, 669/23. *ʾẖy* [sing.]; *ʾʾhw*: (561 bis/1); 566/2; (578/1); 584/9-10,11; 585/1,3,18; (594/4-5); 615/(1), 16; 616/1; 617/[1],7,13; 652/[1-2], 11; 684/[2],9; 690/2; 711/8-9; [718/1]; 738/1; 739/2, 14; 758/2,16; [788/1]; 822/1; cf. also the personal names *ʾlšrḥ*, *yrm*, *šʿrm*. *ʾẖy* [dual]; *ʾʾhw*, 620/1. *ʾẖy* [sing.? dual? pl.?], *ʾʾhw*: 817/1.

ʾẖḏ (A) prisoner, 649/12; 665/20; *ʾʾn* [dual], 649/36; *ʾʾt* [pl.], 578/32; 635/43. *ʾẖyḏt* [pl.], 576/10; 581/10; 616/30; 649/38; 658/17, 26; 665/25,45; 668/8-9.

ʾẖḏ (B) to make prisoner; capture; seize, 560/12; *bʾʾ*, 576/2; *lʾʾ*, 665/20; *ʾʾhw*, 576/2; *ʾʾhmw*, 660/15. *ʾʾw* [pl.], (560/13); 665/35; *ḏʾʾ*, 635/31-32.

ʾẖw [verb], cf. the 4th form *hẖw*.

ʾẖr (A) following, *lʾʾ*, 633/12,15-16.

ʾẖr (B) [verb] [1st form] to go on; *ʾʾn* [inf.], 601/17; 602/17. [2nd form] to put aside; *ʾʾn* [inf.], 853 A/5, B/5,C/5,D/4,E/5,F/5; *ʾʾnh*: 558/7.

ʾẖt sister; *ʾʾhnt*, (786/4-5).

ʾys (A) adversary; opponent, 577/6,7; 578/21; 644/10; *ʾs*, 585/14,15.

ʾys (B) [verb], cf. the 5th form *tʾys*.

ʾk unhappiness, 720/18.

ʾl (A) god, 631/25. *ʾʾy* [dual]; *ʾʾhmw*, 559/18; 561/18; 568/24; (643 bis/10;) *bʾʾhmw*, 606/21; 607/21; 753 (I/8),II/16,III/16. *ʾlʾlt* [pl.]: 643 bis/10; 671/25.

ʾl (B) [negation], 571/8; 576/6,10; 578/42; 614/20; 615/28; 616/40; 617/15; 647/33; 650/35; 651/55; 661/9; 665/48; 691/12; 702/9; 703/11. *ʾldʿw*, 623/24. *ḏʾl*, 572/16; 619/20; 720/13; [739/19]; 758/20. *kʾl*, 643/15; 720/7. [*lqbl*]*y*/*ḏʾl*, (570/3). *lqbly*/*ḏtʾl*, 628/5-6.

ʾl (C) [rel. pron.]; *ḏʾʾ*, 702/4-5, *ʾʾ*/*ḏ*, 651/25-26.

ʾl (D) [?], 763/1-2.

ʾlh (A) adulation; *ʾʾt* [pl.], 578/42.

ʾlh (B) [verb], cf. the 5th form *tʾlh*.

ʾly [pl. masc. relative pron.], 550/1; 555/1; 558/2; 567/(4),23; 576/1; 581/4; 657/3; 692/6; 747/3; 757/2; 818/6; [855/3].

ʾlf thousand, 576/15; 577/4; (608/6); 609/6; 665/39; (680/4); *ʾʾn* [dual], 643 bis/2; *ʾʾʾ* [pl.], 576/15; 577/15; 665/30.

ʾlt [pl. fem. relative pron.], 722/2,3; 734/4; 772/1.

ʾm mother; *ʾʾhmw*, 719/7; *ʾʾhmy*, 594/8.

ʾm[[?], 763/2-3.

ʾmn [verb], cf. the 4th form *hʾmn*.

ʾmr (A) order; command; *bʾʾhw*, 671/16.

ʾmr (B) commanding post. *ʾwmr* [pl.]; *ʾʾhw*, 576/13.

ʾmt maidservant, 700/8; 721/1-2; *ʾʾh*, (764/2-3); *ʾʾhw*, 706/5; 717/4-5; 751/11. *ʾmh* [pl.], 722/3; 731/2; 828/8; *ʾʾhw*, 722/c; 734/4; (786/3).

ʾns man; person, 629/7; 643/16,17,20; 644/5,11. *ʾs*, 649/35; 665/23,49; *ʾʾhw* [fem.]: 700/9; *ʾʾn* [dual], 570/7.

ʾnṯ wife; *ʾʾ* [pl.], 735/9; *ʾʾhw*, 576/7. *ʾʾʾ* [pl.]; *ʾʾhmw*, 575/6. *ʾṯt* [sing.], 700/7; *ʾʾhw*, 655/7; 750/2,14,16; [pl.]: *ʾʾhmw*: 669/15; 738/9; *ʾʾhmy*: 594/8.

ʾs [noun], cf. *ʾys* and *ʾns*.

ʾsd (A) [masc. pl. relative pron.], 564/8; 570/4; 577/6,7; 635/35; 735/1.

ʾsd (B) soldier [pl.], 560/12,13; 576/5,7,15; 577/1,4,13, 14; 586/16,17,19-20; 616/22; 629/17,20,25; 631/31; 643/13,31; 643 bis/2; 644/17,18,19,22,23; 649/11,18, 28,37,38; 651/11; 660/15; 665/15,18,18-19,30,36-37; *ʾʾhw*, 586/22; 651/25; *ʾʾhmw*, 660/12; *ʾʾhmy*, 575/2; 660/16.

ʾswd commanding officer. *ʾʾy* [dual]; *ʾʾhmw*, 665/31.

ʾsy (A) messenger; envoy. [collect.]; *ʾʾhw*, 651/27. *ʾʾn* [dual], 612/12.

ʾsy (B) to send; *fʾʾw* [pl.], 576/16; cf. also the 4th form *hʾsy*.

ʾsy (C) to take refuge; *ʾʾw* [pl.], 578/26.

ʾfs [noun], cf. *nfs*.

ʾfq to reverse. *yʾʾ* [imperf.]; *kʾʾn*, 671/16.

ʾṣ[[?], 586/24.

]*ʾr*[[?], 725/3.

ʾrby locust [collect.], 610/8.

ʾrbʿ (A) four, 577/11, 586/16; 609/5; 631/30; 644/25; 649/38-39; 665/17,36. *ʾʾt* four [fem.], 577/14; 632/2; 689/2; 733/4; 742/6; 853 A/2,B/2,C/2,D/2,E/2,F/2; 854/3.

ʾrbʿ (B) fourth, 653/9; *ʾʾw* [pl.], cf. the clan name *ḏmry*.

ʾrbʿy forty, 576/15; 649/38; 665/38; *bʾʾ*, 586/15-16.

ʾrẖ (A) calamity, 669/23,25-26; *ʾʾʾ* [pl.], 620/6; 623/22; 666/10; 712/6-7,10.

ʾrẖ (B) undertaking; *ʾʾʾ* [pl.], 567/24; 610/14-15; 652/16; 708/10; 733/12-13.

ʾrḍ country; land; ground, 555/4; 560/10,13-14; 576/4, 6,7,8; 578/15,25; 579/7-8; 580/9; 586/15; 590/8; 601/5; 602/5; 612/9; 615/20; 627/8; 629/6; 631/12-13; 635/36; 644/17; 658/10; 665/11; 735/5; 740 A/7; 750/5; 758/8; 821 A/4; *ʾʾhmw*; 561 bis/21; 562/13; 587/11; 601/17; 602/17; 618/23; 627/5,11,22,23; 628/23; 631/40; 650/13,16; 651/48-49; 669/19; 670/27; 704/6; (719/14); (747/16); 799/6; *bʾʾ*, 576/4; 618/19; 645/13-14; 666/6-7; (739/10); *ḏʾʾ*, 616/18-19. *ʾrḍt* [pl.], 561 bis/12,14; 576/6,13; 735/14; *ʾʾhw*, 555/3; *ʾʾhmw*, 563/13; 564/20-21; 567/24; 578/21; (599/8-9); 613/21; 617/8; 623/16; 630/17-18; 645/24; 656/18, 24-25; 657/11; 661/8; 664/16; 703/6,7; *bʾʾ*, 647/29.

ʾśr to fetter; *ʾʾhmw*, 665/22.

ʾ..t[[?], 647/13.

ʾtw to return, 550/2; 578/19; 610/5; 612/11; 628/8; 642/5; 643/30; 649/13,22; 656/6; 665/44,48; 708/8; 758/12; *ḏʾʾ*, 633/5; *fʾʾ*, 643/25; cf. also the 5th form *tʾtw*. *ʾtww* [pl.], 650/22; 656/13-14; *fʾʾ*, 643 bis/3. *yʾtw* [imperf.]; *ʾʾn*, 628/6.

ʾty to return. *y*'' [imperf.]; ''*w* [pl.], 577/11; 601/10; 603/10; *k*''*n*, 580/5.
ʾtyt return, 562/4.
ʾtm to muster; ''*n* [inf.], 643/29; cf. also the 5th and the 8th forms, *tʾtm* and *ʾttm* respectively.
ʾttm to associate; muster (troops); ''*n* [inf.], 665/14-15. *y*'' [imperf.]; ''*w* [pl.], 575/5; ''*nn* [pl.], 631/26.
ʾṯym firm fleshed, 752/11.
ʾṯr tracks; trail. *b*'', 660/11; ''*hmw*, 575/4.
ʾṯt [noun], cf. *ʾnṯ*.

b

b[[?], 577/18; 687/4-5, 9-10; 798/2; 847/1-2.
]*b* [?], 687/10.
]*b*[[?], 746/10.
b (A) [conj.] [causal], cf. *frṭ, šft, tśbb.* [modal], cf. *ʾḫḏ, hbʿl, hsbʿ, hsḥt, hrg, wḏʿ, ḥsm, ḫrʾ, kn, nʿm, nqm, sbṭ, stwfy, qny, qrn, škr, tʾwl, ṯbr.* [temp.], cf. *slm, tʾwl.*
b (B) [mark], 612.
b (C) [prep.] [?]; *bhw*, 702/16. [adversat.]; *bḏbn*, 561 bis/12,14; cf. also the name of god *ʾlmqh*, and *mrʾ*. [causal]; *bhw* [fem.], 751/4; cf. also *ḏ, ḏt, ḥbl, ḫfrt, sbʾt, ʿrb, qḏb, šzb, śn, tnbl.* [instrum.]; *bhwt*, 716/10; cf. also *ʾrbʿ, ḫmsy, yd, kl, msʾl, ʿnt, ṣdġ, qḏb.* [local], 575/8?; *bḏt*, 649/11; *bh*, 643/21; *bhw* there, where, 576/8,9, 13,14; 578/26; 649/18,19; *bhyt*, 577/13; 578/28; 585/11; 643/20-21; *bhmyt*, 574/7; *bmw*, 644/21; cf. also the place names *ʾḏnt, ʾwm, ʾnḥrm, ʾrk, ḥbbḏ, ẓfr, yhdl, ysrn, yfd, yfʿ, kwmnn, klwn(m), m[.]lwn, mslmn, mrb, mryb, nšqm, ʿynm, ṣlyn, ṣnʿw, rḥbtn,* and also *ʾbd, ʾhn, ʾrḍ, ʾṯr, byt, bdʿ, bt, hgr, wsṭ, wṯn, ḥql, ḫlf, ḫms, kbt, kdn, kl, knf, mwṯb, mḥrm, mlk, mfnt, sfl, sr, ʿly, ʿqbt, qr, šʾmt.* [modal], 550/2; 551; 552/4; 555/4; 557; 558/6,7; 559/18; 560/21; 561/17,18; 568/24; 578/43,44; 601/20; 602/20; 643 bis/10; 664/20; [672/2]; 673/2,3; 683/6,7,8; 705/8; 753 I/8,II/15, III/15; 819; 823 A; 831/3; *bhw*, 642/5; 643 bis/6; *bhwt*, 627/7; *bhmw*, 559/9; 561/9; *bhmy*, 651/14; *bhmt*, 643/23; *bmw*, 617/17; cf. also the names of deities *ʾlmw, ʾlmq, ʾlmqh(w), ḏt(/)bʿdn(m), ḏt(/)ḥmym, ḏt/ġḏrn; lmqh, ʿṯtr, rbʿ, šhr, šms,* and *ʾḏn, ʾhn, ʾl, ʾmr, bry, gzyt, ḏ, hbt, hwbl, hwkl, wfy, ḥll, ḥmd, ḥṯʾ, ḫms, kl, mhrg, mwʿd, mlʾ, msg, mqḥ, sḥt, ʿbr, ʿlw, ʿly, ʿlm, ʿm, ṣdq, ṣryt, qht, qrn, rbḫ, rḥl, šym, šʿb, šṣy,*]*t, tbšrt.* [origin.]; *bhw*, 576/6,7,8,13; 577/2; *bhyt* [576/14]; *bhmw*, 576/12; 644/19; cf. also *ḏ, kl, ʿm.* [removal], cf. *hry, kl.* [temp.]; *bhʾ*, 619/7-8; *bhw*, 627/6; *bhwt*, 627/8; 629/20; 643 bis/5,6; 670/14; 751/8-9; *fbmhwt*, 643/18; *bhyt*, 575/3; 610/9; 629/36; *bhmw*, 561 bis/8-9, 581/11-12; 586/13; *bhmt*, 629/39; *bkly*, 644/24; *bmw*, 617/19; 618/10; 653/10,13; *ḏbhw* in which, 616/20; cf. also *ʾhn, brq, wsṭ, wrḫ, ḥbl, ḥrbt, ḫrf, ywm, kl, kn, lly, mgʾt, mlʾ, mnšʾ, msbʾ, mqrn, sbʾt, slm, sqy, ʿsm, ḏbʾ, ḍr, qdm, qdmy, ṯlṯ, ṯny.*
bʾl leadership, 578/39.
bʾs (A) misfortune, 615/26; 670/17. ''*t* [pl.]: 558/5; 561 bis/22; 562/16; 563/14; 564/23; 567/26; 572/10,15; (580/14); 581/18; 587/12; 590/24; 601/18; 602/18; 613/15; 616/38-39; 617/14; 618/31; 620/9; 623/21; (626/14-15); 627/25; 628/25; 629/44; 630/19; 634/11; 640/10; 642/11; 644/13; 645/17-18; 647/32; 650/32; 651/51; 666/9; 667 A/12; 687/11; 702/18-19; 703/7, 10; 706/9; 715/10; (716/12); 717/11; 732/8; 739/17-18; 753 I/5,II/8,III/8; 786/5; 815/8.
bʾs (B) to harm; *ḏ*'', 651/43; cf. also the 4th form *hbʾs*.
bʾr well. ʾ'' [pl.], 577/15; 629/29; 735/7; ''*hmy*, 576/12.
bdʿ novelty; ''*t* [pl.], 647/30.
bhʾ (A) income. ''*t* [pl.]; ''*hmw*, 616/17,18,20.
bhʾ (B) to enter, 700/9; ''*w* [pl.], 644/6.
bhʾ (C) to become friendly; *l*'', 616/17.
bḥḏ (A) sudden attack, 576/6; 578/10; ''*t* [pl.]: 578/10.
bḥḏ (B) to attack abruptly. *y*'' [imperf.]; ''*n*, 576/11; *f*''*n*, 576/4; ''*w* [pl.], 576/5,7; *f*''*w*, 576/12.
bḥr sea, (576/1-2); 577/18; 585/14; 741/8; 756/8; *ḏ*'', 631/7; 635/13; *l*'', 575/4.
bḥt pure object; ''*nhn* [dual], 672/1-2.
byn (A) between, 561 bis/9; 567/8; 576/4,14; 577/2,4; 633/8; 750/14; ''*hw*, 750/14; ''*hmy*, 700/11,13-14.
byn (B) cupola; *ḏ*'', 846/2-3.
byn (C) [verb] [1st form] to be dislocated, 619/8. [2nd form] to separate; *ḏ*''*n*, 671/12; *y*'' [imperf.]; *y*''*nn*: (675/2).
byt house; temple, 559/14; 561/13-14; 562/1,6,7; 564/1; 576/4,13; 577/16; 591/10; 592/5; 615/11,21; 616/3; 643 bis/7-8; 644/9; 651/3,13; 660/19; 670/3; [671/3]; 687/8; 700/15; 716/8; 718/3; 761/2; [788/3]; (847/4-5); 853 A/3,B/3,C/3,D/3,E/3,F/3; 877/14; ''*hw*, 552/3; 555/2,3; [618/16-17]; 832; ''*hmw*, 560/6; 564/7; 591/10; 603/6; 615/11,21; 689/5; 716/8; 730/8-9; *b*'', 644/23; 652/25; *l*'': 559/9; 561/9; 577/19; *l*''*hmw*, 630/16; cf. also the name of deity *ḫgrm*. *ʾbyt* [pl.], 578/12; 644/6,9; ''*hw*, 555/3; ''*hmw*, 644/13; *b*'', 564/19; *b*''*hw*, 619/12. *bythn* [dual], 734/5. *bytnhn* [dual], 651/12-13,14,28; 695/2. *bytnn* [dual], 716/2.
bkl devotees [collect.]; ''*hw*, 692/6.
bl[[?], 643/9-10.
]*bl*[[?], 722/6.
blṭ (*balaṭ*) [coin], 624/5.
blq masonry of hewn stones; ''*hw*, 557.
blt (A) military duty; ''*hmw*, 631/15; *l*'', 578/39; ''*w* [pl.], 560/8. rent, 591/2; (745/11).
blt (B) [verb] to impose a duty; ''*hw*, (560/8-9); 633/6; *f*'' [passive], 578/21-22. to impose a military duty; ''*hmw*, 575/2. Cf. also the 4th and 5th forms, *hblt* and *tblt* respectively.
bltn reward, 750/5.
]*bn* [?], 746/13.
bn (A) [noun] son [sing.], 550/1; 551; 552/1; 553/1; 554; 555/1; 556; 557; 558/6,7; 567/7; 571/6; 577/6,7; 579/1; 580/1,10,[13]; 582/1; (583/1); 603/1; 605/1; 610/6; 611/8; 612/1,16; 613/1,8,10,13; 615/12,13-14; 618/9-10; 632/1; 633/16; 644/4,5,8,11,18; 645/14; 646/1,6; 653/6; 655/[1],7; 660/11,12,15,16; 665/32; 669/9,11; (673/1); 682/1; 684/(1),7,12; 687/1,5; 689/1; 691/1; 692/9; 708/1; 711/1; 721/7; 723/1; 735/4; 740 A/1; 741/1; 749/2; 751/7; 757 bis/1; 758/1, 6,15,19; 768/1; 775/1; (802); 816/1; 824; 831/1,3; 842/1; 846/1; 877/8-9; cf. also the personal names

ʾlšrḥ, *ʾnmrm*, *wtrm*, *yhqm*, *ysrm*, *krbʾl*, *mrʾlqs*, *nšʾkrb*, *sʿdšmsm*, *šmr*, *šʿrm*, *ṯʾrn*. *bnhw*, 555/1; 560/7; 561 bis/2; 568/[1],8,(9-10),15; 584/3-4; 605/5; 606/[1],11-12,17; 607/[1],11,16-17; (629/1); (641/1); 664/7; 670/1-2, 10-11; 693/[1],7,9; 700/9 [*hw*, fem.]; 726/4; 727/7; (732/3-4); 744/3-4; 746/1; 747/1; 753I/[1],6,II/12, III/12; (787/2-3); 831/1; *bnhmw*, 563/6; 705/4,6; 728/ 4; [784/3]; *bnhmy*, 818/4; *lbnhw*, (688/2-3); *lbnhmw*, 759/2-3. [dual]; *bnhw*, 550/1. [pl.]; *bnhw*, 552/2; 555/1; *bnhmw*, 669/15,20. [sing.? dual? pl.?]; *bn*[781/1-2; *bnhw*, 810 A/2. *bnn* [pl.], 736/7. descendant(s) of, people of (+family or clan name), 550/1,2; 552/1; 553/1; 554; 555/1; 561 bis/3; 562/1,9; 563/6; 567/7; 575/(1-2),2; 577/7,10; 578/34; 581/1,9; 587/1; 591/1; 601/1; 602/1; 604/1; 605/2,5; 610/7; 611/9; 613/11; 615/12,14; 618/10; 623/3; 627/4,15; 629/6, 11,15,33,40,41; 630/1,5,8; 631/1,3,11,17,19,23,25,32; 632/1-2,4,6,9; 633/1,17; 634/1; 635/1,17; 637/1; 639/2; 643/12,14,17,24,28,32,33,36; 643 bis/5,6,7,8; 645/[1], 5,9,12,14,17; 649/1; 650/1,9,19,28,31; 653/6; 657/[1],6; 665/1; 667 A/1,6,11; 689/1; 692/1; 693/9; 695/1,[6]; (696/1); 697/1; 700/2,8; 704/2; 705/5; 708/3; 709/1; 713/4,13; 721/2; 726/1-2,4; 730/3; 731/2; 735/4; 744/1,4; 757 bis/3; 759/1; 760; 798/1; 821 A/4; 840/2; 841/1; [846/1]; 877/9; *bn/ḏ*, [588/1].

bn (B) [conj.]; [modal], 631/33; [origin], 570/9; [removal], 562/21; 720/15.

bn (C) [prep.]; [adversat.], 665/40-41; *ʾhmw*, 750/11. [instrum.], 627/5; 643/9; 700/14; 735/7; *ʾhmw:* 665/43. [local], 617/5. [modal], 554; 564/10; 720/ 16; 721/7; 751/8. [origin], 562/7,13; 563/12-13; 564/9,20; 565/15; 567/24; 574/7; 575/3,4,6; 576/1,2,3, 4,5,7,9,10,11,15; 577/1,2,4,7,12,13,14,18; 578/8,13,21; 579/6; 581/6,11; 585/4; 586/17; 590/5,8,12; 599/2,8; 601/17; 602/17; 613/21; 615/9,10,20; 616/22,23,26; 617/4,5; 620/11-12; 627/21; 629/17,18; 630/17; 631/ 16,19,30,33,35; 632/3,4; 633/5; 634/3-4,4; 635/4,19, 38; 636/6; 637/4; (639/5); 640/[1],2; 641/4,4-5; 643/ 6,11,13,16,19,21,24,27,28,33,34; 643 bis/2,3,6; 644/ 16,17,18,22,24-25; 645/24; 649/28,32; 650/5,6; 651/ 12,26; 656/18,24; 657/11; 661/8; 664/16; 665/16,19, 20,37,42,49; 668/10; 671/13; [691/9]; 708/9; 710/4; 734/5; (735/11-12); 738/8-9; 741/7,8; 745/10; 747/16; 756/7,8; 813/1(?); cf. also *ḏ*. *bn/mn*, 735/12. *bnhw* from there, 631/14; 656/7,14; *ʾ/f* [+verb], 575/6; 576/4,5,6,7,7-8,8,9,12,13,14; (577/2-3); 578/20; (586/ 19); 649/26; 665/24,27,28. *bnhmw* from them, 575/7; 576/5,9; 577/5; 586/18; 631/24,34; 649/34-35; 665/34-35. *bnkl*, 628/22; 635/9; 703/6. [removal], 558/5,7; 561 bis/22; 562/(16),21; 563/14; 564/23,24; 567/17,26, 27; 570/14; 571/7; 572/[7],10,14-15,15; 577/8,15,16, 17; 578/10,34,40,42; 579/12; [580/14]; 581/18; 583/8,[9]; 585/10; 587/12; 588/12; 590/24; 591/11; 592/9; 594/11; 597/7; [598/5]; 599/9; 603/12; 610/8; 612/19; 613/8-9,14,15,16; 614/18; 615/26; 616/38,39; 617/14; 618/31; 619/7,12,19; 620/5,6,9,10; [623/21]; 626/14; 627/25,26; 628/25; 629/33,43; 630/19; 631/28,41; 632/9; 633/5,14,20; 634/11; 635/44; 636/17,18; 638/4; (639/5); (640/9-10); 641/15; 642/5,11; 643/5,26; 644/4,13; 645/13,17; 647/32; 648/9; 650/31-32; 651/33,43,51; 652/19; 654/15; 656/26; 658/7; 660/13; 661/5,9; 664/17,18; 665/23; 666/6,9; 667 A/7,12; 668/19; 669/23,25; 670/9,16; 679/3(?); 684/12; 685/3,5; [686/8]; [687/11]; 691/11; 693/13; 695/7; 699/5,8; 700/13; 702/18; 703/7,10,12; 704/7; 705/6,9; 708/7; 711/4,12; 712/6,10,12; 715/10; 716/12; 717/11; 719/12; 720/9,18; 723/4; 725/7; 730/10; 731/6; 732/8; 733/9; 734/7; 736/16-17; 737/3; 739/17; 745/13; 747/5,19; 750/11,13,15,16; 753 I/5,II/8,9,III/8,9; 758/19; [762/5]; [763/5]; 765/3; [786/5]; [803/6]; 804/3; 807/2; 815/8; 839/4; 840/7; *bnkl*, 626/15. [temp.], 565/6; 586/8; 587/3; 631/24; 651/21; 739/9.

bnw [noun] sons [dual], 704/1. descendants of, people of [+family or clan name], 558/[1],3,7; 559/1; 560/2; 561/1; 565/3; 566/3; 569/3; 589/4; 590/2; [592/1]; [614/1]; 616/3; 619/2; 620/2; 621/2; [623/b]; [627/1]; [628/1]; 641/2; [643/1]; 654/3; 656/4; 658/25; 662/2; 669/3; 671/2; 689/4; (693/2); 705/1-2; 712/3; 713/2; 718/2; 719/2; 727/2-3; 730/2; 738/3; 740 A/[2],13; 747/1; 752/4; [767/3]; [788/2]; 815/1. *ʾ/ḏ:* 567/3; 585/1; 603/3; (615/3); 617/1,7,10; 626/2; [642/2-3]; 658/2; 661/[1],6; 664/2; 666/2-3; 668/14; 716/2; 720/14: 733/2; 736/3; 815/5; (817/4).

bny (A) [noun] son [sing.]; *ʾh*, 727/2. *ʾhw*, 588/1; 614/1,8,11; (618/1); 619/1; 708/2; 713/1,4; 729/2-3; 738/2; 745/1; [746/16]; cf. also the personal names *ḏmrʿly*, *ysrm*, *sʾdšmsm*, *ṯʾrn*. *ʾhmw*, 560/1; 563/2; 566/3; 620/2,8-9; (648/1-2); 654/2; 669/3; 715/2,8-9. *ʾhmy*: 666/2. [dual], 594/5; 700/1; 734/3?; *ʾhw*, 567/(1-2),14,16-17; 621/1; 623/[a,2-3],10; 626/1,18; 656/1; 683/4; 701 A/7; 703/1,9; 716/1; 717/8 [*hw*, fem.]; 736/1-2,9; 740 A/[1],9-10; 750/1; cf. also the personal names *ʾlšrḥ*, *sʿdšmsm*, *frʿm*, *šʿrm*; *ʾhmw*, 615/17; *ʾhmy*, 615/2; 822/2. [sing.? dual?]; *ʾhw*, (671/1). [pl.], 576/2; *ʾhw*, 589/1-2; 603/1; 604/2; 616/1; (718/1); 719/1,(7); 733/1; 757/3; [788/1]; (812/1-2); *ʾhmw*, 558/[1],3; 569/1-2; 577/13; 656/2; 707/1; 712/2; 815/4,(7). children [dual], *ʾhw*, 690/6; [pl.]; *ʾhw*, 689/3; *lʾhw* [*hw*, fem.], 742/9. descendants of [+personal name], [561 bis/2]. descendants of, people of [+family or clan name], 555/2; 556; 558/[1],3; 559/15; 561/15; 561 bis/6; 562/14; 563/(2-3),16-17; 568/2,8,10,13,15,18,22; 578/ [1], (35-36); 585/3,18; 590/23; (592/5); 601/15,18; 602/15,18; 604/3; [605/13]; 606/2,12,18; 607/(2),12 17; 616/8,32; 618/2,13,20,21,25-26; 623/11; 626/8; 627/10,13,24; 628/11,14,24; 630/19; 635/35; 642/2,10; 643/3; 643 bis/4,9; 670/2,19; 684/3,9; 690/2,11; 704/9; 713/15; 716/8; 734/3?; 737/2; 739/3; 746/1,(8); 747/(9),10; 753 I/[1],3,7,II/4,12,III/4,12; 757/3-4; 758/3,17; (771); 816/9,(10); 817/1; *ʾ/ḏ:* 557; 561 bis/10; 562/7; 564/22-23,25,26; 567/15; 615/17; 617/ 13; 626/18; 629/1,13,16,24,41-42; (642/16); 666/9; 691/8; 703/4,10; 707/3; 716/6, (11); 747/14.

bny (B) [verb] to build, 557; (675/1); [676/1]; 842/2; [846/2]. *ʾy* [dual]: 554.

bnt daughter, [828/6]; *ʾh*, 764/5; *ʾhw* [fem.]; 731/5. [pl.]: 703/4; 722/2; 735/8; 738/9; 743/5; *ʾhmw*: 577/13.

bʿd (A) after, 575/5; 576/3; 577/4; 629/33; 631/34; 658/13; *ʾhw/f* [+verb], 574/4; 576/6,11; 577/3,4,10, 11; 578/21,24; 586/23; *ʾḏ* [+ verb], 574/10; 721/6.

bʿd (B) [2nd form] to remove; repel; ''*w* [pl.], 631/8; [passive] ''*n* [inf.], 720/17.
bʿdn after; ''*hw/f* [+verb], 658/14; 665/40; 735/14-15.
bʿw (A) crime; felony, treachery; act of treachery, 578/10; ''*hmw*: 643/19; ''*t* [pl.]: 578/10,11.
bʿw (B) to betray; commit a crime; ''*w* [pl.], 631/29; cf. also the 4th form *hbʿy*.
bʿl (A) master, 695/12; (828/7-8); cf. also the names of deities *ʾlmw*, *ʾlmq*, *ʾlmqh(w)*, *wdm*, *ḥgrm*, *lmq*, *ʿṯtr*, *tʾlb*. *ʾbʿl* [pl.], 562/1; (564/1); 616/3; 635/28; 643/22; 651/3; 665/13; 670/3; [671/3]; 689/5; 695/2; 716/2; 718/3; (788/3); ''*hw*: 559/14; 561/14; 576/7; 643 bis/8; 761/3; 853 A/3,B/3,C/3,D/3,E/4,F/3; 877/14-15. *bʿly* [dual], cf. the names of deities *ʾlmqh*, *ʿṯtr*. *bʿlt* [fem.], cf. the names of deities *ḏr/ġḍrn*, *šms*; ''*y* [dual], cf. the name of deity *šmsy*.
bʿl (B) [verb], cf. the 4th form *hbʿl*.
bʿr camel herd; ''*hw*, 709/6; (762/6); ''*hmw*, 644/20; 752/15.
bṣl onion, 720/9-10.
bḍʿ (A) beheaded, 586/22; 649/11,18,35,37; 665/35; *bḍwʿ* [pl.], 631/31.
bḍʿ (B) territory; *b*'', 555/3.
bql [2nd form] to sow; ''*n* [inf.], 821 A/3.
bqr [collect.] bovines, 649/40-41. cows, 665/26.
br wheat, 670/26.
brʾ to build; ''*w* [pl.], 603/5; *l*'', 651/30.
brd cold, 610/8.
brw (A) son, 570/15; ''*hw*: 576/2; 641/8; 648/5. ʾ'' [pl.], 591/9; ''*hw*, (812/7-8). ''*y* [dual]; ''*hw*, 716/7-8.
brw (B) [verb], cf. the 4th and 10th forms, *hbrw*, *hbry*, and *stbrw* respectively.
bry strength, 558/4; 559/12; 561/12; 568/17; 601/16; 602/15-16; 612/14; 613/19; 614/16; 615/25; 616/37; [621/11]; 623/20; 629/43; 631/38; 643 bis/9; 644/27; 650/29; 651/47; 658/29; 661/7; 666/11; 703/8-9; 712/13; 719/10; 733/13-14; 853 A/4,B/4,C/4,D/3,E/4, F/4. ''*t* [pl.], 635/8; *b*'', 612/11.
brq lightning storm; lightning season, 585/7; 610/9; 653/5; 735/4,6,17; 851/4; *b*'', 610/6. ''*n* [dual], 618/7. ʾ'' [pl.], 627/11; 628/12; 658/33; 735/6; *l*'', 610/14.
brr (A) [noun] plain, 576/6,12.
brr (B) to come to an agreement. *y*'' [imperf.]; ''*n*, 631/28; *f*''*n*, 631/31; cf. also the 4th form *hbrr*.
brṯ (A) place, 644/21; 734/(1-2),[5]; ''*hw*, 562/21 [*hw*, fem.]. *ʾbrṯ* [pl.], 559/9; 561/9.
brṯ (B) military campaign, 635/38-39; ʾ'' [pl.], 561 bis/8, 10; 578/39; 635/19,43; 662/17.
brṯ (C) to locate; ''*w* [pl.], 651/27-28.
bšr [verb], cf. the 5th form *tbšr*.
bt (A) house; *b*'', 702/7; ''*nhn* [dual], 651/20.
bt (B) daughter, 706/1; ''*hw*, 694/6-7; [*hw*, fem.] 797 B/2.
bṯ to divulge; communicate. *bṯṯ* [2nd form; passive; fem.]; ''*thw*, 584/10-11.

g

gʾm to cut off; *l*''*n* [inf.], 658/12-13.
gbʾ to return, 643/16,31,34; 656/17-18; cf. also the 4th and 5th forms, *hgbʾ* and *tgbʾ* respectively. ''*w* [pl.], 576/10,14; 577/2; 631/34; *f*'', 577/2. *y*'' [imperf.]; *f*''*w* [pl.], 576/8.
gbḏ to plunder. *y*'' [imperf.]; ''*w* [pl.], (577/14).
gbz to plunder; ''*w* [pl.], 629/28.
gwd excellent, 665/44.
gwz to undertake. *y*'' [imperf.]; ''*n*, 711/11.
gwy to desire intensely. *ygw* [imperf.]; *ḏ*''*nhw*, 567/8.
gwl property, 682/2.
gwʿ famished, 631/35.
gzy to decree, 629/39; ''*w* [pl.], 564/9; *l*'', 629/38;
gzyt edict, 629/37,39; *b*'', 564/9.
gzm (A) oath, 576/3; 577/4.
gzm (B) to declare upon oath, swear; ''*w* [pl.], 576/3. to destroy; *l*''*n* [inf.], 575/2.
gzz [verb], cf. the 4th form *hgz*.
gyr [2nd form] to prostrate, (747/16-17).
gyš troop, 649/13,19,35; 665/41; ''*hmw*, 616/20,21,29; 635/38; 665/15,21,24,27,42,44-45,48,49; ʾ'' [pl.], 577/14.
gml camels [collect.] 576/3; 649/40.
gn [verb], cf. the 5th and 8th form, *tgn* and *gtn* respectively.
gnʾ wall, 550/1; 551; 554; 555/1; 556; 557; ʾ'' [pl.], 651/31.
gnb to battle, 597/1.
gnw garden; ʾ'' [pl.], 574/6.
gnz dead person; ''*t* [pl.], 702/10.
gny garden-fruit [collect.], 650/6.
gʿr [verb], cf. the 5th form *tgʿr*.
grb person; body, 572/5,8; 585/8; 611/17; 613/7,13; 620/5; 645/11,16; 647/31; 651/9,40; 670/16; 740 A/9; 751/11; ''*hw*, 571/4: 633/4; 646/12; 692/5-6; 698/7-8; 699/5; 709/5; 710/4; 751/6 [*hw*, fem.]. ''*t* [pl.]; ''*hmw*. 654/10; 724; 727/8; 736/14; ''*hmy*, 594/7. *grybt* [pl.], 567/14,16; 586/10; 643/16; 651/10; 701 A/7; 703/8; 716/5-6,11; (719/6-7); 815/4,6; 816/8; ''*hmw*, 567/10; 588/11; 656/23; 664/11; 686/6-7; 706/9; 717/10; (719/16); 730/5-6; (732/7); 733/13; 738/11; (820/2-3); *l*''*hmw*, 567/25.
grḥ carnivorous animal, 643 bis/3.
gry deputy; agent; ''*nhn* [dual], 660/12.
grm full-sized skin. ''*y* [dual]; *l*'', 750/7. body; *l*'', 752/9.
gtn to collect garden products. ''*n* [inf.]; l'', 570/8; ''*n*, 570/9.

d

dws to be abused [*maṣdar*], 647/14.
dwr (A) once; *dr*, 576/11; 633/9,11; 711/5.
dwr (B) Bedouin camp; ʾ'' [pl.], 574/7,8.
dyr Bedouin camp; ʾ'' [pl.], 577/4.
dll (A) guide; *dlwl* [pl.], 575/3.
dll (B) to guide; ''*w* [passive], 575/4; *l*'' [inf.], 575/3.
dʿ to know. ''*w* [pl.], 571/8; 572/15-16,16; 578/41,42; 614/19,20; 615/28; 616/40; 617/15; 619/20, 20-21;

623/24; 647/33,(33-34); 650/34,35; 661/9; 691/12, [13]; 703/11; 739/[19],(19-20); 758/20; *d*'', 571/7-8; cf. also *ʾl*.

dʿt daʿat-palm, 610/5; 615/9-10; 617/5; 691/9; 747/16.

dqt fall, 619/7; (745/13).

drk [verb], cf. the 4th form *hdrk*.

dśś fence, receiver of stolen goods, 703/12.

dṯʾ spring (season), 610/14; 615/18; 618/9,15; 623/15; 627/11; 628/12; 650/12; 661/7; 666/16; 704/5; fruits of spring [collect.], 617/8; [719/13-14].

ḏ

ḏ [sing. masc. relative pron.], 550/1; 555/3; cf. the personal name *zbym* and the following clan and place names: *ʾwm*, *ʾws*[, *ʾḥgrm*, *ʾḥdqm*, *ʾẓwr*, *ʾlm*, *ʾlṯwrm*, *ʾmrm*, *ʾʿzz*, *bʾrn*, *bydn*, *bytnhn*, *gblm*, *gdnm*, *gmyln*, *gmʿn*, *grfm*, *drgʿn*, *ḏbyn*, *ḏbn*, *ḏkr*, *ḏnm*, *hgrm*, *hlm*, *hmdn*, *hmy*, *ḥṣbḥ*, *w*[. . .]*bn*, *wdftn*, *zltn*, *ḥbb*, *ḥẓrm*, *ḥywm*, *ḥmln*, *ḥfnm*, *ḥḏnn*, *ḥrwr*, *ḥšdm*, *ẖwln*, *ẖẓfn*, *yhʿn*, *ylrn*, *yʿd*, *yfd*, *kbsyn*, *kbr*, *lḥgm*, *mʾḏnm*, *mḏb*, *mḏrḥm*, *mšqmm*, *mšmn*, *mṯ*[, *nʾsm*, *nzḥt*, *nfʾn*, *shm*, *shrtm*, *sḥr*, *sẖymm*, *smhrm*, *smʿy*, *snfrm*, *ʿblm*, *ʿynwm*, *ʿmd*, *ʿmydm*, *ʿmyṯʿ*, *ʿfm*, *ʿḏdn*, *ʿqbn*, *ġymn*, *fyš*, *ṣwm*, *ṣryhw*, *ṣrfn*, *ḍmdm*, *qb*[, *qy*[, *qtbn*, *rbḥm*, *rgzgzn*, *rydn*, *rydt*, *ryśn*, *rmtm*, *rsmm*, *rfdn*, *šmtn*, *trznn*, *ṯml*, *ṯt*, and also *ʾḥḏ*, *ʾl*, *ʾrḍ*, *ʾtw*, *b*, *bʾs*, *bḥr*, *byn*, *bn*, *bnw*, *bny*, *bʿd*, *gwy*, *dʿ*, *ḏhb*, *ḏkw*, *hʾsy*, *hblt*, *hgr*, *hḥb*, *hḥṯʾ*, *hsbʿ*, *hḏrʿ*, *hrg*, *hrḍ*, *hrḍw*, *hrḍy*, *hšfq*, *wzʾ*, *wkb*, *wld*, *wḏʿ*, *wqh*, *ḥmy*, *ḥml*, *ẖlf*, *ẖrg*, *ẖrf*, *ymnt*, *kdd*, *kwkbt*, *kwn*, *kyn*, *ln*, *lf*, *mdlt*, *mly*, *mnḏ*, *mtʿ*, *sʾl*, *sʾr*, *sbʾ*, *sṭr*, *smy*, *sr*, *stwkl*, *stwšʿ*, *stydʿ*, *stkn*, *stmy*, *stṣr*, *stqy*, *ʿdw*, *ʿdy*, *ʿḏr*, *ʿsm*, *ʿqd*, *ʿšr*, *ʿšrnhn*, *ġwr*, *ġnm*, *fqd*, *frʿ*, *ṣbḥ*, *ṣly*, *ṣrf*, *ḍll*, *qbly*, *qny*, *qrb*, *rḥq*, *rḍw*, *šʾmt*, *šʿb*, *šft*, *šrḥ*, *śf*, *tʾwl*, *tʾlh*, *tlw*, *tmly*, *tnḏʿ*, *tnšʾ*, *tfrq*, *trbʿ*; cf. also some names of months. *ḏbhw* some of it, 653/11; by, in which, 564/3,4; (718/5); 739/5. *ḏbhmy* by both of which, 564/4. *ḏbn* some of, 561 bis/11; 574/5,8: 575/3; 576/4,5,6,7,8,9,10,12,15; 577/4,5,7,8,11; 586/21-22; 616/23; 629/9; 631/29; 635/33,33-34,34; 644/16; 665/21; 712/7; 735/7; cf. also *b*; some part of, 627/8; 735/7; among them, 660/16. *ḏbnhw* some of them, 572/15; 578/41,42; 614/19; 615/27-28,28; 616/40; 617/15; 619/20; 623/23-24,24; 647/33; 650/34; 651/54,55; 661/9; 691/12; 703/11; [739/19]; 758/19-20. *ḏlhmw*, 743/5-6. *bn/ḏ* [+noun] from, by, 575/7; 631/7; 635/12,13. *bḏ*, 584/10; cf. also the proper name *sbʾ*, and *hwfy*, *hwšʿ*, *ḥmd*, *ẖmr*, *rḍw*, *šft*, *ṯbr*. *lḏ*, cf. *hʿn*, *mḥr*.

]*ḏ* [?], 678/2.

][?]*ḏ*[[?], 792/1-2.

ḏbḥ sacrifice; *ʾ*'' [pl.], 851/6.

ḏhb (A) bronze, 558/2; 559/3-4; 561/3-4; 567/(4-5),9; 581/4; 584/8; 585/2; 657/3; 666/5; 693/5; 694/5; 700/4; 703/3; 706/4; 722/5; [732/3]; 733/5; 751/3; 752/8; 757/2; [783/4]; [790/3]; [828/4]; [855/3]. *ḏ*'', 566/5; 578/5; 579/5; 580/4; 582/6; 583/5-6; 584/2; (586/3); 587/2; 588/3; 589/5-6; 590/3; 591/5; 592/2; 600/3; 610/4; 611/5; 612/6; 613/6; 614/6; 615/9; 616/7; 617/4; 618/4; 619/4-5; 620/4; 621/4; 629/3; [631/2]; 632/3; 633/3; 635/3; 637/3; 644/2; 645/4; 646/5; (647/5-6); 648/3; 649/6; 650/4; 651/8; 652/8; (653/2); 654/5; 655/4; 656/6; 658/5; 660/6; 662/6; 664/4; 665/5; 667 A/4; 669/7-8,13; 670/7; 671/7; 684/6; (687/3-4); 688/4; 690/4; 691/4; 692/4; 695/5; 698/6-7; 699/3-4; 705/3; 708/6; 709/4; 711/3; 712/5; 713/7; 715/5; 717/3-4; [718/4-5]; 723/3; 727/9; 729/7-8; 736/5; 738/5; (739/4-5); 740 A/4; 741/5; 744/3; 745/5; (750/4); 755/5; 756/5; 758/4-5; (765/2-3); 815/3; 817/2; 818/2; 840/4-5; 844/4; 877/5. *ḏy*'', 707/6; 735/2.

ḏhb (B) irrigated land; ''*hmw*, (746/8-9); *ʾ*'' [pl.], 735/2.

ḏḥr treasurer, (591/1).

ḏy [dual masc. relat. pron.], 556; 559/3; 561/3; 585/2; 720/2; 722/5; cf. also *ḏhb*.

ḏkw to eradicate; purge out; detach; *ḏ*'', 665/19; ''*n* [2nd form; inf.], 631/27. ''*w* [pl.; passive], 665/17.

ḏkr (A) male [adject.], 588/4; 636/14-15; 654/6-7; 664/5; 669/9; 738/7; (788/4-5). *ʾ*'' [pl.], 564/19; 636/16; 642/13; 650/30; 654/8-9; 655/12; 664/10; 703/4,5; 733/6; 736/7,12; 737/1-2; 738/8; 740 A/5; 743/5; (747/10-11). *ʾ*''*w* [pl.], 561 bis/20; 563/18; 605/11; 704/4; 728/6-7; 757/5; (818/5-6). *ḏkwr* [pl.], 594/9. [noun], 729/10.

ḏkr (B) to invest, 643/14.

ḏll [verb], cf. the 4th and 5th forms, *hḏll* and *tḏll* respectively.

ḏmr [+*bʿm*] to condemn publicly, 669/20-21.

ḏn [masc. demonstr. adject.] [sing.], 550/1; 551; 556; 557; 578/4; 600/2; 611/5; 615/8; 616/6-7; 618/11; 634/3; 655/4; 667 A/9; 684/5; 701 A/3; 710/3; 721/3; 723/2; 758/4; 877/5. [dual], 614/5-6.

ḏnm (A) rain, 651/18,19,21; 653/12; 735/5,12,15.

ḏnm (B) to rain, 651/17.

ḏʿb waves [collect.], 651/33; 671/17; 735/12.

ḏfrʾ stinking herbs [collect.], 720/9.

ḏr spreading far and wide, 735/13.

ḏrr to spread; scatter. *ḏr*; ''*n* [inf.], 702/3-4; cf. also the 4th form *hḏr*.

ḏt (A) [sing. fem.; demonstr. adject.], 567/13; 608/8; 609/8; 626/16; 628/9; 633/12,15; 657/8; 735/6; 743/6; 753 I/6,II/10,III/10; 851/4; *l*'', 633/10; cf. also *b*.

ḏt (B) [sing. fem.; demonstr. pron.], 584/7; 652/22.

ḏt (C) [sing. fem. relat. pron.], 550/2; 551; 555/3; 558/5; 563/15; 567/25; 584/7,8; 640/2; 643 bis/8; 647/14; 706/3; 719/7; 721/1; 731/1; 738/9; [742/2]; 743/1; 751/1,3,4,12; 752/7,8; (783/4); 824/4,[6]; cf. also the list of deities [*passim*], the place name *qrytm*, and also *hg*, *hgn*, *ʿbd*, *ʿdy*, *qbly*. ''*ʾl*, cf. *qbly*. *b*'', 551; 558/4,5; (559/6); 560/5,7,8,16; 561/6-7; 561 bis/15; 564/4; 568/10; 580/9; 585/9,14; 590/7,11; 592/6; 612/6; 616/13,28; (624/6); 629/13,17,19,22,25,29,32,35,37; 631/11,16; 635/13,41; 640/6; 643 bis/4,5; 644/7-8,10, (14); 651/23-24; 656/13; 668/(6),8; 670/8-9,13; 671/15,19; 685/3; 708/7; 715/6; 716/9-10; 725/6; 735/16; 739/6,10; 746/6; 751/5; 758/11; 790/3; cf. also *ḥmd*. *l*'', 561 bis/16; 562/14; 564/26; 565/7; (566/5-6); 576/2; 577/17,19; 587/3; [598/3]; 601/12; 602/12; 606/16; 607/15; 619/11; 626/17; 627/23; 630/6,15; 642/(6),9; 645/7,10,15; 646/5; 650/9,11,30; (710/3); [719/11]; 753 (I/6),II/11,III/11; 761/3.

ḏty [dual fem. relat. pron.], 686/2.

h

h (A) [sing. pers. suffix pron.][masc.], cf. *ʾmt, bny, sʿd.* [fem.], cf. *ʾẖr, b, bnt, hkr, ḏry.*

h (B) [noun plur. ending], cf. *ʾb.*

h (C) [mark], 701 B?

h[(A) [pers. suffix pron.][masc.? fem.? sing.? pl.?], cf. *hʿn, wfy.*

h[(B)[?], 570/4-5,9-10; 746/13-14.

]*h* [?], 850/2.

]*h*[[?], 798/4.

h.tt [?], 569/9.

hʾ (A) [sing. demonst. pron.][masc.], 564/12; 576/11; 584/11; 649/13,[22]; 702/15; 720/13; cf. also *k.* [fem.], cf. *b, ln.*

hʾ (B) [sing. demonstr. adject.; masc.], 585/15.

hʾwl to bring back, (710/3-4); [passive], 670/10.

hʾmn to protect; shelter; "*n* [inf.], 633/13.

hʾsy to take away; *ḏ*", 651/11-12.

hbʾs to act harmfully; "*w* [pl.], 577/13.

hblt to endow; *ḏ*"*w* [pl.; passive], 631/16.

hbʿy to instigate; act corruptly; "*w* [pl.], (750/16); "*n* [inf.], 708/9.

hbʿl to seize, 639/4; "*w* [pl.], 576/13. "*n* [inf.], 576/4,6, 8; 631/8; *b*", (586/17-18?).

hbrw to cut; "*n* [inf.], 631/4.

hbry to cut; "*w* [pl.], 616/20-21.

hbrr (A) to agree; decide, 576/16; "*w* [pl.], 575/3; 576/9,10. *y*" [imperf.]; "*w* [pl.], 576/8; 643/35.

hbrr (B) to liquidate [passive], 644/8.

hbt gift; *b*", 750/7.

hgbʾ to drive back; restore; give over, 651/34; "*w* [pl.], 576/2; "*n* [inf.], 649/34; 670/28; 854/2-3.

hgz to shave, "*n* [inf.], 585/8; 644/17.

hgm unexpected assault, 578/11.

hgr city, 550/2; 560/11,14; 574/10,11; 575/3; 576/3,4,5,6, 7,8,9,(9-10),10,11,12,13,14,15,16; 577/2,3,6,8,11,13, 17; 578/26,28; 585/5,11; 615/11; 616/16,18; 619/9; 629/7,10,23,27-28,30,31,35-36; 631/19,20,21-22,22,23, 25,28; 632/3; 634/4; 635/23,25,28; 636/1,7; 637/4; 640/2; 643/7,10,18,19,20,21,28,29,30,33,35; 643 bis/ 10; 644/16,22; 651/31; 660/19; 668/10; 727/3-4; 730/2; 735/1; 812/4; 816/10; [pl.]: 576/4; 577/14; 629/40; "*hmw*, (777/1-2); *b*", 555/3; 564/9,12; 572/7; 576/2; 577/10; 585/7; 613/9; 619/3,13; 629/38; (642/5-6); 643/9,29,31; 644/7; (651/16-17); 658/12; 660/13-14; 661/5; 662/(8-9),13; 667 A/8; *ḏ*", cf. the clan name *bklm*; *l*", 577/1. *hgrnhn* [dual], 576/4,8,14; 577/2; 578/20; 643/22,23,25,26; 665/20.

hdrk to reach; "*n* [inf.], 629/33. "*hmw*, 575/4; *f*", 574/10; 577/4. "*t* [fem.]; "*hmw*, 576/12. *y*" [imperf.]; "*hmw*, 577/5.

hḏll to reject, 669/21-22.

hḏr to scatter; [passive], "*w*[pl.], 575/4.

hw [sing. pers. suffix pron.][masc.], cf. the name of deity *šms*, and *ʾb, ʾbl, ʾdm, ʾḏn, ʾẖ, ʾẖḏ, ʾmr, ʾmt, ʾnṯ, ʾsd, ʾsy, ʾrḍ, b, byn, byt, bkl, blq, blt, bn, bny, bʿd, bʿdn, bʿl, bʿr, brw, bṯ, gwy, grb, ḏ, hwfy, hwṣt, hẖw, hydʿ, hnwl, hʿn, hqnyt, hrḍw, hrḍy, wld, wfy, wqh, wśf, zẖn,*]*ḥ*[*, ḥlẓ, ḥmd, ḥmy, ḥṣn, ḥqw, ẖms, ẖmr, ẖrg, ẖry, yd, ysr, yfʿ, klʾ, lb, lsn, mʾẖḏ, mdlt, mḏhb, mẖtn, mlʾ, mlk, msʾl, msg, mfsḥ, mṣr, mrʾ, mrr, mtʿ, nbl, nẖl, nẓr, nfs, snt, sʿd, sr, stwkl, stwšʿ, stydʿ, stʿn, ʿbd, ʿbr, ʿdy, ʿwd, ʿlw, ʿly, ʿm, ʿn, ʿḍ, ʿqb, ʿšr, ġyl, fẖḏ, fnwt, frs, ṣdġ, ṣyt, ṣlm, ḍrs, qht, qwl, qny, qrʾ, rʾy, rʾs, rgl, rkb, šwʿ, šʿb, šft, šrḥ, śn, śf, tʾbh, tbšr, twṯb, tlw, tmhrt, tnbʾ, tnḍʿ, tqnʿ,*]*tt, ṯʾr, ṯny*;]*hw*, 647/14; 662/2; 730/1; 753 II/1; *h*]*w*, 577/12-13; 647/9-10; 716/13;](*h*)*w*, 823 A; *lhw*, 550/2; 555/4; 619/10; (647/16); 648/5; 651/32; 655/6,9; 657/6; 664/7; 665/20; 690/6; 693/7; 719/6; 729/10. [fem.], cf. *ʾns, b, bn, bny, bnt, brṯ, grb, hwfy, hnkr, hʿn, wqh, ẖmr, mrʾ, sʾl, ʿyn, thqnyn*; *lhw*, 700/9; 717/6-7; (828/6).

hwʾ (A) [sing. masc. demonstr. pron.], 577/15; 631/14.

hwʾ (B) [sing. masc. demonstr. adjective], 644/10.

hwbl successful pursuit. "*t* [pl.]; *b*", 576/10.

hwkb to force; follow closely; "*n* [inf.], 660/11. *y*" [imperf.]; "*nn* [pl.], 576/14.

hwkl recommendation, 568/6; 653/16; [pl.], 568/13. "*t* [pl.], (611/14); (653/3-4); *b*", 611/6-7.

hwn [2nd form] to soothe, 722/c.

hwsy to undertake; "*hmw*, 647/26; "*w* [pl.], 647/25.

hwfʾ to make ready, 555/4.

hwfy to grant; save; bestow upon, 550/2; 560/5; 568/10; 601/4; 602/4; 614/6; 616/7; (618/12); 627/3; 629/19, 32; 630/4; 644/2; 645/4-5,10-11; 650/19; 658/6; 662/7; 666/6; 671/19; 719/4; 736/10; 739/6; 740 A/6; (746/3-4); 747/4; 758/5,11; (790/3-4). "[, 569/8. *k*", 657/7; 664/7-8; 739/8; (847/3-4); "*w* [pl.]: 656/16. "*hw*, (550/1); 551; 555/3; 581/12; 608/6-7; 609/6-7; 611/6; 632/7-8; 691/5; 701 A/6; 831/2; [*hw*, fem.] 764/4; *bḏ*", 580/5. "*hmw*, 558/5; 560/16; (565/4-5); 566/6; 592/6; 610/7; 618/5; 621/4-5; 627/6; 649/7; 653/3; 701 A/4; 715/6; (746/6); 747/18-19. "*hmy*, 624/6. "*n* [inf.], 561 bis/6; 565/8; 578/10; 580/10; 585/18; 587/6-7; 605/12; 608/10; 609/9-10; 610/10; 611/11; 614/10; 616/32; 620/7; 627/12-13; 628/14; 629/3,25; 630/7; 644/12; 645/8,16; 647/31; 653/15; 657/6; 660/7,20; 662/14-15; 668/7; 701 A/6; 715/7; 716/4-5; 719/6,16; 735/17,18; 736/11; 739/15; 740 A/9; 741/9-10; 756/9-10; (816/7-8); 851/3; "*hw*, 580/13; 587/3; 590/15,18; 612/7-8; 693/11-12; "*hmw*, 561 bis/15; (566/11); 567/18; 584/4; 626/13; 650/25; 716/10; 753 I/4,II/6,III/6; *l*"*hmw*, 650/16-17. *y*" [imperf.]; "*n*, 551; 558/5; *k*"*n*, 647/16.

hwfr to increase (the number of); *l*"*nn* [inf.], 669/14-15.

hwṣl to entrust to, 559/9; 561/9. to intervene, "*w* [pl.], 561 bis/11. to assemble; regroup; "*w* [pl.], 578/25; *f*", 576/4; 665/24.

hwṣt to appoint; "*hw*, 550/2.

hwḍʿ to favor; *l*" [inf.], 652/24-25.

hwrd to conduct, 550/2.

hwšʿ to assist; help, 561 bis/6; 576/1,3; 577/15; 578/5,9, 15; 629/3,13,17,25,29; 631/3,11,16-17; 643 bis/4,5; "*hmw*, 562/4; 576/2; 577/6,8; 586/17; *bḏ*"*hmw*, 577/18. "*n* [inf.], 574/3; 577/17; 585/16; 586/3; 589/6; 635/5,16; 643 bis/7; "*hmw*, 574/12; 642/12.

hwśq to fill up; "*n* [inf.], 557.

hwt (A) [sing. masc. demonstr. adj.], 567/11,12; 576/2 577/7; 590/12; 616/17; 628/8; 629/19; 633/9,14; 635/38; 644/21; 649/41; 651/21; 653/10,13; 671/24;

700/11; 718/6; 734/5; 735/12; 750/15; (807/1); 847/4; cf. also *b*.
hwt (B) [sing. masc. demonstr. pron.], 584/3; 649/27.
hwtw to send back; ”*hmw*, 560/14.
hḥdṯ to renew, 554; 817/3; 854/2.
hḥmd to behave in a praise-worthy way; ”*n* [inf.], 668/12-13.
hẖb to deceive. *ḏ*”, 735/5; ”*t* [fem.], 653/5.
hẖw to associate oneself; ”*hw*, 577/10.
hẖṭʾ to seduce into acting wrongfully, 702/8; ”*n* [inf.], 577/9; 720/15. ”*w* [pl.], 601/8; 602/8; *ḏ*”, 720/5-6.
hẖfr to extend assistance, 576/2.
hẖḏf to soothe, 650/23.
hṭb to make pleasant. ”*w* [pl.]; *k*”, 616/19.
hẓm to inflame with zeal; ”*n* [inf.], 700/6.
hy [sing. fem. pers. suffix pron.], cf. *ẖlf*.
hydʿ to give some information; ”*hw*, 584/9.
hyhr to exalt, 564/7; ”*n* [inf.], 668/13.
hykl palace; ”*t* [pl.], 629/28-29.
hysr to send, 576/5; 577/14; 643/12. ”*n* [inf.]; *l*”, 643/10. *y*” [imperf.]; ”*w* [pl.], 576/6; 577/7.
hyʿ to build up, 643/15; 831/2.
hyt [sing. fem. demonstr. adject.], 576/5,6,13,14; 585/10; 643/25; 669/23,25; 686/5; (735/17); *l*”, 629/21; cf. also *b*.
hkml to act perfectly; ”*n* [inf.], 651/36-37.
hkms to wither, 574/13; 610/17; 611/20-21; 877/16; ”*n* [inf.], 577/18,19; 635/15.
hkn to come to pass, 567/11,12; [*maṣdar*], 567/11,12.
hkr to change. ”*n* [inf.]; ”*h*, 558/7.
hlqḥ to enchain; ”*n* [inf.], 601/9; 602/9; 629/14.
]*hm* [?], 685/2.
hmw (A) [pl. masc. pers. pron.] [suffix], cf. the names of deities *mḏḥ, rbʿ, šms, šmsy*, and *ʾbl, ʾdb, ʾdm, ʾḏn, ʾhb, ʾwl, ʾẖ, ʾẖḏ, ʾl, ʾm, ʾnṯ, ʾsd, ʾswd, ʾrḏ, ʾśr, ʾṯr, b, bhʾ, byt, blt, bn, bny, bnt, bʿw, bʿr, gyš, grb, ḏ, ḏhb, hgr, hdrk, hwsy, hwfy, hwšʿ, hwtw, hmlʾ, hsḥt, hʿn, hfy, hqnyt, hrg, hrḏ, hrḏw, hrḏy, hšʾm, wld, wʿd, wfy, wqḥ, wśy, wśf, ḥyf, ḥyrt, ḥml, ḥmr, ḥṣq, ḥr, ḥrb, ḥrbt, ẖbṭ, ẖms, ẖmr, ẖry, ẓwr, yfʿ, kwn, kl, lb, lfy, mʾdb, mʾẖḏ, mhrt, mwʿd, mẓʾ, mlk, mnẖt, mʿd, mġwn, mfnt, mṣr, mqblt, mqdmt, mqwl, mqyz, mqm, mqtwy, mrʾ, mšm, mšrʿ, mtʿ, nbl, nkl, nfs, nṣr, sbṭ, syt, sʿd, sqy, sr, stnqḏ, stṣr, ʿbd, ʿbr, ʿdy, ʿwf, ʿly, ʿm, ʿnb, ʿṣd, ʿqb, ġyl, ġnm, fẖr, fly, fql, frs, frq, ftḥ, ṣdq, ṣḥb, ṣry, ṣryt, ḍr, qdm, qdmy, qwl, ql, qny, qr, rwt, rkb, rḏw, rqt, šwʿ, šym, šnʾ, šʿb, šʿr, śft, śrʿ, śf,]t, tbql, tbšr, tmnʿ, ṯhb, ṯmr*.]*hmw*, 680/3; 798/2.]*hm*[*w*, 576/16; 577/6. *h*]*mw*, 577/1, 10-11. *hm*]*w*, 719/17; 766/6-7; 799/1-2. ...*hmw*], 735/11. *l*”, 575/4; 576/16; 577/19; 598/4; 616/17-18, 19; 630/15-16; 665/40; 669/8-9,10-11; 670/29; 671/(16-17),19; 730/8; 735/18; 738/7; 752/12; 761/3. [separate], 574/8; 577/10; 616/28; 644/30; 665/48.
hmw (B) [pl. masc. demonstr. adject.], 576/10,16; 577/10, 12; 665/18.
hmḥl to be barren; ”*t* [fem.], 735/6.
hmẓʾ to let arrive, 681/2.
hmy (A) [conj.], cf. *k*.
hmy (B) [dual masc. pers. pron.] [suffix]; *h*]*my*, 570/9; cf. also *ʾb, ʾdm, ʾm, ʾnṯ, ʾsd, bʾr, byn, bn, bny, grb, ḏ, hwfy, hrbb, hrḏw, wld, wqḥ, ẖms, ẖmr, ẖrg, ẖry, mdlt, mġbt, mrʾ, mtʿ, sʿd, ʿm, ḍr, rṯd, šnʾ, šʿb, tʾlh*. [separate], 578/31.
hmy (C) [dual masc. demonstr. adject.], 651/20; cf. also *b*.
hmyt [pl. masc. demonstr. adject.], cf. *b*.
hmlʾ (A) to complete; ”*n* [inf.], 557.
hmlʾ (B) to favor; ”*hmw*, 631/20; 671/16.
hms to break down, 574/13; 577/19; 610/17; 611/20; 877/16; ”*n* [inf.], 577/18.
hmt [demonstr. adject.][pl. masc.], 560/12; 564/15; 574/6; 575/2,4,(4-5),5,6,7; 576/5,10; 577/2,(3),5,12; 586/18; 601/9; 602/9; 644/19,23; 660/15; 665/23. [dual fem.], 643/22; cf. also *b*.
hn (A) [article], cf. *ʿṭwf, rḥl*.
hn (B) [noun dual ending], cf. *byt*.
hn (C) [pl. fem. pers. suffix pron.]; *l*”. 722/c; cf. also *ẖmr, mtʿ*.
hnʾ pleasing, 558/4; 561 bis/20; 563/18; 564/19; 567/23, 24; 570/15; 581/17; 587/10; 588/7; 591/9; 594/10; 599/8; 618/23; 636/16; 642/13; 647/17; 650/30; 654/9,14; 655/12; 656/24; 657/11; 658/29; 661/8; 703/5,6; 704/4; 728/7; 733/6-7; 736/7,13,16; 737/2; 738/8,10; 747/11; 757/5; 818/6.
hnb to replace; ”*w* [pl.], 560/13.
hndʾ to take unaware; ”*n* [inf.], 643/7.
hnwl to lead with care; ”*hw*, (584/11).
hnkr to remove; ”*nhw*, 562/21.
hnqḏ to carry away; ”*n* [inf.], 643 bis/2. to rescue; ”*n* [inf.], 560/(11),12.
hnt (A) [pl. fem. demonstr. adject.], 568/13; 576/4; 577/(15),16; 578/13; (580/11); 636/6; 650/22; 712/10.
hnt (B) [pl. fem. pers. suffix pron.], cf. *ʾẖt*.
hsbʿ to plunder; pillage; *ḏ*”*w* [pl.], 668/11. ”*n* [inf.], 576/4; *b*”, 629/30. *y*” [imperf.]; ”*w* [pl.], 576/7.
hsḥt to destroy; annihilate; ”*hmw*, 576/9,16; 649/34. ”*n* [inf.], 575/7; 576/5; 577/5; 578/6,17; 589/9; 631/5,28; *b*”, (586/17-18?).
hʿmm to let grow; ”*n* [inf.], 627/10; 628/11-12.
hʿn to assist; help; protect; lend assistance, 572/5; 613/7; 620/4; 651/9; 661/4; 665/41; 670/14; 687/9; 699/4; 700/16,16-17; 712/5; 725/6; (745/12); (761/2); ”*hw*, 583/8; ”*hmw*, 694/8; (732/8); (750/12-13); ”*w* [pl.], 629/33; 671/23-24; *k*”, 665/40; 712/9; *k*”*hw* [fem.], 706/7; *l*”, 651/30; 661/8; 702/17; 758/18; *lḏ*”*hmw*, 750/10. *hʿnn* [inf.], 567/15-16; [586/3-4]; 613/12; 631/18; 635/10; 651/42; (695/5); 699/6; 706/8; 731/5; 786/2; ”*hw*, 587/12; 840/7; ”*hmw*, 603/11; 634/10; 737/3; *l*”, (564/21); 576/5; 577/10; 640/4; 643/24; 651/49; 684/11; 706/5; *l*”*h*[, (803/5-6); *l*”*hw*, 597/7; (633/4-5); 711/4,11-12; 739/17; *l*”*hmw*, 579/11: (588/11-12); (598/5); 618/30; 619/18-19; 648/9; 715/9; 717/10-11; 750/13,(15),16. *yhʿn* [imperf.]; ”*w* [pl.], 577/5; ”*nhmw*, 558/4; *l*”*nhw*, (572/9-10); *l*”*nhmw*, 668/18.
hʿsm to continue obstinately; *k*”*w* [pl.], 577/9.
hġr to make a raid; ”*w* [pl.], 576/4; (577/11-12); 616/23; 665/24.
hġṯ to water with rain; ”*n* [inf.], 735/10.
hfy to grant, 752/11. to protect; ”*n* [inf.]; ”*hmw*, 752/14-15.
hfs to cover; *f*”*w* [pl.], 735/15.
hfsḥ to build an annex; *f*”, 618/11.
hfʿ advantage, 651/53.
hṣnʿ to hold; keep back; ”*w* [pl.], 585/6.
hṣr to set out; [+*bʿly*] to fall upon (an enemy); *f*”,

643/21; *''n* [inf.], 576/3; 577/4; 631/21; 643/5. *''w* [pl.], 577/2; *f''*, 576/5,13. *y''* [imperf.], 576/7; *''w* [pl.], 576/7; *f''w*, 576/14; *''y* [dual], 629/8; *''n*, 576/10,11; *k''n*, 643/27; *f''n*, 576/8.

hḏrʿ to subjugate; *ḏ''*, 577/13.

hqḏ to carry away; *''w* [pl.], 665/37. *y''* [imperf.]; *''w* [pl.], 586/22.

hqm to raise up, 557.

hqny to dedicate, 550/1; 551; 552/2; 553/2; 555/1; 557; 564/2; 570/1; 579/4; 580/3; 581/3; 582/5; 583/4-5; 584/1; 587/1; 590/2; 591/4; [600/1]; 604/1; 608/4; 609/3-4; [610/3]; 611/4; 612/5; 613/5; 619/3-4; 630/1-2; 633/2; 634/2; 635/2; 637/2; 644/1; 645/2; 646/4; 649/5; 651/7; 652/22; 655/2; 657/1; 665/4; 667 A/2-3; 672/1; 683/2; 684/4; 687/2; (688/1-2); 689/1; 690/3; 692/2; 694/2-3; 696/2-3; 697/2-3; 698/3; 699/1; 701 A/2; 709/2; 710/2; 711/2; 723/2; 726/2; 729/3-4; (732/1-2); 739/4; 741/3-4; 744/2; 755/2; 756/3-4; 757/1; 757 bis/3; 758/4; [765/1]; (776/2?); (780/1-2?); 787/2; [803/2?]; 816/3; [818/1?]; 831/1; 832; 840/3; 844/2; (849/2?); 853 (A/1-2), B/1-2,(C/1-2),D/1,E/2,[F/1]; 855/2; 877/4. *hqnyw* [pl.], [558/1]; (559/2); 560/3; 561/2; 561 bis/4; 562/3; 563/3; 565/3; 566/4; (567/3); 568/3; 569/4; 586/2; 588/2; 589/4-5; [592/1]; 601/2; (602/2); 603/3; 605/2-3; 606/3; 607/3; 615/8; 616/6; [617/3]; 618/3; 620/3; 621/3; [623/c]; (625/2); 626/3; 627/2; [628/2]; 629/2; (631/1-2); (641/2); 642/3; [643/2]; 647/4; (648/2); 650/3-4; 653/1; 654/3; 656/5; 660/5; (661/3); 662/4; [664/2]; 666/3; 669/4; 670/5; 671/5; 691/3; 695/3-4; 700/3; 703/2; 704/2; 705/2; 707/5; 708/4; 712/4; 713/5; 715/3; 716/3; 718/4; 719/3; 720/2; 727/8; 728/2; 730/3; 733/3; 735/2; 736/3-4; 738/3; 740 A/3; 745/3; (746/2-3); (747/2); 750/3; 752/5; (753 I/1); [761/1]; [766/3]; (767/4-5); [784/2]; [788/3]; 790/1; 812/4-5; [815/2]; [817/1?]; 835; [851/1]; *k''*, 567/12-13. *hqnyt* [fem.], 706/2; 717/2; 721/2-3; 731/3; [742/3]; 743/2; (751/1-2); (777/2-3); (828/3); *''w* [pl.], (686/2-3); (722/3-4); [783/2]; [passive], 584/7; *k''hw*, 584/10. *hqnyy* [dual], 556; 572/3; 574/2; (575/1); [576/1]; 578/4; 585/1-2; 614/5; [624/4]; 632/2; 652/6; (658/3); 693/3. *yhqny* [imperf.]; *kl''nn*, 567/8-9; *f''nn*, 669/11-12,23-24.

hqnyt offering, 554; 559/19-20; 561/19-20; 567/13; (570/10); 608/8; 609/8; 626/16-17; 628/9; 633/10-11, 12,15; 644/30; 647/12; 657/8: 714/1; 743/6; 745/5; 749/1; 753 I/6,II/10-11,(III/10); 755/5; 759/1; 760; 854/3; *''hw*, 664/8; *''hmw*, 558/7; 562/20; 564/32; 568/26; 592/9-10; 601/21; 602/21; 606/23; 607/23; 626/23-24; 627/29-30; 628/29-30; 643 bis/10; 703/12; 753 I/9,II/18, III/18.

hrʾy to show, 567/5.

hrbb to seize upon; *''hmy*, 716/6-7.

hrg (A) to kill, 575/7; 586/21; 612/12; 631/8; 649/10,18, 34; 713/10,14. *b''*, 631/4; [*maṣdar*], 578/11; cf. also the 5th form *thrg*. [passive], 643 bis/2; *f''*, 577/1. *''w* [pl.], 586/18; 631/27; 665/34; [passive] *f''*, 575/6. *y''* [imperf.]; *''n*, 631/30,33; *''w* [pl.], 577/14; 644/23.

hrg (B) to take away; [with *mhrg(t)*] to deprive; *''hmw*, 665/22. *''w* [pl.], 577/1; 643 bis/2; 649/36; *ḏ''*, 635/31. *yhrgw* [imperf. pl.], 575/7; 576/5,9; 577/12; *''hmw*, 644/19.

hrdʾ to assist; *''n* [inf.], 576/1; 578/5,15; (695/9-10).

hry (A) severe cold; *b''*, 751/6.

hry (B) to suffer (from severe cold); *''t* [fem.], 751/6.

hrs to be in command, 550/2.

hrʿl to move forward; *''nn* [inf.], (735/13-14).

hrḍ to please; *ḏ''hmw*, 703/4.

hrḍw to please, 668/9; *''n* [inf.], 650/23-24. *ḏ''*, 577/16; 578/12,33; 590/13; 601/11; 602/11; 616/31; 631/16; 632/6; 653/12;7 39/11; *''hw*, 581/11; *''hmw*, 574/9-10; 576/6; 616/31; 629/18,36; 636/10; 649/23-24; 656/7-8, 14-15; 877/11; *''hmy*, 632/7. *yhrḍw* [imperf.]; *ḏ''n*, 615/22; 626/7; 627/20; 628/21; 753 II/2-3,III/2; *ḏ''nhmw*, 610/15; 623/4-5; 650/15; [799/3-4].

hrḍy to please; *ḏ''hmw*, 649/14. *y''* [imperf.]; *ḏ''n*, 571/5; 580/6; 753 I/3; *ḏ''nhw* 613/20-21; *ḏ''nhmw*, 623/15-16; 645/22,23-24; 658/33-34.

hšʾm to cause to buy; *''hmw*, (734/2).

hšyn to suffer, 620/6.

hšfq to enrich; make abound; *ḏ''*, 665/27; *''n* [inf.], 627/10; 628/11.

hšqr to cover; *''w* [pl.], 671/17; *''n* [inf.], 603/5.

hštʾ to bring about; initiate, 629/6; 656/11; *''w* [pl.], 577/13; 589/11; *''n* [inf.], 643/5.

hśl (A) to empty; *''n* [inf.], 576/7.

hśl (B) to lead; drive (cattle). *y''* [imperf.]; *''nn*, 669/13,24.

]*h.tt* [?], 569/9.

]*ht* [?], 763/2.

hṯb to present, 550/2; 555/4; *''w* [pl.], 716/9.

hṯlʿ to break; *''n* [inf.], 578/6,17; 589/9.

w

]*w* [verb plural ending], 643/8.

]*w*[[?], 725/2.

w (A) [masonry mark]; *w///ṣ*, 740 B.

w (B) [plural ending], cf. *ʾrbʿ*, *frʿ*, and the proper name *kbr*.

wdy wâdî; *ʾ''t* [pl.], 616/26.

wdq (A) familiar; *''t* [pl.], 651/12.

wdq (B) to become allied; *''y* [dual], 651/20.

wdq (C) to occur; happen, 619/7.

whb to give. *''w* [pl.], 574/11; 576/2,2-3; 577/13; *f''*, 574/12.

wzʾ to continue, 559/10-11; 560/17; 561/10; 636/15; 690/7; 728/5; (747/9). *lwzʾ*, (566/10-11); 567/15,21; (568/13-14); 569/8; 574/12; (578/35); 580/12; 581/13; (583/7); 585/16,18; 586/9; 587/6; 588/5; 590/14; 592/7; 600/8; 608/8-9; 609/8; 610/9; 611/9-10; 612/12; 613/11; 614/9; 615/14; 616/31; 617/6; 618/12; 620/7; 626/12; 629/41; 631/36; 641/9; (642/11-12); 650/25,27; 651/41; 653/14; 654/7; 655/10; 656/19; 658/27; 662/14,18; 665/47; 666/7; 667 A/10; 668/11; 669/17; 671/20; 686/7; 693/10; 694/7-8; 699/6; 701 A/6; 703/5; 706/8; 708/9-10; 712/11; 713/13; 716/10; 719/[6],15,[16]; 732/7; 733/7; 735/17; 738/7; 739/11-12,15; 740 A/8,10-11; 741/8-9; (746/7); 753 (I/4),II/5,III/5; 756/8-9; 758/13-14; 765/4; [815/6]; (839/2); 840/6; 877/11. *f''*, 627/9; 628/10; 643 bis/5; 644/14. *lzʾn*, 664/9; 700/16; 752/13. *wzʾw* [pl.], 644/17; 649/15; 651/27; 656/12; 735/13; *f''*, 644/21. *wzʾy* [dual], 629/15-16,21,24,31,34,36. *yzʾ* [imperf.],

(642/9-10); 643 bis/7. *yzʾn*, 561 bis/16-17; 565/7; 577/17; 601/12-13; 602/12; 608/12; 609/12; 611/15; 627/12; 628/13; 630/6; 635/14,41-42,43; 644/12,26; 645/7,10,15; 650/11; 715/6-7; 736/11; 751/10; *ḏ*'', 577/18; *l*'', 584/4; 646/8; 647/30; 657/9; 670/15; 685/4. *yzʾnn*, 567/18-19; 610/13; 614/12; 616/33; 653/16; 735/18.

wzʿ chief, 655/2; 660/14; ''*y* [dual], 662/3; (691/1-2); (715/1-2).

wkb (A) to receive; [passive], 575/8; cf. also the 4th and 10th forms, *hwkb* and *stwkb* respectively. ''*w* [pl.], 567/11; 628/6; (750/8-9).

wkb (B) to meet with; *ykb* [imperf.]; ''*nn*, 576/8,9,15.

wkb (C) [?]; *ḏ*'', 702/15.

wky support (?), 576/16.

wkl [verb], cf. the 10th form *stwkl*.

wld (A) child [sing.], 588/4; 636/14: 647/10; 654/6; 664/5; 686/5; 700/11; 718/6,7; 721/6; 726/5; 727/10; 738/6-7; 740 A/11; 764/3; [788/4]; 799/2; [828/5-6]; *l*'', 550/2; 721/5; cf. also the personal names *bygt*, *grmt*. [pl.], 558/4; 669/18; 717/7; ''*hw*, 550/1; 552/2-3; 553/3; 555/2; 557; 672/2; 831/2; ''*hmw*, 703/7,10; ''*hmy*, (594/8-9); cf. also the name of deity *ʿm*. *ʾwld* [pl.], 561 bis/20; 563/17-18; 564/18; 567/23; 576/7; (588/6-7); 594/9; 605/11; 636/15; (642/13); 647/17; 650/30; 654/8; 655/11-12; 658/29; 664/10; 690/9; 703/4,5; 704/4; 705/7; 728/6; 733/6; 737/1; 738/8; 740 A/5; 743/5; 747/10; 757/4; (810 B); 818/5; ''*hw*, (755/6-7); ''*hmw*, 558/3-4; 567/25; 574/11; 575/5,(5-6); 669/19-20; ''*hmy*, (580/10-11).

wld (B) to be born, 664/6-7; *ḏ*'', 669/8; *k*''*t* [fem.], 752/10. *yld* [imperf.]; ''*n*, 669/10; 729/9-10.

wlw [verb], cf. the 8th form *tlw*.

wsṭ (A) in the center, 631/25.

wsṭ (B) center, 631/28; *b*'', 567/6; 576/15; 577/2; 702/9-10.

wsy [verb], cf. the 4th form *hwsy*.

wʿd to assure; ''*hmw*, 577/9.

wʿl to illustrate; ''*t* [fem. part.], 560/3.

wfʾ [verb], cf. the 4th form *hwfʾ*.

wfy (A) safety, 558/3; 559/5,12,14; 561/5,11-12,13,14; 563/6,7-8; 564/16; 567/22; 571/4; 572/14; 581/14; 588/11; 594/7,[7-8]; 604/2,3; 605/6; 611/17; 616/17; 618/(15-16),18,30; 626/6; 627/19; 628/20; 634/10; 641/10-11; 646/12; 651/39-40; 654/9-10; 656/23; 664/11; 683/4; 704/5; 709/5-6; 730/5; 732/6; 747/7,12; 753 I/3,II/2,III/1-2; 755/6; 757/2-3; [784/3]; 821 A/2; 839/3; 853 A/3,B/3,C/3,D/2-3,E/3,F/3; 854/5; 855/4; ''*hmw*, 744/5; (787/3). *b*'', 574/9; 575/8; 577/1,3,6,7, 11,16,17; 578/32; 579/6; 580/5-6; 581/5,10; 585/4,10; 586/7,(12); 589/14; 590/5,(7-8),12; 601/11; 602/10; 616/29; 629/23,36; 631/14; 632/5; 635/8,18,38; 636/7; 643/18; 643 bis/7; 644/9; 656/7,14; 665/45,48; 708/8; 716/8; 741/7; 756/7; 758/12; 766/8. *l*'', 567/9-10,14; 605/4; 633/4; 641/8; 650/7,8; 652/8,10; 689/3; 698/7; 705/3-4; 709/4-5; 716/5; 726/3-4; 728/3-4; 732/3; 744/3; [784/2-3]; [787/2]; 818/4; 844/4; ''*h*, 803/4; ''*hw*, 604/2; 755/6; 757/2; 810 A/3; 821 A/2; ''*hmw*, 558/3; 563/5; 683/3; 707/7; 728/4-5; 853 A/3,B/3,C/3,D/2,E/3,F/3; 854/5; 855/4.

wfy (B) to protect, 608/13; 609/13; 610/16; 627/22; 643 bis/8; 689/5; 877/14,15; cf. also the 4th forms *hwfy*, *hfy*, and the 10th forms *stwfy*. ''*hw*, 689/4. ''*hmw*, 877/13-14. *lwfy* [inf.], 606/7,10-11; 607/7,10; 643 bis/7; 692/6; 717/9; 738/11; [820/**2**]; ''*hw*, 582/6-7; 608/13; 609/13; ''*hmw*, 610/15-16; 627/22. *wfyn* [inf.], 616/12: (667 A/5-6). *ywfy* [imperf.]; ''*hmw*, (818/6).

wfy (C) to pay off; ''*w* [pl.], 729/11-12; ''*n* [inf.], 647/15.

wfr [verb], cf. the 4th form *hwfr*.

wṣl [verb], cf. the 4th form *hwṣl*.

wṣt [verb], cf. the 4th form *hwṣt*.

wdʿ to make known, 557.

wḍʿ (A) to humiliate, 561 bis/23; 568/20; 577/19; 578/17; 610/17; 611/20; 629/30; 631/38; 635/14; 643 bis/9; (719/15); 853 A/5,(B/5),C/5,D/4,E/5,F/5; [*maṣdar*], 578/11; *b*'' [inf.], 574/12-13; 577/8,18; 585/13,17; 589/9; *l*'' [inf.], 564/24; (586/24); 877/16.

wḍʿ (B) to implore, cf. also the 4th form *hwḍʿ*; *yḍʿ* [imperf.], *ḏ*''*n*: 657/10.

wqh to command; order, 551; 577/13; 643/22; 658/20. ''*hw*, 583/6; 584/10; 630/3; 633/(3-4),10; 651/14-15, 28-29; 652/23; 658/11; 660/9; 662/9; 671/7; 711/3-4; (725/4); [*hw*, fem.], (797 A/2-3). ''*hmw*, 563/4; 564/11,14; 601/5-6; 602/5-6; (606/5); 607/5; 626/4-5; 628/4; (642/13-14); 644/15; 665/6-7,11-12; 753 I/2; 818/3; *ḏ*'', 616/15; 651/37; *f*'', 649/26. ''*hmy*, 616/10. *k*'', 567/13; 568/4; ''*hmw*, 650/6; 877/6. *f*'', 643/23. ''*y* [dual], 586/14; 629/38. *yqh* [imperf.]; ''*n*, 662/17; ''*nhmw*, 578/39; 623/7. *yqhnn*; ''*hmw*, 668/13; ''*hmy*, 578/37-38.

wqm to degrade; debase, 652/20.

wrd to come down; go down; ''*w* [pl.], 575/4; 631/35; cf. also the 4th and 5th forms, *hwrd* and *twrd* respectively.

wrẖ month, 627/8; 633/16; 653/9,13-14; *b*'', 567/6; 613/9; 627/5-6; 642/6; 735/4; (762/4); 877/8; *l*'', 611/7. ''*yn* [dual], 577/9. ''*n* [dual], 577/8. *ʾ*'' [pl.], 564/13,15; 671/24; 720/12.

wśʿ [verb.], cf. the 4th and 10th forms, *hwśʿ* and *stwśʿ* respectively.

wśy [3rd form] to console; comfort, 737/2; ''*hmw*, 737/3.

wśʿ [verb], cf. the 5th form *twśʿ*.

wśf to add; ''*hw*, 757/4; ''*hmw*, 567/21-22; 705/5-6; 784/3. *lwśf*; ''*hw*, (810 B); ''*hmw*, (605/10-11). *yśf* [imperf.]; ''*nhmw*, 558/4.

wśq [verb], cf. the 4th form *hwśq*.

wtw [verb], cf. the 4th form *hwtw*.

wṯb to sit down, 720/8; cf. also the 5th form *twṯb*.

wṯn limit, 576/5; *b*'', 576/4. *ʾ*'' [pl.]; *b*'', 561 bis/11-12; cf. also the name of deity *šmsy*.

wṯq firm pledge; *ʾ*'' [pl.], 574/11,12; 576/2; 577/13; 616/15.

wṯr to level, 629/28; ''*w* [pl.], 576/12. *yṯr* [imperf.]; ''*w* [pl.], 577/15.

z

zʾdʾ provisions [collect.], 750/7.

zʾk to go straight, 720/16.

zʾt constraint, 578/41; 763/5.

zẖn to wound; ''*hw*, 687/6; [passive], 649/19,20-21.

zẖnt wound, 687/7; *zẖn* [pl.], 649/19; 725/7.

ḥ

]*ḥ*[[noun]; ''*hw*, 746/4.
ḥbl (A) deceit; revolt, 667 A/8; *b*'', 576/3,11; 589/11.
ḥbl (B) to deceive, 577/6; ''*w* [pl.], 576/3.
ḥbr (A) to seduce; *y*'' [imperf.], 635/35.
ḥbr (B) [verb], cf. the 7th form *nḥbr*.
ḥbšy Ḥabašite [*nisba*], 577/12; *ʾḥbš* [pl.], 574/3,6; 575/2,5, 6,7; 577/5,8,10; 585/6,7,8; 631/21,24,28,30,32-33,33, 34,35; 635/24.
ḥg so [conj.]; ''*ḏt*, 551.
ḥgk law, ʾ'' [pl.] , 647/13.
ḥgn as; so [conj.], 562/7; 563/4; 564/11; 567/13; 568/13; 583/6; 584/10; 586/14; 605/4; 606/4; 607/4-5; 626/4; [628/3]; 630/3; 631/20; 633/3; 641/7; 642/13; 643/14; 647/17; 650/6; 698/8; 700/10; 711/3; 715/5; 717/4; 735/17; 750/4; 797 A/2; (847/3); ''/*ḏt*, 567/5; 704/3; [818/3]; ''/*k*, 568/4; 577/3; 588/4; 657/8; 740 A/5; 877/5-6.
ḥdṯ [2nd form] to secure; perform; ''*w* [pl.], 643/9; cf. also the 4th form *hḥdṯ*.
ḥḏr to fear; be afraid, 649/21; *l*''*nn* [inf.], 720/14.
ḥwl part, 702/16; 846/2,3.
ḥwr resident, 727/3; ''*w* [pl.], 730/2; (812/3-4).
ḥzb fighting band; ʾ'' [pl.], 574/5; 576/3; 577/3,10; 585/15-16.
ḥẓw to repair; ''*n* [inf.], 603/5.
ḥẓy esteem, 560/18; 561 bis/18; 562/10; 563/8; 564/16; 565/11; 566/8; 567/20,22; 568/19; 569/5; (570/10-11); 571/2; 572/12; 578/36; 579/9; 581/15; 582/7; 583/11; 585/20; 587/7; 588/7; 590/19-20; 591/6; 592/8; 595/2; 597/4-5; 599/5; 600/10; 603/8; 604/5; (605/8); 606/14; 607/14; 612/16; 613/17; 614/14; 615/23; 616/35; 617/11; 618/26,30; 619/14; 620/13; 621/7,11; 623/12; 626/9; 627/15; 628/16; 629/42; 630/11; 631/ 36-37; 632/8; 633/18; 634/6; 635/40; 636/10-11; 640/7; 641/11; 645/20; 647/19,22; 648/6; 650/10; 651/44; 652/13; 653/18; 654/10-11; 655/13; 656/19; 658/30; 661/6; 662/20; 664/12; 666/12; 667 A/15: 668/15; 669/26; 670/20-21; 671/20-21; 684/7; 690/10; 691/7; 692/7; 703/7; 704/8; 711/7; 712/14; 713/15; 719/8; 730/9; 732/9; 736/14; 739/13; 740 A/12; 746/12; (747/12-13); 753 I/4,II/4,III/4; 758/15; (765/ 6-7); [799/4]; [804/3]; [807/4]; 840/8; *l*'', (594/3).
ḥy alive, 635/32.
ḥyw (A) life, 633/14; 693/9; 703/8; 717/8; 733/13; 736/13; (764/5); *l*'', 727/7.
ḥyw (B) [verb] [1st form] to live. *y*'' [imperf.]; ''*n*, 669/11. [2nd form] to grant life, 648/4; 655/6,9; 690/6; 717/6. *y*'' [imperf.]; ''*n*, (693/6-7).
ḥyf (A) injustice, 577/2.
ḥyf (B) to commit (an injustice); ''*hmw*, 577/2.
ḥyr [2nd form] to settle down; ''*w* [pl.], 631/22; 643/21.
ḥyrt camp; encampment, 631/30; ''*hmw*, 576/12,13,15; 631/34.
ḥlẓ (A) oppression, 567/17; 572/10; 585/10; 613/9,14; 633/5,9,15; 711/4-5,5; 762/5; 840/5-6,7; ''*hw*, 720/14.
ḥlẓ (B) to be overwhelmed (by oppression), 567/6; 583/7; 613/9; 633/5; 762/5; 840/6. *y*'' [imperf.]; ''*n*, 633/8.
ḥll animal. ʾ'' [pl.], 574/9; 577/3,6; 586/12; 616/29; 632/5; 635/18-19, 42-43; 636/9; 644/25; 658/26; *b*'', 635/30; 650/22-23.

ḥlm dream, 567/11,12.
ḥlṣ plunder; pillage, 650/32.
ḥmd (A) praise, 574/9; 575/8; 577/1,3,6,11,16; 581/5; 586/7; (589/14-15); 616/29; 635/9; 649/24; 658/16-17; 665/45; *b*'', 725/5-6; ''/*b* [+noun], 649/14-15. ''/*bḏ* [+verb], 577/6,18; 580/4-5; 581/8; 585/3,11; (586/10-11); 589/6; 657/4; 664/4; 701/3-4; (722/5-6). ''/*bḏt*, 559/4; 561/4; 561 bis/5-6; 562/3-4; 564/7-8,13; 565/4; 572/5; 574/2-3,8; 575/8; 576/1,3; 577/6,8,15, 16,18; 578/5,9,15,30,33; 579/5; 581/5,12; 584/3,8-9; (586/3); 588/3; 590/3; 592/3; 600/3; 601/3-4; 602/3-4; 603/4-5; (605/12); 608/6; 609/6; 610/4; 611/5-6; 613/6-7; 614/6; 616/7; 618/4-5; 619/5; 620/4; 621/4; (624/7); 627/3; 629/3; 630/3-4; 632/3-4,6,7; 635/5,16, 28-29,39; 636/5,8,13-14; 642/4; 644/2; 645/4; 647/23; 649/6-7; 650/18-19; 651/8-9; 653/3; 654/5; 655/4-5; 656/6; 658/5-6; 660/7,19-20; (661/4); 662/6; 665/5; 666/5-6; 667 A/5; 690/5; (691/4-5); 695/5; 699/4; 700/4; 703/3-4; 708/6; 712/5; 713/7-8,10; 715/5-6; 716/4; 719/4; 723/3; (731/4-5); 733/5; 734/2; 735/2-3; 738/5-6; 740 A/4,5-6; 743/4; 745/6,8,11-12; (746/3); 747/4,(6); 758/5; [764/1]; [765/3]; 812/7; (815/3-4); (817/2); (828/4-5); [851/2]. ''/*lḏt*, (631/2-3); 686/4. ''/*lqbly*/*ḏt*, (687/4).
ḥmd (B) to praise, [560/5,16]; 564/3; 629/16,21,24,31,34, 37; 643 bis/5; 644/14; 651/22; 656/13; 670/12; [685/2]; 695/8; 739/5; cf. also the 4th form *hḥmd*. *k*'', 758/9-10. *l*'' [inf.]; ''*hw*, (647/6); ''*nn*, 669/16. *f*'', 644/7. ''*w* [pl.], 616/(12-13),27; (640/5-6); [643/3]; 658/23; 665/46; (668/5); 671/14,17-18; 703/5; 718/5; 735/15; (746/5-6). ''*y* [dual], 568/9; 585/8; 629/12; 643 bis/4,6-7. ''*t* [fem.], 751/4,8.
ḥmẓ skinner, 726/1.
ḥmy to protect, (642/4). *y*'' [imperf.]; *ḏ*''*nhw*, 651/33.
ḥml (A) (Ḥamlite); ʾ'' [pl.], 738/3.
ḥml (B) to take up; amass; collect; ''*hmw*, 576/9; *ḏ*''*hmw*, 576/9,16. ''*w* [pl.] [passive], 577/13.
ḥmr (A) ass. ''*t* [pl.]; ''*hmw*, 643 bis/3.
ḥmr (B) Ḥimyarite; ʾ'' [pl.], 576/5,10,16; 586/18; 633/7.
ḥngn as [conj.], 753 I/2.
ḥsm to cut to pieces, 577/3; 643 bis/5; *b*'', 575/7.
ḥf encirclement, 558/5.
ḥṣy esteem, 578/42-43; 647/22; 657/12; 733/8.
ḥṣn stallion. ʾ'' [pl.]; ''*hw*, 619/11-12.
ḥṣq prison-keepers [collect.]; ''*hmw*, 577/15; 586/22-23; 644/20-21.
ḥḍr (A) dwelling; house; ʾ'' [pl.], 629/33; 665/23.
ḥḍr (B) to be present; arrive; *l*'' [inf.], 651/17.
ḥqw buttock. ''*y* [dual]; ''*hw*, 700/13. ''*nhn* [dual], 711/5.
ḥql country; *b*'', 578/7-8,34; 590/10.
ḥr freeman. *ʾḥrr* [pl.], 577/12; ''*hmw*, 616/15.
ḥrb to fight, 616/23; ''*hmw*, 616/26; *l*'' [inf.] 635/34. ''*w* [pl.], 574/4,7; 575/4,6; 577/4; 658/21; 665/27-28. *y*'' [imperf.]; ''*hmw*, 577/11; 635/36; ''*w* [pl.], 574/6.
ḥrbt battle, 575/3; 658/13-14; 685/3; ''*hmw*, 665/40; *b*'', 574/4; 577/4. *ḥryb* [pl.], 650/20,22.
ḥrm (A) interdict, 723/4.
ḥrm (B) to incur (an interdict), 723/4.
ḥšd Ḥâšadite; ʾ'' [pl.], 704/1-2.

ẖ

]*ẖ* [?], 643/5.
ẖbb [verb], cf. the 4th form *hẖb*.
ẖbṭ (A) fullers [collect.]; ''*hmw*, 616/15.
ẖbṭ (B) bad cold in the head, 751/8.
ẖdg to allow; permit, 628/8. to leave, 643/29; ''*w* [pl.], 644/9.
ẖdʿ [verb], cf. the 5th form *tẖdʿ*.
ẖwm pest, 645/13.
ẖẖ passage; ''*nhn* [dual], 552/3.
ẖṭʾ (A); *ẖṭyʾ* [pl.] fines, 720/10. evil deeds; *b*'', 601/8; 602/8.
ẖṭʾ (B) to act wrongfully; ''*w* [pl.], 561 bis/13; cf. also the 4th form *hẖṭʾ*.
ẖybt failure, 567/27.
ẖyl strength, 585/9; 616/13,27; 629/13,16,24,31,34; 651/22; 656/13; 658/23; 665/46; 668/6; 670/12; 671/14; (685/2); [687/6]; [695/8]; 718/5; 735/16; 739/5; [746/6]; 750/8; 751/4; 758/10; *l*'', 611/15; 651/35; 716/9.
ẖytm sown field; ''*t* [pl.], 655/17-18.
ẖlw to act pleasingly for; ''*n* [inf.], 572/5; 651/24.
ẖly to act pleasingly for; ''*n* [inf.], 700/6.
ẖlf (A) gate, 578/25; 643/20.
ẖlf (B) region, 576/5,9,13,16; 586/16,20; 617/6; 629/10, 27,34; 631/35; 635/23; 643/7,13,16,19,20,22,25,26,30, 31-32, 35; *b*'', 576/5; 619/9; 631/22; *b''hy*, 629/29; *ḏ*'', 567/8.
ẖlfn countrymen [collect.], 560/11; 643/10.
ẖms (A) five, 576/15; 577/14; 647/29-30; 649/19; 665/30, 38,41; *b*'', 665/29. ''*t* [fem.], 550/2; 564/13; 574/7; 577/4; 649/11,18; 703/3.
ẖms (B) army, 562/8; 564/5; 577/16,(17),18; 578/7; 612/9; 629/10; 631/29; 643/24; 651/30; 671/10; *b*'', (722/a-b?); ''*hw*, 574/5; 575/3; 576/4,5,8,10,11,12; 577/(1),(5-6),8,9,15,18; 578/8,18,20,26; 608/14; ''*hmw*, 574/8; 576/6,7; 577/4,17; 609/13-14; 610/16; 611/19; 877/15; ''*hmy*, 629/23. ''*nhn* [dual], 633/8. ʾ'' [pl.], 576/1; 635/11; *b*'', (722/a-b?).
ẖmsy fifty, 586/22; 665/15,34; *b*'', 586/19.
ẖmr to vouchsafe, 574/3; 577/18; 578/30,35; 580/12; 581/14; 586/3; 588/6; 590/4,11,14; 612/6,10,13; 615/15; 617/7; (619/5-6); 635/5,16,29,39,42; 646/5; 653/15; 655/11; 657/9; 660/7,20; 661/4; 667 A/5,10; 668/11; 693/8,11; 703/4; 713/13-14; (725/3); 733/5; 735/3,16; [746/8]; 758/14; [764/2]; (812/7); 839/2; ''*hw*, 579/8; 580/(9),13; 584/11; 587/3; 588/3; 600/4,9; 647/10; 648/4; 655/8; 657/10; 664/9-10; 665/5-6; 690/5; 700/4-5; 708/8,10; 713/10; 739/10-11; 740 A/4; ''*hw* [fem.], 686/4-5; 717/8; 721/6; 743/4; 828/5; ''*hmw*, 563/11; 576/5,6,14; 577/3,5,7,16; 580/11; (586/21); 590/7; 592/3,(7-8); 610/4-5; 616/28; 617/5; 618/7; 636/8,14,15; 640/6; 647/23-24; 650/11,27; 654/6,7-8; 656/6,19; 658/16,27-28; 665/47; 668/8; 669/17; 671/15,20; 703/5; 720/10; 729/11; 733/7; 738/6,7-8; (747/7); (788/5-6); [851/2]; 877/12-13; ''*hmy*, 632/6-7. *bḏẖmr*, 581/8; 585/3,11; (586/11); 589/6; 658/24; ''*hw*, 657/4; ''*hmw*, 577/6. *kẖmr*, 589/13; 657/5; 664/6; ''*hw*, 736/8; ''*hmw*, 877/10. *lẖmr*, 623/[1],9; 684/6; ''*hw*, 570/10,(15); [571/1]; 582/7; 587/7,11; 590/17-18, 19; 591/5,9; 597/4; 613/16-17; 633/17; 646/10; 648/5-6; 651/44,46; 654/9; 655/6; 664/5,10-11; 691/6; 692/7; 711/6,10; *hw* [fem.], 743/7; ''*hmw*, 566/7; 567/18,19; 569/5; 585/19; 588/7; (598/4); 599/[5],(7-8); 610/14; 615/22; 617/9-10; (618/20-21,24); 619/13-14; 620/10-11,12; 623/13-14; 647/(16-17),18; 650/29-30; 651/39; 653/17-18; 654/10,12-13; (656/22); 657/11-12; 661/5; 664/11-12,15; 666/14-15; 668/15; 670/25,28; 686/6; 703/6,7, 8; 719/(8,9-10),13; [732/6]; 735/10; ''*hmy*, 614/13; 652/15; ''*hn*, (804/2); ''*nhmw*, 669/26; 670/20; 733/10, 11. *fẖmrhmw*, 653/11-12. *yẖmr* [imperf.]; ''*hmw*, 736/13; ''*nhw*, 736/12; [*hw*, fem.], 717/6; ''*nhmw*, 650/9. *kyẖmrn*, 735/3; ''*hw*, 736/6-7; ''*hmw*, 653/7-8. *lyẖmrn*, 722/b; ''*hw*: 667 A/14; 692/4-5. *flyẖmrn*, 572/(7-8),11.
ẖmrn gracious act, 646/11.
ẖfd grandson; ʾ'' [pl.], (598/4-5).
ẖfr [verb], cf. the 4th form *hẖfr*.
ẖfrt (A) assistance; *b*'', 576/2.
ẖfrt (B) familiars [collect.], 576/3.
ẖḏf [verb], cf. the 4th form *hẖḏf*.
ẖrʾ to oppose; *b''n* [inf.], 576/3.
ẖrg [2nd form] to incite; persuade; ''*hw*, 712/7; *ḏ''hw*, 646/7. *y*'' [imperf.]; ''*nhw*, 646/9; *ḏ''nhmy*, 652/21.
ẖrgt (military) expedition, 665/49. rebellion, 712/7.
ẖrṭ to take away, 700/12.
ẖry to preserve. ''*n* [inf.]: 564/22; 629/43; 630/18; 650/31; 651/49-50; 758/18; (815/6); ''*hw*, [580/14]; 587/12; ''*hmw*, 561 bis/22; 562/15; 563/13; 594/11; 636/16-17; (638/4); 704/7; 730/10; 734/7; 753 I/5; ''*hmy*, 578/40. *lẖryn*, 590/22; 617/13; 628/23; ''*hw*, (570/14); 571/6-7; 581/17; 583/9; (591/10-11); 612/19; 633/20; 635/44; ''*hmw*, 567/26; 592/8; 599/9; 615/26; 616/38; 623/20-21; 626/14; 631/41; 632/9; 640/9; 641/15; 654/14; 656/25; (691/10-11); 693/13; (719/11-12); 753 II/7-8,III/7-8; (815/8); 839/4; ''*hmy*, 572/14; 614/17. *yẖry* [imperf.]; ''*n*, 627/23-24.
ẖrf (A) autumn, 610/6,14; 615/18-19; 618/9,(15); 623/15; 627/12; 628/13; 650/12; 653/5,10; 661/7; 666/16; 704/5; 735/4. fruits of autumn, 617/8.
ẖrf (B) year, 550/2; 618/11; 751/9; *b*'', 633/9,11; 645/14; 711/6; 751/6-7; *ḏ*'', 567/7; 610/6; 611/8; 613/10; 618/9; 633/16; 653/5; 735/4; 877/8; *l*'', 615/12,13. ''*y* [dual], 550/2. ''*n* [dual], 585/7. ''*t* [pl.], 851/4. *ẖryft* [pl.], 647/27.
ẖtn to ally by marriage; ''*w* [pl.], 651/14.

ṭ

ṭwʿ constraint, 614/18; 616/39; 647/32; 651/53; 652/19; 667 A/13; 796/10; [719/13]; 736/17; 804/3; 813/2; (816/10-11).
ṭyb (A) excellent; good, 635/4; 762/2.
ṭyb (B) [verb], cf. the 4th form *hṭb*.
ṭmḥny Ṭamḥânite [*nisba*], 651/32-33.
ṭnf *ṭanuf*, 635/4.
ṭʿm [2nd form] to give the taste of; ''*n* [inf.], 730/7-8.
ṭf plaque, 755/4.
ṭrd to pursue; *l*'', 660/11.

ẓ

ẓwr to besiege; ”*w* [pl.], 629/27. ”*y* [dual]; ”*hmw*, 578/26.
y” [imperf.]; ”*w* [pl.], 577/8.
ẓlm statue, 688/3.
ẓlt room; *ẓll* [pl.], 846/2.
ẓmʾ to become thirsty; ”*w* [pl.], 750/6.
ẓmm [verb], cf. the 4th form *hẓm*.
ẓʿn to flee; run away; ”*w* [pl.], 575/4.

y

]*y* [verb], 734/2-3.
y[[?], 570/8-9; 788/4.
ybs (A) land, 576/2; 577/18; 585/14; 631/7; 635/13.
ybs (B) to dry up, 735/7; ”*w* [pl.], 735/6.
yd hand, 577/8; 700/15; ”*hw*, 570/13; *b*”, 669/20. ”*y* [dual]; ”*hw*, (577/7); 700/14-15.
ydʿ [verb], cf. the 4th and 10th forms, *hydʿ* and *stydʿ* respectively.
yhr (A) exaltation, 616/29.
yhr (B) [verb], cf. the 4th form *hyhr*.
ywm (A) day, 577/12; 616/19-20; 629/19; 631/28,31,35; 643/18; 649/41; 651/19; 653/10, 13; 667 A/9; 685/3; 735/12; *b*”, 570/3; 651/18,19; 652/23; 653/9. *ymt* [pl.], 577/2.
ywm (B) when, 550/1,2; 555/3,4; 640/(2-3),4; 831/2; *b*”, 576/4; [577/11].
ymnt south, 576/1; 577/18; *ḏ*”, 635/12.
ymt to be crippled; ”*n* [inf.], 649/21.
]*yn* [?], 687/8.
yn (noun dual ending], cf. *wrẖ*.
ynhn [noun dual ending], cf. *ś̌ʿb*, *tʾdm*.
ynn [noun dual ending], cf. *ṣlm*.
]*ys* [?], 577/7.
ysr to send, 570/7; 576/14; ”*hw*, 635/32; cf. also the 4th form *hysr*. ”*w* [pl.], 575/3; 616/17; *f*”, 577/10.
yfʿ to raise up, 619/10; 750/8; ”*hw*, 643/16; ”*hmw*, 577/18; 585/13. ”*w* [pl.], 643/13; [passive], 618/18; cf. also the 10th form *styfʿ*.

k

k [conj.]; cf. *ʾl*, *ʾfq*, *ʾty*, *hwfy*, *hṭb*, *hʿn*, *hʿsm*, *hṣr*, *hqny*, *wld wqh*, *ḥgn*, *ḥmd*, *ẖmr*, *khl*, *mhn*, *mlʾ*, *mtʿ*, *nbl*, *nmw*, *sʾl*, *sfh*, *sqy*, *stydʿ*, *styfʿ*, *stmlʾ*, *stṣr*, *ʿthd*, *ṣdq*, *ṣwy*, *ṣry*, *rʾ*, *rʾy*, *ś̌ft*, *śʿʿ*, *tbšr*, *tẖdʿ*. *k*[[?]; 570/7; 647/8. *kbknmw*, 647/11. *khʾ*, 619/10. *khmy*, 567/10-11; (729/9). *kl*, cf. *hqny*, *qdm*. *kmhnmw*, 669/10,22; 736/12. *kmʿnmw*, 693/6; 717/5-6; 736/6. *kʿbrnhmw*, 628/7.
k[[noun], 676/2.
kbr (A) leader, 552/1; 665/1; ʾ” [pl.], (560/2-3); ʾ”*t* [pl.], 576/2; 665/33.
kbr (B) [2nd form] to augment; ”*n* [inf.], 627/5.
kbt hostilities [collect.]; *b*”, 550/2.
kdd to grieve. *kd*; *ḏ*”, 750/12.
kdn ploughed plain; *b*”, 574/6; 577/5; ʾ” [pl.], 574/7.
khl to be able. ”*w* [pl.]; *k*”, 651/36.
khlt might, 559/12; 561/12.
kwkb star, 649/33.
kwkbt great number, 567/23; *ḏ*”, 655/12; 703/5.
kwn to be, 577/4; 610/5; (618/19-20); 628/8; 629/8; 635/35; 644/24; 645/13; 649/36; 666/6; 667 A/8; 751/8; ”*hmw*, 575/5,7; 601/10; 602/10; 629/8,12,15; 635/(23),24-25; 644/5-6,11; *ḏ*”, 575/5,7; 629/12,15; 635/(22-23),24; cf. also the 4th, 5th and 10th forms, *hkn*, *tkwn* and *stkn* respectively, and *kn*. ”*w* [pl.], 561 bis/9; 574/11; 576/13; 618/19; 635/35; 643/6; 644/5,11; *ḏ*”, 633/8. ”*t* [fem.], 626/16; 753 I/6,II/10,III/10. *ykn* [imperf.]; *ḏ*”*n*, 750/14.
kyd to plot; ”*w* [pl.], 585/7-8.
kyn to be; *ḏ*”. 601/10; 602/10; 750/11.
kl all; every, 550/1,2; 551; 552/2,3; 553/3; 555/1,2,4; 557; 561 bis/17,21; 562/13; 563/13; 564/8,14,20,25; 565/15; 567/24,26; 574/13; 575/7; 576/1,7,12,13; 577/2,3,12,13,15,16,17,18,19; 578/7,10,34; 581/6,11; 585/13,17; 586/8; 587/3; 601/17; 602/17; 610/5,8,17; 611/21; 613/21; 615/10,11,20; 616/14,15; 617/8; 618/18; 619/11; 623/16; 627/11,21,26; 628/25; 629/7, 12,14,15,28,30,45; 630/17; 631/14,16; 632/4; 635/11, 15,19,38; 636/18; 643/8,21,26,31,34; 643 bis/2,3,8; 644/20,23,24; 645/17,24; 646/9; 647/25,32; 649/30; 650/13,15; 651/25,43,48,53; 652/21; 656/17; 657/11; 658/7; 661/8; 665/3,15,42-43,44; 668/10; 670/16; 671/12; 672/2; 702/4,18; 703/7,9,10; 719/14; 731/6; 735/6,8,13,14,15,18; 739/9; 746/4; 747/16,17; 753 I/5, II/9,III/9; 762/6; 791/4; 798/3; 831/2; 853 A/5,B/5, C/5,D/4,E/5,F/5; (877/16-17); ”*hmw*, 665/22; cf. also *bn*. *bkl* [instrum.], 627/11; 628/12; [local], 618/23; 635/32; 647/26,27,29; [modal], [560/6]; 561 bis/16; (566/12); 567/18; 581/13; 585/19; 590/18; 592/6; 605/13; 608/11; 609/11; 610/12-13; 611/14; 614/8, 11-12; 616/8,32-33; 618/14; 621/5; 626/13; 627/13; 628/15; 629/20; 630/8; 645/6,9; 651/37; 653/16; 662/15-16; 693/12; 701 A/4; 719/5; 739/7,16; [746/7]; 753 I/4,II/6,III/6; [origin], 559/8-9; 561/9; 561 bis/8, 10; [removal], 580/11; 586/12,13; 618/23; 650/22; [temp.], 550/2; 564/14-15; (570/5-6); 584/5; 590/15; 631/15; 649/7; 650/20,25; 662/17; 740 A/6; 831/2. *kly* [dual], 666/5; cf. also *b*.
klʾ (A) two; ”*y*, 557; ”*ty* [fem.], 672/1.
klʾ (B) young herbage ground; pasture. ʾ” [pl.], 735/7,15; ”*hw*, 653/9; 735/5.
klw terrace, 678/2.
kll to achieve; *kl*, 842/3.
kml [verb], cf. the 4th and 10th forms, *hkml* and *stkml* respectively.
kms [verb], cf. the 4th form *hkms*.
kn [conj.]; *b*”, 567/6; 575/2; 577/8; 578/7,19; 580/6-7; 583/7; 585/5,15; 590/5,8,10; 600/7-8; 601/5; 602/5; 612/8; 616/9; 628/4; 629/3-4,26; 631/7,11,18,20-21; 633/6; 636/(1-2),4; 637/5; [639/3]; 641/5; 643/25;

644/6,15; 651/13,14,28; 656/8,15; 658/19; 660/9,13; 662/9; 665/6; 671/7,11; 702/6; 716/6; 741/6; 745/7,9; (751/7-8); 756/6; 758/7; 767/6; (772/3); 877/7; *''mw*, cf. *k*.
knf border; *b''*, 635/36.
kfḥ unexpected attack, 635/45-46.
kfl steep brink, 575/4.
krb blessing; *''t* [pl.], 567/22-23; 692/10.
krᶜ knee, 619/8.
kśwy garment, 555/4.

l

]*l* [?], 816/6-7.
]*l*[[?], 746/9,12.
l (A) [conj.] that, 559/10,13; 560/17; 561/10,13; 561 bis/18, 19,22,23; 562/8,15; 563/7,11,13,15,17; 565/10, 13,14; 568/20; 578/40; 579/8; [580/14]; 594/6,11; 601/17; 602/17; 603/11; 604/3; 629/43; 630/18; 634/9,10; 636/15,16; [638/4]; 643 bis/8,9; 645/19,22; 658/12; 689/4; 690/7; 702/2,3; 704/7,8; 705/5; 712/14; 726/5; 728/5; 730/6,7,10; 734/6,7; 737/2,3; 747/9,11, 14, [16,18]; 753 I/5; 757/4; 784/3; 853 A/4,[5],B/4, C/4, D/3,4,E/4,5,F/4; cf. also *ʾdn, ʾwl, ʾḫd, bhʾ, brʾ, gʾm, gzy, gzm, gtn, dll, ḏ, ḏt, hwfy, hwfr, hwḏᶜ, hysr, ḥᶜn, wzʾ, wfy, wḏᶜ, wśf, ḥmd, ḥdt, ḥdr, ḥrb, ḫmr, ḫry, ṭrd, k, mtᶜ, nẓr, nṣr, nqm, sbʾ, sᶜd, stwkb, stᶜn, ᶜḏr, ᶜqb, f, ḍbʾ, qdm, qrn, qtdm, rtᶜ, šwᶜ, šym, śrḥ, śf, t.(.)b, tṣry, tqdm, ṯbr*.
l (B) [prep.], for, 558/3; 744/5; 787/3; cf. the names of deity *ʾlmqh, ʾlmqhw*, the personal names *ʾbʾmr, ʾnmrm, ynᶜm, nšʾkrb, swdm, sḫmn, sᶜdšmsm*, the place names *mrb, sbʾ*, and also *ʾdm, ʾḫr, bḥr, byt, blt, bn, bny, brq, grb, grm, ḏ, ḏt, hgr, hw, hyt, hmw, hn, wld, wfy, wrḫ, ḥzy, ḥyw, ḫyl, ḫrf, mʾḫd, mhrg, mḥk, myr, mlk, mngt, mqḥ, mrʾ, nkl, nṣr, ᶜbd, ᶜbr, ᶜzm, ḍr, qbly, tqdm, ṯlṯ*.
lb heart, 632/6; *''hw*, 567/20; 580/6; 722/d; 739/11; 743/7-8. *ʾlbb* [pl.], 577/18; 643 bis/7; 647/20; 650/24; *''hmw*, 615/22; 626/7; 627/20; 628/21; 650/24; 753 (I/3),II/3,III/2-3.
lhm to feast. *''w* [pl.]; *f''*, 665/28.
]*lw* [?], 562/15.
lḫb contentions [collect.], (750/13-14,15-16).
lḫm fitting, appropriate, suitable, 700/11.
lyl night; *''/''*, 649/33.
lly night, 631/24; *b''*, 619/9; 631/30; 665/29; (735/12-13).
lmš to cast; *''w* [pl.; passive], 720/15.
ln (A) [conj.] until; as soon as, 633/12,15; 651/27; 718/7; *''/ḏ*, 633/5; *''hʾ*, 584/7.
ln (B) [prep.] from, 633/16; cf. also *qdm*. *ln*/.../*ᶜd* from...to, 550/1; 554; 555/1; 556; 557. *ln*/.../*ᶜdy* from...to, 551.
lsn tongue; *''hw*, 570/13.
lf crowd, cf. *ḏ* (list of deities).
lfy to bring back; *''w* [pl.], 576/6,9,13; 577/2, (4-5); 644/24; 665/25. *y''* [imperf.]; *''hmw*, 577/12; *''w* [pl.], 576/4,6,7,8,12,[14].
lqḥ [verb], cf. the 4th form *hlqḥ*.

m

m (A) [indefinite pron.], cf. *b*.
m (B) one hundred, 680/2.
m (C) [masonry mark], 724.
m[[?], 576/16.
]*m* [?], 576/16; 681/1; 746/9; 765/6; 782/2.
]*m*[[?], 638/1.
mʾdb beautiful work; *''hmw*, (618/8).
mʾḫd breakwater, 628/8-9. *''hmw*, 618/16; 627/10-11; 628/12; *l''*, 628/5. *''t* [pl.]; *''hw*, 618/17.
mʾḫr destroyer, 703/12.
mʾyl luxuriant garden; *''t* [pl.], 655/17.
mʾn one hundred, 572/4; 576/15; 577/14; (586/17); 609/5; 616/22; 624/5; 631/30-31; 643/12-13; 644/22, 25.
mʾt one hundred, 649/27-28,37,39; 665/15,29-30,31,34-35,36,39.
mbḥr basement, foundation, [846/3].
mbny construction, 552/3; 555/1.
mbᶜl property, 554.
mgʾt occurrence; *b''*, 647/26.
mdlt weight; *''hmy*, 669/6-7; *ḏ''hw*, 572/4; 608/5-6; 609/5; [624/5]; (762/2).
mḏhb passage. *''t* [pl.]; *''hw*, 618/16.
mḏht herd of camels, 600/4.
mḏqnt oratory, 552/3.
mhbʾs malefactor; evil-doer, 739/19.
mhḏr extensive, 851/7.
mhwtn lasting running water, 627/12; 628/13.
mhyᶜ wide wall, 550/1; 551.
mhn (A); *''mw*, cf. *k*.
mhn (B) to shake off; *k''*, 720/13.
mhskn wretched, 576/15.
mhrbḏ favorable, 650/13.
mhrg war trophy, 575/7,8; 576/5,9; 577/1,12; 580/6,11, 13; 590/13; 612/13-14; 631/9; 632/7; 640/6; 643 bis/6; 644/24; 656/7,14; 708/8; 739/11; 758/13; (766/8). *mhrgt* [pl.], 561 bis/7-8; 576/4,6,7,8,9,10,12,13,14; 577/1,(2),5,11,16; 578/12,(32); 581/10; 616/30; 623/4; 649/12,36; 658/17; 665/25,45; 668/8; *b''*, 629/18; 649/13,23; *l''*, 576/10.
mhrt filly, 752/10-11; *''hmw*, 752/9-10.
mhšfq plentiful, 851/7.
mw (A) [indefinite pron.], cf. *ʾhn, b, kn, mhn, mᶜn, ᶜbrn*.
mw (B) water, 750/7,9,10.
mwᶜd gathering, 577/10; *b''hmw*, 577/10.
mwfʾ preparative, 555/4.
mwṣt affray; *''t* [pl.], 831/2.
mwt (A) death, 567/17.
mwt (B) to die, 735/7.
mwtt epilepsy, 645/13.
mwṯb (A) camping [part.]; *''t* [pl.], 575/5.
mwṯb (B) place; *b''*, 600/8.
mḥk quarrel; *l''*, 576/11.
mḥl [verb], cf. the 4th form *hmḥl*.

mḥmy irrigated by the reflector-dam, 550/1.
mḥfd tower, 554; 556; ''*nhn* [dual], 557; ''*t* [pl.], 550/1; 551; 576/13; 651/31.
mḥqr low people, 651/12,28.
mḥr land-surveyor, 666/6.
mḥrm temple, (570/5); 643/32, 34; 669/16; 702/10; 735/8, 12; *b*'', 720/8. ''*nhn* [dual], 577/17. ''*t* [pl.], 629/28.
mḫdn management, 555/4.
mḫr to oppose; combat; *ld*'', 575/6. to occur; *ld*'', 649/41.
mḫtn ceremonial place; ''*hw*, 570/4.
mṭw to take part, 635/10.
mṭr irrigated field; ᵓ'' [pl.], 735/6,(11),13.
mẓᵓ to arrive, 735/12; ''*hmw*, 643/26; cf. also the 4th form *hmẓᵓ*. ''*w* [pl.], 576/6,10,16; 629/33; 643/8,20, 32; (750/9-10). ''*y* [dual], 629/22. *y*'' [imperf.]; ''*w* [pl.], 643/7.
mydᶜ request, 567/18.
mykbt [?]: 702/16.
myqẓ sleeplessness, 572/10; 613/15; 623/22; 650/33.
myr cereal. ᵓ''*t* [pl.], 623/14-15; 661/7; 666/16. ᵓ*mr* [pl.], 627/5; 735/11. ᵓ*mrt* [pl.], 650/12; *l*'', 615/18.
myt to leave one dying [passive], 669/20.
mlᵓ (A) gathering, 558/5. fullness; *b*'', 564/12-13.
mlᵓ (B) favor, 627/7; 660/20; 716/10; ''*hw*, 752/12. *bmlᵓ*, 566/6; 612/8; 627/4; 662/8; 671/19; 758/11; ''*hw*, 588/5; 649/7. ᵓ*mlᵓ* [pl.], (560/6); 561 bis/16,17; 566/12; 567/18; 581/13: 585/19; 590/18; 592/6; (605/13-14); 608/12; 609/11; 610/13; 611/14; 614/8, 12; 616/8,33; 618/14; 621/5; 626/13; 627/13-14; 628/15; 629/20; 630/8; 645/6,9; 653/16; 662/16; 693/12; 701 A/4-5; 719/5; 735/18; 739/7,16; [746/7]; 753 I/5, II/6-7,III/6-7; 877/10-11,13; *b*'', 560/16-17; 565/5,9; 608/7; 609/7; 611/6; (624/6); 630/5; 650/17; 653/3; 660/8; 691/5; 713/9; 758/6.
mlᵓ (C) to complete; fill, 557; 618/8; ''*w* [pl.], 735/13; cf. also the 4th and 10th forms, *hmlᵓ* and *stmlᵓ* respectively, *ymlᵓ* [imperf.]; *k*''*n* [pl.], 618/6.
mly (A) agreeable, 653/8.
mly (B) winter, 615/19; 623/15; 650/13; 661/7; *ḏ*''. 627/5. fruits of winter [collect.], 617/8; 631/41.
mly (C) to enjoy, 649/40; cf. also the 5th and 8th forms, *tmly* and *mtly* respectively.
mlk (A) property, 577/7; 761/3; 877/15; ''*hw*, 608/13-14; ''*hmw*, 609/13; 610/16; 611/19; 853 A/4,B/4,C/4,D/3, E/4,F/4; (854/5); 855/4; 877/15; *b*'', (655/17); *l*'', 816/5; ᵓ'' [pl.], 816/9.
mlk (B) king, 557; 561 bis/14; 566/1-2; 570/1; (575/2-3); 577/9; 584/1; 616/22; 619/3; 629/10; 643/10,12,13,15, 18,21,22,24,25,26,29,31,34; 643 bis/1,2,3,5,9; 644/6,9; 651/29; 658/14; 665/2,13,19; 694/2; 712/8; 723/1; 745/2,7; 749/3; (762/1); [766/5]; 784/1; 791/2; (812/3); 828/8; (847/5); *l*'', 574/11; 643/14; cf. also the name of deity *šms* and the following personal names: ᵓ*lᶜz*, ᵓ*lšrḥ*, ᵓ*nmrm*, *gdrt*, *grmt*, *whbᵓl*, *wtrm*, *yᵓzl*, *ydᶜᵓl*, *yhqm*, *yᶜkrn*, *krbᵓl*, *lḥyᶜṯt*, *lᶜzzm*, *mlkm*, *mrᵓlqs*, *nbṭm*, *nšᵓkrb*, *smhᶜly*, *sᶜdšmsm*, ᶜ*ḏbh*, ᶜ*lhn*, *frᶜm*, *rbᶜt*, *rbšmsm*, *šmr*, *šᶜrm*. ᵓ*mlk* [pl.], 561 bis/9,13; 565/7; 568/19,21; 576/11; 577/3,4,6,8,9,10,14,16; 601/9; 602/9; 629/8; 631/5; 647/25; (668/14); 733/8; 736/15; (747/13); 753 I/4,II/5,III/5; cf. also *ysrm*. *mlky* [dual], cf. the following personal names: ᵓ*lšrḥ*, *ḏmrᶜly*, *ysrm*, *yrm*, *nšᵓkrb*, *sᶜdšmsm*, *šᶜrm*, *šrḥᵓl*, *ṯᵓrn*. *mlknhn* [dual], 576/2,3; 577/11.
mlqḥ chain; ''*t* [pl.], 643/32; 643 bis/4.
mlt riches, 574/9; 575/8; 576/8,12; 577/3,5,6; 578/12,32; 586/12; 616/30; 635/30-31; 643 bis/6; 650/23; 658/18; 758/13.
mn from, 720/13; cf. also *bn*.
mngw (A) security, 564/4; ''*t* [pl.], 626/6; 652/17; 707/8. *mngyt* [pl.], 568/16; 627/19; 630/11; 643/14; 645/21. *mngt* [pl.], 563/8; 564/16; 565/13; 567/24; 581/14-15; 587/10; (588/10-11); 601/11,13-14; 602/11,13; 604/4; 605/6-7; 606/7; 607/7; 610/15; 623/19; 628/21; 643/9,15-16; 655/13; 690/9; 726/5; 732/5; [734/6]; 747/12; 753 I/3,II/2,III/2; 820/2; 839/3; *l*'', 643/11. security measure; *mngt* [pl.], 564/14.
mngw (B) storm; ''*t* [pl.], 645/18-19; *mngt* [pl.], 564/23.
mnḏ in; during; *ḏ*'', (653/10).
mnḏr spy, 643/26.
mnḫt caravan station; ''*hmw*, 618/6.
mnᶜ to hold back, 853 A/5,B/5,C/5,D/4,E/5,F/5.
mnfs distributor; ''*t* [pl.], 735/15.
mnšᵓ military expedition, 643/5; 644/4,(13); *b*'', 644/11.
mnśrt cavalry squadron, 631/29.
msᵓl oracle. *b*'', 551; ''*hw*, 563/5; 568/4-5; 580/5; (583/6-7); (606/5-6); 607/5-6; 626/5; 628/4; 630/3; 632/8; 633/4; 642/14; 647/(8),10-11,18; 650/7,18; 711/4; 725/4-5; (753 I/2); 762/3; (818/3-4); 877/6.
msbᵓ military campaign, 665/20; 750/10; *b*'', 750/6.
msg body guard. ''*t* [pl.], *b*''*hw*, 649/17.
msqyt irrigation canal; *msqy* [pl.], 629/29.
mᶜbr explanation, 669/22.
mᶜd convention place; ''*hmw*, 647/29.
mᶜhd sworn man; ''*y* [dual], 554.
mᶜn; ''*mw*, cf. *k*.
mᶜrb die; ''*t* [pl.], 720/15-16.
mġbt recess; ''*nhn* [dual], 556. *mġbb* [pl.], 550/1; 551; ''*hmy*, 557.
mġwn hiding-place; ''*hmw*, 577/12.
mfgr low ground; ''*t* [pl.], 665/16.
mflq irrigated by sluice-ways, 550/1; 555/3.
mfnt [pl.] lands irrigated by canals, 615/10-11,20. ''*hmw*, 564/21; 617/9; 623/16; 703/6; *b*'', 610/6. *mfnyt* [pl.]; ''*hmw*, 645/25.
mfsḥ annex. ''*t* [pl.]; ''*hw*, 618/17.
mṣnᶜt fortress; *mṣnᶜ* [pl.], 578/12; 629/30.
mṣr expeditionary force, 576/6,9; 578/7; 590/10; 629/14; 631/21; 643/24,27,28,33; 643 bis/2; 665/29; ''*hw*, 577/2; 643/7,18,19,21,26,31,34; 643 bis/1,2,3,5; ''*hmw*, 578/21. ''*nhn* [dual], 643/29. *mṣyrt* [pl.], 576/15,16; 577/1; 581/7; 586/6,9; 589/10. expedition abroad, 643/5.
mṣrᶜ (A) arena; field; ''*y* [dual], 567/8.
mṣrᶜ (B) leaf; ''*t* [pl.], 576/16.
mḍy past [adject.]; ''*t* [fem.], 649/19.
mḍrf construction without cement, 651/32; 671/12.
mqblt (A) meeting place, 647/29.
mqblt (B) peace-offering, tribute; *mqbl* [pl.]; ''*hmw*, 574/12.
mqdmt vanguard, 665/17,18; ''*hmw*, 576/8-9,9; 665/21.
mqwl (A) ruler; ''*hmw*, 577/17.
mqwl (B) resting place. ''*t* [pl.]; ''*hmw*, 647/27.

mqḥ profit; advantage, 601/11; 602/11; *l*'', 643 bis/6. *mqyḥt* [pl.], 559/8; 561/8; 629/36; *b*'', 561 bis/7; 577/18.

mqṭr incense burner, 696/3; 697/3.

mqṭt heat, 649/32-33.

mqyẓ summer settlement; ''*hmw*, 623/17; 631/40-41; 650/14.

mql (mountain) pass, 576/6.

mqm (A) power, 558/4; 559/13; 560/5,16; 561/13; 564/3; 585/9; 612/14; 613/20; 616/13,27; 629/13,16,24,31,34; 643/3; 643 bis/4,5; 644/7,14; 651/23,35; 656/13; 658/23; 665/46-47; 668/6; 669/16-17; 670/12; 685/2; 687/6; [695/8]; 703/5; 716/9; 718/5; 725/6; 735/16; 739/5; (746/6); 751/4-5; 758/10. ''*t* [pl.] 712/13-14. *mqymt* [pl.], 568/17; 601/16; 602/16; 614/16-17; 615/25; 616/37; [621/12]; 623/20; 629/43; 631/38; 643 bis/9; 644/27; 651/47; 658/30; 661/7; 666/12; 703/9; (719/10-11); 733/14; 853 A/4,B/4,C/4,D/4, E/5,F/4; ''*hmw*, 650/29.

mqm (B) place, 633/6.

mqrn military expedition, 578/39; *b*'', (586/24).

mqtw high official, 673/1; ''*t* [pl.], (661/2-3).

mqtwy high official, 579/1; 580/1; 581/1; 582/1; (583/1); 612/1-2; 613/2; 646/2; 649/4; 650/2-3; 651/5; 660/4; 690/1; 708/2; 710/1; (739/1-2); 749/3; 757 bis/2; 758/1; (840/1); ''*hmw*, 577/7. ''*y* [dual], (572/2); 578/2-3; 614/2; [617/1-2]; (624/1); 632/1; 652/3; 700/1-2; 713/3; ''*hmw*, 577/10. *mqtyt* [pl.], (647/1-2); ''*hmw*: 577/7. *mqtt* [pl.], 576/14; 615/5; 616/4; 629/17,20,25-26; (647/1-2).

mrʾ lord, 664/18. ''*hw*, 560/9 [15]; 570/11; 613/18; 633/6-7,18; 635/32,40,44; 639/[2],(4-5); 643 bis/8-9; 646/4,7,8,10,11; 651/15; 652/23; 655/2-3,8; 658/11; 665/4; 670/12-13; 673/2; 692/8; [695/8]; 699/2; 727/5; 831/2,3; 840/9; [*hw*, fem.] 743/2; *l*'', 657/7. ''*hmw*, [558/1]; 559/5,(7),11; 560/18; 561/5,7-8,11; 561 bis/19; 562/4-5,10; 563/9; 564/5,7,10,[16-17]; 566/8; 567/20; 569/6; 571/2; 572/5,8; 575/2; 577/12,13; 578/5; 579/5; 587/4; 590/5-6,9; 601/6,11-12,14; 602/6,11,14; 603/8; 604/4; 605/8; 606/8,(14-15); 607/7-8,14; 612/16; 615/23-24; 616/6,13,15-16,27,31, 34,35; 617/11; 618/26; 619/14-15; 620/13; 621/7; 623/5,7,12; 631/6,7,10,12,14,16,37; 632/4,5,6; 634/6; 635/5-6,12,15-16,20; 636/2,6,11; 637/5; [638/2]; 640/3,7-8; 641/6; (642/7-8); 643/4,15,17,30,35; 643 bis/4, 7,9; 644/3,6,12,16,27; 645/20; (647/4,11-12); 648/7; 649/5,8,15,24,26; 650/3,7,10,21,26; 651/29,35,37-38, 40,45; 652/6-7; 653/4,19; 654/4,11; 655/14; 656/5,8, 11,13,17,20,26; 657/2,12; 658/(3-4),8,16,20,30-31; 660/5,9, 17-18; 661/4,6; 662/4,10,17-18,20; (664/2-3); 665/6,7,12,47; 666/4,7,12-13; 667 A/3,15; 668/(3),6, 15; 669/4-5,21,27; 670/5-6; 671/(5-6),7-8,14,18; 695/4; 703/2-3, 5; 706/4; 712/8,14; 713/5,12; 715/3; 729/4-5,12; 733/3,7,9,10,12; 735/2,10,16; 736/4; 745/3; (746/12-13,14); 752/5-6,13; (766/5); 799/5; [851/1]; *b*'' [adversative], 720/6; *l*'', 564/14; 651/7; 664/8; 735/9; 736/10. *mrʾhmy*, 572/12; 614/14-15; 616/10; 632/8; 652/3,8,13,22; 720/3. *mrʾy* [dual]; ''*hw* 579/9; 582/7-8; (583/11-12); 587/7-8; 591/6-7; [595/2]; 597/(2),5; 600/4-5,10; 646/2; 684/8; (732/9-10); (807/4-5). *mrʾyhmw*, 558/6; 565/11; 577/11; 578/10, 13,16,22,24,26-27,29,36,38,39-40,43,44; (580/7); 581/5,7,12,15; 584/5; 585/5,12,16,17-18,20; 586/(4),7,10, 13,14-15,23; (588/7-8); 589/6,11-12,14; 590/16,20; 592/3,8; 594/4; (598/1-2); 599/5; 626/9; 627/16; 628/17; 629/4,8-9,13,22,26,29,35,38,42; 630/11-12; 641/11; 664/12; 665/9; 670/21; 671/21; 711/8; [739/13]; [747/7]; 758/15-16; *l*'', (599/2-3). *ʾmrʾ* [pl.]; ''*hw*, 713/15; ''*hmw*, 565/6-7; 568/19,20-21; 577/8,9, 10; (621/11); 629/8; (642/15-16); 647/20,25; 668/13-14; 690/11; 691/8; 703/7-8; 704/8-9; (707/8-9); (719/8-9); 730/9-10; 733/8; 736/14-15; 740A/12-13; (747/13); 753 I/4,II/4-5,III/4-5; *bʾmrʾhmw* [adversative], 561 bis/13; 601/8-9; 602/8-9.

mrʾs chiefs [collect.], 576/2; 577/12; 665/37.

mrʾt lady, 686/5.

mrḍ (A) disease, 572/7; 583/8; 585/11; 613/14; 619/12-13; 642/5; 661/5; 670/14,16-17; 699/5; 706/6; 720/12; 807/1; ʾ'' [pl.], 731/6-7.

mrḍ (B) to suffer, 572/7; 585/11; 699/5-6; ''*t* [fem.], 706/6; 731/7; ''*w* [pl.], 619/13; 661/5; ''*y* [dual], [583/8].

mrr to happen; occur. *ymr* [imperf.]; ''*nhw*, 711/5.

mšm arable field. ''*t* [pl.]; ''*hmw*, 650/14. *mšymt* [pl.], 615/10,21; ''*hmw*, (562/13-14); 613/22; 617/5,9; 618/24; 623/18; 704/6; (746/5).

mšrʿ ploughed field; ''*hmw*, 650/16.

mšrq east, 650/16. eastern part; ''*t* [pl.], 576/7.

mśd inscription, 669/6,12.

mśwd incense burner sanctuary, 603/6.

mśwr depredator, 703/12.

mtly to rejoice; ''*n* [inf.], 631/9; [*maṣdar*], 578/11. *y*'' [imperf.]; ''*w* [pl.], 576/7.

mtʾ (A) artifice (?), 664/17.

mtʿ (B) to save, 558/4; 578/33; 651/24; 665/22-23; 668/7; 670/9; 694/6; 723/3; 731/5; 745/8,12; ''*hw*, 584/3; 619/10-11,11; 649/22; 685/3; 708/6; 765/3; *k*''*hmw*, 669/25; *l*''*hn*, [804/3]. *mtʿn* [inf.], 567/16; 572/5,8; 613/7,12; 619/6; 620/4-5,7; 629/32; 642/10; 644/2,12; 645/11; 650/19; 651/9,42,49; 661/(4),8; 666/7-8; 667 A/11; 684/11; 685/4; 687/9; 695/6; 699/5,7; 706/8; 712/5,9,11; 725/6; 751/5,10-11; 765/5; 815/6; ''*hmw*, [562/16]; 567/26; 654/14-15; 668/18; [686/8]; 715/9-10; *l*'', 703/9; *l*''*hmw*, 664/17; 733/9; *l*''*hmy*, 652/18. *ymtʿ* [imperf.], (586/20-21); ''*n*, 650/30; 669/22-23; ''*nhmw*, 736/16; *l*''*n*, 670/18. *ḏmtʿ* [passive], 665/43.

mṯbr ruin, 671/24.

mṯbt reward, 631/16. rescript, 643/14.

mṯkḥ stone tablet (?), 708/5; 713/6.

mṯl image, 817/3; 818/2; ʾ'' [pl.], 558/2.

n

]*n* [?], 763/1; (766/7-8); 839/1; 847/1; 849/2.

](.)*n* [?] [inf.], 643/4.

n[[?], 746/9.

n (A) [mark], 646.

n (B) [noun dual ending], cf. *ʾẖḏ*, *ʾlf*, *ʾns*, *ʾsy*, *brq*, *wrẖ*, *ẖrf*, *ṣlm*, *ṣlmt*, *ṯwr*.

n (C) [noun plural ending], cf. *bn*, *ẖlfn*.

nʾd (A) magnificent, 567/23-24; 666/15; 692/11; 730/6.

nʾd (B) magnificence, 564/20; 594/10; 615/19; 616/37; 617/9; 631/40; 651/47-48; 655/16; 719/13.
nbʾ [verb], cf. the 5th form *tnbʾ*.
nbl to send, 577/6; ''*hw*, 585/5; 631/11-12; *f*'', 576/11. *nblw* [pl.], *k*'', 577/10; *f*'', 577/13. *ynbl* [imperf.]; ''*nhw*, 576/13.
nbʿ [verb], cf. the 8th form *ntbʿ*.
ngšy the Neguš, 577/10; 631/15; cf. also the personal names *bygt*, *grmt*.
ndʾ [verb], cf. the 4th form *hndʾ*.
ndf to scatter, 631/33.
nḏh [verb], cf. the 5th form *tnḏh*.
nhk to inflict, 620/6.
nhn [noun dual ending], cf. *bḥt*, *byt*, *bt*, *gry*, *hgr*, *ḥqw*, *ḫḫ*, *ḫms*, *mḥfd*, *mḥrm*, *mlk*, *mġbt*, *mṣr*, *sbʾt*, *sr*, *ʿr*, *frs*, *ṣlm*, *ṣlmt*, *šʿb*, *ṯr*.
nwb [verb], cf. the 4th form *hnb*.
nwl [verb], cf. the 4th form *hnwl*.
nzʿ to rebel, 577/8. to desert; ''*w* [pl.], 616/20.
nḥb to harass; press, 629/27; ''*w* [pl.], 576/6,14.
nḥbr to be joyful; ''*n* [inf.], (702/3).
nḥl commissioner, 665/33,35,36; [collect.], 665/37.
nḥt beating, 650/32.
nḫl palm grove; ''*hw*, 555/3. *ʾnḫl* [pl.], 735/14; (821 A/2-3); ''*hw*, 550/1; 555/2.
nṭʿ (A) skin cover, 555/4.
nṭʿ (B) bastion, 557.
nẓr (A) subordinates [collect.], 616/22; ''*hw*, 651/11.
nẓr (B) to protect; take care of, 662/12; *l*'', 564/11; 651/16. ''*w* [pl.]; *f*'', 577/10.
nky suffering, 562/16; 563/14; [580/14]; 601/18; 602/18; 626/15; 627/25; 628/25; 629/44; 630/20; 642/11; 644/13; 645/18; 753 I/5,II/8-9,III/8-9. *nkyt* [pl.], 558/5; 567/17,27; 572/10,15; 581/18; 590/24; 613/15; 615/26; 616/39; 617/14; 618/31; 620/9; 623/21-22; 647/32; 650/32,32-33; 651/51; 666/10; 667 A/12-13; 670/17; 687/11; 703/10; 706/10; 715/10; (716/12); 717/11; 739/18; [815/9].
nkl decoration; artistic work; ''*hmw*, 671/17; *l*'', 560/6.
nkf in good order, 576/14; 643/9.
nkr to afflict; [passive], 720/11; cf. also the 4th forms, *hnkr* and *hkr*.
[.]*nm*[[?], 577/1.
nmw to increase; *k*'', 702/1.
nn [noun dual ending], cf. *byt*, *šʿb*.
nʿm to be pleasant; ''*t* [fem.], 562/14; 563/15; 564/26; 567/25; 577/19; [598/3]; 606/16; 607/15-16; 626/17; 630/15; 719/11; 753 I/6,II/11,III/11; 761/3; cf. also the 5th form *tnʿm*. to please; *b*'', 577/18.
nʿmt prosperity, 560/18; 563/7; 564/16; 565/13; 567/22; 568/16; 572/14; 581/14; 587/10; 601/13; 602/13; 603/7-8; 604/3; 605/6; 606/6-7; 607/6-7; 618/30; 623/19; 626/6; 627/19; 628/20; 630/10-11; 634/9; 641/10; 643 bis/9; 645/21; 690/9; 704/5; (707/7); 711/11; 730/5; [732/5]; 733/12; 734/6; (747/11-12); 753 (I/2),II/1,III/1; 820/1-2.
nfs (A) person, 700/6; ''*hw*, 720/18. *ʾnfs* [pl.], ''*hmw*, 558/3. *ʾfs* [pl.]; ''*hmw*, 750/9,12.
nfs (B) [verb], cf. the 4th form *hfs*.
nṣf [verb], cf. the 5th form *tnṣf*.
nṣr (A) support troop, 647/22; ''*hmw*, 577/11; *l*'', 576/11.
nṣr (B) to aid; help; assist, 640/4; *l*'', 577/10; cf. also the 10th form *stṣr*.
nḍʿ (A) hostility, 561 bis/22; 562/16; 563/14-15; 564/24; 567/27; 570/14; 571/7; 572/(10-11),15; 578/40; 579/12; [580/14]; 581/18; [583/9]; 587/12; 588/12; 590/24; 591/11; 592/9; 594/11; 597/7; [598/5]; 599/9-10; 601/18; 602/18; 612/19-20; 613/16; 614/18; 615/26; 616/39; 617/14; 618/31; 619/19; 620/10; 623/22; 626/15; 627/26; 628/25; 629/45; 630/20; 631/41; 632/9; 633/20; 635/45; 636/17; 638/4; 641/15; 645/18; 647/33; 648/9; 650/33; 651/52; 654/15; 656/26; 661/9; 666/10; 668/19; 684/12; 685/5; (686/8); [687/12]; 691/11; 693/13; 699/8; 703/10; 704/7; 708/7; 711/12; (712/12); 719/12; 730/10; 736/17; 737/4; [739/18]; 747/19; 750/16; 753 I/5, II/9,III/9; 758/19; [803/6]; 807/2; (839/4-5).
nḍʿ (B) benefit, 609/11-12.
nḍʿ (C) [verb], cf. the 5th forms, *tnḍʿ* and *tḍʿ*.
nqḏ [verb], cf. the 4th forms *hnqḏ* and *hqḏ*, and the 10th forms *stnqḏ* and *stqḏ*.
nqyḏ captured; seized, 665/45-46.
nqm to take vengeance on, 576/3; 577/6; 646/6,9; 702/11; *b*'', 574/3; *l*'', 575/3; 577/4; 652/20.
nqt she-camel, 665/44.
nšʾ to undertake (an expedition), 643/5; cf. also the 5th form *tnšʾ*.
nšny Našânite [*nisba*]; ''*t* [fem.], 700/8.
ntbʿ to express; ''*n* [inf.], 630/9.

s

s [mark], 701 B?
s[[?], 577/12.
sʾl (A) request, 877/6.
sʾl (B) to ask; require; *ḏ*''*hw*, 721/4; *k*''*hw*, (721/9-10).
sʾr (A) rest, 735/11.
sʾr (B) to remain, 720/10; *ḏ*'', 575/6,(7); 578/21; 643 bis/3.
sbʾ (A) warrior; combatant; *ʾ*'' [pl.], 562/8; 564/5; 629/9; 643/11.
sbʾ (B) to fight, 579/7; 580/7; 586/14; 597/1; 612/8-9; 632/4; 644/17; 649/15; 713/11; 739/9; 740 A/7; 772/3; ''*nn*, 584/5; *ḏ*'', 750/4; *l*'', 576/14; 578/40; 616/12; 635/32; 644/16; 647/13; 651/29; 665/9,12. *sbʾw* [pl.], 565/6; 577/16; 587/4; 590/5,8; 601/5; 602/5; 629/[4],26; 631/18; 635/10,20; 641/5; 643/18; 649/7-8,24; 650/20; 656/15; 658/19; 665/14; 735/7-8; 758/7. *sbʾy* [dual], 578/10; 581/6; 586/8; *ḏ*'', 578/13. *ysbʾ* [imperf.], 586/15; ''*n*, 590/15; ''*nn*, 650/26; *f*'', 586/19,23.
sbʾy Sabaean [*nisba*], 741/2; 756/2; *ʾ*'' [pl.], 693/2; (740 A/2); ''*t* [fem.], 706/1.
sbʾt campaign; encounter; [sing.], 560/8; 565/6; 585/10; 629/21,36; 649/11; *b*'', 649/15; 713/11; [pl.], 578/11, 13; 579/6-7; (580/12); 581/6,11; 584/5; 586/8,(12-13), 13; 587/3-4; 590/15; (597/1); 631/10; 632/4; 635/9; 649/7; 650/20,22,25-26; 658/7; 739/9; 740 A/6-7.

*sby*ʾ [pl.], 577/16. *sb*ʾ*ty* [dual]; *b*'', 601/4-5; 602/4-5. *sb*ʾ*tnhn* [dual], 629/39.
sbb to pierce. *sb*; ''*t* [fem., passive], 700/15.
sbṭ (A) to throw down; *b*'', 578/6; cf. also the 5th form *tsbṭ*.
sbṭ (B) to flagellate; whip; lash; *y*'' [imperf.], 700/11-12.
sbṭ (C) executioners [collect.]; ''*hmw*, 665/34,42.
sby (A) captives [collect.], 574/9; 575/8; 576/4,5,6,7,8, 10-11,12,13,14; 577/[2],3,5,6,11,16; 578/12,32; 586/12; 590/13; 616/30; 631/9; 635/19,30; 636/9; (640/6); 649/14,23,39; 650/23; 658/17-18,26-27; 665/26; 668/9; 758/13. captive; ʾ*sby* [pl.], 577/14.
sby (B) to capture, 631/9; 713/11,14; ''*w* [pl. passive], 575/6. *y*'' [imperf.]; ''*w* [pl.], 576/7.
*sb*ᶜ (A) seven, 577/15; (624/5); 665/15; ''*t* [fem.], (576/1?); 586/18; 647/26; 851/4.
*sb*ᶜ (B) pillager; plunderer; ʾ'' [pl.], (586/19).
*sb*ᶜ (C) to sack (a city); plunder (a man); [passive], 578/28; ''*w* [pl.], 576/13. ''*n* [inf.], (586/6). Cf. also the 4th form *hsb*ᶜ.
*sb*ᶜ*y* seventy, 649/27; 665/16,18,36; 671/13.
sbt reproach; *sb* [pl.], 700/10.
sdm lack of appetite, 619/12.
sdṯ (A) six, 644/25; ''*t* [fem.], 855/3.
sdṯ (B) sixth, 613/11; 615/13.
*sw*ʾ ill; disastrous; devastating, 564/23; 567/17; 623/22; 644/14; 645/19; 666/10; 747/18.
swn toward, 651/32.
sḫt (A) defeat, 578/21; *b*'', 578/20; 643/32.
sḫt (B) to destroy; overthrow; annihilate, 643 bis/4; [passive], 578/8; cf. also the 4th form *hsḫt*.
sṭr inscription, 550/1; 554; 555/1; *ḏ*'', 551; 554; 556; 557.
syb irruption, 567/28.
syṭ (water pond); ʾ'' [pl.], 735/14.
syt work, 647/25,26; ''*hmw*, 647/27-28.
slm (A) peace, 576/3; 577/4; 643/8,9; 652/18; *b*'', 559/10; 561/10.
slm (B) to make peace; bring peace; *b*'', 550/2.
smy [2nd form] to give a name; *ḏ*'', 705/4; cf. also the 8th form *stmy*.
*sm*ᶜ to hear; agree upon, 643/25. *y*'' [imperf.]; ''*w* [pl.], 577/10.
sn [verb], cf. the 5th form *tsn*.
snt sleep; ''*hw*, 567/6.
*s*ᶜ*d* to make happy, 559/7,11; 560/17-18; 561/7,11; 562/8; 568/14; 581/14; 601/13; 602/13; 629/41; 644/26; 690/8; 739/12; [747/9-10]; ''*hw*, 726/5; ''*hmw*, 559/4, 13; 561/4,13; 561 bis/18,19-20; 563/7,17; 565/10,13, 14; 567/22; 604/3; 631/36; 634/9; 641/10; 644/15; 645/19,22; 662/19-20; 704/8; 712/14; 728/6; 730/6; 734/6; 740 A/11; 747/11,(14); 853 A/4,B/4,C/4,D/3, E/4,F/4; ''*hmy*, 594/6; 652/16. *ls*ᶜ*d*, 564/15,18,19; (568/17-18); 601/15; 602/15; 612/14-15; 626/7; 627/14; 630/9; 753 I/3,II/3,III/3; ''*hw*, 571/4; 581/16-17; (583/10); (595/1-2); 692/10; [732/9]; 765/6; (807/3; 840/8; ''*hmw*, (562/11-12); 587/10; 588/10; 603/7; 605/5-6,7; 606/6,13-14; 607/6,13; 616/34; 618/(14-15,17-18),29; 621/6; 623/18; 626/5; 627/18-19,20-21; 628/16,20,21-22; 629/43; 630/16; 631/39; 634/5; 636/10; 640/7; (642/15); 666/11; (691/8-9); 704/4,4-5; 707/7; 712/13; 730/5,9; (732/4); 753 I/2,II/1,III/1; 799/3,4,6; [820/1]; ''*hmy*, 594/9; 632/8; 652/12; ''*nh*, 727/9. *ys*ᶜ*d* [imperf.]; ''*nhw*, 643 bis/8; ''*nhmw*, 642/7; *l*''*nhmy*, 572/14.
*s*ᶜ*s*ᶜ summer, 615/19; 623/15; 650/12-13; 661/7; fruits of summer, [collect.], 617/8; 631/41.
*s*ᶜ*ḏ* [verb][?]. *y*'' [imperf.]; ''*w* [pl.], 586/24.
sfh to act, perform foolishly, 643/28-29; *k*''*w* [pl.], 643/19.
sfḥ (A) to place (under the control of), 578/22.
sfḥ (B) to display sorcery; ''*w* [pl.], 735/8-9.
sfl lower country, (804/1); (821 A/4); 847/2; *b*'', 616/26; 665/28. *sfylt* [pl.], 585/14.
sqh cistern, 603/5-6.
sqy (A) watered, 670/26.
sqy (B) irrigation, 627/7; 628/6,8; 647/30; 653/8,12; 735/5; 851/7; *b*'', 618/9.
sqy (C) *saqay*-palm, 615/9; 617/4; (691/10); [747/15].
sqy (D) to irrigate, 735/4,10,14; cf. also the 8th form *stqy*. *sqyw* [pl.], 735/13. *ysqy* [imperf.]; *k*''*n*, 627/5,10; 628/11; *k*''*nhmw*, 735/11.
sr wâdî-side valley, 574/6; 576/10; 649/16,25; 745/10; 758/8; *b*'', 574/4; 578/19; 658/15,22; *ḏ*'', 577/12. *sry* [dual]; ''*hw*, 577/13; ''*hmw*, 627/7. *srnhn* [dual]; *b*'', 577/11,14. ʾ*srr* [pl.], 615/10,20; 735/6,11,13; ''*hw*, 653/8; 667 B; 735/1,5; ''*hmw*, 561 bis/21; 562/13; 564/21; 565/15; 617/8-9; 618/24; 623/17; 627/22; 628/23; 629/28; 631/40; 645/24-25; 650/13-14; 661/8; 670/27-28,30; [719/15]; 851/5.
st[[noun], 746/4.
*st*ʾ*ḏn* to receive, 643/ 14-15.
*st*ʾ*wl* to bring back; ''*n* [inf.], 577/15.
stbrw to reconnoitre, 649/17.
stwkb to bring back; ''*w* [pl.], (560/12); *l*''*n* [inf.], 560/10.
stwkl to show one's confidence in, 611/7; 655/5; ''*hw*, (558/2); 704/3; *ḏ*''*hw*, 726/3; 816/4; ''*n* [inf.], 611/15; 653/17; ''*w* [pl.], 653/4. to bind oneself, (568/6-7); ''*hw*, 605/4.
stwfy to give, assure protection, 560/7,8; 564/4,8,13; 629/35,37,39; 745/6; [passive], 629/22. *stwfyn* [inf.], 600/4; 610/5; 647/24; 828/6; *b*'', 562/4.
*stwš*ᶜ to request the assistance of. ''*t* [fem.]; *ḏ*''*hw*, 700/7. [passive], 700/10.
*styd*ᶜ to confide in; *k*''*hw*, 740 A/5; ''*n* [inf.], 567/19. ''*t* [fem.]; *ḏ*''*hw*, 721/5. to prove one's reliability to, 564/4-5; 647/15.
*styf*ᶜ to exalt; *k*'', (570/6-7).
stkn to be petitioned; *ḏ*'', (721/6-7).
stkml to terminate happily; ''*n* [inf.], 564/14.
stmy to be named. *y*'' [imperf.]; ''*n*, 828/7; *ḏ*''*n*, 655/9-10.
*stml*ʾ to beseech, 560/17; 566/6; 581/13; 608/7; 609/7; 611/6; 612/8; 614/9; (629/21); 630/5-6; 645/6; 660/8; 662/8; (691/5-6); 713/9; 716/5; 719/5; 739/7; 758/6. *stml*ʾ*n* [inf.], 567/19; 608/12; 609/12; 610/13; 611/15; 614/12-13; 616/33; [624/7]; 645/10; 653/17; 735/19; ''*n*, 565/10; 592/7. *stml*ʾ*w* [pl.], 560/6; 561 bis/16; 565/5; 616/9; 621/5; 627/6,14; 628/15; 653/11; 660/20; 671/19-20; 735/9-10; (746/7); *k*'', 567/10. *ystml*ʾ [imperf.]; ''*n*, 590/18-19; 618/14; 626/13; 630/8-9; 662/16; 693/12; 701 A/5; 739/16-17; ''*nn*, 561 bis/17-18; [566/12]; 585/19; 621/5-6; 627/14; 628/15-16; 650/17-18; 753 I/5,II/7,III/7.

stnqḏ to save; take away. *''n* [inf.]; *''hmw*, 644/20.
stʿn to ask for help; *l'nhw* [inf.], 633/11.
stsyn to protect oneself; *y''* [imperf.], 720/8-9.
stṣr to call for help; *k''hmw*, 577/3. *''w* [pl.]; *ḏ''*, 575/6.
stqbl to call on someone, 762/4.
stqḏ to save; take away; *''w* [pl.], 665/39,42.
stqḥ to draw; *''n* [inf.], 559/8; 561/8; 644/19.
stqy to slake one's thirst (with water). *y''* [imperf.]; *ḏ''nn*, (750/7-8).
strs to be chosen as chief; *''w* [pl.], 561 bis/9.
stṯqf to take along; select, 577/1,7; 643/20.
sṯ six, 577/4; 616/21; 649/29,39; *''t* [fem.], 576/15; 649/37-38; 720/12.
sṯy sixty, 577/14,(14-15).

ʿ

ʿ ten; ʿʿʿ, 680/2.
ʿ... [*nisba*]; ʾ'', 586/2.
ʿbd servant; worshipper, 557; 570/1; 683/1; [684/1]; 694/1-2; 711/1; 723/1; 831/1. *ʿbd/ḏt*, 741/2-3; 756/2-3. *ʿbdhw*, 560/18; 562/9; 564/8,15,18,(19),22; 567/5-6; 568/5,11; 571/5-6; 574/3; 576/1,3; 577/15, 16,18; 578/33; (580/12); 581/9,14; 586/11; 587/7; 588/5,6; 590/11,13,14; 601/4,13; 602/4,13; 608/10; 609/10; 610/10; 611/11,17; 612/7,11,13,15; 613/7,13; 619/6; 620/5; 627/3,9,13,15,24; 628/10,14,23-24; 629/3,17,20,25,32; 630/4,7,10,18; 631/3,11,17; 633/14; 635/17,29,40,42; 643/12,23,36; 643 bis/5; 644/26; 645/5,8,12,16-17; 646/5; 647/31; 650/8,19,28,31; 651/9-10,24,42,50; 655/11; 657/5,9; 660/7-8; 664/6; 667 A/6,11; 670/7-8,9,14,16; 684/6-7,11; (685/4-5); 687/10; 690/8; 693/8-9,11; 695/6; 699/7; 700/5,6-7, 17; 702/11,17-18; 711/7; 712/6,10,11-12; 713/8,14; 716/5; (719/4-5); 720/11; (723/4); 725/7; 733/5; 739/6,8,[12],15-16; 740 A/6,9; 741/6,10; 745/12; [746/4]; [747/4-5]; 756/6,10; 758/5,11,14,18; (763/4-5); (765/5-6); 812/9; 839/2; *l''*, 662/7,15; 720/17. *ʿbdy* [dual]; *''hw*, 568/12,14; 572/11-12; 577/17,(17-18); 578/30-31,33,35; 585/3,18; 590/4,(22-23); 614/7,10-11; 616/7; 617/13; 618/(12-13),25; 629/41; 652/10; 658/6,24; 660/20; 670/18; 716/6,11; *l''hw*, 568/7; *''hmw*, (647/8-9).
ʿbṯ calamity, 567/27; 578/41; 613/15-16; 615/27; *''t* [pl.], (598/5-6); 635/45.
ʿbr (A) for; through; with; toward; *''hw*, 578/21. *b''*, 576/11; 577/2,8,10,11,12; 584/9; 643/8,10,17; 660/17; 668/3; *''hw*, 577/6; 643/10-11; 647/13; *''hmw* 576/11. *l''*, 700/10; *''hw*, 633/11. against, 652/21-22; *b''*, 577/9,10; 585/6; 589/11; 629/8; 631/6,(13); 646/7,9; 656/11; 712/8; 735/8.
ʿbr (B) river-side field. *''t* [pl.]; *''hw*, 555/3; *''hmw*, 617/5; 620/12; 623/17; 730/7.
ʿbr (C) to let someone. *''n* [inf.]; *''hw*, 643/15.
ʿbrn to; toward, 631/23-24,24; *''mw*, cf. *k*.
ʿd against; in; to, 550/2; 555/4; 735/1; cf. also *ln*.
ʿdw to come; go forth, 585/15; 631/21,25; *ḏ''*, 669/18; *f''*, 577/3. *''w* [pl.], *f''*, 577/1. *y''* [imperf.]; *''n*, 576/4; 631/24; 702/6.
ʿdy (A) [conj.] until, 576/2; 578/28; 671/17; 750/(5),9; *''/ḏ*, 576/9,16; *''/ḏt*, 576/5-6,9,10,16; 633/9.
ʿdy (B) [prep.] in; to, 560/10,14; 561/bis/21; 562/6; 574/6,10; 576/3,4,5,6,7,8,9,10,12,13,14; 577/(1),2,3, 6,9,11,13; 578/9,15,20,21,25; (580/8-9); 586/15,16,20; 587/11; 591/10; 601/5; 602/5; 612/9; 616/16,18; 617/8; 623/16; 628/8; 629/6,10,23,27,33,35; 631/12,20, 21,23,40; 635/21,23,25; 636/7; 643/7,13,16,17,18,20, 21-22,25,27,30,32,33,35; 649/9,16,25,32,33; 650/13,15, 21; 651/48; 653/12-13; 656/16; 658/10; 660/19; 665/11,24; 669/16,18-19; 670/27,29; 704/6; 716/8; 719/14; 730/7,8; 735/8; 740 A/7; 745/7,11; 746/5; (750/4-5); 758/8; 766/6; 791/4; 799/6; [821/3-4]; *''hw*, 628/6; *''hmw*, 561 bis/10-11; cf. also *ln*.
ʿdq press, 558/5.
ʿḏr (A) settler, 740 A/12. ʾ'' [pl.], *ḏ''*, 615/4.
ʿḏr (B) to give help. *''n* [inf.]; *l''*, 601/7-8; 602/7-8.
ʿhd [verb], cf. the 8th form *ʿthd*.
ʿhdt (consecutive) rain, 651/18.
ʿwd to bring. *''n* [inf.]; *''hw*, 643/9.
ʿwn [verb], cf. the 4th and 10th forms, *hʿn* and *stʿn* respectively.
ʿws pestilence(?), 645/13.
ʿwf profit; *''hmw*, 616/21.
ʿzm undertaking; *l''*, 763/3.
ʿzt vigor, 559/12; 561/12.
ʿṭwf loving; *''hn*, 735/9.
ʿyn (A) eye; *''hw*, 706/7.
ʿyn (B) spring [water]; ʾ'', 665/28.
ʿyr to overwhelm, 644/10.
ʿlw against; *b''hw*, 643/29.
ʿly (A) against, 649/17; *''hmw*, 620/6. *b''*, 550/2; 551; 561 bis/11; 574/5; 575/4; 576/3,6,7,8,11; 577/3,16; 578/42; 579/7; 635/10,11-12,22,(24,)26,27; 640/5; 644/6; 658/14-15; 665/14; *''hmw*, 575/6; 576/1,(16); 577/5,8,11,12,14,16,17; 643/27,35; 747/18. above; *b''hw*, 708/5; 713/6. because of; *b''*, 700/11; 877/6-7. for; *b''*, 643/16; *b''hmw*, 656/18. in; *b''*, 665/40.
ʿly (B) [2nd form] to cause to overcome; *ʿln* [inf.], 601/17-18; 602/17.
ʿly (C) higher land. *ʿlt* [pl.], 650/16; *b''*, 585/14.
ʿlm mark; *b''*, 700/15.
ʿln to, 618/7; 702/14?
ʿm with, 761/3. from, 665/43. *bʿm* along with; for, 555/4; 570/4; [597/1]; 631/26; 633/7; 643/11; 643 bis/3; 644/23; (656/15); 658/19; 662/13; 665/18; 713/12; 831/2; against, 575/5; 581/7; 586/8,16,20; 590/10; 601/8; 602/8; 629/10; 631/5; 643 bis/1; 644/15,18-19,21-22; 669/19; 739/9; 750/16; 758/9; 772/3; from; because of, 567/10,11; 577/2; 629/21; 631/32; 643/15; 653/7,11; 735/10; 747/6; (750/11-12); in, 653/4; to, 633/10; 718/8; under, (568/8). *bʿmhw* from him, 560/6,17; 561 bis/16,18; 565/5,10; 566/(7), 12; 567/19; 581/13; 585/19; 590/19; 592/7; 608/(7-8), 13; 609/7-8,12; 610/14; 612/8; 614/9,13; 616/9,34; 618/6,14; 621/6; [624/7]; 626/14; 627/6,14; 628/16; 630/6,9; 645/6-7,10; 650/18; 653/17; 657/4-5,7,10; 660/8-9,20; 662/8,16-17; 671/20; 691/6; 693/12-13; 701 A/5; 713/9-10; 716/5; (719/5-6); 735/19; 739/7-8, 17; 753 I/5,II/7,III/7; [746/7]; 877/7-8; from him [separation], 628/5; with him *or* it, 574/5; 576/5,15; 577/3,4,7,11,13; (629/39-40); 643/6,12,14,17,24,27,

31; 651/12; 665/41; in him, 611/7; 655/5; on him, (762/4); under it, 576/7. *bᶜmhmw* against them, 576/5,9; 577/5; 629/19; 669/21; from them, 631/33; 649/32; with them, 577/7; 643/28,33; 649/29; 660/14. *bᶜmhmy* with them both, 629/9.
ᶜmd naturally watered field; ᵓ'' [pl.], 577/15; 735/7.
ᶜmh [2nd form] to wrong; ''*n* [inf.], 722/a.
ᶜmm [verb], cf. the 4th form *hᶜmm.*
ᶜmn from, 574/10; 700/9. against, 631/15.
]*ᶜn* [?], 558/2.
ᶜn away from; ''*hw*, 570/6.
ᶜnb vineyard. ᵓ'' [pl.]; ''*hmw*, 620/12; 730/7.
ᶜnt (A) help; aid; *b*'', 670/11. auxiliary operation, 635/20.
ᶜnt (B) auxiliary troops; troops of reinforcement, 575/7; 577/5,10; 629/33; 643/25.
ᶜsy (A) *ᶜasay* [weight], 669/17.
ᶜsy (B) to acquire, 675/1; [676/1]; 682/1; 842/2; [846/2].
ᶜsm (A) desired, 735/14.
ᶜsm (B) desire, 578/11; 635/42; 658/32; *b*'', 631/5,9-10.
ᶜsm (C) stiffness(?), 585/10.
ᶜsm (D) to desire [passive]; *ḏ*'', 574/9; 575/7,8; 576/4,5,7, 8,9,11,12,13,14; 577/1,[2],3,5,6,11; (589/15); 631/9; 649/14; 651/20; 658/18,27; 668/9; cf. also the 4th form *hᶜsm.*
ᶜṣd gang. ᵓ'' [pl.], 575/3,4; ''*hmw*, 574/5-6.
ᶜṣr [verb], cf. the 6th form *tᶜṣr.*
ᶜḍ woodwork; ''*hw*, 557.
ᶜqb (A) after [conj.], 577/13.
ᶜqb (B) representative, 577/10. ''*t* [pl.], 619/2-3; ''*hw*, 578/22.
ᶜqb (C) to guard; watch; ''*hmw*, 577/12; *l*'' [passive], 577/13; *y*'' [imperf.], 550/2.
ᶜqbt hill-slope; *b*'', 649/31,36.
ᶜqd oath; *ḏ*'', 577/12.
ᶜr citadel; acropolis, 575/4; 578/8; 615/4-5; 631/24; cf. also the name of deity *ᶜṯtr*; ''*nhn* [dual], cf. the name of deity *ḥgrm.*
ᶜrb (A) Arabs [collect.], 560/10; 561 bis/12-13; 629/33; *b*'', 671/10; *ᵓᶜrb* [pl.], 561 bis/11,13; 629/7-8; 635/34; 665/2,3,13; 739/9; 758/9.
ᶜrb (B) [verb], cf. the 4th form *tᶜrb.*
ᶜrbt pledge, 574/11.
ᶜrgl cloud (of flies[?]), 610/8.
ᶜrm dam, 671/11,13.
ᶜšr (A) ten, 576/15; 649/37,39; ''*hw*, 577/11.
ᶜšr (B) tenth, 653/13. tithe, 650/5; 656/17.
ᶜšr (C) [2nd form] to assess as tithe; *ḏ*''*hw*, 615/9; 617/4. to offer as tithe; *y*'' [imperf.]; ''*nn*, 650/5.
ᶜšry twenty, 574/7; 577/4,14; 586/18; 616/21; 649/38; 665/31.
ᶜšrnhn twenty, 853 (A/2),B/2,C/2,D/2,E/3,F/2; *ḏ*'', 653/13.
ᶜšrt group; family, 616/24; (635/34-35); *ᶜšr* [pl.], 616/12, 14,23; 649/31; 658/13,15,21.
ᶜtb ᶜAtabite; ᵓ'' [pl.], 787/4.
ᶜthd to take care of. *y*'' [imperf.]; *k*''*n*, 716/7.

ġ

ġbṭ envy, 615/27.
ġwy to go away, 570/6.
ġwr to plunder, cf. also the 4th form *hġr*. *yġr* [imperf.]; *ḏ*''*w* [pl.], 643/32,34-35.
ġwṯ [verb], cf. the 4th form *hġṯ.*
ġzw (A) raid; ''*y* [dual], 586/14; *ġzt* [pl.], 586/15,19.
ġzw (B) raid-corps; ''*y* [dual], 577/14.
ġzw (C) to make raids, 739/9; 758/7-8.
ġy perdition, 651/51-52.
ġyl (A) stream. *ᵓġyl* [pl.]; ''*hmw*, 670/29. stream bed; ᵓ'' [pl.], 618/18,19; ''*hw*, 555/3; ''*hmw*, 564/21.
ġyl (B) [verb], cf. the 4th form *tġl.*
ġymn Ġaymânite; *ᵓġymn* [pl.], 747/2; (767/4).
ġyr except; without, 665/49.
ġlyt injustice, 664/18.
ġlm youth, 576/2; 655/9; 784/3.
ġnm (A) booty, 574/9; 575/8; 576/4,6,8,11,12,13,14; 577/[2],3,5,6,11,16; 578/12,32; 580/6,11,[13]; 581/11; 586/12; 590/13; 612/14; 616/30; 623/4; 631/9; 632/5-6,7; 635/18,31; 636/9; 649/14,23; 650/23; 656/7,14; 658/18,27; 665/46; 739/11; 758/13; (839/4); ''*hmw*, 632/3; 634/4; 637/4; (640/1-2); 641/4; ''*t* [pl.], 561 bis/8; 629/18; 643 bis/6.
ġnm (B) to plunder, 631/9; 713/11,15. ''*w* [pl.], 649/40; *ḏ*'', 641/4.
ġrb to come from abroad; ''*w* [pl.], 651/54,55.

f

f (A) [mark], 674 A.
f (B) so; then, cf. *ᵓsy*, *ᵓtw*, *b*, *bḥḏ*, *blt*, *bn*, *bᶜd*, *bᶜdn*, *brr*, *gbᵓ*, *hdrk*, *hwṣl*, *hfs*, *hfsḥ*, *hṣr*, *hqny*, *hrg*, *whb*, *wzᵓ*, *wqh*, *ḥmd*, *ḫmr*, *ysr*, *lhm*, *nbl*, *nẓr*, *sbᵓ*, *ᶜdw*, *fḫr*, *ṣbᵓ*, *ṣrḫ*, *ḍbᵓ*, *qfl*, *rṯd*, *šᵓm*, *šwᶜ*, *šft*, *śmk*, *tᵓwl*, *tᵓys*. *fl*, 627/12; 628/13; 643 bis/7; 644/12,26; 702/15; 751/10; cf. also *ḫmr*, *šym.*
fḫḏ thigh. ''*y* [dual]; ''*hw*, 649/20.
fḫr to gather together; ''*hmw*, 576/14. ''*w* [pl.], 577/2,(8); *f*'', 577/12.
fyṣ to depart. *yfṣ* [imperf.]; ''*n*, 631/22.
fyšny Fayšânite [*nisba*], 698/2.
flw [verb], cf. the 5th forms *tflw* and *tfl.*
fly ordinance. ''*t* [pl.]; ''*hmw*, 628/7.
fnwt canal; ''*hw*, 842/3.
fsḥ [verb], cf. the 4th form *hfsḥ.*
fᶜm solid, 730/5.
fqd to loose; *ḏ*''*w* [pl. passive], 651/26; cf. also the 6th form *tfqd.*
fqḥ opening, 676/1-2; 682/1-2.
fql (A) harvest, 727/10. *ᵓfql* [pl.], 561 bis/20-21; 562/12; 563/12; 564/20; 565/14; 571/5; 581/17; 599/8; 601/16-17; 602/16; 615/20; 618/23; 620/11; 627/21; 628/22; 630/17; 645/23; 650/15; 654/13; 664/15; 666/15; 670/26; 692/11; 703/6; 730/8; 733/11; 736/15-16; 738/10; 747/15; ''*hmw*, 656/24.
fql (B) to harvest; ''*w* [pl.], 615/10. *yfql* [imperf.]; ''*nn*, 730/8.
frṭ to outrun; *b*''*n* [inf.], 660/17.

frs (A) horse, 666/4; 745/4,6; ''*hw*, 577/1; 649/20,21-22; ''*nhn* [dual], 745/8-9. ʾ*frs* [pl.], 576/3; 584/1; 635/31; 644/25; 665/38,46; 745/2; ''*hmw*, 643 bis/2; 644/20. mare, 665/44; 752/7.

frs (B). ʾ'' horsemen; cavalry, 576/15; 577/4,11; 616/21; 643/24; 649/29; 665/16,17,31,36,38,42; ''*hw*, 576/4,5,8,10,11,12,12-13; 577/1,8,15; 578/18; ''*hmw*, 574/8-9; 576/7,15; 616/29; 665/37-38.

*fr*ʿ (A) optimum crop, 618/15; 623/14; 650/12; 661/7; 666/15; 704/5; 746/8; ''*w* [pl.], 615/18.

*fr*ʿ (B) great importance, 735/11; *ḏ*'', 649/12,18,35.

frq to deliver; cf. also the 5th form *tfrq*. *frqn* [inf.], 567/16; ''*hmw*, 567/26.

fršt green field, 574/7.

ftḥ (A) edict, 750/11.

ftḥ (B) to open; ''*hmw*, 643/20.

ṣ

ṣ [masonry mark], cf. *w*.

*ṣb*ʾ to proceed. *y*'' [imperf.]; *f*''*w* [pl.], 576/6.

ṣbḥ (A) morning; *ḏ*'', 649/34.

ṣbḥ (B) to make an incursion in the morning; ''*n* [inf.], 616/23.

ṣbn to abstain from; ''*w* [pl.], 720/7-8.

ṣdġ manifestation; *b*''*hw*, 721/4.

ṣdq (A) perfect, 559/8; 561/8; 561 bis/8,21; (562/12-13); 563/8,12; 564/16; 565/13,14-15; 567/23,24; (568/16-17); 571/5; 577/18; 581/15,17; 587/10; 588/11; (591/10); 594/11; 598/5; 599/8; 601/11,14,17; 602/11, 13,16; 604/4; 605/7; 606/7; 607/7; 610/15; 613/20; 620/11; 623/19; 626/6; 627/20,21; 628/21,22; 629/18; 630/11,17; 631/16; (640/6-7); 643 bis/6,9; 645/21-22, 23; 649/12; 650/15; 652/17; 655/13; 657/11; 658/33; 661/8; 690/10; 703/5; 704/6; 707/8; 708/10; 726/5; 732/5; 733/13; [734/6]; 738/10; 747/12,(15); 753 I/3, II/2,III/2; 799/7; 820/2; 839/3; 877/11,13.

ṣdq (B) reality; *b*'', 567/11; *kb*'', 567/12.

ṣdq (C) to bestow, 605/12; 713/8; 716/4,10; ''*hmw*, 561 bis/15; [inf.], 608/9; 609/9; 611/10; 616/32; 618/12 627/12; 628/13-14; 630/7; ''*hmw*, 561 bis/17; 626/12; 753 I/4,(II/6),III/6.

ṣwy to weaken. *y*'' [imperf.]; *k*''*nn*, 577/9.

ṣḥ health, 650/8; 651/39; the best, 567/19-20.

ṣḥb (A) friend; companion. ʾ'' [pl.], 560/11; ''*hmw*, (560/12-13).

ṣḥb (B) to accompany; ''*w* [pl.], 560/11.

ṣyḥ to level, 821 A/3.

ṣyn [verb], cf. the 10th form *stṣyn*.

ṣyt (fame; reputation); ''*hw*, 702/5.

ṣly clay; *ḏ*'', 730/4.

ṣlm statue, 561 bis/5; 562/3; 563/4; 564/3; 565/4; (566/4-5); 568/4; 570/2; 572/4; 578/4-5; 579/4; 581/4; 582/6; 583/5; 584/2; [586/3]; 587/2; 589/5; 590/3; 591/5; 600/3; 603/4; 605/4; 608/5; 609/4; 611/5; 612/6; 613/6; 615/9; 616/7; 617/4; 618/4; 620/4; 624/4; 626/4; 627/3; 628/3; 629/2; 630/3; 633/3; 634/3; 635/3; 637/3; 641/3-4; 642/4; 644/2; 645/3; 646/5; [647/5]; 648/3; 649/6; 650/4; 651/8; 652/7; 654/5; 655/4; 656/5-6; 658/5; 660/6; 662/5; 664/3-4; 665/5; 667 A/4; 669/6,7,12,13; 670/6-7; 671/7; 684/5; 687/3; 690/4; 691/4; 692/3; 698/6; 699/3; 700/4; 701/3; 703/3; 704/3; 705/3; 708/5; 709/3; 710/3; 711/3; 712/4; 717/3; 718/4; [719/4]; 720/4; 721/3-4; 722/4-5; 726/3; 727/8-9; 728/3; 729/7; 730/4; (732/2-3); 736/5; 738/4; 739/4; 744/3; (746/3); 755/5; 757 bis/5; 758/4; 761/2; 765/2; 772/2; 784/2; [790/3]; 812/6; 815/2; [816/3]; 817/2; 840/4; 844/3-4; 877/5; ''*hw*, (647/15-16). *ṣlmynn* [dual], 574/2. *ṣlmnhn* [dual], 559/3; 560/4; 561/3; 585/2; (588/2-3); 592/2; 601/3; 602/3; 606/4; 607/4; 614/6; 619/4; 653/2; 683/3; 693/4-5; (707/6); 715/4; 735/2; (740 A/3-4); 741/5; 747/3; 753 I/2; 756/5; (788/3-4); (821 A/2). *ṣlmn* [dual], 610/4; (631/2); 700/3; 713/7; 716/4; 743/3-4. ʾ*ṣlm* [pl.], 567/4,9; 576/1; 604/2; 632/2; 657/3; 689/2; 703/3; 725/5; 733/4-5; 736/11; 742/6-7; 757/2; (851/2); 853 (A/3),B/3,C/3,D/2,E/3,F/3; 854/3; 855/3.

ṣlmt female statue, 566/5; 569/4-5; 584/8; (624/5-6); 686/3-4; 690/4; 694/4; 706/3; (718/5); 722/5; 731/4; 747/3; 751/3; (783/3); (797 A/2); 828/4; ''*n* [dual], 742/7-8; ''*nhn* [dual], 689/2-3.

*ṣm*ʾ drought, 735/7.

*ṣn*ʿ [verb], cf. the 4th and 5th forms, *hṣn*ʿ and *tṣn*ʿ respectively.

ṣrb fruits of autumn [collect.], 594/10; 617/9; 631/40; 651/48; 655/17; 719/14.

ṣrwḥy Ṣirwâḥite [*nisba*]; ''*t* [fem.], 717/1.

ṣrḥt upper room, 603/6.

ṣrḫ to call; *f*'', 665/40.

ṣry to guard, 633/13; cf. also the 5th and 8th forms, *tṣry* and *ṣtry* respectively. *yṣry* [imperf.]; *k*''*nhmw*, 577/9.

ṣryt counsel, 877/10,13; ''*hmw*, 877/7. *ṣry* [pl.], 560/7; 610/13; 616/9,33; *b*'', 716/5.

ṣrf brass, 576/1; 669/6,12; 693/5; 700/3; *ḏ*'', 572/4; 574/2; 608/5; 609/4-5; [624/5]; 703/3; 716/4; 720/4-5; 755/4-5.

ṣrr [verb], cf. the 4th form *hṣr*.

ṣtry to implore; ''*n* [inf.], 616/9,34.

ḍ

*ḍ*ʾ*n* sheep [collect.], 649/41; 665/26.

*ḍb*ʾ (A) war; engagement, 555/4. ʾ'' [pl.], (586/14); 831/2. *ḍby*ʾ [pl.], 577/[15],16; 579/7; 581/6; 635/9, 19-20; *b*'', 577/14. *ḍb*ʾ*t* [pl.], 635/26; 636/6-7; 658/7-8; 708/9.

*ḍb*ʾ (B) fighting man; ''*t* [pl.], 635/24.

*ḍb*ʾ (C) to wage war; fight, 555/4; 577/14; 578/13; 579/7; 581/6; 635/10; 636/5; 640/4; 658/19; 758/7; *l*'', 575/3; 576/3; 577/14; 658/20-21. *ḍb*ʾ*w* [pl.]; *f*'', 658/14. *ḍb*ʾ*y* [dual]; *f*'', 578/24. *yḍb*ʾ [imperf.]; ''*n*, 577/8; *f*'', 574/4; *f*''*n*, 577/11.

ḍll (A) state of perishing; grave illness, [661/5]; 670/9.

ḏll (B) to lay near death; die; *ḏ"*, 670/10; *"n* [inf.], (661/5).
ḏʿn to be lost; [*maṣdar*], 647/14.
ḏr (A) war, 576/1; 577/3,16; 589/11; 629/20; 631/6; 635/11; *b"*, 550/2; 585/15; 629/6; 652/17; 656/11; *l"*, 561 bis/11. *ʾḏr* [pl.], 577/17; *b"*, 559/10; 561/10; 561 bis/9.
ḏr (B) foe; enemy, 564/25; 568/20,21; 577/18,19; 585/17; 635/15; 643 bis/9; *"hmw*, 561 bis/23; 574/13; 610/17-18; 611/21; 631/39; [719/15-16]; 853 A/5,B/5,C/5, D/4-5,E/5,F/5;877/17; *"hmy*, 581/8. *ʾḏr* [pl.], 585/13.
ḏry to hide. *"n* [inf.]; *"h*, 558/8.
ḏrs molar tooth. *ʾ"* [pl.]; *"hw*, 702/(12),13-14.
ḏrʿ to humble, 610/17; 877/16; *"n* [inf.], 577/19; 611/20; 631/4,(38-39); 635/14-15; cf. also the 4th and 5th forms, *hḏrʿ* and *tḏrʿ* respectively.

q

qbl [verb], cf. the 8th and 10th forms, *qtbl* and *stqbl* respectively.
qbly because of; *l"*, 568/6; 643/9; 840/5; *l"/ḏ*, 653/5; 669/8,18; 693/6; 700/7; 720/5; (721/4-5); 735/5; 750/4; cf. also *ʾl*; *l"/ḏt*, 648/4; 694/5-6; cf. also *ʾl*, *ḥmd*. by means of, 671/24.
qblt fight, 644/4,13.
qdm (A) [*maṣdar*]; *ln"* before, 745/5-6; *b"* before, 649/(12),18-19,35.
qdm (B) commander, 681/3; (816/1-2).
qdm (C) [1st form] to proceed; *"hmw*, 576/5,6; 665/21,29; *"n* [inf.], 665/9; *"nhmw*, 665/12; cf. also the 5th and 8th forms, *tqdm* and *qtdm* respectively. to be in charge; *l"n* [inf.], 633/7. to attack; *"hmw*, 643/30; *l"n* [inf.], 644/17; *yqdm* [imperf.]; *kl"nn*, 576/10.
qdm (D) [2nd form] to move forward. *"t* [fem.]; *"hmw*, 576/13.
qdmy before. *b"*, 608/8; 609/8; 628/9; 667 A/9; 735/6; *"hmw*, 575/3.
qht (A) obedience; docility; *b"*, 565/6.
qht (B) authority, 578/39; *"hw*, 564/12.
qwḥ [verb], cf. the 10th form *stqḥ*.
qwl ruler, 644/1. *ʾqwl* [pl.], (559/1); 561/1; 561 bis/3; 562/2,8; 564/2,5; [568/2-3]; 576/9; 578/2; [601/1]; [602/1]; [606/2]; [607/2]; 612/9; 615/3; 616/3; (618/2); 626/3; [627/1]; (628/1-2); 629/1-2,9,38,39; 631/1,27; 643/[1],11; 643 bis/1; 649/3; 650/1; 651/4; 658/(2-3),19-20; 665/33,37; 666/3; 670/3-4; 671/3; 695/3; 716/3; (718/3); [746/2]; [753 I/1]; *"hw*, 574/5; 575/3; 576/4,5,10,11,12,15; 577/4,[5],8,9,15; 578/18,28; *"hmw*, 574/8.
qwm [2nd form] to manage; take care, 633/7; cf. also the 4th form *hqm*.
qyẓ fruits of summer, 617/9; 631/40; 650/6; 651/48; 655/17; [719/14].
qyn administrator, 550/1; 552/1; 554; 555/1,3; *"y* [dual], 556.
qyf monument; cf. the names of deities *šms*, *šmsy*.
ql ruler; *"hmw*, 559/15; 561/15; 568/15; 606/12-13,18; 607/12,17-18; 626/19; 643 bis/8; 753 I/7, II/13, (III/13).
qll small quantity, 750/9.
qlm insect-pest; *"t* [pl.], 567/27; 610/9; 703/7.
qmʿ to subjugate, 576/4; 629/28; (639/4); *"w* [pl.], 576/12. *yqmʿ* [imperf.]; *"w* [pl.], 576/8; 577/14.
qmt harsh treatment, 558/5.
qny (A) slaves [collect.], 558/4; 576/5; 705/7; *"hw*, 550/1; 552/3; 553/3; 557; *"hmw*, 558/4; 575/5; (680/4). slave, 841/2; *"hw*, 844/5. property; *ʾqnyt* [pl.], 557.
qny (B) to possess; obtain; *b"*, (642/12); *ḏ"*, 844/5-6; cf. also the 4th form *hqny*. *"w* [pl.]; *ḏ"*, 567/25-26; (816/9-10). *"y* [dual]; *ḏ"*, 734/5.
qnʿ (A) satisfaction; contentedness, 643/10.
qnʿ (B) [verb], cf. the 5th form *tqnʿ*.
qsd to revolt; *"w* [pl.], 577/8.
qsdt revolt; rebellion, 577/13; 667 A/8.
qfl to come back; *f"w* [pl.], 665/27.
qṣ fruits of summer, 594/10.
qḏb rod; stick; *b"*, 700/12.
qḏn [verb], cf. the 8th form *qtḏn*.
qr fixed settlements [collect.]; *b"hmw*, 574/4.
qrʾ to call on. *y"* [imperf.]; *"nhw*, 570/7.
qrb (A) near [adject.], 737/4.
qrb (B) to be near, 562/17; 578/41; 591/11; 616/40; 623/23; 626/16; 629/45; 641/16; 647/34; 650/34; 651/54; [691/12]; 699/9; 750/17; 753 I/6,II/10,III/10; *ḏ"*, 649/28; *"w* [pl.], 576/7; 643/31; 644/18.
qryt *qârit*-musk, 635/4.
qrn (A) rebel, 576/13,14. *ʾ"* [pl.]; *b"*, 660/17.
qrn (B) [1st form] to rebel, 643/22; *l"*, 661/4. to attack; *l"/b* [+verb], 643/23.
qrn (C) [2nd form] to head for; *l"*, 662/12.
qtbl to start; *"n* [inf.], 644/4.
qtdm to take command of. *"n* [inf.], 635/33; 651/29-30; *l"*, 671/10.
qtḏn to settle down, 616/14.

r

]*r* [?] 678/1; 850/1.
rʾ [deictic particle], 619/9-10; 693/7; 717/7-8; 721/5-6; 877/9. *rʾ/k* [+verb], 567/10,12; 570/6; 584/10; 589/13; 656/16; 657/5,7; 664/5-6,7; 669/25; 706/7; 712/9; 736/8; 739/8; 758/9; 877/9-10. *krʾ*, 576/15; *"/k* [+verb], 616/19.
rʾy to decide; show; cf. also the 4th form *hrʾy*. *yrʾy* [imperf.]; *"n*, 570/5; 643/15; *k"nhw*, 567/7-8.
rʾs head; *"hw*, 577/7.
rbb [verb], cf. the 4th form *hrbb*.
rbḫ release; *b"*, 633/14.
rbʿ (A) fourth, 618/10; (846/2,3); cf. also the clan name *bklm*.
rbʿ (B) [verb], cf. the 4th form *trbʿ*.
rgl (A) foot; *"hw*, 649/21. *"y* [dual]; *"hw*, 583/7,9; 649/20; 840/6,8.
rgl (B) foot-soldier, 665/24; [pl.], 577/5; *ʾ"* [pl.], 550/2; 576/14.

rgly orderly, aide, 566/1.
*rd*ʾ [verb], cf. the 4th form *hrd*ʾ.
rwt water-carrier beasts [collect.]; ʾʾ*hmw*, 665/43.
rḥl saddle; *b*ʾʾ*hn*, 649/40; 665/39.
rḥq (A) remote [adject.], 737/4.
rḥq (B) to be remote; *ḏ*ʾʾ, (562/17); 578/41; 591/11; 616/39; 623/23; 626/16; [629/45]; 641/16; 647/34; 650/34; 651/54; 691/11; 699/8-9; 750/17; 753 I/6, II/10, III/10.
rym besides, 557.
rys [verb], cf. the 4th and 10th forms, *hrs* and *strs* respectively.
ryt obligation, 564/10.
rkb (A) beasts of burden [collect.], 576/3; 665/46; ʾʾ*hmw*, 586/22; 644/20; 665/43. riding animals [collect.]; ʾʾ*hmw*, 560/13,14. riding camels [collect.], 649/40; 665/39.
rkb (B) cameleer [sing.], 665/23. [collect.] (*also* camelry), 665/16,17,19,30,33; ʾʾ*hw*, 577/15.
rkb (C) saddle; ʾʾ*hw*, 666/4-5; 745/4.
rkb (D) to ride [active]; ʾʾ*hw*, 745/7; [passive] ʾʾ*y* [dual], 745/9-10.
rkbt equitation; riding, 715/2.
*r*ʿ*l* [verb], cf. the 4th form *hr*ʿ*l*.
*rf*ʾ to heal, 700/16.
rḍw (A) grace, 561 bis/18; 562/10; 563/8; 564/16; 565/11; 566/8; 567/20; 568/19; 569/5; (570/11); 571/2; 572/12; 578/36; 579/9; 581/15; 582/7; (583/11); 585/20; 587/7; 588/7; 590/20; 591/6; 592/8; (594/3-4); (595/2); 597/5; 599/5; 600/10; 601/14; 602/14; 603/8; 604/4; 605/7; 606/14; 607/14; 612/16; 613/18; 614/14; 615/23; 616/35; 617/11; 618/26; 619/14; 620/13; 621/7; 623/12; 626/8; 627/15-16; 628/17; 629/42; 630/11; 631/37; 632/8; 634/6; 635/40; 636/11; 640/7; 641/11; 642/7,15; 643 bis/8; 644/27; 645/20; 646/11; 647/19-20,23; 648/6-7; 650/10; 651/44; 652/13; 653/18-19; 654/11; 655/13,18; 656/20; 657/12; 658/30; 661/6; 662/20; 664/12; 666/12; 667 A/15; 668/15; 669/26-27; 670/21; 671/21; 684/7-8; 690/10; (691/7-8); 692/8; 703/7,8; 704/8; 707/8; 711/7-8; 730/9; 733/8; 739/13,14; 740 A/12; 743/7; [746/12]; 747/13; 753 I/3-4,II/4,III/4; 758/15; [765/7]; [799/4]; 804/2; [807/4]; 840/9.
rḍw (B) to please; *bḏ*ʾʾ*hmw*, 586/7-8; cf. also the 4th forms *hrḍ*, *hrḍw* and *hrḍy*. *yrḍw* [imperf.]; *ḏ*ʾʾ*nhmw*, 691/10.
rḍḥ to be bruised; crushed, 647/15; cf. also the 8th form *rtḍḥ*.
rḍy raḍay [weight], 608/6; 609/6.
rḏf raḏaf [weight], 572/4.
rqy to ascend; go up; ʾʾ*w* [pl.], 665/16.
rqt sorcery; ʾʾ*hmw*, 735/9.
ršw priest, 550/1; 703/2.
ršy gift, 702/4; ʾʾ*t* [pl.], 718/9.
*rt*ʿ to establish duly; determine [active]; *l*ʾʾ [inf.], 658/11-12. *yrt*ʿ [imperf.], ʾʾ*nn*, 745/10. [passive], 576/7.
rtḍḥ to slay; sow death; ʾʾ*n* [inf.], 575/5; 578/7,19; 631/5.
rtṯd to preserve; ʾʾ*n* [inf.], 572/8; 586/10; 716/11.
rṯd to entrust to the care of, 841/1; ʾʾ*hmy*, 683/5; *f*ʾʾ, 727/5; cf. also the 8th form *rtṯd*. *rṯdw* [pl.], 558/7; 559/19; 561/19; 562/20; 564/32; 568/26; 592/9; 601/21; 602/21; 606/23; 607/23; 626/23; 627/29; 628/29; 643 bis/10; [644/30]; 703/6, 11; 753 I/9,II/18,(III/18).

š

š [mark], 612.
*š*ʾ*m* to buy; *f*ʾʾ, 720/12-13; cf. also the 4th form *hš*ʾ*m*.
*š*ʾ*mt* north, 576/1; 577/18; 772/4; *b*ʾʾ, 658/22; *ḏ*ʾʾ, 635/12-13.
šh mark, 720/16.
šhr new moon, 651/19.
šwḥṭt šawaḥiṭ [measure]; *šwḥṭ* [pl.], 671/13-14.
*šw*ʿ (A) train; ʾʾ*hw*, 629/17,20,26; ʾʾ*hmw*, 631/14.
*šw*ʿ (B) to assist; help, 586/13; ʾʾ*hw*, 564/8-9. *šw*ʿ*n* [inf.], 580/7; 584/5; 587/4; 590/5,8,16; 612/9; 632/4; 635/20,43; 649/8,15,24; 650/20,26; 740 A/7; *l*ʾʾ, 629/4,26; (641/5-6). *šw*ʿ*w* [pl.], 581/12; 631/7,10; 636/2; 637/5; (640/3); 656/8; *f*ʾʾ, 649/41. *šw*ʿ*y* [dual], 658/8. *yšw*ʿ [imperf.]; ʾʾ*nn*, 623/5.
šwf to take care of; apply one's self, 564/22; 584/7; 666/7; 716/11.
šwft care, 686/6.
šzb branch, 700/13; *b*ʾʾ, 700/14.
šym (A) patron. ʾʾ*hmw*, 561 bis/24; 601/20; 602/20; 631/20; 655/19; *b*ʾʾ, 562/19; 564/30; [598/6]; 618/33; 626/22; 644/29; 747/20. *šymy* [dual]; ʾʾ*hmw*, 578/43.
šym (B) to hide; conceal, 576/13.
šym (C) to assure; *l*ʾʾ [inf.], 651/32. *yšm* [imperf.]; *fl*ʾʾ*n*, 611/16-17. to give; *šm*, 750/6.
šyn to suffer, 578/34; cf. also the 4th form *hšyn*.
škr to defeat, 576/3; 577/6,7; 585/14; *b*ʾʾ [inf.], 576/1; 577/6; (586/6); 643 bis/4; cf. also the 5th form *tškr*.
šlṯ (A) three, 644/22; ʾʾ*t* [fem.], 604/1-2; 757/2.
šlṯ (B) third; cf. the clan name *sm*ʿ*y*.
šms sun, 649/33.
šmt abuse, 581/18; 651/52-53; 652/19.
*šn*ʾ enemy, 558/5; 561 bis/22-23; [562/17]; 563/15; 564/24,25; 567/28; 568/20,21; 570/14; 571/7; 572/11, 15; 577/19; 578/41; 579/12; [580/14]; 581/18-19; 583/10; 585/17; 587/13; 588/12; 590/25; (591/11); 592/9; 594/12; 597/7-8; 598/6; 599/10; 601/19; 602/19; 603/12; 612/20; 613/16; 614/19; 615/27; 616/39; 617/14-15; 618/32; 619/20; 620/6,10; 623/23; 626/15-16; 627/26; 628/26; 629/45; 630/20; 631/42; 632/9; 633/21; 635/15,46; 636/17-18; [638/5]; 640/10; 641/15-16; 643 bis/9; 645/18; 647/33; 648/10; 650/34; 651/53; 654/16; 656/27; 661/9; 664/18; 666/11; 667 A/13; 668/19; 684/12; 685/5; (686/8-9); 687/12; 691/11; 693/13-14; 699/8; 703/11; 704/7; 706/10; 708/7; 711/13; 712/12; 715/11; [719/13]; 730/11; 733/10; 734/7; 736/17; 737/4; 739/19; 747/19; 750/17; 753 I/6,II/9,III/9; 758/19; [803/7]; (804/3-4); [807/3]; [813/3]; (816/11); (839/5); ʾʾ*hmw*, 561 bis/23-24; 574/13; 578/42; 610/18; 611/21; 631/39; (747/17); 853 A/5,B/5,C/5,D/5,E/5-6,F/5; 877/17; ʾʾ*hmy*, 652/20.
*š*ʿ*b* tribe, [559/1]; 560/3; 561/1; 561 bis/3-4,12; 562/2; 564/2,27; [568/3]; 576/2,8; 577/8,9,10,12,14; 578/2; 586/20; 601/1-2; [602/1-2]; [606/2-3]; 607/3; 615/3;

616/3; [618/2]; 626/3; [627/1]; 628/2; 629/2,6,30; (631/1); 635/11; 643/[2],6,13; 643 bis/6; 644/1,10,15, 16,18,21,24,25; 649/3,17; 650/1; 653/1,15; 655/2; 658/3; 660/14; 662/3; 666/3; 668/7,10,12; 670/4; 671/3; 695/3; 716/7; 718/3; 735/[1],3,8,15,18; (746/2); [753 I/1]; 851/1; ''*hw*, 649/13,22-23; 651/11; 712/7; 713/16; (765/7); ''*hmw*, 558/7; 559/2; 561/2; 561 bis/7; 564/9,23,25; (568/15-16,18-19); 606/(13),19; 607/12-13,18; 616/22; 618/22; 626/19; 627/23,25; 628/24; 629/17-18,44; 631/(3-4),18,19,23,25,32; 643 bis/6,8; 644/5,8,(26-27); 647/23; 649/28; 650/24; 655/18; 656/15; 662/13-14; 690/10-11; 703/8; 704/9; 719/9; 730/10; 739/14-15; 740 A/7,13; 753 I/7,II/13,III/13; ''*hmy*, 578/31. ''*ynhn* [dual], 577/7; 651/4. ''*nhn* [dual], 555/3; 577/11. ''*nn* [dual], 716/3. *ʾšʿb* [pl.], 550/2; 561 bis/14; 576/1,3,5,11,[15]; 577/2,16; 578/7; 581/7; 586/6; 589/10; 601/8,10; 602/8,9; 616/12,14, 19; 629/18-19; 631/5-6,27,29; 640/5; 643/6; 643 bis/1; 649/29-30,30-31; ''*hw*, 578/8,18,29; ''*hmw*, 643 bis/8; *ḏ*'', 575/7.

šʿr barley, 670/26-27; 720/13; ''*hmw*, 745/11.

šf appearance, 649/32.

šfʿ invasion, 651/53.

šfq (A) plentiful, 616/30; 649/41; 691/9; 735/14; 747/16.

šfq (B) [verb]; cf. the 4th form *hšfq*.

šft to promise, 627/9; 628/10; 698/9; ''*hw*, 715/5; 750/4; 752/8-9; 755/6; *k*''*hw*, 657/8; *ḏ*'', 767/6; *ḏ*''*hw*, (570/2-3); 582/6; 585/2; 587/3; 592/2; 619/5; 647/6,16; 657/3-4; 658/5; 660/7; 664/8-9, 666/5; 670/7; 684/6; 693/6; 707/6; 709/4; 729/(8-9),14-15; 736/6,10-11; 738/5; 741/5-6; 756/5-6; 815/3; 840/5; *bḏ*''*hw*, (664/4). *šftt* [fem.], 743/6; *ḏ*'', 706/4; 742/8; ''*hw*, 717/4; [783/4-5]. *šftw* [pl.], 641/7-8; 669/9,22; 745/5. to grant; ''*hmw*, 716/7; *f*'', 633/13.

šsy wickedness, 561 bis/22; 562/16; 563/15; 564/24; 567/28; 570/14; 571/7; 572/11,15; 578/41; 579/12; [580/14]; 583/10; 587/12; 588/12; (590/24-25); 591/11; 592/9; 594/12; 597/7; [598/5]; 599/10; 601/19; 602/18-19; 603/12; 612/20; 613/16; 614/18; 615/27: 616/39; 617/14; 618/31-32; 619/19; 620/10; 623/22-23; 626/15; 627/26; 628/25-26; 629/45; 630/20; 631/41; 632/9; 633/21; 635/45; 636/17; [638/5]; 640/10; 641/15; 645/18; (647/33); 648/10; 650/33; 651/52; 652/19; 654/15; 656/27; 661/9; 664/17; 666/10-11; 667 A/13; 668/19; 684/12; 685/5; 686/8; 687/12; 691/11; 693/13; 699/8; 703/10; 704/7; 708/7; 711/13; 712/12; 715/11; 719/12; 730/11; 733/9-10; 734/7; 736/17; 737/4; 739/18-19; 747/19; (750/16-17); 753 I/5-6,II/9,III/9; 758/19; (803/7); [807/3]; (813/2-3); [839/5]; *b*'', 747/18.

šqr (A) top, 550/1; 551; 554; 555/1; 556; 557.

šqr (B) [verb]; cf. the 4th form *hšqr*.

šrḥ to keep healthy, 586/10; 644/12; 670/15; 692/5; (716/10-11); 751/5,10; *ḏ*'', 750/9. to give success, 652/25; *l*'' [inf.], 570/13; cf. also the 8th form *štrḥ*. to make flourish; *y*'' [imperf.]; ''*n*, 702/5. to reinforce; *l*''*hw*, 576/14.

šrḥt squadron, 658/12.

šrʿ brave man; courageous man. *ʾ*'' [pl.]; ''*hmw*, 651/26.

šrʿt charge; office, 555/4.

šrq sunrise, 649/32. rise (of star), 649/33.

štʾ (A) skirmish, 643/5.

štʾ (B) [2nd form] to start; ''*w* [pl.], 631/6; cf. also the 4th form *hštʾ*.

štrḥ to make successful; ''*n* [inf.], 564/13.

ś

śʾd prince, 576/9,10.

śbb to cause; occasion, 702/8-9; cf. also the 5th form *tśbb*.

śyf [verb][?], 702/15-16.

śyq beasts [collect.], 702/9.

śll [verb], cf. the 4th form *hśl*.

śmk [2nd form] to go up. ''*w* [pl.], 576/15; *f*'', 576/6. *y*'' [imperf.]; ''*w* [pl.], 576/3; ''*n*, 576/14.

śn law. *b*'', 687/8; ''*hw*, 576/7.

śny to draw water; ''*w* [pl.], 702/9.

śʿʿ [verb][?]. *śʿ*; *k*'', 570/8.

śf (A) [verb][?]; *ḏ*'', 702/14-15; ''*hmw*, 705/5-6.

śf (B) to adjoin; add; *ḏ*''*hw*, 570/5; *l*''*hmw*, (818/5).

t

]*t* [?], 643 bis/2; ''*hmw*, 778/1-2; *b*'', 643 bis/3-4.

]*t.m*[[?], 558/2.

]*t.mʿ* [?], 636/1.

]*tl*[[?], 791/4-5.

t[[verb][?], 851/3.

t(.)*b* [verb]; *l*''*n* [inf.], 644/16-17.

tʾbh to grant; ''*hw*, 555/3.

tʾdm military enterprise; ''*ynhn* [dual], 644/24.

tʾhr to inflame; ''*n* [inf.], 702/13.

tʾwl to return; go back, 579/5; 585/9; 632/4; 636/5-6; 741/7; 756/7. *tʾwln* [inf.], 577/7; 589/14; 590/4-5,7, 12; 616/28; *b*'', 578/31; 581/10; 585/4; 586/11; 635/8, 18,30; (745/13). *tʾwlw* [pl.], 574/8,10; 576/10; 577/2; 631/13-14; *ḏ*'', 574/10; *f*'', 575/6; 576/9; 577/1,3; 578/20; 631/35. *tʾwly* [dual], 581/5. *ytʾwl* [imperf.]. 635/37-38; ''*w* [pl.], 575/8; 577/16; *f*''*w*, 576/8,9,10; ''*n*, 577/5,9; (586/6-7); *f*''*nn*, 576/7.

tʾys to give help; ''*n* [inf.], 629/35. ''*w* [pl.], 643/17; *f*'', 643/33.

tʾlh to adulate; give (adulations). *y*'' [imperf.]; *ḏ*''*nhmy*, 578/42.

tʾmn testimony of confidence, 550/2; 555/4; 716/9; ''*t* [pl.], 651/34-35.

tʾtw to withdraw; ''*w* [pl.], 735/12.

tʾtm to join, 616/21; ''*w* [pl.], 578/19; (616/13-14).

tblt to serve; ''*n* [inf.], 643/11.

tbql plantation. ''*t* [pl.], 821 A/3; ''*hmw*, 650/14.

tbšr to announce; predict, 643/16; 735/17; ''*hmw*, (647/17-18); ''*n* [inf.], 627/9; 628/10; 633/13; 735/3; *k*'', 588/4-5. to beg; ''*hw*, 627/4; 758/6-7,12;

''*w* [pl.], 618/6; 653/7; ''*n* [inf.], 614/9,13; 616/9,33; 735/10,19; 739/7,17.
tbšrt announcement, 627/4,7; (647/10); 758/6; *b*'', (618/5); *tbšr* [pl.], 610/13; 614/8-9,12; 616/8-9,33; 716/5; 735/18; 758/12.
tgbʾ to give; ''*w* [pl.], 643/13-14.
tgn to collect the garden products, 570/3.
tgʿr to keep under guard; band together, 577/13; 665/14.
tḏll to submit; ''*n* [inf.], 644/8.
tḏr blown, 720/5.
thqnyn offering; ''*hw*, 717/7.
thrg to effect carnage; ''*w* [pl.], 649/32.
twrd to come together; ''*w* [pl.], 665/18.
twśʿ to defeat, 646/7; ''*w* [pl.], 649/30; ''*n* [inf.], 649/29.
twṯb to inflict upon; ''*hw*, 725/8.
tḥbn violence, 578/11.
tḥt under, 578/22,29.
tḥty substructure, 846/3.
tẖdʿ to be without any utility; be lost; *k*''*nn*, 649/21.
tkwn to bring up; make, 633/12,15.
tld birth, 721/8.
tlw to take care of; *ḏy*''*nhw*, 851/6.
tly equerry, 584/1. *ʾtlwt* [pl.], 745/2.
tlf to perish, 700/14.
tlft ruin, 567/27; 636/18; (739/18).
tmhrt trained corps; ''*hw*, 665/12-13.
tmlʾ mass, 550/1; 551; 554; 555/1; 556; 557.
tmly to enjoy; *ḏ*'', 635/3-4; ''*w* [pl.], 576/5.
tmnʿ system of fortifications; ''*hmw*, 643/23.
tnbʾ to promise; ''*hw*, 550/2; 551; 555/3; 558/5.
tnbl messenger. ''*t* [pl.], 574/10; *b*'', 577/6.
tnḏh to graze; pasture, 600/8.
tnʿ Tanaʿite; ʾ'' [pl.], 712/3.
tnʿm to be pleasant; ''*n* [inf.], 562/14; 563/16; 564/26; 567/25; 577/19; (598/3-4); 606/16-17; 607/16; 626/17; 630/15; 719/11; 753 I/6,II/11,III/11; 761/3.
tnṣf to subdue; ''*n* [inf.], 578/40. to preserve; maintain; ''*n* [inf.], 564/11-12; 651/16.
tnḍʿ to implore; ''*hw*, 816/5; *ḏ*'', 657/4,6-7.
tnšʾ to rise up; raise up, 577/17; ''*n* [inf.], 589/11. ''*w* [pl.], 576/1; 635/11; 644/4,11; *ḏ*'', 577/16.
tsbṭ to have an affray, 669/19.
tsn to decree, 720/11.
tsʿ (A) nine, 577/14; ''*t* [fem.], (576/1 ?).
tsʿ (B) ninth, 651/18; 735/5.
tsʿy ninety, 577/15.
tʿṣr to wrestle; ''*w* [pl.], 700/13.
tʿrb to give pledges of submission; ''*n* [inf.], 735/9; [*maṣdar*], 578/22.
tġl to become abundant. *y*'' [imperf.]; ''*n*, 618/18-19.
tfl to turn to [+*bʿm*], 633/9-10.
tflw to go away; separate, 576/6; 628/4-5. to turn to [+*bʿm*], 718/8.
tfqd to seek; search in vain [passive], 665/48-49.
tfrq to drive out; separate. ''*w* [pl.], 660/13; *ḏ*'', 644/22.
tṣnʿ to strengthen; retrench; ''*w* [pl.], 577/2; 644/22-23; ''*n* [inf.], 644/6.
tṣry to ask for advice; ''*w* [pl.], 877/7. to supply with a guard; *l*''*n* [inf.], 577/9,10.
tḍʿ to implore; ''*n* [inf.], 567/19; 590/19; 608/7,12; 609/7, 12. to humiliate; ''*n* [inf.], 581/8.
tḍrʿ to submit; [*maṣdar*], 574/10-11; 577/12; ''*n* [inf. passive], 578/28.
tqdm attack, 590/12; 643 bis/5,6. ''*t* [pl.], 581/6,11; 586/8,13; 631/5; *l*'', 643/33-34. to move forward; +*bʿm*, to attack; assault; *l*'', [inf.], 649/29. *tqdmn* [inf.], 575/5; 576/9; 578/19; 581/7; 586/8,14; 644/15, 21; 649/30; *l*'', 577/2. *tqdmw* [pl.], 578/7; 586/20; 590/10; 629/10,19; 631/5; 643 bis/1; 644/18. *ytqdm* [imperf.]; ''*w* [pl.], 576/5; 577/5; 586/16.
tqnʿ to please; give satisfaction; ''*hw*, 562/7; ''*w* [pl.], 564/4.
trbʿ to arrogate for oneself; *ḏ*'', 586/23.
tšyn disease; ''*t* [pl.], 578/34; 620/5.
tškr to defeat; ''*w* [pl.], 644/10; [passive], 585/15.
tśbb to turn aside; *b*''*n* [inf.], 631/33-34. *y*'' [imperf.]; ''*nn*, 631/32.
]*tt* [noun]; ''*hw*, 721/8.
ttʿt fear, 567/28; 578/41; 581/18; [598/5]; 614/18-19; 615/27; 616/39; 617/14; 623/23; 635/45; 650/33-34; 651/52; 654/15; 661/9; 664/18; 703/11; 719/12.

ṯ

ṯʾr (A) reprisal; ʾ'' [pl.], (725/7-8).
ṯʾr (B) to take vengeance on; ''*hw*, 725/8.
ṯbr (A) loss; ruin, 643 bis/4.
ṯbr (B) to crush; ruin, 561 bis/23; 564/24; 568/20; 574/13; 576/14; 577/5,18; 578/6; 586/(6),18; 589/9; 629/14; 631/4; 635/14; (766/7); 853 A/5,B/5,C/5,D/4,E/5, F/5; *b*'', 578/17; *l*'', 577/19; 610/16; 611/19-20; 631/38. [passive], 671/12,13; ''*t* [fem.], 671/11. *ṯbrw* [pl.], 576/4. *ṯbry* [dual]; *bḏ*'', 581/8. *yṯbr* [imperf.]; ''*w* [pl.], 601/9; 602/9.
ṯhb to return; ''*hmw*, 576/14; 643/8. to satisfy; ''*w* [pl.], 631/14; ''*hmw*, 577/9; 616/18,20.
ṯwb [2nd form] to bestow upon; grant; ''*n* [inf.], 703/4; cf. also the 4th form *hṯb*.
ṯwr bull, 580/4; 621/3; 632/3; 695/5; 713/6; 723/3; 750/3; ''*n* [dual], 669/14,24; *ʾṯwr* [pl.], 581/4; 665/26.
ṯlʿ [verb], cf. the 4th form *hṯlʿ*.
ṯlṯ (A) three, 572/4; 616/21-22; 643/12; 649/39; 735/6; ''*t* [fem.], 567/4,9; 581/4; 657/3; 665/23,30; 671/24; 851/2.
ṯlṯ (B) third, 611/9; 615/14; 653/7; 877/9; *b*'', 577/12; *l*'', 631/28,31; cf. also the clan name *smʿy*.
ṯlṯy thirty, 665/17,38,41-42.
ṯmn eight, 577/14; 665/34; ''*t* [fem.], 558/2.
ṯmny eighth, 570/3.
ṯmr fruit. ʾ'' [pl.], 561 bis/20; 562/12; 563/12; 564/20; 565/14; 567/23; 571/4; 581/17; 587/10; 591/9; 599/8; 601/16; 602/16; 613/20; 615/19; 616/37-38; (618/22-23); 620/11; 627/21; 628/22; 630/17; 645/23; 650/15; 654/13; 657/10-11; 658/33; 661/8; 664/15; 666/15; 670/25; 691/9; 692/10-11; 703/6; 704/6; 730/6; 733/11; 736/15; 738/9-10; 747/15; 799/6; ''*hmw*, 656/24.
ṯny (A) two, 570/7; 577/8,9,14; 585/7; 610/4; 612/12;

631/2; 643 bis/2; 649/35-36; 669/14; 700/3; 713/7; 716/4; 743/3; *b*'', (586/24); 618/7; *ṯty* [fem.], 635/26; 665/39.
ṯny (B) second, 610/7; 631/34; 651/19; *ṯnt* [fem.], 576/11.
ṯny (C) incisor teeth; ''*hw*, 702/14. *ṯn*; ''*hw*, 702/12-13.
*ṯ*ᶜ*d* canalization, 682/2.
ṯqf [verb], cf. the 10th form *sṯṯqf*.
ṯr bull; ''*nhn* [dual], 567/8; 696/3; 697/3.
ṯty, cf. *ṯny*.

Appendix: Glossary of Qat Ja 878

(*Preliminary note:* The numbers refer to the lines of the text)

ʾ*ḏn* understanding; ''*s*, 6.
ʾ*l* god; ''*s*, 2.
b with, cf. ᶜ*m*.
bn (A) son; ''*s*, (6).
bn (B) from, (7).
bnw descendants, (1).
*b*ᶜ*l* master, 2.
brṯ place; ''*s*, [7].
gmlm Gamlum, 1.
ḏ [masc. sing. rel. pron.], cf. *ḥṣbḥ*, *ẓrm*, *rydn*.
*ḏmr*ᶜ*ly* Ḏamarᶜalay; ''/*ḏrḥ*/*mlk*/*sb*ʾ/*wḏrydn*, 5.
ḏrḥ Ḏariḥ, cf. *ḏmr*ᶜ*ly*.
ḏt [fem. sing. demonstr. pron.], cf. *l*.
hwfy to bestow upon, 3.
hmw [masc. pl. pers. pron.], cf. *mr*ʾ.
ḥṣbḥ Haṣbaḥ; *ḏ*'', (1).
wfy [verb], cf. the 4th form *hwfy*.
ḥg according to, 3.
ḫrf Ḫarf, 1.
ẓrm Ẓarum; *ḏ*'', cf. ᶜ*m*.
yḥl[Yuḥal[, 4-5.
kl all, 4.
krb [verb], cf. the 5th form *tkrb*.
l [conj.]; ''*ḏt*, 3.
mlk king, cf. *ḏmr*ᶜ*ly*.
msnkr he who displaces, (7).
*msf*ʾ*y* he who removes, 7.
mqm power; ''*s*, 6.
*mr*ʾ lord; ''*hmw*, 4; ''*s*, 2.
s [sing. masc. pers. pron.]; cf. ʾ*ḏn*, ʾ*l*, *bn*, *brṯ*, *mqm*, *mr*ʾ, *tkrq*.
*sb*ʾ (A) Sabaʾ; cf. *ḏmr*ᶜ*ly*.
*sb*ʾ (B) to fight, 4.
*sb*ʾ*t* fighting, 4.
sqny to dedicate, (2).
ᶜ*m* (A) ᶜAmm, 3; ''/*ḏẓrm*, 2.
ᶜ*m* (B) [prep.]; *b*'' with, 4.
ḍrn Ḍarân, 1, (3-4),4,6.
qny [verb], cf. the 4th form *sqny*.
rydn Raydân; *ḏ*''; cf. *ḏmr*ᶜ*ly*.
rṯd to entrust to the care of, (6).
*šb*ᶜ*n* Šabᶜân, 3.
šy[Šay[, 2.
tkrb to attribute to; ''*s*, 3.

INDEX OF AUTHORS

Preliminary note. 1. The signs "(i)" and "n." mean "(introduction)" and "note(s)" respectively. 2. Most of the entries are followed by two series of references: "Ja" introduces the number of the text(s) published in the first part of the volume and is followed by "(i)" or a figure which refers to the commentary on the line (s) of the inscription; "p." or "pp." refers to the page(s) of the volume.

Abel, Ja 552/1.
Albright, F. P., Ja 681 (i); 682 (i); 759 (i); 823 (i); 824 (i); 825 (i); 838 (i); pp. 3 and n. 1; 275, n. 20; 305, n. 120.
Albright, W. F., pp. 343, n. 197; 359.
AlCAS, Ja 578/22; pp. 262, n. 7; 293, n. 48; 305, n. 120; 343, n. 197.
AlEMY, Ja 550 (i); 557; 682 (i); 748 (i); 761 (i); 824 (i); 825 (i); 831 (i); 832 (i); pp. 3, n. 1; 255 and n. 1, 2; 256; 259, n. 3.
AlETM, Ja 831 (i); 832 (i).
Ansaldi, C., pp. 275, n. 19; 349: 380.
Aramco Handbook, Ja 559 (i).
Arnaud, J., p. 367.
The Assyrian Dictionary, Ja 570/4.

Beeston, A. F. L., Ja 550/1; 558/7; 560/7, 13; 567/5–6, 11; 570/2; 574/9; 576/13–14; 577/7; 578/22; 584/1; 646/7; 682/2; 711/1; 735/2; pp. 4; 295, n. 65; 339, n. 173; 359; 373, n. 122, 124.
BeAIP, Ja 552/2, 3; 559/19; p. 384, n. 25.
BeBAG, Ja 558/4; 560/6; 567/22–23; 576/14; 578/6; 644/4.
BeESACD, Ja 585/7; 594/10; 615/18–19; pp. 326, n. 128; 354, n. 9–11; 359, n. 35, 36, 42, 45, 46, 50, 51; 360 and n. 52.
BeFSTI, Ja 550/1; 558/4, 6; 564/9, 12–13; 567/10; 570/7; 575/5; 576/8; 577/6, 10; 594/5; 644/4–5; 665/25; 683/3, pp. 268, n. 1; 308, n. 1; 328 and n. 141–143.
BeNL II, Ja 669/20–21.—III, Ja 703/12.—IV, Ja 562/8; 567/5–6, 11; 647/29; 660/14; 700/12; p. 355, n. 20.—V, Ja 559/9; 562/8; p. 314, n. 41.—VI, Ja 567/6, 8; 577/6; 585/7–8; pp. 281, n. 21; 363, n. 70. —VII, Ja 610/13.
BeOSA, Ja 563/19–20; 578/1; 735/13.
BePC, Ja 552/1; 584/4; 711/1; 734/4; 832.
BePESA, Ja 550/2; 555/4; 558/4; 561 bis/6; 570/7; 576/1, 15; 577/15; 585/14; 588/4–5; 669/6; 670/11, 26–27; p. 291.
BePSC, pp. 277 and n. 3, 4; 278; 290, n. 31; 305; 308, n. 1; 311, n. 25; 327, n. 135; 344, n. 2; 354, n. 15; 356; 359, n. 35–38, 45; 361 and n. 59; 362; 392, n. 3.
BeSI, Ja 550/1, 2; 551; 555/4; 558/3, 4; 559/1; 560/7, 8–9, 11, 18; 562/13–14, 14; 563/7–8; 564/7, 9, 11–12, 12, 13, 20, 22, 23–24; 567/8, 19–20, 27; 570/2, 3, 4, 7; 571/7–8; 574/5, 9, 13; 576/1, 3, 5, 6, 7, 12, 13, 16; 577/1, 6, 8, 9, 10, 12, 13, 14, 15; 578/8, 22; 584/1, 7; 585/8, 15; 594/10; 610/13; 615/3–4, 9–10, 18–19; 619/9; 624/5; 628/7; 629/17; 631/27; 633/14; 643/9; 645/13–14; 649/19; 653/9; 658/12, 32; 660/11; 665/33; 669/6; 676/1–2; 682/2; 708/5; 720/11–13; 721/4; 821 A/3; 831/2; 842/3; 846/2, 3; pp. 282, n. 24; 291; 355, n. 20.
BeTMS, Ja 558/2, 4; 559/4; 560/18; 561 bis/20, 22; 563/11; 578/34; 590/4; 591/1; 618 (i); 626/2.
Biberstein-Kasimirski, Ja 643/15.
BiSSS I, Ja 577/15.—IV, Ja 562/17; 564/20; 570/4, 6; 577/15.
Boneschi, P., Ja 550/1; 557.
BoAGI, p. 268 and n. 5.
Bowen, R. LeBaron, Jr., p. 318, n. 73.
BoAlADSA, pp. 3, n. 1; 273, n. 17; 275, n. 20; 318, n. 73; 389, n. 2.
van den Branden, A., Ja 550/2; 560/10.
vdBrDSAMW, Ja 630/9; 664/20; p. 280, n. 10.
vdBrHT, Ja 550/2; 560/10; 664/20.
vdBrIT, Ja 550/1; 560/2; 564/31; 566/3–4; 569/3–4; 570/1; 574/7; 576/2, 12; 577/6; 597/1; 601/2; 616/25, 26, 27; 621/1; 631/9; 632/1; 633/2; 649/2; 655/10; 656/3; 657/1; 658/2, 12; 660/11–12, 13; 661/5; 665/32; 681/1; 685/5; 686/1; 692/1; 702/6–7; 721/8; 722/3; 723/1; 734/4; 750/1, 1–2; 816/3.
vdBrTTPN, Ja 570/1; 577/1, 6, 12; 614/1; 616/18, 27; 660/11–12; 661/2; 665/32; 681/1; 692/1; 701 B; 724; 758/1; 837.
vdBrTTPS, Ja 616/18, 24; 646/1; 650/2; 656/2, 4–5; 657/1; 658/12; 660/12; 665/32; 692/1; 693/3; 701 B.
BrBeSIS, Ja 558/7; 567/5–6, 11.
BrDSL, Ja 555/4; 577/9.

Caquot, A. p. 3, n. 3.
Caskel, W., Ja 550/2; 574/7–8; p. 318.
CIH I, Ja 550/1; 557; 559/1, 10, 12, 19; 560/10; 561 bis/1–4; 563/7–8; 564/13, 20, 22; 572/1; 574/5, 9; 576/1, 7; 577/6; 584/7; 610/8; 615/18–19; 617/9; 633/14; 649/19; 738/1–2; 831/2; 878/2; pp. 285; 286, n. 5; 288 and n. 13, 14, 16; 289; 290, n. 33; 291, n. 34, 35; 295, n. 62; 297; 298 and n. 80; 309, n. 7; 310, n. 14, 17, 18; 311 and n. 23; 312; 313 and n. 34; 331 and n. 151; 346; 349; 351; 353 and n. 6; 354 and n. 7, 8; 358, n. 32; 362, n. 61, 63; 363 and n. 66, 67; 365; 366; 367, n. 80, 81; 379; 381 and n. 4, 5; 382, n. 9.—II, Ja 550 (i),/1, 2; 555/4; 558/2; 564/23–24; 567/28; 571/7–8; 576/8; 577/8, 9, 14; 578/12; 615/3–4; 631/27, 36; 633/14; 635/10; 651/32; 656/16; 660/11; 722/1; 752/9–10; 755/4; 846/2; pp. 269, n. 10; 271; 276, n. 26; 283 and n. 25, 28; 291 and n. 42; 292, n. 43; 326; 327; 344, n. 3; 352; 355, n. 20; 360, n. 56; 371 and n. 112; 379; 383, n. 14.—III, Ja 550 (i); 555/2; 559/1; 564/7, 20; 567/8–9; 571/7–8; 576/8; 577/7; 584/1; 631/27; 634/1–2; 649/19; 661/5; 671/5; 701 B; 846/2; pp. 290; 295, n. 63; 310, n. 14; 311, n. 23; 330; 346, n. 13; 347 and n. 15; 353 and n. 5; 354; 358, n. 32; 362, n. 62; 367 and n. 82; 373 and n. 123; 379.
Clark, H., p. 341, n. 186.
CIS, Ja 552/1; 656/2.
Cohen, M., Ja 567/27.
CoRoC, Ja 550/1, 2; 554; 555/3, 4; 557; 558/2, 4, 5; 559/1, 19; 560/3, 6, 7, 8, 8–9, 18; 561 bis/6, 8, 9, 15–16, 20, 20–21, 23–24; 562/7, 13–14, 17; 563/7–8; 564/9, 11–12, 13, 20, 21, 22, 23–24; 567/8; 568/6; 570/7, 13; 571/7–8; 572/4, 7; 574/8–9, 9, 10, 10–11; 575/2, 3, 4, 6; 576/3, 4, 6, 7, 8, 11, 12, 13, 15, 16; 577/2, 7, 8, 10, 12, 14; 578/6, 8, 12, 22, 39; 584/7; 588/4–5; 601/9; 610/8; 614/18; 615/4, 18–19; 616/22, 30; 619/8, 9; 624/5; 627/10, 12; 628/8; 629/7, 33; 631/6, 16, 27; 633/14; 635/4–5, 33, 36; 643/9, 13–14, 15, 20, 32; 643 bis/3; 644/4, 20; 649/19, 32–33, 40–41, 41; 651/18, 26; 658/12; 665/33; 669/6, 20–21, 22; 670/26–27; 671/16, 24; 672/1–2;

INDEX OF TEXTS

Preliminary notes, cf. the index of authors

RÉS 3902, No. 112, Ja 616/24–25; 715/1.
—— 3902, No. 119 (=RÉS 4637), Ja 564/20.
—— 3902, No. 137, Ja 567/5–6.
—— 3902, No. 165, Ja 616/25.
—— 3902, No. 166, Ja 564/30.
—— 3902, No. 177, Ja 649/10.
—— 3902 bis, No. 130, Ja 554.
—— 3902 bis, No. 131, Ja 552/2; 567/1.
—— 3902 bis, No. 138, Ja 558/3.
—— 3903, p. 268, n. 1.
—— 3908, Ja 552/1; 558/2; 567/2.
—— 3910, Ja 550/1; 567/17; 615/9–10; 649/21; 728/1–2; pp. 351; 352; 363 and n. 69; 364; 367–369.
—— 3911, Ja 555/3; 631/1.
—— 3912, Ja 687/8; p. 266, n. 15.
—— 3913, Ja 550/1.
—— 3915, Ja 629/33; 701 A/7.
—— 3921, Ja 616/18.
—— 3924, Ja 731/1.
—— 3929, Ja 567/5–6, 6; 570/15; 618/1; 619/2; pp. 308; 313; 314.
—— 3932, Ja 552/3.
—— 3943, Ja 550/1; 555/4; 616/24–25; 643/7; 643 bis/3; 671/11; 678/2; 832; pp. 348, n. 20; 385.
—— 3945, Ja 550/1; 551; 555/3, 4; 560/3, 4–5, 14; 561 bis/15–16; 567/27; 570/2; 572/4; 574/3; 575/6; 576/4, 5, 5–6; 585/1; 612/1; 615/1–3; 629/29, 31; 643/5; 709/1; 734/4; 745/1; 831/1; p. 317, n. 57.
—— 3946, Ja 557; 558/4; 559/10; 617/6; 629/47; 708/3–4.
—— 3948, Ja 559/19.
—— 3950, Ja 559/19.
—— 3951, Ja 556; 560/8; 575/3; 576/2; 615/9–10; 616/17, 18; 629/17, 38–39; 635/37; p. 272.
—— 3954, Ja 556; 671/12; 846/1–2, 2, 2–3.
—— 3956, Ja 560/2, 18; 735/9.
—— 3957, Ja 613/1.
—— 3958, Ja 559/18; 561 bis/20–21; 577/2; 618/35; pp. 305, n. 122; 324, n. 120; 358; 359 and n. 51; 360 and n. 52; 373.
—— 3959, Ja 559/18; 878/3; p. 335; 344; 345; 347.
—— 3960 (=Vienna 1148), Ja 633/13; 655/9–10; p. 377–381; 384.
—— 3963, Ja 800.
—— 3964, Ja 665/36; 666/1.
—— 3965, Ja 564/31.
—— 3966 (=SE 45), Ja 550/1; 558/3; 559/14; 574/9; 576/7; 584/1; 585/14; 652/2; p. 272.
—— 3968, pp. 308; 331–334.
—— 3972, Ja 558/4; 711/1.
—— 3975, Ja 620/1.
—— 3977, Ja 562/1.
—— 3990, Ja 559/1, 15; 561 bis/4; 562/14; 577/13; pp. 308; 312; 328; 329.
—— 3991, Ja 564/22; 578/34; 583/1; 615/3–4.
—— 3992, Ja 560/5–6; 577/6; 585/7–8; 610/13; pp. 277; 281; 327; 363, n. 70.
—— 3993 (cf. Ja 421), Ja 562/14.
—— 3994, p. 268, n. 1.
—— 3996, Ja 585/1; 667 A/1.
—— 3998, Ja 683/1.
—— 4001, Ja 695/1.
—— 4006, Ja 651/32–33.
—— 4010, Ja 564/10.
—— 4011, Ja 664/18.
—— 4013, Ja 562/13–14; 564/20.
—— 4016, Ja 562/1.
—— 4017, Ja 764/5; 786/4.
—— 4018, Ja 656/3.
—— 4020, Ja 737/1.
—— 4022, Ja 561 bis/4; p. 335.
—— 4031, Ja 665/1.
—— 4033, Ja 591/1; 711/1; 725/1–2.
—— 4038 (136), Ja 563/1.
—— 4043, Ja 570/15.
—— 4050, Ja 560/6.
—— 4052, Ja 567/5–6.
—— 4053, Ja 575/3.
—— 4057, Ja 658/2.
—— 4069, Ja 555/3; 572/1; 576/11; 692/8–9; 821 A/3.
—— 4080, No. 93, Ja 579/1.
—— 4084, Ja 569/2–3; 576/16; 620/2–3; 764/5; 786/4.
—— 4085, Ja 617/6; 772/4; 821 A/3.
—— 4090, Ja 620/6.
—— 4091, Ja 564/32.
—— 4094, Ja 616/25.
—— 4096, Ja 555/3.
—— 4100, Ja 758/8–9; p. 324, n. 120.
—— 4103, Ja 584/4.
—— 4106, p. 387.
—— 4107, Ja 577/6.
—— 4118, Ja 601/1.
—— 4123, Ja 665/43.
—— 4126, Ja 555/2.
—— 4127, Ja 559/1; 560/2.
—— 4128, Ja 562/1.
—— 4130. Ja 615/9–10; pp. 277; 280.
—— 4131, Ja 564/9.
—— 4132, Ja 605/1; pp. 344–346.
—— 4133, Ja 610/6–7; 715/1.
—— 4134, Ja 560/12; 574/11; 576/2; 577/11; 626/1; 721/2; pp. 308; 313.
—— 4135, Ja 567/3.
—— 4136, pp. 308; 312.
—— 4137, Ja 561 bis/6; 574/9; 578/37–38; p. 266, n. 15.
—— 4138, Ja 558/3; 565/6–7; 575/5; 645/13–14; 654/2; pp. 319, n. 74; 349.
—— 4139, Ja 558/7; 567/28; 571/7–8; 581/18; pp. 308; 309; 313; 314.
—— 4142, Ja 585/9.
—— 4143, Ja 633/1.
—— 4145, Ja 660/11; 716/6–7.
—— 4148, Ja 558/2, 3.
—— 4149, Ja 550/2; pp. 284; 300.
—— 4150, Ja 558/3; 560/5–6; 567/19; 670/2; pp. 308; 312; 328.
—— 4151, Ja 603/2; 634/1; 721/4.
—— 4152, p. 284; 300.
—— 4153, Ja 727/3.
—— 4155, pp. 284; 300.
—— 4158, Ja 660/11.
—— 4169, Ja 878/1, 3; pp. 346; 347.
—— 4176 (cf. RÉS 3300), Ja 550/2; 559/1; 560/11; 576/3, 7; 578/8; 618/18–19; 651/17; 816/6; 821 A/3; p. 384, n. 23.
—— 4186, Ja 711/1.
—— 4186 B, Ja 558/2.
—— 4187, Ja 563/7–8.
—— 4188, Ja 590/4; 878/3; p. 347.
—— 4189, Ja 577/13.
—— 4190 (=SE 8), Ja 550/2; 559/1; 561 bis/23–24; 577/13; 671/24; pp. 284; 286; 287 and n. 9; 335.
—— 4191, Ja 556; 572/4; pp. 308; 334–336; 337 and n. 162.
—— 4193, Ja 555/4; 567/8; 576/16; 577/6, 13, 14; 601/5; 644/22.
—— 4194, Ja 560/6; 570/8; 618/8; 630/9.
—— 4196, Ja 576/4, 12; 603/5; pp. 318; 351–353; 355; 357–359; 360 and n. 52; 364.
—— 4197, Ja 563/16.
—— 4197 bis, pp. 359; 360 and n. 52.
—— 4198, Ja 594/4; 671/11; pp. 314; 355.
—— 4198 bis, Ja 712/1.
—— 4200, Ja 687/1.
—— 4202, Ja 640/4–5.
—— 4205, Ja 560/1.
—— 4210, Ja 580/10.
—— 4214, Ja 632/1.
—— 4215, Ja 572/7; pp. 308; 312.
—— 4216, Ja 563/7–8; pp. 284; 290; 292; 293; 328, n. 139.
—— 4217, Ja 567/19.
—— 4219, Ja 702/1–2.
—— 4226, Ja 555/2; 567/1.
—— 4227, Ja 682/1.
—— 4229, Ja 555/2; 613/1; 689/1; p. 298.
—— 4230, Ja 558/7; 567/27; 577/10; 594/10; 610/8; 635/35; 651/7; 750/11; pp. 351; 352; 367–369.
—— 4231, Ja 682/2.
—— 4233, Ja 559/10–11; 576/11; 655/9–10; 723/4; pp. 308; 334–337.
—— 4243, Ja 591/1.
—— 4248, Ja 635/22.
—— 4257 B, Ja 673/1.
—— 4264, Ja 734/4.
—— 4267, Ja 627/8.
—— 4272, Ja 567/27.
—— 4273, Ja 700/8.
—— 4304, Ja 635/26–27.
—— 4324, Ja 578/10; 646/7; 705/4.
—— 4325, Ja 669/14–15.
—— 4326, Ja 703/12.
—— 4329, Ja 695/3.
—— 4330, p. 343, n. 201.
—— 4332, Ja 550/2.
—— 4334, Ja 568/1–2.
—— 4336 (=SE 101), Ja 558/4; 559/9; 576/10; 577/14; pp. 266; 296; 308; 324; 325 and n. 121, 122.

INDEX OF PROPER NAMES

Preliminary notes. 1—See the index of authors. 2—Several names of clans, cities and countries are followed by plural gentilic nouns; some of those nouns are also listed separately when the proper name itself is not mentioned. 3—The names of Sab rulers are followed by one or two of the following signs: *M, KS, KR, KY, KT*, which mean respectively *Mukarrib*, King of Sabaʾ, King of Sabaʾ and Raydân, King of Sabaʾ, Raydân, Ḥaḍramawt and Yamnat, and King of Sabaʾ, Raydân, Ḥaḍramawt, Yamnat, their Arabs on the plateau, and Tihâmat. 4—The kings of Ḥaḍramawt and Qatabân are indicated as such. 5—Individuals belonging to some Sab royal family are listed as such by the addition of "from" followed by the appropriate sign; e.g. "(from *KS*)" means "from the family of a King of Sabaʾ)".

ʾ[. . . *M*, p. 259.
ʾAbʾamar ʾAṣdiq, p. 326.
ʾAbʾanas, pp. 324; 325.
ʿAbdʿaṯtar, p. 312.
ʿAbdulraḥmân, p. 3.
ʾAbfanad, p. 314.
Abha, p. 323, n. 107.
ʾAbkarib, pp. 260; 307; 336; 337.
ʾAbkarib ʾAḥras, pp. 303; 304.
ʾAbkarib ʾAsʿad, pp. 338; 339 and n. 175; 340.
ʾAbkarib ʾAsʿad *KT*, pp. 387; 388; 394.
ʾAbkarib ʾAsʿad (also Abî-kariba Asʿad), *KY*, pp. 386; 387; 393.
ʾAbraha *KT*, p. 363 ,n. 68.
ʿAbrân, p. 375.
ʾAbrataʿ, p. 324.
ʾAbšibâm, Ja 552/4.
ʾAbwân, p. 317.
ʾAbyadaʿ, Ja 557.
Abyssinia (also Abyssinie; Ethiopia), pp. 294; 303.
ʾAbzar, Ja 552/1.
ʿAḏbah, pp. 319; 320; 322.
aḍ-Ḍâlaʿ, p. 321.
ʿAden, Ja 564/27; 576/4; pp. 289, n. 19; 302; 303; 311; 316, n. 45; 318 and n. 73; 319, n. 78; 320–322; 324.
al-ʿÂdîya, p. 298.
al-ʾAʿḍûd, p. 321.
Aelius Gallus, pp. 327 and n. 135; 389; 391.
al-ʿAǧlânîyat, p. 298.
ʾAǧwaṯum, Ja 560/1.
ʾAẖar, p. 316.
ʾAḥdal Ḏîbân, Ja 616/24.
ʾAḥdaqân, p. 322 and n. 105.
ʾAhǧûr, Ja 601/2.
al-ʿAin, p. 316.
ʿAina, Ja 575/6.
ʿAkkum, pp. 316; 340; 370.—ʿAkkites, p. 316.
ʾAksûman, pp. 302; 303; 316; 320; 322.—ʾAksûmites, p. 316.
ʾAkwat, p. 304.
ʿAlam, p. 382.
ʾAlayhân, Ja 552/4.
AlbM I, p. 345.
ʿAlhân, pp. 281; 284–286; 289.
ʿAlhân = ʿAlhân Nahfân *KS, KR*, pp. 273; 275; 278; 284; 285; 288 and n. 12; 289 and n. 24; 290–297; 304; 305; 307; 310; 325, n. 122; 343; 390.
ʾAlw, Ja 615/4–5.
American Foundation for the Study of Man, Ja 578/22; pp. 3, 4.
American Philosophical Society, Ja 550/1.
ʿAmm, pp. 317; 322; 346.
ʿAmmʾamin, Ja 555/4, n. 1.
ʿAmmʾanas, p. 325, n. 123.
ʿAmmḏaẖar (from Ḥaḏr King), pp. 305; 384; 392.
ʿAmr, p. 387.
ʿAmrân, pp. 289 and n. 21; 299; 316; 320, n. 85; 369.
ʿAmšarr, Ja 552/1.
ʾAnbay, p. 325, n. 124.
ʾAnmarum, pp. 282; 283; 285.
ʾAnmarum Yuhaʾmin *KS*, pp. 279–283; 286; 289; 327; 390.
an-Nemârah, pp. 358–361; 389.
ʾAnwadum, p. 384.
ʾAnwiyân, p. 313.
Aqaba, p. 321.
ʿAqbumites, p. 369.
ʾAqyânum (cf. Leader of ʾAqyânum), also p. 316.
Arabia, p. 327.—Arabs, Ja 577/14; pp. 280; 281; 286; 304; 316; 324, n. 118; 385.
ʾArbaʿum, Ja 556.
ʾArak, p. 375.
ʿArieb, Ja 578/26; p. 318, n. 65.
ʿArmân, pp. 293; 294.
ʾArnab, Ja 560/1–2.
ʿArṣum, p. 321.
al-ʿArûš, p. 317.
ʿArwaštân, p. 317.
ʾAsadum ʾAsʿad, pp. 301; 302.
ʾAsʾar, p. 385.
ʾAšʿarân, pp. 303; 304.
ʾAsʾay, p. 317.
ʾAslab, Ja 552/1.
ʾAšš, Ja 552/1.
ʾAšʿûb, p. 294.
ʿAt . . ., p. 353.
ʿAṯay, p. 320.
ʿAṯkalân ʿUsayyat, p. 336.
ʿAṯtar, Ja 550/2; 552/3; 559/18; 564/30; 567/6–7; 576/5; 631/26; 658/15; 742/7–8; pp. 269–271; 279; 280; 290; 295; 314; 326; 328; 371; 372; 382; 383.—ʿAṯtar Baḥr Ḥaṭab, p. 326.—ʿAṯtar Šarqân (also Šariqân), Ja 557; 558/7; pp. 289, n. 24; 369.
Αὔσαρα p. 304.
ʾAwsalat = ʾAwsalat Rafšân, pp. 278 and n. 8; 280; 284–287.
ʾAwsân, pp. 301; 302; 342.
ʾAwsum, p. 337.
ʾAwṭum, Ja 565/1–3.
ʾAwwâm, Ja 550/1; pp. 3; 259; 337; 338.
ʿAyal Saʿîd, p. 317.
ʾAʿyân, pp. 278; 287.
ʾAyḏam (also ʾAyḏamum), Ja 576/7.
ʾAyḏamum, p. 320.
ʿAylal, Ja 585/1.
ʾA[y]nawumites, p. 269.
ʿAynum, p. 316.
ʾAẓwar, pp. 317; 319.
ʿAzzân, p. 387.

Bâb el-Mandeb, p. 303.
Baḏlat, Ja 563/1.
Baẖal (also Baẖâl), p. 324.
Baẖawlum, pp. 324; 325 and n. 121.
Bahîl, pp. 372; 375.
Bahilum, pp. 374; 375.
Bahr as-Safi, p. 304, n. 119.
Baḥrum, pp. 303; 304.
al-Baiḍâ, Ja 555/3; pp. 337; 345; 348.
Bakîlum, pp. 301; 302; 308; 313; 316; 317; 319; 338.—Bakîlites: p. 347.
Balaḥ, Ja 842/3.
Banû Baddâ, p. 342.
Banû beit Qudam, p. 289, n. 21.
Banû Ḥakam, p. 323, n. 108.
Banû Jebr, p. 337.
Banû Maǧîd, p. 348, n. 20.
Banû Merǧamir, p. 317.
Banû Qâsid, Ja 567/8.
Banû Šaddâd, p. 321 and n. 95.
Banû Šuʿayb, p. 319, n. 78.
Banû Šubrumat, p. 318.
Banû Ẓubyân, p. 317 and n. 54.
al-Bâr, p. 340 and n. 182.
Baraʾân, p. 292.
Bararân, Ja 575/5.
Barig, p. 367.
Barig Yaḥmad, p. 277.
Barig Yuharḥib, pp. 278; 281; 284–286.
Bašamum, p. 324.

FIELD STAFF

American Foundation Arabian Expeditions

I & II (BEIḤÂN)
III (YEMEN)
IV (DHOFÂR)

Wendell Phillips	Leader I-II-III-IV
Prof. W. F. Albright	Chief Archaeologist I-II
Dr. Frank P. Albright	Chief Archaeologist III-IV
William B. Terry	Field Director—Director of Photography I
Gladys Terry	Business Manager I
Eileen Salama	Arabist—Secretary II-III-IV
Charles McCollum	Chief of Motor Transport I Field Director II Administrative Director III-IV
George Farrier	Motor Transport Specialist I Administrative Assistant II-III Field Director IV
Robert Carmean	Motor Transport Specialist II Field Director III
Richard Bussey	Business Manager III-IV
Dr. Albert Jamme	Epigrapher I-II-III-IV
Prof. Alexander Honeyman	Archaeologist-Epigrapher I
Dr. Friso Heybroek	Geologist I
Dr. Richard LeB. Bowen	Engineer Archaeologist I
James Swauger	Archaeologist II
Donald Dragoo	Archaeologist II
Ellis Burcaw	Archaeologist II
Robert Shalkop	Archaeologist II
Gus Van Beek	Archaeologist II
Ralf Andrews	Archaeologist III-IV
James Rubright	Archaeologist III-IV
Kenneth Brown	Assistant Archaeologist I
John Simpson	Assistant Archaeologist II
Harry Scarff	Architect III-IV
Dr. Louis Krause	Physician I
Dr. James McNinch	Surgeon I
Dr. Vallentin de Mignard	Surgeon II
Cmdr. C. H. Gilliland	Physician III-IV
Girair Palamoudian	Surveyor-Draftsman II
Octave Romaine	Photographer I
Wallace Wade	Director of Photography II
Chester Stevens	Photographer II Director of Photography III-IV

SUBSTANTIAL CONTRIBUTORS

American Foundation for the Study of Man

GOVERNMENTAL AND ACADEMIC ORGANIZATIONS

American Geographical Society
Carnegie Museum
Leon Falk Trust
Howard Heinz Endowment
Humanities Fund, Inc.
Library of Congress
A. W. Mellon Educational & Charitable Trust
Sarah Mellon Scaife Foundation
United States Navy
Trinity Church (N. Y.)
University of Alexandria
University of California
The Johns Hopkins University
University of Louvain
University of Redlands
St. Andrews University

CORPORATIONS AND COMPANIES

American Anode Company
American Trust Company
Barber-Greene Company
Borden Company
Brush Development Company
Chrysler Corporation
California Texas Oil Co. Ltd.
Cities Service Oil Company
Coca-Cola Corporation
Colgate-Palmolive-Peet Company
Colt's Manufacturing Company
Eastman Kodak Company
Fairbanks Morse & Company
General Foods Corporation
Goodyear Tire and Rubber Company
Graflex, Inc.
Gray Manufacturing Company
Griffin & Howe, Inc.
Gulf Oil Corporation
Hallicrafters Company
H. J. Heinz Company
Geo. A. Hormel & Company
International Business Machines Corp.
International General Electric Co.
Isthmian Steamship Company
R. G. LeTourneau, Inc.
Link Radio Corporation
Lyman Gun Sight Corporation
Marine Transport Line, Inc.
Marlin Firearms Company
Olin Industries, Inc.
Pan American World Airways
Plymouth Oil Company
Remington Rand, Inc.
Richfield Oil Corporation
Royal Typewriter Company, Inc.
Associated Oil Companies in the Royal Dutch Shell Group
Socony-Vacuum Oil Company
Square D Company
E. R. Squibb & Sons
Stokely-Van Camp, Inc.
The Texas Company
United States Steel Corporation
V-M Corporation
Willys Overland Motors, Inc.
Zenith Radio Corporation

INDIVIDUALS

Paul G. Benedum
Helen W. Buckner
Walker G. Buckner
S. Bayard Colgate
W. W. Crocker
Dr. Gilbert Darlington
Walter E. Ditmars
Sidney Ehrman
Clarence Francis

E Roland Harriman
H. J. Heinz II
Samuel S. Himmell
Lester W. Hink
Col. Charles F. H. Johnson
Dr. Harry Katz
†H. H. The Aga Khan
George D. Lockhart
James Lochead
J. K. Moffitt
Lenord Mudge
John I. Moore
H. H. Phillips
Wendell Phillips
Samuel F. Pryor
James C. Rea
Alan and Sarah Scaife
John B. Trevor

BOARD OF DIRECTORS

American Foundation for the Study of Man

Paul C. Aiken
Lawyer, and former
Assistant Postmaster General

William F. Albright
Chairman Emeritus
Oriental Seminary
Johns Hopkins University

S. Bayard Colgate
Board Chairman
Colgate-Palmolive-Peet Co.

Walter E. Ditmars
President
Gray Manufacturing Co.

T. A. McInerny
Pres., T. A. McInerny, Inc.
Washington, D. C.

James K. Moffitt (1949-1955)
Chairman Trustees
Crocker 1st Nat. Bank, S. F.

Charles J. Nager
Member Law Firm
Eagan and Nager

Chester W. Nimitz (1949-1952)
Fleet Admiral, U. S. N.
Regent, Univ. of California

Wendell Phillips
President

Samuel F. Pryor
Vice President
Pan American World Airways

William B. Terry
Vice President

Gladys W. Terry
Secretary

Lowell Thomas
Author
CBS Commentator